Computer Vision

W0036105

Computer Vision

Fundamentals and Applications

Jayanta Mukhopadhyay

Shashaank Aswatha Mattur

CAMBRIDGE
UNIVERSITY PRESS

CAMBRIDGE
UNIVERSITY PRESS

Shaftesbury Road, Cambridge CB2 8EA, United Kingdom

One Liberty Plaza, 20th Floor, New York, NY 10006, USA

477 Williamstown Road, Port Melbourne, VIC 3207, Australia

314–321, 3rd Floor, Plot No. 3, Splendor Forum, Jasola District Centre, New Delhi – 110025, India

103 Penang Road, #05–06/07, Visioncrest Commercial, Singapore 238467

Cambridge University Press is part of Cambridge University Press & Assessment, a department of the University of Cambridge.

We share the University's mission to contribute to society through the pursuit of education, learning and research at the highest international levels of excellence.

www.cambridge.org
Information on this title: www.cambridge.org/9781009330497

© Jayanta Mukhopadhyay and Shashaank Aswatha Mattur 2025

This publication is in copyright. Subject to statutory exception and to the provisions of relevant collective licensing agreements, no reproduction of any part may take place without the written permission of Cambridge University Press & Assessment.

First published 2025

Printed in India by Nutech Print Services, New Delhi 110020

A catalogue record for this publication is available from the British Library

ISBN 978-1-009-33049-7 Paperback

Cambridge University Press & Assessment has no responsibility for the persistence or accuracy of URLs for external or third-party internet websites referred to in this publication and does not guarantee that any content on such websites is, or will remain, accurate or appropriate.

For EU product safety concerns, contact us at Calle de José Abascal, 56, 1°, 28003 Madrid, Spain, or email eugpsr@cambridge.org.

Contents

Preface

The subject, Computer Vision, deals with the science of imparting to a machine or a computer the capability of seeing and understanding the environment as we humans are able to do, and seeks to apply its theories and models in various applications of our life and society. From the late sixties of the last century, there have been efforts in analyzing digital images captured by a scanner or a camera. Initially, it was the 2-D digital geometry in a discrete grid of integral coordinate space which drew primary attention of the researchers. In particular, Prof. Azriel Rosenfeld (1931–2004) of the University of Maryland, USA, took a leading and pioneering role in developing theories of digital picture processing. Subsequently, the area was strengthened by the development and application of theories of mathematical morphology, texture processing, pattern recognition techniques, etc. However, the major development in the theory of computer vision, following the psycho-physiological models of human vision, happened in the seventies of the last century, when Prof. David Marr (1945–1980) of the Massachusetts Institute of Technology (MIT), Cambridge, USA, hypothesized three stages of processing and representation of images by primal sketches consisting of edges, regions, 2.5-D sketches of the scene, and finally 3-D models.

Over the years, theories of computer vision have been developed from different areas of mathematical and physical sciences, such as digital geometry, projective geometry, differential geometry, linear and nonlinear systems, human cognition and psycho-visual perception, color representation and processing, computational learning, pattern recognition, etc. As we see, the theoretical foundation of the subject has been built from different domains, and it requires to learn the fundamentals across these disciplines in a systematic and organized manner in the context of core agenda of computer vision, which is to solve problems related to the understanding of a 3-D scene, static or dynamic, given visual inputs from imaging systems. With this good intention, we proceeded to write this textbook on computer vision. No doubt, it is an extremely challenging task to bring all these foundation topics and their applications to this area under the same basket with the desired technical depth and clarity. Yet, when we were approached by the Cambridge University Press for writing such a textbook, we took the challenge and spent about two years to come up with this draft. But in spite of our best intention and efforts with several rounds of reviews and revision of the text, we do not feel comfortable to make any claim on the fulfilment of our mission. However, as every deadline has its own final dictate, we needed to put an end to this exercise and agree to release the present version. We leave it to our readers for their judgment on our fate accompli. We would appreciate to receive any constructive feedback and suggestions to improve the content and presentation of this book for its future edition, if the need arises.

In our effort to provide a comprehensive coverage of theory and computation related to imaging geometry and scene understanding, we organized the subject matter in such a way as to bring primarily three distinct flavors of theoretical treatments in presenting the concepts and methodologies. These include (i) signal processing based techniques for both linear and nonlinear systems, (ii) geometric analysis with an exposure to digital and projective geometry, and (iii) learning and inference based approaches involving pattern recognition and machine learning techniques. The book is primarily targeted for senior undergraduate and postgraduate students studying in the areas of computer science and engineering, and electrical engineering. However, as the subject covers various interdisciplinary areas, we hope it will be also useful to and of interest to a wider readership in Science and Engineering. Exposure to a first-level image processing course would help the readers. However, in the first chapter, a brief overview of image and video processing techniques is included, which should mostly satisfy the required background in going through the rest of the material.

There are four parts in this book, with eighteen chapters in total. In the first two parts, processing and computation with optical images and videos are discussed. In the first part, there are nine chapters. In these chapters, the concepts of image and video processing are built from the foundation, covering image formation, perceptual models of images, signal processing and digital geometry based processing including alternative representations of images and videos, feature detection, matching and model fitting, and techniques used for higher level understanding of scenes such as clustering and classification. It also includes a chapter on the processing of color images, and topics related to video processing, such as object tracking. Finally, the concepts and applications of deep learning techniques are also introduced in the last chapter of this part.

The second part briefly covers 2-D projective geometry and its applications in understanding and modeling 3-D scenes from single view and stereo imaging systems.

The third part discusses processing and analysis of images obtained from nonoptical/ semi-optical imaging systems, such as range imaging, medical imaging, and remote sensing imaging systems.

In the last part, some of the major applications, such as document processing, biometry, and content based image retrieval, are discussed.

As the book is primarily targeting senior undergraduate and postgraduate students of engineering colleges, technical institutes, and universities, we have included, in most chapters in the first three parts, a few worked out examples, and at the end of every chapter, there are a good number of exercises.

While writing this book, we received much-needed support and encouragements from our friends, colleagues, co-researchers, research collaborators, students, and many other individuals at various stages. We are thankful to Prof. David Noll of the University of Michigan for permitting us to use some of the diagrams and sketches from his lecture slides in the chapter on *Medical Imaging*. Dr Indranil Mullick of the Tata Medical Center, Kolkata is also gratefully acknowledged for sharing an example image for the same chapter. We express our sincere gratitude and appreciation to Prof. Sudeshna Sarkar of IIT Kharagpur for sharing her slides for the purpose of illustrations in the chapter on *Deep Visual Learning*. Many of the former students of the first author, Prof. Rajarshi Pal of IRDBT, Hyderabad; Prof. Debiprasad Dogra of IIT Bhubaneswar; Dr Soumyadeep Dey of Microsoft India, Hyderabad; Dr Jit Mukherjee of BIT, Mesra; Dr M. Sai Phanikumar of

Philips Research, Bangalore; Prof. Sanjoy Pratihar of IIIT, Kalyani; and Ms. Dipannita Podder of IIT Kharagpur, allowed us to use figures and images from their PhD and Master's theses. We sincerely thank all of them for coming forward to help us. We greatly appreciate and acknowledge the efforts put in by Dr Anup Roy of IIT Gandhinagar, Mr Himadri Shekhar Bhunia of Philips Research in Bengaluru, Mr Surajit Kundu, Ms Ankita Chatterjee, and Mr Soumyajit Das of IIT Kharagpur for generating processed images for the purpose of illustrations in this book.

The first author also takes this opportunity to express his deep gratitude from the bottom of his heart to all his students, teachers, colleagues, co-researchers, and research collaborators, from whom he has learned many lessons throughout his academic and research career spanning about four decades. From them he has enriched himself not only in the subject matters of this book but also in various other domains of science and technology. This includes also his deep appreciation for his co-author, Dr Shashaank Mattur Aswatha, who worked with him for more than eight years as a student and has been collaborating with him since then. This textbook is also an outcome of this collaboration. His contributions in writing this book, preparing the manuscript in its present format, writing programs for generating illustrative examples, and creating many diagrams and figures are stupendous. The first author also specially acknowledges his indebtedness to Prof. B.N. Chatterji, his former PhD supervisor, and Prof. Sanjit K. Mitra of the University of California, Santa Barbara, USA, for their guidance and friendship.

Mr Agnibesh Das of the Cambridge University Press had taken the initiative to bring us into this project, and then Mr Ankush Sharma and Ms Shweta Pant extended all possible support and encouragement toward its completion. We express our sincere thanks and gratitude to them for their patience and understanding, in spite of missing many of our deadlines set before, and their regular monitoring of our progress toward the completion of this project.

Finally, no words are sufficient to express our appreciation and thanks to our family members for their understanding, care, and support during our long and busy engagement in preparing this manuscript.

October 29, 2024

Jayanta Mukhopadhyay
Shashaank Aswatha Mattur

Acknowledgements

The authors extend their heartfelt gratitude to the following persons for their invaluable comments and suggestions, generously offered despite their busy schedules. Their contributions have significantly enhanced the quality of this book.

Ankita Chatterjee, Research Scholar, Department of Computer Science and Engineering, Indian Institute of Technology Kharagpur; Aritra Hazra, Assistant Professor, Department of Computer Science and Engineering, Indian Institute of Technology Kharagpur; Arbind Gupta, Professor, Dayananda Sagar College of Engineering, Bengaluru; Bijju Kranthi Veduruparthi, Principal Engineer, Monarch Tractor, Hyderabad; Deepak Mishra, Professor, Department of Avionics, Indian Institute of Space Science and Technology Trivandrum; Deepak Putrevu, Dy Head, Microwave Techniques Development Division, Space Applications Centre (SAC), ISRO, Ahmedabad; Deepti R. Bathula, Associate Professor, Department of Computer Science and Engineering, Indian Institute of Technology Ropar; Jayasree Saha, Post-doctoral researcher, Indian Institute of Information Technology, Hyderabad; Manish Okade, Associate Professor, Department of Electronics and Communication Engineering, National Institute of Technology Rourkela; Mrinal Kanti Bhowmik, Associate Professor, Department of Computer Science and Engineering, Tripura University; Oishila Bandyopadhyay, Assistant Professor, Department of Computer Science and Engineering, Indian Institute of Information Technology Kalyani; Pratik Chattopadhyay, Assistant Professor, Department of Computer Science and Engineering, Indian Institute of Technology (BHU) Varanasi; Rajarshi Pal, Assistant Professor, Institute for Development and Research in Banking Technology, Hyderabad; Ritwik Kumar Layek, Associate Professor, Department of Electronics and Electrical Communication Engineering, Indian Institute of Technology Kharagpur; Sai Phani Kumar M., Research Engineer, Philips Research, Bengaluru; Sanjoy Pratihar, Assistant Professor, Indian Institute of Information Technology Kalyani; Sanjoy Kumar Saha, Department of Computer Science and Engineering, Jadavpur University, Kolkata; Shankho Subhra Pal, Research Scholar, Department of Computer Science and Engineering, Indian Institute of Technology Kharagpur; Suman Deb, Assistant Professor, Department of Computer Science and Engineering, National Institute of Technology Agartala; Vishwanath K., Professor, Department of Telecommunication Engineering, Siddaganga Institute of Technology, Tumkur.

Symbols

Symbol	Description
x	Variable or constant
$\boldsymbol{x}$	Vector (column vector, unless specified otherwise)
$\mathbf{X}$	Matrix
$\mathbf{0}$	Zero column vector or matrix
X	Set
$\mathbb{R}^d$	Real numbers in a d-dimensional space
$\mathbb{P}^d$	d-dimensional projective space
$\mathbb{Z}^d$	d-dimensional integer space
$\hat{f}$	Fourier transform (Discrete Fourier Transform) of the function (sequence) f
$\mathscr{T}$	Transformation operator
$|\mathbf{X}|$	Determinant of a matrix $\mathbf{X}$
$|x|$	Absolute value of a scalar x
$|\boldsymbol{x}|_1$	L_1 Norm of a vector $\boldsymbol{x}$
$|\boldsymbol{x}|_2$	L_2 Norm of a vector $\boldsymbol{x}$
$|\boldsymbol{x}|_p$	L_p Norm of a vector $\boldsymbol{x}$
$\|\mathbf{X}\|$	Frobenius norm of a matrix $\mathbf{x}$
$\mathbf{I}$	Identity matrix
$\mathbf{X}^\top$	Transpose of matrix $\mathbf{X}$
$\overline{x}$	Average value of x
$\sum_{init}(\cdot)$	Summation of terms

Symbol	Description
$\prod_{init}(\cdot)$	Product of terms
$[\mathbf{M}|\boldsymbol{p}]$	A 3×4 projection matrix, where $\mathbf{M}$ is a 3×3 submatrix and $\boldsymbol{p}$ is a 3×1 column vector
$A \cup B$	Union of sets A and B
$A \cap B$	Intersection of sets A and B
A^c	Complement of set A
$\hat{\mathbf{S}}$	Reflection of structuring element $\mathbf{S}$
$\mathbf{S}_{\boldsymbol{t}}$	Translation of structuring element $\mathbf{S}$ by $\boldsymbol{t}$
$\mathbf{I} \oplus \mathbf{S}_{\mathbf{e}}$	Morphological dilation operation on $\mathbf{I}$ using structural element $\mathbf{S}_{\mathbf{e}}$
$\mathbf{I} \ominus \mathbf{S}_{\mathbf{e}}$	Morphological erosion operation on $\mathbf{I}$ using structural element $\mathbf{S}_{\mathbf{e}}$
$\mathbf{I} \star \mathbf{S}_{\mathbf{e}}$	Morphological hit or miss operation on $\mathbf{I}$ using structural element $\mathbf{S}_{\mathbf{e}}$
$\mathbf{I} \cdot \mathbf{S}_{\mathbf{e}}$	Morphological closing operation on $\mathbf{I}$ using structural element $\mathbf{S}_{\mathbf{e}}$
$\mathbf{I} \circ \mathbf{S}_{\mathbf{e}}$	Morphological opening operation on $\mathbf{I}$ using structural element $\mathbf{S}_{\mathbf{e}}$
$f * h$	Linear convolution between f and h
$f \circledast h$	Circular convolution between f and h
$f \circledS h$	Skew circular convolution between f and h
$f \otimes h$	Correlation operation between f and h
$f \bullet h$	Cross correlation between f and h
$\frac{df}{dx}$	Derivative of f with respect to x
$\frac{\partial f}{\partial x}$	Partial derivative of f with respect to x
f_x	Derivative or partial derivative of f with respect to x

Symbol	Description
$f \odot h$	Point-wise multiplication operation between f and h
$\mathbf{X}^{-1}$	Matrix inversion of $\mathbf{X}$
$\mathbf{X}^*$	Complex conjugate of matrix $\mathbf{X}$
j	Complex number, $\sqrt{-1}$
$\boldsymbol{x} \cdot \boldsymbol{y}$	Dot product between vectors $\boldsymbol{x}$ and $\boldsymbol{y}$
$\boldsymbol{x} \times \boldsymbol{y}$	Cross product between vectors $\boldsymbol{x}$ and $\boldsymbol{y}$
$\nabla f(x, y)$	Gradient vector of a function $f(x, y)$
$\nabla^2 f(x, y)$	Laplacian (second order gradient) of a function $f(x, y)$
$[a_{ij}]$	A matrix whose $(i, j)^{\text{th}}$ element is a_{ij}
$\text{Diag}(x_1, x_2, ..., x_n)$	The diagonal matrix of size $n \times n$ with diagonal elements as x_1, x_2, ..., x_n

PART ONE

VISUAL INFORMATION PROCESSING

1

Fundamentals of Image and Video Processing

Computer vision is the science of facilitating a machine or a computer with the human-like capability of seeing and understanding the environment.[1] It is a field of artificial intelligence (AI), which deals with the theory, algorithmic basis, and computation for automatic understanding of visual data acquired from an environment. With the rapid advancement of digital and computing technology, it is possible to capture images and videos of a scene and store the data in the memory of a computer. Computer vision is primarily concerned with the automatic extraction, analysis and understanding of useful information from a single image, a set of images, or a video which is a sequence of images. It has a wide range of applications across the society and various industries, such as in autonomous vehicles, health care, surveillance, augmented reality, robotics, remote sensing, document processing, biometrics, and more. Some of the key tasks of computer vision are acquisition and processing of images and videos, extracting information, and finally, deriving knowledge and description about the scene. In this introductory chapter, we briefly review some of the fundamental aspects of image and video processing which may be sufficient to follow the content of the rest of the book. However, the readers may be advised to go through first level image and video processing textbooks to know more details about it.

1.1 | Image representation

To understand how images are represented in a computer, consider an image shown in Fig 1.1. A small portion of this image, shown by a white rectangle, is zoomed to reveal enlarging details of that portion of the image. We observe that, within this zoomed portion, although the details are better visible, the edges appear jagged. Let us zoom a small rectangular region around a typical segment of jagged edges. In the enlarged rectangular region, small squares of uniform illumination appear. In this figure, the

---

[1] From British Machine Vision Association (BMVA).

3

Figure 1.1 Digital image representation.

integers proportional to the brightness of those small squares are also shown within them. Thus at the lowest level of representation of an image, every point, which is called *pixel*, has an integer associated with it, and that integer represents the brightness value at that pixel. While displaying an image on a screen, each of these pixels covers a small area of the screen with the intensity proportional to the value stored at its corresponding location in the image array.

In computers, an image is represented as a two-dimensional (2-D) array of integers. These integer numbers are arranged in a 2-D array of a specific size. The array size is defined by width and height of the image. For example, in Fig. 1.1, the width of the image is 256 (i.e., 256 pixels along its width) and the height of the image is 384 (i.e., 384 pixels along its height). The image represented by a 2-D array is known as a gray scale image. For representing a color image, it requires three such 2-D arrays, as shown in Fig. 1.2, each representing one of the primary colors: red (R), green (G), and blue (B). At any particular point in an image, these three corresponding array elements with the same array indices represent a color by a combination of the three primary colors. Also, each of these color components of RGB image may be treated individually as a gray scale image that corresponds to a particular color channel. In the example of Fig. 1.2, individual components of an RGB color image are shown using their respective primary colors only. The red component of the image is displayed with only red color. Similarly, the green and blue components of the image are displayed using only green and blue colors for visualization. A color image is displayed on the screen by superimposing these three color channels. So a color image is represented by three 2-D arrays that correspond to three primary colors.

An image is stored in the secondary storage of a computer, e.g., in its hard disk, as a file containing all the relevant information. An image file contains a stream of pixels. To represent an image in a program for computation, other associated information of the image,

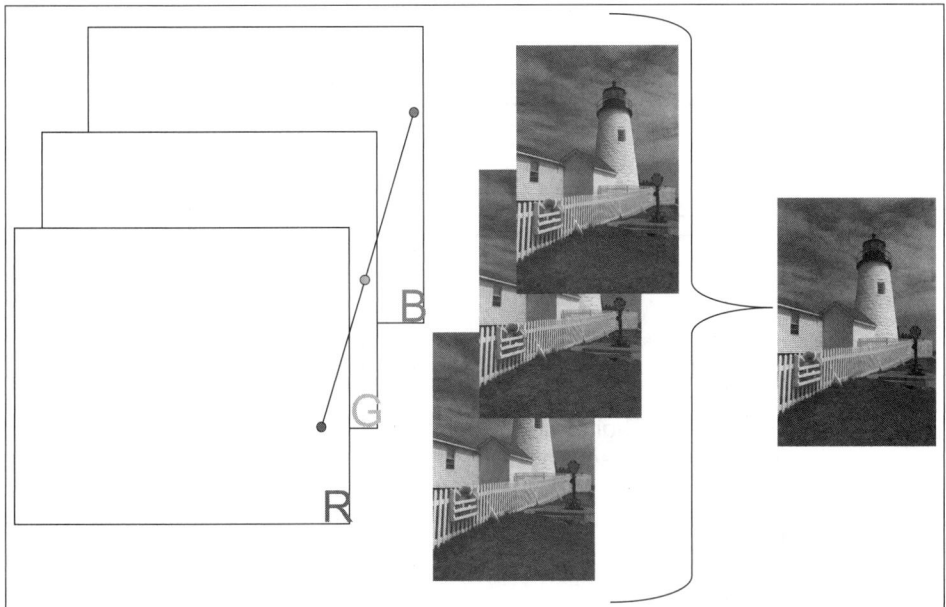

Figure 1.2 Representation of a color image. See Color Plates (page 803).

besides stream of pixels, also are to be stored in the file. Usually, they are stored ahead of the pixel stream in the file in a very predefined format, which is called header of the image file. For example, a simple header may include information such as the width of the image, the height of the image, the number of color components (which is one for a gray scale image and three for a color image), number of bytes per pixel, etc. In a very elementary representation, an image is obtained by *sampling* the signal in two spatial dimensions, where every sampled point is a pixel. A pixel of a gray scale image is *quantized* for representing it by a discrete value in a given range. For instance, a pixel value requiring one byte is usually represented by an 8-bit unsigned integer, which may be of a value between 0 and 255. However, for certain applications, other data types may also be used to represent pixel values, for example, unsigned 16 bit integer, 32 bit floating point number, etc. The resolution of a digital image is usually expressed as the number of pixels per unit length along a direction, unless having other domain specific definitions. There are different standard file formats for an image representation. Each of these standard formats has a particular header structure that are parsed to read an image file. Some of the examples of these formats are: TIFF, BMP, PNG, JPEG, GIF, PGM, PPM, DICOM, etc.

1.1.1 | Video representation

Video is a dynamic form of visual content, which depicts images of objects whose shape and locations may change with time. In the very basic form, a digital video is composed of a sequence of images of a scene that are acquired at regular intervals of time. So, a video consists of a large volume of data requiring larger storage space than an image. This makes the handling of videos more challenging due to their large size and information processing.

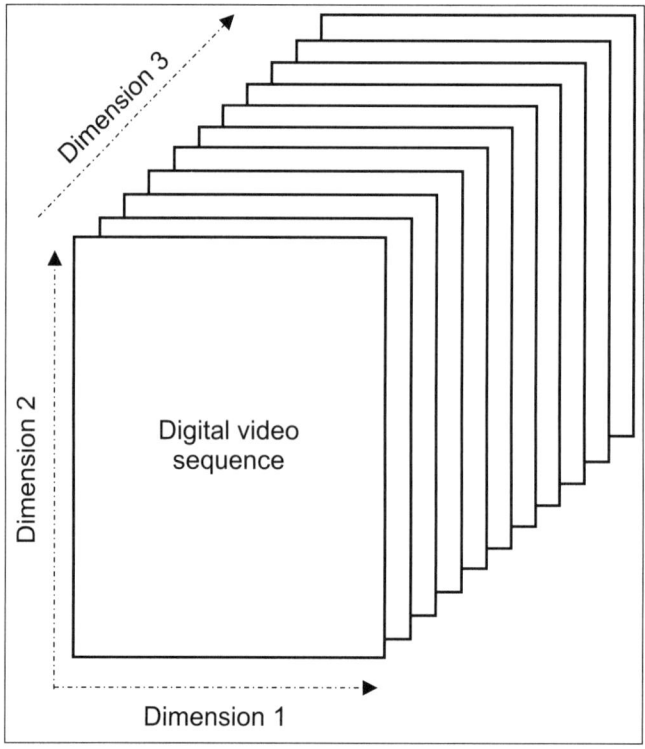

Figure 1.3 Digital video representation.

Videos are represented also as a three-dimensional (3-D) data, as shown in Fig 1.3. In this case, two of them are spatial dimensions, and the remaining one is the temporal dimension. Quantization of a video signal is almost similar to the quantization of images. However, in addition to the sampling in two spatial dimensions as in the images, videos are also sampled along the temporal dimension. So, a video may be represented as a 3-D array of a specific frame size along the two spatial axes and number of frames along the temporal axis. The spatial resolution of a digital video is generally expressed as the number of pixels along the width and the height in each frame. A digital video is called *standard definition*, *high definition*, or *ultra-high definition*, depending on the number of horizontal lines in each frame of the video and number of pixels in each line of the frame. Typical resolutions of various types of digital videos are shown in Fig 1.4. The temporal resolution of a digital video is expressed as the number of frames per second (fps). Most of the videos that are acquired by general purpose cameras have a temporal resolution of 25 or 30 fps. However, with recent advances in camera technology, videos with very high rate of fps are also acquired.

As a video may contain a large number of frames, its processing requires significant amount of storage and computational resources. It consumes more bandwidth for its transmission. So, to make it amenable for a plethora of practical applications, the video data is subjected to compression while storing or transmission. Subsequently, the

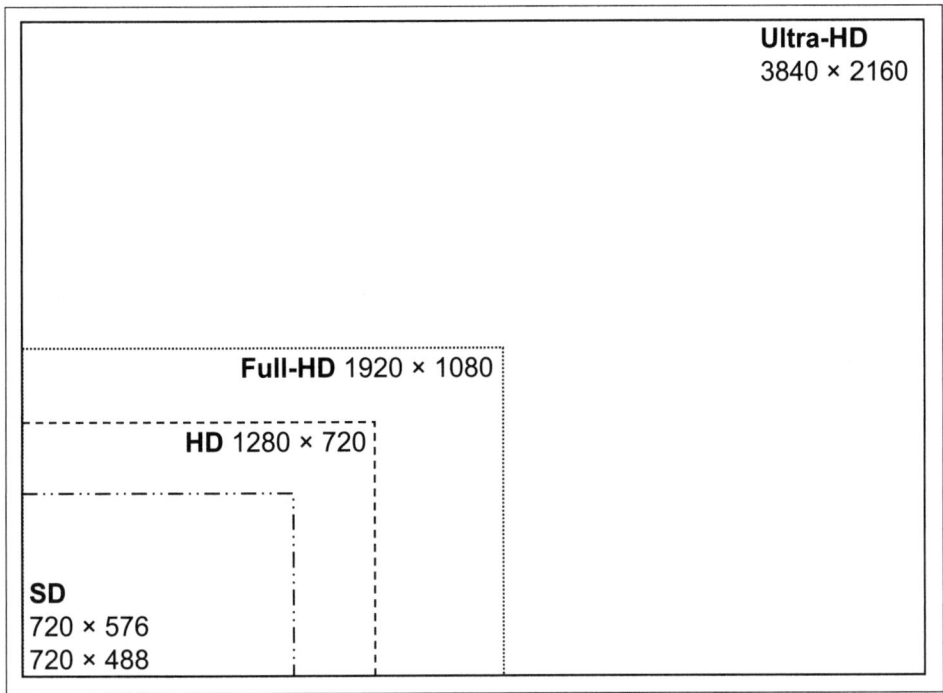

Figure 1.4 Different spatial resolution categories of a digital video.

compressed data is decompressed to recover the videos in their original form of spatio-temporal sequences for further analysis. The data compression may either be lossless or lossy in nature. For a lossless compression, exact reconstruction of the original video after decompression is possible, whereas for a lossy compression, the decompressed video is approximation of the original video. Usually, video compression is lossy in nature as it allows to represent a very close approximation of the original video with a much reduced storage requirement. In many applications this approximation does not make any difference. There are large amounts of statistical redundancies in video data. Besides spatial redundancy, it has a significant temporal redundancy in consecutive frames. Most of the compression algorithms aim at elimination of such redundancies, so that there is a considerable reduction in the size of the video. There are different video compression algorithms that are developed for different kinds of applications. For example, H.26x standards are used in video teleconferencing, while the Motion JPEG (MJPEG) is convenient for video editors as it has easy access to individual frames. There are different standards suggested by the Moving Picture Expert Group (MPEG), an international body of defining standards of videos. Some of the examples of these standards are MPEG-1, MPEG-2, and MPEG-4. Some of the examples of digital video formats are, AVI, MP4, MPEG, 3GP, GIF, FLV, WEBM, VOB, etc., which use different kinds of encoding-decoding formats for different applications.

1.1.2 | Image formation

An image is formed in an optical camera by projecting a 3-D scene on a 2-D plane. The lens of the camera plays a very critical role in acquiring the image of a scene. The points of a 3-D scene are projected onto a 2-D plane through the lens. This 2-D plane is known as the *focal plane* of the camera or the imaging system. The points that are projected on this focal plane are sensed by a 2-D array of image sensors, which are then quantified and digitized to get the final digital representation of the image. To understand how a point in a 3-D space is mapped to an image point in a 2-D space, refer to the diagram in Fig. 1.5. Consider a point P, from where a ray of light is reflected. This ray passes through the center of the camera lens and intersects the plane of projection or the image plane. The point of intersection of the ray of light and the image plane, represented by p, is the image of the scene point P. In this case, since the image is formed by the light that is reflected from a 3-D scene, the image formation has occurred due to the phenomenon of reflection.

Another information that is encoded at an image point is the amount of energy that is received at this point (p), which is reflected from the scene point P. The function of the lens is to collect as much of reflected energy from the scene and put them together on p in the image plane. This is called *focussing*. The collected energy is focused by the lens to the point p. When a proper focusing is achieved, the image of P is formed as a sharp point p. Thus the amount of energy that is reflected from P is received at p and a brightness distribution in a 2-D plane is recorded. Thereby, at each point of the image

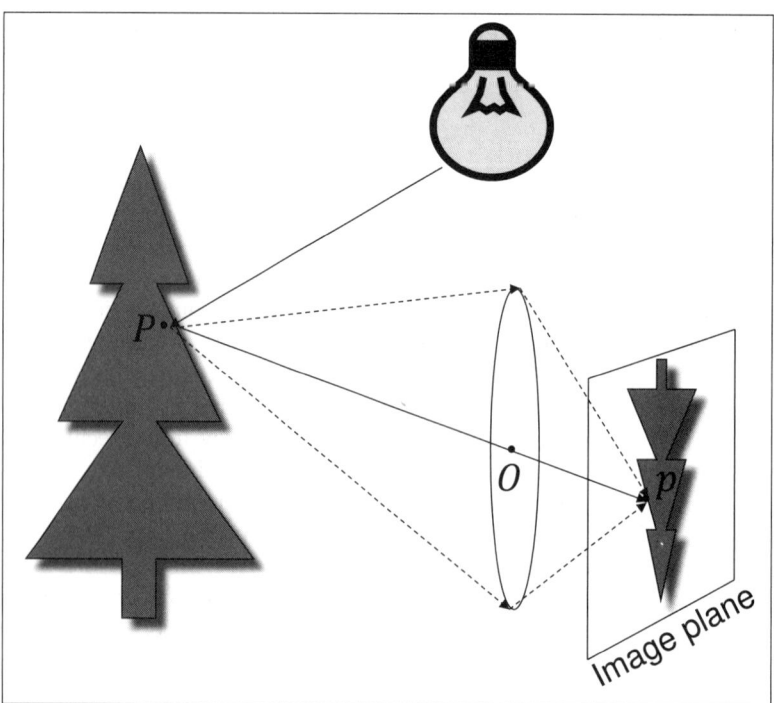

Figure 1.5 Image formation in an optical camera.

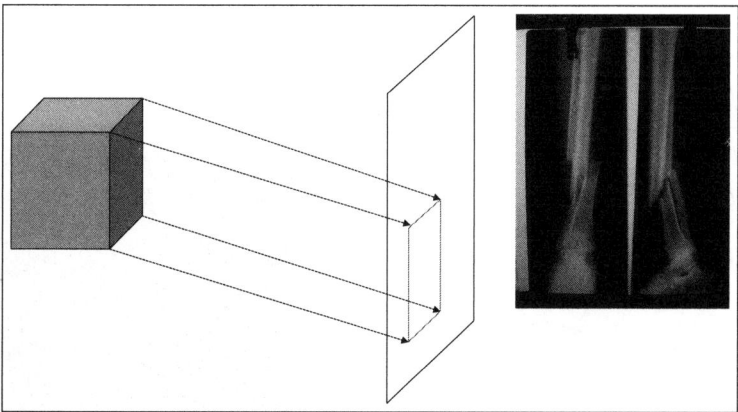

Figure 1.6 Image formed by the intersection of parallel rays from the image plane.

plane, the encoded value is proportional to the amount of energy that is reflected from its corresponding point in the 3-D scene. In the formation of an optical image by a lens, a simple mathematical rule of projection is observed. In the example of Fig. 1.5, a line drawn from P that passes through a fixed point, O, which is the center of the lens, is extended to intersect the image plane. The point of intersection of this line and the image plane defines the 2-D image point, p, of the 3-D scene point P. The center of the lens, O, is also called the *center of projection*, and the plane containing p is the *image plane*. In other words, the image points are formed by intersection of rays from 3-D world points passing through the center of projection with the image plane. This kind of projection is called *perspective projection*.

Perspective projection is not the only way of formation of images. There are other kinds of imaging principles, which may follow different rules of projections. For example, in Fig. 1.6, the image is formed by parallel rays projecting on the image plane. As it is seen in the figure, all the world points are parallely projected onto the image plane. In this case, a particular direction has to be specified for projecting the world points. The projection may either be along normal to the world plane or it may be along any other direction in a 3-D plane. Thus in this case, the image points of corresponding scene points are formed by the intersection of parallel rays coming from those points along a given direction with the image plane. An example of this kind of imaging system is the X-ray imaging, where parallel X-ray beams pass through the tissues and bones of a patient, which then intersect an X-ray plate. The X-ray plate acts like the image plane to form an image. This kind of projection is called *parallel projection*.

In another popular imaging principle, a transmitter is used to transmit electromagnetic or acoustic waves and the reflected waves are received by a receiver, as shown in Fig. 1.7. The waves received at the receiver end are sensed by a sensor to form an image of a 3-D object. The duration of time interval between the transmission and reception of these waves is measured, and the corresponding distance from the reflector is computed by using the velocity of the waves. Usually, this distance is used to form an image. Also, by repeating this process at regular intervals of time over the object surface and by scanning

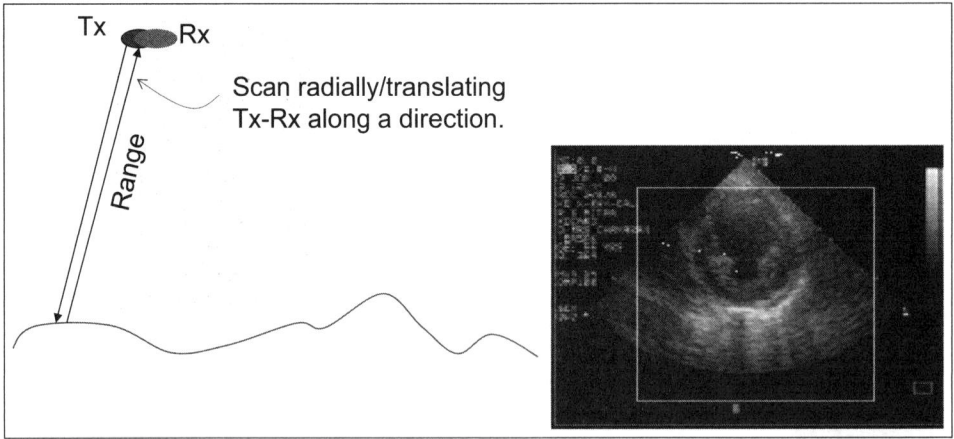

Figure 1.7 Image formed by scanning an object in radial/translation movement with transmission and reception of signals.

it radially along different directions, the orientation and various surface properties of the object are determined. An example of this kind of imaging system is the ultrasonography, where acoustic waves or ultra sound waves are used to scan, analyze, and diagnose various internal body organs. To summarize, an image is defined as an impression of the physical world, which captures the spatial distribution of a measurable quantity by encoding the geometry and material properties of objects.

1.2 | Image histogram

One of the basic techniques of image analysis involves statistical analysis of distribution of pixel values. A simple tool of this analysis is the frequency distribution of the brightness values of pixels in an image, which is called the histogram of the image. In Fig. 1.8, an image of a scanned page from a book written in Bengali is shown. The pixels in this image may be put into two categories, namely, (1) text, which depicts textual content in the image, and (2) background, which depicts nontextual content in the image. Ideally, the intensity histogram of the image is expected to be bimodal. But, as it can be seen in Fig. 1.8, the histogram appears skewed. That is, a prominent peak is present in the zone of white pixels (background pixels' zone) and the distribution in the zone of black pixels (text pixels' zone) appears flat without any prominent peak in the related part of the histogram.

Usually, image analysis using histograms involves estimation of probability distribution of the pixel values. The probability distribution of pixel brightness values is obtained by normalizing the histogram, where each of the frequencies in the image histogram is divided by the total number of pixels of the image. A typical example is shown in Fig 1.8, where, for a pixel of brightness value x (in horizontal axis), the value in normalized histogram corresponding to x is denoted by $p(x) = \frac{n_x}{n}$, where n_x is the number of pixels with brightness value x and n is the total number of pixels.

1.3 | Image binarization

In various applications on digital images, particularly in document images as in Fig. 1.8, the computational problem is to separate the foreground in the image (in this case, the text) from the background region. Both the regions have pixel values of varying intensity values. This process of separating the image into two regions based on pixel values is called *binarization*.

1.3.1 | Thresholding

One of the simple techniques of binarization is to use a threshold value to declare whether the considered pixel belongs to the foreground or the background regions. In the example of a document image shown in Fig. 1.8, the foreground consists of dark pixels belonging to text and the background consists of bright pixels belonging to white region of the image. As seen in the histogram of the image, the pixels in the image have different values without having a discrete separation between the foreground and the background. After binarization, these pixels are set to one of the two preset values that distinguish the foreground and the background pixels discretely. For example, 0 may represent text pixels and the pixels in white region of the document image may have the value 255. A simple algorithm for binarization of an image is as follows.

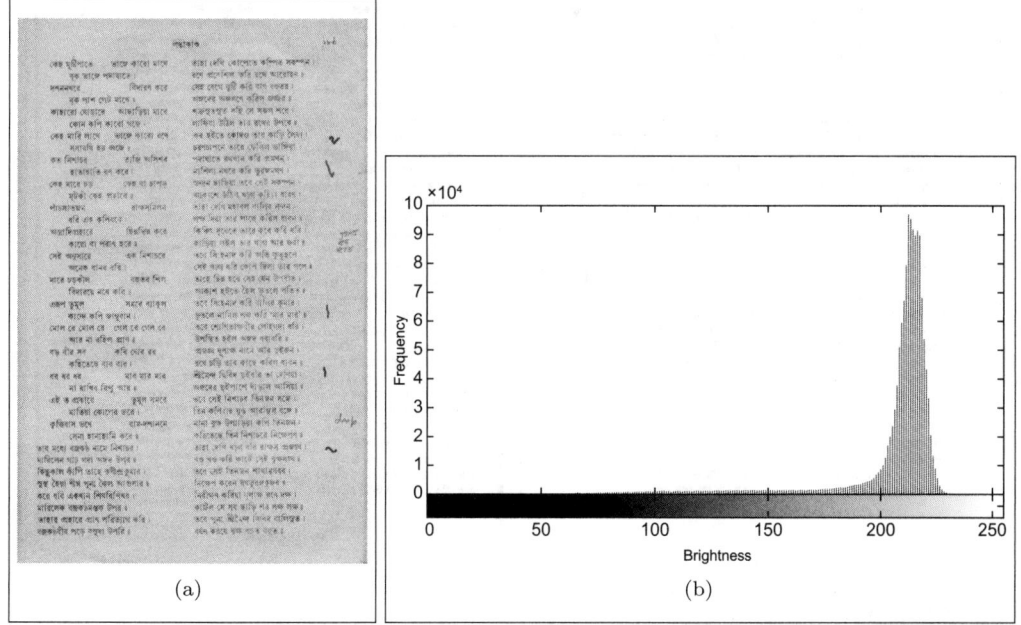

(a)   (b)

Figure 1.8 An example of a document image and its histogram.

Choose a threshold value, T, from one of the possible values in the brightness interval, 0 to 255. Then, set all the pixels greater than T to 255, and the pixels less than or equal to T are set to 0.

In this simple algorithm, the outcome is widely affected by the choice of threshold value, T ($0 \leq T < 255$). The choice of T may be guided by the corresponding histogram of the image. For the document image shown in Fig. 1.8, if the value of T is chosen as 156, all the pixels with values 0 to 156 are set to 0, and the pixels with values greater than 156 are set to 255 in the binarized image. Similarly, if T is chosen as 192, another binarized result on the same document image is obtained, which is different than the result with $T = 156$, as shown in Fig. 1.9. As a trade-off, higher the threshold value, greater is the number of pixels that are set as foreground pixels and the textual content appears bolder. But, with higher threshold values, it produces spurious noise in the background region, which is not desirable. Similarly, if the threshold value is kept low, the background region appears clean without much noise. But, with lower threshold values, a number of foreground textual pixels

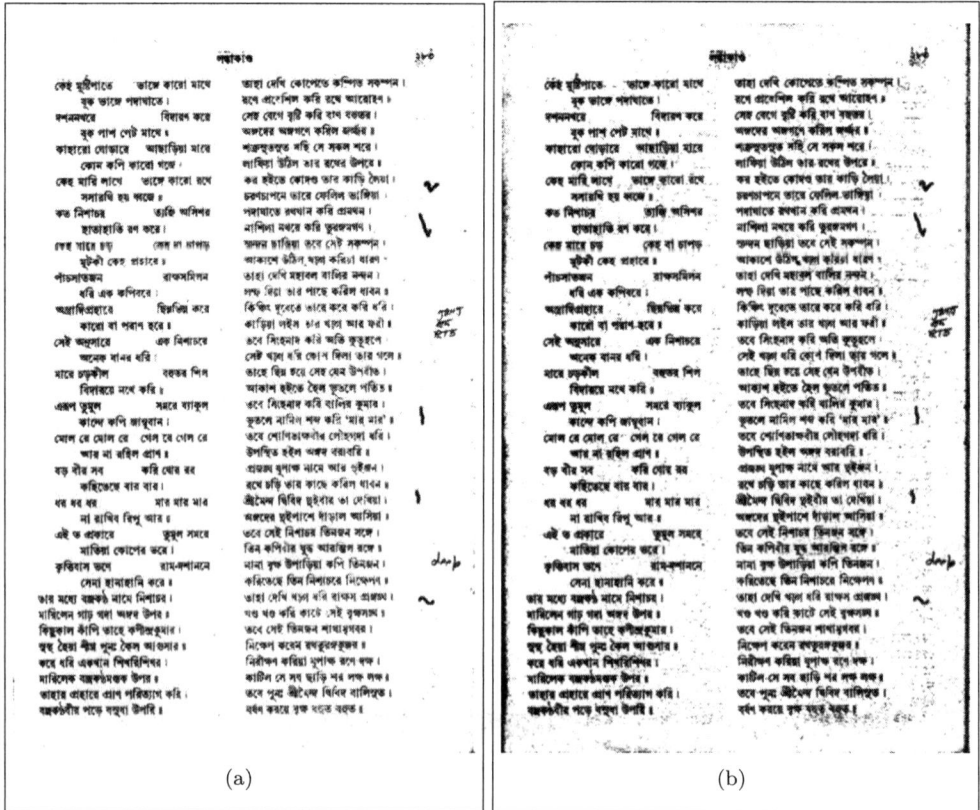

(a)   (b)

Figure 1.9 Results of thresholding operation on the image of Fig. 1.8 with the threshold values: (a) $T = 156$ and (b) $T = 192$.

are labeled as background and corresponding components of text get eroded, which is also not desirable. Therefore, the desirable choice of T is such a value that keeps the foreground text bolder without losing textual pixels, while eliminating the noisy spurious pixels in background.

1.3.2 | Bayesian classification

When a good number of document images are to be processed, manual choice of thresholding for each document image is not viable. Hence it is necessary to automate the choice of T for thresholding. One such technique is to perform Bayesian classification[2] of foreground and background pixels of an image. This approach requires that the histogram of the image is bimodal, as shown in Fig. 1.10. In a bimodal histogram, there are two modes or peaks. Each of these peaks in the bimodal histogram represents one of the regions of foreground or

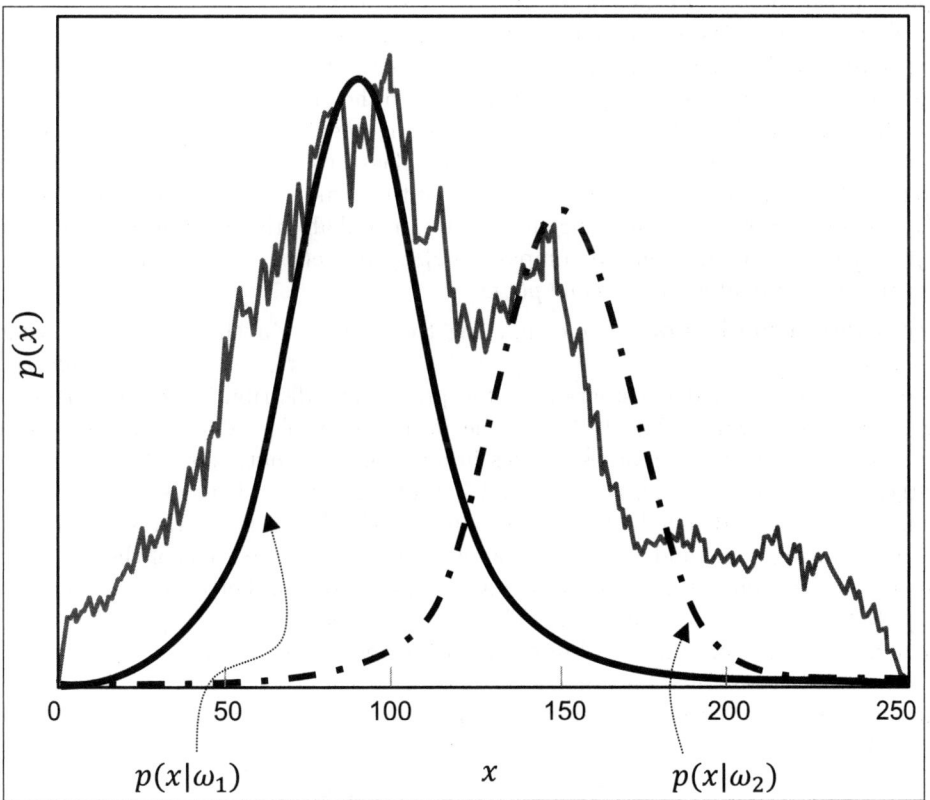

Figure 1.10 A typical bi-modal histogram.

---

[2] This is discussed in detail in Chapter 7.

background. For example, we may observe in the histogram shown in Fig. 1.8 (a), the first peak from the left corresponds to the foreground region, and the second peak corresponds to the background region. So, most of the pixels around the first and second peaks belong to the foreground and the background regions, respectively.

Let the two classes of pixels, namely foreground and background in this case, be denoted by ω_1 and ω_2, respectively. The idea is to compute the *posterior* probabilities of each of the classes, ω_1 and ω_2, given the pixel value x, i.e., $p(\omega_1|x)$ and $p(\omega_2|x)$. Then, from the *Bayesian classification rule*, the pixel x is assigned to the class ω_1 if $p(\omega_1|x) > p(\omega_2|x)$, otherwise, it is assigned to the class ω_2. From the Bayes' theorem, the probability of a class, ω, given the pixel, x, is computed by Eq. 1.1.

$$p(\omega|x) = \frac{p(\omega)p(x|\omega)}{p(x)} \tag{1.1}$$

Moreover, it is simpler to compute $p(x|\omega)$, the *likelihood*, than $p(\omega|x)$. Let us assume that the pixels which are around each of the ω's, the class distributions of ω_1 and ω_2, are coming from the respective classes and form a Gaussian distribution. So, in the bimodal curve of Fig. 1.10, the first peak corresponds to the probability distribution of $p(x|\omega_1)$ for the foreground class, and the second peak corresponds to the probability distribution of $p(x|\omega_2)$ for the background class. These probabilities are the likelihoods that are easy to estimate than computing the posterior probabilities. The class probabilities, $p(\omega_1)$ and $p(\omega_2)$, are computed as the proportional areas under each of the peaks. We may note that, the values of $p(x)$ are not required for comparing class posterior probabilities. Computing $p(x|\omega_1)p(\omega_1)$ and $p(x|\omega_2)p(\omega_2)$ are sufficient to compare $p(\omega_1|x)$ and $p(\omega_2|x)$, since the corresponding values are proportional with the same $p(x)$.

Expectation-maximization   For computing the optimal threshold value following the Bayesian classification approach, we may apply the *expectation-maximization algorithm*.[3] Consider a typical bimodal histogram or the probability distribution of the pixels of an image, which is shown in Fig. 1.11. Let the initial threshold value be around the midpoint in the range of the brightness values in an image, so that, this value partitions the brightness interval into two halves. The first half of this interval belongs to the foreground region, and the second half to the background region. For a given threshold value, the class probabilities, $p(\omega_1)$ and $p(\omega_2)$, are computed by finding the areas of the curves under each interval, and computing proportional areas of each region. Let us assume $p(x|\omega_1)$ and $p(x|\omega_2)$ follow Gaussian distributions. Then, the parameters of $p(x|\omega_1)$ and $p(x|\omega_2)$ are computed by considering the distribution within corresponding intervals.

A *Gaussian distribution* of a random variable, x, is defined by two parameters, namely, the mean of the distribution, μ, and the standard deviation of the distribution, σ, which is given by Eq. 1.2.

$$N(x; \mu, \sigma) = \frac{1}{\sqrt{2\pi\sigma^2}} e^{-\frac{1}{2}\left(\frac{x-\mu}{\sigma}\right)^2} \tag{1.2}$$

Let the parameters of Gaussian distributions corresponding to class ω_1 be μ_1 and σ_1, and class ω_2 be μ_2 and σ_2, respectively. So, to compute the likelihood probabilities, $p(x|\omega_1)$ and

---

[3] See Section 6.4 of Chapter 6 for more details.

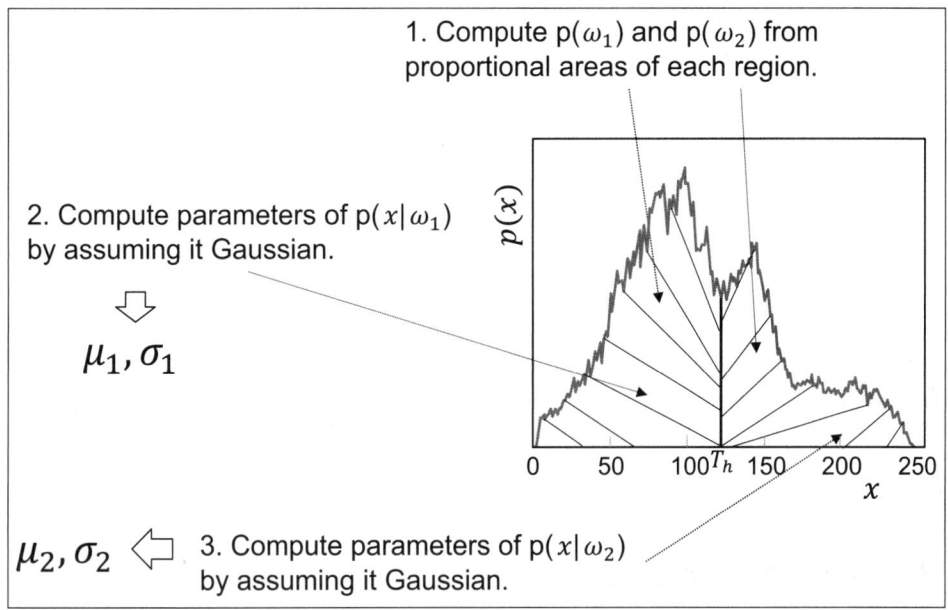

Figure 1.11 A figurative description of computation of parameters of a mixture of Gaussian distributions.

$p(x|\omega_2)$, it is sufficient to estimate the parameters of their respective Gaussian distributions. Also, once these parameters are known, the probability for any value of x may be computed. The parameters of a Gaussian distribution are estimated from the mean and the variance of the data. The expressions of $p(\omega_1)$, $p(\omega_2)$, and the parameters of $p(x|\omega_1)$ and $p(x|\omega_2)$ are given in Eqs. 1.3–1.6, with reference to the histogram shown in Fig. 1.11.

The foreground class probability, $p(\omega_1)$, is computed as area of $p(x)$ under the first interval as follows.

$$p(\omega_1) = \sum_{x-0}^{T} p(x) \qquad (1.3)$$

The background class probability, $p(\omega_2)$, is computed as complementary to $p(\omega_1)$.

$$p(\omega_2) = 1 - p(\omega_1) \qquad (1.4)$$

The parameters of the first Gaussian distribution, μ_1 and σ_1, are computed as the mean and the variance of the distribution in the first interval from 0 to T.

$$\mu_1 = \frac{\sum_{x=0}^{T} x p(x)}{\sum_{x=0}^{T} p(x)}$$

$$\sigma_1^2 = \frac{\sum_{x=0}^{T} x^2 p(x)}{\sum_{x=0}^{T} p(x)} - \mu_1^2 \qquad (1.5)$$

Similarly, the parameters of the second Gaussian distribution, μ_2 and σ_2, are computed as the mean and the variance of the distribution in the second interval from $T + 1$ to 255.

$$\mu_2 = \frac{\sum_{x=T+1}^{255} xp(x)}{\sum_{x=T+1}^{255} p(x)}$$

$$\sigma_2^2 = \frac{\sum_{x=T+1}^{255} x^2 p(x)}{\sum_{x=T+1}^{255} p(x)} - \mu_2^2 \tag{1.6}$$

After computing all the necessary class probabilities and likelihood probabilities for a given threshold, T, a new threshold value, T' is sought such that, $p(\omega_1|x) > p(\omega_2|x)$. The threshold value is updated with this new value, T'. This process of updating the threshold value is iterated till convergence. The final threshold value computed with this iterative process is the optimal threshold value by Bayesian classification method that is used in binarization of the image.

1.3.3 | Otsu thresholding

One more popular and widely used method for image binarization, is the *Otsu thresholding* technique (Otsu, 1979). In this approach too, an objective function of the threshold value is defined whose maximization provides the optimal threshold value. This objective function is defined by the *inter-class variance* (or the *between class variance*) of the considered two classes as given by Eq. 1.7.

$$\sigma_B^2 = p(\omega_1)p(\omega_2)(\mu_2 - \mu_1)^2 \tag{1.7}$$

Given a threshold value, T, σ_B^2 is computed from the probabilities and means of these two classes. As discussed in the previous section, $p(\omega_1)$ and $p(\omega_2)$, and the means, μ_1 and μ_2, are obtained from the probability distributions of pixel values in their respective intervals. In Otsu thresholding algorithm, the value of σ_B^2 is computed at every pixel value in the entire brightness interval of the image, i.e., 0 to 255. Then, the brightness value with the maximum between class variance (σ_B^2) is taken as the optimal threshold value. This method of computing the optimal threshold value for image binarization was proposed by N. Otsu (Otsu, 1979), and hence it is known as the Otsu thresholding technique.

An example of binarization of the document image in Fig. 1.8 is shown in Fig. 1.12 using the Otsu thresholding and the Bayesian classification based binarization methods. The Otsu threshold value for this example is 157, which is incidentally the same value of the threshold obtained by the Bayesian classification based method too. However, we may notice that the results of these two operations are not exactly the same. These differences occur due to an additional preprocessing step associated with the Bayesian classification based method, which is necessary to satisfy its assumption of bimodal characteristics in the image histogram, so that the histogram may have sharper modes in both foreground and background regions. This necessary preprocessing involves contrast stretching, which is explained in the next section.

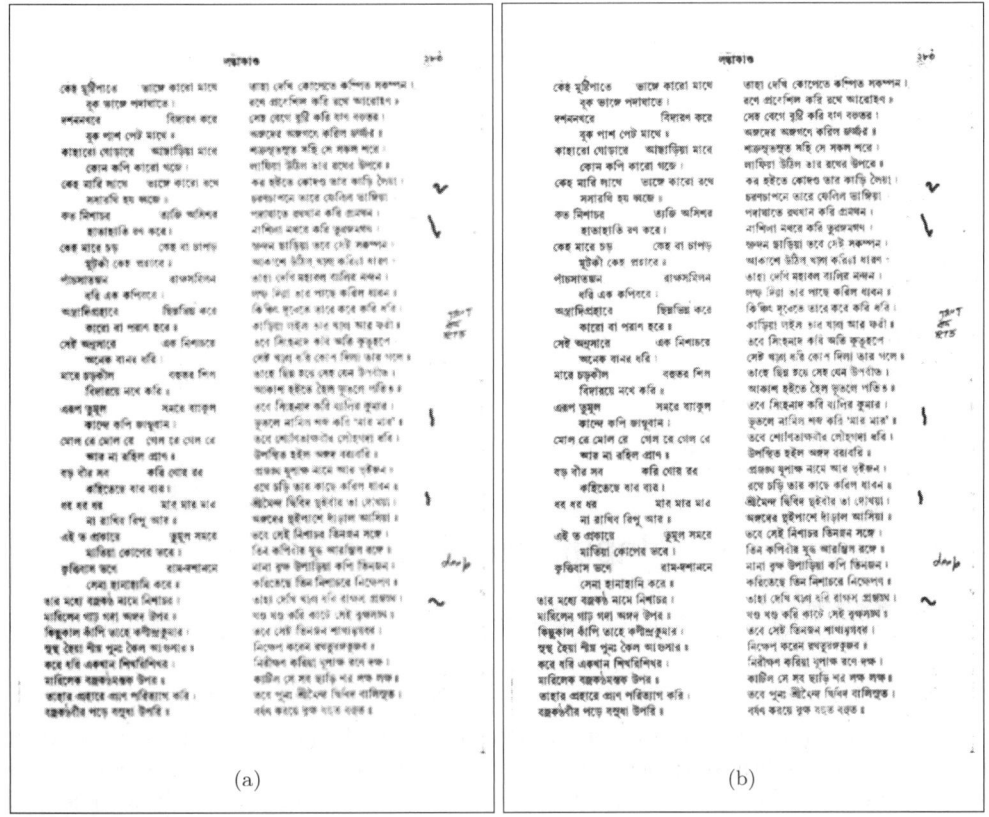

Figure 1.12 Results of thresholding on the document image of Fig. 1.8 by: (a) the Otsu thresholding technique (threshold value: 157), and (b) Bayesian approach (threshold value: 157).

1.4 | Contrast enhancement

In many image processing application, a preprocessing step of contrast adjustment is performed to enhance the image data, both for processing and better visualization. For example, contrast enhancement is performed on images before carrying out the Bayesian classification based binarization to make modes sharper in the histogram. An example of a contrast enhancement method is the *pixel mapping* technique. It is a technique where each brightness value of a pixel is mapped to a value in such a way that the dynamic range of the image increases. The dynamic range refers to the interval of pixel values in a given image. For example, consider a pixel mapping function in Fig. 1.13, where the original dynamic range is an interval from 0 to D, which is nearly half of the entire interval. After mapping, the transformed dynamic range spans from 0 to 255, which makes the image appear sharper in contrast. This processing of an image is called *contrast enhancement*.

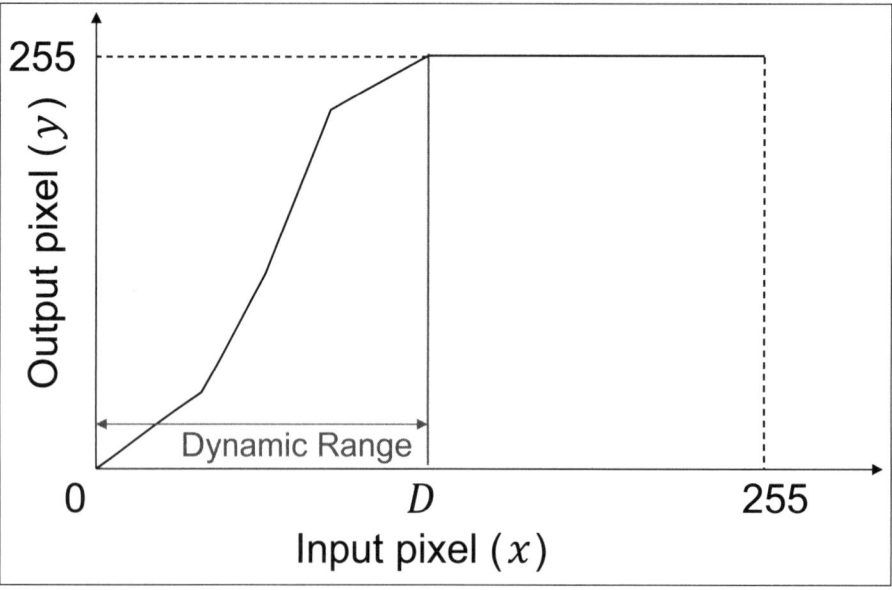

Figure 1.13 An example of pixel mapping function for contrast adjustment.

A necessary condition that such a mapping function should satisfy, is to preserve the relative order of brightness values between any pair of pixels. For instance, consider two pixels, x_1 and x_2. Let y_1 and y_2 be their corresponding mapped values. Then, the mapping should preserve their relative order of values. This implies that, if $x_1 < x_2$, then $y_1 \leq y_2$. A function satisfying this property is called *monotonically increasing function*. This property makes the mapping consistent for displaying the transformed image, so that relatively brighter pixels remain brighter and darker pixels remain darker, both before and after contrast adjustment.

One of the popular contrast mapping function is given in Eq. 1.8, which is the cumulative probability distribution function, of the brightness value x.

$$y = 255 \sum_{i=0}^{D} p(i) \tag{1.8}$$

The processing using the above pixel mapping function is also called *histogram equalization*, as it can be theoretical shown that the histogram of the resulting image tends to follow a uniform distribution. Consider an example of contrast enhancement that is shown in Fig. 1.14 using the mapping function of Eq. 1.8. In the contrast enhanced image, the visual features are more prominent. Also, by comparing the histograms of the image before and after contrast enhancement, the shape of the histograms appears similar, but the dynamic range has been expanded and the modes are more distinct. We may note that this processing is applied to the document image of Fig. 1.8 (a) before computation of the threshold for binarization using the Bayesian classification approach as discussed in Section 1.3.2.

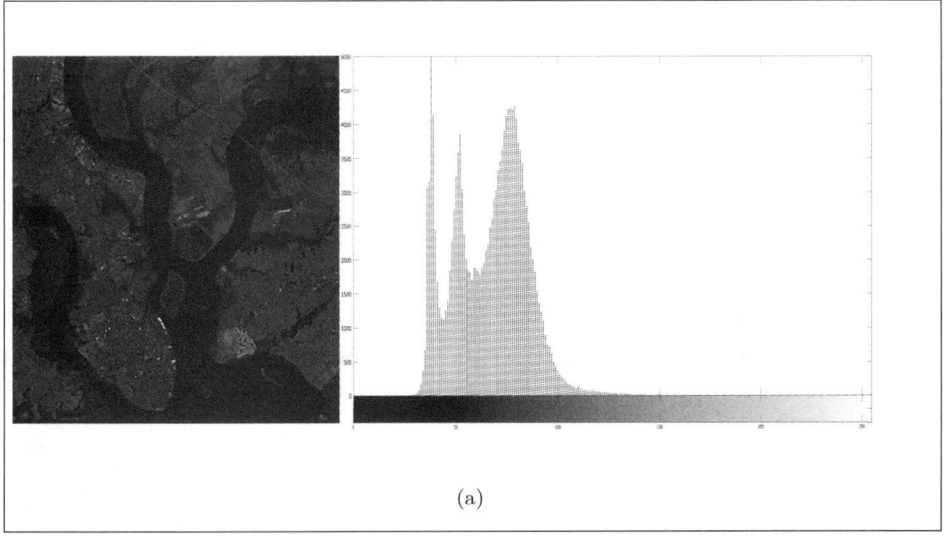

(a)

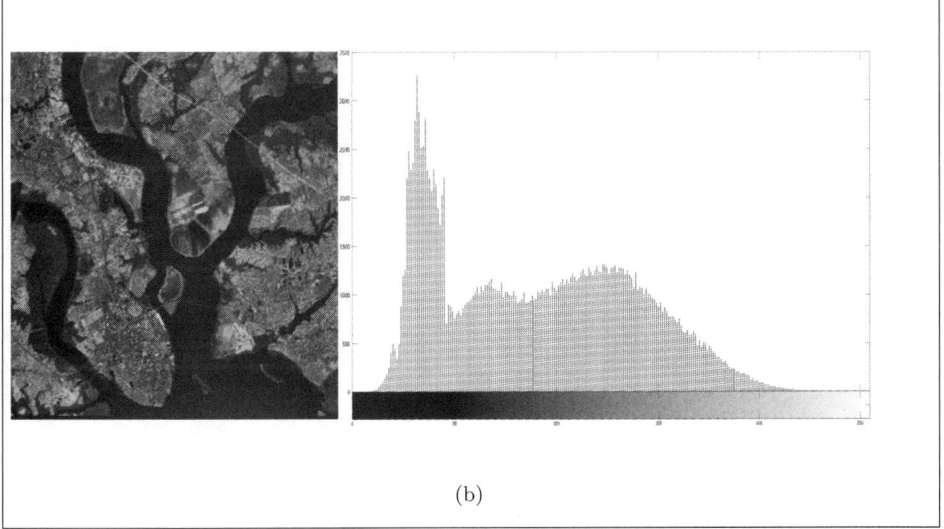

(b)

Figure 1.14 An example of histogram equalization.

Numerical Example

Suppose the brightness values of an image are normalized in $[0, 1]$. Show that the following function could be a pixel mapping function for contrast enhancement of an image.

$$f(x) = x(2 - x)$$

Given the brightness value of a pixel in an image varies between 0 to 255 and is an integer, compute the brightness value of a pixel in the enhanced image using the above function $f(x)$, if the value of that pixel in the original image is 140.

Solution

By differentiating $f(x)$, with respect to x, we get

$$f'(x) = 2 - 2x$$

As $f'(x)$ is nonnegative within $[0, 1]$, $f(x)$ is a monotonically increasing function within that normalized interval. Hence it is suitable to be used as a pixel mapping function.

At the brightness value 140 the normalized value $x = \frac{140}{255} = 0.55$. Hence $f(0.55) = (0.55)(2 - 0.55) = 0.7975$. Hence the mapped pixel value is: $255 * 0.7975 = 203$.

Numerical Example

Consider the following 5×5 image array and answer the following.

$$\begin{bmatrix} 3 & 3 & 3 & 6 & 4 \\ 2 & 2 & 0 & 0 & 4 \\ 1 & 2^* & 4 & 0 & 5 \\ 5 & 1 & 3 & 2 & 1 \\ 5 & 2 & 6 & 6 & 6 \end{bmatrix}$$

What is the value after histogram equalization at location $(2,1)$ shown with asterisk mark in the image array. Consider the top left corner of the matrix as $(0,0)$. Row and column indices increase as we move down and right starting from the $(0,0)$ position, respectively. Use round off operation while converting a continuous value to an integer during pixel mapping.

Solution

Computation of Histogram equalization is shown in the following table.

pixel (x) (x)	frequency $(h(x))$ $(h(x))$	cumulative freq. $(c(x))$ $(c(x))$	Mapped value $(y = 6\frac{c(x)}{25})$	New pixel value $(round(y))$
0	3	3	0.72	1
1	3	6	1.44	1
2	5	11	2.64	3
3	4	15	3.6	4
4	3	18	4.32	4
5	3	21	5.04	5
6	4	25	6	6

According to the above table pixel value 2 becomes 3.

1.5 | Image segmentation

Image segmentation[4] is a process of partitioning the pixels of an image into meaningful and nonoverlapping sets. The binarization of an image, discussed in Section 1.3, is a special case of image segmentation. In binarization, there are only two such sets for partitioning, one each for foreground and background, respectively. But, in general, it may be extended to more than two levels, where multiple groups of pixels are to be formed in an image. As an example, consider Fig. 1.15 to understand the multi-level thresholding scheme, where a satellite image and its corresponding histogram are shown. In case of binarization, there was only a single threshold to determine; whereas in multi-level thresholding, there are more than one thresholds to determine. The threshold values can either be manually chosen by visual inspection of modes in image histogram, or automatically computed using certain algorithms. In order to automate the computation of an optimized set of thresholds, similar techniques (See Section 6.5 of Chapter 6 for details.) may be used as discussed in Section 1.3, particularly the Bayesian classification method to determine a given number of threshold values.

In this particular example, let there be two thresholds at positions 60 and 119, as indicated by brighter lines on the histogram in Fig. 1.15. So, with these two thresholds, the histogram is divided into three intervals: $[0, 60]$, $[61, 119]$, and $[120, 255]$. A particular color is assigned to all the pixels in each of these intervals. Here, the three colors, blue, green, and yellow, represent the three segments formed by intervals, $[0, 60]$, $[61, 119]$, and $[120, 255]$, respectively. By visual inspection, the land cover classes corresponding to these nonoverlapping intervals are as follows:
The darker pixels that are in the interval $[0, 60]$ (blue zone) correspond to water bodies in the landscape. The pixels with values in the middle interval of $[61, 119]$ (green zone)

---

[4] Discussed in detail in Chapter 6.

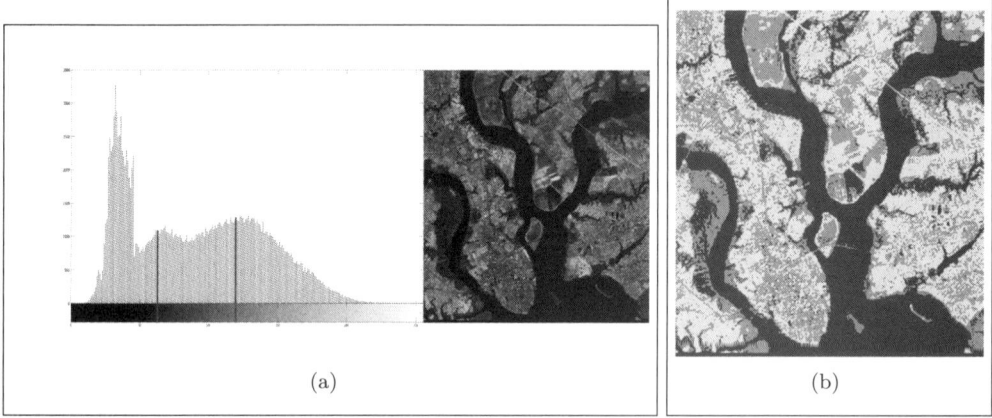

(a)   (b)

Figure 1.15 An example of multi-level threshloding of images. See Color Plates (page 803).

denote most of the vegetation and bare soil regions of the landscape. The brighter pixels that are in the interval of $[120, 255]$ (yellow zone) correspond to human settlement and urban regions of the landscape.

1.5.1 | Component labeling

Even after partitioning the pixels in an image into different groups, the task is often considered incomplete unless these segments are spatially bounded. So, the process of image segmentation is usually followed by a process known as *component labeling*. The objective of component labeling is to connect the similarly labeled image pixels into meaningful and nonoverlapping sets that are partitioned in the image plane. To define connectedness among pixels, various neighborhood relations are specified. Among the pixel neighborhood relations, 4-neighborhood and 8-neighborhood are two of the basic neighborhood definitions.

Consider the pixel layout shown in Fig. 1.16 (a). The pixels at locations that are marked 'o' form a 4-neighborhood of the center pixel. Suppose, (x, y) is the coordinate location of the central pixel, q. Then, the 4-neighborhood of (x, y) consists of pixels in its right, left, top, and bottom locations at $(x + 1, y)$, $(x - 1, y)$, $(x, y - 1)$, and $(x, y + 1)$, respectively. The pixels in the 4-neighborhood of a given pixel, q, are called 4-neighbors of q. If the neighborhood of a pixel, q, also consists of pixels at its diagonal locations, in addition to the 4-neighborhood, it is called 8-neighborhood of q. The pixel layout shown in Fig. 1.16 (b) represents 8-neighborhood of the central pixel.

According to the neighborhood definition that is considered, a connectivity is defined between two pixels in an image. Consider an example shown in Fig. 1.17 (a) to explain components preserving 8-connectivity of pixels. This is a small image of size 4×4 pixels, where each pixel labels are represented by a number. A graph is formed by considering every pixel as a node and an edge is formed between neighboring pixels that have same labels or pixel values. So, in this example, the four pixels with their value of 20, in the top left

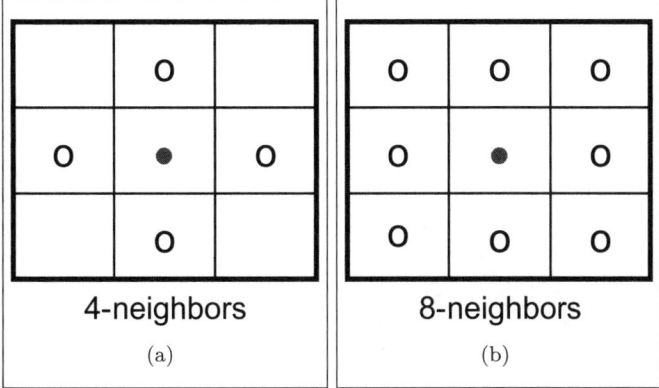

Figure 1.16 Pixel layout of (a) 4-neighborhood and (b) 8-neighborhood configurations.

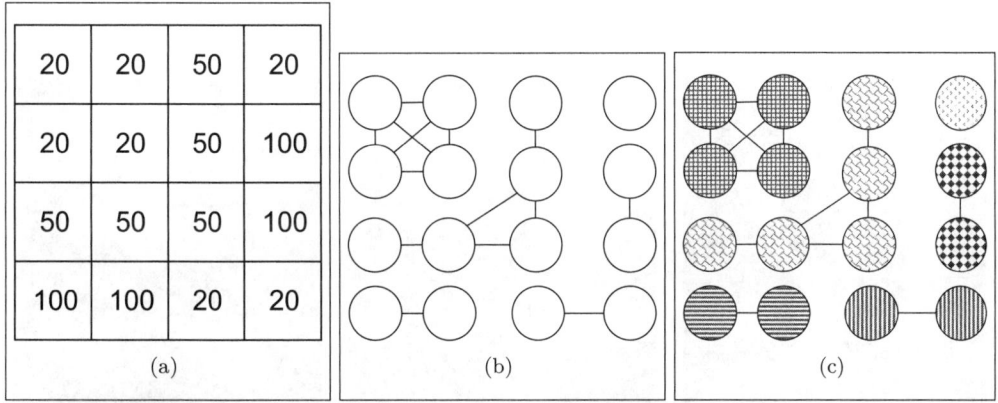

Figure 1.17 Graphical representation of connected pixels in an image according to the neighborhood definitions.

portion of the image, form edges among themselves between these pixels. Edges are formed between the five pixels with their values as 50 that are surrounding the cluster of pixels in the top left portion. Similarly, edges are formed between two pixels with their values of 100, two pixels with their values of 20, and another instance of two pixels with their values of 100. There is also an isolated pixel with the value 20, which does not have any neighbor with the same label. Hence, there is no edge connected to it. This gives a graphical representation of the considered 4×4 image following the neighborhood definitions, which is shown in Fig. 1.17 (b).

The next task is to compute the components of the graph by using any of the graph traversal algorithms, like the breadth first search (BFS) or the depth first search (DFS) algorithms (Cormen et al., 2009). Then, each of these components are declared as a segment of the graph. An example is shown in Fig. 1.17 (c), where each segment of the graph is displayed in a different pattern, which also represents individual components in the graph.

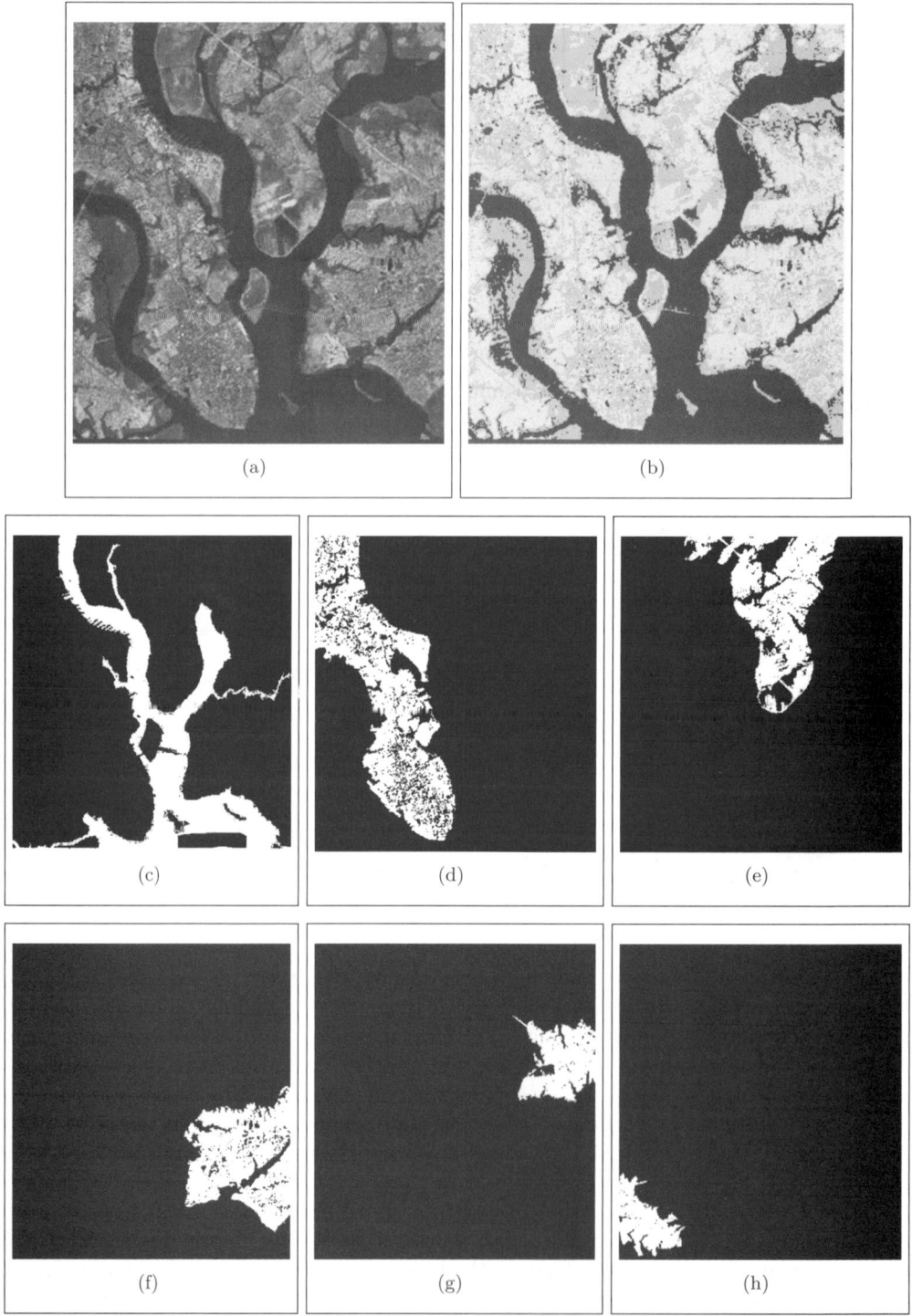

Figure 1.18 An example of extracting connected components from a satellite imagery. (a) Input image. (b) Segmented image. (c)–(h) Different connected components in (a). See Color Plates (page 804).

In fact, it is not necessary to have such explicit graph representation of an image, since the neighborhood definitions that are defined on image arrays are very precise and have a well organized structure. So, the components are computed using only the given image array. However, for the ease of understanding the concept of components, an explicit representation of an image as a graph is illustrated.

Consider the example of a satellite image shown in Fig. 1.15, which is segmented into three segments corresponding to three nonoverlapping intervals. In Fig. 1.18, the connected components that are formed from these segments are shown. Among many components that can be formed in this image, only six prominent components are shown here for reference in the descending order of number of pixels in each connected component. The first connected component, component-1 in the figure, which is the largest component, corresponds to a major part of river channel in the landscape that covers most of the blue zone in the segmented image. The second largest component, component-2, corresponds to large contiguous chunk of vegetation, which is a part of green zone in the segmented image. The third largest component, component-3, consists of some connected portions from the yellow zone of the segmented image that represents human settlement and urban regions. Similarly, various connected components are also retrieved from these segments that correspond to each of blue, green, or yellow zones in the segmented image.

Each component that is retrieved from the segmented image is connected with reference to the definition of pixel connectivity. Even within same segment, if connectivity is not established between some of the pixels, it would result in forming multiple components for the same segment. For example, observe component-1 in Fig. 1.18, particularly near top right portion of the satellite image. The river channel of the landscape is clearly visible in the segmented image as blue zone in that portion of the image, but it is not included in component-1, though it is visibly a large region. This is because, the chunk of pixels in that portion of the image are not connected with the pixels belonging to component-1. So, pixel connectivity could not be established with those pixels and component-1 due to discontinuity in the river channel by the presence of a bridge.

1.6 | Image gradients

One of the fundamental operations in image processing is computation of gradient values at pixels in images. An image is a 2-D function. In a 2-D function, a gradient vector is defined by the corresponding partial derivatives along its two principal directions. Usually, for a 2-D function in rectangular coordinate system, as in images, x and y axes are conventionally used as principle directions. For a function, $f(x, y)$, the partial derivatives with respect to x and y directions are given by Eqs. 1.9 and 1.10, respectively.

$$\frac{\partial f(x, y)}{\partial x} = f(x + 1, y) - f(x, y) \tag{1.9}$$

$$\frac{\partial f(x, y)}{\partial y} = f(x, y + 1) - f(x, y) \tag{1.10}$$

These partial derivatives together form a vector known as the gradient vector, which is given by Eq. 1.11.

$$\nabla f(x,y) = \frac{\partial f(x,y)}{\partial x}\hat{i} + \frac{\partial f(x,y)}{\partial y}\hat{j} \tag{1.11}$$

where $\hat{i}$ and $\hat{j}$ are unit vectors along the x and the y directions, respectively.

As it can be seen, the computation of the gradient is a direct and simple process. For an image, the finite difference method is used to compute the gradients at each pixel location. Along the x direction, it is the difference between the right neighbor of the considered pixel and the pixel itself. Similarly, along the y direction, it is the difference between the bottom neighbor of the considered pixel and the pixel itself. The functional value at every pixel position is a simple difference operation with which the gradient vectors are computed.

These computations may also be described under a general framework by using masks, which extends the understanding and applicability of these operations. For the gradient computation, the difference operation at every pixel is performed by defining a mask, instead of defining the operation at every pixel location. A mask is an array of elements of specified size. For example, consider the mask in Fig. 1.19 (right). It is a mask with 2×1 elements, which is an 1-dimensional (1-D) array, and the values in the mask represent weights. In a 2-D representation, there are two rows and one column in this mask. For computing the image gradients along the vertical direction, at first, this mask has to be placed at every pixel position of the image. One of the points in the mask corresponds to the central pixel position, which is placed at (x,y) location of the image, as shown in Fig. 1.19. After placing the mask at a pixel location, a weighted sum of the values of the underlying image pixels that are defined by the coverage of the mask at every location, is computed.

Here, the functional values at (x,y) and $(x,y+1)$ pixel locations are multiplied with -1, and 1, respectively. The corresponding operation is shown in Eq. 1.12.

$$g(x,y) = (1)f(x,y+1) + (-1)f(x,y) \tag{1.12}$$

where, $g(x,y)$ is the vertical gradient value and $f(x,y)$ is the functional value.

Obtaining the weighted sum of the pixel values as shown in Eq. 1.12, is effectively equivalent to computing the difference between the pixel values at $(x,y+1)$ and (x,y), which provides the gradient values at (x,y). So, for computing the vertical gradients of the

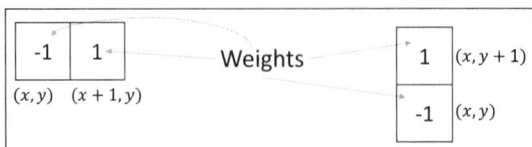

Figure 1.19 A figurative description for computation with mask.

entire image, the same operation is performed at every pixel by scanning the image in a spatial order (e.g., from left-to-right and top-to-bottom).

To summarize the above discussion on the computation with mask, we note the following.

(i) At every point, (x, y), of the image, the mask is placed, and the weighted sum by multiplying the corresponding functional values in image and weights in the mask is computed.

(ii) Then, the central value at each (x, y) is replaced by this weighted sum. With respect to the masks shown in Fig. 1.19, it provides the gradient values at that pixel location.

Using these vertical and horizontal gradients, gradient vectors are computed at each pixel location, (x, y) as in Eq. 1.11.

1.6.1 | Robust computation of gradients

For making a robust gradient computation, a neighborhood region around each pixel is considered for computing finite differences. In this neighborhood region, the statistics of finite differences are computed and the mean of that distribution is taken, instead of computing the differences only with the immediate right/left neighbor or top/bottom neighbor of each pixel.

Prewitt operator

Consider the gradient mask shown in Fig. 1.20 (a). This is a 3×3 mask with its central position at the middle of the mask that is placed over (x, y) location. With respect to this central position, finite differences are computed along horizontal direction using each pair of neighbors that are shown by encircling with ellipses. That is, this 3×3 mask is equivalently expressing the sum of the operations with six 1×2 masks for computing gradients in the horizontal direction. In this way, the finite differences are computed six times around the

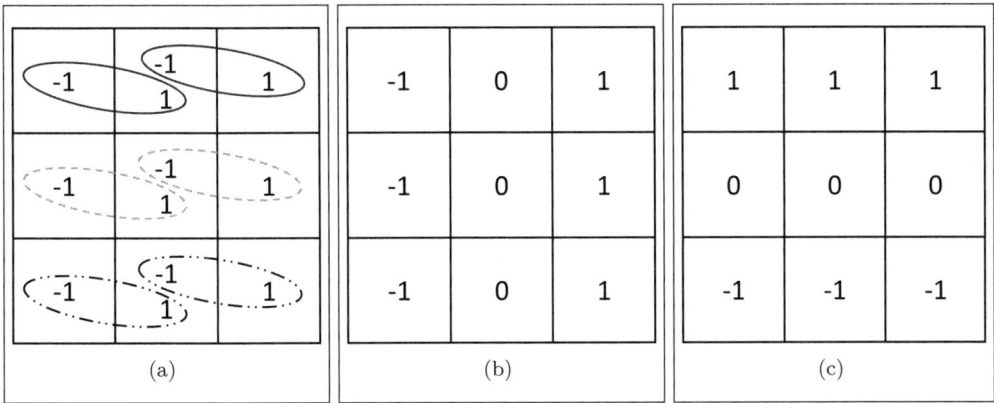

Figure 1.20 Prewitt operator for gradient computation.

neighborhood. So, by taking the average of these computed values, the noise or the error in the gradient computation is reduced. Since the resulting mask (operator) is a linear combination of six elementary masks of computing horizontal gradients, they all may be carried out equivalently operating with a single mask as shown in Fig. 1.20 (b). As it can be seen from the computations, at each cell of the mask in Fig. 1.20 (a), the weights are simply being added. So, in the middle column, the weight at each cell becomes 0 due to addition of 1 and −1. In the same way, the gradients in vertical direction are computed using the 3 × 3 mask shown in Fig. 1.20 (c), which is equivalent to computing the gradient values six times with 2 × 1 masks in vertical direction. The two masks shown in Fig. 1.20 (b) and (c) are called *Prewitt operators*.

Sobel operator

Another example of robust computation of gradients is shown in Fig. 1.21. In this case, central gradients are weighed more than off-centric gradients. For instance, in the mask for computing gradients in the horizontal direction, a central gradient is given a weight of 2, as opposed to an off-centric gradient carrying a weight of 1. Even in this case, every value in the cell under the mask in Fig. 1.21 (a) is computed by the sum of the corresponding pixel values that are multiplied with the respective weights. Thus, the distribution of the weights in a single mask is shown in Fig. 1.21 (b), which is equivalent to computing the gradient values in horizontal direction eight times with 1 × 2 masks. Similarly, for gradients in vertical direction, the mask in Fig. 1.21 (c) is used. These masks in Fig. 1.21 (b) and (c) are known as *Sobel operators*.

Roberts operator

The mask shown in Fig. 1.22 is used to compute the image gradients along the diagonal directions. Here, difference of diagonally adjacent pixels is considered for computing the gradients, as opposed to horizontal and vertical directions. So, instead of having conventional

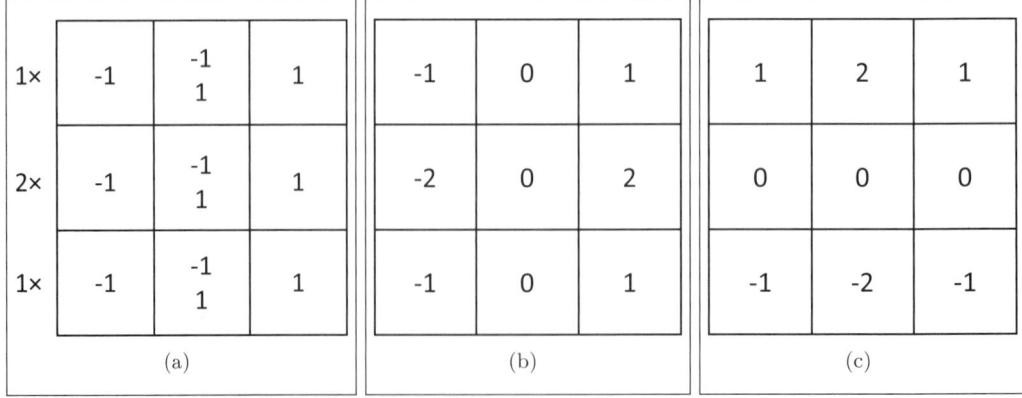

Figure 1.21 Sobel operator for gradient computation.

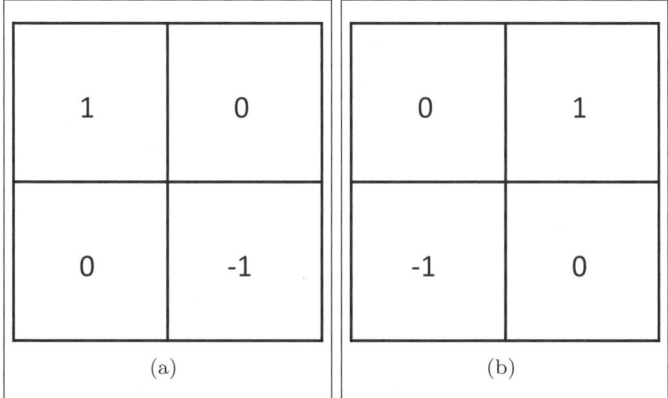

Figure 1.22 Roberts operator for gradient computation along directions with angles with respect to horizontal axis: (a) 135°, and (b) 45°.

x and y directions for gradients, the gradients are computed at 45^0 and 135^0 to x axis, which highlights the changes in images at diagonal directions. Due to its cross directionality, it is also called the *cross operator*. It is similar to computing gradients by taking finite differences between pixels that are immediate diagonal neighbors that is shown in Fig. 1.19, except for the direction in which the neighbors are considered. Unlike Prewitt and Sobel operators, this mask does not show any equivalence with averaging of gradient values obtained as a linear combination of multiple estimates. So, the gradient values resulting from the Roberts operator are comparatively more sensitive to noise.

The results obtained by using the Prewitt operators on an image are shown in Fig. 1.23. The original image is shown in (a), and different gradient images are shown in Fig. 1.23 (b)–(d). The image in Fig. 1.23 (b) shows the horizontal gradients, where the

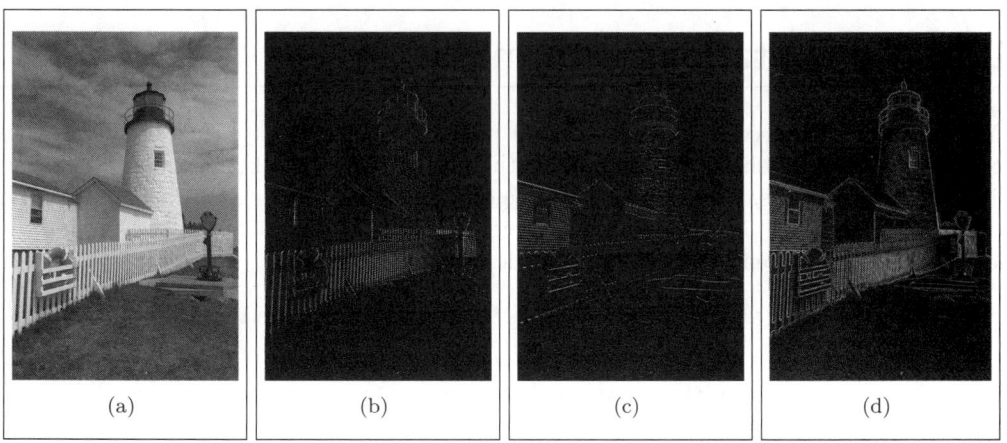

Figure 1.23 Examples of results obtained by using Prewitt gradient operator. (a) Original image, (b) horizontal gradients, (c) vertical gradients, and (d) resultant gradients.

vertical edges in image that are perpendicular to the ground appear prominent. Similarly, the image in Fig. 1.23 (c) shows the vertical gradients, where the horizontal edges in the image that are parallel to the ground appear prominent. We may note that the direction of an edge at a pixel is orthogonal (perpendicular) to the direction of the gradient vector at that pixel. A resultant image is obtained by computing the magnitude of the gradient vector at every pixel. In the resultant image shown in Fig. 1.23 (d), all edge pixels in every direction and the corresponding boundary points of different objects in the image appear prominent.

Numerical Example

Consider the following 5×5 image array and a 3×3 edge operator.

```
3  4  5   6  7
2  1  0*  3  1
5  9  6   0  1        1   2   1
1  4  3   2  1        0   0   0
7  2  1   8  9       -1  -2  -1
```

What is the output of applying 3×3 edge operator at the location shown with the asterisk mark in the image array.

Solution

$1 \times 4 + 2 \times 5 + 1 \times 6 + 0 \times 1 + 0 \times 0 + 0 \times 3 + (-1) \times 9 + (-2) \times 6 + (-1) \times 0 = -1.$

1.7 | Computations with masks

Computations with specific masks to obtain image gradients as explained in the previous section can be generalized to compute with any arbitrary mask having any arbitrary distribution of weights. Consider an example of a 3×3 mask[5] as shown in Fig. 1.24. The computation involved in obtaining the weighted sum of the pixel values around the neighborhood of the central pixel, (x, y), is described in Eq. 1.13.

$$
\begin{aligned}
g(x, y) = {} & w_1 f(x - 1, y + 1) + w_2 f(x, y + 1) + w_3 f(x + 1, y + 1) \\
& + w_4 f(x - 1, y) + w_c f(x, y) + w_5 f(x + 1, y) \\
& + w_6 f(x - 1, y - 1) + w_7 f(x, y - 1) + w_8 f(x + 1, y - 1)
\end{aligned}
\tag{1.13}
$$

where, $f(x, y)$ and $g(x, y)$ are the pixel values of input and output images at (x, y).

---

[5] The mask can be of any dimension.

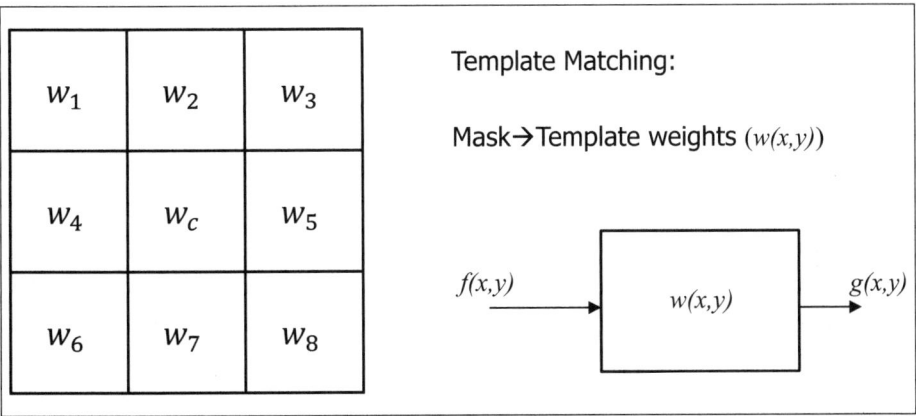

Figure 1.24 Figurative description for computation with masks.

Numerical Example

Suppose the following 3×3 mask is operated with an image of size 4×4 assuming zero padding at the boundary.

	Mask			Image		
0	1	0	4	11	21	6
1	−2	1	12	19	15	5
0	1	0	10	1	p	3
			9	17	12	2

(i) Compute the output image.

(ii) What value of the pixel p would make the value in its corresponding location of the output image to be 15?

Solution

Let the mask and image be denoted by m and I, respectively. After operating the mask on the image I with zero padding in its borders, the output matrix is obtained as,

$$I * m = \begin{bmatrix} 0 & 1 & 0 \\ 1 & -2 & 1 \\ 0 & 1 & 0 \end{bmatrix} * \begin{bmatrix} 4 & 11 & 21 & 6 \\ 12 & 19 & 15 & 5 \\ 10 & 1 & p & 3 \\ 9 & 17 & 12 & 2 \end{bmatrix} = \begin{bmatrix} 15 & 22 & -10 & 14 \\ 9 & 1 & 15+p & 14 \\ 2 & 44+p & 31-2p & 1+p \\ 9 & -12 & p-5 & 11 \end{bmatrix}$$

After the operation,[6] the value in the output matrix at the location corresponding to p of I is $31 - 2p$. So, if $31 - 2p = 15$, the value of p should be 8.

1.7.1 | Correlation and convolution

The computation with any arbitrary mask as discussed in the previous section is known as *correlation operation*. The given mask is placed at every pixel location of the image, and the weighted sum of the neighboring pixel values is the result of this operation. The mathematical expression for the cross correlation of an image $f(x, y)$ with a $(2k + 1) \times (2k + 1)$ mask $w(x, y)$ is given below.

$$g(x, y) = w(x, y) \bullet f(x, y) = \sum_{u=-k}^{k} \sum_{v=-k}^{k} w(u, v) f(x + u, y + v) \qquad (1.14)$$

As we see in the above that the computation with the mask is directly associated with the correlation operation. The operator '$\bullet$' is used to denote the correlation operation between two functions. Here, the correlation operation measures the similarity between $w(x, y)$ and $f(x, y)$.

A closely related operation, which is also performed using a mask almost in the similar fashion is the *convolution operation*. A convolution operation is meant for computing the output function, given an input function to a linear shift invariant system, which is characterized by its *unit impulse response*. The unit impulse response of a linear shift invariant system is its output when the given input is a unit impulse. In discrete system, a unit impulse is represented by the functional value of 1 at the origin of the space, and 0 in every other points. The symbol, $*$ is used for mathematical representation of a convolution operation. The mathematical expression of the linear convolution of an image $f(x, y)$ with a $(2k + 1) \times (2k + 1)$ mask $h(x, y)$ is given below.

$$g(x, y) = f(x, y) * h(x, y) = \sum_{u=-k}^{k} \sum_{v=-k}^{k} f(x - u, y - v) h(u, v) \qquad (1.15)$$

With reference to Fig. 1.24, the processed value, $g(x, y)$, is obtained using the input function $f(x, y)$ and the unit impulse response $h(x, y)$, where $h(x, y) = w(-x, -y)$. If the mask is symmetric, i.e., $w(x, y) = w(-x, -y)$, the results of convolution and correlation operations are the same. Thus computation of gradients using Sobel and Prewitt operators

---

[6] Calculation of each element is given by,

$$= \begin{bmatrix} (4)(-2)+(11)(1)+(12)(1) & (11)(-2)+(4)(1)+(21)(1)+(19)(1) & (21)(-2)+(11)(1)+(6)(1)+(15)(1) & (6)(-2)+(21)(1)+(5)(1) \\ (12)(-2)+(4)(1)+(10)(1)+(19)(1) & (19)(-2)+(11)(1)+(12)(1)+(15)(1)+(1)(1) & (15)(-2)+(21)(1)+(19)(1)+(5)(1)+(p)(1) & (5)(-2)+(6)(1)+(15)(1)+(3)(1) \\ (10)(-2)+(12)(1)+(1)(1)+(9)(1) & (1)(-2)+(19)(1)+(10)(1)+(p)(1)+(17)(1) & (p)(-2)+(15)(1)+(1)(1)+(3)(1)+(12)(1) & (3)(-2)+(5)(1)+(p)(1)+(2)(1) \\ (9)(-2)+(10)(1)+(17)(1) & (17)(-2)+(1)(1)+(9)(1)+(12)(1) & (12)(-2)+(p)(1)+(17)(1)+(2)(1) & (2)(-2)+(3)(1)+(12)(1) \end{bmatrix}.$$

are equivalent to both the correlation and the convolution operations. This process is also known as *filtering*, which is a frequency domain or transform domain terminology that is discussed in Chapter 2. The masks are also referred to as *filters*, and the weights in a mask define a discrete unit impulse response or a *filter response*.

Numerical Example

Consider the mask B of size 3×3 and an image A of size 3×3, as follows.

1	2	3	100	125	50
4	−10	2	50	90	80
1	4	3	70	100	50

Provide the output of convolution and correlation operations between them assuming the boundary of A is zero padded.

Solution

The image after zero padding becomes —

0	0	0	0	0
0	100	125	50	0
0	50	90	80	0
0	70	100	50	0
0	0	0	0	0

Correlation

Mask for correlation —

1	2	3
4	−10	2
1	4	3

Steps —

0×1	0×2	0×3	0	0
0×4	100×-10	125×2	50	0
0×1	50×4	90×3	80	0
0	70	100	50	0
0	0	0	0	0

0	0	0	0	0
0	**−280**	125	50	0
0	50	90	80	0
0	70	100	50	0
0	0	0	0	0

The mask is shifted throughout the image, and the result of correlation is computed at each location. The following result is obtained —

0	0	0	0	0
0	−280	−100	410	0
0	835	580	85	0
0	−130	−150	150	0
0	0	0	0	0

Convolution

Mask for convolution —

3	4	1
2	−10	4
3	2	1

Steps —

0×3	0×4	0×1	0	0
0×2	100×-10	125×4	50	0
0×3	50×2	90×1	80	0
0	70	100	50	0
0	0	0	0	0

0	0	0	0	0
0	**−310**	125	50	0
0	50	90	80	0
0	70	100	50	0
0	0	0	0	0

The mask is shifted throughout the image, and the result of convolution is computed at each location. The following result is obtained −

0	0	0	0	0
0	−310	−440	180	0
0	625	830	355	0
0	−10	−70	290	0
0	0	0	0	0

1.7.2 | Noise filtering

One particular example of filtering operation is noise filtering in images, which is shown in Fig. 1.25. The mask used in filtering the noise in this example is also shown in Fig. 1.25 (a). It can be seen that, all the values of weights in the mask are positive, which gives a weighted combination of neighboring pixel values at every central pixel location. Also, the sum of all the weights in the mask is equal to 1, which makes the operation as weighted average of the neighboring pixel values (including the central pixel). This mask exhibits a kind of low pass filtering action on the input noisy image in Fig. 1.25 (b), when it is applied on the image by performing convolution operation to replace each original noisy pixel by the weighted sum of pixel values around its neighborhood. The processed image, after filtering with the mask, is seen less noisy, as in Fig. 1.25 (c).

Gaussian filtering

A special case of this kind of filtering operation, which is often used in image processing, is *Gaussian filtering or Gaussian smoothing*. While designing the filter or the mask to perform convolution operation on the image, the weights of the mask are computed from the Gaussian distribution, which is given in Eq. 1.16.

$$G(x, y) = \frac{1}{2\pi\sigma^2} e^{-\frac{((x-x_c)^2 + (y-y_c)^2)}{2\sigma^2}} \tag{1.16}$$

where, $G(x, y)$ is the Gaussian function, x_c and y_c are the mean values of the distribution along x and y variables, and σ is the standard deviation of the distribution. With reference to masks, the origin of this distribution lies at the central pixel position of the mask. The standard deviation or the width of the Gaussian distribution determine the size of the mask, such that, most of the significant functional values around the center pixel are captured by it. For example, a processed image, $g(x, y)$, that is obtained by the convolution operation between an image, $f(x, y)$, and a Gaussian mask defined by Eq. 1.16, $G(x, y)$, is expressed as in Eq. 1.17.

$$g(x, y) = f(x, y) * G(x, y) \tag{1.17}$$

The result of this convolution operation is shown in Fig. 1.26 (b) using a Gaussian mask with $\sigma = 2$ and size $= 9 \times 9$.

Median filtering

Another notable noise filtering method is *median filtering*, where computations do not use convolution. It is a simple approach, where the median value among the neighboring pixels within a specified neighborhood of a pixel (x, y) is computed to provide the processed value at that location. An example of median filtering on the image in Fig. 1.25 (a) is shown in Fig. 1.26 (b). It is an example of a nonlinear filter, which is very effective in reducing noise like spot noise and salt-and-pepper noise that appear as random dots scattered over the image.

c	b	c
b	a	b
c	b	c

(a)

(b)

(c)

Figure 1.25 An example of noise filtering. (a) Filter used for denoising. (b) Original image. (c) Filtered image using the mask shown beside. Here, $a = 0.5$, $b = \frac{0.3}{4}$, $c = \frac{0.2}{4}$.

(a) (b)

Figure 1.26 Examples of filtering operations on the noisy image shown in Fig. 1.26 (a). (a) Gaussian smoothing with $\sigma = 2$ and mask size is 9×9. (b) Median filtering with a window size of 5×5.

1.8 | Image morphology

Mathematical morphology is a framework used to analyze and process images. It provides a set of mathematical tools for extracting morphological features from images, enhancing their quality, and analyzing their structure. In this context, it is often referred to as *image morphology*. Image morphological operations are a set of nonlinear operations that relate to the shape or morphology of features in an image. The operations are defined using the concepts of set theory and involve processing of an image by a structuring element. Morphological operations are particularly useful in the preprocessing of images, object extraction, and structure manipulation, which are widely used in various applications. For example,

- Object Segmentation: Morphological operations aid in separating objects from the background, such as, removing small specks and connecting broken regions. In medical imaging, morphological operations are extensively used. They are found to be useful in segmenting anatomical structures, e.g., blood vessels, tumors, etc., from medical images.

- Feature Extraction: By analyzing morphological properties, features like texture, shape, and size may be extracted. Convex hulls and skeletons that are derived from image morphology provide valuable information for object recognition.

- Quality Enhancement: Morphological operations may be used to improve image quality by removing noise and refining edges.

The morphological operations are primarily defined for binary images, and their definitions are also extended to gray scale and color images. The mathematical morphology that focuses on processing only binary images is known as *binary image morphology*. In a binary image, as a convention, pixels with a value of 1 are considered foreground and pixels with a value of 0 are considered background. In binary morphology, an image, $\mathbf{I}$, is represented as a set of points, (x, y), in $\mathbb{Z}^2$. Consequently, two subsets are defined using a set of pixels belonging to the foreground region that represent the object pixels (1's), and another set of pixels that belong to the background region (0's). In this way, an object may be represented by a set of points, where each member of this set represents an object point. Let the set of object pixels be denoted as $\mathbf{I}_{fg}$ and the set of background pixels be denoted as $\mathbf{I}_{bg}$. Any point of the image that does not belong to $\mathbf{I}_{fg}$ falls into its complement set, representing the background. Therefore, it is sufficient to represent only the object points in an image, since $\mathbf{I}_{bg} = \mathbf{I}_{fg}^c$, where the superscript ^{c} indicates the *Boolean complement operator*. So, when an image is represented as a set of points (marked by the value 1), by convention, it represents the set of points belonging to the foreground objects. With this representation of an image as a set of points, all the morphological operations on an image are also defined as set operations.

Here, besides basic operations on sets like, *union, intersection, complement, difference*, etc., two particular set operations are used in the definitions of fundamental morphological operations, namely *reflection* and *translation* of a set. The reflection of a set $\mathbf{S} \in \mathbb{Z}^2$, denoted by $\hat{\mathbf{S}}$, is defined as the set of points obtained by negating the coordinates of the points of $\mathbf{S}$. That is,

$$\hat{\mathbf{S}} = \{\boldsymbol{p} | \boldsymbol{p} = -\boldsymbol{s}, \ \forall \boldsymbol{s} \in \mathbf{S}\} \tag{1.18}$$

The translation of a set $\mathbf{S} = \{\boldsymbol{s} \in \mathbb{Z}^n\}$ by a vector $\boldsymbol{t} \in \mathbb{Z}^n$, represented as $\mathbf{S}_t$, is defined as the set obtained by translating all the points of $\mathbf{S}$ by $\boldsymbol{t}$ implying the coordinates of a point are added with the respective components of the translation vector. That is,

$$\mathbf{S}_t = \{\boldsymbol{q} | \boldsymbol{q} = \boldsymbol{s} + \boldsymbol{t}, \ \forall \boldsymbol{s} \in \mathbf{S}\} \tag{1.19}$$

Particularly, in application to image processing, $\mathbf{S}$ is the set of object or foreground points of an image, $\mathbf{I} = \{\boldsymbol{s} \in \mathbb{Z}^2\}$. Hence, by considering the representation of an image as a set of points in 2-D space, each point may be represented by a 2-D vector, $\boldsymbol{s} = (x, y)$.

The morphological transformations involve binary operations between an image, $\mathbf{I}$ and a smaller image (or template) called *structuring element*, $\mathbf{S_e}$. The computation is similar to the computation with a mask, where the structuring element is described in the mask. Just as with the computation with a mask, morphological transformations involve translating the structuring element across the given image, and transforming the value of the central pixel. The structuring element is also a binary image where object points are denoted by 1 and the background is denoted by 0. It may describe any shape, such as, square, rectangle, disk, etc. For example, in a square structural element of 9×9, all the pixels in a 9×9 array have the value of 1.

The two fundamental morphological operations are,

(i) Dilation: It usually adds pixels to the boundaries of foreground objects in an image, and

(ii) Erosion: It usually removes pixels from the boundaries of foreground objects in an image.

1.8.1 | Dilation

The dilation operation on an image, $\mathbf{I}$, using a structuring element $\mathbf{S_e}$, both in $\mathbb{Z}^2$, is defined as follows.

$$\mathbf{I} \oplus \mathbf{S_e} = \{\boldsymbol{p} | (\hat{\mathbf{S}_e})_{\boldsymbol{p}} \cap \mathbf{I} \neq \emptyset\} \tag{1.20}$$

where, $\oplus$ denotes the dilation operation and $\boldsymbol{p}$ is a point in the set $\mathbf{I}$. The above definition implies that the dilation of $\mathbf{I}$ with the structuring element $\mathbf{S}_e$ provides the set of all points, $\boldsymbol{p}$, such that, the reflection of the structuring element being translated at $\boldsymbol{p}$ hits the image $\mathbf{I}$. This is the same as checking whether the intersection between $\mathbf{I}$ and the set obtained by translation of reflection of $\mathbf{S_e}$ at $\boldsymbol{p}$ results in a nonempty set of points. If at the center of the structuring element, there exists an object point, all the foreground points of the image remain in the dilated image. This implies that, in such a case, $\mathbf{I}$ is a subset of the resulting set obtained from dilation. In this case, all points in the foreground of $\mathbf{I}$ are also the members of $\mathbf{I} \oplus \mathbf{S_e}$. Dilation operation may be applied on an image more than once to repeatedly expand the object boundaries.

An example of dilation operation on a binary image is shown in Fig. 1.27. The image as shown in Fig. 1.27 (a) is dilated by a square structural element of size 9×9. The resulting image is shown in Fig. 1.27 (b), where we observe that the boundary of the foreground object is expanded, while the holes are shrunk in size or get eliminated. In this case, two small holes in the original image get eliminated or filled by object points in the dilated image. This is because of their widths smaller or equal to half the width of the 9×9 structuring element.

1.8.2 | Erosion

The erosion operation on an image, $\mathbf{I}$, using a structuring element $\mathbf{S_e}$, both in $\mathbb{Z}^2$, is defined as follows.

$$\mathbf{I} \ominus \mathbf{S_e} = \{\boldsymbol{p} | (\mathbf{S_e})_{\boldsymbol{p}} \subseteq \mathbf{I}\} \tag{1.21}$$

where, $\ominus$ denotes the erosion operation, $\boldsymbol{p}$ is a point (pixel) in $\mathbb{Z}^2$. In this case, the resulting set consists of all points, $\boldsymbol{p}$, such that, the translation of $\mathbf{S_e}$ at $\boldsymbol{p}$ fits within $\mathbf{I}$. This is the same as checking whether the translated $\mathbf{S_e}$ at $\boldsymbol{p}$ is a subset of $\mathbf{I}$. If at the origin of the structuring element there exists an object point, the eroded image is a subset of the original image. It includes only those points of the image where the foreground pattern of the structuring element is fully embedded in it. Thus, in this case, only a subset of points in the foreground of $\mathbf{I}$ are the members of $\mathbf{I} \ominus \mathbf{S_e}$. Similar to dilation operation, erosion may also be applied on an image more than once to repeatedly shrink the object boundaries.

(a)   (b)   (c)

Figure 1.27 Dilation and erosion operations on a binary image using a square structural element of size 9×9. (a) Binary image, (b) result of dilation operation, and (c) result of erosion operation.

An example of erosion operation on a binary image is shown in Fig. 1.27. The image as shown Fig. 1.27 (a) is eroded by a square structural element of size 9×9. As a result, in Fig. 1.27 (c), the boundaries of the foreground object are shrunk, while the holes among them are expanded in size. In Fig. 1.27 (c), we may observe that a narrow passage between two background regions is eliminated, as its width is less than half the width of the structuring element.

The erosion and dilation operations are duals of each other, with respect to set complement and reflection properties as expressed below.

$$(\mathbf{I} \ominus \mathbf{S_e})^c = \mathbf{I}^c \oplus \hat{\mathbf{S}}_\mathbf{e}$$
$$(\mathbf{I} \oplus \mathbf{S_e})^c = \mathbf{I}^c \ominus \hat{\mathbf{S}}_\mathbf{e}$$

(1.22)

As dilation and erosion operations result in opposite effects in an image, they may be applied back-to-back using the same structuring element for retaining same sizes of objects in an image. Such combinations of erosion and dilation define morphological *opening* and *closing* operations.

1.8.3 | Closing and opening

Consider the binary images shown in Figs. 1.28 (a) and (d). By applying dilation operation using a square structuring element, the holes in the foreground region are filled-up with white pixels, as seen in Figs. 1.28 (b) and (e). However, in this process, the boundaries of the foreground objects have expanded due to dilation. This is an undesired effect, since it is necessary to retain the original shape of the objects. By applying erosion operation using the same structuring element as in the dilation, the boundaries of the objects are shrunk to their original size, but the filled up holes in the dilated image do not appear in the resulting

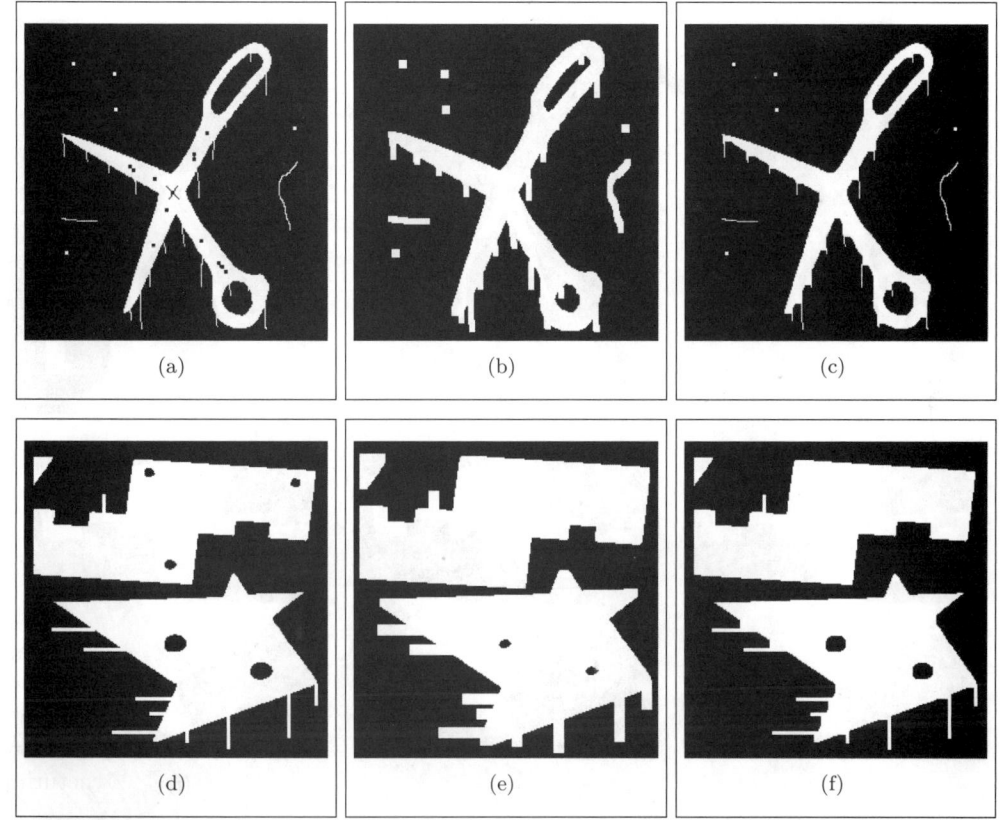

Figure 1.28 Example of closing: (a,d) original noisy images, (b,e) dilation operation on original images, and (c,f) erosion of dilated images.

image (Figs. 1.28 (c) and (f)). However, the noisy streaks in the background region are not eliminated. This sequence of operations, i.e., the dilation followed by the erosion with the same structuring element, is called *morphological closing* operation, which is represented in the following form.

$$\mathbf{I} \cdot \mathbf{S_e} = (\mathbf{I} \oplus \mathbf{S_e}) \ominus \mathbf{S_e} \tag{1.23}$$

In this context, we use the operator $\cdot$ to denote the morphological closing operation. The application of closing operation eliminates the holes that are smaller than $\mathbf{S_e}$, and smooths and fuses narrow gaps in the foreground region.

Similarly, by applying erosion operation using a square structuring element, the protruding streaks from the boundaries of the foreground objects and the noise in the background region are removed, as seen in Figs. 1.29 (b) and (e), while the holes in the foreground region get expanded. However, in this process, the boundaries of the foreground objects are shrunk due to erosion. To retain the original shape of the objects, dilation operation is applied using the same structural element, which brings the shrunk boundaries of the objects to their original size, while removing the noise in the background and foreground streaks. The resulting images are shown in Figs. 1.29 (c) and (f).

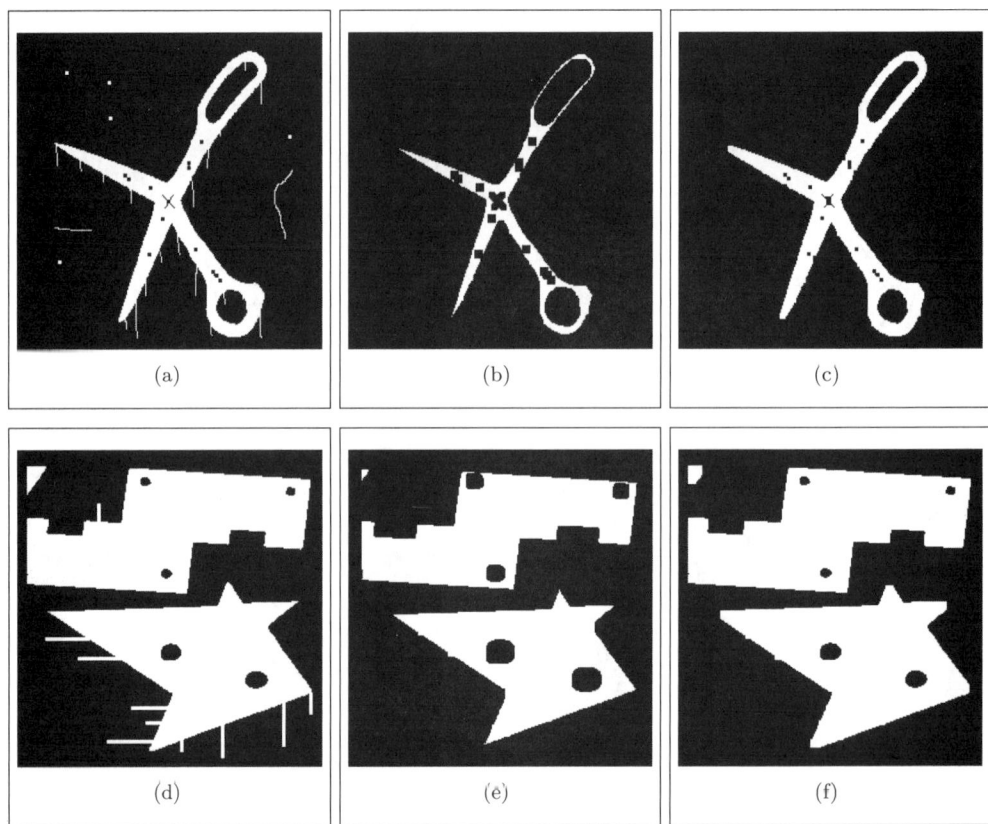

Figure 1.29 Example of opening: (a,d) original noisy images, (b,e) erosion operation on original images, and (c,f) dilation of eroded images.

This sequence of operations, i.e., the erosion followed by the dilation, is called the *morphological opening* operation, which is described below.

$$\mathbf{I} \circ \mathbf{S_e} = (\mathbf{I} \ominus \mathbf{S_e}) \oplus \mathbf{S_e} \tag{1.24}$$

In this context, we use the operator ∘ to denote the morphological opening operation. The application of opening operation eliminates foreground protrusions like spurious streaks, smooths contours, breaks lines with width lesser than $\mathbf{S_e}$, and removes small noisy structures in the background region.

Similar to dilation and erosion operations, opening and closing operations are duals of each other. However, unlike dilation and erosion operations, applying opening and closing operations on an image more than once using the same structuring element do not have any effect beyond the first instance.

By applying the opening and closing operations in a sequence, the holes in the foreground region, spurious foreground streaks, and noise in the background region are removed, which are demonstrated in Fig. 1.30. Here, the morphological opening operation is followed by the morphological closing operation.

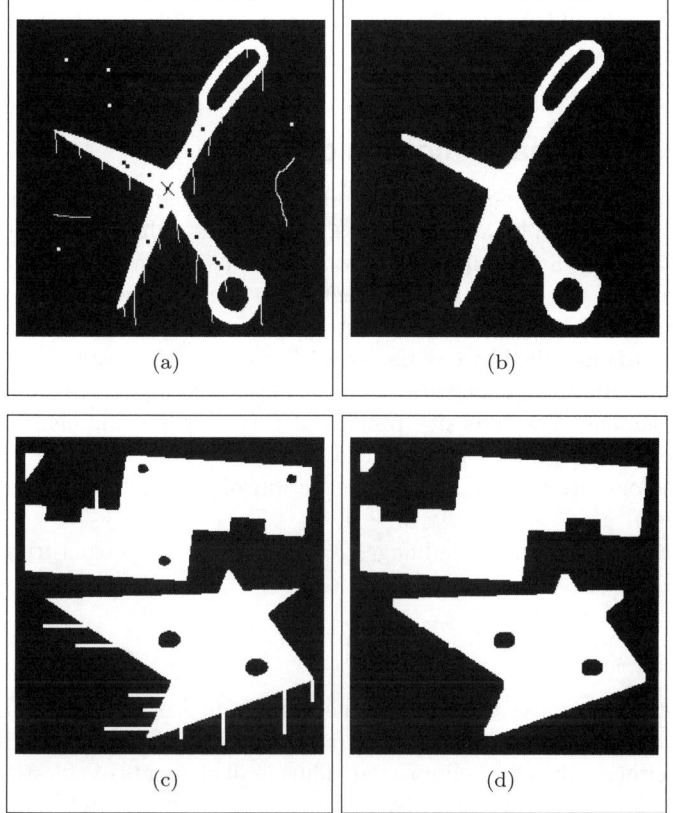

(a)   (b)

(c)   (d)

Figure 1.30 Examples of opening followed by closing operations. (a) and (c): Original images; (b) and (d): Processed images.

1.8.4 | Hit or miss transform

Hit or miss transform is a kind of binary morphological operation that is used to locate a pattern, which is defined by a structural element. In this case, the structuring element defines two nonoverlapping set $\mathbf{S_{e1}}$ and $\mathbf{S_{e2}}$ for checking their containment in foreground and background respectively. Thus The hit or miss transformation on an image, $\mathbf{I}$, using a composite structuring element $\mathbf{S_e} = (\mathbf{S_{e1}}, \mathbf{S_{e2}})$ is defined as follows.

$$\mathbf{I} \bigstar \mathbf{S_e} = (\mathbf{I} \ominus \mathbf{S_{e1}}) \cap (\mathbf{I^c} \ominus \mathbf{S_{e2}}) \qquad (1.25)$$

Consider a structuring element, $\mathbf{S_{e1}}$ that defines a set of object points. It is required to compute the set of foreground points, at which $\mathbf{S_{e1}}$ is fully embedded. Thus the erosion of $\mathbf{I}$ with $\mathbf{S_{e1}}$ provides that set of points. Likewise, we may compute also the set of background points where the structuring element $\mathbf{S_{e2}}$ is fully contained. This is computed by performing erosion of the background points ($\mathbf{I^c}$) with $\mathbf{S_{e2}}$. Hence, the intersection of these two sets provide the set of object points at which both the structures are fully contained in foreground and background, respectively. This is what is expressed in Eq. 1.25 and the operation is called 'Hit-or-Miss' transform. This operation is used for template matching, This operation is illustrated in Fig. 1.31, where the white pixels that do not have any 4-neighboring white pixels are identified.

1.8.5 | Gray scale image morphology

Binary image morphological operations may also be extended to gray scale images. A gray scale image, $\mathbf{I}$, is represented by a set of points, (x, y), in $\mathbb{Z}^2$, whose functional value, $f(x, y)$, varies between 0 and the maximum possible value such as, 255 for an 8-bit image. Similarly, the functional value of the structuring element $\mathbf{S_e}$ at (x, y) is denoted by $s(x, y)$ In a gray scale image, instead of binary values, the intensity of each pixel is used in morphological operations, where it is modified by comparing with its neighbors using structuring elements. Here, two kinds of structuring elements are used, (1) flat structuring element, and (2) non-flat structuring element. The intensity profiles of these structuring elements are shown in Fig. 1.32. In most applications, symmetrical flat structuring elements are used. Similar to binary morphology (refer to Eq. 1.18), reflection of a structuring element is given by $s(x, y) = s(-x, -y)$.

Dilation operation on a gray scale image, $f(x, y)$, using a flat structuring element $s(x, y)$ is defined as in Eq. 1.28.

$$[f \oplus s](x, y) = \max_{(u,v) \in s} \{f(x - u, y - v)\} \tag{1.26}$$

The above operation computes the maximum of pixel values of the neighbors around a pixel (x, y) as defined by the structuring element $s(x, y)$. In gray scale dilation, the darker details in the image get either reduced or eliminated. Thus if all elements of the structuring element are positive, it tends to make the image brighter by enhancing the intensity of darker regions. The dilation of a gray scale image, $f(x, y)$, using a nonflat structuring element $s_n(x, y)$ is given in Eq. 1.29.

$$[f \oplus s_n](x, y) = \max_{(u,v) \in s_n} \{f(x - u, y - v) + s_n(u, v)\} \tag{1.27}$$

In dilation using nonflat structuring element, the values of s_n are added to f at any point. Due to this, the computed values are not bounded by the intensity values of the image.

Similarly, erosion operation on a gray scale image, $f(x, y)$, using a flat structuring element $s(x, y)$ is defined as in Eq. 1.28.

$$[f \ominus s](x, y) = \min_{(u,v) \in s} \{f(x + u, y + v)\} \tag{1.28}$$

That is, the erosion operation results in the minimum value at each pixel location, (x, y), of the image, where the neighborhood is defined by the structuring element centered at (x, y). The gray scale erosion tends to make the image darker by reducing the intensity of brighter regions. So, the brighter details in the image get reduced and the bright regions that are smaller than the structuring element gets eliminated. Erosion of a gray scale image, $f(x, y)$, using a nonflat structuring element $s_n(x, y)$ is given in Eq. 1.29.

$$[f \ominus s_n](x, y) = \min_{(u,v) \in s_n} \{f(x + u, y + v) - s_n(u, v)\} \tag{1.29}$$

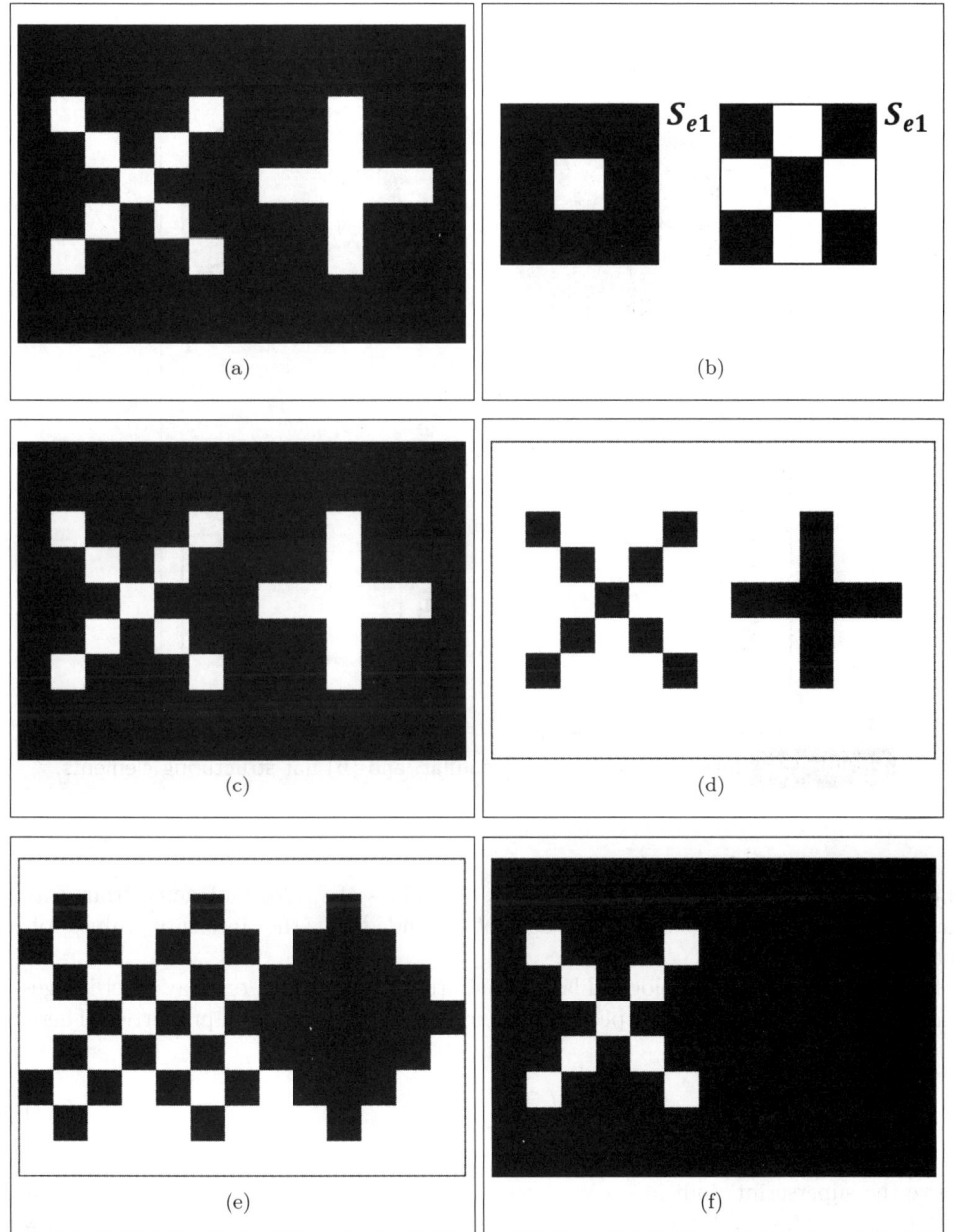

Figure 1.31 Illustration of hit or miss operation on a binary image. (a) Original binary image (**I**), (b) structural elements ($\mathbf{S_{e1}}$ and $\mathbf{S_{e2}}$), (c) erosion of **I** using $\mathbf{S_{e1}}$, (d) $\mathbf{I^c}$, (e) erosion of $\mathbf{I^c}$ using $\mathbf{S_{e2}}$, and (f) hit or miss transformed image.

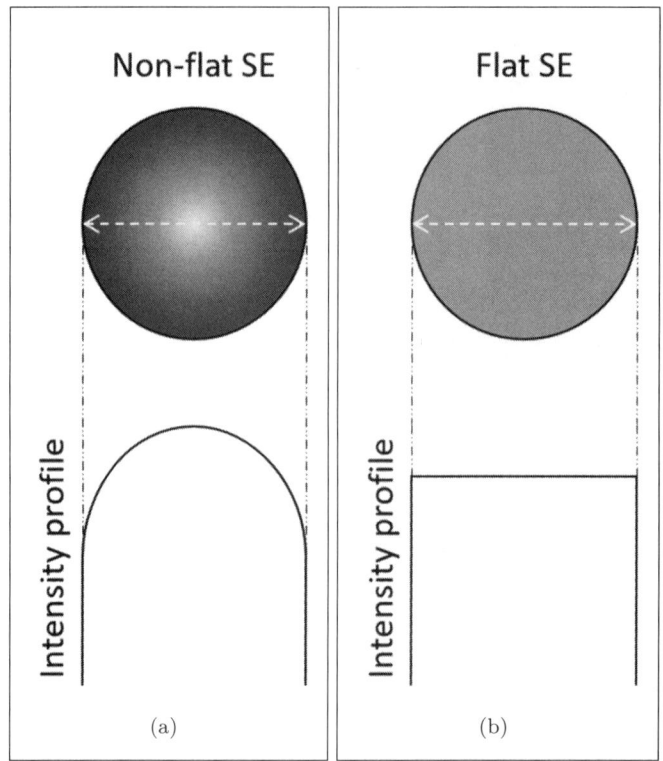

Figure 1.32 Intensity profiles of (a) nonflat, and (b) flat structuring elements.

In erosion using nonflat structuring element, the values of s_n are subtracted from f at any point, which makes the result to be not bounded by the intensity values of the image.

Similar to binary morphology, dilation and erosion operations on gray level images are also duals of each other, with respect to set complement and reflection properties. Therefore,

$$(f \ominus s)^c = f^c \oplus \hat{s}$$
$$(f \oplus s)^c = f^c \ominus \hat{s}$$

(1.30)

where the superscript^c indicates complement operation modified for the gray scale images as $f^c(x, y) = -f(x, y)$. Examples of gray level dilation and erosion operations are shown in Fig. 1.33.

Similarly, morphological closing and opening operations are also defined for gray scale images, which are represented in the following form.

$$f \cdot s = (f \oplus s) \ominus s$$
$$f \circ s = (f \ominus s) \oplus s$$

(1.31)

(a)	(b)	(c)

Figure 1.33 Dilation and erosion operations on a gray scale image using a square structural element of size 5×5. (a) Original image, (b) dilated image, and (c) eroded image.

Examples of applying the closing and opening operations on a gray scale image are shown Fig. 1.34. As seen in the figure, the closing operation removes the darker details that are smaller than $\mathbf{S}_e$ and the opening operation removes the brighter details that are smaller than $\mathbf{S}_e$. Similar to dilation and erosion operations, opening and closing operations are also duals of each other.

1.8.6 | Applications of image morphology

The binary morphological operations are used in various applications like, object boundary extraction, region filling, thinning, skeletonisation, etc. For instance, object boundary, $\beta(\mathbf{I})$, of an image $\mathbf{I}$ is extracted using a structuring element $\mathbf{S_e}$ as follows.

$$\beta(\mathbf{I}) = \mathbf{I} - (\mathbf{I} \ominus \mathbf{S_e}) \tag{1.32}$$

In Fig. 1.35, the detected object boundary of (a) is shown in (b), where a square structuring element of size 3×3 is used.

The gray level morphological operations are used in applications like, image smoothing, noise suppression, gradient detection, image enhancement, etc. For example, morphological filtering is performed by using opening and closing operations in combination, where smaller details in the image (smaller than the structuring element) are removed. Repeated application of such filtering operation is used to achieve alternating sequential filtering. It attenuates both bright and dark artifacts in the images. An example of morphological filtering operation is shown in Fig. 1.36.

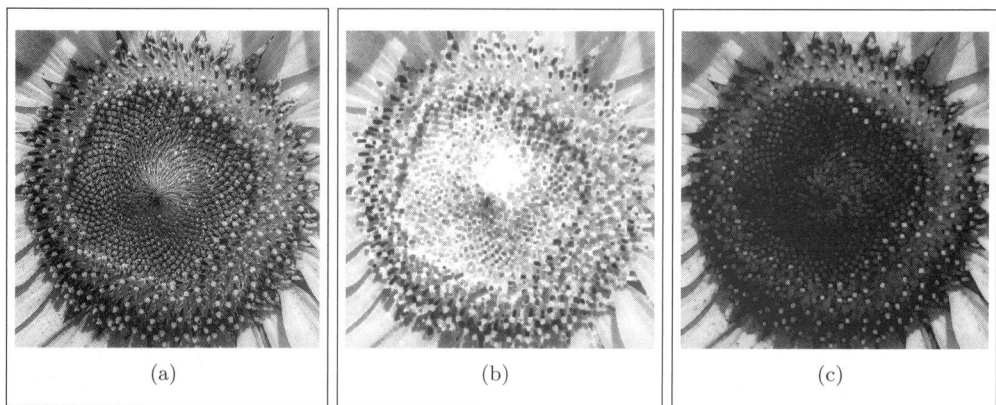

Figure 1.34 Opening and closing operations on a gray scale image using a square structural element of size 7 × 7. (a) Original image, (b) result of closing operation, and (c) result of opening operation.

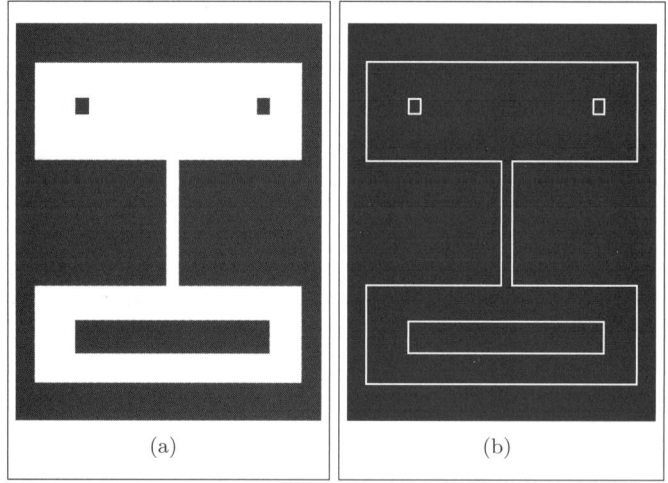

Figure 1.35 Illustration of morphological boundary detection on a binary image.

Morphological gradient, g of an image f using structural element s is computed as follows.

$$g = (f \oplus s) - (f \ominus s) \tag{1.33}$$

Here, a symmetrical structural element is usually used to make it less sensitive of edge direction. The morphological gradient operation highlights sharp gradient transitions in the image, as shown in Fig. 1.37.

Figure 1.36 An example of alternating sequential filtering using morphological opening and closing operations. (a) Original image. (b) Opening–closing sequence on the left image with a 3×3 structural element. (c) Opening–closing sequence on the middle image with a 5×5 structural element.

Figure 1.37 (a) Original image. (b) Morphological gradient image computed using a 3×3 structural element.

1.9 | Video processing

Video processing may be seen as an extension to the processing of images, with an additional temporal dimension to the prevalent spatial dimensions. So, video processing spans spatial, temporal, and/or spatio-temporal domains, which are integral parts of many video analysis and coding problems. Problems like, shot detection, video summarization, video coding and editing, etc. rely more on temporal context of the video, while the problems like, motion estimation, object tracking, surveillance, etc. require spatio-temporal analysis. A typical example of a video processing problem, namely, shot boundary detection is briefly introduced here.

1.9.1 | Shot detection

Along the temporal axis, a *frame* is the basic unit of a video. *Frame numbers* are used to index these spatially identical sized frames, which are usually sampled at a constant rate known as *frame rate* and is measured by *frames per second* (fps). A group of consecutive interrelated frames is called a *video shot*. These shots may be captured by a camera at a single stretch or they may be formed by a set of contiguous frames, that are related by similar characteristics like, illumination, color, objects, etc. Either an individual shot or multiple consecutive shots that are related by certain context, form a *video scene*. Generally, a video is a composite of several such scenes. This structure of videos is depicted in Fig. 1.38. Identification of dissimilarity/similarity between the frames to group them into shots in

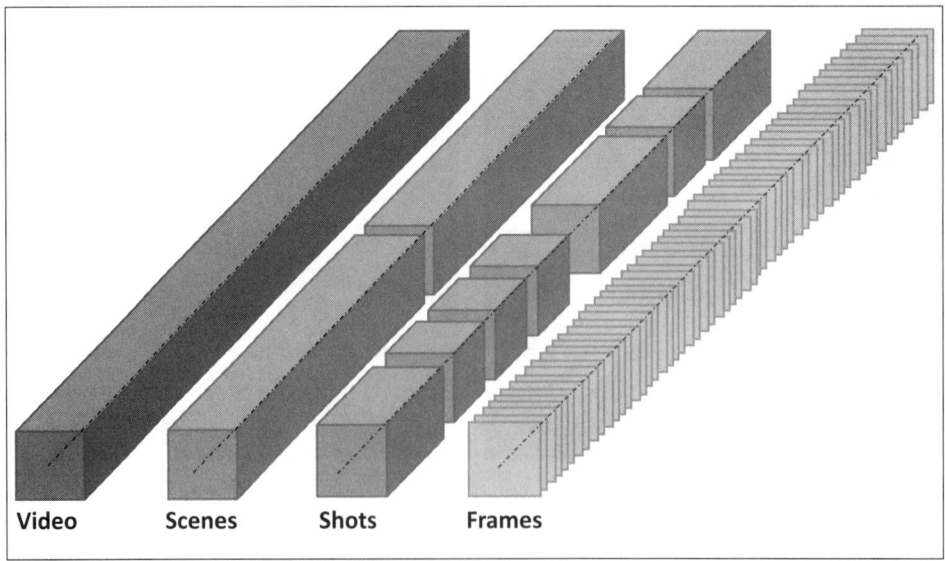

Video   **Scenes**   **Shots**   **Frames**

Figure 1.38 Structure of a video file.

known as *shot detection*. In the context of determining the start and end frames of different shots in a video, this technique is also called *shot boundary detection*.

The visual dissimilarity between the frames during transition of a shot is called *shot transition*, and it may be of various kinds. For example, the change may be an abrupt cut between two frames, as in this case, the two consecutive frames belong to two different shots, or it can be a gradual change, as in this case, in a shot that dissolves gradually to another shot through different kinds of effects. Two such examples, an abrupt detection of change and a gradual fading of shots, are shown in Fig. 1.39. The computation of these changes is the problem of shot detection.

The changes between the consecutive frames of a video may be detected using various measures computed from the brightness distribution in video frames, such as, average luminance, color values, histogram, edge information, transform coefficients, etc (Dey et al., 2015; Huo et al., 2016). Also, these features may be extracted from the entire frame or using a predetermined region of interest. One of the simple approaches for computing the shot boundary in an abruptly cut shot junction is to consider the second derivative of the sum of absolute differences (SAD) vector of pixel values in the consecutive frames. Let there be N_f frames in the video shot, and let $M \times N$ be the size of each frame in the video. The sum of absolute differences between each of the consecutive frames is given by Eq. 1.34.

$$\boldsymbol{d}_a(j) = \sum_{i=1}^{MN} |I_j(i) - I_{j+1}(i)|, \ \text{ where } j = 1, 2, ..., N_f - 1 \tag{1.34}$$

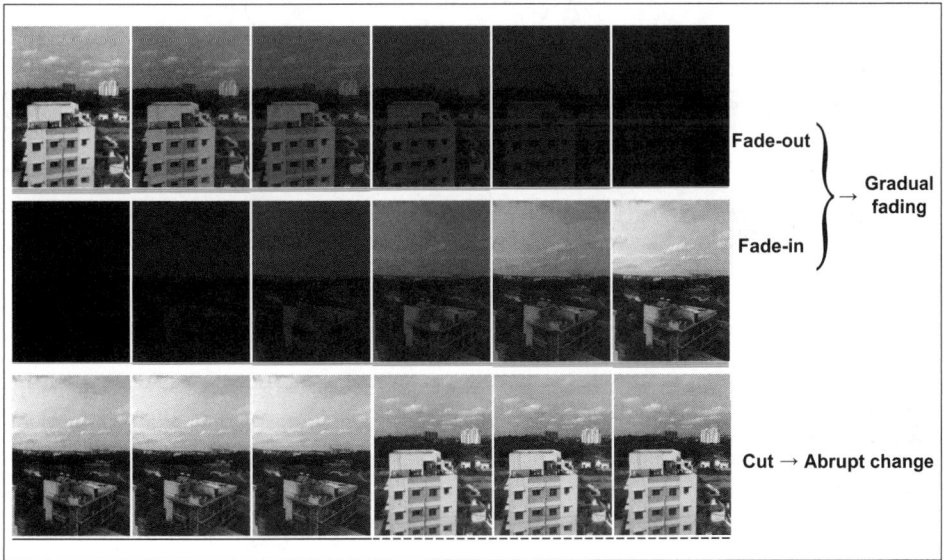

Figure 1.39 Examples of shot transitions.

Given an empirical threshold value, d_{th}, the indices of frames in the second order derivative of $\boldsymbol{d}_a$ that have values lesser than d_{th} denote the shot boundaries. The second order derivative may also be computed by convolving $\boldsymbol{d}_a$ with the 1-D kernel, $[1, -1]$ twice. An example of this method is shown in Fig. 1.40.

Another simple and efficient algorithm for computing abruptly cut shot boundaries uses histogram based statistical measures of the frames (Zhang et al., 1993; Priya and Dominic, 2011). This technique considers a temporal sliding window for identifying the abruptly cut shot boundaries. A sliding temporal window of n_f frames is initialized from the first streaming frame and continuously slid along the temporal axis. If a shot boundary is detected, the shot clip is saved individually and the sliding window is re-initialized to the immediate next frame following the temporal index of the detected shot boundary. Within the field of sliding window, each frame in the video is divided into $m \times m$ uniform nonoverlapping blocks. A frame discontinuity value, L_j, for every frame, j, is computed as,

$$L_j = \sum_{b=1}^{m^2} L_{j_b}, \tag{1.35}$$

where, L_{j_b} denotes the block discontinuity value for the bth block, in the jth frame. This block discontinuity is computed as the average of the histogram differences between corresponding blocks in the jth and the $(j+1)^{\text{th}}$ frames of the video over all the channels of each frame (single channel for a gray scale video, and three channels for a color video), which is expressed in Eq. 1.36.

$$L_{j_b} = \frac{1}{C_n} \sum_{k \in C} \left(\sum_{g_c} |H_{k_j^b}(g_c) - H_{k_{j+1}^b}(g_c)| \right), \tag{1.36}$$

In the above expression, C is the set of channels, C_n is the number of channels,[7] g_c denotes all possible intensity values for each of the channels in the frames, $H_{k_j^b}(g_c)$ and $H_{k_{j+1}^b}(g_c)$ are

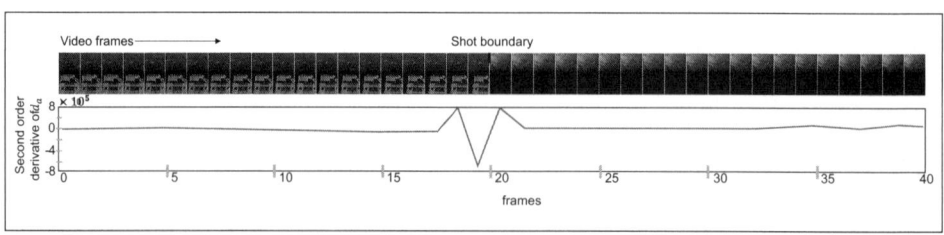

Figure 1.40   An example of shot boundary detection using second order derivative of sum of absolute differences of pixel values in consecutive frames. In this example, the threshold, $d_{th} = -4$.

---

[7] $C = \{R, G, B\}$ (corresponding to red, green, and blue channels) and $C_n = 3$ for a color video, and $C = \{I\}$ (corresponding to gray scale intensity channel) and $C_n = 1$ for a gray scale video.

the histogram values at bin g_c of bth block of kth channel corresponding to the consecutive j^{th} and $(j+1)^{\text{th}}$ frames, respectively.

The jth frame is considered to be at a cut scene, if the discontinuity value at the frame is greater than a threshold value, T_L. The value of T_L is computed from the statistics of the discontinuity values as follows.

The mean of discontinuity values of all the frames in the video is computed as,

$$\bar{L} = \frac{1}{n_f} \sum_{j=1}^{n_f} L_j, \tag{1.37}$$

where, n_f is the number of frames in the sliding window. The absolute deviations of discontinuity values, ρ_j, at each of the frames from their mean value is found as,

$$\rho_j = |L_j - \bar{L}|. \tag{1.38}$$

The mean and standard deviation of the absolute deviations of discontinuity values, $\bar{\rho}$ and σ_ρ, respectively, of all the frames are computed as,

$$\bar{\rho} = \frac{1}{n_f} \sum_{j=1}^{n_f} \rho_j,$$

$$\sigma_\rho = \sqrt{\frac{1}{n_f} \sum_{j=1}^{n_f} (\rho_j - \bar{\rho})^2}. \tag{1.39}$$

Then, the threshold, T_L, is computed as,

$$T_L = \bar{L} + \sigma_\rho \tag{1.40}$$

A frame is declared cut scene, if $L_j \geq T_L$. We may note that if the luminance values of consecutive shots in a scene significantly differ, the estimated shot boundaries are more accurate, since the variation within a shot is relatively small.

Summary

An image is formed by an optical camera by mapping of 3-D points to 2-D points through perspective projection. A straight line from a 3-D scene point passing through the center of projection intersects the image plane at a point to form the corresponding 2-D image point, and this projection is called perspective projection.

Some of the fundamental operations of image processing include,

- Image binarization: Thresholding operation on intensity values, and computation of optimal threshold values.
- Contrast enhancement to improve the information content in the images increasing the dynamic range of pixel values.

- Image segmentation: To obtain groups of pixels related by a common factor, and labeling their components as connected regions in an image.

- Image gradients: Computation of gradients is performed using the principle of finite differences and computation with masks, which are equivalent to correlation.

- Correlation and convolution: These are fundamental linear operations with images. Correlation is used for matching templates defined by a mask. Convolution operation is needed for computing output of a linear shift invariant system given its impulse response.

- Noise filtering: Gaussian filtering is performed by convolving an image with a Gaussian mask. Nonlinear filters such as median filters are also effective in filtering salt and pepper noise in an image.

- Morphological operations: These are performed to process and analyze structure and morphology of an image using a structuring element. The operations are primarily meant for bilevel or binary images. Their extensions for processing gray level images are also found useful. Morphological operations are also nonlinear.

To illustrate a typical example of video processing, shot boundary detection is briefly discussed. Shot boundary detection is used to identify different shots in a given video.

Exercises

(i) Consider a 6 level histogram of a gray scale image of size 6×6. We describe the bin information for the histogram using the notation:

bin[pixel value]=number of pixels.

Accordingly the histogram is described below.

$bin[0] = 8$, $bin[1] = 7$, $bin[2] = 2$, $bin[3] = 6$, $bin[4] = 9$, $bin[5] = 4$.

Partition the pixels in two classes using the threshold value 3 such that $pixel \geq 3$ belongs to class 1 and the rest of the pixels are in class 2.

- What is the probability of class 1.
- What is the probability of class 2.
- What is the between class variance according to Otsu's method?

(ii) Consider the following 5×5 image array.

$$
\begin{array}{ccccc}
3 & 3 & 3 & 6 & 4 \\
2 & 2 & 0 & 0 & 4 \\
1 & 2^* & 4 & 0 & 5 \\
5 & 1 & 3 & 2 & 1 \\
5 & 2 & 6 & 6 & 6 \\
\end{array}
$$

What is the value at location (2,1) of the image (shown with the asterisk mark in the image array) after histogram equalization?

(iii) Consider the following 5×5 image array.

$$
\begin{array}{ccccc}
10 & 20 & 30 & 40 & 50 \\
1 & 5 & 2 & 5 & 1 \\
17 & 27 & 37^* & 47 & 57 \\
11 & 51 & 21 & 51 & 11 \\
15 & 25 & 35 & 45 & 55
\end{array}
$$

What are the 4-neighbors, 8-neighbors, and diagonal neighbors of the pixel position shown by asterisk.

(iv) Consider a simple iterative global thresholding algorithm. Assume that for a given image the histogram is bimodal and furthermore, that the shape of the modes can be approximated by Gaussian functions of the form $A_1 e^{-\frac{(z-m_1)^2}{2\sigma_1^2}}$ and $A_2 e^{-\frac{(z-m_2)^2}{2\sigma_2^2}}$, where m's denote means, σ's denote standard deviations, and A's are constants. Assume that $m_1 < m_2$. What are the constraints on A_1 and A_2 for the algorithm to converge when the threshold is in the interval $(m_1 + m_2)/2 < T < m_2$. Provide with suitable explanation.

(v) Consider an image has a bimodal histogram, one corresponding to its foreground (brighter zones) and the other one to its background (darker zones). Assume that given a class (foreground or background), the probability density functions of pixel values follow Gaussian distributions.

   (a) Given a threshold value Th for delineating the foreground and background pixel values, how do you compute the following from the histogram of the image: (i) Probability of a pixel belonging to foreground, (ii) probability of a pixel belonging to background, and (iii) parameters of the class conditional probability density functions of pixel values.

   (b) Describe the expectation-maximization algorithm for obtaining the threshold value iteratively.

(vi) Consider an image of size 32×32 having pixel values between 0 and 5. The histogram of the image is shown below. In the table a pixel value is denoted by x, and the number of times it occurs in an image is denoted by $h(x)$.

x	0	1	2	3	4	5
$h(x)$	100	400	200	100	200	24

Suppose there are two classes, namely "Background" (denoted by ω_1) and "Foreground" (denoted by ω_2). Choose a threshold value of $T_h = 2$, such that a pixel having values greater than it are in the "Foreground", otherwise it belongs to the "Background". Assume class probability density functions $(p(x|\omega_1)$ and $p(x|\omega_2))$ follow Gaussian distribution. Answer the following questions.

- Compute $p(\omega_1|x = 3)$.
- Compute $p(\omega_2|x = 3)$.
- What would be the updated threshold value?

(vii) Suppose the following 3×3 mask is convolved with an image of size 4×4 assuming zero padding at the boundary.

Mask		
1	2	1
2	-8	2
1	w	1

Image			
1	2	3	4
5	6	7	8
9	10	11*	12
13	14	15	16

What value of w would make the convolved value at the pixel shown by asterisk as 74.

(viii) A gray scale image with its pixel intensities lying in between $i_{min} = 60$ and $i_{max} = 220$, is linearly stretched using a min-max linear function $f(x) = 255 \frac{x - i_{min}}{i_{max} - i_{min}}$. Compute the original pixel value x, given the corresponding stretched pixel value $f(x)$ is 64?

(ix) Consider the following 5×5 image array.

3	4	5	6	7
2	1	0	3	1
5	9	6	0	1
1	4	3	2	1
7	2	1	8	9

Compute values at the pixel location (3, 3), using vertical and horizontal Sobel edge operator, vertical and horizontal Prewitt edge operator, and Robert's cross operators.

(x) Consider the following 5×5 image array.

1	2	3	2	1
1	1	3	4	1
1	2	3	2	1
1	1	3	4*	1
1	2	3	2	1

Compute the pixel value at the location of asterisk after applying a 3×3 median filter.

(xi) Consider initial probability of getting head in A and B as $p = 0.3$ and $q = 0.6$, respectively. Executing expectation-maximization, find the updated "p" and "q" after the first iteration of the algorithm.

(**xii**) Is the following kernel is separable? Explain.

$$
\begin{array}{ccc}
1 & 2 & 3 \\
0 & 0 & 0 \\
-2 & -4 & -6
\end{array}
$$

(**xiii**) Is the Gaussian function separable? Explain.

(**xiv**) Show that, if a digital image $I(x, y)$, where (x, y) is the integral coordinate point, is convolved with the mask given below, it computes an estimate of $\frac{\partial^2 I(x,y)}{\partial x \partial y}$.

$$
\begin{array}{ccc}
-0.25 & 0 & 0.25 \\
0 & 0 & 0 \\
0.25 & 0 & -0.25
\end{array}
$$

(**xv**) For removing unwanted structures in a binary image what morphological operations you need to carry out. State with justification.

(**xvi**) Suppose it is required to eliminate structures of width less than 3. What morphological operations are required to be carried out for that purpose?

(**xvii**) Consider the problem of separating foreground from background in an image and modeling the probability of a pixel value as a mixture of Gaussians, each expressing class likelihood of a pixel value. Formulate the segmentation problem as a Bayesian classification problem. How the parameters of the distributions are computed and updated iteratively using expectation maximization method?

(**xviii**) Define morphological dilation and erosion operations on gray scale images using a nonflat structuring element. Describe an algorithm for sharpening images using above morphological operators.

(**xix**) Given a binary image with black dots scattered over the foreground objects. Which morphological operation should be used to remove them? Can we use the same operation to reduce salt and pepper noise in a binary image?

(**xx**) How gray scale morphological opening and closing could be used to reduce noise in a gray scale image? How it is different from smoothing an image using a mask of low pass filter.

(**xxi**) Define the problem of shot boundary detection in videos. Describe an algorithm for detecting the hard cuts.

2

Alternate Representations of Images and Videos

This chapter provides an insight to some of the general image transforms that offer an alternative representation of images and videos. Few of their properties and applications are also discussed that are related to image compression and reconstruction. Other forms of representation that depend on data, like principal component analysis and sparse representation, are provided as an extension to these representations. Techniques of computing basis functions and dictionary learning are introduced in this chapter.

2.1 | Image transforms

Consider a continuous function, $f(x)$, in one-dimensional (1-D) space, where, $x \in \mathbb{R}$. Consider a set, B, of 1-D basis functions, whose functional values may either be in real or in complex domain. This is represented as in Eq. 2.1.

$$B = \{b_i(x) \mid i = \dots, -1, 0, 1, 2, \dots\} \tag{2.1}$$

where, i is the index of a basis function as given in the set. Let us assume that the given 1-D function, $f(x)$, may be expanded and represented using B as a linear combination of its member basis functions as given by Eq. 2.2.

$$f(x) = \sum_i \lambda_i b_i(x) \tag{2.2}$$

The transform of f, with respect to B, is defined by a set of coefficients, λ_i, called *coefficients* of transform. The function, $f(x)$, is represented as a linear combination of the basis functions using these coefficients.

This indexing may also be multi-dimensional, which is useful in representing multi-dimensional signals. For example, two indices are used to denote a coefficient of linear expansion of a two-dimensional (2-D) function. For an image, consider it as a 2-D function that is known in its functional form as $f(x, y)$. Now, the set, B, consists of 2-D basis functions, whose functional values may either be in real or in complex domain, and a point $(x, y) \in \mathbb{R}^2$. This set of 2-D basis functions is represented as in Eq. 2.3.

$$B = \{b_{ij}(x, y) \mid i, j = ..., -1, 0, 1, 2, ...\} \tag{2.3}$$

Likewise, we assume that the given image may be represented by this alternate description using the basis functions. The image, as a 2-D function, is expanded in the form of a linear combination of 2-D basis functions as given by Eq. 2.4.

$$f(x, y) = \sum_i \sum_j \lambda_{ij} b_{ij}(x, y) \tag{2.4}$$

In other words, the image may simply be represented as an ordered list of these coefficients, which may also be treated functions of indices. One of the major advantages of image transforms lies in extending the properties of basis functions in the analysis of images.

2.1.1 | Orthogonal expansion and one-dimensional transforms

One of the useful properties of basis functions is the property of orthogonality. An expansion of a function in terms of orthogonal basis functions is called *orthogonal expansion*. For the sake of simplicity and understanding, only 1-D transforms are considered to explain the properties of transforms. However, these properties are easily extendable to 2-D transforms as well.

Inner Product   An inner product is a binary operation that takes two functions, $f(x)$ and $g(x)$, as its operands and performs an integration of the product values of these two functions at every point in the space, x, which is given by Eq. 2.5.

$$\langle f, g \rangle = \int_{-\infty}^{\infty} f(x) g^*(x) dx \tag{2.5}$$

In generalized terms, the computation inside the integral operation is a product of function $f(x)$ with the complex conjugate of function $g(x)$. If the functional values of both $f(x)$ and $g(x)$ are in real domain, then the complex conjugate, $g^*(x)$ is the same function $g(x)$ itself. In that case, the product inside the integral operation of Eq. 2.5 may simply be written as $f(x)g(x)$.

An orthogonal expansion is possible by a set of basis functions, as given in Eq. 2.1, only if it satisfies the property of orthogonality, which is given by Eq. 2.6.

$$\langle b_i, b_j \rangle = \begin{cases} 0, & \text{for } i \neq j \\ c_i, & \text{for } i = j, \text{ where } c_i > 0 \end{cases} \tag{2.6}$$

In other words, the inner product of any two different basis functions is 0, whereas the inner product of a basis function with itself is a nonzero (positive) value. If this holds true for any pair of basis functions in the set B, it is said that, all basis functions are orthogonal in that set.

The transform coefficients, λ_i, in an orthogonal expansion of a function, $f(x)$, may easily be computed by exploiting the orthogonality property as given below.

$$\lambda_i = \frac{1}{c_i}\langle f, b_i \rangle \tag{2.7}$$

where, $b_i(x)$s are orthogonal basis functions. If each c_i becomes 1, the expansion is called orthonormal expansion, where, $\lambda_i = \langle f, b_i \rangle$. Since the idea is to express the given function only in terms of transform coefficients, this operation is also called *forward transform* operation.

Using the forward transform operation on a function $f(x)$, the function is represented only by the coefficients, λ_i. The reverse or inverse transform operation is an operation to compute the function back from its transform as the linear combination of the basis functions. This may be performed using Eq. 2.8.

$$f(x) = \int_{i=-\infty}^{\infty} \lambda_i b_i(x) di \tag{2.8}$$

In the above, we replace the discrete summation operations using integration, as we consider even the index of basis function is a continuous variable. The integral operation also expresses the linear combination of basis functions using the coefficients.

2.2 | Fourier transform

One of the special cases of orthogonal expansion is the *Fourier transform*, where the basis functions are given by the form as in Eq. 2.9, where each member of the set is a complex sinusoid.

$$B = \{e^{j\omega x} \mid -\infty < \omega < \infty\} \tag{2.9}$$

Any orthogonal set that is a subset of an orthogonal basis set also remains orthogonal, but a linear combination of the members of the subset may not give a complete reconstruction of the function. The basis set which delivers a complete reconstruction of a function is called the *complete base*. In case of Fourier transform, the basis set that is given in Eq. 2.9 is a complete base, since a given function is completely reconstructed as a linear combination of the basis functions. As it can be seen, Eq. 2.9 is an infinite set, though individually every sinusoid is distinguished in it.

The orthogonality property of this base, B, is given by Eq. 2.10.

$$\int_{-\infty}^{\infty} e^{j\omega x} dx = \begin{cases} 2\pi\delta(x), & \text{for } \omega = 0 \\ 0, & \text{otherwise} \end{cases} \tag{2.10}$$

where, $\delta(x)$ is the *Dirac delta function* whose area is unity centering at $\omega = 0$ and 0 everywhere else. As we observe from Eq. 2.10, the inner product of any two different sinusoids is 0, while that of the same pair is nonzero.

The Fourier transform is defined by Eq. 2.11, which is the forward transform using the Fourier base.

$$\mathcal{F}(f(x)) = \hat{f}(j\omega) = \int_{-\infty}^{\infty} f(x)e^{-j\omega x}dx \qquad (2.11)$$

This is an inner product of the function, $f(x)$, and the complex sinusoid basis, $e^{j\omega x}$ for every radian ω. By definition of inner product, the complex conjugate of the basis function, $e^{-j\omega x}$, is used to compute its product with $f(x)$. In our notation, we use the hat ($\hat{\ }$) operator on top of a function to denote its Fourier transform in this chapter and also in this book. The inverse Fourier transform is defined by Eq. 2.12.

$$f(x) = \frac{1}{2\pi} \int_{-\infty}^{\infty} \hat{f}(j\omega)e^{j\omega x}dx \qquad (2.12)$$

A linear combination of coefficients, $\hat{f}(j\omega)$, and basis functions provides the corresponding inverse transform. This yields a full reconstruction of $f(x)$, since the set of complex sinusoids for radian frequencies ranging from $-\infty$ to ∞ is a complete base.

A complex sinusoid is expanded by its real and imaginary parts as in Eq. 2.13.

$$e^{-j\omega x} = \cos(\omega x) - j\sin(\omega x) \qquad (2.13)$$

In this case, the real part consists of $\cos(\omega x)$ and the imaginary part consists of $-\sin(\omega x)$. By Eqs. 2.11 and 2.13, the forward Fourier transform may also be represented as in Eq. 2.14.

$$\hat{f}(j\omega) = \int_{-\infty}^{\infty} f(x)\left(\cos(\omega x) - j\sin(\omega x)\right)dx \qquad (2.14)$$

From this expression, one of the transform components consists of a real part with its basis functions, C, and the other component consists of an imaginary part with its basis functions S, which are given by Eq. 2.15.

$$\begin{aligned} \text{C} &= \{\cos(\omega x) \mid -\infty < \omega < \infty\} \\ \text{S} &= \{\sin(\omega x) \mid -\infty < \omega < \infty\} \end{aligned} \qquad (2.15)$$

These trigonometric functions in C and S are also orthogonal, but either of the basis sets, C and S, do not form a complete base. Using only one of them with the coefficients it is not guaranteed to reconstruct the full. So, inverse transform with C or S on the coefficients derived from them reconstruct only parts of $f(x)$, but not the full function.

Though C and S are not complete bases in the above case, there are certain functions that use only cosines or sines to reconstruct the functions fully. Such functions are called *even* or *odd* functions, respectively. For a function to be even, the property it has to satisfy is that the function should be *symmetric* about the origin, i.e., at $x = 0$, as given by Eq. 2.16.

$$f(-x) = f(x), \text{ for all } x \qquad (2.16)$$

Whereas for an odd function, the function should be *anti-symmetric* about the origin, as given by Eq. 2.17.

$$f(-x) = -f(x), \text{ for all } x \qquad (2.17)$$

Naturally, for an odd function at $x = 0$, the value of the function has to be 0, i.e., $f(0) = 0$, according to the above definition.

A function may either be even, or odd, or it may be neither of them. If the function is even or odd, it is possible to express it as linear combinations using only cosine or sine functions, respectively. This may be justified as follows.

If a function, $f(x)$, is even, integration of its product with $\sin(\omega x)$ yields 0, as shown in Eq. 2.18.

$$\int_{-\infty}^{\infty} f(x)\sin(\omega x)dx = 0 \tag{2.18}$$

Since all sinusoidal terms are 0 in an even function, it is effectively represented only by the coefficients of cosine terms. Thus in this case (when the function is an even function), only cosine transformations are sufficient to describe all the transform coefficients. Similarly, for an odd function, the coefficients of the cosine terms are 0, shown in Eq. 2.19, and the transform coefficients are computed by only sinusoidal basis functions, which are sufficient for a full reconstruction of the function.

$$\int_{-\infty}^{\infty} f(x)\left(\cos(\omega x)\right)dx = 0 \tag{2.19}$$

These properties (Eqs. 2.18 and 2.19) may be derived by expressing $\cos(\theta)$ and $\sin(\theta)$ in terms of complex exponential quantities, as given by Eq. 2.20.

$$\begin{aligned} \cos(\theta) &= \frac{e^{j\theta} + e^{-j\theta}}{2} \\ \sin(\theta) &= \frac{e^{j\theta} - e^{-j\theta}}{2j} \end{aligned} \tag{2.20}$$

The derivation is left as an exercise. So, a full reconstruction of a function is possible with only cosines if the function is even, and with only sines if the function is odd.

2.3 | Discrete linear transform

In the previous discussion on the transform of a function, the function is considered as a continuous 1-D function. For a discrete representation of a function $f(n)$, it is sampled at periodic intervals, which gives a sequence of functional values. Each position in this sequence is denoted by an integer that is sampled at a specified sampling interval, X_0. A discrete representation of a function is given by Eq. 2.21.

$$f(n) = \{f(nX_0) \mid n \in \mathbb{Z}\} \tag{2.21}$$

In the above definition, $\mathbb{Z}$ is the set of integers. Hence, $f(n)$ may also be considered as a vector in an infinite dimensional vector space. However, in our context, they are represented in discrete domain as a vector in a finite dimensional space. For example, a function may be represented within a certain interval, 0 to $N-1$, as $\{f(n),$

$n = 0, 1, 2, ..., N - 1$}. The sampling interval is implicitly represented in this form, so that, even without an explicit mention of sampling interval, the representation of a function remains valid. Usually, the sampling interval is explicitly used only in interpreting the function with reference to physical terms or physical quantities in the functional space. A discrete function is usually represented in a finite dimensional space (as an N-dimensional vector) by either a row or a column vector. In this book, we consider the representation in the form of a column vector, $\boldsymbol{f} = [f(0) \ f(1) \ f(2) \cdots f(N-1)]^{\mathsf{T}}$.

2.3.1 | A general form of discrete linear transform

To understand a *discrete linear transform* (DLT), consider a simple matrix multiplication as given in Eq. 2.22.

$$\boldsymbol{y}_{m \times 1} = \mathbf{B}_{m \times n} \boldsymbol{x}_{n \times 1} \tag{2.22}$$

where, $\boldsymbol{x}_{n \times 1}$ is an n-dimensional column vector that is multiplied by a matrix, $\mathbf{B}_{m \times n}$, of dimensions $m \times n$, and $\boldsymbol{y}_{m \times 1}$ is the resulting m-dimensional column vector. This is a transformation of a column vector $\boldsymbol{x}$ into another column vector $\boldsymbol{y}$ of a different dimension by the corresponding transformation matrix. This is known as a *linear transformation* or *discrete linear transformation* (DLT), since it has a discrete representation of the transformation. If the *transformation matrix*, $\mathbf{B}$, is a square matrix and invertible, the transform has an inverse transform.

We may note that, analogous to the previous discussion on basis functions, the rows, $\boldsymbol{b}_i$s, of the transformation matrix, $\mathbf{B}$, form the basis vectors in the DLT, as represented in Eq. 2.23

$$\mathbf{B} = \begin{bmatrix} \boldsymbol{b}_0^{*\mathsf{T}} \\ \boldsymbol{b}_1^{*\mathsf{T}} \\ \vdots \\ \boldsymbol{b}_n^{*\mathsf{T}} \end{bmatrix} \tag{2.23}$$

In DLTs, instead of inner products between two functions, inner product of two vectors is performed, which is equivalent to the scalar dot product of two vectors. The row vectors in $\mathbf{B}$ are indicated by transpose operations in Eq. 2.23, which are complex conjugates. This representation is only to keep the consistency with the representation of the inner product. When a scalar dot product or inner product is performed between two vectors, the result is a scalar value. So, the scalar dot product of ith basis vector, $\boldsymbol{b}_i$, with an input vector, $\boldsymbol{x}$, provides the ith element of the transformed vector (and denoted by y_i), which is given in Eq. 2.24.

$$y_i = \boldsymbol{b}_i^{*\mathsf{T}} \boldsymbol{x} \tag{2.24}$$

The orthogonality condition in this case is stated as in Eq. 2.25.

$$\boldsymbol{b}_i^{*\mathsf{T}} \boldsymbol{b}_j = \begin{cases} 0, & \text{if } i \neq j \\ c_i, & \text{otherwise} \end{cases} \tag{2.25}$$

For any pair of basis vectors, $\boldsymbol{b}_i$ and $\boldsymbol{b}_j$, their inner product is 0 if and only if they are distinct, otherwise they have a nonzero value, c_i. With the discrete forms as in Eqs. 2.22 and 2.23, a similar representation of a function as a linear combination of basis vectors is achieved. In the expanded form, $\boldsymbol{x}$ is represented as given below.

$$\boldsymbol{x} = \sum_{i=0}^{N-1} \lambda_i \boldsymbol{b}_i \tag{2.26}$$

where, λ_is are the magnitudes of the components along the direction of $\boldsymbol{b}_i^*$s, which are computed as,

$$\lambda_i = \boldsymbol{b}_i^{*^\top} \boldsymbol{x} \tag{2.27}$$

Accordingly, the transform of $\boldsymbol{x} = [x_0 \ x_1 \ \dots \ x_{n-1}]^\top$ is defined by the vector, $\boldsymbol{y} = [y_0 \ y_1 \ \dots \ y_{m-1}]^\top$, which is expressed in Eq. 2.22. If $\mathbf{B}$ is invertible, $\boldsymbol{x}$ is recovered from $\boldsymbol{y}$, as given by Eq. 2.28.

$$\boldsymbol{x} = \mathbf{B}^{-1} \boldsymbol{y} \tag{2.28}$$

Also, if $\mathbf{B}$ is an orthonormal transformation matrix, then $\mathbf{B}^{-1} = \mathbf{B}^{\mathrm{H}} = (\mathbf{B}^*)^\top$, where $\mathbf{B}^{\mathrm{H}}$ denotes the Hermitian transpose of $\mathbf{B}$.

2.3.2 | Discrete Fourier transform

For the *discrete Fourier transform* (DFT), the basis vectors are represented as in Eq. 2.29. They are defined at N functional points.

$$b_k(n) = \frac{1}{\sqrt{N}} e^{j2\pi \frac{k}{N} n}, \text{ for } 0 \leq n \leq N-1, \text{ and } 0 \leq k \leq N-1 \tag{2.29}$$

where, $b_k(n)$ is the nth element of the kth basis vector. A basis vector is formed by computing each of the elements in it at every integer values within an interval of $n = 0$ to $N-1$. There are N such basis vectors that are indexed by k, and k varies from 0 to $N-1$.

The forward discrete Fourier transform of a discrete sequence, $f(n)$, a finite sequence of length N, is expressed by Eq. 2.30.

$$\hat{f}(k) = \sum_{n=0}^{N-1} f(n) e^{-j2\pi \frac{k}{N} n}, \text{ for } 0 \leq k \leq N-1 \tag{2.30}$$

This is simply an inner product of $f(n)$ and $e^{j2\pi \frac{k}{N} n}$. For computational advantage, instead of including the multiplying term of $\frac{1}{\sqrt{N}}$ in this expression, it has been compensated in the inverse transform expression by multiplying it by $\frac{1}{N}$, which avoids computing square roots.

The inverse discrete Fourier transform is given by Eq. 2.31.

$$f(n) = \frac{1}{N} \sum_{k=0}^{N-1} \hat{f}(k) e^{j2\pi \frac{k}{N} n}, \text{ for } 0 \leq n \leq N-1 \tag{2.31}$$

As it can be seen, it is a linear combination of the corresponding basis vectors used for reconstruction and the coefficients of the forward DFT, $\hat{f}(k)$. After reconstruction, the recovered functional values are the same as the original values.

2.3.3 | Discrete Fourier transform as Fourier series of a periodic function

The expression of the DFT may also be interpreted as a Fourier series of a periodic function. For example, consider a simple finite sequence with $N = 4$ to perform the DFT. There are only four functional values at $n = 0, 1, 2, 3$, as shown in Fig. 2.1 (a). If the functional values outside a given interval are not defined, any definition may be used as per the contextual convenience and other functional values are suffixed to perform the DFT. However, after the inverse transformation, it is necessary to retain the original observation window, which is within an interval from 0 to 3 in this example. Considering a periodic extension of the signal, the functional values in the given interval of 0 to 3 are repeated to satisfy the property of a *periodic signal*: $f(n + N) = f(n)$, where N is the period of the signal $f(n)$. In this example, $N = 4$, and the periodic extension of the signal is shown in Fig. 2.1 (b).

So, in this periodic signal, after every fourth sample, the same functional value keeps repeating. Thus, we may convert a finite sequence to a periodic function as follows. The definition of one period $f_p(x)$, $0 \le x < NX_0$, is given as,

$$f_p(x) = \begin{cases} f(x), & x = 0, X_0, 2X_0, ..., (N-1)X_0, \\ 0, & \text{otherwise.} \end{cases} \tag{2.32}$$

With the foregoing definition, $f(n)$ becomes a periodic sequence of period N such that $f(n + N) = f(n)$. In that case, the *fundamental radian frequency* becomes $\omega_0 = 2\pi \frac{1}{NX_0}$, and the *Fourier series* consists of components of its *harmonics*, say $\frac{k}{NX_0}$ for $k = 0, 1, 2, ...$. They are computed as follows:

$$\lambda\left(\frac{k}{NX_0}\right) = \frac{1}{NX_0} \sum_{n=0}^{N-1} f(nX_0) e^{-j2\pi \frac{k}{NX_0} nX_0} \Delta x,$$

$$= \frac{1}{N} \sum_{n=0}^{N-1} f(nX_0) e^{-j2\pi \frac{k}{N} n} \qquad (\text{Here, } \Delta x = X_0). \tag{2.33}$$

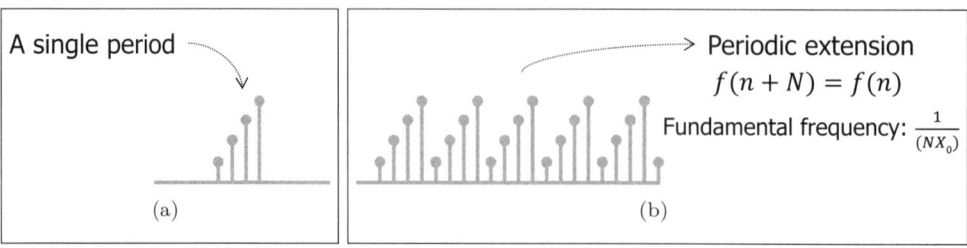

A single period ....⌄   Periodic extension
                                   $f(n + N) = f(n)$
                                   Fundamental frequency: $\frac{1}{(NX_0)}$

(a)   (b)

Figure 2.1 An example of periodic extension. (a) A finite length sequence, and (b) its periodic extension.

Any periodic signal may be represented as a linear combination of complex sinusoids and expressed as its DFT, which is the Fourier series of a periodic function. For example, in the context of the sequence of length 4, while performing the inverse DFT, only these four samples in the original window are considered. Further, the kth harmonic is represented by $\frac{k}{N}$ with an implicit sampling interval of X_0, at which the physical frequency is $\frac{k}{NX_0}$. So, the factor $\frac{k}{N}$ is also called the *normalized frequency* in this representation.

The DFT may be expressed in terms of a discrete linear transform as a matrix multiplication of a column vector with the transformation matrix formed by rows of complex conjugates of basis vectors. This column vector, $\boldsymbol{f}$, is a finite dimensional vector of functional values from which its transform, $\boldsymbol{F}$, is computed using the transformation matrix, as expressed by Eq. 2.34.

$$
\begin{bmatrix} F(0) \\ F(1) \\ \vdots \\ F(N-1) \end{bmatrix} = \begin{bmatrix} 1 & 1 & \cdots & 1 \\ 1 & e^{-j2\pi\frac{1}{N}} & \cdots & e^{-j2\pi\frac{N-1}{N}} \\ \vdots & \vdots & \ddots & \vdots \\ 1 & e^{-j2\pi\frac{N-1}{N}} & \cdots & e^{-j2\pi\frac{(N-1)^2}{N}} \end{bmatrix} \begin{bmatrix} f(0) \\ f(1) \\ \vdots \\ f(N-1) \end{bmatrix}
\tag{2.34}
$$

The transformation matrix formed by rows of conjugated basis vectors is represented in a shorter form with each kth and n^{th} element as in Eq. 2.35.

$$
\mathscr{F}_N = \left[e^{-j2\pi\frac{k}{N}n} \right]_{0 \leq (k,n) \leq N-1}
\tag{2.35}
$$

When the values of k and n range from 0 to $N-1$, it forms an $N \times N$ transformation matrix, $\mathscr{F}_N$.

In the forward transform, this transformation matrix, $\mathscr{F}_N$, is multiplied with a column vector, $\boldsymbol{f}$, the input vector. The output column vector, $\boldsymbol{F}$, represents the coefficients of the DFT, which is given by, $\boldsymbol{F} = \mathscr{F}_N \boldsymbol{f}$. Naturally, the original column vector is reconstructed by performing the inverse transform by multiplying the inverse of $\mathscr{F}_N$ with $\boldsymbol{F}$, which is given by, $\boldsymbol{f} = \mathscr{F}_N^{-1} \boldsymbol{F}$. Using the orthogonal properties of these functions, the inverse of the discrete Fourier transform matrix is computed from the *Hermitian transpose* of the corresponding matrix, i.e., $\mathscr{F}_N^{-1} = \frac{1}{N} \mathscr{F}_N^H$. A Hermitian transpose of a matrix is defined as the transpose of the matrix along with complex conjugate operations on it.

Numerical Example

Define the Discrete Fourier Transform (DFT) matrix for a sequence of length 3. Consider the following 3×3 image **A**.

100	125	50
50	90	80
70	100	50

Show how using the transformation matrix you can compute the DFT of **A**. In your answer to this part, you do not require to provide numerical computation. You should provide only the expressions in terms of matrix operations.

Solution

F is computed as,

1	1	1
1	$e^{\frac{-j\pi}{3}}$	$e^{\frac{-j2\pi}{3}}$
1	$e^{\frac{-j2\pi}{3}}$	$e^{\frac{-j4\pi}{3}}$

DFT of $\mathbf{A} = \mathbf{F}\mathbf{A}\mathbf{F}^{\mathsf{T}}$

2.3.4 | Properties of the DFT

The transform coefficient $\hat{f}(k)$, the DFT of $f(n)$, is N times the frequency component corresponding to the frequency $\frac{k}{NX_0}$. Hence, $\frac{k}{N}$ denotes the *normalized frequency* (considering $X_0 = 1$), so that the *normalized radian frequency* at $k = N$ is 2π. With this observation, the following two useful properties of the Fourier series are extended to the DFT.

(i) $\hat{f}(N + k) = \hat{f}(k)$.

(ii) For real $f(n)$, $\ddot{f}(k) = \hat{f}^*(\frac{N}{2} + k)$ (in this case, $\hat{f}(-k) = \hat{f}^*(k)$ and $\hat{f}(-k) = \hat{f}(N - k)$.)

The above two properties could also be proved from the definition of the DFT by exploiting the properties of complex exponentials. In the following, we briefly discuss the convolution-multiplication property of the DFT. This has been further elaborated in Section 2.5.2.

Linear, periodic, and circular convolutions

The *linear convolution* between two discrete sequences $f(n)$ and $h(n)$ is defined in the following way:

$$f * h(n) = \sum_{m=-\infty}^{\infty} f(m)h(n - m). \tag{2.36}$$

For two periodic sequences of the same period N, the *circular convolution* is defined by considering N functional values within a period only and extending the periodic definition of the function to the samples outside the base interval.

$$f \circledast h(n) = \sum_{m=0}^{N-1} f(m)h(n - m),$$

$$= \sum_{m=0}^{n} f(m)h(n - m) + \sum_{m=n+1}^{N-1} f(m)h(n - m + N). \tag{2.37}$$

It can be proved that the convolution–multiplication property of the Fourier transform holds for the circular convolution operation for DFT, as stated in the following theorem.

Given two finite length sequences $f(n)$ and $h(n)$ and their DFTs as $\hat{f}(k)$ and $\hat{g}(k)$, respectively, the DFT of their circular convolution is the same as the product of their DFTs, that is,

$$\mathbb{F}(f \circledast h(n)) = \hat{f}(k)\hat{h}(k). \tag{2.38}$$

In the same way, we also define circular cross-correlation as follows:
For two periodic sequences of the same period N, the *circular cross correlation* is defined by considering N functional values within a period only and extending the periodic definition of the function to the samples outside the base interval.

$$f \odot h(n) = \sum_{m=0}^{N-1} f(m)h(n+m),$$

$$= \sum_{m=0}^{N-n-1} f(m)h(n+m) + \sum_{m=N-n}^{N-1} f(m)h(n+m-N). \tag{2.39}$$

The relationship in the transform domain is given by the following theorem:
Given two finite length sequences $f(n)$ and $h(n)$ and their DFTs as $\hat{f}(k)$ and $\hat{g}(k)$, respectively, the DFT of their circular cross correlation is the same as the product of the DFT of $f(n)$ and the complex conjugate of the DFT of $h(n)$, that is,

$$\mathbb{F}(f \odot h(n)) = \hat{f}(k)\hat{h}(k)^*. \tag{2.40}$$

Energy preservation

Considering the orthonormal basis vectors that are $\sqrt{N}$ times the basis vectors (see Eq. (2.35)) in the expression of DFT, we can prove the following two properties of the conservation of energy of the function due to (Perseval and Plancherel Frazier, 2005).

$$\vec{x}.\vec{y^*} = \frac{1}{N}\vec{\hat{x}}.\vec{\hat{y^*}}, \tag{2.41}$$

$$||x||^2 = \vec{x}.\vec{x^*} = \frac{1}{N}\vec{\hat{x}}.\vec{\hat{x^*}} = \frac{1}{N}||\hat{x}||^2. \tag{2.42}$$

Please note that, following similar convention of denoting the DFT of a sequence in this text, the DFT of a vector $\vec{x}$ is expressed in the above as $\vec{\hat{x}}$.

Other properties

Other properties remain the same as those of the Fourier transform by considering the translation in the functional domain or frequency domain as the *circular shift* of the sequences. A circular shift of M samples in the sequence $f(n)$ makes it a sequence as $f((n-M) \bmod N)$. Let the operation $x \bmod N$ be denoted as $<x>_N$. In Table 2.1, the different properties of DFT of sequences of length N (Mitra, 2013) are listed.

Table 2.1 Properties of discrete Fourier transforms of sequences of length N.

Name	Given input conditions	Resulting DFT
Linearity	$ax(n) + by(n)$, a and b are arbitrary scalar constants	$a\hat{x}(k) + b\hat{y}(k)$
Circular time shifting	$x(<n - n_0>_N)$	$e^{-j2\pi\frac{k}{N}n_0}\hat{x}(k)$
Circular frequency shifting	$e^{j2\pi\frac{k_0}{N}n}x(n)$	$\hat{x}(<k - k_0>_N)$
Duality	$\hat{x}(n)$	$Nx(<-k>_N)$
Circular Convolution–multiplication property	$x \circledast h(n)$	$\hat{x}(k)\hat{h}(k)$
Multiplication–convolution property	$x(n)y(n)$	$\frac{1}{N}\hat{x} \circledast \hat{h}(k)$
Circular Cross Correlation–multiplication with conjugates property	$x \circledcirc h(n)$	$\hat{x}(k)\hat{h}(k)^*$

2.3.5 | Generalized discrete Fourier transform

There also exist certain kinds of orthogonal basis vectors that are derived or extended from the discrete Fourier transform representation. These are called *generalized discrete Fourier transform* (GDFT). In the DFT, the basis vectors are generated by sampling the complex sinusoidal function in regular intervals between 0 to $N - 1$. By introducing a phase shift of β in this interval, a variation of the DFT may be obtained with a different set of basis vectors. Also, while defining the basis vectors in the DFT, the harmonics are generated at regular intervals. So, by introducing a frequency shift of α in the frequency space, another set of basis vectors is generated. The representation of basis vectors with these shifts is given in Eq. 2.43.

$$b_k^{\alpha,\beta}(n) = \frac{1}{\sqrt{N}}e^{j2\pi\frac{k+\alpha}{N}(n+\beta)}, \text{ for } 0 \leq n \leq N - 1, \text{ and } 0 \leq k \leq N - 1 \tag{2.43}$$

Like the DFT, the above representation also generates N basis vectors of N dimensions which are orthogonal vectors that form an invertible square matrix.

Similar to the DFT, these basis vectors are used to compute transform coefficients from an input column vector. Then, the input vector is reconstructed using the transform coefficients and corresponding basis vectors. The forward and inverse GDFTs are given by Eqs. 2.44 and 2.45, respectively.

$$\hat{f}_{\alpha,\beta}(k) = \sum_{n=0}^{N-1} f(n)e^{-j2\pi\frac{k+\alpha}{N}(n+\beta)}, \text{ for } 0 \leq k \leq N - 1 \tag{2.44}$$

$$f(n) = \frac{1}{N}\sum_{k=0}^{N-1} \hat{f}_{\alpha,\beta}(k)e^{j2\pi\frac{k+\alpha}{N}(n+\beta)}, \text{ for } 0 \leq n \leq N - 1 \tag{2.45}$$

Also, the transformation matrix is expressed in the form of Eq. 2.46

$$\mathscr{F}_{\alpha,\beta,N} = \left[e^{-j2\pi\frac{k+\alpha}{N}(n+\beta)}\right]_{0\leq(k,n)\leq N-1} \tag{2.46}$$

Table 2.2 Examples of transformation matrices.

α	β	Transform Name	Notation
0	0	Discrete Fourier Transform (DFT)	$\hat{f}(k)$
0	$\frac{1}{2}$	Odd Time Discrete Fourier Transform (OTDFT)	$\hat{f}_{0,\frac{1}{2}}(k)$
$\frac{1}{2}$	0	Odd Frequency Discrete Fourier Transform (OFDFT)	$\hat{f}_{\frac{1}{2},0}(k)$
$\frac{1}{2}$	$\frac{1}{2}$	Odd Frequency Odd Time Discrete Fourier Transform (O^{2}DFT)	$\hat{f}_{\frac{1}{2},\frac{1}{2}}(k)$

where, the elements are seen to retain a similar expression as in Eq. 2.35, except for additional parameters of α and β, which generate different sets of transformation matrices.

Some popular transformation matrices are specially defined at particular values of α and β, one of which gives the DFT at $\alpha = 0$ and $\beta = 0$. Four such examples of transformation matrices are illustrated in Table 2.2.

The transformation matrices that are represented in Eq. 2.47 have different properties, and all of them have their respective inverse transforms. Also, there are different relationships of the inverse transforms, some of which are as follows:

$$
\begin{aligned}
\mathscr{F}_{0,0,N}^{-1} &= \frac{1}{N}\mathscr{F}_{0,0,N}^{H} = \frac{1}{N}\mathscr{F}_{0,0,N}^{*} \\[2mm]
\mathscr{F}_{\frac{1}{2},0,N}^{-1} &= \frac{1}{N}\mathscr{F}_{\frac{1}{2},0,N}^{H} = \frac{1}{N}\mathscr{F}_{0,\frac{1}{2},N}^{*} \\[2mm]
\mathscr{F}_{0,\frac{1}{2},N}^{-1} &= \frac{1}{N}\mathscr{F}_{0,\frac{1}{2},N}^{H} = \frac{1}{N}\mathscr{F}_{\frac{1}{2},0,N}^{*} \\[2mm]
\mathscr{F}_{\frac{1}{2},\frac{1}{2},N}^{-1} &= \frac{1}{N}\mathscr{F}_{\frac{1}{2},\frac{1}{2},N}^{H} = \frac{1}{N}\mathscr{F}_{\frac{1}{2},\frac{1}{2},N}^{*}
\end{aligned}
\tag{2.47}
$$

2.4 | Symmetric and anti-symmetric extensions of a finite sequence

Though it is not possible to have cosine and sine transforms for every kind of function in the continuous domain, they may be defined for any finite dimensional sequence in the discrete domain using generalized discrete Fourier transform. To explain this process, it is necessary to understand the concept of symmetric and anti-symmetric extension of a finite sequence. Given a finite sequence with a specific interval, there is a flexibility of defining the functional values beyond its existing interval with contextual convenience. With suitable extension of the sequences, it is made to have certain useful properties for performing transformation on the extended sequences. Two of such extensions are *symmetric* and *anti-symmetric* extensions, which are of interest in relevance to transforms.

Consider an example of a finite sequence, $x(n), 0 \leq n \leq N-1$ of length N, as shown in Fig. 2.2 (a). The sequence may be symmetrically extended at its end point (around the last sample point, $x(N-1)$) in two different ways, symmetric and anti-symmetric extensions. A type of symmetric extension of this sequence is shown in Fig. 2.2 (b), where the center of symmetry lies at the end sample of the original sequence, as denoted by an arrow mark in the figure. Here, for the given four samples ($N = 4$), an additional three samples (i.e., $N - 1$ samples) are appended to maintain the symmetry of samples values, so that the total length of the extended sequence becomes 7 (i.e., $2N - 1$). This type of symmetric extension is called *whole symmetric extension* and the type of symmetry is called *whole symmetry* (WS). In another type of symmetry known as *half symmetry* (HS),

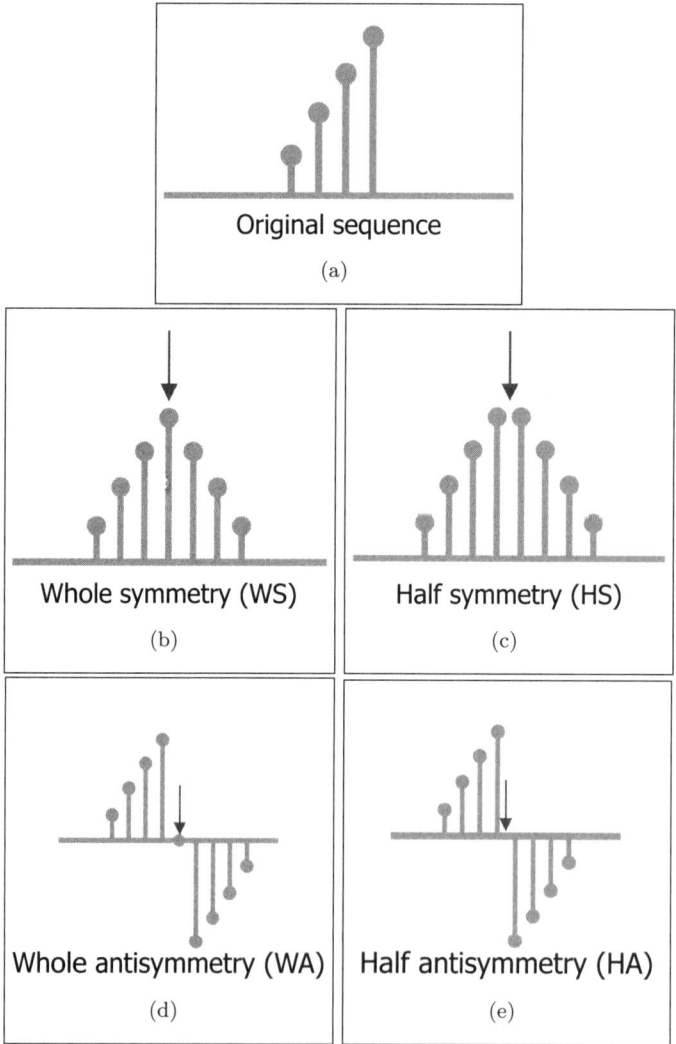

Figure 2.2 Symmetric and anti-symmetric extensions of a finite sequence.
(a) Original input sequence. (b) Whole symmetric extension. (c) Half symmetric extension.
(d) Whole anti-symmetric extension. (e) Half anti-symmetric extension. (b) and (c) are even functions, while (d) and (e) are odd functions.

as shown in Fig. 2.2 (c), the center lies at a separation of an interval of half the sampling period (or sampling interval) from the end sample, which is shown by an arrow in the figure. This type of extension is called *half symmetric extension*. In this case, the symmetric extension may be made centering about the midpoint between the $(N-1)^{\text{th}}$ and the Nth sample. Here, toward the left of the center there are four samples, and toward its right too, there are four samples, so that the total length of extended sequence becomes 8 (i.e., $2N$).

A type of anti-symmetric extension of this sequence is shown in Fig. 2.2 (d), where the center of symmetry lies at a newly introduced sample after the end sample of the original sequence, as denoted by an arrow mark in the figure. The value of this new sample at the center is 0. The subsequent values after the central sample are determined by negation of the corresponding values in the original sequence to make it anti-symmetric, as shown in the figure. Here, the length of the extended sequence becomes 9 (i.e., $2N+1$) that is resulting from 4 ($N = 4$) original sequence values. In this case, there is one new value at the center of the extended sequence, and four subsequent values in a manner to make it antisymmetric. This type of anti-symmetric extension is called *whole anti-symmetric extension* and the type of antisymmetry is called *whole anti-symmetry* (WA). For a WA extension, a zero is introduced at the Nth sample point. Similarly, in a half anti-symmetric extension, instead of introducing a sample with value 0 explicitly after the end sample, the center is assumed to lie at a separation of an interval of half of the sampling period after the end sample, as shown in figure Fig. 2.2 (e). Here, the number of samples in the extended sequence is 8 (i.e., $2N$), similar to half symmetric extension, with a negation of the corresponding values in the original sequence to make it anti-symmetric. This type of anti-symmetric extension is called *half anti-symmetric extension* and the type of antisymmetry is called *half anti-symmetry* (HA).

These extensions from $x(n)$ are mathematically defined below:

(i) For the WS extension at the end sample point,

$$\tilde{x}(n) = \begin{cases} x(n) & 0 \leq n \leq N-1 \\ x(2N-n-2) & N \leq n \leq 2N-2 \end{cases} \tag{2.48}$$

(ii) For the HS extension at the end sample point,

$$\tilde{x}(n) = \begin{cases} x(n) & 0 \leq n \leq N-1 \\ x(2N-n-1) & N \leq n \leq 2N-1 \end{cases} \tag{2.49}$$

(iii) For the WA extension at the end sample point,

$$\tilde{x}(n) = \begin{cases} x(n) & 0 \leq n \leq N-1 \\ 0 & n = N \\ -x(2N-n) & N+1 \leq n \leq 2N \end{cases} \tag{2.50}$$

(iv) For the HA extension at the end sample point,

$$\tilde{x}(n) = \begin{cases} x(n) & 0 \leq n \leq N-1 \\ -x(2N-n-1) & N+1 \leq n \leq 2N-1 \end{cases} \tag{2.51}$$

For a given function or a sequence, its symmetric extension makes the function an even function, considering the center of symmetry as origin. Similarly, an anti-symmetric extension of the function makes it an odd function, whose origin lies at the center of anti-symmetry. Hence, a given sequence is converted to even or odd sequence by making an appropriate extension to it. If these extended sequences further go through a periodic extension, they are suitable for transformation using the DFT and the GDFTs. Effectively the computation becomes equivalent to transformation using either cosine or sine basis functions. For instance, in case of a finite sequence that is extended to become an even function by symmetric extension, transformation with the DFT on it effectively requires only cosine parts. Thereby, it forms a discrete cosine transform (DCT) on using a symmetric extension of the sequence. The original sequence is also reconstructed back using the corresponding discrete cosine transform coefficients and limiting the observation window only to original interval. In this way, the entire original sequence is recovered just by using cosine transforms. Similarly, for an odd function formed by extending a finite sequence using anti-symmetric extension, it is sufficient to use only sine functions in its fully reconstructible transformation. As computation of Fourier transform of an odd function involves only computations of inner products with sine functions from the set of basis functions, it effectively reduces to a discrete sine transform (DST) on using an anti-symmetric extension of the sequence. The existence of discrete sine transforms and discrete cosine transforms for any finite sequence is mainly attributed to the flexibility in using symmetric and anti-symmetric extensions of sequences.

2.5 | Discrete cosine/sine transforms

For a finite sequence, there are different types of symmetric or anti-symmetric extensions at its either ends, and correspondingly the signal may become even or odd. From the very definition of generalized discrete Fourier transforms, there are different kinds of discrete Fourier transforms that may be applied on the extended sequences. Accordingly, there are different DCTs and DSTs. Consider an example of a finite sequence shown in Fig. 2.3 (a). If this sequence is periodically extended by whole symmetric extension on both of its ends, the functional values would be symmetric around a particular value at the center of symmetry, as shown in Fig. 2.3 (a). Here, the original number of values in the sequence is 4. The period of this periodically extended function is the interval of the entire sequence after symmetric extension, which is 7.

It is possible to have cosine transforms for this sequence. Applying the discrete Fourier transform on its symmetric extension results in *type-I even DCT*, whose expression is given in Eq. 2.52.

$$\mathcal{C}_{1e}(x(n)) = X_{Ie}(k) = \sqrt{\frac{2}{N}}\alpha^2(k)\sum_{n=0}^{N} x(n)\cos\frac{2\pi nk}{2N}, \ 0 \leq k \leq N \tag{2.52}$$

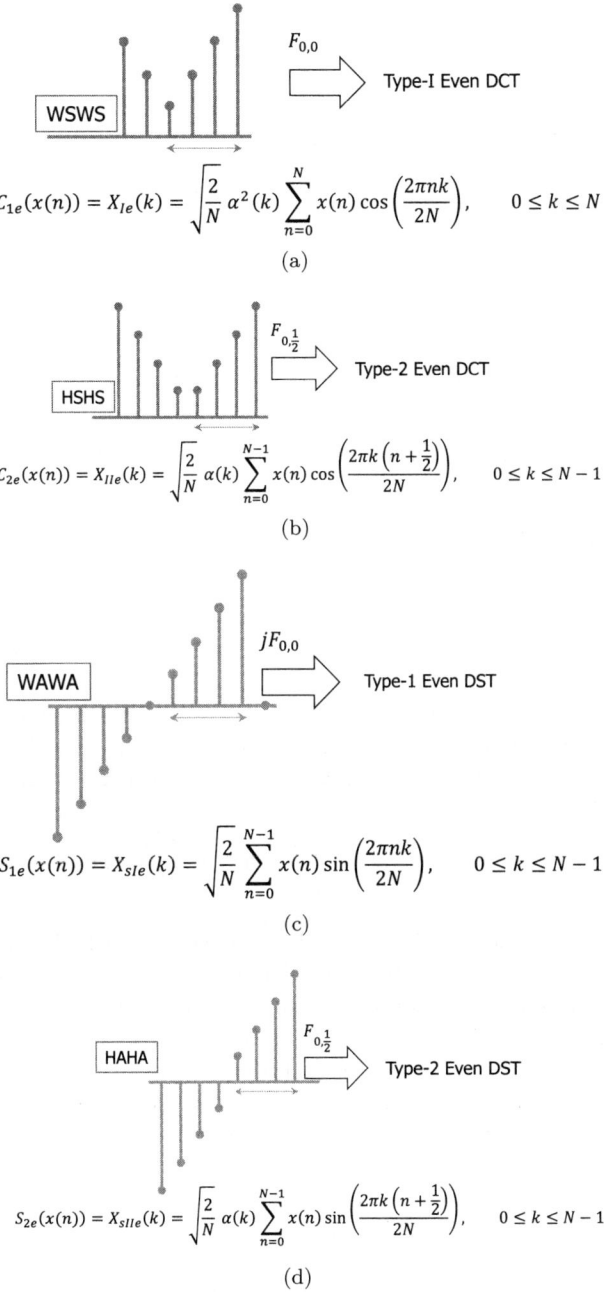

$$C_{1e}(x(n)) = X_{Ie}(k) = \sqrt{\frac{2}{N}}\,\alpha^2(k)\sum_{n=0}^{N}x(n)\cos\left(\frac{2\pi nk}{2N}\right), \qquad 0 \le k \le N$$

(a)

$$C_{2e}(x(n)) = X_{IIe}(k) = \sqrt{\frac{2}{N}}\,\alpha(k)\sum_{n=0}^{N-1}x(n)\cos\left(\frac{2\pi k\left(n+\frac{1}{2}\right)}{2N}\right), \qquad 0 \le k \le N-1$$

(b)

$$S_{1e}(x(n)) = X_{sIe}(k) = \sqrt{\frac{2}{N}}\sum_{n=0}^{N-1}x(n)\sin\left(\frac{2\pi nk}{2N}\right), \qquad 0 \le k \le N-1$$

(c)

$$S_{2e}(x(n)) = X_{sIIe}(k) = \sqrt{\frac{2}{N}}\,\alpha(k)\sum_{n=0}^{N-1}x(n)\sin\left(\frac{2\pi k\left(n+\frac{1}{2}\right)}{2N}\right), \qquad 0 \le k \le N-1$$

(d)

Figure 2.3 Types of symmetric/anti-symmetric extensions at the two ends of a sequence.

Here, only the cosine function is used to form basis vectors. It can be observed in the expression that, for a sequence of length N, the transform generates a period of $2N$. Also, by definition of this transform, for a given value of N, the value of n ranges from 0 to N, requiring $N+1$ number of samples. For the sequence used in our illustration, the total number of samples in the sequence is 4. Since in this case, $N+1=4$, the value of N is 3.

So, the period is found to be $2N = 6$, which is also depicted in Fig. 2.3 (b). In the above equation, the term $\alpha(p)$ is used in normalization operation for making the vectors orthonormal, which are necessary properties to be satisfied for reconstructing the sequence. By definition, $\alpha(k)$ is expressed as in Eq. 2.53.

$$\alpha(k) = \begin{cases} \sqrt{\frac{1}{2}}, & \text{if } k = 0 \text{ or } N \\ 1, & \text{otherwise} \end{cases} \tag{2.53}$$

Likewise, periodically extending both ends of a sequence of length 4 with half symmetric extension would result in an even function of period 8, as depicted in Fig. 2.3 (c). Applying the GDFT with $\alpha = 0$ and $\beta = \frac{1}{2}$, which is the odd time discrete Fourier transform, on this extended sequence, we get a discrete cosine transform (DCT) of the sequence, called the *type-II even DCT*. An expression for type-II even DCT is given by Eq. 2.54, where it can be observed that for given N samples a period of $2N$ is generated by the transform.

$$\mathcal{C}_{2e}(x(n)) = X_{IIe}(k) = \sqrt{\frac{2}{N}}\alpha(k) \sum_{n=0}^{N-1} x(n)\cos\frac{2\pi k(n+\frac{1}{2})}{2N}, \ 0 \leq k \leq N-1 \tag{2.54}$$

This expression of DCT is most widely used in practical applications like image and video compression. When it is generally mentioned as discrete cosine transform in the literature, it refers to the type-II even DCT.

Similarly, discrete sine transforms are defined for anti-symmetric extensions of a finite sequence. Discrete Fourier transform of a whole anti-symmetric extension of a finite sequence with N samples defines *type-I even DST*, whose expression is given in Eq. 2.55.

$$\mathcal{S}_{1e}(x(n)) = X_{sIe}(k) = \sqrt{\frac{2}{N}} \sum_{n=1}^{N-1} x(n)\sin\frac{2\pi kn}{2N}, \ 1 \leq k \leq N-1 \tag{2.55}$$

Here, the number of samples in the original sequence is 4, which makes the number of samples in the extended sequence 9, as depicted in Fig. 2.3 (d). Since this transform generates a period of $2N$ for an original sequence of length N, the value of n in the expression ranges from 1 to $N-1$ in the definition of type-I even DST.

For a *type-II even DST*, general discrete Fourier transform with $\alpha = 0$ and $\beta = \frac{1}{2}$ is applied on a periodically extended half anti-symmetric extension of a finite sequence. An expression for type II even DST is given by Eq. 2.56.

$$\mathcal{S}_{2e}(x(n)) = X_{sIIe}(k) = \sqrt{\frac{2}{N}}\alpha(k) \sum_{n=0}^{N-1} x(n)\sin\frac{2\pi k(n+\frac{1}{2})}{2N}, \ 0 \leq k \leq N-1 \tag{2.56}$$

Apart from these four DCTs and DSTs, many other DCTs and DSTs also exist. Since there are two ends to a finite sequence, and two variations of symmetry and two variations of anti-symmetry are possible at each end, there are sixteen different types of DCTs and DSTs that may be defined for a finite sequence. However, type-II even DCT is mostly used in signal, image, and video compression and related applications.

Numerical Example

Given a 1-D signal $x(n) = \{1, 2, 4, 7\}$. Compute the Type-II Discrete Cosine Transform (DCT) of $x(n)$.

Solution

The matrix form of DCT contains the elements given by $C(u, v) = \sqrt{1/N}\cos((2v + 1)\pi u/2N)$, where $u = 0$, $0 \leq v \leq N - 1$ and $C(u, v) = \sqrt{2/N}\cos((2v + 1)\pi u/2N)$, where $1 \leq u \leq N - 1$, $0 \leq v \leq N - 1$. Thus,

$$
C = \begin{bmatrix}
0.5 & 0.5 & 0.5 & 0.5 \\
0.6533 & 0.2706 & -0.2706 & -0.6533 \\
0.5 & -0.5 & -0.5 & 0.5 \\
0.2706 & -0.6533 & 0.6533 & 0.2706
\end{bmatrix}
$$

Multiply the given signal (as a column vector) with the matrix form representation of DCT to get $\{7, -4.446, 1, -0.317\}$.

2.5.1 | Matrix representation of transformations

All the DCT and DST transformations discussed so far may be expressed as discrete linear transforms. To explain a matrix form of their representation, type-II DCT is taken as an example. Representing an element of this transformation matrix as $(k, n)^{\text{th}}$ element, the transformation matrix is denoted as in Eq. 2.57.

$$
\mathscr{C}_N = \left[\sqrt{\frac{2}{N}}\alpha(k)\cos\left(\frac{\pi k(2n + 1)}{2N}\right) \right]_{0 \leq (k,n) \leq N-1} \tag{2.57}
$$

This matrix is referred to as an *N-point DCT matrix*, which is a type-II DCT matrix. There are certain properties of this matrix, which are interesting and exploited in developing different algorithms using DCT coefficients. One such property is that, each row of this transformation matrix is either symmetric, which is known as even row, or anti-symmetric, which is known as odd row. This property is expressed by Eq. 2.58.

$$
\mathscr{C}_N(k, N - 1 - n) = \begin{cases} \mathscr{C}_N(k, n), & \text{if } k \text{ is even} \\ -\mathscr{C}_N(k, n), & \text{if } k \text{ is odd} \end{cases} \tag{2.58}
$$

The transformation is expressed in terms of its multiplication with the input column vector, $\boldsymbol{x}$, to get the corresponding transformed DCT column vector, $\boldsymbol{y}$, as $\boldsymbol{y} = \mathscr{C}_N\boldsymbol{x}$. The inverse of this transformation is expressed as, $\mathscr{C}_N^{-1} = \mathscr{C}_N^{\mathsf{T}}$. Since the transformation is an orthonormal expansion, the inverse operation is simply computed as a transpose operation.

2.5.2 | Convolution multiplication property

One of the advantages of using Fourier transform is computationally simplifying the convolution operations. The convolution operation that is performed in the functional domain becomes equivalent to multiplication in the transform domain when processed with Fourier transforms, which is depicted in Fig. 2.4. For a given input function and the impulse response of a system, the convolution operation between them is equivalent to the product of the Fourier transform of the input function and the Fourier transform of the impulse function. This property is known as the *convolution multiplication property* (CMP) of Fourier transforms. In Section 2.3.2, the convolutional multiplication property of the DFT is discussed. Here, we elaborate it further in the context of DCTs and DSTs. For the convenience of discussion we summarize definitions of linear convolutions and its special cases here too.

Given two functions, $f(x)$ (an input) and $h(x)$ (the unit impulse response), the convolution between them is defined as in Eq. 2.59.

$$f(x) * h(x) = \int_{-\infty}^{\infty} f(\tau)h(x - \tau)d\tau. \tag{2.59}$$

In discrete domain, the linear convolution operation is expressed by Eq. 2.60.

$$f(n) * h(n) = \sum_{-\infty}^{\infty} f(m)h(n - m) \tag{2.60}$$

Here, accounting to discrete representation, summations are used instead of integrations and shifted unit impulse responses along the corresponding functional domain are taken at integral points. While performing this linear convolution operation, it is assumed that both the input sequence and the impulse response are of infinite length. For performing convolutions with finite sequences, the DFT is applied with necessary modification in the definition of functional values. By the definition of a finite sequence, it is not necessary that

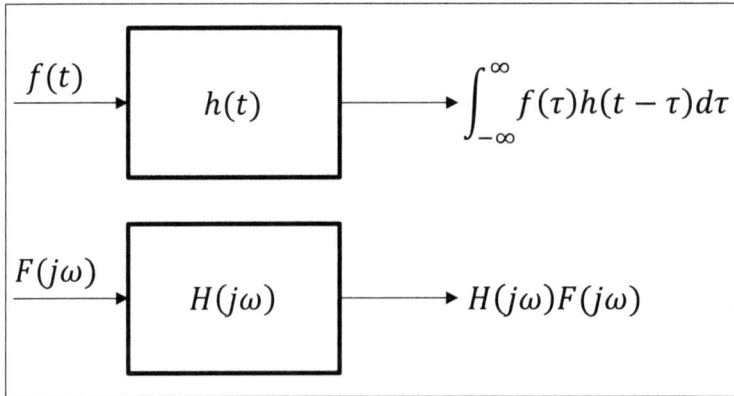

Figure 2.4 Depiction of convolution multiplication property for Fourier transforms.

the corresponding functional domain where the function is not defined in a finite sequence are set to 0.

If the undefined values in the functional domain are set to 0, it is equivalent to a linear convolution. But, by considering a periodic extension of the finite sequences, for example, $f(x + N) = f(x)$, it becomes a periodic convolution of the two finite sequences. A *periodic convolution* of two finite sequences is defined as the convolution between two finite sequences with their periodic extensions. For performing the periodic convolution between two extended sequences, it is necessary that they have the same period. This results in a periodic sequence of the same period. The expression for the periodic convolution with a period N is given in Eq. 2.61. It is also called the *circular convolution* between two periodic sequences.

$$
\begin{aligned}
f \circledast h(n) &= \sum_{m=0}^{N-1} f(m)h(n-m), \\
&= \sum_{m=0}^{n} f(m)h(n-m) + \sum_{m=n+1}^{N-1} f(m)h(n-m+N)
\end{aligned}
\tag{2.61}
$$

The computation of the circular convolution is broken into two parts using the definition of periodicity, which is also shown in Eq. 2.61. It is not necessary to compute in the whole functional domain. Instead, it is sufficient to compute the values of the output sequence for a single period. So, a circular convolution of period N is computed within the interval from 0 to $N - 1$ only. It can be shown that for DFTs, the convolution multiplication property holds for the circular convolution. For an impulse response, $h(n)$, of a system given as a finite sequence of the same length of the input sequence $f(n)$, as expressed by Eq. 2.62, the product of their corresponding coefficients of DFTs are the same as the DFT coefficients of a sequence obtained by circular convolution of the sequences $f(n)$ and $h(n)$. This may be expressed mathematically as follows.

$$
\widehat{f \otimes h}(k) = \hat{f}(k)\hat{h}(k)
\tag{2.62}
$$

where, $\hat{ }$ represents the DFT of a sequence.

There also exists another type of convolution with two finite sequences if we consider their antiperiodic extensions. A function $f(x)$ is said to be an *anti-periodic* function with a period N if $f(x + N) = -f(x)$. An anti-periodic function is also a periodic function with the periodicity the same as twice the anti-period, i.e., an anti-periodic function of anti-period N is a periodic function with period $2N$. So, an anti-periodic extension of a sequence has a periodicity of twice the number of samples in the original sequence. Similar to the circular convolution for periodic extensions of finite sequences, the *skew circular convolution* is defined as convolution between two finite sequences with their anti-periodic extensions, where the extended sequences have the same anti-period. Here too, the convolved output is restricted only to the observation window of the original sequence. A skew circular convolution between two finite sequences is expressed in Eq. 2.63 as a linear convolution between two antiperiodic extensions of two finite sequences of the same length

N and the same anti-period N. After applying the properties of anti-periodic extension, we get the following.

$$
\begin{aligned}
f \circledS h(n) &= \sum_{m=0}^{N-1} f(m)h(n-m), \\
&= \sum_{m=0}^{n} f(m)h(n-m) - \sum_{m=n+1}^{N-1} f(m)h(n-m+N)
\end{aligned}
\tag{2.63}
$$

Different convolution multiplication properties are associated with the use of circular and skew circular convolutions, which hold for DCTs and DSTs too. For example, consider two functions, an input sequence, $x(n)$, and an impulse response, $h(n)$, of same lengths. Let, $u(n)$ and $w(n)$ denote the circular and the skew circular convolution operations between $x(n)$ and $h(n)$, respectively. Processing both of these functions individually with type-I DCTs and computing their product, along with their corresponding multiplication factor by the definition of transform, results in a type-I DCT of the circularly convolved output of the two sequences, as expressed in Eq. 2.64.

$$
\mathcal{C}_{1e}\left(u(n)\right) = \sqrt{2N}\,\mathcal{C}_{1e}\left(x(l)\right)\mathcal{C}_{1e}\left(h(m)\right)
\tag{2.64}
$$

where, $u(n) = x(n) \circledast h(n)$. Thus, the multiplication of two periodic extended sequences in transform domain results in the output of circular convolution in transform domain.

The product of a type-II DCT of the input function and type-I DCT of the impulse response results in a type-II DCT of the corresponding convolved result, which is expressed in Eq. 2.65.

$$
\mathcal{C}_{2e}\left(u(n)\right) = \sqrt{2N}\,\mathcal{C}_{2e}\left(x(l)\right)\mathcal{C}_{1e}\left(h(m)\right)
\tag{2.65}
$$

The number of samples in each term depends upon corresponding type of DCT that is applied on its respective function. Here, N samples define a type-II DCT of periodicity $2N$, and $N+1$ samples define a type-I DCT of periodicity $2N$. Since the two periodic sequences to be convolved should have the same periodicity, N samples are considered in $x(n)$ and $N+1$ samples are considered in $h(n)$, in this particular case, so that the output is defined by a periodicity of $2N$. This consistency in the number of samples and periodicity has to be always cautiously verified while applying these properties.

2.6 | Transforms in 2-D

The concepts of transforms and convolutions that are explained for 1-D functions so far in this chapter are extended to 2-D functions in this section. Consider a 2-D function, $f(x,y)$, that is represented using a set of basis functions, B, as a linear combination of the basis functions, $b_{ij}(x,y)$. It is given by $f(x,y) = \sum_i \sum_j \lambda_{ij} b_{ij}(x,y)$, where, λ_{ij} are the coefficients of transformation. The extension of 1-D transforms to 2-D becomes trivial if the 2-D basis functions are separable. In this case, according to separability property, a set of 2-D basis functions are represented in a form of two separable sets of 1-D functions, as in Eq. 2.66.

$$
\text{B} = \{b_{ij}(x,y) = g_i(x) \cdot h_j(y)\}
\tag{2.66}
$$

where, $g_i(x)$ and $h_j(y)$ are 1-D basis functions. Thus, a 2-D basis function is expressed as a product of two 1-D basis functions. If both the sets of these 1-D basis functions are orthogonal, the corresponding set of 2-D basis functions is also orthogonal. In such a case, the 2-D transform coefficients are expressed by reusing the 1-D transform computations as given in Eq. 2.67.

$$\lambda_{ij} = \sum_y h_j^*(y) \left(\sum_x f(x,y) g_i^*(x) \right) \tag{2.67}$$

Here, first the transforms are computed with respect to variation over x at a given value of y. Then, the transform with respect to y is computed.

The computations performed in Eq. 2.67 may also be expressed in terms of matrix operations. The sequence of computations involves, first, the transformation of columns, and then, the transformation of rows. Consider a 1-D transformation matrix, $\mathbf{B}$ and a corresponding 2-D input image, $\mathbf{X}$, of dimensions $M \times N$. So, first the columns are transformed in the input image data. Since the dimension of each column is M, a corresponding transformation matrix that deals with M-dimensional vectors is considered, which is of dimensions $M \times M$, as given by Eq. 2.68.

$$[\mathbf{Y_1}]_{M \times N} = \mathbf{B}_{M \times M} \mathbf{X}_{M \times N} \tag{2.68}$$

After this transformation, the M-dimensional columns of the input image are transformed into another set of N M-dimensional columns by the transformation matrix to get a matrix of dimensions $M \times N$. Then the N-dimensional rows are transformed by a corresponding N-point transformation matrix, i.e., of dimensions $N \times N$, to get the final transformed image of size $M \times N$, as given in Eq. 2.69.

$$\begin{aligned} \mathbf{Y}_{M \times N} &= [\mathbf{B}_{N \times N} \mathbf{Y_1}^\top]^\top \\ &= \mathbf{Y_1} \mathbf{B}_{N \times N}^\top \end{aligned} \tag{2.69}$$

From Eqs. 2.68 and 2.69, the whole operation is expressed in a composite form by Eq. 2.70.

$$\mathbf{Y}_{M \times N} = \mathbf{B}_{M \times M} \mathbf{X}_{M \times N} \mathbf{B}_{N \times N}^\top \tag{2.70}$$

Using the above processing, a 2-D discrete transformation is represented by a 2-D input image and a corresponding transformation matrix toward its right and toward its left to get the corresponding transformed image in the transformed domain.

Consider the DFT as a typical example for applying the separable form of 2-D transforms on an image, $f(x,y)$ of size $M \times N$. The forward and inverse DFTs are also expressed using the summation operations as in Eqs. 2.71 and 2.72, respectively, as the basis functions or basis vectors are separable.

$$\begin{aligned} \hat{f}(k,l) &= \sum_{m=0}^{M-1} \sum_{n=0}^{N-1} f(m,n) e^{-j2\pi \frac{km}{M}} e^{-j2\pi \frac{ln}{N}} \\ &= \sum_{m=0}^{M-1} e^{-j2\pi \frac{km}{M}} \sum_{n=0}^{N-1} f(m,n) e^{-j2\pi \frac{ln}{N}} \end{aligned} \tag{2.71}$$

$$f(m,n) = \frac{1}{MN} \sum_{k=0}^{M-1} \sum_{l=0}^{N-1} \hat{f}(k,l) e^{j2\pi \frac{km}{M}} e^{j2\pi \frac{ln}{N}} \tag{2.72}$$

It is observed that, this is a simple extension of the 1-D DFT that is discussed in Section 2.3.2. Also, using the matrix representation of DFT matrix and separability property, the transformation of $\boldsymbol{f}$ is expressed by Eq. 2.73.

$$\hat{\boldsymbol{f}} = \mathscr{F}_M \boldsymbol{f} \mathscr{F}_N^{\top} \tag{2.73}$$

where, $\mathscr{F}_M$ is an $M \times M$ transformation matrix and $\mathscr{F}_N$ is an $N \times N$ transformation matrix, which are simply called the M-point DFT matrix and the N-point DFT matrix, respectively.

Similar to 2-D DFTs, 2-D DCTs of a 2-D function, $\boldsymbol{x}$, are defined in Eqs. 2.74 and 2.75 for type-I and type-II 2-D DCT, respectively.

$$\mathbf{X}_I(k,l) = \frac{2}{N} \alpha^2(k) \alpha^2(l) \sum_{m=0}^{M} \sum_{n=0}^{N} \left(\boldsymbol{x}(m,n) \cos\left(\frac{m\pi k}{M}\right) \cos\left(\frac{n\pi l}{N}\right) \right), \tag{2.74}$$
$$0 \le k \le M; \; 0 \le l \le N$$

$$\mathbf{X}_{II}(k,l) = \frac{2}{N} \alpha(k) \alpha(l) \sum_{m=0}^{M-1} \sum_{n=0}^{N-1} \left(\boldsymbol{x}(m,n) \cos\left(\frac{(2m+1)\pi k}{2M}\right) \cos\left(\frac{(2n+1)\pi l}{2N}\right) \right), \tag{2.75}$$
$$0 \le k \le M-1; \; 0 \le l \le N-1$$

Also, the matrix representation of 2-D DCT, as an extension of 1-D DCT representation, is expressed in Eq. 2.76.

$$\mathbf{X} = \mathrm{DCT}(\boldsymbol{x}) = \mathscr{C}_M \boldsymbol{x} \mathscr{C}_N^{\top} \tag{2.76}$$

2.7 | Wavelet transforms

Wavelets are the functions that have ideally finite support, in both their original domain (i.e., time or space) and the transformed domain (i.e., the temporal or spatial frequency domain). The wavelets also act as basis functions. Theoretically, due to their finite support in both original and transformed domains, wavelets have a very good localization property. However, in reality, no such function exists that truly satisfies such properties having finite support in both the original and transform domains. So, attempts are made to define functions that match these properties as far as possible. For example, consider the Dirac-delta function, $\delta(t)$, which is an impulse, as shown in Fig. 2.5 (a). One of the definitions of this function is that its functional value is infinite at $t = 0$ and zero everywhere else, and its integral over time is unity. The Fourier transformation of $\delta(t)$ is shown in Fig. 2.5 (b), which contains every frequency component of the function. It may be observed that, $\delta(t)$ is very much localized in time domain, but it has an infinite support in frequency domain. Similarly, consider another function, $\cos(8\pi t)$, which is a sinusoidal function, as shown in Fig. 2.6 (a). The Fourier transformation of $\cos(8\pi t)$ is shown in Fig. 2.6 (b). It may be observed that,

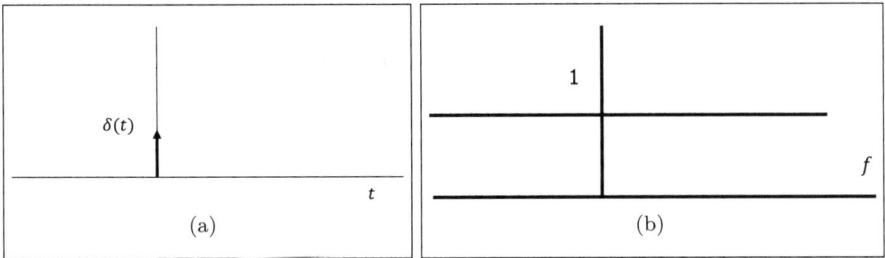

Figure 2.5 Dirac-delta function and its transform.

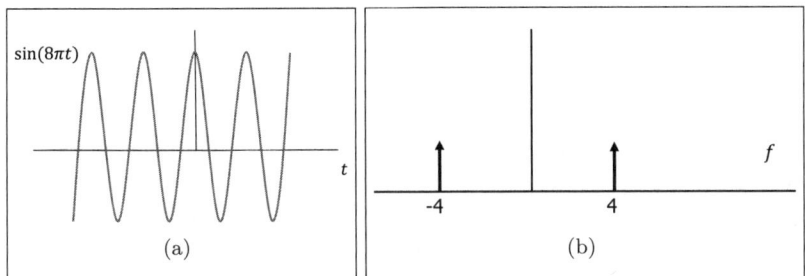

Figure 2.6 A sinusoidal function and its transform.

this function has a finite support in frequency domain, but it has an infinite support in time domain. These are the two contrasting examples, where one of the functions has a finite support in time domain and an infinite support in frequency domain, and the other function has it vice versa.

Consider a Gaussian function, which has the same form in both time and frequency domains. The Gaussian function is one of the most useful functions that has a wide applicability in statistics, function analysis, and various other domains. The functional form of the Gaussian function in time domain is given by Eq. 2.77.

$$g(t) = \frac{1}{\sigma_t \sqrt{2\pi}} e^{-\frac{t^2}{2\sigma_t^2}} \tag{2.77}$$

where, the parameter σ_t controls the width of the Gaussian pulse in time domain. The shape of a Gaussian pulse in time domain is shown in Fig. 2.7 (a), which has an infinite support, i.e., $g(t) \to 0$ as $t \to \infty$. The Fourier transform of the Gaussian function is also a Gaussian function (in frequency domain), which is given by Eq. 2.78.

$$G(\omega) = e^{-\frac{\omega^2 \sigma_f^2}{2}} \tag{2.78}$$

where, the parameter σ_f controls the width of the Gaussian pulse in frequency domain. The shape of the Gaussian pulse in the frequency domain is shown in Fig. 2.7 (b), which also

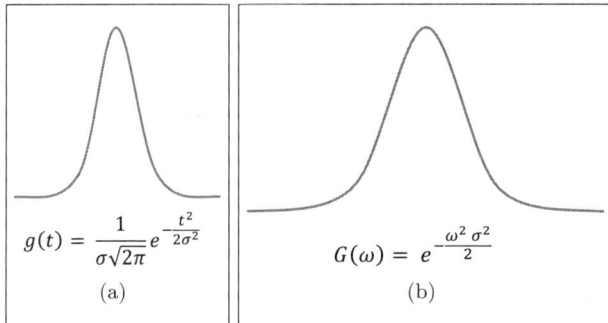

Figure 2.7 A Gaussian function in (a) time and (b) frequency domains.

has an infinite support, i.e., $G(\omega) \to 0$ as $\omega \to \infty$. The widths of the Gaussian pulses in time and frequency domains are inversely proportional. That is, if the width of a Gaussian pulse is σ in time domain, the corresponding width of its transformed function is $\frac{1}{\sigma}$.

As a physical interpretation of this, if the width of the Gaussian pulse is smaller in time domain, the corresponding width of the transformed function (called frequency spectrum) becomes larger in the frequency domain, and vice versa. The analogy of the relationship between the widths, σ, in the time and frequency domains may also be drawn from Heisenberg's uncertainty principle of quantum physics (Heisenberg, 1927). In the time domain, σ_t^2 is the variance of time, t weighted by $g^2(t)$. Similarly, σ_f^2 is the variance of ω weighted by $G^2(\omega)$ in the frequency domain. Then, it can be shown that $\sigma_t^2 \sigma_f^2 \geq \frac{1}{4}$, which is analogous to Heisenberg's uncertainty principle of momentum and position of a particle. The uncertainty associated in the measurement of exact position and momentum of a particle in quantum theory is analogously extended to the representation of signals in time (t) and frequency (ω). As it may be seen, it is not possible to localize the function in both the original domain and the transform domain.

2.7.1 | Wavelets

A square pulse, which is a time limited signal, is shown in Fig. 2.8. The square pulse has a finite support, but its transform is a *sinc* function, which has an infinite support in the frequency domain. A sinusoidal signal, which is a band limited signal, as shown in the figure. The sinusoidal signal has the finite support in the frequency domain, but it has an infinite support in the time domain. The signal obtained as a product of these two signals, the square pulse and the sinusoidal signal, as seen in Fig. 2.8, has a better localization property in both the domains than the individual signals. The product signal may not be exactly finite in both the domains, but most of the signal strength spans over a finite support. This kind of a function is known as a *wavelet*. The DC component of a wavelet should be zero.

Consider an example of a Gabor wavelet in 1-D, which is shown in Fig. 2.9. A Gabor wavelet is obtained by multiplying a Gaussian pulse with a complex sinusoid. Since the Gabor wavelet is also complex, it has both real and imaginary parts, as shown in the figure.

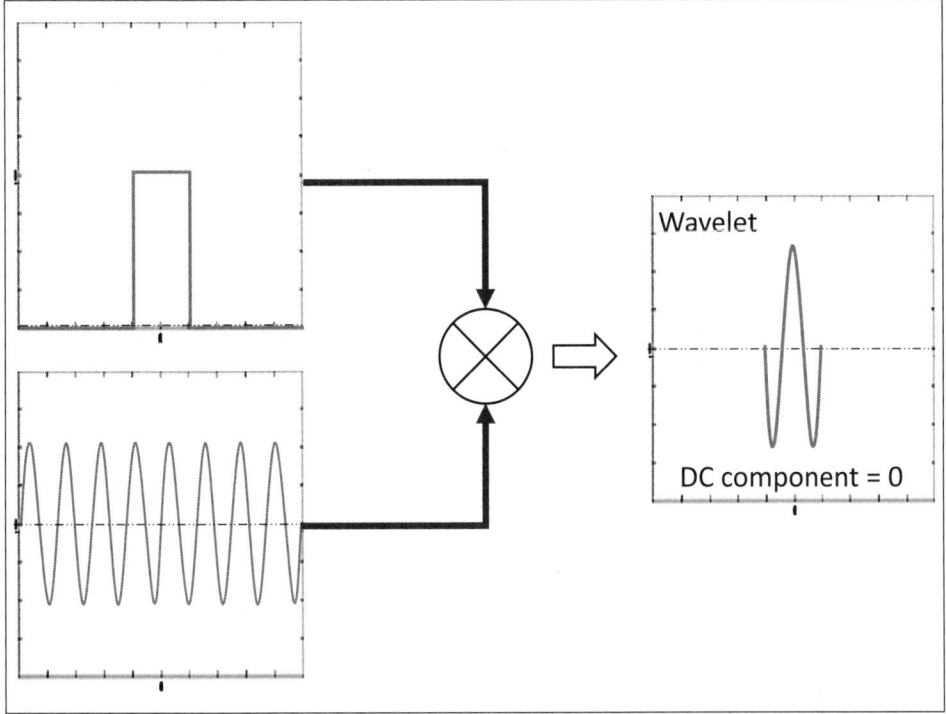

Figure 2.8 A wavelet formed by the product of a square pulse and a sinusoidal signal.

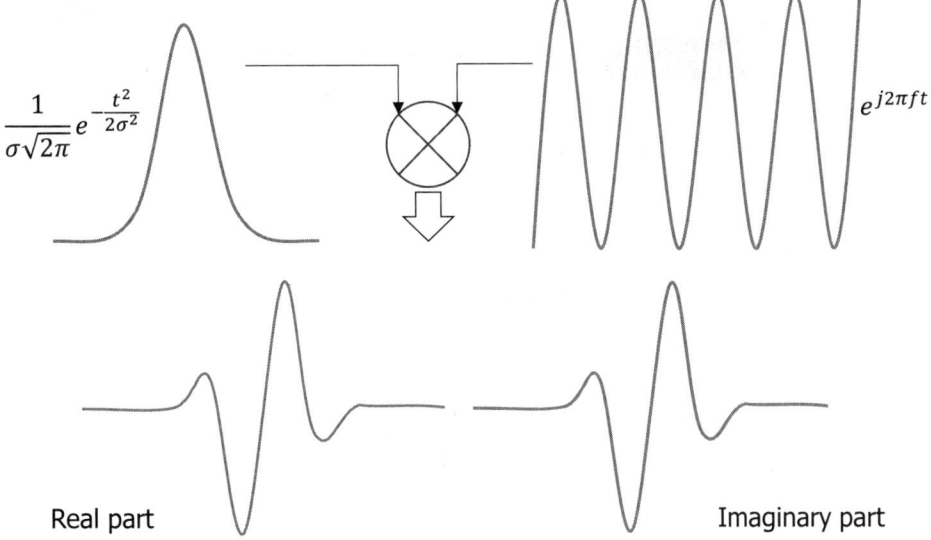

Figure 2.9 Illustration of a 1-D Gabor wavelet.

As it may be seen, the functional support is mostly confined to a finite interval, though it is not strictly finite. This function still has nonzero values through infinity. But, most of the energy is confined over a finite interval. Another example is shown in Fig. 2.10, which is known as a *Shannon wavelet*. The signal in Fig. 2.10 (a) is the same sinc function as discussed before. The Shannon wavelet in time domain is given by Eq. 2.79.

$$h(t) = 2B\frac{\sin(2\pi Bt)}{2\pi Bt} = 2B\text{sinc}(2Bt) \tag{2.79}$$

where, B is the pulse width in the transformed domain. Its corresponding frequency transform is a square pulse that is shown in Fig. 2.10 (b). The Haar wavelet, which is shown in Fig. 2.11, is also a popular wavelet that is defined by Eq. 2.80.

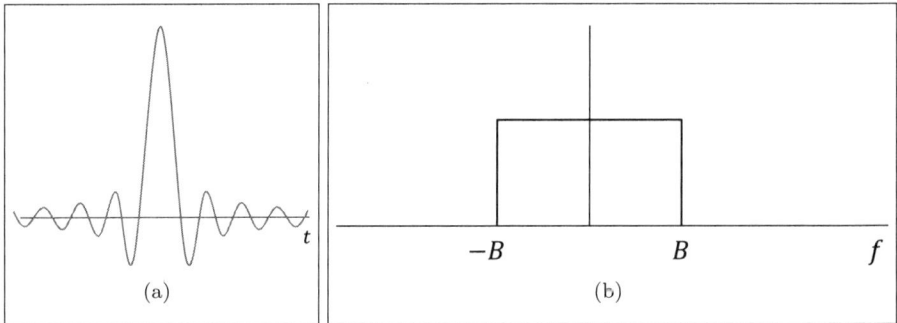

Figure 2.10 Illustration of a 1-D Shannon wavelet.

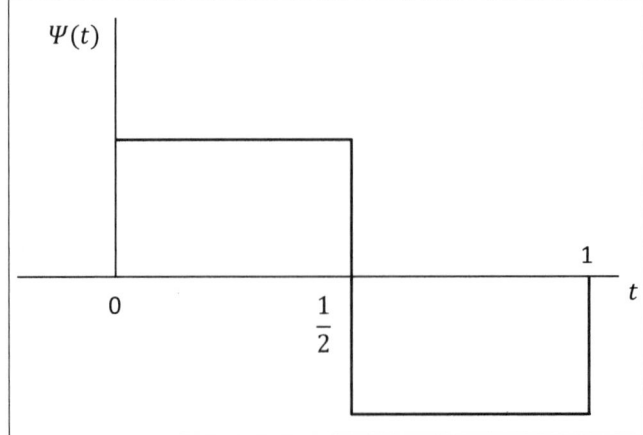

Figure 2.11 Illustration of a 1-D Haar wavelet.

$$\psi(t) = \begin{cases} 1, & 0 \leq t < \frac{1}{2} \\ -1, & \frac{1}{2} < t \leq 1 \\ 0, & \text{otherwise} \end{cases} \tag{2.80}$$

The Haar wavelet is a square pulse followed by an inverted square pulse. It also has a finite support in time domain, but an infinite support in frequency domain.

In a wavelet transform, a function is decomposed into factors of a set of wavelets, which act like basis functions. One of the primary characteristics of these wavelets is that they may be derived from a single wavelet function by translating and dilating it in its domain. In translation, the wavelets are translated to different points in the domain of the function, so that, each one of them acts as a distinct basis function, as shown in Fig. 2.12 (a). In dilation, the wavelets are scaled along their support to obtain another basis wavelet function, as shown in Fig. 2.12 (b). For example, dilation in time means scaling of time axis, implying that, the dilated function has more low frequency components after scaling. Using these two operations, namely, translation and dilation, a family of wavelets is defined from a single *mother wavelet function*. This transformation is mathematically expressed by Eq. 2.81.

$$\psi_{\tau,s}(t) = \frac{1}{\sqrt{s}} \psi\left(\frac{t-\tau}{s}\right) \tag{2.81}$$

where, $\psi(t)$ is the mother wavelet function, $\psi_{\tau,s}(t)$ is the transformed wavelet function, τ is the parameter of translation, and s is the parameter for dilation or scaling operation.

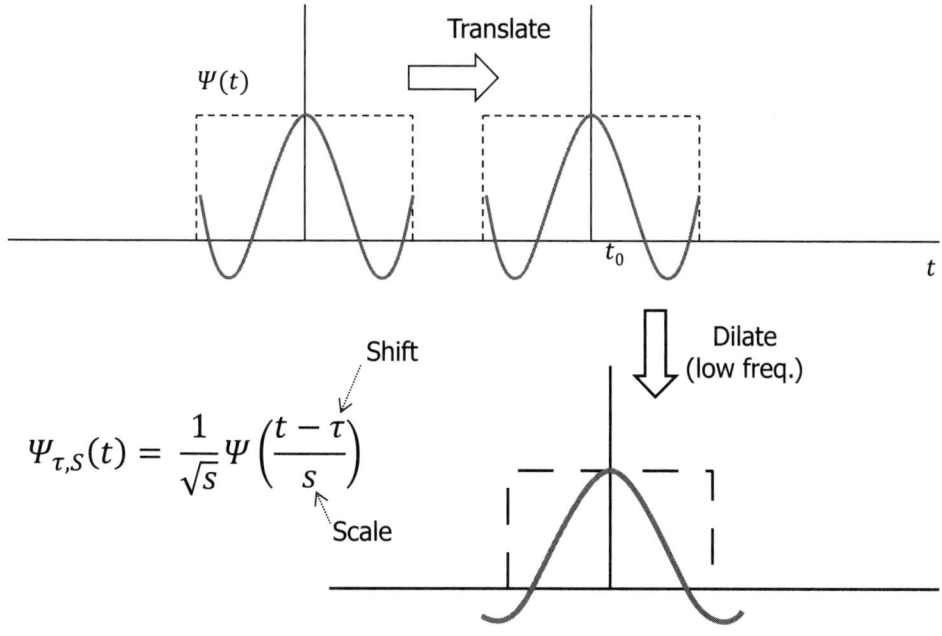

Figure 2.12 Translation and dilation operations on wavelets.

This transformation defines a family of wavelets, which are effectively a set of basis functions. The transform coefficients are obtained by the inner product of the given function and the wavelet function.

The forward wavelet transform, $W(s, \tau)$, of a function, $f(t)$, in continuous time and frequency domains is defined as in Eq. 2.82, which is a 2-D transform representation of a 1-D function.

$$W(s, \tau) = \int_{-\infty}^{\infty} f(t) \frac{1}{\sqrt{s}} \psi^* \left(\frac{t - \tau}{s} \right) dt \qquad (2.82)$$

Also, the inverse transform of $W(s, \tau)$ is defined as in Eq. 2.83.

$$f(t) = \frac{1}{C_\psi} \int_0^{\infty} \int_{-\infty}^{\infty} W(s, \tau) \frac{\psi(t)}{s^2} ds d\tau \qquad (2.83)$$

where, $C_\psi = \int_{-\infty}^{\infty} \frac{|\widehat{\psi}(\omega)|}{|\omega|} d\omega$, and $\widehat{\psi}(\omega)$ is the Fourier transform of $\psi(t)$.

By the definition and formulation of the wavelet functions, they reveal the structure of functions at multiple resolutions. For example, with a translated wavelet in the time domain, the computation of the inner product provides, the component or structure of a signal at a time interval centering the point of translation. This is the localization of the corresponding component at a particular time instant. Likewise the computation of factors using the dilated and translated wavelet, is equivalent to the localization of the corresponding components over multiple resolutions. This multi-resolution representation is one of the key properties of the wavelet transformation. In fact, it is an over complete representation of the function. Not every wavelet transform provides an exact complete representation of a function. So, there may be many redundant coefficients that are not required to reconstruct the function.

2.7.2 | Multi-resolution representation

One of the very popular multi-resolution representations in image processing is the *Gaussian pyramid representation*. The computation of a Gaussian pyramid, as illustrated in Fig. 2.13, is as follows.

The building of the pyramid starts with a base image, which is the input image, $I^{(0)}$. The input image is convolved with a Gaussian kernel (i.e., Gaussian filtering of the input image). Then, the filtered image is down-sampled, for example, to half the original size, in both of the spatial dimensions. The down-sampled image is denoted by $I^{(1)}$ in the figure. The image, $I^{(1)}$, gives the representation of $I^{(0)}$ in a reduced resolution. The difference image, $d^{(1)}$, is computed as the difference between the $I^{(0)}$ and the up-sampled $I^{(1)}$,

$$d^{(1)} = I^{(0)} - \text{upsampled}(I^{(1)}).$$

The up-sampling may be achieved by any of the interpolations, like bi-linear interpolation technique. The image, $I^{(0)}$, is decomposed into $I^{(1)}$ and $d^{(1)}$ and could be reconstructed from them as given below.

$$I^{(0)} = \text{upsampled}(I^{(1)}) + d^{(1)}.$$

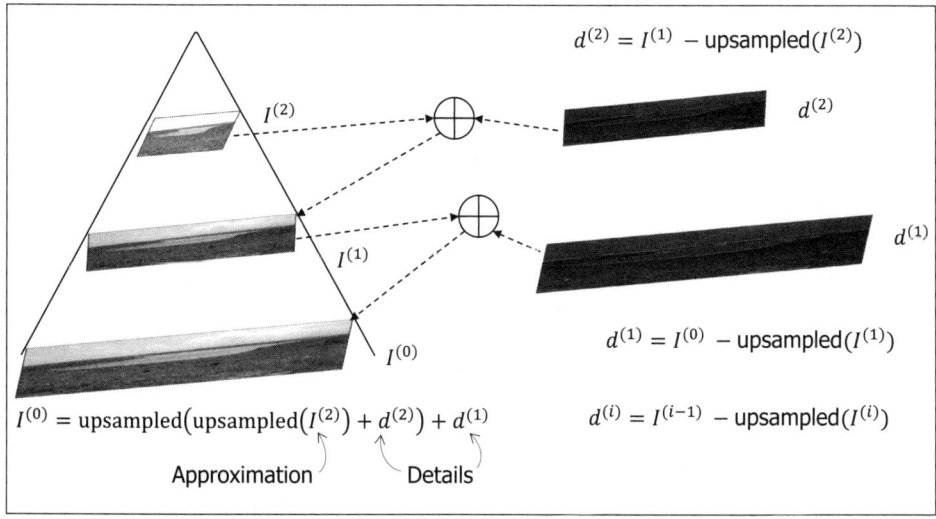

$$d^{(2)} = I^{(1)} - \text{upsampled}(I^{(2)})$$

$$d^{(1)} = I^{(0)} - \text{upsampled}(I^{(1)})$$

$$d^{(i)} = I^{(i-1)} - \text{upsampled}(I^{(i)})$$

$$I^{(0)} = \text{upsampled}\big(\text{upsampled}(I^{(2)}) + d^{(2)}\big) + d^{(1)}$$

Approximation   Details

Figure 2.13 An example of a Gaussian pyramid representation.

Similarly, at the second level, $I^{(2)}$ and $d^{(2)}$ are obtained from $I^{(1)}$. In general, the ith difference image, $d^{(i)}$, is computed from $I^{(i-1)}$ and upsampled($I^{(i)}$) as,

$$d^{(i)} = I^{(i-1)} - \text{upsampled}(I^{(i)}).$$

This process of down-sampling the filtered image and obtaining the difference image is carried out at different levels to obtain the representation of the original image in multiple scales in a Gaussian pyramid. For representing a two-level Gaussian pyramid that is shown in Fig. 2.13, $I^{(2)}$, $d^{(2)}$, and $d^{(1)}$ are sufficient. The original image, $I^{(0)}$, is computed from them as,

$$I^{(0)} = \text{upsampled}(\text{upsampled}(I^{(2)}) + d^{(2)}) + d^{(1)}.$$

Here, the up-sampled images are the *approximations* of the original image, and the difference images represent the *details*. With this multi-resolution description, the original image may be represented in more compact form that reduces the space requirement to represent the whole image. Also, such a representation may simplify certain operations at a later processing pipeline for different applications. Wavelet transforms are characterized by these kind of multi-resolution representations. In the above example, only one mother wavelet has been considered (the input image, $I^{(0)}$). Here, $I^{(2)}$ may also be computed using another mother wavelet, which would give certain approximations in a form of low resolution.

The images of the pyramid illustrated in Fig. 2.13 are shown side-by-side in Fig. 2.14. The $I^{(i)}$s are the approximations of the image at different resolutions, and the $d^{(i)}$s are the corresponding details at different levels of the pyramid. The Gaussian wavelet that is used in convolution to perform filtering is given by Eq. 2.84.

$$G(x,y) = \frac{1}{2\pi\sigma^2} e^{\frac{-((x-x_c)^2 + (y-y_c)^2)}{2\sigma^2}} \tag{2.84}$$

where (x_c, y_c) denote the position of the center pixel of the Gaussian kernel and σ is the scaling parameter. The difference images are simply the differences between the subsequent Gaussian filtered images that are down-sampled at the corresponding levels of the pyramid. In the same way, for filtering a time varying signal, the Gaussian function in time domain is repeatedly used to obtain the approximations of the signal. The difference of Gaussian (DoG) is another wavelet, which is also used repeatedly, and then down-sampled to obtain the details of signal. The scaling function is used for filtering and the wavelet function is used to compute difference image, which is down-sampled, as shown in Fig. 2.14. Another interpretation of the wavelet transform is sub-band approximation of a function. Gaussian filtering effectively performs the smoothing operations on the function, which is a low-pass filtering. Similarly, performing difference of Gaussian filtering is equivalent to a high-pass filtering. The function is decomposed into two components, a low-pass component and a high-pass component, at each level of the pyramid. So, at different levels, different kinds of frequency bands are obtained from the input signal. These bands of functional representation are called sub-band representation of a function. Here, the filtering and transformation operations are equivalent. In other words, wavelet transform may also be considered as simple subband filtering operations.

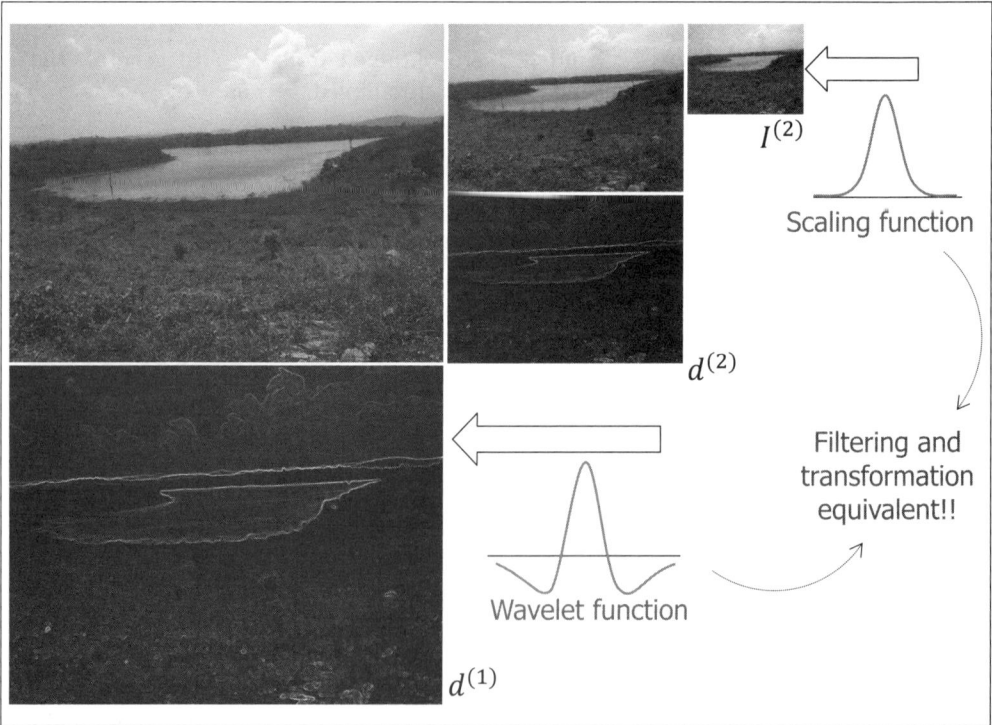

Figure 2.14 The images of approximation and details of an input image in the Gaussian pyramid.

2.7.3 | Discrete wavelet transform

When the operations of dilation and translation are performed with finite number of basis functions, it is known as *discrete wavelet transform* (DWT). Unlike continuous domain, the mother wavelets are translated only at discrete grid points, $k = 0, \pm 1, \pm 2, \ldots$ Similarly, the scaling is also performed only at discrete scales, usually by powers of 2, 2^j, $j = 0, 1, 2, \ldots$ Effectively, scaling or down-sampling takes care of the dilation of the wavelets and allows to use the same functions or mother wavelets at a particular level of the pyramid. These operations provide a family of dilated and translated wavelet functions in the form of sequences of length N, as given in Eq. 2.85.

$$\phi_{j,k}(n) = 2^{-\frac{j}{2}} \phi \left(2^{-j} n - k \right), \quad j = 0, 1, \ldots, \quad k = 0, 1, \ldots, M$$
$$\psi_{j,k}(n) = 2^{-\frac{j}{2}} \psi \left(2^{-j} n - k \right), \quad j = 0, 1, \ldots, \quad k = 0, 1, \ldots, M$$
(2.85)

where, scaling functions are represented by $\phi(\cdot)$, and wavelet functions are represented by $\psi(\cdot)$, and $M \leq N$.

Similar to computation of multi-resolution representation as discussed in the previous section, in this case also an image is filtered by these two functions, namely the scaling function $\phi(n)$ and the wavelet function $\psi(n)$ as successive stages of down-sampled images. The scaling function behaves as a low pass filter, and the wavelet function as a high pass filter. The set of filters is called a *filter bank*. A representation of filtering and reconstruction processes is shown in Fig. 2.15. Here, $x(n)$ is the original signal. There are only two filters, $h(n)$ and $g(n)$, which perform low-pass filtering and high-pass filtering, respectively. These are followed by down-sampling operations. These stages may be repeated on the approximation coefficients to get multi-level decompositions, which are not shown in the example. So, $h(n)$ results in approximation of the signal and $g(n)$ gives the corresponding details. Using the approximation and details, the original signal is reconstructed as $x'(n)$, by up-sampling and filtering by $h'(n)$ and $g'(n)$. To obtain an exact reconstruction of the original signal, it is possible to design the filters, $h(n)$, $g(n)$, $h'(n)$, and $g'(n)$, in such a way that the signal is fully reconstructed (i.e., $x'(n) = x(n)$, for all n). The process related to the computation of approximation and details is called the *analysis*, and the process related to reconstruction is called the *synthesis*. Two typical

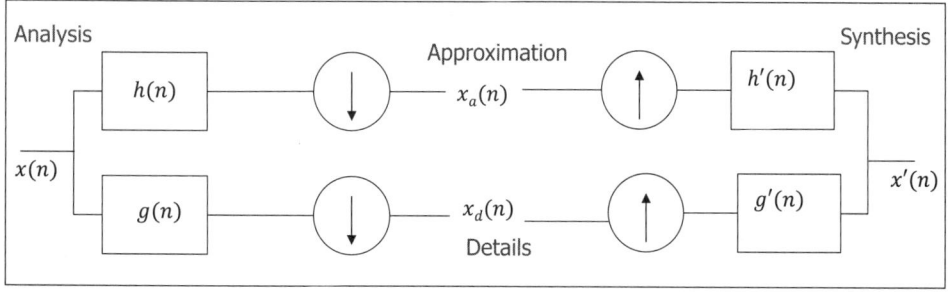

Figure 2.15 Representation of filtering and reconstruction processes of a signal.

wavelet filters, viz. Daubechies 9/7 filters and Le Gall 5/3 filters, are given in Tables 2.3 and 2.4, respectively (Mukhopadhyay, 2011). In each of them, one filter bank is used for analysis and the other filter bank is used for synthesis.

Haar wavelet transform

Consider the Haar wavelet transform, whose scaling and wavelet functions are shown in Fig. 2.16 (a) and (b), respectively. Here, the scaling function is a simple square pulse, which performs smoothing or averaging. The processes of dilation and translations are performed

Table 2.3 Daubechies 9/7 filters.

n	Analysis filter bank		Synthesis filter bank	
	$h(n)$	$g(n-1)$	$h'(n)$	$g'(n+1)$
± 0	0.603	1.115	1.115	0.603
± 1	0.267	-0.591	0.591	-0.267
± 2	-0.078	-0.058	-0.058	-0.078
± 3	-0.017	0.091	-0.091	0.017
± 4	0.027			0.027

Table 2.4 Le Gall 5/3 filters.

n	Analysis filter bank		Synthesis filter bank	
	$h(n)$	$g(n-1)$	$h'(n)$	$g'(n+1)$
± 0	$\frac{6}{8}$	1	1	$\frac{6}{8}$
± 1	$\frac{2}{8}$	$-\frac{1}{2}$	$\frac{1}{2}$	$-\frac{2}{8}$
± 2	$\frac{1}{8}$			$-\frac{1}{8}$

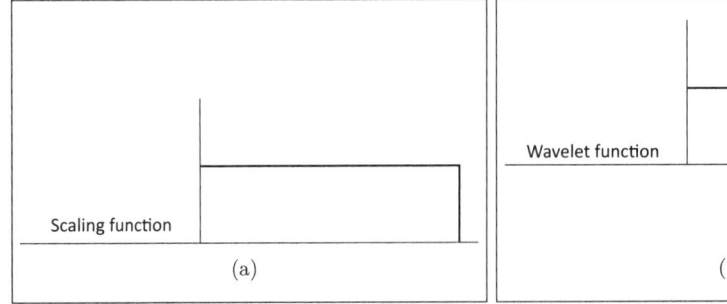

Scaling function

(a)

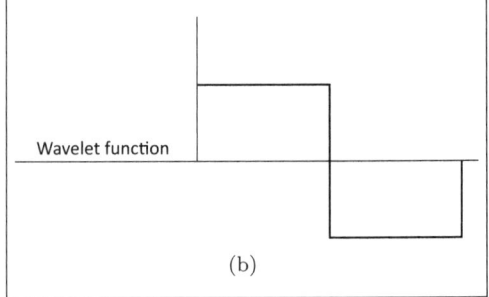

Wavelet function

(b)

Figure 2.16 Scaling and wavelet functions for a typical Haar wavelet transform.

on these two mother wavelets. The scaling function, $\phi(n)$, and the wavelet function, $\psi(n)$, corresponding to discrete Haar wavelets of $N = 8$ are given in Eq. 2.86.

$$\phi(n) = \frac{1}{\sqrt{2}}(1,1,0,0,0,0,0,0)$$
$$\psi(n) = \frac{1}{\sqrt{2}}(1,-1,0,0,0,0,0,0)$$
(2.86)

These functions are translated by using a transformation matrix, $\mathbf{W}_8$, which is given by Eq. 2.87 (Mukhopadhyay, 2011).

$$\mathbf{W}_8 = \frac{1}{\sqrt{2}}\begin{bmatrix} 1 & 1 & 0 & 0 & 0 & 0 & 0 & 0 \\ 0 & 0 & 1 & 1 & 0 & 0 & 0 & 0 \\ 0 & 0 & 0 & 0 & 1 & 1 & 0 & 0 \\ 0 & 0 & 0 & 0 & 0 & 0 & 1 & 1 \\ 1 & -1 & 0 & 0 & 0 & 0 & 0 & 0 \\ 0 & 0 & 1 & -1 & 0 & 0 & 0 & 0 \\ 0 & 0 & 0 & 0 & 1 & -1 & 0 & 0 \\ 0 & 0 & 0 & 0 & 0 & 0 & 1 & -1 \end{bmatrix}$$
(2.87)

In Eq. 2.87, the first four rows of $\mathbf{W}_8$ are the translated versions of $\phi(n)$, and its last four rows are the translated versions of $\psi(n)$. Here, the scaling is automatically applied when these operations are performed repeatedly with down-sampling. So, they are only translated, and not scaled, since scaling is not explicitly required. The transformation matrix depends upon the number of data points considered. In this case, the functions are defined by an 8×8 transformation matrix, since there are eight points, $N = 8$. This transformation matrix defines an orthonormal transformation. That is, the scalar dot product of any two distinct rows is zero, and the scalar dot product of any row with itself is unity.

Dyadic decomposition

The form of decomposition that is shown in Fig. 2.17 is called *dyadic decomposition*. Here, the filtering operations are performed iteratively at every level of the pyramid, which is

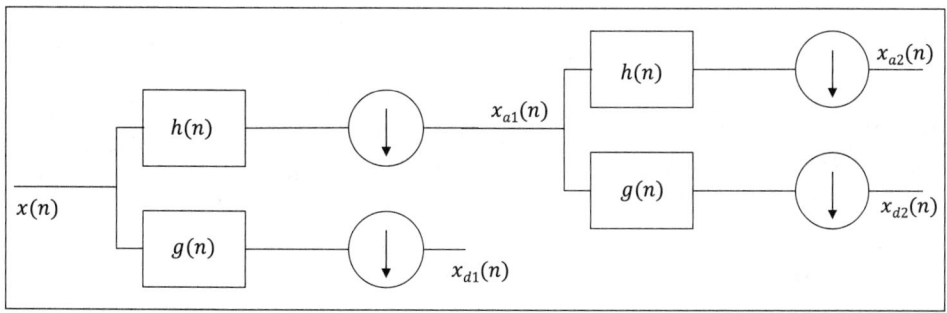

Figure 2.17 Representation of a dyadic decomposition form.

followed by the corresponding down-sampling. At each level, the sample size is halved, an equivalent of scaling by 2, so that, the total number of samples remains the same. In dyadic decomposition, only the last approximation at the highest level and all the details at every level of the pyramid are retained. That is, in the example shown in the figure, $x_{a2}(n)$, $x_{d2}(n)$, and $x_{d1}(n)$ are retained.

DWT in 2-D

The property of separability is used to extend the discrete wavelet transforms to 2-D space. The basis functions are formed as a product of two wavelet basis functions in 1-D, and then the transformation of rows and columns are performed individually. Performing the transformation using Le Gall 5/3 analysis filters, those are given in Table 2.4, on a 2-D image, is shown in Fig. 2.18. The filtering is performed along the rows and columns to get different components of the signal. Since the signal is in 2-D, there are four components in the decomposed signal because of the four different combinations, unlike only two components in 1-D signal.

Figure 2.18 Example of applying Le Gall 5/3 analysis filters on a 2-D image.

2.8 | Application of image transforms

Image transforms provide alternative representation of images, instead of their representation in functional domains. Such representation in different domains gives various information about an image, that are not always vivid in its functional domain. For example, the Fourier transform provides frequency domain representation, where an image may be factored into low frequency and high frequency components. After transformation, only a few transform coefficients may be used to get an approximation of the functional representation of the image, which are useful in providing more compact representation of the image. By considering the effect of coefficients on human visual perception, the representation may be made more precise and brief by performing selective quantization of the coefficients. Multi-resolution representations and wavelet transforms are widely used in various application of image and video processing tasks, like, compression, noise filtering, image enhancement and restoration, feature representation, image fusion, etc.

In certain applications of image and video processing, like compression, their alternative representations are mainly sought for their requirement of less storage space compared to their representations in the original space. Consider an analogy of representing a rectangle, which may be represented by a set of points in a 2-D coordinate space. However, only four points are sufficient to uniquely represent the rectangle. So, all the points in excess to the four corner points are redundant, which may be removed to reduce the storage requirement. Alternatively, a rectangle may also be represented by its center, and height and width, which also require significantly lesser storage than its representation as a set of points in the 2-D space. In some cases, such a representation may not always be exact, unlike the representation of a rectangle. For example, representation of complex structures and closed curves or contours by approximate ellipses. By considering certain approximations in the representations, a significant amount of reduction may be achieved in the storage requirement. These types of approximations may be employed in applications where they are acceptable. Mostly, images and videos are handled with approximate representations of the original data that are captured by the cameras. Compression schemes dealing with approximate representations of objects are known as *lossy compression* schemes, while the schemes with exact representation are known as *lossless compression* schemes.

For any compression scheme, its alternative representation of images (or data) should have the features of reconstructibility, low redundancy, and factorization into substructures. They are briefly discussed below.

- Reconstructibility: Since an alternative representation of data is a type of encoding, it is desirable to decode or reconstruct the data from its encoded form. However, the reconstruction may be partial or approximate for a lossy compression.

- Low redundancy: The alternative representation should have low redundancy in its information content. The redundancy may occur in various forms. For example, in images, the redundancies are due to spatial correlation among the pixels and their color components. In videos, in addition to the redundancies within its frames (images), there are temporal correlations among consecutive frames. There may be other context dependent redundancies, such as symmetry of objects, bias in intensity and color distributions, etc.

- Factorization into substructures: Another desirable feature of an alternative representation scheme is the decomposition of the object into its different components or substructures. This is particularly useful for approximate representation of objects. In this case, the components that have insignificant contribution to the reconstruction of an object are removed, which results in a lossy representation. However, this reduces the storage requirement of the representation.

These alternative representations may be realized in various ways. The image transforms may be used to represent the images by a set of coefficients corresponding to a given set of basis functions. These coefficients may be real numbers (e.g., DCT, DWT, etc.) or complex numbers (DFT), as discussed in this chapter. Toward this, there are several other techniques of representation that depend on the data, like principal component analysis (PCA) and sparse representation techniques. In this context, an image, **I**, of size $M \times N$ (i.e., M rows and N columns) is considered as a data point, $\boldsymbol{I}$, of MN dimensions (i.e., a MN-D column vector). In subsequent sections, we discuss a few such schemes of alternative representation.

2.9 | Principal component analysis

Let us understand how the dimension of the data distributed over a space could be different from the dimension of the space itself. Consider a set of data points, $S = \{\boldsymbol{x}_i \mid \boldsymbol{x}_i \in \mathbb{R}^n\}$, where $\boldsymbol{x}_i$ is a data point in n-dimensional real space. This does not imply that the dimension of S is also n. For example, Fig. 2.19 depicts a 3-D space with four data points. These four data points may be arranged in such a way that they lie on a plane, as seen in Fig. 2.19. Now, a coordinate system is defined for the plane that contains these data points, and this

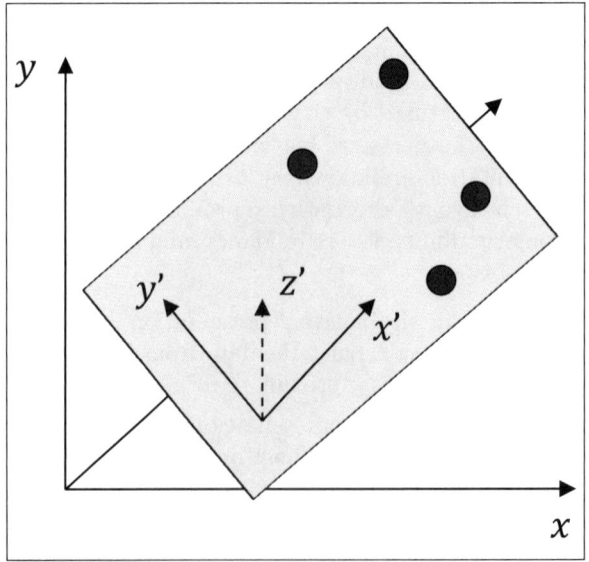

Figure 2.19 Depiction of four data points for PCA.

coordinate convention is used to represent every point in that plane. In the example of Fig. 2.19, all the data points are represented as a set of points in the 2-D real space. So, it is not necessary that the dimension of data points in a given set are the same as the dimension of the space. The dimension of data points may also be lower than the dimension of the space, as illustrated in this example. The *principal component analysis* (PCA) is a method to find the minimum dimensional subspace for representing the given data using coordinate transformation. The basic idea of PCA is to compute a new set of orthogonal axes that is used to define new coordinates with respect to the representation of data.

2.9.1 | Maximizing variance of a component

Given a set of data points, principal component analysis maximizes the variance of a component computed by projecting this data point along a direction out of all possible directions in the space. The feature vector representation of a data point, x, in an n-dimensional space is represented as, $x = (x_1, x_2, ..., x_n)$, which denotes the n components or n fields of this vector. Let there be N data points, $S = \{x_1, x_2, ..., x_N\}$. The variance of the ith component, x_i, is defined as in Eq. 2.88.

$$\text{var}(x_i) = \frac{1}{N} \sum_{j=1}^{N} (x_{ij} - \overline{x_i})^2 \tag{2.88}$$

where, $\overline{x_i}$ is the mean value of the ith component over all data points. For a feature vector x_j, its ith component is denoted by x_{ij}. Among these n components, a component is said to be dominant if the variance of that component is the maximum of all the components. The PCA computes the transformation of feature vectors so that it maximizes the variance of the dominant component.

To understand this further, consider a n-dimension unit vector, w. In order to have a convenient coordinate convention, the coordinates are transformed in such a way, so that, the origin of the coordinates is at the mean of the feature vectors. Let, $\overline{S}$ be the mean of N feature vectors in S, which is given by Eq. 2.89.

$$\overline{S} = \frac{1}{N} \sum_{j=1}^{N} x_j \tag{2.89}$$

After computing the mean vector, $\overline{S}$, every vector, x_j, in S is translated by the mean vector, and its component along w, y_j, is computed by Eq. 2.90.

$$y_j = (x_j - \overline{S}) \cdot w \tag{2.90}$$

For example, consider Fig. 2.20. There are four 2-D data points, $\{x_1, x_2, x_3, x_4\}$, represented by plus marks, and their mean is represented by a point, $\overline{S}$. As depicted in the figure, origin of the original coordinate space, O, is first translated to $\overline{S}$. Then, a unit vector, w, is defined at the translated origin. The components of every data point, $\{x_1, x_2, x_3, x_4\}$, along w is computed as the scalar dot product between w and each of the data points, which are denoted by $\{y_1, y_2, y_3, y_4\}$.

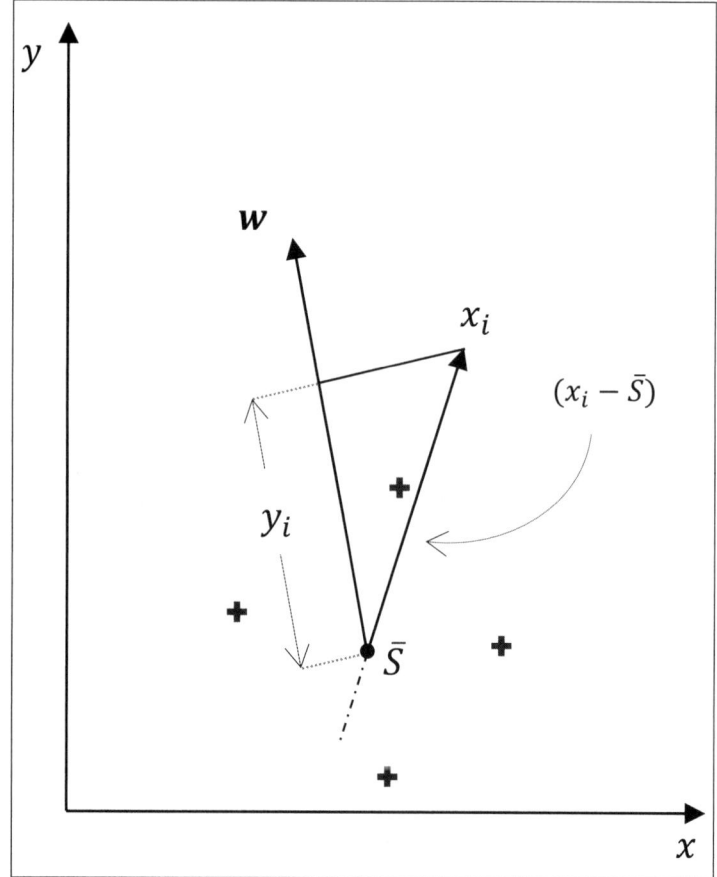

Figure 2.20 Representation of four 2-D data points and their mean.

The optimization problem of the PCA is formulated as to find out the direction $\boldsymbol{w}$, where the variance of the projections of all the data points centered at its mean is maximized. Once such a direction is obtained, the process is repeated for the residuals of data points. The residual vectors are obtained by subtracting the component along $\boldsymbol{w}$ from a data point $\boldsymbol{x}_j$. This means, $\boldsymbol{r}_j = \boldsymbol{x}_j - y_j\boldsymbol{w}$. It goes on till the residuals of all the data points become zero. Computation of directions of principal components may be carried out in various ways by exploiting the relationships among the directions of principal components. In the following a description of such a computation is provided.

Continuing further with our notations of representing a set of N data points, S, if $\boldsymbol{x}_j$ is the jth vector of S, the ith component of $\boldsymbol{x}_j$ is represented as x_{ij}. In this representation, each vector in the set of data points is indexed as the jth vector, and each component in a vector is a variable that is indexed as the ith component. This is represented as, $S = \{\boldsymbol{x}_j = (x_{1j}, x_{2j}, ..., x_{ij}, ..., x_{nj}) \mid \boldsymbol{x}_j \in \mathbb{R}^n\}$, where $j = 1, 2, ..., N$. Here, each vector has n components, usually, $n \leq N$, unless specified otherwise. The mean vector, $\overline{\boldsymbol{S}}$, given by Eq. 2.89, is represented as $\overline{\boldsymbol{S}} = (\overline{x}_1, \overline{x}_2, ..., \overline{x}_n)^\top$. Similarly, the transformation that is defined in Eq. 2.90 is represented as in Eq. 2.91, by which, every vector in S is translated to their mean, $\overline{\boldsymbol{S}}$, by taking their components along a unit vector $\boldsymbol{w}$.

$$\boldsymbol{y} = \begin{bmatrix} y_1 \\ y_2 \\ \vdots \\ y_j \\ \vdots \\ y_N \end{bmatrix} = \begin{bmatrix} (\boldsymbol{x}_1 - \overline{\boldsymbol{S}})^{\mathsf{T}} \\ (\boldsymbol{x}_2 - \overline{\boldsymbol{S}})^{\mathsf{T}} \\ \vdots \\ (\boldsymbol{x}_j - \overline{\boldsymbol{S}})^{\mathsf{T}} \\ \vdots \\ (\boldsymbol{x}_N - \overline{\boldsymbol{S}})^{\mathsf{T}} \end{bmatrix} \begin{bmatrix} w_1 \\ w_2 \\ \vdots \\ w_i \\ \vdots \\ w_n \end{bmatrix} = \widetilde{\mathbf{X}}^{\mathsf{T}} \boldsymbol{w} \tag{2.91}$$

where, $\widetilde{\mathbf{X}}$ denotes a matrix formed by the column vectors, $\boldsymbol{x}_j$s, in S after translating them toward their mean.

Translating a data point or vector in S and computing its corresponding component along the unit vector gives the projection of the considered data point. So, by transforming all vectors in S along $\boldsymbol{w}$ by centering the mean of their vectors, N observations or projections are obtained. Since all the vectors are centered at their mean vector, the mean of the projected values, y_js, is 0, as given by Eq. 2.92.

$$\text{mean}(\boldsymbol{y}) = \frac{1}{N} \sum_{i=0}^{N} y_i = 0 \tag{2.92}$$

Accounting to mean$(\boldsymbol{y}) = 0$, the variance of components of $\boldsymbol{y}$ is the mean of squares of components of $\boldsymbol{y}$. So, the optimization problem involves maximizing the sum of squares of the magnitudes of the projection vector, $\boldsymbol{y}$, which is given by Eq. 2.93.

$$\text{var}(\boldsymbol{y}) = \frac{1}{N} \boldsymbol{y}^{\mathsf{T}} \boldsymbol{y} = \frac{1}{N} \sum_{i=1}^{N} y_i^2 \tag{2.93}$$

Effectively, this is maximizing the variance of the components in $\boldsymbol{y}$. By the definition of $\boldsymbol{w}$, it is a unit vector. Hence, a condition of $\boldsymbol{w}^{\mathsf{T}} \boldsymbol{w} = 1$ (which is equivalent to $||\boldsymbol{w}|| = 1$) is imposed in Eq. 2.93.

Furthermore, by Eqs. 2.91 and 2.93, an expansion of the maximizing term is given by Eq. 2.94.

$$\frac{1}{N} \boldsymbol{y}^{\mathsf{T}} \boldsymbol{y} = \left(\frac{1}{N} \widetilde{\mathbf{X}}^{\mathsf{T}} \boldsymbol{w} \right)^{\mathsf{T}} \widetilde{\mathbf{X}}^{\mathsf{T}} \boldsymbol{w} = \boldsymbol{w}^{\mathsf{T}} \frac{\widetilde{\mathbf{X}} \widetilde{\mathbf{X}}^{\mathsf{T}}}{N} \boldsymbol{w} \tag{2.94}$$

The quantity, $\mathbf{C} = \frac{\widetilde{\mathbf{X}} \widetilde{\mathbf{X}}^{\mathsf{T}}}{N}$ is called the covariance matrix. In general, by definition of the covariance matrix, an element, c_{kl}, i.e., the value at the kth row and the lth column, of a covariance matrix, $\mathbf{C}$, denotes the covariance between the kth component and the lth component of the vectors or data points. This is represented by Eq. 2.95.

$$c_{kl} = \frac{1}{N} \sum_{i=1}^{N} (x_{ki} - \overline{x}_k)(x_{li} - \overline{x}_l), \ 1 <= k, l <= N \tag{2.95}$$

The idea is to compute w that maximizes this covariance matrix. So, for maximizing the variance, an objective function, which is a function of the unit weight vector, w, is considered, as in Eq. 2.96.

$$\mathcal{L}(w) = w^\top C w - \lambda(w^\top w - 1) \tag{2.96}$$

Since w is constrained of being a unit vector, the constraint is added to the objective function using a Lagrange multiplier, λ, as the second term in Eq. 2.96.

Taking derivative of $\mathcal{L}(w)$ with respect to λ enforces the constraint over w, as given by Eq. 2.97.

$$\frac{\partial \mathcal{L}}{\partial \lambda} = 0 \implies w^\top w = 1 \tag{2.97}$$

Taking derivative of $\mathcal{L}(w)$ with respect to the unit vector, w, gives a system of equations as Eq. 2.98.[1]

$$\frac{\partial \mathcal{L}}{\partial w} = 0 \implies 2Cw - 2\lambda w = 0 \implies Cw = \lambda w \tag{2.98}$$

This is an eigen equation in C, and λ is an eigenvalue. Since the task of optimization is to maximize the objective function, the eigenvector corresponding to the maximum eigenvalue is computed in the solution to Eq. 2.98. Also, accounting to the constraint on w as a unit vector, unit eigenvector is considered in the solution.

2.9.2 | Principal components and dimension reduction

The eigenvector corresponding to the maximum eigenvalue of the covariance matrix, C, computed using Eq. 2.98, is the dominant principal component of the considered data. For a covariance matrix of dimension $n \times n$, which is a symmetric matrix, n eigenvectors are formed corresponding to the n eigenvalues. In fact, all of these n eigenvectors provide the maximum variances along the residuals one after another. That is, the set of eigenvectors corresponding to decreasing eigenvalues provide the directions of subsequent principal components. We call these directions *principal directions* and the components along them *principal components*. Suppose, the n eigenvectors are represented by, $E_v = \{e_1, e_2, \ldots, e_n\}$, that correspond to the respective eigenvalues in decreasing order, $\{\lambda_1, \lambda_2, \ldots, \lambda_n\}$. So, e_1 is the unit vector with the maximum eigenvalue, λ_1, and e_n corresponds to unit vector with the minimum eigenvalue, λ_n. We may note that, all these eigenvectors that are represented by E_v are unit vectors of the principal directions.

The ith principal component is defined as the projection of the data point vectors, that are centered at the mean of the data points, along the ith eigenvector. This is computed as in Eq. 2.99.

$$y_{ij} = (x_j - \overline{S}) \cdot e_i \tag{2.99}$$

where, x_j is the jth data point or column vector in S. The dimension reduction is achieved by ignoring the eigenvectors corresponding to small eigenvalues. The eigenvalues represent

---

[1] Similar properties or similar rules of differential calculus for 1-D variables can be extended to matrix operations and linear operations in multi-dimensional space.

the variances of the residuals at that point. So, if all the eigenvectors corresponding to the first k eigenvalues are retained for representing the data, the data is approximated by k-dimensional vectors as, $\boldsymbol{y}_j = (y_1, y_2, \ldots, y_k)^\top$. As it may be observed, an n-dimensional data is lying on a k-dimensional subspace. In other words, the dimension of data is not necessarily the dimension of the space. Using the principal component analysis, coordinate transformations are performed. So, the coordinate axes after transformation are given by the eigenvectors or the directions of principal components, and the center of the coordinates lie at the center of the data point. The components are computed as the projection of the data points along each of the eigenvectors.

After dimension reduction, the data is represented by the first k components in decreasing order of eigenvalues, which are sufficient to capture the variances of the data. This is represented as in Eq. 2.100.

$$\mathbf{Y} = \left((\mathbf{X} - \overline{\boldsymbol{S}})^\top \cdot \boldsymbol{e}_1, (\mathbf{X} - \overline{\boldsymbol{S}})^\top \cdot \boldsymbol{e}_2, \ldots, (\mathbf{X} - \overline{\boldsymbol{S}})^\top \cdot \boldsymbol{e}_k \right)^\top, \text{ where } k \leq n \tag{2.100}$$

The total variance of data is computed as the sum of variances of each component. Since there are n components, the sum of the variances of each of these n components would give the total variance of data, which is given by Eq. 2.101.

$$V = \sum_{j=1}^{n} \left(\frac{1}{N} \sum_{i=1}^{N} (x_{ij} - \overline{x}_j)^2 \right) \tag{2.101}$$

The total variance is also the same as the sum of all the eigenvalues, which is given in Eq. 2.102.

$$V = \sum_{j=1}^{N} \lambda_j \tag{2.102}$$

Since very small eigenvalues do not contribute to the data variance significantly, the corresponding components may be ignored while retaining only larger eigenvalues. The ratio of the sum of k eigenvalues to the total sum of all eigenvalues is the fraction of total variance of data that is accounted by the dimension reduction. In dimension reduction, higher this fraction is, better is the information content retained in the data. So, a high value of this fraction, nearly 1.0, is desirable for representing the data. Mathematically, the statistics for rejected variances is expressed by Eq. 2.103.

$$R^2 = \frac{\sum_{j=k+1}^{n} \lambda_j}{V} \tag{2.103}$$

The R^2 statistic captures the sum of all the variances that are not accounted in the representation of the data, and the value of R^2 should be as small as possible.

2.9.3 | PCA algorithm

An algorithm for the PCA is given in Algorithm 1.

Algorithm 1 PCA algorithm

Input: A set of N data points, $S = \{\boldsymbol{x}_j = (x_{1j}, x_{2j}, \dots, x_{nj}) \mid \boldsymbol{x}_j \in \mathbb{R}^n\}$.
Output: A set of k eigenvectors, $\mathbf{E_v} = \{\boldsymbol{e}_1, \boldsymbol{e}_2, \dots, \boldsymbol{e}_k\}$.

1: Compute the mean of data points.
2: Translate all data points to their mean.
3: Compute the covariance matrix of the set.
4: Compute eigenvectors and eigenvalues (in decreasing order).
5: Choose k such that the fraction of accounted variance is more than specified threshold.
6: Use those k components for representing the data points.

The input is a set of data points, where each data point is represented in an n-dimensional space. The output is a set of k eigenvectors. The value of k is determined by a threshold on the fraction of variances that account for the data representation. This threshold is also a parameter to this algorithm. For example, if we keep this threshold as 0.95, at least 95 percent of the variance is accounted by k components for representing the data points.

Numerical Example

Consider the following set of data points.

$$\{(5,3,2),\ (4,6,0),\ (3,-7,14),\ (2,5,3),\ (3,13,-6)\}$$

Perform PCA and, if applicable, reduce the dimension of the data.

Solution

Let $\mathbf{X}$ be the matrix of given data points, which are represented as column vectors, and $\overline{\mathbf{X}}$ be the mean of given set of data points.

$$\mathbf{X} = \begin{bmatrix} 5 & 4 & 3 & 2 & 3 \\ 3 & 6 & -7 & 5 & 13 \\ 2 & 0 & 14 & 3 & -6 \end{bmatrix}$$

$$\Rightarrow \overline{\mathbf{X}} = \begin{bmatrix} 3.4 \\ 4 \\ 2.6 \end{bmatrix}$$

Let $\widetilde{\mathbf{X}}$ be the matrix of mean translated data points, which is given by,

$$\widetilde{\mathbf{X}} = \mathbf{X} - \overline{\mathbf{X}} = \begin{bmatrix} 1.6 & 0.6 & -0.4 & -1.4 & -0.4 \\ -1 & 2 & -11 & 1 & 9 \\ -0.6 & -2.6 & 11.4 & 0.4 & -8.6 \end{bmatrix}$$

Then, compute the covariance matrix, $\mathbf{C}$, which is given by,

$$\mathbf{C} = \tfrac{1}{5}\widetilde{\mathbf{X}}\widetilde{\mathbf{X}}^{\mathsf{T}} = \begin{bmatrix} \mathbf{1.04} & -0.2 & -0.84 \\ -0.2 & \mathbf{41.6} & -41.4 \\ -0.84 & -41.4 & \mathbf{42.24} \end{bmatrix}$$

To perform PCA, the eigenvectors and eigenvalues of this $\mathbf{C}$ are to be computed. Since $\mathbf{C}$ is a 3×3 symmetric covariance matrix, there will be three eigenvalues and, correspondingly, there will be three eigenvectors. The diagonal elements of the covariance matrix represent the variances of components, which shown in bold in the above expression. That is, the variance of first, second, and third components are 1.04, 41.6, and 42.24, respectively. Also, the total variance is the sum of all these diagonal terms, which is also the sum of eigenvalues, is given by,

Total variance: Trace$(\mathbf{C}) = 1.04 + 41.6 + 42.24 = 84.88.$

The eigenvalues of $\mathbf{C}$ in descending order:

$$(83.3238,\ 1.5562,\ 0)$$

One of the eigenvalues is 0, which is the minimum, and the maximum eigenvalue is 83.3238, which is significantly higher than the other two values. So, the component corresponding to the maximum eigenvalue captures almost all the variance of the data. However, since the second Eigenvalue is 1.5562, the second component also captures some variance of the data. So, the given data may be represented using only two of the components, since the third component is 0. The eigenvectors, e_1, e_2 and e_3, corresponding to the eigenvalues, 83.3238, 1.5562 and 0, respectively, are computed as,

$$e_1 = \begin{bmatrix} -0.0055 \\ -0.7043 \\ 0.7099 \end{bmatrix},\ e_2 = \begin{bmatrix} -0.8165 \\ 0.413 \\ 0.4034 \end{bmatrix},\ \text{and } e_3 = \begin{bmatrix} -0.5774 \\ -0.5774 \\ -0.5774 \end{bmatrix}$$

These eigenvectors are considered as basis vectors, $\mathbf{B}$, which is given by,

$$\mathbf{B} = [e_1\ \ e_2\ \ e_3] = \begin{bmatrix} -0.0055 & -0.8165 & -0.5774 \\ -0.7043 & 0.413 & -0.5774 \\ 0.7099 & 0.4304 & -0.5774 \end{bmatrix}$$

Then, the dimension reduction is performed as follows.

$$\left(\widetilde{\mathbf{X}}^{\top} \cdot \mathbf{B}\right)^{\top} = \begin{bmatrix} 0.2696 & -3.2576 & 15.8421 & -0.4126 & -12.4415 \\ -1.9615 & -0.7128 & 0.3825 & 1.7175 & 0.5742 \\ 0 & 0 & 0 & 0 & 0 \end{bmatrix}$$

In this new set of data points, which are translated and projected, one of the components is zero. So, the transformed data points are represented in a 2-D space, since the third dimension is redundant here. The dimension reduction is performed by considering projections along e_1 and e_2 only.

In this exercise, the original set of points is chosen such that, the points lie in the plane, $x + y + z = 10$, which is a 2-D plane. Principle component analysis provides the plane on which these points are lying. In fact, the third eigenvector is normal to that plane.

2.9.4 | Applications of PCA

Out of several applications of principal component analysis, three specific applications are discussed in this section, viz., data compression, component decorrelation, and factor analysis.

Data compression   As discussed in the previous section on the PCA, the given data may not always require the original number of dimensions for representation. In such a case, the data may be represented with fewer dimensions using some of the principal components of the data. This provides a more compact way of representing the data, since it requires less storage than the original data. As discussed in Section 2.1.1, orthonormal basis vectors are very convenient to transform any data point into another space. If the basis vectors are chosen properly, the redundancy in the representation of data is reduced considerably. The PCA provides an optimal set of orthonormal basis vectors for transforming a set of data points. But, the basis vectors computed by the PCA are data dependent. For every set of data points, the PCA is performed individually and a new set of orthonormal basis vectors are computed. Since the basis vectors are specific to each set of data points, the information of basis vectors also has to be conveyed along with the compressed data, which is inconvenient from the point of view of data compression.

The basis vectors computed using the PCA are known as Karhunen-Loeve basis, and this respective transform is called *Karhunen-Loeve transform* (KLT), which is an optimal representation of the data. In fact, many standard basis vectors can be shown as the eigenvectors of certain statistical representation of signals or images. For example, type-II DCT basis vectors are approximately the eigenvectors of a 2-D matrix with $(j, k)^{\text{th}}$ entry as $r^{|j-k|}$. The r is a value (such that, $r \le 1$) that represents a measure of correlation between the adjacent samples, j and k. So, if j and k deviate more from their locations, the magnitude, $|j - k|$, increases, which reduces the value of $r^{|j-k|}$. So, with less adjacency between j and k, the correlation between them decreases. The samples with higher adjacency between them are expected to be highly correlated. For functions like audio signals, images, etc., it has been shown that the basis vectors or the eigenvectors of the covariance matrix are almost similar to the type-II DCT basis vectors. This is the reason for type-II DCT being more efficient in representing a large class of natural signals and natural images with the kind of statistics it models the data.

Decorrelation of components   The PCA is used in many applications for its property of decorrelating the components. A covariance matrix of data may exhibit high correlation between different components in the original data. After performing the PCA, the correlations between the components are largely reduced, and ideally their values are expected to be 0. An application of this property of decorrelating the components is found in representing the color images using different color spaces (Ohta et al., 1980). When color images are represented in the RGB color space, they are highly correlated. The eigenvectors that are computed by performing the PCA using different blocks of color images give a new data dependent transformation space. For example, on a particular set of color images, the PCA of the color components, R, G, and B in the RGB space[2] provides the eigenvectors, $\frac{(R+G+B)}{3}$, $R - B$, and $\frac{(2G-R-B)}{2}$. Using them, the decorrelated color components are obtained. These components are obtained by performing the PCA over the distribution of color vectors in the RGB space for a large set of images. The first component provides the brightness value and the other two components are the chromatic components.

This application of the PCA is extended to images with more number of components. Simple RGB color images have only three bands or components, red, green, and blue, whereas remote sensing images may have a very large number of components. Depending on the electromagnetic wavelengths used in acquiring the images, remote sensing images in different spectral bands are acquired. Among some of these bands there may exist high correlation. The number of bands widely vary in different types of remote sensing images such as multi-spectral images, hyper-spectral images, and ultra-spectral images. In such cases, the PCA is performed to get an efficient representation of data and highlight the correlated information. The decorrelated components of images with reduced dimensions are also used in various kinds of image analysis (Li et al., 2011). As an example, the first eight principal components of a multi-spectral image from Landsat-8 satellite are shown in Fig. 2.21. The principal components in the figure are sorted in descending order of their variances, where Fig. 2.21 (a) corresponds to maximum variance. As it may be observed from the figure, the details in the principal components are reduced gradually in the components that correspond to lower variances; hardly any details are visible in the eighth component, since it accounts to a very small fraction of the total variance. Using the PCA, a prioritization of bands in the transformed image can be achieved by giving more preference to the bands having more information content.

Factor analysis   The third application of PCA that is considered here is, factor analysis, which relates to highlighting the decorrelated factors. The principal components are related to certain factors in the original image. Even the decorrelated color components of an RGB image relates to the factors like intensity and chromatic factors in the color image. The factor analysis is one of the important aspects of image classification and segmentation processes.

---

[2] Color spaces are discussed in Chapter 3.

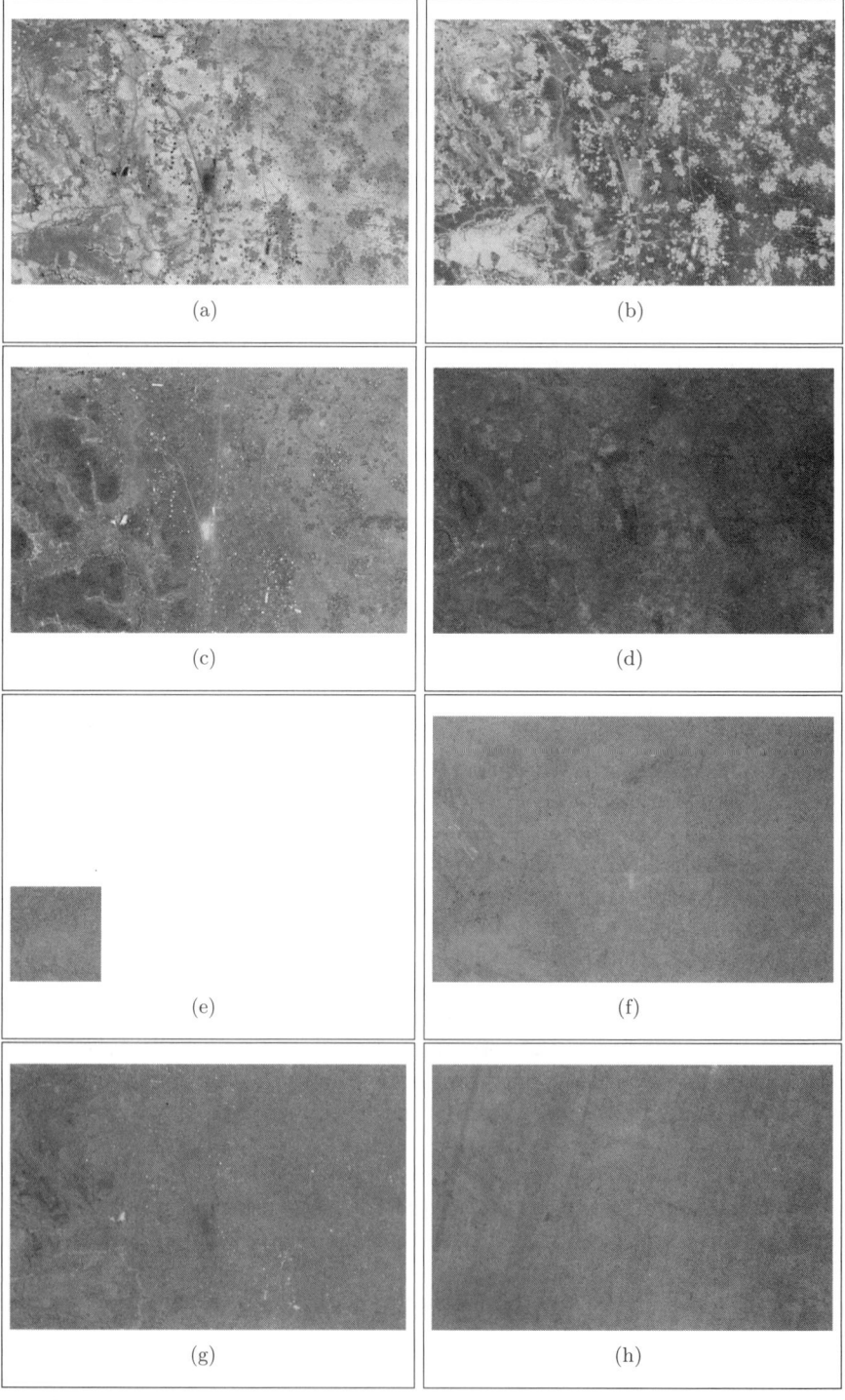

Figure 2.21 Example of an application of principal component analysis on a multi-spectral image.

Eigenface representation of human faces is considered as an example to explain the application of factor analysis (Turk and Pentland, 1991). In eigenface representation, at first, a large set of images of human faces are cropped to the same size and certain rules are followed, like maintaining relative spatial positions of different parts of the face in all the images at similar distances from the borders. Then, by performing the PCA on this set of face images, a set of eigenvectors are computed, which are known as eigenfaces. Any arbitrary face may be expressed as a linear combination of these eigenfaces. Thus, coefficients of linear combination of the eigenfaces may represent any arbitrary image of a face. A simple example with four eigenfaces is shown in Fig. 2.22. This representation of faces by factor analysis is further used in other high level processing, such as face recognition.

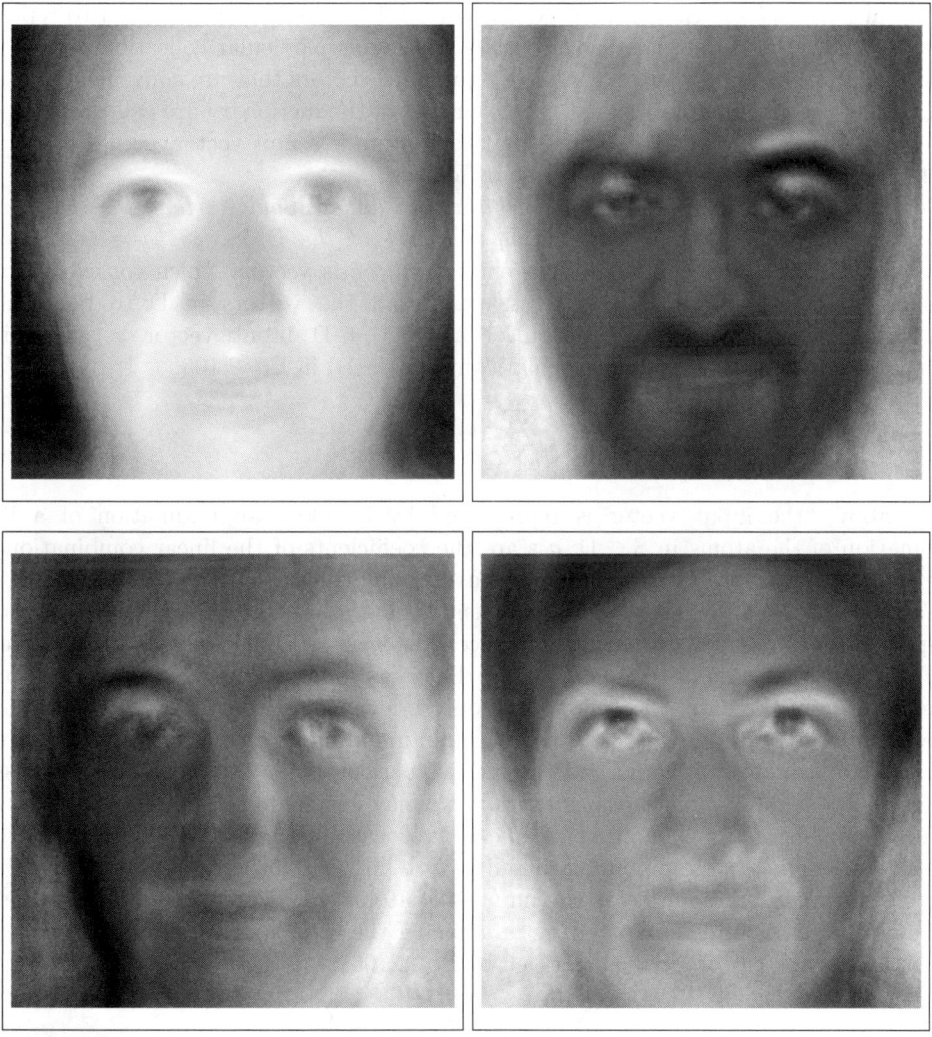

Figure 2.22 Example of an application of principal component analysis in factor analysis.

2.10 | Sparse representation

Sparse representation is also a concept related to data representation. In order to understand the problem statement of the sparse representation, consider a dictionary, D, of N elementary n-dimensional vectors, which is represented by,

$$D = \{\boldsymbol{d}_i \mid \boldsymbol{d}_i \in \mathbb{R}^n \text{ and } i = 1, 2, \dots, N\}, \text{ where, } N > n \qquad (2.104)$$

In this context, a dictionary is similar to a set of basis vectors. In the set of basis vectors, only those basis vectors are included which are sufficient to represent the given data. But in a dictionary, a redundant set of basis vectors is considered, which consists of more number of basis vectors than necessary, and only a few of them are required to represent the data. Instead of calling it a set of basis vectors, this particular collection of vectors is called a *dictionary*, since there are a lot of redundant vectors that are conveniently used in representing the given data or signal. The elements of the dictionary are called *atoms*, e.g., $\boldsymbol{d}_i$ in Eq. 2.104 is an atom. We assume that each atom is a unit vector, i.e. $\|\boldsymbol{d}_i\| = 1$. The problem of sparse representation is stated as follows.

Given a dictionary D *and any arbitrary n-dimensional vector, the best linear approximation has to be computed using a subset of the* D, S, *as basis vectors.* The dictionary, D, is an over-complete representation of basis vectors which consists of many redundant vectors, and it is not necessary for all the vectors in D to be used for representing the data. Representation of a given n-D input vector $\boldsymbol{x}$ as a linear combination of a subset of D is mathematically expressed in Eq. 2.105.

$$\boldsymbol{x} \approx \sum_{\boldsymbol{d}_j \in S \subset D} a_j \boldsymbol{d}_j, \ |S| \leq n \qquad (2.105)$$

In the above, the input vector is represented by its close approximation of a linear combination of the atoms in $S \subset D$, a_js are the coefficients of the linear combination and the elements, $\boldsymbol{d}_j$s are the corresponding atoms forming the subset S of D.

We know that, in an n-D space, it is sufficient to have n linearly independent basis vectors to represent any arbitrary vector in that space. The sparsity considered in this formulation is to have a desirable number of vectors, m, that is as small as possible for an appropriate representation of the data. In other words, only a few atoms from D may be sufficient to represent $\boldsymbol{x}$. The objective here is to have the minimum number of atoms from D, so that, the cardinality of S is minimum and the reconstruction of the data is as close as possible to the original data. For exact reconstruction, we may formulate the problem as to find the minimum number of atoms required for an exact reconstruction of the data. In this case, the task is to determine the minimum cardinality of S, $|S|_{min}$, for the expression in Eq. 2.105. In an approximate representation, the number of atoms, m, is preset to a fixed value and the best representation is computed by minimizing the error between approximation of $\boldsymbol{x}$ with m atoms and the original $\boldsymbol{x}$, as given by Eq. 2.106.

$$\boldsymbol{x} \approx \sum_{\boldsymbol{d}_j \in S \subset D} a_j \boldsymbol{d}_j, \ |S| \leq m < |S|_{min} \qquad (2.106)$$

The desirable properties of such sparse approximation are (Tropp, 2004):

- The representation should be optimal/near optimal.
- Computation of the best representation (linear combination) should be fast.
- The dictionary should be optimal, both in size and representation.

A mathematical formulation for optimal representation is to minimize the approximation error using L_2 norm. The L_2 norm of a vector, $\boldsymbol{x} - (x_1, x_2, \dots, x_n)$, in an n-D space is expressed by Eq. 2.107.

$$L_2(\boldsymbol{x}) = \|\boldsymbol{x}\|_2 = \sqrt{(x_1^2 + x_2^2 + \dots + x_n^2)} \qquad (2.107)$$

For a dictionary in n-D space, $D = \{\boldsymbol{d}_i \mid i = 1, 2, \dots, N\}$, $N > n$, the task is to find a set of coefficients, a_k, corresponding to m number of atoms such that the L_2 norm of the error vector is minimum. This is mathematically expressed by Eq. 2.108.

$$\min_{|S|=m} \ \min_{\{a_k\}} \left\| \boldsymbol{x} - \sum_{\boldsymbol{d}_{i_k} \in S} a_k \boldsymbol{d}_{i_k} \right\|_2 \qquad (2.108)$$

where, $S \subset D$.

Sparse reconstruction A set of m atoms, $S = \{\boldsymbol{d}_{i_1}, \boldsymbol{d}_{i_2}, \dots, \boldsymbol{d}_{i_m}\}$, is formed as a subset of the dictionary D. The best reconstruction of any arbitrary vector, $\boldsymbol{x}$, is obtained in terms of linear combination of the atoms in S by formulating it as a least-squares error optimization problem. A matrix, $\mathbf{B}$, is constructed by considering all atoms in S as the set of basis vectors, $\mathbf{B} = [\boldsymbol{d}_{i_1} | \boldsymbol{d}_{i_2} | \dots | \boldsymbol{d}_{i_m}]$. So each column vector in $\mathbf{B}$ corresponds to an atom of $\mathbf{S}$, and the dimension of $\mathbf{B}$ is $n \times m$ accounting to m vectors of n-dimensions. A data vector, $\boldsymbol{x}$, represented as a linear combination of the atoms in S is expressed by Eq. 2.109.

$$\boldsymbol{x} = \left[\boldsymbol{d}_{i_1} | \boldsymbol{d}_{i_2} | \dots | \boldsymbol{d}_{i_m} \right] \begin{bmatrix} a_1 \\ a_2 \\ \vdots \\ a_m \end{bmatrix} = \sum_{k=1}^{m} a_k \boldsymbol{d}_{i_k} \qquad (2.109)$$

By denoting the column vector of coefficients as $\boldsymbol{y}$, $\boldsymbol{x}$ is represented by a product of the matrix of basis vectors and $\boldsymbol{y}$ as in Eq. 2.110.

$$\boldsymbol{x} = \mathbf{B}\boldsymbol{y} \qquad (2.110)$$

Here, $\boldsymbol{y}$ is desired to be as sparse as possible with a best approximation for m elements. Given the matrix of basis vectors, $\mathbf{B}$, and the data vector $\boldsymbol{x}$, $\boldsymbol{y}$ is computed as a solution to a least squares estimation problem, which is given by Eq. 2.111.

$$\hat{\boldsymbol{y}} = \min_{\boldsymbol{y}} \|\boldsymbol{x} - \mathbf{B}\boldsymbol{y}\|^2 \qquad (2.111)$$

where, $\hat{\boldsymbol{y}}$ is the optimal representation of $\boldsymbol{x}$ with respect to the least-squares constraints. The solution to of the above optimization problem is given by,

$$\boldsymbol{y} = \left(\mathbf{B}^\top \mathbf{B}\right)^{-1} \mathbf{B}^\top \boldsymbol{x} \qquad (2.112)$$

2.11 | Pursuit approaches

Sparse representation discussed in the previous section is based on least-squares error estimation method to get a representation, $\boldsymbol{y}$, for a particular $\boldsymbol{x}$, given the set of m basis vectors, S. The primary task here is the selection of a list of m optimal atoms from the dictionary of N elements, $\boldsymbol{d}_i$s, to form S. To address this issue, a particular list of m atoms has to be chosen for sparse representation that provides the minimum reconstruction error. There are various approaches to select such an optimal or suboptimal set of atoms which derives the sparse representation of data. These approaches are called pursuit approaches. The two major pursuit approaches are *orthogonal matching pursuit* (OMP) and *basis pursuit* (BP).

2.11.1 | Orthogonal matching pursuit (OMP)

The orthogonal matching pursuit is an iterative greedy algorithm. The OMP selects a dictionary element at each iteration that is best correlated with the residual part of the input vector, thereby refining the representation by successive approximations. For example, consider an input data vector, $\boldsymbol{x}$. At first, a basis vector from a given set of vectors is chosen for which the component of $\boldsymbol{x}$ is maximum. As this basis vector, among all other vectors present in the dictionary, accounts for the maximum part of the signal, it is included into the set of basis vectors, S. In the next iteration, the part of $\boldsymbol{x}$ that is represented by the first basis vector is subtracted from $\boldsymbol{x}$, which is called the *residual* part. The subsequent basis vector is selected by carrying out similar operation of finding maximum component of the residual vector. The basis vector along which the residual has maximum component is included into S. Then using the selected set of basis vectors the least squares estimation as described in the previous section is carried out to get the optimal linear combination out of them. This process continues iteratively as long as the required representation of data is achieved, or for specified m number of times to get a set of m basis vectors for representing $\boldsymbol{x}$. This approach produces a new approximation by projecting the residual onto the dictionary elements that are to be selected. At each iteration, the residual part of the input vector is projected on the vectors of dictionary elements that are not yet included into the set of basis vectors. The dictionary element that gives the maximum value of projection is included into S, which is used in an efficient representation of $\boldsymbol{x}$. The OMP extends the trivial greedy algorithm that succeeds for an orthonormal system. In the following subsections, we discuss the algorithm for computing the OMP based sparse representation.

Matching pursuit algorithm

Before visiting the OMP algorithm, a simple matching pursuit algorithm is discussed as a precursor to the OMP. The idea of matching pursuit algorithm is to look at only those elements of the dictionary which correspond to maximum residual components, and use those elements to represent the data vector. The objective is to minimize the approximation error with m terms using L_2 norm, which is expressed in Eq. 2.108. Let r_k and a_k represent the residue and approximate representation of the input data vector, x, at k^{th} iteration, which is expressed by Eq. 2.113.

$$r_k = x - a_k \qquad (2.113)$$

As an initialization of the algorithm, $r_0 = x$ and $a_0 = 0$. Then, at every k^{th} iterative step, an element of the dictionary, D, is found along which the projected component of residual, r_{k-1}, is maximum. The index, $i^\#$, of the element in dictionary with maximum projected component of residual vector that is used to represent the input signal is given by Eq. 2.114.

$$i^\# = \operatorname*{argmax}_{j} \langle r_{k-1}, d_j \rangle \qquad (2.114)$$

In the above equation, we represent $< a, b >$ as the inner product or scalar dot product of vectors a and b. The approximation of x, a_k, at k^{th} iteration is incrementally updated over the previous approximation, a_{k-1}, by a magnitude of r_{k-1} along the direction of $d_{i^\#}$, which is given by Eq. 2.115.

$$a_k = a_{k-1} + \langle r_{k-1}, d_{i^\#} \rangle d_{i^\#} \qquad (2.115)$$

Also, the corresponding residue, r_k, at the kth step, which is given in Eq. 2.113, is incrementally updated over the residue from previous iteration, r_{k-1}, using Eq. 2.116.

$$r_k = r_{k-1} - \langle r_{k-1}, d_{i^\#} \rangle d_{i^\#} \qquad (2.116)$$

This iterative process is repeated till a good approximation of x is obtained.

With this kind of iterative approach, the residue gradually tends to become 0 and approximation tends to become x. When the residue becomes 0, it provides the exact representation of the input data vector. With approximate representation using m vectors, the balance residual error is accounted for the error of approximate representation. The problem with matching pursuit algorithm is that, no restrictions are put on choice or selection of elements from the dictionary. So, the whole dictionary is searched for selecting a basis vector at each iteration, which may select the same dictionary elements multiple times in the process.

The OMP algorithm

In the OMP algorithm, selecting same dictionary elements multiple times is avoided. The OMP algorithm is similar to the matching pursuit algorithm, except for a few additional operations. Here, the approximation of the function at each iteration is performed as a least squares estimation (LSE) from the selected set of vectors, which makes the residue to be always orthogonal to the selected set of dictionary atoms. The orthogonality property is ensured by the LSE method.

Similar to the matching pursuit algorithm, the initialization of the OMP algorithm is made by assigning the residue, $r_0 = x$, and approximation, $a_0 = 0$, at 0th iteration. Additionally, a subset of dictionary elements at every k^{th} iteration, S_k, that is used for reconstructing the signal is included, initialized as a null set, $S_0 = \{\}$. At k^{th} iterative step, the direction or index of the dictionary element along which the component of residue is maximum is found, which is given by Eq. 2.117.

$$i^{\#} = \underset{j \in D - S_{k-1}}{\text{argmax}} \langle \boldsymbol{r}_{k-1}, \boldsymbol{d}_j \rangle \qquad (2.117)$$

The dictionary element corresponding to maximum residual component at k^{th} iteration is included into the set of atoms selected previously for representing the input vector, $\boldsymbol{x}$, which is expressed as in Eq. 2.118.

$$S_k = S_{k-1} \bigcup \{\boldsymbol{d}_{i\#}\} \qquad (2.118)$$

The best linear approximation of $\boldsymbol{x}$, $\{\boldsymbol{a}_k^{\#}\}$, at the kth step is computed as a minimization problem using the least-squares error estimate, which is given by Eq. 2.119.

$$\{\boldsymbol{a}_k^{\#}\} = \underset{\{\boldsymbol{a}_k\}}{min} \left\| \boldsymbol{x} - \sum_{\boldsymbol{d}_{i_k} \in S_k} \boldsymbol{a}_k \boldsymbol{d}_{i_k} \right\|_2 \qquad (2.119)$$

This minimization is performed at every step of incremental update of the selected set of atoms using any of the standard least-squares techniques. The residue, $\boldsymbol{r}_k$, is given by Eq. 2.120.

$$\boldsymbol{r}_k = \boldsymbol{x} - \sum_{\boldsymbol{d}_{i_k} \in S_k} \boldsymbol{a}_k^{\#} \boldsymbol{d}_{i_k} \qquad (2.120)$$

This is the major difference of OMP algorithm from matching pursuit algorithm. The LSE method ensures that all the atoms selected in S_k are orthogonal to the residue, $\boldsymbol{r}_k$ at the kth iteration. So, in $(k+1)^{\text{th}}$ iteration, only those elements in D are chosen which are the remaining elements that are not in S_k. This selection strategy of dictionary elements ensures that there is no possibility of repeating existing atoms in S_k. Repeating this iterative process to select m terms results in the best m-terms approximation of the input vector.

2.11.2 | Basis pursuit (BP)

The basis pursuit computation is different from the OMP technique. The BP is a more sophisticated approach that replaces the original sparse approximation problem by a linear programming problem. The BP minimizes the approximation error using the L_1 norm on the coefficients of representation or the coefficients of linear combination. It is represented by a convex function, which is minimized in polynomial time, which is expressed by Eq. 2.121.

$$\underset{\{\boldsymbol{a}_k\}}{min} \sum_{k=1}^{N} |\boldsymbol{a}_k| \quad \text{subject to} \quad \boldsymbol{x} = \sum_{k=1}^{N} \boldsymbol{a}_k \boldsymbol{d}_k \qquad (2.121)$$

The problem statement corresponds to minimizing the sum of coefficients that represent the input signal. The solution to this minimization problem achieves a sparse representation, which is solved by different advanced approaches, which are not discussed in this book.

Numerical Example

Consider a dictionary in a 3-D space consisting of following atoms:

$$\{[1 \ \ 1 \ \ 1]^{\mathsf{T}}, [1 \ \ -1 \ \ 1]^{\mathsf{T}}, [-1 \ \ -1 \ \ 1]^{\mathsf{T}}, [-1 \ \ 1 \ \ 1]^{\mathsf{T}}\}$$

Derive the best representation of the vector $[1 \ \ 2 \ \ 3]^{\mathsf{T}}$ using two atoms of the above dictionary following orthogonal matching pursuit (OMP).

Solution

Since the magnitude of all the atoms of the dictionary are the same, we ignore the normalization of those atoms to solve this problem. To apply the orthogonal matching pursuit algorithm, consider the first selection of an atom along which the scalar dot product value or component value is maximum. In this example, $\langle [1 \ \ 2 \ \ 3]^{\mathsf{T}} \cdot [1 \ \ 1 \ \ 1]^{\mathsf{T}} \rangle = 6$, is the maximum component values. The corresponding residual, $\boldsymbol{r}_1$, is given by,

$$\boldsymbol{r}_1 = [1 \ \ 2 \ \ 3]^{\mathsf{T}} - 6[1 \ \ 1 \ \ 1]^{\mathsf{T}} = [-5 \ \ -4 \ \ -3]^{\mathsf{T}}$$

For the selection of the second atom, consider the scalar dot product of $\boldsymbol{r}_1$ and an atom from the remaining set of atoms along which the component value is maximum. This is obtained as, $\langle [-5 \ \ -4 \ \ -3]^{\mathsf{T}} \cdot [-1 \ \ -1 \ \ 1]^{\mathsf{T}} \rangle = 6$. So, the two atoms that are selected from the given dictionary are, $[1 \ \ 1 \ \ 1]^{\mathsf{T}}$ and $[-1 \ \ -1 \ \ 1]^{\mathsf{T}}$.

The best linear combination representation of the vector $[1 \ \ 2 \ \ 3]^{\mathsf{T}}$, approximated by LSE solution, $\boldsymbol{a}_2$, is given by the following form.

$$\boldsymbol{a}_2 = x[1 \ \ 1 \ \ 1]^{\mathsf{T}} + y[-1 \ \ -1 \ \ 1]^{\mathsf{T}}$$

where, $\boldsymbol{a}_2 \approx [1 \ \ 2 \ \ 3]^{\mathsf{T}}$ In matrix form, this is represented as,

$$\begin{bmatrix} 1 \\ 2 \\ 3 \end{bmatrix} \approx \begin{bmatrix} 1 & -1 \\ 1 & -1 \\ 1 & 1 \end{bmatrix} \begin{bmatrix} x \\ y \end{bmatrix}$$

where, $\mathbf{A} = \begin{bmatrix} 1 & -1 \\ 1 & -1 \\ 1 & 1 \end{bmatrix}$ is the matrix formed by selected atoms of the dictionary. The LSE solution to the above form is given by,

$$\begin{bmatrix} x \\ y \end{bmatrix} = \left(\mathbf{A}^{\mathsf{T}}\mathbf{A}\right)^{-1} \mathbf{A}^{\mathsf{T}} \begin{bmatrix} 1 \\ 2 \\ 3 \end{bmatrix}$$

This is solved as follows.

$$\mathbf{A}^{\top}\mathbf{A} = \begin{bmatrix} 3 & -1 \\ -1 & 3 \end{bmatrix}, \quad \Longrightarrow \quad \left(\mathbf{A}^{\top}\mathbf{A}\right)^{-1} = \frac{1}{10}\begin{bmatrix} 3 & 1 \\ 1 & 3 \end{bmatrix}$$

So,

$$\begin{bmatrix} x \\ y \end{bmatrix} = \frac{1}{10}\begin{bmatrix} 3 & 1 \\ 1 & 3 \end{bmatrix}\begin{bmatrix} 1 & 1 & 1 \\ -1 & -1 & 1 \end{bmatrix}\begin{bmatrix} 1 \\ 2 \\ 3 \end{bmatrix} = \begin{bmatrix} \frac{18}{10} \\ \frac{6}{10} \end{bmatrix}$$

Therefore, the best representation of the vector $\begin{bmatrix} 1 & 2 & 3 \end{bmatrix}^{\top}$ using two atoms of the given dictionary is given by,

$$\begin{bmatrix} 1 \\ 2 \\ 3 \end{bmatrix} \approx \frac{18}{10}\begin{bmatrix} 1 \\ 1 \\ 1 \end{bmatrix} + \frac{6}{10}\begin{bmatrix} -1 \\ -1 \\ 1 \end{bmatrix}.$$

Numerical Example

Consider the following set of basis vectors.

$$\begin{bmatrix} \frac{1}{\sqrt{3}} \\ -\frac{1}{\sqrt{3}} \\ \frac{1}{\sqrt{3}} \end{bmatrix}, \begin{bmatrix} \frac{1}{\sqrt{2}} \\ \frac{1}{\sqrt{2}} \\ 0 \end{bmatrix}, \text{ and } \begin{bmatrix} -\frac{1}{\sqrt{6}} \\ \frac{1}{\sqrt{6}} \\ \frac{2}{\sqrt{6}} \end{bmatrix}$$

(i) Show that they form an orthonormal set of basis vectors.

(ii) Decompose a vector, $\begin{bmatrix} 1 & 2 & 3 \end{bmatrix}^{\top}$ as a linear combination of the above set.

Solution

Consider every pair of vectors from the set and perform their dot product. For every pair, if their dot product is zero and the magnitude of the vectors is unity, then they form a set of orthonormal basis vectors. In the given set of three vectors, the scalar dot product of any two vectors is zero, and the magnitude of each of the vectors is unity. So, they form an orthonormal set of basis vectors.

To represent an arbitrary vector, $\begin{bmatrix} 1 & 2 & 3 \end{bmatrix}^{\top}$, as a linear combination of the above basis vectors, consider its components along each of the orthonormal basis vectors.

$$\begin{bmatrix} 1 \\ 2 \\ 3 \end{bmatrix} \cdot \begin{bmatrix} \frac{1}{\sqrt{3}} \\ -\frac{1}{\sqrt{3}} \\ \frac{1}{\sqrt{3}} \end{bmatrix} = \frac{2}{\sqrt{3}}, \quad \begin{bmatrix} 1 \\ 2 \\ 3 \end{bmatrix} \cdot \begin{bmatrix} \frac{1}{\sqrt{2}} \\ \frac{1}{\sqrt{2}} \\ 0 \end{bmatrix} = \frac{3}{\sqrt{2}}, \quad \text{and} \quad \begin{bmatrix} 1 \\ 2 \\ 3 \end{bmatrix} \cdot \begin{bmatrix} -\frac{1}{\sqrt{6}} \\ \frac{1}{\sqrt{6}} \\ \frac{2}{\sqrt{6}} \end{bmatrix} = \frac{7}{\sqrt{6}}$$

So, the decomposition of $[1 \ 2 \ 3]^{\top}$ as a linear of combination of the given basis vectors is expressed using the coefficients that are obtained by above products as,

$$
\begin{bmatrix} 1 \\ 2 \\ 3 \end{bmatrix} = \frac{2}{\sqrt{3}} \begin{bmatrix} \frac{1}{\sqrt{3}} \\ -\frac{1}{\sqrt{3}} \\ \frac{1}{\sqrt{3}} \end{bmatrix} + \frac{3}{\sqrt{2}} \begin{bmatrix} \frac{1}{\sqrt{2}} \\ \frac{1}{\sqrt{2}} \\ 0 \end{bmatrix} + \frac{7}{\sqrt{6}} \begin{bmatrix} -\frac{1}{\sqrt{6}} \\ \frac{1}{\sqrt{6}} \\ \frac{2}{\sqrt{6}} \end{bmatrix}.
$$

2.12 | Learning a dictionary

In the previous section, we discuss how to obtain a sparse representation of an n-D input data vector using a given dictionary of m atoms. An extension to the problem of sparse representation is to learn an optimal dictionary using a given set of data vectors. In other words, given a set of data points, $\mathrm{X} = \{\boldsymbol{x}_i \mid i = 1, 2, \ldots N, \boldsymbol{x}_i \in \mathbb{R}^n\}$, the task is to find a dictionary, D, of K atoms, so that, D gives the best possible sparse representation for each member of X. Learning the dictionary makes it adaptive to certain classes of signals or data of interest. Since the dictionary is learnt from exemplars, it is expected to provide the sparse representation of the respective data.

2.12.1 | Problem statement

Let $\mathbf{X}$ represent a set of N data points as a matrix, where each data point is a column with an n-D vector. This is represented in a matrix form as in Eq. 2.122.

$$
\mathbf{X} = \begin{bmatrix} \boldsymbol{x}_1 & \boldsymbol{x}_2 & \ldots & \boldsymbol{x}_N \end{bmatrix}_{n \times N}, \text{ where } \boldsymbol{x}_i \in \mathbb{R}^n \tag{2.122}
$$

Here, $\mathbf{X}$ is an $n \times N$ matrix with each column, $\boldsymbol{x}_i$, representing an input vector of dimension n. Consider a dictionary, D, of K atoms, where each atom is of dimension n, as shown in the following.

$$
\mathrm{D} = \begin{bmatrix} \boldsymbol{d}_1 & \boldsymbol{d}_2 & \ldots & \boldsymbol{d}_k \end{bmatrix}_{n \times K}, \text{ where } \boldsymbol{d}_i \in \mathbb{R}^n \tag{2.123}
$$

We note that, in order to represent the data, $\mathbf{X}$, as a linear combination of the atoms of D, the dimensionality of atoms are required to be the same as the input data vectors. Let the sparse representation of $\mathbf{X}$ be given by the linear combination of the atoms with the corresponding coefficients in $\mathbf{Y}$, which is given by Eq. 2.124.

$$
\mathbf{Y} = \begin{bmatrix} \boldsymbol{y}_1 & \boldsymbol{y}_2 & \ldots & \boldsymbol{y}_N \end{bmatrix}_{K \times N}, \text{ where } \boldsymbol{y}_i \in \mathbb{R}^K \tag{2.124}
$$

The columns, $\boldsymbol{y}_i$s, of the matrix, $\mathbf{Y}$, provide the sparse representation of $\boldsymbol{x}_i$s of $\mathbf{X}$ in K-D real space, which is expressed as $\mathbf{X} = \mathrm{D}\mathbf{Y}$ or $\mathbf{X} \sim \mathrm{D}\mathbf{Y}$. This represents the linear combination of dictionary atoms for each data point, and the coefficients of linear combination form the columns of $\mathbf{Y}$. Such a sparse representation factorizes the input data matrix, $\mathbf{X}$, into two matrices, (1) a dictionary, D, of K atoms, and (2) N sparse representations in $\boldsymbol{y}_i$s, corresponding to N data points, $\boldsymbol{x}_i$s.

The dimensions of $\mathbf{X}$ and D are $n \times N$ and $n \times K$, respectively, where n is the dimensionality of column vectors of $\mathbf{X}$ and D. In other words, $\mathbf{X}$ has N columns corresponding to N data points, and D has K columns corresponding to K atoms of the dictionary. Here, K is the dimension of sparse representation of $\mathbf{X}$ ($K < N$), which implies that only a few of the elements in column vectors of $\mathbf{Y}$ are nonzero. The sparsity is characterized by the presence of a few nonzero elements of $\mathbf{Y}$ accounting for the contributions of the corresponding columns of D. To interpret the above representation, consider the reconstruction of $\boldsymbol{x}_i$s of $\mathbf{X}$ using the coefficient vectors and the dictionary as given by Eq. 2.125.

$$[\boldsymbol{x}_1 \ \ \boldsymbol{x}_2 \ \ ... \ \ \boldsymbol{x}_N] = [\boldsymbol{d}_1 \ \ \boldsymbol{d}_2 \ \ ... \ \ \boldsymbol{d}_K] \begin{bmatrix} a_{11} & a_{12} & ... & a_{1N} \\ a_{21} & a_{22} & ... & a_{2N} \\ \vdots & & & \\ a_{K1} & a_{K2} & ... & a_{KN} \end{bmatrix} \tag{2.125}$$

$$\implies \boldsymbol{x}_1 = \sum_{i=1}^{K} a_{i1}\boldsymbol{d}_i \ , \quad \boldsymbol{x}_2 = \sum_{i=1}^{K} a_{i2}\boldsymbol{d}_i \ , \quad ... \boldsymbol{x}_N = \sum_{i=1}^{K} a_{iN}\boldsymbol{d}_i$$

where, $[a_{1i} \ \ a_{1i} \ \ ... \ \ a_{Ki}]^\top$ corresponds to the ith column of $\mathbf{Y}$, $\boldsymbol{y}_i$. That is, $\boldsymbol{x}_1$ is obtained by multiplying each of the coefficients, a_{ji}, in the ith column of $\mathbf{Y}$ with the column vector, $\boldsymbol{d}_j$. Similarly, $\boldsymbol{x}_2$ is also computed as given in Eq. 2.125, and so on. The linear combinations of each column vector of $\mathbf{X}$ is expressed as the product of the columns of D and the elements in corresponding column of $\mathbf{Y}$.

2.12.2 | Sparsity constraints

There are various sparsity constraints which may be imposed on the sparse representation of $\mathbf{Y}$. These constraints impose a limit on the number of nonzeros elements of $\mathbf{Y}$, such that, it optimizes the sparse representation of the input data matrix $\mathbf{X}$. An example of such a constraint is to consider the 0th norm of $\mathbf{Y}$ to be minimum, which is given by Eq. 2.126.

$$\min_{\boldsymbol{y}} \ ||\boldsymbol{y}||_0 \ \text{subject to} \ \boldsymbol{x} = \mathrm{D}\boldsymbol{y} \tag{2.126}$$

The above implies that, the number of nonzero elements of $\mathbf{Y}$ should be minimum, subject to the satisfaction of the constraint as shown in Eq. 2.126. This objective limits the number of dictionary atoms and the number of nonzero elements of each sparse represented vector. Another example of constraint is to consider the L_2 norm as an optimization problem for reconstructing the elements of $\mathbf{X}$ with a tolerance of ϵ, which is given by Eq. 2.127.

$$\min_{\boldsymbol{y}} \ ||\boldsymbol{y}||_0 \ \text{subject to} \ ||\boldsymbol{x} - \mathrm{D}\boldsymbol{y}||_2 \leq \epsilon \tag{2.127}$$

Here, a widely used dictionary forming algorithm, *K-Singular Value Decomposition* (*K*-SVD) is discussed (Aharon et al., 2006). It computes the dictionary of K elements that leads to the best possible representation for each member in the input data set with strict sparsity constraints. In the case of the 0th norm, a tolerance, T_0, is imposed in its optimization problem, so that $||\boldsymbol{y}||_0 \leq T_0$. The principle of this algorithm is based on generalizing the K means clustering problem (discussed in Chapter 6). In this context, the K representatives for each of the K groups of data vectors act like atoms. This results in an extreme sparse representation, if the representative of a group is represented by a single atom of a dictionary formed by the K mean vectors as obtained by the K-means clustering algorithm. In the K-SVD algorithm, instead of considering a single atom representation of the K means clustering, a sparse linear combination of K atoms is considered. Here, a dictionary of K atoms is chosen and the atoms in the dictionary are updated to get a better sparse representation. Once a sparse representation using these atoms is obtained, it is rechecked whether any sparser representation is further possible by updating some of atoms with better approximation of the input signal. The atoms are updated only if a better approximation is available, which is repeated till no such improvements are possible anymore.

2.12.3 | K-singular value decomposition (K-SVD)

The K-SVD algorithm derives a code book from the training examples. Consider a $n \times K$ code book dictionary, $\mathrm{D} = \{\boldsymbol{d}_i\}_1^K = [\boldsymbol{d}_1 \ \boldsymbol{d}_2 \ ... \ \boldsymbol{d}_K]_{n \times K}$. Here, n is the dimensionality of the training samples, and the set of training examples is, $\mathbf{X} = \{\boldsymbol{x}_i\}_{i=1}^N$. The extreme sparse vector, $\boldsymbol{e}_j$, is given by $\begin{bmatrix} 0 & 0 & ... & 0 & 1 & 0 & ... & 0 \end{bmatrix}^\top$, where, only the jth term of the K-D vector is 1 and the rest of the elements are 0. This j^{th} element of the extreme sparse vector, whose value is 1, denotes the jth atom that is assigned to the input vector. Since $\boldsymbol{e}_j$ has only one nonzero element, it is called the extreme sparse vector. Initial dictionary and extreme sparse vectors may be obtained using the K-means clustering algorithm (refer to Chapter 6). In this case, the mean of the ith cluster is taken as $\boldsymbol{d}_i$ and the data point belonging to that cluster is represented by the extreme sparse vector $\boldsymbol{e}_i$. The sparse representation of $\mathbf{X}$, $\mathbf{Y} = [\boldsymbol{y}_1 \ \boldsymbol{y}_2 \cdots \boldsymbol{y}_N]_{K \times N}$, is a matrix of dimension $K \times N$, where each of its K-D column vectors, $\boldsymbol{y}_i$, is one of the sparse vectors, $\boldsymbol{e}_j$.

Let the set of N training examples be represented by $n \times N$ matrix, $\mathbf{X} = \{\boldsymbol{x}_i\}_{i=1}^N$. Let the $K \times N$ matrix, $\mathbf{Y}$, represent the sparse representation, where each column is a sparse representation of K data vectors. Then, the optimization problem is formed as minimizing the L_2 norm of $\mathbf{X} - \mathrm{DY}$, subject to the number of nonzero elements for each sparse representation to be less than a threshold, T_0. This is expressed in Eq. 2.128.

$$\text{Minimize } ||\mathbf{X} - \mathrm{DY}||_\mathrm{F}^2, \text{ subject to } ||y_i||_0 \leq T_0 \ \forall i \tag{2.128}$$

The optimization function (L_2 norm of $\mathbf{X} - \mathrm{DY}$) is rewritten in Eq. 2.129 so that the contribution of a single dictionary element (say the kth atom) is isolated from the rest of the atoms.

$$
\begin{aligned}
||\mathbf{X} - \mathrm{DY}||_\mathrm{F}^2 &= ||\mathbf{X} - \sum_{j=1}^K \boldsymbol{d}_j \boldsymbol{y}_T^j||_\mathrm{F}^2 \\
&= ||(\mathbf{X} - \sum_{j \neq k} \boldsymbol{d}_j \boldsymbol{y}_T^j) - \boldsymbol{d}_k \boldsymbol{y}_T^k||_\mathrm{F}^2
\end{aligned}
\tag{2.129}
$$

where, $\boldsymbol{y}_T^j$ represents j^{th} row of $\mathbf{Y}$. We may note that, $\mathbf{X}$ may be represented as the sum of rank 1 matrices, where the ith component is obtained by the outer product of the ith atom of the dictionary and the ith row of $\mathbf{Y}$, as in Eq. 2.130.

$$\mathbf{X} = \sum_{i=1}^{K} [\boldsymbol{d}_i][\boldsymbol{y}_T^i] \tag{2.130}$$

In the above expression, on the right hand side of the equation, for any particular value of i, a matrix of dimension $n \times N$ is obtained, which is the same as the dimension of $\mathbf{X}$. The sum of all such matrices, for all i, would result in $\mathbf{X}$, which is equal to $\mathbf{DY}$. Hence, every atom, $\boldsymbol{d}_k$, contributes to the reconstruction of $\mathbf{DY}$. Thus, the contribution of every atom, $\boldsymbol{d}_k$, may be independently identified.

To optimize the L_2 norm, it is necessary to find out which of the $\boldsymbol{d}_k$s and $\boldsymbol{y}_T^k$s best fit the error term, $E_k = (\mathbf{X} - \sum_{j \neq k} \boldsymbol{d}_j \boldsymbol{y}_T^j)$. Given the input data, $\mathbf{X}$, the error of approximation, E, is computed using all the atoms of the dictionary, except the kth atom. Since this approximation happens iteratively, the sparse representation is computed using only $k - 1$ atoms, and the error term is computed without using the kth atom. Therefore, the selection of $\boldsymbol{d}_k$ and $\boldsymbol{y}_T^k$ are made such that, E_k is minimized. This is done by making the best rank-1 approximation of E_k. The computation is performed by decomposing E_k into $\mathbf{U}$, $\boldsymbol{\Sigma}$ and $\mathbf{V}$ matrices using the technique of singular value decomposition (SVD) as follows:

$$E_k = \mathbf{U} \, \mathbf{V}^{\top}$$

where $\boldsymbol{\Sigma}$ is a diagonal matrix with the singular values in the diagonal in a nonincreasing order. The column vectors of $\mathbf{U}$ and $\mathbf{V}$ correspond to the singular vectors of E_k. The columns of $\mathbf{U}$ and $\mathbf{V}$ are called the left-singular vectors and right-singular vectors of E_k, respectively. The first column of both $\mathbf{U}$ and $\mathbf{V}$ correspond to the same maximum singular value of E_k. The normalized column of $\mathbf{U}$ is considered as the updated atom of the dictionary (i.e., $\boldsymbol{d}_k$) and the first column of $\mathbf{V}$ is the residual contribution by the updated $\boldsymbol{d}_k$. Also, the product of the columns of $\mathbf{V}$ and the maximum singular value, $\boldsymbol{\Sigma}(1, 1)$, results in $\boldsymbol{y}_T^k$. Though this representation may not be exactly equal to E_k, this is the closest approximation by a rank-1 matrix. However, the sparsity of $\boldsymbol{y}_T^k$ is not ensured here.

The sparsity is enforced on $\mathbf{X}$ by considering only those samples of the input that make nonzero contributions toward the dictionary atoms, $\boldsymbol{d}_k$. Suppose there are m nonzero elements in $\boldsymbol{y}_T^k$. Hence only m column vectors of the data matrix $\mathbf{X}$ would be selected and the error of reconstruction would be computed with respect to a reduced dimensional data matrix of $n \times m$. Accordingly E_{kR} would be also of dimension $n \times m$. This also ensures that the coefficients, y_ks, would be nonzero. Such a sparsity enforcement results in a reduced dimensional error, E_{kR}, matrix. Thereby, performing SVD of E_{kR} provides the best possible results for $\boldsymbol{d}_k$ and $\boldsymbol{y}_T^k$. This process is continued for evaluating all the other dictionary atoms, $\boldsymbol{d}_j$, and the updated $\boldsymbol{y}_T^k$ until convergence. This algorithm for obtaining both the sparse representation and the dictionary of K atoms for a set of N data points $\mathbf{X}$ is provided in Algorithm 2.

There are various applications of the K-SVD algorithm. Since the input data is factorized, only the important factors are retained and the other information are rejected,

---

Algorithm 2 K-SVD algorithm

Input: $\mathbf{X} = \{\boldsymbol{x}_i | i = 1, 2, \dots, N\}$, where, $\boldsymbol{x}_i \in \mathbb{R}^n$.
Output: $\mathrm{D} = \{\boldsymbol{d}_i | i = 1, 2, \dots, K\}$, where, $\boldsymbol{d}_i \in \mathbb{R}^n$, and $\mathbf{Y} = \{\boldsymbol{y}_i | i = 1, 2, \dots, N\}$, where, $\boldsymbol{y}_i \in \mathbb{R}^K$.

1: Form an initial dictionary of K atoms using K-means clustering technique.
2: Obtain an initial sparse representation, $\mathbf{Y}$, using any of the pursuit algorithms, like OMP.
3: Iterate for updating j^{th} atom and the sparse representation associated with the jth atom (i.e., j^{th} row of $\mathbf{Y}$).

---

thereby achieving compression of the data. Sparse representation may be used in learning dictionaries for representation of a signal in different resolutions. The mapping that is established between two dictionaries corresponding to different resolutions of data representation may help in estimating a higher resolution representation from the low resolution signal. This approach finds uses in the task of deriving an image of super resolution. The other applications of sparse representation in image processing include image denoising, image deblurring, etc.

2.13 | Alternative representation of a video

In its original form, a video is a sequence of frames of images. Hence, like images, in a video, every frame may be independently represented using the techniques discussed in previous sections of this chapter. However as the consecutive frames are highly correlated, there are efficient representations of a sequence of frames. Various compression standards (Mukhopadhyay, 2011) such as MPEG-2, MPEG-4, H.263, HEVC, etc., use both image transforms and dependencies and similarities among a group of frames to represent videos. Instead of detailing all such compression schemes, here we discuss a few typical approaches for deriving alternate representation of a video.

2.13.1 | Group of pictures

For exploiting both spatial and temporal redundancy in a video, it is partitioned into groups of consecutive frames or pictures, called a *group of pictures* (GOP) (Mukhopadhyay, 2011). Usually the length of the GOP is fixed. There are three types of frames in a GOP, namely, *Intra-frames* (*I-Frames*), *Predicted frames* (*P-Frames*), and *Bidirectional frames* (*B-Frames*). The starting frame must be of an 'I-frame.' A typical GOP structure is shown in Fig. 2.23.

I-frames, are represented independently using the content of the picture itself. Hence the techniques of alternate representation of images may be used directly for these frames. I-frames are also synchronization points in the represented stream.

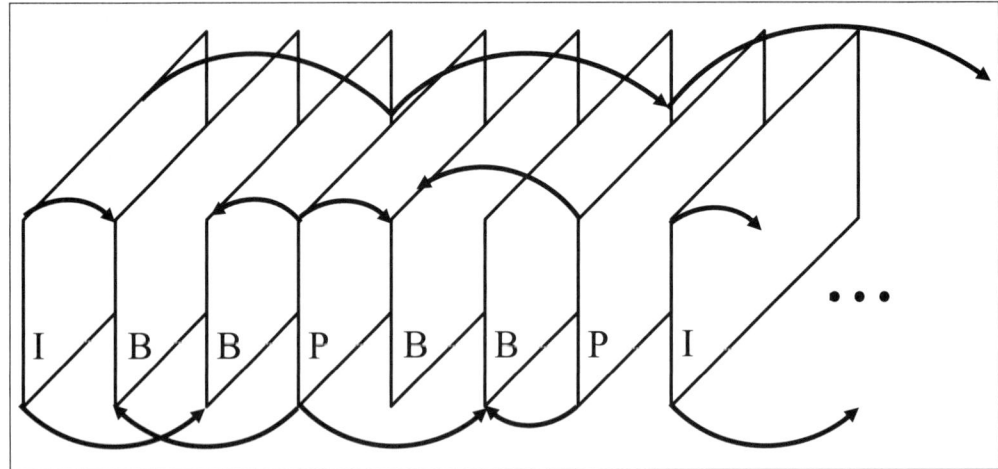

Figure 2.23 Prediction of pictures in a GOP sequence.

P-frame, is represented with reference to its nearest previous I- or P-frame. Usually a P-frame keeps record of the offsets of highly similar collocated neighboring blocks of its reference frame in the form of *motion vectors*. It also encodes the errors of prediction in a transform domain, such as using DCT.

B-frames, are frames that use both a past and a future frame as references. Hence, in this case, the frame is encoded with bidirectional prediction.

2.13.2 | Blocks and macroblocks

Every frame of a video is partitioned into a set of nonoverlapping *blocks*. The typical size of a block is 8×8. A group of blocks form a *macroblock*. For example, a macroblock of size 16×16 consists of 4 blocks. Blocks and macroblocks are used for efficient encoding of frames. For an I-frame, each block is represented in a transform domain (DCT), whereas for a P-frame and a B-frame, motion vectors of macroblocks are recorded, providing the neighboring regions of the same size in the reference frames, from where the predictions to be made. The differences of predicted values and the true values of the macroblock of the frame are encoded. This kind of prediction is called *motion compensation*.

2.13.3 | Motion vectors

For prediction of pixels within the current frame, a region in the reference frame is searched, and the respective offset or translation vector is recorded. This translation vector is called *motion vector*. Computation of this motion vector is called *motion estimation*. In forward prediction of a P-frame, each macroblock (MB) is predicted from the previous frame with the underlying assumption that every pixel within that MB undergoes the same amount of translational motion. This motion vector is represented by a 2-D displacement vector. As the blocks of a given size in two frames are to be compared, *block-matching* algorithms are applied in computing this vector. A schematic diagram of this computation is shown in

Fig. 2.24. As it is shown, each block in the current frame is matched at every pixel location within the search window of the previous frame. For optimizing the search, an error function is defined between the candidate block of the reference frame, and the target block of the current frame. There are different error functions used for this purpose, such as, mean of absolute differences (MAD), sum-of-absolute-differences (SAD), mean-square-error (MSE), etc. The SAD is widely used for this task. It is defined as follows.

$$SAD_{i,j}(u,v) = \sum_{p=0}^{N-1} \sum_{q=0}^{N-1} |c_{i,j}(p,q) - r_{i-u,j-v}(p,q)|. \qquad (2.131)$$

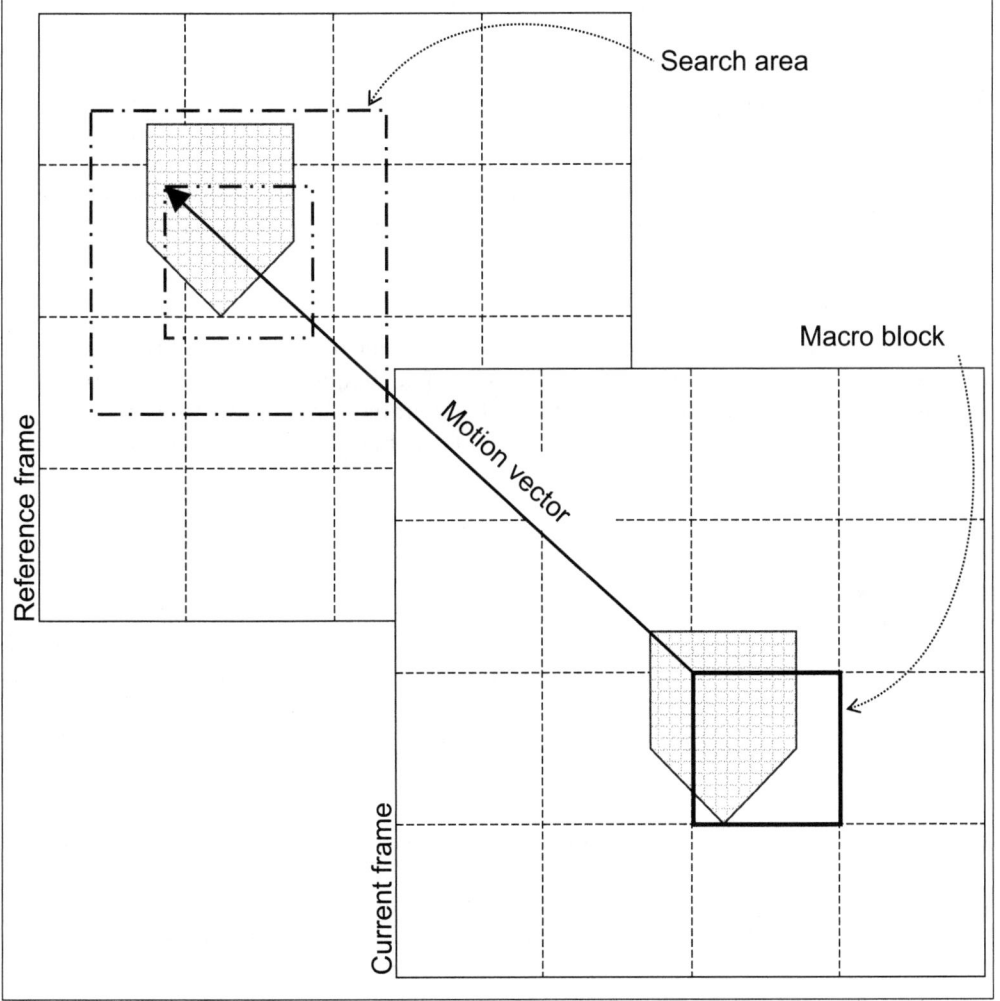

Figure 2.24 Motion estimation for MPEG-2 video encoder.

where $SAD_{i,j}(u,v)$ represents the SAD between the $(i,j)th$ block and the block at the $(u,v)th$ location in the search window $W_{i,j}$ of the $(i,j)th$ block. Here, $c_{i,j}(p,q)$ represents the $(p,q)th$ pixel of an $N \times N$ $(i,j)th$ MB $C_{i,j}$, from the current picture and $r_{i-u,j-v}(p,q)$ represents the $(p,q)th$ pixel of an $N \times N$ MB from the reference picture displaced by the vector (u,v) within the search range of $C_{i,j}$.

To find the MB producing the minimum mismatch error, the SAD is to be computed at several locations within the search window. The simplest but the most computationally intensive search method, known as the full search or exhaustive search method, evaluates SAD at every possible pixel location in the search area. Using full search, the motion vector is computed as follows:

$$\boldsymbol{MV}_{i,j} = \{(u',v')|SAD_{i,j}(u',v') \leq SAD_{i,j}(u,v), \forall (u,v) \in W_{i,j}\}, \qquad (2.132)$$

where $\boldsymbol{MV}_{i,j}$ expresses the motion vector of the current block $C_{i,j}$ with minimum SAD among all search positions. Motion vectors may be computed at varying resolution. For example, for a *full pixel* estimation, MBs are defined from the locations of the reference frame in its original resolution, but for *half pixel* motion vectors, the reference image is first upsampled (say, using bilinear interpolation) to double its resolution in both the directions. Then using the locations of upsampled image motion vectors are computed.

2.13.4 | Video object layer

There are also other forms of representation of a video. Some of them use additional layers of information on top of basic representation using motion compensated prediction. To derive this representation segmentation algorithms in video frames are applied to extract objects and the sequence of these objects in the overall video defines a *video object* (VO) or a *video object layer* (VOL). Individual VOs are independently coded bearing information related to *shape*, *motion*, and *texture*.

Summary

Transforms provide an alternative representation of images and videos, which are useful in different image and video processing applications, like data compression. There are various techniques for transforming or factorizing an image as a linear combination of orthogonal or orthonormal basis functions. For a finite discrete image, the number of these discrete basis functions is also finite, and transformations are invertible. Some of the properties of these transforms, particularly, the properties of discrete Fourier transforms, generalized discrete Fourier transforms, trigonometric functions, discrete cosine transforms, and discrete wavelet transforms are discussed.

Wavelets provide a multi-resolution representation of an image. Their computation is very fast, since both the forward and inverse transformation may be performed by simple filtering. Multi-resolution representation of images in useful in progressive and scalable processing. Both lossy and lossless reconstruction are possible using wavelets, which is useful in several applications, including image compression, like JPEG2000 compression scheme.

In dimension reduction, the principal component analysis (PCA) is found to be effective. One of the objectives of the PCA is to represent data in a minimal subspace and it involves coordinate transformation. In the PCA, a direction that maximizes the variance of dominant components is obtained and the data across different dimensions are decorrelated. In sparse representation different pursuit algorithms, like matching pursuit, orthogonal matching pursuit, and basis pursuit may be applied. The techniques for dictionary learning and using it to derive sparse representation of data are illustrated, particularly using the K-SVD algorithm.

With reference to videos, group of pictures and motion vectors are discussed, which are the basics of alternative representation of a video signal.

Exercises

(i) Consider the following set of data points.

$$\mathbf{X}_1 = \{(5, 3, 2),\ (4, 6, 0),\ (3, -7, 14)\}, (-2, -5, 17),\ (3, -13, 10),\ (-4, -2, 16)\}$$

Perform the PCA on the data set and get the dominant principal direction. Represent the data points by their principal components in the order of increasing variances.

(ii) Consider the algorithm for principal component analysis (PCA). Suppose there are N feature vectors in an n-dimensional feature space. Let $\mathbf{X}$ be the matrix whose column vectors are those feature vectors. Let $\bar{\mathbf{X}}$ be the mean feature vector. Answer the following.

  (a) What is the form of covariance matrix $\mathbf{C}$, which obtained from $\mathbf{X}$?

  (b) How is the total variance of data computed from $\mathbf{C}$?

  (c) What is the direction of the maximum variance of the projected data set?

(iii) A continuous time signal is given by $x(t) = e^{-2t}u(t)$. Compute its Fourier transform, $X(j\omega)$.

(iv) Compute the N-point DFT of $x(n) = 7\delta(n - n_0)$

(v) Compute the 4-point Discrete Fourier Transform of $X(k)$, $k = 0, 1, 2, 3$ of a discrete time sequence $x(n) = (1, 0, 2, 3)$.

(vi) Consider 3 data points in the 2D space: $(-1, -1)$, $(0, 0)$, $(1, 1)$.

  (a) What will be the principal components for this data?

  (b) What are the coordinates of the given data points in the projected 1D subspace?

(vii) Consider the data points: $((5, 3, 2), (4, 6, 0), (2, 5, 3))$. Compute the covariance matrix of the set using PCA.

(viii) For the data points $((4, 1, 2), (3, 2, 8), (2, 4, 3))$, perform PCA and compute the projected data points with redundant dimension.

(ix) Consider a dictionary in 2D space consisting of following atoms: $((1, 1), (-1, 1), (1, -1))$.
  Perform normalization of the atoms of the dictionary. For a given vector $(2, 3)$, evaluate its representation using two normalized atoms of the above dictionary following orthogonal matching pursuit (OMP).

(x) Let the type-II N-point DCT matrix be defined as $\mathbf{C}_N$. Answer the following questions.

   (a) Enumerate $\mathbf{C}_2$.

   (b) Transform the image block X of size 2×2, as given below, into type-II DCT.

$$X = \begin{bmatrix} 30 & 45 \\ 20 & 50 \end{bmatrix}$$

(xi) Let the type-I and type-II N-point DCT matrices be denoted as $\mathbf{C}_N^{(I)}$ and $\mathbf{C}_N^{(II)}$, respectively. Answer the following questions.

   (a) Enumerate $\mathbf{C}_2^{(I)}$ and $\mathbf{C}_2^{(II)}$.

   (b) State the convolution multiplication property involving the above two transforms, and discuss how it is useful in performing filtering in the type-II block DCT domain.

(xii) Consider a dictionary of 4 column vectors as follows.
$\{[1,0,0]^T, [0,1,0]^T, [0,0,1]^T, [\frac{1}{\sqrt{2}}, \frac{1}{\sqrt{2}}, 0]^T\}$.

   (a) Verify if they form an orthogonal set of basis vectors.

   (b) Decompose a vector $[1, 2, 1]^T$ as the best approximation of a linear combination of any two atoms of the dictionary following the method of Orthogonal Matching Pursuit (OMP).

(xiii) Explain K-SVD algorithm for learning a dictionary of m elements (atoms), given N data points in $\mathbb{R}^n$, for their sparse representation.

(xiv) How motion compensation is used in video compression? Describe the computational steps for computing motion vectors and residuals in this process?

(xv) Consider the following transformation matrix A for transforming a column vector of dimension 4.

$$A = \begin{bmatrix} \frac{1}{2} & \frac{1}{2} & \frac{1}{2} & \frac{1}{2} \\ \frac{1}{2} & \frac{1}{2} & -\frac{1}{2} & -\frac{1}{2} \\ \frac{1}{\sqrt{2}} & -\frac{1}{\sqrt{2}} & 0 & 0 \\ 0 & 0 & \frac{1}{\sqrt{2}} & -\frac{1}{\sqrt{2}} \end{bmatrix}$$

   (a) Show that the transformation matrix is orthonormal.

   (b) Given the transformed column vector $[3 \quad 4 \quad 5 \quad 6]^T$, compute the vector whose transformation it is.

(xvi) Given a 1D signal $x(n) = \{1, 2, 4, 7\}$. Compute the Discrete Cosine Transform (DCT) of $x(n)$.

(xvii) (a) Write the set of basis functions of the Fourier series of a periodic 1-D function $f(x)$.

(b) Show how they can provide the set of orthogonal basis vectors of discrete Fourier transform (DFT) of a finite sequence of length N. Justify whether there can be many such sets of orthogonal basis vectors.

(c) Explain why cosine transform of any arbitrary function does not exist in continuous domain, but that exists for finite sequences in the form of a discrete cosine transform.

(d) Explain why wavelet transform of a 1-D transform is 2-D.

(xviii) What are the set of basis functions of the Fourier series of a periodic 1-D function $f(x)$. Show how they can provide the set of orthogonal basis vectors of discrete Fourier transform (DFT) of a finite sequence of length N. Justify whether there can be many such sets of orthogonal basis vectors.

(xix) Explain why cosine transform of any arbitrary function does not exist in continuous domain, but does exist for finite sequences in the form of a discrete cosine transform.

(xx) Find the 2D DCT for a 4x4 matrix $\mathbf{A} = \begin{bmatrix} 1 & 2 & 2 & 1 \\ 2 & 1 & 2 & 1 \\ 1 & 2 & 2 & 1 \\ 2 & 1 & 2 & 1 \end{bmatrix}$.

3

Color Processing

Color is a psycho-physiological property of human visual experiences when the eyes look at objects and light. Color is not a physical property of those objects or light, rather, it is the result of an interaction between physical light in the environment and human visual system (Palmer, 1999). For processing color images, it is required to develop an understanding on how colors are represented following human perception.

3.1 | Light sources

A broad range of electromagnetic spectrum, shown in Fig. 3.1, consists of electromagnetic waves ranging from very long wavelengths at radio waves to very high frequency at gamma waves. A very narrow interval in this spectrum, toward the higher end of spectral frequencies, accounts for the visible rays and it is called the *visible spectrum*. The light and colors that a human eye perceives relate to the frequencies of waves that fall under the visible spectrum. A pictorial representation of the correspondence of wavelengths in the visible range of the spectrum to different perceived colors has been shown in Fig. 3.1. There are seven distinguishable colors in the figure, violet, indigo, blue, green, yellow, orange, and red, usually known in order of their increasing wavelengths by the acronym of VIBGYOR. The luminance sensitivity function that is shown as a curve in Fig. 3.1 is a function of the wavelength. It is empirically observed that the sensitivity of the human visual system is maximum in the green zone of the visible spectrum. The luminance sensitivity function gradually decays toward violet (higher frequencies) and red (lower frequencies) from the green zone, as shown in the figure by the white curve.

Usually, light in the visible spectrum is not characterized by uniform energy distributions over all the wavelengths in visible range. Any light that causes the sensation of color in the eyes is physically described by its spectrum using spectral power as a signature of the light source. *The spectral power is defined as the power (or the amount of energy emitted per unit time) at each wavelength in the visible band (400–700 nm) of the electromagnetic spectrum.*

127

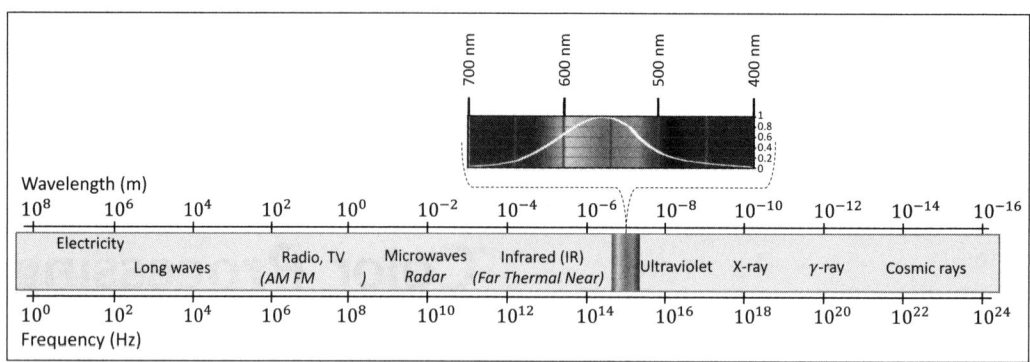

Figure 3.1 A broad range of electromagnetic spectrum and human luminance sensitivity function in the optical range of the spectrum. See Color Plates (page 804).

3.1.1 | Black body radiators

A particular characterization of a luminance source is a black body radiator, which is a near ideal energy emitter. A black body is a hot body with near-zero albedo that does not reflect the light from the environment. Hence, it cannot be seen. One of the easiest ways to observe a black body is to build a hollow metal object with a tiny hole in it and look through the hole. The inside of the hollow body behaves as an ideal blackbody radiator. The spectral power distribution of a black body radiator is a function of temperature. The relationship between the temperature (T), wavelength (λ), and the distribution of energy with respect to wavelength $(E(\lambda))$, is given by Eq. 3.1.

$$E(\lambda) \propto \frac{1}{\lambda^5} \frac{1}{e^{\frac{hc}{k\lambda T}} - 1} \tag{3.1}$$

where, c is the speed of light, k is the Boltzmann constant, and h is the Planck's constant. This leads to the notion of a *color temperature. It is the temperature of a black body radiator whose energy spectrum matches with that of a light source with a specific energy emission distribution over the wavelengths. In other words, the equivalent representation of a light source is a black body radiating at its color temperature.*

3.2 | Human visual system

Let us have a brief understanding of the human visual system, which responds to the optical stimuli from the environment.

3.2.1 | Interaction of light and surfaces

The objects in the environment are perceived by our visual system primarily due to the phenomenon of reflection of light. The light reflected from the surface of an object in a

3-D space falls on the retina of the eyes to stimulate the image of the scene. The observed color is the result of interaction of the light source spectrum with the surface reflectance. The nature of the reflected energy mainly depends on the kind of surfaces that reflect it. For example, a tomato appears as a red surface because the energy reflected from its surface points have content of higher wavelengths in the optical region of the electromagnetic (EM) spectrum. Likewise, a banana, which is yellow, reflects light in different wavelengths, with a prominent reflectance value in yellow and red zones, and blueberries reflect light in the blue range of the visible spectrum. Every surface absorbs a part of the incident energy and reflects a part of it in different wavelengths that gives a sense of color, which is figuratively shown in Fig. 3.2. The percentage of light reflected across different wavelengths depends on the material property of reflecting surface that imparts the appearance of color to the surface. At every wavelength, the energy ($\mathcal{E}$) received by the human visual system is the product of two factors, viz., the power of illumination ($\mathcal{I}$) or the relative energy of the particular wavelength (λ), and the reflectance value ($\mathcal{R}$) of that wavelength. Thus, $\mathcal{E}(\lambda) = \mathcal{I}(\lambda)\,\mathcal{R}(\lambda)$.

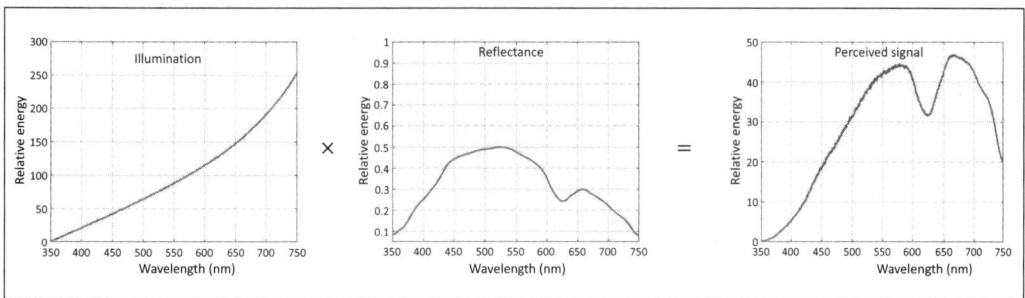

Figure 3.2 Components of a perceived signal. See Color Plates (page 805).

3.2.2 | Eye as a camera

The eye in the human visual system acts as a camera, which has a *lens* that projects a three-dimensional (3-D) scene points onto a two-dimensional (2-D) semi-spherical screen, known as *retina*. The projected points on retina impart a sensation that is carried through the nervous system of the brain leading to perception of color. The amount of optical energy that is transmitted through the lens is controlled by radial muscles known as *iris*. An anatomy of the human eye is shown in Fig. 3.3. The conventional camera has a direct analogy with the human visual system. In the primitive form, it consists of (1) a lens, similar to the lens in an eye, (2) an image plane, similar to the retina of the eye, and (3) photo-sensitive sensors that convert photon energy into electrical signal, similar to the photo-receptor cells in eyes that send signals via nervous system to brain.

There are two kinds of photo-receptor cells in the retina, namely *rods* and *cones*. The rods and cones are attached with the corresponding optical nerves which are linked directly to the brain. The nomenclature of the photo-receptor cells is based on their shapes. The cone cells, which are responsible for the perception of color and high illumination, are in conical shape, and the rod cells, which are responsible for the perception of low illumination, are in

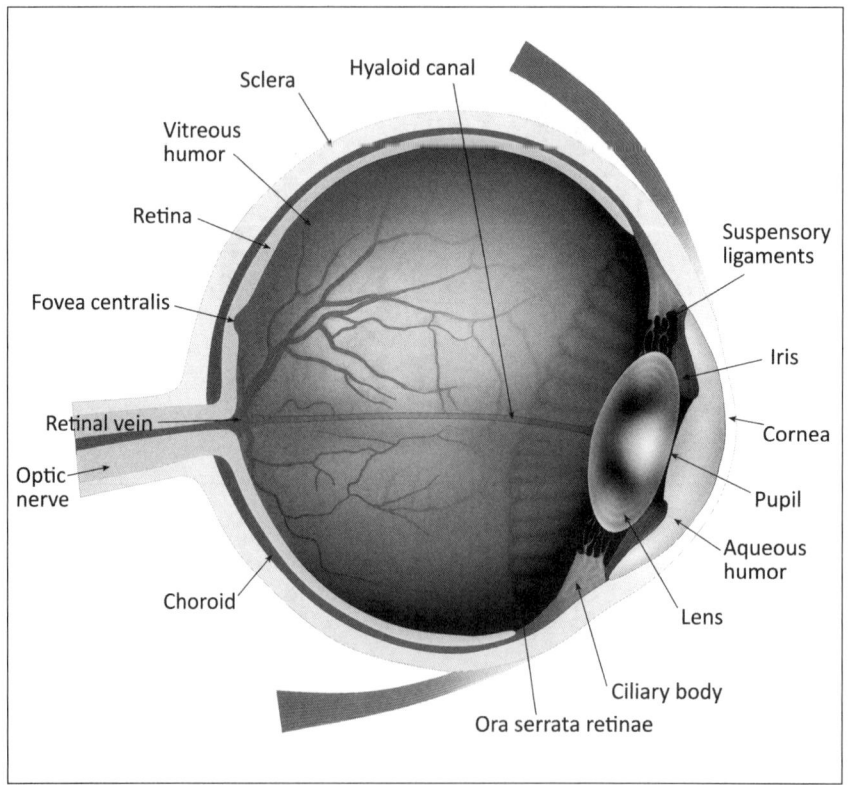

Figure 3.3 Basic anatomy of the human eye. (Courtesy: Getty Images/MARK GARLICK/SCIENCE PHOTO LIBRARY.) See Color Plates (page 805).

cylindrical form (Fig. 3.4 (b)). The distribution of rods and cones is not uniform over the retina, as shown in Fig. 3.4 (a). The cones are highly concentrated in a narrow region in the retinal part, whereas the rods are distributed widely outside this region. The narrow region of high visual acuity, which is approximately 1° to 2° at the center of the visual field, that

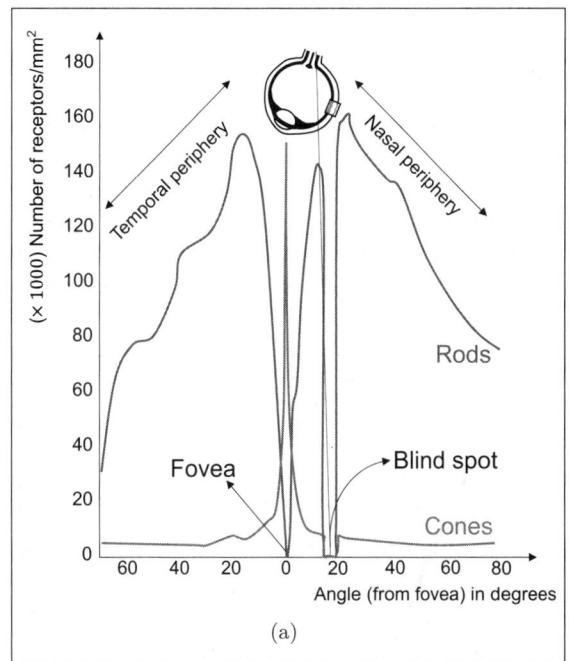

(a)

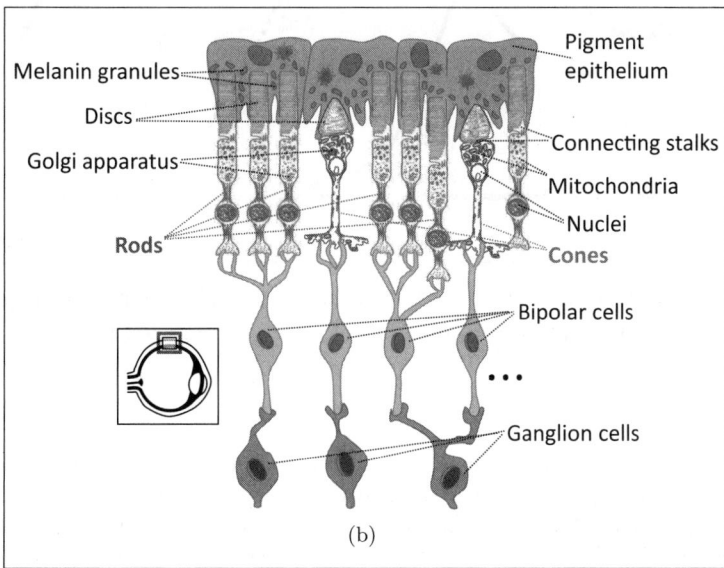

(b)

Figure 3.4 Distribution of rod and cone cells in human eye. See Color Plates (page 806).

contains the highest density of cones is called *fovea*. The visual acuity is comparatively less in peripheral region of retina, where rods are distributed.

The vision by rods is sensitive in the low illumination environment, while the vision by cones is more sensitive in a bright or well illuminated environment.[1] At high intensity object points, human eyes perceive through cones, whereas low intensity vision is enabled by rods. The difficulty to read in low illumination is due to low visual acuity zone of rod cells.

3.2.3 | Color perception

There are three kinds of cone cells in the human visual system, as shown in Fig. 3.5. In the figure, the responses of different cone cells are indicated as S, M, and L, which indicate their sensitivity to short wavelength (blue zone), medium wavelength (green zone), and long wavelength (red zone), respectively. The numbers of cones corresponding to long wavelength, medium wavelength, and short wavelength also widely vary. The number of long wavelength cones is more than the number of medium wavelength cones, and the number

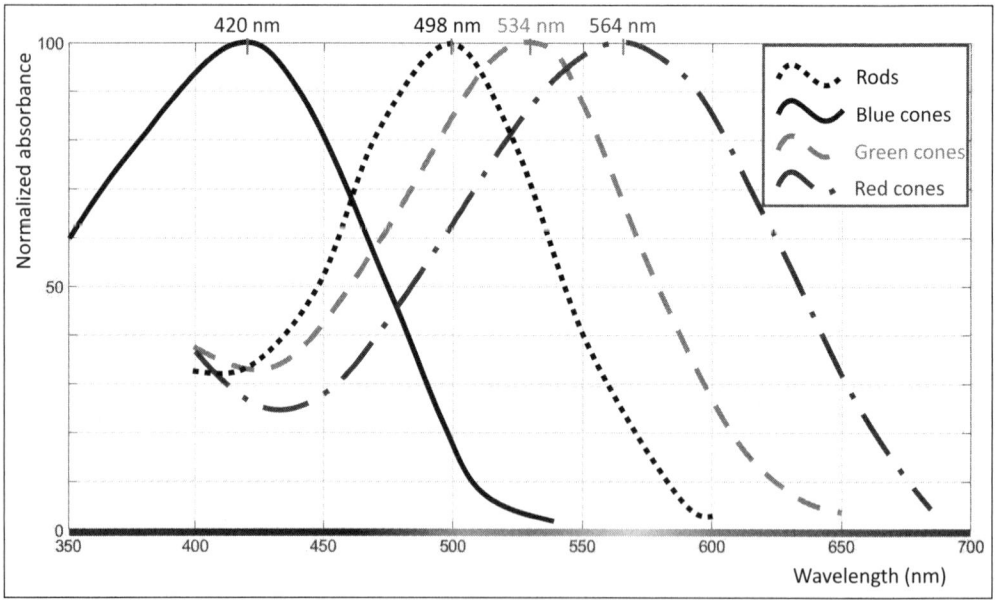

Figure 3.5 Responses of different cone cells in human visual system to a range wavelengths in visible spectrum. See Color Plates (page 806).

---

[1] The intensity of light that is reflected from different objects is expressed in lamberts, which is defined as $\frac{1}{\pi}$ candela per square centimeter $\left(\text{i.e, } 0.3183 \text{ cd/cm}^2 \text{ or } \frac{10^4}{\pi} \text{ cd m}^{-2}\right)$, where candela is the unit of luminous intensity. One candela is the luminous intensity, in a given direction, of a source that emits monochromatic radiation of frequency 540×10^{12} hertz, and that has a radiant intensity in that direction of $\frac{1}{683}$ watt per steradian.

of short wavelength cones are the least. The ratios of long, medium and short wavelength cones are 10 : 5 : 1. In fact, S cones are hardly present in the center of the fovea.

The color perception is explained only by using cone vision, and not by considering the rod vision, since the color perception is primarily a phenomena due to the sensations in cone cells. Though the sensation created or energy received by different kinds of cones is the same, their responses to different wavelengths vary. We may consider a simple mathematical model in expressing the processing involved in color perception. The incident energy on the retina is characterized by its spectral power distributions. Let the total received energy at retina be $E(\lambda)$, corresponding to a wavelength λ. Let the filter responses of long, medium and short wavelength cones be represented by $L(\lambda)$, $M(\lambda)$ and $S(\lambda)$, respectively. In that case the received energy at the wavelength λ at long, medium, and short wavelength cone cells are given by, $E(\lambda)L(\lambda)$, $E(\lambda)M(\lambda)$, and $E(\lambda)S(\lambda)$, respectively. Then, individual responses from these cones are obtained as follows.

$$C_L = \int_\lambda E(\lambda)L(\lambda)d\lambda$$

$$C_M = \int_\lambda E(\lambda)M(\lambda)d\lambda \qquad (3.2)$$

$$C_S = \int_\lambda E(\lambda)S(\lambda)d\lambda$$

From the above, we see that, through an optical stimulation from the environment, the responses in our visual system are coded into three factors, one each from long, medium, and short wavelength cones. These sensations are carried to the brain through the nervous systems, enabling the perception of color. In other words, color is perceived as an effect of the sensations of different cone cells in response to optical stimulation. This forms the basis of *trichromatic theory* of color vision. The entire spectrum of reflected energy from an object or energy of an illuminant is encoded by three numbers that correspond to red, green, and blue colors. However, different spectra may lead to the same representation of color triplets due to different responses from various cone cells and their integration or accumulation over wavelengths. This may make different spectra indistinguishable in perception, and such spectra are called *metamers*. For example, the spectra of white petal and the white flower are mostly the same for human perception, which is similar as a white sensation. But, their relative spectral power distributions over the wavelengths are quite different.

3.3 | Standardizing color perception

Calibrating the color perception with respect to sources to understand the color response from any arbitrary color source is referred to as standardizing color perception or experience. This requires experiments on *color matching*, which provide information of different spectra producing similar color sensation under similar viewing conditions. The color experience is standardized by performing these color matching experiments.

3.3.1 | Color matching experiments

To understand the process of conducting color matching experiment, consider its typical setup, as shown in Fig. 3.6. In the setup shown in the figure, there are three primary sources of light that correspond to the wavelengths of red (R), green (G), and blue (B). These three colors, red, green, and blue, are called primary colors, because any color may be represented by a combination of these three color components. Also, there is a test light, T, which is pure monochromatic color source of a particular wavelength, that needs to be calibrated as factors of the three primary sources. The test color and superimposed primary colors are displayed on a screen to highlight their differences. The projection is designed in such a way that these differences, if any, are easily visible. For example, the test color and the combination of primary colors are projected in a rectangular region, as shown in Fig. 3.6. Also, there may be a surrounding field to provide a contrast around the observation region. The relative strengths of the primary energy sources are varied and the proportions of their mixing or superposition are noted. The proportion of primary colors is varied in such a way that the color of T and the combination of R, G, and B, do not have any distinction between them. This proportion of primary colors that imitates the color of the test light represents their factors for T. This experiment is known as color matching experiment. In subsequent subsections, two scenarios of color matching experiments are discussed.

Color matching experiment for additive mixing

The first scenario of color matching experiment involves superposition or mixing of all the three primary colors on a portion of the display screen as shown in Fig. 3.7. A hypothetical color matching experiment is diagrammatically shown in the figure. In each of the sub-figures, left portion of the color display is projected by the test light source, and the right portion of the display is projected by a particular combination of three primary color sources

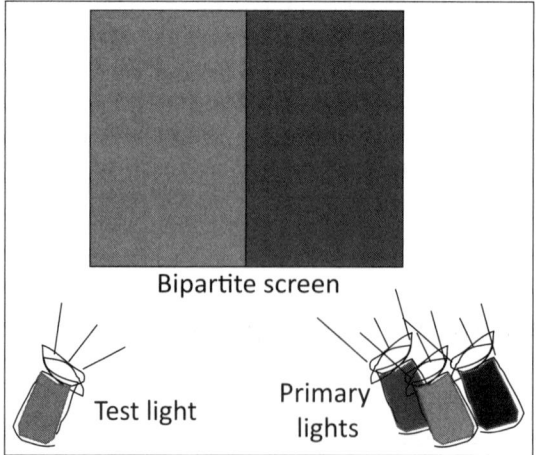

Figure 3.6 A typical setup for conduction of color matching experiments. See Color Plates (page 807).

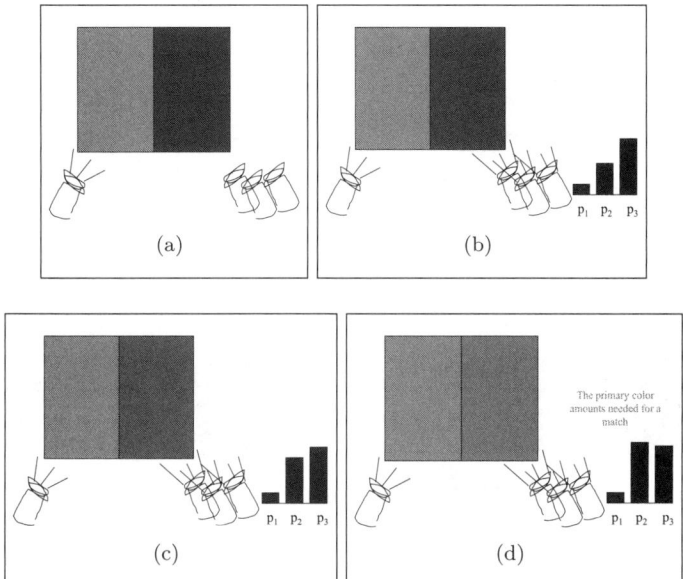

Figure 3.7 Diagrammatic illustration of the color matching experiment for additive mixing. See Color Plates (page 807).

that are denoted by p_1, p_2, and p_3. If any one of the primary colors varies, then the resultant color projected on the screen also varies. The resultant of primary colors is matched with the test source color by varying their proportions, as shown in the figure in lexicographic order. A particular combination of p_1, p_2, and p_3, as shown in the bottom right figure, matches the test color. By using this experiment, any light source is standardized with respect to primary colors.

Color matching experiment for subtractive mixing

Consider another scenario that is shown in Fig. 3.8. Here, the left portions in each of the sub-figures of the color display are projected by the test light source, and the right portions of the display are projected by a particular combination of three primary color sources, p_1, p_2, and p_3. By varying the combinations of the primary colors, the closest match is obtained as in Fig. 3.8 (c), which is still not the same as the color of the test source. Here, instead of projecting all the three primary colors, one of the primary colors is added with the test color and the other two are projected as before. For instance, after adding a primary color, p_2, to the test source, the colors on the display match each other, as shown in Fig. 3.8 (d). This is equivalent to subtracting the corresponding proportion of p_2 from the combination of source colors, p_1 and p_3, that best matches the test source, which produces the same sensation. That is, a negative amount of p_2 is required to achieve the match in colors, where negative addition of primary color components is also considered along with additive superposition.

In the color matching experiments, by considering all proportions of each of the primary wavelengths, including both addition and subtraction of primary sources, a chart is obtained for different colors, which is used to represent a color in a trichromatic model.

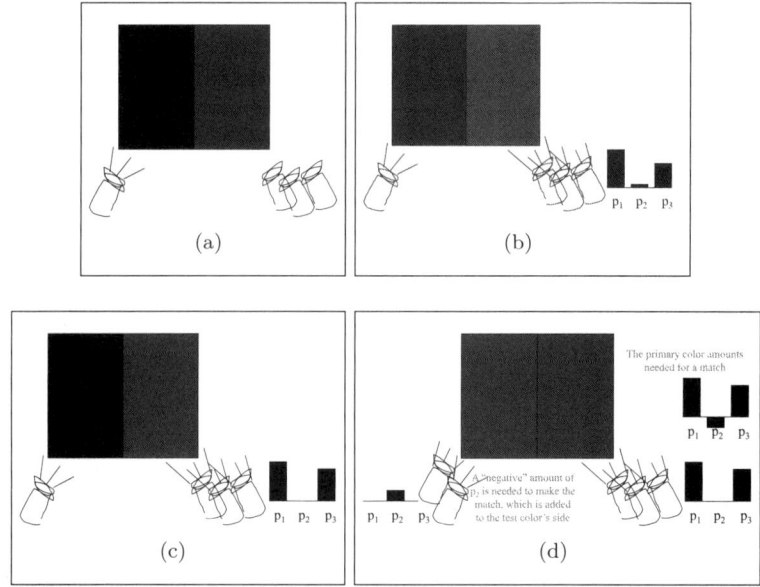

Figure 3.8 Diagrammatic illustration of the color matching experiment for subtractive mixing. See Color Plates (page 808).

3.3.2 | Trichromacy

By standardizing the color matching chart, a trichromatic representation of any color may be obtained. This feature of representing any color by using three independent primary colors is known as *trichromacy*. Experimentally, it is observed that most of the observers match a given light with almost the same combination of three primary colors. The three primary colors are strictly independent, i.e., any combination of two of the primary colors does not produce the third primary color. The uniqueness of color representation in the human visual perceptual system across different human subjects is established through this empirical study of color matching. However, anomalies like color blindness are exception to this generalization. Under normal human vision, a given color is uniquely represented by the same proportion of independent primary color by different subjects. This characteristic is known as *the trichromatic color theory*, which suggests that *three primary colors are mostly sufficient for encoding any color*. This theory was proposed by Thomas Young in the early 19th century (Young, 1802).

3.3.3 | Grassman's laws

There is a strong analogy between a linear space and the color space. Grassman proposed three laws of color matching using the property of linearity (Reinhard et al., 2008). They are summarized below.

(1) If two test lights are matched with the same set of weights for the primary colors, they match each other. For example, let the three primary colors be represented by P_1, P_2, and P_3.

To produce a color, A, let the weights of primary colors be, u_1, u_2, and u_3, respectively. If, another color, B, is perceived through superposition of the same amounts of components, i.e., u_1, u_2, and u_3, of the primary colors, A and B are perceived as the same color. This rule is mathematically expressed in the following.

$$\text{If} \quad A = u_1 P_1 + u_2 P_2 + u_3 P_3, \text{ and}$$
$$B = u_1 P_1 + u_2 P_2 + u_3 P_3 \tag{3.3}$$
$$\text{Then,} \ A = B$$

(2) If two lights, A and B, are mixed, the corresponding mixing of the matches of the combination of primary colors that represent A and B matches the mixed light, $A + B$, as expressed mathematically below.

$$\text{If} \quad A = u_1 P_1 + u_2 P_2 + u_3 P_3, \text{ and}$$
$$B = v_1 P_1 + v_2 P_2 + v_3 P_3 \tag{3.4}$$
$$\text{then,} \quad A + B = (u_1 + v_1)P_1 + (u_2 + v_2)P_2 + (u_3 + v_3)P_3$$

(3) If the color of the test light, A, is scaled, then scaling the weights of the primary colors that are combined to match the test light by the same amount matches the scaled test light, which is expressed in Eq. 3.5.

$$\text{If} \quad A = u_1 P_1 + u_2 P_2 + u_3 P_3$$
$$\text{then,} \quad kA = (ku_1)P_1 + (ku_2)P_2 + (ku_3)P_3 \tag{3.5}$$

These three laws of Grassman show that a color may be represented in a linear space.

3.4 | Linear color spaces

A linear color space is defined by three primary colors. There may be different color spaces corresponding to distinct sets of primary colors that result in different vectorial representations. The RGB color space with three primary colors namely, red, green, and blue, is one of the common choices, but there may also be other choices of primary colors. The coordinates of any color are given by the weights of the primary colors that are used to match it. The corresponding weights of matching combination may be represented as a 3-D vector by using its respective matching function. If a given color requires mixing of more than one primary colors for its representation, the primaries are mixed by the principle of linear superposition, and the mixing proportions are noted. A mixing of any two colors, i.e., a linear combination of the two colors, is represented as a point on a straight line that connects the two colors being superimposed, as shown in Fig. 3.9 (left). Similarly, any combination of three colors is represented by a point in a triangle that is formed by the three superimposed colors as vertices. If the considered weights are positive and the sum of all the weights is unity, then it is a convex combination of the colors used in mixing, and the resulting color, as a point, lies within the respective triangle, as shown in Fig. 3.9 (right).

3.4.1 | Color matching functions

In the experiments of color matching, a test light source is mostly a pure color or an electromagnetic radiator of monochromatic wavelength, which is represented by a 3-D vector using the set of three primary colors. But, a test color signal may also be composed of a linear combination of different wavelengths at different proportions, as depicted in Fig. 3.10. In such a case, for each of the monochromatic lights in the test signal, its 3-D vector representation by the three primaries, $p_1(\lambda)$, $p_2(\lambda)$ and $p_3(\lambda)$, is noted. For each wavelength, λ_i, in the test color light, the amounts of each of the three primaries to represent the monochromatic light, $t(\lambda_i)$, is given by $c_1(\lambda_i)$, $c_2(\lambda_i)$ and $c_3(\lambda_i)$. That is, the amount of each primary color that is required to match every monochromatic light in the test color signal is measured.

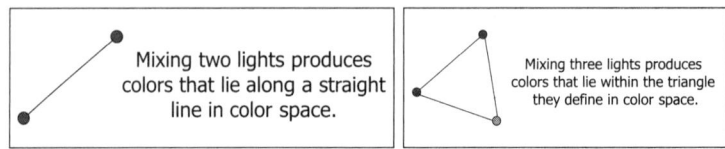

Figure 3.9 Representation of the linear combination of primary colors. See Color Plates (page 808).

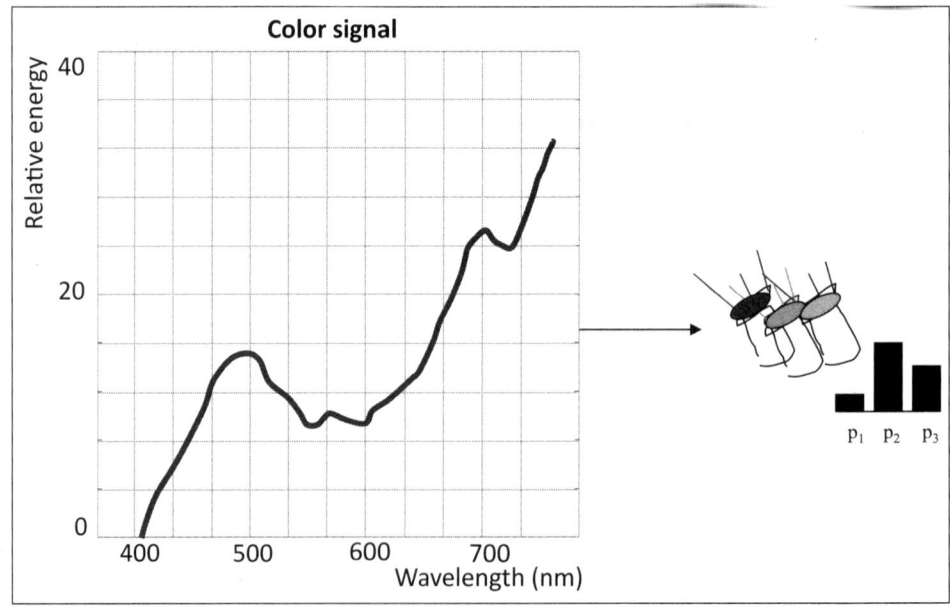

Figure 3.10 Representation of a test color signal as a linear combination of primary color signals. See Color Plates (page 808).

The test optical signal may be modeled as a linear combination of different such monochromatic lights, whose coefficients are given by the spectral power at each wavelength, as given by Eq. 3.6.

$$\boldsymbol{t} = \begin{pmatrix} t(\lambda_1) \\ t(\lambda_2) \\ \vdots \\ t(\lambda_N) \end{pmatrix} \tag{3.6}$$

where, $t(\lambda_1)$, $t(\lambda_2)$, ..., $t(\lambda_N)$ are the coefficients corresponding to the wavelengths λ_1, λ_2, ..., λ_N, respectively, and N is the number of monochromatic lights in the test signal. Then, the matching 3-D vectors of primaries corresponding to individual wavelengths are mixed in specific proportions to obtain the 3-vector representation of the test color signal. The color matching functions of each of the wavelengths are stored as a matrix, which is given by Eq. 3.7.

$$\mathbf{C} = \begin{pmatrix} c_1(\lambda_1) & c_1(\lambda_2) & \cdots & c_1(\lambda_N) \\ c_2(\lambda_1) & c_2(\lambda_2) & \cdots & c_2(\lambda_N) \\ c_3(\lambda_1) & c_3(\lambda_2) & \cdots & c_3(\lambda_N) \end{pmatrix} \tag{3.7}$$

In the above representation, a column of $\mathbf{C}$ provides the matching combination of primary colors for its corresponding optical wavelength. The amounts of each of the primaries that are needed to match $\boldsymbol{t}$ are given by Eq. 3.8.

$$\boldsymbol{e} = \mathbf{C}\boldsymbol{t} \tag{3.8}$$

where, $\boldsymbol{e} = \begin{pmatrix} e_1 & e_2 & e_3 \end{pmatrix}^{\mathsf{T}}$ describe the proportional components of primary colors, whose superposition would provide the same perception of the color of $\boldsymbol{t}$. If some other spectral signal, $\boldsymbol{s}$, matches $\boldsymbol{t}$ perceptually, by Grassman's laws, the corresponding e_1, e_2, and e_3 of $\boldsymbol{t}$, would be the same that of $\boldsymbol{s}$, i.e., $\mathbf{C}\boldsymbol{t} = \mathbf{C}\boldsymbol{s}$.

3.4.2 | Additive and subtractive colors

There are two different types of technologies available for rendering colors. The representation of a color as superposition of primary colors may either be an additive mixing or a subtractive mixing. But, only one of these representations may be used in the principle of color mixing technology, i.e., either the rendering could be only on additive mixing, or it could be only on subtractive mixing. They form the two types of systems for color renditions, (1) an additive system, and (2) a subtractive system.

An additive system of color mixing is shown in Fig. 3.11 (a), where red, green, and blue colors are the chosen primary colors. Different proportions of these primary colors are positively added to produce different kinds of colors like yellow, cyan, magenta, etc., as shown in the figure. The principle of additive superposition is used to display colors in a computer monitor, display screen, or television screen that use cathode ray tubes, etc.

On the other hand, in the subtractive system, as shown in Fig. 3.11 (b), the corresponding primary colors are magenta, yellow, and cyan. Here, the absorption of red color produces a

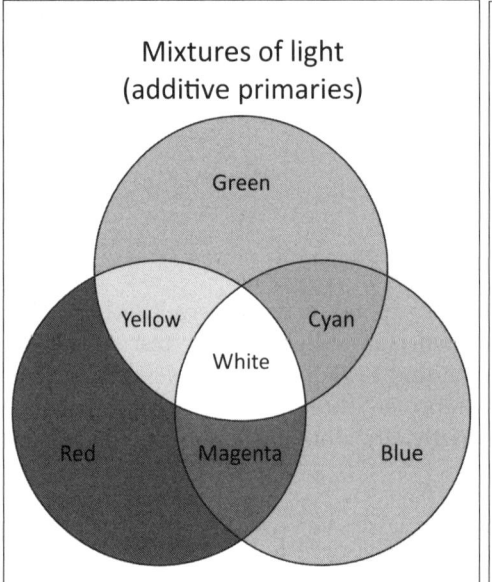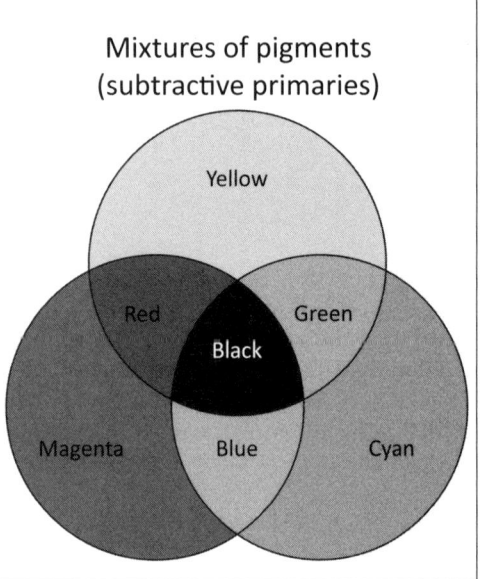

Figure 3.11 (a) Additive system of color mixing that depict mixtures of light. (b) Subtractive system of color mixing that depict mixtures of pigments. The labeled colors correspond to both primary and secondary colors of light and pigments. See Color Plates (page 809).

sensation of magenta, absorption of green color produces the sensation of yellow, and the absorption of blue produces the sensation of cyan. Similarly, different kinds of colors are produced by absorption principle of corresponding primaries in different proportions. This principle is known as subtractive principle of color production. An example of a system that uses subtractive principle for color production is the printing system using color dyes, where the colors are printed on white pages.

3.4.3 | RGB model

One of the most common linear color spaces is the *RGB color space*, which is appropriate for most of the image displays. It is an additive model, where an image consists of three bands, one for each primary color, red (R), green (G), and blue (B). The color information of a point in cameras is also usually captured in the RGB color space by applying red, green, and blue filters over the optical energy that is incident on a lens. The color is represented by the energy in each of the red, green, and blue zones (corresponding to red, green, and blue filters) of the spectrum that is independently captured by three respective sensors for the same incident energy. This space of color representation in red, green, and blue components, is known as the RGB color space.

The RGB matching function, which is a function of wavelength, is shown in Fig. 3.12, where the corresponding wavelengths representing red, green and blue appear as peaks in the plot. As seen in the figure, the mixing is not always additive for every wavelength. For example, for some wavelengths of around 500 nm, the red matching response is subtractive.

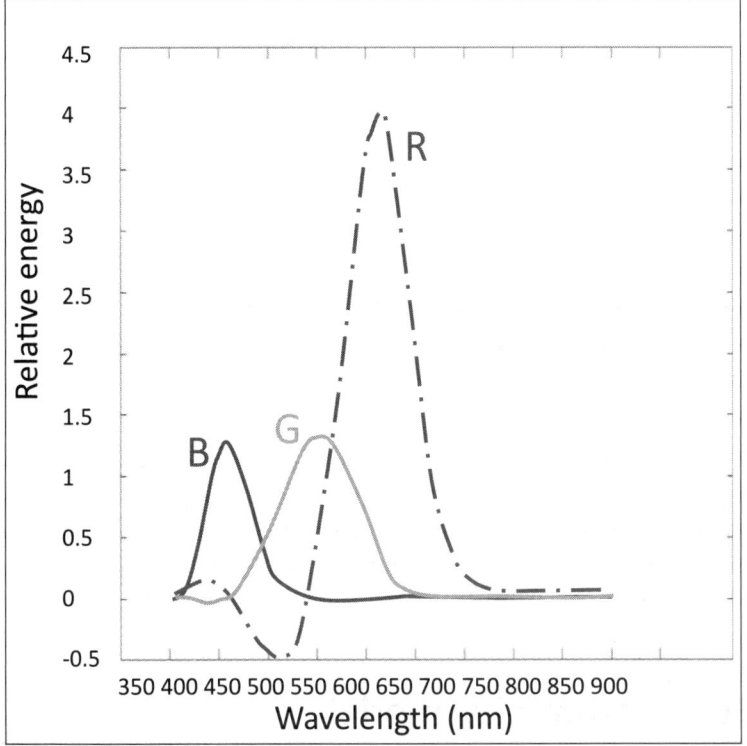

Figure 3.12 Curves of RGB matching function with respect to wavelengths. The curves labeled as "R", "G", and "B" correspond to the wavelengths of red, green, and blue, respectively. See Color Plates (page 809).

Thus, in the RGB color space, it is not possible to produce all colors only by additive mixing. Since some sets of colors require subtractive mixing to be rendered, which is not possible by the display technology based on additive mixing, producing such colors for perception is not possible. The RGB model may also be represented in a normalized form, as shown in Fig. 3.13 (a), where 1 denotes highest intensity values and 0 denotes lowest intensity value. Every color vector is represented within this normalization cube, as shown in Fig. 3.13 (b).

3.4.4 | CMY model

The *CMY model* is a subtractive color model, where an image consists of three bands, one for each primary color, cyan (C), magenta (M), and yellow (Y). In fact, the primary colors of this model are complementary colors of red, green, and blue, which is represented as in Eq. 3.9.

$$\begin{bmatrix} C \\ M \\ Y \end{bmatrix} = 1 - \begin{bmatrix} R \\ G \\ B \end{bmatrix} \tag{3.9}$$

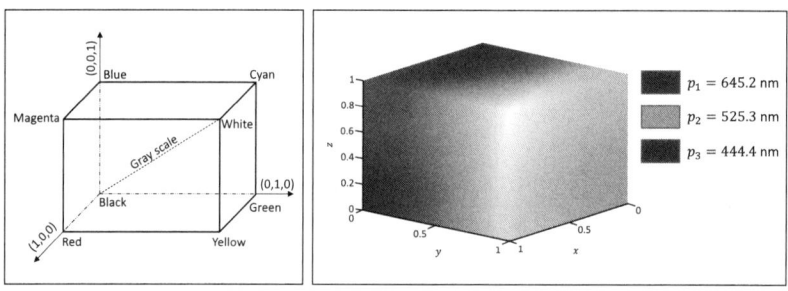

Figure 3.13 (a) RGB model in normalized form. (b) Representation of color vectors with the normalization cube. See Color Plates (page 809).

So, if the red, green and blue are represented as additive model, as in Fig. 3.13 (a), by normalizing them within the range of 0 to 1, cyan, magenta and yellow are represented correspondingly from the RGB representation using the subtractive model. That is, in the subtractive model, producing a particular amount of cyan is equivalent to absorption of a proportional amount of red. The CMY model is appropriate for producing color for paper printing.

3.5 | CIE chromaticity model

The *CIE chromaticity model* defines another standard color space that is provided by an international body for color standards known as *Commission Internationale de l'Eclairage* (CIE), which is established in 1931. The CIE chromaticity model uses three hypothetical primary colors with an objective of producing all the colors using only additive mixing, and not requiring any subtractive mixing. As it is a hypothetical space, there are no light sources that produce such primary colors. But, mathematically, the three hypothetical primary colors, X, Y, and Z, are defined in such a way that the color matching function corresponding to Y component matches the sum of the three human cone responses.

In Eq. 3.10, the linear transformation of RGB primaries to CIE-primaries, X, Y, and Z, is shown.

$$\begin{bmatrix} X \\ Y \\ Z \end{bmatrix} = \begin{bmatrix} 0.6067 & 0.1736 & 0.2001 \\ 0.2988 & 0.5868 & 0.1143 \\ 0.0000 & 0.0661 & 1.1149 \end{bmatrix} \begin{bmatrix} R \\ G \\ B \end{bmatrix} \tag{3.10}$$

As observed in Eq. 3.10, X, Y, and Z components are different linear combinations of R, G, and B components of the RGB color space. The factors for producing the primaries, X, Y, and Z, are greater than 1, which is not possible since the RGB components are normalized between 0 to 1. So, the transformation that is defined mathematically in Eq. 3.10 cannot be physically realized to produce the respective primary colors, X, Y, and Z. In practical applications, this transformation is used to transform the same matching functions that are obtained by the matching experiments of RGB primaries, which are transformed to comply with fully additive principle. All the RGB components, though some of them are negative in the original matching functions, become positive after the transformation of Eq. 3.10, and the resulting color space is known as *CIE XYZ space* or *XYZ color space*. Since the transformation is linear, the corresponding transformed color space is also linear. This transformation is an invertible transformation, so that, color representation in the XYZ color space may be transformed back to the RGB color space using Eq. 3.11.

$$\begin{bmatrix} R \\ G \\ B \end{bmatrix} = \begin{bmatrix} 1.9107 & -0.5326 & -0.2883 \\ -0.9843 & 1.9984 & -0.0283 \\ 0.0583 & -0.1185 & 0.8986 \end{bmatrix} \begin{bmatrix} X \\ Y \\ Z \end{bmatrix} \tag{3.11}$$

The matching functions using X, Y, and Z are positive throughout the color spectrum, as shown in the plot of matching functions across wavelengths in Fig. 3.14. From Grassman's law, scaling a color vector does not change the sensation of the color, but only its intensity changes. So, separating the intensity component provides normalized color components with

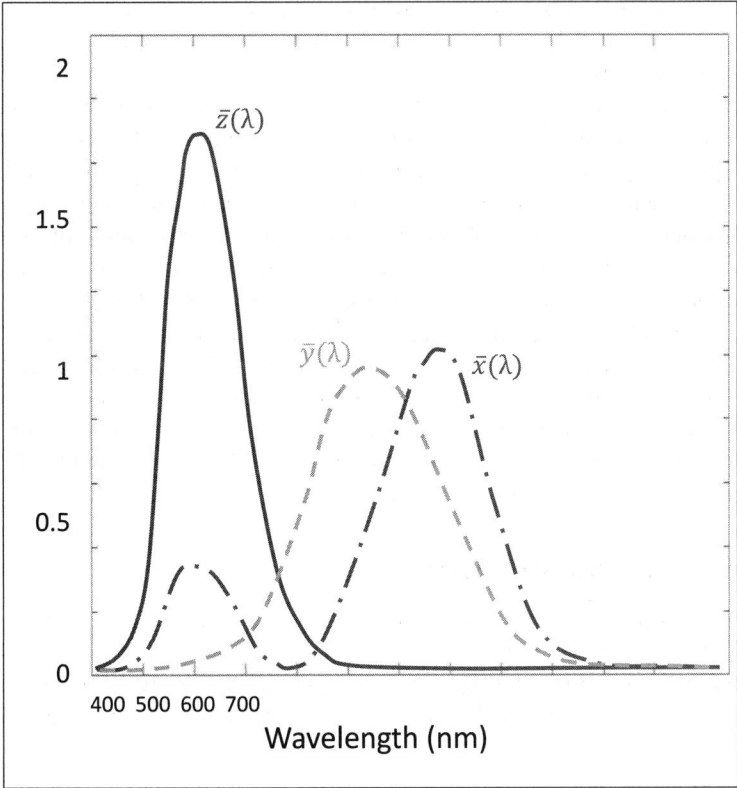

Figure 3.14 Curves of matching function of XYZ color space across wavelengths. Note that the functions are positive throughout the space, unlike the RGB matching functions. See Color Plates (page 810).

respect to intensity, which motivates to represent color in a 2-D space. The normalization of the color components of the XYZ color space are given by Eq. 3.12.

$$x = \frac{X}{X + Y + Z}$$

$$y = \frac{Y}{X + Y + Z}$$

(3.12)

where x and y represent the normalized X and Y components, respectively. A normalized representation of all colors is obtained by converting them to their respective normalized x, y and z coordinates for a given range of wavelengths, in a 2-D space as shown in Fig. 3.15. The space spanned by x and y coordinates is normalized x-y space, and every color dot in this space represents the corresponding coordinates. This space is called the *CIE x-y chromaticity space*, because it represents color information without explicitly considering the intensity information. In fact, the relative representation of two components is sufficient to identify a color uniquely, as in the CIE x-y chromaticity space.

To understand the 2-D representation of this color space, the *CIE chromaticity model* is used. As shown in Fig. 3.15, the wavelength of the electromagnetic wave in the optical band decreases (or the frequency increases) along the boundary, with 700 nm at the red zone to 360 nm at the blue zone. In the inner regions of the chromaticity chart, there are other components of colors. The *white point*, a point where all the color components are present with equal magnitudes, is represented by the point $\left(\frac{1}{3} \ \frac{1}{3} \ \frac{1}{3}\right)$ in the 3-D form, or by $\left(\frac{1}{3} \ \frac{1}{3}\right)$ in the 2-D form. Also, a curve, as shown in the figure, represents a particular color in human visual perception, whose sensation remains almost the same all along the curve, while only the purity of the color varies. In this case, the curve represents the locus of the same chromatic sensation, where only the whiteness of the color differs.

The spectral loci of monochromatic lights and heated black bodies are also shown in Fig. 3.15. The representations of different light sources of different wavelengths are shown in this figure. For example, at noon, the Sun is equivalent to a blackbody radiator of 4870 Kelvin, whose energy spectrum is almost like a white source with uniform distribution. But, during sunrise and sunset, the sunlight appears reddish, and this trend of perception is captured by the curve shown in Fig. 3.15.

3.5.1 | CIE chromaticity chart

The *CIE chromaticity chart* provides a simple representation of color using two particular components that are known as *hue* and *saturation*. Any achromatic color, which is perceived as a white sensation, is represented by the *white point*, $\left(\frac{1}{3} \ \frac{1}{3}\right)$, and the saturated spectral colors or pure colors appear at the boundary of the chromaticity diagram or chromaticity chart, as shown in Fig. 3.16.

Chromaticity chart: hue and saturation

With reference to Fig. 3.16, a straight line connecting the white point, $\boldsymbol{W}$, to any point on the periphery, $\boldsymbol{B}$, represents the same color or wavelength corresponding to the peripheral

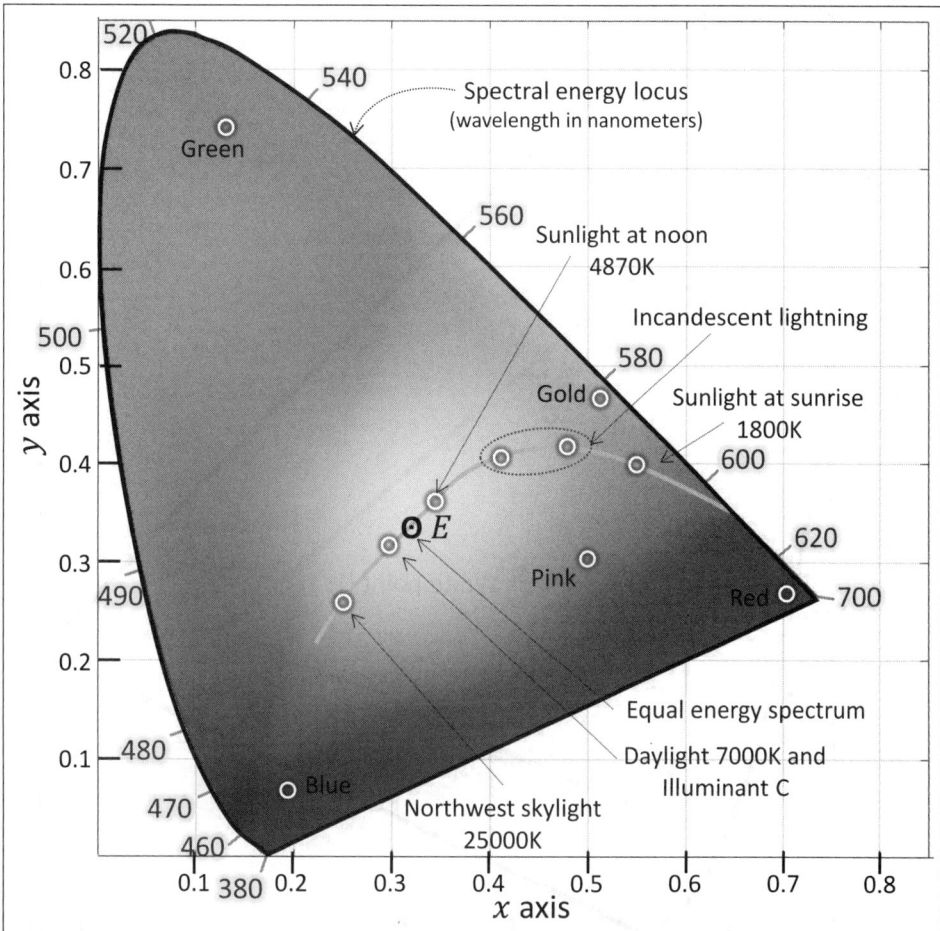

Figure 3.15 Normalized representation of all colors in a 2-D space. The wavelengths are shown at the periphery of the curve, and **E** represents the white point. See Color Plates (page 810).

point. Only the whiteness of the color varies along this radial line. The color or wavelength is measured by *hue*, which is represented by a direction from the white point toward a particular point on the periphery. Thus, the hue is represented by an angle with respect to a reference direction, which denotes the dominant wavelength along that direction.

The color becomes more purer, i.e., the whiteness decreases, toward the periphery of the chromaticity chart, and the whiteness increases toward the white point. This measure of purity of the color is the *saturation*. In other words, lesser the whiteness of the color, more is its saturation. The saturation of a point, **P**, along a particular hue angle is represented by the relative proportion of the two lengths, a and b, as shown in Fig. 3.16. Thus, the relative distance of a point, from the white point, determines its saturation or purity, which is computed at the ratio, $\frac{a}{b}$. The value of this ratio increases by moving more outwards

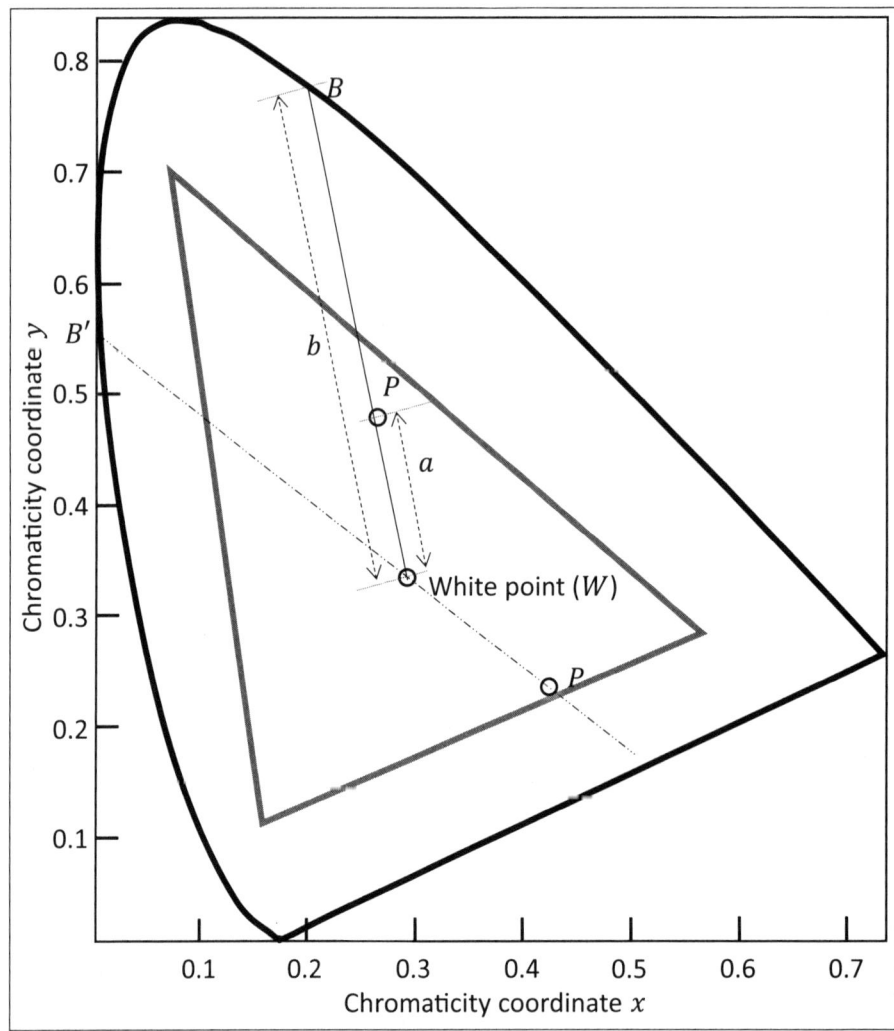

Figure 3.16 Chromaticity chart depicting the hue and saturation, with respect to the white point, W.

from the white point. A point with purity of 1 (when $a = b$) implies a spectral color with maximum saturation.

Numerical Example

Given the coordinates in the normalized x-y chromaticity space of three primary colors as $G = (1/3, 2/3)$, $R = (3/4, 1/5)$, and $B = (1/10, 1/6)$, compute the corresponding maximally saturated color in the x-y chromaticity space preserving the same hue and intensity for the given point $(0.29, 0.21)$ in x-y chromaticity space.

Solution

Here, three primary colors are given by $R = (3/4, 1/5)$, $G = (1/3, 2/3)$, and $B = (1/10, 1/6)$ in x-y chromaticity space. We have white point $w = (0.33, 0.33)$ and a given point $q = (0.29, 0.21)$. If the point is moved radially to the gamut edge, it reaches at a maximum saturation given a hue. In this case, the intersection of the radial line, wq with an edge of the triangle, is the required answer.

In the following we use operations from the 2-D projective geometry (discussed in Chapter 10) for computing lines of the gmut triangle and the intersection of a pair of line segments. The resulting edges of the triangle and the intersecting point are given below.

$BG = (5/6, 7/30, 2/90)$
$BR = (-1/30, 13/20, -21/200)$
$GR = (-7/15, -5/12, 13/30)$
$wq = (0.04, -0.12, 0.025)$
$BG \times wq = (0.0085, -0.01994, -0.10933) \rightarrow$ Not a point within the x-y space.
$GR \times wq = (0.04158, 0.029, 0.07266) \rightarrow$ maximally saturated point $(0.57, 0.40)$
$BR \times wq = (0.00365, -0.00336, -0.022) \rightarrow$ Not a point within the x-y space.

Numerical Example

Consider the following transformation matrix of color spaces (from RGB to XYZ).

$$\begin{bmatrix} X \\ Y \\ Z \end{bmatrix} = \begin{bmatrix} 0.49 & 0.31 & 0.20 \\ 0.18 & 0.81 & 0.01 \\ 0.00 & 0.01 & 0.99 \end{bmatrix} \begin{bmatrix} R \\ G \\ B \end{bmatrix}$$

   (i) Given a color value in RGB space as (100, 80, 200), compute its corresponding point in the normalized x-y chromaticity space.

  (ii) Given the coordinates in the normalized x-y chromaticity space of three primary colors as $\left(\frac{2}{3}, \frac{1}{3}\right)$, $\left(\frac{1}{5}, \frac{3}{4}\right)$, and $\left(\frac{1}{6}, \frac{1}{10}\right)$, compute the corresponding maximally saturated color in the RGB space preserving the same hue and intensity for the RGB point (100, 80, 200). (*White point*: $\left(\frac{1}{3}, \frac{1}{3}\right)$).

Solution

Substitute the values of (100, 80, 200) for RGB in the given transformation to obtain the corresponding values of XYZ.

$$\begin{bmatrix} X \\ Y \\ Z \end{bmatrix} = \begin{bmatrix} 0.49 & 0.31 & 0.20 \\ 0.18 & 0.81 & 0.01 \\ 0.00 & 0.01 & 0.99 \end{bmatrix} \begin{bmatrix} 100 \\ 80 \\ 200 \end{bmatrix} = \begin{bmatrix} 113.8 \\ 84.8 \\ 198.8 \end{bmatrix}$$

Then, the values of normalized x and y are computed as,

$$x = \frac{X}{(X+Y+Z)} = \frac{113.8}{397.4} = 0.2864$$

$$y = \frac{Y}{(X+Y+Z)} = \frac{84.8}{397.4} = 0.2134$$

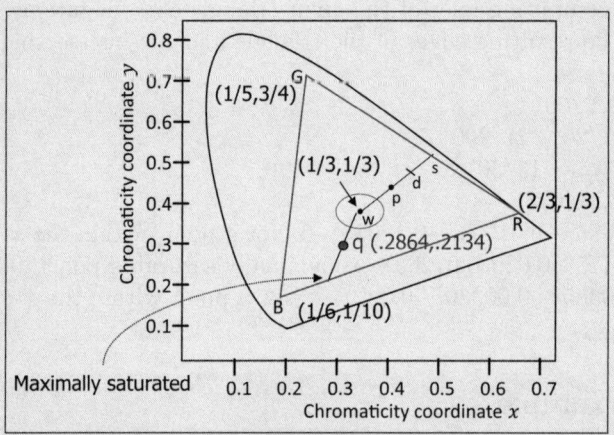

Figure 3.17

Consider the color gamut, as shown in Fig. 3.17. Here, q is the corresponding point of (100, 80, 200) in normalized x-y chromaticity space, as computed above, and w is the white point. The three primary colors form the three vertices of the gamut triangle, which are denoted by R, G, and B in the figure. For a given hue, maximum saturation is obtained by radially moving q to the edge of the gamut. That is, the intersecting point of the line formed by an edge of the gamut triangle and the line wq is the corresponding maximally saturated point in x-y space. Using the concepts of projective space,[2] check if the edge BG and line wq intersect each other within the x-y space. The line, wq is computed as,

$$wq = \left(\frac{1}{3} \quad \frac{1}{3} \quad 1\right) \times (0.2864 \quad 0.2134 \quad 1) = (0.1199 \quad -0.0469 \quad -0.0234).$$

The edge, BG is given by,

$$BG = \left(\frac{1}{6} \quad \frac{1}{10} \quad 1\right) \times \left(\frac{1}{5} \quad \frac{3}{4} \quad 1\right) = (-0.6500 \quad 0.0333 \quad 0.1050).$$

[2] Refer to Chapter 10.

So, the intersection of BG and wq is computed as,
$BG \times wq = (-0.0041 \quad 0.0032 \quad -0.0265)$.
That is, in nonhomogeneous coordinates, the intersection point BG and wq is $(0.1553 \quad -0.1216)$, which does not lie within the x-y space.

Similarly, check if the edge BR and line wq intersect each other within the x-y space.

$$BR = \left(\frac{1}{6} \quad \frac{1}{10} \quad 1\right) \times \left(\frac{2}{3} \quad \frac{1}{1} \quad 1\right) = (-0.2333 \quad 0.5000 \quad -0.0111)$$

So, intersection of BR and $wq = BR \times wq = (0.0127 \quad 0.0070 \quad 0.0490)$.

That is, in nonhomogeneous coordinates, the intersection point BR and wq is $(0.2592 \quad 0.1429)$, which lies within the x-y space. So, the point, $(0.2592 \quad 0.1429)$, is the maximally saturated point in x-y space.

Then, convert the maximally saturated point in x-y space to XYZ space by keeping the same intensity as before (i.e., by using the same value of $(X + Y + Z)$ that is used in normalizing to x-y space).

$$X = (X + Y + Z)\, x = (397.4)(0.2592) = 103.0061$$

$$Y = (X + Y + Z)\, y = (397.4)(0.1429) = 56.7885$$

$$Z = (X + Y + Z) - (X + Y) = 397.4 - (103.0061 + 56.7885) = 237.6054.$$

As the final step, the XYZ values is transformed to RGB values by using the inverse of the transformation matrix.

$$\begin{bmatrix} R \\ G \\ B \end{bmatrix} = \begin{bmatrix} 0.49 & 0.31 & 0.20 \\ 0.18 & 0.81 & 0.01 \\ 0.00 & 0.01 & 0.99 \end{bmatrix}^{-1} \begin{bmatrix} X \\ Y \\ Z \end{bmatrix}$$

$$\begin{bmatrix} R \\ G \\ B \end{bmatrix} = \begin{bmatrix} 2.37 & -0.90 & -0.47 \\ -0.52 & 1.44 & 0.09 \\ 0.01 & -0.01 & 1.01 \end{bmatrix} \begin{bmatrix} 103.0061 \\ 56.7885 \\ 237.6054 \end{bmatrix} = \begin{bmatrix} 81.42 \\ 49.06 \\ 239.51 \end{bmatrix}$$

So, in RGB space, the required maximally saturated color of $(100, \; 80, \; 200)$ is $(81, \; 49, \; 240)$.

Color reproduction

A color gamut represents a set of reproducible colors, given a set of primaries. The reproduction of color depends upon the choice of primary colors, because any color may be represented as a 2-D vector in the x-y chromaticity chart using the chosen set of primaries. The three chosen primary colors form a triangle (Fig. 3.16). Any additive linear combination of the primaries is represented by a point within the interior or on the edges of this triangle. These edges define limits of representation of colors by the chosen set of primaries. Thus, projecting a 3-D color gamut on the set of primaries results in a triangular representation of their combination, which is also called a 2-D color gamut or *color gamut triangle*. The 2-D color gamut may vary depending on the choice of the primaries. If more saturated colors are chosen as primary colors, the points representing the primaries lie toward the periphery of the chromaticity chart. This increases the area of the triangle of 2-D color gamut to accommodate more colors. However, color gamuts do not have any information related to luminance.

The scope of color gamut for displaying colors is enhanced by using various sets of primaries. In fact, in certain kinds of displays there are more than three primaries. In this case, the set of colors used to produce the gamut of colors may not be independent, unlike the set of primaries. They may also be dependent set of colors whose combinations are considered to increase the range of color reproducibility. For example, a multiple laser source digital light processing (DLP) projection system consists of multiple primaries. Each gamut is obtained by different sets of primary color sources. A linear combination of one set of primaries may produce a color, which is not possible to be rendered by additive mixing of another set of primary colors. In this way, color reproducibility gets expanded even outside the gamut of a single set of primary colors.

3.5.2 | Saturation and de-saturation of colors

Saturation and *de-saturation* operations are two interesting operations of color processing (Lucchese et al., 2001). Given a color image in the RGB space, the color of any pixel may be represented within the color gamut in the CIE XYZ space, as shown in Fig. 3.18, where the primaries of the corresponding color system are represented by the points, $\boldsymbol{R}$, $\boldsymbol{G}$, and $\boldsymbol{B}$. Consider a true color point, $\boldsymbol{p}$, as shown in the figure, which is a color in the source image. Using the CIE chromaticity model, a straight line from the white point, $\boldsymbol{W}$ (at the point (0.33, 0.33) in the figure), to $\boldsymbol{p}$, is further extended to intersect the edge of the color gamut at $\boldsymbol{s}$. The intersecting point provides the maximum possible saturation for the reproduction of the color of the same hue as of $\boldsymbol{p}$. In other words, in the direction of $\boldsymbol{p}$ from $\boldsymbol{W}$, $\boldsymbol{s}$ is the maximally saturated color possible. After computing the saturated point, $\boldsymbol{s}$, its representation is converted back to the RGB space to get the corresponding RGB component of $\boldsymbol{s}$. Similarly, maximum saturation points of all the colors in the given image may be obtained. All the points along the straight line from $\boldsymbol{W}$ to $\boldsymbol{s}$ represent colors of the same hue or wavelength that is represented by a direction from $\boldsymbol{W}$ to $\boldsymbol{p}$.

However, saturation may not always provide a pleasing sensation. It is not always true that more saturated colors are always pleasing for human perception. A comfortable feel is experienced with a right balance of colors and their saturations, which are accustomed to human visual system by perception of different phenomena of nature. So, it is often

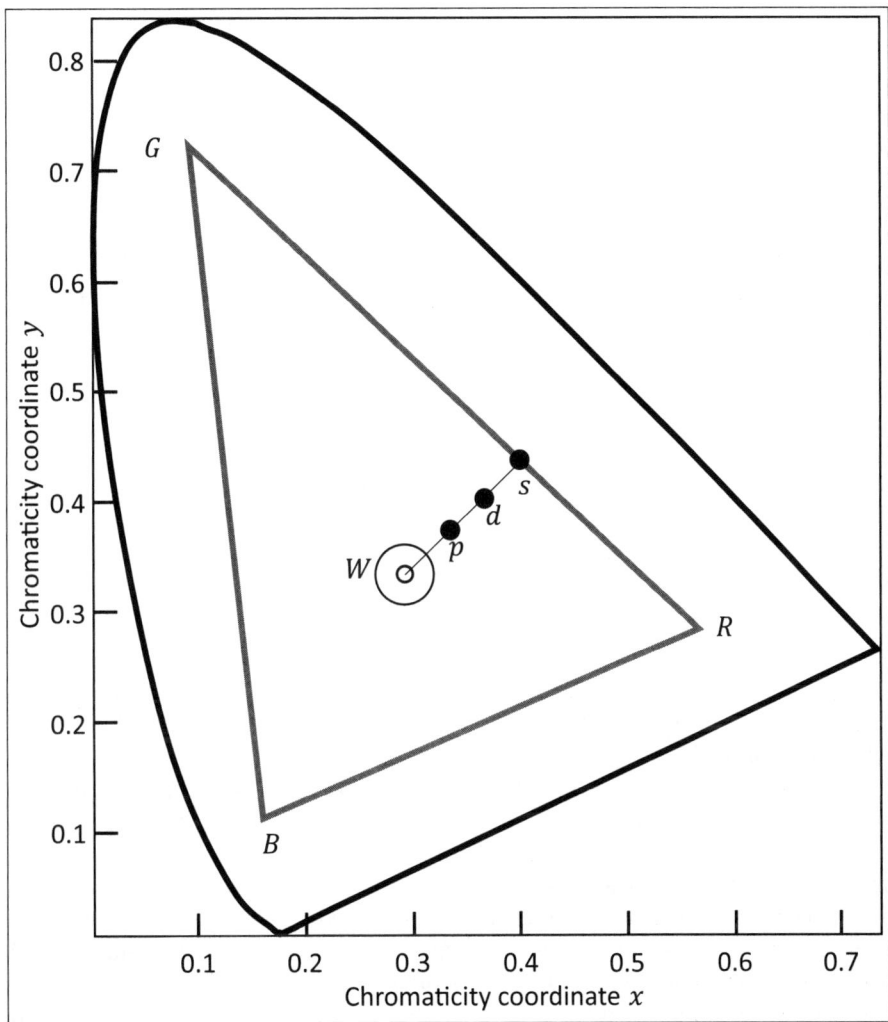

Figure 3.18 Color gamut for illustrating the operations of saturation and de-saturation of colors.

necessary to reduce the saturation of color and move its representative point inwards in the gamut toward the white point along the same line between W to s. This process is called *de-saturation operation*. With reference to Fig. 3.18, if the point p, which is the color of a pixel, is extended along the line from W to p to intersect with the edge BG, the point of intersection represents the *maximal saturation point*. If the point s is moved inwards along the same line toward W to the point d, it is a de-saturation point. Also, the colors with a circle around W, as shown in the figure, are mostly whitish in appearance. Usually, the colors are not visually pleasing if the points within the circle are disturbed. So, while processing the points with saturation and de-saturation operations, the points that are very close to W are left out. The threshold radius that defines these points that are left out from processing are usually chosen empirically in the model.

Desaturation using center of gravity law   There is an intuitive way of obtaining a weighted combination of saturation and white points to achieve de-saturation process (Hunt and Pointer, 2011). In a 3-D representation, let $\boldsymbol{W} = (x_W,\ y_W,\ Y_W)$ be the white point, $\boldsymbol{S} = (x_S,\ y_S,\ Y_S)$ be the maximal saturation point, and $\boldsymbol{D} = (x_D,\ y_D,\ Y_D)$ be the target point of de-saturation. In this representation, the third dimension refers to the intensity value of the color. Given $\boldsymbol{W}$ and $\boldsymbol{S}$ in the x-y chromaticity space, the de-saturation point, $\boldsymbol{D}$, which is desaturated with respect to $\boldsymbol{S}$, is obtained by a property called center of gravity law as a weighted combination of $\boldsymbol{W}$ and $\boldsymbol{S}$. The weights for $\boldsymbol{W}$ and $\boldsymbol{S}$ are, $\frac{|Y_W|}{y_W}$ and $\frac{|Y_S|}{y_S}$, respectively. So, the weighted combination of $\boldsymbol{W}$ and $\boldsymbol{S}$ for computing $\boldsymbol{D}$ is given by Eq. 3.13.

$$x_D = \frac{x_W \frac{|Y_W|}{y_W} + x_S \frac{|Y_S|}{y_S}}{\frac{|Y_W|}{y_W} + \frac{|Y_S|}{y_S}}$$

$$y_D = \frac{|Y_W| + |Y_S|}{\frac{|Y_W|}{y_W} + \frac{|Y_S|}{y_S}} \tag{3.13}$$

$$Y_D = |Y_W| + |Y_S|$$

Also, the intensity of the white point is estimated as a fraction, k, of the average of Y components, Y_{avg}, of all the pixels in the image, which is given as $Y_W = kY_{avg}$. The value of k is chosen empirically.

The operations of saturation and de-saturation are used for enhancing color images. Examples of saturation and de-saturation processes on the image of the `Alps` are shown in Figs. 3.19 and 3.20. Fig. 3.19 (a) is the original image, and a plot of colors of its pixels in x-y chromaticity chart is also shown. From the distribution of the values in the chromaticity chart, a triangular gamut may be perceived that contains all the color points of the image, where the primaries are taken at three suitable points in the x-y chromaticity space considering the properties of the display. In Fig. 3.19 (b), the image of the Alps after saturating its color points, excluding the points that are close to white point, and its corresponding plot of colors in x-y chromaticity chart is shown. The image after de-saturation operation using center of gravity law, and its distribution of colors in the chromaticity chart are shown in Fig. 3.19 (c). The image in Fig. 3.19 (d) is the result of performing de-saturation operation on the saturated image.

Also, some variations may be considered subjectively in enhancing the images using saturation and de-saturation operations. For example, a negative value of k may be taken in the expression of $Y_W = kY_{avg}$ to compute the intensity of white point, which is then used in Eq. 3.13 for saturation and de-saturation processes. While computing, as k is negative, Eq. 3.13 is redefined by ignoring the modulus operation to accommodate the negative values. The effect of this operation is shown in Fig. 3.20 (a). In Fig. 3.20 (b), the effect of shifting the white point from $\left(\frac{1}{3}, \frac{1}{3}\right)$ to $(0.5, 0.2)$, toward the reddish zone of chromaticity diagram, is shown. Similarly, shifting the white point toward the greenish zone at $(0.5, 0.4)$ and bluish zone at $(0.2, 0.5)$ of the chromaticity diagram are shown in Figs. 3.20 (c) and (d), respectively.

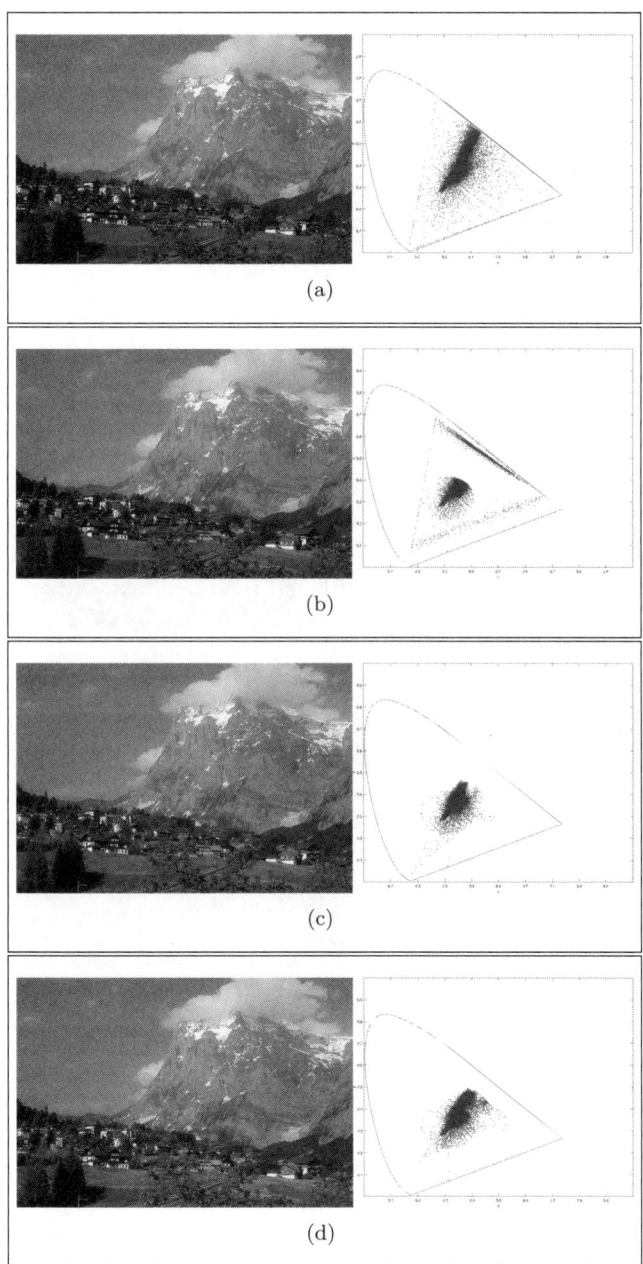

(a)

(b)

(c)

(d)

Figure 3.19 Examples of saturation and de-saturation processes on the image of the Alps.
(a) Original image and its color gamut. (b) Saturated image and its color gamut.
(c) De-saturated image and its color gamut. (d) Saturated–de-saturated image and
its color gamut. See Color Plates (page 811).

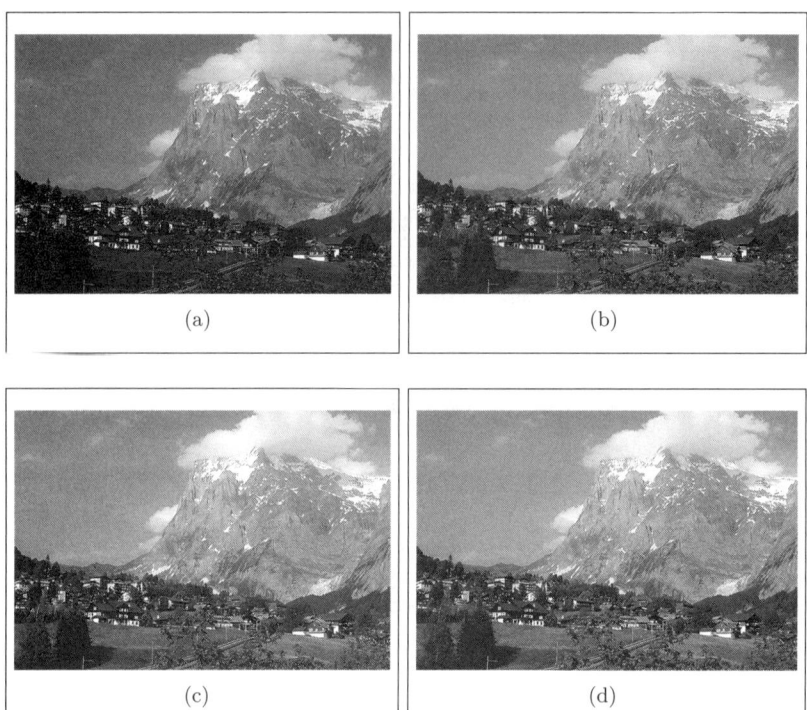

(a)

(b)

(c)

(d)

Figure 3.20 Examples of saturation and de-saturation processes on the image of the Alps (continued from Fig. 3.19). (a) De-saturated image with a negative value of k. (b) De-saturation by shifting the white point to $(0.5, 0.2)$. (c) De-saturation by shifting the white point to $(0.5, 0.4)$. (d) De-saturation by shifting the white point to $(0.2, 0.5)$. See Color Plates (page 812).

3.6 | Uniform color spaces

In the chromaticity space, a color is represented as a superposition of three primary colors, particularly, when it is captured as red, green and blue components. Then the color point is converted into a 2-D chromaticity space, i.e., x-y chromaticity space. In such a representation, there are several regions that are almost similar in color sensation within them, and the span of such regions where the colors are almost indistinguishable are approximated by ellipses, as shown in Fig. 3.21 (a). These ellipses may be larger or smaller, depending upon the wavelengths in their regions. Centering an ellipse at a point, all the colors covered by the chromatic points in it generate the same sensation for human perception. These ellipses are known as *McAdam ellipses* or *just noticeable differences* in color (JND) ellipses. The perception of color from all the points within each of the JND ellipses is almost similar in human visual system.

In Fig. 3.21 (a), where the colors are shown within the semi-elliptic region, the points in the periphery of the curve correspond to different wavelengths of spectral colors. For example, the wavelength at the right most corner in the red zone is 700 nm, the wavelength

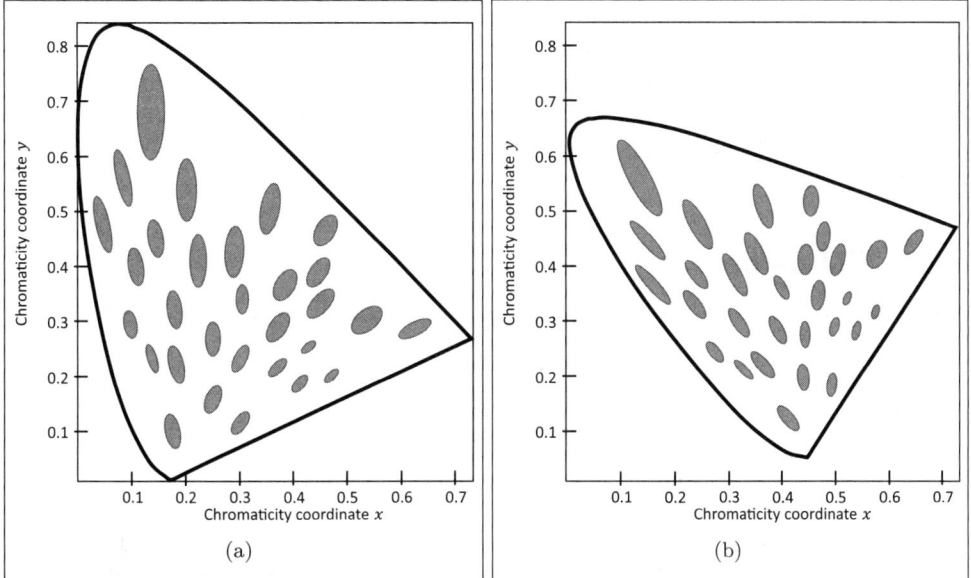

Figure 3.21 McAdam ellipses or JND ellipses in, (a) x-y chromaticity space, and (b) $u'v'$ chromaticity space. The ellipses in $u'v'$ chromaticity space appear more uniform in their size than in x-y chromaticity space.

at a point in the top portion of the curve in green zone is 520 nm, and the wavelength at the bottom most corner in the blue zone is 380 nm. Traversing across the periphery of the curve from the vertex in the red zone to the vertex in the green zone, the wavelengths are in the decreasing order. Each of these wavelengths correspond to a particular pure color that is sensed by the human visual system when the energy from electromagnetic wave of a specific wavelength is received by eyes.

As seen in Fig. 3.21 (a), some of the ellipses are large, and some of them are very small, comparatively, when are represented in the x-y chromaticity space. A proposition of another color space called *uniform color space* is to make the sizes of the ellipses more or less uniform. The sizes of ellipses may not be exactly uniform in every place, but the variation in their sizes is kept small. The adjective "uniform" is added from the perspective of trying to make the sizes of ellipses uniform as far as possible by applying some transformation directly on the enclosed points. One example of such transformation is shown in Fig. 3.21 (b), which is known as $u'v'$ space. The CIE $u'v'$ chromaticity space is a projective transformation of the CIE x-y space to make the ellipses more uniform in representing the chromatic components, which is given by Eq. 3.14.

$$(u',\ v') = \left(\frac{4X}{X + 15Y + 3Z},\ \frac{9Y}{X + 15Y + 3Z} \right) \tag{3.14}$$

As seen in the figure, the differences in the sizes of ellipses in different zones are reduced, so that the transformed space is more suitable to compare colors, in terms of defining certain distances. Since the ellipses are not transformed to circles, Euclidean distance may not be very appropriate in this space in a strict sense. However, the $u'v'$ space is more effective for distinguishing colors than x-y space, since the sizes of the neighborhoods have less variation in $u'v'$ space.

3.6.1 | YIQ model

The YIQ color space is obtained by linear transformation of the RGB color space, which is given by Eq. 3.15.

$$\begin{bmatrix} Y \\ I \\ Q \end{bmatrix} = \begin{bmatrix} 0.299 & 0.587 & 0.114 \\ 0.596 & -0.275 & -0.321 \\ 0.212 & -0.532 & 0.311 \end{bmatrix} \begin{bmatrix} R \\ G \\ B \end{bmatrix} \tag{3.15}$$

where, Y is the luminance component, and I and Q are chrominance components. The YIQ color space has the property of better compressibility of information. The chromatic components, I and Q, require lesser bandwidth to represent color variations. A color television signal, if represented in the YIQ space, requires less bandwidth than its equivalent representation in the RGB color space. So, the YIQ space conversion is particularly used in transmission of color television signal, to keep the bandwidth of transmission low. Since humans are more sensitive to the intensity or luminance, Y, it is encoded using more bits that require more bandwidth, whereas the chrominance values, I and Q, are coded at lower rate and with less number of bits. The YIQ model is very effective for sending information by factorizing the data into the three channels.

3.6.2 | YCbCr space

The YCbCr space is mainly used for image compression in JPEG and many other similar standards. The transformation from the RGB space to the YCbCr space is given in Eq. 3.16.

$$\begin{bmatrix} Y \\ Cb \\ Cr \end{bmatrix} = \begin{bmatrix} 0.256 & 0.502 & 0.098 \\ -0.148 & -0.290 & 0.438 \\ 0.438 & -0.366 & -0.071 \end{bmatrix} \begin{bmatrix} R \\ G \\ B \end{bmatrix} + \begin{bmatrix} 0 \\ 128 \\ 128 \end{bmatrix} \tag{3.16}$$

where, Y represents the luminance, and Cb and Cr represent the chrominance components, which are called *complementary blue* and *complementary red*, respectively. Accounting to better compression properties of this space, it is used in different image and video compression schemes. The transformation in Eq. 3.16 has a linear part and a translatory or additive part, which makes the transformation affine. The translation of linearly transformed values is performed with the motivation to make all the values positive. This is convenient for storing information in the unsigned format of representation of integers. For the values of red, green, and blue components in the range of 0 to 255, their corresponding values in Cb and Cr transformation vary from 0 to 240.

3.7 | Nonlinear color spaces

There are nonlinear color spaces, where the hue and saturation components are factored out from the achromatic information, like intensity. The hue, saturation, and intensity are usually considered as perceptually meaningful dimensions for representation. One such example is shown in Fig. 3.22, which is a conical shaped representation of a space. Here, the intensity, V, is varying along the vertical direction and the saturation, S, of colors is varying along the horizontal plane in radial direction from the center. The hue, H, is represented by angular movement of the radial line around the center, as shown in the figure. For example, if the reference direction is toward the color red, increasing the angle of radial line from red gives a transition from red to green, cyan, blue, magenta, and back to red, which is represented as a circle or a hexagon.

3.7.1 | HSI model

The HSI stands for hue, saturation, and brightness or intensity, respectively. The mathematical form of transformation to the HSI space from the RGB space is given by Eq. 3.17.

$$
\begin{aligned}
I &= \frac{R+G+B}{3} \\
S &= 1 - \frac{\min(R,\ G,\ B)}{I} \\
H &= \begin{cases}
\cos^{-1}\left[\dfrac{\frac{1}{2}[(R-G)+(R-B)]}{\sqrt{[(R-G)^2+(R-B)(G-B)]}}\right] & \text{if } B <= G \\[4mm]
360 - \cos^{-1}\left[\dfrac{\frac{1}{2}[(R-G)+(R-B)]}{\sqrt{[(R-G)^2+(R-B)(G-B)]}}\right] & \text{if } B > G
\end{cases}
\end{aligned} \tag{3.17}
$$

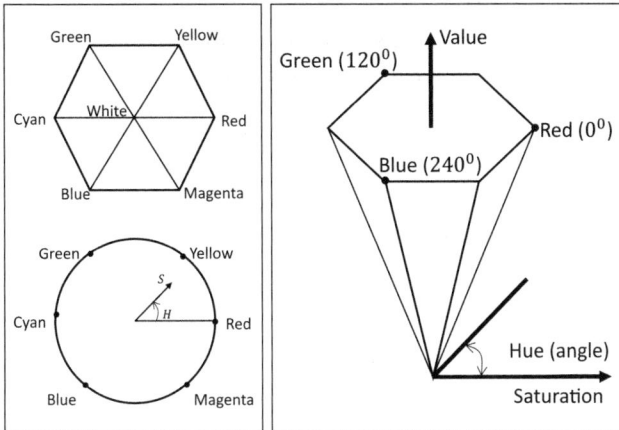

Figure 3.22 Representation of hue, saturation, and intensity values in a nonlinear color space.

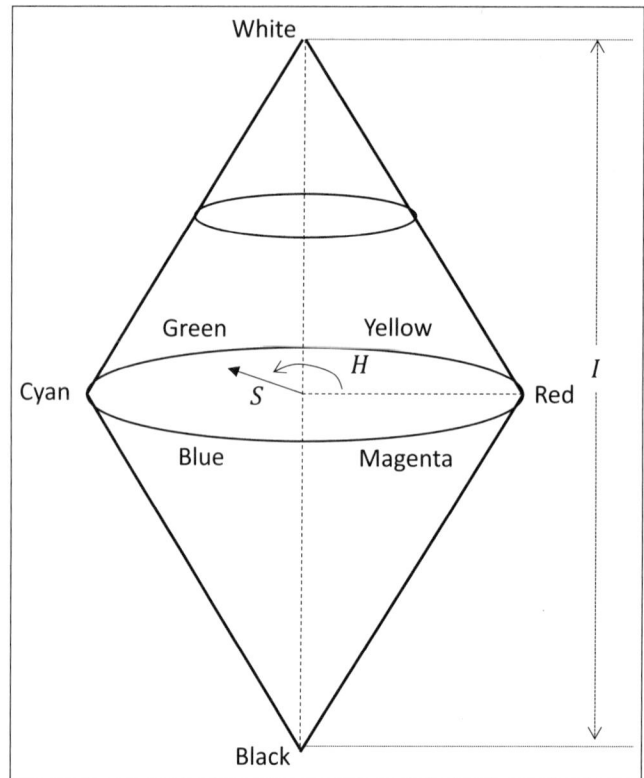

Figure 3.23 A 3-D representation of hue relations in HSI model.

In the above representation R, G and B are expressed in a normalized form so that they vary from 0 to 1. The hue relations are naturally expressed in a circle, as shown in Fig. 3.23, which is 3-D representation of HSI model. As an implication of the HSI model, it is uniform in its representation of colors, so that, small and equal steps have similar effect in changes of color perception. It has a uniform representation of nondistinguishable colors in the neighborhood. So, in the double conical region that is shown in the figure, small spheres or spherical neighborhood around a point appear uniform in HSI space. Here, hue is encoded as an angle that ranges from 0 to 2π. Saturation is the distance to the vertical axis radially, and intensity is the height along the vertical axis. The values of both saturation and intensity vary from 0 to 1. The inverse computation of R, G and B in their normalized forms from hue $H \in [0°, 360°)$, saturation $S \in [0, 1]$, and intensity $I \in [0, 1]$ are given below.

$$H' = \frac{H}{360}$$
$$Z = 1 - |(H \bmod 2) - 1|$$
$$C = \frac{3\,I\,S}{1 + Z}$$
$$X = C\,Z$$

$$(R_1, G_1, B_1) = \begin{cases} (0,0,0) & \text{if } H \text{ is undefined} \\ (C,X,0) & \text{if } 0 \le H' \le 1 \\ (X,C,0) & \text{if } 1 \le H' \le 2 \\ (0,C,X) & \text{if } 2 \le H' \le 3 \\ (0,X,C) & \text{if } 3 \le H' \le 4 \\ (X,0,C) & \text{if } 4 \le H' \le 5 \\ (C,0,X) & \text{if } 5 \le H' \le 6 \end{cases} \tag{3.18}$$

$$m = I\,(1 - S)$$
$$(R, G, B) = (R_1 + m, G_1 + m, B_1 + m)$$

Numerical Example

Consider a pixel whose RGB components are given by $(10, 20, 30)$. What is the saturation value of this pixel in HSI color space?

Solution

$I = \frac{R+G+B}{3} = 30$

saturation, $S = 1 - \frac{min(R,\ G,\ B)}{I} = 0.66.$

3.7.2 | CIE *Lab* ($L^*a^*b^*$) model

The Lab^3 space or $L^*a^*b^*$ space is also a color space that is proposed by the CIE. In this color space, Euclidean distance is more effective in distinguishing colors, since the JND ellipses are transformed to almost circular shapes in the a^*b^* chromatic space. In the *Lab* space, L^* represents luminance channel, and a^* and b^* represent the color channels. The transformation to $L^*a^*b^*$ space is given in Eq. 3.19, which is a nonlinear transformation of XYZ space representation of colors that are normalized with respective to the reference white point.

$$L^* = 116 \left(\frac{Y}{Y_n}\right)^{\frac{1}{3}} - 16$$

$$a^* = 500 \left[\left(\frac{X}{X_n}\right)^{\frac{1}{3}} - \left(\frac{Y}{Y_n}\right)^{\frac{1}{3}} \right] \tag{3.19}$$

$$b^* = 200 \left[\left(\frac{Y}{Y_n}\right)^{\frac{1}{3}} - \left(\frac{Z}{Z_n}\right)^{\frac{1}{3}} \right]$$

---

[3] Pronounced as *el-a-bee*.

where, X_n, Y_n, and Z_n are the coordinates of the white point. Usually, the white is represented by the coordinates of $(\frac{1}{3}, \frac{1}{3})$ in the x-y chromaticity chart, where almost all the components of X and Y are equal. However, in many practical situations, they may not be exactly equal. So, a normalization of the XYZ representation, with respect to white point, is performed and then the normalized values are used to derive L^*, a^*, and b^*, as given in Eq. 3.19, to calibrate the system.

After the transformation to the *Lab* space, the color differences that are perceived by human vision can be better approximated by Euclidean distances. This representation also reduces the problem of distinguishing colors in the uniform color space. The variations of colors and intensities in *Lab* space is diagrammatically shown in Fig. 3.24. The variation of hue along a^* axis extends from green region in negative direction to red region in positive direction. Similarly, the variation of hue in b^* axis extends from blue region in negative direction to yellow region in positive direction. Also, along the L^* axis, which is shown in Fig. 3.24 as a vertical line that is perpendicular to a^* and b^* axes, the intensity varies from white to black from top to bottom ends.

3.7.3 | Opponent color processing

A color space is also proposed from the theory of the opponent processing of colors, while modeling the human visual system. Consider the representation of the responses of three

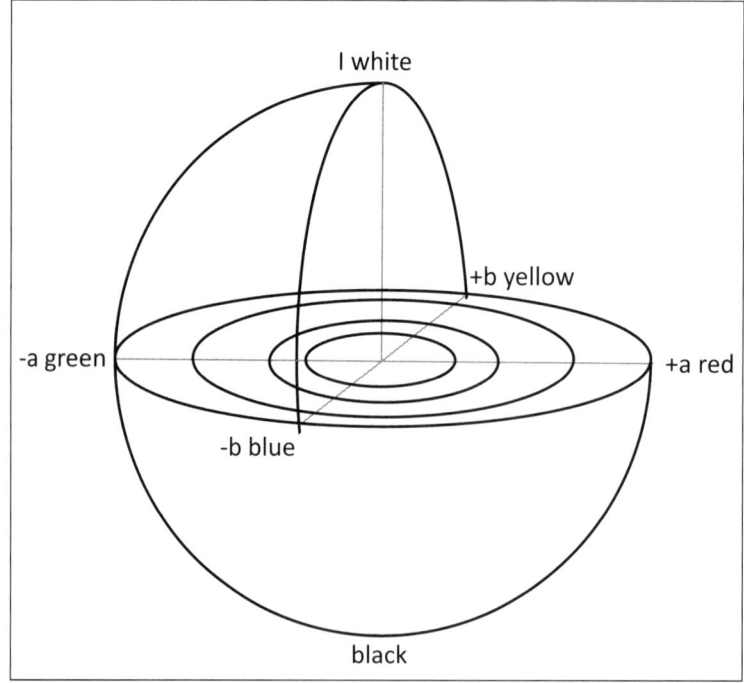

Figure 3.24 Depiction of variations of colors and intensities in *Lab* space.

types of cones in the overlapping spectral zone. The spectral response from long, medium, and short wavelength zone cones are called L, M, and S, respectively. The L, M, and S types of cones define the color perception in human visual system, which considers the differences between the responses of these cones, rather than their individual responses. That is, when a color signal is sensed by the visual system, the received energy is processed in terms of three stimulation corresponding to red, green, and blue in three primary forms. These primary forms of red, green, and blue are not directly processed for the interpretation of the color, but their differences are processed. This is supported by psycho-visual phenomena, which explain why there is hardly any perception like reddish-green and bluish-yellow in our color sensing. This forms the motivation for opponent color processing theories. The representation is diagrammatically shown in Fig. 3.25. Here, R, G, B, and Yl represent red, green, blue, and yellow, respectively.

As shown in the figure, L and M cones participate in an antagonistic manner that provides the component C_1 as $R - G$. In this case, the excitations of red and green oppose each other. Similarly, L, M, and S cones participate to provide the component $C_2 - C_3$ as $Yl - B$, where Yl is equivalent to $R + G$. Here, the excitations of yellow and blue oppose each other. Similarly, rods and all the three types of cones participate in producing the brightness value as $\frac{R+G+B}{3}$, where the black opposes white. There are three factors of the color, two from chromatic part as C_1 and $C_2 - C_3$, and one from luminance part by cones and rods.

The linear part of the YCbCr transformation, which is given in Eq. 3.16, follows the principle of opponent color processing. From the formulation of the YCbCr space, the luminance, Y, is a weighted average of red, green, and blue components. The complementary blue, Cb component, is similar to subtracting the addition of R and G components from B component. Similarly, the complementary red, Cr component, is similar to subtracting

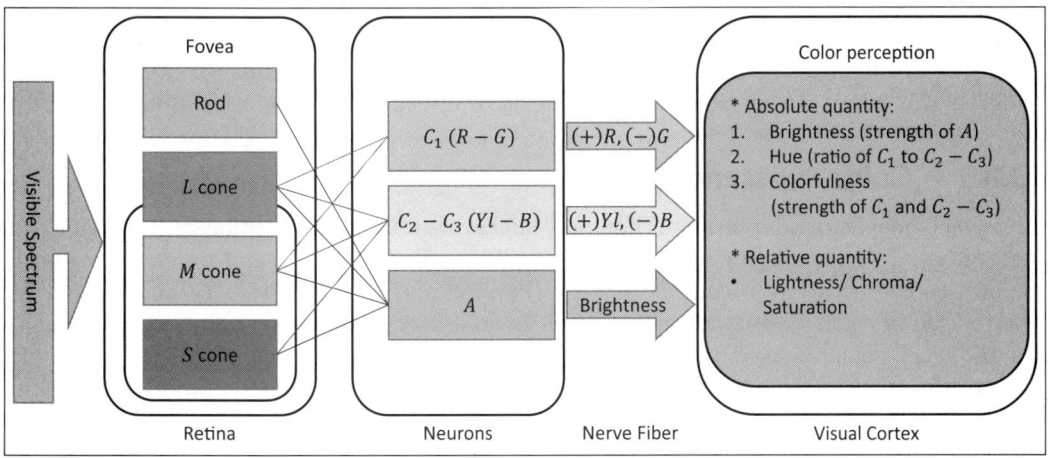

Figure 3.25 Representation of opponent processing of colors in human visual system.

G component from R component. The YCb$'$Cr$'$ model, a linear representation of Eq. 3.16, which follows opponent color space representation, is given by Eq. 3.20.

$$\begin{bmatrix} Y \\ Cb - 128 \\ Cr - 128 \end{bmatrix} = \begin{bmatrix} 0.256 & 0.502 & 0.098 \\ -0.148 & -0.290 & 0.438 \\ 0.438 & -0.366 & -0.071 \end{bmatrix} \begin{bmatrix} R \\ G \\ B \end{bmatrix} \tag{3.20}$$

In the above, $Cb' = Cb - 128$ and $Cr' = Cr - 128$. This color space is also known as the YUV space, where Cb' and Cr' are denoted by U and V, respectively.

3.8 | Effect of illumination

The variation of environmental illumination has a very strong influence on perceived color. For example, the photographs of the same subject that are taken in varying illuminations widely vary in their composition of red, green, and blue components. So, the superposition of these primary colors that produce different kinds of other colors in the image also vary significantly with varying illumination. An example is shown in Fig. 3.26, where the same scene is captured using three different illuminations, white light, off-white light, and orange light. Interestingly, humans adapt naturally to such illumination variations. Even with largely varying illuminations, humans understand true red, which implies that, illumination does not have much effect on human color perception. But, in photographs, there is a large variation of red, green, and blue component, when captured under varying illumination. In this case, the lighting conditions of the scene have a large effect on the recorded colors.

Knowing just the RGB values is not sufficient to know everything about an image. So, image interpretation becomes difficult in this case. The primaries, red, green, and blue components, that are used by different devices are usually different. So, for scientific applications, the camera and light source are well calibrated before processing and analysis. For multimedia applications, it is more difficult to organize such calibrations. To address this issue, various algorithms are devised for estimating the color of illuminants.

3.8.1 | Color constancy

The phenomenon of adaptation of human visual system to the perception of the same color or true color under varying illumination is called *color constancy*, and its computation is known as computation of color constancy (Forsyth and Ponce, 2011). To understand the perception of colors and its reproduction, it is necessary to know the reflected components of the color signal that is recorded, which occurs from the surface of object. There are two components of reflected light, as shown in Fig. 3.27, (1) a diffuse component, which is the product of spectral power density and the reflectance, and (2) a specular component, which is similar to the reflection by a shining surface. In the latter case, almost the same color of an illuminant gets reflected from the surface points that behave like mirror points. So, these points actually provide the color of the illumination or the color of the incident light sources. When a light falls on a diffuse surface, the color of the surface is reflected.

(a)

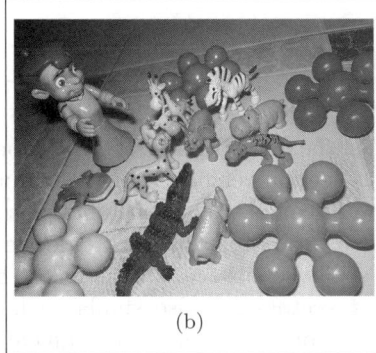

(b)

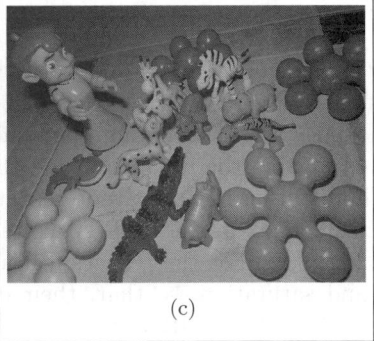

(c)

Figure 3.26 An example depicting the effect of illumination on the captured scene. (a) Image captured using the white camera flash. (b) Image captured using off-white LED light. (c) Image captured using orange filament light. See Color Plates (page 812).

When the same light falls on a specular surface, the specular reflections represent the color of the illumination or the color of the light source. Thus, two different kinds of colors are perceived from the same scene.

In a diffuse reflection, the incident energy is reflected in all possible directions. In an ideal diffuse surface, the reflected energy is equal in all the directions. The amount of the reflected energy depends on material property of the surface (*reflection coefficient*) and the angle of incidence. It is proportional to the cosine of the angle of incidence. In the mirror like specular reflection, the reflected energy at a particular direction is captured by the sensors or recording media, if they are positioned in that direction. The specular reflection occurs in specific directions with a very narrow angular conical spread around that direction. It almost

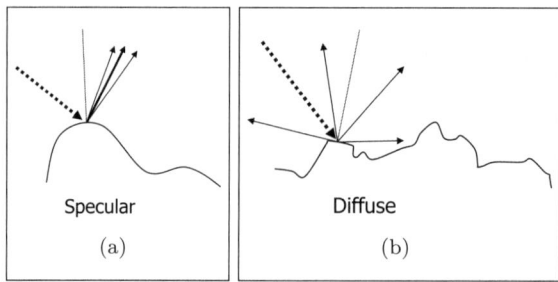

Figure 3.27 Components of reflected light. (a) Specular component, and (b) Diffuse component.

follows Newton's law of reflection, like mirror reflections. When the received energy from a signal is perceived or recorded at a point, a weighted sum of these two reflection components is captured.

3.8.2 | Finding specularities

In a computational model providing both the diffuse and specular components, specular reflection bears the signature of the color of the illuminating light, while the diffuse reflection is characteristics of illuminant and surface properties. It is a product of the intensity received from the illuminant and the reflection coefficient of the surface. In order to have an illumination invariant representation of colors, color constancy is computed. A plot of the color points in the RGB space takes a form of characteristic dog leg structure, as shown in Fig. 3.28. For the reflection from a diffuse surface, all the colors have almost similar hue and saturation, so that, their color vectors are also similar, which are only scaled by intensities. In the RGB space, the color points form a linear segment originating from the origin of the color space. The specular reflection from a shiny surface, which is related to the color of the illuminant, provides a linear segment branching out that of the diffuse reflection. Since the net reflection is a superposition of both diffuse and specular reflections, there are shifts in the directions, and a dog legged structure is observed.

3.8.3 | Computation of color constancy

There are three factors of image formation to produce an image from the sensory information that are obtained from the optical energy of the environment through reflection from a surface point. These three factors are,

(i) the reflection from objects, i.e., the surface reflectance spectrum,

(ii) the illumination from light sources, i.e., the spectral power distribution, and

(iii) the sensing by sensors, i.e., the spectral response of sensors.

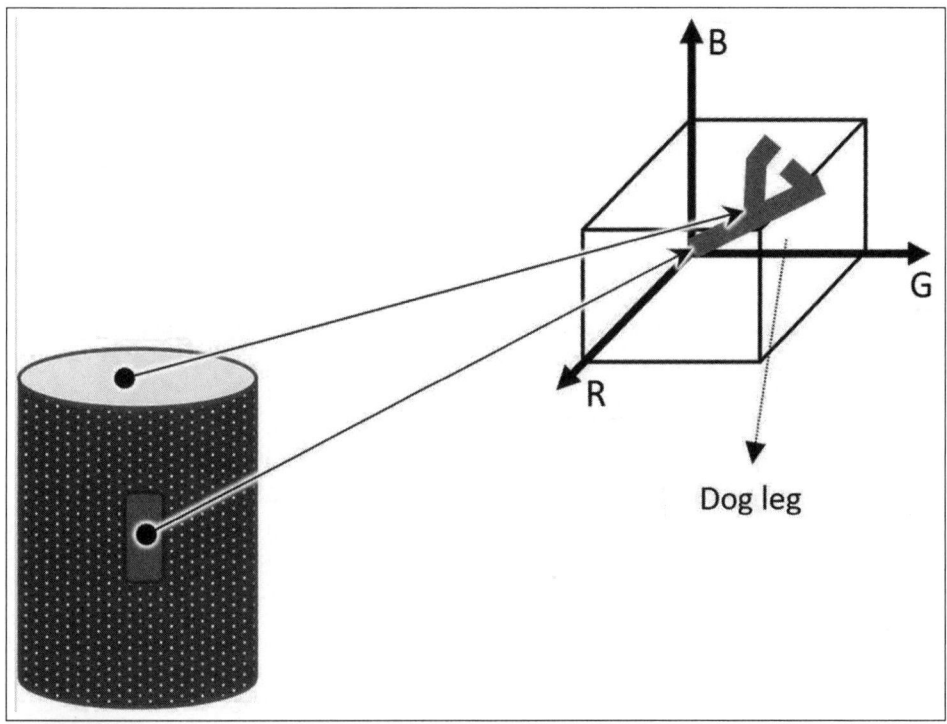

Figure 3.28 The characteristic a dog leg structure that is observed by plotting the color points in RGB space.

This is mathematically represented as in Eq. 3.21.

$$I(x) = \int_{\lambda} E(\lambda) R_x(\lambda) S(\lambda) d\lambda \qquad (3.21)$$

where, $I(x)$ is the intensity or brightness value at a point x in the image, $E(\lambda)$ is the spectral power distribution, $R_x(\lambda)$ is the surface reflectance spectrum at x, $S(\lambda)$ is the spectral response of sensor, and λ is the wavelength of light. Thus, an image is formed as an accumulation of these responses over all the wavelengths in the spectrum of the illuminating light for each type of sensor. For example, if there are three different sensors that are having three different types of spectral responses, there are three such components. In Fig. 3.29, three different scenes are shown that are captured under two different illumination conditions (Barnard et al., 2002). The problem of color constancy is to derive an illumination independent representation of color. The solution requires also to address the transferring of colors from one illumination to the other.

The computation of color constancy requires an estimation of spectral power density of the light source. This estimate is then used to normalize the colors that are obtained as sensory responses. The process of this color normalization is known as *color correction*. One of the methods used for this purpose is called *diagonal correction*. Consider a scene that

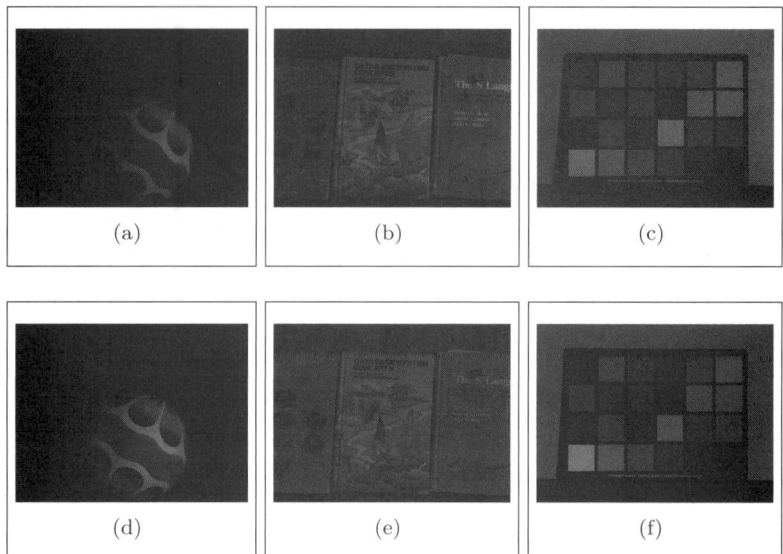

Figure 3.29 Examples of three different scenes that are captured under two different illumination conditions. Scenes: (a, d) `ball`, (b, e) `books`, and (c, f) `macbeth`. Scenes in (a, b, c) are captured by some reference illuminations, and their corresponding scenes in (d, e, f) are captured by different illuminations. (*Source*: Images obtained from `https://www2.cs.sfu.ca/~colour/data/colour_constancy_test_images/mondrian/index.html` (Barnard et al., 2002)). See Color Plates (page 813).

is illuminated by a light source, (R_s, G_s, B_s). The task is to transfer all the colors in the scene, as if, they are illuminated by another light, (R_d, G_d, B_d). The diagonal correction is given by Eq. 3.22.

$$k_r = \frac{R_d}{R_s}, \quad k_g = \frac{G_d}{G_s}, \quad k_b = \frac{B_d}{B_s}$$
$$f = \frac{R + G + B}{k_r R + k_g G + k_b B} \tag{3.22}$$

where, k_r, k_g and k_b are the proportion factors of the primary spectral components of color vectors corresponding to the target illuminant, (R_d, G_d, B_d), and the source illuminant, (R_s, G_s, B_s). The intensity values are normalized by the factor, f, so that, the same intensity values are obtained irrespective of the illumination. The updated color values, (R', G', B'), of (R, G, B) are then computed by Eq. 3.23.

$$R' = f k_r R, \quad G' = f k_g G, \quad B' = f k_b B \tag{3.23}$$

3.8.4 | Estimation of color of the illuminant

The two tasks that are identified in computing color constancy are, (1) to estimate the color of the source illuminant, and (2) to transform the colors from the source image to a target image, where the illumination by a target illuminant is desired. There are different approaches of estimating the color of the illuminant. One of the techniques assumes that the *world is gray* (Buchsbaum, 1980; Gershon et al., 1987). Under this assumption, the average of red, green, and blue components, $(R_{avg}, G_{avg}, B_{avg})$, gives the color of the illuminant. The assumption in another similar technique is called *white-world assumption*, where the color of the illuminant is given by the maximum of red, green, and blue components, $(R_{max}, G_{max}, B_{max})$, which is almost like white (Land, 1977). This is also a very simple computation, which is obtained by finding independently the maximum values in red, green, and blue components.

3.8.5 | Estimation from edge pixels

Unlike, the two simple techniques of computing color constancy, there are other methods which use more extensive computations and complex assumptions. In edge based estimation, it is assumed that the pixels that lie on the edges in the image capture more information of the color of the illuminant. When colors are reflected by the boundaries of objects, it happens mostly due to specular reflection that contains the information of color of the illuminant. One of the methods to estimate the color of the illuminant from edge based assumption is to extend the pixel based methods to incorporate derivative information. That is, to accumulate the intensity values or their derivatives from all the pixels in the image, as given by Eq. 3.24.

$$e^{n,p,\sigma} = \left(\int \left| \frac{\partial^n f_{c,\sigma}(\boldsymbol{x})}{\partial \boldsymbol{x}^n} \right|^p d\boldsymbol{x} \right)^{\frac{1}{p}} = ke_c \tag{3.24}$$

where, the function $f(x)$ represents the intensity value at a point $\boldsymbol{x}$ of an image, n is the order of derivative of function $f_{c,\sigma}(\cdot)$, p denotes the type of norm, σ is the scale, c is the color channel, e_c is the color image component of channel c, k is a constant, and $\left(\int \left| \cdot \right|^p d\boldsymbol{x} \right)^{\frac{1}{p}}$ is the *Minkowki's norm*. This aggregated form denotes a proportional color representation of the illuminant for a particular channel, c. By performing this computation on red, green, and blue channels, three proportional values that represent the color of the illuminant, corresponding to the primaries, are obtained, which may be represented in the form of a 3-D vector. Then, a particular intensity of the estimated illuminant can be adjusted or the color can be transferred using the color correction.

3.8.6 | Selection from a set of canonical illuminants

There are some data driven methods, which bypass the computation of colors by accumulating the responses of the perceived specularities in pixels. One of these methods use models of different canonical illuminants using distributions in a color space. The color space may be any of the available choices, such as the RGB space, the XYZ space, etc. Given an image, the distribution of its colors in the considered space is computed. Then, the similarity of the computed distribution of the image with a set of known distributions from different illuminants indicate the kind of illumination present in the scene. That is, from a set of known illuminants, the illumination whose distribution is the most similar to the distribution of the image is considered. The spectral power density of the illuminant that is nearest to the distribution of image points in 2-D chromatic space is assigned to the image. The distribution may also be considered in 3-D space by using both chromatic and luminance components. Assigning an illumination by the closest approximation of the known distribution to a given scene is achieved by defining a set of canonical illuminants.

Gamut mapping is one of the approaches in which the points are considered in x-y chromaticity chart, in which a gamut is defined (Forsyth and Ponce, 2011). The distribution of points that lie in a triangular space or gamut is compared with the distribution of the canonical illuminants to find the most similar illuminant. Here, the existence of chromatic points is critical. Color by correlation is another approach, where the relative strength over the distributions is considered (Finlayson et al., 2001). An example of color constancy computation from different approaches is shown in Fig. 3.30.

(a)

(b)

(c)

(d)

Figure 3.30 Examples of color correction. (a) Original image. (b) Color constancy computation using max-world assumption. (c) Color constancy computation using gray-world assumption. (d) Color constancy computation using gamut mapping approach. See Color Plates (page 813).

Here, the target image is illuminated by a reddish hue. Color correction of the target image using gray-world assumption, white-world or max-world assumption, and gamut mapping approach are shown in the figure.

Numerical Example

Consider that the color of a source illuminant is represented by an RGB vector, (200, 240, 180), whereas the target color is given by, (240, 240, 240). Given a color vector (100, 150, 200) in the source image, compute the corresponding color corrected vector using diagonal correction rule.

Solution

The color of source illuminant is, $(R_s, G_s, B_s) = (200, 240, 180)$. The color of target illuminant is, $(R_d, G_d, B_d) = (240, 240, 240)$. Given color vector is, $(R, G, B) = (100, 150, 200)$. The proportion factors for diagonal correction are given by,

$$k_r = \frac{R_d}{R_s} = \frac{240}{200} = 1.2$$

$$k_g = \frac{G_d}{G_s} = \frac{240}{240} = 1$$

$$k_b = \frac{B_d}{B_s} = \frac{240}{180} = 1.33$$

$$f = \frac{R+G+B}{k_r R + k_g G + k_b B} = \frac{100+150+200}{(1.2)(100)+(1)(150)+(1.33)(200)} = 0.8396.$$

The corrected components of color are given by,

$$R' = f k_r R = (0.8396)(1.2)(100) = 100.75$$

$$G' = f k_g G = (0.8396)(1)(150) = 125.94$$

$$B' = f k_b B = (0.8396)(1.33)(200) = 223.33.$$

So, using diagonal correction rule, the color corrected vector of (100, 150, 200) is (101, 126, 223). It may also be verified that, the sum of the original vector and the corrected vector remains the same.

3.9 | Color transfer

Color transfer is a more generalized form of color correction. Consider a source image that has a particular color distribution, and consider a target image that has a different color distribution from the source image. Transferring the distribution of the target image to the

(a)   (b)   (c)

Figure 3.31 An example of color transfer between two images of different illuminations. (a) Source image with reddish illumination, (b) target image with day light illumination, and (c) color transferred image (color transfer from target to source). See Color Plates (page 814).

source image in the rendition of the source image is the task of color transfer (Reinhard et al., 2001). For example, consider the images shown in Fig. 3.31. Here, the source image is illuminated by a reddish illuminant, which also affects all the objects present in the image. The target image, that defines the target illumination or color distribution, is seen to be completely different from the source image in the context of objects present in the images and appearance of colors and illuminants in them. Transferring the color distribution of target image to the objects of source image results in a different appearance of the source image, as shown in the figure. That is, the colors in the source image are similar to the target illumination, as if they are illuminated by the illuminant of target image.

3.9.1 | Color transfer algorithm

We discuss here a typical color transfer algorithm proposed in (Reinhard et al., 2001). At first, all the pixels in the given image are converted to a different color space, where the chromatic components are separable from the luminance component. For example, if the color values of the pixels are captured in the RGB color space, they are converted into another space, which is called the LMS cone space. LMS cone model is based on human retinal sensitivity to different cones cells. This model tries to provide a natural perception, as if the sensations are generated in human cones. The mathematical form of this model is given in Eq. 3.25, which is a linear transformation of RGB space.

$$\begin{bmatrix} L \\ M \\ S \end{bmatrix} = \begin{bmatrix} 0.3811 & 0.5783 & 0.0402 \\ 0.1967 & 0.7244 & 0.0782 \\ 0.0241 & 0.1288 & 0.8444 \end{bmatrix} \begin{bmatrix} R \\ G \\ B \end{bmatrix} \tag{3.25}$$

where, L, M, and S represent long, medium, and short wavelengths, respectively. Then, the logarithm of LMS values are computed, since some of the perceptual models consider human perception to be proportional to the logarithm of the received energy at the sensory units. These logarithmic LMS values are used to separate out the chroma and luminance components by another linear transformation, which is given in Eq. 3.26.

$$
\begin{bmatrix} l \\ \alpha \\ \beta \end{bmatrix} = \begin{bmatrix} \frac{1}{\sqrt{3}} & 0 & 0 \\ 0 & \frac{1}{\sqrt{6}} & 0 \\ 0 & 0 & \frac{1}{\sqrt{2}} \end{bmatrix} \begin{bmatrix} 1 & 1 & 1 \\ 1 & 1 & -2 \\ 1 & -1 & 0 \end{bmatrix} \begin{bmatrix} L' \\ M' \\ S' \end{bmatrix}
\tag{3.26}
$$

where, $L' = \log(L)$, $M' = \log(M)$, $S' = \log(S)$, and $l - \alpha - \beta$ is a color space that is similar to an opponent color space model. This is a variant of processing a particular opponent color space, where the chroma and luminance components are separated. Then, these chromatic components are further processed, so that, the distribution of colors in the target image may be transferred to the source image.

Before modifying the chromatic and luminance components, they are mean normalized by subtracting the mean of each of these components in the source image, as given in Eq. 3.27.

$$
l^* = l - \langle l_s \rangle, \quad \alpha^* = \alpha - \langle \alpha_s \rangle, \quad \beta^* = \beta - \langle \beta_s \rangle
\tag{3.27}
$$

where, l_s, α_s, and β_s represent the $l - \alpha - \beta$ components of the source image, $\langle \cdot \rangle$ denotes the averaging operation, and l^*, α^*, and β^* represent their corresponding mean normalized components. Then, the subtracted values are scaled up, so that, the variances of the transferred color components become the same as those of the target distribution. So, subtracted values are scaled proportional to their ratios of standard deviations in source and target distributions, which is given by Eq. 3.28.

$$
l' = \frac{\sigma_t^l}{\sigma_s^l} l^*, \quad \alpha' = \frac{\sigma_t^\alpha}{\sigma_s^\alpha} \alpha^*, \quad \beta' = \frac{\sigma_t^\beta}{\sigma_s^\beta} \beta^*
\tag{3.28}
$$

where, l', α', and β' are the scaled values of l^*, α^*, and β^*, and σ_s^l, σ_s^α, and σ_s^β are the standard deviations of $l - \alpha - \beta$ components of source image, respectively, and σ_t^l, σ_t^α, and σ_t^β are the standard deviations of $l - \alpha - \beta$ components of target image, respectively.

Then, the mean values of $l - \alpha - \beta$ components of the target distribution are added to l', α', and β' to transfer the corresponding mean values, which is given by Eq. 3.29.

$$
l_m = l' + \langle l_t \rangle, \quad \alpha_m = \alpha' + \langle \alpha_t \rangle, \quad \beta_m = \beta' + \langle \beta_t \rangle
\tag{3.29}
$$

where, l_t, α_t and β_t represent the $l - \alpha - \beta$ components of the target image, and l_m, α_m and β_m represent transferred $l - \alpha - \beta$ components from target to source images. The transferred $l - \alpha - \beta$ components of the distribution have the means and variances of the colors produced by the target illumination, while retaining the objects of the source image.

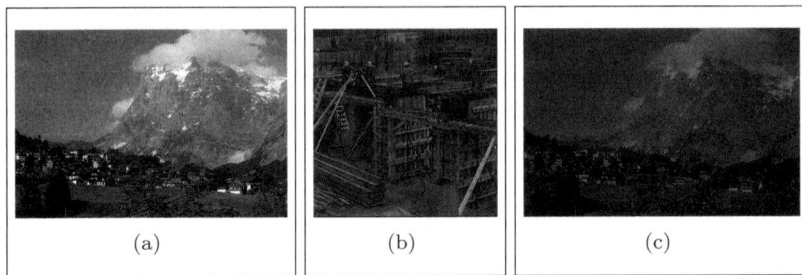

(a)   (b)   (c)

Figure 3.32 Another example of color transfer between two images of different illuminations. (a) Source image with day light illumination, (b) target image with reddish illumination, and (c) color transferred image (color transfer from target to source). See Color Plates (page 814).

As a final stage of processing, the modified $l - \alpha - \beta$ components, which are represented by l_m, α_m and β_m, are converted back to the RGB domain using corresponding inverse transformations, which are given in Eq. 3.30.

$$
\begin{bmatrix} \tilde{L}' \\ \tilde{M}' \\ \tilde{S}' \end{bmatrix} = \begin{bmatrix} 1 & 1 & 1 \\ 1 & 1 & -1 \\ 1 & -2 & 0 \end{bmatrix} \begin{bmatrix} \frac{1}{\sqrt{3}} & 0 & 0 \\ 0 & \frac{1}{\sqrt{6}} & 0 \\ 0 & 0 & \frac{1}{\sqrt{2}} \end{bmatrix} \begin{bmatrix} l_m \\ \alpha_m \\ \beta_m \end{bmatrix}
$$

$$
(3.30)
$$

$$
\begin{bmatrix} \tilde{R} \\ \tilde{G} \\ \tilde{B} \end{bmatrix} = \begin{bmatrix} 4.4679 & -3.5873 & 0.1193 \\ -1.2186 & 2.3809 & -0.1624 \\ 0.0497 & -0.2439 & 1.2045 \end{bmatrix} \begin{bmatrix} \tilde{L} \\ \tilde{M} \\ \tilde{S} \end{bmatrix}
$$

where, $\tilde{L}'$, $\tilde{M}'$, and $\tilde{S}'$ represent modified components of L', M', and S', $\tilde{L} = e^{\tilde{L}'}$, $\tilde{M} = e^{\tilde{M}'}$, and $\tilde{S} = e^{\tilde{S}'}$, and $\tilde{R}$, $\tilde{G}$, and $\tilde{B}$ are the corresponding values of RGB components, respectively.

An example of color transfer of a source image using the characteristics of the distribution of a target image is shown in Fig. 3.32. The source image is captured in a well lit natural day light, whereas the target image is captured using a reddish illumination. After performing the color transfer operation, the source image appears unnatural from the sense of human perception. However, given two images of different illuminations and compositions, transfer of colors between them may be performed as a means of processing them.

3.10 | Color demosaicing

A normal camera requires three types of color optical filters to capture three primary components of a color signal. This kind of sensing is called *full color sensing*. In this case, when a color signal is captured by sensors of a camera, the same signal is received by three different sensors, each capturing distinct primary component of a color, for example, red, green, and blue components. There are different techniques by which the same optical signal is divided into three different parts and guided to three different sensors, where the signal components are sensed independently. But, the divided signal components must belong to the same coherent source, and the coherency has to be maintained in order to represent the color of a particular object that is received by the signal. Accounting to the complexity of such a technology, the signal is triplicated in different ways, for example, by using an optical divider like prisms, etc. Since three different sensors are used for each pixel, these cameras are called *three chip color camera* or *three chip sensors.* Manufacturing of these kinds of cameras requires high technological innovations, which is economically very expensive.

However, there is a cost effective technology for sensing color images, which uses only one of the sensors, instead of three sensors. In this case, at each pixel, either red or green, or blue is captured. When the camera is supposed to record a signal that is coming from a particular point, it captures only one of the components at each pixel, which is done in an interleaved fashion. For example, let only the red value be recorded at a particular point of the sensor forming an image. Then, the green value is recorded at the adjacent point of the red pixel of the sensor in horizontal direction. The blue value is recorded at the adjacent point of the green pixel of the sensor in vertical direction. In this way, the energies corresponding to different color channels are captured, as illustrated in the patterns shown in Fig. 3.33. But, with this method, the spatial resolution of the image suffers, in comparison with a sensor layout that senses all the color components simultaneously at every point. If a coarser spectral resolution is assumed, the neighboring blue, red and green pixels may have been sufficient to form a full RGB image. In this case, pixels that are in an immediate neighborhood of each other are assumed to have the same RGB values. This is

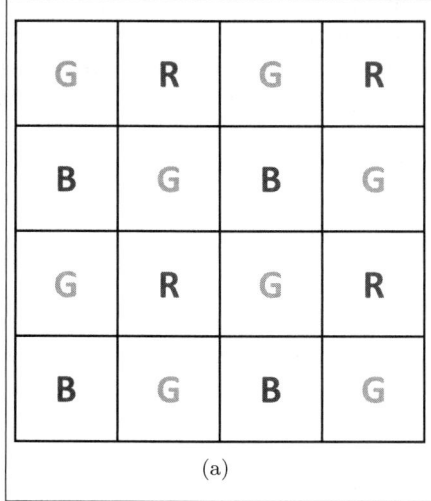
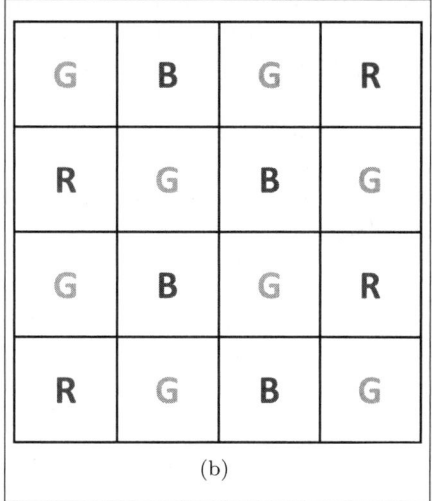

Figure 3.33 Popular patterns of color filter arrays. (a) Bayer's pattern, and (b) Kodak pattern.

a very crude method of estimating the colors, because the values of missing components are assigned by simple transfer of the values from the neighboring pixels by considering the spatial correlation of the spectral channels.

There exist many solutions to address this problem of interpolating the missing components in color channels. For example, at a particular point, if only red value is recorded, the corresponding green and blue components are missing at that point. Similarly, in its neighboring pixels, if green or blue values are recorded, the other two components of color are missing. Each color channel may be visualized as a lattice with missing values at intermediate points. Estimating these missing components from the neighborhood pattern or neighborhood information is the computational task that we need to perform. The image that is sensed or recorded in an interleaved fashion, as discussed above, by recording one of the spectral components at each pixel location is called a *color filter array* (CFA). The task of performing these computations to obtain full RGB color values at each pixel of the image is known as *color demosaicing* or *color interpolation*. The term, 'demosaicing', is used in the context of unfolding an interleaved pattern, which is also called a *mosaic pattern*, with different color components.

In this problem, color filter array of a *single chip* CCD camera is used to generate a dense pixel map of all the color components. The motivation of this technique is its technological simplicity to design and manufacture the cameras that work on this principle. Also, this technique does not require to ensure any spectral coherency of the received signals. Simply using color filters of necessary patterns in front of the lens a CFA can be captured. At each pixel, only the energy from a particular spectral band that is defined by its corresponding filter is received. Different patterns are proposed to design these filters. Two examples of such patterns are shown in Fig. 3.33. Fig. 3.33 (a) is called the *Bayer's pattern*, which is a very popular and extensively used pattern. Here, in one of the rows, red and green components are interleaved, and in the next row, green and blue components are interleaved. These two rows are repeated in turns throughout the sensor matrix. In the Bayer's pattern, green is sampled at twice the rate of the red and blue in the color filter array. This strategy is adopted due to the fact that the human eye is more sensitive to the green channel (Serway and Faughn, 2003). So, having more information of the green channel than the other two components is useful in obtaining good perceptual quality of reconstruction of the full color image. Another pattern is shown in Fig. 3.33 (b), which is adopted by Kodak. In the *Kodak pattern*, filters corresponding to red, green, and blue occur in the same row, one after another. In this pattern too, green components are sampled twice than red and blue components.

From these patterns, it should be noted that, given the color of the filter at the starting row and column, whole pattern of the filter array may be deduced. The positions may be encoded by two different indexing schemes, one by row, and the other by column. For example, in the Bayer's interleaved pattern, if a row has alternations of green and red values in the pixels, the next row alternately holds values of blue and green in the pixels. The rows where red and green samples are available, are called *red rows*, and the rows where blue and green samples are available, are called *blue rows*. Similarly, the columns are denoted as either *green column* or *nongreen column*, depending whether the pixel under consideration is a green sample. Using this periodic spatial arrangement of color filters, it is possible to know the type of row and column of a pixel in the color filter array and the spectral component captured at that location. For example, (1) if the position is given by red row and nongreen column, it is a red pixel location, (2) if the position is given by blue row and nongreen column, it is a blue pixel location, and (3) any position with a green column is always a green pixel. In the color demosaicing problem, the pattern remains fixed. So, given a color filter array, all the missing spectral components of each pixel in the image are computed. The major advantage of using regular patterns to describe a color filter array is the ability of describing the spectral components of all the pixels in the array by having the information of color of a filter at just one precise location.

In summary, the pattern of the color filter array by which a color image array is sensed is known. In the given pattern, at every pixel, only one spectral component is captured. The interleaved pattern of channels is standardized with respect to the pixel coordinates. So, at every pixel of the color filter array, the information of the spectral component at that coordinate locations is available. The problem of color interpolation or color demosaicing is to compute the missing components at every pixel by taking care of its neighboring distributions.

3.11 | Color interpolation algorithms

In this section we discuss a few algorithms of color interpolation or demosaicing. In describing this algorithm, we consider that the CFA follows the Bayer's pattern. There are two key observations which are useful in developing algorithms of color interpolation. These are as follows.

- There is a high correlation between red, green, and blue channels. Given the information of any of these channels, the correlation between them may be exploited to derive the information of other channels. They are very likely to have the same texture and edge locations. Particularly, the cross channel gradient estimation is useful in this regard.

- In the color filter array, green channel is sampled at a higher rate than the red and blue channels. Usually, green channel is akin to intensity values, while the chromatic information is more embedded in red and blue channels than green channel. In the context of color interpolation, green is sometimes considered as synonymous to luminance. So, in estimations requiring luminance, the green channel is first interpolated, which is then used as luminance values in subsequent processing. This is also another reason why the sampling rate is high in green channel. Having a higher quality of reconstruction of green channel is an obvious choice to have its higher sampling rate. This also explains why green channel is less likely to be aliased, and the image details are preserved better in green channel than the other two chromatic channels.

3.11.1 | Bilinear interpolation

Since an image is a 2-D distribution, linear interpolation in both the directions has been considered, which is a simple and direct technique called *bilinear interpolation*. For example, to interpolate the green pixels, i.e., to get the information of green pixels at the locations

G_1	R_2	G_3	R_4	G_5
B_6	G_7	B_8	G_9	B_{10}
G_{11}	R_{12}	G_{13}	R_{14}	G_{15}
B_{16}	G_{17}	B_{18}	G_{19}	B_{20}
G_{21}	R_{22}	G_{23}	R_{24}	G_{25}

Figure 3.34 An example of Bayer's pattern for illustrating bilinear interpolation.

where green samples are not available, the available information from the neighboring green samples are used that form a four-neighborhood. An example of such locations is shown in Fig. 3.34, where, the pixel locations that are denoted by R or B with an index in subscript have missing green values. As observed in the figure, the neighboring information of green samples are available in the form of 4-neighbors.[4] For instance, to compute the green value at the pixel location of B_8 in the figure, the corresponding 4-neighbors are G_3, G_7, G_9, and G_{13}. The interpolated green value G_8 at B_8 may be computed as the average of its 4-neighbors, which is given by,

$$G_8 = \frac{G_3 + G_7 + G_9 + G_{13}}{4}.$$

Similarly, to interpolate red or blue values of pixels, only their neighboring samples that contain true values of red or green are considered. Unlike the case of missing green values, there are three scenarios where the red component has to be interpolated. They are as follows.

(i) a pixel location at red row and green column,

(ii) a pixel location at blue row and green column, and

(iii) a pixel location at blue row and nongreen column.

For example, at the pixel location of G_7, which corresponds to blue row and green column, only two red samples, R_2 and R_{12}, are available in its 4-neighborhood. Then, the interpolated red sample, R_7, at that location is computed as the average of the two neighboring samples, which is given by,

$$R_7 = \frac{R_2 + R_{12}}{2}.$$

[4] Neighborhood definitions of pixels in a discrete grid are discussed in Chapter 1 on fundamentals of image and video processing.

At the pixel location of G_{13}, which corresponds to red row and green column, two red samples, R_{12} and R_{14}, are available only in its 4-neighborhood. Then, the interpolated red sample, R_{13}, is given by,

$$R_{13} = \frac{R_{12} + R_{14}}{2}.$$

If the pixel location is at B_8, which corresponds to blue row and nongreen column, there are no red samples available in the 4-neighborhood. In this case, all its diagonal neighbors, R_2, R_4, R_{12}, and R_{14}, are considered to interpolate the respective red sample, R_8, which is given by,

$$R_8 = \frac{R_2 + R_4 + R_{12} + R_{14}}{4}.$$

Similar operations are carried out for interpolating the blue values. For example, at the pixel location of G_7, which corresponds to blue row and green column, its left and right neighboring samples, B_6 and B_8, are considered for interpolating B_7, which is given by,

$$B_7 = \frac{B_6 + B_8}{2}.$$

At the pixel location of G_{13}, which corresponds to red row and green column, its top and bottom neighboring samples, B_8 and B_{18}, considered for interpolating B_{13}, which is given by,

$$B_{13} = \frac{B_8 + B_{18}}{2}.$$

If the pixel location is at R_{12}, which corresponds to red row and nongreen column, its diagonal neighbors, B_6, B_8, B_{16}, and B_{18}, are considered to interpolated B_{12}, which is given by,

$$B_{12} = \frac{B_6 + B_8 + B_{16} + B_{18}}{4}.$$

The above illustration may be summarized as follows. To interpolate a color value at a particular pixel location, the type of the location in color filter array has to be identified. In the case of interpolating red values, if the type of pixel location corresponds to blue row and green column, the average value of the top and bottom neighbors is assigned as the interpolated value. If the type of pixel location corresponds to red row and green column, the average value of the left and right neighbors is assigned as the interpolated value. And, if the type corresponds to blue row and nongreen column, the average value of the diagonal neighbors is assigned as the interpolated value. These are the three cases that are encountered while interpolating red values. In this way, bilinear interpolation is carried out to get the full color values at each pixel of the given image.

3.11.2 | Interpolation by averaging red and blue hues

There are other methods of interpolation that exploit the correlation of the green samples with red and blue samples. One such technique considers the average value of the hue values, which are estimated at every point of the array. At first, all the pixel values with missing green samples are interpolated using the bilinear interpolation, so that, green values are available at every pixel locations. Then, blue and red hues are computed at the pixel positions wherever the respective blue and red samples are available. The blue hue is computed as the ratio of blue and green components at the considered pixel location. The red hue is computed as the ratio of red and green components at the considered pixel location. The computation of blue and red hues are given by Eq. 3.31.

$$\text{Blue hue} = \frac{B}{G} \quad \text{and} \quad \text{Red hue} = \frac{R}{G} \tag{3.31}$$

While performing the interpolation of missing blue component at a pixel, the interpolated blue value is computed as the product of the respective green value at that pixel and the average of blue hues in its neighborhood. Similarly, the interpolated red value at a pixel where red sample is missing, is computed as the product of the respective green value at that pixel and the average of red hues in its neighborhood. That is, the bilinear interpolation of red and blues hues are converted to the corresponding color values at their respective pixel locations by multiplying them with the green component at that pixel.

For example, consider the interpolation of blue values at the pixel locations of G_7, G_{13}, and R_{12} in the Bayer's pattern that is shown in Fig. 3.34. The pixel, G_7, belongs to a blue row and a green column, where its left and right neighbors, B_6 and B_8, are blue samples. The pixel, G_{13}, belongs to a red row and a green column, where its top and bottom neighbors, B_8 and B_{18}, are blue samples. The pixel, R_{12}, belongs to a red row and a nongreen column, where its diagonal neighbors, B_6, B_8, B_{16}, and B_{18}, are blue samples. Since green components are already interpolated at this stage, the green values are available for all the pixel positions in the color filter array. To compute the values of B_7, B_{13}, and B_{12}, the average value of the hues of their respective neighboring pixels are multiplied with G_7, G_{13}, and G_{12}, respectively, which are given by,

$$B_7 = \frac{G_7}{2} \left(\frac{B_6}{G_6} + \frac{B_8}{G_8} \right), \qquad B_{13} = \frac{G_{13}}{2} \left(\frac{B_8}{G_8} + \frac{B_{18}}{G_{18}} \right), \quad \text{and}$$

$$B_{12} = \frac{G_{12}}{4} \left(\frac{B_6}{G_6} + \frac{B_8}{G_8} + \frac{B_{16}}{G_{16}} + \frac{B_{18}}{G_{18}} \right).$$

Similarly, the red components in the color filter array are also computed using the interpolated green values and the hues of available red values.

3.11.3 | Laplacian corrected edge correlated interpolation (LCEC)

Another effective technique of interpolation uses the gradients. The interpolation technique that exploits the information of gradients is one of the commonly used methods, which interpolates the pixels along the directions of the least gradient. Consider a region, where one of its side has a brightness value I_0 and the other side has a brightness value I_1, as depicted in Fig. 3.35. Each block in the image represents a pixel position. Consider the interpolation of pixel values along the vertical line, as shown in the figure, between the regions of different intensities. If the interpolation is performed along the direction of

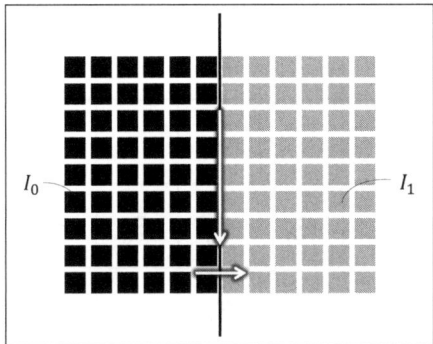

I_0 I_1

Figure 3.35 An example of interleaved color filter array to illustrate Laplacian corrected edge correlated interpolation.

maximum gradient, which is denoted by horizontal arrow in the figure, the interpolated values are in between I_0 and I_1. Also, there will be some blurriness in the corresponding pixel values on the edge. If the interpolation is performed along the direction of minimum gradient, which is denoted by vertical arrow in the figure, then the edge is preserved, since the neighbors used in interpolation are more similar. It is inferred that, interpolating along the direction of least gradient change results in a better reconstruction of edges.

There are four natural directions of gradients that are defined in a neighborhood of a pixel in an array pattern, horizontal, vertical, and two diagonal gradient directions. Though other directions may also be defined, in this context depending upon the availability of samples only horizontal, vertical, and diagonal neighbors are taken to compute the corresponding gradients. Whenever there is a possibility of choosing samples among these directions, the choice is made by considering the direction along minimum gradients. Consider the case of interpolating a green value in an arbitrary position of a color filter array. The interpolated green value may be computed as the average of its left and right neighbors along horizontal direction, or the average of its top and bottom neighbors along vertical direction. In this case, if the vertical gradient is significantly smaller than the horizontal gradient, then there exists a vertical edge, and the interpolation along vertical direction is preferred. If the horizontal gradient is significantly smaller than the vertical gradient, then there exists a horizontal edge, and the interpolation along horizontal direction is preferred. If there is no significant change in the gradients along both horizontal and vertical directions, then all the four samples in the neighborhood may be used for interpolation. If the neighbors are available in the diagonal directions, which are also two perpendicular directions along the two diagonals of the array, then the same principle of choosing pixels along the minimum gradient direction is followed.

Here, the estimation of gradient is a key factor. The estimation is further refined by considering the second order derivative of the distributions.[5] The principle of considering

---

[5] Given a discrete 1-D function, $f(x)$, the first order derivative is given by, $x' = f(x+1) - f(x)$, and the second order derivative is given by, $x'' = (f(x+1) - f(x)) - (f(x) - f(x-1)) = f(x+1) + f(x-1) - 2f(x)$.

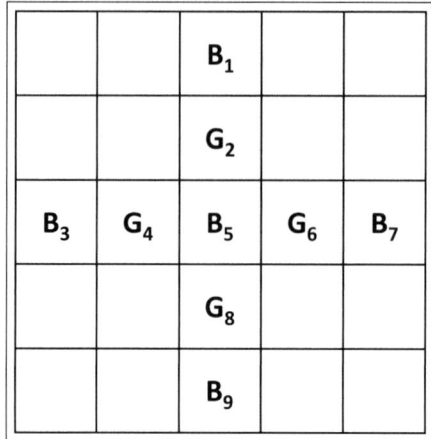

Figure 3.36 An example of Bayer's pattern to illustrate LCEC interpolation of the green value, G_5.

the direction of minimum gradient is used to interpolate the green components at all the pixel locations of the color filter array. For example, consider the array shown in Fig. 3.36, where the green value, G_5, is required to be interpolated. The horizontal gradient, ΔH, and the vertical gradient, ΔV, are computed as,

$$\Delta H = |G_4 - G_6| + |B_5 - B_3 + B_5 - B_7|$$
$$\Delta V = |G_2 - G_8| + |B_5 - B_1 + B_5 - B_9|$$

where, G_4 and G_6 are the horizontal neighbors of G_5, G_2 and G_8 are the vertical neighbors of G_5. Also, B_3, B_5 and B_7 are the blue samples that are used to estimate second order derivatives along horizontal direction, and B_1, B_5 and B_9 are the blue samples that are used to estimate second order derivatives along vertical direction. Here, the absolute values are considered, since the magnitude of change is the required factor. In the above computations, the first term is the gradient of green values, and the second term, that is added to the gradient of green values, is the difference of difference of pixel values, which is equivalent to the second order derivative. The second order derivatives are estimated using the blue values, accounting to a high correlation in the higher order derivatives across the channels. So, the estimated derivatives from blue samples is proportional to the derivatives of green samples. This is a cross channel refinement of the estimated value using the Laplacian operation.

The next step is to estimate the value of G_5 along the direction in which the gradient is minimum. By using the above estimated gradients, G_5 is computed as follows.

If $\Delta H < \Delta V$,

$$G_5 = \frac{G_4 + G_6}{2} + \frac{B_5 - B_3 + B_5 - B_7}{4}$$

else if $\Delta H > \Delta V$,

$$G_5 = \frac{G_2 + G_8}{2} + \frac{B_5 - B_1 + B_5 - B_9}{4}$$

else,

$$G_5 = \frac{G_2 + G_4 + G_6 + G_8}{4} + \frac{B_5 - B_1 + B_5 - B_3 + B_5 - B_7 + B_5 - B_9}{8}$$

Here, the estimation of G_5 is computed as the average value of its neighbors with an additional refinement by the second order derivative or the Laplacian value that is estimated from the blue channel. This correction or refinement is particularly interesting because, the use of Taylor series expansion suggests the addition of second derivative as correction term. However, during interpolation, the addition of the second derivative term performs poorly in achieving plausible results. But, the correction step obtained by subtracting the second derivative term is found to be a more effective technique (Adams and Hamilton [United State Patent 5 629 734]).

After interpolating the green pixels, the red and blue pixels are also interpolated in similar fashion by using the interpolated green pixels. For interpolating red and blues pixels, the green values that are available at every location of the color filter array are used as cross channel estimation of Laplacian. For example, consider the interpolation of red values at pixel locations where they are missing in the color filter array. The relevant part of the Bayer's pattern is shown in Fig. 3.37. There are three different possible cases while interpolating a red sample. In the first case, consider the location of a pixel where a red value is missing, and the true red samples are available only in its vertical neighbors. This corresponds to the location of G_4 in the figure. Then, only its vertical neighbors, R_1 and R_7, are used for interpolating the value of R_4, since the true information of red values is available in only vertical direction. So, the interpolated red value, R_4, is computed by

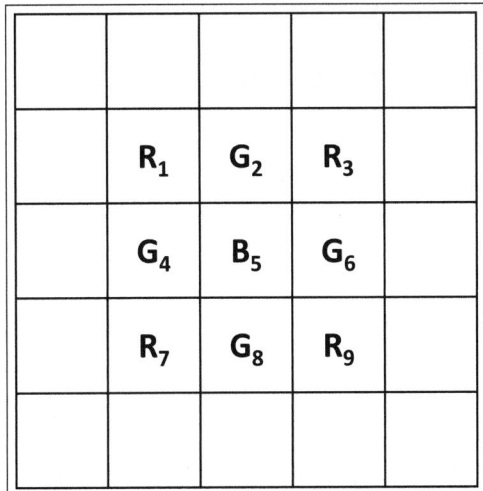

Figure 3.37 An example of Bayer's pattern to illustrate LCEC interpolation of the red value, R_5.

the average of the vertical neighbors, which is then refined by its cross channel Laplacian estimate of the green components, as given by,

$$R_4 = \frac{R_1 + R_7}{2} + \frac{G_4 - G_1 + G_4 - G_7}{4}.$$

In the second case, consider the location of a pixel where the red value is missing, and only its horizontal neighbors are available that are true red samples. This corresponds to the location of G_2 in the figure. Then, only its horizontal neighbors, R_1 and R_3, are used for interpolating the value of R_2, which is then refined by its respective cross channel Laplacian estimate of the green components, as given by,

$$R_2 = \frac{R_1 + R_3}{2} + \frac{G_2 - G_1 + G_2 - G_3}{4}.$$

In the third case, the location of a pixel where the red value is missing, and neighboring red samples are available only in the diagonal directions. This corresponds to the location of B_5 in the figure. Here, the same technique of performing interpolation in the least gradient direction is followed. The only difference in the computation to previous instance on the interpolation of green samples is the directions of estimation of gradients, which are along the two perpendicular diagonal directions, unlike horizontal and vertical directions. Let the gradients along the two perpendicular diagonal directions, $R_1 - R_9$ and $R_3 - R_7$, be denoted by ΔN and ΔP, respectively, which are given by,

$$\Delta N = |R_1 - R_9| + |G_5 - G_1 + G_5 - G_9|$$
$$\Delta P = |R_3 - R_7| + |G_5 - G_3 + G_5 - G_7|.$$

That is, the gradients are refined by the corresponding Laplacian estimates from the green channel along the respective directions of ΔN and ΔP. Then, the interpolated value of R_5 is computed by along the direction of minimum gradient, which are given as follows.

If $\Delta N < \Delta P$,

$$R_5 = \frac{R_1 + R_9}{2} + \frac{G_5 - G_1 + G_5 - G_9}{4}$$

else if $\Delta N > \Delta P$

$$R_5 = \frac{R_3 + R_7}{2} + \frac{G_5 - G_3 + G_5 - G_7}{4}$$

else

$$R_5 = \frac{R_1 + R_3 + R_7 + R_9}{4} + \frac{G_5 - G_1 + G_5 - G_9 + G_5 - G_3 + G_5 - G_7}{8}$$

In Fig. 3.38, examples of demosaic patterns on a color image using bilinear technique (BI), averaging of red and blue hue interpolation (ARBH), and Laplacian corrected edge correlated interpolation (LCEC) are shown. Here, the color filter array has been extracted from the original color image using the Bayer's pattern for demonstrating the interpolation effects. That is, the color filter array is simulated from the original image, so that, the interpolation results using BI, ARBH, and LCEC may be compared with each

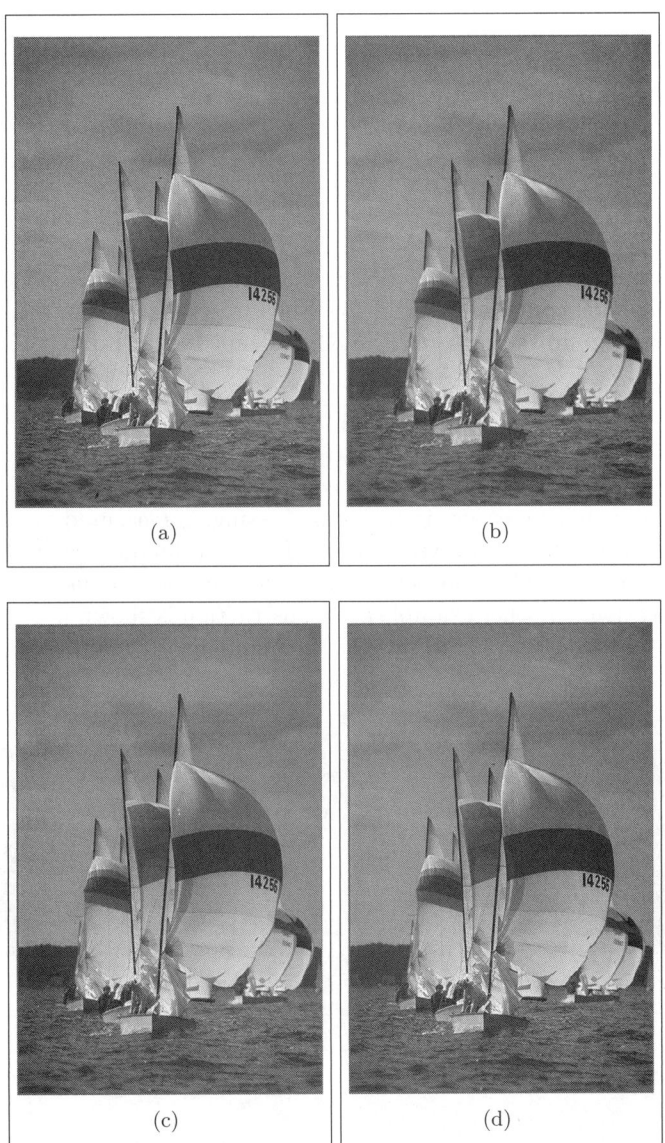

(a)   (b)

(c)   (d)

Figure 3.38 Example of demosaicing a color image. (a) Original color image, (b) bilinear interpolation, (c) averaging of red and blue hue interpolation, and (d) LCEC interpolation techniques. See Color Plates (page 814).

other. As seen in the figure, visually, the results from all the three interpolation techniques look almost similar. However, on a closer examination, some color artifacts and blurriness may be observed in certain cases, which are evaluated by a objective quality measure. Consider a reconstructed image, for example, the image processed by the BI method, and the original image. Let the pixel value at a certain location, (x, y), in the processed image be $(\hat{I}_R(x,y),\ \hat{I}_G(x,y),\ \hat{I}_B(x,y))$, and the pixel value at the corresponding location in the original image be $(I_R(x,y),\ I_G(x,y),\ I_B(x,y))$, where the pixel values are represented by the three color components. Then the error between the pixel values in the two considered images is given by Eq. 3.32.

$$E = \frac{1}{3N} \sum_C \sum_x \sum_y (I_C(x,y) - \hat{I}_C(x,y))^2 \qquad (3.32)$$

where, N is the number of pixels, C is the channel identity corresponding to red (R), green (G), and blue (B) components, and E is the error value. Then, the objective quality measure, *peak signal to noise measure* (PSNR), is defined as in Eq. 3.33.

$$\text{PSNR} = 20\log\left(\frac{255}{\sqrt{E}}\right) \text{dB} \qquad (3.33)$$

where, the signal strength is considered as a constant $(= 255)$ for convenience. The PSNR, which is one of the popular measure in image processing, is measured in dB. On evaluating with this measure, it has been observed that the LCEC technique scores the highest PSNR value, which indicates LCEC to be better than the other techniques, in terms of PSNR, for image interpolation. Another example of reconstruction is shown in Fig. 3.39, which are experimented in the same way as in Fig. 3.38, and similar observations were made.

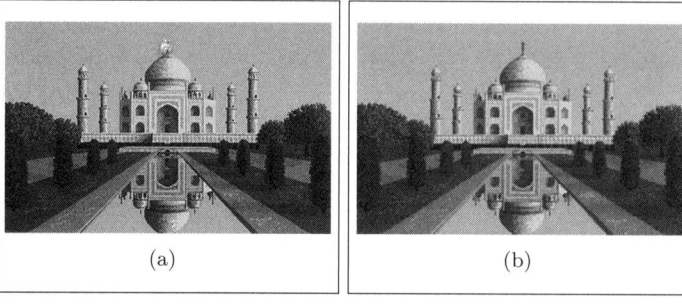

(a)   (b)

(c)   (d)

Figure 3.39 Another example of demosaicing a color image. (a) Original color image, (b) bilinear interpolation, (c) averaging of red and blue hue interpolation, and (d) LCEC interpolation techniques. See Color Plates (page 815).

Numerical Example

Interpolate G_5 by laplacian corrected edge correlated interpolation using the given Bayer's pattern.

$$\text{Bayer's Pattern} = \begin{bmatrix} & & B_1 & & \\ & & G_2 & & \\ B_3 & G_4 & B_5 & G_6 & B_7 \\ & & G_8 & & \\ & & B_9 & & \end{bmatrix}$$

$$\text{Corresponding CFA values} = \begin{bmatrix} & & 30 & & \\ & & 48 & & \\ 24 & 65 & 212 & 225 & 168 \\ & & 124 & & \\ & & 200 & & \end{bmatrix}$$

Solution

$\Delta H = |G_4 - G_6| + |B_5 - B_3 + B_5 - B_7| = 392$

$\Delta V = |G_2 - G_8| + |B_5 - B_1 + B_5 - B_9| = 270$

As $\Delta H > \Delta V$

$G_5 = \frac{G_2 + G_8}{2} + \frac{B_5 - B_1 + B_5 - B_9}{4} = 134.5$

3.11.4 | Problems of image reconstruction

There are two major problems of image reconstruction, (1) blurred edges, and (2) appearance of false colors. Though blurriness of edges is reduced by using interpolation along the direction of minimum gradients, blurred edges still exist in the reconstructed image. An example is shown in Fig. 3.40, where a zoomed portion of the interpolated image of the dome of Taj Mahal is displayed, which shows significant blur in its edges. Appearance of false colors may also be observed in the images. The appearance of false colors is particularly very severe, when the content of the image includes very high frequency transitions and the color is white, as observed in Fig. 3.41. Since, the representation of white color requires the components of red, green, and blue to be estimated very accurately, even slight error in their estimation causes appearance of different kinds of false colors. Such appearances are called *false color artifacts*, which are quite visible in the kind of images shown in Fig. 3.41. The particular image shown in this

Figure 3.40 An example of a zoomed portion of an interpolated image (from LCEC technique in Fig. 3.38) that shows blurred edges and appearance of false colors.
See Color Plates (page 815).

Figure 3.41 Another example depicting a severe appearance of false colors after reconstruction. (a) Original image. (b) Reconstructed using LCEC interpolation technique.
See Color Plates (page 815).

figure is known for studying such artifacts, and this image is also heavily used in testing different algorithms for evaluating the quality of interpolated results. For removing blur from images, there are different filtering and post processing techniques (Jain, 2015). For removing/reducing false colors, a very simple and effective technique using median filtering is employed, which is discussed below.

The median filtering is performed by converting the images from the RGB space to a different color space, where the luminance and chroma components are separable. Any color space that represents an image with separated luminance and chroma components may be used in this context. As an example, the YUV space has been considered to demonstrate the effect of median filtering. The U and V components, which are the chroma components of YUV space, are the modified complementary blue (Cb) and complementary red (Cr) components of YCbCr transformation (refer to Section 3.6).

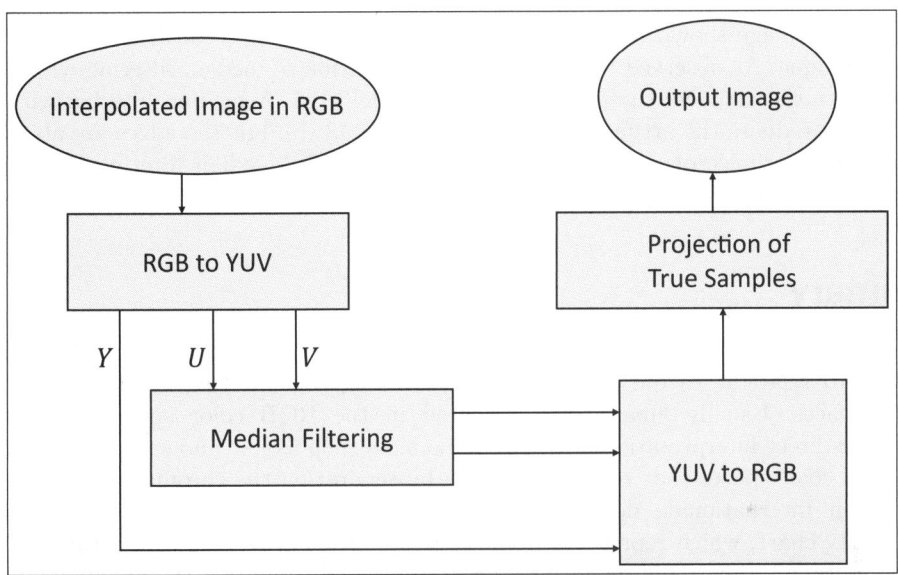

Figure 3.42 Processing pipeline for suppressing false colors in reconstructed images.

Figure 3.43 An example of suppressing false colors in reconstructed images using the pipeline depicted in Fig. 3.42. (a) Reconstructed image using LCEC interpolation, (b) LCEC with median filtering using 3×3 neighborhood, and (c) LCEC with median filtering using 5×5 neighborhood. See Color Plates (page 816).

The median filtering is performed on the chroma components, U and V, and then the filtered components are transformed back to the RGB space. This processing pipeline is figuratively represented in Fig. 3.42. Since the median filtering also modifies the true pixel values in the image, the true pixel samples are projected back to their respective locations after the filtering operation to get the final output image. An example that shows the effect of performing the median filtering operation is shown in Fig. 3.43. The original reconstructed image shown in Fig. 3.43 (a) corresponds to the reconstructed image using LCEC technique. As observed from the figure, application of median filtering with a 3×3 mask reduces the artifacts significantly, as in Fig. 3.43 (b). A median filtering with 5×5 mask further reduces the artifacts, as shown in Fig. 3.43 (c), but the edges are also visibly blurred. So, the choice of the size of mask that is used for median filtering is a trade-off between artifact suppression and blurriness of edges.

Summary

Color carries vital information for interpreting images and videos. Representation of color is crucial to relate it to our semantic understanding and relating to the properties of object surfaces. Usually, images are captured in the RGB color space, which is not suitable for direct interpretation of color components such as hue and saturation. So, there are various color spaces that represent images by separating the chroma components. The Commission Internationale de l'Eclairage (CIE) has recommended a chart called the chromaticity chart, which represents colors in a 2-D space according to tri-stimulus model of color representation. This representation is capable of providing the gamut triangle for reproducing colors, which standardizes the representation of colors. There are various other colors spaces, like the YUV space, the XYZ space, etc., that are used for processing color images. For example, an image may be converted from the RGB space to the XYZ space at first, then from the XYZ space to normalized the x-y chromaticity space, and then its hue and saturation components are processed to analyze different kinds of information.

The color in an image may be enhanced through saturation and desaturation operations, which are performed using the CIE chromaticity chart. For illumination invariant representation of colors, color constancy is computed. There are two specific steps for computing the color constancy, (1) estimation of the color of illuminant, and (2) correcting the colors using the estimated color of illuminant. A more generalized computation of this problem is on transferring the colors between two different images, a source image and a target image. The source and target images are usually composed of seemingly different illuminations in them. The color of the illumination in the target image is transferred to the source image, as if the source image is illuminated by the target illumination.

Color demosaicing is another necessary process for color images that are captured using a color filter array (CFA), which is the most generally used technique in the present day digital cameras that are relatively less expensive. This technique follows the principle of imaging which consists of an interpolation process that is built with the imaging system. It is necessary to interpolate an image for obtaining the full color information, when the image is captured in the form of color filter array. These are some of the typical examples of processing of color images.

Exercises

(i) Consider the following Bayer's pattern and the corresponding color filter array (CFA).

$$\text{Bayer's Pattern} = \begin{bmatrix} G_1 & R_2 & G_3 & R_4 & G_5 \\ B_6 & G_7 & B_8 & G_9 & B_{10} \\ G_{11} & R_{12} & G_{13} & R_{14} & G_{15} \\ B_{16} & G_{17} & B_{18} & G_{19} & B_{20} \\ G_{21} & R_{22} & G_{23} & R_{24} & G_{25} \end{bmatrix}$$

$$\text{Corresponding CFA values} = \begin{bmatrix} 10 & 20 & 30 & 40 & 50 \\ 12 & 28 & 48 & 102 & 220 \\ 24 & 65 & 212 & 225 & 168 \\ 65 & 87 & 124 & 100 & 144 \\ 34 & 112 & 200 & 235 & 245 \end{bmatrix}$$

Estimate the components G_{14}, R_{19}, G_8, and B_{12} of the pattern using bilinear interpolation to the nearest integer.

(ii) Consider the saturation-desaturation operation using CIE chromaticity chart. The transformation matrix from RGB to XYZ is given below.

$$\begin{bmatrix} 0.49 & 0.31 & 0.2 \\ 0.18 & 0.81 & 0.01 \\ 0 & 0.01 & 0.99 \end{bmatrix}$$

Suppose the three primary colors in RGB are $\boldsymbol{R} = (240, 0, 0)$, $\boldsymbol{G} = (0, 240, 0)$ and $\boldsymbol{B} = (0, 0, 240)$, and the input color vector, $\boldsymbol{C}$, is given by $(120, 130, 25)$. Answer the following.

   (a) Compute the chromaticity point of $\boldsymbol{C}$ in the normalized x-y chromaticity space.

   (b) Compute the angle in degree formed by $\boldsymbol{C}$ at the white point $\boldsymbol{W}$, when the reference axis is formed by $\boldsymbol{W}$ and $\boldsymbol{R}$ in the normalized x-y chromaticity space.

   (c) For performing saturation operation, explain how the chromaticity point of a color vector should be shifted?

(iii) Consider a pixel whose RGB component is given as $(10, 30, 20)$. What are the hue and saturation values of this pixel in HSI color space?

(iv) Consider that the color of a source illuminant is represented by a RGB vector $(100, 200, 100)$, whereas the target color is given by $(200, 200, 200)$. Given a color vector $(100, 150, 200)$ in the source image, compute the color corrected vector using diagonal correction rule.

(**v**) Given the coordinates in the normalized x-y chromaticity space of three primary colors as $G = (1/3, 2/3)$, $R = (3/4, 1/5)$, and $B = (1/10, 1/6)$, compute the corresponding maximally saturated color in the x-y chromaticity space preserving the same hue and intensity for the given point $(0.29, 0.21)$ in x-y chromaticity space.

(**vi**) Consider the following Bayer's pattern and corresponding CFA.

$$\text{Bayer's Pattern} = \begin{bmatrix} & & B_1 & & \\ & & G_2 & & \\ B_3 & G_4 & B_5 & G_6 & B_7 \\ & & G_8 & & \\ & & B_9 & & \end{bmatrix}$$

$$\text{Corresponding CFA values} = \begin{bmatrix} & & 30 & & \\ & & 48 & & \\ 24 & 65 & 212 & 225 & 168 \\ & & 124 & & \\ & & 200 & & \end{bmatrix}$$

Interpolate G_5 using Laplacian corrected edge correlated interpolation.

(**vii**) Consider the following Bayer's pattern.

$$\text{Bayer's Pattern} = \begin{bmatrix} R_1 & G_2 & R_3 \\ G_4 & B_5 & G_6 \\ R_7 & G_8 & R_9 \end{bmatrix}$$

Using laplacian corrected edge correlated interpolation, answer the following.
(**a**) What should be the form of R_4?
(**b**) What should be the form of R_2?
(**c**) What should be the form of R_5 if,

   i) $|R_1 - R_9| + |G_5 - G_1 + G_5 - G_9| > |R_3 - R_7| + |G_5 - G_3 + G_5 - G_7|$

   ii) $|R_1 - R_9| + |G_5 - G_1 + G_5 - G_9| < |R_3 - R_7| + |G_5 - G_3 + G_5 - G_7|$

   iii) $|R_1 - R_9| + |G_5 - G_1 + G_5 - G_9| = |R_3 - R_7| + |G_5 - G_3 + G_5 - G_7|$

(viii) Estimate B_{13} using averaging hues for the below given Bayer's pattern and the corresponding CFA.

$$\text{Bayer's Pattern} = \begin{bmatrix} G_1 & R_2 & G_3 & R_4 & G_5 \\ B_6 & G_7 & B_8 & G_9 & B_10 \\ G_{11} & R_{12} & G_{13} & R_{14} & G_{15} \\ B_{16} & G_{17} & B_{18} & G_{19} & B_{20} \\ G_{21} & R_{22} & G_{23} & R_{24} & G_{25} \end{bmatrix}$$

$$\text{Corresponding CFA values} = \begin{bmatrix} 10 & 20 & 30 & 40 & 50 \\ 12 & 28 & 48 & 102 & 220 \\ 24 & 65 & 212 & 225 & 168 \\ 68 & 88 & 124 & 100 & 144 \\ 34 & 112 & 200 & 235 & 245 \end{bmatrix}$$

(ix) Consider the following transformation matrix of color spaces (from RGB to XYZ).

$$\begin{bmatrix} X \\ Y \\ Z \end{bmatrix} = \begin{bmatrix} 0.49 & 0.31 & 0.2 \\ 0.18 & .81 & .01 \\ 0 & 0.01 & .99 \end{bmatrix} \begin{bmatrix} R \\ G \\ B \end{bmatrix}$$

Answer the following.

(a) What is the advantage of above transformation from the point of view of color mixing law?

(b) Explain whether the primary colors, X, Y, and Z, can be physically reproduced.

(c) Given a color value in RGB space as $(100, 80, 200)$ compute its corresponding point in the normalized x-y chromaticity space.

(d) Explain how the hue and saturation can be measured for the above point using the x-y chromaticity chart.

(e) Given the coordinates in the normalized x-y chromaticity space of three primary colors as $(\frac{2}{3}, \frac{1}{3}), (\frac{1}{5}, \frac{3}{4})$, and $(\frac{1}{5}, \frac{1}{10})$, compute the corresponding maximally saturated color in the RGB space preserving the same hue and intensity for the above point. Discuss whether there is any approximation involved in the computation.

(f) Given the primary colors as $(240, 10, 5)$, $(10, 240, 5)$, and $(5, 10, 240)$, compute the maximum saturation color vector (in the RGB color space) of the color represented by $(50, 100, 120)$ in the same (RGB) color space. Discuss whether there is any approximation involved in the computation.

(x) What is computed in the computation of color constancy? Why is it required for processing a color image?

(xi) Interpolate R_{19} using bilinear interpolation using given Bayer's pattern.

$$\text{Bayer's Pattern} = \begin{bmatrix} G_1 & R_2 & G_3 & R_4 & G_5 \\ B_6 & G_7 & B_8 & G_9 & B_10 \\ G_{11} & R_{12} & G_{13} & R_{14} & G_{15} \\ B_{16} & G_{17} & B_{18} & G_{19} & B_{20} \\ G_{21} & R_{22} & G_{23} & R_{24} & G_{25} \end{bmatrix}$$

$$\text{Corresponding CFA values} = \begin{bmatrix} 10 & 20 & 30 & 40 & 50 \\ 12 & 28 & 48 & 102 & 220 \\ 24 & 65 & 212 & 225 & 168 \\ 65 & 87 & 124 & 100 & 144 \\ 34 & 112 & 200 & 235 & 245 \end{bmatrix}$$

(xii) Why a color corresponding to a single optical wavelength may be produced by mixing three primary colors, say Red, Green and Blue in different ratios? Why it is not possible to produce all the colors by superposing (mixing additively) these three primary colors?

(xiii) Consider the following transformation matrix of color spaces (from RGB to XYZ)

$$\begin{bmatrix} X \\ Y \\ Z \end{bmatrix} = \begin{bmatrix} 0.49 & 0.31 & 0.2 \\ 0.18 & .81 & .01 \\ 0 & 0.01 & .99 \end{bmatrix} \begin{bmatrix} R \\ G \\ B \end{bmatrix}$$

Given the primary colors as $(240, 10, 5)$, $(10, 240, 5)$, and $(5, 10, 240)$, compute the maximum saturation color vector (in the RGB color space) of the color represented by $(10, 50, 100)$ in the same (RGB) color space. Discuss whether there is any approximation involved in the computation.

(xiv) Given a color pixel $(100, 20, 50)$ in the RGB color space, and the primary colors of the display device are given by $(200, 0, 200)$, $(200, 200, 0)$, $(0, 200, 200)$, show mathematically whether the color pixel is displayable by additive mixing of primary colors?

(xv) Explain how color information is made available from the chromaticity chart.

(xvi) Describe the features of a CIE chromaticity chart with a schematic diagram of the chart.

(xvii) Write an algorithm for computing hue and saturation from a pixel value in the RGB color space following the chromaticity chart.

(**xviii**) State the problem of color interpolation (or demosaicing) for single chip optical camera. Describe an algorithm which takes care of edge reconstruction during interpolation. Explain the principle and motivation behind the computation.

 (**xix**) Describe an algorithm for transferring colors from one image to another.

  (**xx**) Discuss the limitations of technology in rendering all possible colors perceived by a human being.

 (**xxi**) Explain the use of the CIE chromaticity chart in deriving perceptual attributes of color from its representation in RGB space.

(**xxii**) Consider the color filter array shown in Fig. 3.44, whose first row corresponds to the red (R) row and first column of that row corresponds to a green (G) pixel of the Bayer pattern.

30	40	37	43	40
20	35	25	60	30
32	45	**45**	48	55
30	38	27	55	33
45	48	47	50	46

Figure 3.44

 (**a**) What are the missing components of the central pixel?

 (**b**) Compute the missing components using Bilinear and ARBH interpolation techniques.

(**xxiii**) Discuss how to obtain the measures of hue and saturation of a color pixel using the CIE chromaticity chart. Can additive mixture of any three colors produce all possible colors of this physical world? Justify with proper reasoning.

(**xxiv**) What is meant by color constancy? Identify the tasks for solving the problem of color constancy and suggest a solution for each of the tasks.

4

Feature Detection, Matching, and Model Fitting

In various applications of computer vision and image processing, it is required to detect points in an image, which characterize the visual content of the scene in its neighborhood and are distinguishable even in other imaging instances of the same scene. These points are called key points of an image and they are characterized by the functional distributions, such as distribution of brightness values or color values, around its neighborhood for an image. For example, in the monocular and stereo camera geometries, various analyses involve computations of transformation matrices such as, homography between two scenes, fundamental matrix between two images of the same scene in a stereo imaging setup, etc. These transformation matrices are computed using key points of the same scene point of a pair of images. The image points of the same scene point in different images of the scene are called *points of correspondence* or *corresponding points*. Key points of images are good candidates to form such pairs of corresponding points between two images of the same scene. Hence detection and matching of key points in a pair of images are fundamental tasks for such geometric analysis.

Consider Fig. 4.1, where images of the same scene are captured from two different views. Though the regions of structures in the images visually correspond to each other, it is difficult to precisely define points of correspondences between them. Even an image of a two-dimensional (2-D) scene, such as 2-D objects on a plane, may go through various kinds of transformations, like rotation, scale, shear, etc. It may be required to compute this transformation among such a pair of images. This is also a common problem of image registration. To solve this problem, it is necessary to detect points of correspondences, which in turn translates into the problem of detection and matching of key points in both the images. There are several challenges involved in automatically detecting a set of corresponding points between two different views of an image, like variations in scales, rotation, viewing angle, etc. In such scenarios, characterizing or detecting unique structural landmarks in images help in establishing the correspondence between two views of a scene. Usually, statistics of a region (neighborhood of a pixel location) are used as feature vectors to define the corresponding points. These feature vectors are further used to establish matching among the key points of a different image.

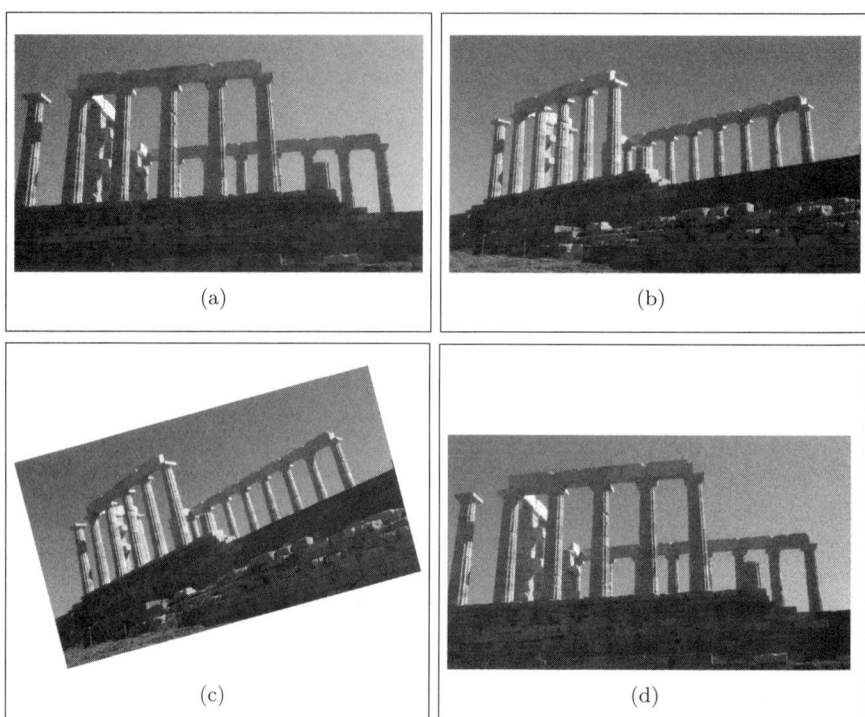

(a)

(b)

(c)

(d)

Figure 4.1 Image of the same scene captured at different views, like (a) captured from front (b) captured from a side (c) rotated, and (d) scaled.

4.1 | Key point detection

A key point represents local characteristics of an image region that uniquely defines its presence with respect to other image locations and regions.[1] Ideally, key points are expected to be preserved even under different kinds of transformations like translation, rotation, scaling, etc. Several local measures are defined by considering the local statistics of image regions for unique identification of key points. In Fig. 4.2, an example of such a region is shown as a shaded block that is used for characterizing the local statistics of a neighborhood around a pixel location. At different points in an image, it computes different measures, which may be captured and represented by sliding this block all over the image. Here, the structural properties in the neighborhood of a location are identified for its characterization. In a flat region with no significant changes in local statistics, a uniform distribution of intensities is observed. Also, for a sliding block that moves along the isophotic lines or edges, there may be no significant changes in statistics. However, if the movement is in a direction perpendicular to the edges, considerable changes in the local statistics are observed due to significant structural variations in the neighborhood. These changes are more prominent at the corners where two edges meet and hence, the structural changes are very significant.

---

[1] In a more general perspective, any such characteristic representation of the visual content of an image is called a *feature*.

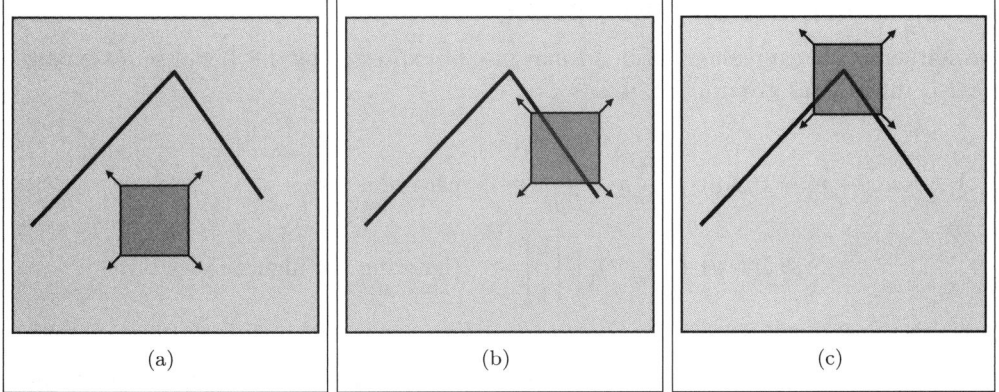

Figure 4.2 Kinds of regions encountered within a window. (a) *Flat* region: no change in any of the directions, (b) *edge*: no change along the edge direction, and (c) *corner*: significant change in all directions.

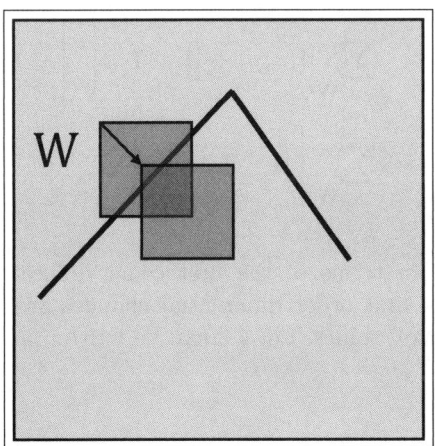

Figure 4.3 Illustration of a sliding window in an image.

Consider shifting a sliding window $\mathbf{W}$ by (u, v) on an image, as shown in Fig. 4.3. To understand how the intensity distribution between these neighborhoods change, the sum of squared differences (SSD) of all the pixel values within these two blocks is computed. After shifting the window, every pixel in it is shifted in a particular direction by (u, v). The squared differences between the intensities of pixels in the window before shifting and the intensities of the pixels in the window at the shifted position are computed and accumulated. This SSD function is given by Eq. 4.1.

$$\mathcal{E}(u, v) = \sum_{(x,y)\in\mathbf{W}} \left(\mathbf{I}(x + u, y + v) - \mathbf{I}(x, y)\right)^2 \tag{4.1}$$

where $\mathbf{W}$ represents the window region and $\mathcal{E}$ represents the error function as SSD.

4.1.1 | Small motion assumption

The mathematical expression in Eq. 4.1 may also be expressed by the Taylor series expansion of a 2-D function as given in Eq. 4.2.

$$\mathbf{I}(x+u, y+v) = \mathbf{I}(x,y) + \frac{\partial \mathbf{I}}{\partial x}u + \frac{\partial \mathbf{I}}{\partial y}v + \text{ higher order terms}$$

$$\approx \mathbf{I}(x,y) + \begin{bmatrix} \mathbf{I}_x & \mathbf{I}_y \end{bmatrix} \begin{bmatrix} u \\ v \end{bmatrix} \qquad \text{(ignoring the higher order terms)} \tag{4.2}$$

where $\mathbf{I}_x = \frac{\partial I}{\partial x}$ and $\mathbf{I}_y = \frac{\partial I}{\partial y}$ represent the rates of intensity variations along x and y, respectively. The SSD of Eq. 4.1 is rewritten using Eq. 4.2, as given below.

$$\mathcal{E}(u,v) = \sum_{(x,y) \in \mathbf{W}} \left(\mathbf{I}(x+u, y+v) - \mathbf{I}(x,y) \right)^2$$

$$\approx \sum_{(x,y) \in \mathbf{W}} \left[\mathbf{I}(x,y) + \begin{bmatrix} \mathbf{I}_x & \mathbf{I}_y \end{bmatrix} \begin{bmatrix} u \\ v \end{bmatrix} - \mathbf{I}(x,y) \right]^2 \tag{4.3}$$

$$\approx \sum_{(x,y) \in \mathbf{W}} \left[\begin{bmatrix} \mathbf{I}_x & \mathbf{I}_y \end{bmatrix} \begin{bmatrix} u \\ v \end{bmatrix} \right]^2$$

Eq. 4.3 expresses Eq. 4.1 in terms of the first order differential changes along certain directions. Hence, only the first order differential changes are needed for computing the SSD, unlike the absolute pixel values. Eq. 4.3 can be written in the form $\sum \mathbf{A}^\top \mathbf{A}$, where, $\mathbf{A} = \begin{bmatrix} \mathbf{I}_x & \mathbf{I}_y \end{bmatrix} \begin{bmatrix} u \\ v \end{bmatrix}$.

By further expanding Eq. 4.3, we rewrite the local change along a direction $[u \ v]$ as,

$$\mathcal{E}(u,v) = \sum_{(x,y) \in \mathbf{W}} \begin{bmatrix} u & v \end{bmatrix} \begin{bmatrix} \mathbf{I}_x^2 & \mathbf{I}_x \mathbf{I}_y \\ \mathbf{I}_y \mathbf{I}_x & \mathbf{I}_y^2 \end{bmatrix} \begin{bmatrix} u \\ v \end{bmatrix} = \sum_{(x,y) \in \mathbf{W}} \begin{bmatrix} u & v \end{bmatrix} \mathbf{H} \begin{bmatrix} u \\ v \end{bmatrix} \tag{4.4}$$

where $\mathbf{H} = \begin{bmatrix} \mathbf{I}_x^2 & \mathbf{I}_x \mathbf{I}_y \\ \mathbf{I}_y \mathbf{I}_x & \mathbf{I}_y^2 \end{bmatrix}$ is a 2×2 matrix. The differential changes along x and y directions are computed and used to obtain $\mathbf{H}$ for evaluating the local statistics in the neighborhood around a pixel. It is necessary to understand how $\mathbf{H}$ changes as the window moves to a new location. This may be traced by performing the eigen analysis of the matrix $\mathbf{H}$. It gives two eigenvalues: (1) the larger eigenvalue corresponds to the direction in which the largest change occurs, and (2) the smaller eigenvalue corresponds to the direction of the smallest change. These two directions (the respective eigenvectors) are orthogonal to each other.

A quick review of eigenvalue/eigenvector

As a quick review of computation of eigenvalues and eigenvectors under the present context, consider a 2×2 matrix $\mathbf{A}$, whose eigenvectors are the vectors $\vec{x}$ that satisfy

$$\mathbf{A}\vec{x} = \lambda\vec{x} \tag{4.5}$$

The characteristic equation of Eq. 4.5 is given as,

$$\text{determinant}(\mathbf{A} - \lambda\mathbf{I_d}) = 0 \tag{4.6}$$

where $\mathbf{I_d}$ is 2×2 identity matrix. Using matrix $\mathbf{H} = \begin{bmatrix} h_{11} & h_{12} \\ h_{21} & h_{22} \end{bmatrix}$, where h_{11}, h_{12}, h_{21}, and h_{22} are the four elements of $\mathbf{H}$, in Eq. 4.6,

$$\text{determinant}(\mathbf{H} - \lambda\mathbf{I_d}) = \text{determinant} \begin{bmatrix} h_{11} - \lambda & h_{12} \\ h_{21} & h_{22} - \lambda \end{bmatrix} = 0 \tag{4.7}$$

In Eq. 4.7, the eigenvalue λ corresponds to the scaled vector $\vec{x}$ in Eq. 4.5. The solution to λ has two values for it. If the matrix is symmetric, both of them would be real values. The scalar values for λ are found by solving Eq. 4.8.

$$\lambda_{\pm} = \frac{1}{2}[h_{11} + h_{22} \pm \sqrt{4h_{12}h_{21} + (h_{11} - h_{22})^2}] \tag{4.8}$$

where λ_{+} and λ_{-} denote the amount of change in the direction of the largest and the smallest change in $\mathcal{E}$. The corresponding eigenvectors are denoted by $\vec{x}_{+}$ and $\vec{x}_{-}$, respectively, which are computed using Eq. 4.7. The eigenvectors and the eigenvalues are used in characterizing a pixel location as a feature point. The larger eigenvalue gives the eigenvector along which the direction of the largest increment in $\mathcal{E}$ occurs. And the smaller eigenvalue shows the direction in which the smallest increment in $\mathcal{E}$ occurs.

Ideally, for defining a unique feature point, $\mathcal{E}$ should be large for small shifts in the window position in all directions around a particular location. That is, considerable changes in local statistics would occur even with small disturbances in the window position at a feature point. Therefore, $\mathcal{E}(u, v)$ should be large for small shifts in all directions. That is, (1) the minimum value of $\mathcal{E}(u, v)$ should be relatively large over all the unit vectors $[u\ v]$, and (2) this minimum value is given by the smaller eigenvalue (λ_{-}) of $\mathbf{H}$.

For instance, in Fig. 4.4, a chess board pattern is shown for illustrating the distribution of eigenvalues. At every pixel location, the largest eigenvalue shows the highlighted edges. Also, the smallest eigenvalue shows the highlighted points of intersection of perpendicular edges. This demonstrates that the largest eigenvalue at the uniform regions is approximately equal to 0. The corner points that are prominently visible are represented by the smallest eigenvalue at that pixel location.

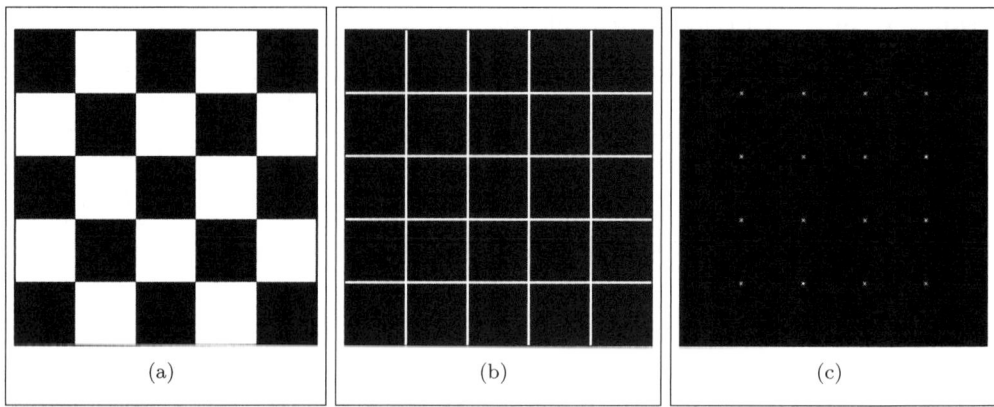

Figure 4.4 Eigenvalues in a chessboard pattern. (a) The image, $\mathbf{I}$, (b) λ_+, and (c) λ_-.

4.1.2 | Algorithm for key point detection

The algorithm for detecting key points is described below. The threshold mentioned in this algorithm is usually set empirically and the local maximum of the distribution is computed to provide corner points.

Algorithm 3 Algorithm for key point detection

   Input: An image.
   Output: Detected feature points.
   1: Compute gradients $\mathbf{I}_x$ and $\mathbf{I}_y$, at each pixel location in the image.
   2: Perform averaging of the gradient measures, $\overline{\mathbf{I}_x}$, $\overline{\mathbf{I}_y}$, $\overline{\mathbf{I}_x^2}$, and $\overline{\mathbf{I}_y^2}$.
   3: Obtain $\mathbf{H}$ matrix from the entries in the gradient values as,

$$\mathbf{H} = \begin{bmatrix} \overline{\mathbf{I}_x^2} & \overline{\mathbf{I}_x \mathbf{I}_y} \\ \overline{\mathbf{I}_y \mathbf{I}_x} & \overline{\mathbf{I}_y^2} \end{bmatrix}.$$

   4: Compute eigenvalues λ_+ and λ_- of $\mathbf{H}$.
   5: Locate values with large response ($\lambda_- >$ threshold).
   6: Select points where λ_- is a local maximum as features.

The computation of λ_- is similar to a popular feature point detection operator known as the *Harris operator* (Harris and Stephens, 1988). The Harris operator provides a proportional quantity that is very much similar to λ_-, which is given by Eq. 4.9.

$$h = \frac{\lambda_1 \lambda_2}{\lambda_1 + \lambda_2} = \frac{\text{determinant}(\mathbf{H})}{\text{trace}(\mathbf{H})} \tag{4.9}$$

where the determinant of $\mathbf{H}$ provides the product of its eigenvalues and the trace of $\mathbf{H}$ is the same as the sum of its eigenvalues. The measure in Eq. 4.9 has similar variation of λ_-, but computationally it is less expensive, as it does not require to perform square root operation. The Harris operator is also known as the *Harris corner detector*. In Fig. 4.5, the detected feature points from the Harris operator and λ_- are shown. They almost appear equivalent. The feature points detected using the Harris operator appears to be more scattered in comparison with the features computed using λ_-, but the local maxima are retained without any changes. An example of detecting feature points on a natural image using the Harris operator is shown Fig. 4.6.

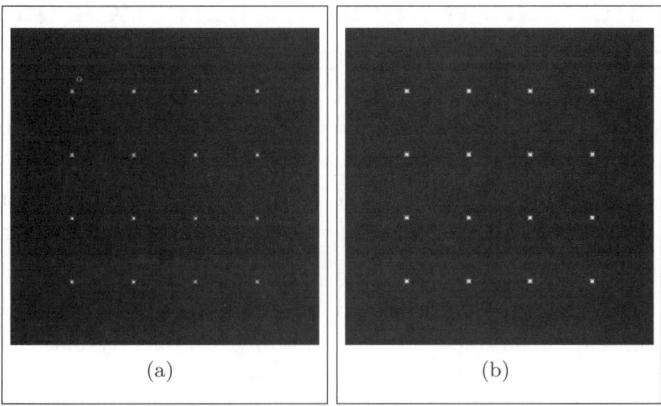

(a)   (b)

Figure 4.5 Comparison between feature point detected by (a) λ_-, and (b) Harris operator.

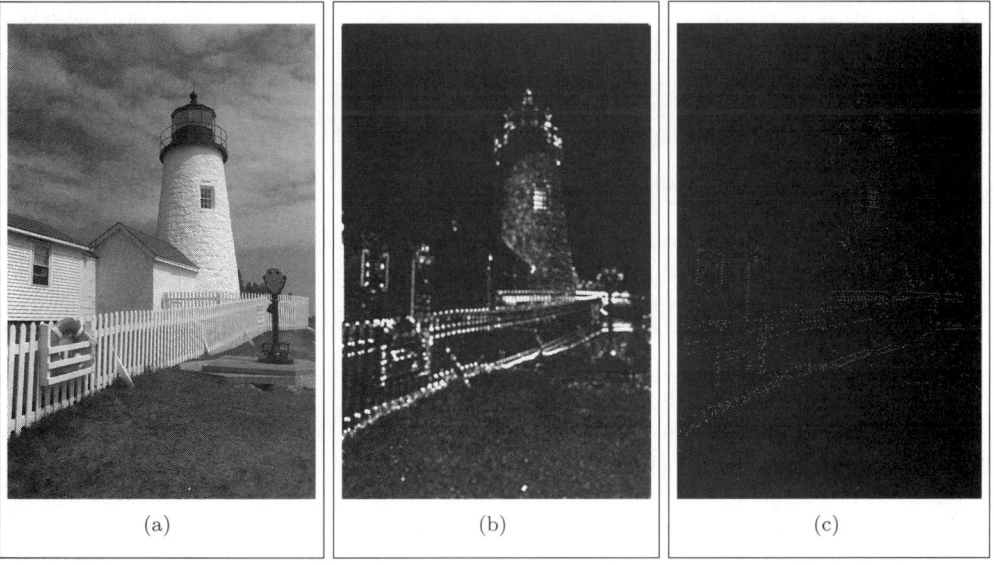

(a)   (b)   (c)

Figure 4.6 An example of using Harris operator for feature point detection. (a) Input image, (b) h-value, and (c) local maxima.

After detecting feature points from two images of the same scene, the next step is to match the detected features to establish point correspondences between the images. There are three stages of computation for matching features between two images:

(i) Detect feature points in both the images (feature detection)

(ii) Identify and describe the features by local statistics (feature description)

(iii) Find the corresponding pairs of feature points (feature matching)

4.2 | Transformation invariant detection and description of features

The transformation invariant detection of features implies that the features with its locations and descriptions are to be preserved and detected even after transformations like translation, rotation, scale, reflection, nonuniform scaling, illumination, view-point changes, etc. It is necessary that both the feature detector and descriptor should be invariant to such transformations.

- For instance, Harris corner detection approach is invariant to translation and rotation. Incorporating scale invariance requires handling of multi-resolution representation of images. Features at multiple scales may be computed by using a Gaussian pyramid of the given image (refer to Section 2.7.2 of Chapter 2). Every image in this pyramid is filtered by a Gaussian mask with different kernel sizes and then sub-sampled to create its representation at multiple resolutions. Then, a more precise computation is performed to locate features at the best scale possible.

- A transformation invariant feature descriptor must capture the information in a region around the detected feature point consistently. An example of such feature descriptor is the normalized histogram of gradient directions in a square window centering a feature point.

4.2.1 | Scale invariant feature detection

Usually, most of the local descriptors vary at different resolutions around a given feature point. For example, consider the image of a letter 'a', as shown in Fig. 4.7 (a). It is evident from different concentric circles in the image that the description of regions in different circles changes. The letter is entirely missed in the smallest circle, and the largest makes its fractional coverage smaller. The amount of information available in circles of different radii is shown notionally as a plot in Fig. 4.7 (b).

A Gaussian pyramid resembles a three-dimensional (3-D) structure with stacked 2-D images at different scales. There are different methods for building a Gaussian pyramid, the popular choices being Laplacian of Gaussian (LoG) and Difference of Gaussians (DoG), which are mathematically represented in Eq. 4.10 and Eq. 4.11.

$$\text{Laplacian:} \ \mathcal{L} = \sigma^2(\mathcal{G}_{xx}(x,y,\sigma) + \mathcal{G}_{yy}(x,y,\sigma)) \tag{4.10}$$

$$\text{Difference of Gaussians:} \ DoG = \mathcal{G}(x,y,k\sigma) - \mathcal{G}(x,y,\sigma) \tag{4.11}$$

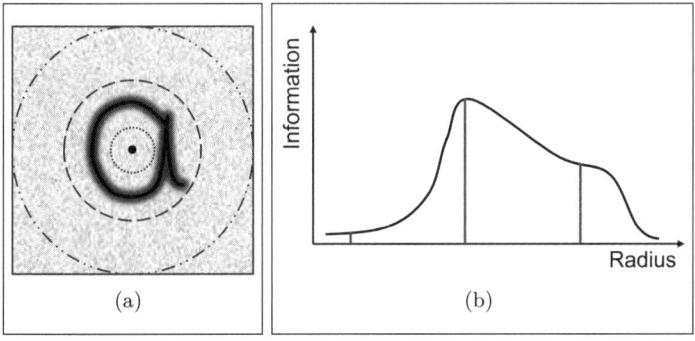

Figure 4.7 Importance of scale in feature detection.

where $\mathcal{G}(x, y, \sigma) = \frac{1}{2\pi\sigma^2} e^{-\frac{x^2+y^2}{2\sigma^2}}$ is a 2-D Gaussian function with uniform standard deviation σ along all the directions, k is the increment factor of scale, and $\mathcal{G}_{xx}(x, y, \sigma)$ and $\mathcal{G}_{yy}(x, y, \sigma)$ are the second order derivatives of $\mathcal{G}(x, y, \sigma)$ along x and y directions, respectively. For determining the scale, the kernels are convolved with the image to obtain the Gaussian pyramid, which is then searched for extrema at each feature point in 3-D image stack. If a mask of a particular size is chosen (for example, a 10×10 mask), the weights of the center element and other elements of the mask depend on the standard deviation considered. To maintain consistency over the choice of size of mask and standard deviation, one of the criteria is to have a mask of size $2\sqrt{2}\sigma$.

In Fig. 4.8, plots of 1-D kernels for LoG and DoG functions are shown, where both are invariant to scale and rotation. To understand the relationship between LoG and DoG operators, consider the following equations.

$$\frac{\partial \mathcal{G}}{\partial \sigma} = \sigma \nabla^2 \mathcal{G}$$

$$\frac{\mathcal{G}(x, y, k\sigma) - \mathcal{G}(x, y, \sigma)}{k\sigma - \sigma} = \sigma \nabla^2 \mathcal{G} \qquad (4.12)$$

$$\mathcal{G}(x, y, k\sigma) - \mathcal{G}(x, y, \sigma) = (k - 1)\sigma^2 \nabla^2 \mathcal{G}$$

Here, the factor $(k - 1)$ is kept constant across all the scales, so that it does not influence the locations of local extrema (i.e., either maxima, or minima).

For discrete processing of these formulations with matrix operations, the convolving functions are also considered in their discrete representations. In Fig. 4.9, the computation for detecting scale invariant features using DoG operator is illustrated. At each stage (also known as octave), the original image is convolved with a Gaussian mask, and two such images from consecutive scales are subjected to difference operation. Also, the original image is downsampled to compute the DoG operations in the next octave, and this sequence of processes is repeated till the desired depth of scale-space representation is derived. This forms a 3-D space of scale and positions, as seen in the figure, from which the local extrema are computed as feature points. This method is used in the scale invariant feature transformation (SIFT) technique of feature detection (Lowe, 2004).

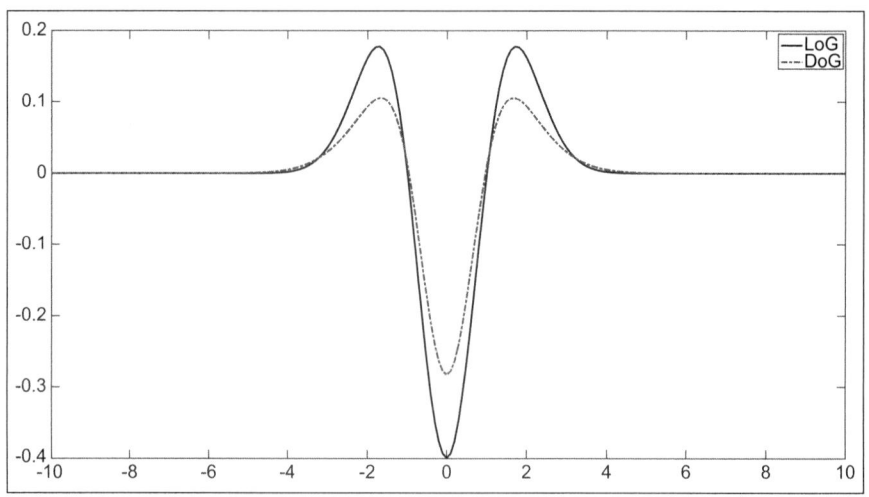

Figure 4.8 1-D kernels for LoG and DoG operation.

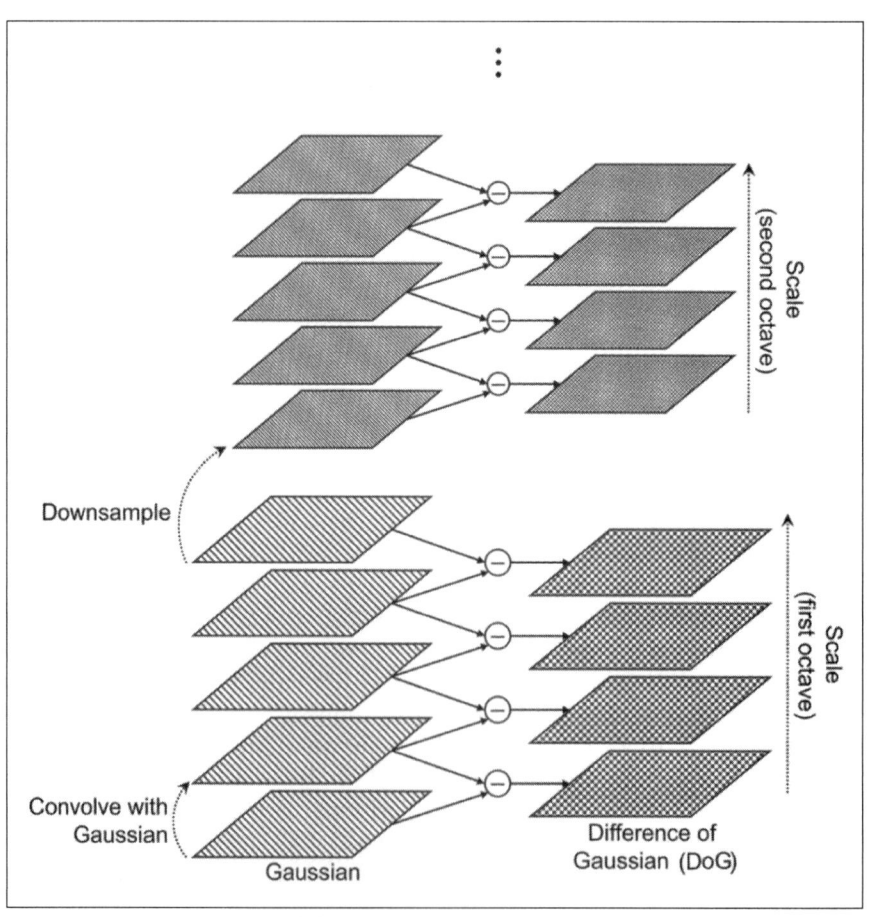

Figure 4.9 Gaussian pyramid.

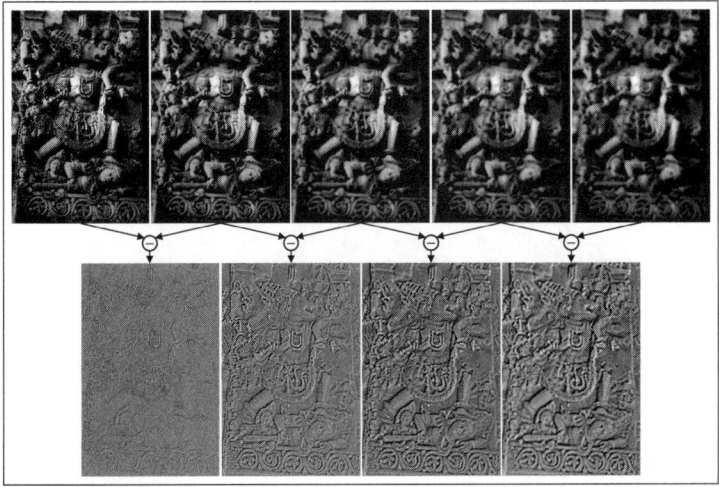

Figure 4.10 An example of filtered images using DoG operator.

A typical example of filtered images at a particular octave using the DoG operator is shown in Fig.4.10.

As a summary of the above discussion, we noted that, given two images of the same scene with a considerable difference in the scales of their acquisition, two kinds of feature detectors are widely used in the literature to find the same interest points independently in each image.

(i) Difference of Gaussians (used in the SIFT feature detection (Lowe, 2004)): Here the feature points are detected by finding the local maximum of the DoG convolved image representations across both space and scale.

(ii) Harris-Laplacian (Mikolajczyk and Schmid, 2001): The Harris operator is applied over the Laplacian pyramid representation. Here, Laplacian operator is applied with varying scales, and then the feature points are detected by finding the local maxima of the response of the Harris corner detector across both scale and space.

Both of these techniques provide scale invariant detection of feature points (also called key points). The best scale of a feature point is determined by searching for a local maxima of suitable functions in scale and space over the image. In either of the cases, it results in a lot of key points which further needs to be filtered for identifying the stable feature points.

4.2.2 | Key point localization

From the set of identified key points, a few of them are chosen which are more robust to image transformations. For instance, key points on edges are relatively less robust than those on corners. Also, some edge points give a high response as well as may relate to local maxima, which needs to be eliminated. For verifying whether to eliminate or retain a key point, the curvature value at the key point location is computed. For this, the Hessian operator $\mathcal{H}$ is applied at the specific point.

$$\mathcal{H} = \begin{bmatrix} \mathcal{D}_{xx} & \mathcal{D}_{xy} \\ \mathcal{D}_{yx} & \mathcal{D}_{yy} \end{bmatrix} \tag{4.13}$$

where $\mathcal{D}_{xx}$, $\mathcal{D}_{xy}$, $\mathcal{D}_{yx}$, and $\mathcal{D}_{yy}$ are the double derivatives of DoG operator, and $\mathcal{D}(\cdot)$ is the DoG of the function.

The eigenvalues of the matrix $\mathcal{H}$ may be used to compute the principal curvatures, whose values are large across the direction of edges and small in the corresponding perpendicular directions. Since the eigenvalues of $\mathcal{H}$ are proportional to the principal curvatures, the two eigenvalues do not differ significantly if it is not an edge point. This characterization of edge points is given in Eq. 4.14.

$$\frac{\text{trace}(\mathcal{H})^2}{\text{determinant}(\mathcal{H})} > \frac{(r+1)^2}{2}, \text{ for a high value of } r \text{ (e.g., } r = 10) \qquad (4.14)$$

A key point is eliminated as an edge point, if the ratio is greater than a threshold defined by r.

Further, each key point is assigned with an orientation to characterize it. The dominant orientation of the neighborhood of the key point is used to make the description of local statistics around the key point rotationally invariant. Given the orientation of the key point, the image patch centering the key point is rotated, so that the reference axis of the local coordinate system gets aligned with the dominant direction. Then a histogram of local oriented gradients at the selected scale characterizes the local statistics around the key point. With this, each key point is specified by a set of parameters, namely its location (x and y coordinates), scale, and orientation. For orientation characterization, the gradient orientations around a key point are binned by discretizing the angles from 0 to 2π into a few intervals, as shown in Fig. 4.11. Then, the peak of the histogram provides the dominant orientation. In certain cases, two major orientations may occur at a key point, wherein both of them are retained as its dominant orientations.

An example of key point localization and orientation is shown in Fig. 4.12, where a set of 3312 initial key points on an image are reduced to 1072 after applying gradient threshold and ratio threshold on $\mathcal{H}$ matrix. Here, each key point is drawn as circle centered at its spatial location and radius proportional to its magnitude. The orientation of the key point is denoted by a radial line from the center to the circumference along its direction.

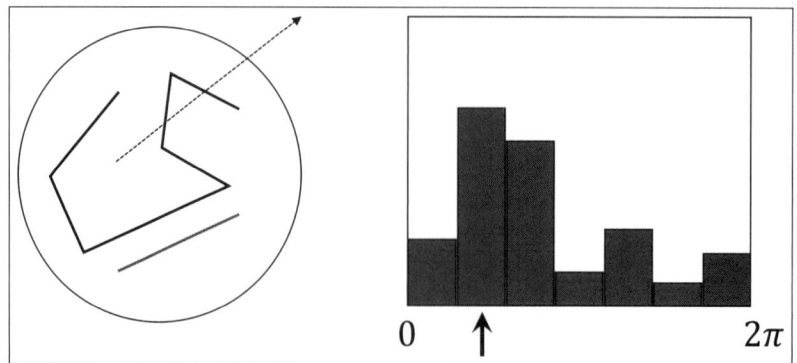

Figure 4.11 Key point orientation assignment.

(a)

(b)

(c)

(d)

Figure 4.12 An example of pruning key points. (a) Input image, (b) initial 3312 key points, (c) pruned 2106 key points after gradient threshold, and (d) further pruned 1072 key points after ratio thresholding. See Color Plates (page 816).

Numerical Example

Given a Hessian matrix $\mathcal{H} = \begin{bmatrix} 0.2 & 0.05 \\ 0.05 & 0.2 \end{bmatrix}$ at an edge pixel in an image, compute the ratio of its largest and smallest eigenvalues.

Solution

The eigenvalues are calculated as $\begin{vmatrix} 0.2 - \lambda & 0.05 \\ 0.05 & 0.2 - \lambda \end{vmatrix} = 0.$

After computing the eigenvalues, their ratio is obtained as 1.66.

Numerical Example

Suppose a histogram contains 9 bins corresponding to angles (in degree) 10, 30, 50, 70, 90, 110, 130, 150, 170. Each bin covers an interval of 20° centering the bin angle. Consider a 4 × 4 image **X** as given below.

100	125	50	60
50	90	80	70
70	100	50	80
80	50	100	50

Consider the central 2 × 2 block of the above image. Compute a vector representing histogram of gradients corresponding to the block using Sobel operators. Assume the direction of a vector and its opposite direction is equivalent and thus it is always possible to express the directions in the first and the second quadrants of the 2-D coordinate space.

Solution

Sobel kernels along the horizontal and the vertical directions are as follows.

$$\mathbf{S}_x = \begin{array}{|c|c|c|} \hline -1 & 0 & 1 \\ \hline -2 & 0 & 2 \\ \hline -1 & 0 & 1 \\ \hline \end{array} \text{ and } \mathbf{S}_y = \begin{array}{|c|c|c|} \hline 1 & 2 & 1 \\ \hline 0 & 0 & 0 \\ \hline -1 & -2 & -1 \\ \hline \end{array}$$

The central 2 × 2 block is considered as reference points (shown highlighted)-

100	125	50	60
50	**90**	**80**	70
70	**100**	**50**	80
80	50	100	50

Using the kernel $\mathbf{S}_x$ and $\mathbf{S}_y$, the gradients along the horizontal and the vertical directions, G_x and G_x, respectively, are computed.

$$\mathbf{G}_x = \begin{array}{|c|c|} \hline -10 & -125 \\ \hline 10 & -60 \\ \hline \end{array} \text{ and } \mathbf{G}_y = \begin{array}{|c|c|} \hline -80 & -5 \\ \hline -30 & -20 \\ \hline \end{array}$$

Angle (θ) is calculated as $\theta = tan^{-1}\dfrac{G_y}{G_x}$

$$\theta = \begin{array}{|c|c|} \hline 82° & 2° \\ \hline 108° & 18° \\ \hline \end{array}$$

Magnitude (μ) is calculated as $\mu = \sqrt{G_x^2 + G_y^2}$

$$\mu = \begin{array}{|c|c|} \hline 81 & 125 \\ \hline 32 & 63 \\ \hline \end{array}$$

Vector obtained using direction $= [2, 0, 0, 0, 1, 1, 0, 0, 0]$.
Replacing the magnitude in vector,
final vector $= [125 + 63, 0, 0, 0, 81, 32, 0, 0, 0] = [188, 0, 0, 0, 81, 32, 0, 0, 0]$.

4.3 | Key point descriptors

As discussed in the previous section, each key point has its location, scale, and orientation. The next step is to compute a descriptor for the local image region about each key point that is highly distinctive and as invariant as possible to transformations. There are several popular feature descriptors toward this end, a few of which will be discussed in this section.

4.3.1 | Scale invariant feature transform (SIFT)

After identifying a feature, its descriptor has to be computed such that it is unique to the feature. Scale invariant feature transform (SIFT) (Lowe, 2004) is one of such operations. Here, a 16×16 orientation corrected square window (or a local image patch) is considered around each detected key point, as shown in Fig. 4.12. Orientation correction is a process of aligning the local reference axis along the dominant orientation of the image patch. The edge orientation of every pixel in the window is obtained by computing its gradients along x and y directions and subtracting 90° from it (because, edge orientation is perpendicular to gradient directions). Then, by thresholding over gradient magnitudes, the weak edges are discarded. Using the orientations of the surviving edges after thresholding of gradient magnitudes, a histogram is formed by dividing the range of 0° to 360° into 8 equal bins or intervals. The 16×16 image patch is further divided into a 4×4 grid of cells (an example of 2×2 grid is shown in Fig. 4.12) and a histogram of 8 bins is computed for each of these

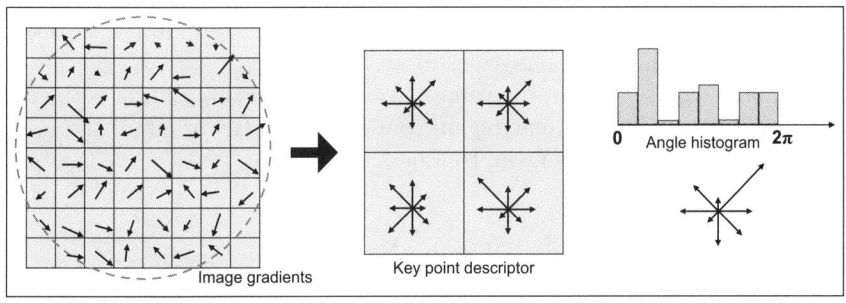

Figure 4.13 Illustration of SIFT key point description.

16 cells. By concatenating all the histograms from each of the cells, a feature descriptor of 128 dimensions is computed (16 cells × 8 bins = 128-D).

The SIFT feature descriptor has certain properties, in terms of its robustness to handle different transformations. It is capable of handling changes in viewpoint to a certain extent. It is seen that, SIFT is invariant up to about 60° of out of plane rotation. Also, the SIFT descriptor is found to handle significant changes in illumination and contrast in the scene. Sometimes, the descriptor is also seen to be invariant even with day versus night views.

4.3.2 | Speeded-up robust features (SURF)

Since its invention in 2006, the SURF feature descriptor (Bay et al., 2008) has evolved over time to gain a significant increase in its speed of computation of the descriptor. In the SIFT feature description, the major operations involved are Gaussian convolutions, which are relatively slower to compute. The SURF feature detection technique mostly employs box filters to speed up the computations, which are considerably faster to execute using integral image representation. The values of elements of a box filter (or mask) are 1 or −1. Unlike the SIFT technique, where the DoG operation is used to exploit scale, the SURF technique uses the Hessian operator on the images. This operation is performed at multiple resolutions of the image using masks of different sizes. By increasing the size of the mask, the scale of the image gets coarser, since larger scales smoothen the image more. For incorporating the orientation, orientation corrected Haar wavelet responses are accumulated, which is also computed efficiently using box filters.

The Hessian operator in an image is defined as in Eq. 4.15.

$$\mathcal{H} = \begin{bmatrix} \mathcal{D}_{xx}(\mathbf{I}, \sigma) & \mathcal{D}_{xy}(\mathbf{I}, \sigma) \\ \mathcal{D}_{yx}(\mathbf{I}, \sigma) & \mathcal{D}_{yy}(\mathbf{I}, \sigma) \end{bmatrix} \tag{4.15}$$

where the double derivatives, $\mathcal{D}_{xx}$, $\mathcal{D}_{xy}$, $\mathcal{D}_{yx}$, and $\mathcal{D}_{yy}$, of DoG operator, $\mathcal{D}(\cdot)$, with standard deviation σ, are applied on the image $\mathbf{I}$. It requires to perform convolution of the second order derivative of a 2-D Gaussian function with the image. Here, a key point is detected by computing the local maximum of the determinant of this matrix, $\mathcal{H}$, over scale and space, which is approximated as $\mathcal{D}_{xx}\mathcal{D}_{yy} - (w\mathcal{D}_{xy})^2$, where w is empirically set at 0.9. To simplify the computations, the Gaussian operators used in computing $\mathcal{H}$ in Eq. 4.15 are approximated by box filters, as shown in Fig. 4.14. Particularly, 9 × 9 box filters are an approximation of Gaussian function of width 1.2. This approximation of the Gaussian filters by box filters is useful for achieving fast computations using integral image representation of the input images as discussed below.

In integral image representation, the value at each image pixel location is the cumulative sum of pixel values over a rectangular region spanning from the origin of the image to the considered pixel location, which is given by Eq. 4.16.

$$\mathbf{I}_{\sum}(\boldsymbol{x}) = \sum_{i=0}^{i \leq x} \sum_{j=0}^{j \leq y} \mathbf{I}(i, j) \tag{4.16}$$

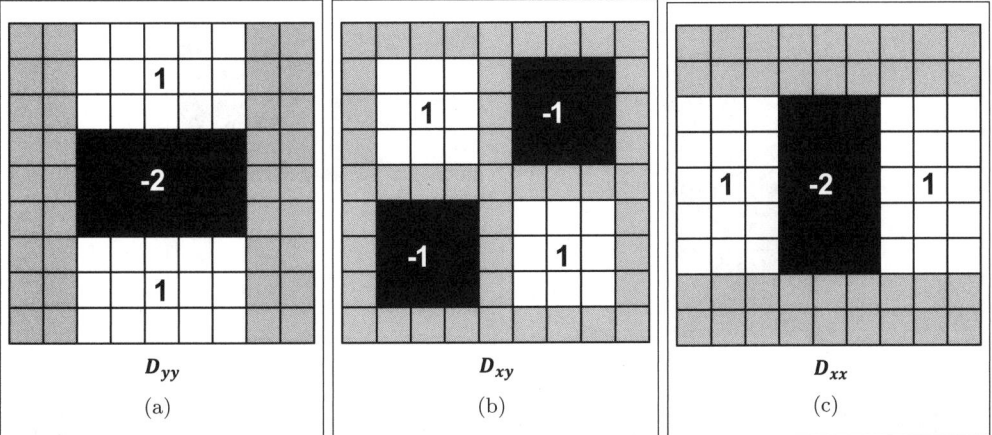

D_{yy}

(a)

D_{xy}

(b)

D_{xx}

(c)

Figure 4.14 Approximation of derivatives of Gaussian width of 1.2 with 9×9 box filters.

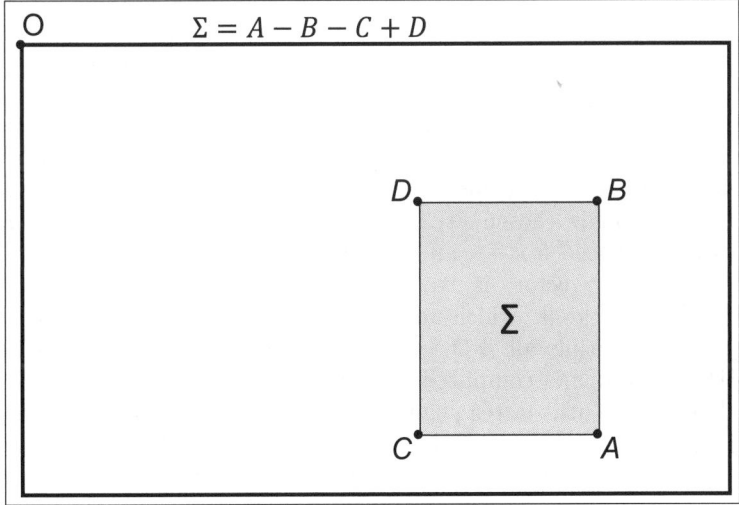

Figure 4.15 Integral image representation.

where, $\mathbf{I}_{\sum}(\boldsymbol{x})$ is the integral image, and $\boldsymbol{x} = (x, y)$ denotes the pixel location. An integral image is obtained with a single scan of the input image. Given an integral image, the integral image value (sum of pixel values in the input image) over a rectangular region defined by four points, A, B, C, and D in Fig. 4.15 is computed using only three additions and four memory accesses as given by $\sum = A - B - C + D$. This property is used with box filter approximation of Gaussian filters to harness fast computation in the SURF technique. Here, the box responses are obtained by simply adding scaled integral values of different rectangular regions that are defined by approximated masks, whose examples are shown in Fig. 4.14.

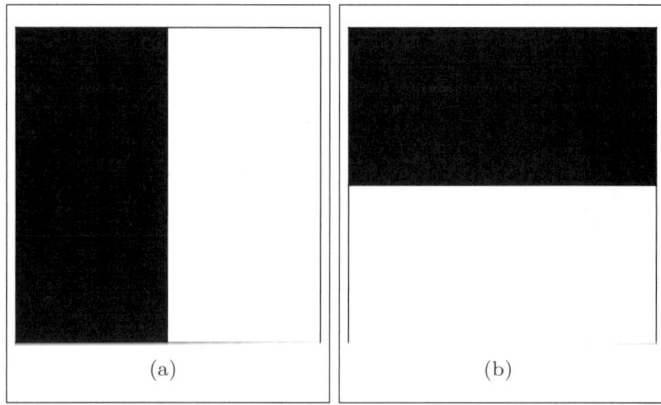

Figure 4.16 Examples of Haar wavelets. (a) Horizontal, and (b) vertical Haar wavelets.

The orientations of the descriptors are evaluated by Haar wavelets (discussed in Section 2.7.1 of Chapter 2) using box filters. Dominant orientations are computed by accumulating Haar responses in both horizontal and vertical directions in a rotating sliding window (wedge of width 60°) at the scale of key point centered at its location. Typical Haar filters in horizontal and vertical directions are shown in Fig. 4.16. The longest vector provides the dominant direction. The box filter implementation and Haar filters need only 6 operations for computing each filter response using an integral image. Here, each image region is partitioned into 4×4 square sub-regions. The size of the window for a sub-region is chosen at 20×scale. Then, the Haar wavelet responses are captured at regularly spaced 5×5 sample patches in each sub-region and summed up to form features. A 4-D vector is computed from each of these sub-regions as $[\sum dx, \sum |dx|, \sum dy, \sum |dy|]$, which are obtained from Haar responses at x and y directions. By concatenating all 4-D vectors from each of the sub-regions, a feature descriptor of 64 dimensions is computed (16 sub-regions × 4-D vector = 64-D). Though the SURF technique executes faster than the SIFT technique, both of these descriptors are computationally quite intensive and not well suited for real time applications. In real time, it is necessary to have much faster computational speeds.

4.3.3 | Features from accelerated segment test (FAST)

The FAST algorithm (Rosten et al., 2010) also detects a feature point that computes with an image patch centering the candidate point for describing local statistics. A step-by-step procedure for detecting the key points using the FAST algorithm is described below.

- Select a pixel p in the image which is yet to be identified as an interest point or not. Let its intensity be $\mathbf{I}_p$.
- Select an appropriate threshold value t, empirically.
- Consider a circle of 16 pixels around the pixel under test, as shown in Fig. 4.17.
- The pixel p is a corner pixel, if there exists a set of n contiguous pixels in the circle of 16 pixels, where all n pixels are all either brighter than $\mathbf{I}_p + t$, or darker than $\mathbf{I}_p - t$. The value of n is usually set at 12.

Figure 4.17 Illustration of FAST descriptor.

- To make the algorithm fast, the intensity of pixels numbered 1, 5, 9, and 13 of the circle in Fig. 4.17 are first compared with $\mathbf{I}_p$. With reference to the figure, at least three of these four pixels should satisfy the threshold criterion to qualify as interest point

- If the values of at least three of the four pixels numbered 1, 5, 9, and 13 are not above or below $I_p \pm t$, p does not qualify as a corner point, and it is rejected as a possible interest point. If the values of at least three of these four pixels are above or below $\mathbf{I}_p \pm t$, all 16 pixels on the circle are further checked to see if $n = 12$ contiguous pixels satisfy the threshold criterion. If 12 contiguous pixels are found to satisfy the threshold criterion, p is identified as a key point.

- The above procedure is repeated for all the pixels in the image.

The strategy of FAST algorithm is further modified using machine learning algorithms. The modification involves partitioning of points on the circle around p and training a decision tree classifier (Rokach and Maimon, 2005) to classify a point as a key point or not. At first, a set of images for training (preferably from the target application domain) is selected. The FAST algorithm is applied on every image in the set to extract feature points. For every point p, the considered 16 pixels around it by the FAST technique are stored and represented as a vector. This is performed for all points in all the images to get a set of feature vectors, $\boldsymbol{f}_p$. Among the 16 pixels in each vector of this set, each pixel, $\boldsymbol{x}$, is classified into one of the following three states:

$$
S_{\boldsymbol{p} \to \boldsymbol{x}} = \begin{cases} d & I_{\boldsymbol{p} \to \boldsymbol{x}} \leq I_{\boldsymbol{p}} - t & \text{(darker)} \\ s & I_{\boldsymbol{p}} - t < I_{\boldsymbol{p} \to \boldsymbol{x}} < I_{\boldsymbol{p}} + t & \text{(similar)} \\ b & I_{\boldsymbol{p}} + t \leq I_{\boldsymbol{p} \to \boldsymbol{x}} & \text{(brighter)} \end{cases} \tag{4.17}
$$

Corresponding to these three states of pixels, the feature vectors $\boldsymbol{f_p}$ are subdivided into three partitions, $\boldsymbol{f_{p_d}}, \boldsymbol{f_{p_s}}, \boldsymbol{f_{p_b}}$, respectively. Then, a variable, $K_{\boldsymbol{p}}$, is defined, which is TRUE if $\boldsymbol{p}$ is an interest point, and FALSE if $\boldsymbol{p}$ is not an interest point. Finally, a decision tree classifier (for example, ID3 algorithm (Rosten et al., 2010)) is trained to query each partition using the variable $K_{\boldsymbol{p}}$ for the knowledge about the true class. It should be noted that the FAST feature detector does not handle scale and rotation transformations in an image.

4.3.4 | Binary robust independent elementary features (BRIEF)

To describe a key point using the BRIEF technique (Calonder et al., 2010), at first, a set of n_d pairs of pixel locations $(\boldsymbol{x_i}, \boldsymbol{y_i})$ in a patch centered around a point $\boldsymbol{p}$ are generated randomly. Using these pairs, a boolean test, as in Eq. 4.18, is performed.

$$\tau(\boldsymbol{p}; \boldsymbol{x}, \boldsymbol{y}) = \begin{cases} 1 & \text{if } \boldsymbol{p}(\boldsymbol{x}) < \boldsymbol{p}(\boldsymbol{y}) \\ 0 & \text{otherwise} \end{cases} \tag{4.18}$$

where $\boldsymbol{p}(\boldsymbol{x})$ and $\boldsymbol{p}(\boldsymbol{y})$ represent pixel values at $\boldsymbol{x}$ and $\boldsymbol{y}$ around $\boldsymbol{p}$, respectively. This boolean comparison of the values at two pixel locations results in a binary value to the function $\tau(\cdot)$. Since there are n_d pairs of pixels around each patch, it requires n_d boolean comparisons resulting in a n_d-D feature descriptor, which is computed using Eq. 4.19

$$\boldsymbol{f}_{n_d} = \sum_{1 \leq i \leq n_d} 2^{i-1} \tau(\boldsymbol{p}; \boldsymbol{x_i}, \boldsymbol{y_i}) \tag{4.19}$$

Typical dimensions of the BRIEF feature descriptors are 128, 256, and 512. The BRIEF descriptor does not have the properties of rotational and scale invariance. A combination of both the FAST and BRIEF techniques, the Oriented FAST and Rotated BRIEF descriptor (Rublee et al., 2011) takes care of scale and rotational invariance.

4.3.5 | Oriented FAST and rotated BRIEF (ORB)

The ORB descriptor (Rublee et al., 2011) extends the techniques of the FAST detector and the BRIEF descriptor to handle scaling and rotation. Originally, the FAST detector does not operate across scales. In the ORB technique, the FAST detector is applied on a pyramid of smoothened images. In a patch selected from the image around a key point detected using the FAST algorithm, its orientation is computed as the vector from the center of the patch and to a centroid considering the intensity distribution in the patch. Thus it requires to compute the intensity weighted center of the patch, which is approximately the geometric center of it. Then, the patch is rotated by the angle of rotation obtained by its orientation, and the BRIEF descriptor is computed from it. This is referred to as the steered BRIEF, which is found to be computationally more efficient when compared to the SIFT and the SURF descriptors.

4.4 | Region descriptors

The region descriptors considered for defining and matching images may be based on local patches, local texture, or global description of images/sub-images.

4.4.1 | Patch descriptor

The *histogram of gradients (HoG)* descriptor (Dalal and Triggs, 2005) is a popular and generic form of a patch descriptor. In the HoG descriptor, the horizontal and vertical gradients are computed over a patch of an image without any smoothing. The gradients include both magnitude and orientations. For color image, the gradients are computed on the channel with the highest magnitude of gradient at each pixel. For an image (or a patch) of size[2] $N \times M$, it is divided into 16×16 blocks of 50% overlap between them, which results in 105 blocks in total. Then, each block is further divided into 2×2 cells, with each cell of size 8×8 pixels. Similar to the SIFT technique, the gradient orientations are quantized into 9 bins spanning a range of $0° - 360°$ or $0° - 180°$ and voted by their respective gradient magnitudes. The votes are further weighed by a Gaussian function to down-weight the pixels near the edges of a block. The concatenation of all the histograms from 105 blocks results in a feature descriptor of 3780 dimensions (105 blocks $\times$ 4 cells $\times$ 9 bins) for a patch of size 64×128.

There are various applications of patch descriptors, where HoG has been used. Primary applications include object detection problems like, pedestrian detection, character recognition, template matching, etc. With some additional modifications, the HoG descriptor can also be used in solving the classification problem. In the case of classification, instead of using a distance function, a classifier (e.g., nearest neighbor, SVM, random forest, etc.) is trained using a set of labeled sample feature descriptors. After building a classification model, it can be used to label an unknown patch.

Nonmaximal suppression

When a particular patch in an image is detected with a matching score by using a reference patch descriptor, there are high chances among the neighboring patches also to be detected with similar higher scores. Natural images usually exhibit a significant degree of spatial coherency, particularly in the vicinity of a given region. So, there is a tendency to have similar descriptions of patches that are close to each other. To resolve such ambiguities among spatially close patches, the patch with locally maximum score is selected during matching. This process is known as *nonmaximal suppression*. A greedy approach for nonmaximal suppression is as follows.

- Select the best scoring window that is expected to cover the target object
- Suppress all the other windows that are spatially too close to the selected window.
- Search for the next top-scoring windows out of the rest, and repeat until all windows are exhausted.

---

[2] The original work on HoG (Dalal and Triggs, 2005) considered images of size 64×128.

4.4.2 | Texture descriptor

Texture is the spatial arrangement of the colors or intensities in an image. As an example, consider the image in Fig. 4.18, where distinct textures can be observed, like the sky, sunflower bed, and the mountain. Describing a texture involves defining a quantitative measure of the arrangement of intensities in the region that can distinctly be identified. There are various techniques for describing texture in regions. The following techniques are briefly discussed here.

- Edge density and direction,
- Local binary pattern (LBP),
- Co-occurrence matrix, and
- Laws' texture energy features.

Edge density and direction

Here, the normalized histograms of magnitudes and directions of gradient are computed over a region around each pixel. The histograms are normalized with respect to its area, so that it has a unit area, which gives a probability density function. This gives two histograms, a normalized histogram of magnitudes ($H_R(\text{mag})$) and a normalized histogram of directions ($H_R(\text{dir})$), that are normalized independently. Typically, the number of bins in histogram are kept small (e.g., 10 bins). For computing similarity between any two feature vectors, a distance measure, like L_1 norm (refer to Section 4.5), between them is computed. If a library of textures in available, such distance functions may be used to determine the label of the given texture.

Figure 4.18 An example of a natural image exhibiting various texture information.

Local binary pattern

The *local binary pattern* is another texture representation technique (Ojala et al., 1996) that uses the spatial arrangement of pixels values in a region. Consider an indexing scheme of a patch $\mathbf{I}$ of 3×3 pixels centered around pixel $\boldsymbol{c}$, to denote the locations of the neighbors. Then a binary pattern is coded as follows.

$$\boldsymbol{b}(i) = \begin{cases} 1 & \text{if } (\mathbf{I}(i) > \mathbf{I}(\boldsymbol{c})) \\ 0 & \text{otherwise} \end{cases} \tag{4.20}$$

where $i = 0, 1, 2, \dots, 7$. This binary coded pattern of integers around the center pixel c is used to compute the LBP feature, $\text{LBP}(c)$, as in Eq. 4.22

$$\text{LBP}(c) = \sum_{i=0}^{7} \boldsymbol{b}(i) 2^i \tag{4.21}$$

This is a binary pattern that is represented in an aggregated form by the value of a binary string that ranges from 0 to 255. This is found to be invariant to illumination and contrast, but not to rotation, since different ordering of neighbors changes the pattern.

As an example, consider the index matrix, $\begin{bmatrix} 3 & 2 & 1 \\ 4 & c & 0 \\ 5 & 6 & 7 \end{bmatrix}$ providing the index of a neighbor

of the central pixel at $\boldsymbol{c}$. Consider a 3×3 neighborhood of a pixel, $\begin{bmatrix} 45 & 60 & 80 \\ 35 & 70 & 90 \\ 25 & 19 & 27 \end{bmatrix}$. Then, the binary pattern following the above indexing scheme is, 0 0 0 0 0 0 1 1. So, the LBP of the pixel having the value 70 is 3.

To make the LBP rotational invariant, a circular neighborhood of radius R, with P pixels, is considered at equal intervals of orientation angles. The selected neighbors are indexed in the same way discussed before. The choice of a circular neighborhood, instead of a fixed 3×3 neighborhood, is made to handle rotational transformations. Then, the LBP at each of these P pixels is computed using Eq. 4.22.

$$\text{LBP}_{P,R}(\boldsymbol{c}) = \sum_{i=0}^{P-1} \boldsymbol{b}(i) 2^i \tag{4.22}$$

Since it is a discrete grid, there are possibilities that few pixels may not coincide with the discrete P locations. In that case, such pixels are interpolated. When the radius is fixed at $R = 1$ and the number of pixels are set to $P = 8$, a specific case of the original definition of the LBP (without rotational invariance) is obtained (i.e., $\text{LBP}_{8,1} \leftrightarrow \text{LBP}$). However, when rotational invariance in incorporated, the rotation of the binary string of P pixels is performed. At each of these rotated locations, the LBP is computed and the minimum of them is chosen as the resulting value, which is given by Eq. 4.23.

$$\text{LBP}_{P,R}^{ri}(\boldsymbol{c}) = \min\{\text{ROR}(\text{LBP}_{P,R}(\boldsymbol{c}), i) | i = 0, 1, 2, .., P-1\} \tag{4.23}$$

where $\text{LBP}_{P,R}^{ri}(\boldsymbol{c})$ is the final descriptor, $\text{ROR}(\boldsymbol{x}, i)$ performs a circular bit-wise right shift operation on the P-bit number $\boldsymbol{x}$, i times. This approach makes the LBP rotation invariant. For the rotation invariant $\text{LBP}_{8,1}^{ri}$, there are only 36 distinct values obtained from all possible binary strings of 0 and 1.

Another variation of the LBP is to count the number of spatial transitions in a string. In this variation, instead of choosing every possible LBP, only those patterns that are considered uniform are chosen, and the rest of them are put in the same class or in a separate class, as in Eq. 4.24

$$\text{LBP}_{P,R}^{riu2}(\boldsymbol{c}) = \begin{cases} \sum_{i=0}^{P-1} \boldsymbol{b}(i)2^i & \text{if } U(\text{LBP}_{P,R}(\boldsymbol{c})) \leq 2 \\ P+1 & \text{otherwise} \end{cases} \tag{4.24}$$

Here, the function $U(\cdot)$ denotes the number of transitions in the binary string and $riu2$ in the superscript denotes that not more than two spatial transitions are allowed in the bit sequence. That is, if there are more than 2 transitions, it is not considered as a uniform pattern. For example, the pattern $U(11111111)$ has zero transitions from 1 to 0 or vice versa. Hence, it is a uniform pattern. Similarly, the pattern $U(11101111)$ has two transitions from 1 to 0 or vice versa. So, it is also a uniform pattern. Whereas, the pattern $U(10001001)$ has 4 transitions from 1 to 0 or vice versa. Hence, it is not a uniform pattern. Here, the rotational invariance is achieved by considering only those patterns that are uniform. By using rotation invariant value and computing the minimum by applying the ROR operator, exactly $P+1$ uniform patterns are obtained. Hence, if the rest of the patterns are put in a separate class, there could be at most $P+2$ distinct values.

It has been shown that there are nine uniform patterns of $\text{LBP}_{8,1}^{riu2}$ (Ojala et al., 2002). All other patterns except these nine uniform patterns are nonuniform patterns. The numbers inside nine uniform patterns correspond to their unique codes, which are shown in Fig. 4.19. Therefore, in the histogram of these LBPs, there are only 10 bins, corresponding to patterns shown in Fig. 4.19. This is further augmented by other measures which makes them invariant to intensities. The local variance of intensities of a uniform pattern is taken into consideration for this, as given by Eq. 4.25.

$$\text{var}_{P,R} = \frac{1}{P} \sum_{p=0}^{P-1} (\boldsymbol{g}_p - \mu)^2$$

$$\mu = \frac{1}{P} \sum_{p=0}^{P-1} \boldsymbol{g}_p \tag{4.25}$$

where $\boldsymbol{g}_p$ is the intensity value of the pixel corresponding to the LBP value p. The normalized histogram of local variances, $\text{var}_{P,R}$ is another feature based on the LBP. Another robust representation is the ratio of the LBP and the normalized histogram of the LBP or normalized histogram of the local variances, which is given by $\frac{\text{LBP}_{P,R}^{riu2}}{\text{var}_{P,R}}$. There are multiple ways the robust representation of a region using the LBP is possible, such as, the histogram of the rotational invariant LBP, the histogram of the local variances, or the histogram of ratios of the LBP and the variance of intensities.

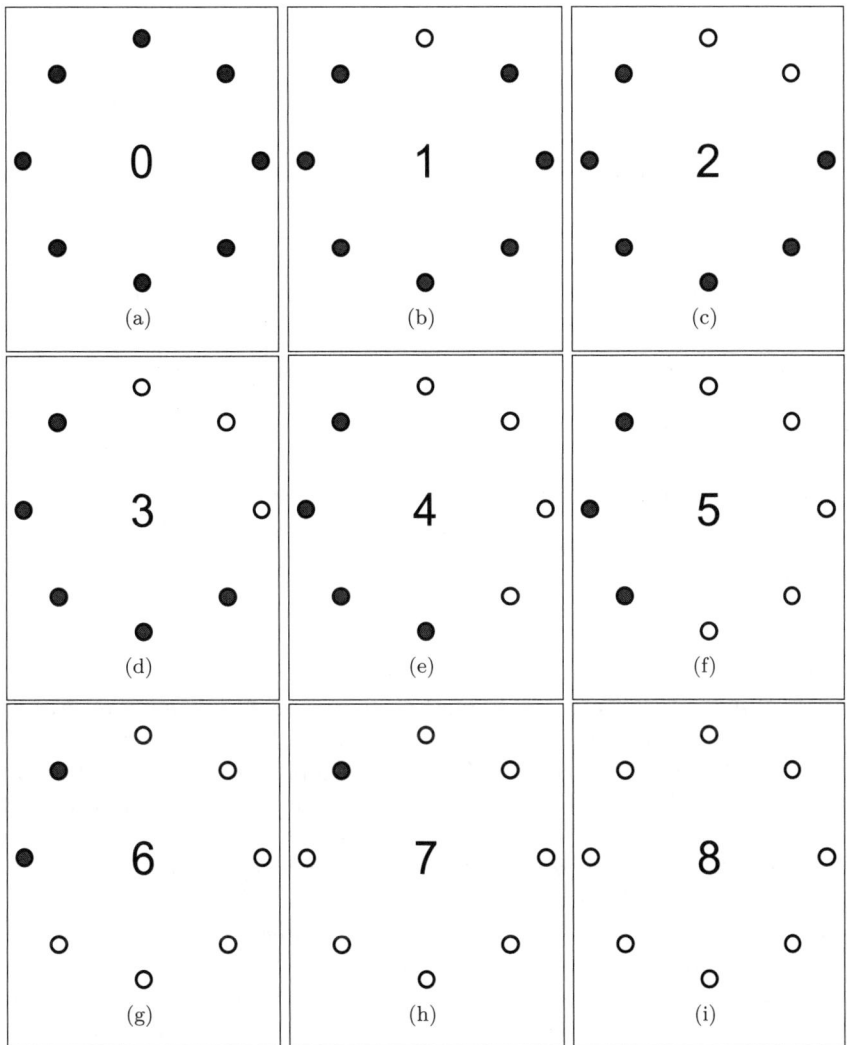

Figure 4.19 The nine uniform patterns of $\text{LBP}_{8,R}^{riu2}$.

Numerical Example

Let the array of weight to be used for computing the LBP from its 8-neighbors is given as $\begin{bmatrix} 2^6 & 2^7 & 2^0 \\ 2^5 & & 2^1 \\ 2^4 & 2^3 & 2^2 \end{bmatrix}$, where top right corner is considered as the first neighbor and this order moves clockwise.

Consider a 3×3 neighborhood with grey scale pixel values $\mathbf{A} = \begin{bmatrix} 90 & 200 & 140 \\ 180 & 172 & 100 \\ 170 & 181 & 152 \end{bmatrix}$.

Compute a single LBP code for this pattern considering the center pixel as reference.

Solution

Since the value of center pixel is 172, matrix elements greater than 172 become 1 and 0

otherwise. Hence, after this operation, matrix becomes $\begin{bmatrix} 0 & 1 & 0 \\ 1 & & 0 \\ 0 & 1 & 0 \end{bmatrix}$. Now, multiplying

these values with a weight table $\begin{bmatrix} 2^6 & 2^7 & 2^0 \\ 2^5 & & 2^1 \\ 2^4 & 2^3 & 2^2 \end{bmatrix}$ and summing up the corresponding

values gives 168.

Co-occurrence matrix

A *co-occurrence matrix*, $\mathbf{C}_r(x, y)$, of an image or a region of an image captures how many times the elements x and y occur as a pair of pixels that are spatially related by r. For convenience, in subsequent description, $\mathbf{C}_r(x, y)$ is simply written as $\mathbf{C}_r$. It is a count of how many times the pixel values x and y occur together with respect to certain spatial relationships, r. For instance, consider $\boldsymbol{prq}$, which denotes a pixel $\boldsymbol{q}$ is shifted from a pixel $\boldsymbol{p}$ by a translation of $\boldsymbol{t} = (a, b)$, i.e., $\boldsymbol{q} = \boldsymbol{p} + \boldsymbol{t}$. This relation is represented in the co-occurrence matrix as $\mathbf{C}_{(a,b)}(x, y)$, which defines the number of cases in an image where $\mathbf{I}(\boldsymbol{p}) = x$ and $\mathbf{I}(\boldsymbol{q}) = \mathbf{I}(\boldsymbol{p} + \boldsymbol{t}) = y$. If there are L intensity levels in an image, the co-occurrence matrix is of size $L \times L$. So, an image with pixel values ranging from 0 to 255 results in a co-occurrence matrix of size 256×256. Each element in the co-occurrence matrix represents the number of occurrences of a pair of intensity values in the input image which gives a frequency distribution of these paired occurrences.

As an example of computation of a co-occurrence matrix, consider a small binary image, $\mathbf{I}_b$, of size 4×4, which has only two intensity levels, 0 and 1.

$$\mathbf{I}_b = \begin{bmatrix} 0 & 0 & 1 & 1 \\ 0 & 0 & 1 & 1 \\ 1 & 1 & 0 & 0 \\ 1 & 1 & 0 & 0 \end{bmatrix}.$$

Here, three 2×2 co-occurrence matrices, $\mathbf{C}_{(0,1)}$, $\mathbf{C}_{(1,0)}$, and $\mathbf{C}_{(1,1)}$, represent the spatial relationships of (a, b) as $(0, 1)$, $(1, 0)$, and $(1, 1)$, respectively. To compute $\mathbf{C}_{(0,1)}$, count the number of occurrences of all possible intensity level pairs in the direction $(a, b) = (0, 1)$, which is a unit shift along the horizontal direction. As seen in $\mathbf{I}_b$, the number of paired occurrences of intensity levels 0 and 0 is four. That of levels 0 and 1, 1 and 0, and 1 and 1 are 2, 2 and 4, respectively. This is represented in the matrix form as $\mathbf{C}_{(0,1)} = \begin{bmatrix} 4 & 2 \\ 2 & 4 \end{bmatrix}$.

Similarly, $\mathbf{C}_{(1,0)}$ and $\mathbf{C}_{(1,1)}$ are computed as, $\mathbf{C}_{(1,0)} = \begin{bmatrix} 4 & 2 \\ 2 & 4 \end{bmatrix}$ and $\mathbf{C}_{(1,1)} = \begin{bmatrix} 2 & 2 \\ 2 & 3 \end{bmatrix}$. This set of co-occurrence matrices represent the texture feature. Depending upon the definition of the paired locations of pixels, different co-occurrence matrices are obtained.

A co-occurrence matrix, $\mathbf{C}_r$, may be converted to a normalized co-occurrence matrix, $\mathbf{N}_r$, by dividing each element of $\mathbf{C}_r$ by the sum of elements in $\mathbf{C}_r$. With respect to the image $\mathbf{I}_b$, the normalized cooccurrence matrices corresponding to $\mathbf{C}_{(0,1)}$, $\mathbf{C}_{(1,0)}$, and $\mathbf{C}_{(1,1)}$ are given by, $\mathbf{N}_{(0,1)} = \begin{bmatrix} \frac{1}{3} & \frac{1}{6} \\ \frac{1}{6} & \frac{1}{3} \end{bmatrix}$, $\mathbf{N}_{(1,0)} = \begin{bmatrix} \frac{1}{3} & \frac{1}{6} \\ \frac{1}{6} & \frac{1}{3} \end{bmatrix}$, and $\mathbf{N}_{(0,1)} = \begin{bmatrix} \frac{2}{9} & \frac{2}{9} \\ \frac{2}{9} & \frac{1}{3} \end{bmatrix}$, respectively.

Similarly, a co-occurrence matrix, $\mathbf{C}_r$, may also be represented as a symmetric co-occurrence matrix, $\mathbf{S}_r$, which is computed as $\mathbf{S}_r = \mathbf{C}_r + \mathbf{C}_{-r}$, where $\mathbf{C}_{-r}$ represents the relation between x and y pixels in the opposite direction. The symmetric occurrence matrices corresponding to $\mathbf{C}_{(0,1)}$, $\mathbf{C}_{(1,0)}$, and $\mathbf{C}_{(1,1)}$ are given as follows.

$$\mathbf{S}_{(0,1)} = \mathbf{C}_{(0,1)} + \mathbf{C}_{(0,-1)} = \begin{bmatrix} 1 & 4 \\ 4 & 8 \end{bmatrix}, \quad \mathbf{S}_{(1,0)} = \mathbf{C}_{(1,0)} + \mathbf{C}_{(-1,0)} = \begin{bmatrix} 1 & 4 \\ 4 & 8 \end{bmatrix}, \quad \text{and} \quad \mathbf{S}_{(1,1)} =$$

$$\mathbf{C}_{(1,1)} + \mathbf{C}_{(-1,-1)} = \begin{bmatrix} 4 & 4 \\ 4 & 6 \end{bmatrix}, \text{ respectively.}$$

The normalized co-occurrence matrix is used to compute various features or normalized measures of texture attributes (Haralick et al., 1973) like correlation, energy, entropy, contrast, and homogeneity. The expressions of these measures are given below.

$$\text{Correlation} = \frac{\sum_x \sum_y (x - \mu_x)(y - \mu_y)\mathbf{N}_r(x,y)}{\sigma_x \sigma_y} \tag{4.26}$$

$$\text{Energy} = \sum_x \sum_y \mathbf{N}_r^2(x,y) \tag{4.27}$$

$$\text{Entropy} = -\sum_x \sum_y \mathbf{N}_r(x,y)\log_2(\mathbf{N}_r(x,y)) \tag{4.28}$$

$$\text{Contrast} = \sum_x \sum_y (x-y)^2 \mathbf{N}_r^2(x,y) \tag{4.29}$$

$$\text{Homogeneity} = \sum_x \sum_y \frac{\mathbf{N}_r^2(x,y)}{1 + |x-y|} \tag{4.30}$$

where μ_x and μ_y are the means of x and y, respectively, and σ_x and σ_y, standard deviations of x and y, respectively. Sometimes, μ_x and σ_x may also be computed as mean and standard deviation of sum of rows of the co-occurrence matrix, which is given by the function $f(x)$ as in Eq. 4.31.

$$f(x) = \sum_y \mathbf{N}_r(x, y) \tag{4.31}$$

Similarly, μ_y and σ_y are computed as mean and standard deviation of sum of columns of the co-occurrence matrix, which is given by the function $g(y)$ as in Eq. 4.32.

$$g(y) = \sum_x \mathbf{N}_r(x, y) \tag{4.32}$$

Laws' texture energy features

Laws' texture energy measures (LTEM) consider a set of nine 5×5 masks, which are used to compute the texture energy. In the base level, there are four 1-D FIR filters, which are given in Eq. 4.33

$$\text{L5 (Level): } \begin{bmatrix} 1 & 4 & 6 & 4 & 1 \end{bmatrix}^\top$$

$$\text{E5 (Edge): } \begin{bmatrix} -1 & -2 & 0 & 2 & 1 \end{bmatrix}^\top$$

$$\text{S5 (Spot): } \begin{bmatrix} -1 & 0 & 2 & 0 & -1 \end{bmatrix}^\top \tag{4.33}$$

$$\text{R5(Ripple): } \begin{bmatrix} 1 & -4 & 6 & -4 & 1 \end{bmatrix}^\top$$

An outer product of any pair of these 1-D filters results in a 2-D mask that is used in convolution operations.

For example, a 5×5 mask, E5L5 is computed as,

$$\text{E5} \cdot \text{L5}^\top = \begin{bmatrix} -1 \\ -2 \\ 0 \\ 2 \\ 1 \end{bmatrix} \begin{bmatrix} 1 & 4 & 6 & 4 & 1 \end{bmatrix} = \begin{bmatrix} -1 & -4 & -6 & -4 & -1 \\ -2 & -8 & -12 & -8 & -2 \\ 0 & 0 & 0 & 0 & 0 \\ 2 & 8 & 12 & 8 & 2 \\ 1 & 4 & 6 & 4 & 1 \end{bmatrix}.$$

Using all combinations of pairing these 1-D filters, 16 such 5×5 masks can be obtained. Among these 16 masks, some of them provide symmetric measures, like L5E5 and E5L5, etc. Such symmetric occurrences of the 1-D filters are combined by taking average of responses of two masks. There are 12 such masks that provide symmetric responses, which are combined to 6 masks. They are, L5E5 and E5L5, L5R5 and R5L5, E5S5 and S5E5, L5S5 and S5L5, E5R5 and R5E5, and S5R5 and R5S5. So, a resultant number of nine 5×5 masks are obtained, including S5S5, R5R5, and E5E5. A block diagram of computing Laws' texture

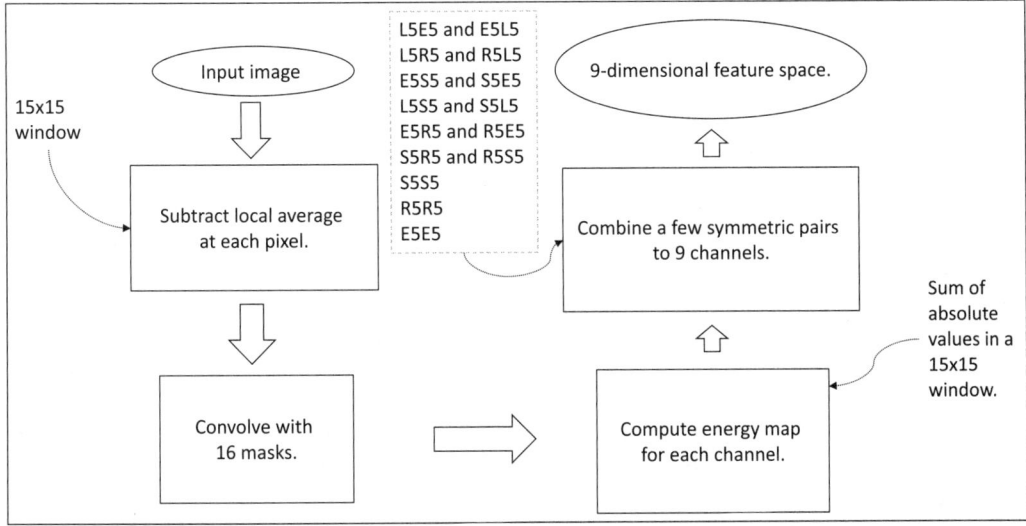

L5E5 and E5L5
L5R5 and R5L5
E5S5 and S5E5
L5S5 and S5L5
E5R5 and R5E5
S5R5 and R5S5
S5S5
R5R5
E5E5

Figure 4.20 A block diagram representation of computing Laws' texture energy.

energy from an input image in 9-D feature space is shown in Fig. 4.20. These measures represent the sum of absolute values in a 15×15 window. Texture descriptors have found profound uses in several applications, such as, detection of object patches represented by textured patterns, segmentation of images, classification and matching, etc.

4.4.3 | Global descriptors

There are also a few image descriptors that consider the entire visual content in the input image in the representation. Such descriptors are known as global descriptors. Two typical examples are, (1) bag of visual words, and (2) vector of locally aggregated descriptors.

Bag of visual words (BoVW)

The *bag of visual words (BoVW)* (Sivic et al., 2005) representation requires a library of images. The idea is to construct visual words from a set of images and then use those visual words as a dictionary to describe any image. The motivation of forming bag of visual words is to find whether the visual words are present in the image, and if present, then to what extent they occur. This information is represented by a feature vector. The analogy of this approach came from the domain of information retrieval; document retrieval in particular. Textual documents contain certain words, known as keywords, that play distinctive roles on the nature of the documents. A document can be represented by a feature vector, where the presence of such textual words are captured quantitatively. Similar concept is extended to describe the visual content of an image, which is the BoVW. But the problem here is, unlike documents, images do not have any precisely defined set of visual words. In document processing, the dictionaries are independently created by linguists, which are used to represent any document in terms of the words in the dictionary.

For images, the first task is to create a dictionary of visual words, which should be dependent on the visual content or local visual features in the library of images. This task is addressed by computing the key points in the images, since the key points play a very important role in defining transformation invariant features in an image. The key-point based feature descriptors are computed from all the images in the library. The descriptors of these key points are the possible candidates of visual words. Key points may be detected and their descriptors are computed using any robust technique, like SIFT, SURF, FAST, BRIEF, etc. These key points provide the locations or landmark regions in the images that may be invariant to certain kinds of transformations. The computed descriptors that describe the region around these key points also should have the property of certain transformational invariance. But there would be a wide variety of large number of descriptors from a library of images, and it is very difficult to represent an image with so much of variations. In order to get some representatives of these visual words, the key point descriptors have to be quantized.

For performing vector quantization, the visual words are clustered with similar descriptors, and each cluster is represented by a representative vector, which is usually the mean of the cluster. This task, which is performed in a vector space, is called *clustering*, where similar visual words or similar feature vectors are bucketized into a group and a representative is chosen from each group. There are different algorithms for clustering. For example, using the technique of K-means clustering (refer to Chapter 6), which partitions the descriptors into K sets. In K-means clustering technique, from a set of feature vectors, the mean of those feature vectors is chosen as the representative of that set. Here, the parameter K denotes the number of representatives to be chosen or the number of partitions to be created. Hence, K also denotes the number of visual words in the dictionary, which are used to describe an image. Likewise, the dimension of the BoVW feature descriptor is also determined by K, and it remains the same for describing every kind of image under consideration.

For any given image, the key points and their descriptors are computed using the same technique that is used to construct the dictionary of visual words. Then, the nearest visual word corresponding to the extracted feature descriptors is computed, and its description is associated with that word. The task is performed by simply counting the number of representative visual words and their number of occurrences in the given image. This is analogous to counting the number of keywords from a dictionary that occur in a document, and is represented as a frequency distribution of keywords. The feature vector is represented by a histogram or frequency distribution of the visual words in the visual dictionary. The number of bins in this histogram is fixed by the number K. This provides a K dimensional feature representation for an image, and this is called the *bag of visual words* (BoVW) representation of the image.

Vector of locally aggregated descriptors (VLAD)

Another global image descriptor, viz., *vector of locally aggregated descriptors* (VLAD) (Jégou et al., 2010), is an extension of the BoVW. However, the summarization of the visual content and the nature of description is a bit different from the BoVW. The first step of computing the VLAD is similar to the BoVW, where a code book of visual words is generated using a library of images. That is, from a set of images, key points are identified to extract feature descriptors, which are clustered by the K-means clustering technique to get a bag of K visual words that define the visual dictionary. Here, these representative visual words are denoted by K vectors (or codes) and the resulting set of codes is called the visual codebook. For example, the K vectors may be denoted by $\boldsymbol{C}_1$, $\boldsymbol{C}_2$, ..., $\boldsymbol{C}_K$. These codes are simply the cluster centers of dimension D, where D is the dimension of the feature descriptors. For example, the SIFT feature vector and the SURF feature vector have $D = 128$, and $D = 64$, respectively. Then, the feature vectors are subjected to aggregation operation with respect to the cluster centers. Consider a local descriptor $\boldsymbol{x}$ in an image, which is associated to one of the visual words. The difference of $\boldsymbol{x}$ with respect to corresponding cluster center is accumulated by a summation operation, which is given by Eq. 4.34

$$v_i = \sum_{\boldsymbol{x} \text{ assigned to } \boldsymbol{C}_i} (\boldsymbol{x} - \boldsymbol{C}_i) \tag{4.34}$$

where $\boldsymbol{C}_i$ is the ith cluster center. These accumulated differences are concatenated to form a vector $\boldsymbol{V} = [\boldsymbol{v}_1 \ \boldsymbol{v}_2 \ \cdots \ \boldsymbol{v}_K]$. The vector $\boldsymbol{x}$ is assigned to $\boldsymbol{C}_i$ if it is the closest cluster center to $\boldsymbol{x}$. That is, $d(\boldsymbol{x}, \boldsymbol{C}_i) \le d(\boldsymbol{x}, \boldsymbol{C}_j)$, where $i \ne j$ and $d(\cdot)$ denotes a distance function. So, if $\boldsymbol{x}$ is assigned to $\boldsymbol{C}_i$, the distances with all other cluster centers become either greater than or equal to $d(\boldsymbol{x}, \boldsymbol{C}_i)$. This process is known as aggregating the differences of $\boldsymbol{x}$ with respect to a cluster center $\boldsymbol{C}_i$.

Since the dimension of $\boldsymbol{v}_i$ is D and there are K cluster centers, the dimension of the concatenated feature vector, $\boldsymbol{V}$ is KD. The VLAD descriptor is the normalized vector of this representation of aggregated differences or concatenated aggregated differences, which is given by the operation, $\frac{\boldsymbol{V}}{\|\boldsymbol{V}\|}$. Here, it can be seen that the dimension of feature representation increases in the VLAD descriptor, in comparison with the BoVW. However, in reality, the value of K is kept so small in the VLAD representation, that its dimension remains comparable with a BoVW descriptor. The advantage of the VLAD representation is that the formation of dictionary is less computationally intensive with a small K. The VLAD descriptor is also found to be efficient in discriminating images.

Applications of global image descriptor

One of the important applications of global image descriptor is in the domain of the content based image retrieval (CBIR).[3] It is an image search operation based on visual content, where a query image is given to a search engine and it fetches the images from the repository that are similar to the query image. For this, the set of images in library need to be represented as descriptors and the query image is also converted to a descriptor. Then, the query descriptor is matched with the descriptors in code book and a few closest images are ranked and retrieved. The search is run through a curated dataset of images of heritage sites of India (Podder et al., 2018).[4] An example is shown in Fig. 4.21 (a), where the query image is a chariot from Vitthala temple in Hampi, India. The retrieved images also contain chariots of various kinds. Another example of image query is shown in Fig. 4.21 (b), which is an image from a temple in Bishnupur, India.

---

[3] Refer to Chapter 18.
[4] http://www.facweb.iitkgp.ac.in/~jay/ihird/index.html.

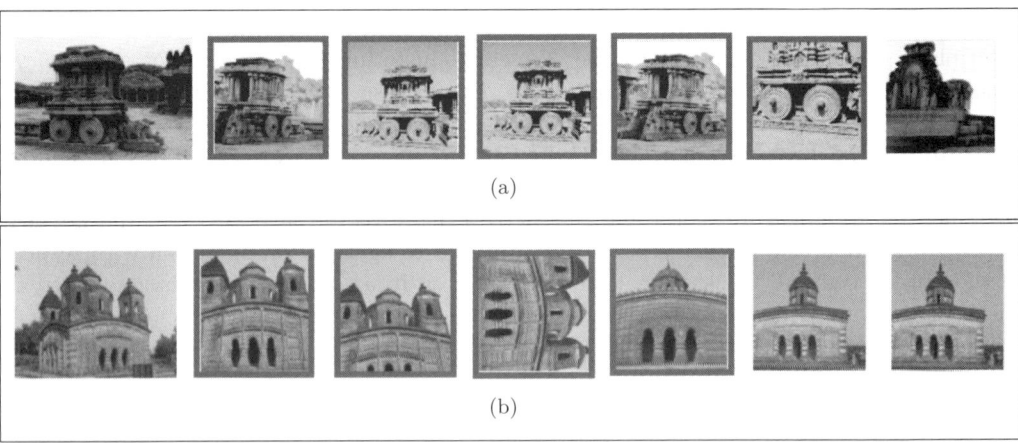

(a)

(b)

Figure 4.21 An example of image retrieval. (*Source*: Dipannita Podder, Indian Institute of Technology, Kharagpur, for sharing images from her thesis (Podder, 2018).)

4.5 | Feature matching and model fitting

Given multiple images of a 3-D scene, the extracted features from the images are matched appropriately to get pairs of corresponding points, which would then provide information about 3-D structures in the scene. A holistic view of a solution for a typical feature matching problem involves the following steps (refer to Chapters 10 and 12 for the details about these concepts.).

- Forming a set of corresponding points,
- Computation of fundamental matrix,
- Deriving the individual camera matrices, and
- Solving for 3-D coordinates of scene points for each pair of corresponding points.

For matching features to understand the 3-D structure in a scene, it requires a set of pairs of corresponding points, which may be provided either by visually selecting them or by using an automated process. The automated process is the sequence of key point detection and feature description techniques that are accomplished using the transformation invariant approaches, like SIFT detector, Harris corner detector, etc. For example, consider the Harris corner detector that computes the feature locations by finding out the local maxima from a set of corner points. This is performed on two views of the same scene that are acquired from different view points. When these detected points are described using some transformation invariant feature descriptor, it is expected that the change of view in the imaging does not significantly change the descriptors of the detected set of points. Then, the relation between these feature points from the two images are established to find a set of pair of correspondences between the two views. The relation is about determining if they belong to the same structure of the scene or not. By precisely locating the feature points, robust point

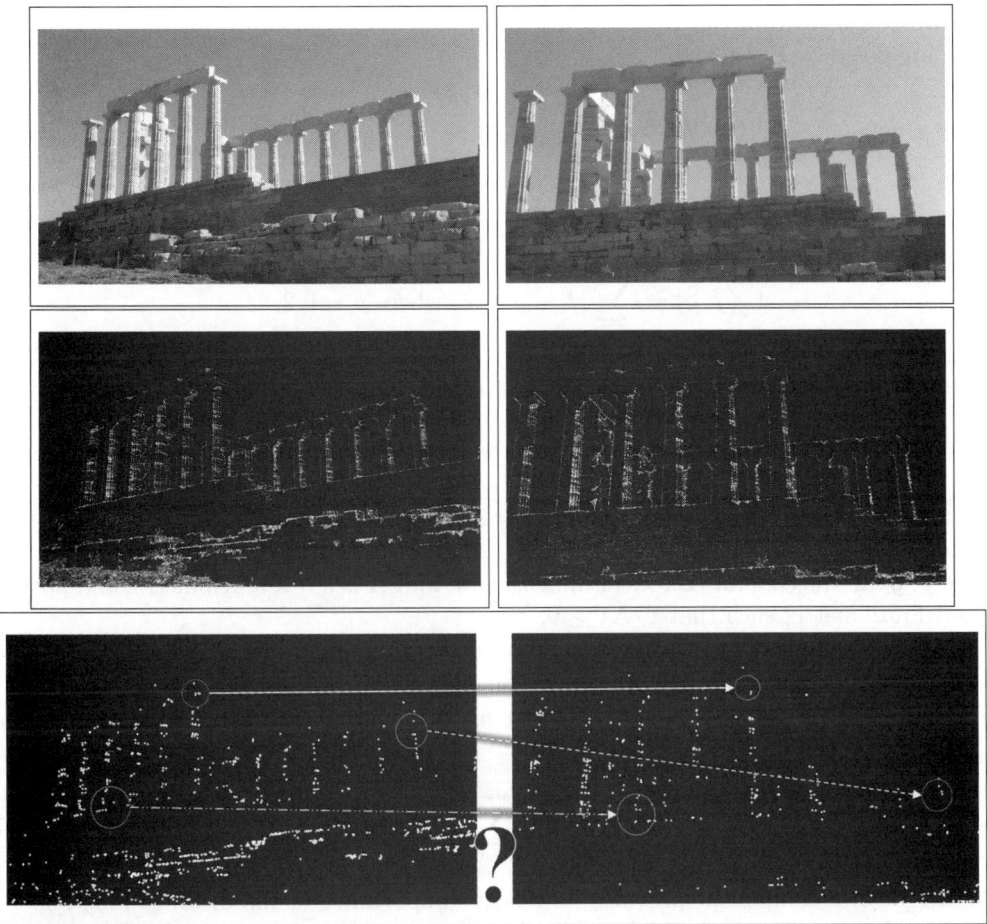

Figure 4.22 An example of feature matching between two images of the same scene.

correspondences are established. The computation that involves pairing these feature points or getting the pairs of corresponding points is known as *feature matching*. As a process, it is required to first find out the interesting points or key points in two images as features in scale and transformation invariant manner. Then, the features in both the images are matched to build correspondences. An example of feature matching task between two images of the same scene is illustrated in Fig. 4.22.

4.5.1 | Matching feature descriptors

In our context, a feature is described as a feature vector, $\boldsymbol{f} = [f_0, f_1, \ldots, f_{n-1}]^\top$. In our notation, it is a column vector. To define the proximity or distance between two feature vectors, some distance function is used. A few of the distance functions that are generally used are obtained from the L_1 norm, L_2 norm, and their generalization as the L_p norm, which are given by Eq. 4.35.

$$L_1(\boldsymbol{f}, \boldsymbol{g}) = \sum_{i=0}^{n-1} |f_i - g_i|$$

$$L_2(\boldsymbol{f}, \boldsymbol{g}) = \left(\sum_{i=0}^{n-1} |f_i - g_i|^2\right)^{\frac{1}{2}} \tag{4.35}$$

$$L_p(\boldsymbol{f}, \boldsymbol{g}) = \left(\sum_{i=0}^{n-1} |f_i - g_i|^p\right)^{\frac{1}{p}}, \text{ where } p = 1, 2, 3, ...$$

The above distance functions weigh all the vector components uniformly, irrespective of their importance. A weighted distance function is used to weigh the important and reliable components more than others. For example, a weighted distance function is given by Eq. 4.36

$$d_w(\boldsymbol{f}, \boldsymbol{g}) = \sqrt{(\boldsymbol{f} - \boldsymbol{g})^\top \mathbf{A}(\boldsymbol{f} - \boldsymbol{g})} \tag{4.36}$$

where $\boldsymbol{f}, \boldsymbol{g}$ are the column vectors of dimension n, and $\mathbf{A}$ is a $n \times n$ symmetric and positive semi-definite matrix such that $\boldsymbol{v}^\top \mathbf{A} \boldsymbol{v} \geq 0, \ \forall \boldsymbol{v}$.

A typical example of the matrix $\mathbf{A}$ is given by, $diag(w_0, w_2, ..., w_{n-1})$, where $w_i \geq 0$. This is a diagonal matrix where the diagonal element at i^{th} row and i^{th} column is given by w_{i-1} and all other elements are zero. Using this diagonal matrix, Eq. 4.36 is simplified as in Eq. 4.37.

$$d_w(\boldsymbol{f}, \boldsymbol{g}) = \sqrt{\sum_{i=0}^{n-1} w_i (f_i - g_i)^2} \tag{4.37}$$

The weight of a component provides its relative importance in the distance function. For example, the components may be weighted by inverse of their variances. In that case, the weights are given by, $w_i \propto \frac{1}{\sigma_i^2}$, where σ_i is the standard deviation of the ith component of the vectors. Intuitively, if a component of a vector has more variability, it is assigned lesser weight while defining the distance measure.

Using distance-based metrics, two feature vectors are identified as similar if the distance between them is small. There are also a few similarity measures to compare two feature vectors. The distance measure and similarity measure have an inverse relationship: the distance measures are smaller between a pair of similar features, whereas similarity measures are larger between them. Examples of similarity measures include the *normalized cross-correlation*, the *cosine similarity*, etc. The mathematical expressions for the normalized cross-correlation (ρ) is given by Eq. 4.38.

$$\begin{aligned} \rho(\boldsymbol{f}, \boldsymbol{g}) &= \frac{\text{cov}(\boldsymbol{f}, \boldsymbol{g})}{\text{std}(\boldsymbol{f}) \ \text{std}(\boldsymbol{g})} \\ &= \frac{\frac{1}{n} \sum_{i=0}^{n-1} (f_i - \bar{f})(g_i - \bar{g})}{\sqrt{\frac{1}{n} \sum_{i=0}^{n-1} (f_i - \bar{f})^2} \sqrt{\frac{1}{n} \sum_{i=0}^{n-1} (g_i - \bar{g})^2}} \end{aligned} \tag{4.38}$$

where $\text{cov}(\boldsymbol{f}, \boldsymbol{g})$ is the covariance of the two vectors, $\boldsymbol{f}$ and $\boldsymbol{g}$, and $\text{std}(\cdot)$ is the standard deviation of the respective components of a feature vector. $\bar{f}$ and $\bar{g}$ are their means. The value of ρ varies from -1 to 1. Highly similar vectors give a measure close to 1. The expression for cosine similarity is given by Eq. 4.39,

$$\text{Cosine similarity } = \frac{\boldsymbol{f} \cdot \boldsymbol{g}}{||\boldsymbol{f}|| \, ||\boldsymbol{g}||} \tag{4.39}$$

The cosine similarity value is close to 1 if the vectors are similar.

Numerical Example

Calculate cosine similarity between $[7, 8, 2]$ and $[3, 5, 1]$.

Solution

Cosine similarity between vectors a and b is $\frac{a \cdot b}{||a|| \, ||b||} = 0.984$.

Matching criteria

There are different matching criteria to establish point correspondences. In the distance based matching, smaller distances indicate better matching between the two given vectors. One of the ways of selecting distance based matches is to define a fixed threshold value on distances and report all the matches within that threshold distance. This policy is not only used to declare a pair of feature vectors similar, but it is also used to provide candidate feature vectors, given a reference feature vector. In that case, some post processing is required to select the fittest or the best matching feature vector corresponding to the query feature.

If a precise selection of the corresponding feature vector is required, the *nearest neighbor* (NN) definition is more useful, since there is no fixed hard threshold on distance values. Here, the feature vector nearest to the query vector is declared a match. However, by definition, the NN technique does not consider whether the distance between them is high thus often leading to a poor match between the two feature vectors. For example, consider a set of N feature vectors, $\mathbf{X} = [\boldsymbol{x}_1, \boldsymbol{x}_2, \ldots, \boldsymbol{x}_N]$ in one image, which are the candidate feature vectors to be matched with the feature vector $\boldsymbol{y}$ in another image. To find the nearest neighbor of $\boldsymbol{y}$, $\boldsymbol{x}^*$, the distances between each of the N feature vectors in $\mathbf{X}$ and $\boldsymbol{y}$ are computed and the feature corresponding to the smallest of them is selected as $\boldsymbol{x}^*$. But, it may happen that the distance between $\boldsymbol{x}^*$ and $\boldsymbol{y}$ is too high to declare it a close match of $\boldsymbol{y}$. Hence, another predetermined threshold value may be used to ensure that the distance of a matched pair remains small.

Another strategy, which is found to be more robust, uses the *nearest neighbor distance ratio* (NNDR). Here, the ratio of distances between the nearest neighbor and the second nearest neighbor is computed while matching the feature vectors. In this approach, it is judged whether $\boldsymbol{x}^*$ is distinctly nearest to $\boldsymbol{y}$. This means that the next neighbor of $\boldsymbol{y}$ in

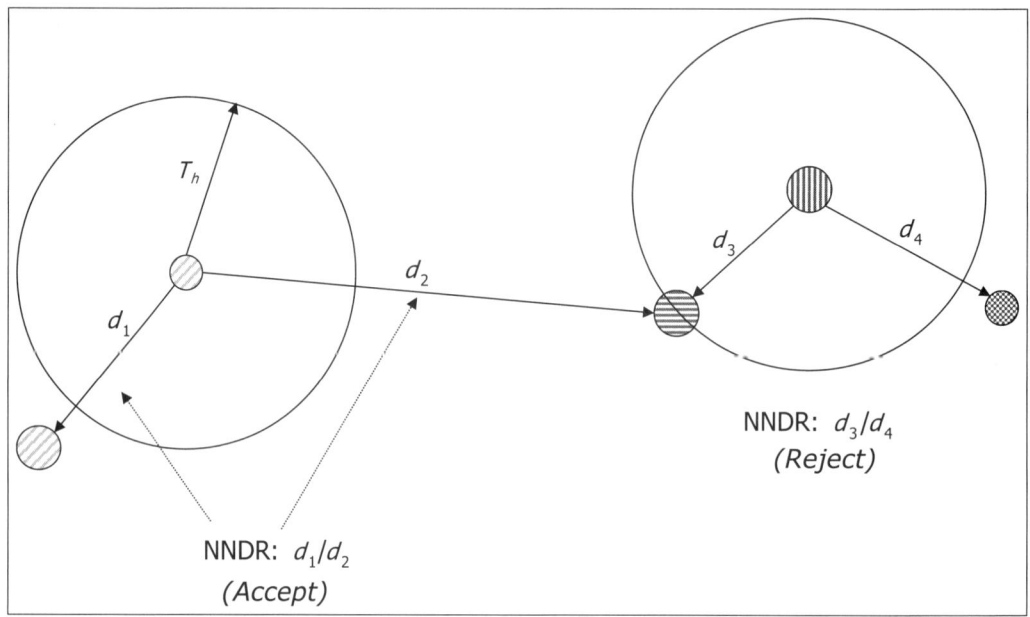

Figure 4.23 Illustration of nearest neighbor based matching strategies.

X is quite far away. To get a good matching point, it evaluates the ratio of the distance between the nearest neighbor and the second nearest neighbor. If the ratio is very small, x^* is accepted as a reliable matching vector with y.

As an example, consider Fig. 4.23, where similar feature vectors are identified by their patterns, depending on the ratio of distances between its first and second nearest neighbors. Here, the 2-D feature vectors (represented by balls with different patterns) that are actually closer in the space have the same pattern. In this 2-D space, if a threshold, T_h is used, all the feature vectors within a circular region around the query vector, a point denoted by the slant-striped ball within the circle, are searched. For an N-D space, the threshold defines a N-D hyper sphere around the query vector. In this example, since no features are present within the chosen threshold distance, use of a fixed threshold rejects a match. Using the nearest neighbor principle, its closest match is selected, which is the point denoted by another slant-striped ball outside the circle at a distance of $d_1 > T_h$. According to this particular configuration in the figure, this match corroborates with the ground truth as well. If the NNDR strategy is adopted, the ratio of the distances between the query point and the first nearest neighbor (point denoted by slant-striped ball outside the circle), and the query point and second nearest neighbor (point denoted by horizontal-striped ball), $\frac{d_1}{d_2}$ is found to be very small. So, the match is accepted in either cases of the NN technique.

Similarly, using the nearest neighbor principle to fetch the closest point to the point denoted by vertical-striped ball matches with the point denoted by the horizontal-striped ball at a distance of d_3. But, as per the ground truth, it is not the corresponding matching point, since they are shown with the different patterns. So, though it is the nearest neighbor, it should not be considered as a valid match. Here, the first nearest neighbor is the point denoted by the horizontal-striped ball and the second nearest neighbor is the point denoted by the checkered ball. Then the ratio of the distances between the query point and the first nearest neighbor, and the query point and second nearest neighbor, $\frac{d_3}{d_4}$ is found to be relatively higher. So, the match is rejected.

4.5.2 | Matching histograms

The key points are usually matched using the distance or similarity measures on the feature descriptors. If the images or regions of images are represented using histograms of certain measurable quantity, it is required to use histogram based measures. Histograms can also be considered as feature vectors, where each bin represents a component of that feature vector. The distance functions like L_1, L_2, and L_p norms can also be used for identifying feature similarities, as discussed earlier. However, as histogram depicts the frequency distribution of the entity and provides its probability distribution, it is more appropriate to use measures to reflect similarity or dissimilarity of these two distributions. One such measure is *Kullback-Leibler divergence* (KL-divergence) measure, which computes the dissimilarity between two given probability distributions, $P(x)$ and $Q(x)$, as expressed in Eq. 4.40,

$$\mathcal{D}_{\mathrm{KL}}(\boldsymbol{P}||\boldsymbol{Q}) = -\sum_x P(x) \ln\left(\frac{P(x)}{Q(x)}\right) \tag{4.40}$$

where $\boldsymbol{P}$ and $\boldsymbol{Q}$ are the histograms.

Another distance function for measuring histogram similarity is called *earth mover's distance* (EMD). Here, the idea is to measure the minimum accumulated cost of transferring masses from any bin of $\boldsymbol{P}$ to any bin of $\boldsymbol{Q}$, so that the histogram $\boldsymbol{P}$ gets transformed into histogram $\boldsymbol{Q}$. In a histogram, which is a frequency distribution of some quantity, every bin represents a certain amount of mass. If a portion of a mass in one bin of a histogram is transferred to another bin, the histogram gets transformed. Such transfer of mass has a cost. This cost is defined as the product of transferred mass and the distance between the involved bins. The cost of transferring mass m from i^{th} bin of $\boldsymbol{P}$ to j^{th} bin of $\boldsymbol{Q}$ is given as, $(|i - j|)m$. This results in the transformation of the histograms $\boldsymbol{P}$ and $\boldsymbol{Q}$ as, $\boldsymbol{P}[i] = \boldsymbol{P}[i] - m$ and $\boldsymbol{Q}[j] = \boldsymbol{Q}[j] + m$ In this context, the total mass of $\boldsymbol{P}$ and $\boldsymbol{Q}$ remains the same. By performing such transfer of masses, the histogram $\boldsymbol{P}$ is transformed to histogram $\boldsymbol{Q}$. As a measure, the accumulated cost for achieving the transformation of $\boldsymbol{P}$ to $\boldsymbol{Q}$ is normalized with respect to the total transfer of mass. The minimum cost required for the transformation is measured by the EMD. The naming of the EMD is due its similarity of transferring mass by digging earth from one place to another place, which are analogous to bins.

For computing the EMD, it is required to solve an optimization problem. Since the masses of two distributions should be the same, the first step is to normalize the two given histograms or distributions. The histograms are normalized such that their sum of areas is equal to 1. Let $\boldsymbol{P} = p_i$ and $\boldsymbol{Q} = q_i$, where $i = 0, 1, ..., N - 1$, represent two normalized histograms with N bins. Let m_{ij} be the mass transferred from i^{th} bin of $\boldsymbol{P}$ to j^{th} bin of $\boldsymbol{Q}$, and d_{ij} be the distance between the two involved bins. The minimum normalized work (transfer of masses) required for transforming the P into Q, EMD(P, Q), is given by, Eq. 4.41,

$$\text{EMD}(P, Q) = \min_{M = \{m_{ij}\}} \left(\frac{\sum_{i,j} m_{ij} d_{ij}}{\sum_{i,j} m_{ij}} \right) \tag{4.41}$$

$$m_{ij} \geq 0, \quad \sum_j m_{ij} \leq p_i, \quad \sum_i m_{ij} \leq q_j, \quad \text{and} \quad \sum_i \sum_j m_{ij} \leq min(\sum_i p_i, \sum_j q_j)$$

This is a constraint optimization problem where the numerator is the cost of transfer of mass m_{ij} from i^{th} bin of P to j^{th} bin of Q and the denominator is the total mass. The constraints specified in the form of several inequalities are explained below.

The constraint, $m_{ij} \geq 0$, indicate that every mass should be greater than or equal to 0. That is, if there is a transfer it has to be only a positive transfer.

The constraint, $\sum_j m_{ij} \leq p_i$, indicate that the transfer from i^{th} bin of P should not exceed the content of that bin. Thus, there is a capacity to the mass that can be transferred from a bin. If all the transfer of masses from i^{th} bin is accumulated, then it should not exceed the original mass of that bin in the histogram of P.

The constraint, $\sum_i m_{ij} \leq q_j$, indicate that the transfer to j^{th} bin of Q should not exceed the content of that bin. That is, there is a capacity to the mass that can be transferred to a bin.

The constraint, $\sum_i \sum_j m_{ij} \leq min(\sum_i p_i, \sum_j q_j)$ indicate that the overall transfer of masses should be less than or equal to total mass of the minimum of two histograms. There are efficient computations of $\mathcal{O}(N)$ time complexity to solve the above problem (Ling and Okada, 2007).

Numerical Example

Find KL distance between A and B with probability distribution $(0.2, 0.05, 0.6, 0.15)$ and $(0.3, 0.1, 0.4, 0.2)$, respectively.

Solution

$D_{KL}(P||Q) = -\sum_x P(x) \, ln(\frac{P(x)}{Q(x)}) = 0.0844.$

4.5.3 | Efficient search of neighbors in the feature space

As we see, that computing a close match of a given feature vector (query) among a set of candidates is equivalent to searching neighbors around the query point in the feature space. In a multidimensional feature space, this type of query is called *range query*, where, instead of finding a single feature vector, it results in a set of possible candidates in its proximity. Then, the retrieved vector against the query is obtained from this set which satisfies some criteria to declare it as the close match. A simple solution is to consider all the nearest neighbors of the query. Or, for a range query, all the features within a particular distance from the query may be reported. This process requires to compute the distances between a query vector and all the vectors in the candidate set. If there are N candidate feature vectors in the database, the distance with the query vector has to be computed N times. This makes the operation to have linear time complexity of order $\mathcal{O}(N)$. However, for performing this task efficiently, there exist various indexing and hashing techniques. In our discussion, we consider two such popular techniques, namely (i) K-D tree indexing technique, and (ii) locality sensitive hashing (LSH) technique.

4.5.4 | K-D tree indexing

In a K-D *tree*, the set of candidate vectors are indexed in an organized manner, so that the search time reduces to a sub-linear time complexity. The process of organizing the storage of data elements in an ordered form is known as *indexing*. In a K dimensional tree (K-D tree), K is the same as the dimension of feature vectors. For example, for a 2-D feature vector, it is a 2-D tree, for 3-D features, it is a 3-D tree, and so on. The K-D tree is an extended form of a binary search tree (BST). A BST operates on scalar data points. But a K-D tree is used for searching over multidimensional feature representations.

In a K-D tree, every node contains a key feature vector, instead of a single key value. Each node behaves like a node of a BST corresponding to the key value of a specific (say, i^{th}) dimension. The root of the tree starts with a predefined dimension, and also with any arbitrary element from the set of candidates. Along a path of a tree the dimensions (or ordinal position of the vector) attached to its nodes alternate one after another in a predetermined periodic order. The sequence of key values from the root to a node determines the partition of the feature space. The dimension based on which the partitioning takes place is called the *cut dimension*. Like a BST, the order of values of the tree structure is determined. When the feature vectors are considered, they are kept in a node, which appears in the search path along the tree following the same traversal rule.

NN search using a K-D tree

A K-D tree partitions the space and locates a query into a particular cell. As a strategy for the nearest neighbor search using a K-D tree, with respect to a query vector, the current smallest distance and its respective feature point should always be maintained. No sub-tree should be ignored while traversing a node for searching a key feature, unless all the key vectors within that sub-tree are at a distance greater than the minimum distance in the feature space. This is the reason the current smallest distance and the respective feature point to be maintained. Then, the sub-trees are pruned by comparing the minimum distance with the corner nodes of the hyper volume (or bounding boxes) represented by the sub-tree. Their corner points may also be considered to compare the distances. If the distances of all the corner points are greater than the minimum distance, searching of any key values in that region is avoided. While taking a decision to move to the next sub-tree, the sub-tree should be searched to maximize the chance of pruning. Thus, the sub-tree which is closer to the query has to be selected. Here, unlike a BST, no sub-tree is removed from the search space immediately. Also, in a K-D tree, unlike a BST, the decision to go either left or right is not taken at every node. Sub-trees are pruned only when all the corner points of the partitions covered by it are at a distance greater than the smallest distance observed till that stage.

Otherwise, it requires to traverse all the nodes of the tree. All the feature vectors in the remaining sub-trees are compared to obtain the neighboring vectors.

For the above process of walking through the tree nodes for NN search, the time complexity for the worst case is $\mathcal{O}(N)$. But, in practice, the complexity is close to: $\mathcal{O}(\log(N) + 2^d)$, where d is the dimension of the feature space. That is, $\log(N)$ to find the cell near the query point and 2^d to search along cells in the neighborhood.

Locality sensitive hashing (LSH)

For hashing multidimensional feature points, the *locality sensitive hashing* (LSH) technique (Andoni and Indyk, 2008) is widely used. In order to get the feature vectors within a certain locality of the query feature vector, the concept of geometric hashing is used. In general, hashing is a technique for simple matching of a random point using a function which has certain properties in generating a number or index. The data points which are hashed to the same number are kept in a linear order of their storage. We call the unit of such linear storage as a bucket. In the case of feature matching, a group with corresponding candidate set that are closely spaced in the feature space should ideally belong to the same bucket. If the candidate data point is close to the query and it is found in the same hashed bucket of the query, we call the event as the hit (success). If there is no point sufficiently close to it, it is considered that there is no such data point in the storage. However, the hashed index of a query may also miss the data point as it may belong to a different bucket. A good hashing function should have a high probability of a successful hit. One of the ways to increase probability is by using multiple hashing functions, and by considering each independently providing buckets for searching the data point within them. The LSH is an approach that ensures a high probability of placing closely spaced feature points in the same hashed bucket by exploiting geometry based computation of multiple hash functions.

A hash function of the LSH preserves the locality of feature vectors by placing feature vectors having low distances among them in the same bucket (i.e. by mapping to them to the same index of the bucket) with a high probability. Mathematically, it should satisfy the following property.

For a LSH function, $h(\cdot)$, the probability of $h(\boldsymbol{x}) = h(\boldsymbol{y})$ should be high, if $d(\boldsymbol{x}, \boldsymbol{y})$ is small, where $\boldsymbol{x}$ and $\boldsymbol{y}$ are feature vectors, and $d(\boldsymbol{x}, \boldsymbol{y})$ is the distance function. Otherwise, the probability should be small.

The above property ensures that the similar features stay in the same group and the distant features stay apart so that they are in different groups or bins or buckets.

As an example, consider the selection of a random unit vector $\boldsymbol{r}$ of dimension n (e.g., following Normal distribution ($\mathcal{N}(0, 1)$) independently in each dimension). For any vector $\boldsymbol{x}$ of dimension n, a hash function is defined using $\boldsymbol{r}$ as follows.

$$h_{\boldsymbol{r}}(\boldsymbol{x}) = \begin{cases} 1 & \text{if } \boldsymbol{x} \cdot \boldsymbol{r} > 0 \\ 0 & \text{otherwise} \end{cases} \tag{4.42}$$

The above is a two-valued hash function. It can be shown that (Tsai and Yang, 2014) for any $\boldsymbol{x}$ and $\boldsymbol{y}$, $P[h_r(\boldsymbol{x}) = h_r(\boldsymbol{y})] = 1 - \frac{\theta(\boldsymbol{x}, \boldsymbol{y})}{\pi}$, where $\theta(\boldsymbol{x}, \boldsymbol{y})$ is the angle between $\boldsymbol{x}$ and $\boldsymbol{y}$

in radians. This represents that the feature vectors are close to each other when the angle between them is small.

Using this property, a new scheme of multidimensional bucketing is designed by considering K random vectors. A set of K random vectors are used to generate K independent hash values. Then, a scheme of multidimensional bucketing is defined for the LSH to place the input vector $\boldsymbol{x}$, as shown below.

$$H(\boldsymbol{x}) = [h_{r1}(\boldsymbol{x}) \ \ h_{r2}(\boldsymbol{x}) \ \ \cdots \ \ h_{rK}(\boldsymbol{x})] \tag{4.43}$$

where, $h_{ri}(\cdot)$ is the ith hash value. Here, K such hash values are generated. Each hashing of a feature vector $\boldsymbol{x}$ gives a K-dimensional binary string, which is a multidimensional index of a bucket. If there are K hash values, there can be 2^K buckets. An input vector is placed in the same bucket that matches with the same binary string. Likewise, there may be L multiple buckets (corresponding to L sets of K random vectors) for the same input as $H_1(\boldsymbol{x})$, $H_2(\boldsymbol{x})$, ..., $H_L(\boldsymbol{x})$. Given a query $\boldsymbol{y}$, L bucket values are computed and the nearest neighbors are gathered from all of them. Since this is repeated L times, such multidimensional vectors are also generated L times. For a given query, the nearest neighbor is searched in all those buckets, increasing the probability of the success of the hashing scheme. This makes locality sensitive hashing more efficient and the chance of missing a nearest neighbor is reduced.

4.6 | Model fitting

In our context, given a set of feature points, and sometimes a set of corresponding pairs of feature points, deriving a mathematical model to establish the relationship among the data points is the computational problem of model fitting. Examples of such mathematical models include homography matrix, fundamental matrix, a polynomial function, etc. For example, a homography matrix represents the relationship between pixels in two images of the same scene point in a plane. A fundamental matrix depicts the relationship between corresponding points in two stereo images. Examples of model fitting also include fitting of a straight line, a parabolic curve, a circle, or a high degree polynomial curve among a set of points. Thus, to fit an appropriate model, it is necessary to obtain relevant data points. In images, these data points may be obtained using the pipeline of feature detection-description-matching, as discussed in previous sections of this chapter.

For model fitting, a prior knowledge of the mathematical form of the model is a necessity. For instance, the mathematical form of a homography is a 3×3 nonsingular matrix. The form of a fundamental matrix in a stereo geometry is a 3×3 singular matrix, which relates to the corresponding points and it is used while fitting a model. Similarly, a 3×4 projective matrix maps a 3-D scene point to an image point in the projective space or in the homogeneous coordinate systems.

The choice of a model is a very important factor that depends on the knowledge of a particular system or analysis of how the data are related. However, there are situations where it is not possible to precisely define a structure of a model. Precisely knowing the number of independent parameters for building a model is quite challenging. To ascertain if a chosen model is appropriate in data fitting, one of the measures that become useful, is the error of fitting. There are various kinds of errors that can be used. Consider a measurement,

y, a scalar quantity, that depends upon a feature vector, $\boldsymbol{x}$. That is, y is a function of $\boldsymbol{x}$. An appropriate choice of a model establishes a functional relationship between the feature vectors and their measurements. On applying the model over the data, predicted values are obtained corresponding to each observed value in the data. The error between observation and prediction may be simply defined as the average of squares of their differences, since the measured and observed values are scalars, in this case.[5] The mean squares error (MSE) is mathematically expressed in Eq. 4.44.

$$\text{MSE} = \frac{1}{N} \sum_{i=1}^{N} (y_i - y'_i)^2 \tag{4.44}$$

where, y_i and y'_i are the observed and predicted values, respectively. So one of the technique of model fitting is to choose that set of parameters of a model which minimizes the MSE.

There are also probabilistic approaches for fitting a model. The strength of a model can be evaluated by computing the likelihood of the data, given the model. The likelihood is the probability of occurrence of the data, given a model. Since this is a probability measure, it lies between 0 and 1. The model fitting is good if the probability is very high. That is, a probability value close to 1 indicates that the data fits to the model more appropriately. This measure can also be used to determine the goodness of fitting a model, when there are comparative models to consider. In situations requiring to apply intuitive or intelligent guesses about the form of a model, observing the error of fitting or likelihood of data based on a model becomes useful to decide if that model can be accepted or not.

Another important aspect of model fitting is the size of a model, which is determined by the number of independent parameters involved in the model. If there are more number of independent parameters, the size of the model is higher, and is considered to be more complex. So, it is critical to choose an appropriate size. A simple linear relationship between the components of a feature vector $\boldsymbol{x} = (x_1, x_2, \dots, x_n)$ with n components is expressed in a linear form as, $y = a_1 x_1 + a_2 x_2 + \dots + a_n x_n$, where a_is denote weights or parameters and y is the measurement. To establish if the parameters are independent or not, it requires deeper study and analysis of the relationship among the input and output, or analysis of the process by which the input data gets transformed into the output. If a nonlinear model is considered, there are coefficients or parameters relating to the nonlinear terms, which usually increase the size of the model compared to a linear model. In a way, the size also determines the complexity of a model.

For evaluating the performance of a model, there are two particular type of errors to be considered: (1) *training error*, and (2) *test error*. Fitting a model using a set of data is the training operation, and verifying the model with another set of data that is outside the training set is the testing operation. Even for the test set, the ground truth values are known, so that the predicted values are compared with them. The error associated with training process is called training error and the error associated with testing process is called test error. A model fitting is assessed by observing the amount of training and test errors. For example, if the training error is very large, the model is weak and does not explain the data properly. This is a case of *under fitting*, and it indicates that the number of parameters in

---

[5] This concept may also be extended to a vector. In the case of vectors, norm of the differences is considered for error computation.

the model should be increased. If the training error is reasonably small, but the test error is large, the model has become very specific to the training data. This is the case of *over fitting*, and most likely, there are too many parameters involved than required. In an ideal situation, both training error and test error should be small, which gives the confidence of having a good fit of model.

4.6.1 | Fitting straight lines

For illustrating various challenges and issues in model fitting, we discuss here the problem of fitting a straight line over a set of 2-D points under various contexts.

4.6.2 | Line fitting

Consider the data in the form of a set of n 2-D points, whose coordinates are denoted as (x_1, y_1), (x_2, y_2), ..., (x_n, y_n). The relationship between these coordinates, in the model, is given by an equation of a straight line, $y_i = mx_i + c$, where c is the intercept. In fact, the straight line is an affine relationship, and not strictly a linear relationship. However, colloquially, it is called a *linear model*. Then, the error of fit is expressed as given by Eq. 4.45.

$$E = \sum_{i=1}^{n} (y_i - mx_i - c)^2 \tag{4.45}$$

where (x_i, y_i) represents the data point coordinates with the line equation $y_i = mx_i + c$. The task is to optimize the parameters m and c in this case.

Consider the straight line representation shown in Fig. 4.24. Here, the deviations in y are measured by the vertical shifts or vertical differences, as seen in the figure. This is called vertical error, and the squares of these deviations gives the mean squares error. Since the mean squares vertical error is being minimized, it is called *vertical least squares*. The goal is to find a straight line with appropriate values of m and c, which minimizes the sum of squares of these errors.

The expression in Eq. 4.45 can be represented in a matrix form, as given in Eq. 4.46.

$$E = \sum_{i=1}^{n} \left(y_i - \begin{bmatrix} x_i & 1 \end{bmatrix} \begin{bmatrix} m \\ c \end{bmatrix} \right)^2 = \left\| \begin{bmatrix} y_1 \\ \vdots \\ y_n \end{bmatrix} - \begin{bmatrix} x_1 & 1 \\ \vdots & \vdots \\ x_n & 1 \end{bmatrix} \begin{bmatrix} m \\ c \end{bmatrix} \right\|^2 = \| \boldsymbol{Y} - \boldsymbol{X}\boldsymbol{C} \|^2 \tag{4.46}$$

where $\boldsymbol{Y} = \begin{bmatrix} y_1 \\ \vdots \\ y_n \end{bmatrix}$, $\boldsymbol{X} = \begin{bmatrix} x_1 & 1 \\ \vdots & \vdots \\ x_n & 1 \end{bmatrix}$, and $\boldsymbol{C} = \begin{bmatrix} m \\ c \end{bmatrix}$.

The Eq. 4.46 is rewritten as,

$$E = (\boldsymbol{Y} - \boldsymbol{X}\boldsymbol{C})^{\top}(\boldsymbol{Y} - \boldsymbol{X}\boldsymbol{C}) = \boldsymbol{Y}^{\top}\boldsymbol{Y} - 2(\boldsymbol{X}\boldsymbol{C})^{\top}\boldsymbol{Y} + (\boldsymbol{X}\boldsymbol{C})^{\top}(\boldsymbol{X}\boldsymbol{C}) \tag{4.47}$$

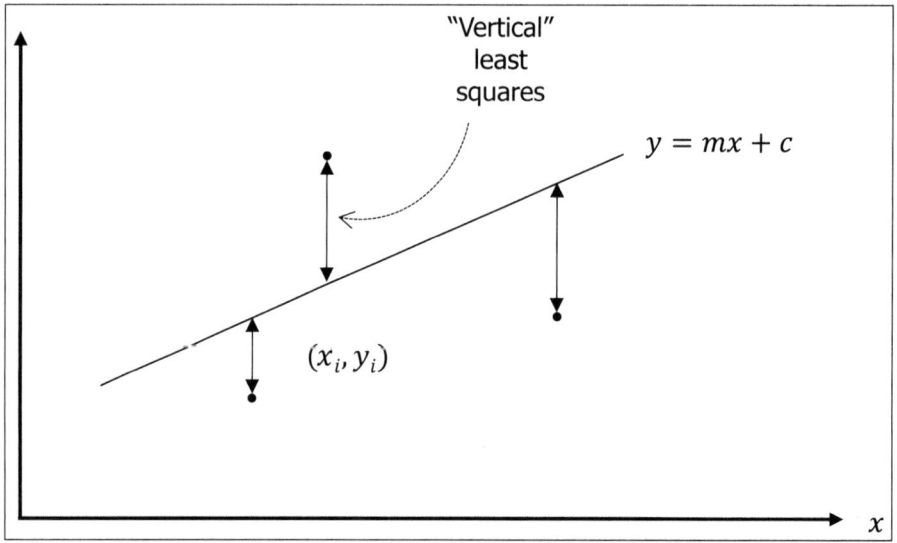

Figure 4.24 Vertical distances in straight line representation.

Taking derivatives of Eq. 4.47, i.e, independently taking derivative of E with respect to each component of C,

$$\frac{dE}{dC} = 2X^\top XC - 2X^\top Y = 0 \tag{4.48}$$

From Eq. 4.48, the solution to C is obtained as a pseudo inverse relationship, as given in Eq. 4.49.

$$C = (X^\top X)^{-1} X^\top Y \tag{4.49}$$

Fitting the model, $Y = XC$, solves for the parameters C, given Y and X, which is the result of minimization of the error E.

The relationship in Eq. 4.49 can be expanded in a more granular level of data elements to get the solution of m and c. An expression of m, as a ratio, is given as in Eq. 4.50.

$$m = \frac{\text{cov}(x,y)}{\text{var}(x)} = \frac{\frac{1}{n}\sum_i x_i y_i - \overline{xy}}{\frac{1}{n}\sum_i x_i^2 - \bar{x}^2} \tag{4.50}$$

where, $\bar{x}$ and $\bar{y}$ are the mean values of x_is and y_is, respectively. The $\text{cov}(x,y)$ denotes the covariance of x and y and $\text{var}(x)$ denotes the variance of x. Similarly, c is expressed as in Eq. 4.51.

$$c = \bar{y} - m\bar{x} \tag{4.51}$$

Using the expressions of m and c in Eq. 4.50 and 4.51, the error is expressed as in Eq. 4.52.

$$E = n(\text{var}(y) - m^2\text{var}(x)) \tag{4.52}$$

For this model fitting, a goodness of fit, R^2, is measured as in Eq. 4.53.

$$R^2 = 1 - \frac{\sum_{i=1}^{n}(y_i - \hat{y})^2}{\sum_{i=1}^{n}(y_i - \bar{y})^2} = 1 - \frac{E}{n \, \text{var}(y)} \tag{4.53}$$

where $\hat{y} = m \, x_i + c$. The value of R^2 lies between 0 and 1. A high value of R^2 (usually greater than 0.8) signifies a good model fit. This criterion compares the variability in the measurement that is not explained by the model to the total variability in the measurements. This goodness of fit, R^2, is also called the *coefficient of regression*. However, this approach of line fitting does not achieve rotational invariance. Also, it completely fails in the case of vertical lines, since the slope becomes infinite.

There is a technique which takes care of these situations. It is called the *total least squares*. Here, the distance between a point (x_i, y_i) and the line $px + qy = d$ is used for measuring error, which is expressed as, $|px_i + qy_i - d|$ given $p^2 + q^2 = 1$. Here, d is the length of the perpendicular drop from the point to the straight line, and is measured as the deviation of the point from the line, as shown in Fig. 4.25. In this case, for n points, the error term is given by Eq. 4.54.

$$E = \sum_{i=1}^{n}(px_i + qy_i - d)^2 \tag{4.54}$$

Since the vertical distances are to be minimized, the derivative of E is performed with respect to d, which is given by Eq. 4.55.

$$\frac{\partial E}{\partial d} = \sum_{i=1}^{n} -2(px_i + qy_i - d) = 0 \tag{4.55}$$

$$\implies d = p\bar{x} + q\bar{y}$$

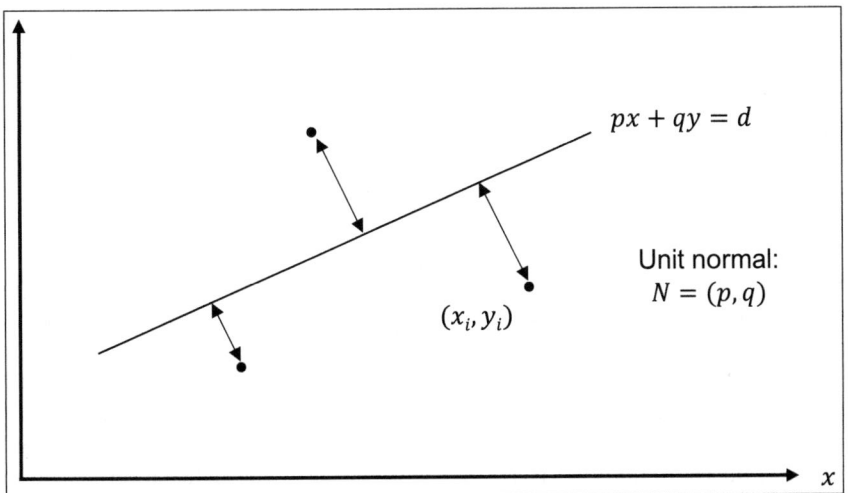

Figure 4.25 Vertical distance between a point and a line.

Using Eq. 4.55, Eq. 4.54 can be expressed as in Eq. 4.56.

$$E = \sum_{i=1}^{n}(p(x_i - x) + q(y_i - y))^2 \tag{4.56}$$

The choice of p and q is such that, it minimizes E under the constraint $p^2 + q^2 = 1$.

The expression of error term in Eq. 4.56 can be represented in matrix form as given in Eq. 4.57.

$$\left\| \begin{bmatrix} x_1 - \bar{x} & y_1 - \bar{y} \\ \vdots & \vdots \\ x_n - \bar{x} & y_n - \bar{y} \end{bmatrix} \begin{bmatrix} p \\ q \end{bmatrix} \right\|^2 = (\mathbf{UN})^{\top}(\mathbf{UN}) \tag{4.57}$$

where, $\mathbf{U} = \begin{bmatrix} x_1 - \bar{x} & y_1 - \bar{y} \\ \vdots & \vdots \\ x_n - \bar{x} & y_n - \bar{y} \end{bmatrix}$ and $\mathbf{N} = \begin{bmatrix} p \\ q \end{bmatrix}$.

Solving for this requires taking derivatives of E with respect to $\mathbf{N}$, subject to $||\mathbf{N}|| = 1$, which is given by Eq. 4.58.

$$\frac{dE}{d\mathbf{N}} = 2(\mathbf{U}^{\top}\mathbf{U})\mathbf{N} = 0 \tag{4.58}$$

The solution to this is the zero vector of $\mathbf{U}^{\top}\mathbf{U}$. There are several ways of computing this solution. One of the simple approaches is to compute the smallest eigenvalue and the corresponding eigen vector of the matrix $\mathbf{U}^{\top}\mathbf{U}$, which is a 2×2 symmetric matrix as given below.

$$\mathbf{U}^{\top}\mathbf{U} = \begin{bmatrix} \sum_{i=1}^{N}(x_i - \bar{x})^2 & \sum_{i=1}^{n}(x_i - \bar{x})(y_i - \bar{y}) \\ \sum_{i=1}^{n}(x_i - \bar{x})(y_i - \bar{y}) & \sum_{i=1}^{N}(y_i - \bar{y})^2 \end{bmatrix} \tag{4.59}$$

For a better understanding, consider Fig. 4.26, which provides a notion of geometry. As seen in the figure, the direction of the normal, $\mathbf{N}$, is perpendicular direction of the fitted line, $px + qy = d$. The parameter, d is interpreted as the perpendicular distance from the origin to that line.

4.6.3 | Random sample consensus (RANSAC)

Consider the problem of line fitting when there may be noisy data much deviated from the true line passing through these points. For fitting the data with a straight line in such a situation, the *random sample consensus* (RANSAC) technique (Fischler and Bolles, 1981) is more suitable. The approach provides a generic framework for model fitting in the presence of outliers. It can be used for computing homography matrix, fundamental matrix, or projection matrix, from their respective sets of corresponding points. In this technique, initially, a small subset of points is chosen uniformly at random. Then, a model is fit to this subset, and all the remaining points that are close to the fitted model are found. The points that are not close to the model are rejected as outliers. This process is repeated for a preset number of times and the best model among them is chosen.

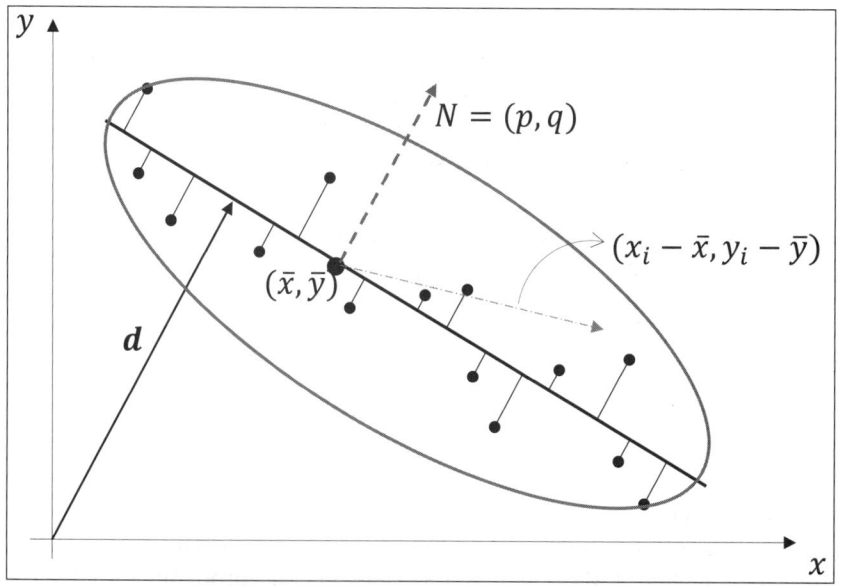

Figure 4.26 Geometric interpretation of line fitting.

Let us illustrate this approach for fitting a straight line among 2-D points. In this set, there may be a few outliers that deviate from the true straight line model fit on this set. Then the conventional least squares error method tries to minimize the error with respect to the outliers, which degrades the quality of the fit. To handle this situation, a set of reliable points called inlier points is first identified, and then model fitting is performed using only these points. The steps involved in RANSAC for solving the problem of fitting a straight line, given a set of points as input, is described in the following algorithm.

Algorithm 4 RANSAC algorithm for line fitting

   Input: A set of 2-D points, P.
   Output: A straight line fitted to the given set of points.
1: Select s points uniformly at random ($s < P$).
2: Fit a line using the least squares error method.
3: Find inliers to this line as the points whose distance from the line is less than the threshold, t.
4: For sufficient number of inliers, d, accept the line and refit using all inliers.
5: Repeat the above steps N times and choose the best model which has the least error of the fit.

There are a number of parameters involved in this process that affects the fitting of the model using the RANSAC technique. These parameters and their choices are as follows.

- Initial number of points, s: A small number of initial set of points is a good start. Typically, a minimum number of points needed to fit the model is chosen.
- Distance threshold, t: A threshold value is chosen such that the probability of the point becoming an inlier point, p, is high (e.g., 0.95). In practice, if the noise is observed to be zero-mean Gaussian noise with a standard deviation of σ, the threshold is set at $t = 1.96\sigma$.
- Number of trials, N: It is the number of iterations in the RANSAC process to obtain a good number of inliers for terminating the process. The value of N is usually chosen such that, with probability p, at least in one of the trials, random selections are free from any outlier. The degree of presence of outliers is given by the outlier ratio, e, which is the fraction of data that are outliers.
- Size of consensus set, d: It represents the number of points required to be declared as sufficient inliers for deciding about a model. This is expected to match the inlier ratio, $(1 - e)n$.

Here, one important issue is about the choice of the number of trials, N. A probabilistic analysis has been made to study the relation between N and the outlier ratio e, which is given by a plot in Fig. 4.27. It is deduced that, (1) the probability that all s samples are inliers is $(1 - e)^s$, (2) the probability that at least one sample is an outlier in a trial is $(1 - (1 - e)^s)$, and (3) the probability that all N trials have an outlier is $(1 - (1 - e)^s)^N$. So, given the probability p, probability of at least one random sample being free from outliers

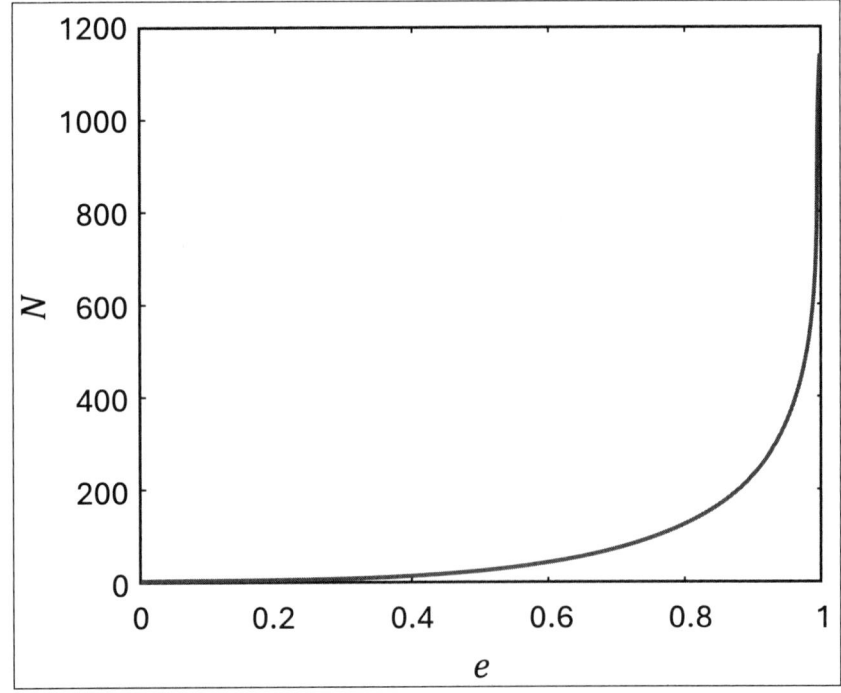

Figure 4.27 Relation between number of trials and outlier ratio.

is $(1 - p) = (1 - (1 - e)^s)^N$. By solving this equation, the expression for number of trials is computed as in Eq. 4.60.

$$N = \frac{log(1 - p)}{log(1 - (1 - e)^s)} \tag{4.60}$$

The advantages of the RANSAC technique are as follows.

(i) This technique is a simple and general approach to obtain reliable fitting of a model.

(ii) As an approach, it is applicable to many different problems of model fitting.

(iii) The RANSAC technique often works well in practice to get a model with least error of the fit, given a set of points.

It also suffers from a few limitations as listed below.

(i) The RANSAC technique has many parameters to tune, which may become tricky and nontrivial.

(ii) It may not always be possible to get a good initialization of the model based on the minimum number of samples.

(iii) In order to get a good number of inliers, too many iterations may be required in some cases.

(iv) This technique is not suitable if the ratio of inliers in the dataset is very low.

4.6.4 | Voting schemes

Given a set of data points, there are a few techniques of model fitting that are based on voting schemes. Particular to line fitting, these voting based approaches are more useful in cases where multiple straight lines are present. In a general approach of voting scheme, multiple instances of similar models are estimated from the data points. Then, the votes of each of the feature points compatible with these models are counted. It is assumed that, the noisy points do not vote consistently for any single model. Since the votes from reliable feature points are considered to be consistent, as an overall effect, the most voted model describing the given set of points is chosen. This method is also found to handle the missing data points. When some of the data points are missing, they do not contribute any vote to a model. But for a consistent model, votes are accumulated only from the available and reliable feature points.

This voting scheme can be realized using a technique called *Hough transform* (Duda and Hart, 1972). As a model is described by a set of parameters, every point in the parametric space represents an instance of a model. The approach involves accumulation of votes for all instances of fitted models on the given set of data points to get a distribution of votes in the parametric space. So, the parameter values where these votes are maximal are the possible descriptions of a model supported by these data points. In general, the following are the steps of Hough transform.

(i) Discretize parameter space into bins.

(ii) For each feature point in the image, put a vote in every bin in the parameter space that generates this point.

(iii) Find bins that have the most votes.

Consider this approach for the line fitting from a set of points, as shown in Fig. 4.28 (left). Evidently, a straight line passes through these points. In Hough transform, at every point, all possible straight lines that could pass through that point are computed. The parametric representation of a straight line is given using m (slope) and b (intercept), where a line is described as $y = mx + b$. In the parametric space of straight line representation, each pair of m and b that describe a straight line at any point, are recorded in a discrete grid, as shown in Fig. 4.28 (right). So, every combination of (m, b) is a cell in the parametric space, and a grid of these cells accumulates the votes for all possible combinations of (m, b) that provide straight lines. This grid provides a distribution of votes in the parametric space. The cells corresponding to the values of parameters with higher number of votes provide the possible descriptions of models through these data points.

Given a straight line, $y = m_1 x + b_1$, in an image, it is represented in the Hough space as a point, (m_1, b_1), as shown in Fig. 4.29. A family of combinations of (x, y) gives all the lines that correspond to a particular (m_1, b_1). Similarly, in the parametric form of representation, a point in the image corresponds to a line in the Hough space, as shown in Fig. 4.30. In the Hough space, an equation of a straight line with parameters of m and b is represented as $b = -x_1 m + y_1$, where (x_1, y_1) is a point in the image space. In fact, all possible (m, b) lying in the straight line represent all lines passing through (x_1, y_1).

Two points in the image space entail two lines in the Hough space. Thus, the line joining these two points in the image space is given by the intersecting point of the two lines in the Hough space, as shown in Fig. 4.31. In the grid of parametric space, if votes are collected at every cell of parameter combinations, (m, b), the votes in the cell corresponding to this point of intersection of two lines will have a higher count than in other cells. So, this point in the parametric space, denoted by the cell with highest votes, is chosen as a solution or final model. This is the principle behind the model fitting using the Hough transform.

However, for fitting a straight line, there remain two main issues with its parametric space representation. First, it is based on discretizing the space of m and b, but the ranges of values of m and b are not bounded. The second issue is the case of vertical lines, which requires representation of the infinite slope (m), in the parametric space. Toward this,

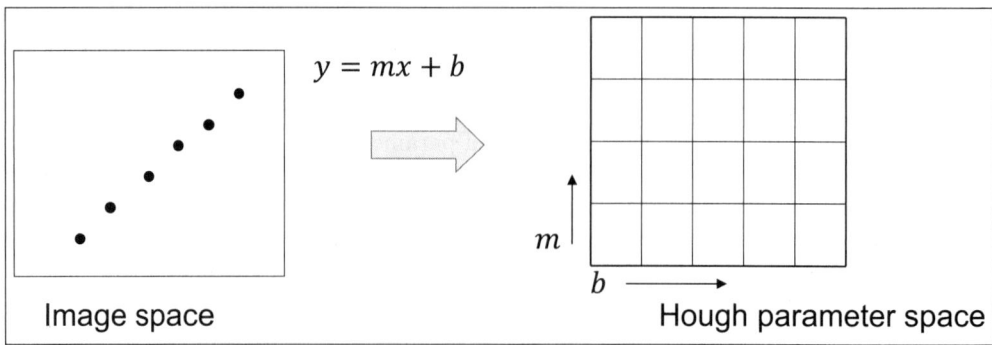

Figure 4.28 Discretization of parametric space in Hough transform.

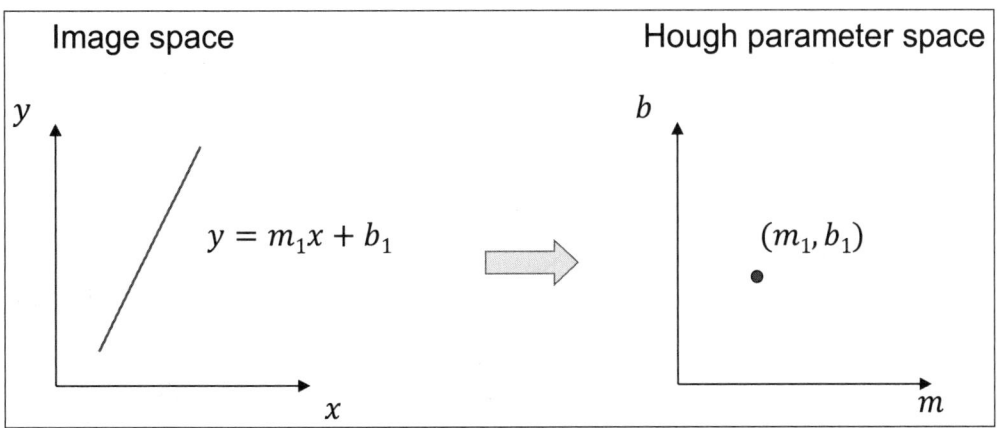

Figure 4.29 Parametric representation of a line in an image, in Hough transform space.

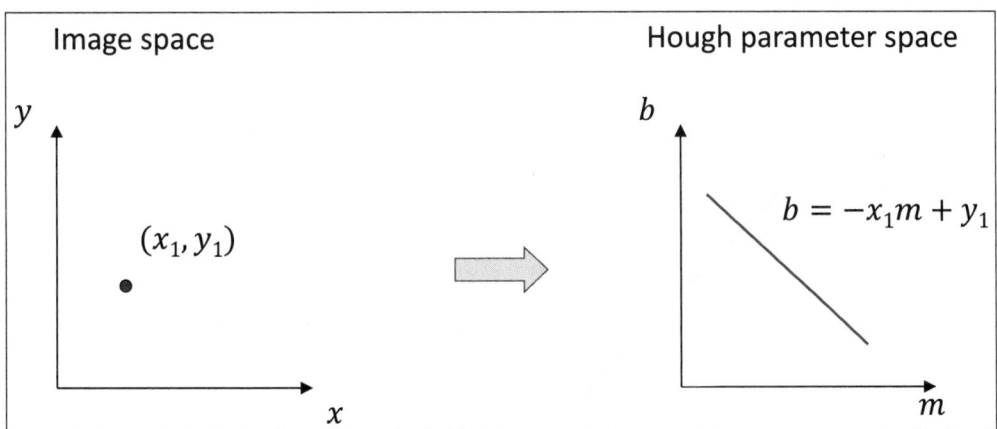

Figure 4.30 Parametric representation of a point in an image, in Hough transform space.

there are other representations of straight lines that are more convenient to handle these cases, like polar representation. The polar representation of a straight line is given by Eq. 4.61.

$$x \cos(\theta) + y \sin(\theta) = \rho \qquad (4.61)$$

where ρ is the perpendicular distance from the origin to the straight line and θ is the angle of the perpendicular from the origin to the straight line with the x-axis, as shown in Fig. 4.32. So, in the polar representation, the parameters are (ρ, θ), instead of (m, b). As an advantage of this representation, the ranges of ρ and θ span a finite range. The value of ρ varies from 0 to the length of the diagonal of the image grid and the value of θ varies from $0°$ to $180°$.

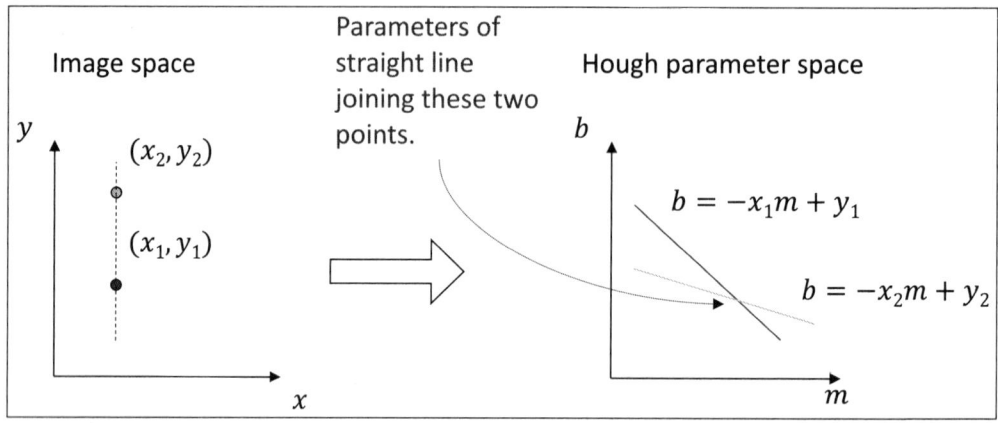

Figure 4.31 Representation of a line joining two points in image space as point of intersection of two lines in Hough transform space.

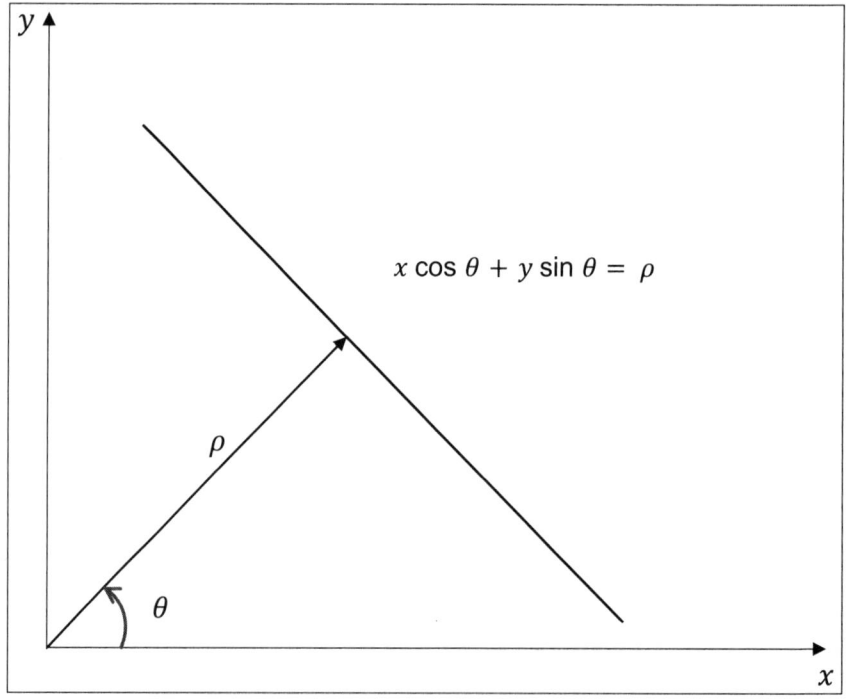

Figure 4.32 Polar space representation of a straight line.

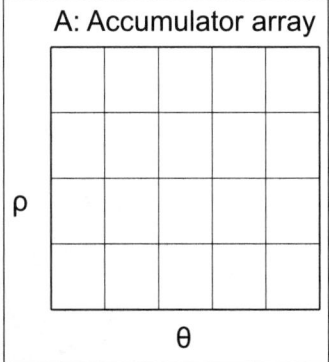

Figure 4.33 Accumulator array in the polar parametric space.

Due to the finite ranges, discretization becomes more convenient to design an algorithm. An algorithm of the Hough transform for line fitting in the polar representation is given in Algorithm 5.

Algorithm 5 Hough transform for line fitting

    Input: An image with at least one straight line.
    Output: A model of the detected line in the image in polar representation.
1: Initialize accumulator $\mathbf{A}$ to all zeros (discretized parametric space in polar form, as in Fig. 4.33).
2: For each edge point (x, y) in the image, do,
3:     For $\theta = 0°$ to $180°$, do,
4:         Compute, $\rho = x \cos(\theta) + y \sin(\theta)$.
5:         Accumulate, $\mathbf{A}(\theta, \rho) = \mathbf{A}(\theta, \rho) + 1$.
6: Find the value/values of (θ^*, ρ^*), where $\mathbf{A}(\theta^*, \rho^*)$ is a local maximum.
7: Detect the line in the image as $\rho^* = x \cos(\theta^*) + y \sin(\theta^*)$.

A basic illustration of the voting scheme in the Hough transform is shown in Fig. 4.34. The image in the left is a very precise straight line that passes through all the given set of points. As an implication, only one point may be seen with high illumination in the right image presenting visualization of votes. Here, the brightness values show the amount of voting. Since there is a single line, a very short peak is seen in the parametric space of Hough transform, as expected. In a complex image (for example, an image with complex structures), where there are multiple lines, each line results in a local maxima, as shown in Fig. 4.35. As a result, there may be multiple peaks due to multiple votings from the points lying on each of the straight lines. As an example, one of the lines is shown on the image by a white dotted line in Fig. 4.35, which corresponds to one of the local maxima.

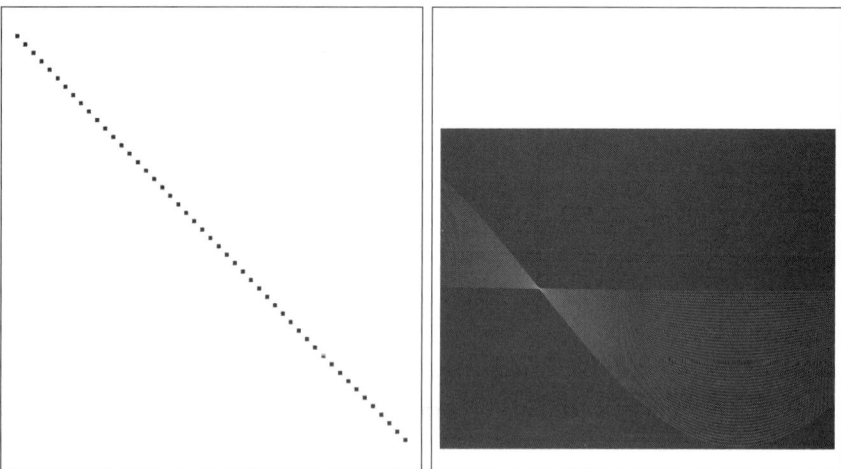

Figure 4.34 Illustration of the Hough transform voting scheme for a straight line. (a) Features, and (b) votes.

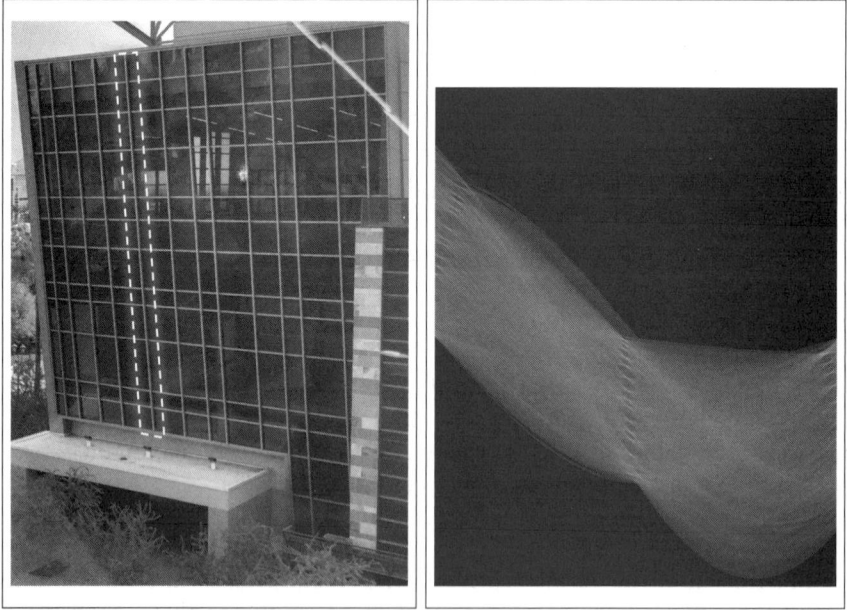

Figure 4.35 Illustration of the Hough transform voting scheme for multiple lines in an image. (a) Input image, and (b) votes.

If the data points representing the line are noisy, the sharpness or preciseness of the support region of the corresponding local peak would be lost, causing a blurred peak region in the Hough space, as shown in Fig. 4.36. Dealing with noise requires an appropriate resolution of discretization of the grid in the parametric space. If the resolution is too

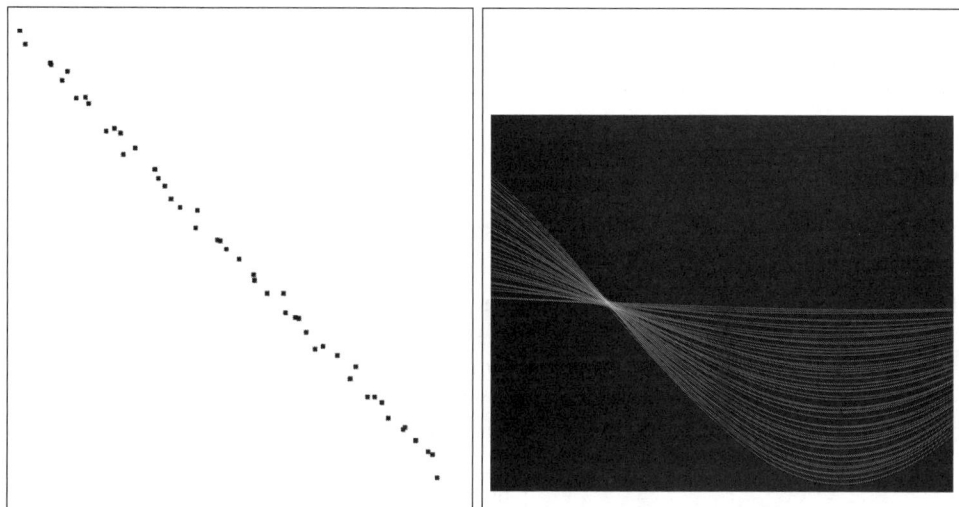

Figure 4.36 Illustration of Hough transform voting scheme for a straight line in noisy image. (a) Input image, and (b) votes.

coarse, large votes in a cell are accumulated due to multiple lines corresponding to a single bucket. If the resolution is too fine, some lines may be missed due to a few data points that are not exactly collinear and voted into different buckets. To address this, it is necessary to have an appropriate choice of resolution. Also, the accumulator array should be smoothened to reduce the effect of rippling of local maxima. Getting rid of irrelevant features also helps in better handling of noise, which is done by considering only edge points with significant gradient magnitude for fitting.

Summary

In various applications of computer vision such as image registration, object recognition, understanding 3-D structure of a scene etc., feature detection, representation, and matching with a candidate feature point are identified as key tasks. There exist several techniques for detection and representation of a feature point such as Harris corner detection, SIFT, SURF, FAST, BRIEF, etc. There exist also descriptors of image patches and regions such as HOG, and texture descriptors as well as global image descriptors such as BoVW, VLAD, etc. For matching a pair of feature vectors, distance functions such as L_1 and L_2 norms, and similarity measures such as correlation coefficient, cosine similarity, etc. are used. For reducing the time of search among a candidate set, geometric indexing and hashing schemes such as K-D tree and LSH are used.

The feature points are also used to study the geometry and establish relationships among them. The task involved in this process is fitting models describing the relationship among the data points, such as fitting geometric curves, estimating transformation matrices, etc. Least squares error (LSE) techniques are used for deriving mathematical functions describing such relationships. There exist also various strategies to take care of outliers and noisy data. The RANSAC is one such technique. Hough transforms are also used for making the estimation robust and fitting multiple models jointly by identifying the subsets of data points supporting them.

Exercises

(i) Given two features each of dimension 4 as $f = (4, 1, 2, 4)$ and $g = (9, 1, 2, 2)$. Compute L_1 and L_2 norms between f and g, respectively.

(ii) Consider the following 3×3 patch in an image centered around a pixel with the intensity value 60. If a LBP is formed starting at the pixel in the south-east location valued 75 with clockwise traversal, what would be the decimal value of the binary pattern? Assume the bit value to be 0 when the intensity of the pixel being compared is less than the intensity of the central pixel, otherwise it is 1.

56	66	65
50	60	70
62	60	75

(iii) Given two feature vectors $f = (1, 2, -1, -2)$ and $g = (1, -1, 1, -1)$ in R^4, compute L_3 norm of their difference vector.

(iv) Consider the *random sample consensus* (RANSAC) algorithm for fitting a model. It is an iterative trial and error method to select a good set of data points by keeping aside outliers in the given set of input data. Suppose there are N data points, with estimated m fraction of them are outliers or noisy. Consider s is the number of data points chosen to fit a model initially, and there are at most k trials.

  (a) What is the probability that none of chosen s samples is an outlier?

  (b) What is the probability that none of the k trials is free from an outlier?

  (c) What is the expected number of inliers in the data set?

(v) Using Random Sample Consensus, compute the number of trials (N) required which gives a 99% gurantee of getting a pure inlier sample provided the minimal sample size $s = 2$, total number of points $n = 12$.

(vi) If an octave in SIFT operator has 12 images, then determine the scale factor by which each image in octave differs from the next image.

(vii) Assume that we are fitting a circle to a set of points using RANSAC. Consider that 20% of the points are outliers, then how many random samples (N) of 5 points are needed to detect the circle with 85% probability. Answer by rounding it to the closest integer.

(viii) Write the mathematical expression of the operator used for detecting key points of SIFT descriptor. On which criteria a key point is chosen?

(ix) Define Hessian matrix for a 2-D function and how it is used in choosing robust key points.

(x) How does the SIFT descriptor maintain rotation and scale invariance?

(xi) Explain how the scale variation is handled in the following feature descriptors.

    (a) SIFT

    (b) SURF

    (c) ORB

    (d) HOG

(xii) Define integral image of a 2-D digital image. Show how it could be used for computing the response of a box filter.

(xiii) Write the RANSAC algorithm for fitting a straight line on a set of 2-D points. Given the fraction of outlier points in the dataset 0.2, what would be the number of trials to guarantee that at least one of them will provide the seed points free from outliers with probability 0.95 with the minimum number of seed points required to get a model?

5

Visual Saliency and Cognitive Processing

In images, some objects in the visual scene stand out from their neighboring or other regions grabbing immediate attention of a human observer. Those objects are called *visually salient objects*. The distinct perceptual quality of these objects compared to other objects in the scene is called *visual saliency*. This quality is attributed to the behavior of an observer, and hence it is subjective. The mechanism by which the visually salient objects are selected is called *visual attention*. It is a key perceptual function in human visual system (HVS) for processing information from complex natural scenes (Pinker, 1986). The visual attention mechanism extracts essential features from redundant data aiding the information processing in human brain. Our nervous system has a limited ability for simultaneous processing of all the incoming sensory information. The attention mechanism thus accelerates this processing by selecting and modulating the most relevant information. There exist multiple perceptive and cognitive operations under a hierarchical control process to establish global priorities to highlight some locations, objects or features in the visual field. A powerful approach to study visual saliency is to analyze eye gaze data of a viewer of a given scene, as the visual saliency is associated with its corresponding gaze information of human beings. In this chapter we develop an understanding of visual attention, saliency and cognitive processing in the HVS.

5.1 | Visual cognition

The way an individual acquires and processes the visual information is called *visual cognition*. It involves interpretation of visual sensation and identification of object, such as, recognition of face, scene and object, visual attention and search, recognition of visual words and reading, control of eye movement and active vision, short-term and long-term visual memory, visual imagery, etc.

To understand the kind of processing that takes place in the visual cognition system of the human body, consider the schematic diagram of the human visual pathway shown in Fig. 5.1. The human visual sensory organs are the two eyes, through which the visual

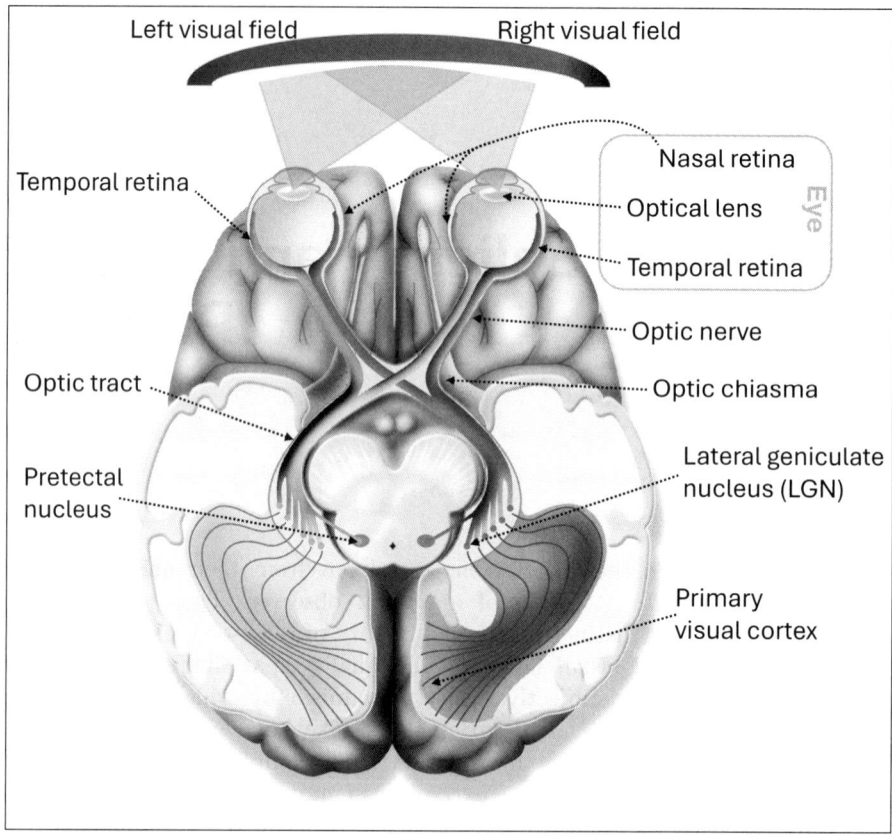

Left visual field · Right visual field

Temporal retina

Nasal retina

Optical lens

Temporal retina

Eye

Optic nerve

Optic chiasma

Optic tract

Pretectal nucleus

Lateral geniculate nucleus (LGN)

Primary visual cortex

Figure 5.1 Representation of human visual pathway. (Courtesy: Getty Images/BSIP/Contributor.) See Color Plates (page 817).

information from the external world enters a particular region of the brain, known as *visual cortex*, that is at the rear portion of the brain. The optical signal received by each of the eyes is incident on the respective retina, which is then carried by two different tracks in each eye. A part of the information on the retina of the left eye is processed in the right side of it, and the other part is processed in the left side of it. Similarly, a part of the information in the right eye is processed in the left side of it, and the other part is processed in the right side of it. Thus, the visual sensation is processed by two parallel pathways in the brain, which occurs in both the sides of the brain corresponding to left and right eyes. There are also other smaller pathways that exist in the visual system at other portions of the brain, like the pathway to the *superior colliculus*. These pathways that carry visual information are called *optical nerves*. The tract that surround the optical nerves in called *optic tract*. The optical nerves from the left and the right eyes cross each other at a particular point known as *optic chiasma*. The information through the optical nerves are processed in an intermediate processing center, known as *lateral geniculate nucleus* (LGN), before the visual cortex.

5.1.1 | Visual attention

Visual attention is the result of a set of cognitive operations that processes the information from the visual stimuli. A selective visual attention enables selection and filtering of various attributes while processing the visual information in the scene. It directs the gaze rapidly toward objects of interest in the visual environment, which provides the ability to orientate rapidly toward salient objects in a cluttered visual scene. That is, among a wide variety of information that are available from the environment, the focus of attention of human vision is restricted to certain zones of regions.

To interpret the visual attention, a two component framework is used, which is shown in Fig. 5.2. Here, primarily, two tasks are involved when the selective visual attention process takes place. The first stage is called *pre-attentive stage*, where the processed information from the activities of human sensory organs and their corresponding cells on the optical pathway are carried to the brain. The second stage is called *focused attention stage*, where the brain gives a feedback or control signal to the organs that control the visual process, which facilitates to make eye movements for shifting the attention. The pre-attentive stage uses bottom-up image-based saliency cues, which is driven by the physiological process. The focused attention stage uses top-down task-dependent cues, which is responsible for shifting of attention, movements of eyes, perception of various objects in the scene and their relationships, etc.

Visual saliency is a kind of highlight of certain information on the retinal map that correspond to the zones where the visual tasks are more oriented. A visually salient region in a scene automatically attracts the viewer due to the reflex action of human senses. Visual attention to salient regions in a scene is driven in a top-down manner. *Bottom-up* and *top-down* approaches are the two different ways of processing a stimuli. In bottom-up approach, the stimulus from the scene drives the perception, without involvement of any cognitive process. Whereas in a top-down approach, the cognitive processing in brain and the preconceived knowledge drives the visual phenomenon to interpret the scene. The bottom-up processing, involving visual saliency, is a pre-attentive processing that operates rapidly (around 25 to 50 millisecond per item) across the entire visual field. This involves processing huge information, which are taken care of by different cells and pathways that act in parallel to process them and highlight the respective salient regions. The formation of saliency maps is independent of the nature of the task. In contrast, selective attention is task oriented, which is controlled by voluntary mechanisms in the brain for directing the attention. Selective attention is a top-down process, which makes it comparatively slow

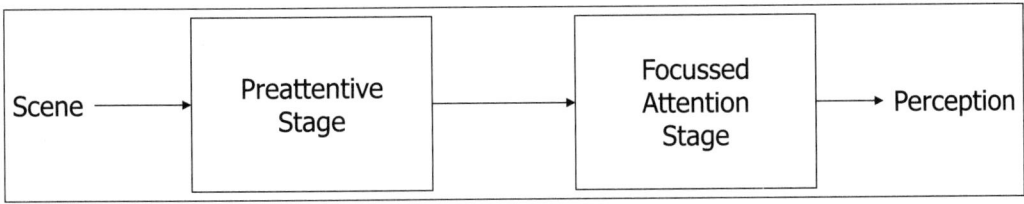

Figure 5.2 Block diagram of the two component framework for visual attention interpretation.

(greater than 200 millisecond per item). Also, it allows only a small part of the incoming sensory information to reach short-term memory. Unlike saliency, selective attention is processed sequentially. In this process, the salient regions are processed and interpreted sequentially in the order of their importance.

5.1.2 | Neuronal mechanisms for the control of attention

To understand the neuronal mechanisms that control the visual attention, consider the block diagram shown in Fig. 5.3 (Itti and Koch, 2001). As shown in the figure, the visual information is processed through two parallel streams. Different segments of human brain and their associated actions or tasks that are processed in the respective areas are shown in the sketch of fronto-parallel position of the brain in Fig. 5.4. At a very high level, as shown in the figure, there are four primary segments in the human brain: *occipital, parietal, frontal,* and *temporal* segments. The optical nerve carries the stimuli from the visual cortex

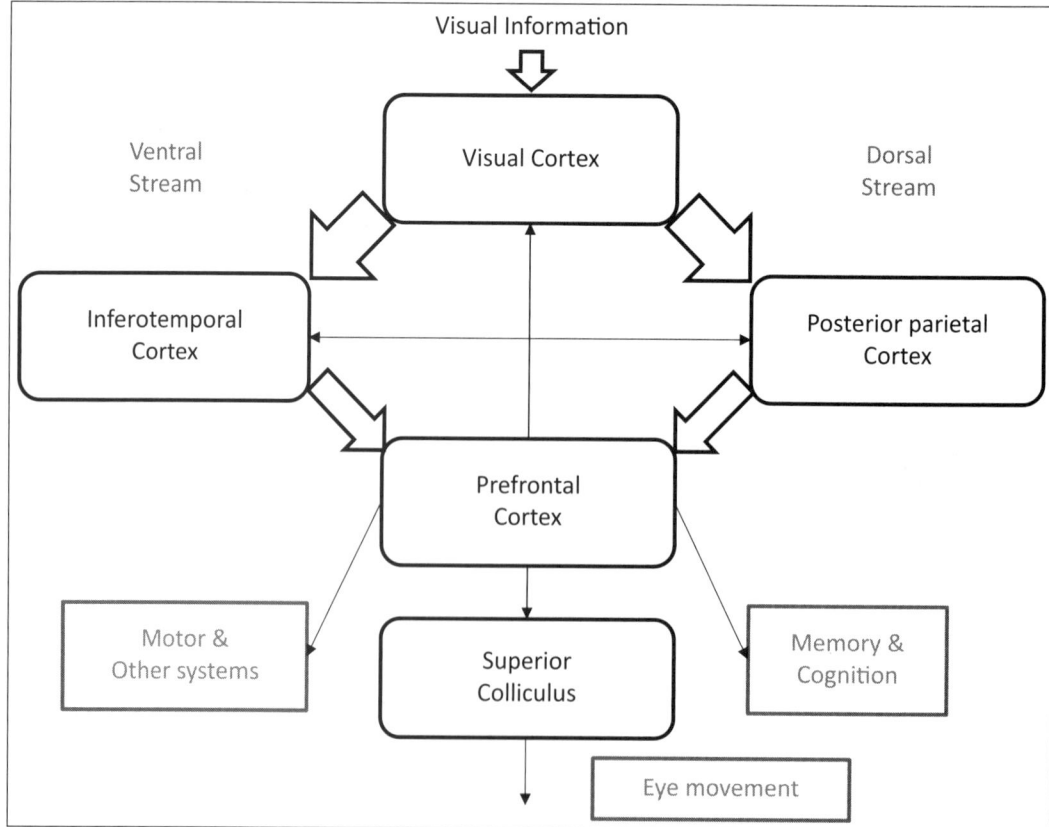

Figure 5.3 Block diagram of processes that control the attention.

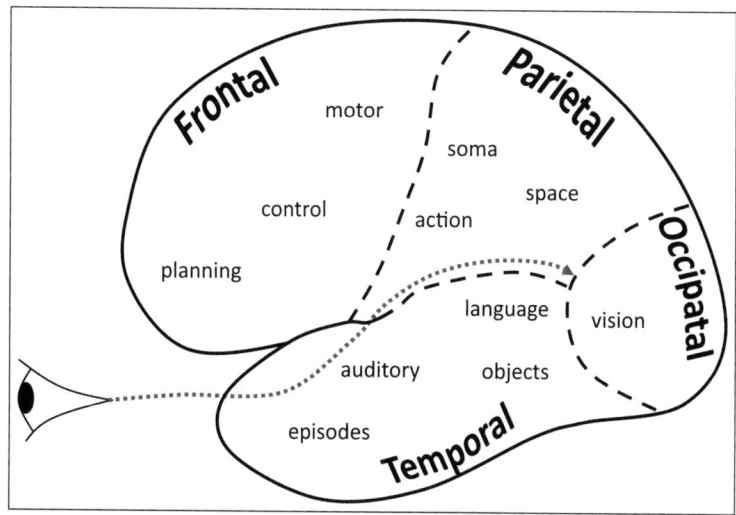

Figure 5.4 Different segments of human brain and their associated processing tasks in visual cognition.

in the optical retina of the eye to the location of the *occipital cortex*, which is responsible for processing the information for vision. Then, this processed information progress through two parallel streams, known as *ventral stream* and *dorsal stream*. In the ventral stream, the information is further processed by *inferotemporal cortex*, where detection and recognition of objects take place. In the dorsal stream, the information is processed by *posterior parietal cortex*, where space (or location information) and action are understood. The two processed streams are then carried through the *prefrontal cortex*, which processes to infer actions on motor, planning, control, memory and cognition. The *superior colliculus* in the frontal location of the brain is driven by this processed information to control the eye movements. This roughly depicts the information pathway and the processing pathway in the human brain. Several computational models that try to mimic the respective biological system and biological processes, are based on the understanding of these neuronal mechanisms. For modeling the visual saliency task, it is necessary to understand the processing of information in the visual cortex as carried away through the optic nerves from the retina, which is a pre-attentive process.

In the retina of the human eye, there are two primary types of optical sensors, rods and cones, that are sensitive to the optical sensations. The rods are responsible for interpreting low illumination scene and the cones are responsive to bright scenes and color. There are three types of cones that are sensitive to three different regions of the optical wavelengths, which direct the perception of colors. There are two components of color perception, chroma (color) component and the luminance component. These aspects are discussed in detail in Chapter 3 on color image processing. One of the color models that considers this physiology of optical sensation is called *color opponency*. Color opponency is the interaction between the spectral information in such a way that sensations from different types of cone cells act in an opponent way, where one of the sensations inhibits the other. For example, in green minus red (G–R) opponency, the cells that are sensitive to green sensation get excited, whereas the cells that are sensitive to red sensation are inhibited. Consider the schematic diagram of synapse between rods and cones in Fig. 5.5. As seen in the figure, besides rods and cones, there are various other cells that are involved in the visual sensation, such as *horizontal cells, bipolar cells, amacrine cells*, and *ganglion cells*. A horizontal cell sums up the inhibitory signals and activates the inhibition through the bipolar cells. The bipolar cells act with the inhibitory signals from the horizontal cells and the excitation signals from cones. The processes of inhibition and excitation take place jointly. This information is then carried to the ganglion cells where certain *center surround spatial processing* takes place. The information from ganglion cells is further processed to perceive the sensation by the optical nerve.

A brief summary of the pathways and synapses between various kinds of cells in the HVS is schematically shown in Fig. 5.6. Here, different kinds of photo receptors include the cones and rods, which are sensitive to light. The horizontal cells aggregates spatial receptions of specific type of cones, and produce inhibitory signals. These signals excite a bipolar cell via inhibitory indirect pathway from the horizontal cells. Some of the cones directly excite the bipolar cells by their respective pathways known as excitatory direct pathway. The inhibitory

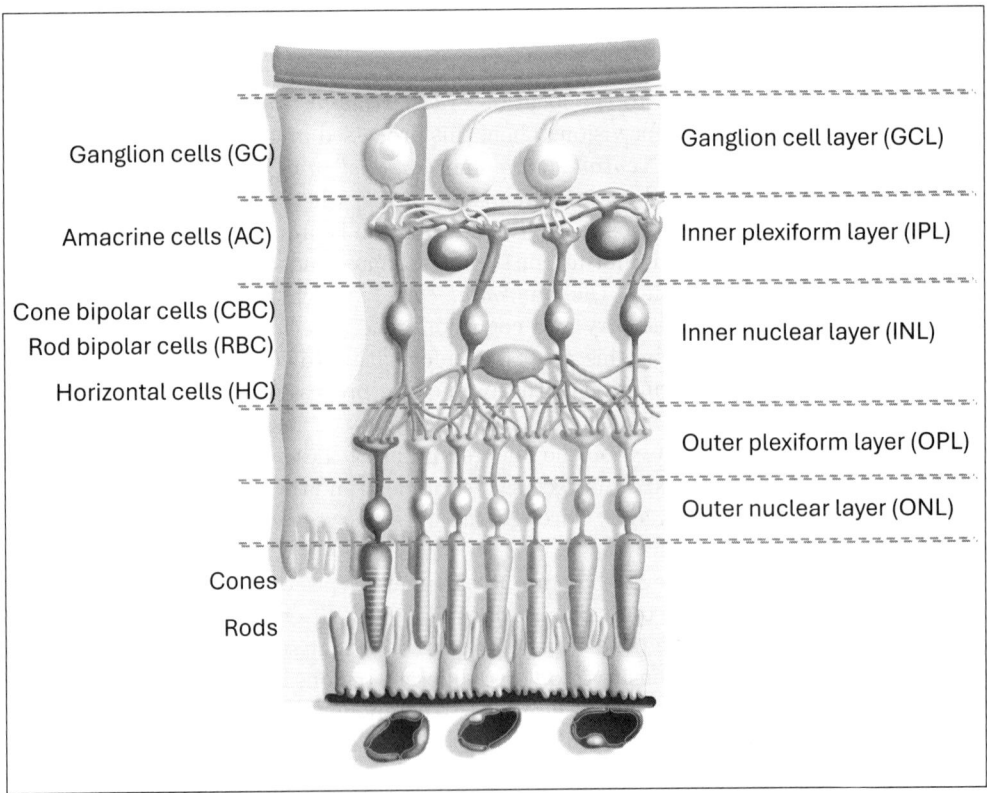

Ganglion cells (GC)

Amacrine cells (AC)

Cone bipolar cells (CBC)
Rod bipolar cells (RBC)

Horizontal cells (HC)

Cones

Rods

Ganglion cell layer (GCL)

Inner plexiform layer (IPL)

Inner nuclear layer (INL)

Outer plexiform layer (OPL)

Outer nuclear layer (ONL)

Figure 5.5 Synapse of rods and cones. (Courtesy: Getty Images/BSIP/Contributor.)
See Color Plates (page 817).

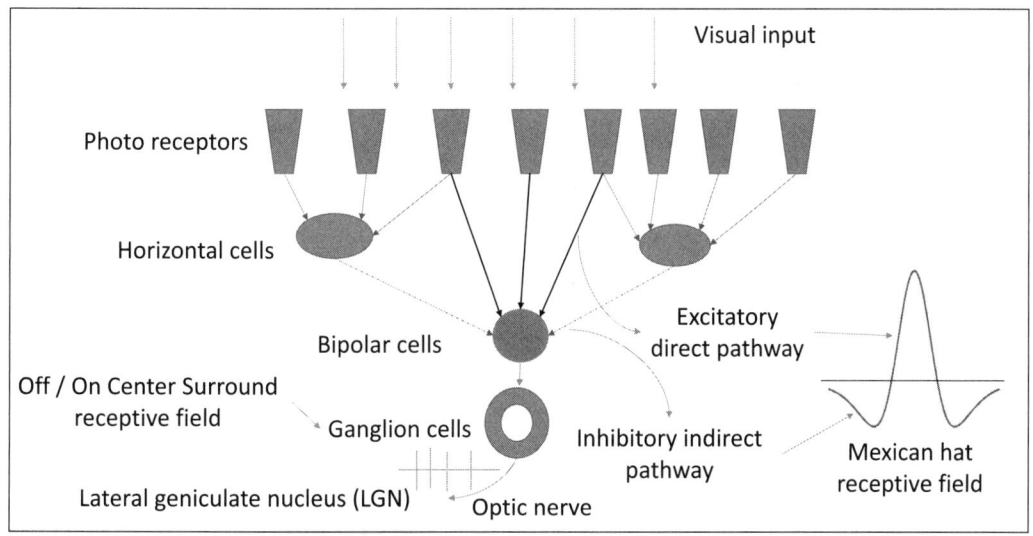

Figure 5.6 Cells and pathways in retina.

pathways result in some kind of subtraction of the sensation from the excitatory pathways. This is modeled by Laplacian of Gaussian (LoG) operation or difference of Gaussian (DoG) operation, which provides a Mexican hat receptive field, as shown in the figure. The ganglion cell has an off/ on center surround receptive field, where the surrounding disc portion of the cell is exciting and the inner part is inhibiting or vice versa. Before this information is carried out to the visual cortex by optical nerves, there is a kind of intermediate processing node called *lateral geniculate nucleus*. Roughly, this is the pipeline of processing that takes place from the sensors of retina to the optical nerve through LGN cells.

The sensations in the LGN cells capture the spatial orientation by an *orientation selective simple cell*. Certain LGN cells act together to understand the notion of orientation in receptive field at the *striata cortex*, as depicted in Fig. 5.7. This receptive field may be modeled by Gabor receptive field to capture the feature of orientation selectivity. Mathematically, it is given by Eq. 5.1.

$$G(x, y) = \frac{1}{2\pi\alpha\beta} e^{-\pi\left(\frac{(x-x_0)^2}{\alpha^2} + \frac{(y-y_0)^2}{\beta^2}\right)} e^{i(\zeta_0 x + \nu_0 y)} \tag{5.1}$$

where, x and y are spatial parameters, x_0 and y_0 correspond to the center of the receptive field, α and β are scale parameters, ζ_0 and ν_0 are spatio-frequency modulation parameters, and $G(\cdot)$ is the two-dimensional (2-D) Gabor function. The expression in Eq. 5.1 is with respect to a complex sinusoid. In modeling response of a physical system, we may decompose the function by both sine and cosine components that model the temporal phase variations also. One of the interesting aspects of Gabor field is that, it is a Gaussian function, whose shape is a Gaussian bell curve in both spectral (frequency) and spatial domains. When this function is multiplied by a sinusoidal signal, in the frequency domain, the base band

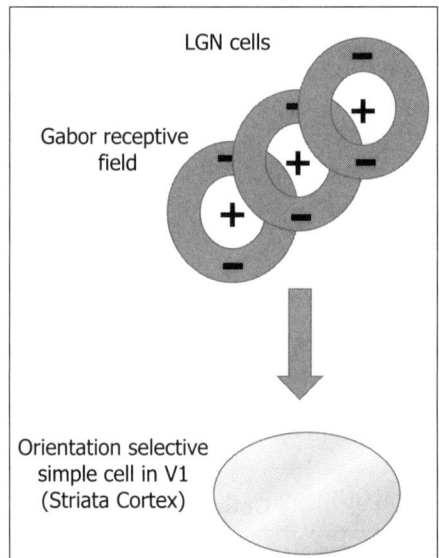

Figure 5.7 Response of LGN to edges and their orientations.

Gaussian spectrum gets translated in the frequency domain and acts like a bandpass filter. The translated response is active at a certain orientation in the spectral zone. When this process operates at different scales, the response becomes equivalent to a wavelet transform. In this transform, the wavelets are Gabor wavelets. This theory was proposed in 1962 by David Hubel and Torsten Wiesel (Hubel and Wiesel, 1962).

5.2 | An early model of visual attention and saliency

A computational model and its architecture for controlling visual attention was proposed by C. Koch and S. Ullmann in 1985 (Koch and Ullman, 1985). An outline of this bottom up process is shown in Fig. 5.8. This architecture models the pre-attentive stage that highlights salient regions. Here, the input is an image and the output is the saliency map. The concept of the visual saliency and the saliency map were introduced in this model. The *saliency map* is an explicit 2-D topographical map that encodes stimulus conspicuity, or saliency, at every location in the visual scene. This map gives an idea of how discriminating is the salient objects from its background in a visual scene. This model considers that the visual input, like an image in retina, is processed by various pathways and its features are extracted from various channels. These features are generated at multiple scales. As an example, in the figure, only three planes of features are shown. But, there can be many number of such feature channels or feature planes that actually gets extracted through the processing and several maps are created. Also, there are center surround difference operations that take place in ganglion cells. The architecture models all the operations from sensing to the generation of response from the ganglion and LGN cells. In the pipeline of this processing, different types of information get processed such as, colors, intensity, orientations, shape,

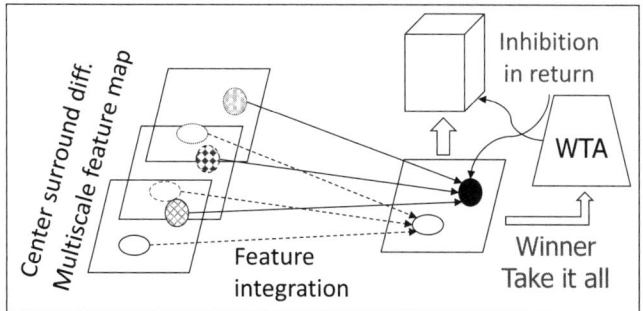

Figure 5.8 Computational architecture for controlling visual attention.

motion, disparity, etc. The feature map is also similar to a saliency map. Further, all these features are integrated to one particular feature map.

The feature integration also involves a processing with top-down attention bias and training. This is not always an automatic process. After processing the feature maps, only the most conspicuous zones or the portions of the individual maps that contain most salient zones are selected for processing. This module hypothesizes that this process also takes place in a pyramidal architecture, as shown in Fig. 5.8 by a pyramid shaped winner take all (WTA) architecture. This pyramidal architecture is used to compare localized regions or pixels and select a winner with the maximum saliency. In the lower levels of the pyramid, the localized spatial regions of all the individual saliency maps are compared. The spatial regions with higher activities among all the maps are chosen. These comparisons are performed at various levels and the region, known as the *winner*, with maximum saliency reaches the top of the pyramid. In this process, the winner (region with maximum saliency) inhibits the other regions. The inhibition also takes place repeatedly in the pyramidal fashion. With such repeated inhibitions, all the individual maps are integrated into a final feature saliency map.

While performing this kind of saliency selection, there is a shifting of visual attention within the saliency map. In the process of comparing and selecting the regions along the pyramid, after the most conspicuous location is detected and examined, its output decays due to inhibition. Then, by the mechanism of winner take it all, the attention shifts to the next most salient location. The time needed to find the next location depends on the distance between the locations of subsequent salient regions. If the distance is shorter, a smaller time is required. Otherwise, a larger time is consumed. According to this model, it is hypothesized that the processing takes place in ganglion cells. But another conjecture states that the saliency map may be localized either within the LGN or within the striate cortex (VI).

This architecture only discusses a possible model, and it may not exactly happen in the optical pathways and the brain. The architecture tries to postulate a model by exploiting some of the features that are known so far and get some plausible output which looks reasonable to our understanding. A combined model of attentional selection and object recognition is shown in Fig. 5.9. The incoming visual scene is processed by a pre-attentive

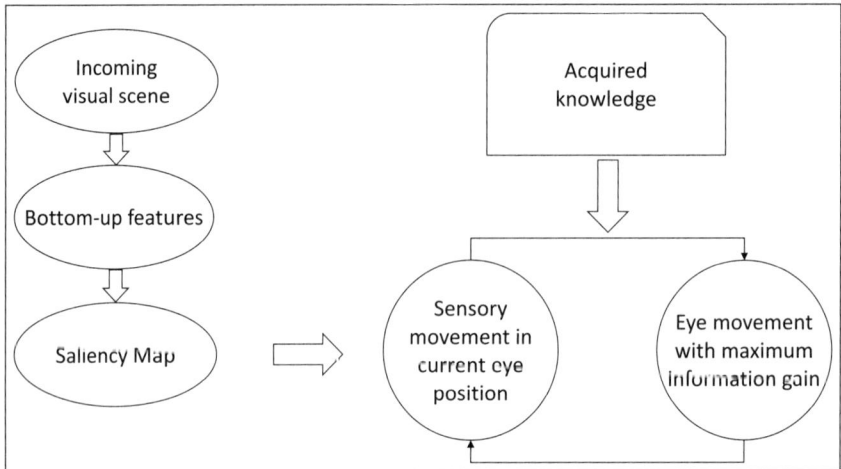

Figure 5.9 A combined model of attentional selection and object recognition.

stage to extract bottom-up features. These feature maps are integrated to produce a saliency map. The saliency maps then drive the sensory movement in current eye position, and control the eye movement of the pupils and shift the visual attention or gaze to gain maximum information. These eye movements are further influenced by the acquired knowledge and learning.

5.2.1 | The computational model

In the computational model that was proposed by L. Itti, C. Koch, and E. Niebur in 1998, there are different stages of processing where various features are extracted from the input image (Itti et al., 1998). In this computational model, the process of feature extraction is carried out using linear filters. There are mainly three different kinds of information that are considered for extracting features, viz., image channels (primarily, the colors), pixel intensities, and the local orientations. The model derives multi-channel and multi-scale feature representations, by using a *dyadic Gaussian pyramid* of nine scales. A dyadic Gaussian pyramid is an image pyramid constructed by blurring and subsampling the images by a factor of 2 repeatedly for the considered number of scales.[1] For example, consider a Gaussian filter with standard deviation, $\sigma = 0.8$. This filter is initially applied on the input image. In the next stage of repeated application, the standard deviation of the filter is increased by two times. Computationally, instead of applying a different Gaussian filter mask corresponding to 2σ, the image is downsampled by a factor of 0.5 and the same initial filter is applied. In effect, it becomes the same as applying a filter of 2σ on the image of the original scale. This method forms the dyadic computation with a Gaussian filter. Since the model considers a dyadic Gaussian pyramid of nine scales, there are nine stages of filtering.

---

[1] Please refer to Section 2.7.2 of Chapter 2 for related discussion.

The features are extracted in the following information channels.

- *Color*: There are four color channels and each channel is used to form an image pyramid.
- *Intensity*: The intensity or brightness channel is an average of all the color channels, which is also subjected to pyramid processing.
- *Orientation*: This model uses an oriented Gabor pyramid, where four discrete orientations, θ are considered, namely, $\theta = \{0°, 45°, 90°, 135°\}$. The filtered images at these orientations are also considered at multiple scales for the processing.

The features that are extracted from these channels are processed through the center surround difference model across multiple scales that generate another set of feature maps. This operation is to mimic the process that takes place in the ganglion cells. In this model, the proposed scaling factor at the center region is $c = \{2, 3, 4\}$, and scaling at the surround region is $s = c + d$, where $d = \{3, 4\}$. That is, if the scaling at the center region is at 2σ, then the scaling of the surrounding region is at 5σ, when $d = 3$, where σ is the standard deviation of the filter used for scaling. The resulting scaling operation is performed as, $I(c, s) = I(c) \ominus I(s)$, where $\ominus$ represents difference operation across scales, and $I(c)$ and $I(s)$ are the scaled images at center and surround regions, respectively. The difference operation of images at different scales is performed by interpolating the regions at the coarser scale to match the resolution of the finer scale. This brings the surround region to the same resolution of the image at the central region. All the resulting feature maps are normalized to bring them under the same dynamic range so that they become comparable. By pairing different feature maps for comparisons, various planes of feature components are generated. For example, in the proposed model, there are 12 feature maps for color, 6 feature maps for intensity, and 24 feature maps for orientations, which are composed across scales. All these feature maps are normalized and considered at different pairing combinations to perform the feature integration and get the final saliency map. This computational model is illustrated in Fig. 5.10.

The summary of operations in Fig. 5.10 are as follows.

(i) The color channels are normalized, as given by Eq. 5.2, to bring them under the same dynamic range.

$$r = \frac{R}{I}, \ g = \frac{G}{I}, \ b = \frac{B}{I} \tag{5.2}$$

where, R, G and B are the red, green and blue color channels, respectively, $I = \frac{R+G+B}{3}$ is the intensity image, and r, g and b are the normalized red, green and blue channels, respectively.

(ii) The four color channels, R_o, G_o, B_o and Y_o, are generated, as given by Eq. 5.3, using the concept of opponent colors.[2]

$$R_o = r - \frac{g+b}{2}, \ G_o = g - \frac{r+b}{2}, \ B_o = b - \frac{r+g}{2}, \ Y_o = \frac{r+g}{2} - \frac{|r-g|}{2} - b \tag{5.3}$$

---

[2] Please refer to Section 3.7.3 of Chapter 3.

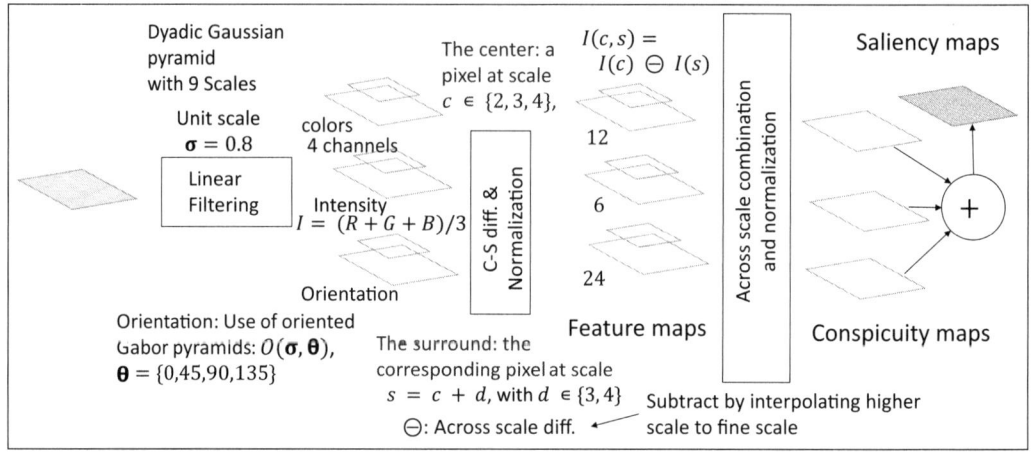

Figure 5.10 A combined model of attentional selection and object recognition.

(iii) These four color channels are then used to create four Gaussian pyramids, $R_o(\sigma)$, $G_o(\sigma)$, $B_o(\sigma)$ and $Y_o(\sigma)$, of nine scales.

(iv) These pyramids are then used to compute the center surround feature maps by considering the center pixels at three scales and the surrounding pixels at a coarser scale than the center pixels.

(v) The center surround maps are computed by subtracting the images across scale by interpolating the coarser scale to finer scale. For the intensity image, the center surround operation is given by $I(c,s) = I(c) \ominus I(s)$, where $c = \{2,3,4\}$, $s = c + d$, and $d = \{3,4\}$. For the color channels, the enter surround operations reduce the number of color channels to two, as given in Eq. 5.4.

$$R_oG_o(c,s) = |(R_o(c) - G_o(c)) \ominus (R_o(s) - G_o(s))|, \text{ and}$$
$$B_oY_o(c,s) = |(B_o(c) - Y_o(c)) \ominus (B_o(s) - Y_o(s))| \tag{5.4}$$

(vi) Then, for the orientations, oriented Gabor pyramids, $O(\sigma, \theta)$, are computed with $\theta = \{0°, 450°, 900°, 1350°\}$ to extract features across different scales and orientations.

(vii) Finally, all these feature maps are integrated to form the saliency map.

5.2.2 | Normalization of feature maps

For combining the feature maps of different modalities, the values in each map are normalized to a fixed range, say $[0 \ldots M]$. This normalization is performed to eliminate any modality-dependent amplitude differences. Then the local peaks in each map are found and the average, μ, of all such local peaks is computed. The maps are further scaled by globally multiplying them with $(M - \mu)^2$. This gives more weight to those maps that are

 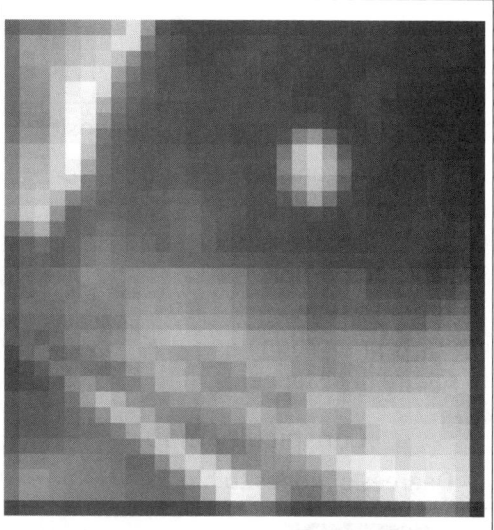

Figure 5.11 An example of the saliency map generated using the model proposed in Itti et al. (1998). (*Source*: Prof. Rajarshi Pal, Institute of Development and Research in Banking Technology (IDRBT), Hyderabad, India, for sharing the images form his PhD work (Pal, 2011).)

more contrastive. For individual maps, higher the difference of $(M - \mu)^2$, higher its weight of the saliency map. These feature maps are combined into three conspicuity maps, corresponding to color, intensity, and orientation by performing *across scale addition* of all feature maps for individual modality. Here, across scale addition is performed by downsampling the maps at higher resolution to the resolution of the map at a lower resolution. This begets maps at lower resolution for each of the three modalities. Then the three conspicuity maps are normalized and averaged to get the saliency map. With this process, given an image, its saliency map is computed. This model of saliency map is mostly driven by the corresponding neuronal mechanisms and biological processes. An example of the saliency map obtained by this model is shown in Fig. 5.11.

5.3 | ViSaNet: a graph based computational model

Another model for saliency, known as *Visual Saliency Network* (ViSaNet), is proposed in Pal et al. (2010). The principle behind the development of the model is to capture the interaction of the salient regions with other regions. The salient regions compete with various other regions during processing of visual information in our visual system. The representation of these interactions is considered in pairs of homogeneous regions, which is modeled in the form of a graph. The nodes of the graph are the homogeneous blocks and the edges represent the strength of interaction between the corresponding two blocks. The graph is constructed as an unweighted graph by allowing edges whose weights are greater

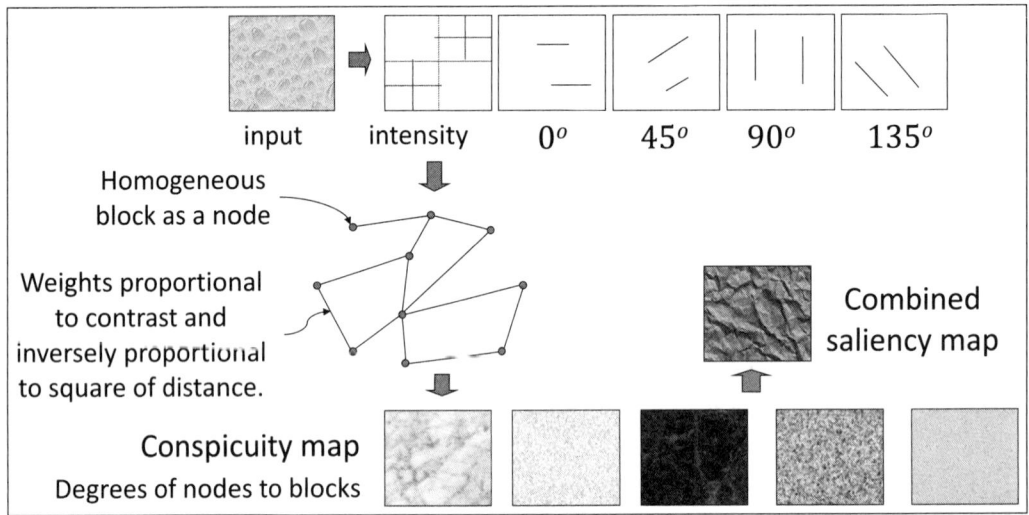

Figure 5.12 Illustration of ViSaNet model. (*Source*: Adapted from Pal (2011).)

than a threshold value. A simple count of the number of regions that interact with a particular node gives the *degree of the node*. It is hypothesized that the salient regions interact more with the other regions. This intuition is based on a measurement of the centrality of a node. According to this intuition, the salient zones are those regions which have high degree centrality. Due to the high degrees of the salient regions, they are connected to different zones. This hypothesis about salient regions is called the *degree centrality hypothesis*. Here, each graph corresponds to a feature map. There are different feature maps corresponding to homogeneous blocks in different feature planes. These feature planes are driven by intensity and orientations, as depicted in Fig. 5.12.

In this model, four orientations are considered at $\{0°, 45°, 90°, 135°\}$ in the luminance component of the image. A Gabor filter, $G_\theta(x, y)$, is used to extract the orientation features, whose functional form is given by Eq. 5.5.

$$G_\theta(x, y) = e^{-\frac{x'^2 + \gamma^2 y'^2}{2\sigma^2}} \cos\left(2\pi \frac{x'}{\lambda} + \phi\right) \tag{5.5}$$

where σ is the standard deviation of the function, x' and y' define the orientation of the filter along θ, and γ is the spatial aspect ratio that specifies the ellipticity of the Gabor filter. The x' and y' are given by Eq. 5.6.

$$\begin{aligned} x' &= x\cos(\theta) + y\sin(\theta) \\ y' &= -x\sin(\theta) + y\cos(\theta) \end{aligned} \tag{5.6}$$

Here, the real component of the Gabor filter response is used by performing rotation of image patches about their centers by an angle θ with respect to x-axis. Thus, it is defined only by the cosine function, where $\frac{1}{\lambda}$ denote the spatio-frequency modulation and ϕ is the phase. This filter is circular when the value of $\gamma = 1$. In general, it is an orientated filter whose receptive field is aligned with the direction θ with respect to the x-axis. Thus the shape of the response is an ellipse, whose spatial aspect ratio is defined by γ and the orientation is captured through the transformation angle θ. In this model, the multi-scale orientation feature maps are constructed only on the intensity image, and the color features are not considered.

The graphs are formed from each of the feature maps. While defining a graph, homogeneous blocks are chosen as the nodes. A homogeneous block is defined by considering the distribution of the feature values in the block whose standard deviation is very small. A block of a feature map is said to be homogeneous, if the dynamic range of the block is within a certain limit, say 5.88% of the global dynamic range of the feature map. The dynamic range is the difference between maximum and minimum values in a considered block or image. Such homogenous blocks define the nodes of a graph and each pair of nodes is connected by a weighted edge. These weights are computed such that they are proportional to the contrast between the two zones and are inversely proportional to the squares of the distances between them. The weight between two nodes is computed by Eq. 5.7.

$$w_{i,j} = \frac{|\mu_i - \mu_j|}{\max\limits_{\forall l,m}|\mu_l - \mu_m|} e^{-\frac{D_{i,j}^2}{2\sigma^2}} \tag{5.7}$$

where $\mu_{\{i,j,l,m\}}$ is the average value of the block $\{i, j, l, m\}$, $D_{i,j}$ is the distance between block i and block j. The difference between the average values of two blocks, $|\mu_i - \mu_j|$, denotes the contrast between them, which is a relative measure. The denominator of Eq. 5.7, $\max\limits_{\forall l,m}|\mu_l - \mu_m|$, computes the maximum among all pairs of blocks in a feature map. A threshold value is set on these weights to accept certain edges in the graph. The conspicuity map is generated for each type of feature map at the early stage by knowing the degrees of nodes that are assigned to the blocks at each node. In each conspicuity map, the degree of the respective node is assigned to all the pixels of the corresponding block. Then, different conspicuity maps are normalized and combined to get the final saliency map.

Typical examples of computing the saliency map of input images are shown in Fig. 5.13. For the input images shown in the left column, the saliency maps obtained by the models of Itti et al. (1998) and ViSaNet (Pal et al., 2010) are shown in the middle and right columns, respectively. In these saliency maps, the brighter regions represent the most salient zones. Also, there are certain hierarchies or sequences for the most salient zone. The ViSaNet model is more computationally intensive. However, these examples do not really validate the model. For validating a model, there should be some reference output that is obtained by the human input stimulus. This reference output needs to be compared with the results obtained by the models to be validated. So, for testing models, it is crucial to have reference saliency maps. In other words, for a set of input images, it is necessary to have their ideal saliency maps from an independent method of map creation using some human-centric subjective or objective techniques.

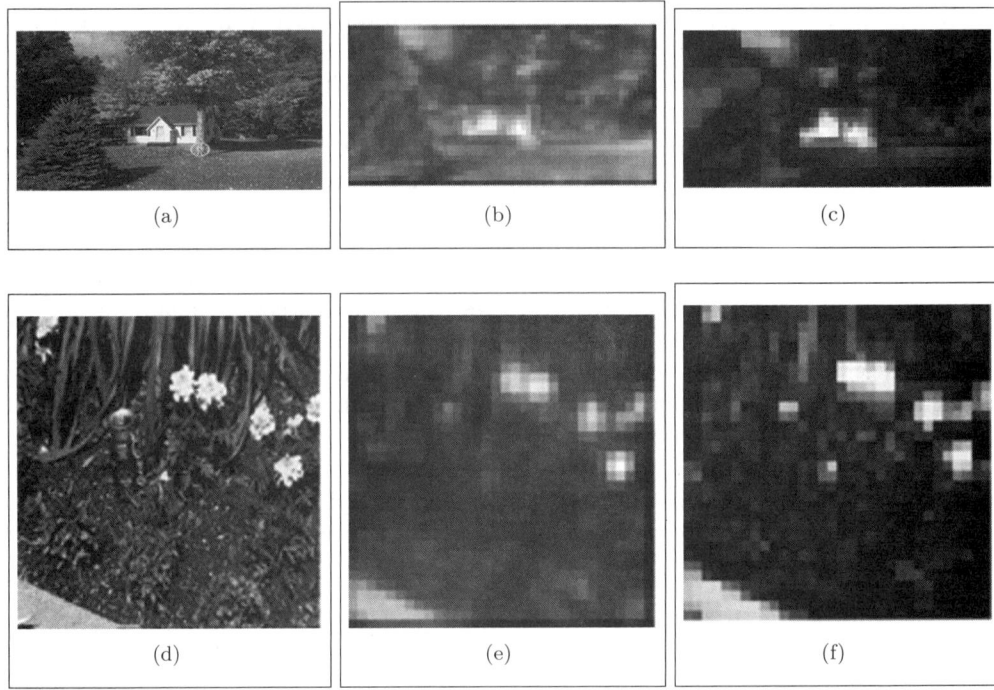

Figure 5.13 Example of saliency map on a natural scene. (a) Input image. (b) Saliency result of Itti et al. (1998) (Itti and Koch, 2001). (c) Saliency result of ViSaNet (Pal et al., 2010). Their zoomed portions are shown in (d), (e), and (f), respectively. (*Source*: Prof. Rajarshi Pal, Institute of Development and Research in Banking Technology (IDRBT), Hyderabad, India, for sharing the images form his PhD work (Pal, 2011).)

5.4 | Validation of saliency models

Obtaining the ground truth data for validating saliency models is a very challenging task, since it primarily depends on the subject viewing an image or a scene. Although there can be an average behavior of the viewers, individually each viewer may vary on forming saliency maps. There are two main approaches by which the experiments are designed to get the salient regions with respect to viewers. One approach is to collect the feedback from each of the viewers. In this technique, each viewer would look at every image which is displayed on a screen for a certain duration. Then viewers mark the salient regions on a blank canvas that replaces the image. After collecting this data from several viewers, their responses are aggregated. The viewers may also suggest their preferred ranking of salient regions. Since this is subjective to each viewer's preference, the average behavior of the viewers is taken as the final ground truth. This approach is more simple and requires relatively less resource as it does not require any special device other than display monitor and a general purpose computer for a viewer's interaction. In the earlier days of studying visual saliency, particularly when the technology was not so advanced, this was a more common means of capturing the ground truth data. Though there are some processes to make this approach more objective, essentially, it is still a subjective process.

On the other hand, there is another approach, which utilizes certain devices that track the gaze of human eyes. Here, the viewers do not have to explicitly suggest their preferred salient regions. The viewers would simply view the scene and the tracking device captures the respective gaze locations for each viewer. The device also provides the information regarding which points in the image are being viewed by the viewer. These devices are called *eye gaze trackers*, or simply, *eye trackers*. After analyzing the gaze information, a visual saliency map is obtained for each viewer. This approach is more objective in its process. In the recent days, eye trackers have become very prevalent and accurate due to advancement in technology. So, the eye tracking devices are usually used to create visual saliency maps. Gaze tracking of viewers by eye tracking devices require the devices to be calibrated to record sequence of gaze points in images. This facilitates the analysis of recorded data to obtain salient regions of images. Similar to the subjective approach, every viewer has a distinct sequence of gaze points, which is aggregated to create a saliency map reflecting average behavior of our visual system.

5.4.1 | Evaluation metrics

In either of the approaches of collecting ground truths, some kind of aggregations of the data from different viewers (and hence, different perspectives) is required, to obtain the average response of viewers. For validating the saliency model, the computed saliency map is to be evaluated with respect to the ground truth acquired by one of the above approaches. There exist several measures or metrics for evaluating the performance of a technique. Some of the measures that are commonly used in the literature are discussed here.

Let the ground truth be denoted by $G(x, y)$. Let the saliency map be denoted by $M(x, y)$. Certain regions in the ground truth data are identified as salient or nonsalient, depending on some preset threshold value. Let R_s and R_{ns} denote the salient and nonsalient regions in the ground truth, respectively. Some of the metrics used in evaluating these models are as follows.

- *Average discrimination ratio* (ADR): It computes the proportion of saliency values as a ratio of the average saliency over the salient region of the predicted saliency map to the sum of the averages of saliency over salient and nonsalient regions in the same predicted map. In a saliency map, it is desired to have higher average value in salient regions and a lower average value in nonsalient regions. The mathematical expression for the ADR is given by Eq. 5.8.

$$\text{ADR} = \frac{\frac{1}{|R_s|} \sum_{(x,y) \in R_s} M(x, y)}{\frac{1}{|R_s|} \sum_{(x,y) \in R_s} M(x, y) + \frac{1}{|R_{ns}|} \sum_{(x,y) \in R_{ns}} M(x, y)} \tag{5.8}$$

  where $|R_s|$ and $|R_{ns}|$ represent the number of points in R_s and R_{ns}, respectively. Higher the ADR, better is the discrimination power of the saliency map.

- *Kullback–Leibler distance* (KLD): It is a measure of dissimilarity between two probability distributions. One of the distributions, $p(x, y)$, corresponds to the computed saliency map and the other distribution, $h(x, y)$, corresponds to the ground truth. The distributions, $p(x, y)$ and $h(x, y)$, are computed from $M(x, y)$ and $G(x, y)$, respectively, by normalizing their values as, $p(x, y) = \frac{M(x,y)}{\sum_{\forall x, y} M(x,y)}$ and

$h(x, y) = \frac{G(x,y)}{\sum_{\forall x, y} G(x,y)}$. Then, the KLD between $p(x, y)$ and $h(x, y)$ is expressed by Eq. 5.9.

$$\text{KLD} = \sum_{\forall x, y} p(x, y) \frac{\log p(x, y)}{\log h(x, y)} \tag{5.9}$$

- *Correlation coefficient* (CC): It is a standard statistical measure of computing the correlation between two random variables, which is normalized by their corresponding standard deviations. The correlation between the ground truth and the computed saliency map is possible since they have one-to-one correspondences at each location. Here, the two random variables are the ground truth, G, and the predicted saliency map, M. The CC between them is defined by Eq. 5.10.

$$\text{CC} = \frac{\text{Cov}(G, M)}{\sigma_G \sigma_M} \tag{5.10}$$

where σ_G and σ_M are the standard deviations of G and M, respectively, and $\text{Cov}(G, M)$ is the covariance between them. This is the standard definition of Pearson's correlation coefficient, whose value varies from -1 to 1. A good saliency model is desired to have a high positive CC.

A saliency detection can also be viewed as a classification problem, that categorizes whether a pixel is salient or not. In this case, the ground truth provides the true classification label at every pixel. Besides the above three metrics, a few other measures can also be defined with respect to the classification problem, like, precision, recall (or sensitivity), and specificity. The definition of these metrics[3] is given in Eq. 5.11.

$$\text{Precision} = \frac{\text{TP}}{\text{TP} + \text{FP}}$$
$$\text{Recall} = \frac{\text{TP}}{\text{TP} + \text{FN}} \tag{5.11}$$
$$\text{Specificity} = \frac{\text{TN}}{\text{TN} + \text{FP}}$$

where *TP* is the number of *true positive* pixels that are labeled as salient in both computed saliency map and ground truth, *TN* is the number of *true negative* pixels that are labeled as nonsalient in both computed saliency map and ground truth, *FP* is the number of *false positive* pixels that are labeled salient in computed saliency map but nonsalient in ground truth, and *FN* is the number of *false negative* pixels that are labeled nonsalient in the computed saliency map, but salient in the ground truth. *Precision* indicates the proportion of the computed salient pixels that are actually salient, *recall* indicates the proportion of actual salient pixels that are computed as salient, and *specificity* indicates the proportion of the computed nonsalient pixels that are actually not salient. Sometimes a combination of these metrics are used to assess the performance of a classifier. Ideally, the values of all these measures are desired to be high, close to 1. These evaluation metrics are also used in validating the performance of computational models of visual saliency.

---

[3] Their definitions are also given in Section 7.6 of Chapter 7.

5.4.2 | Subjective feedback

There are several methodologies for obtaining the ground truth by subjective feedback of viewers for validating the saliency models. A typical example of one such methodology is discussed here. In Pal et al. (2009), an experiment was designed where the images are initially shown to the viewers on a display device. After a certain duration of time, those images are withdrawn and only the blank screen is shown. The viewers are asked to identify the regions of saliency from their short term memory and mark those regions. In this way, the saliency maps are obtained using a subjective feedback from various viewers that are finally aggregated. However, in this process, the nature of the viewer is pre-assessed to check if she/he is capable of providing an appropriate map. This pre-assessment is made using *hand-eye coordination* technique, which tests the ability of a viewer to follow up the respective stimulus. In this technique, the blank computer screen is illuminated at some spot and shown to the viewer for a certain duration of time. Then, the illumination is withdrawn and the viewer is asked to identify the point of illumination. The actual point of illumination and the response of the viewer are recorded, and the deviation of the distance between them is noted. This process is repeated for a fixed number of times and the average error is computed. If the viewer is able to provide the feedback within a certain range (i.e., if the average error lies within a preset tolerance interval), the viewer is selected. The threshold values on the average error and standard deviations are fixed through experiments on different viewers. Besides testing, this hand-eye coordination stage acclimatizes the viewers to the process of identifying salient regions.

The selected users then participate in identifying the salient regions in the given set of images. In this stage, the volunteer (viewer) is shown an image for a duration of 15 milliseconds. It is necessary to maintain the limit of a time interval, since this primarily is a bottom-up process of attention. Physically, the changes in the scene that stays for less than 100 milliseconds cannot be perceived. That is, it has lesser role for the top down component of attention. After the image is withdrawn, the volunteers are asked to mark the center of the salient regions on a background mask. The background mask is adaptive to the input image. Though this does not emphasize precise marking of the whole region, it is a very simple way of capturing salient locations. The process is repeated for each image in the set. This is one example of getting the saliency map using a subjective feedback. In one of the experiments, the dataset[4] consisted of 100 images and 65 volunteers, where 20 volunteers marked each image. A typical example of this data is shown in Fig. 5.14. After seeing the input image, several viewers identify the salient locations. The average response of all the viewers is aggregated and those points that are mostly agreed upon are identified as salient points. The salient points corresponding to each of the input images in the left are marked in the masked image in the right in Fig. 5.14. One of the main bottleneck of this method is the representation of the salient region is made through a representative set of salient points, which usually belong to the central zones of the salient regions. This form of ground truth does not provide much information about the spread of the saliency map. However, it can be improved (Pal et al., 2012) by identifying object segments, region boundaries, etc.

---

[4] IIT-KGP Visual Saliency Dataset: `http://www.facweb.iitkgp.ac.in/~jay/VS/Groundtruth.html`.

Figure 5.14 An example from IIT-KGP Visual Saliency Dataset. (*Source*: Prof. Rajarshi Pal, Institute of Development and Research in Banking Technology (IDRBT), Hyderabad, India, for sharing the images from his PhD work (Pal, 2011).)

5.5 | Eye tracking

In the recent days, eye trackers have become a very popular choice due to better precision and reliability of the devices. They record the gaze positions at regular intervals in an image viewed by an observer. The sequence of these points also provides the gaze path. The data is usually in the form of X-Y or X-Y-Z coordinates with respect to the image, along with the corresponding time stamp. The ranges of the coordinates are made compatible with the resolution of the associated display device. Through appropriate calibration of the tracker, the pixels in the images that are viewed by the viewers can be identified. A typical example of eye tracking is shown in Fig. 5.15. As seen in the figure, the eye gaze path is traced by the white curve along with the transitions from different parts shown by blue arrows. From eye tracking devices trajectories of both right and left eyes are obtained. However, in the figure, only one trajectory corresponding to the binocular vision is depicted, combining the left and the right eyes.

5.5.1 | 2-D gaze

One of the popular techniques to capture 2-D gaze data is called *pupil center cornea reflection* (PCCR) technique (Hutchinson et al., 1989; Morimoto et al., 2000). In the

 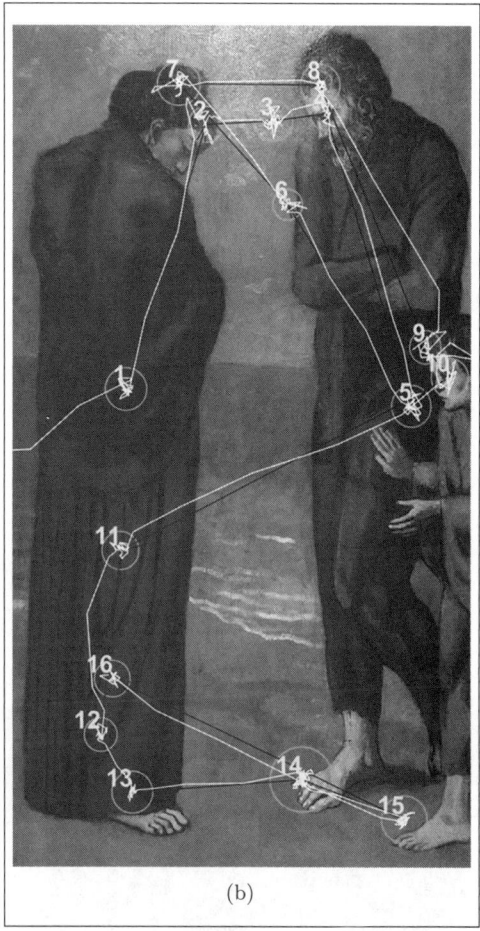

(a)   (b)

Figure 5.15 An example of eye tracking. (a) An image of painting by Picasso: Tragedy, and (b) its corresponding eye gaze. (*Source*: Dr. Anup Kumar Roy, Post Doctoral Fellow, IIT Gandhinagar.) See Color Plates (page 818).

human eye, the pupil is relatively easier to detect, since it has a very distinct contrast with its surrounding region. Depending upon the illumination used, the pupil is either very dark or white, as shown in Fig. 5.16. This technique uses a controlled illumination with an infrared LED (IR-LED) source, which does not affect the viewing experience of the viewer, and the image of reflection of the IR-LED source is recorded by an infrared sensor. This virtual image of the light source on convex cornea is called *glint*, which is a distinguishable bright spot that is clearly identifiable, as shown in the figure. The gaze location, the point where the viewer is looking at, is then determined using the position of the glint and the location of the center of the pupil of each eye. The glint provides a fixed reference position of the light source, because the light source is fixed relative to the pupil. Also, it is assumed that the viewer is also stationary. When looking at a particular object,

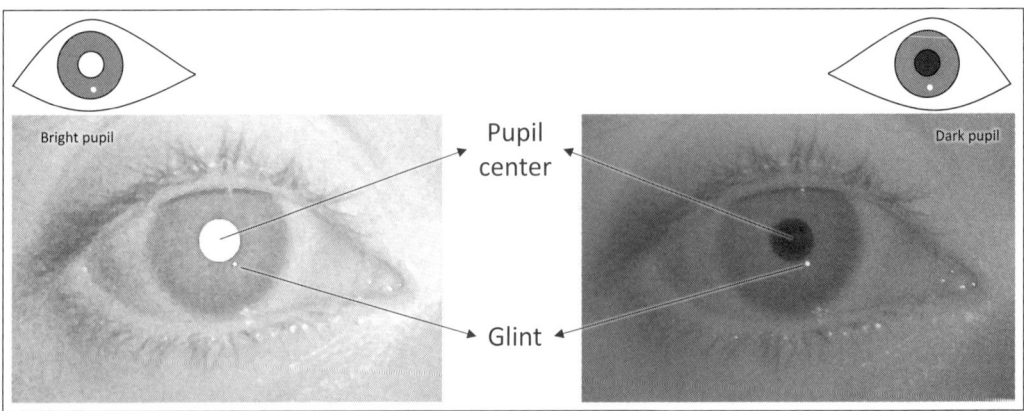

Figure 5.16 Appearance of pupil in different illuminations.

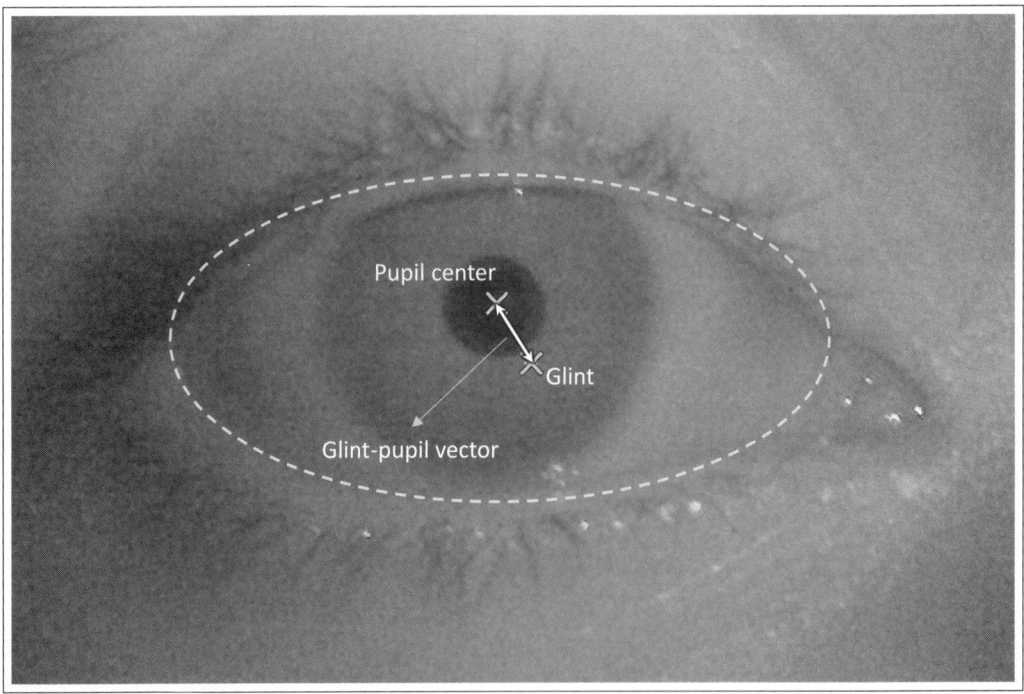

Figure 5.17 Glint-pupil vector.

the pupil moves with respect to the light source. That is, the location of the pupil changes relative to the glint. The center position of the pupil changes depending on the direction of the gaze of the eye. So, the locations of center of pupil and the glint are the functions of the respective gaze direction in the image.

The locations of center of pupil and the glint are used to form a vector, $\boldsymbol{v} = (v_x, v_y)$, called *glint-pupil vector*, which is directed from the glint to the center of the pupil, as shown in Fig. 5.17. The gaze points are modeled using different computational models, whose coefficients are estimated by the measurements. For example, a quadratic model is given in Eq. 5.12.

$$x_g = a_0 + a_1 v_x + a_2 v_y + a_3 v_x v_y$$
$$y_g = b_0 + b_1 v_x + b_2 v_y + b_3 v_x v_y$$

(5.12)

where x_g and y_g are the x and y coordinates of the gaze location, and $\{a_0, b_0, a_1, b_1, a_2, b_2, a_3, b_3\}$ are the coefficients There are two equations and eight unknowns in Eq. 5.12, which requires a minimum of four points or measurements to solve the coefficients. The 2-D eye gaze trackers usually have a calibration phase for every viewer. The position of the gaze points are calibrated by measuring them on a set of points with known coordinates that are displayed on a reference screen. Then, by measuring the glint-pupil vectors for each of the known points, a regression model is fit to the measurements to generalize the eye gaze estimations. This model is further applied for various measurements in different scenarios. This is the principle behind recording 2-D gaze points.

5.5.2 | 3-D gaze

A three-dimensional (3-D) gaze tracker captures the respective 3-D positions of the gaze data, with respect to a defined coordinate system. Usually, the coordinate system is defined relative to the viewer, which is known as *egocentric system*. In a typical egocentric camera system (Zhu and Ji, 2007), the viewer either has a head mounted camera pair or a spectacle in which a pair of cameras are mounted. These mounted cameras are fixed in a certain way such that the eye gaze information can be captured. To understand the gaze information, consider a very simplistic model of human eye, as shown in Fig. 5.18. This model shows eyeball, cornea, fovea, and pupil. The cornea is similar to a convex structure where the light through the lens is refracted to create its image. The light gaze from a target enters the eye via the pupil, passes through the cornea, and projected on the retina at a particular location of fovea to create the image of the target. Here, the location of the pupil and cornea define the 3-D gaze point.

To measure the 3-D locations of cornea and the gaze point, a stereo camera is used. In this case, the 3-D position of the pupil, O_{pu}, is obtained using infrared stereo imaging.[5] Also, by using the IR-LEDs at known locations, the corresponding virtual image of the glint at each eye can be captured. This 3-D position of the image of the glint acts as a fixed reference position in the cornea. Suppose, L_1' and L_2' are the images of the glint obtained by the two IR-LEDs in the stereo setup, L_1 and L_2, respectively. Then, since both the rays, $L_1'L_1$ and $L_2'L_2$, pass through the center of cornea, the point of intersection of these two lines gives an estimation of the center of cornea, O_{co}. The visual axis or gaze can be now defined by the location of pupil (obtained by the position of the image of the target) and

---

[5] Please refer to Section 12.7 of Chapter 12 for a detailed discussion on computing 3-D scene points using stereo imaging.

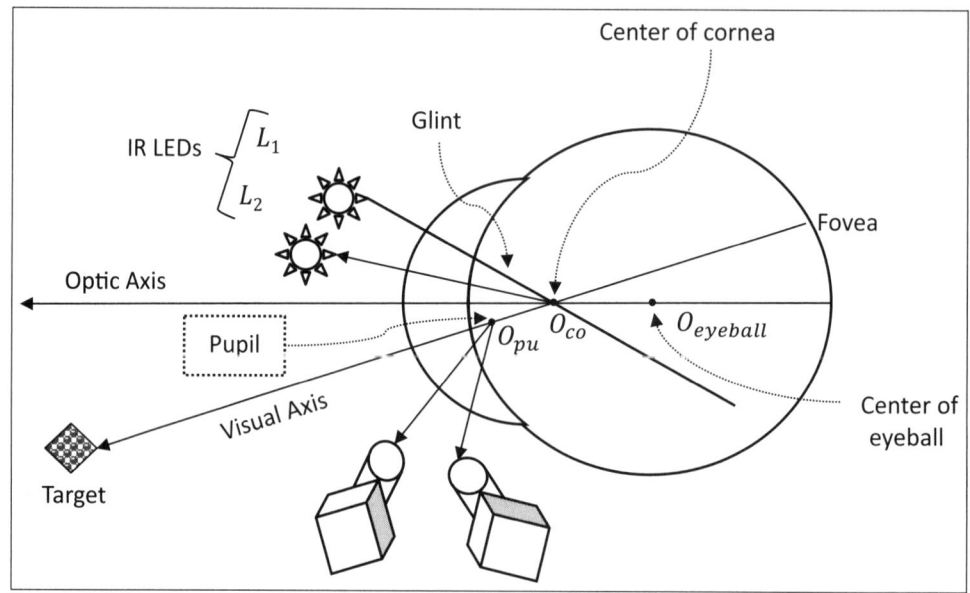

Figure 5.18 A technique for determining 3-D eye gaze direction of a viewer.

the location of cornea (obtained by the IR-LEDs and glints). That is, the 3-D direction of the gaze is computed by the vector, $\overrightarrow{O_{co}O_{pu}}$.

A 3-D eye tracker provides the 2-D gaze locations and the associated 3-D information, with respect to a world coordinate system defined relative to the viewer. The 3-D gaze data primarily consist of the following information.

(i) Sequence of 3-D gaze location in an image. Additionally, for a video, the corresponding time stamps are also included.

(ii) Normalized 2-D gaze location, which is similar to the data provided by the 2-D gaze trackers. The gaze locations are normalized to the eye tracking camera resolution.

(iii) The gaze direction vector and the pupil centers of both the eyes, which provides the information about where the viewer is looking in an image.

The egocentric video eye trackers usually perform the gaze recording at a higher frequency at each frame. These trackers are mostly available in two forms: desktop mounted 3-D eye trackers and head mounted 3-D eye trackers. Desktop mounted trackers require a static position of viewers who would see the scene that is displayed on a monitor. Head mounted trackers or eye-glass based trackers can get the 3-D gaze information from the scene and the objects that the viewer sees around. These wearable trackers can record the video of the world scene and do not require the viewer to be static while recording the gaze data. Here, the motion of the viewers, particularly the head movements, are also captured by accelerometer and gyroscope, which can be used for correcting the respective gaze data or for co-registering the coordinate systems. The gaze data provides opportunities to explore and understand the visual cognitive processes that occur in the visual processing system of our brain.

5.6 | Eye movements

In human vision, the eye movements are usually not automatic or reflexive actions. They arguably represent the most frequent decision process carried out by the brain. This conscious perception depends on the trajectory of the *fixated locations*. There are three types of eye movements that are characterized by the nature of the points in the gaze locations. These movements also provide some understanding about the mechanism of the visual perceptual process. The three types of eye movements are as follows.

(i) *Fixation*: Fixation occurs when the eye stops to collect visual data. Here, the gaze locations of the eye movements remain stable at a focused region for certain time interval. During fixations, the eye locations move only around the fixated region. When the eye gaze changes from one region of fixation to another, there can be a sequence of fixated regions.

(ii) *Saccade*: Saccades or saccadic movements occur when the fovea is moved rapidly from one fixation (point of interest) to another fixation. These saccadic movements are due to the transition of the regions of selective attention. In visual cognition, after detecting the most salient zones in a saliency map, the attention moves to the next salient zones.

(iii) *Microsaccade*: Human visual system has some amount of randomness and our attention may not be perfectly controlled to always remain at the same point of fixation. Except for professionally trained individuals, like shooters and archers, whose attention are more stable at the locations of fixation, the fixated attention usually drifts around the target location in common people. A corrective function brings back the attention to the fixated location through rapid eye movements called microsaccades. Similar to saccade, microsaccade is also a mechanism where the gaze does not remain stationary at a particular point. Microsaccades occur as a corrective function to bring the fovea back to the target fixation from which the eye gets drifted. These movements are mostly localized around the fixation.

With respect to the computational model discussed in Section 5.2.1, the salient zones in a saliency map are the zones of fixation. When the gaze moves from one salient region to another, and saccadic movements corroborate to the transition of the fixation states (i.e., attention to the salient zones).

An example is shown in Fig. 5.19, where the regions of fixation and saccadic movements between them are shown on an image of a *Rorschach test card*, which is used to study psychological behavior of a subject. Here, the regions marked with circles indicate the fixation regions and the saccades are marked by thick lines, which are the transitions from one fixation to another. The microsaccades are observed at the fixation regions. An example of microsaccades around a fixation point is also shown by enlarging a portion of the image. Another interesting example is shown in Fig. 5.20, where the gaze locations of a reader are observed using an eye tracker while reading a few lines of text. As seen in the figure, more attention is given to some of the portions of certain words and a few words are skipped without holding the gaze for significant duration. In viewing a scene, the fixations focus on visually salient parts with a higher variability in saccades. That is, there is some kind of relation between the gaze sequences and the salient regions.

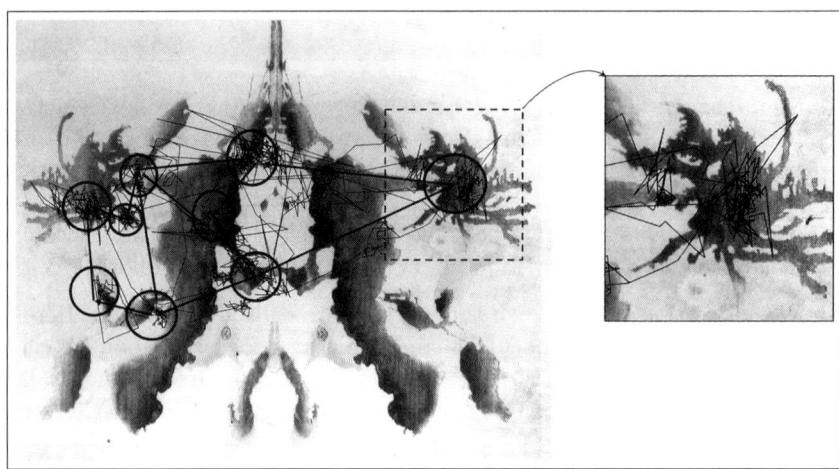

Figure 5.19 Fixations and saccades of eye gaze trajectory on an image of Rorschach test card. (*Source*: Dr Anup Kumar, Post Doctoral Fellow, IIT Gandhinagar; Image in Public domain, via Wikimedia Commons
`https://commons.wikimedia.org/wiki/File:Rorschach_blot_10.jpg.`)
See Color Plates (page 818).

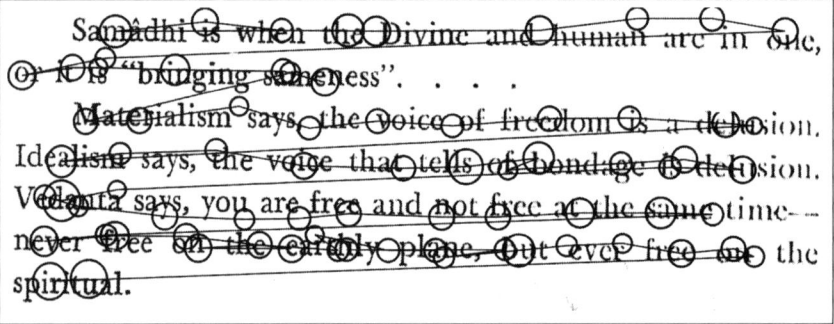

Figure 5.20 An example of a scene showing fixations and saccades. (*Source*: Dr Anup Kumar, Post Doctoral Fellow, IIT Gandhinagar.)

A fixation is not a single point in an image. Instead, it is a region that is made up of multiple gaze points. The movement of the eye ball is restricted around that region. A fixated view implies that looking at a particular region (not a particular point) where the gaze points are spread. The gaze points scan the visual scene within the region of fixation. The strength of a fixation zone is determined by duration spent by the viewer on that region and the number of times the viewer returns back to that region. Since this scan is limited to a very small region, it appears the gaze locations are fixated to that region. Some evident object in a scene may fix the gaze locations faster, while a scene with more details may take more time to settle the gaze. Though the range of duration for fixation is 50–600 milliseconds, a typical natural scene usually takes 100–300 milliseconds to fix the gaze locations. Practically, unless a static scene is momentarily stationary for more than 100 milliseconds, it does not make much impact on our cognition process. However, if it is a video, the saliency also has to account for the motion of the objects involved in the frames. So, the viewing angle has to be considered to characterize the fixation regions. Typical ranges of angular velocities for a system mounted eye tracker and wearable eye tracker are 0−10 degrees per second and 50−80 degrees per second, respectively. In fact, the higher angular velocities in wearable eye trackers is to compensate for the head movements as well. Intuitively, a higher duration of average fixation on a target implies putting more effort to understand the scene (i.e., the scene is more engaging).

Saccades are triggered either voluntarily or involuntarily during viewing a scene. Saccades are fast movements and their range of duration is 20−120 milliseconds. For typical natural scenes, the usual duration for a saccade is 20 to 40 milliseconds. Larger jumps in fixation zones produce longer durations of saccades. While saccades play an important role in selective attention, the microsaccades are critical in keeping the gaze locations stable in the fixated region. Unlike saccades, which move the gaze from one salient zone to another, microsaccades bring the attention back to the same fixation point when it is drifted away for it. Microsaccadic movement is like a feedback mechanism to correct the fixated points. Microsaccades are faster than saccades. The peak angular velocity of microsaccades is in the range of 90−200 degrees per second. From the trajectory of eye gaze on a painting of Picasso (`Tragedy`, Fig. 5.15), we observe that the saccadic movements are mainly the transitions between the faces, the limbs, and to a few other weaker fixation areas. The rapid movements in fixation zones, as observed in the zoomed portion of the figure, near the toe of a person (Fig. 5.21), are the microsaccades. We observe that, in this cognitive process, human faces attract long-duration fixations and they are the primary focus of microsaccades.

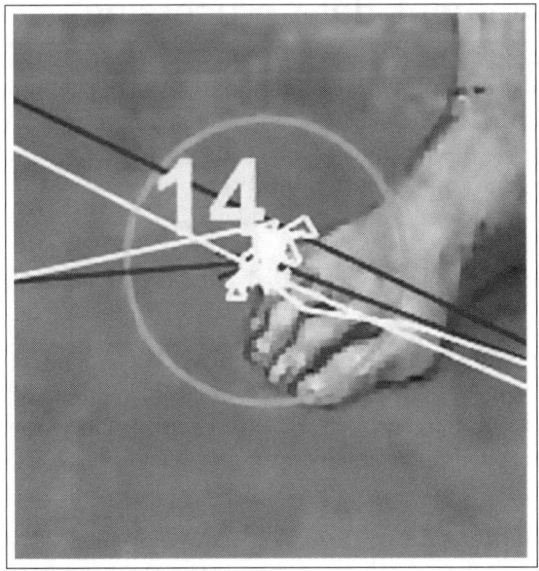

Figure 5.21 A portion of Fig. 5.15 showing saccades and microsaccades. (*Source*: Dr Anup Kumar, Post Doctoral Fellow, IIT Gandhinagar.)

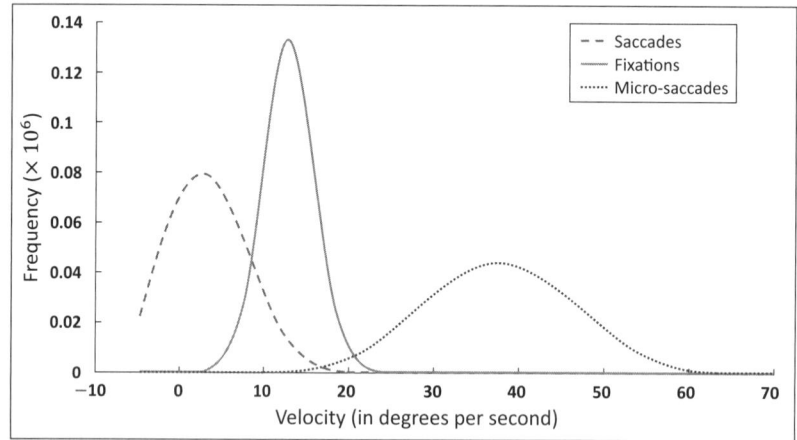

Figure 5.22 Velocity distribution of fixation, saccade, and microsaccade movements. (*Source*: Dr M. Sai Phani Kumar for sharing the figure from his PhD work (Malladi, 2022).)

An interesting statistics of these movements is shown in Fig. 5.22, where the distribution of the angular velocities of the three states, fixation, saccades, and microsaccades, is plotted (Malladi, 2022). As seen in the figure, the velocity for fixation is the least with an average of around 4 degrees per second. For saccadic movement, the average velocity is around 13 degrees per second. The microsaccade movement has the highest velocity with an average of around 38 degrees per second.

5.7 | Eye movement data processing

The eye gaze data needs to be post processed due to some of the limitations of the tracking devices. There can be various kinds of noise in the acquired data, which may not always provide absolutely reliable observations. Also, some of the data samples may be missed in the processing pipeline due to hardware limitations. To account for the data quality, some of the high-end and sophisticated eye trackers, like Tobii™ eye trackers and devices, provide a measure of quality of the data as a metric. In such devices, only the data samples with sufficiently good quality measures can be used. Few of the common processing steps are discussed here.

Correction of practical sampling frequency It is observed that the practical sampling frequency in most of the trackers is not always equal to the manufacturer's designed frequency and the number of records in each second is found to be inconsistent. Besides, the issues in synchronization of eye movement data also create difficulties in processing them.

Selection of eye movement data Selection of eye movement data is very much essential when there are instances where both the left and the right eyes are tracked, but they do not function equally. In such a scenario, two cases are usually considered:

(i) Case 1: The binocular data is used. This is more relevant for understanding the visible scene.

(ii) Case 2: Dominant/auxiliary eye's data is considered. Here, the missing data of the eye is set to blank or zero for further processing.

Filling-in of small gaps   Gaps in the gaze data are usually caused by the blinking of eyes of the viewer and frequency correction of the samples in the device. Such gaps are typically filled-in by using linear or spline interpolation techniques. Since the gaze data is characterized by some trajectory, different interpolations of the data can be used to compensate for the missing samples.

Data filtering   A high sampling frequency provides better tracking of the gaze, but it is prone to contamination of noise in the samples. So to tackle the high frequency noise, though the gaze data is acquired at a high sampling rate, it is brought down to a lower sampling rate for better handling of the data. The data is downsampled by smoothening it using the methods like moving average, moving median etc.

Identification of fixation, saccade, and microsaccade   Identification of fixation, saccadic, and microsaccadic intervals is one of the major tasks of eye gaze analysis. One of the approaches is by using the angular velocity profile of the gaze data. However, this is not a straight and simple process, since the ranges of these movements vary with use cases and there are overlapping ranges of velocities. So, the behavior of the trajectory has to be considered. If the gaze locations are stably concentrated in a small zone in the image without significant jumps, they are mostly the fixations. Saccades are usually observed with long jumps from one fixation zone to the another with a relatively lower velocity profile. If the velocity is very high and the movements are randomly distributed around the fixation region, then they are microsaccades. Thus, all the characteristics of the movements, by definition, should be exploited to identify these zones. Angular velocity is one of the major cues in identifying the types of movements. Other important cues are the distribution or spatial proximity characteristics of clusters and length of the duration or interval of the movements. Further, the fixation zones may be merged based on the longer durations and lower velocities, since very close fixations are usually required to be merged to larger regions.

Use of the processed data   There are several uses of processing the gaze data. Generally, the processed data reflects the interests of the observers through obtained gaze targets. This helps in understanding the behavior of the viewer. One of the major objectives of gaze analysis is to study the behavior of an observer. In the recent days, it is increasingly being used to analyze the mental health by psychiatrists to understand the behavior of their subjects.

5.8 | Applications of eye movement data

The applications of gaze data span various domains of science and technology, like computer science, neuroscience, industrial engineering, advertising media, etc. Relevance to some of these fields is briefly discussed here.

Computer science   There are various applications of gaze data in the domain of computer science. *Attentive user interfaces* is one of the primary applications, where the eye contact as attentional cue engages the users in a more sociable process of turn-taking, such as, use of an eye contact sensor to turn on/off a light. Similarly, any user interface that uses the eye movements to drive the environment by understanding user's intentions and performs necessary actions will require gaze data. The gaze data is also used in *collaborative systems* to aid multiparty mediated communication, since eye gaze is also a mode of communication. For example, the gaze information can be used as screen pointers by only using the movements of eye. *Cognitive modeling* is another major application where this data is used to predict better models for accuracy and ease of learning. An example of this includes the eye-mouse movement relationship.

Neuroscience and psychology   Processed gaze data is extensively used in *scene perception* to develop a set of tasks to uniquely locate the interaction of context with object. For example, initial fixations provide a gist of the scene, and the rest of the fixation zones mostly fill-up the details. Another application is in assisting with certain *natural tasks* to analyze how our visual system takes part in performing those tasks.

Industrial engineering and human factors   The gaze data is extensively used in *aviation* industry, from testing procedural training to evaluation of increasingly sophisticated deployment of new displays. For example, it is used in training of new pilots. In automotive industry, the eye movement data is used to train and assess driving skills. Deficiency in attention is found to be significant cause for large proportion of accidents. Through eye tracking, an intelligent vehicle management system can analyze the driver's eye movement and trigger a warning system which will make the driver aware and motivate to pay more attention.

Marketing and advertising   Marketing and advertising see profound applications of gaze data, since it is very much necessary for the business units to understand the interested buyers whose interests are analyzed by their attention over boards and hoardings. In *advertisements* the eye trackers help to gain insight into the attentive processes over advertisement bills. For example, to know whether an increased advertisement repetition of a particular commodity diminishes the attentional devotion. In *marketing sector*, the gaze data is used to furnish and render product label designs. Eye gaze data helps in explaining the noted increase in speed during tasks of visual search over newly redesigned labels. For instance, newer designs for a product may require lesser fixation duration than for existing ones.

Summary

There are two component frameworks for interpreting visual attention, viz., (1) a bottom-up processing, which performs the saliency computation and (2) a top-down processing, which shifts the visual attention. There exist various computational models for visual saliency. In this chapter we discuss two typical models namely, a model based on psychological and neurological basis of visual saliency and a graph based model on degree centrality. The latter model assumes that the salient regions capture the centrality of the interactions of several regions. It is required to use reference or ground truth data of visual saliency for validating these models. The ground truths are primarily generated by two approaches, namely by techniques of recording subjective feedback from viewers, and recording eye gaze movements of a viewer using eye trackers. The study of eye movements aid in understanding the cognitive processes. There exist 2-D and 3-D eye tracking devices. Typically, 2-D gaze trackers use regression models using locations of pupil and glint, and 3-D gaze trackers determine a 3-D eyegaze vector joining the center of the cornea and the pupil position using stereo imaging and a pair of IR-LED for illumination. There are three types of eye gaze movements, namely fixations, saccades, and microsaccades. It is hypothesized that in the early stages of eye movements, the fixations occur in salient regions in an image.

Exercises

   (i) Describe briefly the visual pathway for processing the visual signal received at retinal cells of Eyes.

  (ii) Explain how modeling visual saliency is distinct from the selective attention.

 (iii) Describe how visual information processing proceeds in two pathways from the visual cortex to other parts of our brain.

  (iv) How trichromacy and color opponency theories are used in modeling the processing of information received in retinal cells by identifying roles of different types of cells that take part in processing information in the visual pathway.

   (v) What is a saliency map of an image? Describe the model and computation proposed by Koch and Ullman for obtaining the saliency map.

  (vi) Briefly describe the computational model to obtain saliency map as proposed by Itti, Coch and Niebur.

 (vii) Briefly describe the VisaNet, a model for computing the saliency using the degree centrality feature of a graphical representation.

(viii) Describe the methods of validating computational models with experimentally obtained ground truth of salient regions of an image.

  (ix) Define the metrics ADR, KLD, and CC for evaluating performance of a model for computing visual saliency.

   (x) Describe an experimental methodology for obtaining ground truth of salient regions of an image from subjective feedback.

  (xi) What is meant by a 2-D eye gaze sequence? Describe the PCCR technique for obtaining 2-D eye gaze data.

 (xii) Define fixations, saccades and micro saccades of eye movement in a sequence of eye gaze data. How they could be identified in the sequence?

(xiii) How do you define the visual axis of 3-D eye gaze? Describe how this axis could be obtained using stereo infra-red imaging.

6

Clustering and Segmentation

Clustering is a task of organizing objects into groups whose members are similar in some way. A *cluster* is a collection of objects that are similar to each other, but dissimilar to the objects belonging to other clusters. In other words, a cluster is a group of objects with loosely defined similarity among them, which may have the potential to form a class. A *class* is a known group of objects that are described by similar characteristics, and *classification* is the task of assigning a defined class to an object.[1] *Image segmentation* is also a problem that is similar to clustering, where the clusters are formed by groups of pixels that are similar in some context. In image segmentation, homogeneous regions in an image may be clustered to derive segments in the image. These segments represent clusters. An example of image segmentation is shown in Fig. 6.1, where the foreground is represented by mushroom and the background is represented by humus substance around it. In this case, the image is primarily clustered into two regions, which are shown by white solid contour (foreground) and white dashed contour (background).

The main motivations of clustering techniques are as follows.

- To find representative samples of homogeneous groups in the given data, which would reduce the data transmission and storage requirements in certain applications. Here, the data is represented by a smaller set of representative samples that capture the characteristics of total data.

- To discover natural groups or categories in the data, which may be used to describe the data samples by their unknown properties.

- To find relevant groups in the data, which facilitates to draw attention toward major groups of the data in the distribution. These groups form the major clusters in a given context, like segments in an image.

- To detect unusual data objects, which are the outliers in the data, that deviate from the collective characteristics of groups of data in a given context.

---

[1] Details of classification techniques are discussed in Chapter 7.

(a)   (b)

Figure 6.1 An example of image segmentation.

General processing pipeline In the context of image processing, and computer vision, the general processing pipeline is shown in Fig. 6.2. As seen in the figure, the clustering and classification stages are placed at a very high level of this pipeline. The lower level of the pipeline consists of stages like image preprocessing and feature extraction. At the feature extraction stage, the objects or image patches are represented by feature descriptors or feature vectors, which capture relevant information in images. These feature vectors are representative of the corresponding classes or groups of objects that are used for classification or clustering to assign them with known or unknown groups, respectively, by contextual similarity. In the figure, the end results (clusters with not well defined characteristics or known classes) are represented by different patterns to denote different groups.

Learning problems The approaches of clustering and classification tasks are essentially learning problems. There are two approaches to the learning problem, viz., supervised and unsupervised learning. Here, the learning is about groups or categories in the given data. Clustering is an *unsupervised learning* approach, where the learning is accomplished in the absence of almost[2] any prior knowledge on the groups in the data. Classification is a *supervised learning* approach, which exploits knowledge about the data, such as exemplar instances of classes. For example, in the case of classification, training samples with class labels are provided for finding appropriate features that are suitable for predicting classes of unknown data samples.

There are also other variations in the learning framework, like the *semi-supervised learning* and the *reinforcement learning*. In the semi-supervised learning, the system learns by using unlabeled data for majority of portion in training, in conjunction with a smaller set of labeled data. The size of unlabeled data is usually much larger than the size of the

---

[2] Sometimes, the information of number of groups or categories in the data is required.

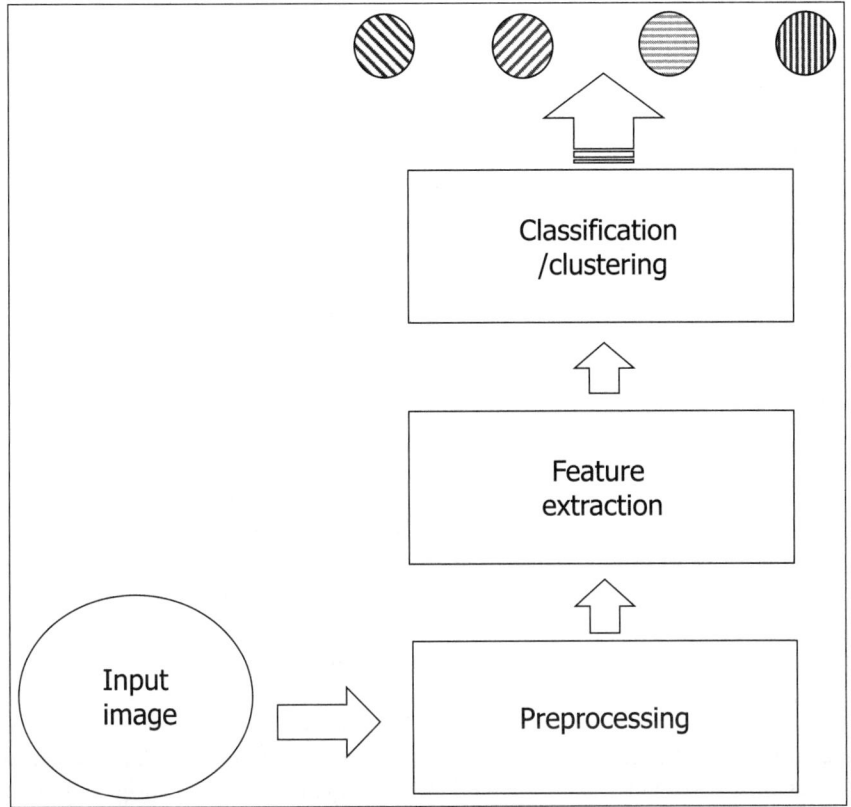

Figure 6.2 General processing pipeline for classification and clustering.

labeled data. This mechanism of the semi-supervised learning falls between the unsupervised and the supervised learning. In the reinforcement learning, the learning is achieved by appropriate feedback from a teacher or a critique (e.g., a human expert) in the form of reward or punishment, which is usually in the binary form like yes or no, true or false, etc. The feedback facilitates in gradually refining the learning process.

6.1 | Components of clustering technique

There are three major components in a clustering approach, which are as follows.

(i) A similarity (or distance) measure between any two data samples: For defining similarity between data samples, different distance measures are used, for example, L_1 norm, L_2 norm, or generalized L_p norm.

(ii) Criterion or objective function to evaluate clustering outcome: To evaluate a clustering solution, two particular properties are looked for, viz., intra-cluster cohesion and inter-cluster separation. A good clustering solution is expected to have a good homogeneity property within the members of the cluster, which represents high intra-cluster cohesion. Toward this, one of the popular measures is the sum of squares errors (SSE) measuring deviations from the homogeneity property. A clustering solution is also characterized by well separated or well discriminated groups or clusters, which represents large inter-cluster separation.

(iii) The clustering algorithm: There are various algorithms to solve the clustering problem such as, K-means, K-medoids, mixture of Gaussians, graph-based techniques, hierarchical clustering, etc.

6.1.1 | Homogeneity and separation principles

Homogeneity is a property that measures how close are the elements to each other within a cluster. For example, the average distance of the elements of a cluster from its cluster center is a measure to compute homogeneity. If this average distance is small, the cluster satisfies a good homogeneity property. By separation property in clusters, the elements in different clusters should be significantly apart from each other than the elements in the same clusters. For example, the average distance between pairs of cluster centers is a popular measure to compute separation. If this distance is large, the clustering solution satisfies a good separation property, where the cluster centers are placed sufficiently apart from each other. The clustering or partitioning is a non trivial problem, which may have several choices of solutions. As an example, consider the distribution of 2-D data points in Fig. 6.3 (a) that are shown by circles in a 2-D coordinate space. Consider one kind of partition as in Fig. 6.3 (b), and another kind of partitioning as in Fig. 6.3 (c). By considering the properties of homogeneity and separation, the solution shown in Fig. 6.3 (b) is found to be a bad clustering example, whereas the solution in Fig. 6.3 (c) is a good clustering example.

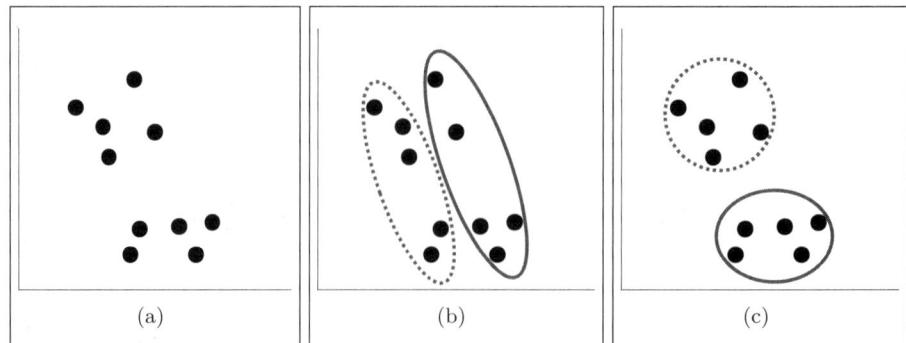

(a)	(b)	(c)

Figure 6.3 An example of clustering. (a) Given data points. (b) Bad clustering. (c) Good clustering.

6.2 | *K*-means clustering

The *K-means clustering* technique computes K partitions or clusters, given N data points such that, the sum of square of distances between any data point and the center of its respective partition or cluster is minimized. The objective function for minimization in this algorithm is formulated below.

$$E = \sum_{k=1}^{K} \sum_{\forall \boldsymbol{x} \in \boldsymbol{C}_k} ||\boldsymbol{x} - \boldsymbol{c}_k||^2, \text{ where } \boldsymbol{c}_k = \frac{1}{|C_k|} \sum_{\forall \boldsymbol{x} \in \boldsymbol{C}_k} \boldsymbol{x} \tag{6.1}$$

Here, $\boldsymbol{x}$ is a data point, and $\boldsymbol{c}_k$ denotes the mean of the kth partition, C_k. The function, E, represents the sum of square of deviations or distances from $\boldsymbol{c}_k$ to the points which are included in C_k. The objective is to minimize this error function, E. Since there are K partitions, all the components from K partitions are summed up in the optimization function. This problem is an NP-hard problem, provided $K > 1$.

6.2.1 | The Lloyd algorithm

A popular algorithm for obtaining an approximate solution of the K-means clustering is known as *Lloyd algorithm* (Lloyd, 1982), named after Stuart Lloyd of Bell Labs, USA (1957), the inventor of the algorithm. The Lloyd algorithm is summarized in Algorithm 6. Given the number of clusters, K, the initial centers of K clusters may be randomly chosen.

Algorithm 6 Lloyd algorithm for K-means clustering

Input: A set of data points and their K initial cluster centers
Output: K final cluster centers
1: Given K initial centers, assign each data point to the cluster represented by its center, if it is the closest among them.
2: Update the cluster centers as the mean of the data points in each of them.
3: Iterate above two steps, till the centers do not change their positions by a tolerance margin, ϵ_t.
4: Compute the final K cluster centers.

The data points are partitioned by these K initial centers by assigning each data point to the cluster of its nearest center. Then, the cluster centers are updated by computing the mean of the data points in each of the K partitions. The newly computed cluster centers are mostly different from the chosen initial centers. These steps of computing cluster centers and assigning each data point to its nearest cluster center are iterated till the centers do not change their position by a small tolerance margin, ϵ_t. This is a very simple yet effective approach for computing the cluster centers. Mathematically, this technique tries to minimize the energy function defined by the sum of divergence, which is given by Eq. 6.1, to compute the clusters. Though this technique is seen to work well in practice, it has two major issues: (1) it does not guarantee the convergence of the cluster centers, and (2) the algorithm may get stuck at a local minimum.

6.2.2 | Greedy K-means algorithm

The Lloyd algorithm is fast, but it does not necessarily result in optimal solution. A more conservative approach is to move one data point at a time iteratively, provided overall cost is reduced. An example of such an approach is a greedy algorithm that chooses the transfer of a data point from a class (say, c_i) to another class (say, c_j), which causes a maximal cost reduction at that step. Here, similar to Lloyd algorithm, the data points are initially subjected to an arbitrary partition, P, into K clusters. At first, the reduction in cost is initialized with 0. Then, for every cluster, the difference between the cost of the current P and a new partition after the transfer of every element that is not in the considered cluster is computed. This difference in the costs is its reduction, and at each iteration, the reduction in the cost is checked. The partition resulting the maximum reduction in the cost is accepted. That is, the centers and the partitions are recomputed. This can be efficiently performed by considering only those clusters that are affected by the accepted transfer by recomputing their means. The cluster labels of the elements that are not affected by the transfer remains unchanged. The iterations last till the convergence of the cost function, when there is no reduction further, or the algorithm is stopped after some preset number of iterations. The Greedy K-means algorithm is summarized in Algorithm 7.

Algorithm 7 Greedy K-means algorithm

    Input: A set of data points and their K initial cluster centers
    Output: K final cluster centers
1: Select an arbitrary partition P into K clusters.
2: Iterate the following steps till convergence of cost.

        maxReduction = 0

3: For every cluster c_k, where $k = 0, 1, 2, ..., K$,

        For every element p_i not in c_k,
- reduction = cost(P) - cost($P_{p_i \rightarrow c_k}$).
- If (reduction $\geq$ 0),
  - If reduction $\geq$ maxReduction,
    - ○ maxReduction = reduction.
    - ○ Move p_i to c_k.
    - ○ Update centers of c_k and the cluster containing p_i.

4: Compute the final cluster centers.

Similar to the Lloyd algorithm, this algorithm also does not guarantee to converge at global minimum, but it is seen to converge to a relatively better local minimum. However, this greedy algorithm is very slow in comparison with the Lloyd algorithm.

Numerical Example

Assume, you want to cluster 12 observations into 4 clusters using K-means clustering algorithm. After first iteration clusters, C_1, C_2, C_3, C_4 has following observations:

$C_1 : \{(2,2),(1,4),(9,9)\}$

$C_2 : \{(5,5),(-1,4),(10,40)\}$

$C_3 : \{(4,4),(2,-2),(-22,-20)\}$

$C_4 : \{(6,6),(4,0),(0,0)\}$

What will be the cluster assignment for the point $(5,5)$ in the next iteration?

Solution

We need to compute centroids of clusters and assign the cluster whose center is the nearest to $(5,5)$. For example, centroid of $C_1 = ((2+1+9)/3, (2+4+9)/3)$, $C_2 = ((5-1+10)/3, (5+4+40)/3)$, $C_3 = ((4+2-22)/3, (4-2-30)/3)$ and $C_4 = ((6+4+0)/3, (6+0+0)/3)$. Therefore, $(5,5)$ is assigned to C_1.

6.3 | K-medoids clustering

The K-medoids clustering is a particular variation of the K-means clustering technique. A *medoid* is defined as the representative element of a set of data points with minimal average dissimilarity with the other data points in the set. That is, for a set of points, its medoid is the point in the set that has the minimum average of the distances from the other points in the set. So, the medoid is always restricted to be a member of the data set. Given a set of points, $\mathrm{X} = \{\boldsymbol{x}_i | i = 1, 2, \dots, n\}$, where n is the number of points in X, the definition of medoid is mathematically given as in Eq. 6.2.

$$\boldsymbol{x}_{\text{medoid}} = \underset{\boldsymbol{x}_k}{\operatorname{argmin}} \frac{1}{n-1} \sum_{\forall j, j \neq k} ||\boldsymbol{x}_j - \boldsymbol{x}_k|| \qquad (6.2)$$

This is similar to the median vector of the set. Similar to the Eq. 6.1 in K-means clustering, the cost to be minimized in K-medoids clustering is given by Eq. 6.3.

$$E = \sum_{k=1}^{K} \sum_{\forall \boldsymbol{x} \in \boldsymbol{C}_k} ||\boldsymbol{x} - \boldsymbol{m}_k||^2, \text{ where } \boldsymbol{m}_k \text{ is the medoid of } C_k. \qquad (6.3)$$

The function, E, computes the sum of square of deviations or distances from $\boldsymbol{m}_k$ to the points which are included in C_k.

The K-medoids clustering algorithm is almost similar to the K-means clustering algorithm, except for the measure used in updating the cluster centers. The K-medoids algorithm is given in Algorithm 8.

One of the problems of K-medoids clustering is that of updating of the medoids, which is computationally very expensive. For every cluster, the corresponding median vector has

---

Algorithm 8 Algorithm for K-medoids clustering

   Input: A set of data points and their K initial cluster centers
   Output: K final cluster centers
1: Given K initial centers, assign each data point to the cluster represented by its center, if it is the closest among them.
2: Update the centers as the medoid of the data points in each of them.
3: Iterate above two steps, till the medoids do not change their positions.
4: Compute the final K cluster centers.

---

to be computed at each iteration, which is a very slow process. One of the variations of K-medoids technique to make this computation faster is known as *partitioning around medoids* (PAM). Here, in an iteration, the medoids of only two clusters are computed, instead of all of them. A randomly chosen element of a cluster is swapped with the medoid element of another cluster. The swap is accepted and the medoid is updated if the swap decreases the cost. This operation of swapping is continued till the algorithm converges. The convergence criteria may be the number of iterations or when there is no further decrease in the cost. The PAM algorithm (Kaufman and Rousseeuw, 2008) is given in Algorithm 9.

Algorithm 9 Partitioning around medoids algorithm

   Input: A set of data points and their K initial cluster centers
   Output: K final cluster centers
1: Given K initial centers, assign each data point to the cluster represented by its center, if it is the closest among them.
2: For each cluster, randomly choose an element of a different cluster and swap with the medoid element. Update the medoids.
3: If the cost decreases, accept the swap.
4: Iterate above two steps, till convergence.
5: Compute the final K cluster centers.

6.4 | Probabilistic modeling by mixture of Gaussians

Segmentation of images by probabilistic modeling is performed by considering the data as a mixture of probability densities. One of the popular techniques of analyzing the probability density functions of the data is by representing them as a mixture of Gaussians. Similar to the K-means clustering technique, this is also an iterative method of clustering a given set of data points. Here, a cluster center is augmented by its covariance matrix, along with the mean of the data points in the cluster. In this iterative technique, at every iteration, both the means and covariance matrices of all clusters are updated. The distance of every data point with each of the clusters is computed using Mahalanobis distance function, which is given by Eq. 6.4.

$$d_M(\boldsymbol{x}, \boldsymbol{\mu}_k; \boldsymbol{\Sigma}_k) = (\boldsymbol{x} - \boldsymbol{\mu}_k)^\top \boldsymbol{\Sigma}_k^{-1}(\boldsymbol{x} - \boldsymbol{\mu}_k) \tag{6.4}$$

where, $d_M(\cdot)$ represents the *Mahalanobis distance function*, $\boldsymbol{x}$ is the data point, and $\boldsymbol{\mu}_k$ and $\boldsymbol{\Sigma}_k$ are the mean or the cluster center and the covariance matrix of the kth cluster, respectively.

Though this appears to be similar to the K-means clustering technique at the outset, the clusters are not updated by simple distance based assignments in mixture of Gaussians. Instead of crisply defining the membership of a cluster for every data point, a probability of belongingness of the data points to all the clusters is maintained at each iteration. This process is iterated till a good estimation of probability density functions that consistently describes the corresponding distribution is achieved. The parametric probability density function of a data point $\boldsymbol{x}$ is described by the weighted sum of normal distributions or mixture of Gaussian distributions, which is given by Eq. 6.5.

$$p(\boldsymbol{x}|\{\pi_k, \boldsymbol{\mu}_k, \boldsymbol{\Sigma}_k\}) = \sum_{k=1}^{K} \pi_k \mathcal{N}(\boldsymbol{x}|\boldsymbol{\mu}_k, \boldsymbol{\Sigma}_k) \tag{6.5}$$

where, K is the number of clusters and $\mathcal{N}$ is the kth normal distribution, which is given by Eq. 6.6.

$$\mathcal{N}(\boldsymbol{x}|\boldsymbol{\mu}_k, \boldsymbol{\Sigma}_k) = \frac{1}{\sqrt{(2\pi)^n|\boldsymbol{\Sigma}|}} e^{-\frac{1}{2}d_M(\boldsymbol{x}, \boldsymbol{\mu}_k; \boldsymbol{\Sigma}_k)} \tag{6.6}$$

where, π_k represents the mixing coefficients that weigh multiple K distributions, and $\boldsymbol{\mu}_k$ and $\boldsymbol{\Sigma}_k$ are the mean (or cluster center) and covariance matrix of the kth normal distribution. To compute the mixture of Gaussian distributions, these parameters are estimated using an algorithm known as the *expectation-maximization* (EM) algorithm.

6.4.1 | Expectation-maximization algorithm

Expectation-maximization is a two stage process, an expectation stage and a maximization stage. At first, the K distributions are initialized with a set of randomly chosen parameters over the given set of data points. In the expectation stage, the likelihood probabilities of all the data points to each of the K Gaussian clusters are computed. The kth cluster posterior, z_{ik}, is computed as the product of the probability distribution function (i.e., corresponding probability of each data point, $\boldsymbol{x}_i$, belonging to the kth normal distribution) and the respective mixture coefficient, π_k. This is mathematically given by Eq. 6.7.

$$z_{ik} = \frac{1}{Z_i} \pi_k \mathcal{N}(\boldsymbol{x}_i|\boldsymbol{\mu}_k, \boldsymbol{\Sigma}_k) \tag{6.7}$$

where, Z_i is the normalizing coefficient, i.e. $Z_i = \sum_k \pi_k \mathcal{N}(\boldsymbol{x}_i|\boldsymbol{\mu}_k, \boldsymbol{\Sigma}_k)$. The posterior probabilities for each cluster are computed for every data point, $\boldsymbol{x}_i$, in the given set. This is the expectation stage.

Then, $\boldsymbol{x}_i$ is assigned to the cluster whose posterior is the maximum. This implies that cluster of $\boldsymbol{x}_i$ is $\underset{k}{\mathrm{argmax}}\ z_{ik}$. However, this assignment is an optional step at each iteration and it does not reflect the final assignment. The cluster assignment at the last iteration of the expectation stage is the valid assignment.

By using the cluster posteriors of data points, reestimation of parameters is performed for all the K clusters. This reestimation is carried out following the maximum likelihood approach. Hence this stage is called the maximization stage. This process of expectation and maximization stages is iterated till convergence. For a given data point, $\boldsymbol{x}$, its posterior probability of belongingness to the kth cluster, $(P(k|\boldsymbol{x}_i) = z_{ik})$ is computed by Eq. 6.7 as the product of the kth component of Gaussian distribution (probability density function) and the corresponding mixture coefficient, which is then normalized with respect to all the K clusters. These probabilities are taken as the strengths that represent the number of points in their respective clusters. The sum of posteriors of all the data points to a cluster N_k provides an estimate of the size of the cluster, which is not a discrete number. In other words, it is the expected number of feature vectors in the kth cluster. Then, the mean of the kth distribution or cluster is computed by considering the corresponding posteriors of data points in it as their weights. Thus, the weighted mean of the data points belonging to the kth cluster is given by Eq. 6.8.

$$\boldsymbol{\mu}_k = \frac{1}{N_k} \sum_{i=1}^{N} z_{ik} \boldsymbol{x}_i \tag{6.8}$$

where, $N_k = \sum_{i=1}^{N} z_{ik}$ is the number of data points in the kth cluster. Similarly, the covariance matrix of the cluster is computed as in Eq. 6.9.

$$\boldsymbol{\Sigma_k} = \frac{1}{N_k} \sum_{i=1}^{N} z_{ik} (\boldsymbol{x}_i - \boldsymbol{\mu}_k)(\boldsymbol{x}_i - \boldsymbol{\mu}_k)^{\top} \tag{6.9}$$

Also, the mixture coefficients, π_k is computed as the fraction of the total number of data points, N, which is given by Eq. 6.10.

$$\pi_k = \frac{N_k}{N} \tag{6.10}$$

The mixture coefficient represents the prior probability of the kth cluster.

The EM algorithm is given Algorithm 10. In this way, the set of parameters, $\{\pi_k, \boldsymbol{\mu}_k, \boldsymbol{\Sigma}_k\}$, is computed. After iterating the redistribution of data and re-estimation of parameters till convergence, each data point is assigned to the cluster that is represented by the corresponding Gaussian distribution component which has the highest posterior probability. This probabilistic modeling technique is also known as mixture of Gaussian method or Gaussian mixture model (GMM), which is used for clustering of images.

Algorithm 10 Expectation-maximization algorithm for data clustering

---

Input: A set of data points and an initial set of its parameters, $\{\pi_k, \boldsymbol{\mu}_k, \boldsymbol{\Sigma}_k\}$, that represent K clusters
Output: Final set of parameters that define the K final clusters
1: Start with the initial set of $\{\pi_k, \boldsymbol{\mu}_k, \boldsymbol{\Sigma}_k\}$.
2: E-step (expectation stage)

- Compute the posterior probability (z_{ik}) of $\boldsymbol{x}_i$ belonging to the kth Gaussian cluster.
- Assign $\boldsymbol{x}_i$ to the mth cluster whose posterior is the maximum (optional step; decision is taken at the end).

3: M-step (maximization stage)

- Re-estimate the parameters $(\{\pi_k, \boldsymbol{\mu}_k, \boldsymbol{\Sigma}_k\})$ of the clusters using the maximum likelihood approach (Eqs. 6.7 - 6.10).

4: Iterate the above E-step and M-step till the convergence.
5: Compute the final parameters for the K clusters.

6.5 | Segmentation of images

The segmentation of an image is the task of partitioning of image pixels into meaningful non overlapping sets or regions, which may or may not be connected. By a subsequent task, it may be required to extract the connected regions as subsets of those nonoverlapping sets. The latter task is called *component labeling*.

Let R be the entire spatial region occupied by the image. Segmentation is a process to partition R into n sub-regions, R_1, R_2, ..., R_n, so that

$$\bigcup_{i=1}^{n} R_i = R$$

$$R_i \cap R_j = \emptyset, \ \forall i, j, \ i \neq j \qquad (6.11)$$

$$Q(R_i) = \text{TRUE}, \ \forall i$$

$$Q(R_i \cup R_j) = \text{FALSE, if } i \text{ and } j \text{ are adjacent}$$

where $Q(R_i)$ is a logical predicate over R_i.

The logical predicate states some homogeneity property of a region which is true for all the pixels lying in the region. For example, consider the following definition of a logical predicate Q.

If the brightness values of all the pixels of a region are such that either all of them lie within the interval $[0, 50)$, or they lie within $[50, 255]$, then the value of the predicate is true, else it is false.

The above definition of the logical predicate partitions a gray level image whose pixel values lie within $[0, 255]$, in two regions in the following way.

(i) R_1: All the pixels of the image, whose brightness values lie within $[0, 50)$.

(ii) R_2: All the pixels of the image, whose brightness values lie within $[50, 255]$

For each of the above regions (or their subsets), the values of the logical predicates $Q(R_1)$ and $Q(R_2)$ are true. For any other region sharing pixels from both of them, the value of the predicate is false.

There are two ways to compute the segments. It may be carried out by detecting edge pixels, and linking them to define the boundaries of regions or segments. The other segmentation approach is a region based approach, where regions of a group of similar pixels are computed, each defining a segment.

6.5.1 | Edge based segmentation

In Chapter 1, it is briefly discussed how gradient operators are used in computing edge pixels. Mathematically, an edge point is characterized by the presence of discontinuity of the function. Thus, the behavior of first order and second order derivatives of a function at points of discontinuity may be modeled to design an edge detector. Let us illustrate these characteristics with an example in 1-D as shown by an intensity plot in Fig. 6.4. Different segments of changes of functional values are illustrated in the figure, such as segments of a constant value (flat), gradual descent or ascent (ramp), sharp changes in slope (isolated point), and abrupt (or sharp) transition from one level to another level (step). The slopes of the line segments are also shown close to them in the figure. Accordingly the

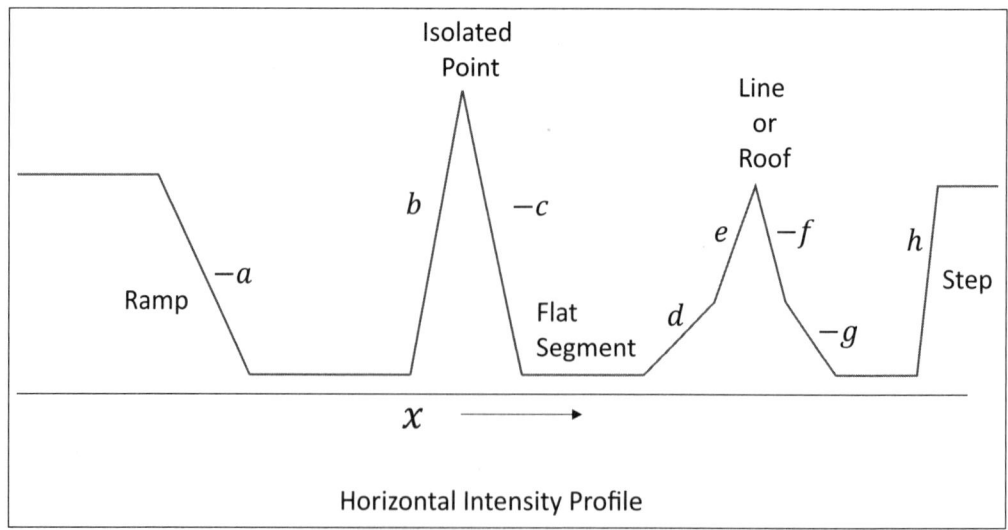

Figure 6.4 Horizontal intensity profile.

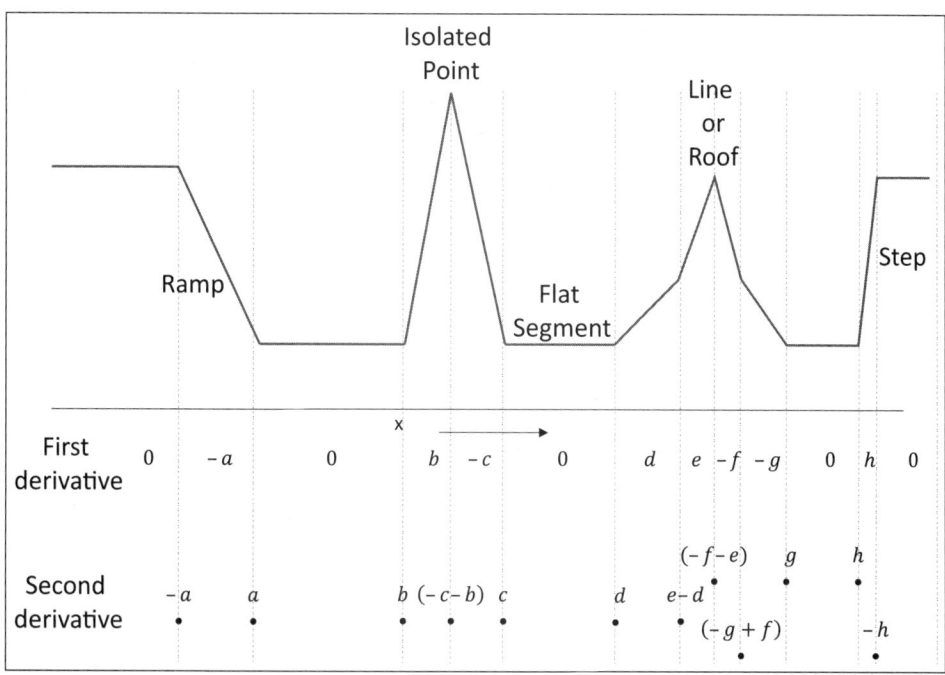

Figure 6.5 First and second derivatives of the horizontal intensity profile shown in Fig. 6.4.

point where one of these types of discontinuity takes place is called a *ramp edge* or an *isolated point* (not an edge) or a *step edge*. In Fig. 6.5, the values of first and second derivatives of the intensity profile are shown. For the first derivative values of the function, the values are shown for each segment of the plot, as they remain constant throughout the segment. But for the second derivative, only nonzero values at the points of discontinuities are shown. In all other points its value remains zero. From these we may observe the following:

(i) The magnitudes of first derivatives are high at the intervals of transitions. Sharper the ascent or descent, higher is the magnitude. At all the points belonging to the whole interval of ascent or descent, the magnitudes are high and hence, the detection using first derivative operation (such as Sobel and Prewitt, as discussed in Chapter 1) provide thick edges.

(ii) For the second derivative, the magnitude is high only at the point of transition. But for each segment of ascent or descent, a change of sign takes place from its one end to the other end. This produces two values at closely spaced points. However, due to the phenomenon of the change of sign, the point of zero-crossing within the interval provides a good localization of the edge point. In this case, edges are thin, and isolated points are also detected as edge points. The estimation of second derivative is done by computing the difference of differences. Hence the detector is very sensitive to noise.

The edge detectors are designed using the above principles. In Chapter 1, it is discussed how the first derivatives of images are computed using edge operators, such as Sobel and Prewitt operators. Likewise we may compute the second derivative at a point by computing the difference of differences along a particular direction. This is illustrated below. Consider the estimation of the partial second derivative of $f(x, y)$ with respect to x. It is defined as in Eq. 6.12.

$$\frac{\partial^2 f(x, y)}{\partial x^2} = \frac{\partial f(x, y)}{\partial x} - \frac{\partial f(x-1, y)}{\partial x} \tag{6.12}$$

Now $\frac{\partial f(x,y)}{\partial x}$ is estimated by the difference operation as follows.

$$\frac{\partial f(x, y)}{\partial x} = f(x+1, y) - f(x, y) \tag{6.13}$$

Hence the difference of differences along x provides the estimate of the partial second derivative as follows.

$$\frac{\partial^2 f(x, y)}{\partial x^2} \approx f(x+1, y) - f(x, y) - (f(x, y) - f(x-1, y))$$
$$= f(x+1, y) - 2f(x, y) + f(x-1, y) \tag{6.14}$$

Hence for computing the *Laplacian* of $f(x, y)$, $\frac{\partial^2 f(x,y)}{\partial x^2} + \frac{\partial^2 f(x,y)}{\partial y^2}$, the mask as shown in Fig. 6.6 (a) may be used. If we consider the estimation using the two diagonal directions, the mask is designed as shown in Fig. 6.6 (b). For a robust computation, a weighted combination of these may be used, for example using the mask in Fig. 6.6 (c). After computing the Laplacian of an image, the zero crossings are detected in Laplacian operated image to obtain the edge pixels. Typical results are shown in Fig. 6.7.

0	1	0
1	−4	1
0	1	0

(a)

1	0	1
0	−4	0
1	0	1

(b)

4	1	4
1	−20	1
4	1	4

(c)

Figure 6.6 Masks for computing Laplacian. (a) Laplacian-1, (b) Laplacian-2 (diagonal), and (c) Laplacian-3 (mixed).

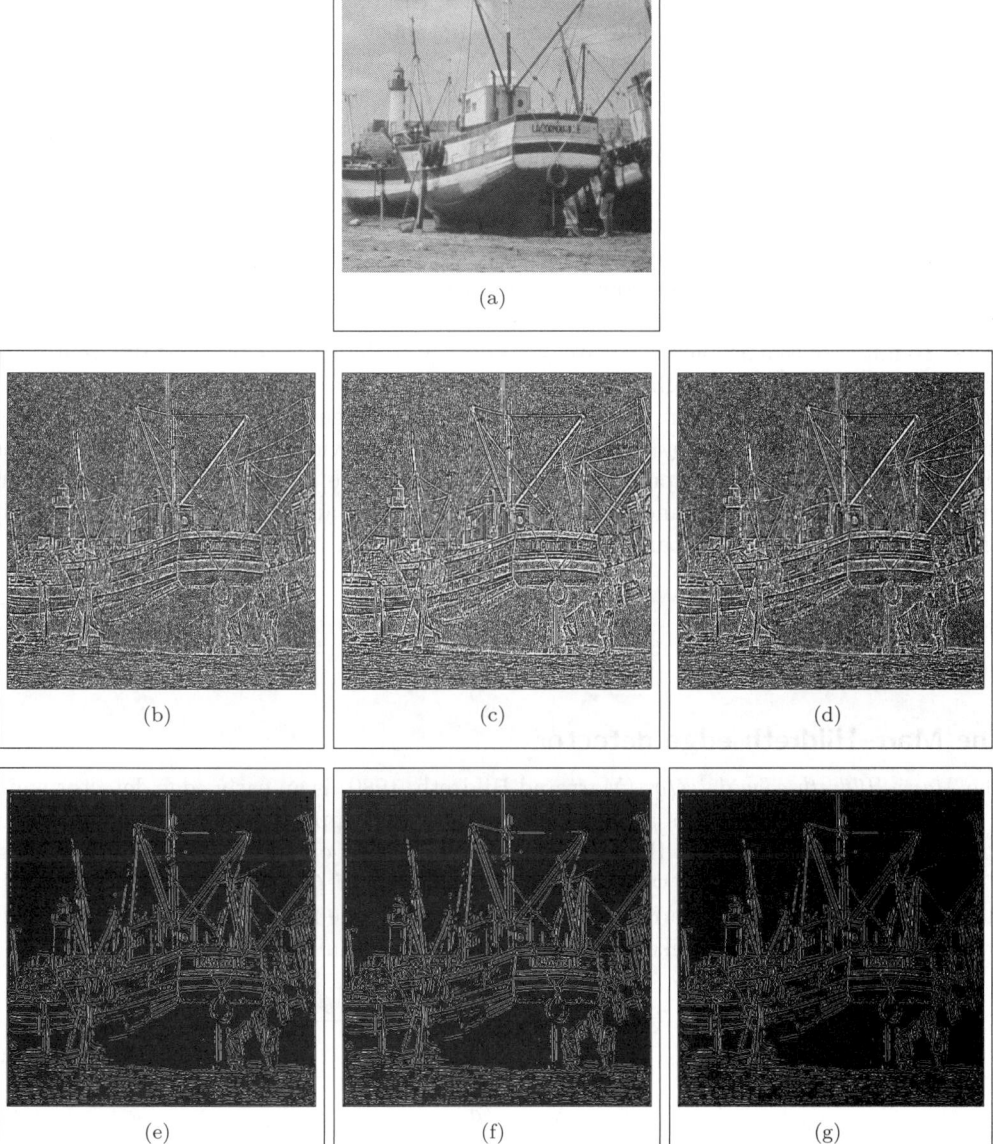

Figure 6.7 Masks for computing Laplacian. (a) Input image, "boat", (b) Laplacian-1, (c) Laplacian-2 (diagonal), (d) Laplacian-3 (mixed), (e) zero-crossings from Laplacian-1, (f) zero-crossings from Laplacian-2, and (g) zero-crossings from Laplacian-3.

Effect of noise and blur

The presence of noise and blur in images affect the detection of the edges. The noise introduces spurious discontinuities, many local spikes and errors in estimating the derivatives. In particular it affects the estimation of second derivatives more, which causes suppression of weak edges.

The blur dampens the changes due to a discontinuity and thus, reduces the strength of the response of the detectors at edge points. Thus step edges tend to become ramp edges, and the slope of ramp edges decreases. The degree of dampening is proportional to amount of blur. It also causes shifts in the locations of transitions. Hence the localization of edge points becomes imprecise in presence of a blur.

To handle noise, an image is smoothed or low pass filtered. But this introduces blur in the image, which not only suppresses weak edges, but also causes shift and dampening of strong edges. To mitigate this problem, a strategy is adopted to detect edge pixels at different scales and track its location from higher scales to lower scales. The approach is called *scale space tracking of edge pixels* (Witkin, 1983). The detection of edge pixel at any scale, σ, implies that the image is smoothed by a low pass filter of a bandwidth proportional to the scale. Then the derivatives are computed on the smoothed image for detecting the edge pixels. Larger the scale, higher the bandwidth. For example, in a Gaussian filter, $G_\sigma(x, y)$ with the following filter response, the parameter σ denotes the scale.

$$G_\sigma(x, y) = \frac{1}{2\pi\sigma^2} e^{-\left(\frac{x^2+y^2}{2\sigma^2}\right)} \tag{6.15}$$

The Marr–Hildreth edge detector

The *Marr–Hildreth edge detector* (Marr and Hildreth, 1980) is an early edge detector which is robust to handle noise. It is a Laplacian operator and applied on a Gaussian smoothed image at an appropriate scale. However, since the Laplacian on a Gaussian smoothed image is the same as the operation with a mask of *Laplacian of Gaussian (LoG)* function, the Marr–Hildreth operator uses a mask designed from the same function. The LoG function is given below and its shape is like a Mexican hat, as shown in Fig. 6.8 (a).

$$\begin{aligned} \nabla^2 G(x, y) &= \frac{\partial^2 G(x, y)}{\partial x^2} + \frac{\partial^2 G(x, y)}{\partial y^2} \\ &= \left(\frac{x^2 + y^2 - 2\sigma^2}{\sigma^4}\right) e^{-\frac{x^2+y^2}{2\sigma^2}} \end{aligned} \tag{6.16}$$

We may note here in the plot we consider the negation of the LOG operator. The half-width of the mask implementing this function should be at least $2\sqrt{2}\sigma$. A typical approximation with integer values in a mask, at $\sigma = 1$, is shown in Fig. 6.9.

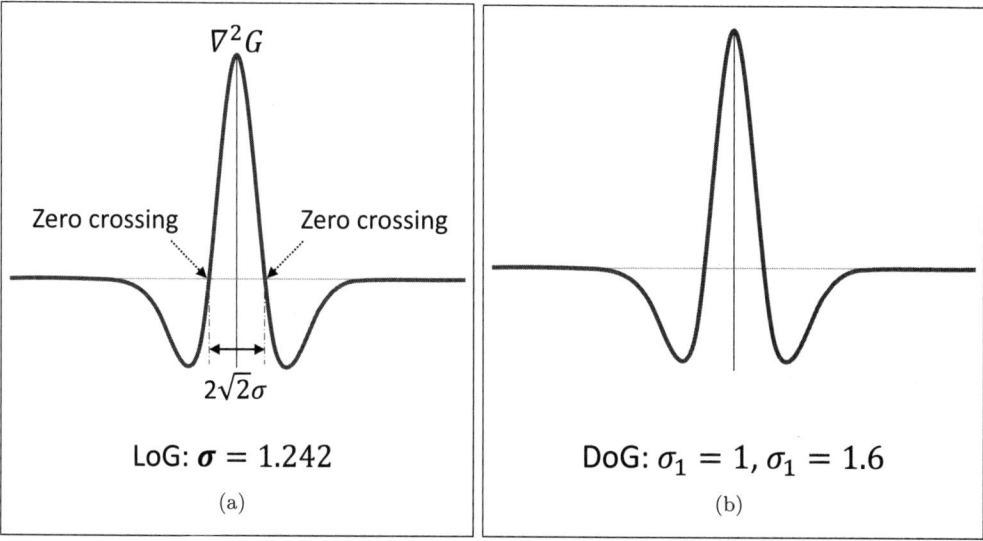

Figure 6.8 Plot of a 1-D LoG function.

0	0	−1	0	0
0	−1	−2	−1	0
−1	−2	16	−2	−1
0	−1	−2	−1	0
0	0	−1	0	0

Figure 6.9 Approximation of LoG with integer values in a mask.

The LoG function can also be approximated by a difference of Gaussian (DoG) functions, where differences of two Gaussian functions at two different scales, σ_1 and σ_2 are computed as shown in the following expression.

$$\text{DoG}(x,y) = \frac{1}{2\pi\sigma_1^2}e^{-\frac{x^2+y^2}{\sigma_1^2}} - \frac{1}{2\pi\sigma_2^2}e^{-\frac{x^2+y^2}{\sigma_2^2}} \tag{6.17}$$

We may observe that the DoG acts like a bandwidth filter, as its response is the difference of two low pass filters. It can be shown that the LoG is approximated by DoG when $\sigma_1 : \sigma_2 = 1.6 : 1$, as shown in Fig. 6.8 (b). At this condition, the zero-crossings of the DoG is the same as that from an LoG with σ, which is given by,

$$\sigma^2 = \frac{\sigma_1^2\sigma_2^2}{\sigma_1^2 - \sigma_2^2}\ln\left(\frac{\sigma_1^2}{\sigma_2^2}\right) \tag{6.18}$$

Typical examples of edges computed from the Marr–Hildreth operator and its approximation using an equivalent DoG are shown in Fig. 6.10. We may note also that certain channels of the human vision system are selective with respect to frequency and orientation, and may be modeled by the DoG with a ratio of $\sigma_1 : \sigma_2 = 1.75 : 1$.

(a)   (b)   (c)

Figure 6.10 Example of edge computation. (a) Original image. (b) Edges computed from Marr–Hildreth operator. (c) Edges computed using equivalent DoG operator.

The Canny edge detector

Another widely used operator was proposed in 1986 by Joseph Canny. This operator is designed through optimization of certain objective function which attempts to achieve, (i) low error rate, (ii) good localization, and (iii) single edge response. By keeping the error rate low, the detector attempts to detect all true edges and reject spurious edges that occur due to noise. A good localization means that the location of the edge point should not deviate much due to smoothing, and by designing the detector to give only a single edge point per occurrence of a true edge point. Canny (Canny, 1986) obtained an optimal detector in an empirical form for an ideal step edge in 1-D. The response is found to be closely approximated by the first order derivative of a Gaussian function as expressed below.

$$\frac{d\,e^{-\frac{x^2}{2\sigma^2}}}{dx} = -\frac{x}{\sigma^2}e^{\frac{-x^2}{2\sigma^2}} \tag{6.19}$$

For computing edges in an image, the analysis has been extended to 2-D. A brief outline of the Canny edge detection is shown in the block diagram of Fig. 6.11. In this case, the same computation may have been performed at a given direction at a point. However, there is no a priori knowledge of the direction of the edge at that point. Hence, the computation is carried out by using a 2-D gradient operator of the first order partial derivative of the Gaussian function along x and y directions, as they are used for any ordinary gradient operator, and computing the magnitude $M(x,y)$ and edge directional angle $\theta(x,y)$ at the point (x,y). Then non-maximal suppression is carried out in the following manner.

First a discrete direction among $0°$, $45°$, $90°$ and $135°$ is chosen, which is closest to $\theta(x,y)$. If the neighbor at its orthogonal direction has a greater magnitude, $M(x,y)$ is set to zero,

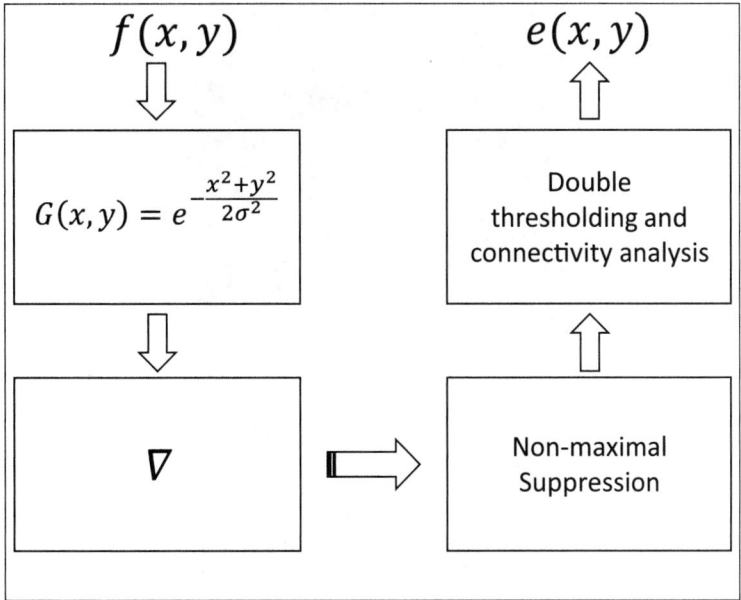

Figure 6.11 Canny edge detection pipeline.

implying the pixel is excluded from the set of candidate edge points. In this way the edges become thinner.

In the next stage of detection of edge pixels from the magnitudes, two threshold values are used following a strategy called *Hysteresis thresholding*. In this approach, a high threshold value T_h is used to detect strong edge points and thus, restraining noisy edge points to be included in the set. Then, another lower threshold value T_l is used to give consideration to the pixels whose magnitudes lie between T_l and T_h. If the pixel is found to be connected to a strong edge point (magnitude $> T_h$), it is chosen as an edge pixel. In this way, at the second stage, weaker edges get detected, yet not allowing spurious noisy edges, which are expected to have isolated occurrences in the image. Typical examples of results from the Canny edge detection are shown in Fig. 6.12.

Edge linking Once the edges are computed, they need to be linked to represent the boundaries and contours of regions. There are global and local linking methods. The example of a global linking method is the use of the Hough transform techniques as discussed in Chapter 4 to obtain geometric lines and curves linking the edge pixels. There exist edge linking techniques (Canny, 1986) which exploit local connectivity and orientations of edges. For example, in a local linking technique, we may link an edge pixel with another pixel in its neighborhood having similar magnitude and direction. However, it is computationally expensive. In another technique, we may perform the computation in the following way.

Figure 6.12 Example of Canny edge detection.

(i) Set an edge pixel to 1 if it is of specific direction with a tolerance and having sufficient magnitude. Else set it to 0.

(ii) Fill small gaps along that direction and compute connected components.

6.5.2 | Region based segmentation

Among region based segmentation approaches, analysis of histogram of images is found to be very useful. There are various approaches to compute the modal intervals of a histogram, such as, mixture of Gaussians approach, K-means, mean shift, etc.

Histogram analysis using a Gaussian mixture model (GMM)

The estimation of parameters of a probability distribution following the GMM using EM technique is discussed in Section 6.4. It is demonstrated for binary segmentation of images in Section 1.3 of Chapter 1, which partitions the image into two segments. The same technique may be applied to the analysis of histograms of images to obtain an appropriate modal intervals of a histogram, which are subsequently used to segment the image. For partitioning the histogram of an image, $h(x)$ into K segments, ω_1, ω_2, ..., ω_K, their respective posterior probabilities are computed by estimating the parameters of their respective Gaussian distributions. An example of segmentation of an image by this approach is shown in Fig. 6.13.

Histogram analysis using K-means clustering

In Section 6.2, the K-means clustering technique is discussed. In this section, its use in the analysis of histograms to compute its modal intervals and thus, performing segmentation of images is illustrated. In this case, K-means clustering algorithm is applied in the 1-D space,

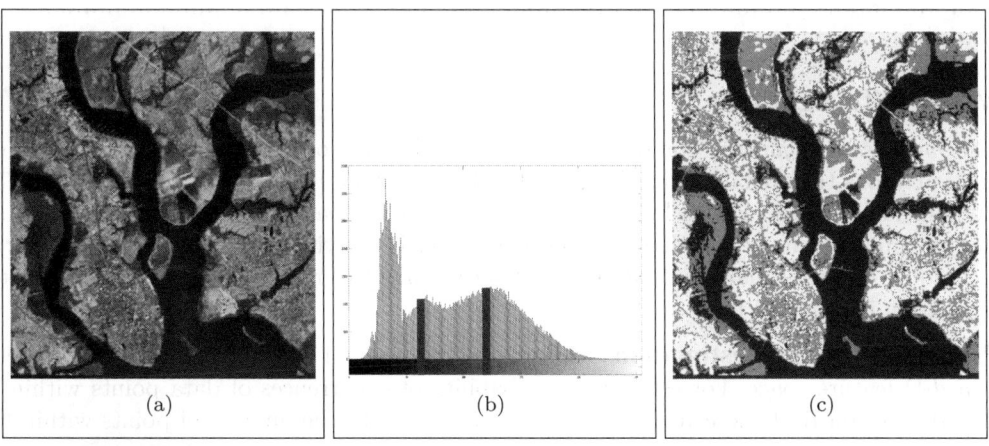

Figure 6.13 Example segmentation using expectation-maximization technique.
(a) Input image, (b) histogram of the input image, and (c) segmented image with intervals [0, 60] as blue, [61, 119] as green, and [120, 255] as yellow.
See Color Plates (page 818).

where the feature values are the intensity values. The histogram provides the frequency of occurrences of those values. Let us denote $h(x)$ as the frequency of x. Hence, we need to compute an ordered set of K values $m_1, m_2, \ldots, m_K$, such that they represent the weighted means of the brightness values lying within K nonoverlapping intervals. We note that the partition represented by m_k defines an interval within $\left[\frac{m_{k-1}+m_k}{2}, \frac{m_k+m_{k+1}}{2}\right]$ in the brightness intervals. The mean m_k of that interval is computed by the following expression using $h(x)$ as the weight of x.

$$m_k = \frac{\sum_{\frac{m_{k-1}+m_k}{2}}^{\frac{m_k+m_{k+1}}{2}} x h(x)}{\sum_{\frac{m_{k-1}+m_k}{2}}^{\frac{m_k+m_{k+1}}{2}} h(x)}, \ \forall k \tag{6.20}$$

The algorithm The algorithm for image segmentation using K-means clustering is described below. A typical example of K-means clustering based histogram analysis and the segmentation of the image in Fig. 6.13 (a) is shown in Fig. 6.14.

Algorithm 11 Algorithm for histogram-based image segmentation using K-means clustering

---

    Input: A gray scale image of N intensity levels
    Output: K cluster centers
  1: Compute the histogram $h(x)$, $x = 0, 1, 2, \ldots, N$.
  2: Choose initial K brightness levels for the set of means, $m_1, m_2, \ldots, m_k$, such that $0 < m_1 < m_2 < \ldots < m_k < N$.
  3: Update the kth mean, $\forall\ k$.
  4: Iterate till convergence.

Mean shift algorithm

The *mean shift algorithm* computes modes or local peaks of a function over its domain, and partitions the domain using those modes (Cheng, 1995; Fukunaga and Hostetler, 1975; Comaniciu and Meer, 2002). In this case, given a feature space, it computes the modes on the probability density function over the space, which is estimated using a nonparametric technique, *Parzen window method*. A brief description of this method for probability density estimation is provided here.

Probability density estimation Consider a finite set of N data points $x_1, x_2, \ldots, x_N$ in a d-D feature space. For estimating probability of occurrences of data points within a bounded region R of the feature space, we may first count the number of points within R, say n_R. Then we estimate the probability of occurrence of a data point in R, p_R, as $p_R = \frac{n_R}{N}$. Suppose the volume of the region is V_R. In that case, the estimate of the probability density at every point in R is $\frac{p_R}{V_R}$. We may refine this computation instead of the discrete count of a data point x_i (as 1), by using a continuous function which distributes the contribution of its evidence over all the points in the space in such a way that,

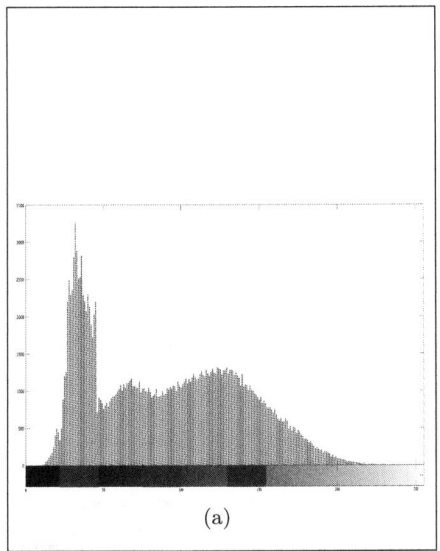 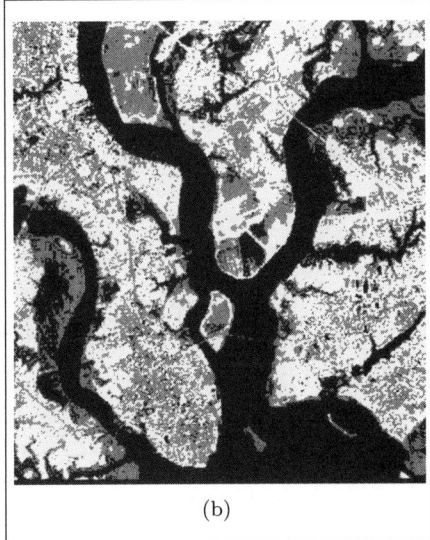

(a)　　　　　　　　　　　　　(b)

Figure 6.14 Example of K-means clustering based segmentation using histograms. (a) Histogram of the input image, and (c) segmented image with $K = 3$. The cluster centers are $m_1 = 39$, $m_2 = 90$, and $m_3 = 147$, with their corresponding intervals at [0, 65] as blue, [66, 119] as green, and [120, 255] as yellow. See Color Plates (page 819).

(i) The closer the point to $\boldsymbol{x}_1$, the higher is its contribution,

(ii) The maximum contribution is accounted for the point $\boldsymbol{x}_i$ itself, and

(iii) The accumulated contribution over the space is 1.

Suppose $K(\boldsymbol{x})$ is a function, which satisfies the above for the point at the origin in the space. In that case $K(\boldsymbol{x} - \boldsymbol{x}_i)$ also satisfies for the point $\boldsymbol{x}_i$. $K(x)$ is called a *Kernel function* that should satisfy the following properties, which include the above conditions as well.

- Normalized: $\int_{\mathbb{R}^d} K(\boldsymbol{x}) d\boldsymbol{x} = 1$
- Symmetric: $\int_{\mathbb{R}^d} \boldsymbol{x} K(\boldsymbol{x}) d\boldsymbol{x} = 1$
- Exponential weight decay: $\lim_{||\boldsymbol{x}|| \to \infty} K(\boldsymbol{x}) = 0$

Hence the probability density function modeled by the set of data points using the kernel function is given by Eq. 6.21.

$$P(\boldsymbol{x}) = \frac{1}{N} \sum_{i=1}^{N} K(\boldsymbol{x} - \boldsymbol{x}_i) \tag{6.21}$$

A few examples of Kernel functions are given below.

- Epanechnikov: $K_e(\boldsymbol{x}) = \begin{cases} c\left(1 - ||\boldsymbol{x}||^2\right), & ||\boldsymbol{x}|| \leq 1 \\ 0 & \text{otherwise} \end{cases}$

- Uniform: $K_u(\boldsymbol{x}) = \begin{cases} c, & \|\boldsymbol{x}\| \leq 1 \\ 0 & \text{otherwise} \end{cases}$

- Gaussian: $K_g(\boldsymbol{x}) = c e^{-\frac{1}{2}\|\boldsymbol{x}\|^2}$

Mode selection   From the above expression of $P(x)$ in Eq. 6.21, we compute its gradient as,

$$\nabla P(\boldsymbol{x}) = \frac{1}{N} \sum_{i=1}^{N} \nabla K(\boldsymbol{x} - \boldsymbol{x}_i) \tag{6.22}$$

Here, since $K(\boldsymbol{x} - \boldsymbol{x}_i) = c k \left(\left\| \frac{\boldsymbol{x} - \boldsymbol{x}_i}{h} \right\| \right)$, where h is the size of window, Eq. 6.22 can be written expressed as follows.

$$\nabla P(\boldsymbol{x}) = \frac{c}{N} \sum_{i=1}^{N} \nabla k_i = \frac{c}{N} \left[\sum_{i=1}^{N} g_i \right] \left[\frac{\sum_{i=1}^{N} \boldsymbol{x}_i g_i}{\sum_{i=1}^{N} g_i} - \boldsymbol{x} \right]_{g(\boldsymbol{x}) = -k'(\boldsymbol{x})} \tag{6.23}$$

The mode of this distribution occurs where the gradient value becomes zero. This is true at a point where the following criterion is satisfied.

$$\nabla P(\boldsymbol{x}) = 0 \implies \boldsymbol{m}(\boldsymbol{x}) = \left[\frac{\sum_{i=1}^{N} \boldsymbol{x}_i g \left(\frac{\|\boldsymbol{x} - \boldsymbol{x}_i\|^2}{h} \right)}{\sum_{i=1}^{N} g \left(\frac{\|\boldsymbol{x} - \boldsymbol{x}_i\|^2}{h} \right)} - \boldsymbol{x} \right] = 0 \tag{6.24}$$

The above expression implies that the weighted mean of the data points, considering the weights computed from the derivative function of the kernel function centering the point $\boldsymbol{x}$, should be the point $\boldsymbol{x}$ itself. This provides an iterative method to arrive at a local peak from any arbitrary point $\boldsymbol{x}$. The iterative update is carried out as follows.

$$\boldsymbol{x}^{(i+1)} = \boldsymbol{x}^{(i)} + \boldsymbol{m}(\boldsymbol{x}^{(i)}) \tag{6.25}$$

The algorithm   The algorithm of the mean shift technique for selection of modes and subsequently partitioning the feature space is described in Algorithm 12.

Algorithm 12 Mean shift clustering algorithm

Input: An image to be segmented
Output: Segmented image
1: Choose a search window (width and location).
2: Compute the mean of the data in the search window.
3: Center the search window at the new mean location.
4: Repeat until convergence (converged point is a mode).
5: Follow the above steps from every point (the set of points arriving at the same mode forms a segment).

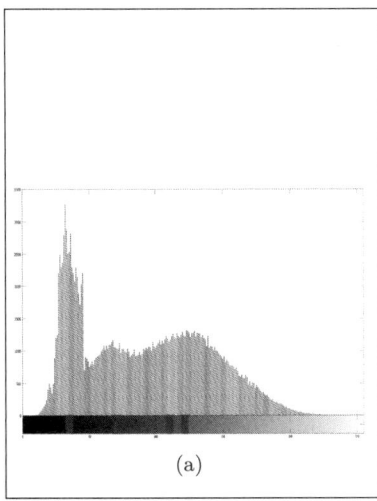

(a)   (b)

Figure 6.15 Example of mean shift clustering based segmentation using histograms.
(a) Histogram of the input image, and (c) segmented image with modes at 32, 67, 117, and 130. The corresponding intervals are [0, 51] as yellow, [52, 82] as red, [83, 128] as blues, and [129, 255] as white. See Color Plates (page 819).

Mean shift analysis of histogram

The mean shift technique may be applied for selection of modes of a histogram of an image to subsequently obtain the intervals corresponding to each mode. Unlike the K-means clustering based analysis, the mean shift analysis does not require any prior knowledge of the number of partitions (K). It also estimates modes of partitions, whereas the K-means technique computes means of clusters. But there is a challenge in this computation, as there may occur various spurious noisy modes. These are to be detected and suppressed. Toward this a few objective criteria have been set to accept a mode obtained in this process. A mode is accepted only when, (i) it has sufficient support implying a wide brightness interval, (ii) a sufficient gap between adjacent distinct pair, and (iii) a sufficient strength to have a good number of pixels belonging to its partition. For each of the above, empirically chosen threshold values are used.

The algorithm of this computation is summarized in Algorithm 13. The result of mean shift analysis of histogram of the image in Fig. 6.13 (a) is shown in Fig. 6.15.

Summary

The clustering of a set of data points is to partition them into meaningful groups or clusters, so that they are similar to each other if they belong to the same group, but distinct from any member of a different group. There are various clustering approaches, namely K-means clustering, K-medoid clustering, GMM driven clustering, etc. The task of segmentation involves meaningful partitioning of image pixels. There are primarily two approaches for obtaining segments, namely (i) by computing edges and (ii) by obtaining regions of similar pixels. First order and second order derivative operators are used for computing edges. Examples of two such robust edge operators are the Marr–Hildreth, and

---

Algorithm 13 Algorithm for histogram-based segmentation of images using mean shift clustering

---

    Input: An image to be segmented
    Output: Segmented image
1: Compute the histogram $h(x)$, $x = 0, 1, 2, \ldots, N$.
2: For each x determine the mode $m(x)$ in the histogram.
3: Ensure monotonicity in $m(x) = 0, 1, 2, \ldots, N$, so that $m(x_1) < m(x_2)$, for $x_1 < x_2$.
4: Prune spurious modes to retain the modes with,

- sufficient support (brightness interval),
- sufficient gap between adjacent distinct pair, and
- sufficient strength (number of pixels)

5: Get brightness interval for each mode.

---

the Canny operators. The Marr–Hildreth operator uses LoG function to compute second order derivatives and obtain edges from the zero-crossings of the resulting operations. The Canny edge operator uses Gaussian derivative function and hysteresis thresholding of the magnitudes of the resulting operations. In region based segmentation approaches, analysis of histogram of images is found to be very useful. There are various approaches to compute the modal intervals of a histogram, such as use of GMM and estimating its parameters using EM technique, K-means clustering technique and mean shift algorithm for selecting modes.

Exercises

(i) Consider the K-means clustering algorithm, where the dimension of the feature space is 100 and the number of feature vectors is 1000. What value of K minimizes the objective function used in this algorithm?

(ii) Assume, you want to cluster 7 observations into 3 clusters using K-means clustering algorithm. After first iteration clusters, C1, C2, C3 has following observations:

    C1: (2,2), (4,4), (6,6)

    C2: (0,4), (4,0)

    C3: (5,5), (9,9)

    What will be the cluster centroids if you want to proceed for second iteration?

(iii) Design a Laplacian operator by using difference operations where the weights along vertical and horizontal directions are three times of that of diagonal directions. How edges are detected using Laplacian operators?

(iv) How the LoG operator using the parameter σ can be approximated by a DoG operator? Describe the algorithm of edge detection using the Marr–Hildreth operator.

(v) Describe the hysteresis thresholding for detecting edges using Canny edge operation. Explain how spurious edge points get removed by this process.

(vi) Describe the algorithm for segmenting images by K-means clustering of its histogram.

(vii) Explain how mean shift algorithm is used for estimating mode of a distribution. Describe the algorithm for finding modal intervals using mean shift algorithm.

7

Classification

Classification is a task of assigning a known category or class to an object. A *class* is a well studied group of objects that is identified by their common properties or characteristics. For example, consider the image in Fig. 7.1, where an instance of a region in the image is denoted by a rectangular bounding box. Here, the task is to classify different regions in the image by considering various patches, as illustrated by a few bounding boxes, to two classes, "human" or "nonhuman". Likewise a few other examples of image classification problem are, detection of pedestrians in an image patch, recognition of a letter given a two-dimensional (2-D) image pattern, assigning a pixel of an image to its foreground or background, finding whether an image captured indoor or outdoor, etc. We may observe here the diversified nature of classification problems and by solving them, different types of tasks are performed. Mostly, the classification problem falls under the supervised learning framework, where training samples with appropriate features and class labels are used to learn a model that is suitable for predicting classes of the given data. There are various approaches for addressing the classification problem like probabilistic approach, distance based approach, discriminant

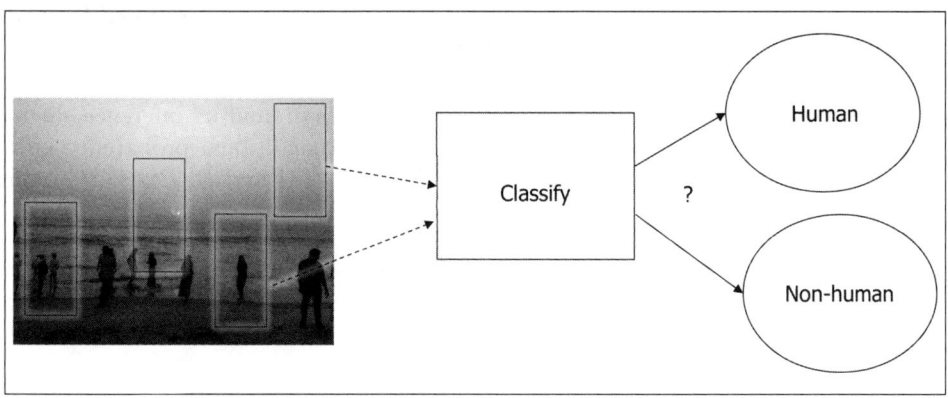

Figure 7.1 Example of a general classification problem.

analysis based approach, artificial neural network (ANN) based approach, etc. This chapter introduces four specific techniques from these approaches, namely, Bayesian classification technique (particularly, naive Bayesian classifier), K-nearest neighbor (K-NN) classifier, use of linear discriminant functions, and artificial neutral network, respectively.

7.1 | The formal description of the problem

For a given data set of N points, $\{(\boldsymbol{x}_i, y_i)\}$, $i = 1, 2, \ldots, N$, such that $\boldsymbol{x}_i \in \mathbb{R}^n$ and y_i is the class of $\boldsymbol{x}_i$, derive a mathematical model or a classifier which assigns the class y to any arbitrary input vector $\boldsymbol{x}$ in $\mathbb{R}^n$, and should largely satisfy the training examples.

Each data point, $\boldsymbol{x}_i$, is represented as an n-dimensional feature vector in real space for every object in an abstract way and y_i is an element of a finite set of classes. Here, y_i may also be any categorical data, names of classes, or numerical representations of the classes that distinctly identify the classes. For example, for a two class problem, y_i may be denoted as $+1$ and -1. In this case, the classifier, $\mathcal{C}$, assigns a class, y_i (output in the form of either $+1$ or -1), to the data points, $\boldsymbol{x}_i$ (input). A *loss* is always associated with a classification task, which is defined as the fraction of misclassified data, as given by Eq. 7.1.

$$\text{Loss}(\mathcal{C}) = \frac{1}{N} \sum_i 1_{y_i \neq \mathcal{C}(\boldsymbol{x}_i)} \tag{7.1}$$

There are several classification techniques for minimizing the loss, and Bayesian classification is one such technique that is discussed in the following section.

7.2 | Bayesian classification

Bayesian classification is based on a theoretical framework that was proposed by Thomas Bayes (published in 1763 AD) in the form of *Bayes' theorem*.

Bayes' theorem and Bayesian Inference   Bayes' theorem and its inference elucidates the concept of conditional probability. By definition, the conditional probability between two events, A and B, is defined from the joint probability of A and B, $P(A \cap B)$, which is given by Eq. 7.2.

$$P(A|B) = \frac{P(A \cap B)}{P(B)}$$
$$P(B|A) = \frac{P(B \cap A)}{P(A)} \tag{7.2}$$

where, $P(A)$ and $P(B)$ are the prior probabilities of observing the events A and B, respectively, without any given conditions. $P(B|A)$ is a conditional probability corresponding to the occurrence of B given A, and $P(A|B)$ is the conditional probability corresponding to the occurrence of A given B. Bayes' theorem states that

$$P(B|A) = \frac{P(A|B)P(B)}{P(A)} \tag{7.3}$$

The above Eq. 7.3 is easily derived from the definitions of conditional probabilities. It is directly used in drawing probabilistic inference, called the *Bayesian inference*, for the task of classification.

Consider H, which denotes a hypothesis that the data $\boldsymbol{X}$ belongs to a class y. In that case, by applying Bayesian theorem, we may compute the probability that H is true given the occurrence of $\boldsymbol{X}$ by Eq. 7.4.

$$P(H|\boldsymbol{X}) = \frac{P(H)P(\boldsymbol{X}|H)}{P(\boldsymbol{X})} \tag{7.4}$$

Here, the quantity, $P(H|\boldsymbol{X})$, is the *posterior probability*, the probability of the hypothesis (assigning a class to the data), given the data. The quantity, $P(H)$, is the *prior probability*, the probability of the hypothesis on previous knowledge. The probability, $P(\boldsymbol{X}|H)$, is known as the *likelihood*, which describes the likelihood of occurrence of $\boldsymbol{X}$ under the given hypothesis, H. The probability, $P(\boldsymbol{X})$, is the unconditional or marginal probability of the data, which is a normalizing constant that ensures the sum of posterior probabilities to be unity. In other words, the sum of all the probabilities that lead to the occurrence of $\boldsymbol{X}$ for all the possible hypotheses is equal to $P(\boldsymbol{X})$. Let there be M hypotheses, so that, H_m denotes that $\boldsymbol{X}$ belongs to the mth class, where $m = 1, 2, ..., M$, the unconditional probability of data is given by Eq. 7.5.

$$P(\boldsymbol{X}) = \sum_{m=1}^{M} P(\boldsymbol{X}|H_m)P(H_m) \tag{7.5}$$

In the context of classification problem, the data $\boldsymbol{X}$ may be defined by certain features of images, like color or intensity values, texture elements, patch descriptors, etc., which are either scalar values or vectors. The hypothesis may be defined as whether a given data point belongs to a particular class or not.

In Bayesian classification, given the data, $\boldsymbol{X}$, the posterior probability of hypothesis H is computed and then the decision on class assignment takes place by comparing these posterior probability values among classes. The class with the highest posterior probability is assigned to the data point. That is, the ith class label, C_i is assigned to $\boldsymbol{X}$, if and only if the probability $P(C_i|\boldsymbol{X})$ is the maximum among all the probabilities, $\{P(C_1|\boldsymbol{X}), P(C_2|\boldsymbol{X}), ..., P(C_M|\boldsymbol{X})\}$, for M classes. This is what is known as *Bayesian inference* for the task of classification. However, the challenge involved in this computation is the requirement of prior knowledge of probabilities of classes and their distributions in multi-dimensional feature spaces.

In a multi-dimensional feature space, a training set consists of n-D feature vectors. Typically, a feature vector is represented, $\boldsymbol{X} = (x_1, x_2, ..., x_n)$. Let there be M classes, $C_1, C_2, ..., C_M$. For the given data, the class with maximum posterior probability is assigned to the data by computing the posterior probabilities of each class using Bayes' theorem as given in Eq. 7.6.

$$P(C_i|\boldsymbol{X}) = \frac{P(C_i)P(\boldsymbol{X}|C_i)}{P(\boldsymbol{X})} \tag{7.6}$$

The prior probability of class C_i, $P(C_i)$, is computed using the given data as the proportion of times each class instance occurs among all the classes. The prior probability may also be computed using other acquired information from a different knowledge source. The probability, $P(\boldsymbol{X}|C_i)$, or the likelihood is computed by using the data distribution within the class C_i. Sometimes, the denominator of Eq. 7.6, $P(\boldsymbol{X})$, is ignored for computational purposes, since it is essentially a constant for every class, given the data $\boldsymbol{X}$. So, it is sufficient to compute only the numerator, $P(C_i)P(\boldsymbol{X}|C_i)$, which forms the basis of comparison. Here, by ignoring $P(\boldsymbol{X})$, the comparison of the probability values is made in relative sense, since the actual probability values are not needed in the comparisons. But for attributing to the confidence on the decision of class assignment, it is required to compute the posterior probabilities and then the classes are assigned by the following.

$$i^* = \underset{i}{\operatorname{argmax}}\ P(C_i|\boldsymbol{X}) \tag{7.7}$$

The classifier following the above inference mechanism is called the *Bayesian classifier*. A simple Bayesian classifier, the *naive Bayes classifier*, is discussed here, which is a probabilistic prediction of belongingness of a data point to a class. An advantage of the naive Bayes classification technique is that, each training example contributes to increase or decrease in the probability of a predicted class, so that, the classifier learns the classification model incrementally. Also, prior knowledge, when available, is combined with the observed data in this technique.

7.2.1 | Naive Bayes classifier

The *naive Bayes classifier* works on a simplified assumption that the attributes are conditionally independent (Mitchell, 2017). With such an assumption, the likelihood of $\boldsymbol{X}$, given a class C_i, is expressed as the product of all likelihood probabilities of its individual attributes or feature components. This relationship is depicted in Eq. 7.8.

$$P(\boldsymbol{X}|C_i) = \prod_{k=1}^{n} P(x_k|C_i) = P(x_1|C_i)\ P(x_2|C_i) \cdots\ P(x_k|C_i) \tag{7.8}$$

Thus, in this case, the computation of the likelihood, $P(\boldsymbol{X}|C_i)$, is carried out as a simple product of likelihoods of individual attributes. The simplicity of naive Bayes classifier lies in computing with the likelihood functions in one dimension, instead of multi-dimensional representation of probability density functions. This further simplifies the handling of multi-dimensional data for modeling the probability density functions. Also, the computational cost is significantly reduced in this technique, since it requires only class distributions in a single dimensional feature space. So, it is convenient to estimate the probability of every attribute, given a particular class.

For categorical or discrete variables, the number of occurrences of considered values of attributes is counted, given all occurrences of all values of the attributes. The fraction of these occurrences over the total number of occurrences gives an estimate of the required probability value. For a continuous variable, the probability is computed by modeling the function by any of the known probability density functions. For instance, if the parametric modeling is performed by using a Gaussian distribution, the probability is computed by the estimated parameters of the distribution. For example, for a Gaussian distribution, $g(x; \mu, \sigma)$, of variable x in one-dimensional (1-D) feature space, which is given by Eq. 7.9, there are only two parameters, the *expectation* of the distribution or mean, μ, and the *standard deviation* of the distribution, σ.

$$g(x; \mu, \sigma) = \frac{1}{\sigma\sqrt{2\pi}} e^{-\frac{(x-\mu)^2}{2\sigma^2}} \tag{7.9}$$

The parameters, mean and standard deviation, of the Gaussian distribution are estimated from the given data as follows.

$$\mu = \frac{1}{N}\sum_{i=1}^{N} x_i$$
$$\sigma^2 = \frac{1}{N-1}\sum_{i=1}^{N}(x_i - \mu)^2 \tag{7.10}$$

where N is the number of samples.

The probability, $P(\boldsymbol{X}|C_i)$, of the n-D feature, $\boldsymbol{X}$, given the class C_i, is then computed by Eq. 7.11.

$$P(\boldsymbol{X}|C_i) = \prod_{j=1}^{n} g(x_j; \mu_j, \sigma_j) \tag{7.11}$$

To illustrate a simple naive Bayes classifier, consider an example of classifying big-teethed and water-dwelling large lizards into two category of reptiles, Alligators and Crocodiles, based on the attributes of "size" and "weight". The training set, $\boldsymbol{X}$ for this example is given in Table 7.1. Here, let the two classes, Alligator and Crocodile, be denoted by C_1 and C_2, respectively. By the training data, the parametric model obtained by using Gaussian distribution is given by mean and variance values of each class, as in Table 7.2. In this example, the number of occurrences of each of the two classes is the same. So, the two classes are equiprobable, i.e., $P(C_1) = P(C_2) = \frac{5}{10} = 0.5$. Using the above training data, consider classifying a new test sample data of a specimen, which is given in Table 7.3, as belonging to class Alligator or Crocodile. Using Eqs. 7.6 and 7.8, the posterior probability of $P(C_1|\boldsymbol{X})$ is given by Eq. 7.12 (where the denominator term will be ignored).

$$P(C_1|\boldsymbol{X}) = \frac{P(C_1)P(\text{size}|C_1)P(\text{weight}|C_1)}{P(\boldsymbol{X})} \tag{7.12}$$

Table 7.1 An example training set for naive Bayes classifier.

Reptile category	Size (feet)	Weight (pounds)
Alligator	10	500
Alligator	11.2	560
Crocodile	19.2	1800
Crocodile	17.6	1680
Alligator	12.7	620
Crocodile	15.4	1500
Alligator	14.2	680
Crocodile	16.2	1570
Alligator	13.4	640
Crocodile	15.0	1480

Table 7.2 Parameters estimated from the training data of Table 7.1.

Reptile category	Size (feet)		Weight (pounds)	
	mean (μ_{size})	variance (σ^2_{size})	mean (μ_{weight})	variance (σ^2_{weight})
Alligator (C_1)	12.3	2.8700	600	5000
Crocodile (C_2)	16.68	2.9720	1606	17880

By the parametric model of Gaussian distribution given in Table 7.2, the likelihood components are given by Eq. 7.13.

$$P(\text{size}|C_1) = \frac{1}{\sqrt{2\pi\sigma^2_{\text{size}_{C_1}}}} e^{\left(\frac{-(14.3-\mu_{\text{size}_{C_1}})^2}{2\sigma^2_{\text{size}_{C_1}}}\right)} = 0.1173$$

$$P(\text{weight}|C_1) = \frac{1}{\sqrt{2\pi\sigma^2_{\text{weight}_{C_1}}}} e^{\left(\frac{-(1300-\mu_{\text{weight}_{C_1}})^2}{2\sigma^2_{\text{weight}_{C_1}}}\right)} = 2.9580 \times 10^{-24}$$

(7.13)

Therefore, the posterior probability, $P(C_1|\boldsymbol{X})$ is given by Eq. 7.14.

$$P(C_1|\boldsymbol{X}) = (0.5)(1.102 \times 10^{-1})(1.5825 \times 10^{-29}) = \frac{1.7350 \times 10^{-25}}{P(\boldsymbol{X})}$$

(7.14)

Table 7.3 An example test sample for naive Bayes classifier.

Reptile category	Size (feet)	Weight (pounds)
New sample	14.3	1300

Similarly, the likelihood components and posterior probability for class C_2 are given by Eq. 7.15.

$$P(\text{size}|C_2) = \frac{1}{\sqrt{2\pi\sigma^2_{\text{size}_{C_2}}}} e^{\left(\frac{-(14.3-\mu_{\text{size}_{C_2}})^2}{2\sigma^2_{\text{size}_{C_2}}}\right)} = 0.0892$$

$$P(\text{weight}|C_2) = \frac{1}{\sqrt{2\pi\sigma^2_{\text{weight}_{C_2}}}} e^{\left(\frac{-(1300-\mu_{\text{weight}_{C_2}})^2}{2\sigma^2_{\text{weight}_{C_2}}}\right)} = 2.1754 \times 10^{-4} \qquad (7.15)$$

$$P(C_2|\boldsymbol{X}) = \frac{P(C_2)P(\text{size}|C_2)P(\text{weight}|C_2)}{P(\boldsymbol{X})}$$

$$= (0.5)\ (7.86\ 10^{-2})\ (1.2639 \times 10^{-4}) = \frac{9.7059 \times 10^{-6}}{P(\boldsymbol{X})}$$

From Eqs. 7.13, 7.14, and 7.15, it may be observed that, $P(C_2|\boldsymbol{X}) > P(C_1|\boldsymbol{X})$. Therefore, the given test sample is classified as in to class C_2, i.e., the features of the test specimen resemble a Crocodile.

The advantages of naive Bayes classifier are (i) its ease of implementation, and (ii) its ability to achieve good results in many cases. However, a major disadvantage of using naive Bayes classifier is the assumption of conditional independence. The assumption of class conditional independence may not be true for all realistic data, which results in loss of accuracy on deviating from the assumption. Practically, dependencies exist among many of the attributes or variables in real life. For example, in hospitals, patients' profile (age, family history, lifestyle, etc.) and disease symptoms (diabetes, asthma, cancer, etc.) are usually related. Such dependencies cannot be modeled by a naive Bayes classifier.

7.3 | *K*-nearest neighbor classification

The *nearest neighbor* (1-NN) classification is a very simple classification approach, where the learning is carried out by simply storing the training data (Hastie et al., 2017). Unlike Bayesian classification that requires parametric modeling of the processed data to get the probability distributions, just storing the training examples is sufficient for nearest neighbor classification. In its simplest form, the training examples are stored as $(\boldsymbol{x}_i, y_i)$, $i = 1, 2, \ldots, N$, where $\boldsymbol{x}_i$ and y_i denote the ith training data point and its corresponding label, respectively, and N is the number of training examples. Then, the class label of a new data sample, $\boldsymbol{x}$, is predicted by finding the training example that is nearest to $\boldsymbol{x}$, $\boldsymbol{x}_j$. Correspondingly, the class label of $\boldsymbol{x}$, y, is assigned by the class label of $\boldsymbol{x}_j$, y_j.

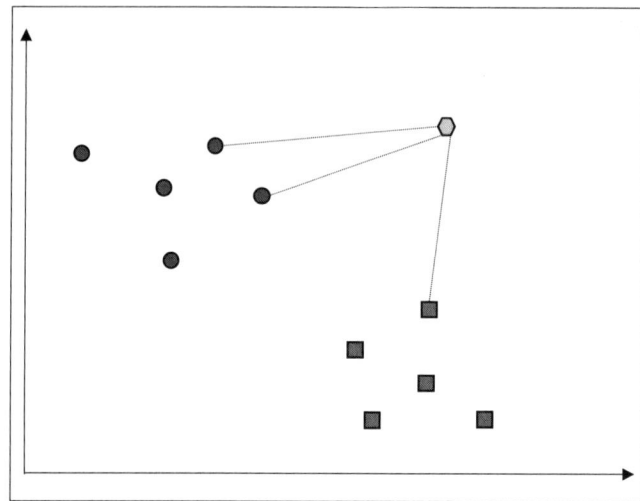

Figure 7.2 K-nearest neighbors of a query point (shown by the hexagon). Here, $K = 3$.

One particular method of efficient nearest neighbor classification is known as *K-NN* method. In this method, instead of observing a single nearest neighbor, a set of K closest neighbors is observed. These top K close neighbors are called K-NNs. To classify a new data point, x, the K-NNs or K closest training data points of x are examined, and then x is assigned to the most frequently occurring class among them. This technique is known as K-NN classification.

This approach is explained using an example of a set of 2-D data points, which is illustrated in Fig. 7.2. There are two classes of data points, whose labels are represented by two different shapes of a square and a circle. For a given query data point, which is shown by a hexagon in the figure, its distance with each of the training samples is computed. These distance values are sorted in ascending order, and K data points corresponding to the top K minimum distances are chosen. They are the K-NN of the query data point. Then, the class which comprises of maximum number of data points among the nearest neighbors is assigned to the query point. In the illustrated example, $K = 3$. So, 3-nearest neighbors are selected, which are shown by dotted lines connecting the respective data points and the query point. Here, two data points among the 3-nearest neighbors belong to the class "circle", and one data point belongs to class 'square'. So, the query point is assigned with the label of "circle".

Numerical Example

Consider the set of samples from different people that measure blood density and body temperature for assessment of a particular disease, as given in Table 7.4. Check if a new sample with blood density of 106.5×10^{-2} g/mL and body temperature of 100.1°F is normal or abnormal using 3-NN classification technique with Euclidean distance measure.

Table 7.4 Example data for K-NN classification.

Blood density ($\times 10^{-2}$ g/mL)	Body temperature (°F)	Health (Normal/ Abnormal)
106.0	97.8	N
105.5	99.1	N
105.9	99.6	N
105.7	98.4	N
105.6	98.2	N
107.5	101.7	A
108.7	104.1	A
109.0	99.8	A
108.8	103.4	A
108.7	101.6	A
108.4	102.7	A

Solution

The computation of the distance of every sample in the data and the test sample is shown in Table 7.5. As seen in the table, among the three nearest neighbors, two sample belong to class "normal" and one sample belongs to class "abnormal". Hence, by consensus, the test sample is classified as "normal".

Table 7.5 Solution to numerical example.

Blood density ($\times 10^{-2}$ g/mL)	Body temp. (°F)	Health	Distance (Euclidean)	Ranking of neighbors
106	97.8	N	2.35	6
105.5	99.1	N	1.41	4
105.9	99.6	N	0.78	2
106.9	100.0	N	0.41	1
105.6	98.2	N	2.10	5
107.0	100.9	A	0.94	3
108.7	104.1	A	4.56	11
109	100.8	A	2.59	8
108.8	103.4	A	4.02	10
108.6	101.6	A	2.58	7
108.8	102.7	A	3.47	9

Though K-NN classification is computationally simple, it has a very sound theoretical basis in following Bayesian classification principles. It is explained by a nonparametric estimation of probability density at $\boldsymbol{x}$, given K-NNs. Let N be the number of training samples. Let us also assume that the size of hypervolume containing K-NN of a sample $\boldsymbol{x}$ is V. Let p be the probability of a data point in the volume, V. This is modeled by following the binomial distribution. Here we assume that the sampling of data point in V occurs with a probability p, which is repeated N times. Thus, it follows the binomial distribution. Following the property of a binomial distribution, the expected number of data points in the volume is given by Eq. 7.16,

$$\text{E(No. of data points in V)} = Np = K \tag{7.16}$$

Hence, $p = \frac{K}{N}$ is the estimation of the probability that the volume, V, around $\boldsymbol{x}$ contains a data point, which is also expressed as the fraction of times it has occurred out of N trials. Assuming a continuous space, the probability density at $\boldsymbol{x}$, $P(\boldsymbol{x})$ is given by Eq. 7.17.

$$P(\boldsymbol{x}) = \frac{p}{V} \tag{7.17}$$

Let a class, ω_1, contain n_1 number of neighbors out of K neighbors. The joint probability of $\boldsymbol{x}$ and ω_1, $P(\boldsymbol{x}, \omega_1)$, which is the ratio of the fraction of times the n_1 neighbors occur out of N trials to the data hypervolume, is given by Eq. 7.18.

$$P(\boldsymbol{x}, \omega_1) = \frac{\left(\frac{n_1}{N}\right)}{V} \tag{7.18}$$

Then, from the Bayesian rule, the posterior probability, $P(\omega_1|\boldsymbol{x})$, is given by Eq. 7.19.

$$P(\omega_1|\boldsymbol{x}) = \frac{P(\boldsymbol{x}, \omega_1)}{P(\boldsymbol{x})} = \frac{n_1}{K} \tag{7.19}$$

If there are n_1 nearest neighbors, out of K-NN, in class ω_1, then the quantity, $\frac{n_1}{K}$, measures the posterior probability of ω_1 for a given data point. Then, the data point is assigned to a particular class by maximizing the posterior probability value, which follows the Bayesian inference rule.

Some of the critical issues of nearest neighbor classification technique are as follows.

- The choice of distance measure: It may become critical for some applications. Euclidean distance is one of the most commonly used distance measure.

- The choice of K: Increasing the value of K beyond a reasonable limit reduces the variance while increasing the bias, which causes class prior to dominate.

- Dimension of the data points: For high-dimensional space, the nearest neighbor model may not be close to acceptable performance at all. On empirical observations, it is advisable to use this technique with not more than 20 dimensions or attributes.

- Prohibitively slow for a large training set: It is a memory based technique. So, for each classification, it has to make a pass through all the data points. So, it is prohibitive for large data sets.

The advantages of K-NN classification are as follows.

- Fast training: since a given query data point is classified by directly comparing with all the training data points, training is comparatively faster with fewer data points.

- Learn complex target functions: though the method is simple for implementation, the functions that are learnt by the method are not simple. A more detailed analysis in understanding the decision boundaries that are learnt by the K neighbors show that such boundaries are quiet complex.

- The information is not lost: since the whole set of training data represents the model, no information is lost in approximating or pruning.

The model learnt by the nearest neighbor method may be easily fooled by irrelevant attributes due to its consideration on all the available training data points. That is, if there are outliers (or irrelevant data points that are not related to target function), they are also considered in establishing the relationships with a query point, which may be erroneous.

7.4 | Classification by discriminant functions

The approach of classification using discriminant functions is usually considered for two-class problems. Although it can be extended to multi-class problems, discriminant functions are mostly illustrated with two-class problems in this book. Consider a labeled data set of N points, $\{(\boldsymbol{x}_i, y)\}$, $i = 1, 2, \ldots, N$, where $\boldsymbol{x}_i \in \mathbb{R}^n$ is a n-D data point with label $y = +1$ or -1. There are two classes, ω_1 and ω_2, which are represented by $+1$ and -1, respectively. The problem of designing the classifier using a discriminant function is to design a function, $g(\boldsymbol{x})$, such that, at $\boldsymbol{x}_i$, the sign of $g(\boldsymbol{x})$, either positive or negative, should be the class identity. Here, the decision boundary is given by $g(\boldsymbol{x}) = 0$, which geometrically partitions the space of data points into two regions. The evaluation of the discriminant function on one side of this partition is $+1$, and on the other side of the partition, it is -1. Only on the boundaries, the function is evaluated to 0. This analysis is called *linear discriminant analysis* (LDA), when the function, $g(\cdot)$, is in a linear form (Duda et al., 2000). If $g(\cdot)$ takes a quadratic form, the analysis is known as *quadratic discriminant analysis*. When $g(\cdot)$ is in linear form, the degree of polynomial of $\boldsymbol{x}$ is 1. That is, every term in the polynomial contains at most one attribute, whose degree is 1 in the linear form. In quadratic form of $g(\cdot)$, the degree of polynomial of $\boldsymbol{x}$ is 2. So, that every term in the polynomial contains at most two different attributes, whose sum of degrees do not exceed 2 in the quadratic form. In the following sections we discuss various approaches for obtaining linear discriminant function. We begin our discussion with a class of classifier which is called a *perceptron*.

7.4.1 | Perceptron classifier

A perceptron classifier is a discriminant function based classifier. It is modeled as a directed graph, having a single node with edges for connecting to inputs and an output. In its simplest form, a node of a classifier is shown in Fig. 7.3. The input of a node is an n dimensional feature vector, $\boldsymbol{X} = [x_1, x_2, \ldots, x_n]$. Each attribute of $\boldsymbol{X}$ is associated with a

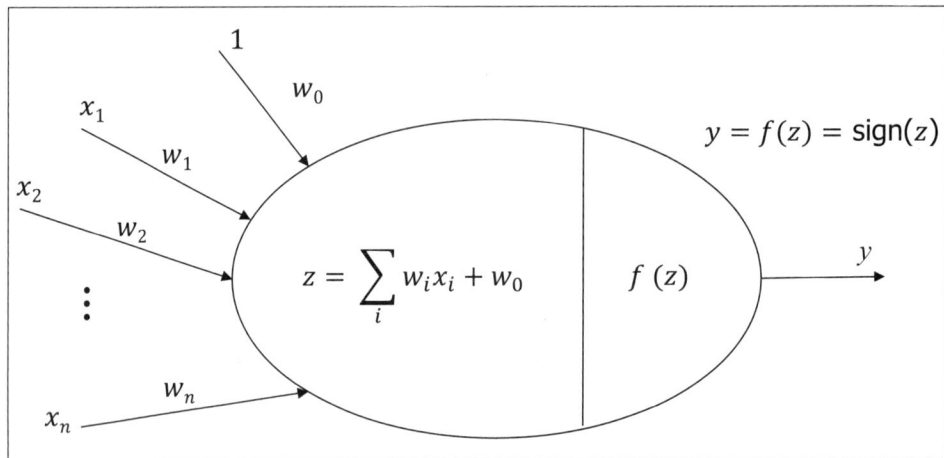

Figure 7.3 A perceptron node, whose input, X, is an n-dimensional vector, and output y is a scalar value.

weight, so that, the input to this computational block is a weighted combination of the attributes of X. The input may be considered to be augmented by an additional dimension, w_0, with value 1, which, as a whole, is considered as a linear classifier. These weights are represented by a $(n + 1)$ dimensional vector, $W = [w_1, w_2, \ldots, w_n, w_0]$, where w_0 is a bias value and the remaining n values, $w_1, w_2, \ldots, w_n$, are the weights corresponding to the attributes $x_1, x_2, \ldots, x_n$, respectively. The functional form of a perceptron is given in Eqs. 7.20 and 7.21.

$$z = \sum_{i=1}^{n} w_i x_i + w_0 \tag{7.20}$$

where z is a linear functional form that behaves like a discriminant function. For a two-class classification, the sign of the function z is considered, which is expressed by Eq. 7.21.

$$y = f(z) = \text{sign}(z) \tag{7.21}$$

The classification output varies with respect to the functional value of $f(z)$. In this case, the function, $f(\cdot)$, is a *signum* function or sign function. If z is positive, the class label is assigned as $+1$, and if z is negative, the class label is -1. Although a value of 0 is ambiguous, for the sake of completeness of the function, let us assume that a class label of $+1$ is assigned when its value is 0.

Numerical Example

In a recruitment drive to hire a candidate for a clerk's position, x months of experience get y grade points. The recruitment is based on a minimum and maximum threshold for acceptance. The recruitment condition is based on a discriminant function, $y = f(x) = \frac{9}{25}x - 56$. Consider two competing candidates, Harry and Henry, who have 12.4 and 13.2 years of experience, respectively. Verify if the two candidates get the same result, "Selected" (for +ve grade point) or "Rejected" (for −ve grade point), based on signs of grade points obtained by them using the provided discriminant function.

Solution

Number of months of experience of Harry $= (12.4)(12) = 148.8$ months. Number of months of experience of Henry $= (13.2)(12) = 158.4$ months. Based on the discriminant function, let y_1 and y_2 be the grade points obtained by Harry and Henry, respectively.

$$y_1 = f(148.8) = \frac{9}{25}(148.8) - 56 = -2.432$$

$$y_2 = f(158.4) = \frac{9}{25}(158.4) - 56 = 1.024$$

Since the signs of $f(x)$ for the two candidates are different, Harry and Henry have got different selection results. So, Henry is selected and Harry is rejected.

Linear separability of classes

Considering the augmented input with the additional dimension, the input vector is an $(n + 1)$ dimensional vector, X, where the $(n + 1)^{\text{th}}$ dimension is set to 1. The corresponding weight vector is also an $(n + 1)$ dimensional vector, W, where the bias, w_0, is included as the $(n + 1)^{\text{th}}$ dimensional value. The representations of X and W are given in Eq. 7.22.

$$X = \begin{bmatrix} x_1 \\ x_2 \\ \vdots \\ x_n \\ 1 \end{bmatrix}, \qquad W = \begin{bmatrix} w_1 \\ w_2 \\ \vdots \\ w_n \\ w_0 \end{bmatrix} \qquad (7.22)$$

With these representations of input and weight vectors, the function, z, is expressed as a simple linear operation of matrix multiplication.

$$z = W^\top X \qquad (7.23)$$

The output is a functional value of the net input, z, which is a signum function, $\text{sign}(z)$, in the case of the two-class problem. Given (X_i, y_i), where y_i is the label of the corresponding input vector, X_i, the objective here is to compute an optimum W that minimizes the classification error. This computational problem is the same as deriving a classifier using a linear discriminant function.

Consider the illustration, shown in Fig. 7.4, where a hyperplane, $W^\top X = 0$, separates the two samples, X and X', in the space into two classes, ω_1 and ω_2, respectively. Here,

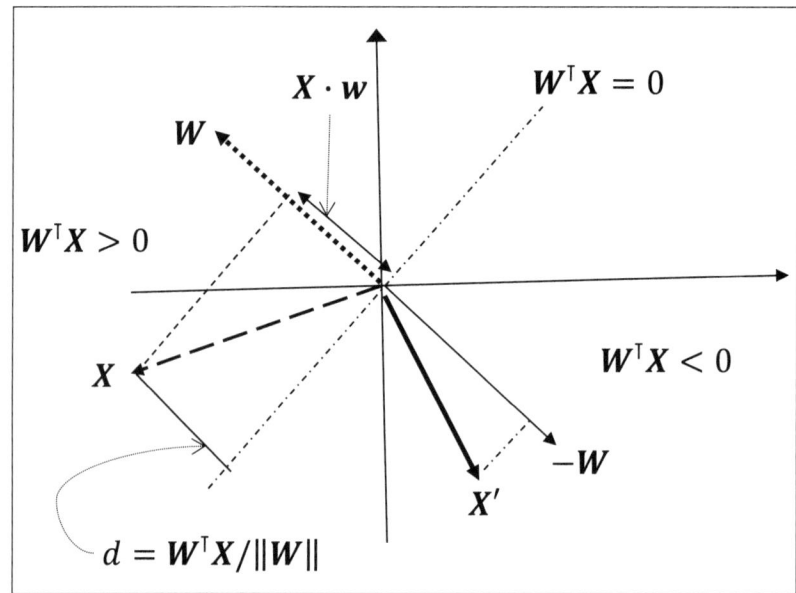

Figure 7.4 Illustration of linearly separable classes.

W is the normal to the hyper-plane, as shown in the figure. In this form of representation, the hyper-plane passes through the origin of the corresponding space. In this illustration, only two dimensions are shown for simplicity, but any arbitrary dimension, n, may be considered for applications. The dot product of a sample from ω_1, X, with W, $W^\top X$, represents the projection of X along the direction of W. In the representative figure, since the vector normal, W, and X are lying in the same partition, the dot product is positive, i.e., $W^\top X > 0$. This is proportional to the distance, d, of X from the hyper-plane, $W^\top X$. From the analytical geometry this distance function is computed as in Eq. 7.24.

$$d = \frac{W^\top X}{\|W\|} \tag{7.24}$$

Similarly, for a sample from ω_2, X', which lies on the other side of the hyper-plane, the corresponding dot product is negative, i.e., $W^\top X < 0$, since W is the reference direction.

In this illustration of an ideal case, the considered hyper-plane discriminates the two samples, X and X', of two different classes. The classifier correctly classifies two classes, ω_1 and ω_2, if the samples of ω_1 lie in one side of the hyper-plane, and the samples of ω_2 lie in the other side of the hyper-plane. If this condition is satisfied and the data is given in such a way that there exists a hyper-plane which divides the input data into separate partitions in a form similar to Fig. 7.4, the considered classes are said to be *linearly separable*. In other words, when the objective is to find a hyper-plane that separates the given data points of two classes, if a solution exists, the classes are called linearly separable.

Error functions

To design an error function, a data normalization is considered, where the data is transformed in a certain way, so that, the problem gets simplified. Let the samples be considered as it is, for example, $\boldsymbol{X}$, if they belong to ω_1. If the samples belong to ω_2, they are transformed by negating them, i.e., $-\boldsymbol{X}$. This data normalization is expressed in Eq. 7.25.

$$\boldsymbol{Y} = \begin{cases} \boldsymbol{X}, & \text{if } \boldsymbol{X} \in \omega_1 (\text{the class label as } 1) \\ -\boldsymbol{X}, & \text{if } \boldsymbol{X} \in \omega_2 (\text{the class label as } -1) \end{cases} \tag{7.25}$$

With this process, all the data samples, from both the classes, are intentionally brought into the same partition of the hyper-plane. In this kind of normalization, all input samples satisfy the property of lying in one part of the hyper-plane. So, for a correct classification, $\boldsymbol{W}^\top \boldsymbol{Y}$, for all $\boldsymbol{Y}$, is always a positive value. This particular normalization ensures that all the input samples lie in the positive half of the hyper-plane, as shown in Fig. 7.5. After data normalization, an error function, $J_p(\boldsymbol{W})$, is defined, which is of the form given in Eq. 7.26.

$$J_p(\boldsymbol{W}) = \sum_{\boldsymbol{Y} \text{ misclassified}} -\boldsymbol{W}^\top \boldsymbol{Y} \tag{7.26}$$

Here, the error value is computed only if a $\boldsymbol{Y}$ is misclassified. This makes the error always a positive quantity or zero. The classifier is designed by using the error function, $J_p(\boldsymbol{W})$. The problem is to obtain the weight vector that minimizes this error function.

Gradient descent method for iterative optimization

Gradient descent method for iterative optimization is one of the efficient techniques to obtain an optimum weight vector by minimizing $J_p(\boldsymbol{W})$. The process is started by using an initial

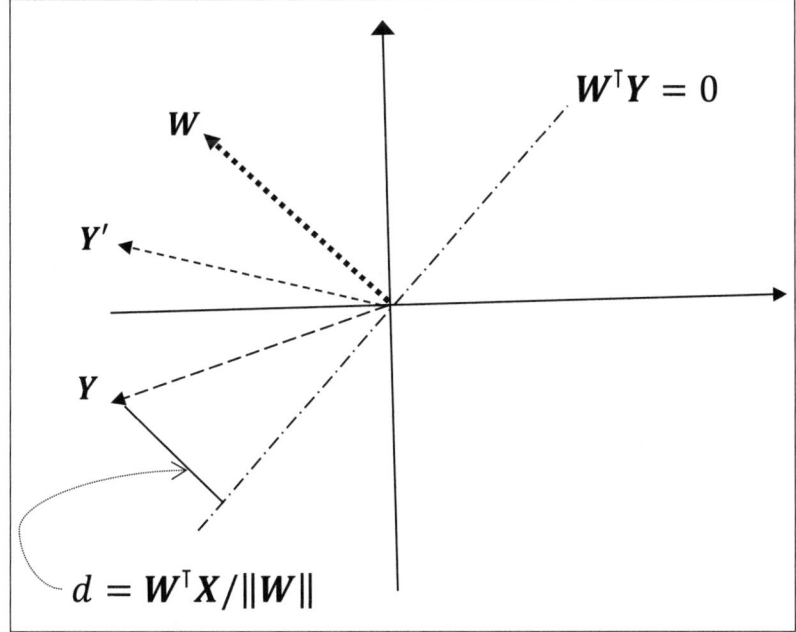

Figure 7.5 Illustration of data normalization for classification.

vector, $\boldsymbol{W}_0$. Then, the gradient vector is computed by applying differential operators over $J_p(\boldsymbol{W})$, which is represented by $\nabla J_p(\boldsymbol{W}_0)$, i.e., $\nabla J_p(\boldsymbol{W})$ at $\boldsymbol{W} = \boldsymbol{W}_0$. Here, the functional value is $\boldsymbol{W}_0$. By updating $\boldsymbol{W}$, the computation moves toward the minimum error. By following the rules of gradient descent method, the direction of change is opposite to the steepest gradient direction. It implies that the weight updates should move along $-\nabla J_p(\boldsymbol{W}_0)$ The movement toward an optimal value is achieved by a certain step size, which may vary depending on the error value, $J_p(\boldsymbol{W})$, to update the weights. This step size is called the positive scale factor or learning rate in the weight update process.

After initializing the process of iterative optimization using gradient descent with $\boldsymbol{W}_0$, the weight vector, $\boldsymbol{W}$, at the ith iteration, is updated using the values from the previous iteration in the form as given in Eq. 7.27.

$$\boldsymbol{W}^{(i)} = \boldsymbol{W}^{(i-1)} - \eta(i)\nabla J_p(\boldsymbol{W}^{(i-1)}) \tag{7.27}$$

where, $\eta(i)$ is the positive scale factor or the learning rate that is used to move along the direction opposite to the steepest gradient. Since $\nabla J_p(\boldsymbol{W})$ is the gradient of the function given in Eq. 7.26, the expression in Eq. 7.27 is analytically simplified by computing the derivative of $\sum_{\boldsymbol{Y} \text{ misclassified}} -\boldsymbol{W}^{\top}\boldsymbol{Y}$ with respect to $\boldsymbol{W}$, as given in Eq. 7.28.

$$\boldsymbol{W}^{(i)} = \boldsymbol{W}^{(i-1)} + \eta(i) \sum_{\boldsymbol{Y} \text{ misclassified}} \boldsymbol{Y} \tag{7.28}$$

As it can be seen from the above analysis, the computation is simple. The process may be initiated by using any $\boldsymbol{W}$, and the learning rate, $\eta(i)$, may either be a constant or it may vary with iterations. Then, the samples that are misclassified using the initialized $\boldsymbol{W}$ are used to update the weights. The weights are updated by adding the sum of misclassified samples with a proportional value. These steps are repeated till a convergence is achieved when the updates are no more significant.

Other forms of error functions

There are also other forms of the error function. For example, in the function given by Eq. 7.29, which is quite similar to Eq. 7.26, $(\boldsymbol{W}^{\top}\boldsymbol{Y})^2$ is used instead of $-\boldsymbol{W}^{\top}\boldsymbol{Y}$.

$$J_q(\boldsymbol{W}) = \sum_{\boldsymbol{Y} \text{ misclassified}} (\boldsymbol{W}^{\top}\boldsymbol{Y})^2 \tag{7.29}$$

As an advantage, this error function is continuous, unlike the function in Eq. 7.26. However, there are a few limitations with the error function of Eq. 7.29, such as, (1) it is very smooth in the boundary, which may result in arbitrary values if gradient descent is applied there, (2) the process may get stuck at some local minima, if the function is not convex where it has only a global minimum, and (3) the value of this error function is dominated by long $\boldsymbol{Y}$s. To resolve the issues of this error function, it requires some kind of normalization with respect to $\boldsymbol{Y}$.

To take care of this factor, another error function is proposed as given below. It also imposes more restriction in the form of the solution.

$$J_r(\boldsymbol{W}) = \frac{1}{2} \sum_{\substack{\boldsymbol{Y} \text{ misclassified} \\ \boldsymbol{W}^\top \boldsymbol{Y} \leq b}} \frac{(\boldsymbol{W}^\top \boldsymbol{Y} - b)^2}{\|\boldsymbol{Y}\|^2} \tag{7.30}$$

In this case, the hyper-plane is further moved toward the positive side by a distance of $\frac{b}{\|\boldsymbol{W}\|}$. So, it is a more stringent criteria for satisfying the linear separability of the classes. The gradient of this function is computed by using the expression given in Eq. 7.31.

$$\nabla J_r(\boldsymbol{W}) = \sum_{\boldsymbol{W}^\top \boldsymbol{Y} \leq b} \frac{\boldsymbol{Y}(\boldsymbol{W}^\top \boldsymbol{Y} - b)}{\|\boldsymbol{Y}\|^2} \tag{7.31}$$

In Fig. 7.6, the characteristic of stringent separability due to the use of an offset that moves the separating hyper-plane further toward positive partition by a distance of b is shown.

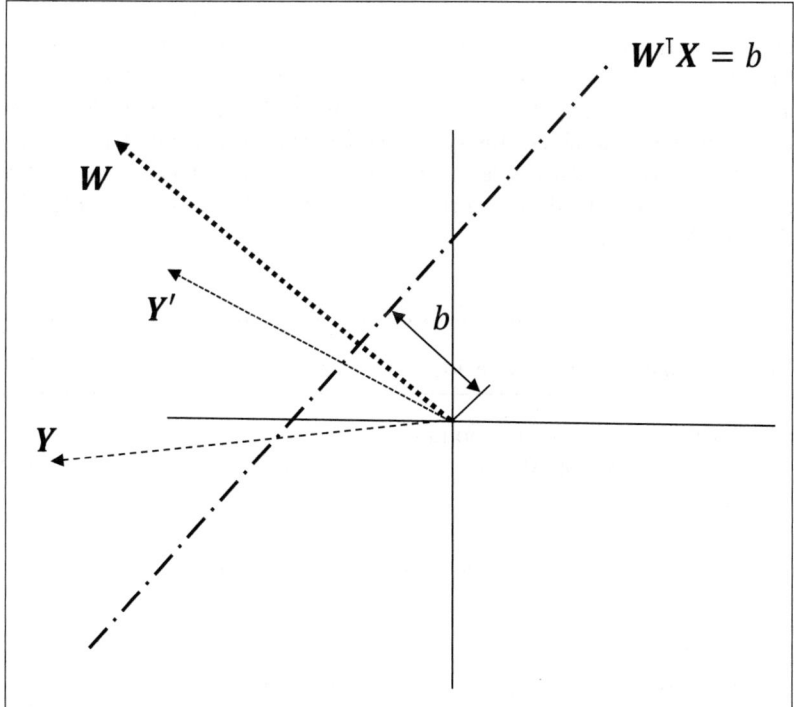

Figure 7.6 Illustration of a more stringent criteria for linear separability of the classes.

The algorithms for linear classification

In view of above notations and representations, these processes are summarized in an algorithm called batch relaxation with margin, as discussed in Algorithm 14

Algorithm 14 Batch relaxation with margin

Input: A set of two-class data points.

Output: A weight vector, $\boldsymbol{W}$, that linearly separates the given set of data points.

1: Initialize $\boldsymbol{W}$ to $\boldsymbol{W}^{(0)}$.

2: Iterate the following steps till convergence.

3: Compute the set of misclassified samples, M, with a margin b, so that, M = $\{\boldsymbol{Y} | \boldsymbol{W}^{\top} \boldsymbol{Y} \leq b\}$.

4: Compute the gradients using Eq. 7.31.

5: Update $\boldsymbol{W}$ as, $\boldsymbol{W}^{(i)} = \boldsymbol{W}^{(i-1)} - \eta(i) \nabla J_r(\boldsymbol{W}^{(i-1)})$, at every iteration, i.

Batch relaxation means that the classification is performed on all samples in a batch, and then the gradient function is computed. As a simplification of these computations for a batch, the weight vector, $\boldsymbol{W}$, is immediately updated by considering every single sample whenever it is misclassified, instead of considering the whole batch at a time. This simplification, known as *single sample relaxation with margin*, has been found to be faster than the batch relaxation, while delivering a similar performance. An algorithm of this scheme is given in Algorithm 15.

Algorithm 15 Single sample relaxation with margin

Input: A set of two-class data points.

Output: A weight vector, $\boldsymbol{W}$, that linearly separates the given set of data points.

1: Initialize $\boldsymbol{W}$ to $\boldsymbol{W}^{(0)}$.

2: Iterate the following steps till convergence.

3: Perform the update on $\boldsymbol{W}$ by considering samples one by one en every iteration, i.

4: For k^{th} sample, $\boldsymbol{Y}_k$, in i^{th} iteration, do

- If $(\boldsymbol{W}^{\top} \boldsymbol{Y}_k \leq b)$,

- Update $\boldsymbol{W}$ as, $\boldsymbol{W}^{(i)} = \boldsymbol{W}^{(i-1)} - \eta(i) \frac{b - \boldsymbol{W}^{\top} \boldsymbol{Y}_k}{\|\boldsymbol{Y}_k\|^2} \boldsymbol{Y}_k$.

5: Stop if very little changes in updates at the end of an iteration.

7.4.2 | Linear discriminant analysis from Bayes classifier

Bayesian classification and deriving linear discriminant functions from Bayesian classification approaches is discussed here. In Section 7.2, it is discussed that for a given input $\boldsymbol{x}$, the posterior probabilities are estimated as, $P(C_i|\boldsymbol{X})$, where, $i = 1, 2, \ldots, l$, l is the number of classes. For the simplicity of representation, let C_i be denoted by k, which represents class labels. Then, the given data point, $\boldsymbol{x}$, is assigned with the class label of a class with the maximum posterior probability value. Since it is practically difficult to estimate $P(k|\boldsymbol{x})$ directly, the class likelihood, $P(\boldsymbol{x}|k)$, and class prior, $P(k)$, are computed, so that, the posterior probability is estimated using Eq. 7.32.

$$P(k|\boldsymbol{x}) = \frac{P(\boldsymbol{x}|k)P(k)}{P(\boldsymbol{x})} \implies P(k|\boldsymbol{x}) \propto P(\boldsymbol{x}|k)p_k \qquad (7.32)$$

where, p_k is the prior probability of the class k (also denoted by $P(k)$). It is also noted that, $P(\boldsymbol{x})$ is not required to be computed since it is the same for all classes, so that, Eq. 7.32 may be simplified as, $P(k|\boldsymbol{x}) \propto P(\boldsymbol{x}|k)P(k)$. In our context the number of class is 2 ($l = 2$), and the labels (k) are denoted either by $+1$ or by -1.

As an assumption, let the likelihood distributions follow a normal distribution. Unlike naive Bayes classifier that considers categorical attributes in discrete domains, here we consider continuous attribute values in a continuous domain for parametric modeling. In other words, the combined set of attributes represented by an n-D feature vector is assumed to follow a normal distribution. In addition, unlike a naive Bayes classifier, the independence of attributes sets are not considered. Let the normal distribution in a multi-dimensional space be denoted by, $\mathcal{N}(\boldsymbol{x}; \boldsymbol{m}_k, \mathbf{S}_k)$. Analogous to 1-D representation, there are two parameters corresponding to the mean and the variance. However, in multi-dimensional representation, the mean of the distribution corresponds to the n-D mean vector, $\boldsymbol{m}_k$, for the class k, and the variance of the same class corresponds to the covariance matrix, $\mathbf{S}_k$, which is a $n \times n$ symmetric matrix. For simplification, we assume that the covariance matrices of all classes are the same, that is, $\mathbf{S}_k = \mathbf{S}$, for all k. Thus the probability density function of the likelihood of class k in multi-dimensional space is given by,

$$\mathcal{N}(\boldsymbol{x}|\boldsymbol{m}_k, \mathbf{S}) = \frac{1}{\sqrt{(2\pi)^n |\mathbf{S}|}} e^{-\frac{1}{2}(\boldsymbol{x}-\boldsymbol{m}_k)^{\top}\mathbf{S}^{-1}(\boldsymbol{x}-\boldsymbol{m}_k)} \qquad (7.33)$$

In the above, $|\mathbf{S}|$ denotes the determinant of $\mathbf{S}$. To simplify the expression, the denominator in Eq.7.33 is considered as a normalizing constant, $C = \sqrt{(2\pi)^n |\mathbf{S}|}$, that is independent of any class. With reference to Eq. 7.32, the term $P(\boldsymbol{x}|k)$ corresponds to $\mathcal{N}(\boldsymbol{x}|\boldsymbol{m}_k, \mathbf{S})$.

It is convenient to use logarithm of these measures for comparisons, as logarithm of a variable x ($x > 0$) is a monotonically increasing function.[1] There are a few advantages of using logarithm operations. Since the logarithm of a quantity is proportional to the original quantity, the comparisons of different values in either domain remain similar. As it can be seen in the expression of normal distribution in Eq. 7.33, one of the factors is in an exponential form. The use of logarithm operation on such factors makes the expression in a linear or a quadratic polynomial form. This is more convenient for mathematical treatment.

---

[1] Since the measure expresses a probability value, this is true for any nonzero probability value.

Applying logarithm operations over the posterior probability values, using Eq. 7.32 and 7.33, the log-probability or the log-likelihood is given by $\log(P(k|\boldsymbol{x})) \propto \log(p_k \mathcal{N}(\boldsymbol{x}|\boldsymbol{m}_k, \mathbf{S}))$, as expressed in Eq. 7.34.

$$\begin{aligned} \log(p_k \mathcal{N}(\boldsymbol{x}|\boldsymbol{m}_k, \mathbf{S})) &= \log(p_k) + \log(\mathcal{N}(\boldsymbol{x}|\boldsymbol{m}_k, \mathbf{S})) \\ &= \log(p_k) - \log(C) - \frac{1}{2}(\boldsymbol{x} - \boldsymbol{m}_k)^\top \mathbf{S}^{-1}(\boldsymbol{x} - \boldsymbol{m}_k) \end{aligned} \tag{7.34}$$

The constant term, $\log(C)$, is ignored while comparing the log-likelihood values since it is not dependent on classes. So, the log-likelihood values are compared using the expression $\log(p_k) - \frac{1}{2}(\boldsymbol{x} - \boldsymbol{m}_k)^\top \mathbf{S}^{-1}(\boldsymbol{x} - \boldsymbol{m}_k)$ to find the class with a maximum value of posterior probability, and its corresponding class label is assigned to the input data vector, $\boldsymbol{x}$.

To understand how logarithm operation transforms the proportional measure to a linear form, consider the expression of Eq. 7.34, whose value is to be maximized. Here, the term, $\log(p_k)$, is the prior component and the other term is the likelihood part. An expansion of this expression, by ignoring the constant terms, is given in Eq. 7.35.

$$\begin{aligned} &\log(p_k) - \frac{1}{2}(\boldsymbol{x} - \boldsymbol{m}_k)^\top \mathbf{S}^{-1}(\boldsymbol{x} - \boldsymbol{m}_k) \\ &= \log(p_k) - \frac{1}{2}(\boldsymbol{x}^\top \mathbf{S}^{-1}\boldsymbol{x} - \boldsymbol{x}^\top \mathbf{S}^{-1}\boldsymbol{m}_k - \boldsymbol{m}_k^\top \mathbf{S}^{-1}\boldsymbol{x} + \boldsymbol{m}_k^\top \mathbf{S}^{-1}\boldsymbol{m}_k) \end{aligned} \tag{7.35}$$

In the above expression, the term $\boldsymbol{x}^\top \mathbf{S}^{-1}\boldsymbol{x}$ is independent of classes. Its value is the same for all the classes for a given data, $\boldsymbol{x}$. So it is ignored and the simplified expression becomes as follows.

$$\log(p_k) - \frac{1}{2}(-\boldsymbol{x}^\top \mathbf{S}^{-1}\boldsymbol{m}_k - \boldsymbol{m}_k^\top \mathbf{S}^{-1}\boldsymbol{x} + \boldsymbol{m}_k^\top \mathbf{S}^{-1}\boldsymbol{m}_k) \tag{7.36}$$

Further, in Eq. 7.36, $\boldsymbol{x}^\top \mathbf{S}^{-1}\boldsymbol{m}_k = \boldsymbol{m}_k^\top \mathbf{S}^{-1}\boldsymbol{x}$, since $\mathbf{S}$ is a symmetric matrix. Therefore, the expression is further simplified, in the following form.
$\log(p_k) + \boldsymbol{m}_k^\top \mathbf{S}^{-1}\boldsymbol{x} - \frac{1}{2}(\boldsymbol{m}_k^\top \mathbf{S}^{-1}\boldsymbol{m}_k) = g_k(\boldsymbol{x})$.
In the above, we observe that $g_k(\boldsymbol{x})$ is a function of variable $\boldsymbol{x}$, which is in its linear form. This acts as the linear discriminant function for the task of classification. In this case, the discriminant function, $g(\boldsymbol{x})$, is expressed using the individual linear functions, $g_k(\boldsymbol{x})$, $k = +1$ or -1, which is a linear form, as given by Eq. 7.37.

$$g(\boldsymbol{x}) = g_{+1}(\boldsymbol{x}) - g_{-1}(\boldsymbol{x}) \tag{7.37}$$

When $g_{+1}(\boldsymbol{x}) > g_{-1}(\boldsymbol{x})$, the sign of $g(\boldsymbol{x})$ is positive, and $\boldsymbol{x}$ is assigned to class $+1$. Similarly, when $g_{+1}(\boldsymbol{x}) < g_{-1}(\boldsymbol{x})$, the sign of $g(\boldsymbol{x})$ is negative, and $\boldsymbol{x}$ is assigned to class -1.

A summary of the derivation of linear discriminant function from Bayesian classification approach is as follows.

- Given the training data, estimate the class priors, p_k, using the number of instances in class k, N_k, and the total number of instances, N, as $p_k = \frac{N_k}{N}$.
- Estimate the means of classes, $\boldsymbol{m}_k$s, and the covariance of the data, $\mathbf{S}$ as, $\boldsymbol{m}_k = \frac{1}{N_k}\sum_{\boldsymbol{y} \in k} \boldsymbol{y}$ and $\mathbf{S} = \frac{1}{N-1}\sum_{\forall \boldsymbol{y}}(\boldsymbol{y} - \boldsymbol{m})(\boldsymbol{y} - \boldsymbol{m})^\top$, where $\boldsymbol{y}$ is a data sample in training set and $\boldsymbol{m}$ is the mean of the whole training data.

- Obtain the discriminant function, $g(\boldsymbol{x})$, as in Eq. 7.37, and perform the LDA of the given data points.

7.4.3 | Fisher linear discriminant analysis

Using the PCA (refer to Chapter 2), images may be represented by a few principal components, which may be useful in a task of classification. But, dimension reduction and representation by factors or principal components using the PCA is not a very efficient approach for classification tasks, particularly if we use linear discriminant functions. This is due to the fact that the class distribution of principal components may not be well separable. There exists an efficient dimensional reduction method which also takes account of the class distribution of the factors for obtaining linear discriminant functions. In this case, linear discrimination of data points becomes simpler by reducing the features to just 1-D component. This discriminant is known as the *Fisher linear discriminant* (FLD) (Fisher, 1938), invented by the renowned statistician, Ronald Fisher (1890−1962) in 1938.

Let us first discuss why the PCA may not be suitable for providing a feature space, which is well separable. The separability property is required for the existence of a linear discriminant function. This has been elaborated in Section 7.4. In Section 2.9 of Chapter 2, we discuss how the PCA captures the direction of the maximum variance of a given data set. But, for a labeled data set, the PCA does not capture the direction of maximum separation between the groups of data points of different labels. For example, consider a labeled set of six points that belong to two different groups, as shown in Fig. 7.7, where the points in one of the groups are shown in triangles and the points in the other group are shown in ellipses. In Fig. 7.7 (a), the direction of maximum variance, obtained by the PCA, is shown by a dotted line, where the projections of all the data points along this line has the maximum variance. The projected points over the principal component, represented by the dotted line, are intermingled along its direction and they cannot be discriminated by a simple rule of linear separation. Whereas, in Fig. 7.7 (b), the points are projected on a line in another direction, where the projected points are linearly separable. That is, the points from each of the groups lie within specific nonoverlapping intervals along this new direction, so that, they can be separated by a simple threshold value. As we observe from the figures, the direction of the principal component is not providing a good separation between different groups of data points. However, the data points can be well separated, but in a different direction, and not along the direction of the principal component.

To understand the computational problem involved in the FLD analysis, consider a set of N data points, $S = \{\boldsymbol{x}_i \mid \boldsymbol{x}_i \in \mathbb{R}^n\}$. Let there be N_1 data points that belong to class ω_1 and N_2 data points that belong to class ω_2, such that $N_1 + N_2 = N$. Since the objective is to find a direction where the separation between the groups of data points belonging to these two classes is maximum, consider projection of the data point, $\boldsymbol{x}_i$, on a line with a direction, $\boldsymbol{u}$. This projection operation is expressed as a dot product of two vectors, $\boldsymbol{x}_i$ and $\boldsymbol{u}$, or in the matrix operation. It is denoted by Eq. 7.38.

$$y_i = \boldsymbol{x}_i^\top \boldsymbol{u} \qquad (7.38)$$

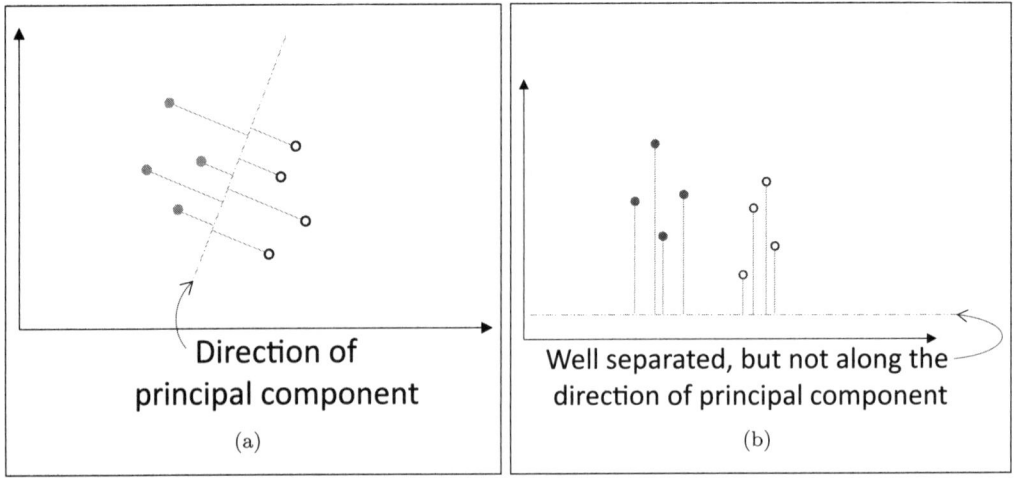

Figure 7.7 Linear separability on projected data points.

The projection of the data points is a 1-D sub-space representation of the data and all the points lie on that line.

Separation between projected data of different classes

To formulate a problem of separating the data well, it is necessary to define a measure of separation of projected data, so that, maximizing this measure becomes the objective of the computational problem. Let, $\boldsymbol{m}_1$ and $\boldsymbol{m}_2$ be the mean vectors of data points in classes ω_1 and ω_2, respectively. The projection of these mean vectors, m_{y_1} and m_{y_2}, along the direction of $\boldsymbol{u}$ are computed by Eq. 7.39.

$$\begin{aligned} m_{y_1} &= \boldsymbol{m}_1^\top \boldsymbol{u} \\ m_{y_2} &= \boldsymbol{m}_2^\top \boldsymbol{u} \end{aligned} \tag{7.39}$$

In Fig. 7.8, these projected means are figuratively shown for the data points corresponding to Fig. 7.7 (b). One of the measures of separation between the groups of data points is the separation of these two projected means. For a well separated groups of data points, this value is expected to be large. For example, a measure of separation of the means can be computed as the absolute difference between the two projected mean values, which is given by Eq. 7.40.

$$D = |m_{y_1} - m_{y_2}| \tag{7.40}$$

But, such a measure of an absolute difference does not capture the variance of data. Certain groups of data points could be widely spread around the projected mean, while some groups of data points may be very closely spaced around the mean after projection. Ideally, it is

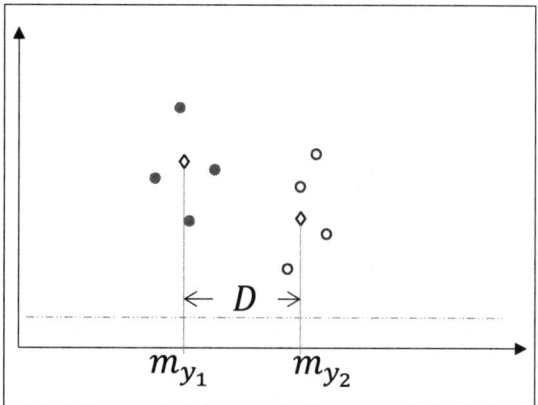

Figure 7.8 Representation of a measure of separation between two groups of data points.

preferred to have the data points in each group to be very closely spaced around their mean, and the mean values to be largely separated from each other. These desirable cases for projection of data points are not captured by using only the value of D.

A measure of separation

In order to incorporate the information of spread of projected data points around their projected means in each class, the measure, D, is normalized by a factor proportional to the class variances. This factor is called *scatter*. The scatter, s_C^2, of data belonging to a class C is defined by Eq. 7.41.

$$s_C^2 = \sum_{y \in C} (y - m_C)^2 \tag{7.41}$$

where, y represents projected data and m_C represents the mean of projected data points in class C. That is, the scatter is the sum of squares of mean deviations of data points from the projected mean of the data points. The scatter is a proportional factor with variance because, by Eq. 7.41, s_C^2 is simply the product of class variance and number of samples in class C. A better measure of separation between the two groups of data points is given by Eq. 7.42.

$$J(\boldsymbol{u}) = \frac{D^2}{(s_1^2 + s_2^2)} \tag{7.42}$$

where, s_1^2 and s_2^2 are the scatters of the data points in classes ω_1 and ω_2, respectively. Here, D^2 is normalized by the sum of the scatters of the two projected groups. To make the measure unitless, the square of the separating distance between two projected means is used in the expression. So, the objective is to maximize the value of $J(\boldsymbol{u})$ to get a direction so that the scatter of the projected samples are comparatively smaller along that.

Scatter matrix

Similar to the scatter that is defined on the projected data in 1-D sub-space, scatter matrix is defined on the original data in a multi-dimensional space. The scatter matrix, $\mathbf{S}_C$ of a sample of class C in the original space is given by Eq. 7.43.

$$\mathbf{S}_C = \sum_{x \in C} (\boldsymbol{x} - \boldsymbol{m}_C)(\boldsymbol{x} - \boldsymbol{m}_C)^\top \tag{7.43}$$

where, $\boldsymbol{m}_C$ is the mean of data points in class C.

Within the class scatter matrix is defined as the sum of individual scatter matrices in the given data. For the example of two classes, within the class scatter matrix is given by Eq. 7.44.

$$\mathbf{S}_\omega = \mathbf{S}_1 + \mathbf{S}_2 \tag{7.44}$$

where, $\mathbf{S}_1$ and $\mathbf{S}_2$ are the scatter matrices of classes ω_1 and ω_2, respectively. For the class, ω_1, from Eq. 7.38 and 7.41, the scatter, s_1^2, is expressed by Eq. 7.45.

$$
\begin{aligned}
s_1^2 &= \sum_{y \in \omega_1} (y - m_{y_1})^2 = \sum_{x \in \omega_1} (\boldsymbol{u}^\top \boldsymbol{x} - \boldsymbol{u}^\top \boldsymbol{m}_1)(\boldsymbol{u}^\top \boldsymbol{x} - \boldsymbol{u}^\top \boldsymbol{m}_1)^\top \\
&= \sum_{x \in \omega_1} \boldsymbol{u}^\top (\boldsymbol{x} - \boldsymbol{m}_1)(\boldsymbol{x} - \boldsymbol{m}_1)^\top \boldsymbol{u} \\
&= \boldsymbol{u}^\top \left(\sum_{x \in \omega_1} (\boldsymbol{x} - \boldsymbol{m}_1)(\boldsymbol{x} - \boldsymbol{m}_1)^\top \right) \boldsymbol{u}
\end{aligned}
\tag{7.45}
$$

where, s_1^2 and $\boldsymbol{m}_1$ are the scatter and the mean of data points in class ω_1. From Eq. 7.43 and 7.45, the relation between s_1^2 and $\mathbf{S}_1$ are given by Eq. 7.46.

$$s_1^2 = \boldsymbol{u}^\top \mathbf{S}_1 \boldsymbol{u} \tag{7.46}$$

Similarly, s_2^2 and $\mathbf{S}_2$ are related by Eq. 7.47.

$$s_2^2 = \boldsymbol{u}^\top \mathbf{S}_2 \boldsymbol{u} \tag{7.47}$$

So, from Eq. 7.44, 7.46, and 7.47, the relation between within the class scatter matrix and class scatters is expressed by Eq. 7.48.

$$s_1^2 + s_2^2 = \boldsymbol{u}^\top \mathbf{S}_\omega \boldsymbol{u} \tag{7.48}$$

Between the class scatter matrix is defined by the difference between the two mean vectors of data points from each of the classes in original space, which is given by Eq. 7.49.

$$\mathbf{S}_B = (\boldsymbol{m}_1 - \boldsymbol{m}_2)(\boldsymbol{m}_1 - \boldsymbol{m}_2)^\top \tag{7.49}$$

The relation between D^2 and $\mathbf{S}_B$ is expressed by Eq. 7.50.

$$\begin{aligned} D^2 = (m_{y_1} - m_{y_2})^2 &= (\boldsymbol{u}^\top \boldsymbol{m}_1 - \boldsymbol{u}^\top \boldsymbol{m}_2)(\boldsymbol{u}^\top \boldsymbol{m}_1 - \boldsymbol{u}^\top \boldsymbol{m}_2)^\top \\ &= \boldsymbol{u}^\top(\boldsymbol{m}_1 - \boldsymbol{m}_2)(\boldsymbol{m}_1 - \boldsymbol{m}_2)^\top \boldsymbol{u} \\ &= \boldsymbol{u}^\top \mathbf{S}_B \boldsymbol{u} \end{aligned} \tag{7.50}$$

From Eq. 7.42, 7.48 and 7.50, the optimization function, $J(\boldsymbol{u})$, is rewritten in the form as expressed by Eq. 7.51.

$$J(\boldsymbol{u}) = \frac{D^2}{s_1^2 + s_2^2} = \frac{\boldsymbol{u}^\top \mathbf{S}_B \boldsymbol{u}}{\boldsymbol{u}^\top \mathbf{S}_\omega \boldsymbol{u}} \tag{7.51}$$

This is a constrained optimization problem, where $J(\boldsymbol{u})$ is to be maximized with a constraint of $\boldsymbol{u}$ as a unit vector. Provided, $\mathbf{S}_\omega$ is an invertible matrix, this can be formed as an eigenvalue problem, as given in Eq. 7.52.

$$\mathbf{S}_\omega^{-1} \mathbf{S}_B \boldsymbol{u} = \lambda \boldsymbol{u} \tag{7.52}$$

where, λ is the eigenvalue. As a solution to this problem, $\boldsymbol{u}$ is the eigenvector of the matrix, $\mathbf{S}_\omega^{-1} \mathbf{S}_B$. Since the problem is on maximization, the eigenvector corresponding to the maximum eigenvalue is chosen as the solution.

It is interesting to note that, $\mathbf{S}_B \boldsymbol{u}$ already has an eigenvector along $(\boldsymbol{m}_1 - \boldsymbol{m}_2)$. Using a particular expansion of $\mathbf{S}_B \boldsymbol{u}$ that is given in Eq. 7.53, it can be interpreted as a dot product of the difference of mean vectors with respect to $\boldsymbol{u}$, which is a scalar value, k.

$$\mathbf{S}_B \boldsymbol{u} = (\boldsymbol{m}_1 - \boldsymbol{m}_2)(\boldsymbol{m}_1 - \boldsymbol{m}_2)^\top \boldsymbol{u} = k(\boldsymbol{m}_1 - \boldsymbol{m}_2) \tag{7.53}$$

where $k = (\boldsymbol{m}_1 - \boldsymbol{m}_2)^\top \boldsymbol{u}$. Therefore, $(\boldsymbol{m}_1 - \boldsymbol{m}_2)$ is also an eigenvector of $\mathbf{S}_B$. Hence, the solution can be further simplified as in Eq. 7.54

$$\boldsymbol{u} = \mathbf{S}_\omega^{-1}(\boldsymbol{m}_1 - \boldsymbol{m}_2) \tag{7.54}$$

This expression gives the direction along which the maximum separation of projected samples is achieved, so that we may find a linear discriminant function which separates the data points.

Numerical Example

Consider the following two sets of data points.

$$\mathbf{X}_1 = \{(5, 3, 2),\ (4, 6, 0),\ (3, -7, 14)\}$$
$$\mathbf{X}_2 = \{(-2, -5, 17),\ (3, -13, 10),\ (-4, -2, 16)\}$$

Perform LDA and get the optimum direction. Check separability in the line of projection.

Solution

Consider the given sets of data points in the matrix form, where each column represents a data point, given by,

$$\mathbf{X}_1 = \begin{bmatrix} 5 & 4 & 3 \\ 3 & 6 & -7 \\ 2 & 0 & 14 \end{bmatrix}$$

$$\mathbf{X}_2 = \begin{bmatrix} -2 & 3 & -4 \\ -5 & -13 & -2 \\ 17 & 10 & 16 \end{bmatrix}$$

The mean vectors of $\mathbf{X}_1$ and $\mathbf{X}_2$, $\overline{\mathbf{X}_1}$ and $\overline{\mathbf{X}_2}$, are computed as,

$$\overline{\mathbf{X}_1} = \begin{bmatrix} 4 \\ 0.67 \\ 5.33 \end{bmatrix} \quad \text{and} \quad \overline{\mathbf{X}_2} = \begin{bmatrix} -1 \\ -6.67 \\ 14.33 \end{bmatrix}$$

The scatter matrices of $\mathbf{X}_1$ and $\mathbf{X}_2$, $\mathbf{S}_1$ and $\mathbf{S}_2$, are computed as,

$$\mathbf{S}_1 = \left(\mathbf{X}_1 - \overline{\mathbf{X}_1}\right)\left(\mathbf{X}_1 - \overline{\mathbf{X}_1}\right)^\top = \begin{bmatrix} 2 & 10 & 12 \\ 10 & 92.66 & -102.67 \\ -12 & -102.67 & 114.67 \end{bmatrix}$$

$$\mathbf{S}_2 = \left(\mathbf{X}_2 - \overline{\mathbf{X}_2}\right)\left(\mathbf{X}_2 - \overline{\mathbf{X}_2}\right)^\top = \begin{bmatrix} 26 & -41 & -25 \\ -41 & 64.67 & 39.67 \\ -25 & 39.67 & 28.66 \end{bmatrix}$$

Also, the within class scatter matrix, $\mathbf{S}_\omega$, is computed as,

$$\mathbf{S}_\omega = \mathbf{S}_1 + \mathbf{S}_2 = \begin{bmatrix} 28 & -31 & -37 \\ -31 & 157.33 & -63 \\ -37 & -63 & 143.33 \end{bmatrix}$$

Then, the optimum direction, $\boldsymbol{u}$, is obtained as,

$$\boldsymbol{u} = \mathbf{S}_\omega^{-1}\left(\overline{\mathbf{X}_1} - \overline{\mathbf{X}_2}\right) = \begin{bmatrix} 3.2070 \\ -1.1952 \\ 1.2904 \end{bmatrix}$$

The separability in the line of projection may be verified by computing $\boldsymbol{Y}_1$ and $\boldsymbol{Y}_2$, the projections of all the data points in $\mathbf{X}_1$ and $\mathbf{X}_2$ with respect to $\boldsymbol{u}$, respectively, which are given by,

$$\boldsymbol{Y}_1 = \mathbf{X}_1^\top \boldsymbol{u} = \begin{bmatrix} 22.2 \\ 19.99 \\ 19.31 \end{bmatrix} \quad \text{and} \quad \boldsymbol{Y}_2 = \mathbf{X}_2^\top \boldsymbol{u} = \begin{bmatrix} 9.55 \\ 6.99 \\ 5.43 \end{bmatrix}$$

It may observed that, the range of $\boldsymbol{Y}_1$ is between 19.31 to 22.2, and the range of $\boldsymbol{Y}_2$ is between 5.43 to 9.55. That is, the intervals of $\boldsymbol{Y}_1$ and $\boldsymbol{Y}_2$ are well separated.

7.4.4 | Linear support vector machine

A *linear support vector machine* (SVM) is a linear discriminant classifier, which maximizes the separability of training samples of two linearly separable classes. In this case, the computational problem is stated as follows.

Computational problem

Let $X = \{(\boldsymbol{x}^t, r^t) | t = 1, 2, \ldots, N\}$ be a set of N training samples, where $\boldsymbol{x}^t \in R^d$ is a data point in the d-dimensional data point and r^t is its class label, which can be either $+1$ or -1. Find a linear discriminant function $g(\boldsymbol{x}) = \boldsymbol{w}^\top \boldsymbol{x} + w_0$, where $\boldsymbol{w} \in R^d$ and $w_0 \in R$, which maximizes the distance between the class margins $g(\boldsymbol{x}) = +1$ and $g(\boldsymbol{x}) = -1$, and satisfies the following condition for every tth sample:

$$\begin{aligned} \boldsymbol{w}^\top \boldsymbol{x}^t + w_0 &\geq +1 \text{ if } r^t = +1 \\ \boldsymbol{w}^\top \boldsymbol{x}^t + w_0 &\leq -1 \text{ if } r^t = -1 \end{aligned} \tag{7.55}$$

We may note here that the conditions imposed by the linear SVM for the training sample is much harder than the usual classification criterion of a discriminant function, where it is sufficient to declare a class label for a sample $\boldsymbol{x}$, by determining the sign of $g(\boldsymbol{x})$. During the design of the classifier these harder restrictions (Eq. 7.55) are imposed, and a margin is kept between the training sample and the class boundary. But during class assignment of any test sample, it is sufficient to assign its class by checking the sign of $g(\boldsymbol{x})$.

We may note that Eq. (7.55) may be written in a more concise form in the following manner.

$$r^t(\boldsymbol{w}^\top \boldsymbol{x}^t + w_0) \geq +1 \text{ for all } t \tag{7.56}$$

The optimization problem

Consider the two class margin functions $g_1(\boldsymbol{x})$, and $g_2(\boldsymbol{x})$ as given below.

$$\begin{aligned} g_1(\boldsymbol{x}) &: \boldsymbol{w}^\top \boldsymbol{x} + w_0 - 1 = 0 \\ g_2(\boldsymbol{x}) &: \boldsymbol{w}^\top \boldsymbol{x} + w_0 + 1 = 0 \end{aligned} \tag{7.57}$$

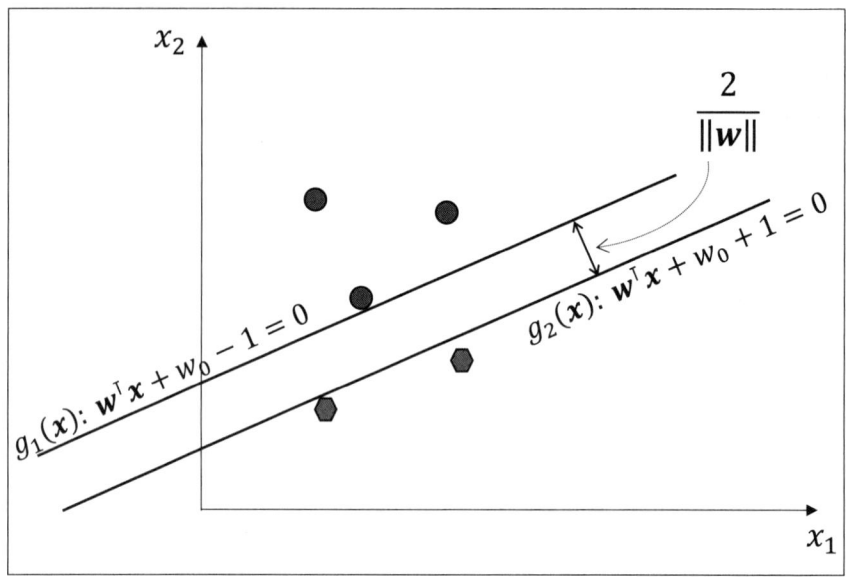

Figure 7.9 Class margins and distance between them.

Each of the above functions define a hyper-plane in the feature space, and they are parallel. A typical illustration in a 2-D feature space is provided in Fig. 7.9. The distance between these two hyper-planes is given by $\frac{2}{\|\boldsymbol{w}\|}$. Hence for maximizing the distance, it is sufficient to minimize $\|\boldsymbol{w}\|$. Hence the optimization problem for the linear SVM is formulated as follows:

Given the training samples $X = \{(\boldsymbol{x}^t, r^t) | t = 1, 2, \ldots, N\}$, obtain $\boldsymbol{w}$ and w_0, which minimize $\frac{1}{2}\|\boldsymbol{w}\|^2$ subject to $r^t(\boldsymbol{w}^\top \boldsymbol{x}^t + w_0) \geq +1$ for all t.

Constraint optimization

The optimization problem as stated above is an example of a constrained optimization problem. In this case, the objective function is convex with linear constraints. To make it unconstrained, we use Lagrange multipliers, α^t's to modify the objective function in the following form.

$$
\begin{aligned}
L_p &= \frac{1}{2}\|\boldsymbol{w}\|^2 - \sum_t \alpha^t [r^t(\boldsymbol{w}^\top \boldsymbol{x}^t + w_0) - 1] \\
&= \frac{1}{2}\|\boldsymbol{w}\|^2 - \sum_t \alpha_t [r^t(\boldsymbol{w}^\top \boldsymbol{x}^t + w_0)] + \sum_t \alpha^t
\end{aligned}
\tag{7.58}
$$

Dual problem

The optimization problem for minimizing the objective function as expressed in Eq. (7.58) with respect to $\boldsymbol{w}$ and w_0 may be solved using an equivalent dual form. In this form, the objective function is transformed to a function of Lagrange multipliers subject to setting the partial derivatives of the primary objective function to zero, and the transformed function is to be maximized with respect to the Lagrange multipliers, which are either positive or zero.

Hence,

$$\frac{\partial L_p}{\partial \boldsymbol{w}} = 0 \implies \boldsymbol{w} = \sum_t \alpha^t r^t \boldsymbol{x}^t \tag{7.59}$$

$$\frac{\partial L_p}{\partial w_0} = 0 \implies \sum_t \alpha^t r^t = 0 \tag{7.60}$$

By using the above relations, the dual objective function with respect to maximization by the Lagrange multipliers is derived below.

$$L_p = \frac{1}{2} \boldsymbol{w}^\top \boldsymbol{w} - \sum_t \alpha_t [r^t (\boldsymbol{w}^\top \boldsymbol{x}^t + w_0)] + \sum_t \alpha^t$$

$$= \frac{1}{2} \boldsymbol{w}^\top \boldsymbol{w} - \boldsymbol{w}^\top \left(\sum_t \alpha^t r^t \boldsymbol{x}^t \right) - w_0 \sum_t \alpha^t r^t + \sum_t \alpha_t \tag{7.61}$$

Using Eq. (7.59) and Eq. (7.60)) in the above expression we get the dual objective function.

$$L_d = \frac{1}{2} \boldsymbol{w}^\top \boldsymbol{w} - \boldsymbol{w}^\top (\boldsymbol{w}) - w_0 \times 0 + \sum_t \alpha_t$$

$$= -\frac{1}{2} \boldsymbol{w}^\top \boldsymbol{w} + \sum_t \alpha_t \tag{7.62}$$

Further using Eq. 7.59, we replace $\boldsymbol{w}$ in the above expression, and the dual optimization problem reduces to a quadratic optimization problem with respect to Lagrange multipliers to maximize the following objective function.

$$L_d = -\frac{1}{2} \sum_t \sum_s \alpha^t \alpha^s r^t r^s (\boldsymbol{x}^t)^\top \boldsymbol{x}^s + \sum_t \alpha_t \tag{7.63}$$

The solution

The above optimization problem is a quadratic optimization problem and could be solved in $O(N^3)$, and $O(N^2)$ time and space complexities, respectively. It is found that in the solution the values of most of the lagrange multipliers are zero. Only for samples lying at the boundary of class margin, values are nonzero and positive. From Eq. 7.59, we find that $\boldsymbol{w}$ is a linear combination of all these samples only, called *support vectors*. In other words, training samples with positive (nonzero) Lagrange coefficient are the support vectors.

Once we get a support vector (say $\boldsymbol{x}^k$), from them we obtain w_0 by using the following condition.

$$r^k (\boldsymbol{w}^\top \boldsymbol{x}^k + w_0) = 1 \implies w_0 = r^k - \boldsymbol{w}^\top \boldsymbol{x}^k \tag{7.64}$$

As there may be many such support vectors, for the numerical stability we may take the average of estimates from each of them.

Testing with SVM

Once the discriminant function $g(\boldsymbol{x})$ is obtained. For classifying any unknown or test sample $\boldsymbol{x}$, it is sufficient to check the sign of the discriminant value for assigning a class. Thus, if $g(\boldsymbol{x}) > 0$, the label $+1$ is assigned to $\boldsymbol{x}$, otherwise its class label becomes -1.

7.5 | Artificial neural network

In biological interpretations, the perceptron classifier (Section 7.4.1) tries to model a neuron as a biological function. In this particular classifier, the output is expressed as a function of its weighted inputs. A biological neuron consists of several synapses that are excited from these inputs. A net response from the inputs, similar to a weighted function, is processed and propagated through an appropriate path of our nervous system of the neuron. A diagrammatic depiction of analogy between a biological neuron and a perceptron is shown in Fig. 7.10. Also, this excitation propagates through other neurons along its path that are connected in the same manner. Likewise, a perceptron node is

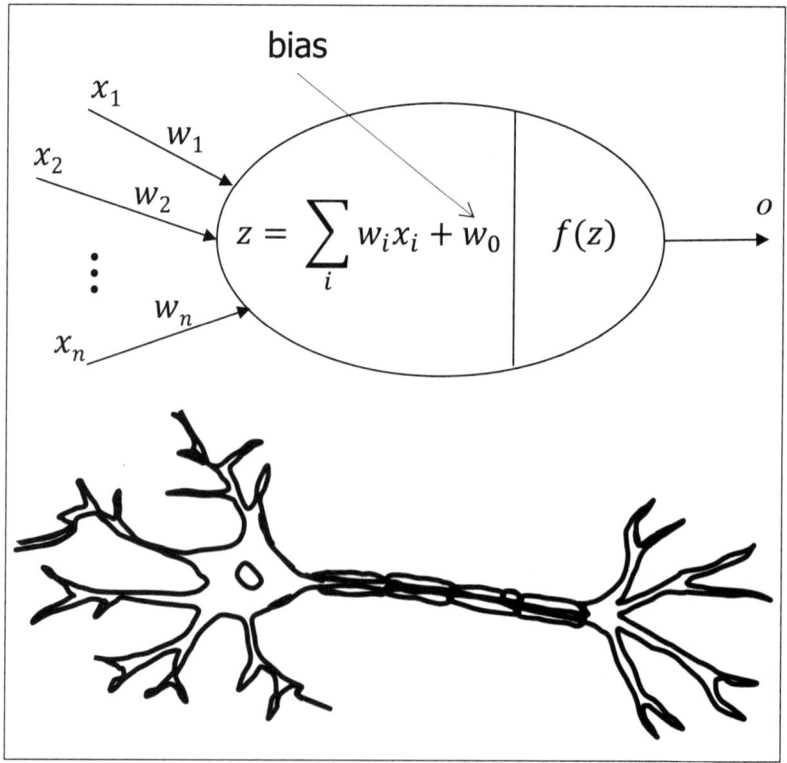

Figure 7.10 Analogy between a biological neuron and a perceptron.

considered as an individual neuron, which collects excitations from different synapses in its input and propagates the corresponding output response through a path that is connected further to other nodes. A model of a system as a network of these neurons or perceptrons that propagates a weighted combination of its inputs and generates an output by propagating the responses along their path is known as a neural network (NN) or an ANN model (Haykin, 1998). Such a strong generalized model is used in depicting various kinds of input-output relationships. In Fig. 7.11 an example of an ANN is shown. In this example, both input and output are vectors. Usually, the input to an ANN is a vector, and the output may be a vector or a scalar. If there are multiple neurons at the output, it is a vector. If there is a single output neuron, the output is a scalar.

7.5.1 | Feed-forward network

One of the special cases of this kind of network is known as feed-forward network, where there is no feedback or loop in the network. A loop in the network indicates feedback from the output to one or more of its input neurons. If the network does not contain such loops, the network is called a *feed-forward neural network*. A very general form of feed-forward neural network is a *multilayered feed-forward neural network*, as shown in Fig. 7.12. Apart from the input and output layers, there may be several intermediate layers that are known as hidden layers. In the example shown in the figure, only one hidden layer exists, which is followed by an output layer. In this form of the network, every layer has a certain number of neurons, which may vary in numbers for different layers. However, this model ensures that every neuron in a particular layer is connected to all the neurons in the next higher layer. Thus, a function of weighted sum of the outputs of neurons in a layer is the input of a neuron in the next layer. A nonlinear function processes this weighted sum of the

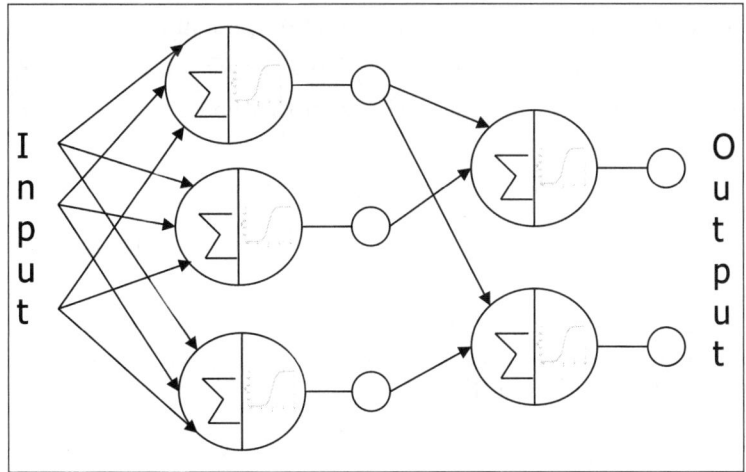

Figure 7.11 Example of an artificial neural network.

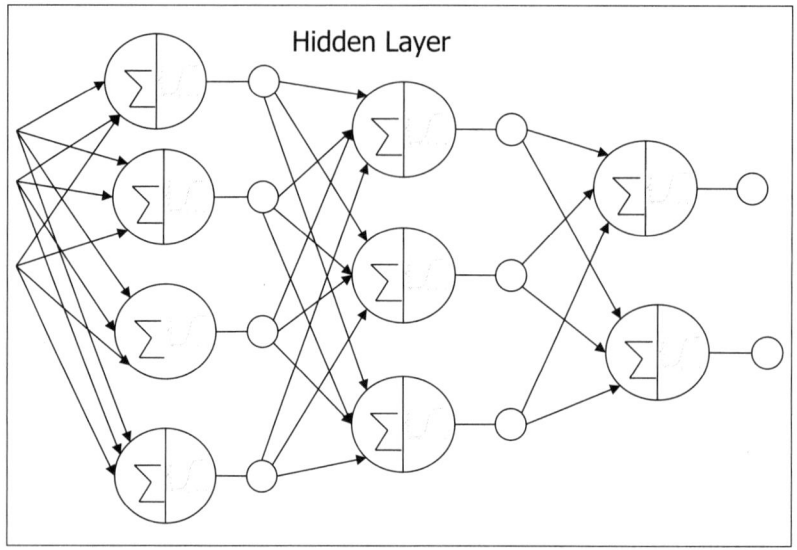

Figure 7.12 Example of a feed-forward neural network.

responses, whose corresponding output further propagates and excites the neurons of the subsequent layers. This network performs a layer wise processing, where the ith layer takes input from the $(i-1)^{\text{th}}$ layer and forwards its output to the input of the next layer. In this model, since all the neurons in a layer are fully connected by the neurons of its previous layers, this kind of network is also known as *fully connected neural network* (FCNN).

To describe this model mathematically, consider a weight vector in a particular layer that is connected to the outputs of the all the neurons of previous layers. Let, the jth neuron of the ith layer be denoted by $ne_j^{(i)}$. Let the number of outputs in the $(i-1)^{\text{th}}$ layer be n_{i-1}. The $ne_j^{(i)}$ node is connected by the weight $w_{kj}^{(i)}$ from the kth output node of the $(i-1)^{\text{th}}$ layer. We express the set of connecting weights to this node by a vector $\boldsymbol{W}_j^{(i)}$, as given below.

$$\boldsymbol{W}_j^{(i)} = [w_{1j}^{(i)}, w_{2j}^{(i)}, \dots, w_{n_{i-1}j}^{(i)}]^\top \tag{7.65}$$

Let the bias term of $\boldsymbol{W}_j^{(i)}$ be represented by $w_{0j}^{(i)}$. That is, n_{i-1} is the dimension of input to the neuron $ne_j^{(i)}$ which is also the number of neurons in the output layer for a fully connected network. Let the number of outputs in the ith layer be n_i. Then, at the jth neuron in the ith layer, the net response is expressed as the product of a weighted combination of its weight vector and input vector, as given in Eq. 7.66.

$$y_j^{(i)} = f(\boldsymbol{W}_j^{(i)^\top} \boldsymbol{X}^{(i-1)} + w_{0j}^{(i)}) \tag{7.66}$$

where, $\boldsymbol{X}^{(i-1)}$ is the vector that is generated by the $(i-1)^{\text{th}}$ layer. The product term, after adding a bias term, is fed as an input to a nonlinear function that generates the output response of that neuron.

The relation between the inputs and outputs at i^{th} layer is expressed by Eq. 7.67.

$$\boldsymbol{Z}^{(i)} = \begin{bmatrix} \boldsymbol{W}_1^{(i)^\top} \\ \boldsymbol{W}_2^{(i)^\top} \\ \vdots \\ \boldsymbol{W}_{n_i}^{(i)^\top} \end{bmatrix} \boldsymbol{X}^{(i-1)} + \begin{bmatrix} w_{01}^{(i)} \\ w_{02}^{(i)} \\ \vdots \\ w_{0n_i}^{(i)} \end{bmatrix} \tag{7.67}$$

$$\Longrightarrow \boldsymbol{Z}^{(i)} = \mathbf{W}^{(i)} \boldsymbol{X}^{(i-1)} + \boldsymbol{b}^{(i)}$$

$$\boldsymbol{Y}^{(i)} = f(\boldsymbol{Z}^{(i)})$$

where, $\mathbf{W}^{(i)}$ is the weight matrix at the ith layer. The $f(\boldsymbol{Z}^{(i)})$ denotes pointwise nonlinear operation for each element of $\boldsymbol{Z}^{(i)}$. Given an input at the input layer, the parameters $\mathbf{W}^{(i)}$ and $\boldsymbol{b}^{(i)}$ are used to generate the output, $\boldsymbol{Y}^{(i)}$ for the next hidden layer. This propagates with similar operations at each layer till the end of the output layer. At each layer, the description of the parameters is represented as in Eq. 7.65 to 7.67.

7.5.2 | Optimization problem

An optimization problem is considered to model a neural network in such a way that it satisfies the input-output specifications. Let the set of all the parameters, $\mathbf{W}^{(i)}$s and $\boldsymbol{b}^{(i)}$s, be denoted by $\mathscr{W}$. That is, if an input-output specification is provided in the form of $\{(\boldsymbol{X}_i, \boldsymbol{O}_i)\}$, $i = 1, 2, \ldots, N$, N is the number of samples, the objective is to find a $\mathscr{W}$ that produces $\boldsymbol{O}_i$ for the given input, $\boldsymbol{X}_i$, for all i. Toward this, an error function, $J_n(\mathscr{W})$, is defined, which is of the form as in Eq. 7.68.

$$J_n(\mathscr{W}) = \frac{1}{N} \sum_{i=1}^{N} \|\boldsymbol{O}_i - \mathscr{F}(\boldsymbol{X}_i; \mathscr{W})\|^2 \tag{7.68}$$

where, $\mathscr{F}(\boldsymbol{X}_i; \mathscr{W})$ is the predicted output. This is, in fact, the mean squared error between the predicted output, $\mathscr{F}(\boldsymbol{X}_i; \mathscr{W})$, and the actual output, $\boldsymbol{O}_i$. The problem is to find a particular $\mathscr{W}$ for which the error, $J_n(\mathscr{W})$, is minimized.

The optimization procedure follows the same gradient descent approach. The process is initialized with an arbitrary weight matrix, $\mathscr{W}_0$, which is updated iteratively. Here, the representation of the weight matrix, $\mathscr{W}$, is a collective term that is used to describe weights and biases of every layer of the ANN. The corresponding weight update scheme at the ith iteration for the kth sample is given by Eq. 7.69.

$$\mathscr{W}_i = \mathscr{W}_{i-1} + \eta(i) \sum_k (\boldsymbol{O}_k - \mathscr{F}(\boldsymbol{X}_k; \mathscr{W}_{i-1})) \nabla \mathscr{F}(\boldsymbol{X}_k; \mathscr{W}_{i-1}) \tag{7.69}$$

where, $\eta(i)$ is the scaling factor. Also, for efficiency, stochastic gradient descent may be used to immediately update the weights for every sample, instead of considering the sum over a batch. For stochastic gradient descent scheme, the weight update scheme at the ith iteration for the kth sample is given by Eq. 7.70.

$$\mathscr{W}_i = \mathscr{W}_{i-1} + \eta(i) (\boldsymbol{O}_k - \mathscr{F}(\boldsymbol{X}_k; \mathscr{W}_{i-1})) \nabla \mathscr{F}(\boldsymbol{X}_k; \mathscr{W}_{i-1}) \tag{7.70}$$

When the weights converge, that is, little changes in the values of weights are observed, the process completes.

7.5.3 | Chain rule of computing gradients

One of the primary tasks of optimization is the computation of gradients. Let us discuss this computation with respect to a single neuron or a single perceptron. Consider a neuron, as shown in Fig. 7.12, whose functional description is given by Eq. 7.71.

$$o = f(z), \text{ and}$$
$$z = \sum_i w_i x_i + w_0 \tag{7.71}$$

where, x_i and w_i are the ith attributes of input vector and weight vector, respectively, w_0 is the bias term, z is the weighted sum of the attributes of the input vector, o is the neuron output, and $f(\cdot)$ is a nonlinear function. If t is the target response, then the error function is given by, Eq. 7.72.

$$E = (t - o)^2 \tag{7.72}$$

Here, a squared error is considered. To update the weights, it is necessary to compute the derivative of E with respect to the individual weights. After computing the gradient, the weights should be updated such that, the error is minimized.

The derivative of E with respect to w_i is computed by applying the chain rule, which is given by Eq. 7.73.

$$\frac{\partial E}{\partial w_i} = \frac{\partial E}{\partial o} \frac{\partial o}{\partial z} \frac{\partial z}{\partial w_i} \tag{7.73}$$

By using this chain rule, all the necessary gradients are computed. From Eq. 7.71 and 7.72, $\frac{\partial E}{\partial o}$ and $\frac{\partial z}{\partial w_i}$ are computed, which are given by Eq. 7.74.

$$\frac{\partial E}{\partial o} = -2(t - o), \qquad \frac{\partial z}{\partial w_i} = x_i \tag{7.74}$$

Let $\frac{\partial o}{\partial z}$ be represented by $f'(z)$. Assuming $f(z)$ to be the sigmoid function, which is one of the widely used form, $f'(z)$ is computed as given in Eq. 7.75.

$$f(z) = \frac{1}{1 + e^{-z}}$$
$$\implies f'(z) = \frac{e^{-z}}{(1 + e^{-z})^2}$$
$$= \frac{1}{1 + e^{-z}} \left(1 - \frac{1}{1 + e^{-z}} \right) \tag{7.75}$$
$$= f(z)(1 - f(z))$$

Eq. 7.75 also shows one of the interesting simplifications with the use of sigmoid function. Because of this property of sigmoid function, it is used in many cases in neural networks for computations. Similarly, $\frac{\partial E}{\partial x_i}$, the derivative of the error with respect to input, is computed as in Eq. 7.76.

$$\frac{\partial E}{\partial x_i} = \frac{\partial E}{\partial o}\frac{\partial o}{\partial z}\frac{\partial z}{\partial x_i} = -2(t-o)f'(z)w_i \tag{7.76}$$

The purpose of computing $\frac{\partial E}{\partial x_i}$ is discussed in subsequent sections. Interestingly, the whole process of computations uses only analytical methods. Any numerical solution is not necessary in the above computations. Unlike prevalent approaches that require the ratio of changes in output and input values to compute gradients of a complicated function, here, the functional values are directly used in computations. Only the weights and inputs are used to compute the functional values which are again used to compute the derivatives. This is the advantage of this approach.

7.5.4 | Back propagation method of computing gradients

The same chain rule is used to compute the gradients of a multilayered feed forward network. But, in this case, since there are layered computations, the chain rule is applied by following the layered architecture. The gradients are computed from the output layer toward the input layer. So, all the partial derivatives at the output end, with respect to individual weights and biases, are computed, and then these computations proceed toward the input end for successive derivatives. The partial derivatives of weights at the $(i-1)^{\text{th}}$ layer are computed from the corresponding derivatives of the ith layer.

Consider an example shown in Fig. 7.13 for understanding the concept of back propagation. Here, the weight notation, $w_{jk}^{(i)}$, denotes the weight multiplying the output of the jth neuron in the $(i-1)^{\text{th}}$ layer that is fed to the kth neuron in the ith layer. For instance, in the figure, $w_{31}^{(2)}$ denotes the weight between the connectivity of the output of the third neuron of the first layer and the first neuron of the second layer. Similarly, $y_j^{(i)}$ denotes the output of the jth neuron in the ith layer. To explain concept of back

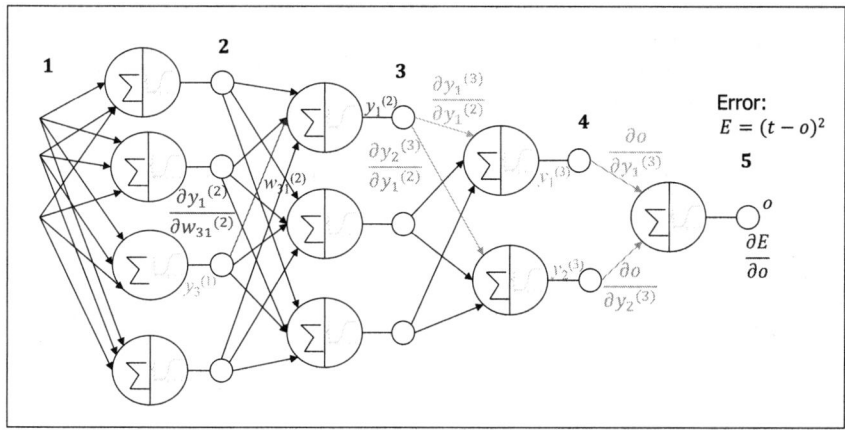

Figure 7.13 Example of a multilayered feed forward network.

propagation, the effect of $w_{31}^{(2)}$ on the change of output response is discussed as an example. In Fig. 7.13, all the outputs and weights that are affected by $w_{31}^{(2)}$ are explicitly shown. Using the chain rule, the derivative of the error function in Eq. 7.72 with respect to $w_{31}^{(2)}$, which is denoted by $\Delta w_{31}^{(2)}$, is given by Eq. 7.77.

$$\Delta w_{31}^{(2)} = \frac{\partial E}{\partial w_{31}^{(2)}} = \frac{\partial E}{\partial o} \left(\frac{\partial o}{\partial y_1^{(3)}} \frac{\partial y_1^{(3)}}{\partial y_1^{(2)}} + \frac{\partial o}{\partial y_2^{(3)}} \frac{\partial y_2^{(3)}}{\partial y_1^{(2)}} \right) \frac{\partial y_1^{(2)}}{\partial w_{31}^{(2)}} \tag{7.77}$$

In similar conventions, $\frac{\partial y_1^{(2)}}{\partial w_{31}^{(2)}}$ and $\frac{\partial y_2^{(3)}}{\partial y_1^{(2)}}$ are given by Eq. 7.78.

$$\frac{\partial y_1^{(2)}}{\partial w_{31}^{(2)}} = f'(z_1^{(2)})y_3^{(1)}$$
$$\frac{\partial y_2^{(3)}}{\partial y_1^{(2)}} = f'(z_2^{(3)})w_{12}^{(3)} \tag{7.78}$$

where, the notation in the form of $f'(z_j^{(i)})$ represent the derivative of the output of the jth neuron in the ith layer, $f(z_j^{(i)})$.

7.5.5 | Delta rule of back propagation

The rule by which the gradients are propagated from the output toward the input direction is called *delta rule*. Delta rule is used to organize the computations of gradients. The error, E, is defined as the square of the deviation of output, o, from the target response, t, which is given by Eq. 7.72. The notations of representing the weight, $w_{jk}^{(i)}$, and the output of a neuron, $y_j^{(i)}$, in each of the layers is the same as already discussed. Consider Fig. 7.14, a reproduction of Fig. 7.13 with simplified representation of variables for convenience of explanation. In the neural network shown in the figure, there are four neurons in first layer, three neurons in the second layer, two neurons in the third layer, and a single neuron in the fourth layer. Fifth layer has the output response, which is denoted only by the output response variable, o. Here also, the effect of the weight $w_{31}^{(2)}$ on the output is considered for analysis. In this figure, all the output variables that play role in determining the gradient of the error, E, with respect to $w_{31}^{(2)}$ are shown. The expression for computing the updates of $w_{31}^{(2)}$, $\Delta w_{31}^{(2)}$, is already given in Eq. 7.77. Also, in Eq. 7.78, the expressions for computing $\frac{\partial y_1^{(2)}}{\partial w_{31}^{(2)}}$ and $\frac{\partial y_2^{(3)}}{\partial y_1^{(2)}}$ are provided. Here, the gradient of the output, o, with respect to $y_1^{(3)}$ is denoted by $\delta_1^{(3)}$. So, the $\delta_1^{(3)}$ represents the accumulated gradients till the output of the first neuron of the third layer. That is, in general, $\delta_j^{(i)}$ is defined as the accumulated gradients till the output of the jth neuron of the ith layer. Similarly, the gradient of o with respect to $y_2^{(3)}$ is denoted by $\delta_2^{(3)}$.

In Eq. 7.77, consider the gradient of $y_1^{(3)}$ with respect to $y_1^{(2)}$, which may be expressed as a linear combination of the derivative of nonlinear function, $f'(z_1^{(3)})$, and the corresponding weight, $w_{11}^{(3)}$. So, the expression for the term, $\frac{\partial y_1^{(3)}}{\partial y_1^{(2)}}$, using the defined conventions, is given in Eq. 7.79.

$$\frac{\partial y_1^{(3)}}{\partial y_1^{(2)}} = f'(z_1^{(3)})w_{11}^{(3)} \tag{7.79}$$

Similarly, gradient of $y_2^{(3)}$ with respect to $y_1^{(2)}$ in Eq. 7.78 is expressed as in Eq. 7.80.

$$\frac{\partial y_2^{(3)}}{\partial y_1^{(2)}} = f'(z_2^{(3)})w_{12}^{(3)} \tag{7.80}$$

From Eq. 7.77, 7.79, and 7.80, $\Delta w_{31}^{(2)}$ is expressed as in Eq. 7.81.

$$\Delta w_{31}^{(2)} = \frac{\partial E}{\partial w_{31}^{(2)}} = \frac{\partial E}{\partial o}\left(\frac{\partial o}{\partial y_1^{(3)}}f'(z_1^{(3)})w_{11}^{(3)} + \frac{\partial o}{\partial y_2^{(3)}}f'(z_2^{(3)})w_{12}^{(3)}\right)\frac{\partial y_1^{(2)}}{\partial w_{31}^{(2)}} \tag{7.81}$$

Similar to gradient changes at nodes using notations for weights, gradient changes along edges are expressed using the δ notations in the same conventions. For example, in Fig. 7.14, the gradient change at the output edge of first neuron of third layer is represented by $\delta_1^{(3)}$, and the gradient change at the output edge of second neuron of third layer is represented by $\delta_2^{(3)}$. Similarly, the gradient change at the input edge of the first neuron of third layer is represented by $\delta_{11}^{(3)}$, and the gradient change at the input edge of the second neuron of third layer is represented by $\delta_{12}^{(3)}$. Using the δ representations, terms in Eq. 7.81 are expressed as in Eq. 7.82.

$$\delta_{11}^{(3)} = \frac{\partial o}{\partial y_1^{(3)}}f'(z_1^{(3)}), \text{ and } \delta_{12}^{(3)} = \frac{\partial o}{\partial y_2^{(3)}}f'(z_2^{(3)}) \tag{7.82}$$

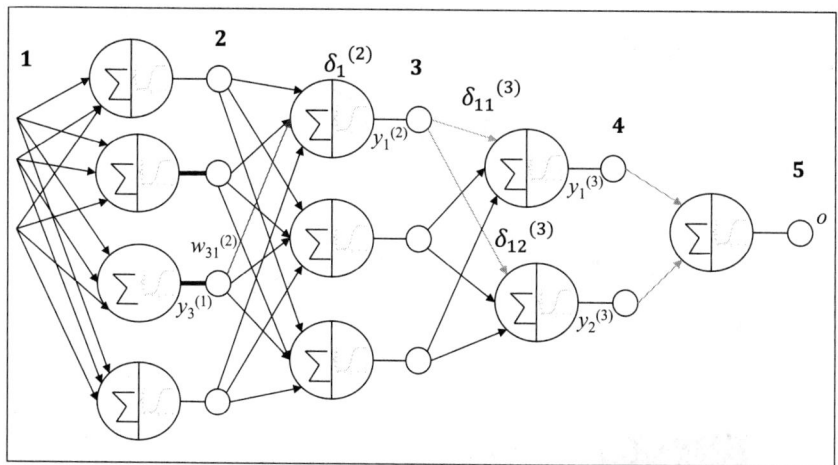

Figure 7.14 Example of a multilayered feed forward network explaining the delta rule.

The sum of the product of $\delta_{11}^{(3)}$ and $w_{11}^{(3)}$, and the product of $\delta_{12}^{(3)}$ and $w_{12}^{(3)}$ is the gradient change at the output edge of first neuron of second layer, $\delta_1^{(2)}$, and this is known as δ rule. That is, by δ rule, $\delta_1^{(2)}$ is expressed as in Eq. 7.83.

$$\delta_1^{(2)} = \delta_{11}^{(3)} w_{11}^{(3)} + \delta_{12}^{(3)} w_{12}^{(3)} \tag{7.83}$$

Therefore, from Eqs. 7.77 to 7.83, the required update of the weight, $\Delta w_{31}^{(2)}$, is computed as in Eq. 7.84.

$$\Delta w_{31}^{(2)} = \frac{\partial E}{\partial o} \delta_1^{(2)} f'(z_1^{(2)}) y_3^{(1)} \tag{7.84}$$

To give a more clear picture of these concepts, consider a portion of a network, as shown in Fig. 7.15. As shown in the figure, the accumulated gradient values from the output to the respective points in the ith layer are computed as, $\{\delta_1^{(i)}, \ldots, \delta_j^{(i)}, \ldots, \delta_{n_i}^{(i)}\}$. Then all these accumulated gradient values are propagated backwards. For instance, $\delta_{k1}^{(i)} = f'(z_1^{(i)})\delta_1^{(i)}$, $\delta_{kj}^{(i)} = f'(z_j^{(i)})\delta_j^{(i)}$, and so on. A weighted sum of all these terms gives the accumulated gradient value from the output to a point at the output edge of kth node in $(i-1)^{\text{th}}$ layer, which is represented by $\delta_k^{(i-1)}$. This is propagated backwards in a similar fashion. Finally, the update of the weight, Δw_{mk} in this case, is obtained as a product of $\frac{\partial E}{\partial o}$ and $\delta_{mk}^{(i-1)} y_m^{(i-2)}$. In this way, the updates of weights are computed at all branches of the network.

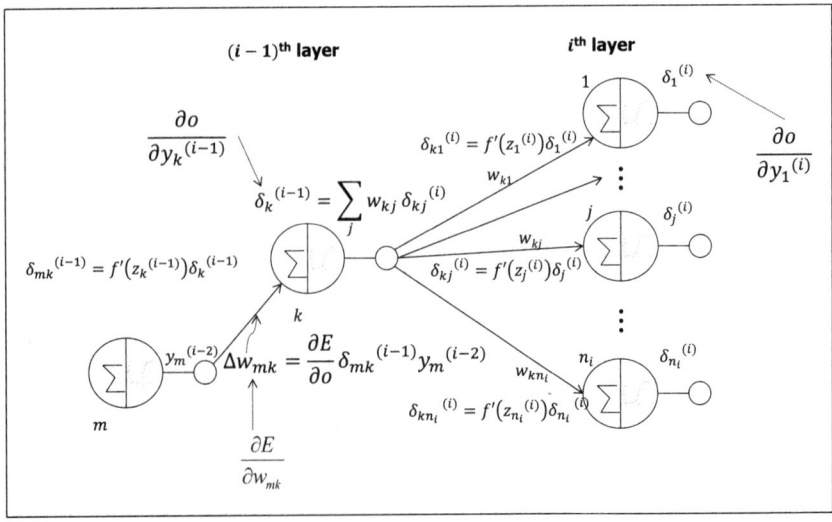

Figure 7.15   Portion of a multilayered feed forward network.

7.5.6 | ANN training

The algorithm for training an ANN follows the same sequence of steps discussed so far. The algorithmic steps are summarized in Algorithm 16.

Algorithm 16 ANN training algorithm

Input: A set of data vectors.
Output: A weight vector, $\boldsymbol{W}$, that linearly separates the given set of data points into specified classes.

1: Initialize the weight vector, $\boldsymbol{W}_0$.
2: Iterate the following steps till convergence.
3: For each training sample $(\boldsymbol{x}_i, o_i)$, **do**

  (i) Compute the functional values of each neuron in the forward pass.

  (ii) Update the weights of each link, starting from the output layer, using back propagation.

Classification or regression?   These ANN models are primarily regression models. ANNs usually build a model to predict functional values, $f(\boldsymbol{x})$, given an input, $\boldsymbol{x}$. But, these models may also be used as a classifier by converting the output responses as probability distribution of classes to which the input sample may belong to. In this case, the error function is defined by considering the divergence between the true distribution and the observed distribution. Examples of such measures are KL-divergence (KLD), cross entropy function, etc. Refer to Chapter 9 (on deep learning) for a more elaborate discussion on this matter. One typical true probability distribution of classes for a sample is equivalent to use one hot encoding of classes. In one hot encoding, if there are n classes, they are represented by n binary variables or bits, where only one of them would be 1 for a particular class, and the rest are 0s. For example, if there are two output neurons for a training sample, one of them will be 1 and the other will be 0, for a two-class problem.

7.6 | Evaluation of a classifier

When a classifier is designed, it is necessary to evaluate it. Toward this, there are several measures of evaluation. Consider a two-class problem that has *positive* and *negative* classes. After classification of a given set of data points, there are several possibilities of outcomes. Table 7.6 depicts possible outcomes of the classification results that are predicted by a trained model. Since it is a binary classification problem, there are two possible predictions: predicted positive and predicted negative. It may happen that, a sample is actually positive and it is also predicted positive. Such an instance is called a *true positive* (TP). If a sample is actually negative, but it is predicted as positive, it is called a *false positive* (FP). Similarly, if the sample is actually positive, but it is predicted as negative, it is called a *false negative* (FN), and if it is actually negative that is predicted as negative, it is a *true negative* (TN).

Table 7.6 Confusion matrix of a binary classifier.

	Actual Positive	*Actual Negative*
Predcited Positive	Number of TPs	Number of FPs
Predicted Negative	Number of FNs	Number of TNs

The numbers of these occurrences are usually shown in a table (refer to Table 7.6), which is also known as *confusion matrix*. For a perfect classifier, only TP and TN occurrences are expected and there should not be any FP and FN. So, a high number of TP and TN occurrences, and a low number of FP and FN occurrences are desirable for a good classifier. There are several measures to assess a classifier that use these numbers. Some of these measures are described below. For simplicity, in these expressions, we use TP, TN, FP, and FN to denote their numbers of occurrences respectively.

- Accuracy: The accuracy of a classifier is defined as the fraction of total number of predictions that are true, either positive or negative, which is expressed in Eq. 7.85.

$$\text{Accuracy} = \frac{\text{TP} + \text{TN}}{\text{TP} + \text{TN} + \text{FP} + \text{FN}} \tag{7.85}$$

- Precision: The precision of a classifier is defined as the fraction of predicted positives that are actually positive, which is expressed in Eq. 7.86.

$$\text{Precision} = \frac{\text{TP}}{\text{TP} + \text{FP}} \tag{7.86}$$

- Recall: The recall of a classifier is defined as the fraction of total positives that are predicted as positive, which is expressed in Eq. 7.87.

$$\text{Recall} = \frac{\text{TP}}{\text{TP} + \text{FN}} \tag{7.87}$$

- Sensitivity: The sensitivity of a classifier is the same as recall, which is expressed in Eq. 7.87. Usually, the term, sensitivity, is used in medical domain.
- Specificity: The specificity of a classifier is defined as the fraction of total negatives that are predicted as negative, which is expressed in Eq. 7.88.

$$\text{Specificity} = \frac{\text{TN}}{\text{TN} + \text{FP}} \tag{7.88}$$

Table 7.7 Evaluation of a multi-class classifier.

* F-Score: The F-score is defined as the harmonic mean of precision and recall, which is expressed in Eq. 7.89. It is combination of the two measures, precision and recall.

$$\text{F-Score} = \frac{2}{\frac{1}{\text{Precision}} + \frac{1}{\text{Recall}}} = \frac{2 \times \text{Precision} \times \text{Recall}}{\text{Precision} + \text{Recall}} \tag{7.89}$$

For evaluation of multi-class problems, similar confusion matrix is used, which is shown in Table. 7.7 for a three-class example. Here, the classes are ω_1, ω_2, and ω_3. In the table, darker shades indicate higher numbers and lighter shades indicate smaller numbers. Also, the values considered in the tabulation are with respect to true classes along the columns and predicted classes along the rows. Here, the diagonal elements represent proper classifications and off-diagonal elements represent misclassification. So, for an ideal classifier, only nonzero positive values in diagonal positions of the table are expected. High values of the diagonal elements and low numbers of off-diagonal elements are desirable for a good classifier. In this case, the accuracy measure is expressed as the ratio of the sum of diagonal elements to the sum of all elements of the matrix, which is the same as the fraction of total number of predictions that are correct.

Numerical Example

A binary classification algorithm resulted in a confusion matrix as follows. Determine the precision, recall, accuracy, and F-Score of the classifier.

		True Class	
		True	False
Predicted Class	True	35	15
	False	20	70

Solution

In this example,

$$\text{number of true positives (TP)} = 35.$$
$$\text{number of true negatives (TN)} = 70.$$

$$\text{number of false positives (FP)} = 15.$$
$$\text{number of false negatives (FN)} = 20.$$

$$\text{Precision} = \frac{\text{TP}}{\text{TP} + \text{FP}} = \frac{35}{35 + 15} = 0.7$$

$$\text{Recall} = \frac{\text{TP}}{\text{TP} + \text{FN}} = \frac{35}{35 + 20} = 0.6364$$

$$\text{Accuracy} = \frac{\text{TP} + \text{TN}}{\text{TP} + \text{TN} + \text{FP} + \text{FN}} = \frac{35 + 70}{35 + 70 + 15 + 20} = 0.75$$

$$\text{F-Score} = \frac{2 \times \text{Precision} \times \text{Recall}}{\text{Precision} + \text{Recall}} = \frac{0.8909}{1.3364} = 0.6666$$

7.6.1 | Cross validation

There are some of the standard methods of testing the performance of a classifier. One such method is called *cross validation*. In cross validation, the data is partitioned into training and test data sets. Then, the model is trained using the training data set and evaluated on the test data set using some evaluation metric.

One of the most used cross validation methods is k-fold cross validation. Here, the data is divided into k sets of equal size, usually as random partitions. Then, the network is trained with $k - 1$ data partitions, and tested on the remaining data partition. This process is performed repeatedly by considering every single partition as the test data partition, and the average of performance on each data partition set is reported. Further, the variance of the performance measure is also computed for checking the statistical range of this estimate.

Summary

In this chapter, some of the basic concepts of classification are discussed. Classification is the task of assigning a known category or class to an object, which is mostly a supervised process. Some of the classification techniques that are considered are naive Bayesian classification scheme, K-nearest neighbor classification scheme, linear discriminant analysis, support vector machine, and artificial neural network models. In Fisher's linear discriminant analysis, the task is to project the data in a 1-D subspace and then use it for classification. Also, a few measures and techniques for assessing the performance of a classifier are briefly introduced.

Exercises

(i) Consider a single perceptron node, which takes weighted sum of 2-D input and adds bias to it to provide net input to a nonlinear sigmoid function. The resulting operation produces an output response. Let the input vector be denoted by $(x_1, x_2) \in \mathbb{R}^2$, corresponding weights as $(w_1, w_2) \in \mathbb{R}^2$, the bias w_0 and the output of the node o. In the following table, values of input, weights, bias, and the target response (t) have been provided. If the error is defined as $E = \frac{1}{2}(t - o)^2$, compute $\frac{\partial E}{\partial w_2}$.

w_1	w_2	w_0	x_1	x_2	t
1	2	1	1	$\frac{1}{2}$	1

(ii) Suppose the input to the *sigmoid* activation function is 2. what would be the output obtained from it?

(iii) Consider the given samples for two class problem:

$X_1 = ((4, 2), (2, 4), (2, 3), (3, 6), (4, 4))$ and $X_2 = ((9, 10), (6, 8), (9, 5), (8, 7), (10, 8))$.

  (a) Compute both the within-class ($\mathbf{S}_w$) and between-class ($\mathbf{S}_B$) scatter matrices.

  (b) Compute the projection vector such that it provides maximum separability between data of two classes following Fisher's LDA.

(iv) Assume there are seven persons identified by letters from A to G, who are friends of X. Degree of friendship to X is measured by a distance measure. Smaller the distance stronger the friendship between a person and X. Each of them love to play either Football (f) or Cricket (c). In the following, these are shown in a Table. Predict which sport X would love to play from this data using K-NN method, where the value of $K = 5$, along with its corresponding posterior probability.

Persons	A	B	C	D	E	F	G
Degree (distance) of friendship	10	100	20	40	70	5	15
Sports	f	f	c	c	f	c	c

(v) Assume there are six different people from various states. We want to identify the mother tongue of a new person X, given the distances between two states where they are born. Also, mother tongue of those people are given in a symbolic notation in the following table.

	A	B	C	D	E	F
Distances from X	10	100	20	40	70	5
mother tongue	1	4	2	4	4	1

Determine what is the mother tongue of X using K-NN classifier where $K = 3$ along with the corresponding posterior probability.

(vi) Assume a game where a person can invest x dummy coins and get y rewards according to an investment. Consider A and B are two players who have invested 6 and 3 dummy coins. Classify the two players into one of the same classes, "YES" or "NO", based on the reward collected by considering the following LDA functions with proper reasoning.

  (a) $f(x) = -\frac{4}{3}x + 5$

  (b) $f(x) = -\frac{5}{3}x + 4$

(vii) Consider a perceptron that has two inputs. With proper reasoning, determine which logical function does the perceptron compute in each of the following cases.

(a) If both the inputs are weighted by 3 and the overall bias is 4.

(b) If both the inputs are weighted by 5 and the overall bias is -4.

(c) If the inputs are weighted by 7 and -7, respectively, and the overall bias is 0.

(viii) The task is to design a classifier using multi-layer perceptron that will process 100, 16×16 images. Each image contains only one digit. How many input and output neurons will be in multi-layer perceptron for this problem?

(ix) A record of cars sold by a company "XYZ" is given as follows.

Instances	Color	Type	Origin	Sold
1	Blue	Sports	Domestic	Yes
2	Blue	Sports	Domestic	No
3	Blue	Sports	Domestic	Yes
4	Black	Sports	Domestic	No
5	Black	Sports	Imported	Yes
6	Black	SUV	Imported	No
7	Black	SUV	Imported	Yes
8	Black	SUV	Domestic	No
9	Blue	SUV	Imported	No
10	Blue	Sports	Imported	Yes

Determine whether blue domestic SUV is sold by the company. Explain with proper reasoning.

(x) Consider the following confusion matrix for a given dataset where a binary classification algorithm is executed.

		True Class	
		yes	no
Predicted Class	yes	50	10
	no	5	100

(a) Identify total number instances in the dataset.

(b) Identify TP, FP, TN, and FN.

(c) Compute the accuracy of the classifier.

(d) Compute the recall of the classifier.

(e) Compute the precision of the classifier.

8

Object Tracking

Object tracking deals with the estimation of the trajectory of a moving object in the image plane. The tracking takes place in a temporal sequence of images or frames in a given input video. The task of object tracking is performed in various contexts. Accordingly the computational problems are formulated with varying set of objectives. For example, the tracking may be required for either a single object or multiple objects. It can either be a trajectory in two-dimensional (2-D) space, as in the image space, or it can be a three-dimensional (3-D) trajectory, where the object is moving in a world coordinate system. It can either be a tracking of a set of points, or it can be tracking of the entire body of an object. The motion involved with the object can either be a rigid body motion, or it can be a deformable body motion. The processing can either be performed offline on recorded videos, or it may be required to process the video in real-time or quasi real-time, while capturing the videos. On the other hand, it could be an online tracking, which means tracking results are obtained within a very short time interval of capturing of video frames. The choice and design of a tracking algorithm depends on the context and application. A few examples of applications of tracking are shown in Fig. 8.1. The Fig. 8.1 (a) illustrates tracking of the vehicles and pedestrians to check if they are on the correct lane. In (b), visitors of a monument in crowd are being tracked and in (c), cars are being tracked to ensure the speed limit.

8.1 | Optical flow

Optical flow in a video sequence is the distribution of apparent velocities of movement of brightness pattern in images or frames. It is assumed that the brightness value of pixels remain almost constant across consecutive frames due to apparent motion of image point for a moving object. Such pixels with constant brightness values provide clues to compute the projected velocity field at their respective points. Consider an image, $\mathbf{I}$, which represents a spatial distribution of intensity values, captured at a particular time instant. The intensity value of $\mathbf{I}$ at any point, (x, y), at a time instant t is represented as a function of 3-D variables of x, y, and t. This 3-D function representing the motion between consecutive images is

(a)

(b)

(c)

Figure 8.1 Examples of application of tracking.

assumed to be a smooth function. Due to the motion, the pixel value at a time instant of $t + \Delta t$ at location $(x + \Delta x, \ y + \Delta y)$ is given by the Taylor series expansion in terms of the functional value at (x, y, t), and the approximation of their first order derivatives, as shown in Eq. 8.1.

$$\mathbf{I}(x + \Delta x, y + \Delta y, t + \Delta t) = \mathbf{I}(x, y, t) + \left(\frac{\partial \mathbf{I}}{\partial x}\right)\Delta x + \left(\frac{\partial \mathbf{I}}{\partial y}\right)\Delta y + \left(\frac{\partial \mathbf{I}}{\partial t}\right)\Delta t + \text{ higher orders}$$

$$(8.1)$$

Since the higher order terms are numerically very small, for the convenience of computation and simplicity they are ignored. So, the expansion of Eq. 8.1 contains only the first order derivative terms. The changes in brightness due to motion are ideally expected to be zero. This constraint expresses the relationship in the form an equation, which is approximated with only first order terms as given by Eq. 8.2.

$$
\begin{aligned}
\left(\frac{\partial \mathbf{I}}{\partial x}\right) \Delta x + \left(\frac{\partial \mathbf{I}}{\partial y}\right) \Delta y + \left(\frac{\partial \mathbf{I}}{\partial t}\right) \Delta t &= 0 \\
\implies \left(\frac{\partial \mathbf{I}}{\partial x}\right) \frac{\Delta x}{\Delta t} + \left(\frac{\partial \mathbf{I}}{\partial y}\right) \frac{\Delta y}{\Delta t} + \left(\frac{\partial \mathbf{I}}{\partial t}\right) &= 0 \\
\implies \mathbf{I}_x v_x + \mathbf{I}_y v_y + \mathbf{I}_t &= 0
\end{aligned}
\tag{8.2}
$$

where, $\mathbf{I}_x = \frac{\partial \mathbf{I}}{\partial x}$, $\mathbf{I}_y = \frac{\partial \mathbf{I}}{\partial y}$ and $\mathbf{I}_t = \frac{\partial \mathbf{I}}{\partial t}$ are the partial derivatives of $\mathbf{I}$ with respect to x, y and t, respectively, and $v_x = \frac{\Delta x}{\Delta t}$ and $v_y = \frac{\Delta y}{\Delta t}$ are the x and y components of the approximated velocity field in the projected space, respectively. The equation in Eq. 8.2 is rewritten by using a short vector representation, as shown in Eq. 8.3.

$$
\nabla \mathbf{I} \cdot \boldsymbol{v} = -\mathbf{I}_t
\tag{8.3}
$$

where, $\nabla \mathbf{I} = [\mathbf{I}_x\ \mathbf{I}_y]^\top$ is a column vector of partial derivatives of $\mathbf{I}$ and $\boldsymbol{v} = [v_x\ v_y]^\top$ is a column vector of the velocity field. This scalar dot product results in a scalar component that represents the change of intensity values along the temporal dimension.

At each point in the image, an equation, as in Eq. 8.3, is obtained. There are two unknowns, v_x and v_y, for each equation. Since the number of unknowns is greater than the number of equations, an under-determined set of equations is obtained. One strategy to solve this is to consider a few more points around each point. For motion of a rigid body, assuming the nearby points to have the same velocity is a pragmatic assumption. So, there are two equations to solve for two variables. That is, with at least two points, the velocity equation can be solved by constrained observations. Here, all the required values are computed from the data or image sequences to solve the equation. However, this is not a robust solution, since the computations are susceptible to noise. Also, the higher derivative terms in Eq. 8.1 may not be exactly zero, which fails the assumption of the solution. Alternatively, this problem can be formulated as an optimization problem where an error term is minimized. Here, the velocity profile is assumed to be smooth. This constraint of smoothness is enforced by minimizing higher order derivatives of functions. For example, this may be performed by minimizing the magnitude of the Laplacian (i.e., sum of magnitudes of second order derivatives of functions) of the variables v_x and v_y, which is given by $|\nabla^2 v_x| + |\nabla^2 v_y|$. Instead of Laplacian one may also use the squares of norms of gradient vectors, such as, $||\nabla v_x||^2 + ||\nabla v_y||^2$.[1]

A technique to solve this problem using these constraints was first proposed by B.K.P. Horn and B.G. Schunck in 1980 (Horn and Schunck, 1981). There could be various ways to

---

[1] Please note the following definitions of the Laplacian and the gradient of a vector v.
$\nabla^2 v = \frac{\partial^2 v}{\partial x^2} + \frac{\partial^2 v}{\partial y^2}$ and $||\nabla v||^2 = \left(\frac{\partial v}{\partial x}\right)^2 + \left(\frac{\partial v}{\partial y}\right)^2$.

define an error in this context. For example, two such error terms of minimization, E_1 and E_2, are given by Eq. 8.4.

$$
\begin{aligned}
E_1 &= \sum \left((\mathbf{I}_t + \mathbf{I}_x v_x + \mathbf{I}_y v_y)^2 + k(\|\nabla v_x\|^2 + \|\nabla v_y\|^2) \right) \\
E_2 &= \sum \left((\mathbf{I}_t + \mathbf{I}_x v_x + \mathbf{I}_y v_y)^2 + k(|\nabla^2 v_x| + |\nabla^2 v_y|) \right)
\end{aligned}
\tag{8.4}
$$

where, k is a constant. In each of the above equations, the summation is taken over all the pixel locations of an image frame.

In this discussion, we consider the E_1 error definition for the optimization problem. Our objective is to get the velocities at all the pixels in the images, which minimize E_1. Let us compute partial derivatives of E_1 with respect to v_x and v_y, and equating them to zero, the expressions in Eq. 8.5 are obtained.

$$
\begin{aligned}
\frac{\partial E_1}{\partial v_x} &= 0 \implies \mathbf{I}_x^2 v_x + \mathbf{I}_x \mathbf{I}_y v_y = k\nabla^2 v_x - \mathbf{I}_x \mathbf{I}_t \\
\frac{\partial E_1}{\partial v_y} &= 0 \implies \mathbf{I}_x \mathbf{I}_y v_x + \mathbf{I}_y^2 v_y = k\nabla^2 v_y - \mathbf{I}_y \mathbf{I}_t
\end{aligned}
\tag{8.5}
$$

Following the similar approach, equations can be obtained by using the error term E_2, which is left as an exercise. As seen above (Eq. 8.5), there are two equations. Though there are two equations, there is a neighborhood information that is required to compute the derivatives and Laplacians. So, it is not really independent in an absolute sense, since it also requires the neighborhood velocity profile. Thus the computation involves solving a set of linear equations toward minimizing the objective function, where each point has its own velocity profile.

In Eq. 8.5, the Laplacian of a variable v is approximated in a form given by Eq. 8.6.

$$
\nabla^2 v \approx c \, (v_m - v)
\tag{8.6}
$$

where, c is a constant, usually taken as 3 in 2-D, and v_m is the mean of v in the neighborhood. In fact, subtracting v from its average v_m gives the discrete form of Laplacian of the variable. By replacing $\nabla^2 v_x$ and $\nabla^2 v_y$ in Eq. 8.5 with the form in Eq. 8.6 and rearranging the terms,

$$
\begin{aligned}
(k + \mathbf{I}_x^2 + \mathbf{I}_y^2)v_x &= (k + \mathbf{I}_y^2)v_{x,m} - \mathbf{I}_x \mathbf{I}_y v_{y,m} - \mathbf{I}_x \mathbf{I}_t \\
(k + \mathbf{I}_x^2 + \mathbf{I}_y^2)v_y &= -\mathbf{I}_x \mathbf{I}_y v_{x,m} + (k + \mathbf{I}_x^2)v_{y,m} - \mathbf{I}_y \mathbf{I}_t
\end{aligned}
\tag{8.7}
$$

where, $v_{x,m}$ and $v_{y,m}$ are the average v_x and v_y, in the neighborhood, respectively. Since averaging requires a neighborhood information, the two equations in Eq. 8.7 are not really independent equations.

If there are N points in the image, it requires to solve $2N$ simultaneous equations to get the solution of optical flow in the entire image. This is solved using an iterative method by which the values are updated at each iteration and by keeping a check on the reduction of the objective function. The equations used in this iterative approach are given by Eq. 8.8.

$$v_x^{(n+1)} = v_{x,m}^{(n)} - \frac{\mathbf{I}_x(\mathbf{I}_x v_{x,m}^{(n)} + \mathbf{I}_y v_{y,m}^{(n)} + \mathbf{I}_t)}{k + \mathbf{I}_x^2 + \mathbf{I}_y^2}$$

$$v_y^{(n+1)} = v_{y,m}^{(n)} - \frac{\mathbf{I}_y(\mathbf{I}_x v_{x,m}^{(n)} + \mathbf{I}_y v_{y,m}^{(n)} + \mathbf{I}_t)}{k + \mathbf{I}_x^2 + \mathbf{I}_y^2}$$

(8.8)

where, n is the iteration index. When the iterations converge to reflect no further changes in the values, the process stops. Using this method of the optical flow, the velocity profile of the points in a particular space are computed. For example, if there are two image frames that has an object which has moved between the frames, this method models a translation for each point in the image by considering the velocity profiles. If there is another moving object in the images, there will be another velocity profile to the set of pixel locations corresponding to the moving object. The optical flow is computed by using these flow distributions between two consecutive images. An example is shown in Fig. 8.2, where the detected flow vectors

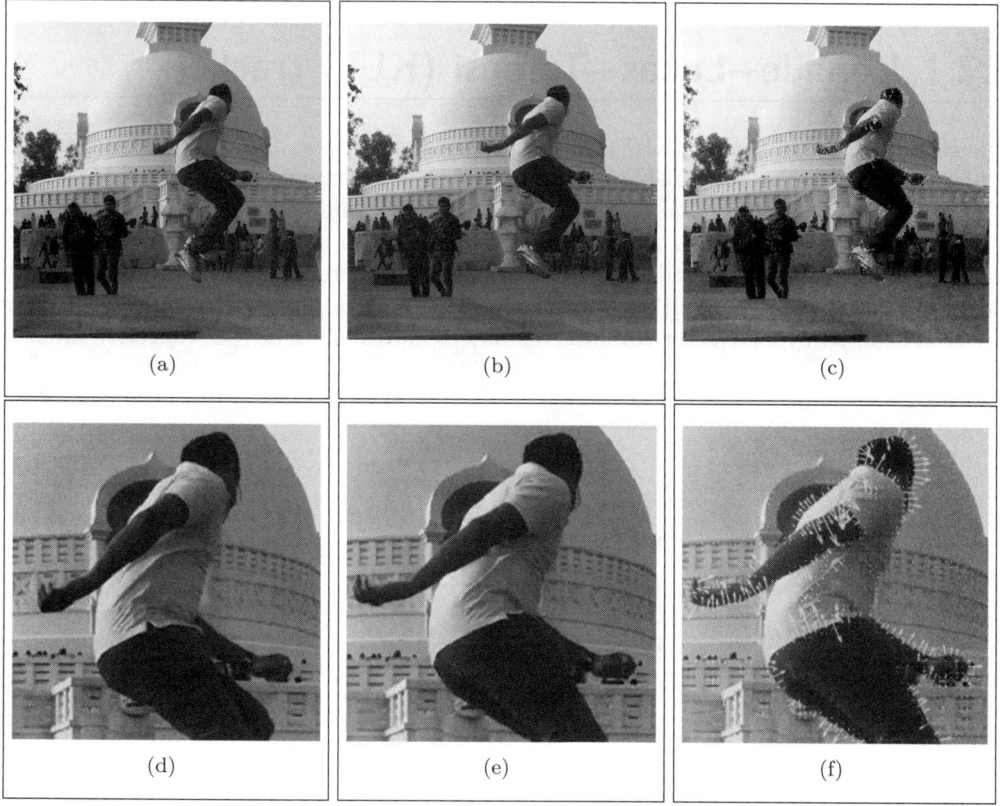

(a)   (b)   (c)

(d)   (e)   (f)

Figure 8.2 Computation of optical flow between two frames with moving objects. Zoomed portions from (a, b, c) are shown in (d, e, f) for better visibility.

between the two consecutive frames are shown by arrows pointing their respective directions of vectors and their lengths represent the magnitudes. Here, most of the flow vectors are concentrated around the region of movement due to a jumping stuntman.

One of the main advantages of this optical flow based solution to the object tracking problem is not having any assumption about the shape and motion of the objects in the video. Therefore, it is generic in approach, since the appearance of objects is not modeled. Aggregation of optical flows of pixels of an object may be performed for the tracking of objects at a later stage of processing. Also, it is applicable for both rigid body and deformable motion to understand the motion of different particles in a 3-D world on the projected space. On the other hand, there are some of the disadvantages as well, which are as follows.

- In this approach, the optical flow is computed for every pixel in the frames, but it does not model the whole-body motion.
- The approach does not give the motion of the objects directly.
- This approach is computationally intensive, since the flow is computed almost for every pixel.
- Due to pixel-wise computation, this technique is more susceptible to noise.

8.2 | Kanade–Lucas–Tomasi (KLT) tracker

The *Kanade–Lucas–Tomasi* (KLT) tracker (Lucas and Kanade, 1981; Tomasi and Kanade, 1991) follows a similar principle as of the optical flow technique that assumes a constant intensity levels in the direction of movement of an object in an image sequence. Consider a scenario where an object is moved from one position to another position between two consecutive frames, as depicted in Fig. 8.3. Here, **I** and **J** represent the intensities at the location x in the two consecutive frames, respectively. The direction of movement of the object is denoted by the vector d. Since the object moves along d, the respective intensity

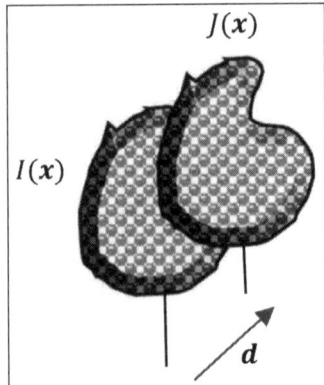

Figure 8.3 Movement of an object between two frames.

values due to the displacement remain constant along that direction, which is given by Eq. 8.9.

$$\mathbf{J}(\boldsymbol{x}) = \mathbf{I}(\boldsymbol{x} - \boldsymbol{d}) \tag{8.9}$$

The equation in Eq. 8.9 can be expressed with the Taylor series expansion, which is given in Eq. 8.10.

$$\mathbf{J}(\boldsymbol{x}) = \mathbf{I}(\boldsymbol{x} - \boldsymbol{d}) = \mathbf{I}(\boldsymbol{x}) - \nabla\mathbf{I} \cdot \boldsymbol{d} + \text{ higher order terms} \tag{8.10}$$

By ignoring the higher order terms and rearranging the Eq. 8.10, similar to Eq. 8.3,

$$\mathbf{I}(\boldsymbol{x}) - \mathbf{J}(\boldsymbol{x}) = h = \nabla\mathbf{I} \cdot \boldsymbol{d} \tag{8.11}$$

where, $\mathbf{I}(\boldsymbol{x}) - \mathbf{J}(\boldsymbol{x})$ is proportional to the temporal derivative and $\nabla\mathbf{I} \cdot \boldsymbol{d}$ is the spatial derivative along the direction of motion.

To minimize an error function obtained using Eq. 8.11, a neighborhood of $\boldsymbol{x}$ is considered. This minimization problem is spatially weighted by $w(\boldsymbol{x})$, where the central pixels are given more weights than the points in peripheries. The error function is given by Eq. 8.12.

$$E = \frac{\sum_{\boldsymbol{x} \in N_{\boldsymbol{x}}} w(\boldsymbol{x})(\mathbf{I}(\boldsymbol{x}) - \mathbf{J}(\boldsymbol{x}) - \nabla\mathbf{I} \cdot \boldsymbol{d})^2}{\sum_{\boldsymbol{x} \in N_{\boldsymbol{x}}} w(\boldsymbol{x})} \tag{8.12}$$

where, $N_{\boldsymbol{x}}$ is the defined neighborhood around $\boldsymbol{x}$. In this minimization operation, a particular $\boldsymbol{d}$ that minimizes E has to be computed. Taking the derivative of E with respect to $\boldsymbol{d}$ and equating it to zero,

$$\frac{\partial E}{\partial \boldsymbol{d}} = 0 \implies \sum_{\boldsymbol{x} \in N_{\boldsymbol{x}}} w'(\boldsymbol{x})(h - \nabla\mathbf{I} \cdot \boldsymbol{d})\nabla\mathbf{I} = 0 \tag{8.13}$$

where, $w'(\boldsymbol{x}) = \frac{w(\boldsymbol{x})}{\sum_{\boldsymbol{x} \in N_{\boldsymbol{x}}} w(\boldsymbol{x})}$ represents the normalized weights. The term, $\nabla\mathbf{I} \cdot \boldsymbol{d}$ can also be expressed as in Eq. 8.14.

$$\nabla\mathbf{I} \cdot \boldsymbol{d} = \nabla\mathbf{I}^{\top}\boldsymbol{d} \tag{8.14}$$

which is the representation of Eq. 8.14 in matrix notations, where $\nabla\mathbf{I}^{\top}$ is the transpose of $\nabla\mathbf{I}$. Using Eq. 8.14 in Eq. 8.13,

$$\sum_{\boldsymbol{x} \in N_{\boldsymbol{x}}} w'(\boldsymbol{x})(h\nabla\mathbf{I} - \nabla\mathbf{I}\nabla\mathbf{I}^{\top}\boldsymbol{d}) = 0 \tag{8.15}$$

From Using Eq. 8.15, the optimal $\boldsymbol{d}$ is computed, which is given by Eq. 8.16.

$$\boldsymbol{d} = \left(\sum_{\boldsymbol{x} \in N_{\boldsymbol{x}}} w'(\boldsymbol{x})\nabla\mathbf{I}\nabla\mathbf{I}^{\top} \right)^{-1} \left(\sum_{\boldsymbol{x} \in N_{\boldsymbol{x}}} w'(\boldsymbol{x})h\nabla\mathbf{I} \right) \tag{8.16}$$

Here, though explicitly not shown, $\boldsymbol{d}$ is a function of $\boldsymbol{x}$, since the matrix $\mathbf{I}$, which represents pixel values, is also a function of $\boldsymbol{x}$.

Though its concept of tracking is the same as the optical flow, the KLT tracker is applicable only for rigid body motion. So, only those points in the images where the changes are more perceptible are considered here. As discussed in Chapter 5 on feature detection, corners in the images are more suitable for detecting such perceptible changes. A similar principle of Harris operator may be used to identify the corners in the images and the motions along those corners are used for tracking by computing their displacements. In Harris corner detection, the eigenvalues obtained by the singular value decomposition at the spatial points of the image denote the changes along the directions of their corresponding eigenvectors at their respective locations. If the minimum eigenvalue is greater than some preset threshold, the respective point is a corner point. Only at such corner points, the $\boldsymbol{d}$ is estimated, which is used to estimate the motion of the corresponding object.

8.3 | Object tracking approaches

Optical flow and KLT techniques are typical examples of computing the motion vectors at the image points. Though the computations are carried out at a pixel level in these approaches, the physical movement is associated with a particular object that is moving. A generalized pipeline of processing for object tracking is shown in Fig. 8.4. For tracking an object, it requires to have a representation of the object, which is followed by identifying the presence of the object in subsequent frames. Thus, it is a two-step process.

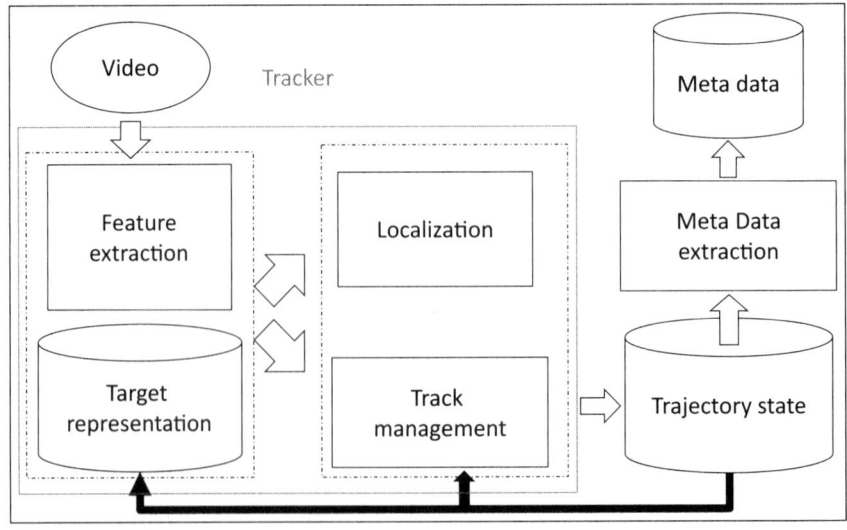

Figure 8.4 A generalized pipeline of processing for object tracking.

(i) **Derive a representation of an object**: This may be accomplished by extracting features and describing the object using them.

(ii) **Localization of the object in the sequence of frames**: This task involves identification of the presence of objects in the subsequent frames and also computing its location in that frame.

The task of object localization is to determine the presence and location of the object (or objects) in the window of visibility. This also includes determining whether the object has disappeared or made an exit in the video frames. With this information, the trajectory state for the object is generated as a metadata related to the state information. A *trajectory state* is the information about the trajectory of the object, i.e., the location of the object, its profile, and states of motion such as, velocity, acceleration, etc.

There are different tracking approaches which may be broadly categorized as follows (Chen et al., 2022).

- Generative tracker: Here, at first, an appearance model for the target is established. Then, the region most similar to the target object in a successive frame is searched. In this case, learning the appearance model is a very critical process, which is performed using various techniques such as, subspace learning, sparse representation, spatio-temporal motion energy, Boolean map, etc.

- Discriminative tracker: In this approach, the tracking problem is formulated as a binary classification problem. A binary classifier is trained to distinguish the target from the background. An object is localized by considering each candidate block or candidate window to be classified as background or a part of the target by the classifier. Correlation filter based tracker is an example of discriminative tracker.

- Collaborative tracker: This is a collaborative approach that takes the advantage of both generative and discriminative approaches.

- Deep learning based tracker: This approach combines the deep features with traditional tracking algorithms. There are two strategies here: (1) extract features using a deep learning model and then use a traditional tracking algorithm, and (2) design a model that accomplishes an end-to-end learning of a deep neural network for tracking.

Only the generative and discriminative tracking approaches are discussed in this chapter.

8.4 | Generative tracker

In generative trackers, an appearance model of the target is generated for its use to search for the presence of objects and locations in the frames of a video. The appearance model can be described in various ways such as, using points, kernels, silhouettes, moment invariants, etc. Some of the descriptors that are used to model appearances of localized objects are as follows:

- Distribution based descriptors like, histogram of pixel intensities, histogram of oriented gradients (HOG), scale invariant feature transform (SIFT), gradient location and orientation histogram (GLOH), histogram of optical flow velocities, etc.

- Differential descriptors computed using operations such as, steerable filters and Gaussian derivatives.
- Binary descriptors like, binary robust independent elementary features (BRIEF), oriented fast and rotated BRIEF (ORB), binary robust invariant scalable keypoints (BRISK), fast retina keypoint (FREAK), etc.
- Spatial-frequency based descriptors like, Gabor/Haar wavelet responses, speeded-up robust features (SURF), etc.

Using one or more of the above feature descriptors, an appearance model of the target is built.

These feature descriptors are represented as vectors, which are used to search the target in a frame of a video. At each frame, a similarity measure is used for matching with the generated description of the target (appearance model) with that of candidate objects to compute the object location in a subsequent frame. One of the popular choices of similarity measure is the *normalized correlation coefficient* (NCC). Consider a region $\mathcal{R}$ in the tth frame, I_t, and let $\boldsymbol{x}$ be a pixel in $\mathcal{R}$. The NCC between $\boldsymbol{x}$ and another pixel, $(\boldsymbol{x} + \boldsymbol{u})$, in a region of the same size as $\mathcal{R}$ in the $(t+1)^{\text{th}}$ frame, I_{t+1}, is given by Eq. 8.17.

$$\text{NCC}(\boldsymbol{u}) = \frac{\left(\sum_{\forall \boldsymbol{x} \in \mathcal{R}} I_t(\boldsymbol{x}) I_{t+1}(\boldsymbol{x} + \boldsymbol{u}) \right)}{\left(\left(\sum_{\forall \boldsymbol{x} \in \mathcal{R}} I_t(\boldsymbol{x})^2 \right) \left(\sum_{\forall \boldsymbol{x} \in \mathcal{R}} I_{t+1}(\boldsymbol{x} + \boldsymbol{u})^2 \right) \right)^{\frac{1}{2}}} \tag{8.17}$$

The NCC between the two considered image blocks is computed by making correspondences between the respective image points in the blocks. It is used for identifying the object location in the next frame. Wherever the value of this coefficient is high and at a local peak, that corresponds to a match and the velocity of the object can be estimated by the change in the location of the target within the time interval between two frames. The expression in Eq. 8.17 is expressed in terms of intensity values. But, this can also be defined in the feature space. This is one of the types of generative tracking approach where an appearance model is used to establish the presence of an object by computing the correlation between the blocks of two subsequent frames.

8.4.1 | Bayesian tracking

The *Bayesian tracking* approach (Arulampalam et al., 2002) considers a state space representation of an object at every time instant. The *state* of an object may be described by various attributes, like location, velocity, acceleration, etc. The transition of objects from one state to another state takes place due to the movement as the time progresses. Let $\boldsymbol{x}_k$ denote the state of the object at a time instant k. The state changes from the $(k-1)^{\text{th}}$ instant to the kth instant are governed by the motion dynamics, which is expressed by a function $f_k(\cdot)$ as in Eq. 8.18.

$$\boldsymbol{x}_k = f_k(\boldsymbol{x}_{k-1}, \boldsymbol{v}_{k-1}) \tag{8.18}$$

where $\boldsymbol{v}_{k-1}$ denotes independent and identically distributed (i.i.d) noise. When an object is moving, it moves from one state to another state which is described by a set of measurements, like image locations, orientations, etc., associated with it. Let $\boldsymbol{z}_k$ be the observed measurement at the kth time instant. The relationship between the presence of an object at the kth instant with $\boldsymbol{z}_k$ is expressed by the functional form, $h_k(\cdot)$, in Eq. 8.19.

$$\boldsymbol{z}_k = h_k(\boldsymbol{x}_k, \boldsymbol{u}_k) \tag{8.19}$$

$\boldsymbol{u}_k$ is i.i.d. noise. Here, the function $f_k(\cdot)$ expresses the state of the object and the function $h_k(\cdot)$ provides the related measurement of the object for its given state.

Recursive Bayesian tracking

In the Bayesian tracking approach, a series of such measurements is considered. For example, the locations and velocities of the considered object in certain windows in the projected space are obtained by a series of measurements. Let $\boldsymbol{z}_{1:k}$ represent this series of measurements from the first frame of the video sequence till the frame at the kth instant. The objective here is to compute the state of the object at the kth instant, $\boldsymbol{x}_k$, given the measurements $\boldsymbol{z}_{1:k}$. For the Bayesian tracking, the posterior probability of the state at the kth instant, given all the measurements till the kth instant, is expressed by the probability $p(\boldsymbol{x}_k|\boldsymbol{z}_{1:k})$. Estimation of this posterior probability is the computational problem, which is solved by assuming that the initial state, $\boldsymbol{x}_0$, is known. Let the probability of $\boldsymbol{x}_0$ be given by $p(\boldsymbol{x}_0)$. We may note that the initial state of the object does not involve any measurement. Then, by applying the Bayes' rule, given the probability of the $(k-1)^{\text{th}}$ instant of a state and the measurements till the $(k-1)^{\text{th}}$ instant, the probability $p(\boldsymbol{x}_k|\boldsymbol{z}_{1:k})$ is computed by a recursive process. It implies that, given $p(\boldsymbol{x}_{k-1}|\boldsymbol{z}_{1:k-1})$, we need to compute $p(\boldsymbol{x}_k|\boldsymbol{z}_{1:k})$ by applying the state transition and measurement functions as given in Eqs. 8.18 and 8.19.

This is similar to a prediction problem, where $\boldsymbol{x}_k$ is predicted from $p(\boldsymbol{x}_{k-1}|\boldsymbol{z}_{1:k-1})$, the probability of the state at the $(k-1)^{\text{th}}$ instant and the past $k-1$ measurements. We understand that, there are always some uncertainties associated with the state of the object in the probabilistic interpretation. For example, the position of the object in the state $\boldsymbol{x}_{k-1}$ may not be precise or the measurements made at the $(k-1)^{\text{th}}$ instant may have some error. There are two components, (1) the probability of the state for each state transition, and (2) the probability of the state for all the measurements.

By integrating their product over all possible states in the space, we obtain the probability of the state $\boldsymbol{x}_k$, which is given by the *Chapman Kolmogorov* equation (Arulampalam et al., 2002).

$$p(\boldsymbol{x}_k|\boldsymbol{z}_{1:k-1}) = \int p(\boldsymbol{x}_k|\boldsymbol{x}_{k-1}, \boldsymbol{z}_{1:k-1})p(\boldsymbol{x}_{k-1}|\boldsymbol{z}_{1:k-1})d\boldsymbol{x}_{k-1} \tag{8.20}$$

Following the first order Markovian principle, we simplify $p(\boldsymbol{x}_k|\boldsymbol{x}_{k-1})$ as follows:

$$p(\boldsymbol{x}_k|\boldsymbol{x}_{k-1}, \boldsymbol{z}_{1:k-1}) = p(\boldsymbol{x}_k|\boldsymbol{x}_{k-1}) \tag{8.21}$$

Thus Eq. 8.20 is simplified as follows.

$$p(\boldsymbol{x}_k|\boldsymbol{z}_{1:k-1}) = \int p(\boldsymbol{x}_k|\boldsymbol{x}_{k-1})p(\boldsymbol{x}_{k-1}|\boldsymbol{z}_{1:k-1})d\boldsymbol{x}_{k-1} \tag{8.22}$$

Then, Bayesian rule is applied to compute $p(\boldsymbol{x}_k|\boldsymbol{z}_{1:k})$, as given by Eq. 8.23.

$$p(\boldsymbol{x}_k|\boldsymbol{z}_{1:k}) = \frac{p(\boldsymbol{z}_k|\boldsymbol{x}_k)p(\boldsymbol{x}_k|\boldsymbol{z}_{1:k-1})}{p(\boldsymbol{z}_k|\boldsymbol{z}_{1:k-1})} \tag{8.23}$$

where $p(\boldsymbol{z}_k|\boldsymbol{z}_{1:k-1}) = \int p(\boldsymbol{z}_k|\boldsymbol{x}_{k-1})p(\boldsymbol{x}_{k-1}|\boldsymbol{z}_{1:k-1})d\boldsymbol{x}_{k-1}$.

The expression in Eq. 8.23 is an update equation where $\boldsymbol{x}_k$ is conditionally independent of $\boldsymbol{z}_{1:k-1}$. Thus, after estimating $\boldsymbol{x}_k$ from the past $k-1$ observations, the value of $\boldsymbol{x}_k$ is updated with the current measurement, $\boldsymbol{z}_k$.

8.4.2 | Kalman filtering

A particular form of the recursive Bayesian tracking approach, known as *Kalman filtering*, assumes the posterior density at every time step to be a Gaussian density function. Here, $p(\boldsymbol{x}_{k-1}|\boldsymbol{z}_{1:k-1})$, the probability of state $\boldsymbol{x}_{k-1}$, given all the measurements till the $(k-1)^{\text{th}}$ instant, is assumed to be Gaussian. It can be mathematically proved that if $p(\boldsymbol{x}_{k-1}|\boldsymbol{z}_{1:k-1})$ is Gaussian, the prediction state, $p(\boldsymbol{x}_k|\boldsymbol{z}_{1:k-1})$, is also Gaussian for linear functional relationships of states and measurements with Gaussian noises. These linear relationships of states and measurements are expressed in the form as given by Eq. 8.24.

$$\begin{aligned} \boldsymbol{x}_k &= F_k\boldsymbol{x}_{k-1} + \boldsymbol{v}_{k-1}; \quad \boldsymbol{v}_{k-1} \sim \mathcal{N}(0, \mathbf{Q}_{k-1}) \\ \boldsymbol{z}_k &= H_k\boldsymbol{x}_k + \boldsymbol{u}_k; \quad \boldsymbol{u}_k \sim \mathcal{N}(0, \mathbf{R}_k) \end{aligned} \tag{8.24}$$

where F_k is the linear transformation matrix that relate current state to previous state, H_k is the linear transformation matrix that relate measurement and state, $\boldsymbol{v}_{k-1}$ is the noise associated with the state $\boldsymbol{x}_{k-1}$, and $\boldsymbol{u}_k$ is the noise associated with measurement $\boldsymbol{z}_k$. The terms $\boldsymbol{v}_{k-1}$ and $\boldsymbol{u}_k$ are from normal distributions with zero mean and covariance of $\mathbf{Q}_{k-1}$ and $\mathbf{R}_k$, respectively. $\mathcal{N}(\boldsymbol{\mu}, \boldsymbol{\Sigma})$ denotes normal distribution of mean $\boldsymbol{\mu}$ and the covariance matrix $\boldsymbol{\Sigma}$. Using this model, given a movement of the object, its current state can be predicted from its past state and the associated measurement of the current state can also be obtained.

The posterior densities with respect to the state and measurements are given by Eq. 8.25.

$$\begin{aligned} p(\boldsymbol{x}_{k-1}|\boldsymbol{z}_{1:k-1}) &\sim \mathcal{N}(\boldsymbol{m}_{k-1|k-1}, \mathbf{P}_{k-1|k-1}) \\ p(\boldsymbol{x}_k|\boldsymbol{z}_{1:k-1}) &\sim \mathcal{N}(\boldsymbol{m}_{k|k-1}, \mathbf{P}_{k|k-1}) \\ p(\boldsymbol{x}_k|\boldsymbol{z}_{1:k}) &\sim \mathcal{N}(\boldsymbol{m}_{k|k}, \mathbf{P}_{k|k}) \end{aligned} \tag{8.25}$$

Here, $p(\boldsymbol{x}_{k-1}|\boldsymbol{z}_{1:k-1})$ is the probability of the state at the $(k-1)^{\text{th}}$ instant, given the observations till the $(k-1)^{\text{th}}$ instant. This probability is denoted by the parameters of the normal probability density function, $\mathcal{N}(\boldsymbol{m}_{k-1|k-1}, \mathbf{P}_{k-1|k-1})$, where $\boldsymbol{m}_{k-1|k-1}$ is the mean and $\mathbf{P}_{k-1|k-1}$ is the covariance matrix. The notations for parameters, $\boldsymbol{m}_{k-1|k-1}$ and $\mathbf{P}_{k-1|k-1}$, indicate that, given the observations till $k-1$, we are estimating the state at $k-1$. Similarly, $p(\boldsymbol{x}_k|\boldsymbol{z}_{1:k-1})$ is the probability of the state at the kth instant, given the observations till the $(k-1)^{\text{th}}$ instant, and $p(\boldsymbol{x}_k|\boldsymbol{z}_{1:k})$ is the probability of the state at the kth instant, given the observations till the kth instant. The means of the normal probability density functions for $p(\boldsymbol{x}_k|\boldsymbol{z}_{1:k-1})$ and $p(\boldsymbol{x}_k|\boldsymbol{z}_{1:k})$ are described by $\boldsymbol{m}_{k|k-1}$ and

$m_{k|k}$, respectively, which are to indicate that they are not the same as $m_{k-1|k-1}$. Similarly, their corresponding covariance matrices are also different. These parameters essentially denote the distributions that qualify for a particular state from their corresponding observations. In a general situation, the state and measurement equations are time varying. That is, F_k and H_k are time varying, since they depend on k, the time instant.

Given the functional relationships, density functions and the measurements (or observations) till the kth instant, the problem of Kalman filtering is to compute x_k from all the available measurements. This is performed by estimating the parameters of the probability density functions as given in Eq. 8.25. Given the probabilistic mean state of the distribution at the $(k-1)^{\text{th}}$ instant, m_{k-1}, the mean or expected state at the kth instant is predicted by using the linear model, F_k, as in Eq. 8.26.

$$m_{k|k-1} = F_k m_{k-1} \tag{8.26}$$

Similarly, the covariance matrices are also predicted by a linear operation in the quadratic fashion, which is given by Eq. 8.27.

$$\mathbf{P}_{k|k-1} = F_k \mathbf{P}_{k-1|k-1} F_k^{\top} + \mathbf{Q}_{k-1} \tag{8.27}$$

where $\mathbf{Q}_{k-1}$ represents the noise associated with the prediction. The values of $m_{k|k-1}$ and $\mathbf{P}_{k|k-1}$ are the estimations of the expected state and the covariance matrix at the new k^{th} position that are predicted using the values at the $(k-1)^{\text{th}}$ position.

Furthermore, at the kth instant, an observation (measurement) of the object is made, which is used to update the predicted values. Let $z_k^{(o)}$ be the observation at the kth instant. Then, the update to the mean and the covariance is given by Eq. 8.28.

$$
\begin{aligned}
m_{k|k} &= m_{k|k-1} + K_k(z_k^{(o)} - H_k m_{k|k-1}) \\
\mathbf{P}_{k|k} &= \mathbf{P}_{k|k-1} - K_k H_k \mathbf{P}_{k-1|k-1}
\end{aligned}
\tag{8.28}
$$

where K_k is a gain factor called *Kalman gain*. When the relationship of the estimated position and the measurement is applied, the product of the Kalman gain and the difference in measurements are used to compensate the error with the update as given in Eq. 8.28. The Kalman gain is computed by Eq. 8.29.

$$
\begin{aligned}
K_k &= \mathbf{P}_{k|k-1} H_k^{\top} \mathbf{S}_k^{-1} \\
\text{where } \mathbf{S}_k &= H_k \mathbf{P}_{k-1|k-1} H_k^{\top} + \mathbf{R}_k
\end{aligned}
\tag{8.29}
$$

This is the recursive solution of the Kalman filtering. These update equations in Eq. 8.28 are derived using the Bayesian recursive approach.

Another perspective of Kalman filtering

The Kalman filtering may also be interpreted as a decision fusion process, which handles uncertainties. In the process of tracking, there are two kinds of estimations, (1) based on the prediction of the position, and (2) based on the measurement or observation. Both of these estimations are associated with some uncertainties, which are considered in the update operation using the Kalman gain. Consider the observations as multiple pairwise uncorrelated noisy estimates, $f(\boldsymbol{x}_{k-1})$, and $h(\boldsymbol{z}_k)$. The estimation at the kth instant is based on the state at the previous $(k-1)^{\text{th}}$ instant and the measurement is performed on the state at the kth instant. In Kalman filtering, a linear combination of the estimates and measurements is considered, as given in Eq. 8.30, which minimizes the variance of prediction after the decision fusion.

$$\boldsymbol{x}_k = \alpha f(\boldsymbol{x}_{k-1}) + \beta h(\boldsymbol{z}_k) \tag{8.30}$$

where α and β are the coefficients of linear combination.

In Eq. 8.30, the two different observations are, (1) $\boldsymbol{x}_k^{(1)}$: the prediction of state of motion from the previous instant, which is given by $f(\boldsymbol{x}_{k-1})$, and (2) $\boldsymbol{x}_k^{(2)}$: the measurement of state of motion at the current instant, which is given by $h(\boldsymbol{z}_k)$. Here, the noise terms are not shown for the sake of brevity of representation. The objective is to achieve a correction of $\boldsymbol{x}_k$ through a decision fusion of $\boldsymbol{x}_k^{(1)}$ and $\boldsymbol{x}_k^{(2)}$. Intuitively, higher the variance of the estimates, smaller the values of the coefficients in Eq. 8.30. That is, the coefficients α and β are inversely proportional to the variances of estimates and measurements, respectively. The final updated decision, based on corrected $\boldsymbol{x}_k$, is taken after the decision fusion.

Kalman filtering in 1-D

Consider the case of 1-D Kalman filtering. Let $x_1 \sim p_1(\mu_1, \sigma_1^2)$, ..., $x_n \sim p_n(\mu_n, \sigma_n^2)$ be a set of pairwise uncorrelated random variables, where μ_i and σ_i^2 denote the mean and the variance of the probability density function, p_i. The aggregation of the individual decisions is performed by fusing the decisions as a linear combination of these estimates (Pei et al., 2019). Let, y be a random variable, which is a linear combination of x_i's, as given in Eq. 8.31.

$$y = \sum_{i=1}^{n} a_i x_i \tag{8.31}$$

where a_i's are the coefficients. The mean and variance of y are related with the set of random variables from which the fusion of estimates is performed. Since x_1, ..., x_n, are pairwise independent and uncorrelated, the mean, μ_y, and variance, σ_y^2, of y are given by Eq. 8.32.

$$\mu_y = \sum_{i=1}^{n} a_i \mu_i$$
$$\sigma_y^2 = \sum_{i=1}^{n} a_i^2 \sigma_i^2 \tag{8.32}$$

where μ_i and σ_i^2 are the mean and variance of x_i, respectively. Also, if a random variable z is pairwise uncorrelated with x_1, ..., x_n, it is also uncorrelated with y.

The objective here is to find the optimal linear combination of x_i's. In other words, it is to find the coefficients of the linear combination that results in the minimum variance of y. These coefficients are called *optimal coefficients*. Since this combination is a convex combination, the sum of the coefficients is unity, all the coefficients are nonnegative, and the coefficients are inversely proportional to the variance of corresponding same random variable. Mathematically, these are given by Eq. 8.33.

$$\sum_{i=1}^{n} a_i = 1$$

$$a_i^* = \frac{(1/\sigma_i^2)}{\sum_{j=1}^{n}(1/\sigma_j^2)}$$

$$(8.33)$$

The optimal estimate, y_{opt}, of the linear combination of x_i's with the set of optimal coefficients, a_i^*'s, is expressed by Eq. 8.34.

$$y_{\text{opt}} = \sum_{i=1}^{n} a_i^* x_i \qquad (8.34)$$

Multi-dimensional Kalman filtering

The Kalman filtering in multi-dimensional space is an extension of the 1-D Kalman filtering. Naturally, the computations are more complex, since quadratic modifications of matrices are involved in computing variances. Let $\boldsymbol{x}_1 \sim p_1(\boldsymbol{\mu}_1, \boldsymbol{\Sigma}_1)$, ..., $\boldsymbol{x}_n \sim p_n(\boldsymbol{\mu}_n, \boldsymbol{\Sigma}_n)$ be a set of pairwise uncorrelated multi-dimensional random variables, where $\boldsymbol{\mu}_i$ and $\boldsymbol{\Sigma}_i$ denote the mean and covariance matrix of the probability density function, p_i. Let, $\boldsymbol{y}$ be a random variable, which is a linear combination of $\boldsymbol{x}_i$'s, as given in Eq. 8.35.

$$\boldsymbol{y} = \sum_{i=1}^{n} \mathbf{A}_i \boldsymbol{x}_i \qquad (8.35)$$

where $\mathbf{A}_i$'s are the coefficient matrices. The mean, $\boldsymbol{\mu_y}$, and covariance, $\boldsymbol{\Sigma_y}$, of $\boldsymbol{y}$ are given by Eq. 8.36.

$$\boldsymbol{\mu_y} = \sum_{i=1}^{n} \mathbf{A}_i \boldsymbol{\mu}_i$$

$$\boldsymbol{\Sigma_y} = \sum_{i=1}^{n} \mathbf{A}_i \boldsymbol{\Sigma}_i \mathbf{A}_i^{\top}$$

$$(8.36)$$

where $\boldsymbol{\mu}_i$ and $\boldsymbol{\Sigma}_i$ are the mean and covariance of $\boldsymbol{x}_i$, respectively. Here, the covariance matrix, $\boldsymbol{\Sigma_y}$, is modified by the quadratic term, $\mathbf{A}_i \boldsymbol{\Sigma}_i \mathbf{A}_i^{\top}$. In this multi-dimensional case, the matrix operations are equivalently showing the linear operations for the decision fusion. Similar to 1-D Kalman filtering case, if a multi-dimensional random variable $\boldsymbol{z}$, is pairwise uncorrelated with $\boldsymbol{x}_1$, ..., $\boldsymbol{x}_n$, it is also uncorrelated with $\boldsymbol{y}$.

Here, the problem is to minimize the mean square error (MSE) of $\boldsymbol{y}$, which is given by the expectation of the covariance matrix of $\boldsymbol{y}$, $\mathrm{E}((\boldsymbol{y} - \boldsymbol{\mu_y})^{\top}(\boldsymbol{y} - \boldsymbol{\mu_y}))$. Since this is performed in a multi-dimensional perspective, the MSE actually represents a scalar valued distance estimate, which is minimized in the optimization process. Similar to 1-D Kalman filtering, this is equivalent to convex combination of the random variables, x_i's. For the optimal estimate of the coefficient matrices, the sum of the coefficient matrices is an identity matrix and the inverse of the covariance matrices dictate the linear term of transformation matrices or coefficient matrices to transform from x to the respective random variable. This is expressed by Eq. 8.37.

$$\sum_{i=1}^{n} \mathbf{A}_i = \mathbf{I}$$

$$\mathbf{A}_i = (\mathbf{\Sigma}_i)^{-1} \left(\sum_{i=1}^{n} (\mathbf{\Sigma}_j)^{-1} \right)^{-1} \tag{8.37}$$

The optimal estimate, y^*, of the linear combination of x_i's with the set of optimal coefficients, $\mathbf{A}_i^*$'s, is expressed by Eq. 8.38.

$$y^* = \sum_{i=1}^{n} \mathbf{A}_i^* x_i \tag{8.38}$$

For two variables, corresponding to two conditions, (1) prediction from the motion model, and (2) measurement from observation, there are two estimates. From the notations defined in Eq. 8.24, let x_1 be the estimate with the model F and x_2 be the estimate from measurement, z, with transformation H (i.e., $x_2 = Hz$). The correction on the final estimate, y, is given by Eq. 8.39.

$$y = x_1 + \mathbf{K}(x_2 - x_1) \tag{8.39}$$

where $\mathbf{K} = \mathbf{\Sigma}_1 \left(\mathbf{\Sigma}_1 + \mathbf{\Sigma}_2 \right)^{-1}$ is the Kalman gain. The covariance matrices may not always be invertible, from the point of view of relationships. In such cases, some other means of estimations to compute the gain has to be considered. We may note that, Eq. 8.39 is the same as Eq. 8.38, where the linear combination form is rewritten to explicitly incorporate the Kalman gain. The measure of uncertainty in y is given by Eq. 8.40.

$$\mathbf{\Sigma}_y = (\mathbf{I} - \mathbf{K}) \mathbf{\Sigma}_1 \tag{8.40}$$

8.4.3 | Graph based method

In generative tracking approaches, besides the probabilistic models, there are also some of the nonprobabilistic approaches. Any nonprobabilistic approach has a very close relationship with probabilistic models. One of the very popular techniques is the *graph based method*. Consider the objects in motion in the consecutive frames. From the measurements of observations and predictions, there are certain possible positions of the objects in the subsequent frames. Among them, some of the positions may be considered as *candidate positions* to perform the computations for searching the object. These candidate positions are selected on the basis of some scores that are used during the estimation of the motion. For example, the NCC may be used as the scores.

Corresponding to an object of interest in the first frame, suppose the kth frame consists of several similar objects. The position of each of the objects in the latter frame may be a candidate position with a particular correlation score between the window of the object in the first frame. Except for the window of the genuine object to be tracked, windows of other objects that may look similar to the object of interest are expected to have relatively lower scores, so that, they can be discarded as candidate positions. In this way, the possible connections are established between subsequent frames, where the relationships are expressed in the form of a graph. The objects in the frames form the nodes of the graph. Between two correlated windows of objects in different frames, an edge is formed, which is the connection between the nodes. Since the association of the objects occurs between different frames of a video, there is a notion of direction along temporal axis. So, the formed graph is a directed graph, where the weights of the edges are provided by the measure of correlation between respective windows.

The problem here is to compute the trajectory, which is the longest path in a graph. In this approach (Vajinepalli et al., 2008), the evidence gets accumulated over several frames. In each frame, there may be several candidates with respective scores. Collectively, this forms a chain of nodes that are connected by directed edges of appropriate weights, which is represented as a graph. Since there are multiple nodes, the destination node may also not always be known. By considering all the possible candidates at the last frame and computing the length of paths from source to each of the destinations, the longest path is determined. This longest path in the graph is the trajectory for the considered object. These computations are mostly offline computations or buffered computations, which are used to compute the trajectory.

For the sake of explanation of computing object trajectory, consider the pictorial illustration shown in Fig. 8.5. The source object is represented by a single node in the first frame. In the second frame, there are three candidate objects, as shown in the figure. With kernel correlation of the source object, the edges of the nodes in the second frame have weights of 0.5, 0.4, and 0.6, respectively, as seen in the figure. Similarly, all the edges have some weights, which are computed by correlations. In this directed and weighted graph,

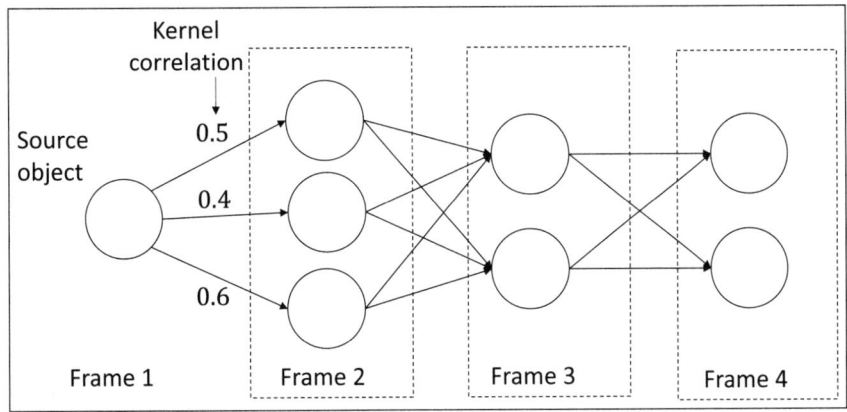

Figure 8.5 Pictorial illustration of object trajectory detection.

Figure 8.6 Example of ball detection in long shots. (*Source*: Dr Pallavi Vajinepalli for sharing the figure from her PhD work (Vajinepalli, 2007).)

the edges are directed from the nodes in a frame to the nodes in the next frame. From the source node to the destination node, the longest path is computed as the object trajectory, which is obtained by dynamic programming (Bellman, 2010).

This technique is applied for ball detection (Vajinepalli et al., 2008) in a broadcast video, whose sample frames are shown in Fig. 8.6. Relative to the scene in the frame, the ball is a very small object, as seen in the left image. So, several possible candidates of ball can be detected in the subsequent frames due to factors like noise, blur, etc., as shown in the middle image. Because of elimination and accumulation that are associated with the nodes, the graph is formed by considering each of the candidates. Then, the valid candidate is selected, as seen in the right image, by considering the overall accumulation of the evidence while recovering the trajectory.

Multipath tracking

The graph based method can be also considered for real time or pseudo real time applications, where accumulating the evidences for too many frames is not required. In such cases, the evidences can be dynamically accumulated by judiciously increasing the number of nodes by expanding the graph or selectively choosing single path tracking. This is called *multi-path tracking*. At a certain point, it is simplified to the single path tracking. When there is a very strong evidence, the corresponding candidate is selected unambiguously. But, when there are more than one evidences that are equally strong, there is a confusion in selecting the candidate. In such cases, all the candidates are considered for exploring each of the respective spaces till a certain point where one of the evidences becomes stronger than others. Then, only the path defined by that particular (strongest) evidence is selected for exploring further and all the rest are discarded. This is a kind of online processing that is almost in real time.

This approach is pictorially summarized in Fig. 8.7. This is a greedy on-the-fly approach that uses the maximum kernel correlation score, C_{max}, to find the location of the object of interest in the subsequent frame. If C_{max} is stronger than a preset threshold, T_{MPT}, the approach is the same as the single path tracking. If $C_{max} < T_{MPT}$, each of the top K candidate nodes is further explored till the point where $C_{max} > T_{MPT}$ (i.e., one particular evidence is unambiguously stronger than the others).

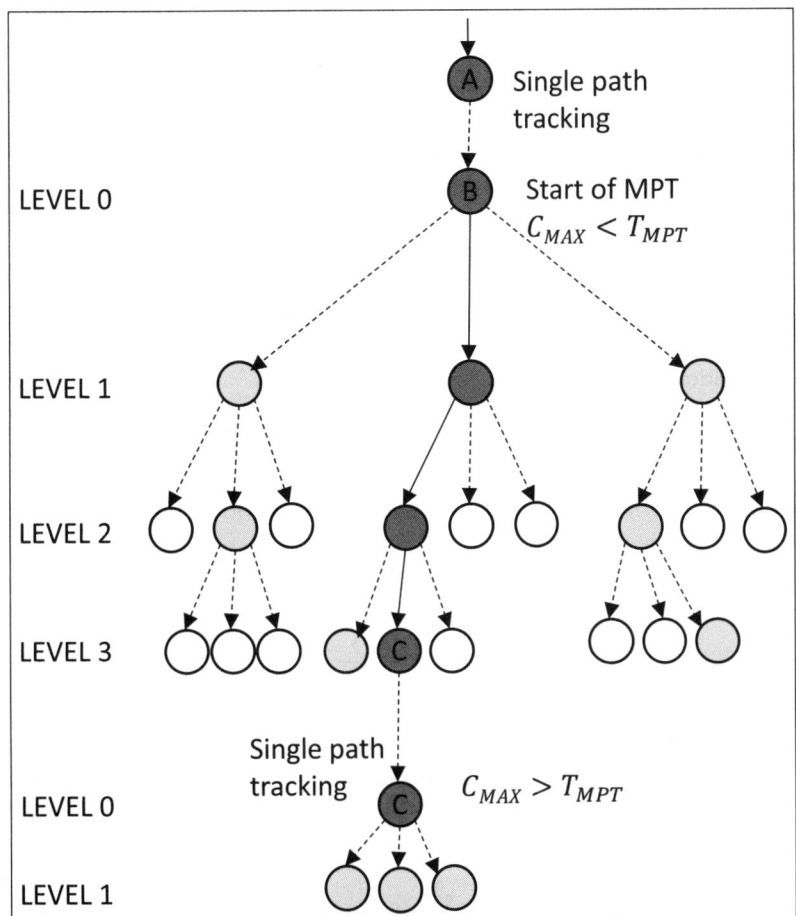

Figure 8.7 Illustration of multi-path tracking approach. (*Source*: Adapted from the PhD thesis (Dogra, 2012) of Prof. Debi Prosad Dogra, Indian Institute of Technology, Bhubaneswar.)

8.5 | Discriminative tracker

In discriminative tracking approach, the tracking problem is posed as a classification problem. That is, if an object of interest is present in a particular frame, the task is to classify the regions in the image as foreground or background. This is usually performed by considering candidate windows in the image. Here, the object is considered as the foreground. It is assumed that the image would consist of only one possible strong candidate. For example, for classifying the objects, a linear classifier may be designed, which is almost similar to computation of correlation, as it computes essentially a scalar dot product of the coefficient vector of the classifier with the feature vector of the object.

The regions in the image are represented by a vector, so that the classifier learns the discrimination among the candidate regions.

The discriminative tracker requires some labeled data to design the tracker. Similar to the classification problem, there is a training stage to compute the coefficients in a discrimination model. As noted before, this computation is modeled by the *correlation* operation. Most of the discriminative trackers are similar to correlation filters in their respective contexts. Since the tracking problem is posed as a detection problem, to design the classifier, the training data is required in pairs, (f_i, g_i), where f_i is a training image and g_i is its label. The output of the classifier is in the form of $0/1$ or $-1/+1$, or it may also be a regression with a range of values. The input to the classifier is a feature vector describing the visual content of the region, such as, texture, histogram, etc. This also depends on the choice of the classifier considered in the process.

To illustrate this computation, let us consider the correlation operation between the candidate window and the template appearance model. The candidate windows are sampled from the image and the template model is learnt from the training data. The correlation, $g(x)$, of a function, $f(x)$, with a template, $h(x)$, in temporal/spatial domain is formally defined as in Eq. 8.41.

$$g(x) = f(x) \otimes h(x) = \sum_{i=-K}^{K} f(x+i)h(i) \tag{8.41}$$

where $\otimes$ is the correlation operation and $(2K + 1)$ is the length of the template $h(\cdot)$. This operator is also referred to as the correlation filter. For an image, Eq. 8.41 is extended to 2-D space, which is given by Eq. 8.42.[2]

$$g(m, n) = \sum_{i=-K}^{K} \sum_{j=-K}^{K} f(m+i, n+j)h(i, j) \tag{8.42}$$

where the considered windows are of sizes $(2K + 1) \times (2K + 1)$. The correlation operation is performed at every point of the function in space/time and wherever the object that matches with the template is present, the correlation value would shoot to a very high value at that point. As we noted before, within the zone of the considered window, the correlation operation is the simple scalar dot product of the two functions.

In Fourier transform domain, the mathematical forms of correlation and convolution are very much similar. For a function, $y(x) = f(x) * h(x)$, which is the convolution of $f(x)$ and $h(x)$, its representation in Fourier domain is given by Eq. 8.43.

$$Y = \mathscr{F}(y(x)) = \mathscr{F}(f(x) * h(x)) = \mathscr{F}(f(x)) \odot \mathscr{F}(h(x)) = F \odot H \tag{8.43}$$

---

[2] Though the mathematical representation of correlation operation appears similar to the convolution operation, they are not the same. Note that, in convolution, the template/mask is spatially/temporally inverted, whereas in correlation, the template/mask is used as it is.

where $\mathscr{F}(\cdot)$ denotes Fourier transform operator, $F = \mathscr{F}(f(x))$, $H = \mathscr{F}(h(x))$, and $\odot$ denote point-wise multiplication operation. For a function, $g(x) = f(x) \otimes h(x)$, which is the correlation of $f(x)$ and $h(x)$, its representation in Fourier domain is given by Eq. 8.44.

$$G = \mathscr{F}(g(x)) = \mathscr{F}(f(x) \otimes h(x)) = \mathscr{F}(f(x)) \odot \mathscr{F}(h(x))^* = F \odot H^* \tag{8.44}$$

where H^* is the complex conjugate of H. Here, the problem is to learn the optimal representation of the filter, H, given a set of labeled data of tracking (i.e., object locations in consecutive frames or a set of frames). The filter, H, provides the appearance model, which can be used as a template for object classification. The optimization function used in this case to compute H is of the following form.

$$E = \sum_i |F_i \odot H^* - G_i|^2 \tag{8.45}$$

An optimal H minimizes the square of the error, given in Eq. 8.45, for every observation i.

8.5.1 | Linear regression method

The correlation operation is a linear operation, as observed in Eq. 8.44. The optimization problem in estimating the correlation filter is also the same as the computation involved in linear regression, where the template used for correlation corresponds to the coefficients of regression. Thus, given the pairs, $(\boldsymbol{x}_i, y_i)$, $i = 1, 2, \ldots, N$, where $\boldsymbol{x}_i$ is a column vector and y_i is the corresponding scalar value, the objective is to get the filter coefficients, $\boldsymbol{w}$, in the form of a vector, such that Eq. 8.46 is true for all the N examples.

$$\boldsymbol{w}^\top \boldsymbol{x}_i = y_i \tag{8.46}$$

Here, the regression target, y_i, may assume any value in general, without the restriction of being a discrete label.

Let $\mathbf{X} = [\boldsymbol{x}_1 \ \boldsymbol{x}_2 \ \ldots \ \boldsymbol{x}_N]^\top$ represent the data in the form of a data matrix, where each data point $\boldsymbol{x}_i$ is a column vector. We may note that each row of $\mathbf{X}$ is a data point here. Their corresponding observations are represented by the column vector, $\boldsymbol{y} = [y_1 \ y_2 \ \ldots \ y_N]^\top$. Using matrix multiplication, Eq. 8.46 can be expressed as a set of equations, which is given by Eq. 8.48.

$$\mathbf{X}\boldsymbol{w} = \boldsymbol{y} \tag{8.47}$$

For the ridge regression (Rifkin et al., 2003), the error term, $E = ||\mathbf{X}\boldsymbol{w} - \boldsymbol{y}||^2 + \lambda ||\boldsymbol{w}||^2$, has to be minimized , as given in Eq. 8.48, along with regularization of $\boldsymbol{w}$.

$$\min_{\boldsymbol{w}} E = \min_{\boldsymbol{w}} ||\mathbf{X}\boldsymbol{w} - \boldsymbol{y}||^2 + \lambda ||\boldsymbol{w}||^2 \tag{8.48}$$

where λ is the regularization parameter that controls overfitting. This can be solved algebraically by using the least squares error technique. Taking the partial derivatives of E

with respect to the individual components of w as a system of equations and equating it to zero, we get the form given by Eq. 8.49.

$$\frac{\partial E}{\partial w} = 0 \implies 2(\mathbf{X}w - y)^\top \mathbf{X} + 2\lambda w^\top = 0$$
$$\mathbf{X}^\top(\mathbf{X}w - y) + \lambda w = 0 \qquad (8.49)$$
$$(\mathbf{X}^\top \mathbf{X} + \lambda \mathbf{I})w = \mathbf{X}^\top y$$

Solving Eq. 8.49, the expression for w is given by Eq. 8.50.

$$w = \left(\mathbf{X}^\top \mathbf{X} + \lambda \mathbf{I}\right)^{-1} \mathbf{X}^\top y \qquad (8.50)$$

The expression in Eq. 8.50 provides the optimal weight for the correlation filter. Here, the term $\mathbf{X}^\top \mathbf{X}$ is the covariance matrix with respect to the data matrix.

8.5.2 | Kernelized correlation filters (KCF)

The core component of the discriminative tracker is a discriminative classifier, which distinguishes between the target and the background. Usually, the classifier is trained with scaled and translated versions of the image patches to cope with the changes in the natural scene. The design of the filter for classifying the images requires a set of training images. The filter coefficients may change with changes in the training set in a sequence of video frames. The computed filter coefficients can be made more robust to such changes by using some of the data augmentation strategies.

One of the early works (Henriques et al., 2015) in this regard is the *kernelized correlation filter*. In the KCF technique, many versions of an input sample are generated using a single observation. Operations like translation and rotation, are used to get several observations from a single input observation, which can be represented as a *circulant data matrix*. Certain properties of circulant data matrix are useful to simplify the compute operations for estimating the filter coefficients using ridge regression efficiently.

Circulant matrix

Consider a row, $x = [x_1 \; x_2 \; \dots \; x_n]$, of the data matrix, where n is the dimension of the data vector. Its circulant matrix is formed by rotating x by circularly right shifting its position incrementally n times to obtain a matrix. That is, the first row is x, the second row is circularly shifted version of x by one element, the third row is circularly shifted version of x by two elements, and so on till the nth row. Let $\mathbf{X} = \mathcal{C}(x)$, where $\mathcal{C}$ is the circulant matrix operator. Then, $\mathbf{X}$ is given by Eq. 8.51.

$$\mathbf{X} = \mathcal{C}(x) = \begin{bmatrix} x_1 & x_2 & x_3 & \cdots & x_n \\ x_n & x_1 & x_2 & \cdots & x_{n-1} \\ x_{n-1} & x_n & x_1 & \cdots & x_{n-2} \\ \vdots & \vdots & \vdots & \ddots & \vdots \\ x_2 & x_3 & x_4 & \cdots & x_1 \end{bmatrix} \qquad (8.51)$$

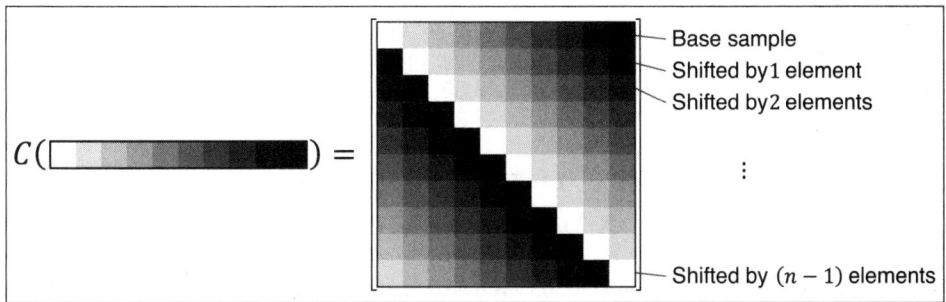

Figure 8.8 Illustration of formation of circulant matrix.

This is pictorially illustrated in Fig. 8.8.

The circulant matrix has an interesting relationship with the Fourier transform space. Consider the circulant matrix, $\mathbf{X} = \mathcal{C}(\boldsymbol{x})$, as given in Eq. 8.51. The inverse Fourier transform of the diagonal matrix formed by the Fourier transform of $\boldsymbol{x}$ would result in the same form of the circulant matrix, $\mathbf{X}$. Mathematically, this is given by Eq. 8.52.

$$\mathbf{X} = \mathbf{F}\mathrm{diag}(\widehat{\boldsymbol{x}})\mathbf{F}^{\mathcal{H}} \tag{8.52}$$

where $\mathbf{F}$ is the DFT matrix, the superscript $^{\mathcal{H}}$ indicates Hermitian transpose, and $\widehat{\boldsymbol{x}} = \mathscr{F}(\boldsymbol{x}) = \sqrt{n}\mathbf{F}\boldsymbol{x}$ is the Fourier transform[3] of $\boldsymbol{x}$ with a normalization of $\sqrt{n}$. Though the solution obtained in Eq. 8.50 is more intuitive and concise, it is computationally very intensive, since it requires matrix inversion operation. To avoid matrix inversion, these computations can be performed in Fourier domain representation. It is seen that, in some cases, they are more convenient for computation and representation.

KCF: The solution of linear regression

Consider the expression for ridge regression, which is given by Eq. 8.53.

$$\min_{\boldsymbol{w}} \sum_i (f(\boldsymbol{x}_i) - y_i)^2 + \lambda ||\boldsymbol{w}||^2 \tag{8.53}$$

where $f(\boldsymbol{x}) = \boldsymbol{w}^{\top}\boldsymbol{x}$, the data vector $\boldsymbol{x} \in \mathbb{R}^n$, and n is the dimension of $\boldsymbol{x}$. The solution to this is given in Eq. 8.50. However, assuming a general case of the data matrix to have complex entities, $\boldsymbol{x} \in \mathbb{C}^n$, Eq. 8.50 can be equivalently represented using the Hermitian transpose, which given by Eq. 8.54.

$$\boldsymbol{w} = \left(\mathbf{X}^{\mathcal{H}}\mathbf{X} + \lambda\mathbf{I}\right)^{-1}\mathbf{X}^{\mathcal{H}}\boldsymbol{y} \tag{8.54}$$

Here, the covariance matrix, $\mathbf{X}^{\mathcal{H}}\mathbf{X}$, in the complex domain, is expressed by Eq. 8.55.

$$\begin{aligned}\mathbf{X}^{\mathcal{H}}\mathbf{X} &= \mathbf{F}\mathrm{diag}(\widehat{\boldsymbol{x}}^*)\mathbf{F}^{\mathcal{H}}\mathbf{F}\mathrm{diag}(\widehat{\boldsymbol{x}})\mathbf{F}^{\mathcal{H}} \\ &= \mathbf{F}\mathrm{diag}(\widehat{\boldsymbol{x}}^* \odot \widehat{\boldsymbol{x}})\mathbf{F}^{\mathcal{H}}\end{aligned} \tag{8.55}$$

---

[3] Refer to Section 2.2 of Chapter 2.

In estimating $\boldsymbol{w}$, it is required to compute the inverse of the diagonal matrix, which is a matrix of real numbers, formed by the point-wise multiplication of the Fourier transform of $\boldsymbol{x}$ and its complex conjugate. Similar to Eq. 8.55, the expressions for $\mathbf{X}^{\mathcal{H}}\mathbf{X} + \lambda\mathbf{I}$ and $\mathbf{X}^{\mathcal{H}}\boldsymbol{y}$ are given by Eq. 8.56

$$
\begin{aligned}
\mathbf{X}^{\mathcal{H}}\mathbf{X} + \lambda\mathbf{I} &= \mathbf{F}\mathrm{diag}(\widehat{\boldsymbol{x}}^* \odot \widehat{\boldsymbol{x}} + \lambda)\mathbf{F}^{\mathcal{H}} \\
\mathbf{X}^{\mathcal{H}}\boldsymbol{y} &= \mathbf{F}\mathrm{diag}(\widehat{\boldsymbol{x}}^* \odot \widehat{\boldsymbol{y}})\mathbf{F}^{\mathcal{H}}
\end{aligned}
\tag{8.56}
$$

As observed in Eqs. 8.55, and 8.56, all the terms of Eq. 8.54 are represented using some form of diagonal matrices, whose inverse will provide the respective quantities. In the transformed domain, these inversion operations are computed as element-wise division operations to obtain the coefficients of the filter Fourier domain, which is given by Eq. 8.57.

$$
\widehat{\boldsymbol{w}} = \left(\frac{\widehat{\boldsymbol{x}}^* \odot \widehat{\boldsymbol{y}}}{\widehat{\boldsymbol{x}}^* \odot \widehat{\boldsymbol{x}} + \lambda} \right)
\tag{8.57}
$$

where the fraction is element-wise fraction operation. Then, the weight vector, $\boldsymbol{w}$ is computed as $\mathrm{IDFT}(\widehat{\boldsymbol{w}})$, the inverse Fourier transform of $\widehat{\boldsymbol{w}}$. After computing the filter, $\boldsymbol{w}$, it is applied for finding the learnt pattern in images.

KCF: Nonlinear regression

In a general scenario, the KCF approach of solving the regression problem may also accommodate the nonlinear models using the kernel trick. Here, the given feature vector, $\boldsymbol{x}_i$, is mapped to a higher dimensional space, $\boldsymbol{x}_i \to \phi(\boldsymbol{x}_i)$, where $\phi(\boldsymbol{x}_i)$ represents the higher dimensional space. For using the kernel trick effectively, an explicit representation of this mapping is not really necessary. In fact, this can be computed by performing simple scalar dot products of different quantities. That is, higher dimensional vectors can be obtained by essentially computing the scalar dot products of the respective pairwise elements of the input vectors. Also, the weights of the filter can be considered as a linear combination of the high dimensional training vectors. This is expressed in Eq. 8.58.

$$
\boldsymbol{w} = \sum_i \alpha_i \phi(\boldsymbol{x}_i)
\tag{8.58}
$$

Here, α is the dual representation.

The correlation filter in the form of Eq. 8.59 can be expressed as in Eq. 8.58, which is similar to computing the dot product of two vectors.

$$
f(\boldsymbol{z}) = \boldsymbol{w}^{\top} \phi(\boldsymbol{z})
\tag{8.59}
$$

where $\boldsymbol{z}$ is a vector. The kernel trick leads to the simplification of the problem, where it is now sufficient to model only the dot products. This requires a definition of a kernel, which can provide the desired values of $\boldsymbol{w}$ directly. Using Eqs. 8.58 and 8.59,

$$
f(\boldsymbol{z}) = \sum_i \alpha_i \phi^{\top}(\boldsymbol{x}_i)\phi(\boldsymbol{z})
\tag{8.60}
$$

The expression in Eq. 8.60 is a functional form, where $\phi(\boldsymbol{x}_i)^\top \phi(\boldsymbol{z})$ is not explicitly computed. Rather, it is computed by a kernel function, κ (which can be a Gaussian, a polynomial, etc.), which is given in Eq. 8.61.

$$K_{ij} = \phi^\top(\boldsymbol{x}_i)\phi(\boldsymbol{x}_j) = \kappa(\boldsymbol{x}_i, \boldsymbol{x}_j) \tag{8.61}$$

where K_{ij}s are the elements of the $n \times n$ kernel matrix, $\mathbf{K} = [K_{ij}]$, which is composed of scalar dot products between all pairs of vectors. From Eqs. 8.60 and 8.61, the functional form can be expressed as in Eq. 8.62.

$$f(\boldsymbol{z}) = \sum_i \alpha_i \kappa(\boldsymbol{x}_i, \boldsymbol{z}) \tag{8.62}$$

For example, the Gaussian and linear kernel functions are given in Eqs. 8.63 and 8.64, respectively.

$$\kappa(\boldsymbol{x}_i, \boldsymbol{x}_j) = e^{\left(-\frac{1}{\sigma^2}(\|\boldsymbol{x}_i - \boldsymbol{x}_j\|^2)\right)} \tag{8.63}$$

$$\kappa(\boldsymbol{x}_i, \boldsymbol{x}_j) = \boldsymbol{x}_i^\top \boldsymbol{x}_j \tag{8.64}$$

KCF: Kernel regression

Using Eq. 8.62, the optimization problem given in Eq. 8.53 is converted using the kernel values, which has to be now minimized by α, as given by Eq. 8.65.

$$\min_{\boldsymbol{\alpha}} \sum_j \left(\sum_i \alpha_i \kappa(\boldsymbol{x}_i, \boldsymbol{x}_j) - y_j \right)^2 + \lambda \|\boldsymbol{w}\|^2 \tag{8.65}$$

Here, it is required to satisfy the fact that the functional value should be invariant to the ordering of dimension. That is, $\mathbf{K} = \mathcal{C}(\boldsymbol{k}^{\boldsymbol{xx}})$, where $\boldsymbol{k}^{\boldsymbol{xx}}$ is the first row of the kernel. If the functional value of the kernel is invariant to the ordering of the dimensions, the kernel derived from the columns of the circulant matrix is also circulant. For example, computaiton of the Euclidean distance between two data points is free from any ordering of dimensions. This is valid for Gaussian function also. Thus, if the functional value of the kernel is invariant to the ordering of the dimensions, it satisfies the circulant matrix property as well. All the theories that are discussed on KCF are valid only when the kernel is derived from a circulant matrix. This is because, the formation of respective diagonal matrices for simplifying the computations using Fourier transform of the base vector is valid only for circular matrices.

KCF: Solution of nonlinear regression

The solution for the nonlinear regression are evaluated using Eqs. 8.61 and 8.62, with reference to the weight vector, $\boldsymbol{w} = \sum_i \alpha_i \phi(\boldsymbol{x}_i)$. The computed solution, $\widehat{\boldsymbol{\alpha}}$, in Fourier transform domain is given in form as expressed by Eq. 8.66.

$$\widehat{\boldsymbol{\alpha}} = \frac{\widehat{\boldsymbol{y}}}{\widehat{\boldsymbol{k}}_{\boldsymbol{xx}} + \lambda} \tag{8.66}$$

By taking the inverse Fourier transform of Eq. 8.66, the required solution is obtained. After computing the $\boldsymbol{\alpha}$, the functional values of $f(\boldsymbol{z})$ can be obtained using $\boldsymbol{\alpha}$ in Eq. 8.62, along with the considered kernels.

Summary

The object tracking involves estimation of the object trajectory in an image plane, as the object moves. A flexible computational model for tracking points in images is the optical flow. It provides the distribution of apparent velocities of movement $\boldsymbol{v}$ of brightness ($\mathbf{I}$) pattern in an image, which are governed by the equation, $\nabla \mathbf{I} \cdot \boldsymbol{v} = -\mathbf{I}_t$. At any point, the scalar dot product of the gradient of $\mathbf{I}$ in the space and its apparent velocity $\boldsymbol{v}$ in the 2-D image plane negates the temporal change of the pattern. Similar concept is exploited in tracking group of pixels such as rectangular patches by using the KLT tracking algorithm. In the KLT tracker, the tracking problem is solved by finding the displacement, $\boldsymbol{d}$, of the moving object. There exist also probabilistic approaches for solving the tracking problem. In recursive Bayesian tracking, probabilities of states of an object at the kth instant is computed by applying state transition and measurement models. The Kalman filtering, a special case of this Bayesian tracking framework, assumes the linear models with additive Gaussian noise.

The tracking problem can also be formulated as a longest path finding problem in a directed graph, whose nodes are probable object locations at discrete time points and weighted edges are formed from its time points to the present time point. Though this method is primarily meant for offline analysis of object trajectory, an on-the-fly greedy method using multi-path tracking may also be adapted for its wider application.

An example of discriminating object tracking approach is the use of correlation filters, which are learnt from the examples formed from the regions around a moving object. To make the learning efficient, data augmentation methods are used, in particular, the augmented data in the form of a circulant matrix formed from a single feature vector is found to provide computational advantages, as it exploits the properties of circulant matrix in the Fourier domain. A more powerful model using KCF improves the quality of solutions for the problem of object tracking.

Exercises

(i) Specify the assumption in the computation of optical flow from successive frames of a video. Derive the equations related to optical flow and define the objective function to compute optical flow at every point in a frame of a video.

(ii) Formulate the optimization criterion for obtaining rigid body displacement in the KLT tracker. Provide the expression after minimization of the function and discuss how the computation could be made more robust.

(iii) Explain how NCC is used in computing rigid body translation of an object.

(iv) Formulate the mathematical problem of Bayesian inference for tracking an object from the past observations of its locations in images. Provide a recursive computational framework for solving the problem.

(**v**) What are assumptions involved in Kalman filtering to track an object? Formulate the computational model following the assumptions and describe the computation to solve it.

(**vi**) Suppose there are N number of estimates $\hat{\mathbf{x}}_1, \hat{\mathbf{x}}_2, \dots \hat{\mathbf{x}}_N$ of a new position $\mathbf{x} \in \mathbf{R}^n$ of the object. The covariance matrix for the ith measurement is represented as $\sigma_i^2 I$, where I is an identity matrix of dimension $n \times n$. Show that the optimal estimate with minimum uncertainty (determinant of the covariance matrix of the estimate) is

$$\mathbf{x_{opt}} = \frac{1}{\sum_{i=1}^{N} \frac{1}{\sigma_i^2}} \sum_{i=1}^{N} \frac{1}{\sigma_i^2} \hat{\mathbf{x}}_i$$

(**vii**) Formulate the problem of computing the trajectory of an object in a video sequence as the computation of longest path in a directed path. Describe an algorithm to solve the problem.

(**viii**) Describe the multi-path tracking algorithm of an object. How the computation can be modeled under the Bayesian tracking framework.

(**ix**) What is a correlation filter? How it is learnt in a discriminative tracker? How the computation can be made efficient using the property of a circulant matrix.

(**x**) Derive the equation for optical flow relating the temporal changes and spatial gradients of intensity in a video. Describe the computation of KLT tracker for tracking image patches.

9

Deep Visual Learning

An artificial neural network (ANN) is a network of neural nodes or perceptual nodes.[1] In a feed forward neural network, each node is fed with a weighted input vector and the net sum of the weighted vectors from several such nodes is passed through a nonlinear function, whose response is the output of that node. The layers formed by the input nodes and the output nodes are known as the input layer and the output layer, respectively. The layers formed by other nodes are known as hidden layers. A network of several such layers (along with input and output layers) forms an ANN, as shown in Fig. 9.1.[2] The conventional ANNs have very few hidden layers, usually not more than three. Using only one or two hidden

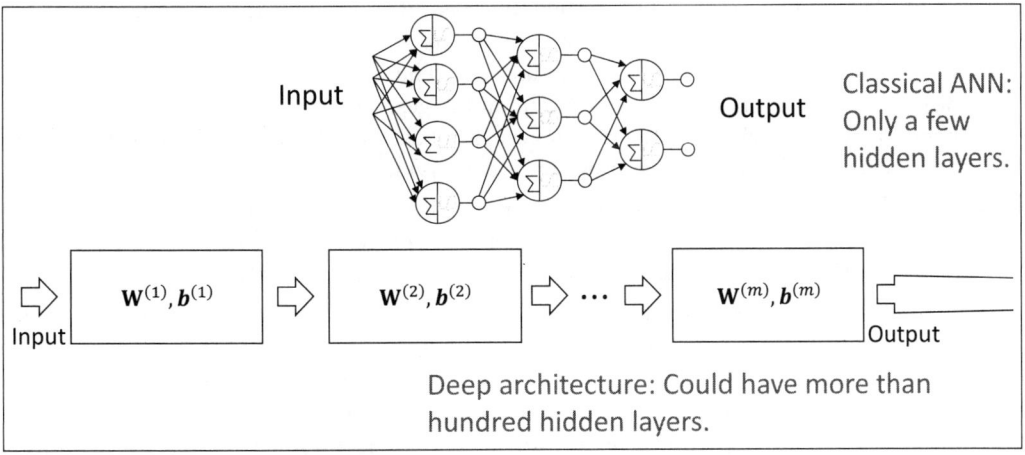

Figure 9.1 An artificial neural network.

---

[1] Please refer to Chapter 7 for detailed discussion on ANNs.
[2] Please refer to Eq. 7.67 of Chapter 7 for the description of the mathematical model with the parameters shown in the figure.

layers is also common in many applications. In contrast, *deep neural architectures* have relatively more number of layers. Even more than 100 hidden layers is not uncommon. This is one of the distinguished characteristics of deep neural networks (DNN) from an ordinary ANN.

The concepts used in deep neural computations are decades older. In fact, they involve the same neural network computations as in a simple ANN model. These concepts were introduced in 1980's and their basic principles still remain the same. However, a boom in using deep architectures after almost three decades of their proposition is mainly attributed to the advancement in technology and science. There are mainly two reasons for this:

(i) Capacity of generating large scale annotated data, and their ease of availability to masses and dissemination due to penetration of internet and smart-phones, which enable widespread use of social networking, online shopping, etc.

(ii) Advancement of computing power, which makes it possible to train a large neural network using graphics processing units (GPUs).

Many applications using deep learning models and architectures solving many critical problems are increasingly reported day by day. To accelerate the process various research groups publish large volumes of annotated datasets inviting solutions for performing challenging tasks on them. A few examples of such research problems and data sets are illustrated below.

- *Image classification*: One of the main tasks identified for the development of deep neural models is image classification. Toward this, a public data set of images, viz., *ImageNet large scale visual recognition challenge data set* (ILSVRC) (Russakovsky et al., 2015), was created for testing the classification algorithms to improve them. For more than a decade, various researchers have been reporting the performance of their classification algorithm on this data set. The ImageNet data set consists of 1000 object classes assigned to about 1.4 million images. The major algorithms, which have been found to provide good performances, are based on deep features. In other words, deep neural architectures are used while classifying the data.

- *Object recognition and localization*: In this application, a system localizes one or more object(s) in the given image. While performing localization, it also performs the task of recognition or classification of the object (Girshick et al., 2014).

- *Object segmentation*: Object segmentation is another generalized problem. With respect to deep neural architectures, it is usually called semantic segmentation, since the problem involves knowing what is detected and classifying each and every pixel of the image (Dai et al., 2016). It equivalently performs object localization, where the declarations of presence of an object, are made at pixel level, i.e., computing segments containing a specific type of objects.

- *Pose estimation*: Pose estimation is a problem of describing the human body using skeleton representation. Skeletons are 3-D graphical information of lines representing limbs, hands, body, etc., like human skeleton, that are joined by their edges at 3-D coordinate vertices, like skeletal joints. Depending upon images of different persons, the skeleton configurations are estimated for each kind of stances, which capture their poses (Cao et al., 2017). An estimated pose is further used to determine different attributes like, whether a person is standing, or performing certain activity, etc.

- *Image and video captioning*: This is an example of multimodal information processing that needs understanding of images and videos that are described using natural languages. That is, when different scenes are processed for detecting various objects, they are described using a semantic sentence (Karpathy and Fei-Fei, 2015).

- *Image super-resolution*: There are several deep architectures that are proposed for accomplishing the task of image super-resolution. They are seen to perform better than the classical cubic interpolation algorithm (Ledig et al., 2017).

- *Image art generation and style transfer*: Using deep neural architectures, different kinds of artistic images are synthesized by rendering on an arbitrary photograph (Gatys et al., 2016). Using a photograph of a scene from a camera, its painting from different painters can be rendered in their style of strokes and color cues using these architectures.

- *Applications not related to processing images*: There are also many other applications of deep neural architectures, which range from solving chemical equations to estimating astronomical events. Some of the widely used areas in day-to-day applications include machine translation and text synthesis, speech recognition and synthesis, navigating autonomous vehicles, playing different kinds of games like chess, alpha go, etc.

9.1 | Deep feature representation

To understand the differences between classical and deep learning algorithms, consider the problem of image classification as an example. In classical image classification an image is generally represented by a set of handcrafted features. In this case, the distinct features that characterize images under some context are well studied and computational algorithms to extract those are developed. Since the features are identified by the understanding of the data, they are called *handcrafted*. The classical approach also requires explicit design and development of algorithms to extract such features. Examples of such features include SIFT/SURF descriptors at key points, HOG patch descriptors, motion features, etc. The feature representation of images is the input to classification algorithms (classifiers), such as, Bayesian classifier, discriminant functions, support vector machine, K-NN classifier, etc. Here, in the classical approach, the feature representation and classification are two independent tasks that are cascaded in a pipeline of processing for deriving a model, as shown in Fig. 9.2. The trained model is then used to classify any arbitrary image. Thus it is required to define appropriate feature by analyzing its role and contribution in distinguishing a class, and then to develop computation algorithms to obtain it from an input image. This kind of a well defined feature, useful for discriminating classes, is called a *handcrafted feature*.

Developing handcrafted features to handle various challenges in capturing relevant information is a very tedious and costly process. In general, there is a large variation in appearances of the same object in a natural world. There can be different kinds of variations on imaging, like, view point variation, deformation, occlusion, interclass variation, illumination, clutter, instances, scale, etc. It is very difficult to account for all

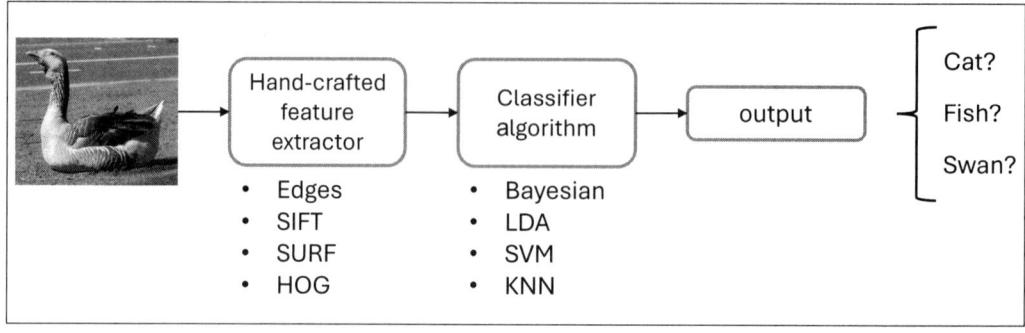

Figure 9.2 The classical approach.

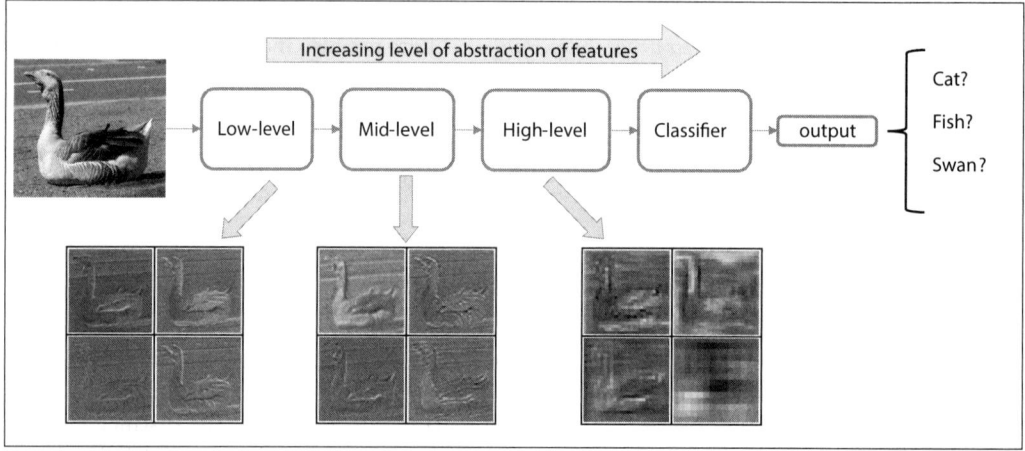

Figure 9.3 Example of deep features. (*Source*: Ankita Chatterjee, Research Scholar, IIT Kharagpur.)

such kinds of variations while designing handcrafted features and to develop computational algorithms for extracting them. So, the handcrafted features are usually limited to and depend on some particular application, and it may not be reusable to other applications or generic use cases.

In a deep learning based model, the feature representation is jointly learnt with the task of classification. Features are also computed under the similar multilayered feed forward neural computing framework and processed in subsequent layers to provide the output of the model. During training the weights of the whole model including the layers involving feature extraction and followed by classification are learnt through end to end minimization of a loss or error function. Here, the extracted features are not handcrafted, instead, the feature representations are directly learnt by the neural network. There may be different levels of feature representations in deep architectures. The initial layers of the network provide low-level features. As the level of abstraction increases with the depth of the network, mid-level features and high-level features are learnt, which is illustrated in Fig. 9.3. The classifier is trained using a composite of these features. Unlike the classical approach, where the feature representation is independent of classification scheme, the feature representation and classification tasks go hand-in-hand in deep learning paradigm, as shown in Fig. 9.3. In deep networks, rich hierarchical representations are learnt through multiple stages of feature learning process, which provide different levels of data abstraction (Zeiler and Fergus, 2014). Also, such learned deep features are easier to adapt depending on the context of applications. However, to learn appropriate deep features, a large volume of labeled data for training are needed.

9.2 | Supervised learning of deep neural networks

Most of the classification applications of deep neural architectures come under supervised learning framework. The network is trained using sufficient volume of annotated training data for the classification task, which is a typical supervised classification setup. Different kinds of problems like classification, regression, object detection, semantic segmentation, image captioning, etc. can be mapped to this learning framework. The classification task and different methodologies on deriving a classifier or a model from training examples are discussed in Chapter 7. This is under the category of supervised learning. We revisit this problem again under the context of deep learning. Given a set of data $\mathbf{X}$ and corresponding labels $\mathbf{Y}$, the goal here is to determine a function f, which maps the data to the labels. In the task of image classification, the computational problem is to learn what class an image belongs to. In this case, it is desired to learn the parametric function f, which is described by weight parameters of the deep learning model to classify an image $\boldsymbol{x}$ with a class label y.

9.2.1 | Steps in supervised learning

Supervised learning is a data driven approach to learn the model in three steps.

(i) **Define the model**: The model, in this case, is in the form of a mathematical function, described by a set of parameters $\boldsymbol{w}$, which maps an input sample $\boldsymbol{x}$ to output y. For instance, as in Eq. 9.1.

$$\hat{y} = f(\boldsymbol{x}, \boldsymbol{w}) \tag{9.1}$$

where $\hat{y}$ is the predicted output (image label), $\boldsymbol{x}$ is the input image, and $\boldsymbol{w}$ represents model weights. Since a DNN is similar to ANN, except for having more number of hidden layers, the structure of the model almost remains the same, where the image pixels are the input data that pass through the model described by parameters (or weights) to compute the predicted output or image label.

(ii) **Collect data for learning the model**: Since this is supervised learning of the model, it is important and necessary to gather sufficient volume of annotated data,

$\{(\boldsymbol{x}_i, y_i)\}_{i=1}^{N}$, where $\boldsymbol{x}_i$ is a training sample, y_i is the corresponding true output, and N is the number of data samples in the training set.

(iii) **Learn the model**: A mapping function between the data samples and their outputs (e.g., labels) is learnt. Toward this, it is necessary to assess the performance of the model or weights for improving the learning. A loss function is defined for this purpose. The learning involves a mechanism of selection or updates of weights so that it gets progressively reduced toward its minimization. The optimization problem using a loss function for deriving a model is given in the form as in Eq. 9.2.

$$\boldsymbol{w}^* = \underset{\boldsymbol{w}}{\text{argmin}} \; \frac{1}{N} \sum_{i=1}^{N} \ell(f(\boldsymbol{x}_i, \boldsymbol{w}), y_i) + \mathcal{R}(\boldsymbol{w}) \tag{9.2}$$

where $\boldsymbol{w}^*$ represent learned weights, $\ell(\cdot)$ is the data loss function (or measure of failure of prediction), and $\mathcal{R}(\cdot)$ is a function called regularizer to penalize complex models. For a set of N training samples, the loss is accumulated to minimize the average loss over the training set. In Eq. 9.2, the total loss to be minimized over the training set is the sum of data loss and the regularization loss, which is given by $\ell(\cdot) + \mathcal{R}(\cdot)$.

9.2.2 | Loss functions

A *loss function* assesses the performance of a classifier at a particular stage of learning. Data loss is representative of the deviation of the model prediction from the training data. Ideally, the model predictions should match the desired output in the training data, thus making the loss almost negligible. There are different kinds of loss functions accounting different factors of deviations from desirable properties of a classifier.

Hinge loss

Hinge loss accounts for a quantitative loss value for each wrongly classified sample. This loss is the difference of the predicted functional values of a data sample by the model and the true functional value of the data sample. The functional form of Hinge loss is given in Eq. 9.3.

$$\mathcal{L} = \frac{1}{N} \sum_{i=1}^{N} \sum_{j \neq y_i} \max(0, f(\boldsymbol{x}_i; \mathbf{W})_j - f(\boldsymbol{x}_i; \mathbf{W})_{y_i} + 1) \tag{9.3}$$

where $\mathbf{W}$ is the weight matrix of the model, and $f(\boldsymbol{x}_i; \mathbf{W})_j$ and $f(\boldsymbol{x}_i; \mathbf{W})_{y_i}$ represent the predicted value and true value for the data sample $\boldsymbol{x}_i$, respectively. It may be noted that for a multi-class classification scheme using a set of discriminant functions, a class is assigned to a sample $\boldsymbol{x}$, if its corresponding discriminant function returns higher value compared to any other discriminant function. This policy is also followed in a multi-class support vector machine (SVM). That is why these deviations are accumulated only for misclassified samples in the loss function. The loss function in the above considers only positive differences between the functional values between an incorrect class and the true class.

Softmax loss

The functional form of the *softmax loss* or *multinomial logistic regression loss* is as given in Eq. 9.4.

$$\mathcal{L} = -\log(P(Y = y_k | X = x_i)) = -\log\left(\frac{e^{f_k(x_i; \mathbf{W})}}{\sum_j e^{f_j(x_i; \mathbf{W})}}\right) \tag{9.4}$$

where y_k is the true label of x_i, and $f_k(x_i; \mathbf{W})$ is the output corresponding to the k th class from the model. The exponentiation of the latter provides a proportional value to softmax probability, which is normalized by taking sum of these values from outputs of all the classes. We may note here the functional value $f_k(.)$ may be treated as the log of the posterior probability of a class y_k given a sample x, i.e. $log(P(y_k|x))$. Thus, if this probability for the true class is very high, the value of the loss becomes less.

Cross-entropy loss

The *cross entropy loss* is another form of softmax loss. When there are only two classes in data (for example, foreground and background classes), a 2-class entropy loss is used, which is given by Eq. 9.5.

$$\mathcal{L} = -(y \log(p) + (1 - y) \log(1 - p)) \tag{9.5}$$

where p is the softmax probability of foreground class and y is the true class label of the sample. It is 1 for the foreground class and 0 for the background class.

If there are multiple classes (more than two), then the 2-class entropy formulation is extended to compute the loss as given in Eq. 9.6.

$$\mathcal{L} = -\sum_{c=1}^{K} y_{o,c} \log(p_{o,c}) \tag{9.6}$$

where c represents a class, K is the number of classes, $p_{o,c}$ is the probability of the sample o belonging to c, and $y_{o,c}$ is a binary indicator (1 if o belongs to c, else 0). In a more general framework, probability distribution of the true class labels is considered, which is not always binary. That is, instead of binary $y_{o,c}$, the true probability, $q_{o,c}$, of o belonging to c is used, which is used to provide the loss function as shown in Eq. 9.7.

$$\mathcal{L} = -\sum_{c=1}^{K} q_{o,c} \log(p_{o,c}) \tag{9.7}$$

Regularization loss

The regularization loss introduces a factor to keep the model simple. For the model to be simple, the size of $\mathbf{W}$ is desired to be as small as possible. There are different kinds of regularization functions, which put constraints on the values of the $\mathbf{W}$. Let us denote the combined set of weights $\mathbf{W} = \{w_i | i = 1, 2, \dots M\}$, where M is the total number of weights in the model. Some of the typical examples of, regularization function, $\mathcal{R}(\mathbf{W})$, for minimization are as follows:

- L$_2$ regularization (weight decay): $\mathcal{R}(\mathbf{W}) = \sum_{i=1}^{M} w_i^2$.

- L$_1$ regularization: $\mathcal{R}(\mathbf{W}) = \sum_{i=1}^{M} |w_i|$.

- Elastic net (L$_1$ + L$_2$) regularization: $\mathcal{R}(\mathbf{W}) = \sum_{i=1}^{M} (\kappa w_i^2 + |w_i|)$, where κ is a constant.

Numerical Example

The output of a neural network is $[1, 2, 7, 4]$. Find the softmax probability for the class whose output is 7.

Solution

The softmax probability of the class with 7 as the output $[1, 2, 7, 4]$ is
$\frac{e^7}{e^1 + e^2 + e^7 + e^4} = 0.94$.

Numerical Example

Suppose for a single training sample, the true label is $[0\ 0\ 1\ 0\ 0\ 0\ 0]$ while the predictions are $[0.1\ 0.1\ 0.4\ 0.1\ 0.2\ 0.05\ 0.05]$. Calculate the cross entropy loss for this sample (use natural logarithm).

Solution

$L = -\sum y.log(p)$
where, y is the true label and p is the predicted probability. In this case we calculate it as
$L = -[1.log(0.4)] = 0.92$.

9.2.3 | Computing optimal weights

For training a network, the optimization problem given in Eq. 9.8 needs to be solved.

$$\boldsymbol{w}^* = \underset{\boldsymbol{w}}{\operatorname{argmin}}\ g(\boldsymbol{w}) \tag{9.8}$$

where, $g(\boldsymbol{w}) = \sum_{i=1}^{N} l(f(\boldsymbol{x}_i, \boldsymbol{w}), y_i) + \mathcal{R}(\boldsymbol{w})$. Given the objective function of Eq. 9.8, the data loss and regularization loss terms are to be minimized with respect to a set of chosen weights. One way of achieving this may be by using a random search, where some guesses of $\boldsymbol{w}$ iteratively compute the loss, and the minimum out of them is chosen. However, this is a very inefficient way, particularly in higher dimensions. A standard technique used for this purpose is the use of *gradient descent algorithms*.

In a gradient descent algorithm, at first, $\boldsymbol{w}$ is randomly initialized. Then the gradient of $\boldsymbol{w}$, $\nabla g(\boldsymbol{w})$, is computed at the current point at each iteration. For updating the weights, the current point is moved downhill in little steps at each iteration in the space of $\boldsymbol{w}$ as $\boldsymbol{w} = \boldsymbol{w} - \alpha \nabla g(\boldsymbol{w})$, where α is the learning rate that controls the step size for updates. The direction of descent is opposite to the direction of the steepest increase of the gradient, which gives the steepest descent of the gradient values. The term, $\alpha \nabla g(\boldsymbol{w})$ is called the learning factor. This is an iterative process of updating the weights. While training a feed forward network, usually the back propagation algorithm is used, which has two passes: a forward pass and a backward pass. In the forward pass, the network is traversed forward to compute the losses, and in the backward pass the traversal takes place backward to compute the gradients with respect to the loss. This method is particularly found to be efficient in computing the gradients for big and complex models.

9.2.4 | Neural networks for linear regression

Supervised learning may also be considered as a linear regression problem, where both the input and output are vectors. In a linear regression problem, given the input vector $\boldsymbol{x}$, a weighted linear combination of the input with a matrix $\mathbf{W}$ gives another vector $\boldsymbol{y}$, which is expressed by Eq. 9.9.

$$\boldsymbol{y} = f(\boldsymbol{x}, \mathbf{W}) = \mathbf{W}\boldsymbol{x} \tag{9.9}$$

This is a linear model, which is defined by simple matrix multiplication. If the input, $\boldsymbol{x}_i \in \mathbb{R}^{D_{in}}$ and the output, $\boldsymbol{y}_i \in \mathbb{R}^{D_{out}}$, the weight matrix $\mathbf{W} \in \mathbb{R}^{D_{out} \times D_{in}}$. The Euclidean distance may be used as the loss function, which is the norm of the deviations, as given by Eq. 9.10.

$$\ell(\hat{\boldsymbol{y}}, \boldsymbol{y}) = \frac{1}{2}||\hat{\boldsymbol{y}} - \boldsymbol{y}||^2 \tag{9.10}$$

As a linear regression learning problem, the Frobenius norm (sum of squares of elements of the matrix) of $\mathbf{W}$ is used for regularization, which is given by Eq. 9.11.

$$\mathcal{R}(\mathbf{W}) = \lambda||\mathbf{W}||^2_{\text{Frobenius}} \tag{9.11}$$

The corresponding objective function of the learning problem is given by Eq. 9.12.

$$\mathbf{W}^* = \underset{\mathbf{W}}{\text{argmin}} \; \frac{1}{2N} \sum_{i=1}^{N} ||\mathbf{W}\boldsymbol{x}_i - \boldsymbol{y}_i||^2 + \lambda||\mathbf{W}||^2_{\text{Frobenius}} \tag{9.12}$$

This supervised learning may also be performed using the neural network. However, if the network is only a cascade of a sequence of linear layers, the learning problem remains almost the same. Consider an example of a simple network with only two layers. Then, the model is expressed as in Eq. 9.13.

$$\boldsymbol{y} = f(\boldsymbol{x}, \mathbf{W}_1, \mathbf{W}_2) = \mathbf{W}_2\mathbf{W}_1\boldsymbol{x} \tag{9.13}$$

where the weights in the first and second layers are $\mathbf{W}_1 \in \mathbb{R}^{H \times D_{in}}$ and $\mathbf{W}_2 \in \mathbb{R}^{D_{out} \times H}$, respectively, and H is number of nodes in the hidden layer. The net weight matrix may also be represented as, $\mathbf{W} = \mathbf{W}_2\mathbf{W}_1$, since they are linear operations. Hence the model is equivalent to a single layered model and there is not much of advantage having two cascaded layers. Increasing more number of layers also does not make any difference. But, this is not the case if we introduce a nonlinearity in the processing after every layer in the model, as in Eq. 9.14. In this way, the capacity of solving the problem is increased by adding complexity to the model.

$$\boldsymbol{y} = f(\boldsymbol{x}, \mathbf{W}_1, \mathbf{W}_2) = \mathbf{W}_2 \sigma(\mathbf{W}_1 \boldsymbol{x}) \qquad (9.14)$$

where $\sigma : \mathbb{R}^H \to \mathbb{R}^H$ is the introduced element-wise nonlinearity.

9.2.5 | Activation functions

Activation functions are the nonlinear functions (usually, element-wise operations) present in the neural networks. As mentioned in Chapter 7, one of the very often used activation functions in the ANN is the *sigmoid function*, which is given by Eq. 9.15.

$$f(x) = \sigma(x) = \frac{1}{(1 + e^{-x})} \qquad (9.15)$$

where, x is the input value and $\sigma(x)$ is the sigmoid function. A plot of sigmoid function is shown in Fig. 9.4 (a). One of the key properties of this function is that, it squashes the numbers to the range $[0, 1]$. As a result, it kills gradients when the values saturate, where the gradient becomes almost 0. Also, it is not a zero-centered function. Sigmoid function is found to be very appropriate for learning logical functions, which have binary inputs.

Another activation function, called *tan-hyperbolic* ($f(x) = \tanh(x)$) function, has similar saturating properties of the sigmoid function, but it is zero-centered, which is a desirable property (Lecun et al., 1998). This also squashes the gradients to the range $[-1, 1]$ A plot of tan-hyperbolic function is shown in Fig. 9.4 (b).

A very popular activation function in convolution neural network among different neural architectures is the *rectified linear unit* (ReLU) (Krizhevsky et al., 2012). Its functional form is given by $f(x) = \max(0, x)$. So, it is linear for only positive inputs and 0 for negative inputs, as shown in plot of ReLU function in Fig. 9.4 (c). As seen in the figure, there is a nonlinearity as a first order discontinuity at the value 0. As an advantage, the ReLU function does not saturate in the positive region. Also, it converges faster than sigmoid and tanh functions on image data (found to be around six times faster on the average (Krizhevsky et al., 2012)). ReLu function is also found to be computationally very efficient. But, it is not zero-centered function. It is not found to be suitable for modeling logical functions and for control in recurrent nets. If the function is to operate in the negative region (refer to the plot), it never activates since the gradient becomes zero for $x < 0$. So, the parameters (weights and biases) of the network may not get any updates. In such a case, it is a dead zone, and the function stops operating there.

To avoid the case of dead zone in the ReLU, *leaky ReLU* function is used, where a very small increase in the negative region is present to yield small gradients for negative inputs (Maas et al., 2013). The functional form is slightly modified version of ReLU, which is given by $f(x) = \max(0.01x, x)$. A plot of the leaky ReLU function is shown in Fig. 9.4 (d). As advantages of the leaky ReLU, it does not saturate and pushes convergence faster than sigmoid and tanh functions on image data, and the gradients do not die.

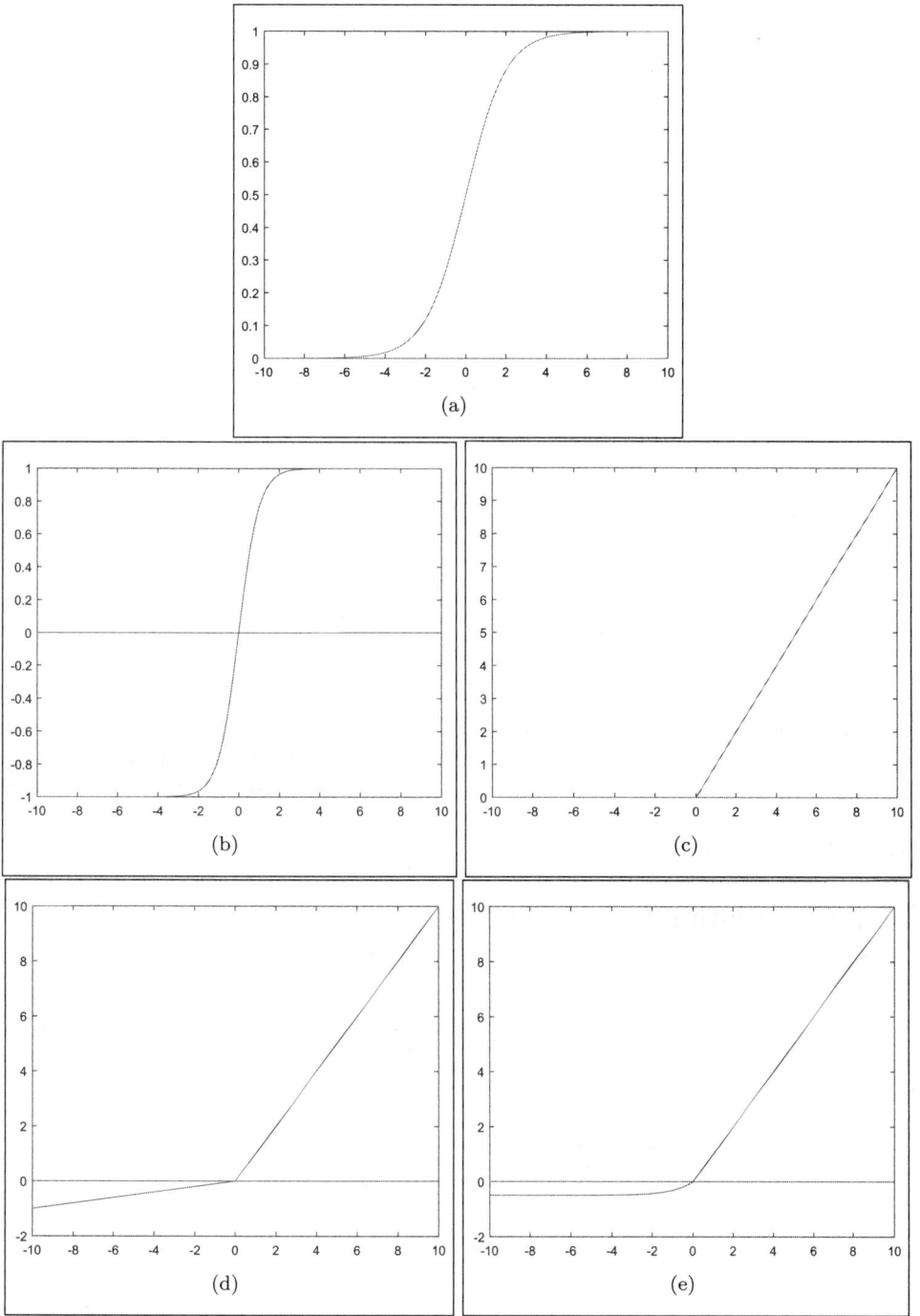

Figure 9.4 Plots of different activation functions: (a) sigmoid function, (b) tanh function, (c) rectified linear unit (ReLU) function, (d) leaky ReLU function, and (e) exponential linear unit function (ELU).

Another widely used activation function, like the ReLU, is the *exponential linear unit* (ELU) (Clevert et al., 2016). The functional form of the ELU is given by Eq. 9.16.

$$f(x) = \begin{cases} x & \text{if } x > 0 \\ \alpha(e^x - 1) & \text{if } x \leq 0 \end{cases} \tag{9.16}$$

The ELU function carries all the benefits of the ReLU, while remaining closer to zero mean outputs and the gradients do not die.

A nonlinear activation function called *maxout neuron* computes the output as maximum of two linear parts, i.e., maximum of two linear combinations of the inputs, which is given by Eq. 9.17 (Goodfellow et al., 2013).

$$f(x) = \max(\boldsymbol{w}_1^\top \boldsymbol{x} + b_1, \boldsymbol{w}_2^\top \boldsymbol{x} + b_2) \tag{9.17}$$

It does not have the basic form of dot product, which shows its nature of nonlinearity. The maxout neuron generalizes the ReLU and the leaky ReLU. As an advantage, this function neither saturates nor dies. But, it increases the complexity of the model as it doubles the number of parameters per neuron.

9.3 | Convolutional neural networks (CNN)

The concepts discussed so far are the general features of neural networks, which are also applicable to deep neural architectures. A specific deep neural architecture, called *convolutional neural network* (CNN), is very popular and extensively used in various applications of image processing and computer vision. The main elements of a typical CNN are, convolution layer, nonlinear layer, pooling layer, fully connected layer, batch normalization (BN), and drop out, which are discussed in this section.

9.3.1 | Convolution layer (CONV)

In a CNN, a *convolution layer* is a hidden layer. For an image of size $W \times H \times D$, a convolution layer is defined with a *filter* (or *kernel*) of size $F_w \times F_h \times d$, which performs convolution operation over the input image with a stride of (S_w, S_h). In this case, S_w and S_h are strides along the directions of width and height, respectively. This filter usually extends the full depth of the input volume, D (therefore, $d = D$), except for certain specific implementations that operate by splitting the channels. So, for simplicity, the filters are usually represented only by their spatial size, $F_w \times F_h$, and it is assumed to extend the full depth of its input volume. Consider an example, as illustrated in Fig. 9.5. Here, in the convolution layer, the input is an image of size $32 \times 32 \times 3$. The depth of three channels may correspond to red, green, and blue channels for an RGB image, or it may be any other three components for other kinds of images represented by three channels. The filter, **w**, that performs the convolution operations over this image is of size $5 \times 5 \times 3$, as shown in the figure. In this example, the depth is 3. This filter spans over points of input, so that it is fully contained within the image, and computes the weighted sum of the pixel values in the neighborhood of the pixel of the same size of the filter by

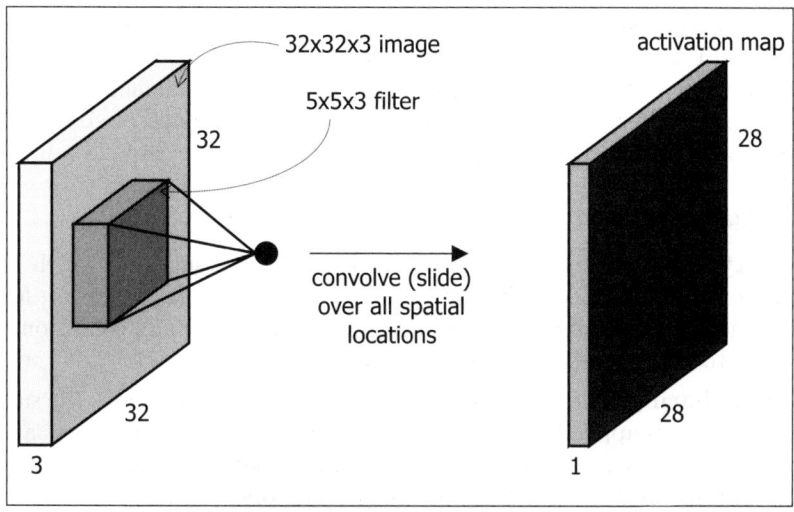

32x32x3 image

5x5x3 filter

32

32

3

convolve (slide)
over all spatial
locations

activation map

28

28

1

Figure 9.5 Convolution layer.

sliding over in steps of S_w and S_h along the directions of width and height of the image, respectively. Effectively, the filter performs scalar dot products with the neighborhood distribution centering the point with the filter weights to produce an output at location of the central pixel of the filter. Though this layer is called convolution layer, the operation is a correlation as discussed in Chapter 1. After performing this operation the weighted sum is added with a bias term, which is also a parameter of the convolution layer. In this typical example, since the filter is of size $5 \times 5 \times 3$, it is a 75-D scalar dot product. Each neuron is associated with a bias term. So, the sum of the bias term and the scalar dot product of the filter is the output at that point. We call this output as the activation of the neuron and the 2-D arrangement of neurons providing this output is called activation map. The output of the convolution layer using a single filter is the 2-D activation map of depth 1. Since the network produces a 2-D activation map, we also call it 2-D CNN (2-D CNN). When multiple filters operate on the same input and produces multiple activation maps of the same size, we refer to each of them as a channel and the stack of channels is taken as the output from the convolution layer.

Let us typically illustrate this computation with the same input and filter sizes. As the computation takes place at only those pixels that are fully embedded within the image, the filter or the convolution mask reduces the size of the activation map of the convolution layer. In the example, since the filter is of size 5×5, two pixels have to be left out at each of the borders along the height and width of the image. These pixels at the border are not fully embedded with respected to the filter placement over them. The step sizes of sliding over the image are $S_w = 1$ and $S_h = 1$. So, the size of the activation map, which is the output of the convolution layer, is 28×28. Also, along depth, other planes are not coming into picture since they are not fully embedded. That is, the convolutions for only the central pixels in the central plane (or channel) are considered here, because full embedding is available only for those pixels. As there can be more than one convolution filters in a convolution layer, for K

number of convolution filters, there are K activation maps in the convolution layer. In the example shown in Fig. 9.6, consider six filters that are of the same size, $5 \times 5 \times 3$. However, their weights are different. Then each of these six filters produces an activation map. Hence, if there are six such filters, there are six separate activation maps of size 28×28. These six activation maps are stacked to get the output image of size $28 \times 28 \times 6$, as shown in Fig. 9.6.

The following are the main features of a convolution layer.

(i) **Locality**: The objects tend to have a local spatial support, which is exploited using convolution (effectively, the operation is correlation.[3] However, following the convention in the literature of deep learning for avoiding any confusion, henceforth we refer to this operation as convolution).

(ii) **Weight sharing**: The units connected to different locations have the same weights, and each unit is applied to all the locations. The weights of the filters are invariant. Since the convolution is performed over all the spatial locations, same weights are used that are shared at each scalar dot product operation.

(iii) **Translation invariance**: The appearance of objects is independent of location, since convolution operation yields the same response irrespective of their spatial position in the image.

(iv) **Receptive field**: Each unit output of filter is connected to a local rectangular area in the input, which is called *receptive field*.

In our subsequent discussion while describing an architecture we use the short keyword CONV to denote a convolution layer.

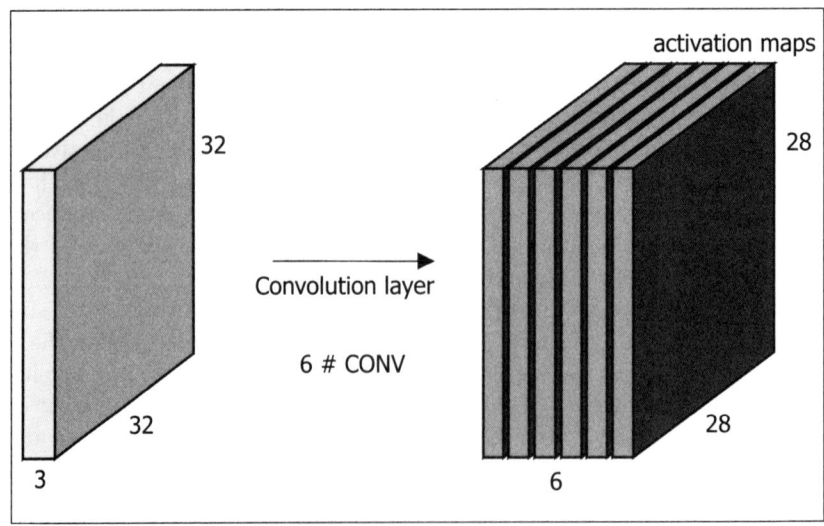

Figure 9.6 Activation maps.

---

[3] The convolution with a filter which is formed by the reflection of weights such as $w(i, j) = w(-i, -j)$, where the center of the filter is $(0, 0)$, provides the same output as the correlation operation does here. Hence, mathematically we may also relate to the activation map to a true convolution operation.

Numerical Example

Consider a 3-channeled input to a convolutional layer with 64 kernels. The size of the input is 50×30. The input is convoluted using stride 2 with 2×2 kernels. What is the dimension of the feature map?

Solution

$(\frac{50-2}{2}+1) \times (\frac{30-2}{2}+1) \times 64 = 25 \times 15 \times 64$

Numerical Example

Consider a model with three convolutional layers, CONV1, CONV2 and CONV3. The specifications of the layers are given below:
CONV1: It takes 8 input channels. It has 16 kernels of dimension 3×3.
CONV2: It is stacked after CONV1. It has 32 kernels of dimension 5×5.
CONV3: It is stacked after CONV2. It has 4 kernels of dimension 3×3.
Find the number of input channels of CONV2.

Solution

The number of input channels of CONV2 = the number of output channels of CONV1 = number of kernels in CONV1 = 16.

Numerical Example

Consider a 3-channeled input to a convolutional layer with 4 kernels. The size of the input is 32×40. The input is convoluted using stride 2 with 2×2 kernels. What is the dimension of the feature map?

Solution

width of activation map $= \frac{\text{width of input layer-width of kernel} + 2 \times \text{padding}}{\text{stride}} + 1$

height of activation map $= \frac{\text{height of input layer-height of kernel} + 2 \times \text{padding}}{\text{stride}} + 1$

output channel = number of kernels

Consider the dimension of the activation map to be $W \times H \times D$. Then each of the following is given by:

$W = \frac{32-2}{2} + 1$

$H = \frac{40-2}{2} + 1$

$D = 4$. Hence the dimension of the feature map $= 16 \times 20 \times 4$.

Number of parameters involved in a convolution layer

Let the input image be of size $W_1 \times H_1 \times D_1$. Let there be K number of filters, each of size $F_w \times F_h \times D_1$. Since the filter needs to have the same number of channels (the depth) as in the input image, the depth, D_1 is the same in the image and the filters. Also, since the operation in a convolution layer requires to have a filter fully embedded within the input image, each filter provides only a single channel output. The stride parameters control the grid points, where convolutions are performed. If convolutions are performed at every adjacent pixel locations along both width and height of the image, the stride is $(1, 1)$. If convolutions are performed at every alternate pixel locations along both width and height of the image, the stride is $(2, 2)$. Similarly, when the convolutions are performed by leaving $S_w - 1$ pixel locations along width and $S_h - 1$ pixel locations along height between every stride of the filter, the stride is (S_w, S_h). If the activation maps are desired to have the same width and height of the input image, the input image is zero-padded on the borders before filtering. Thus, if the boundary pixels of the image are to be included in the convolution operation, the input image is padded with required number of 0s at the borders and then the convolution operation is performed. Let the padding along the width and height of the input image be (P_w, P_h). This makes the resulting size of the output channel as $(W_1 + 2P_w) \times (W_2 + 2P_h)$. Let the size of the output volume be $W_2 \times H_2 \times D_2$

The output dimensions are related to the values of input sizes, number of filters, filter sizes, strides, and padding sizes. The values of W_2, H_2, and D_2 are given by Eq. 9.18.

$$
\begin{aligned}
W_2 &= \frac{W_1 - F_w + 2P_w}{S_w} + 1 \\
H_2 &= \frac{H_1 - F_h + 2P_h}{S_h} + 1 \\
D_2 &= K
\end{aligned}
\tag{9.18}
$$

So, the number of parameters involved in a convolution layer depends on the number of weights in each of the filters and the number of filters. The number of weights in each filter is $F_w \times F_h \times D_1$. Since there are K number of filters, there will be K times the weights and K number of bias terms (one bias term from each neuron). Assuming all the filters in the convolution layer to be of the same size, the number of parameters in the convolution layer is given by Eq. 9.19.

$$
\text{Number of parameters} = (F_w F_h D_1)K + K
\tag{9.19}
$$

In the output image of the convolution layer, its dth depth slice of is the result of convolution of dth filter over the padded input volume with a given stride, and then the filtered values are added by the dth bias.

9.3.2 | Nonlinearity layer (NL)

There is a nonlinear function in each neuron. After a convolution layer, the nonlinearity at every point is considered as a response of a layer from the system, known as the *nonlinearity layer*. The input to the nonlinearity layer is the output of the convolution layer. Here, every pixel undergoes through a stage of nonlinear operation. This introduces element-wise

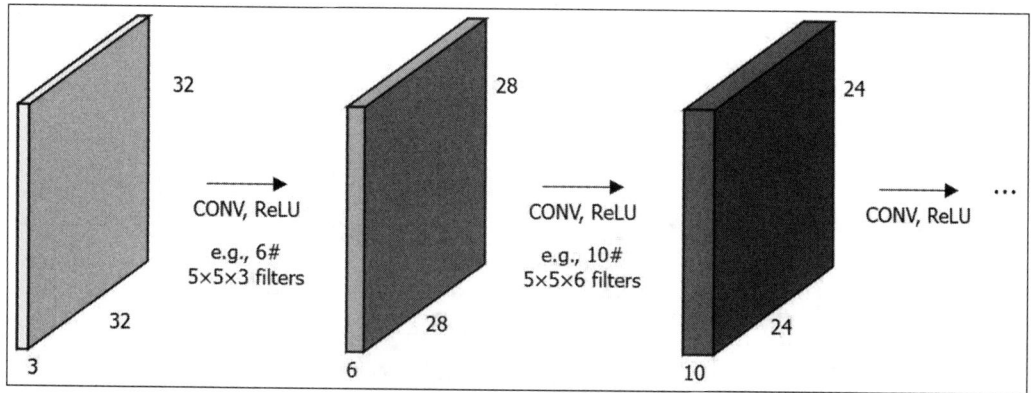

Figure 9.7 Nonlinear layer.

nonlinearity, which increases overall nonlinearity of the entire network architecture without affecting the respective fields of convolutional layer. It helps in further generalizing the model. In the processing of a CNN on image data, ReLU is the commonly used nonlinearity function. In its simplest form, a CNN is a sequence of convolution layers and nonlinearities. An example is shown in Fig. 9.7, where each layer is composed of a convolution layer and a ReLU. In our subsequent discussion while describing an architecture, we use the short keyword NL to denote a nonlinear layer.

9.3.3 | Pooling layer (POOL)

There is another kind of layer in a CNN called the *pooling layer*. The pooling layer is used to progressively reduce the spatial size of the representation, as illustrated in Fig. 9.8. The reduction in the spatial representation is mainly done for two reasons: (1) to reduce the size of activation map leading to reduction of number of parameters and computation in successive stages of the network, and (2) to perform operations at a larger scale of neighborhood processing. The reduction in the number of parameters also controls over-fitting of the model. The pooling operation partitions the input image into a set of non-overlapping rectangles. For each sub-region of the image, an aggregated value of the features in that region is computed.

In the example shown in Fig. 9.8, the input is of size $224 \times 224 \times 64$, which is max pooled with a 2×2 filter. This is equivalent to having a stride of 2 (leaving every alternate sample), which results in an output spatial size of half of the input size, $112 \times 112 \times 64$. It should be noted that the number of depth channels remains the same after pooling operation. This aggregation may be performed in two ways:

(**i**) Max pooling, which considers the maximum value of the region.

(**ii**) Average pooling, which takes the mean value of the region.

An example of max pooling is shown in Fig. 9.9, where a small block of image is considered with each partitioned sub-region coded in the same shade before pooling. The pooling layer operates over each of the activation maps independently.

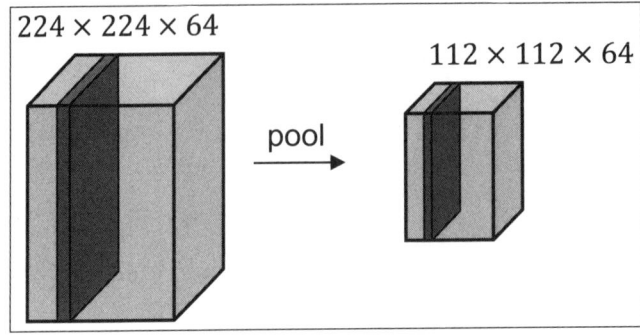

Figure 9.8 Pooling layer.

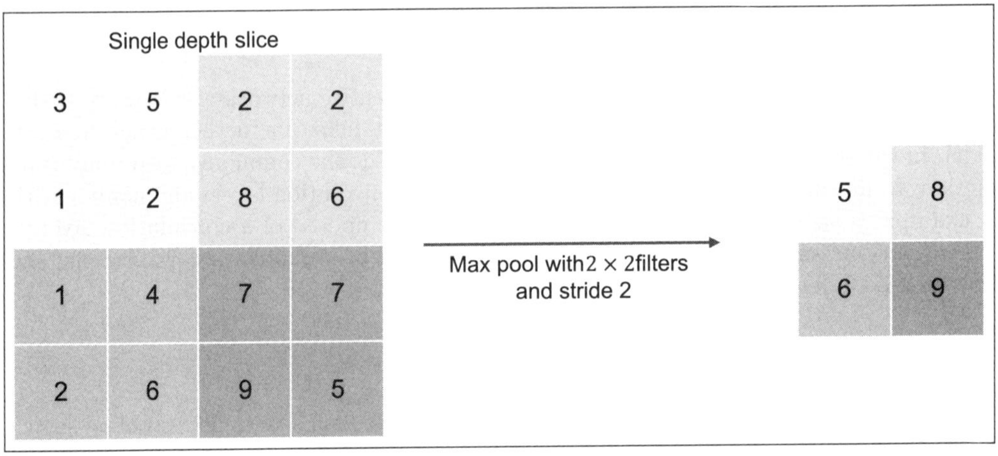

Single depth slice			

3 5 2 2

1 2 8 6   5 8

1 4 7 7   Max pool with 2 × 2 filters   6 9
                   and stride 2

2 6 9 5

Figure 9.9 Example of max pooling.

Consider an input volume of size $W_1 \times H_1 \times D_1$. Let the pool size be $F_w \times F_h$ with stride (S_w, S_h). Let the output volume size be $W_2 \times H_2 \times D_2$. The output dimensions are related to the input dimensions, pool size, and strides, as given by Eq. 9.20.

$$W_2 = \frac{W_1 - F_w}{S_w} + 1$$
$$H_2 = \frac{H_1 - F_h}{S_h} + 1 \qquad (9.20)$$
$$D_2 = D_1$$

In this case, the number of depth channels remains the same as in the input. It is very uncommon to use any padding in a pooling layer. Since there are no weights or bias involved in this computation, there are no parameters involved in this operation. So, the number of parameters in the pooling layer is 0. In our subsequent discussion while describing an architecture we use the short keyword POOL to denote a pooling layer.

Numerical Example

Suppose a convolution layer C has number of input channel $= 3$, number of output channel $= 32$ and a kernel size $= 3 \times 3$ and a pooling layer P has a kernel of size $= 2 \times 2$. Compute the number of parameters for each of these layers.

Solution

Number of parameters in convolution layer $=$ (input channel $\times$ kernel height $\times$ kernel width $\times$ output channel) $+$ output channel $= 896$ Number of parameters in the pooling layer $= 0$.

9.3.4 | Fully connected layer (FC)

A *fully connected layer* follows the last convolution layer of a CNN toward the output end of the network. The output activation maps of the final convolution layer of size $W \times H \times D$ is unfolded to form a vector of length WHD. This becomes the input to a fully connected neural network (FCNN) which is the fully connected layer of the model. The input to the fully connected layer may be interpreted as follows:

(i) The input vector may be treated as deep features.

(ii) The input vector may also be treated as an embedding vector, a representation of an instance of the class in a feature space.

In our subsequent discussion while describing an architecture we use the short keyword FC to denote a fully connected layer.

9.3.5 | Batch normalization (BN)

Various operations are required for efficient training and testing of a CNN, which support effective computations of CNN. One of such operations is known as *batch normalization*, which conditions the input and the intermediate responses. It normalizes the input activation map to a layer by considering its distribution over a batch of training samples. Using BN, the gradient flow through the network may be improved. This allows for higher learning rates, so that, the convergence becomes faster. Also, BN reduces the strong dependence on initialization and acts as a form of regularization of the network. BN is usually inserted after a fully connected or convolution layer, before the nonlinearity.

Computationally, normalization is achieved by subtracting the mean of responses of a batch and dividing it by their standard deviation. Then, the resultant output operation is transformed by scaling and translation by parameters, γ and β, respectively. These parameters are also learned by the gradient descent algorithm. During test time, running averages and standard deviations of the activation maps are used, along with learnt parameters γ and β, for each channel at a layer. The algorithm for the BN may be described as given below. In our subsequent discussion while describing an architecture we

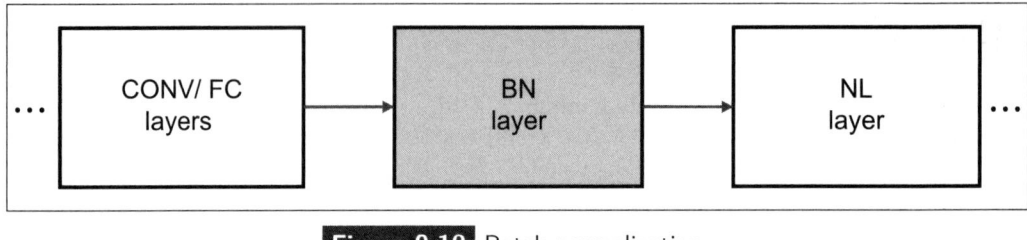

Figure 9.10 Batch normalization.

use the short keyword BN to denote BN. A BN layer takes input from CONV or FC layers and processes it for the NL layer as shown in Fig. 9.10.

Algorithm 17 Algorithm for batch normalization.

    Input: Values of x over a mini-batch of size m: B $= \{x_{1\ldots m}\}$; parameters to be learned: γ, β

    Output: $\{y_i = \text{BN}_{\gamma,\beta}(x_i)\}$

1: Compute mean of mini-batch: $\mu_\text{B} \leftarrow \frac{1}{m}\sum_{i=1}^{m} x_i$.

2: Compute variance of mini-batch: $\sigma_\text{B}^2 \leftarrow \frac{1}{m}\sum_{i=1}^{m}(x_i - \mu_\text{B})^2$.

3: Normalize the values of x: $\hat{x}_i \leftarrow \frac{x_i - \mu_\text{B}}{\sqrt{\sigma_\text{B}^2 + \epsilon}}$. ϵ is a small positive constant to handle very low variance in a mini-batch.

4: Scale and shift $\hat{x}$: $y_i \leftarrow \gamma\hat{x}_i + \beta$.

9.3.6 | Drop out

Another operation that is commonly used for improving the generalization of the model is known as *drop out* (Srivastava et al., 2014). It randomly drops out the nodes of the network at hidden and visible layers during the training phase. The dropping out is achieved by temporarily removing a node from the network, along with all its incoming and outgoing connections. This is done to regulate over-fitting, which is found to be more effective for smaller datasets. This operation simulates the learning of sparse representation in hidden layers. In implementation of dropout, output of a node is retained with a probability p, which is typically in $[0.5, 1]$ at hidden layers and in $[0.8, 1]$ in visible layers (input and output layers).

While learning the weights with drop out, the weights become larger due to the effect of drop out. So, the weights are to be scaled at the end of the training phase. As a simple heuristic, if the outgoing weights of a unit node are retained with probability p during training, they have to be multiplied by p at the test time. This scaling operation may be performed during the training time at each weight update, so that, it is not required to rescale the weights for the test network.

Numerical Example

Consider a model with two convolution layers, CONV1 and CONV2. The CONV2 layer is followed by a MAXPOOL layer. The specifications of the three layers are given below:
CONV1: It takes 3 input channels. It has 8 kernels of dimension 3×3.
CONV2: It is stacked after conv1. It has 16 kernels of dimension 5×5.
MAXPOOL: Pooling layer with kernel size of 2×2.

   (i) Compute the number of input channels of CONV2.

   (ii) Compute the number of parameters in CONV2.

   (iii) Number of parameters in the pooling layer.

Solution

   (i) The number of input channels of CONV2 = the number of output channels of CONV1 = number of kernels in CONV1 = 8.

   (ii) The number of parameters in CONV2 = $8 \times 5 \times 5 \times 16 + 16 = 3216$

   (iii) No parameter required for a pooling layer. Hence it is 0.

9.4 | CNN architectures

There are various CNN architectures that are developed for different computer vision applications. In this chapter we cover a few such applications, namely image classification, object localization and recognition, and image segmentation. Some of the popular architectures under each of these applications are briefly discussed in the following sections.

9.4.1 | CNN architectures for image classification

In this section we discuss architectures of CNNs used for image classification and their evolution.

LeNet

One of the very first DNNs that was reported in 1998 for the application of image classification is called *LeNet* (Lecun et al., 1998). This network was particularly proposed for document image processing or character recognition. This network demonstrated the gradient based learning in application to document recognition. The architecture of the LeNet consists of two convolution layers, two pooling layers, and two fully connected layers, which are stacked as shown in Fig. 9.11. Here, the pooling layers are adjacent to the convolution layers. The output layer follows two fully connected layers. The number of parameters in the LeNet is 60000 and the number of floating point operations per inference is 341000. Here, sigmoid function is used as a nonlinearity function with CONV.

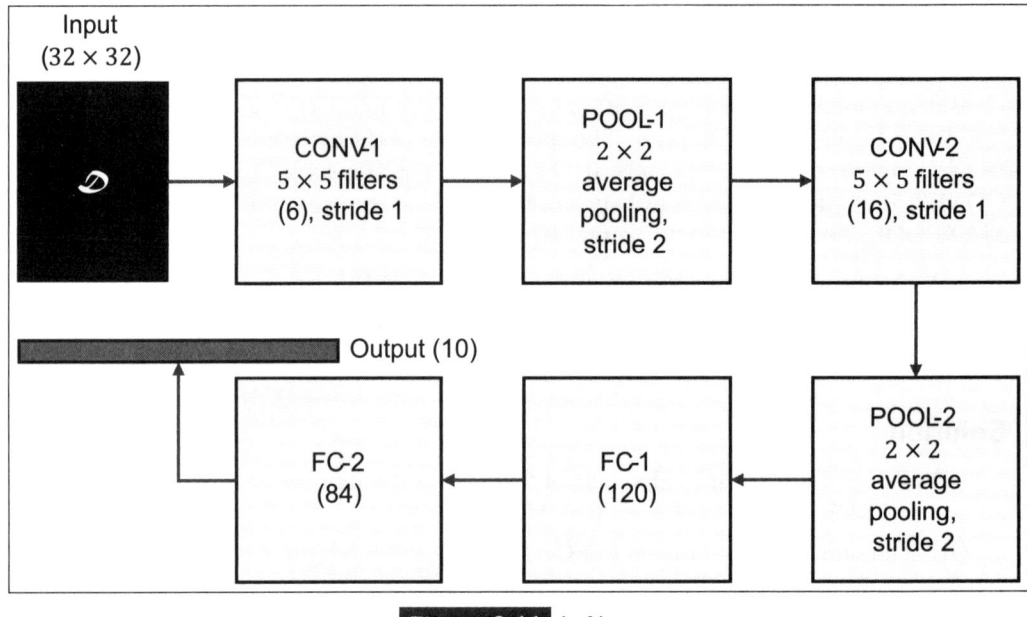

Figure 9.11 LeNet.

AlexNet

In 2012, another network was reported, known as *AlexNet* (Krizhevsky et al., 2012), which provided very good results for image classification problem. This network uses local response normalization (LRN) in its functionality. The architecture of AlexNet consists of five convolution layers and three pooling layers, which is shown in Fig. 9.12. Here, by design, the first two pooling layers are adjacent to their convolution layers, but the last pooling layer operates after getting the processed data through three consecutive convolution layers. The normalization operations are performed after the first and the second pooling layers. The output is tapped after three fully connected layers. It processes inputs of size $227 \times 227 \times 3$. The filters are of size 11×11 and the max pooling is performed using 5×5 kernel. The feature representation is of 4096 dimensions, which are classified for the 1000 nodes at the output. The number of weights in the AlexNet is 61 million, and the number of floating point operations is 724 million. In comparison to the primitive LeNet, the AlexNet is a very large network. Here, as one of the major change in nonlinear functions in neural network, the *ReLU* has been used for nonlinearity with a CONV layer.

ZFNet

The *ZFNet* (Zeiler and Fergus, 2014) is a deep network that is very much similar to the AlexNet. In fact, the ZFNet came from the AlexNet, with some modifications to the size and the number of filters used in the CONV layers. In the architecture of the AlexNet, the filter size in CONV1 is reduced from 11×11 with stride of 4 to 7×7 with stride of 2.

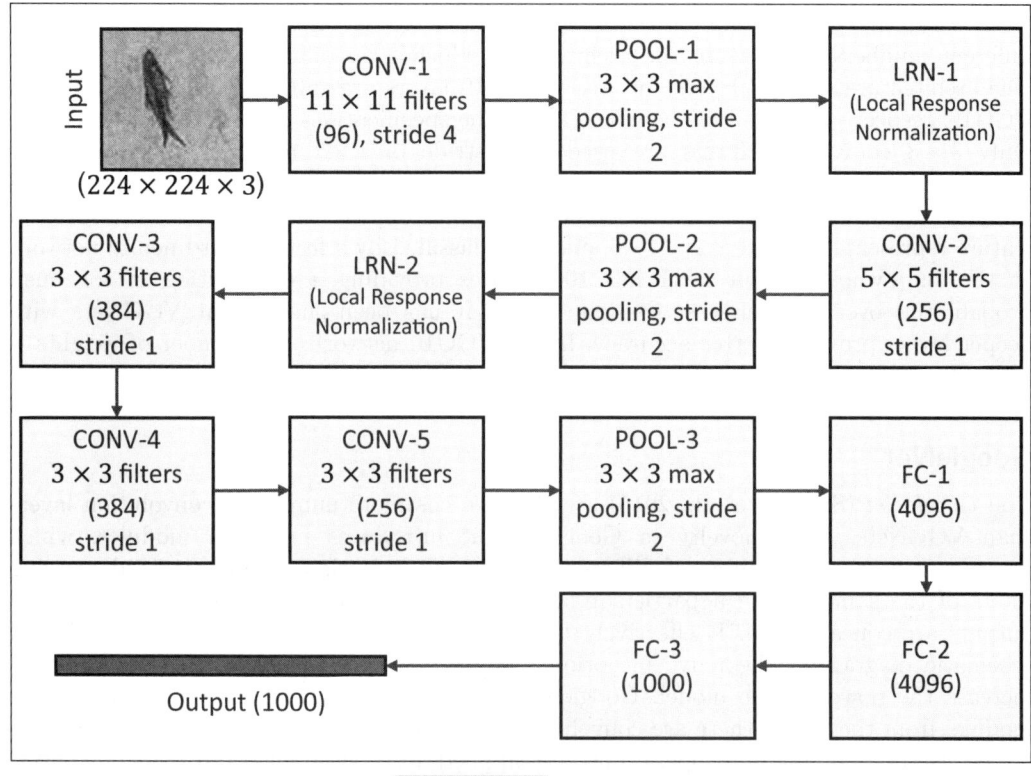

Figure 9.12 AlexNet.

In CONV-3, CONV-4, and CONV-5 of AlexNet, the number of filters were increased from 384, 384, and 256 filters to 512, 1024, and 512 filters, respectively. These changes on AlexNet formed the ZFNet, which is found to improve the accuracy of the image classification on the ImageNet dataset. The top-5 error in ImageNet dataset was reduced from 16.4% to 11.7% using the ZFNet.

VGGNet

In the evolution of CNN architectures, the next significant improvement was brought by the *VGGNet* (Simonyan and Zisserman, 2015). In this architecture, the number of deep layers is increased considerably. Here, the idea is to have smaller filters and deeper layers. For example, a stack of three convolution layers with 3×3 filters has the same receptive field as that of a convolution layer operated with 7×7 filter. This is done by successively applying three convolution operations on an image with 3×3 filter to equivalently produce the same receptive field of a 7×7 filter operating at a single convolution. But, as an advantage, using smaller filters increase the depth of the network, which introduces more nonlinearities in the network. Also, successive use of smaller filters requires fewer number of parameters than an equivalent filter of larger size. For example, for C channels per layer, with the use of three 3×3 filters, the number of parameters is $3(3^2C^2) = 27C^2$. Whereas, using one 7×7 filter requires $(7^2C^2) = 49C^2$ number of parameters.

By this, the performance of the image classification is improved further. There are different numbers of layers in the architecture, which form different kinds of VGGNets. The architecture with 13 layers, 16 layers, and 19 layers are called VGG13, VGG16, and VGG19, respectively. In all of these VGGNets, the specifications of filters are very simple. Only 3×3 convolution filters are used with stride of 1×1 and the max pooling is performed with 2×2 kernels with stride of 2×2. The typical size of input for VGG16 network starts from $224 \times 224 \times 3$, which is down-sampled till 7×7. This provides a feature representation of $1 \times 1 \times 4096$, and it is classified by a feed forward neural network at the end, whose output layer has 1000 nodes providing a distribution of soft max probabilities over 1000 classes. Experimentally, it has been shown that VGGNets with deeper layers provided better accuracy. In the VGG16 network, the number of weights is 138 million and the number of floating point operations is 15.5 billion.

GoogleNet

The *GoogleNet* (Szegedy et al., 2015) architecture has more number of convolution layers than VGGNets. As a novelty in GoogleNet, it introduces inception modules, which concatenates output of filters of different sizes. In an inception module, instead of using filters of the same size in a particular layer, filters of different sizes are used and their outputs are concatenated. It effectively facilitates learning features at different scales. A schematic diagram of the naive inception module is shown Fig. 9.13. This is found to increase the power of the model. GoogleNet has only one fully connected layer. In this module, from the input, there are convolution filters of three sizes: 1×1, 3×3, and 5×5 filters. Here, parallel filter operations are applied on the input from previous layer. Different sizes of filters correspond to sizes of multiple receptive fields for convolution. Here, 1×1 filter performs filtering only along the depth. The number of filters with different sizes are also different. There are 128 1×1 filters, 192 3×3 filters, and 96 5×5 filters in the shown example. Besides, there is a 3×3 pooling, which does not require any

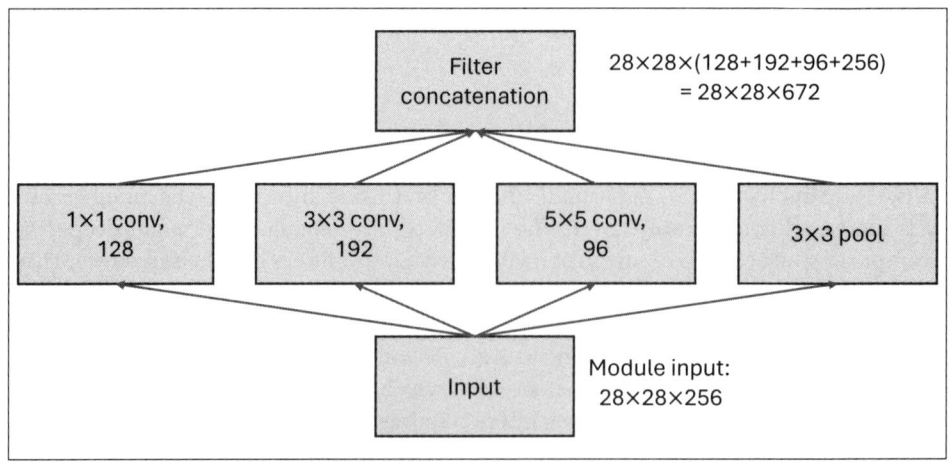

Figure 9.13 Naive inception module.

number of filters. The pooling retains the same depth value as in the input. The output of convolution from 128 1×1 filters is a $28 \times 28 \times 128$ image. Similarly, for 192 3×3 filter and 96 5×5 filters, the output of convolution yields images of size $28 \times 28 \times 192$ and $28 \times 28 \times 96$, respectively. Here, in this inception module, the convolutions are performed with zero-padding of the input to keep the output sizes same as the input size. The output of the 3×3 pooling, with no stride, is of size $28 \times 28 \times 256$, which is the same as input size. The output of the inception module is obtained by concatenation of all the filter outputs together, depth-wise. So, the total output size, after concatenation of all the individual outputs, is $28 \times 28 \times 672$. In the inception model, the number of channels keep varying at different points of operation.

The naive inception module concatenates the outputs of filters with multiple receptive fields, which increases the number of channels in the output of the module. Also, it is very expensive to compute all the convolutions with original depth of the input. Since the pooling layer also preserves the feature depth, the total depth after concatenation only grows at every layer in the naive inception module, which increases parameter count and computations. To tackle this problem, *bottleneck* layers are included, which use 1×1 convolutions to reduce the feature depth while preserving the spatial dimensions. Bottleneck is mainly used for the purpose of reducing the depth of data by reducing the feature representations. A schematic diagram of an inception module with bottleneck is shown Fig. 9.14. Here, the depth of the input data is projected to lower dimension by combination of feature maps, which is achieved by 1×1 convolution filters. In this example, the bottleneck reduces the depth from 256 to 64 using 64 1×1 filters, which is then used in convolution operations using filters of different sizes. A bottleneck is also used after the pooling layer to reduce the number of feature maps further. By using bottlenecks, the number of computations is also reduced, in comparison with the naive inception module.

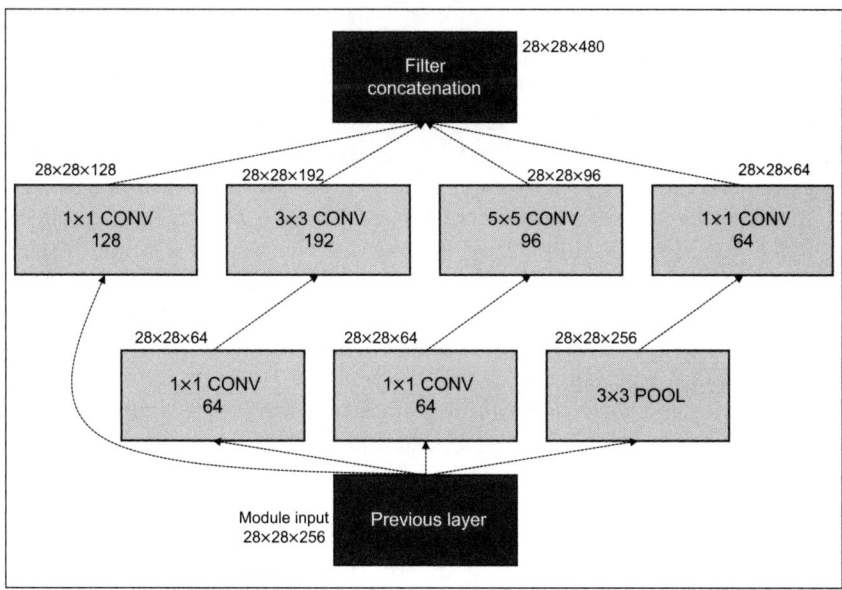

Figure 9.14 Inception module with bottleneck.

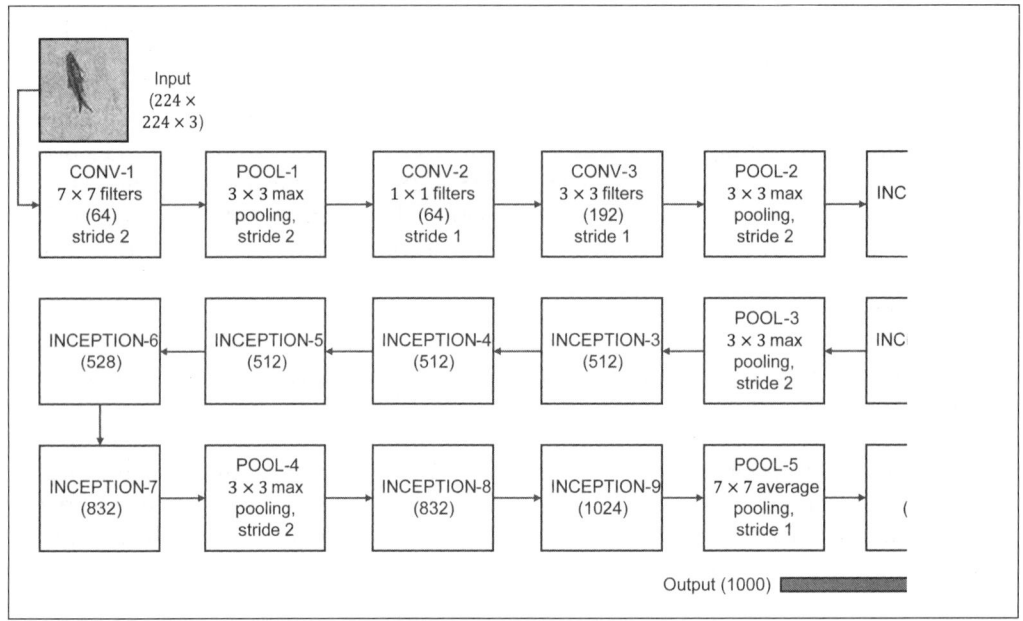

Figure 9.15 GoogleNet.

An example of GoogleNet architecture with 9 inception modules consists of convolution layers, pooling layers, inception layers, and pooling of inception layers, which are stacked as shown in Fig. 9.15. The number of weights in GoogleNet is 7 million and the number of floating point operations is 1.43 billion. GoogleNet is seen to provide a very good performance in image classification with a top-5 error of 6.7%.

ResNet

Residual network or *ResNet* (He et al., 2016) was proposed to address some of the problems observed in deeper models. In deeper models, increase in the number of layers causes over-fitting of the model. Also, as the network gets deeper, the gradients get vanished. It became harder to optimize the network because of the vanishing gradients. As an effect of over-fitting, though a good (low) training error is observed, the test error would be significantly higher. To tackle this issue, a residual network learns the residual errors. In ResNet, network layers are used to fit a residual mapping, instead of directly trying to fit a desired underlying mapping or data. A typical ResNet unit is shown in Fig. 9.16. As seen in the figure, it is learning the residual part. In the figure, the identity connection from the input $\mathbf{x}$ to the addition operator is called *skip connection*. As shown in the figure, due to the skip connection, the input $\mathbf{x}$ is added with its residual part $F(\mathbf{x})$ to get the output $H(\mathbf{x})$. That is, in composing $H(\mathbf{x})$, $F(\mathbf{x})$ is learnt by the network, which is the residual part that is computed as $H(\mathbf{x}) - \mathbf{x}$.

The number of residual layers can go beyond 100. ResNet architectures with varying number of layers such as 34, 50, 101, 152, etc., are tested for the image classification problems.

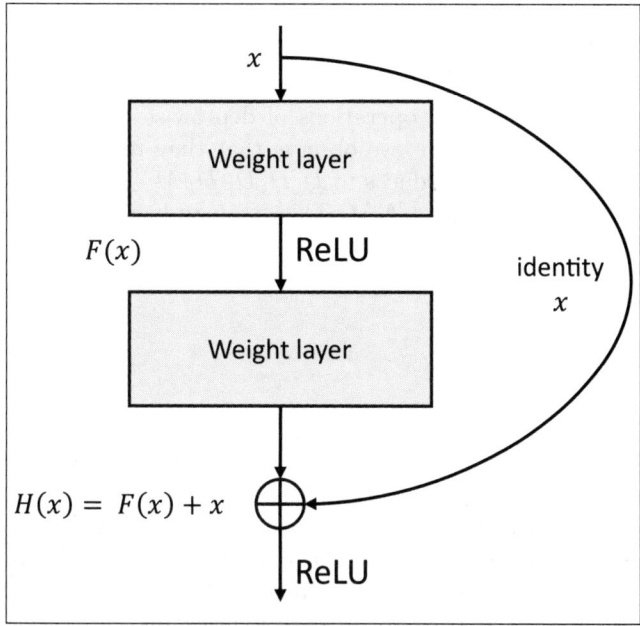

Figure 9.16 ResNet unit.

9.4.2 | MobileNet

The MobileNet architecture (Howard et al., 2017) uses 3×3 depthwise separable convolution, followed by 1×1 pointwise convolution to bring down the number of parameters significantly at the cost of marginal drop in the performance. Let us discuss how the depthwise separable convolution is performed.

Depthwise separable convolution

Suppose, we have $D_F \times D_F \times M$ input feature map. By applying a conventional convolution filters of size $D_k \times D_k \times M$, we obtain an output feature map of dimension $D_F \times D_F$ by assuming appropriate zero padding at the boundaries of the input feature map. Here, we note that, in the conventional convolution layer, the depth of a filter is always kept as the number of channels (or the depth) of the input feature map. Therefore, while mentioning the depth of the input feature map, we may not always explicitly mention the depth of the filter, and denote its dimension as $D_k \times D_k$ as well. If we use N such filters, the output feature map has N channels, and the dimension of the feature map becomes $D_F \times D_F \times N$. The computational cost of this operation is $D_k D_k M D_F D_F N$, and the number of parameters involved is $D_k D_k M N$.

We may also obtain M channels of the output feature map by independently filtering each channel by using a distinct filter of size $D_k \times D_k$. Thus, this operation provides an output feature map of size $D_F \times D_F \times M$. This is known as *depthwise separable convolution*. In this case, sizes of both the input and the output feature maps remain the same after the operation. The cost of this computation is $D_k D_k D_F D_F M$. This output is processed by performing 1×1 pointwise convolution with a filter size of $1 \times 1 \times M$. Hence, the output feature map becomes $D_F \times D_F$. If we use N such 1×1 filters, we have an output feature map of $D_F \times D_F \times N$. Hence, if we compare the size of output feature map of the conventional convolution layer and the combined operations of depthwise convolution and 1×1 point wise convolution, as described before, we observe that they remain the same, though the number of operations in the latter reduces to $D_k D_k D_F D_F M + N D_F D_F M$. The number of parameters also reduces to $D_k D_k M + NM$. This strategy has been adopted in MobileNet architecture providing a feature descriptor of the same dimension using significantly less number of parameters.

The architecture

The MobileNet architecture performs computations using simple CNN layers. It consists of a number of alternate layers of depthwise separable convolution layer and 1×1 pointwise convolution layer. In many of these layers, it also uses strided convolution of stride 2 to reduce the dimensions of the feature map. In the MobileNet V1 (Howard et al., 2017) architecture the first layer is a conventional convolutional layer with 32 3×3 filters with an input image size of $224 \times 224 \times 3$. It is followed by a series of 19 pairs of 3×3 depthwise and 1×1 pointwise convolutional layers. This is followed by an average pooling layer to provide the feature descriptor of size $7 \times 7 \times 1024$, which is fed to a FC layer for the task of classification.

If all the pairs of depthwise separable convolutional layers and 1×1 pointwise convolutional layers are replaced by conventional full convolutional layers, the number of parameters in the model becomes 29.3 Millions. Whereas, for the MobileNet architecture, it is 4.2 Millions. But in the latter model, the drop in accuracy for the ImageNet classification task is very marginal (approximately 1%). The computational cost also significantly reduces from 4.966 billions of operations to 569 millions. In the MobileNet, further reduction of parameters takes place by scaling down the number of channels at each layer. Similarly, the computational cost is reduced by scaling down the resolution of the input and output feature maps in each layer. However, these cause degradation of the performance of the model. But in a resource constraint scenario, there are techniques for deriving optimal scaling down parameters that are obtained to meet a desired performance level, which is a function of accuracy, number of parameters, and computational cost.

EfficientNets (Tan and Le, 2020) are examples of such models, which includes balancing all dimensions of the network, i.e., width, depth and image resolution, against the available resources to get the best overall performance. This is particularly useful in performing a grid search to find the relationship between different scaling dimensions of the baseline network under a fixed resource constraint. Then, the computed coefficients are applied to scale up the baseline network to the desired target model size or computational budget.

There are many other networks in the literature that are proposed for the application of image classification such as,

- Network in Network (NiN)
- Wide Residual Networks
- Aggregated residual transformations for deep neural networks (ResNeXt)

- DenseNets: Provides denser features that are aggregated from several consecutive layers
- SqueezeNet: Provides accuracies similar to AlexNet with fifty times fewer parameters. The model size can be squeezed to < 0.5Mb
- ShuffleNet: Performs grouped convolutions for better feature representations
- FractalNet: Ultra-deep neural networks without any residuals

9.4.3 | Training of neural networks

For training a neural network, the training dataset needs to be pre-processed. There are different kinds of pre-processing operations on the data for the purpose of computation, which depends on the application. Typical stages of pre-processing are briefed here.

At first, the data is normalized with respect to the variances in the data. During normalization, the data is divided by its variances, which normalizes the range. Also, to normalize the mean, the mean of the data is subtracted from the entire dataset. The normalized data is decorrelated by diagonalization of the covariance matrix. Conceptually, this is similar to the principal component analysis. Then, whitening of data is performed by computing the identity covariance matrix.

It may also be required to generalize the dataset because, the labeled dataset (i.e., training dataset) may not capture variances in each of the classes. This step is called *data augmentation*, which is the process of generating more data from the given set of data by performing certain simulations on them. These simulations are performed by different kinds of geometric operations on data, images in particular, like, horizontal flips, vertical flips, random crops, spatial scaling, color jitters by adding different kinds of color variations, adding simulated noise with different variances and distributions, image distortions, geometric transformations, etc. Using such different kinds of simulations on the given input dataset, more data are generated and used in the training process. Then, the weights in the network are initialized by different policies, and the network is trained by updating the weight parameters iteratively.

While training a model, it is better to start with small regularization and with an appropriate learning rate that makes the loss go down. The net loss function is a combination (usually, a linear combination) of the regularization term and the data loss function. While beginning to train the network, it is preferred to keep the regularization component small and tune the learning rate such that, it reduces the net loss with the progress in the training. The network may overfit a small portion of the training data in the initial stages of the training. In the first few epochs of the training, it is good to train the network with few samples from the training set to initiate the hyper-parameters. An introspection of the behavior of the model would help to select those parameters that provide good directions of convergence. Since parameter tuning is very time consuming process, only those selected parameters may be considered for tuning empirically by observing the behavior of the model. This reduces the time of experimentation considerably. If there is a big gap between the training accuracy and the validation accuracy, it is a sign of an overfitting case. In such a case, increasing the regularization term is suggested. If there is no significant gap in the accuracy, the model capacity may be increased.

Transfer learning

One of the policy for initialization of the weights is called *transfer learning* (Donahue et al., 2014; Razavian et al., 2014). Usually deep learning requires a lot of data to train a network. Transfer learning makes it possible to work with deep learning paradigm, even if the data set is not exhaustive. In this case, a large dataset may not be required to train a CNN. This is achieved by using a pre-trained network (or model), which has been trained using a very large data set for some applications, for initialization of the network at the early stage of the training. That is, the feature representation of a pre-trained network is used in the new network that needs to be trained. For example, consider training a network shown in Fig. 9.17 (a) that is trained on a large dataset. As shown in Fig. 9.17 (a), in this network, there are two cascaded CNN layers (CNN1 and CNN2) followed by two cascaded FC layers (FC1 and FC2) toward the output end.

For the same network to be trained on a small dataset, B, the portion of the network, the FC2, shown in a dashed bigger rectangular box in the Fig. 9.17 (b) is considered for retraining. This layer provides inference on the feature representations of the data. Since the architecture is the same, the entire feature representation in the network trained by the dataset A is kept fixed and frozen for any further changes, and its learnt weights are transferred directly to the new network. Here, the constraint is to have the same architectures, so that the weights can be transferred and used to learn the features. Then, only the output layer is trained. That is, in the final classifier, only the reinitialized part (the final layer) of the network is trained for the classification problem defined on the small dataset.

If the dataset B is large, then other different kinds of policies are used to suit the application. For example, all the fully connected layers of the network shown in Fig. 9.17 (c),

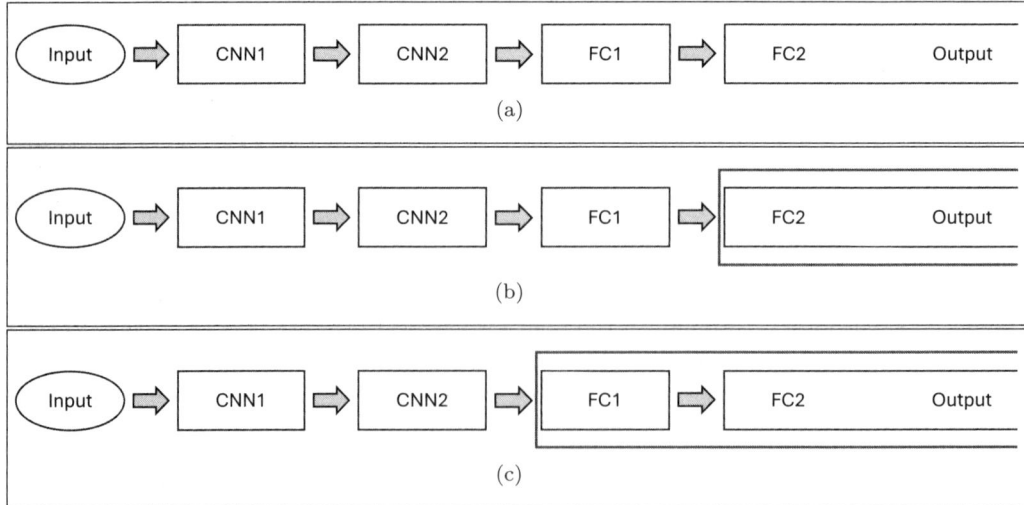

Figure 9.17 Illustration of transfer learning. (a) Trained on a large dataset, A. (b) FC2 retrained keeping weights of other layers fixed on a small dataset B. (c) FC1 and FC2 retrained keeping weights of other layers fixed on a relatively larger dataset.

are retrained by keeping the feature representations frozen from the learnt network. After achieving convergence of the weights, then the network can be fine-tuned with a relatively lower learning rate. For example, one-tenth of the original learning rate is a good starting point, which can be varied empirically. These are a few pragmatic policies and heuristics that are used while training a DNN, which takes a lot of time and resources.

9.4.4 | Object localization and recognition

The problem of object localization and recognition is to identify the label of an object in the image and detect where the object lies in the image, which is illustrated in Fig. 9.18. Identifying the presence of an object in the image is known as object recognition, which is realized as labels of the objects. Identifying the portion in the image where the object lies, is known as localization, which is realized in the form of a closed polygon or a rectangular box around the object. In most of the works, objects are localized using rectangular boxes, which can be specified by the two diagonal corners of the rectangle in pixel coordinates.

There are various conventional or non-deep learning based methods to localize a probable object. The task of finding the probable regions that contain the object of interest and then

Figure 9.18 Illustration of object localization and recognition. (*Source*: Himadri S. Bhunia, Philips Research, Bengaluru.)

analyzing what object is present in those regions, is called *region proposal*. In general, the stages of object detection and localization are as follows.

- Propose the probable regions.
- Extract and describe those regions by features.
- Use those features to classify the objects of interest in the regions, if present. Otherwise, discard the regions since they do not contain any objects of interest.

Trivially, every type of rectangular block (region) in the image may be searched exhaustively. But this is combinatorially a hard problem. To handle this, some heuristics are used. To form heuristic criteria on a proposed region containing an object, some of the handcrafted features may be used that consider the classes of objects. For example, SIFT or SURF operators, shape descriptors, or any kind of key point detectors and descriptors can be used. The extracted features are then aggregated to define object-level features. These features are then fed to different classification algorithms, like linear classifier, SVM, etc. for recognizing the objects.

In Table 9.1, several proposed approaches combining conventional and deep learning based methods are summarized for performing this task. The first technique is called *Region-based Convolutional Neural Network* (RCNN) (Girshick et al., 2014). It considers the task of region proposals from conventional methods. For this, features are learnt and extracted using CNNs, and then classification is performed using classical learning algorithms like SVM. Here, any handcrafted design of features is not required. In the second technique, known as fast RCNN, conventional techniques are used to obtain the region proposals, and both feature extraction and classification are performed by a DNNs. The third technique is called faster RCNN, where the entire pipeline is performed in a deep neural architecture in an end-to-end fashion.

RCNN with CNN feature extractor

Fig. 9.19 illustrates the computations involved in the *RCNN* as a flow diagram. As shown in the figure, region proposals are extracted over an input image, as depicted by bounding boxes. These regions are proposed using conventional methods, which are extracted and fed to the CNN. The proposed regions are of the same size, since the CNN assumes a fixed input size. Using these regions, features are computed by the CNN, where the last layer of the CNN represents the feature descriptor that is used in a classifier. The classifier is one of

Table 9.1 Different techniques for object localization and recognition.

	Region proposal	Feature extraction	Classification
Pre-CNN	Exhaustive	Handcrafted	Linear
RCNN	Region proposal	CNN	Linear SVM
Fast RCNN	Region proposal	Deep learning	Deep learning
Faster RCNN	Deep learning	Deep learning	Deep learning

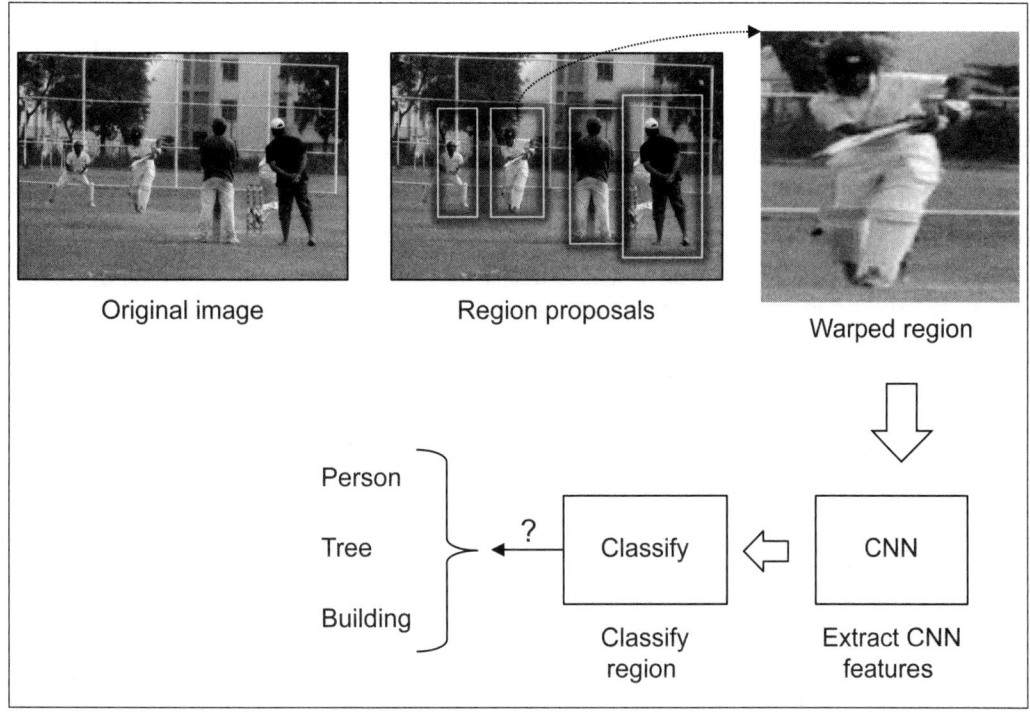

Figure 9.19 Illustration of RCNN.

the conventional classifiers, which is trained to predict the class of the input image, based on the considered target classes in the classifier.

One of the popular conventional techniques for proposing regions is a method based on selective search, which uses hierarchical grouping of image attributes like, color, texture, object size, etc. It performs bottom-up segmentation by merging regions at multiple scales. Based on the properties of these regions, whether any object is contained in it or not is decided by the classifier using extracted feature by the CNN. The inference time, T_{inf} in the RCNN is computed as in Eq. 9.21.

$$T_{\text{inf}} = T_{\text{prop}} + (N_{\text{prop}}T_{\text{CNN}}) + (N_{\text{prop}}T_{\text{Cl}}) \tag{9.21}$$

where, T_{prop} is the time taken for generating all proposals, N_{prop} is the number of proposals generated, T_{CNN} is the time taken to compute the features, and T_{Cl} is the time taken to identify an object in the image.

Fast RCNN

A *fast RCNN* (Girshick, 2015) network is an improvement over the RCNN approach. Here, instead of using a CNN for feature extraction and an SVM for classification, both classification and feature extraction are carried out sequentially using a CNN. That is, every region passes through the feature extraction and classification stages, which are parts of the same network, at the same go. Similar to the RCNN, the regions are proposed using conventional methods. The fast RCNN network takes an entire image and a set of region proposals in the form of bounding boxes of the object proposals as input. The CNN computes a feature map for the whole image. The feature maps in the region of interests (ROIs), formed from the region proposals are processed and pooled to pass it through the classification stage. This is summarized in Fig. 9.20. Given the image, fast RCNN computes the feature set for the whole image using feature extraction stage of the CNN, which are then pooled using the region proposals to feed the classification stage of the CNN to classify the objects.

The inference time in the fast RCNN is computed as in Eq. 9.22.

$$T_{\text{inf}} = T_{\text{prop}} + (1)(T_{\text{CNN}}) + (N_{\text{prop}} T_{\text{Cl}}) \tag{9.22}$$

In the feature extraction stage, since all the features are computed at once, the network uses the convolution only once, unlike RCNN. In fast RCNN, each feature vector is fed to a sequence of fully connected (FC) layers and two sibling output layers. The two sibling output layers are, (1) a layer with softmax probability estimates over K target object classes

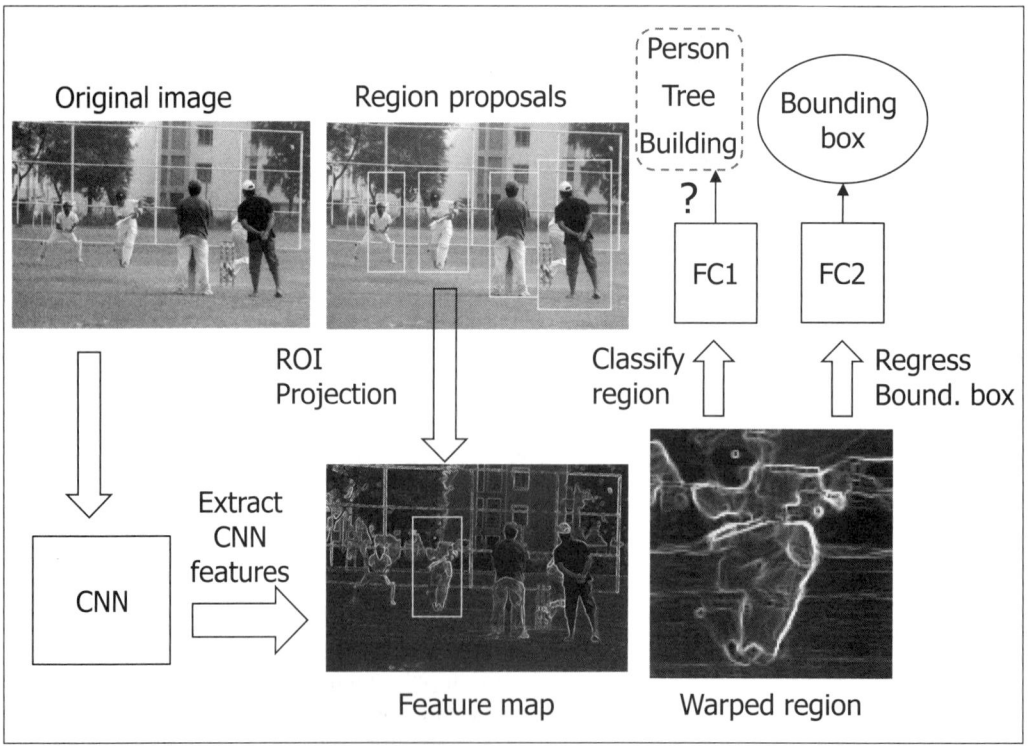

Figure 9.20 Illustration of fast RCNN.

and a catch-all background class, and (2) another layer producing four real-valued numbers, that define a bounding box, for each of the K object classes. This is effectively performing regression of the regions. In the fast RCNN, the CNN is used to generate all the features only one time, which also consists of the proposed regions. These regions in the feature map are used for classification by feeding them to the fully connected layers. Here, the classifier is usually a fully connected feed forward neural network (FCNN) classifier, which is used for both the tasks of classifying the object and finding out the respective region.

The loss that is used in the classification stage, where the fully connected layer is classifying the object while detecting the box (rectangular area) that contains the object, is given by Eq. 9.23.

$$L(p, u, t^u, v) = L_{cls}(p, u) + \lambda[u \geq 1]L_{loc}(t^u, v) \tag{9.23}$$

where u is the true class score, p is the predicted class score, t^u denotes true box coordinates, v denotes predicted box coordinates, $L_{cls}(\cdot)$ is the classification loss, $L_{loc}(\cdot)$ is the smooth L_1 loss, $[u \geq 1]$ evaluates to 1 when $u \geq 1$ and 0 otherwise. $L_{cls}(\cdot)$ and $L_{loc}(\cdot)$ correspond to two components of the loss function for regressing the bounding box of the region containing the object: (1) component due to classification, and (2) component due to the regression, respectively. The hyper-parameter λ controls the balance between two types of losses. It is typically set to 1. Here, only those samples whose classes are object classes, are considered for computing the loss function.

Faster RCNN

Faster RCNN (Ren et al., 2017) is an improvement over the fast RCNN, where the whole task of classification is performed in a convolution network, including the region proposal. Here, a *region proposal network* (RPN) is inserted after the last convolution layer. The RPN is trained to produce region proposals directly, which does not require any provisions for external region proposals. Thus, the features that are generated by the convolution layers are directly used for generating region proposals. These region proposals are pooled and the features in these proposed regions are used for classification. After the RPN, similar to the fast RCNN, RoI pooling, and an upstream classifier and bounding box (bbox) regressor are used. The architecture and the processing pipeline of the faster RCNN is shown in Fig. 9.21. Here, the first stage is to generate a feature map, which is then used to propose regions, classify objects, and regress the rectangular boxes. This is the reason why the faster RCNN is capable of fast processing.

In the RPN, a small window is slided over the feature map to build a small network for, (1) classifying object or non-object, and (2) regressing bounding box locations. Position of the sliding window with respect to the given image is the initial localization. These positions are used to compute finer location at the final stage of classification and regression. The box regression performs the finer localization with respect to the sliding window. The inference time in the faster RCNN is computed as in Eq. 9.24.

$$T_{\text{inf}} = T_{\text{prop}} + (1)(T_{\text{CNN}}) + (N_{\text{prop}}T_{\text{Cl}}) \tag{9.24}$$

In the faster RCNN, there is no separate proposal time, since it is computed by the CNN along with classification and regression. The RPN is depicted in Fig. 9.22. Here, the sliding

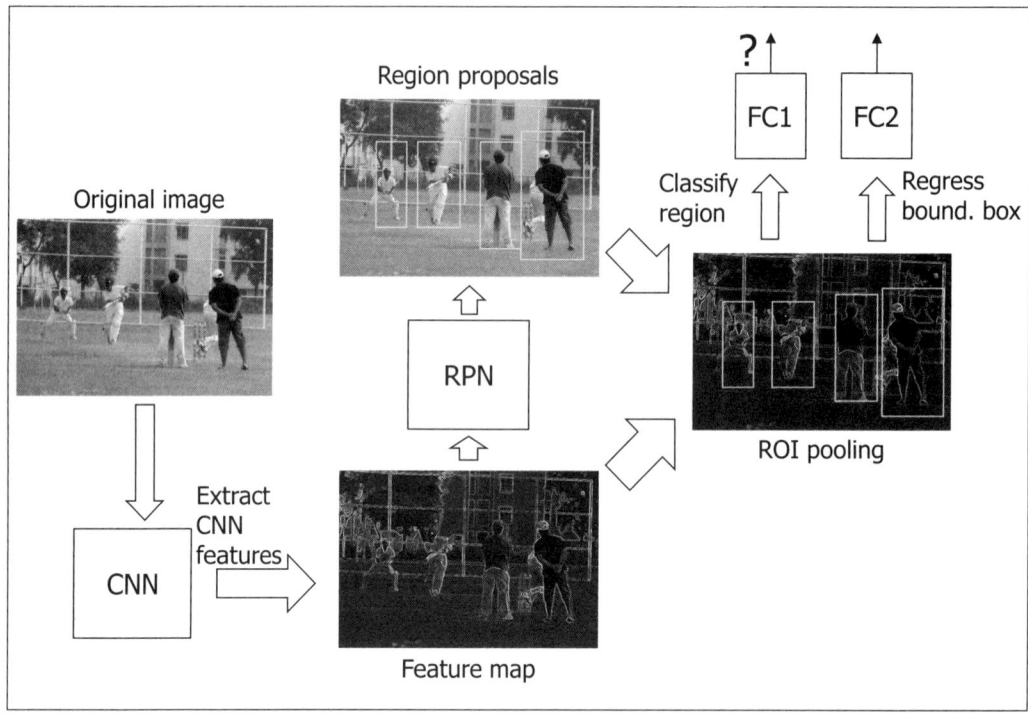

Figure 9.21 The architecture of the faster RCNN.

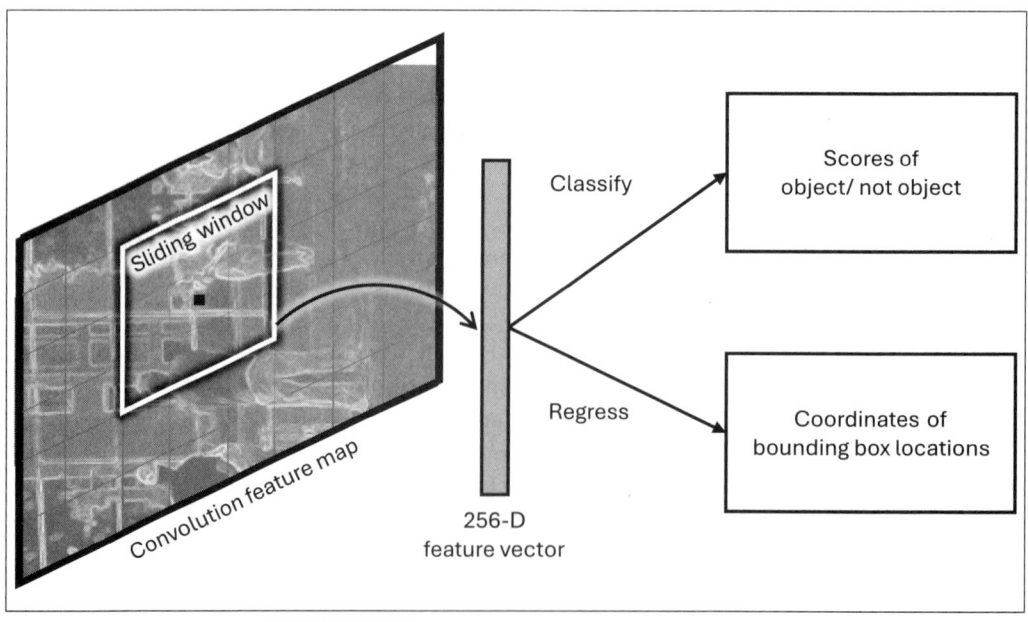

Figure 9.22 Final layer of the faster RCNN.

window in the feature map provides a 256 dimensional feature descriptor. This is used to classify a region as object or non-object and regress the box location.

The loss function for RPN is given by Eq. 9.25.

$$L(\{p_i\}, \{t_i\}) = \frac{1}{N_{cls}} \sum_i L_{cls}(p_1, p_i^*) + \lambda \frac{1}{N_{reg}} \sum_i p_i^* L_{reg}(t_i, t_i^*) \qquad (9.25)$$

where, p_i is the true class score, p_i^* is the predicted class score, t_i denotes true box coordinates, t_i^* denotes predicted box coordinates, $L_{cls}(\cdot)$ is the two class softmax cross entropy loss, $L_{reg}(\cdot)$ is the regression loss, λ is a regression parameter, and N_{cls} and N_{reg} are the numbers of regions contributing to classification and regression losses, respectively. In this loss function, the sliding window may consist of different shapes of windows that may contain a box or an object. If there are k anchor boxes, each of them is tested to check whether it contains an object or not. If the object is present, this box provides the coordinates that are output of this region.

YOLO

YOLO (You Only Look Once) architecture (Redmon et al., 2016) provides a framework of a single stage processing for object localization and recognition. It performs an end to end training for predicting both the bounding boxes (containing an object) and object classes (Fig. 9.23). Thus the network is trained to optimize a loss function taking care of both the errors of localization (a regression loss) and object recognition (a classification loss). The network has 24 convolution layers, followed by two FC layers. A few of the convolution layers are followed by 2×2 max pool layers and 1×1 convolution layers to reduce the size of the feature maps. The training of the model proceeds in the following manner.

(i) It divides the input image into $S \times S$ nonoverlapping grid.

(ii) For each grid, it predicts B boxes containing objects (x, y, w, h) with the confidence scores. A box is specified by its coordinates of the leftmost and bottommost corner point (x, y), width (w), and (h).

(iii) Get soft-max probabilities of n_C object classes using a pre-trained network for the box.

The confidence score in the above is computed as,

$$\text{confidence score} = P(\text{Object}) \text{ IOU-score}$$

Figure 9.23 An example of YOLO processing. (*Source*: Himadri S. Bhunia, Philips Research, Bengaluru.)

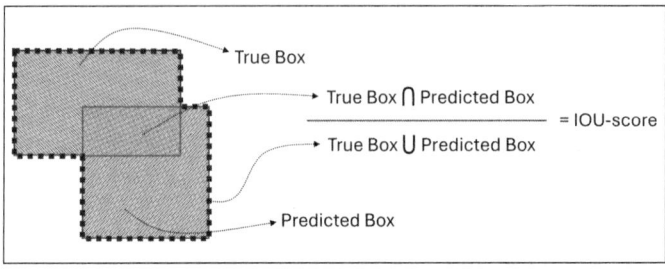

Figure 9.24 Depiction of IOU-score.

Here, $P(\text{Object})$ is the probability of the bounding box being a part of background or an object, and the IOU-score is computed as illustrated in Fig. 9.24 and is defined as follows.

$$\text{IOU-score} = \frac{\text{predicted boxes} \cap \text{true boxes}}{\text{predicted boxes} \cup \text{true boxes}} \tag{9.26}$$

If the box does not contain any object, confidence score is 0. The confidence score is used to filter bounding boxes of low score and also select the box with locally maximum score. The process is known as *non-maximal suppression*. Each bounding box is represented by 4 parameters (x, y, w and h), and it is associated with a confidence score (C) and class probability ($p(c)$) for class c. If n_C is the number of classes, there are ($5 + n_C$) number of output parameters predicted for a box. Since there are B boxes for each grid, the total number of output parameters is $S^2(5B + n_C)$. For example, in Redmon et al. (2016), it is reported that on PASCAL VOC, the values of the hyper parameters are $S = 7$, and $B = 2$. As the PASCAL VOC dataset has 20 labeled classes, the value of n_C is 20. Hence the number of output parameters predicted are $7 \times 7 \times (5 \times 2 + 20) = 1470$.

Loss function Optimization of the YOLO model takes care of three types of loss functions, namely, localization loss, confidence loss, and classification loss. All of these components use the mean squared error (MSE) losses. The expression for the loss function is given below:

$$\begin{aligned}
\text{Loss function: } & \lambda_{\text{coord}} \sum_{i=0}^{S^2} \sum_{j=0}^{B} \mathbb{1}_{ij}^{\text{obj}} \left[(x_i - \hat{x}_i)^2 + (y_i - \hat{y}_i)^2 \right] + \\
& \lambda_{\text{coord}} \sum_{i=0}^{S^2} \sum_{j=0}^{B} \mathbb{1}_{ij}^{\text{obj}} \left[\left(\sqrt{w_i} - \sqrt{\hat{w}_i} \right)^2 + \left(\sqrt{h_i} - \sqrt{\hat{h}_i} \right)^2 \right] + \\
& \sum_{i=0}^{S^2} \sum_{j=0}^{B} \mathbb{1}_{ij}^{\text{obj}} \left(C_i - \hat{C}_i \right)^2 + \\
& \lambda_{\text{noobj}} \sum_{i=0}^{S^2} \sum_{j=0}^{B} \mathbb{1}_{ij}^{\text{noobj}} \left(C_i - \hat{C}_i \right)^2 + \\
& \sum_{i=0}^{S^2} \mathbb{1}_{i}^{\text{obj}} \sum_{c \in \text{classes}} (p_i(c) - \hat{p}_i(c))^2
\end{aligned} \tag{9.27}$$

(a)   (b)

Figure 9.25 An example of object localization and recognition using YOLO. (a) Input image, (b) predicted boxes with confidence scores and object classes. (*Source*: Himadri Bhunia, Philips Research, Bengaluru.)

where 1_i^{obj} denotes the presence of the object cell i and 1_{ij}^{obj} denotes the attribution of the prediction of jth bounding box in cell i. The hyper-parameters λ_{coord} and λ_{noobj} account for the weights of losses from bounding boxes containing objects and the loss from confidence score predictions for boxes that do not contain objects. respectively. Typical values of λ_{coord} and λ_{noobj} are 5 and 5, respectively.

Testing of the network During testing of network the bounding boxes with high confidence scores are selected. As there could be closely spaced bounding boxes for a large object, non-maximal suppression is carried out by selecting a box whose predicted confidence score is locally maximum. The confidence score is weighted by the probability of a class before its use. Thus it becomes a class specific confidence score. Thus the score encodes both the probability of a class and that class specific confidence for the predicted bounding box to fit the object. A typical example of object localization and recognition are shown in Fig. 9.25.

9.4.5 | Semantic segmentation

In semantic segmentation, the task is to label the pixels in an image with a label, similar to the classification problem. However, in semantic segmentation, instead of classifying the image as objects or a group of pixels, each pixel is classified with an appropriate label. Here, only pixels are independently classified and individual instances of object classes are not differentiated. For example, if there are multiple human profiles whose pixels are all connected in an image, it is sufficient to denote a segment with all the connected human profiles together. This kind of segmentation is called *semantic segmentation*. If instance level semantic segmentation is required, the task is to further differentiate the individual instances in a connected segment.

The building blocks of a network for semantic segmentation are as follows.

- An *encoder* network consisting of successive stages of convolution and down-sampling layers. The down-sampling operation may be performed by various techniques such as max pooling, average pooling, strided convolution (with stride, $S > 1$), etc.

- A *decoder* network consisting of successive stages of up-sampling and convolution layers. Typical approaches for up-sampling are unpooling and up-convolution.
- An output layer with K 1×1 filters for labeling each pixel of the output image in one of K classes. This layer effectively implements a set of linear discriminant functions.

The purpose of down sampling task is to learn the features with aggregations at different resolutions. It provides the intermediate feature representation at each image locations of multiple resolutions. These are used for labeling in the next stage. In the result of segmentation, the sizes of the input and the output images are to be the same, since every pixel of the input needs to have a semantic label. Hence the down-sampled intermediate feature vectors are filtered and up-sampled to the size of the input image in the up-sampling stage. The up-sampling task learns the features, their labels, and their projection in the semantic space. In the following, we discuss two typical techniques of up-sampling, namely *unpooling* and *up-convolution*.

Max unpooling To understand the unpooling operation, max unpooling in particular (Noh et al., 2015), consider an example as shown in Fig. 9.26. In this example, the input image is a 4×4 matrix, as shown in top left matrix in Fig. 9.26. This matrix is subjected to max pooling operation by 2×2 filters. Here, while performing max pooling operation, the index of the positions of the pooled values is also generated. For example, in the top left 2×2 sub-block of the input matrix, $\begin{bmatrix} 1 & 2 \\ 4 & 5 \end{bmatrix}$, the maximum value is 5. Similarly, other three 2×2 sub-blocks in the input image have their maximum values as, 6, 7, and 8, respectively. The down sampled matrix after max pooling operation, $\begin{bmatrix} 5 & 6 \\ 7 & 8 \end{bmatrix}$, is shown in top middle matrix of the figure. Also, the positions of each of the max pooled

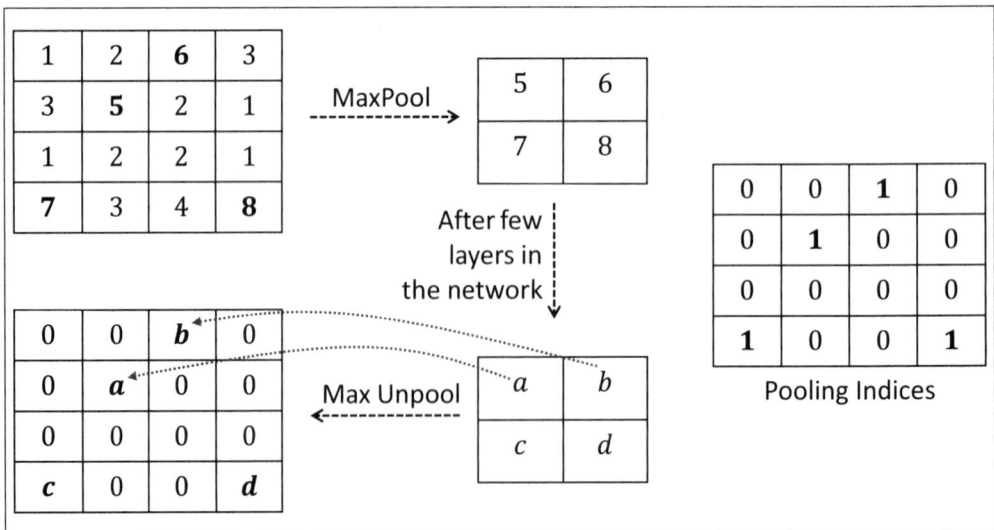

Figure 9.26 Illustration of max unpooling operation.

values in their corresponding 2×2 sub-blocks are stored as pooling indices. The pooling indices of all the positions of max pooled values are shown in the right most matrix in Fig. 9.26. The pooling index is stored in the form of a binary mask, where 1s indicate the positions of considered max pooled values and 0s are filled in all the other positions. These indicator function is known as *pooling index*. This information in pooling index is used during the unpooling operation. For the unpooling operation, the values of max pooling operation are taken as input. The down sampled image from max pooling operation after a few layers in the network and the pooling indices are used in max unpooling the image to generate the unpooled output. By the processing pipeline, since the unpooling layer appears after a few layers in the network, the pooling indices from max pooling layer are tagged to the unpooling layer. For example, the 2×2 matrix with values a, b, c, and d, as shown in bottom middle matrix of Fig. 9.26, is the input to the unpooling layer. This matrix is not the same as the output of max pooling layer, since the network layers change the values of max pooled matrix with several convolutions. Using this 2×2 matrix, $\begin{bmatrix} a & b \\ c & d \end{bmatrix}$, and the tagged pooling indices, the max unpooling operation is performed by placing the matrix values in the corresponding positions indicated by indices of 1s. This is shown in bottom left matrix in the figure. In this way, the image is up-sampled using max unpooling operation.

Up-convolution   Consider a 2×2 matrix as input to an up-sampling block, as shown in Fig. 9.27. Here, the up-convolution is performed using a 3×3 filter. For each input element, the filter is multiplied by pivoting its central position and the overlap region is summed up to get the output. That is, the up-convolved output contains the copies of the filter weighted by the input. Let the 2×2 matrix be given by, $\mathbf{A} = \begin{bmatrix} a & b \\ c & d \end{bmatrix}$. Let a 3×3 filter be given by,

$\mathbf{L} = \begin{bmatrix} x & y & z \\ u & v & w \\ p & q & r \end{bmatrix}$, where v is the value of central location of the filter. Consider up-sampling the input matrix using the filter $\mathbf{L}$ with a stride of 1. Here, the filter values are placed at

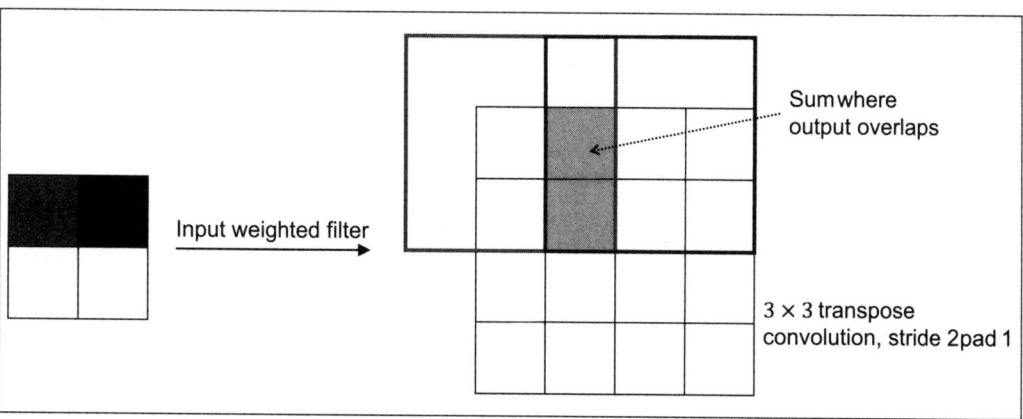

Sum where output overlaps

Input weighted filter

3×3 transpose convolution, stride 2pad 1

Figure 9.27   Illustration of up-convolution.

the locations of each of the elements of the input matrix and the values at the overlapping locations are summed up to obtain the up-convolved output. At first, using the element a, the output of multiplying $\mathbf{L}$ with a generates the matrix $\mathbf{A}_a$ as,

$$\mathbf{A}_a = \begin{bmatrix} ax & ay & az & 0 \\ au & av & aw & 0 \\ ap & aq & ar & 0 \\ 0 & 0 & 0 & 0 \end{bmatrix}.$$

Then, using the element b, the output of multiplying $\mathbf{L}$ with b and summing the corresponding overlapping values with $\mathbf{A}_a$ generates the matrix $\mathbf{A}_{ab}$ as,

$$\mathbf{A}_{ab} = \begin{bmatrix} ax & ay + bx & az + by & bz \\ au & av + bu & aw + bv & bw \\ ap & aq + bp & ar + bq & br \\ 0 & 0 & 0 & 0 \end{bmatrix}.$$

Similarly, using the element c, the output of multiplying $\mathbf{L}$ with c and summing the corresponding overlapping values with $\mathbf{A}_{ab}$ generates the matrix $\mathbf{A}_{abc}$ as,

$$\mathbf{A}_{abc} = \begin{bmatrix} ax & ay + bx & az + by & bz \\ au + cx & av + bu + cy & aw + bv + cz & bw + dz \\ ap + cu & aq + bp + cv & ar + bq + cw & br + dw \\ cp & cq & cr & 0 \end{bmatrix}.$$

Finally, weighing $\mathbf{L}$ with d and summing the corresponding overlapping values generates the final 4×4 up-sampled matrix as,

$$\mathbf{A}_{abcd} = \begin{bmatrix} ax & ay + bx & az + by & bz \\ au + cx & av + bu + cy + dx & aw + bv + cz + dy & bw + dz \\ ap + cu & aq + bp + cv + du & ar + bq + cw + dv & br + dw \\ cp & cq + dp & cr + dq & dr \end{bmatrix}.$$

This is an example of 2-D up-convolution of matrix $\mathbf{A}$ using a filter $\mathbf{L}$ with a stride of 1 and padding of 1. This kind of operation is also called *transpose convolution*, *fractionally strided convolution*, *backward strided convolution* and *deconvolution*.

Numerical Example

Up-convolve the following input $\mathbf{x}$ using the filter $\mathbf{h}$. What is the value at (3, 1) and (2, 2) in the up-convolved feature map? We assume index of first cell of any 2-D matrix is (0,0).

$\mathbf{x}$

1	3
3	2

$\mathbf{h}$

0	0.1	0
0.1	0.2	0.1
0	0.1	0

Solution

The up-sampling computation is done as,

0	0.1 + 0	0 + 0.3	0
0.1 + 0	0.2 + 0.3 + 0.3 + 0	0.1 + 0.6 + 0 + 0.2	0.3 + 0
0 + 0.3	0.1 + 0 + 0.6 + 0.2	0 + 0.3 + 0.3 + 0.4	0 + 0.2
0	0.3 + 0	0 + 0.2	0

This will give the following result:

0	0.1	0.3	0
0.1	0.8	0.9	0.3
0.3	0.9	1	0.2
0	0.3	0.2	0

Hence the values at $(3, 1) = 0.3$, and at $(2, 2) = 1$.

Fully convolutional neural network (FCN)

A *fully convolutional neural network*, which is used for performing semantic segmentation (Long et al., 2015), does not have any FC layer. Every operation is performed by a convolution layer coupled with downsampling and upsampling. That is, all the layers of the network are used as convolution layers. The output of this architecture is also an image of a certain number of channels, whose size (number of pixels in the output) is the same as the number of pixels in the input. Here, the prediction of the class is performed at every pixel in the image. This kind of prediction is called *dense prediction*. The segmentation is performed by determining the semantics associated with each pixel, which captures the association of a pixel to every class. For predicting the classes at pixel level, the convolutions on the input image are carried out at several layers of the network. The network consists of one or more down-sampling operations, usually by pooling operations, that result in the down-sampled processed tensors (or arrays). To make the size of the output the same as of the input of the network, the processed images are up-sampled by one or more layers of unpooling or strided convolutions. Although the input and output are of the same size, the number of channels at the last convolution layer (previous to the prediction layer) may be different.

Let there be d number of channels in the layer before the dense prediction. Let the size $M \times N$ of the output at this layer. The objective is to predict the label of every pixel. So, convolution operation is performed with a 1-D filter of length d, i.e., $1 \times 1 \times d$. Each $1 \times 1 \times d$ filter gives a response per pixel in the output. If there are k such filters, then there are k responses at each pixel. Each of these k filters is associated with a certain class. That is, there are k classes or labels. By using the softmax principle, the probability of a pixel belonging to a particular class is computed. A class with highest probability is assigned at each pixel.

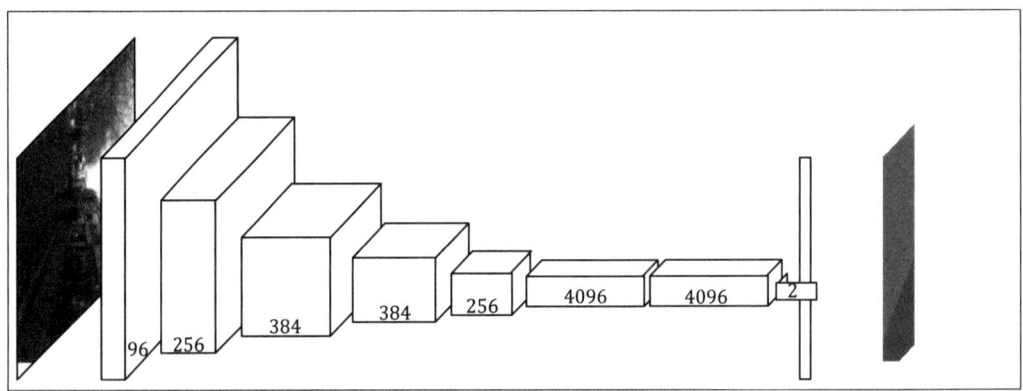

Figure 9.28 A typical FCN architecture. (*Source*: Soumyajit Das, Research Scholar, IIT Kharagpur for providing images.)

There are many parameters associated with prediction of class at each pixel that are to be learned. Since there are d channels before the output layer and k filters are used to form the output, the number of parameters in the output layer is $k \times d$. The number of channels at the output layer (i.e., the number of filters in the output layer), k, should be equal to number of classes considered. Since this network is meant for semantic labeling of the pixels, this restriction on the number of classes and filters has to be followed. For performing the optimization, cross entropy as a loss function is a natural choice here, since the task is to classify each pixel. This is a general way of using a fully convolutional neural network for labeling every pixel at the output for performing semantic segmentation.

There are several variations of this architectures for specific segmentation applications. A typical architecture is shown in Fig. 9.28. In this architecture, the convolution operations and corresponding down-sampling operations are performed at multiple layers. Then, after a certain stage, the up-sampling operations are performed, as seen in the figure, to bring the output to the same size as the input image for pixel-wise prediction. Here, while performing up-sampling, the initialization of the up-sampling filters is done by using bilinear interpolation filter weights. It is a very standard interpolation filter whose weights are predetermined by bilinear operations. The optimization is performed after the initialization to update these weights.

Convolutional encoder decoder network

In a convolutional encoder decoder architecture, at the encoder stage of the network, it takes an input image and generates a high dimensional feature vector. Also, this process aggregates features at multiple levels. At the decoder stage, it takes a high dimensional feature vector and generates a semantic segmentation mask. The decoder stage performs reverse operation of encoder stage by decoding the features that are aggregated by encoder at multiple levels,. Here, instead of using up-sampling filters, unpooling operations are used to perform up-sampling. By using unpooling operations, the spatial location information is preserved. So, the information of high responses that are observed in the encoder stage are passed to the decoder stage, which is found to improve the segmentation performance. The

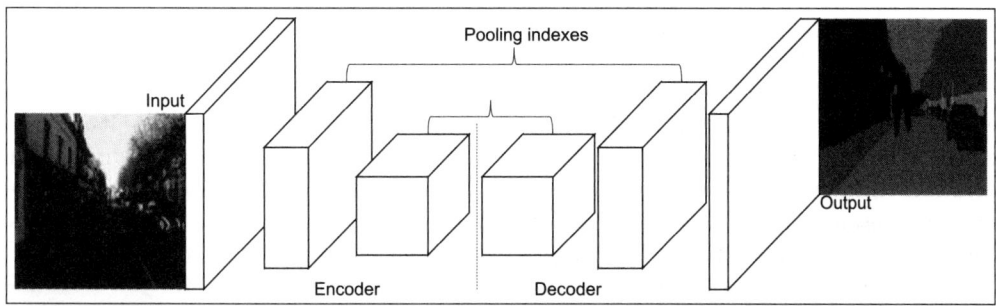

Figure 9.29 A typical convolutional encoder decoder architecture. (*Source*: Soumyajit Das, Research Scholar, IIT Kharagpur for providing images.)

decoder semantically projects the discriminative features (lower resolution) learnt by the encoder onto the input pixel space (higher resolution) to get a dense classification.

A typical encoder decoder architecture is shown in Fig. 9.29. The encoder stages comprises of convolutional layers and max pooling layers. At every pooling layer, the pooling indices are passed to the corresponding unpooling layers of the decoder stage. The final output is the same size as the input image. The d layers in the last convolution layer are convolved with k 1×1 filters to generate k labels in the segmentation output. There are two stages in the semantic segmentation process: (1) a learning stage that represents the image as a features, and (2) up-convolutions to project the learnt features to the semantic domain. In the second stage, the learned low resolution semantic feature maps are up-sampled by up-convolutions using bilinear interpolation filter weights as initialization of weights. Finally, the class labels are predicted for each pixel. Here, with a defined input-output specification, the network is trained through down-sampling and up-sampling layers using encoder decoder structure. The Segnet is an example of such an architecture for performing semantic segmentation of images (Badrinarayanan et al., 2017).

This kind of encoder decoder architecture, sometime referred to as pix-to-pix model, is used for various other applications of image processing, such as inpainting, superresolution, denoising, colorization, etc. Usually models are trained by using a pair of original image and a processed image. The processed image is obtained by simple image processing operations such as conversion from color to gray level, addition of simulated noise, downsampling of images, etc. The processed image acts as the input to the model and the ground truth becomes the original image. Hence the purpose of a generic encoder decoder model is to learn to transform a processed image to a target image the same as the original image. This kind of learning is known as self-supervised learning.

UNet architecture

The *UNet* architecture is one of the very popular architectures used for semantic segmentation (Ronneberger et al., 2015). In the UNet architecture, the computations are carried out in two successive stages, similar to a convolutional encoder decoder architecture. A typical architecture is shown in Fig. 9.30. The two stages[4] are: (1) contracting path for down-sampling, and (2) expansive path for up-sampling. In the contracting path, there are repeated processing of two consecutive convolution layers (typically with a filter size of 3×3) that are followed by a rectified linear unit and max pooling operation (typically of size 2×2) with stride 2. Also, at each down-sampling operation, the number of feature channels is doubled. In the expansive path, there are repeated up-sampling by up-convolution with half the number of feature channels, which is followed by concatenation with the correspondingly cropped feature map from the contracting path and two consecutive convolutions (of typical size 3×3) with a rectified linear unit.

In this network, the size of the output image becomes the same as the size of the input image. However, cropping is required to keep this constraint of size due to the loss of border pixels in every convolution operation. At the final layer, when all the pixels at the output are generated, each pixel is classified into a defined number of classes. For example, in the UNet architecture shown in Fig. 9.30, every pixel in the final layer is represented by a D-dimensional feature vector. These D-dimensional feature vectors are the input to the classifier, where they are mapped by K 1×1 convolutions to the K number of classes. Typical examples of semantic segmentation using a UNet architecture are shown in Fig. 9.31. The images are taken from BRATS 2020 data set. They are typical cross sections of Brain MRI images for cancer patients. In this case the task of segmentation is to identify regions of various parts of the tumor in the slices. The ground truth of segmentation regions as annotated by expert oncologists are also shown in Figs. 9.31 (c) and (d). The segmentation results obtained from a UNet model are shown in Figs. 9.31 (e) and (f). We observe that the predicted labels of the pixels in the tumor region strongly match with the annotated labels (visually distinguished by distinct colors).

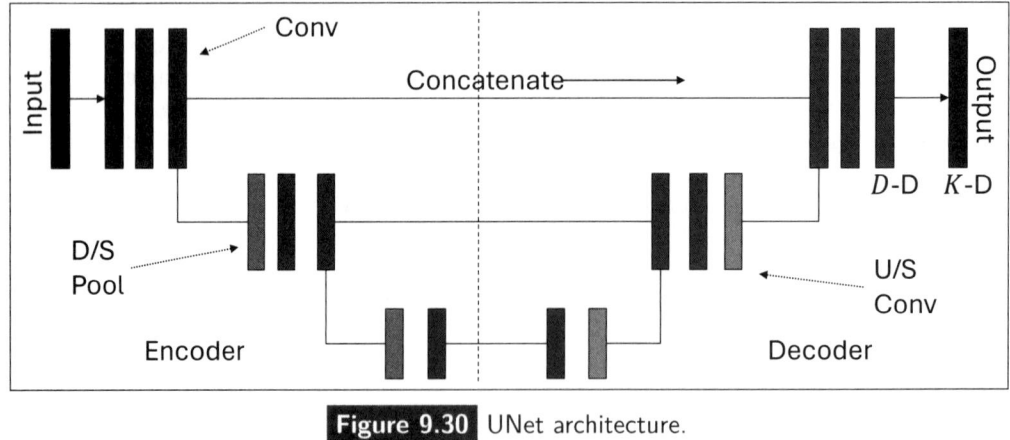

Figure 9.30 UNet architecture.

---

[4] The processing in UNet architecture is analogous to wavelet analysis and synthesis as discussed in Section 2.7.3 of Chapter 2.

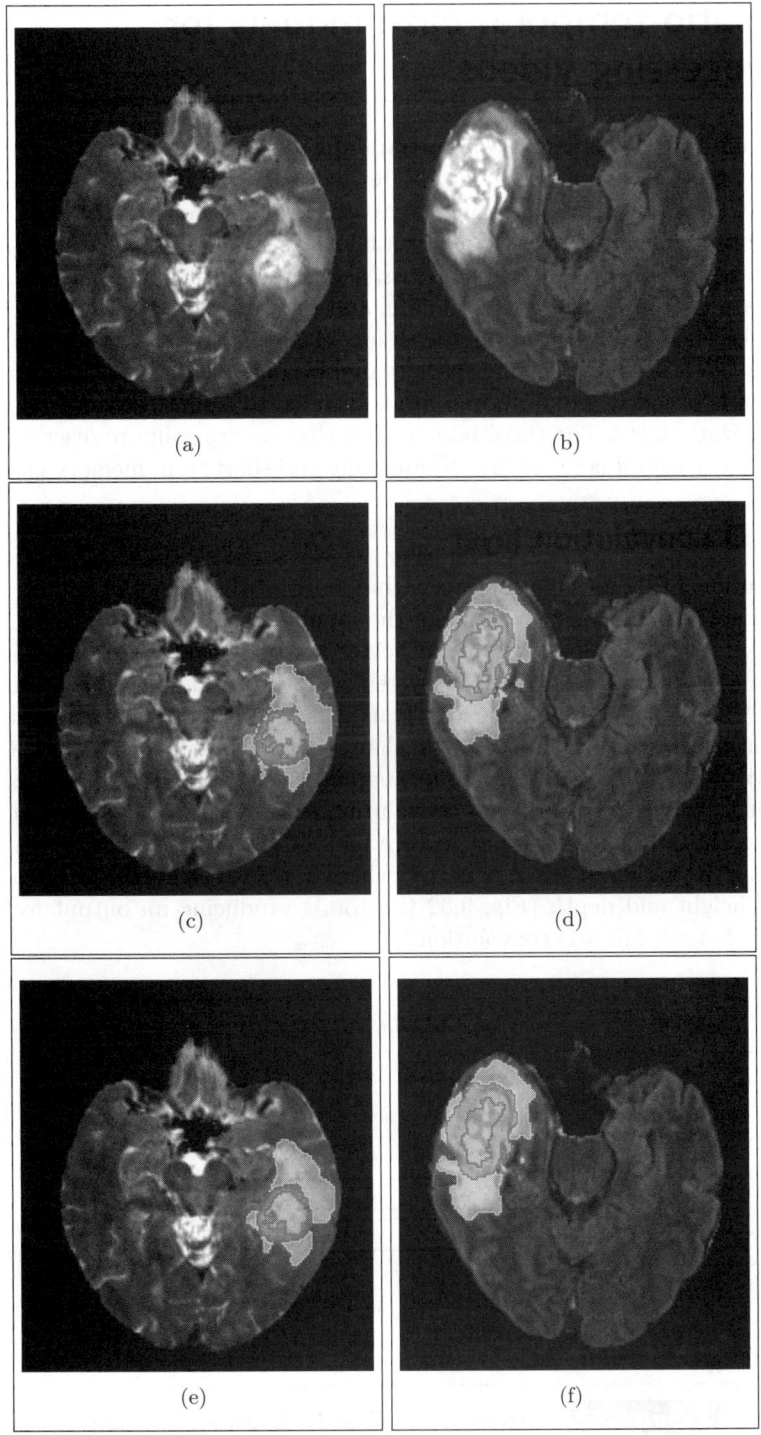

Figure 9.31 Example of image segmentation using UNet. (a, b) Original images, (c, d) ground truth images, and (e, f) segmentation results. (*Source*: Surajit Kundu, Research Scholar, IIT Kharagpur.) See Color Plates (page 820).

9.5 | Spatio-temporal base models for processing videos

The video is an example of a spatio-temporal data. It is a function in a three dimensional space. A pixel in a video is a point in a discretized 3-D grid, including two coordinates to denote a pixel in a frame corresponding to its spatial dimensions and the other dimension expresses the time instances, which are given by the frame numbers. For processing videos using a deep neural architecture, we discuss here three base models which are used for extracting features from spatio temporal data, and subsequently the feature map is used for high level tasks, such as, classification, regression, clustering, etc. The feature map may also be used to encode the context of the spatio-temporal data, and in the later stage, encoded representation is decoded into a desired form, such as, to a short description of the video, video summarization, etc. The three base models that we are going to discuss here are 3-D convnet, recurrent neural network (RNN) and long and short term memory (LSTM) model.

9.5.1 | 3-D convolution layer

In the conventional 2-D convolution layer, the depth of the kernel of a filter remains the same as the depth (number of channels) of the input feature map. Effectively the kernel is of 3-D. The kernel moves along width and height at the central plane of the input feature map and the computation is performed by replacing the value of the pixel in the central plane, where the kernel center is moved. Thus in a 2-D convolution layer, the output of this operation is a feature map of a single channel (Fig. 9.32 (top)). Hence, for an image of size $H \times W \times D$ with a kernel of size $h \times w$ (effectively in 3-D it is $h \times w \times D$), the size of the output feature map from a full convolution is of size $H \times W$. In a 3-D convolution layer (Tran et al., 2015), for an input feature map of $H \times W \times D$, the kernel is explicitly mentioned as a 3D kernel of size $h \times w \times d$, where $d < D$. The kernel moves at each point along width, height and depth (Fig. 9.32 (bottom)) producing an output feature map of size $H \times W \times D$ for a full 3-D convolution.

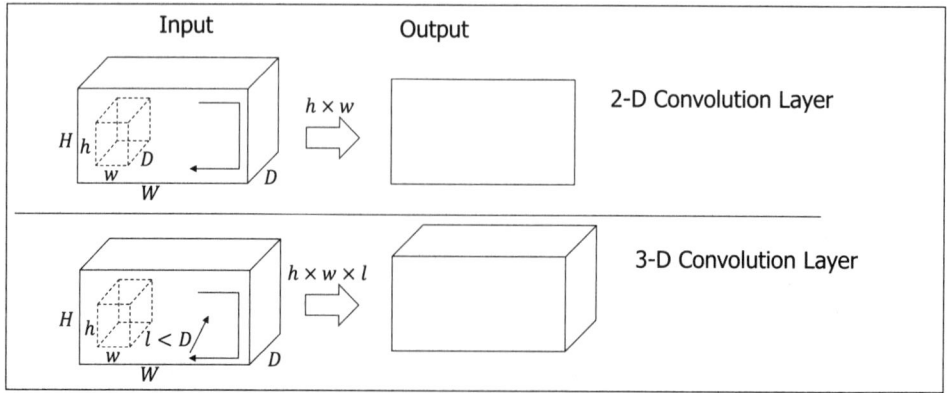

Figure 9.32 Illustration of 2-D and 3-D convolution layers.

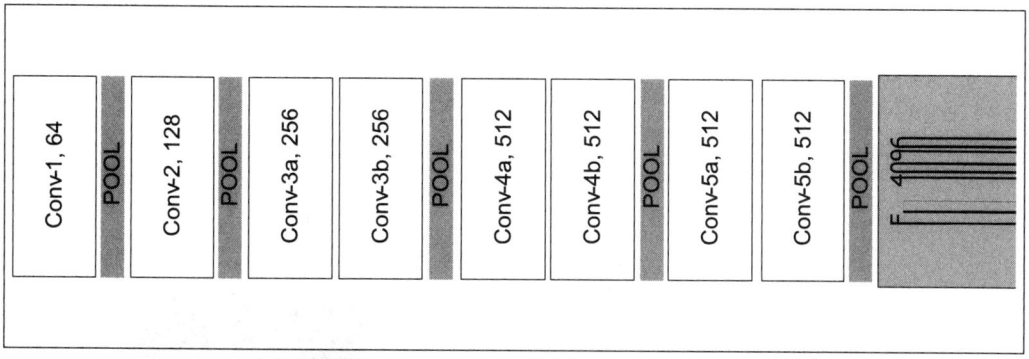

Figure 9.33 Architecture of C3D network.

By drawing the same analogy from a 2-D convolution layer, instead of a feature plane, we refer to it as a feature volume. When M number of kernels operate at a 3-D convolution layer, the output feature map becomes a 4-D tensor of size $H \times W \times D \times M$. Hence the 3-D kernel operating on a 4-D tensor is also effectively a 4-D tensor having the same value in the 4th dimension. For example, if the input feature map is a 4D tensor of size $H \times W \times D \times M$, a 4-D kernel has M number of 3-D kernels of size $h \times w \times d$, and effectively making the size of 4-D kernel as $h \times w \times d \times M$. The operation with this kernel with the 4-D input feature map, produces a single 3-D feature map (volume), whose size for a full convolution is $H \times W \times D$.

The other kinds of layers, such as pooling, nonlinearity, BN, etc., in a CNN using 3-D convnet remains similar to a conventional CNN layer. A typical example of an architecture using 3-D convnet for handling videos is the C3D network (Fig. 9.33) (Tran et al., 2015). The architecture has eight 3-D convolution layers and five max pooling layers. Each filter in a convolution layer is of size $3 \times 3 \times 3$, with stride $1 \times 1 \times 1$. The first pooling layer has a mask of $1 \times 2 \times 2$ with stride $1 \times 2 \times 2$, and the remaining pooling layers use $2 \times 2 \times 2$ mask with stride $2 \times 2 \times 2$. The number of output nodes in each FC layer is 4096. The model has been used for classifying sports videos. The trained model is also used for extracting a feature descriptor from a video clip of size $112 \times 112 \times 16$ from the final FC layer. Thus the dimension of this descriptor is 4096 and it is L_2 normalized. For example, the feature descriptors from video clips are used in an SVM classifier to classify human actions (Tran et al., 2015).

The 3-D convnet is used also for processing 3-D image data such as medical images, CT, MRI, etc. The conventional CNN and pooling layers are replaced by 3-D CNN and 3-D pooling layers in 2-D architectures of classification, semantic segmentation, etc.

9.5.2 | Recurrent neural networks (RNN)

Recurrent neural networks (RNN) (Lipton et al., 2015) are used to process a sequence of vectors $\boldsymbol{x}_t$ by applying a recurrence formula at every time step, t. In this architecture, the output from the layer of recurrence nodes (hidden recurrence layer) $\boldsymbol{h}_t$ are fed back to their

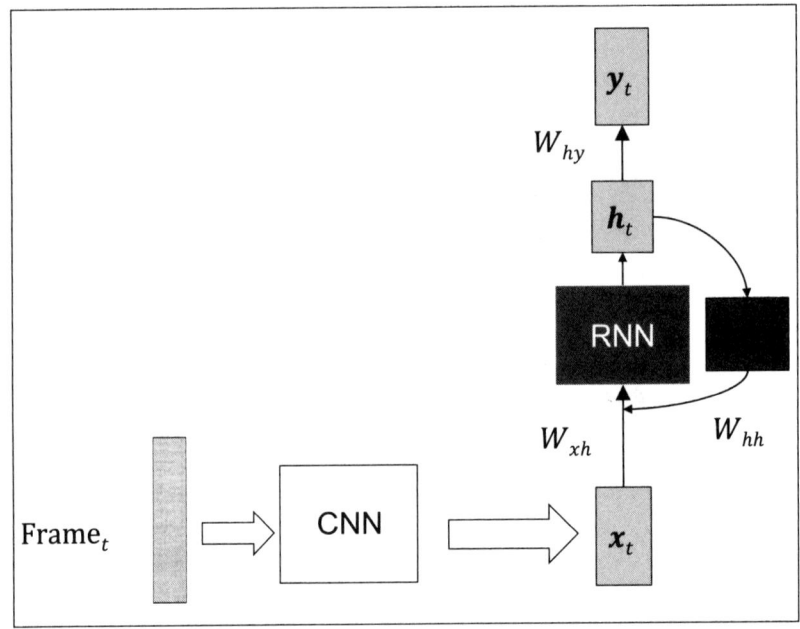

Figure 9.34 Feedback in RNN architecture.

inputs with a delay of one time step as shown in Fig. 9.34. The mathematical relationship among the input $\boldsymbol{x}_t$ and output $\boldsymbol{y}_t$ are shown by the following equations.

$$\boldsymbol{h}_t = \tanh(W_{hh}\boldsymbol{h}_{t-1} + W_{xh}\boldsymbol{x}_t)$$
$$\boldsymbol{y}_t = W_{hy}\boldsymbol{h}_t \tag{9.28}$$

where W_{hx}, W_{hh} and W_{hy} are the parameters of the RNN. Usually the nonlinearity in the hidden recurrence layer uses the $\tanh(\cdot)$ function as shown in Eq. 9.29.

The RNN may be used for prediction of a vector at some time steps. It may also be considered as the feature descriptor of a sequence capturing its dynamics and context. The feature descriptor may be used for the desired task in the next stage, such as, classification, translation to another sequence, etc. For a video, feature descriptors from its frames are captured independently, and they are used as the input to the RNN as shown in Fig. 9.34.

Training of RNN

The RNN is equivalent to an unfolded feedforward network of infinite number of layers. For a stable network, the output practically converges after a few time steps. Thus the training of RNN is carried out by unfolding the input output processing in successive time steps for a finite number of times. The training algorithm for the unfolded network becomes the same as that what is applied to a feed forward network. The output of the final layer of the unfolded network is taken as the feature vector capturing the dynamics or context of the sequence as shown in Fig. 9.35.

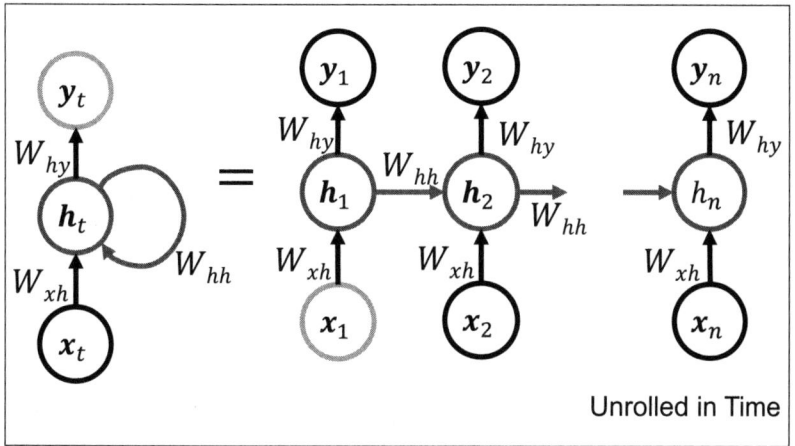

Figure 9.35 Unfolded RNN. (*Source*: Adapted from a slide from Prof. Sudeshna Sarkar, Department of Computer Science and Engineering, IIT Kharagpur.)

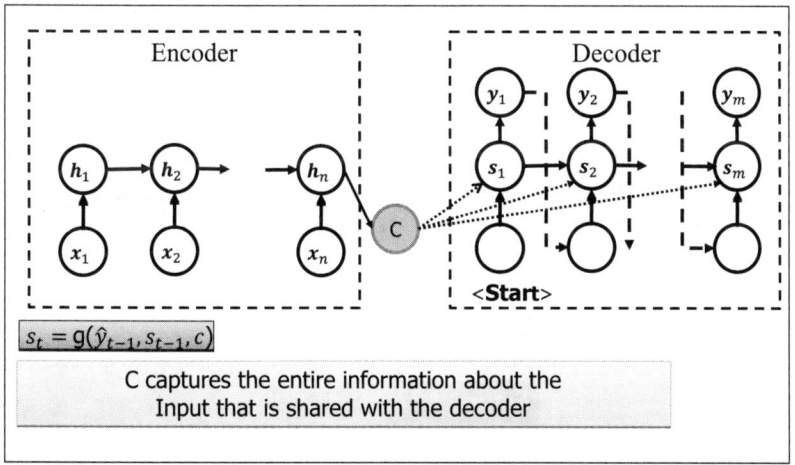

Figure 9.36 Encoder decoder using RNN. (*Source*: Adapted from a slide from Prof. Sudeshna Sarkar, Department of Computer Science and Engineering, IIT Kharagpur.)

Encoder decoder using RNN

A typical application of sequence processing in RNN is to encode a sequence and decoding (Cho et al., 2014) it into another sequence as shown in Fig. 9.36. Some of the applications of this kind of architecture are image and video captioning, video summarization, etc. The bottleneck with the RNN is that, with the progression of iterative processing in the feedback mechanism, the influence of distant past instances in the input sequence decays fast in the generation of the output. This is called *memory fading*, as if the memory of the past instances gets faded away. To circumvent this problem, another architecture is proposed to capture both long and short term contexts of a sequence as discussed in the next section.

9.5.3 | Long short term memory (LSTM) network

As the RNN is unable to learn long term dependency, the *long short term memory* (LSTM) network architecture is proposed to avoid this problem (Hochreiter and Schmidhuber, 1997; Greff et al., 2017). An LSTM architecture too processes a sequence of feature vectors x_t. An LSTM node or cell maintains two states, e.g., C_t, a long term memory state, called *cell state*, and h_t, a short term memory state, called *hidden state*, as shown in Fig. 9.37. The output from a node is captured from the short term memory state.

The LSTM architecture processes a finite sequence of input feature vectors and produces a finite sequence of output feature vectors as a function of long and short term contexts from the previous instances in the input sequence. The processing in an LSTM node is shown schematically in Fig. 9.38.

The current instance x_t of the input sequence is concatenated with the short term context h_{t-1} carried from the previous cell. The output from this node is a function of the modified input and a part of it is modified by the long term context C_t carried from the previous cell. A part of this long term context gets faded away and a part of it influences the

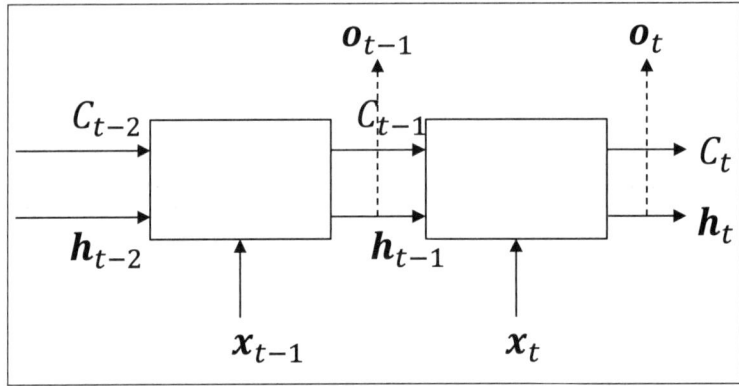

Figure 9.37 LSTM cell.

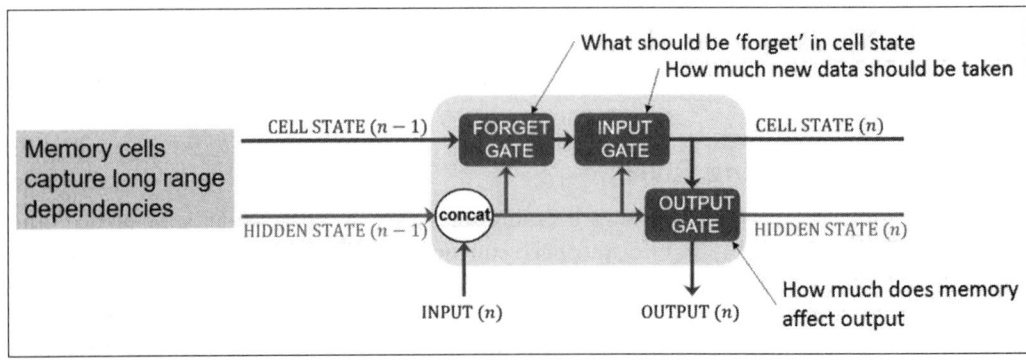

Figure 9.38 Processing in an LSTM memory cell. (*Source*: Adapted from a slide from Prof. Sudeshna Sarkar, Department of Computer Science and Engineering, IIT Kharagpur.)

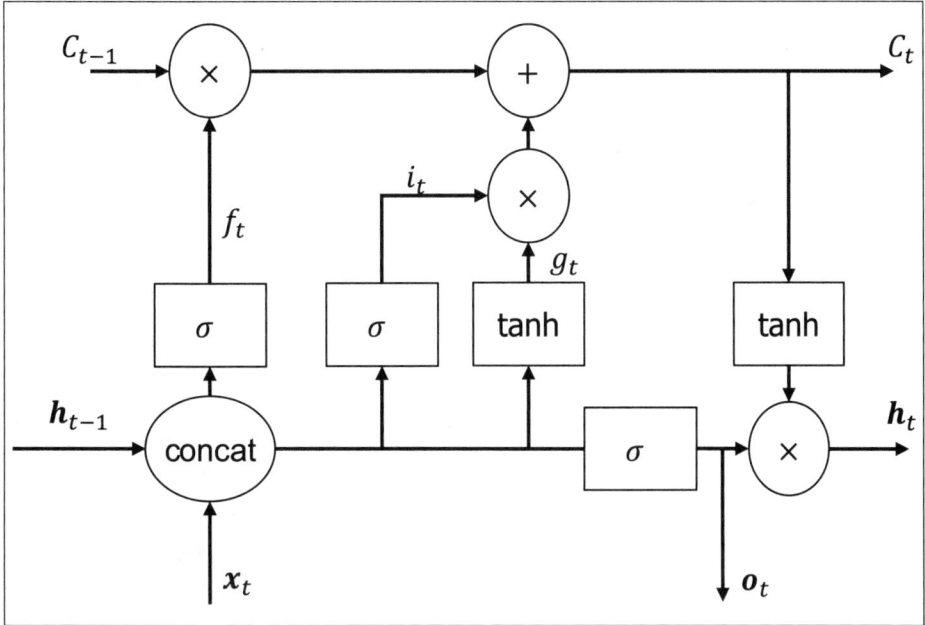

Figure 9.39 Functional relationships among different constituents of an LSTM cell.

outcome. There are three gates in an LSTM node, which modulates the influence of long and short term contexts, namely *forget gate, input gate* and *output gate*. The forget gate determines how much should be allowed or what should be forgotten of the long term context or cell state. The input gate determines how much new data should be taken from the modulated input instance, which also becomes the long term context of the next cell. The output gate determines how the long and short term contexts affect the output, which also becomes a short term context for the next cell. The functional relationships among different constituents of this computation, as shown in Fig. 9.39, are given below.

$$
\begin{aligned}
\text{New cell content: } g_t &= \tanh(U_g \boldsymbol{h}_{t-1} + W_g \boldsymbol{x}_t) \\
\text{Input: } i_t &= \sigma(U_i \boldsymbol{h}_{t-1} + W_i \boldsymbol{x}_t) \\
\text{Forget: } f_t &= \sigma(U_f \boldsymbol{h}_{t-1} + W_f \boldsymbol{x}_t) \\
\text{Output: } o_t &= \sigma(U_o \boldsymbol{h}_{t-1} + W_o \boldsymbol{x}_t) \\
\text{Cell state: } C_t &= f_t \odot C_{t-1} + i_t \odot g_t \\
\text{Hidden state: } \boldsymbol{h}_t &= o_t \odot \tanh(C_t)
\end{aligned}
\tag{9.29}
$$

In Eq. 9.29 $\odot$ denotes the element-wise multiplication or *Hadamard product* operation. We observe that an LSTM node has three learnable gates. Each of them use the sigmoid activation function, as indicated by $\sigma(.)$ in Eq. 9.29. In addition, there are learnable parameters for computing new cell content or cell input activation vector to determine how much information to be carried forward to the subsequent cell state.

A variation of the LSTM architecture is the Bi-LSTM architecture, which considers long and short term dependencies from both the directions of the sequence, as shown in Fig. 9.40.

A typical architecture using the LSTM network is shown in Fig. 9.41 for the task of classification, such as recognition of human action out of a set of candidate actions. The network processes a video of K frames. Each frame in the sequence is represented by a feature vector by processing it using a 2-D CNN. The sequence of these feature vectors is processed by an LSTM network to provide the feature descriptor (from the last node of the LSTM network) to the classifier.

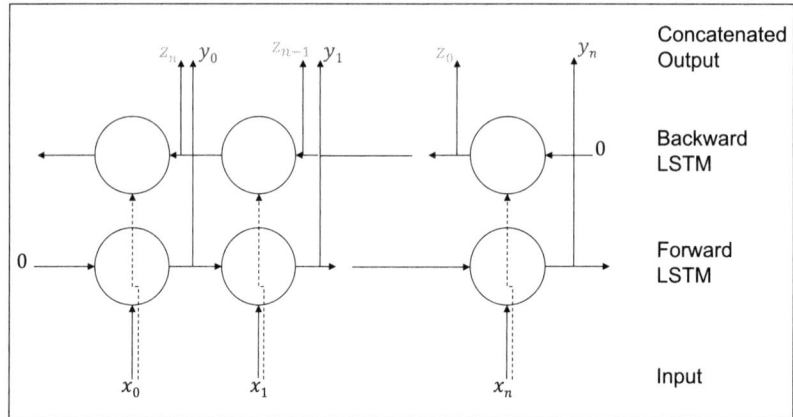

Figure 9.40 Bi-LSTM architecture.

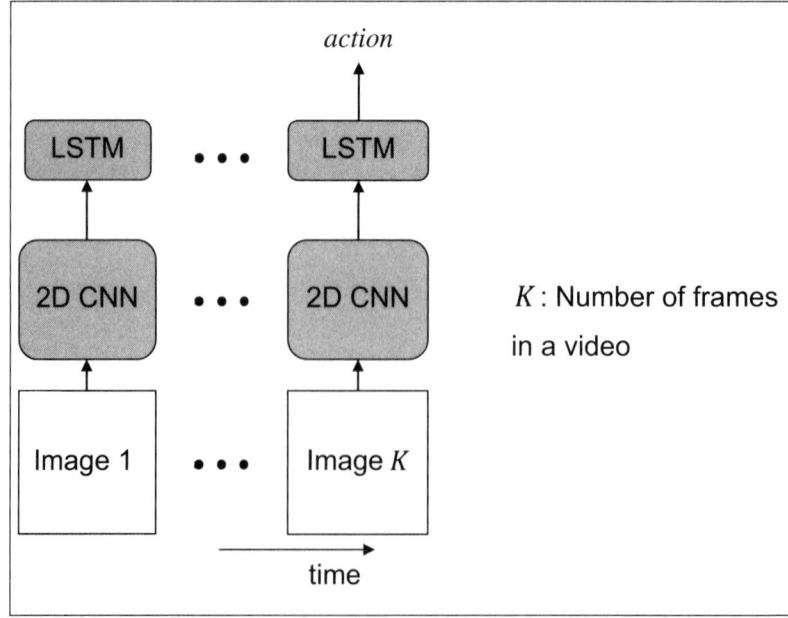

Figure 9.41 Human action recognition using LSTM.

9.6 | Two stream video descriptor architectures

For processing videos, the additional information of optical flow computed separately may improve the performance of the model. As the optical flow has two components, namely horizontal and vertical velocity components, each may be represented by a sequence of as many frames of the input video. Hence for a video sequence of K frames, there are K frames for horizontal components, and vertical components providing effectively $2K$ frames for the optical flow. In various architectural combinations of 2-D and 3-D CNNs, these two streams are used to compute a video descriptor, which is used in a classification network (Carreira and Zisserman, 2017). Let us consider N $(< K)$ consecutive frames in a sequence form a part of the video. The task that of classification may be considered as independently processing $\frac{K}{N}$ such groups and aggregate the classification results from them. For representing a video descriptor from a group, its first frame is processed by a 2-D CNN and the sequence of optical flow of N frames is processed by a 3-D CNN. Then the two feature vectors are concatenated to provide the video descriptor of that group of frames (Fig. 9.42).

In another variation, we consider a sequence of these concatenated feature descriptors from the $\frac{K}{N}$ groups and process them with a 3-D CNN to provide the final video descriptor (Fig. 9.43).

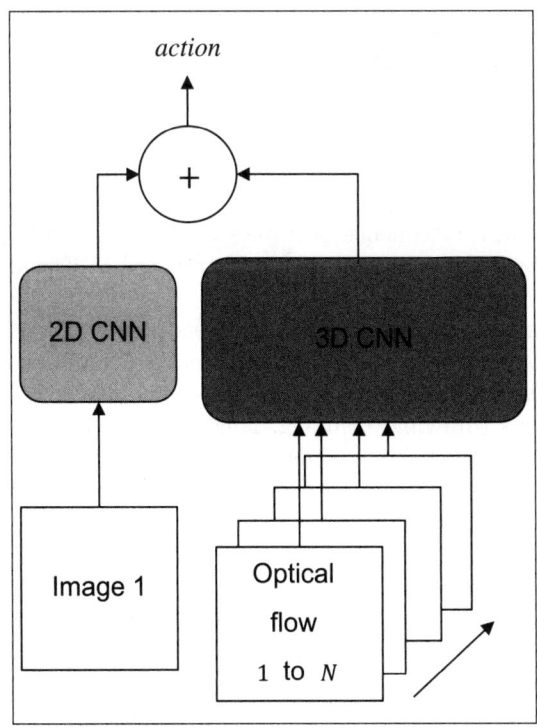

Figure 9.42 Two stream descriptor.

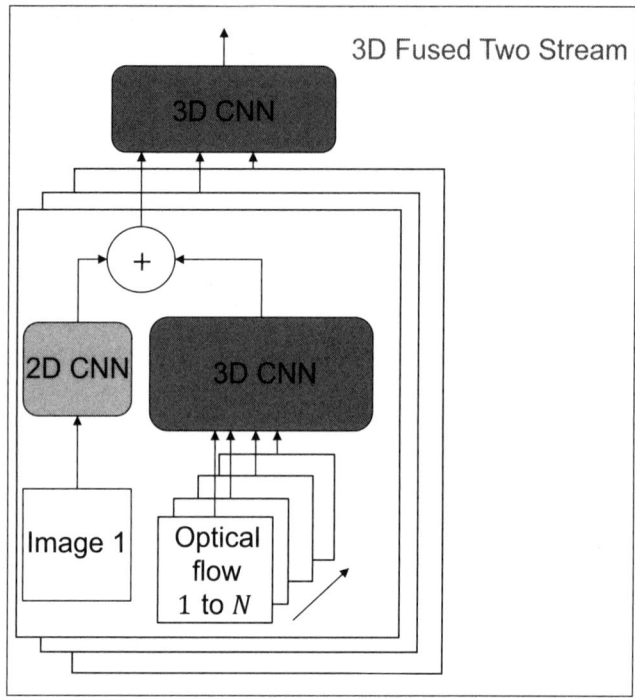

Figure 9.43 3-D fused two stream descriptor.

In the third variation, the sequence of frames in the video and optical flow frames are processed separately by 3-D CNNs and then concatenated to provide the video descriptor (Fig. 9.44).

Here, as an illustration, we discuss a comparative study on The Kinetics Human Action video dataset on the performance of above architectures including the LSTM and Convnet (3-D CNN) based architectures (Carreira and Zisserman, 2017). Different types of actions such as personal actions (drawing, drinking, laughing, punching, etc.), person to person interaction (hugging, kissing, shaking hands, etc.), and person-object interaction, (opening presents, mowing lawn, washing dishes, etc.) are included in it. The dataset contains 400 action classes. The training dataset consists of 240 thousand video clips and more than 400 per class. The test set has more than 100 video clips per class. The top-1 accuracy in percentages are shown in Table 9.2.

We may observe that the two stream feature descriptors which include information from optical flow are very effective in performing the task requiring relatively less number of parameters, but higher accuracy, compared to single stream (information only from the video frames) representations. In Table 9.2, we may also observe the baseline performances of a single stream component for the architectures using two streams, highlighting the benefits of use of both the types of information in combination.

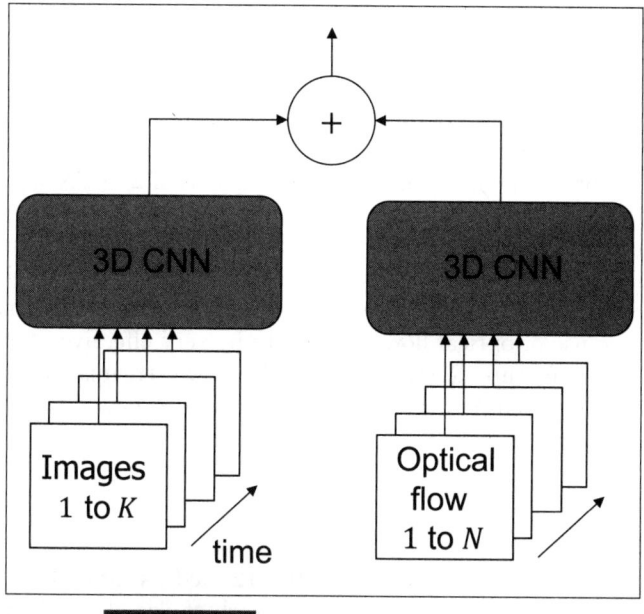

Figure 9.44 Two stream 3-D convnet.

Table 9.2 Experimental Results (Carreira and Zisserman, 2017) of The Kinetics Human Action Video dataset.

Architecture	# of params (in Millions)	RGB	Optical Flow	RGB + Opt. Flo.
LSTM + 2D CNN	9	63.3	–	–
3D CNN	79	56.1	–	–
Two stream	12	62.2	52.4	65.6
3D Fused Two Stream	39	–	–	67.20
Two Stream 3D CNN	25	**71.1**	**63.4**	**74.2**

Summary

Deep architectures work with the same principle of ANNs, but consists of a large number of hidden layers. Hence, a DNN has a large number of parameters. One of the very popular deep neural architectures is convolution neural network (CNN). A CNN learns filter weights and share them for fine tuning to fit different applications. Different types of layers in a CNN are, convolution, pooling, nonlinearity, BN, etc. For the task of classification, there are two stages of the network, viz., the feature extraction stage and the classification stage. In the classification stage, usually FCNNs are used. There are several variations in the architectures of CNNs for image classification, like ResNet (which processes residual errors), GoogleNet (which uses inception module), VGGNet, etc.

For object detection and recognition, RCNN and its variants are used. A Faster RCNN model uses an RPN that proposes bounding boxes of objects for classification. There are fully convolutional networks (FCN), such as convolutional encoder decoder networks, which are used for image segmentation. The UNet is also another variation of FCN, which is found to be very effective in semantically segmenting images.

3-D CNN (or 3D convnet) models are simple extensions of 2-D CNNs and are effective in processing spatio-temporal data and 3-D images. For sequence processing RNN and LSTM models are more effective. But in a RNN, long term contexts of a sequence are not properly captured, which may play a critical role in encoding the description in a video sequence. That is why LSTM architectures are more useful. In classifying videos of dynamic events such as human action, the use of optical flow is found to be very effective. Accordingly different architectures combining feature descriptors from these two streams (RGB and optical flow) are found to provide improved performances in various tasks related to processing of videos, such as recognizing human actions.

Exercises

(i) Consider a 6-channel tensor of size 120×120 fed as input to a convolution layer producing a 10-channel tensor with filters each of size of 3×3. What would be the number of parameters associated with this layer.

(ii) What is the number of parameters learned in a convolution layer with an input image size of $240 \times 240 \times 3$ and filter size of 5×5 producing a 6 channel output?

(iii) Suppose the input to ReLU activation function is -6, what would be the output obtained from it

(iv) Consider a maxpooling operation is performed on the following matrix using an operator of size 2×2 with stride 1 and no padding. What would be the output?

34	45
27	46

(v) Consider the following represents a set of output from a neural network. Compute the cross-entropy loss after softmax nonlinearity is applied on the output. Use natural logarithm in your computation for any function of logarithm.

Sample Id	Class Label	Class 1 Neuron	Class 2 Neuron
1	1	2	1
2	1	1	2
3	1	1	2
4	2	2	1

(vi) Consider a fully convolutional neural network for semantic labeling of 3 classes. The input to its last layer is of size $240 \times 240 \times 16$. What will be the size of the output from the last layer, and how many parameters are involved in this layer?

(**vii**) A loss function is designed which has a component of regularization loss that gets multiplied with a hyper-parameter λ and added with the other components. Consider a 3×3 filter for a single channel input of a CNN. What would be its contribution to regularization loss if the square of the Frobenius norm of the filter mask is used as a measure. Assume that the value of λ is 1.

1	2	1
2	−4	2
1	2	1

(**viii**) Consider an input image of dimension $19 \times 15 \times 3$. It passes through a convolution layer with 64 kernels of dimension $5 \times 5 \times 3$. The image has been zero padded on both sides with 1×1 padding and convoluted using 2×2 stride. What is the dimension of the activation map?

(**ix**) Describe the working of the depthwise separable convolution layer. How it is used in tandem with 1×1 pointwise convolution for producing the same size of the output tensor as in a conventional convolution layer? Given an input size of $112 \times 224 \times 16$, and 10 filters of size 3×3, what are the number of operations and parameters involved in computing with the depthwise separable convolution layer and conventional convolution layer for producing an output of dimension $112 \times 224 \times 10$.

(**x**) Consider a 3-D CNN with a filter of size $3 \times 3 \times 3$. Suppose the input feature map is of size $117 \times 117 \times 117 \times 10$. What would be the size of the output while computing with strides $2 \times 2 \times 2$. What is the number of parameters involved in this operation.

(**xi**) How does a 3-D convolution layer differ from a 2-D convolutional layer? Briefly describe a deep learning architecture which uses optical flow and the video frames for recognizing actions.

(**xii**) Describe the RNN architecture for processing a sequence of vectors. How the training of the network is carried out? What is the memory fading problem in this architecture?

(**xiii**) Describe the LSTM network for processing a finite sequence of vector. How does encoding-decoding take place using this architecture? Describe a model for video classification using the LSTM network.

(**xiv**) Consider a 6-channel tensor of size 120×120 fed as input to a convolution layer with a filter size of 3×3 and convolution operated with stride $= 2$. What would be the size of the corresponding output channel if there is no zero padding to the input.

(**xv**) What is meant by a two stream descriptor of a video? Describe a model which is used to learn a two stream descriptor from a video clip.

PART TWO

VISION GEOMETRY

10

Two-dimensional Projective Geometry

In Chapter 1 on introduction of image processing, image formation in a camera has been briefly described. Consider the image in Fig. 10.1. As a basic rule of projection, for a given scene point, $\boldsymbol{P}$, a ray from $\boldsymbol{P}$ that passes through the center of projection, $\boldsymbol{O}$, intersects the image plane at its image point, $\boldsymbol{p}$. This is a mapping, $\boldsymbol{P} \to \boldsymbol{p}$, of a three-dimensional (3-D)

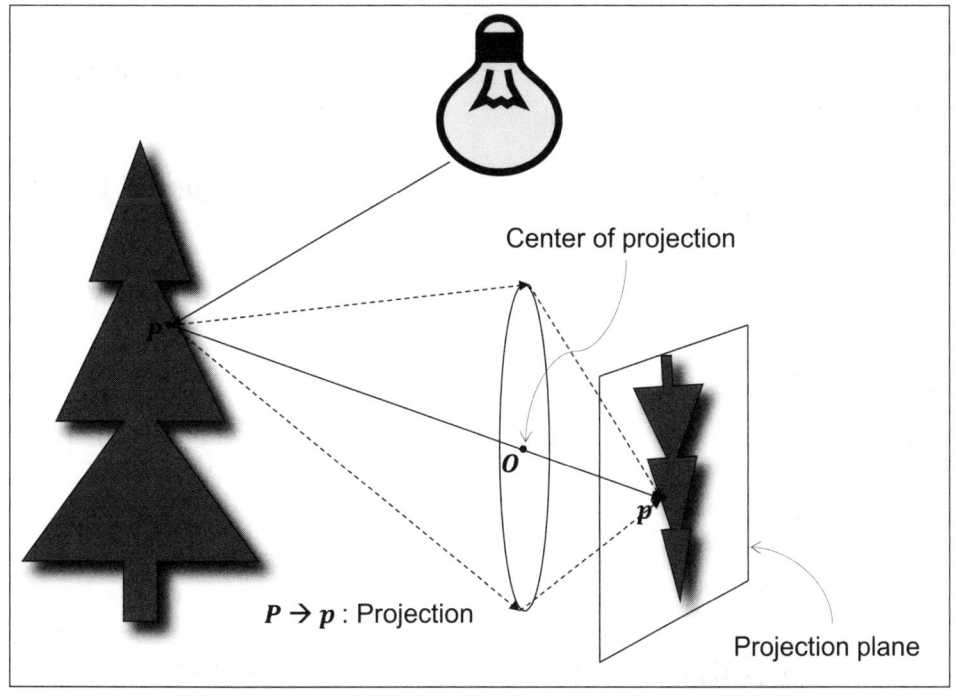

Figure 10.1 Image formation in a projective camera.

scene point to its two-dimensional (2-D) image point. This rule of perspective projection is applied for getting the image point of any scene point, in general. This particular geometry is the basis of *projective geometry* in our context.

10.0.1 | Real and projective spaces

Consider a 2-D space, where a point, p, is denoted by a pair of coordinates, (x, y), as shown in Fig. 10.2. Since it is a cartesian product in real axis, the 2-D space is also denoted as $\mathbb{R}^2$, and the point p belongs to the 2-D coordinate space. Following the coordinate conventions, these coordinates are defined corresponding to an origin, O, and two perpendicular axes meeting at the origin, namely, x-axis and y-axis. The considered projective space, although defined in a 2-D space, implicitly includes a 3-D space behind its definition. For example, though all the points in an image are in a 2-D plane, they are related to 3-D points of a scene which are lying on the ray of projection. This is the abstraction of a 2-D projective space. Consider a 3-D space, as shown in Fig. 10.2. If a ray passes through the origin, O, and the considered point, p, p is said to be the representative of the ray. Every point in this projected plane represents a ray. In this case, the set of projection points, each representing a ray or straight line passing through the origin, is known as a *2-D projective space*, $\mathbb{P}^2$.

The representation of a projection point in a 3-D coordinate form as $p(x, y, 1)$ is known as its canonical representation in the projective space. The plane of projection in the projective space with this representation in a 3-D coordinate system may be seen as a

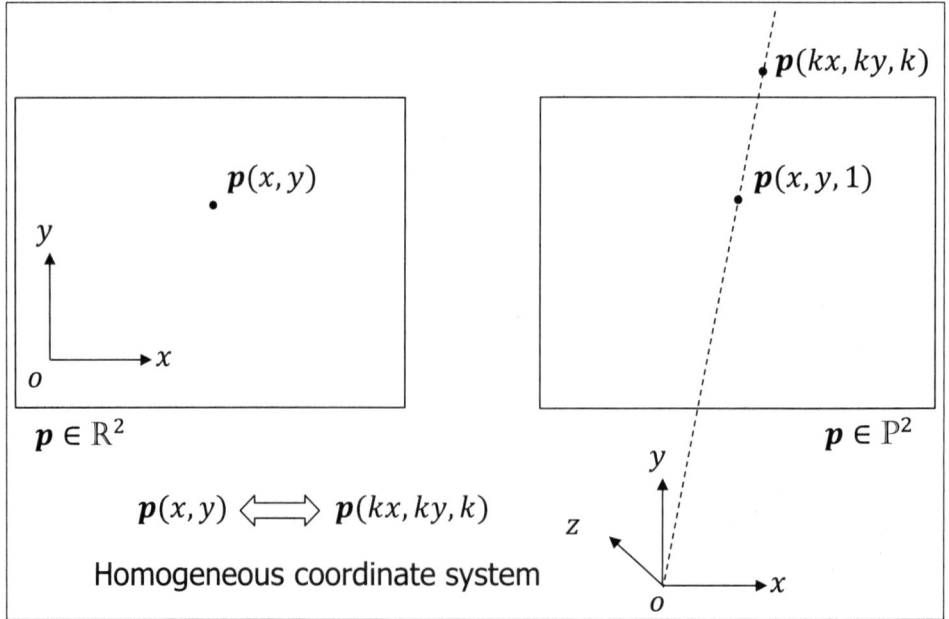

Figure 10.2 Illustration of 2-D real and projective spaces.

plane parallel to the XY plane at a unit distance along the z direction. All the coordinate axes in this plane at unit distance are parallel to the corresponding coordinates of the implicit coordinate system of the 3-D plane. Any point in this plane along the considered straight ray is also represented by a proportional factor of k as $\boldsymbol{p}(kx, ky, k)$, where k is a parameter, as shown in Fig. 10.2 (right). So, a point, $\boldsymbol{p}(x, y) \in \mathbb{R}^2$, in a 2-D real space is equivalently represented in a 2-D projective space as a set of points, $\boldsymbol{p}(kx, ky, k) \in \mathbb{P}^2$, where k varies. This is the relationship between an image in a 2-D real space and its representation in 2-D projective space, under the imaging perspective of projection. This coordinate system is called homogeneous coordinate system, where an additional dimension denotes the scale of the coordinate system. So, if first two coordinates of a point, $\boldsymbol{p}(kx, ky, k)$, are divided by its scale, k, we obtain the nonhomogeneous representation of the point, $p(x, y)$, as a point in the 2-D plane.

Homogeneous coordinate representation of points To formally define the conventions of representation, consider a point, $\boldsymbol{x}$, in $\mathbb{R}^2$ space, which is a 2-D real space.[1] Let the corresponding point in $\mathbb{P}^2$, the 2-D projective space, be denoted as $\boldsymbol{X}$, which has a 3-D vector representation. These points are denoted as in Eq. 10.1.

$$
\boldsymbol{x} \equiv \begin{bmatrix} x \\ y \end{bmatrix} \in \mathbb{R}^2 \quad \Leftrightarrow \quad \boldsymbol{X} \equiv \begin{bmatrix} kx \\ ky \\ k \end{bmatrix} \in \mathbb{P}^2 \tag{10.1}
$$

The additional dimension denotes the scale, which is multiplied with all other coordinates of the system. These two notations, $\boldsymbol{x}$ and $\boldsymbol{X}$, with respect to an image, are equivalent representations. Thus, a point in an image is either denoted in 2-D real space with two coordinate dimensions or it is denoted in a 2-D projective space with three coordinate dimensions. We may note that in this projective space, the origin of that space, $[0 \ 0 \ 0]^\top$, is not included among the set of points in the space. So, the origin is a singular point that cannot be used to form a projection ray at itself. Also, any point in the 3-D real space, excluding the origin, may have a representation of a point in the 2-D projective space. This equivalence of representation of these two spaces is expressed in the following form.

$$
\mathbb{P}^2 = \mathbb{R}^3 - \begin{bmatrix} 0 \\ 0 \\ 0 \end{bmatrix} \tag{10.2}
$$

However, the elements in the projective space are not mere points. They are rays that pass through the origin and each ray is mapped to a point in a particular plane in that space.

---

[1] The bold case notation of a variable denotes a column vector or a tuple of coordinates. In this case, it is a two-tuple coordinate system. This representation is followed throughout this book, unless mentioned to mean otherwise.

10.0.2 | Points and lines in the 2-D projective space

Consider a point, $\boldsymbol{p} \in \mathbb{R}^2$, and a line through this point that is represented by the equation of a straight line, as given in Eq. 10.3.

$$ax + by + c = 0 \tag{10.3}$$

where a, b, and c are the parameters of the straight line. Since a straight line is uniquely identified by the proportional ratios of a, b, and c, the straight line may be sufficiently represented using only two parameters, instead of three parameters. Such a space is also a projective space, $\mathbb{P}^2$, which represents only lines. A line in a 2-D space is represented by a point in this projective space, as shown in Fig. 10.3. There is also an implicit 3-D coordinate system, similar to the representation of any projective space. Any element in this 2-D projective space is a ray passing through the origin that also passes through a particular point, $\boldsymbol{l}(a/c, b/c, 1) \in \mathbb{P}^2$, which is a representation of a straight line. Thus, each element in this space, irrespective of its representation as (a, b, c) or (ka, kb, kc), represents a straight line. The 3-D in this representation of an element, a straight line, denotes the scale. This relationship between a straight line and a point is expressed as a scalar dot product or matrix multiplication of the two vectors, namely, the transpose of the column vectors of the projective point and its corresponding straight line vector, which is given in Eq. 10.4.

$$\begin{bmatrix} x & y & 1 \end{bmatrix} \begin{bmatrix} a \\ b \\ c \end{bmatrix} = 0 \tag{10.4}$$

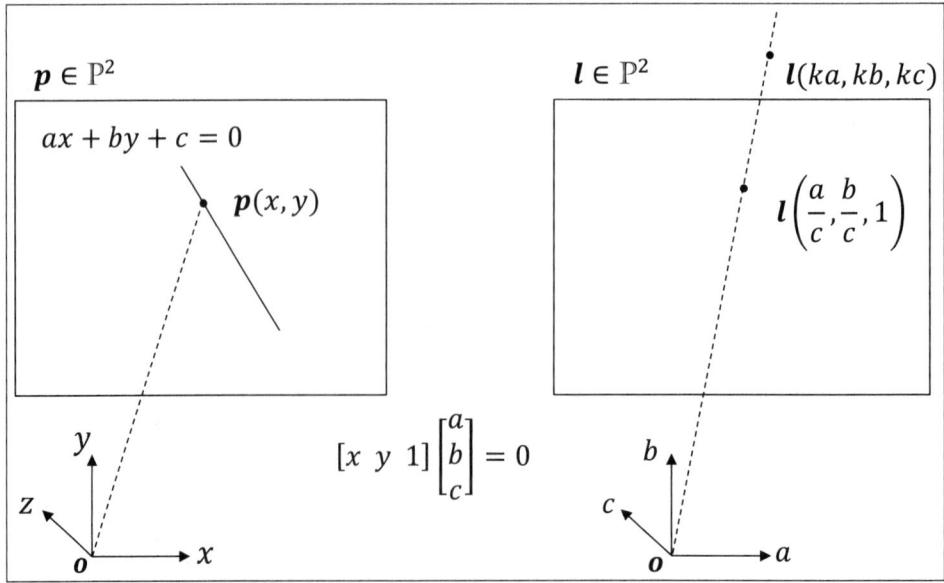

Figure 10.3 Homogeneous representation of a line in a plane.

This relationship is known as point containment relationship, which is expressed in a simpler form, along with an equivalent representation, as in Eq. 10.5.

$$\boldsymbol{X}^\top \boldsymbol{l} = 0 \quad \Leftrightarrow \quad \boldsymbol{l}^\top \boldsymbol{X} = 0 \tag{10.5}$$

where, $\boldsymbol{X}$ and $\boldsymbol{l}$ are the corresponding point and line, respectively.

Any line in the real space is uniquely defined by two points, as shown in Fig. 10.4 (a). Mathematically, this line is computed as a cross product of the two 3-D vectors that represent points. Let, $\boldsymbol{X}_1(x_1, y_1, 1)$ and $\boldsymbol{X}_2(x_2, y_2, 1)$ be the projective homogeneous representations of the points, $\boldsymbol{X}_1$ and $\boldsymbol{X}_2$, respectively. Since $\boldsymbol{X}_1$ and $\boldsymbol{X}_2$ are 3-D vectors and $\boldsymbol{l}$ is orthogonal to each of them (from the point containment relation), their cross product yields the straight line, $\boldsymbol{l}$, as expressed in Eq. 10.6.

$$\boldsymbol{l} = \boldsymbol{X}_1 \times \boldsymbol{X}_2 \tag{10.6}$$

where, the cross product between $\boldsymbol{X}_1$ and $\boldsymbol{X}_2$, $\boldsymbol{X}_1 \times \boldsymbol{X}_2$, is expressed in a 3-D vector form as,[2] $\boldsymbol{X}_1 \times \boldsymbol{X}_2 = [(y_1 - y_2), \ (x_2 - x_1), \ (x_1 y_2 - x_2 y_1)]^\top$. Also, similar to the real space, a point, $\boldsymbol{P}$ is defined as an intersection of two straight lines, $\boldsymbol{l}_1$ and $\boldsymbol{l}_2$, as shown in Fig. 10.4 (b). As $\boldsymbol{P}$ is orthogonal to both of them, their relationship in the projective space is expressed as in Eq. 10.7.

$$\boldsymbol{P} = \boldsymbol{l}_1 \times \boldsymbol{l}_2 \tag{10.7}$$

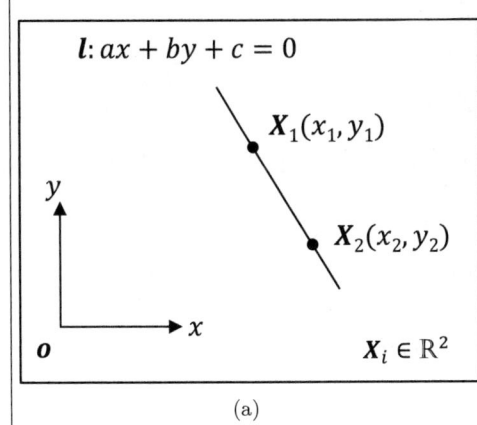 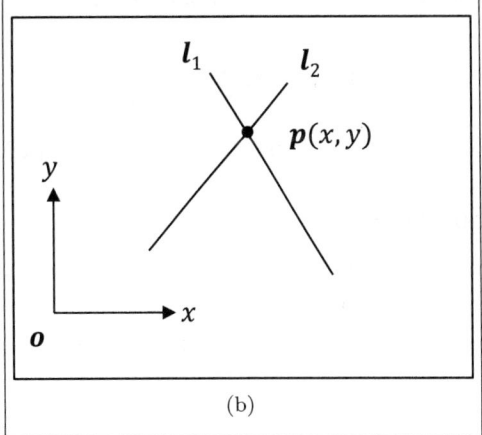

(a)   (b)

Figure 10.4 Illustration of points and lines in $\mathbb{P}^2$.

---

[2] Cross product between two vectors, $\boldsymbol{X}_1$ and $\boldsymbol{X}_2$, is defined as, $\boldsymbol{X}_1 \times \boldsymbol{X}_2 = \begin{vmatrix} i & j & k \\ x_1 & y_1 & 1 \\ x_2 & y_2 & 1 \end{vmatrix}$. The determinant,

$|\boldsymbol{X}_1 \times \boldsymbol{X}_2|$, represents the required form of the line.

That is, the cross product of two lines that are represented in their projective form yields their corresponding point of intersection, which is also represented in the homogeneous coordinate system as an element of the projective space.

In simple terms, only one line passes through given two points and exactly one point lies at the intersection of two lines, and their relationships in projective space are similar. The straight line may be expressed as a cross product of the two corresponding points in the projective space, and a point may be expressed as a cross product of its two intersecting straight lines in the projective space. The points and lines in the projective space have a complementary relationship, and satisfy the duality principle as explained below.

Duality principle   The relationship between the points and lines that are represented in the projective space are complemented by each other. For instance, a containment relationship of $X^\top l = 0$ implies also $l^\top X = 0$. An interchange between l and X does not disturb the validity of the relationship, which is expressed in Eq. 10.5. This is known as the duality principle. Similarly, Eq. 10.8 also conforms the duality principle, where the cross product of two lines, l and l', results in their corresponding point of intersection, X, and the cross product of two points, X and X', results in the corresponding line between them, l.

$$l = X \times X' \quad \Leftrightarrow \quad X = l \times l' \tag{10.8}$$

The duality theorem states that, *to any theorem of 2-D projective geometry involving points and lines, there exists a dual theorem, which may be derived by interchanging the roles of points and lines in the original theorem.*

Numerical Example

Compute the line passing through two points, (3, 5) and (5, 0), in a plane.

Solution

Consider the given points in their homogeneous representation. Let the points be,

$x_1 = \begin{bmatrix} 3 \\ 5 \\ 1 \end{bmatrix}$ and $x_2 = \begin{bmatrix} 5 \\ 0 \\ 1 \end{bmatrix}$. The line, l, passing through x_1 and x_2 is given by,

$$l = x_1 \times x_2 = \begin{bmatrix} 3 \\ 5 \\ 1 \end{bmatrix} \times \begin{bmatrix} 5 \\ 0 \\ 1 \end{bmatrix} = \begin{bmatrix} 5 \\ 2 \\ -25 \end{bmatrix}.$$

Numerical Example

Compute the point of intersection of the lines, $l_1 : 5x - 2y + 4 = 0$ and $l_2 : 6x - 7y - 3 = 0$.

Solution

The point of intersection, p, of two lines, l_1 and l_2, is given by,

$$p = l_1 \times l_2 = \begin{bmatrix} 5 \\ -2 \\ 4 \end{bmatrix} \times \begin{bmatrix} 6 \\ -7 \\ -3 \end{bmatrix} = \begin{bmatrix} 34 \\ 39 \\ -23 \end{bmatrix}.$$

So, the point of intersection in nonhomogeneous representation is given by, $\left(-\frac{34}{23}, -\frac{39}{23}\right)$.

10.0.3 | Intersection of parallel lines

Though the elementary knowledge of geometry provides an understanding that two parallel lines intersect at infinity, the nature of this point at infinity is not qualified in a normal 2-D real space. One of the interesting properties of a projective space lies in a theoretical explanation for expressing the point of intersection of parallel lines. Consider two parallel lines, l_1 and l_2, as shown in Fig. 10.5 (a), which are given by Eq. 10.9.

$$\begin{aligned} l_1 &: & ax + by + c_1 = 0 \\ l_2 &: & ax + by + c_2 = 0 \end{aligned} \tag{10.9}$$

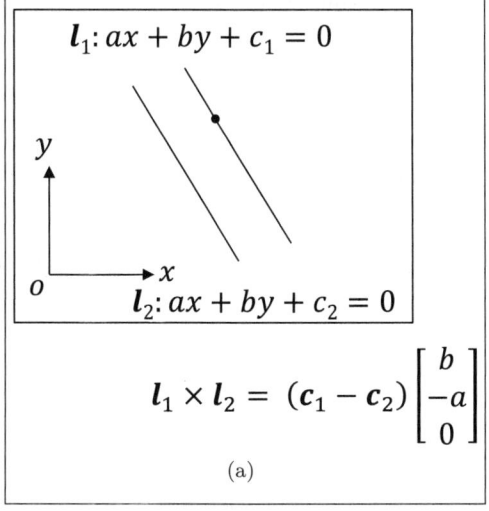

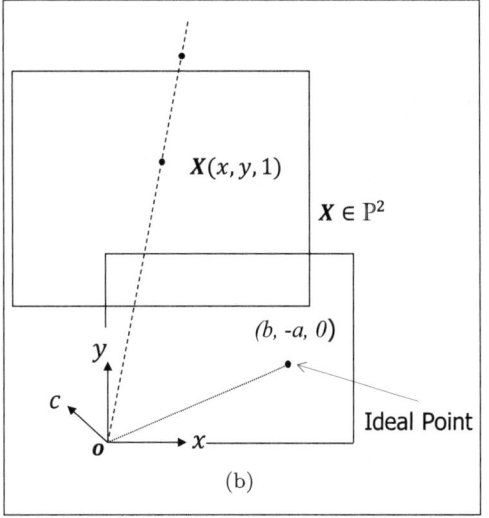

(a)   (b)

Figure 10.5 Depiction of intersection of parallel lines in $\mathbb{P}^2$.

The coefficients, a and b, are the same for both l_1 and l_2, since they are parallel lines. The intersection of these two parallel lines is computed by the cross product of 3-vectorial representation of l_1 and l_2, which is expressed as in Eq. 10.10.

$$l_1 \times l_2 = \begin{bmatrix} a \\ b \\ c_1 \end{bmatrix} \times \begin{bmatrix} a \\ b \\ c_2 \end{bmatrix} = \begin{vmatrix} i & j & k \\ a & b & c_1 \\ a & b & c_2 \end{vmatrix} \tag{10.10}$$

$$= i(bc_2 - bc_1) - j(ac_2 - ac_1) + k(ab - ab)$$

where i, j, and k are the unit vectors along the three orthogonal axes. The expression of the intersection point in Eq. 10.10 is further simplified and expressed in a vectorial form, as given by Eq. 10.11.

$$l_1 \times l_2 = \begin{bmatrix} b(c_2 - c_1) \\ -a(c_2 - c_1) \\ 0 \end{bmatrix} = (c_2 - c_1) \begin{bmatrix} b \\ -a \\ 0 \end{bmatrix} \tag{10.11}$$

Here, if the coordinates are divided by the scale factor, which is 0, to represent the point of intersection in real 2-D space, the two coordinates become infinite. However, in the projective space, the nature of infinity is captured, because it is qualified by the two values, b and $-a$.

The point of intersection that is expressed in Eq. 10.11, $p_i = \begin{bmatrix} b & -a & 0 \end{bmatrix}^\top$, is represented as a point in a plane which is parallel to the canonical projection plane, as shown in Fig. 10.5(b). The plane that contains this point of intersection is known as the *principal plane*, since it contains the x-axis and y-axis through origin of the implicit 3-D coordinate system of the 2-D projective space. In fact, by the representation of elements in the projective space, the entire ray that passes through p_i and the origin, O, is represented by p_i. The point, p_i, is called an *ideal point*. The plane where all such points (i.e., the points with third coordinate as 0) lie, is called the *ideal plane*, which is the principal plane of this representation.

Ideal points

Ideal points are the points on the $x - y$ plane or principal plane, which is parallel to the projection plane. For a canonical coordinate system, ideal points are of the form $\begin{bmatrix} x & y & 0 \end{bmatrix}^\top$, where the 3-D, which represents the scale, is 0. As an implication of an ideal point, it denotes a direction toward infinity.

Consider a 2-D plane, as shown in Fig. 10.6, where two parallel lines, and the x-axis and the y-axis are shown with respect to origin, O. Let one of the straight lines, the bottom line in the figure, be represented by Eq. 10.12.

$$ax + by + c = 0 \tag{10.12}$$

This straight line may also be represented in analytical geometric form, which is given by Eq. 10.13.

$$y = -\frac{a}{b}x + \frac{c}{b} = \tan(\theta)x + c' \tag{10.13}$$

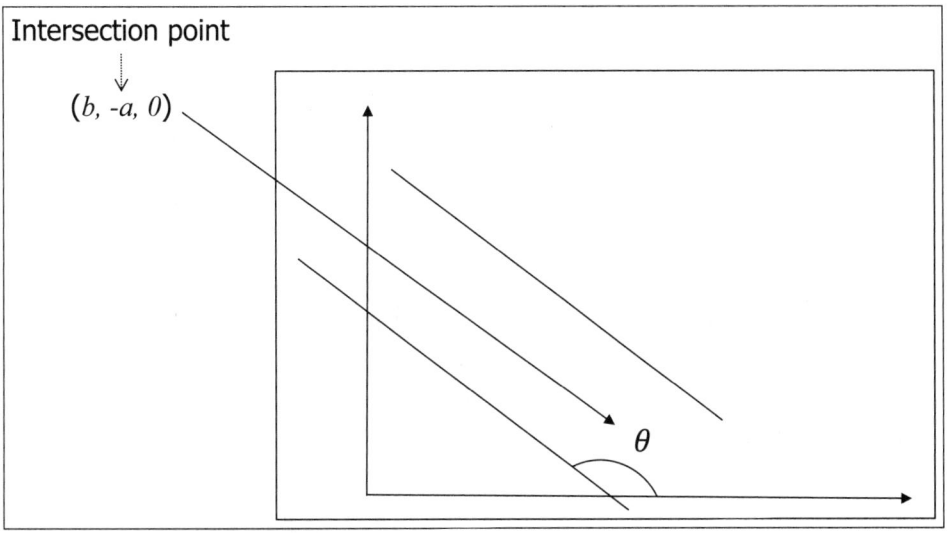

Figure 10.6 An ideal point representing a direction.

where, $\tan(\theta) = -\frac{a}{b}$ represents the slope of the considered straight line with x-axis, and $c' = \frac{c}{b}$ represent interception of the straight line with y-axis. That is, the point of intersection of the two parallel lines, $\boldsymbol{p}_i = [b \ \ -a \ \ 0]^\top$, is related with the slope, $\tan(\theta)$. In other words, it is a point at infinity at the direction making an angle $\theta (= tan^{-1}(\frac{-b}{a}))$ with the x-axis.

Line at infinity

Another concept in the projective space is the *line at infinity*. Consider Fig. 10.7, where an axis is extended toward the direction of parameter c, and is represented by $\boldsymbol{l}_\infty = [0 \ \ 0 \ \ 1]^\top$. This also corresponds to an element in the 2-D projective space. Consider the point-containment property of an ideal point and the line, $\boldsymbol{l}_\infty$, as given in Eq. 10.14.

$$[x \ \ y \ \ 0] \begin{bmatrix} 0 \\ 0 \\ 1 \end{bmatrix} = 0 \qquad (10.14)$$

The above equation shows that all the ideal points lie on the line at infinity.

10.0.4 | A model for projective plane

All the points in the projective plane are represented using a geometric model, as shown in Fig. 10.8. As in the figure, the projection plane is represented by the symbol π. All the points in the real space that have correspondence in the projective space directly lie on this projection plane. Also, every point in π corresponds to a ray passing through the respective point and the origin. Similarly, any point in the principal plane or ideal plane is also an element of the projective space. The points in the ideal plane span all the ideal points that represent directions with respect to the planar observation. And any straight line on the

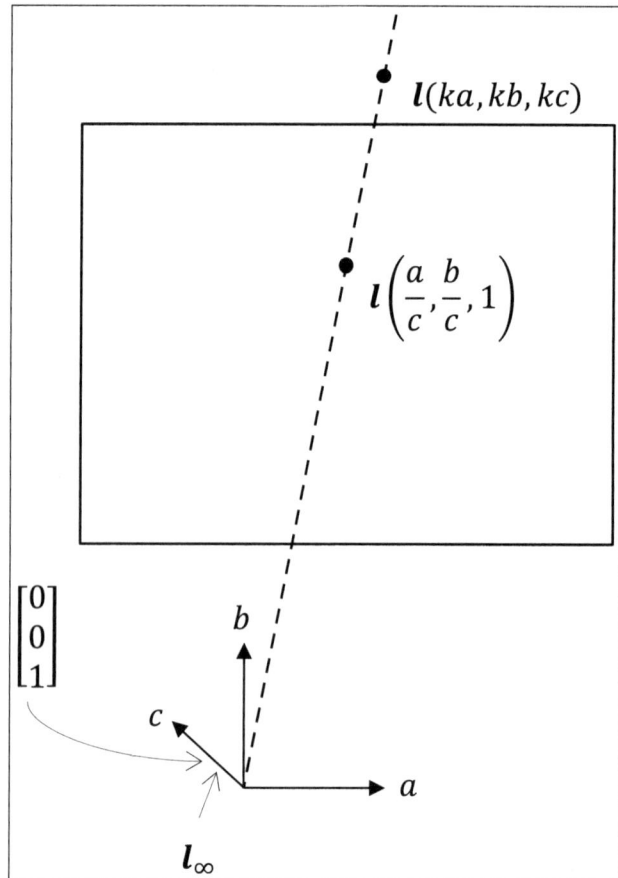

Figure 10.7 Depiction of the line at infinity.

projective plane, π, is geometrically interpreted as an intersection of a plane containing the origin and the plane of projection. That is, any line in the projection plane actually represents a plane of implicit 3-D coordinate system that passes through the origin. This forms a geometric model that is used to illustrate the 2-D projective space.

Mathematically, the set of all points in a projective space is equivalent to the set of all points in the 3-D real space, excluding the origin, as the origin is a singular point of the projective space. Similarly, the set of all points in a projective space is also equivalent to the set of points in 2-D real space, in addition to another plane that is parallel to the real space in the canonical representation, i.e., the ideal plane. Instead of expressing it as a plane that contains all the points, it may also simply be represented by all those points that lie on a particular line, the line at infinity. These equivalences of representations are expressed as in Eq. 10.15.

$$\mathbb{P}^2 = \mathbb{R}^3 - \begin{bmatrix} 0 \\ 0 \\ 0 \end{bmatrix} = \mathbb{R}^2 \cup \boldsymbol{l}_\infty \qquad (10.15)$$

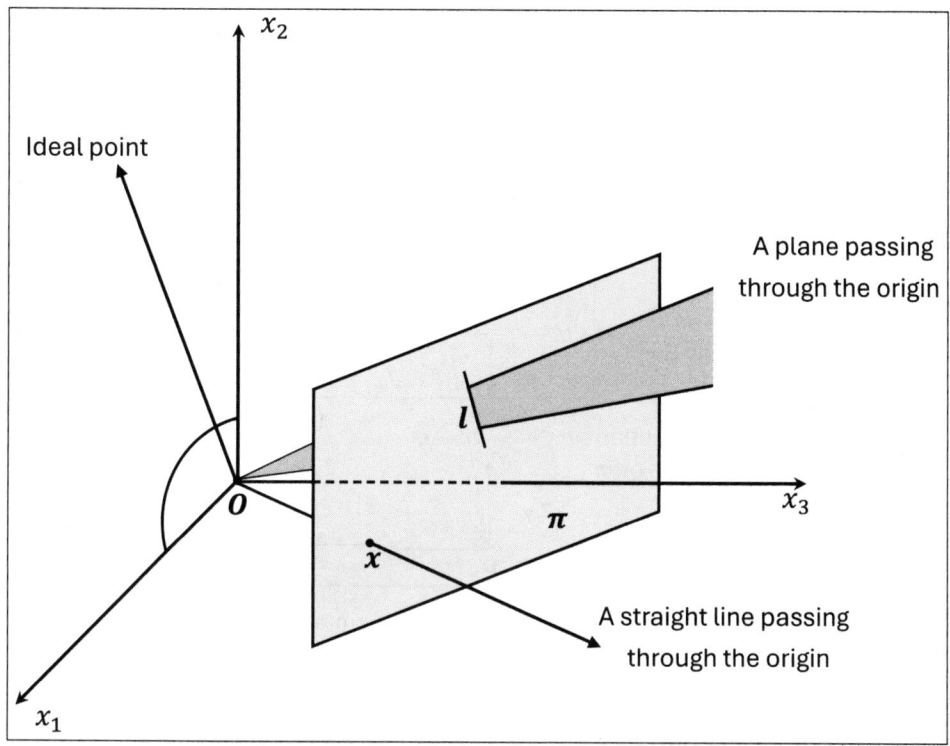

Figure 10.8 A model of the projective plane.

Projection of parallel lines from any arbitrary plane

Consider a projective space, as shown in Fig. 10.9, which carries an implicit 3-D representation. The figure shows an ideal plane and a plane of projection, where any point in the projective space is represented through this plane of projection in canonical form. Consider an arbitrary plane, π, and two parallel lines in it. These two parallel lines are projected on the canonical plane, which are represented for each of the lines lying on the plane π by two rays that pass through any two points on them. The rays from each of the parallel lines intersect the plane of projection, and these intersections form two straight lines that lie on the plane of projection. Though the lines are parallel in plane π, they meet each other at a definite point in the canonical projection plane. This point of intersection is called *vanishing point*.

Vanishing points and vanishing lines

A vanishing point is the point of intersection of parallel lines that are projected on the canonical plane. To understand the implications of vanishing points, consider Fig. 10.10. Consider groups of parallel lines in different directions that lie on the plane, π. As an example, three sets of parallel lines in three different directions are shown in the figure. After projecting the parallel lines on the canonical projection plane or the plane of projection, each set of parallel lines in a particular direction appear to be meeting at some point, which

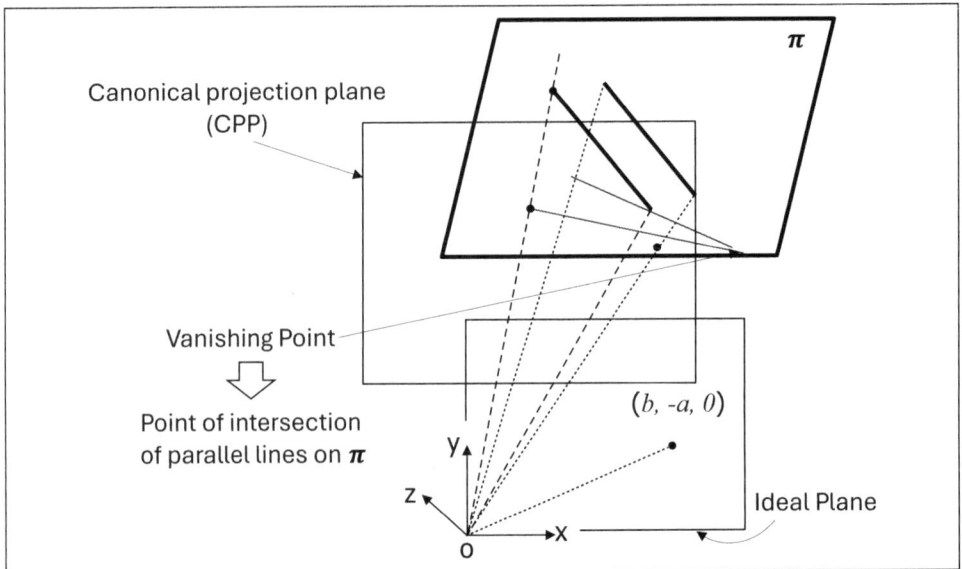

Figure 10.9 Projection of parallel lines from any arbitrary plane.

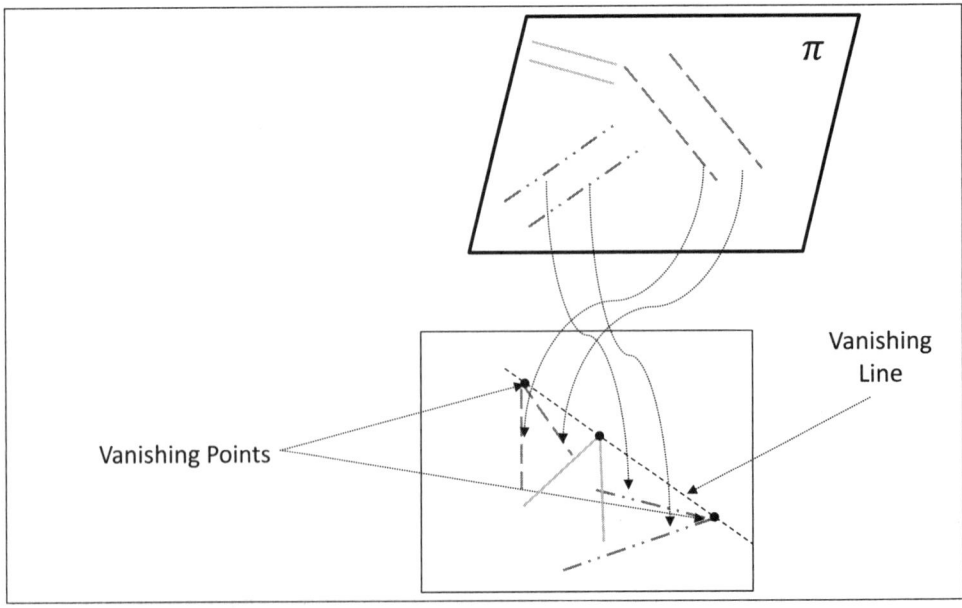

Figure 10.10 Illustration of vanishing points and vanishing lines.

is their vanishing point. So, each of the three sets of parallel lines in three different directions meet at three distinct points, which are their respective vanishing points. The line obtained by joining these three vanishing points is called the *vanishing line*. We may note that all of them lie on a straight line. Likewise, any set of parallel lines in any direction in plane π has their vanishing point on the vanishing line in the plane of projection. That is, the vanishing points corresponding to different sets of parallel lines of a plane lie on a line that is known as the vanishing line.

This is illustrated with a real world example in Fig. 10.11. As observed in the figure, the edges in the horizontal direction meet at some point, which is the vanishing point of horizontal lines. Here, the text also behaves like a horizontal edge. Similarly, the vertical edges also meet at some point, which is the vanishing point of the vertical lines. The vanishing line is obtained by connecting these two vanishing points. A visual demonstration of the vanishing point is shown in Fig. 10.12, which illustrates an image of a road that is captured from the dashboard of a car. It may be perceptually sensed from the image that the edges of the road are meeting at a point at infinity, but it remains ever illusive. Philosophically, the journey is toward infinity, which is sensed from the point of

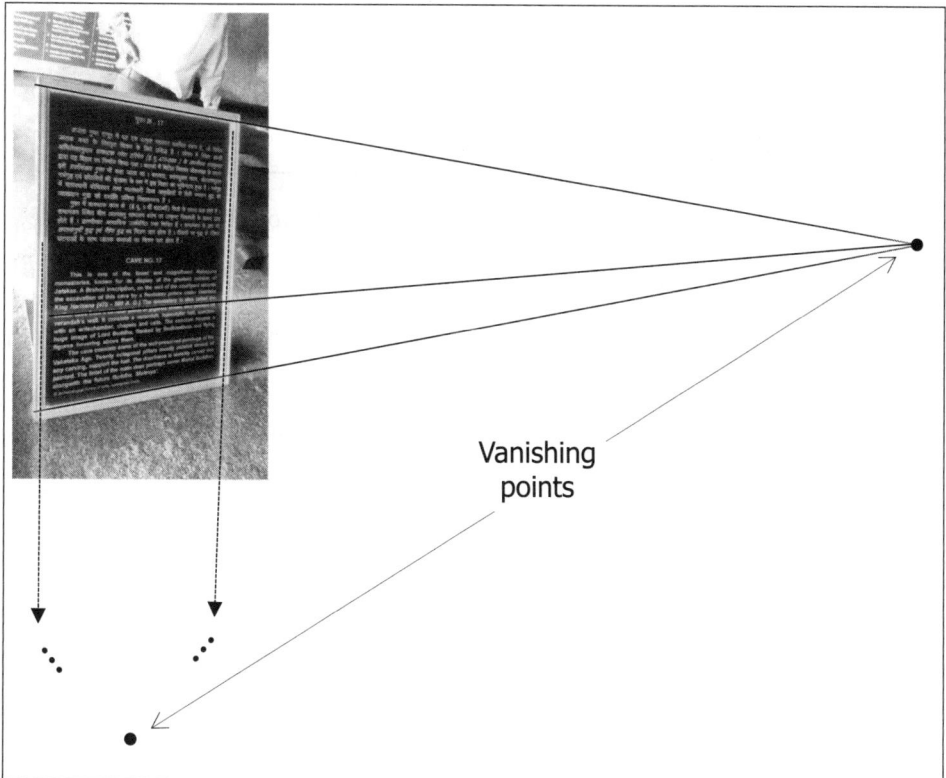

Vanishing
points

Figure 10.11 An example of vanishing points in real world image of a description board from archaeological survey of India, Aurangabad region, India.

Figure 10.12 A visual demonstration of the vanishing point in an image of a road that is captured from the dashboard of a car.

view of perspective projections, but the point at infinity can never be reached. This is how we may interpret a vanishing point.

10.1 | Conics in $\mathbb{P}^2$

Conics are also one of the elementary concepts in the 2-D projective space (Hartley and Zisserman, 2003). They are curves that are described by a generalized second degree equation, as given in Eq. 10.16.

$$ax^2 + bxy + cy^2 + dx + ey + f = 0 \tag{10.16}$$

For a point in homogeneous coordinate representation, (x_1, x_2, x_3), its corresponding 2-D real coordinates are given by, $(x, y) = \left(\frac{x_1}{x_3}, \frac{x_2}{x_3}\right)$. Substituting this in Eq. 10.16, the representation of conics in homogeneous coordinates is given as in Eq. 10.17.

$$a\left(\frac{x_1}{x_3}\right)^2 + b\left(\frac{x_1}{x_3}\right)\left(\frac{x_2}{x_3}\right) + c\left(\frac{x_2}{x_3}\right)^2 + d\left(\frac{x_1}{x_3}\right) + e\left(\frac{x_2}{x_3}\right) + f = 0$$
$$\implies ax_1^2 + bx_1x_2 + cx_2^2 + dx_1x_3 + ex_2x_3 + fx_3^2 = 0 \tag{10.17}$$

The expression in Eq. 10.17 is a general form of representation of a conic. This is more concisely represented in a matrix form, as given in Eq. 10.18.

$$\boldsymbol{x}^\top \mathbf{C} \boldsymbol{x} = 0, \quad \text{where,} \quad \mathbf{C} = \begin{bmatrix} a & \frac{b}{2} & \frac{d}{2} \\ \frac{b}{2} & c & \frac{e}{2} \\ \frac{d}{2} & \frac{e}{2} & f \end{bmatrix}, \quad \text{and} \quad \boldsymbol{x} = \begin{bmatrix} x_1 \\ x_2 \\ x_3 \end{bmatrix} \tag{10.18}$$

Here, the matrix, $\mathbf{C}$, is a symmetric matrix of dimensions 3×3. Also, in Eq. 10.18, if $\mathbf{C}$ is multiplied by a factor of k, still it remains the same conic. Hence, it is an element of a projective space. In this representation of conics, though there are six parameters, a, b, c, d, e, and f, the degree of freedom is five, as one of them may be deemed as a scale parameter.

Since the degree of freedom is five, naturally, at least five points are necessary to uniquely define a conic in a 2-D projective space as in Eq. 10.16, which is expressed in Eq. 10.19.

$$[x_i^2 \ x_i y_i \ y_i^2 \ x_i \ y_i \ 1][a \ b \ c \ d \ e \ f]^{\mathsf{T}} = 0, \quad i = 1, 2, 3, 4, 5$$

$$\implies \begin{bmatrix} x_1^2 & x_1 y_1 & y_1^2 & x_1 & y_1 & 1 \\ x_2^2 & x_2 y_2 & y_2^2 & x_2 & y_2 & 1 \\ x_3^2 & x_3 y_3 & y_3^2 & x_3 & y_3 & 1 \\ x_4^2 & x_4 y_4 & y_4^2 & x_4 & y_4 & 1 \\ x_5^2 & x_5 y_5 & y_5^2 & x_5 & y_5 & 1 \end{bmatrix} \mathbf{c} = 0 \qquad (10.19)$$

where, $\mathbf{c} = [a \ b \ c \ d \ e \ f]^{\mathsf{T}}$. As one of the parameters may be taken as the scale parameter, the other parameters can be represented in proportion to the scale parameter. In this case, the conic in Eq. 10.16 may be solved by setting the scale parameter to a fixed value.

10.1.1 | Dual line conics

For a conic, $\mathbf{C}$, its tangent lines, l, are functionally related with the points, $\boldsymbol{x}$, that are lying on that conic in a linear form, as in Eq. 10.20.

$$l = \mathbf{C}\boldsymbol{x} \qquad (10.20)$$

That is, the conic itself acts as a transformation matrix for transforming its point to the tangent at that point. This kind of transformation (from a point to a line) is also called *correlation* in this geometric context. We note here that $\mathbf{C}$ is invertible (except a few degenerate cases, that we discuss elsewhere (Section 10.1.2)). Hence for a point $\boldsymbol{x}$ on the conic, there exists a unique tangent l (up to scale). By the definition of a tangent, it passes through a single point of the conic. Thus we get one to one correspondence between l and $\boldsymbol{x}$. Hence,

$$l = \mathbf{C}\boldsymbol{x} \implies \boldsymbol{x} = \mathbf{C}^{-1}l \qquad (10.21)$$

This provides a conic representation known as the *dual representation of a conic*. A conic may be represented by all its tangential lines that forms an envelope of the conic. Similar to the expression of the conic in Eq. 10.18, in this case, the conic is represented by Eq. 10.22.

$$l^{\mathsf{T}} \mathbf{C}^* l = 0 \qquad (10.22)$$

where, $\mathbf{C}^*$ is a 3×3 matrix that is different than $\mathbf{C}$ in Eq. 10.18, and l is the tangent. The relationship between the original conic representation and the dual conic representation is obtained using Eqs. 10.18–10.22.

From Eqs. 10.18 and 10.21, the expression for dual conic is derived as,

$$x^\top \mathbf{C} x = 0$$
$$\Longrightarrow \left(\mathbf{C}^{-1} l\right)^\top \mathbf{C} \left(\mathbf{C}^{-1} l\right) = 0$$
$$\Longrightarrow l^\top \left(\mathbf{C}^{-1}\right)^\top \mathbf{C} \mathbf{C}^{-1} l = 0 \qquad (10.23)$$
$$\Longrightarrow l^\top \mathbf{C}^{-\top} l = 0$$

From Eqs. 10.21 and 10.23, $\mathbf{C}^*$ is determined as shown in Eq. 10.24.

$$\mathbf{C}^* = \left(\mathbf{C}^{-1}\right)^\top \mathbf{C} \mathbf{C}^{-1} = \left(\mathbf{C}^{-1}\right)^\top \mathbf{I} = \mathbf{C}^{-\top} \qquad (10.24)$$

where, $\mathbf{I}$ is an identity matrix. In Eq. 10.24, $\mathbf{C}^{-\top} = \mathbf{C}^{-1}$, since $\mathbf{C}$ is a symmetric matrix. That is, the dual conic representation of $\mathbf{C}$ is its inverse, $\mathbf{C}^{-1}$.

Numerical Example

Find the line l which is the tangent to the conic $\mathbf{C}$ at a point $(x, y) = (2, -2)$, where $\mathbf{C} : 2x^2 + 3xy + 2y^2 + 2x + 4y = 0$

Solution

Check the point, whether it lies in the conic. $(2, -2)$ lies on $\mathbf{C}$. Hence, the line l tangent to $\mathbf{C}$ at a point x on $\mathbf{C}$ is given by $l = \mathbf{C} x$, where

$$\mathbf{C} = \begin{bmatrix} a & b/2 & d/2 \\ b/2 & c & e/2 \\ d/2 & e/2 & f \end{bmatrix}$$

In this problem,

$$\begin{bmatrix} 2 & 3/2 & 2/2 \\ 3/2 & 2 & 4/2 \\ 2/2 & 4/2 & 0 \end{bmatrix} \begin{bmatrix} 2 \\ -2 \\ 1 \end{bmatrix} = \begin{bmatrix} 2 \\ 1 \\ -2 \end{bmatrix}$$

10.1.2 | Degenerate conics

In representing the conic as in Eq. 10.18, there may be some rank deficiency in $\mathbf{C}$, where the degree of freedom is less than 5. If the rank of matrix $\mathbf{C}$ is less than 3, it is considered to have some degenerate conditions of representation. Such rank deficient conics are called *degenerate conics*. For example, a point conic $\mathbf{C}$ may be formed by two lines of rank 2 and by a repeated line of rank 1. Similarly a dual conic (or line conic) $\mathbf{C}^*$ of rank two are described by two points and that of rank one by a single point. For example, a degenerate point conic is represented using two lines, l and m, which is given by $\mathbf{C} = lm^\top + ml^\top$, where, l and m are 3-vectors, so that $\mathbf{C}$ is a 3×3 matrix. Points lying on l and m satisfy the conic relationship i.e. $x^\top(lm^\top + ml^\top)x = 0$. Similarly, the degenerate dual conic is represented by two points, s and t, as $\mathbf{C}^* = s\,t^\top + t\,s^\top$. In this case, lines passing through s and t satisfy the dual conic relationship. We may note that as the degenerate point conic and degenerate dual line conic are singular, they are not invertible and they do not have their corresponding duals.

10.2 | Projective transformation

The transformation of a point in a projective space to a point in another projective space is known as projective transformation, $h : \mathbb{P}^2 \to \mathbb{P}^2$, if it satisfies that, (i) the transformation, h, is invertible, and (ii) it preserves the collinearity of every 3 points. Satisfying the collinearity property implies that, for a given set of three points, x_1, x_2, and x_3, that lie on a line, their corresponding transformed points also lie on a line in the same order in the transformed projective space. This is shown figuratively in Fig. 10.13, where a set of three collinear points are shown by different shapes. After transformation, the corresponding transformed points are also shown in the same shapes in another projective space, whose mapping are shown by arrows. The transformed points are related by a one-to-one mapping function, which are invertible. For a transformation to be a projective transformation, these properties have to be satisfied for every configuration of three collinear points. In summary, a projective transformation preserves the properties of (i) collinearity of points, (ii) invertibility of the transformation in one-to-one mapping of points, and (iii) belongingness of the transformed points in a 2-D projective space.

There are various examples of projective transformation. For instance, consider the image shown in Fig. 10.14, which depicts a case of change of coordinate convention. In the figure,

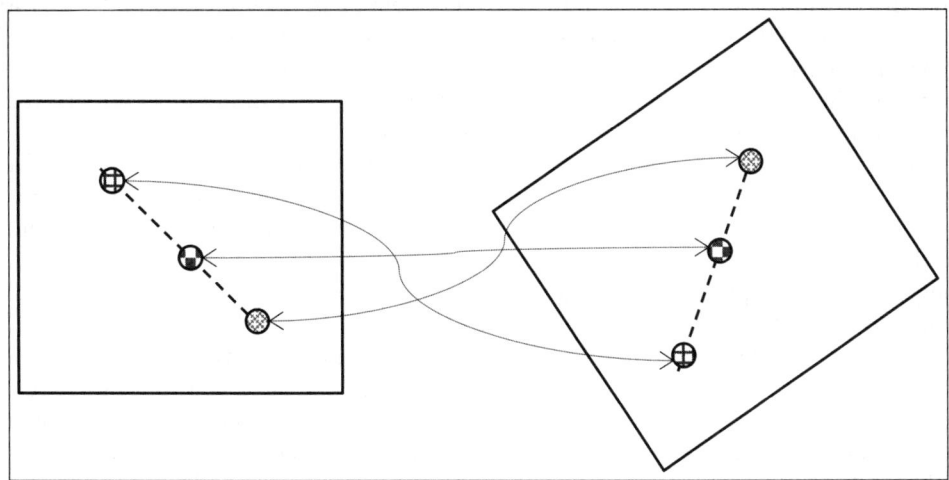

Figure 10.13 Illustration of collinearity of three points in projective transformation.

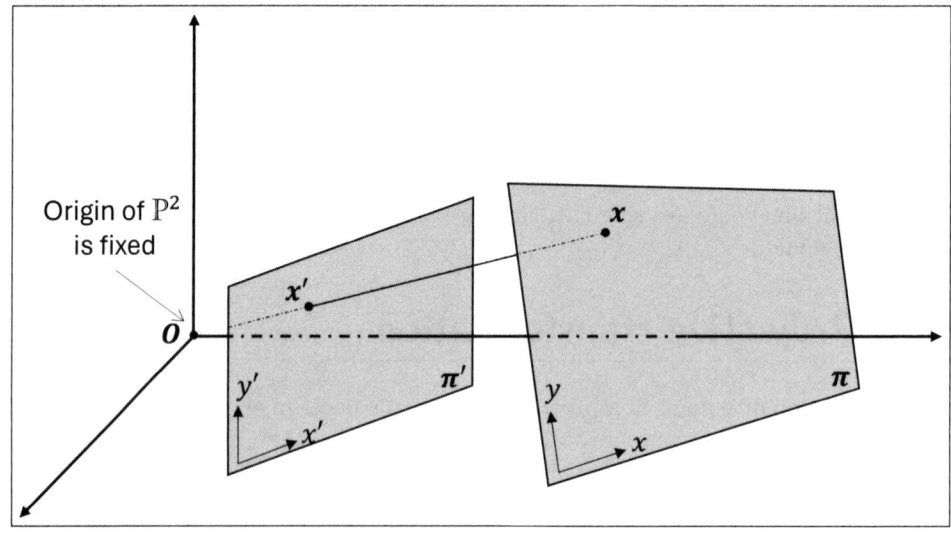

Figure 10.14 An example of projective transformation as a change of coordinate convention.

a point, $\boldsymbol{x}' = (x' \ y' \ 1)^{\top}$, in a plane, π', is mapped to another point, $\boldsymbol{x} = (x \ y \ 1)^{\top}$, in another plane, π, where the points are represented in their canonical form. A ray connecting $\boldsymbol{x}'$ and the center of coordinates, $\boldsymbol{O}$, which is the center of projections in this case, also connects $\boldsymbol{x}$, the corresponding transformed point, when extended toward the corresponding plane of projection. Similarly, every point in the plane π' of a 2-D projective space is mapped to its corresponding point in the plane π of another 2-D projective space by a geometric rule. There may be individual coordinate conventions, i.e., the coordinate axes may be in different orientations in the considered projective spaces. In the example shown in the figure, the coordinates axes of π' and π are represented by $x' - y'$ axes and $x - y$ axes, respectively. The individual coordinate axes in the projective spaces need not be parallel to the coordinate axes of the implicit 3-D space. Also, any straight line in plane π' is projected as a straight line in plane π, which implies that the collinearity of points is preserved after the transformation. So, it is a projective transformation.

There may be several other examples of projective transformations, like, rotation of axes, change of scale, and translation of origin in the planar coordinate system. These examples are shown in Fig. 10.15. In Fig. 10.15 (b), the plane of projections is rotated about an axis. Here, the two planes are related by a rotation, where the intersection of a ray passing through the center of projections and a point in one of the planes with another plane defines the corresponding transfer point. In Fig. 10.15 (a), the corresponding points, $\boldsymbol{x}$ and $\boldsymbol{x}'$, in two different planes have two different centers of projections, but they are formed by the rays that connect to the same point, $\boldsymbol{X}$, on a particular planar surface. In Fig. 10.15 (c), the shadow formation depicts a case of projection where the scale of the image in the plane of shadow is different from the plane of the object. Although each of these operations results in a different set of coordinates for the transformed points, geometrically, all the properties of a projective transformation are preserved.

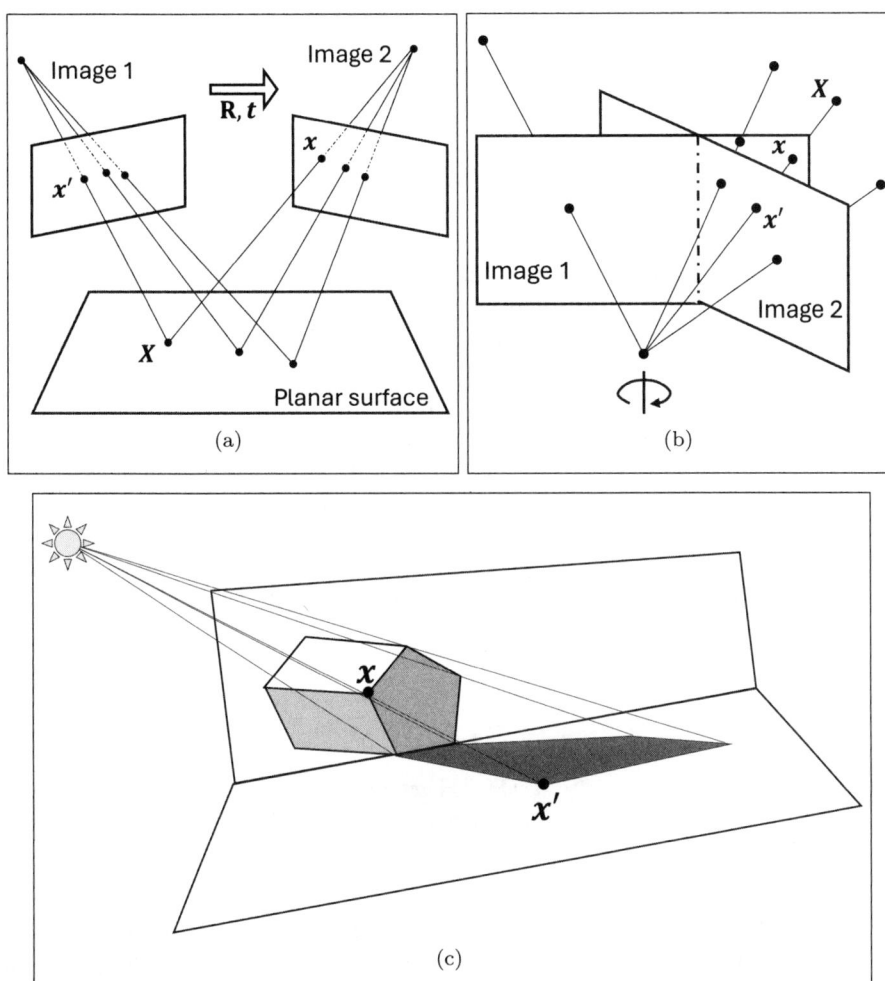

Figure 10.15 Other examples of projective transformation. (a) Shift of origin in the planar coordinate system, (b) rotation of axes, and (c) change of scale.

10.2.1 | Form of projective transformation

It can be mathematically proved that, only one form of the projective transformation, $\boldsymbol{x}' = h(\boldsymbol{x})$, is possible, as expressed in Eq. 10.25, which is a linear form.

$$
\begin{bmatrix} x'_1 \\ x'_2 \\ x'_3 \end{bmatrix} = \begin{bmatrix} h_{11} & h_{12} & h_{13} \\ h_{21} & h_{22} & h_{23} \\ h_{31} & h_{32} & h_{33} \end{bmatrix} \begin{bmatrix} x_1 \\ x_2 \\ x_3 \end{bmatrix}
\tag{10.25}
$$

Here, the 3×3 transformation matrix is an invertible matrix that maps a point, $\boldsymbol{x} = (x_1 \ x_2 \ x_3)^\top$, to another point, $\boldsymbol{x}' = (x_1' \ x_2' \ x_3')^\top$. This 3×3 transformation matrix is represented by $\mathbf{H}$, and Eq. 10.25 is represented in matrix notations as in Eq. 10.26.

$$\boldsymbol{x}' = \mathbf{H}\boldsymbol{x} \equiv k\mathbf{H}\boldsymbol{x} \tag{10.26}$$

where, k is any arbitrary nonzero real value. The projective relationship is not disturbed by the multiplication of k (called scale factor) because a point, $\boldsymbol{x}'$, and $k\boldsymbol{x}'$ correspond to the same element in the projective space. So, the multiplication of the transformation matrix with any scalar constant is equivalent to the same transformation matrix. Hence, the projective transformation matrix with its nine elements is also an element of a 8-D projective space. Though there are nine elements in $\mathbf{H}$, it has eight degrees of freedom, since one of the elements may be used as the scale factor. The matrix, $\mathbf{H}$, is called *homography matrix*, and its corresponding transformation is named *homography*.

Consider a line, $\boldsymbol{l}$, in the 2-D projective space, $\mathbb{P}^2$. A point, $\boldsymbol{x}$, on $\boldsymbol{l}$ satisfies the point containment relationship, which is given by $\boldsymbol{l}^\top \boldsymbol{x} = 0$. Using the matrix property of $\mathbf{H}^{-1}\mathbf{H} = \mathbf{I}$, where $\mathbf{I}$ is an identity matrix, this point containment relationship is further expanded, as given in Eq. 10.27.

$$\begin{aligned} \boldsymbol{l}^\top \boldsymbol{x} &= 0 \\ \boldsymbol{l}^\top (\mathbf{I})\boldsymbol{x} &= 0 \\ \boldsymbol{l}^\top (\mathbf{H}^{-1}\mathbf{H})\boldsymbol{x} &= 0 \\ (\mathbf{H}^{-\top}\boldsymbol{l})^\top \mathbf{H}\boldsymbol{x} &= 0 \end{aligned} \tag{10.27}$$

In the above equations, $\mathbf{H}^{-\top}$ denotes transposition of $\mathbf{H}^{-1}$. Here, $(\mathbf{H}^{-\top}\boldsymbol{l})$ is the transformed line of $\boldsymbol{l}$. That is, $(\mathbf{H}^{-\top}\boldsymbol{l})$ is a line in the transformed space where all the points of $\boldsymbol{l}$ are lying, which are collinear. This proves the property that homography preserves collinearity. The proof for $\mathbf{H}$ being the only form of homography requires much complex arguments, and it is not provided here.[3] However, the fact that $\mathbf{H}$ is the only form of homography used in relevant mathematical treatment and analysis in this book, which have the following implications.

- If there is a homography, there exists a unique $\mathbf{H}$ (up to a nonzero scale factor k) that is a 3×3 invertible matrix.

- It is easier to estimate $\mathbf{H}$, since its functional form is known.

- The equivalence of $\mathbf{H}$ and $k\mathbf{H}$ may be directly used in applications, where k is a scalar constant.

- The number of unknowns in $\mathbf{H}$ is eight, as one of its elements can be used as the scale factor, so that, all other elements are expressed in proportion to its value.

---

[3] Interested readers may refer to Hartley and Zisserman (2003) for a detailed analysis of the proof.

Numerical Example

Consider the following homography matrix $\mathbf{H}$ from image $\mathbf{I}_1$ (source) to $\mathbf{I}_2$ (target) of the same scene captured by a pair of cameras.

$$\mathbf{H} = \begin{bmatrix} 1 & 3 & 5 \\ 4 & 3 & 7 \\ 5 & -4 & 2 \end{bmatrix}$$

Suppose an image point in $\mathbf{I}_1$ given by $(5, 6) \in \mathbb{R}^2$. Find the corresponding point in $\mathbf{I}_2$.

Solution

$$\begin{bmatrix} 1 & 3 & 5 \\ 4 & 3 & 7 \\ 5 & -4 & 2 \end{bmatrix} \begin{bmatrix} 5 \\ 6 \\ 1 \end{bmatrix} = \begin{bmatrix} 28 \\ 45 \\ 3 \end{bmatrix}$$

Therefore, transformed point is $\left(\frac{x_1}{x_3}, \frac{x_2}{x_3}\right)$, i.e., $\left(\frac{28}{3}, \frac{45}{3}\right)$

10.2.2 | Estimation of $\mathbf{H}$

To compute the homography matrix, a set of point correspondences is necessary. A typical point correspondence between a point $\boldsymbol{x} = [x \ y \ 1]^\top$ in the original space (here, the scale is assumed to be 1 for simplicity) and its corresponding point, $\boldsymbol{x}' = [x_1' \ x_2' \ x_3']^\top$, in the transformed space is defined by a projective transformation relationship, $\boldsymbol{x}' = \mathbf{H}\boldsymbol{x}$, where, $\mathbf{H}$ is the homography matrix. Here, the computational problem is to estimate $\mathbf{H}$. From Eq. 10.25 and 10.26, the representation of the point, $\boldsymbol{x}'$, in 2-D real coordinate space, (x', y'), is expressed by dividing the coordinates, x_1' and x_2', by the scale factor, x_3', which are given in Eq. 10.28.

$$\begin{bmatrix} x_1' \\ x_2' \\ x_3' \end{bmatrix} = \begin{bmatrix} h_{11} & h_{12} & h_{13} \\ h_{21} & h_{22} & h_{23} \\ h_{31} & h_{32} & h_{33} \end{bmatrix} \begin{bmatrix} x \\ y \\ 1 \end{bmatrix}$$

$$\implies x' = \frac{x_1'}{x_3'} = \frac{h_{11}x + h_{12}y + h_{13}}{h_{31}x + h_{32}y + h_{33}}$$

$$\text{and}$$

$$y' = \frac{x_2'}{x_3'} = \frac{h_{21}x + h_{22}y + h_{23}}{h_{31}x + h_{32}y + h_{33}}$$

(10.28)

Here, the point, x, whose scale factor is 1, is transformed using $\mathbf{H}$ that is defined in Eq. 10.25. As it can be seen in Eq. 10.28, there are eight unknowns in $\mathbf{H}$. Since a single point correspondence gives only two independent equations, four point correspondences are required to compute $\mathbf{H}$, as there are eight degrees of freedom, excluding the scale factor. Thus, a minimum of four point correspondences are necessary to solve for $\mathbf{H}$.

10.2.3 | Application of homography to remove projective distortion

Consider the example shown in Fig. 10.11, where the horizontal parallel lines are not appearing as horizontal in the projective space and they look like oblique lines that are meeting at a finite point, the vanishing point. In such cases, homography may be used to remove the projective distortions, so that, the horizontal lines appear as horizontal and the vertical lines appear as vertical after correction. To solve for eight unknowns in $\mathbf{H}$, four points with known coordinates are selected to form eight equations. The selections are shown as the corner points in the figure. The objective is to fix the oblique lines that are supposed to be parallel in the horizontal direction, so that, the selected quadrilateral appears as a rectangle. That is, the corner points of the selected quadrilateral are mapped to the corner points of a rectangle, as shown in the figure. Since the coordinates of the four corresponding points, which are mapped, are known in both of the considered projective spaces, four pairs of equations, i.e., eight equations, are formed using Eq. 10.28. These equations are expressed in a linear form with respect to the elements of the transformation matrix, $\mathbf{H}$, as given by Eq. 10.29.

$$
\begin{aligned}
x'(h_{31}x + h_{32}y + h_{33}) &= h_{11}x + h_{12}y + h_{13} \\
y'(h_{31}x + h_{32}y + h_{33}) &= h_{21}x + h_{22}y + h_{23}
\end{aligned}
\tag{10.29}
$$

The set of eight equations that are in the form as in Eq. 10.29 is solved by considering h_{33} as the scale element and assigning it to a value of 1. This transformation produces a result, as shown in Fig. 10.16, where all the horizontal lines are parallel. Also, as observed from the figure, the text in the image is better readable after the correction. The advantage of this method is its simplicity, where the projective distortion is corrected by the coordinate definitions, and it does not require any prior calibration of the cameras. However, as a caution to this method, this approach is applicable only if the scale factor, h_{33}, is a nonzero element. In cases where $h_{33} = 0$, a different method is applied, viz., *direct linear transformation*, which is generally applicable to any kind of homography matrix.

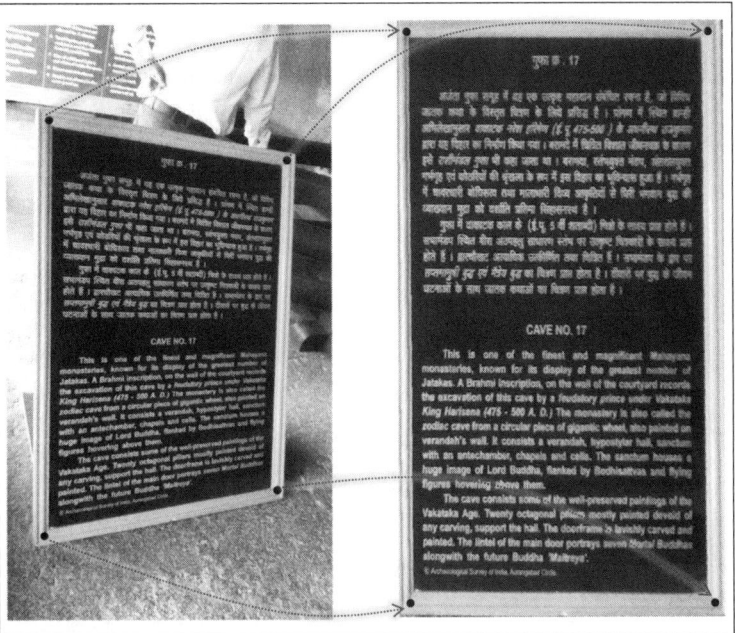

Figure 10.16 A real world example of application of homography to remove projective distortion.

Numerical Example

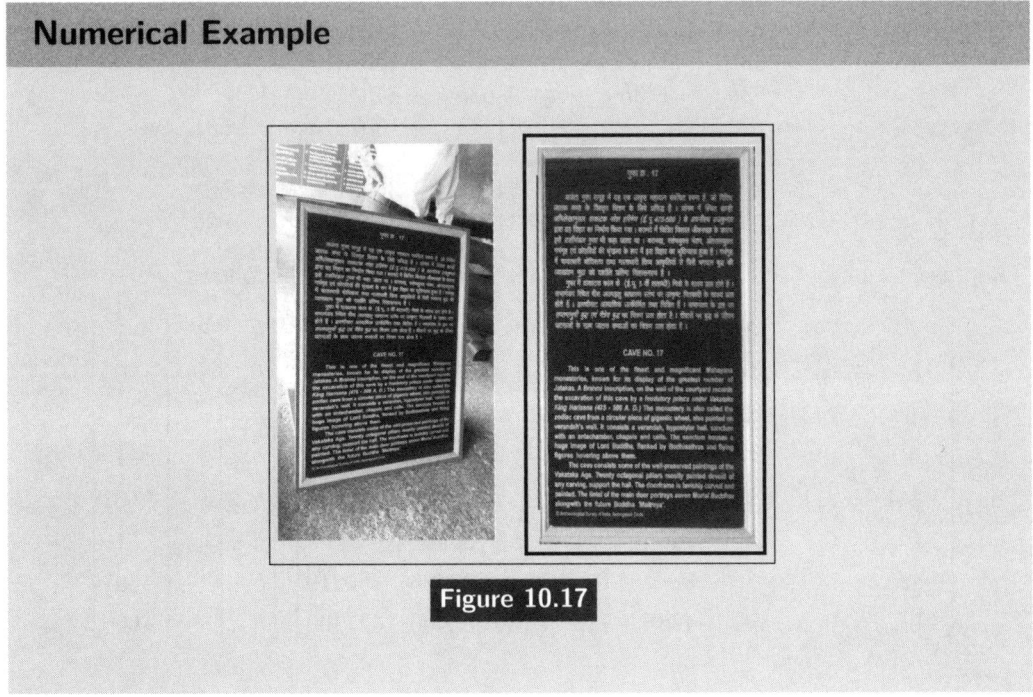

Figure 10.17

Consider the images shown in Fig. 10.17. The four points in a plane in Fig. 10.17 (left), which are the corner points of the marked quadrilateral, are given as, $(51, 791)$, $(63, 143)$, $(444, 211)$, and $(426, 791)$. The corresponding points in Fig. 10.17 (right) are given as, $(1, 900)$, $(1, 1)$, $(501, 1)$, and $(501, 900)$, respectively. Compute the transformation matrix between Fig. 10.17 (left) and (right) images.

Solution

Let the homography matrix be of the form,

$$\mathbf{H} = \begin{bmatrix} h_{11} & h_{12} & h_{13} \\ h_{21} & h_{22} & h_{23} \\ h_{31} & h_{32} & h_{33} \end{bmatrix}$$

For a point correspondence, $\boldsymbol{x} = (x, y) \Leftrightarrow \boldsymbol{x}' = (x', y')$, two equations may be obtained in the following form.

$$x'(h_{31}x + h_{32}y + h_{33}) = h_{11}x + h_{12}y + h_{13}$$
$$y'(h_{31}x + h_{32}y + h_{33}) = h_{21}x + h_{22}y + h_{23}$$

Here, the value of h_{33} is set to 1. The four given point correspondences are, $(51, 791) \Leftrightarrow (1, 900)$, $(63, 143) \Leftrightarrow (1, 1)$, $(444, 211) \Leftrightarrow (501, 1)$, and $(426, 791) \Leftrightarrow (501, 900)$. Using these four point correspondences, eight equations may be formed, which are as follows.

$$-51h_{11} - 791h_{12} - h_{13} + 51h_{31} + 791h_{32} = -1$$
$$-51h_{21} - 791h_{22} - h_{23} + 45900h_{31} + 711900h_{32} = -900$$
$$-63h_{11} - 143h_{12} - h_{13} + 63h_{31} + 143h_{32} = -1$$
$$-63h_{21} - 143h_{22} - h_{23} + 63h_{31} + 143h_{32} = -1$$
$$-444h_{11} - 211h_{12} - h_{13} + 222444h_{31} + 105711h_{32} = -501$$
$$-444h_{21} - 211h_{22} - h_{23} + 444h_{31} + 211h_{32} = -1$$
$$-426h_{11} - 719h_{12} - h_{13} + 213426h_{31} + 360219h_{32} = -501$$
$$-426h_{21} - 719h_{22} - h_{23} + 383400h_{31} + 647100h_{32} = -900$$

Representation of the above set of equations in matrix form is as follows.

$$\begin{bmatrix} -51 & -791 & -1 & 0 & 0 & 0 & 51 & 791 \\ 0 & 0 & 0 & -51 & -791 & -1 & 45900 & 711900 \\ -63 & -143 & -1 & 0 & 0 & 0 & 63 & 143 \\ 0 & 0 & 0 & -63 & -143 & -1 & 63 & 143 \\ -444 & -211 & -1 & 0 & 0 & 0 & 222444 & 105711 \\ 0 & 0 & 0 & -444 & -211 & -1 & 444 & 211 \\ -426 & -719 & -1 & 0 & 0 & 0 & 213426 & 360219 \\ 0 & 0 & 0 & -426 & -719 & -1 & 383400 & 647100 \end{bmatrix} \begin{bmatrix} h_{11} \\ h_{12} \\ h_{13} \\ h_{21} \\ h_{22} \\ h_{23} \\ h_{31} \\ h_{32} \end{bmatrix} = \begin{bmatrix} -1 \\ -900 \\ -1 \\ -1 \\ -501 \\ -1 \\ -501 \\ -900 \end{bmatrix}$$

The solution to the above set of equations is obtained by solving it by matrix inversion. The transformation is computed as,

$$\mathbf{H} = \begin{bmatrix} 0.9791 & 0.0181 & -63.3104 \\ -0.2303 & 1.2874 & -168.6295 \\ -0.0005 & -0.0001 & 1.0000 \end{bmatrix}$$

10.3 | Direct linear transformation

Direct linear transformation (DLT) is a general method to compute homography, which is more robust in the estimation of the homography matrix, $\mathbf{H}$. Only 4 point correspondences may affect in erroneous estimation of $\mathbf{H}$ in the presence of noise that heavily influences the quality of the result. With more number of observations, the effect of such noise may be reduced and the estimation will be more robust. The DLT is a method that considers more number of observations (more than 4 points) to compute the homography. Let the transformed coordinate of a point, $\boldsymbol{x}_i = (x_i, y_i, w_i)^\top$, be represented as, $\boldsymbol{x}_i' = (x_i', y_i', w_i')^\top$, where, $i = 1, 2, \ldots, N$ and N is the number of pairs of corresponding points. Let the homography matrix be represented in the form as given in Eq. 10.30.

$$\mathbf{H} = \begin{bmatrix} \boldsymbol{h}^{1\top} \\ \boldsymbol{h}^{2\top} \\ \boldsymbol{h}^{3\top} \end{bmatrix} \tag{10.30}$$

where, $\boldsymbol{h}^{1\top}$, $\boldsymbol{h}^{2\top}$, and $\boldsymbol{h}^{3\top}$ are the row vector that denote the first, second, and third rows of $\mathbf{H}$, respectively. From the expression of $\mathbf{H}$ in Eq. 10.30, the term, $\mathbf{H}\boldsymbol{x}_i$, is represented in sub-matrix form, as given by Eq. 10.31.

$$\mathbf{H}\boldsymbol{x}_i = \begin{bmatrix} \boldsymbol{h}^{1\top}\boldsymbol{x}_i \\ \boldsymbol{h}^{2\top}\boldsymbol{x}_i \\ \boldsymbol{h}^{3\top}\boldsymbol{x}_i \end{bmatrix} \tag{10.31}$$

Here, the scale is involved within the representations, and hence, it is difficult to carry on the computations with an equality sign that is expressed in Eq. 10.26. But, since both $\boldsymbol{x}_i'$ and $\mathbf{H}\boldsymbol{x}_i$ are 3-D vectors, they are related with scale factor and they have the same direction. So, as expressed in Eq. 10.32, the cross product of $\boldsymbol{x}_i'$ and $\mathbf{H}\boldsymbol{x}_i$ is equal to $\mathbf{0}$, a 3×1 zero vector, because they are parallel vectors.

$$\boldsymbol{x}_i' \times \mathbf{H}\boldsymbol{x}_i = \mathbf{0} \tag{10.32}$$

From Eq. 10.31 and 10.32, the transformed point, $\boldsymbol{x}'_i$, is represented as in Eq. 10.33.

$$\boldsymbol{x}'_i \times \mathbf{H}\boldsymbol{x}_i = \begin{bmatrix} y'_i \boldsymbol{h}^{3^\top} \boldsymbol{x}_i - w'_i \boldsymbol{h}^{2^\top} \boldsymbol{x}_i \\ w'_i \boldsymbol{h}^{1^\top} \boldsymbol{x}_i - x'_i \boldsymbol{h}^{3^\top} \boldsymbol{x}_i \\ x'_i \boldsymbol{h}^{2^\top} \boldsymbol{x}_i - y'_i \boldsymbol{h}^{1^\top} \boldsymbol{x}_i \end{bmatrix} = \mathbf{0} \tag{10.33}$$

In Eq. 10.33, each of the rows is equated to 0. However, there is a redundancy in this representation. In Eq. 10.33, the sum of x'_i times the first row and y'_i times the second row is equal to the third row. So, though the representation has three rows, only two equations are formed with each point correspondence due to redundancy.

The expression in Eq. 10.33 is written in a matrix form, as in Eq. 10.34.

$$\begin{bmatrix} \mathbf{0}^\top & -w'_i \boldsymbol{x}_i^\top & y'_i \boldsymbol{x}_i^\top \\ w'_i \boldsymbol{x}_i^\top & \mathbf{0}^\top & -x'_i \boldsymbol{x}_i^\top \\ -y'_i \boldsymbol{x}_i^\top & x'_i \boldsymbol{x}_i^\top & \mathbf{0}^\top \end{bmatrix} \begin{bmatrix} \boldsymbol{h}^1 \\ \boldsymbol{h}^2 \\ \boldsymbol{h}^3 \end{bmatrix} = \mathbf{0} \tag{10.34}$$

In the DLT method, only the first two rows of the matrix in Eq. 10.34 are considered, as the third row provides a redundant equation. Thus the set of two independent equations formed from a point correspondence is given by the following.

$$\mathbf{A}_i \mathbf{h} = \mathbf{0}$$

$$\text{where, } \mathbf{A}_i = \begin{bmatrix} \mathbf{0}^\top & -w'_i \boldsymbol{x}_i^\top & y'_i \boldsymbol{x}_i^\top \\ w'_i \boldsymbol{x}_i^\top & \mathbf{0}^\top & -x'_i \boldsymbol{x}_i^\top \end{bmatrix} \text{ and } \mathbf{h} = \begin{bmatrix} \boldsymbol{h}^1 \\ \boldsymbol{h}^2 \\ \boldsymbol{h}^3 \end{bmatrix} \tag{10.35}$$

Here, the dimension of $\mathbf{A}_i$ is 2×9, where each element in a row represents transpose of a 3-D column vector.

10.3.1 | DLT: Nonhomogeneous equations

One approach to solve the set of equations, as in Eq. 10.35, is by solving a set of non-homogeneous equations. Let, the parameter h_{33} in $\mathbf{H}$ be set to 1 and $\mathbf{h}$ in Eq. 10.35 be represented as $\mathbf{h} = \begin{bmatrix} \tilde{h} \\ 1 \end{bmatrix}$, so that $\tilde{h}$ consists of a column vector representation of the rows of matrix $\mathbf{h}$, excluding h_{33}. Then, an expansion of the elements of $\mathbf{A}_i$ in Eq. 10.35 results into the following.

$$\begin{bmatrix} 0 & 0 & 0 & -x_i w'_i & -y_i w'_i & -w_i w'_i & x_i y'_i & y_i y'_i \\ x_i w'_i & y_i w'_i & w_i w'_i & 0 & 0 & 0 & -x_i x'_i & -y_i x'_i \end{bmatrix} \tilde{h} = \begin{bmatrix} -w_i y'_i \\ w_i x'_i \end{bmatrix} \tag{10.36}$$

$$\implies \mathbf{A}_i \tilde{h} = \boldsymbol{b}_i$$

where, the dimensions of $\mathbf{A}_i$, $\tilde{\boldsymbol{h}}$, and $\boldsymbol{b}_i$ are 2×8, 8×1, and 2×1, respectively. It may be noted that the values of w_i and w_i' in x_i and x_i' are taken as 1 while directly using non-homogenous coordinates of corresponding points in these equations. Since the considered number of point correspondences is more than four, a stack of two rows for each point correspondence, as in Eq. 10.36, forms a composite matrix, $\mathbf{A}$, which is of a higher dimension than the matrix of four points. If there are n point correspondences, the dimension of $\mathbf{A}$ is $2n \times 8$, so that, the stacked rows of Eq. 10.36 are expressed as in Eq. 10.37.

$$\mathbf{A}\tilde{\boldsymbol{h}} = \boldsymbol{b} \tag{10.37}$$

where, the dimensions of $\mathbf{A}$, $\tilde{\boldsymbol{h}}$, and $\boldsymbol{b}$ are $2n \times 8$, 8×1, and $2n \times 1$, respectively.

Here, the least squares error estimate method is used to solve for the eight unknowns in $\tilde{\boldsymbol{h}}$, since there are more than eight equations. The solution to Eq. 10.37 is obtained by minimizing the term,[4] $||\mathbf{A}\tilde{\boldsymbol{h}} - \boldsymbol{b}||^2$. To solve this, consider equating partial derivatives of the error term with respect to each element of $\tilde{\boldsymbol{h}}$. By solving this set of equations, $\tilde{\boldsymbol{h}}$ is obtained. A simple way to look at this solution is also presented in Eqs. 10.38 and 10.39. Multiplying both the sides of Eq. 10.37 by $\mathbf{A}^\top$,

$$\mathbf{A}^\top \mathbf{A}\tilde{\boldsymbol{h}} = \mathbf{A}^\top \boldsymbol{b} \tag{10.38}$$

In the above equation, $(\mathbf{A}^\top \mathbf{A})$ is a square matrix, and assuming it to be invertible, Eq. 10.39 is obtained as follows.

$$\tilde{\boldsymbol{h}} = (\mathbf{A}^\top \mathbf{A})^{-1} \mathbf{A}^\top \boldsymbol{b} \tag{10.39}$$

Here, $(\mathbf{A}^\top \mathbf{A})^{-1} \mathbf{A}^\top$ is known as the pseudo-inverse of $\mathbf{A}$, which is denoted by $\mathbf{A}^+$. So, the solution to the considered least squares problem is given by, $\tilde{\boldsymbol{h}} = (\mathbf{A}^+)\boldsymbol{b}$. To this solution of $\tilde{\boldsymbol{h}}$, the element, $h_{33} = 1$, is appended to obtain the required transformation matrix, $\mathbf{H}$. But, similar to the method discussed in Section 10.2.3, the assumption of $h_{33} = 1$ may not always be valid, as when $h_{33} = 0$, this approach is not applicable. To address this issue, a generalized approach is considered by solving a set of homogeneous equations.

10.3.2 | DLT: Homogeneous equations

A generally applicable method for estimating the homography from a set of more than four point correspondences is by solving a set of homogeneous equations. In this case, unlike the previous approach, no assumptions are made on the value of any elements or parameters of $\mathbf{H}$ in setting them to a constant so that $\boldsymbol{h}$ is a vector of all the nine elements of $\mathbf{H}$. The problem is formulated as solving a stack of equations formed by two rows for each point correspondence, as in Eq. 10.35, as expressed in Eq. 10.40.

$$\mathbf{A}\boldsymbol{h} = \mathbf{0} \tag{10.40}$$

---

[4] $||\boldsymbol{h}||$ denotes L_2 norm of the vector $\boldsymbol{h}$, which is simply the magnitude of the vector. For example, if $\boldsymbol{h} = [h_1 \ h_2 \ h_3]^\top$, then $||\boldsymbol{h}|| = \sqrt{h_1^2 + h_2^2 + h_3^2}$.

where, **A** is the matrix formed by stacking the n point correspondence matrices as in Eq. 10.41.

$$\mathbf{A} = \begin{bmatrix} \mathbf{A}_1 \\ \mathbf{A}_2 \\ \mathbf{A}_3 \\ \vdots \\ \mathbf{A}_n \end{bmatrix} \qquad (10.41)$$

where, $\mathbf{A}_1$, $\mathbf{A}_2$, ..., $\mathbf{A}_n$ correspond to the matrix form of equations of each of the n point correspondences. In this case, the dimensions of **A**, $\boldsymbol{h}$, and **0** are $2n \times 9$, 9×1, and $2n \times 1$, respectively, since there are no assumptions on the value of any parameter. Here, the objective is to minimize $||\mathbf{A}\boldsymbol{h}||$, subject to the condition of $||\boldsymbol{h}|| = 1$. Since a scale factor is involved in this set of equations, a constraint on $\boldsymbol{h}$ is necessary to minimize $||\mathbf{A}\boldsymbol{h}||$, so that the problem becomes a constrained optimization problem, where $||\boldsymbol{h}||$ is constrained to 1. The solution to this constrained optimization problem is the *unit eigenvector of the smallest eigenvalue* of $\mathbf{A}^{\top}\mathbf{A}$. The derivation of this solution is left for the interested readers to workout.

10.3.3 | Different error criteria

There are several other error criteria to consider in solving the problem of estimation of homography. Using the least squares error estimate for a set of homogeneous or nonhomogeneous equations, as in the DLT, is one of the ways of solving it. This is a kind of *algebraic error*. The error, e, may also be a kind of *geometric error*. For example, it may be the sum of the squares of distances between the observed points in the transformation space and the estimated transformed points. It is expressed in Eq. 10.42.

$$e = \sum d_e^2(\boldsymbol{x}', \mathbf{H}\boldsymbol{x}) \qquad (10.42)$$

where, $d_e(\cdot)$ is the Euclidean distance function. Minimizing the sum of distances between each pair of estimated and observed points in the projected space is the task formulated in this case. In addition, the error may also consider another component of geometric error with re-projection, where inverse transformations of projected points are also in the estimation of error. In this case, the inverse transformation is applied to the estimated transformed point and its distance with the observed point in the original space is computed for considering it in error estimation. The error function in this case is expressed in Eq. 10.43.

$$e = \sum \left(d_e^2(\boldsymbol{x}', \mathbf{H}\boldsymbol{x}) \right) + \left(d_e^2(\mathbf{H}^{-1}\boldsymbol{x}', \boldsymbol{x}) \right) \qquad (10.43)$$

Nonlinear iterative optimization techniques (Hartley and Zisserman, 2003; Bazaraa et al., 2006; Nocedal and Wright, 2006; Ryaben'kii and Tsynkov, 2006) such as, *Newton iteration*, *Levenberg–Marquardt* (LM) method, etc., may be used in solving this problem.

10.3.4 | Transformation invariance and normalization of data

It is possible to estimate the homography, $\mathbf{H}$, after applying an invertible transformation on the set of corresponding points that are observed in each of the two projective spaces independently. Consider two invertible transformations, $\mathscr{T}$ and $\mathscr{T}'$, on the set of points in two projective spaces, $\boldsymbol{x}_i$ and $\boldsymbol{x}'_i$, as given by Eq. 10.44.

$$\boldsymbol{y}_i = \mathscr{T}\boldsymbol{x}_i$$
$$\boldsymbol{y}'_i = \mathscr{T}'\boldsymbol{x}'_i \tag{10.44}$$

where, $\boldsymbol{y}_i$ and $\boldsymbol{y}'_i$ are the transformed points. The transformations, $\mathscr{T}$ and $\mathscr{T}'$ are applied in two spaces, both in the original space and the projective transformed space. The problem is to estimate $\mathbf{H}$ from $\mathbf{G}$, where $\mathbf{G}$ is the transformation matrix between the set of transformed points, $\boldsymbol{y}_i$ and $\boldsymbol{y}'_i$.

Consider the relationship between the points, $\boldsymbol{x}_i$ and $\boldsymbol{x}'_i$, and Eq. 10.44 to compute $\mathbf{G}$, which is given by Eq. 10.45.

$$\boldsymbol{x}'_i = \mathbf{H}\boldsymbol{x}_i$$
$$\implies \mathscr{T}'^{-1}\boldsymbol{y}'_i = \mathbf{H}\mathscr{T}^{-1}\boldsymbol{y}_i \tag{10.45}$$
$$\implies \boldsymbol{y}'_i = \mathscr{T}'\mathbf{H}\mathscr{T}^{-1}\boldsymbol{y}_i$$

Here, the transformation matrix between $\boldsymbol{y}_i$ and $\boldsymbol{y}'_i$ is given by $\mathbf{G} = \mathscr{T}'\mathbf{H}\mathscr{T}^{-1}$. Since $\mathscr{T}$ and $\mathscr{T}'$ are known transformations, $\mathbf{H}$ is computed from $\mathbf{G}$ using the respective relation between them. However, using the least squares estimate in this case may result in a close estimate of $\mathbf{H}$, but it is not equivalent to the result obtained by this technique. That is, if $\mathbf{H}$ is originally estimated without the transformation and $\mathbf{G}$ is estimated after the transformation, both using least squares estimate, $k\mathbf{H} \neq \mathbf{G}$, for some $k \neq 0$.

One of the examples of such transformations, which is very often used, is the transformation on the set of points to center them at the origin of the plane with an average distance of the points from the center as $\sqrt{2}$. This processing is achieved by subtracting every point, (x_i, y_i), in the set by the mean of the set of points, $(\bar{x}, \bar{y})$, and then dividing them by the standard deviation of the set, (σ_x, σ_y), which is expressed in Eq. 10.46.

$$x_i^{(n)} = \frac{x_i - \bar{x}}{\sigma_x}$$
$$y_i^{(n)} = \frac{y_i - \bar{y}}{\sigma_y} \tag{10.46}$$

where, $(x_i^{(n)}, y_i^{(n)})$ denotes the normalized set of points, and the values of σ_x and σ_y are the standard deviations of the respective x and y coordinates. This computation makes it robust, since it does not allow to form the large values that appear at different coefficients in the set of equations.

10.4 | Vanishing points and vanishing line of a projective transformation

To understand the characteristics of vanishing points in the transformed space, consider a pair of parallel lines as shown in Fig. 10.18, where one of the lines is denoted by l. Let l' be the corresponding line of l in the transformed space, as shown in the figure, so that, their relation is represented by $l' = \mathbf{H}^{-\top} l$, where $\mathbf{H}$ is the 3×3 homography transformation matrix. Similarly, the other line among the parallel lines in the figure is mapped to another straight line in the projected space. Incidentally, the lines that are parallel in the original projective space, may not remain parallel in the transformed space, as shown in the figure, where they appear converging straight lines in the right image and they meet at a certain point. This is the transformed point of the intersecting point of the two parallel lines in the original projective space which happens to be an ideal point (the value at the third dimension or scale is zero). This transformed point of intersection of the two transformed parallel lines is the vanishing point of these straight lines (shown by a thick circular point in the figure). For example, if the straight line, l, is represented by $ax + by + c = 0$, all the lines that are parallel to this straight line intersect at a point in the original projective space that is given by $\boldsymbol{v}_p = (b, -a, 0)$ in the homogenous coordinate representation (see Section 10.0.3). We may note that, $\boldsymbol{v}_p$ is an ideal point, as its scale value is 0. The vanishing point of the set of parallel lines in the transformed space is computed as the transformation of $\boldsymbol{v}_p$ into the transformed projective space, which is given by, $\boldsymbol{v}'_p = \mathbf{H}\boldsymbol{v}_p$. That is, $\boldsymbol{v}'_p$ is the transformation of the corresponding coordinates of $\boldsymbol{v}_p$ in the projective space. This forms the interpretation of the vanishing point in the transformed space.

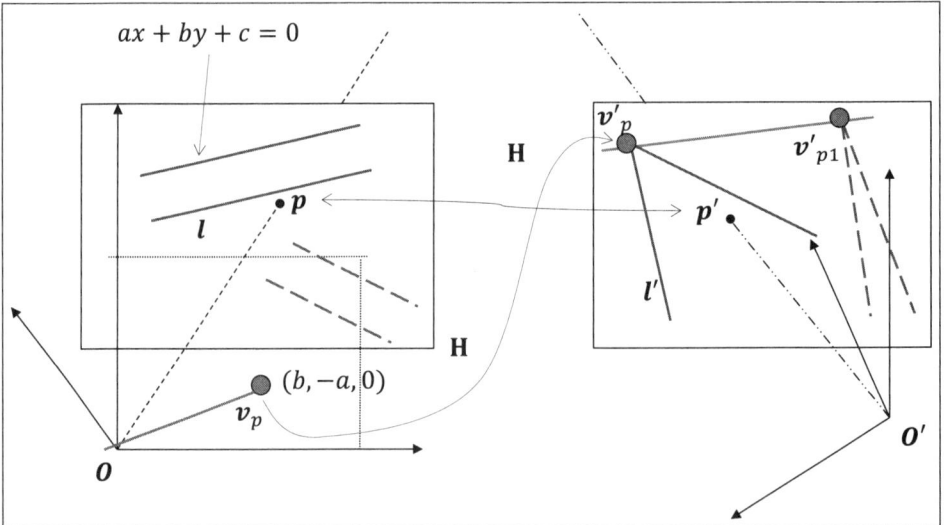

Figure 10.18 Illustration of vanishing point and vanishing line in the transformed space.

If another set of parallel lines in a different direction in the original projective space is considered, their transformed lines in the transformed projective space also meet at some other point, v'_{p_1}, which is the vanishing point of this set of parallel lines. The line formed by these two vanishing points, v'_p and v'_{p_1}, is the vanishing line and all the vanishing points in the transformed space lie on this line. It is noted before that all the ideal points in the original projective space lie on the line at infinity, $l_\infty = (0\ 0\ 1)^\top$. As vanishing points are transformations of ideal points, they also lie on a line, which is the transformation of the line at infinity. This line is the vanishing line l_v and it is given by, $l_v = \mathbf{H}^{-\top} l_\infty$.

A brief summary of the properties of projective transformation or homography is as follows.

- Point transformation: $x' = \mathbf{H}x$.
- Line transformation: $l' = \mathbf{H}^{-\top} l$.
- Vanishing point of lines parallel to $l = (a, b, c)^\top$: $v_p = \mathbf{H}(b, -a, 0)^\top$.
- Vanishing line: $l_v = \mathbf{H}^{-\top} l_\infty = \mathbf{H}^{-\top}(0, 0, 1)^\top$.

Here, all the elements are represented in the homogeneous coordinate form.

Numerical Example

Consider the following homography, $\mathbf{H}$, between two projective spaces.

$$\mathbf{H} = \begin{bmatrix} 3 & 4 & -6 \\ 1 & 3 & -8 \\ 0 & 5 & 1 \end{bmatrix}$$

(i) Compute the transformation of the line formed by two points $(2, 4, 2)$ and $(6, 9, 3)$ in $\mathbb{P}^2$.

(ii) Compute the vanishing line in the transformed space.

Solution

The computation of the transformation of the line between the given two points may be solved by two methods.

(i) Compute transformed points of $(2, 4, 2)$ and $(6, 9, 3)$. Then, compute their cross product to obtain the transformed line.

(ii) Compute the line between the points, $(2, 4, 2)$ and $(6, 9, 3)$, and then transform the computed line.

In either of the cases, consider the equivalent form of the given points as follows.

$$\boldsymbol{x}_1 = \begin{bmatrix} 2 \\ 4 \\ 2 \end{bmatrix} \equiv \begin{bmatrix} 1 \\ 2 \\ 1 \end{bmatrix} \quad \text{and} \quad \boldsymbol{x}_2 = \begin{bmatrix} 6 \\ 9 \\ 3 \end{bmatrix} \equiv \begin{bmatrix} 2 \\ 3 \\ 1 \end{bmatrix}$$

Method-1

The transformed points, $\boldsymbol{x}_1'$ and $\boldsymbol{x}_2'$, of $\boldsymbol{x}_1$ and $\boldsymbol{x}_2$, respectively, are computed as,

$$\boldsymbol{x}_1' = \mathbf{H}\boldsymbol{x}_1 = \begin{bmatrix} 5 \\ -1 \\ 11 \end{bmatrix}$$

$$\boldsymbol{x}_2' = \mathbf{H}\boldsymbol{x}_2 = \begin{bmatrix} 12 \\ 3 \\ 16 \end{bmatrix}$$

Then, the line, $\boldsymbol{l}'$ between $\boldsymbol{x}_1'$ and $\boldsymbol{x}_2'$, which is the transformed line between $\boldsymbol{x}_1$ and $\boldsymbol{x}_2$, is obtained as,

$$\boldsymbol{l}' = \boldsymbol{x}_1' \times \boldsymbol{x}_2' = \begin{bmatrix} 5 \\ -1 \\ 11 \end{bmatrix} \times \begin{bmatrix} 12 \\ 3 \\ 16 \end{bmatrix} = \begin{bmatrix} -49 \\ 52 \\ 27 \end{bmatrix}$$

Method-2

The line, $\boldsymbol{l}$, between $\boldsymbol{x}_1$ and $\boldsymbol{x}_2$ is computed as,

$$\boldsymbol{l} = \boldsymbol{x}_1 \times \boldsymbol{x}_2 = \begin{bmatrix} 1 \\ 2 \\ 1 \end{bmatrix} \times \begin{bmatrix} 2 \\ 3 \\ 1 \end{bmatrix} = \begin{bmatrix} -1 \\ 1 \\ -1 \end{bmatrix}$$

Then, the transformation of $\boldsymbol{l}$, $\boldsymbol{l}'$, is computed by,

$$\boldsymbol{l}' = \mathbf{H}^{-\top}\boldsymbol{l}$$

$$\mathbf{H}^{-1} = \frac{1}{95} \begin{bmatrix} 43 & -34 & -14 \\ -1 & 3 & 18 \\ 5 & -15 & 5 \end{bmatrix}$$

$$\Rightarrow \boldsymbol{l}' = \frac{1}{95} \begin{bmatrix} -49 \\ 52 \\ 27 \end{bmatrix}$$

The vanishing line, $\boldsymbol{l}_v'$, is obtained by the transformation of the line at infinity, $\boldsymbol{l}_\infty = \begin{bmatrix} 0 & 0 & 1 \end{bmatrix}^\top$. This is given by,

$$l'_v = \mathbf{H}^{-\top} l_\infty$$

$$\mathbf{H}^{-\top} l_\infty = \frac{1}{95} \begin{bmatrix} 43 & -1 & 5 \\ -34 & 3 & -15 \\ -14 & 18 & 5 \end{bmatrix} \begin{bmatrix} 0 \\ 0 \\ 1 \end{bmatrix}$$

$$\Rightarrow l'_v = \begin{bmatrix} 5 \\ -15 \\ 5 \end{bmatrix}.$$

10.5 | Projective linear group

Projective transformations form a group of linear transformations, which is called *projective linear group*. Consider three different projective spaces as shown in Fig. 10.19. Let $\mathbf{H}_1$ denote the transformation of points from the first projective space to the points in the second projective space, as shown in the figure. Also, let $\mathbf{H}_2$ denote the transformation of points from the second projective space to the points in the third projective space. Then, the equivalent transformation of the points in the first projective space to the points in the third space is given by $\mathbf{H} = \mathbf{H}_1 \mathbf{H}_2$. That is, a cascade of transformations is replaced by a single transformation, which is one of the implications of the property of projective linear group.

Consider another similar series of transformations, as shown in Fig. 10.20. In this figure, there are four projective spaces, where the transformations between the first and the second, the second and the third, and the third and the fourth projective spaces are given by $\mathbf{H}_1$, $\mathbf{H}_2$, and $\mathbf{H}_3$, respectively. So, the transformation between the first and the third projective space

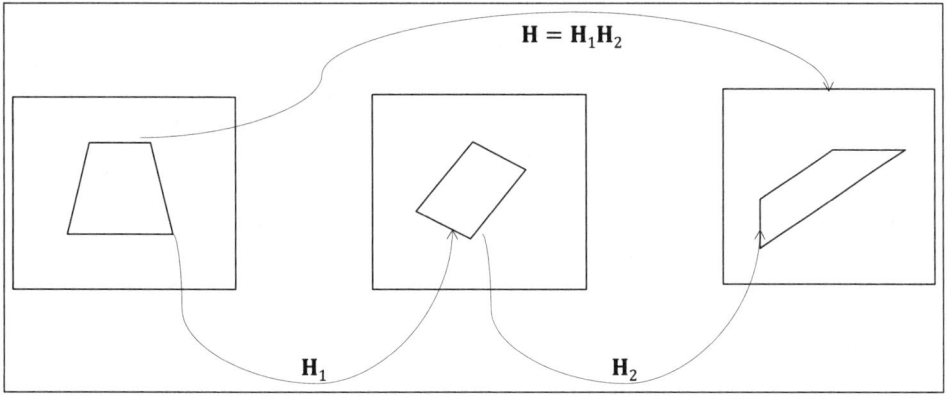

Figure 10.19 Depiction of a cascade of transformations being represented as a single transformation in a projective linear group.

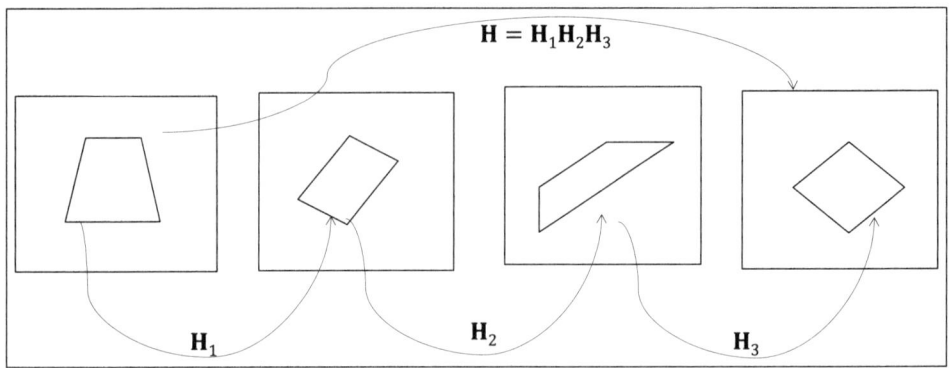

Figure 10.20 Another depiction of a cascade of transformations being represented as a single transformation, which is possible because of the group property.

is given by $\mathbf{H} = \mathbf{H}_1\mathbf{H}_2\mathbf{H}_3$. Since the matrix multiplications are associative in nature, the computation of $\mathbf{H}$ is invariant to the order of performing the multiplications of individual transformation matrices. That is, $\mathbf{H} = \mathbf{H}_1(\mathbf{H}_2\mathbf{H}_3) = (\mathbf{H}_1\mathbf{H}_2)\mathbf{H}_3$.

10.5.1 | Subgroups and hierarchy

Within the projective linear group, there are subgroups and there is also a hierarchy among the subgroups. However, the parent group is the projective linear group. All the projective transformations fall under the generalized category of projective linear group. All the properties of projective transformations that are discussed in this chapter so far hold true for all kinds of transformations under the projective linear group. Let the matrix, $\mathbf{H}$, be a transformation matrix under projective linear group, which is represented as in Eq. 10.47.

$$\mathbf{H} = \begin{bmatrix} h_{11} & h_{12} & h_{13} \\ h_{21} & h_{22} & h_{23} \\ h_{31} & h_{32} & h_{33} \end{bmatrix} \tag{10.47}$$

A special case of projective transformation is *affine projective transformation*. One of the key properties of the transformations in the affine group is that, the last row of the transformation matrix is $(0, 0, 1)$ or any scaled factor of $(0, 0, 1)$. So, a transformation under the affine group is easily distinguishable by observing the last row of $\mathbf{H}$, $(h_{31}\ \ h_{32}\ \ h_{33})$, to be a scaled factor of $(0, 0, 1)$. A special class of affine group is called *Euclidean group* if the upper left 2×2 sub-matrix of the transformation matrix under affine group is orthogonal. That is, $\mathbf{H}$ is a transformation under the Euclidean group if $(h_{31}\ \ h_{32}\ \ h_{33})$ is a scaled factor of $(0, 0, 1)$, and $\begin{bmatrix} h_{11} & h_{12} \\ h_{21} & h_{22} \end{bmatrix}$ is orthogonal. So, for a transformation under the Euclidean group, the scalar dot product of two different rows is 0 and the scalar dot product of a row with itself is a nonzero value, where the rows are considered from the upper left 2×2 sub-matrix. A special class of Euclidean group is called *oriented Euclidean group* if the determinant of the orthogonal sub-matrix of the transformation under Euclidean group is equal to unity. Thus, **H** is a transformation under oriented Euclidean group if $(h_{31} \quad h_{32} \quad h_{33})$ is a scaled factor of $(0, 0, 1)$, $\begin{bmatrix} h_{11} & h_{12} \\ h_{21} & h_{22} \end{bmatrix}$ is orthogonal, and $\begin{vmatrix} h_{11} & h_{12} \\ h_{21} & h_{22} \end{vmatrix} = \pm 1$.

The hierarchy of the projective transformation space is as follows: Oriented Euclidean group is a sub-class of Euclidean group, Euclidean group is a sub-group of affine group, and affine group is a sub-group of projective linear group. The properties of different subgroups are discussed below.

10.5.2 | Projective group

The parent group of the subgroups, which is a projective group, is represented in the form of a 3×3 matrix, $\mathbf{H}_P$, which is given by Eq. 10.48.

$$\mathbf{H}_P = \begin{bmatrix} h_{11} & h_{12} & h_{13} \\ h_{21} & h_{22} & h_{23} \\ h_{31} & h_{32} & h_{33} \end{bmatrix} = \begin{bmatrix} \mathbf{A} & \boldsymbol{t} \\ \boldsymbol{v}^{\mathsf{T}} & v \end{bmatrix} \tag{10.48}$$

where, **A** is a 2×2 sub-matrix, $\boldsymbol{t}$ is a 2×1 vector, v is a scalar quantity, and $\boldsymbol{v} = (v_1, v_2)^{\mathsf{T}}$ is a column vector. The form in Eq. 10.48 represents any projective transformation matrix in general, where the parallelism is not necessarily preserved. An example of the effect of this transformation on the shape of a rectangle or a parallelogram is shown in Fig. 10.21. We observe that the sides of the transformed object are not parallel. In the group of transformation expressed by Eq. 10.48, there are eight degrees of freedom, i.e., the number of independent parameters is eight, which correspond to two scales, two rotations, two translations, and two parameters for transformation of the line at infinity.

The transformation, $\mathbf{H}_P$, of an ideal point, $\boldsymbol{x} = (x_1, x_2, 0)$, where the third coordinate is 0, is given by Eq. 10.49.

$$\boldsymbol{x}' = \mathbf{H}_P \boldsymbol{x} = \begin{bmatrix} \mathbf{A} & \boldsymbol{t} \\ \boldsymbol{v}^{\mathsf{T}} & v \end{bmatrix} \boldsymbol{x} = \begin{bmatrix} \mathbf{A} & \boldsymbol{t} \\ \boldsymbol{v}^{\mathsf{T}} & v \end{bmatrix} \begin{pmatrix} x_1 \\ x_2 \\ 0 \end{pmatrix} = \begin{bmatrix} \mathbf{A} \begin{pmatrix} x_1 \\ x_2 \end{pmatrix} \\ v_1 x_1 + v_2 x_2 \end{bmatrix} \tag{10.49}$$

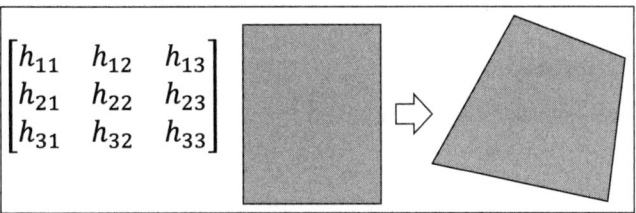

Figure 10.21 Representation of a projective transformation matrix, and an example of the transformation under projective group.

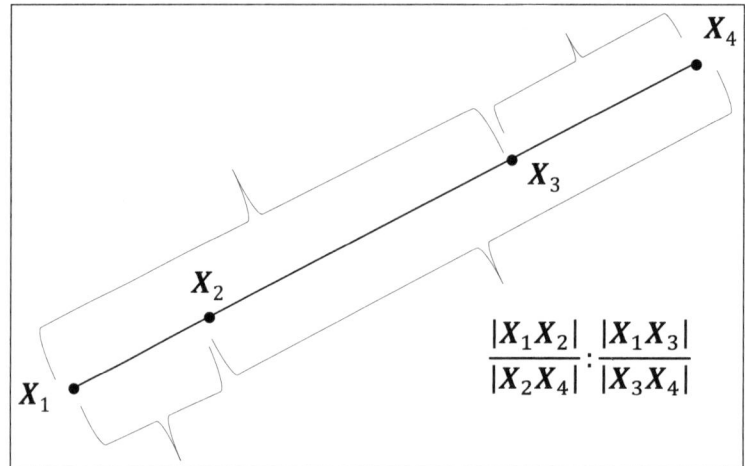

$$\frac{|\boldsymbol{X}_1\boldsymbol{X}_2|}{|\boldsymbol{X}_2\boldsymbol{X}_4|} : \frac{|\boldsymbol{X}_1\boldsymbol{X}_3|}{|\boldsymbol{X}_3\boldsymbol{X}_4|}$$

Figure 10.22 Illustration of cross ratio of four points that are lying on a straight line.

The transformation of an ideal point may not always be another ideal point in the projected space. That is, if the third coordinate, $v_1x_1 + v_2x_2$, is nonzero, the transformed point is a finite point in the transformed projective space, which is not an ideal point. Also, the transformed line at infinity has a finite representation of a line in the transformation space. Since the line at infinity is transformed to a vanishing line in the transformation space, it contains all the vanishing points and appears like a horizon in the transformed space. The properties that are preserved in this projective group are, (i) co-linearity of any three points, (ii) order of contacts of points, and (iii) the cross ratio of four points, as defined below.

Consider four points that are lying on a straight line, as shown in Fig. 10.22. The cross ratio is defined as the ratio of ratios of distances between the points, as given by Eq. 10.50.

$$\text{Cross ratio} := \frac{|\boldsymbol{X}_1\boldsymbol{X}_2|}{|\boldsymbol{X}_2\boldsymbol{X}_4|} : \frac{|\boldsymbol{X}_1\boldsymbol{X}_3|}{|\boldsymbol{X}_3\boldsymbol{X}_4|} \tag{10.50}$$

where, the numerator of the ratio of ratios is the ratio of lengths between $\boldsymbol{X}_1$ and $\boldsymbol{X}_2$; and, $\boldsymbol{X}_2$ and $\boldsymbol{X}_4$. and the denominator of the ratio of ratios is the ratio of lengths between $\boldsymbol{X}_1$ and $\boldsymbol{X}_3$; and $\boldsymbol{X}_3$ and $\boldsymbol{X}_4$. The cross ratio of the points that lie on a same line is preserved in a projective transformation.

10.5.3 | Affine group

An affine group is represented in the form of a 3×3 matrix, $\mathbf{H}_A$, which is given by Eq. 10.51.

$$\mathbf{H}_A = \begin{bmatrix} a_{11} & a_{12} & t_x \\ a_{21} & a_{22} & t_y \\ 0 & 0 & 1 \end{bmatrix} = \begin{bmatrix} \mathbf{A} & \boldsymbol{t} \\ \boldsymbol{0}^\top & 1 \end{bmatrix} \tag{10.51}$$

where, $\mathbf{A}$ is a 2×2 sub-matrix, t is a 2×1 vector. Since the third row of the affine transformation is a scaled factor of $(0, 0, 1)$, for the sake of convenience, the minimal representation of $(0, 0, 1)$ is sufficient to uniquely define a affine homography. The effect of affine transformation on the shape of a rectangle or a parallelogram is figuratively shown in Fig. 10.23, where, a parallelogram is transformed into another parallelogram after applying affine transformation. That is, one of the invariants of this transformation is parallel lines. It is easy to show that affine transformation of an ideal point is also an ideal point. Hence the intersection of parallel lines in the original space is transformed into a point which also lies at infinity. So, parallel lines remain parallel in the transformed space.

The sub-matrix $\mathbf{A}$ is further decomposed by a set of operations, which is expressed as in Eq. 10.52.

$$\mathbf{A} = \mathbf{R}(\theta)\mathbf{R}(-\phi)\mathbf{D}\mathbf{R}(\phi) \tag{10.52}$$

where, $\mathbf{R}(\cdot)$ is a rotation matrix, θ and ϕ are the rotation angles of $\mathbf{R}$, and $\mathbf{D}$ is a diagonal matrix. The operations in Eq. 10.52 may be physically related as if a deformation is applied in the corresponding directions that are perpendicular to the axes. At first, a rotation aligns the parallelogram with the axis where the deformation is intended to be applied. Then, it is subjected to the deformation in two perpendicular directions, which is given by the diagonal matrix, $\mathbf{D} = \begin{bmatrix} \lambda_1 & 0 \\ 0 & \lambda_2 \end{bmatrix}$, where, λ_1 and λ_2 are scale parameters. Thus, the deformation is introduced by using two different scales on the coordinate measurements at two oblique axes. So, the initial rectilinear coordinate representation is transformed into a nonrectilinear representation after projection, but all parallel lines are preserved with their respective parallelism. In this way, the transformation results in an oblique axis representation, instead of the conventional rectilinear coordinate representation.

In affine transformation, the co-ordinate transformation happens because the unit scales, before transformation, are scaled by different factors along different axes. The co-ordinate axes are rotated by the parameter ϕ, and rotated back after scaling, which is wholly rotated by parameter θ, which is figuratively represented in Fig. 10.24. Then, there is a translation by $t = \begin{bmatrix} t_x & t_y \end{bmatrix}^\top$. So, in the affine group of transformation, there are six degrees of freedom, as there are six independent parameters in $\mathbf{H}_A$, corresponding to two translation parameters, two rotation parameters, and two scale parameters. Along with the properties of projective

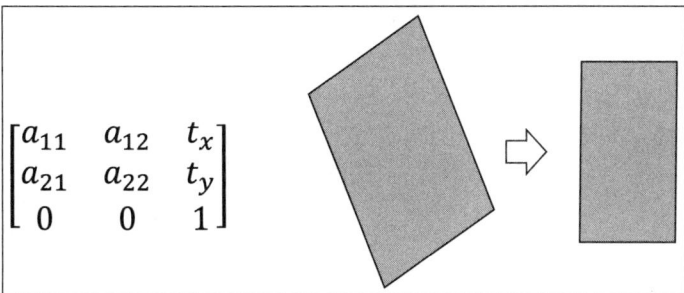

Figure 10.23 Representation of an affine transformation matrix, and an example of the transformation under affine group.

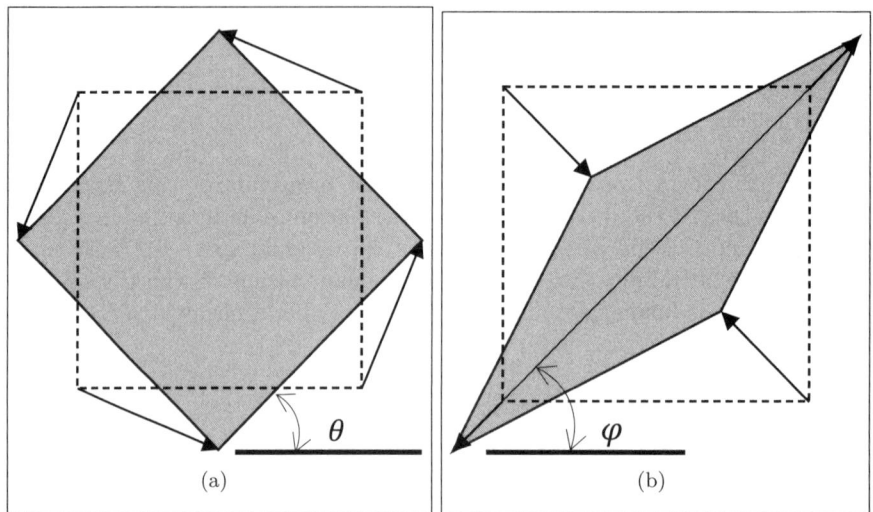

Figure 10.24 Illustration of (a) rotation and (b) deformation effects in the affine group of transformation.

transformation, the properties that are preserved in the affine group are, (i) the parallelism of lines, (ii) the ratio of areas, (iii) the ratio of lengths on parallel lines, for example, midpoints, (iv) linear combination of vectors, for example, centroids, and (v) the line at infinity, $\boldsymbol{l}_\infty$.

10.5.4 | Similarity group

The Euclidean group is also known as the *similarity group*, because it maintains the similarity property of shapes. For example, in rectangles, as all the edges are parallel, their aspect ratios are preserved. In this case the ratios of distances are preserved, as figuratively shown in Fig. 10.25. A similarity group is represented in the form of a 3×3 matrix, $\mathbf{H}_S$, which is given by Eq. 10.53.

$$\begin{bmatrix} sr_{11} & sr_{12} & t_x \\ sr_{21} & sr_{22} & t_y \\ 0 & 0 & 1 \end{bmatrix}$$

Figure 10.25 Representation of a similarity transformation matrix, and an example of the transformation under Euclidean group.

$$\mathbf{H}_S = \begin{bmatrix} sr_{11} & sr_{12} & t_x \\ sr_{21} & sr_{22} & t_y \\ 0 & 0 & 1 \end{bmatrix} = \begin{bmatrix} s\mathbf{R} & t \\ 0^{\mathsf{T}} & 1 \end{bmatrix} \tag{10.53}$$

where, $\mathbf{R}$ is a 2×2 orthonormal matrix for rotation of axes, s is a scalar quantity for scaling, and t is a 2×1 column vector for translation of the origin. Since $\mathbf{R}$ is an orthonormal matrix, $\mathbf{R}^{\mathsf{T}}\mathbf{R} = \mathbf{I}$, where $\mathbf{I}$ is the identity matrix. The transformation matrix, $\mathbf{H}_S$, is a special case of an affine transformation matrix, with an additional constraint to satisfy the property that makes the sub-matrix, $\mathbf{R}$, to be orthonormal. Here, there are four degrees of freedom corresponding to one rotation, one scale, and two translation parameters.

Consider two special points, $\boldsymbol{I}$ and $\boldsymbol{J}$, which are given in the form as in Eq. 10.54.

$$\boldsymbol{I} = \begin{pmatrix} 1 \\ i \\ 0 \end{pmatrix} \quad \text{and} \quad \boldsymbol{J} = \begin{pmatrix} 1 \\ -i \\ 0 \end{pmatrix} \tag{10.54}$$

Here, instead of a real space, a projective space with complex coordinate systems is considered. A 2-D projective space is represented by simple complex numbers by considering one of the two axes as the imaginary axis. The similarity transformation of $\boldsymbol{I}$ is given by Eq. 10.55.

$$\boldsymbol{I}' = \mathbf{H}_S \boldsymbol{I} = \begin{bmatrix} s\cos(\theta) & -s\sin(\theta) & t_x \\ s\sin(\theta) & s\cos(\theta) & t_y \\ 0 & 0 & 1 \end{bmatrix} \begin{pmatrix} 1 \\ i \\ 0 \end{pmatrix} = se^{i\theta} \begin{pmatrix} 1 \\ i \\ 0 \end{pmatrix} \equiv \boldsymbol{I} \tag{10.55}$$

As it is observed above, after applying the similarity transformation, $\boldsymbol{I}$ remains the same point, except for the multiplication by a scale factor. Similarly, the similarity transformation of point $\boldsymbol{J}$ also results in the same point, $\boldsymbol{J}$. The points, $\boldsymbol{I}$ and $\boldsymbol{J}$, are called the *circular points*, which are invariants of similarity transformation. Along with the properties of affine transformation, the properties that are invariant in the similarity group are, (i) the ratios of lengths, (ii) angles, and (iii) the circular points, $\boldsymbol{I}$ and $\boldsymbol{J}$.

10.5.5 | Isometry

The oriented Euclidean group is also known as the *isometry*, since it preserves the length between any two points. An example of isometry is shown figuratively in Fig. 10.26 using the shape of a rectangle. An isometry is represented in the form of a 3×3 matrix, $\mathbf{H}_I$, which is given by Eq. 10.56.

$$\mathbf{H}_I = \begin{bmatrix} \epsilon\cos(\theta) & -\sin(\theta) & t_x \\ \epsilon\sin(\theta) & \cos(\theta) & t_y \\ 0 & 0 & 1 \end{bmatrix} = \begin{bmatrix} \mathbf{R} & t \\ \mathbf{0}^{\mathsf{T}} & 1 \end{bmatrix} \tag{10.56}$$

$$\begin{bmatrix} r_{11} & r_{12} & t_x \\ r_{21} & r_{22} & t_y \\ 0 & 0 & 1 \end{bmatrix}$$

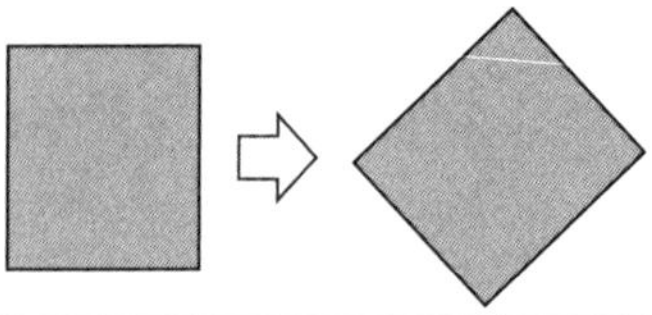

Figure 10.26 Representation of a isometry transformation matrix, and an example of the transformation under oriented Euclidean group.

where, $\epsilon = \pm 1$, so that, the determinant of the left 2×2 sub-matrix is equal to 1. Here, the number of parameters are three, which correspond to one rotation parameter, θ, and two translation parameters, t_x and t_y. So, the degree of freedom is only three. Isometry is an orientation preserving transformation when $\epsilon = 1$, otherwise it is an orientation reversing transformation, like reflection. In this case, lengths between the points are also invariants. Along with the properties of similarity transformation, the properties that are invariant in the isometry are, (i) the lengths, (ii) the angles, and (iii) the area.

10.5.6 | Decomposition of projective transformations

Any projective transformation may be decomposed as a cascade of all sub-group transformations. A cascade of similarity transformation, affine transformation, and general projective transformation is given in Eq. 10.57.

$$\mathbf{H} = \mathbf{H}_S \mathbf{H}_A \mathbf{H}_P = \begin{bmatrix} s\mathbf{R} & t \\ \mathbf{0}^\top & 1 \end{bmatrix} \begin{bmatrix} \mathbf{K} & 0 \\ \mathbf{0}^\top & 1 \end{bmatrix} \begin{bmatrix} \mathbf{I} & 0 \\ v^\top & v \end{bmatrix} = \begin{bmatrix} \mathbf{A} & t \\ v^\top & v \end{bmatrix} \tag{10.57}$$

where, $\mathbf{K}$ is an upper triangular matrix with determinant$(\mathbf{K}) = 1$. It should be noted that $\mathbf{K}$ does not form an orthogonal matrix, but it has a unit determinant. In Eq. 10.57, among the three cascaded transformation matrices that are being multiplied, the first matrix represents the similarity transformation, the second matrix represents the affine transformation, and the third matrix represents the projective transformation. The first and second matrices are forms of affine transformation, which is inferred by their last rows, $(0, 0, 1)$. In the third matrix, which is a projective transformation, $\mathbf{I}$ is a 2×2 identity matrix, $v^\top$ a 1×2 row vector, and v a scalar quantity. In relation with the original transformation matrix that is decomposed as in Eq. 10.57, the last row of the third matrix defines the component of projective transformation and the translation matrix, t, is used in the first matrix that defines the similarity transformation.

Also, the matrix, $\mathbf{A}$, is decomposed as expressed by Eq. 10.58.

$$\mathbf{A} = s\mathbf{R}\mathbf{K} + tv^\top \tag{10.58}$$

Here, t and $v^\top$ are the known components. So, the decomposition is performed on $\mathbf{A} - tv^\top$. Since, one of the matrices, $\mathbf{R}$, is orthonormal, and the other matrix, $\mathbf{K}$, is an upper triangular matrix, the matrix decomposition may be performed to derive the corresponding components using any QR-decomposition method, a standard technique in linear algebra (Lay et al., 2015). If s is a positive value, this decomposition is unique. As the scale factor matters in a projective transformation, s is restricted to be a positive value. In this way, any projective transformation matrix may be decomposed as a cascade of similarity, affine, and general projective transformation matrices.

10.5.7 | Affine rectification

The affine properties of transformation are used for rectifying the images and it is called the process of image rectification. As shown in Fig. 10.27, consider an image in plane π_1, which is projected on plane π_2. The image borders that are parallel in π_1 do not appear parallel in π_2 due to the transformation. Thus, a square shape in the original space, which has parallel borders, is transformed into a quadrilateral after applying 2-D general projective transformation, $\mathbf{H}_p$, that makes the borders meet at a vanishing point. One of the key tasks is to retrieve the seemingly parallel lines that are identified as parallels from the human experience by applying another transformation, $\mathbf{H}'_p$, that is projected on plane π_3. This process may not give the original shape of the square, as the properties of perpendicular corners and equal edges may not be preserved, but the parallelism of the edges are restored using this particular transformation. Here, the corresponding edges are computed using the transformation from π_1 to π_2. Though the transformation from π_1 to π_2 is a general projective transformation, the transformation from the original space, π_1, to π_3 is an affine transformation. In fact, $\mathbf{H}'_p$ is also a general projective transformation. However, the cascade of these two transformations, $\mathbf{H}_p$ and $\mathbf{H}'_p$, is an affine transformation, $\mathbf{H}_A = \mathbf{H}_p \mathbf{H}'_p$. So, the problem is to compute the transformation, $\mathbf{H}'_p$. Let the vanishing line in π_2 be represented

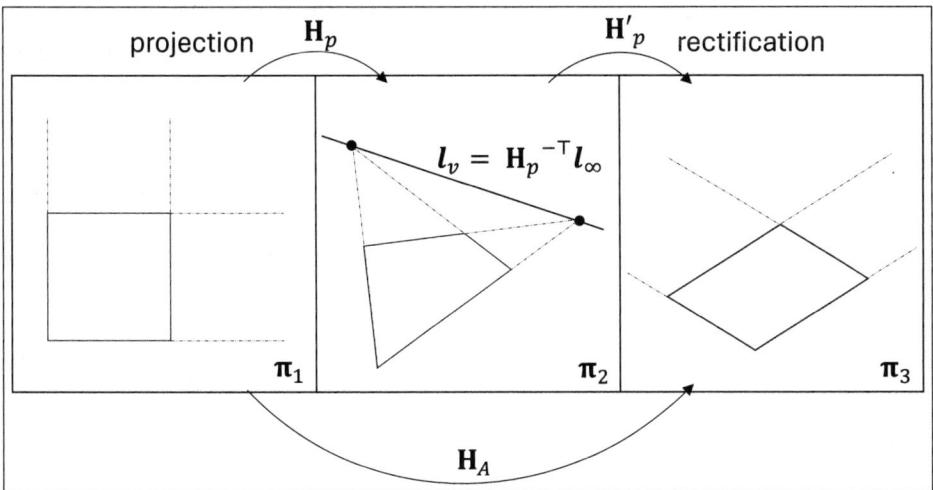

Figure 10.27 Diagrammatic illustration of a projective transformation of an image and its affine rectification.

by $\boldsymbol{l}_v = \mathbf{H}_p^{-\top} \boldsymbol{l}_\infty$, where, $\boldsymbol{l}_v = [l_1 \ l_2 \ l_3]^\top$ is the vanishing line in $\boldsymbol{\pi}_1$, and $l_3 \neq 0$. Then a projective transformation may be defined in the form as in Eq. 10.59.

$$\mathbf{H}'_p = \mathbf{H}_A \begin{bmatrix} 1 & 0 & 0 \\ 0 & 1 & 0 \\ l_1 & l_2 & l_3 \end{bmatrix} \tag{10.59}$$

The form in Eq. 10.59 is a general projective transformation because the last row is not $[0 \ 0 \ 1]$, but $\mathbf{H}_A$ is an affine transformation. So, the product of a general projective transformation matrix with any affine transformation matrix is a general projective transformation matrix. By the property of this transformation, the line at infinity is obtained by transforming the vanishing line. In this case, the vanishing points in $\boldsymbol{\pi}_2$ are transformed to ideal points after the transformation by $\mathbf{H}'_p$, so that, the converging lines in $\boldsymbol{\pi}_2$ that were supposed to be parallel appear like parallel lines in the transformed space, $\boldsymbol{\pi}_3$. By this process of image rectification, the converging but seemingly parallel edges in the image are made parallel.

Consider an example that is shown in Fig. 10.28 to further understand the process of affine rectification. As observed in Fig. 10.28 (a), sets of seemingly parallel edges in the considered image are meeting at some finite points. Two such sets of parallel lines are considered, as shown the figure, and each set of lines meet at a vanishing point. So, two vanishing points are obtained by two sets of parallel lines, which are used to compute the vanishing line. The corresponding projective transformation is computed from the representation of the vanishing line, which is the transformation of the line at infinity. The steps of rectification process, in the considered example of Fig. 10.28, are summarized below.

- Identify two sets of seemingly parallel lines, $\boldsymbol{l}_1$ and $\boldsymbol{l}_2$, and $\boldsymbol{l}_3$ and $\boldsymbol{l}_4$.
- Compute two vanishing points, $\boldsymbol{v}_1 = \boldsymbol{l}_1 \times \boldsymbol{l}_2$ and $\boldsymbol{v}_2 = \boldsymbol{l}_3 \times \boldsymbol{l}_4$.
- Compute the vanishing line, $\boldsymbol{l}_v = \boldsymbol{v}_1 \times \boldsymbol{v}_2$, which is the corresponding line at infinity.
- Apply the computed transformation to the image to make the edges appear parallel, as shown in Fig. 10.28 (c).

As seen in the figure, the rectangular shapes may not become perfect rectangles after transformation, but, at least they appear as parallelograms.

Consider another example of image rectification in Fig. 10.29. The borders of the image in Fig. 10.29 (a) do not really appear parallel, which are supposed to form a rectangle. The first set of parallel lines, $\boldsymbol{l}_1$ and $\boldsymbol{l}_2$, are formed in horizontal directions by two pairs of points, as given in Eq. 10.60.

$$\begin{aligned} \boldsymbol{l}_1 &= (104, 69, 1) \times (380, 71, 1) = (-2, 276, -18836) \\ \boldsymbol{l}_2 &= (122, 226, 1) \times (366, 228, 1) = (-2, 244, -54900) \end{aligned} \tag{10.60}$$

Similarly, the second set of parallel lines, $\boldsymbol{l}_3$ and $\boldsymbol{l}_4$, are formed in vertical directions by two pairs of points, as given in Eq. 10.61.

$$\begin{aligned} \boldsymbol{l}_3 &= (88, 254, 1) \times (62, 49, 1) = (-2, 276, -18836) \\ \boldsymbol{l}_4 &= (390, 250, 1) \times (406, 53, 1) = (197, 16, -80830) \end{aligned} \tag{10.61}$$

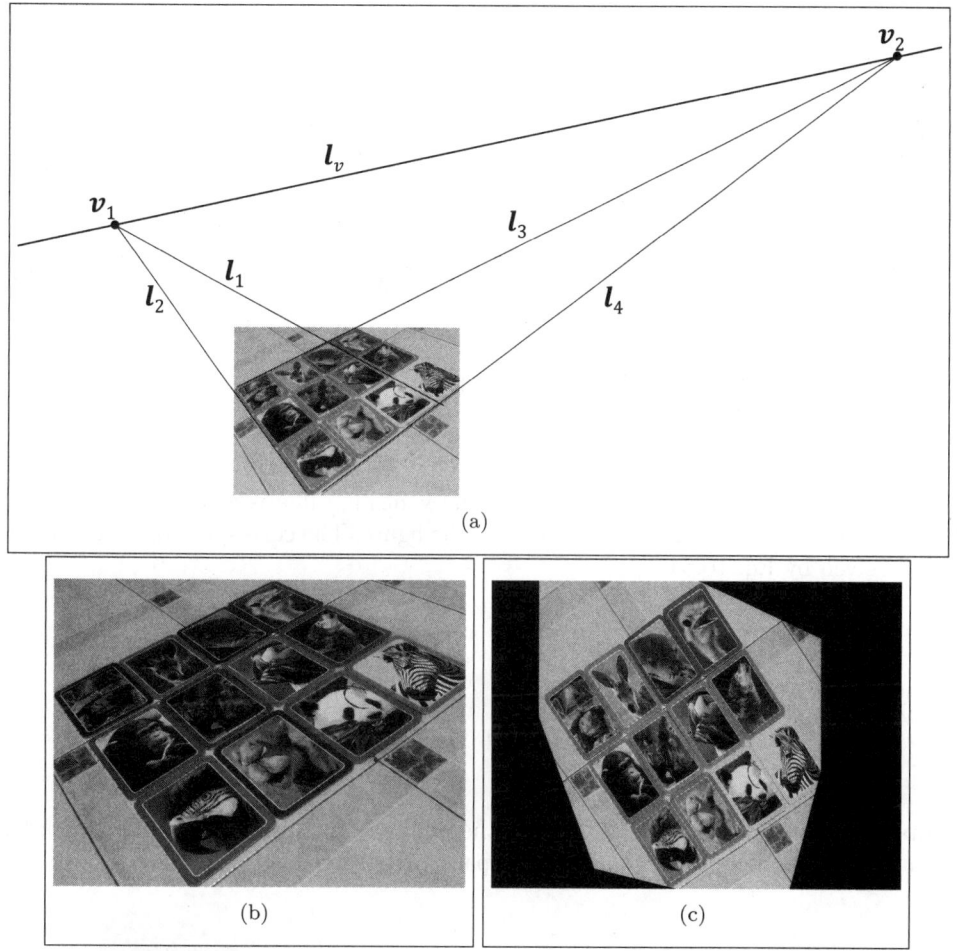

(a)

(b)   (c)

Figure 10.28 Depiction of affine rectification on a real world image.

The vanishing points, v_1 and v_2, are computed from these lines, which are given by Eq. 10.62.

$$v_1 = l_1 \times l_2 = (-10556416, -72128, 64)$$
$$v_2 = l_3 \times l_4 = (2284556, 14317258, 8402) \tag{10.62}$$

Though big numbers appear due to numerical computations, by taking out the associated scale factor, the vanishing line is represented as in Eq. 10.63.

$$l_v = v_1 \times v_2 = 10^{14}(0.000015, -0.0009, 1.5097) \tag{10.63}$$

By making the 3-D of the vanishing line in Eq. 10.63 as 1, it is scaled and represented as $l_v = (0.00001, -0.0006, 1)$. The vanishing line in Eq. 10.63 is scaled and represented as $l_v = (0.00001, -0.0006, 1)$ by making the 3-D as 1. Actually, a very small value of almost

(a)

(b)

Figure 10.29 An example of image rectification.

zero of the first element of l_v indicates that the vanishing line is at a very large distance, such as to appear almost horizontal, as seen in the figure. The corresponding transformation matrix is given by Eq. 10.64.

$$
\mathbf{H} = \begin{bmatrix} 1 & 0 & 0 \\ 0 & 1 & 0 \\ 0.00001 & -0.0006 & 1 \end{bmatrix} \tag{10.64}
$$

On applying this transformation matrix on the points in the image, the opposite borders of the image look parallel in the transformed space, as observed in Fig. 10.29 (b).

10.6 | Transformation of conics under homography

As discussed in Section 10.1, a general representation of conics in a nonhomogeneous coordinate representation is given by, $ax^2 + bxy + cy^2 + dx + ey + f = 0$. In a homogeneous coordinate representation, this is represented in a simple quadratic structure as $\boldsymbol{x}^\top \mathbf{C}\boldsymbol{x} = 0$, where $\mathbf{C} = \begin{bmatrix} a & \frac{b}{2} & \frac{d}{2} \\ \frac{b}{2} & c & \frac{e}{2} \\ \frac{d}{2} & \frac{e}{2} & f \end{bmatrix}$.

The matrix, $\mathbf{C}$, which is also an element of the projective space, is a 3×3 symmetric matrix with five independent parameters. By the dual representation of conics, it is also given by $l\mathbf{C}^*l = 0$, where l is its tangent and $\mathbf{C}^*$ is the dual conics representation, so that, $\mathbf{C}^* = \mathbf{C}^{-1}$.

To understand conics under transformation, consider a point, $\boldsymbol{x}$, that is transformed by $\mathbf{H}$, which is given by $\boldsymbol{x}' = \mathbf{H}\boldsymbol{x}$. Also, if $\boldsymbol{x}$ lies on conics $\mathbf{C}$, $\boldsymbol{x}^\top \mathbf{C}\boldsymbol{x} = 0$. From the expression of transformation of $\boldsymbol{x}$, $\boldsymbol{x} = \mathbf{H}^{-1}\boldsymbol{x}'$. Substituting this in the equation of conics is expressed in Eq. 10.65.

$$\left(\mathbf{H}^{-1}\boldsymbol{x}'\right)^{\top} \mathbf{C}\left(\mathbf{H}^{-1}\boldsymbol{x}'\right) = 0$$

$$\implies \boldsymbol{x}'^{\top}\mathbf{H}^{-\top}\mathbf{C}\mathbf{H}^{-1}\boldsymbol{x}' = 0 \qquad (10.65)$$

$$\implies \boldsymbol{x}'^{\top}\mathbf{C}'\boldsymbol{x}' = 0$$

where, $\mathbf{C}' = \mathbf{H}^{-\top}\mathbf{C}\mathbf{H}^{-1}$ is the transformed conics. The 3×3 matrix, $\mathbf{C}'$, in Eq. 10.65 is a representation of another conics. Thus, a conic remains as a conic under homography transformation. So, conics are invariants of this transformation. Since a dual of conic is the inverse of the conic in its point representation, the inverse operation on a transformed conic results in the corresponding dual conic.

Numerical Example

Compute the transformation of a conic $\mathbf{C}$ Under a point transformation $\boldsymbol{x}' = \mathbf{H}\boldsymbol{x}$, where $\mathbf{C}$ and $\mathbf{H}$ are given below.

$$\mathbf{C} = 2x^2 + 3xy + 2y^2 + 2x + 4y = 0, \text{ and } \mathbf{H} = \begin{bmatrix} 1 & 1 & 0 \\ 1 & 0 & -2 \\ 2 & 1 & -1 \end{bmatrix}.$$

Solution

We know $\boldsymbol{x}' = \mathbf{H}\boldsymbol{x}$.

The conic equation in matrix form is $\boldsymbol{x}^{\top}\mathbf{C}\boldsymbol{x} = 0$,

where, $C = \begin{bmatrix} 2 & 3/2 & 1 \\ 3/2 & 2 & 2 \\ 1 & 2 & 0 \end{bmatrix}.$

Therefore, after transformation it becomes $\boldsymbol{x}'^{\top}\mathbf{C}'\boldsymbol{x}' = 0$.

$\boldsymbol{x}^{\top}\mathbf{C}\boldsymbol{x} \to (\mathbf{H}^{-1}\boldsymbol{x}')^{\top}\mathbf{C}\mathbf{H}^{-1}\boldsymbol{x}' \to \boldsymbol{x}'^{\top}\mathbf{H}^{-\top}\mathbf{C}\mathbf{H}^{-1}\boldsymbol{x}'$

Therefore, $\mathbf{C}' = \mathbf{H}^{-\top}\mathbf{C}\mathbf{H}^{-1} = \begin{bmatrix} 0 & -5/2 & 1 \\ -5/2 & -1 & 1 \\ 1 & 1 & 0 \end{bmatrix}.$

10.6.1 | Circular points

In Section 10.5.4, it has been discussed that two specific points that are known as circular points, $\boldsymbol{I}$ and $\boldsymbol{J}$, are invariants of similarity transformation. The circular points are the fixed points under the projective transformation, $\mathbf{H}$, if and only if $\mathbf{H}$ is a similarity. These points are also on the line at infinity, $\boldsymbol{l}_{\infty}$. If the plane of complex number is treated as a 2-D projective space, where one of the axes is the imaginary axis and the other axis is the real axis, the circular points are represented by $\boldsymbol{I} = (1, i, 0)^{\top}$ and $\boldsymbol{J} = (1, -i, 0)^{\top}$. As discussed in Section 10.5.4, after transformation, these points are transformed to points in a complex space. Under similarity transformation the circular points still remain the same. Since the scale factor of these points is 0, they lie on the line at infinity. So, they satisfy the point containment relationship with $\boldsymbol{l}_{\infty}$. This may also be verified by the following operations.

$$[1 \quad i \quad 0] \begin{bmatrix} 0 \\ 0 \\ 1 \end{bmatrix} = 0, \quad \text{and} \quad [1 \quad -i \quad 0] \begin{bmatrix} 0 \\ 0 \\ 1 \end{bmatrix} = 0 \tag{10.66}$$

Consider the representation of a circle in homogeneous coordinate system, as given in Eq. 10.67.

$$x_1^2 + x_2^2 + dx_1x_3 + ex_2x_3 + fx_3^2 = 0 \tag{10.67}$$

In this representation, the coefficients of x_1^2 and x_2^2 are the same, so that, only three parameters, d, e, and f, are needed to represent the circle. Further, the intersection of the circle and $\boldsymbol{l}_{\infty}$ is computed by setting $x_3 = 0$, because, any point, whose third coordinate is 0, lies on $\boldsymbol{l}_{\infty}$. If $x_3 = 0$, then the expression of the circle is given by Eq. 10.68.

$$x_1^2 + x_2^2 = 0 \tag{10.68}$$

The circular point, $\boldsymbol{I}$, satisfies Eq. 10.68, since $x_1^2 + x_2^2 = 1^2 + i^2 = 0$. So, $\boldsymbol{I}$ lies on both the circle and the line at infinity. Similarly, $\boldsymbol{J}$ also lies on both the circle and the line at infinity. Therefore, every circle intersects the line at infinity at $\boldsymbol{I}$ and $\boldsymbol{J}$.

A conic dual representation may be defined using the two circular points, as given in Eq. 10.69.

$$\mathbf{C}_{\infty}^* = \boldsymbol{I}\boldsymbol{J}^{\top} + \boldsymbol{J}\boldsymbol{I}^{\top} \tag{10.69}$$

This degenerate conic in a 3×3 matrix form is shown in Eq. 10.70.

$$\mathbf{C}_{\infty}^* = \begin{bmatrix} 1 & 0 & 0 \\ 0 & 1 & 0 \\ 0 & 0 & 0 \end{bmatrix} \tag{10.70}$$

This is a typical dual conic that is formed by the two circular points, and this dual conic remains fixed under similarity, since the circular points are fixed under similarity. The determinant of this transformed *dual conic at infinity* is 0, and its degree of freedom is four. Also, the line at infinity, $\boldsymbol{l}_{\infty}$, is the null vector of $\mathbf{C}_{\infty}^*$.

10.6.2 | Measurement of angle under homography

Consider two straight lines, $\boldsymbol{l} = (l_1, l_2, l_3)$ and $\boldsymbol{m} = (m_1, m_2, m_3)$, as shown in Fig. 10.30, with an angle of θ between them. The directions of $\boldsymbol{l}$ and $\boldsymbol{m}$ are given by (l_1, l_2), and (m_1, m_2), respectively, in the projective space, since the first two components provide the

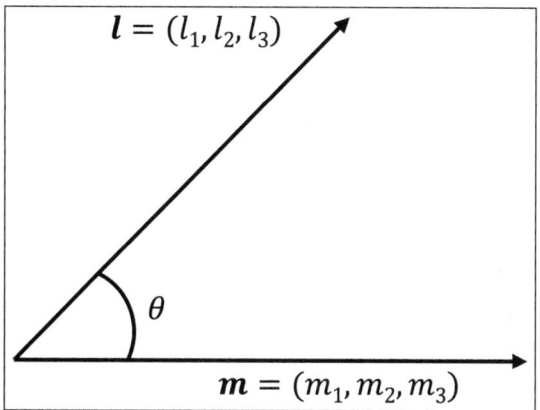

Figure 10.30 Illustration for measurement of angle under homography.

corresponding direction ratio of a 3-D vector. The angle between l and m are measured using the expression given in Eq. 10.71.

$$\cos(\theta) = \frac{l_1 m_1 + l_2 m_2}{\sqrt{(l_1^2 + l_2^2)(m_1^2 + m_2^2)}} \tag{10.71}$$

The expression in Eq. 10.71 is the cosine of the dot product of two unit vectors that represent the directions along l and m.

The above expression may also be written in the following form.

$$\cos(\theta) = \frac{l^{\mathsf{T}} \mathbf{C}_\infty^* m}{\sqrt{(l^{\mathsf{T}} \mathbf{C}_\infty^* l)(m^{\mathsf{T}} \mathbf{C}_\infty^* m)}} \tag{10.72}$$

where, $\mathbf{C}_\infty^*$ is the dual conic at infinity, which is given by Eq. 10.70. There is a transformation invariance associated with this measure, particularly with the term, $l^{\mathsf{T}} \mathbf{C}_\infty^* m$, as discussed below.

(i) The dual conic at infinity under transformation of $\mathbf{H}$ is given by $\mathbf{C}_\infty^{*\prime} = \mathbf{H}\mathbf{C}_\infty^*\mathbf{H}^{\mathsf{T}}$.

(ii) The line l' in the transformed space under $\mathbf{H}$, given the line in the original space, l, is computed as $l' = \mathbf{H}^{-\mathsf{T}} l$.

Using these properties, the quantity, $l'\mathbf{C}_\infty^{*\prime} m'$, may be expressed as in Eq. 10.73.

$$\begin{aligned} l'^{\mathsf{T}} \mathbf{C}_\infty^{*\prime} m' &= (\mathbf{H}^{-\mathsf{T}} l)^{\mathsf{T}} (\mathbf{H}\mathbf{C}_\infty^*\mathbf{H}^{\mathsf{T}})(\mathbf{H}^{-\mathsf{T}} m) \\ l^{\mathsf{T}} \mathbf{H}^{-1} \mathbf{H} \mathbf{C}_\infty^* \mathbf{H}^{\mathsf{T}} \mathbf{H}^{-\mathsf{T}} m &= l^{\mathsf{T}} \mathbf{C}_\infty^* m \end{aligned} \tag{10.73}$$

Thus given the transformed dual conic at infinity, $\mathbf{C}_\infty^{*\prime}$, the value of $\cos(\theta)$ remains the same in both the original and the transformed spaces, which is an invariant under homography.

Given an image under homography, at first, $\mathbf{C}_\infty^{*\prime}$, the transformed dual line conic at infinity, is computed. Then relationship of expressions in Eqs. 10.71 and 10.72 may be used to obtain the original angle formed by any two considered lines in the original space. For example, if there are two perpendicular lines in the original space, they may not remain perpendicular after the transformation under homography. But, this relationship between these representations still holds. Hence, if the lines, l and m, are orthogonal, $l'^{\mathsf{T}} \mathbf{C}_{\infty}^{*}{}' m' = 0$, since the cosine of a right angle is 0, where, the quantities, l', $\mathbf{C}_{\infty}^{*}{}'$, and m', are in the transformed space. This relation is used to perform rectilinear corrections.

10.6.3 | Estimation of $\mathbf{C}_{\infty}^{*}{}'$

To estimate the dual line conic at infinity under transformation, $\mathbf{C}_{\infty}^{*}{}'$, a set of pairs of orthogonal lines is used. For the given two orthogonal lines, $l = (l_1, l_2, l_3)$ and $m = (m_1, m_2, m_3)$, from the invariant property of cosine angle we get, $l'^{\mathsf{T}} \mathbf{C}_{\infty}^{*}{}' m' = 0$. This gives an equation as expressed in the following.

$$\begin{bmatrix} l_1 m_1 & \frac{1}{2}(l_1 m_2 + l_2 m_1) & l_2 m_2 & \frac{1}{2}(l_1 m_3 + l_3 m_1) & \frac{1}{2}(l_2 m_3 + l_3 m_2) & l_3 m_3 \end{bmatrix} \mathbf{C} = 0 \tag{10.74}$$

where, $\mathbf{C}$ is represented by a column vector $\begin{bmatrix} a & b & c & d & e & f \end{bmatrix}^{\mathsf{T}}$ following a general conic representation. Since there are five independent variables in $\mathbf{C}$, a minimum of five such orthogonal pairs of lines are necessary to form five different equations to solve it.

Since this is a set of linear homogeneous representation with six parameters and five unknowns, they are solved by applying DLT technique. Thus, by representing the set of equations in a matrix form, $\mathbf{AC} = 0$, where $\mathbf{A}$ is formed by stacking each of the equations of the form in Eq. 10.74, it is solved by using least squares estimate method when number of equations is more than five by minimizing $||\mathbf{AC}||^2$, subject to the constraint of $||\mathbf{C}||^2 = 1$. The solution to this set of equations is the eigenvector corresponding to the minimum eigenvalue of $\mathbf{A}^{\mathsf{T}} \mathbf{A}$.

Alternatively, the set of equations may also be converted into a set of nonhomogeneous equations and solved. In this case, one of the variables is set to 1 (e.g., $f = 1$) to get the solution. But, if f happens to be 0 in the representation of conic, this approach is not applicable. Once the solution $\mathbf{C}$ is obtained, we need to make it singular as the transformed dual conic at infinity is also a rank deficient matrix of rank 2. For this we may consider the nearest rank 2 approximation of $\mathbf{C}$. For this, a singular value decomposition (SVD) is applied on $\mathbf{C}$ and the minimum singular value is set to 0 and then the matrix is reconstructed from the SVD components. The computation is illustrated below.

Let the SVD of $\mathbf{C}$ be represented as in Eq. 10.75.

$$\mathbf{C} = \mathbf{U} \mathbf{D} \mathbf{V}^{\mathsf{T}} \tag{10.75}$$

where, $\mathbf{U}$ and $\mathbf{V}$ are 3×3 matrices, and $\mathbf{D}$ is a diagonal matrix whose singular values are its diagonal entries, which is given by Eq. 10.76.

$$\mathbf{D} = \begin{bmatrix} \lambda_1 & 0 & 0 \\ 0 & \lambda_2 & 0 \\ 0 & 0 & \lambda_3 \end{bmatrix} \tag{10.76}$$

The singular values are arranged in the order of, $\lambda_1 > \lambda_2 > \lambda_3$, and λ_3 is set to 0. Let $\widetilde{\mathbf{D}}$ be the modified diagonal matrix that is obtained by setting $\lambda_3 = 0$ in $\mathbf{D}$, so that, it becomes a rank-2 matrix. Then, $\widetilde{\mathbf{D}}$ is used to estimate $\mathbf{C}$ as, $\mathbf{C} = \mathbf{U}\widetilde{\mathbf{D}}\mathbf{V}^{\mathsf{T}}$.

10.6.4 | Recovery of metric properties

To recover the metric properties, it is necessary to estimate the homography from $\mathbf{C}_\infty^{*}{}'$ up to similarity transformation, since the dual line conic is preserved under the similarity transform. The estimation obtained in the previous section corresponds to the dual line conic at infinity. To obtain the homography matrix that corresponds to the transformed dual line conic, matrix decomposition method is applied to $\mathbf{C}_\infty^{*}{}'$. A decomposition of $\mathbf{C}_\infty^{*}{}'$ into a form of $\mathbf{H}\mathbf{C}_\infty^{*}\mathbf{H}^{\mathsf{T}}$, as expressed in Eq. 10.77, indicates homography.

$$\mathbf{C}_\infty^{*}{}' = \mathbf{U}\begin{bmatrix} 1 & 0 & 0 \\ 0 & 1 & 0 \\ 0 & 0 & 0 \end{bmatrix}\mathbf{U}^{\mathsf{T}} \tag{10.77}$$

where, $\mathbf{U}$ is a 3×3 matrix. Since conic is a symmetric matrix, similar to the matrix decomposition in Eq. 10.77, the singular values of the form in Eq. 10.76 may be adjusted in such a way that the first two quantities are unity, and subsequently, the columns of $\mathbf{U}$ and $\mathbf{U}^{\mathsf{T}}$ are accordingly adjusted. After this decomposition, the middle matrix in Eq. 10.77 satisfies the structure of $\mathbf{C}_\infty^{*}$, the dual line conic at infinity. The $\mathbf{U}$ may be considered a homography performing the transformation of the dual conic at infinity to $\mathbf{C}$ and the inverse of $\mathbf{U}$ is applied to an image for its *rectification* or to recover the metric properties, like ratios of distances. We may note also that $\mathbf{H}_S\mathbf{U}$ is also a solution of the above problem, where $\mathbf{H}_S$ is a similarity transformation.

Summary

A point in a 2-D projective space is represented by a ray passing through the origin of an implicit 3-D space. It requires an additional dimension for its representation in homogeneous coordinates. A straight line in 2D real space is also represented as an element of the 2D projective space, which is the space that represents lines of 2-D real space. Points and lines hold duality theorem. Conics in 2D projective space are represented by a 3×3 symmetric matrix. Every nondegenerate conic represented by nonsingular 3×3 symmetric matrix has a dual conic or line conic, which is an envelope of its tangents.

A projective transformation is a transformation of a point in projective space to a point in another projective space. Properties of a projective transformation are, (i) it is invertible, (ii) it preserves collinearity, and (iii) it is always in a linear form. The linear model of projective transformation provides applicability of convenient techniques for estimating it. The product of an original line with the inverse of transpose of the transformation matrix, corresponds to the line in the transformed space. Computationally, homography is estimated by establishing a set of point correspondences. The minimum number of point correspondences required to solve for homography is four. If there are more than four point correspondences, a robust computation of homography is obtained by applying least squared error techniques, like DLT.

The conics remain as conics after projective transformation. Likewise, the dual conic transformation has the same property in the projective transformation space. There are various groups of projective transformation, which are hierarchical, viz., projective linear group (8 degrees of freedom), affine group (6 degrees of freedom), Euclidean group or similarity transformation (4 degrees of freedom), and oriented Euclidean group or isometric transformation (3 degrees of freedom). Conic dual and circular points are invariant under similarity transformation. The line at infinity is a zero vector of conic dual and it preserves the cosine of angle of two lines under transformation. By using the transformed dual conic, the cosine of the angle between the lines in original space may be computed. This property is used for rectifying the images. There are two types of rectifications, an affine rectification, and stratification or rectilinear rectification. Image rectification helps in recovering the metric properties. Particularly, the proportionate distances may be recovered by applying estimated homography exploiting these properties.

Exercises

(i) Given two straight lines $(1, 2, 3)$ and $(3, 2, 1)$ in $\mathbb{P}^2$.

   (a) Compute their point of intersection in $\mathbb{R}^2$.

   (b) Compute their point of intersection in $\mathbb{P}^2$.

(ii) Consider the following homography matrix $\mathbf{H}$ between two images I_1 to I_2 of the same scene.

$$\mathbf{H} = \begin{bmatrix} 1 & 3 & 5 \\ 4 & 3 & 7 \\ 5 & -4 & 2 \end{bmatrix}$$

Suppose an image point in I_1 given by $(5, 6) \in \mathbb{R}^2$. Find the corresponding point in I_2.

(iii) Consider the following projection matrix of a camera.

$$\begin{bmatrix} 10 & 8 & 7 & 2 \\ 4 & -3 & -2 & 0 \\ 3 & 4 & 1 & 1 \end{bmatrix}$$

   (a) Compute, in $\mathbb{R}^2$, the vanishing point of the x-axis of the world coordinate system.

   (b) Compute, in $\mathbb{R}^2$, the image point of the world coordinate point $(5, 6, 10) \in \mathbb{R}^3$.

(iv) Compute dual conic, C^*, of the conic $C = \begin{bmatrix} 1 & 2 & 1 \\ 2 & 1 & -1 \\ 1 & -1 & 1 \end{bmatrix}$.

(v) Consider the following homography matrix, **H**, for mapping points from image I to the corresponding points in image I'.

$$\begin{bmatrix} 1 & -2 & 1 \\ 2 & 1 & 2 \\ 1 & 1 & -2 \end{bmatrix}$$

(a) Compute the transformed line in I' formed by the points $(1, 3)$ and $(3, 1)$ in I.

(b) Compute the transformed dual conic at infinity under **H**.

(c) Compute the transformed point $q \in I'$ of $(1, 2) \in I$.

(vi) Consider the following homography matrix, **H**, for mapping points from image I

to those in I'. $\begin{bmatrix} 1 & 2 & 1 \\ 2 & 1 & 2 \\ 1 & 1 & 2 \end{bmatrix}$ Note: Line at infinity containing all ideal points is given

by $l_\infty = (0, 0, 1)$

(a) Compute the vanishing line in I'.

(b) Compute the vanishing point in I' of the lines parallel to a straight line $(1, 2, 1) \in \mathbb{P}^2$ in I.

(vii) Consider a projective transformation $\mathbf{H} = \begin{bmatrix} 1 & -1 & 1 \\ -1 & 1 & 1 \\ 1 & 1 & 1 \end{bmatrix}$ and a conic

$\mathbf{C} = \begin{bmatrix} 1 & 2 & 1 \\ 2 & 1 & -1 \\ 1 & -1 & 1 \end{bmatrix}$. Find the transformation of conic **C** under **H**?

(viii) Compute the homography induced by plane at infinity $\mathbf{H}_\infty$ for camera matrices

$$\mathbf{P} = \begin{bmatrix} 1 & 0 & 0 & 0 \\ 0 & 1 & 0 & 0 \\ 0 & 0 & 1 & 0 \end{bmatrix} \text{ and } \mathbf{P'} = \begin{bmatrix} 4 & 4 & 6 & 1 \\ 3 & 5 & 7 & 7 \\ 2 & 6 & 9 & 2 \end{bmatrix}.$$

(ix) The matrix **A** is formed from the following equations relating a point $\mathbf{X}_i$ and its transformed point $\mathbf{X}'_i$ in 2D projective spaces.

$$\begin{bmatrix} \mathbf{0}^\mathsf{T} & -w'_i\mathbf{X}_i^\mathsf{T} & y'_i\mathbf{X}_i^\mathsf{T} \\ w'_i\mathbf{X}_i^\mathsf{T} & \mathbf{0}^\mathsf{T} & -x'_i\mathbf{X}_i^\mathsf{T} \\ -y'_i\mathbf{X}_i^\mathsf{T} & x'_i\mathbf{X}_i^\mathsf{T} & \mathbf{0}^\mathsf{T} \end{bmatrix} \begin{pmatrix} h^1 \\ h^2 \\ h^3 \end{pmatrix} = 0$$

where $\mathbf{X}'_i = (x'_i, y'_i, w'_i)^\mathsf{T}$ and $\mathbf{X}_i = (x_i, y_i, w_i)^\mathsf{T}$, $i = 1, 2, \cdots n$. Compute the dimensions and rank of all the involved matrices for solving $\mathbf{A}h = 0$ using DLT for a set of nonhomogeneous equations.

(Note: DLT algorithm for nonhomogeneous equation $Ah = 0$)

(x) Compute the tangent to the conic $\mathbf{C}$ at a point $p = (2,3)$, where

$$\mathbf{C} = \begin{bmatrix} 1 & 2 & 1 \\ 2 & 1 & 3 \\ 1 & 1 & 5 \end{bmatrix}$$

(xi) Consider the following homography matrix $\mathbf{H}$ from image I_1 (source) to I_2 (target) of the same scene captured by a pair of cameras.

$$\mathbf{H} = \begin{bmatrix} 1 & 3 & 5 \\ 4 & 3 & 7 \\ 5 & -4 & 2 \end{bmatrix}$$

Suppose a line in I_1 given by $(2, 3, 1)$. Find the corresponding line in I_2.

(xii) An image point in I_1 given by $(5,6) \in \mathbb{R}^2$. Compute the following.

(a) If the image is rotated by $90°$ and translated by $(t_x = 1$ and $t_y = 2)$, compute the new coordinates of I_1, given the isometry is orientation-preserving.

(b) If the image is rotated by $90°$ and translated by $(t_x = 1$ and $t_y = 2)$, compute the new coordinates of I_1, given the isometry is reverses the orientation.

(c) If similarity transformation is applied on the image, where isotropic scaling $(s = 2)$, translation $(t_x = 2$ and $t_y = 3)$, and rotation $(\theta = 90°)$, compute the new co-ordinates of I_1.

(xiii) Consider the points, $x_1 = (1,1), x_2 = (1,2), x_3 = (2,1), x_4 = (2,2)$. Compute the cross ratio, $\mathrm{Cross}(x_1, x_2, x_3, x_4)$.

(xiv) Compute the transformation of the point, $\begin{pmatrix} 1 \\ i \\ 0 \end{pmatrix}$, under similarity transformation?

(xv) Compute the angle between the two lines, $\boldsymbol{l} = (1,1,1)$ and $\boldsymbol{m} = (1,-1,4)$, in Euclidean geometry?

(xvi) Consider the following homography matrix $\mathbf{H}$ from image I_1 to I_2 of the same scene.

$$\mathbf{H} = \begin{bmatrix} 4 & 3 & 6 \\ 9 & 1 & 2 \\ 3 & 8 & 1 \end{bmatrix}$$

(a) Discuss the constraints on imaging and the matrix $\mathbf{H}$. Verify whether $\mathbf{H}$ satisfies these constraints.

(b) Given a pixel $(3,5)$ in I_1, compute its corresponding pixel in I_2.

(c) Given the equation of a straight line, $y = 4x + 1$, in image I_2, compute the equation of the corresponding straight line in image I_1 using the dual representation of line and point in a 2-D projective space.

(d) Given a circle C in image I_1 with equation: $x^2 + y^2 - 8x + 4y - 16 = 0$, compute the corresponding conic section and its dual conic in image I_2. Compute the intersection of the circle C with the line at ∞ in image I_1.

(**xvii**) For two straight lines l and m in $\mathbb{P}^2$, prove that their point of intersection is given by $l \times m$. Show that the point of intersection of these two straight lines lies on the line at infinity, if $l \parallel m$.

(**xviii**) Prove that under projective transformation (homography), two parallel lines may intersect at a finite point in $\mathbb{P}^2$. Under what condition does the intersecting point lies at infinity?

(**xix**) Define a conic and dual conic in P^2. Prove that under homography a conic remains a conic.

(**xx**) Form the equations for solving homography between two images I_1 and I_2 of a 3-D plane, given a pair of corresponding points, $x_1 \in I_1$ and $x_2 \in I_2$. What is the minimum number of point correspondences required for solving the homography. Explain why a solution of nonhomogeneous equations is not preferred in this case.

(**xxi**) Use projective geometry to compute the following:

(**a**) Equation of the straight line passing through the points $(4, 5)$ and $(9, 10)$ in $\mathbb{R}^2$.

(**b**) Point of intersection of the straight lines given by the equations
(i) $3x + 8y + 11 = 0$, and (ii) $4x + 7y + 15 = 0$.

(**c**) Consider the following homography $\mathbf{H}$ between two projective spaces.

$$\mathbf{H} = \begin{bmatrix} 6 & 4 & 5 \\ 2 & 8 & 0 \\ 4 & 2 & 1 \end{bmatrix}$$

(**1**) Compute the vanishing line in the transformed space.

(**2**) Compute the conic dual at ∞ ($\mathbf{C}_\infty$) in the transformed space.

(**3**) Given two lines, $(1, 2, 3)$ and $(4, 5, 6)$, in $\mathbb{P}^2$, compute the angle formed by them in the canonical space.

(**d**) How affine homography matrix is distinguished from a general projective matrix?

(**xxii**) Consider the following homography $\mathbf{H}$ between two projective spaces.

$$\mathbf{H} = \begin{bmatrix} 3 & 4 & -6 \\ 0 & 2 & -8 \\ 0 & 0 & 1 \end{bmatrix}$$

Answer the following questions with respect to homography $\mathbf{H}$.

(a) Show that parallel lines remain parallel under **H**.

(b) Given a circle of radius 5 with center at $(-3, 2) \in \mathbb{R}^2$, find the transformed conic under **H** in $\mathbb{P}^2$.

(c) Define the conic dual at ∞ ($\mathbf{C}_\infty$) identifying the set of straight lines lying on this conic, and compute its transformation under **H**. What is the property of an angle between two straight lines that remains invariant under **H**?

(d) Compute a nontrivial fixed point (other than the zero vector) of **H**. (A fixed point of any transformation is a point, which remains the same after being transformed.)

(e) Compute the transformed point of intersection of the straight lines given by the equations $3x + 4y + 2 = 0$ and $4x + 3y + 5 = 0$ in $\mathbb{R}^2$.

(xxiii) Using the concepts of projective geometry, compute the following:

(a) Compute the straight line formed by the points $(5, 2)$ and $(7, 8)$.

(b) Compute the point of intersection of straight lines given by the equations $3x + 4y + 5 = 0$ and $7x + 5y + 9 = 0$.

(xxiv) Consider the following homography **H** between two projective spaces.

$$\mathbf{H} = \begin{bmatrix} 7 & 5 & -1 \\ 0 & 1 & -8 \\ 0 & 5 & 1 \end{bmatrix}$$

(a) Compute the vanishing line in the transformed space.

(b) Given two points $(2, 4)$ and $(3, 7)$ compute the corresponding dual line conic in $\mathbb{P}^2$.

(c) Find the transformed dual line conic with the homography **H**.

(xxv) What is the minimum number of point correspondences required for computing homography between two projective spaces? Form the set of equations considering these point correspondences.

(xxvi) Given three concurrent straight lines, l_1, l_2, and l_3 in 2-D projective space $\mathbb{P}^2$, prove that they satisfy the following: $[l_1 \cdot (l_2 \times l_3) = 0]$.

(xxvii) Suppose the nonsingular homography matrix between fronto-parallel view of a 3-D plane and for any arbitrary projective space (Π) of the same scene is given as follows:

$\begin{bmatrix} a & b & 0 \\ c & d & 0 \\ e & f & g \end{bmatrix}$ Compute the vanishing line in the transformed projective space (Π).

(xxviii) Provide the forms of homography matrices representing the hierarchy of projective transformation. Show that the line at infinity is fixed under similarity. Explain how this fact is used in affine rectification.

(xxix) Compute the transformation of a conic C under a point transformation $x' = Hx$, where $C = 2x^2 + 3xy + 2y^2 + 2x + 4y = 0$ and the projective transformation matrix **H** as follows.

$$\mathbf{H} = \begin{bmatrix} 1 & 1 & 0 \\ 1 & 0 & -2 \\ 2 & 1 & -1 \end{bmatrix}.$$

(xxx) While driving on the highway, why do the two parallel sides and also parallel white markers beside them of a straight metal road appear to be meeting the horizon at the same point? Explain how the horizon appears to a viewer.

(xxxi) Consider the following homography **H** between two projective spaces.

$$\mathbf{H} = \begin{bmatrix} 3 & 4 & -6 \\ 1 & 2 & -8 \\ 10 & 0 & 0 \end{bmatrix}$$

Answer the following questions with respect to homography **H**.

(a) Compute the transformed point of intersection of the straight lines given by the equations $3x - 4y + 2 = 0$, and $4x - 3y + 5 = 0$ in $\mathbb{R}^2$.

(b) Given a circle of radius 7 with center at $(0, 2) \in R^2$, find the transformed conic under **H** in $\mathbb{P}^2$.

(c) Define the conic dual at ∞ (C_∞). Compute its transformation under **H**.

(d) Compute the vanishing line in the transformed space. Show that it is the right null vector of the transformed C_∞.

(xxxii) Define projective transformation or homography in 2-D projective geometry. Consider the following homography matrix **H**.

$$\mathbf{H} = \begin{bmatrix} 1 & 10 & 2 \\ 3 & 9 & 4 \\ 5 & 8 & 1 \end{bmatrix}$$

Compute the following in the transformed space:

(a) The transformation of the point of $(5, 1) \in \mathbb{R}^2$.

(b) The algebraic equation of the transformation of the straight line given be $3x + 2y = 5$.

(c) The algebraic equation of the transformation of the circle given by $x^2 + y^2 = 16$.

(d) The vanishing point of the X-axis.

(e) The vanishing line.

11

Single View Camera Geometry

In this chapter, the theory and properties of single view camera geometry are discussed. We consider the principle of image formation in optical cameras in this case and apply it to relate the three-dimensional (3-D) world with the image points on a two-dimensional (2-D) plane.

11.1 | Pinhole camera

A mapping of a point in a 3-D coordinate space to a point on a 2-D plane has been already discussed in the previous chapter while explaining the canonical configuration of a 2-D projective space. We relate these concepts with respect to a pinhole camera based imaging system. Consider a 3-D scene point, P, as shown in Fig. 11.1. The corresponding image point, p', is the point of intersection of the image plane and the straight line from P that passes through the center of the lens, O. In the same analogy, consider the formation of an image in front of the camera center, where the corresponding image plane is placed at the same distance as the sensor is placed behind the lens. In this case, the images obtained on the image plane that is placed in front of the lens are of the same size as on the sensor, and there is a logical transformation of coordinates from point p' to point p. Thus we may directly relate the scene point P with the image point p. This is a convenient way of handling coordinate system of image points by placing it in front of the camera in the same side of the viewing objects.

The configuration shown in Fig. 11.2 is a typical set-up that is used to represent a mapping from a 3-D scene onto a 2-D image plane using a pinhole camera. The camera center, C, is the center of projection through which all the rays from the points in the 3-D real world pass and intersect the image plane to form the images of their corresponding 3-D real world points. With respect to projective geometry, the image point, p, represents the 3-D ray formed by the camera center and the 3-D world point, P.

In order to formulate an association between the world coordinate point, P, and its image, p, it is assumed that the camera center, C, is the origin of the world coordinate system. The coordinate systems of the 3-D world and the image plane are referred to as the *world coordinate system* (represented by X, Y, and Z axes) and the *image coordinate*

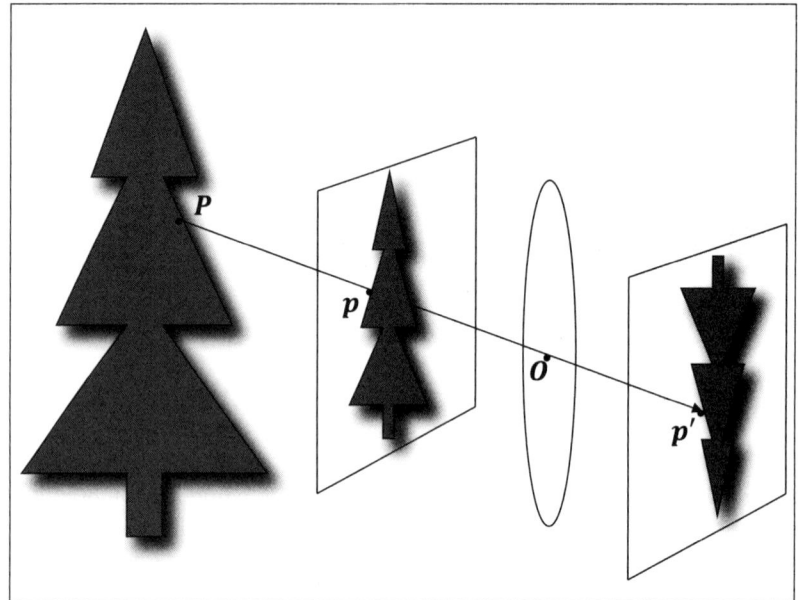

Figure 11.1 Optical imaging in a pinhole camera.

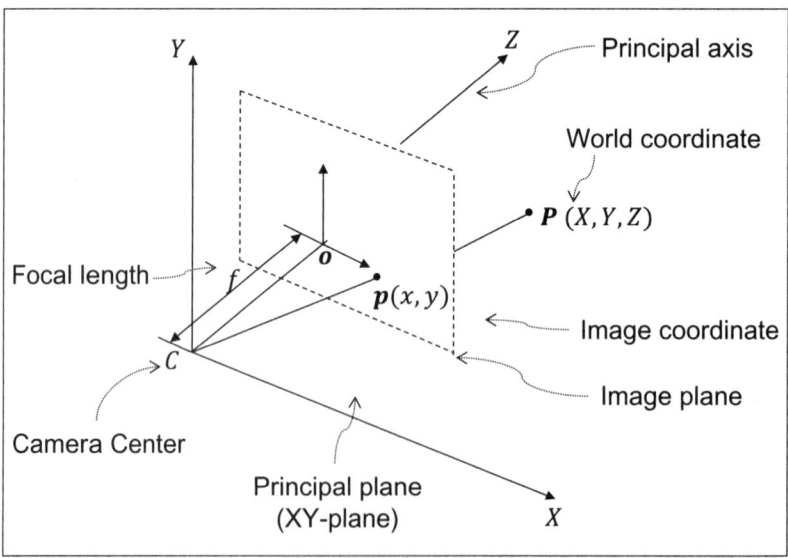

Figure 11.2 Coordinate conventions in a pinhole camera imaging system.

system (represented by x and y axes), respectively. It is assumed that the coordinate axes, X-axis and Y-axis, of the 3-D world coordinate system are parallel to the coordinate axes, x-axis and y-axis, of the image plane. The image plane is located at a distance of f from the camera center $\boldsymbol{C}$, where f is the focal length of the camera. The XY-plane and the Z-axis of the world coordinate system are referred to as the *principal plane* and the *principal axis*, respectively. The point of intersection of the Z-axis of the world coordinate system with the image plane is taken as the origin, $\boldsymbol{o}$ of the image coordinate system. This point which is the intersection of the principal axis with the image plane is called the *principal point*.

The camera center, $\boldsymbol{C}$, the image point, $\boldsymbol{p}(x, y)$, and the origin, $\boldsymbol{o}$, form a triangle, as observed in the figure. Similarly, the world point, $\boldsymbol{P}(X, Y, Z)$, its projection onto YZ-plane, and the camera center, $\boldsymbol{C}$, form another triangle. By applying the law of similar triangles, the projected image coordinates, x and y, are expressed as in Eq. 11.1.

$$x = \frac{fX}{Z}, \quad \text{and} \quad y = \frac{fY}{Z} \tag{11.1}$$

Given a 3-D world point, its projection onto an image plane at a distance of f from the camera center is evaluated using Eq. 11.1. However, the inverse computation is not possible since an image point, $\boldsymbol{p}$, is represented by a ray passing through $\boldsymbol{C}$. In this case, a scene point may be any of the 3-D points lying on the ray. In an optical image, the information of the particular point along this ray is available in the form of received energy in the image. The point along this path, from where this energy is received, is considered as the object point for the respective image point. Thus in an image of an optical camera, identification of the object point lying on the projection ray may be resolved by using other information such as, of texture, color, structure, etc., from the image.

The projection of a 3-D world point onto a 2-D image plane is mathematically represented by a linear transformation using homogeneous coordinate systems as given by Eq. 11.2.

$$\begin{bmatrix} x \\ y \\ 1 \end{bmatrix} \equiv \begin{bmatrix} fX \\ fY \\ Z \end{bmatrix} = \begin{bmatrix} f & 0 & 0 & 0 \\ 0 & f & 0 & 0 \\ 0 & 0 & 1 & 0 \end{bmatrix} \begin{bmatrix} X \\ Y \\ Z \\ 1 \end{bmatrix} \tag{11.2}$$

The transformation matrix in the above expression is called the *projection matrix*. Given the image point $\boldsymbol{x}$ and the scene point $\boldsymbol{X}$ in 2-D and 3-D homogeneous coordinates, respectively, the projection matrix $\mathbf{P}$ transforms $\boldsymbol{X}$ to $\boldsymbol{x}$ such that, $\boldsymbol{x} = \mathbf{P}\boldsymbol{X}$. We may note here that the image point belongs to a 2-D projective space, whereas the scene point belongs to a 3-D projective space in the above expression. Hence to get the coordinates in real space the coordinates are to be divided by the last dimension (corresponding to scale).

The projection matrix, $\mathbf{P}$, may be decomposed as given by Eq. 11.3.

$$\mathbf{P} = \begin{bmatrix} f & 0 & 0 \\ 0 & f & 0 \\ 0 & 0 & 1 \end{bmatrix} \begin{bmatrix} 1 & 0 & 0 & 0 \\ 0 & 1 & 0 & 0 \\ 0 & 0 & 1 & 0 \end{bmatrix} = \text{Diag}(f, f, 1)[\mathbf{I}|\mathbf{0}] \tag{11.3}$$

In the above, $\text{Diag}(a, b, c)$ represents a diagonal matrix of dimension 3×3 with the diagonal elements as a, b, and c, respectively. $\mathbf{I}$ is the 3×3 identity matrix, and shown here as a submatrix of the composition. Here, $\mathbf{0}$ is the zero column vector of dimension 3×1. We may note here that for the convenience of notation a separator ($|$) is used to distinctly identify 3×3 submatrix and 3×1 column vector of the 3×4 matrix here. This notation is used for camera matrices in this book. Eq. 11.3 describes the linear transformation of a point in a 3-D projective space corresponding to the scene point to a point in a 2-D projective space corresponding to its image point. Thus, when the 3-D point, $\mathbf{X}$, in the homogeneous coordinate system is left multiplied by the projection matrix $\mathbf{P}$, we get the 2-D image point $\boldsymbol{x}$ in homogeneous coordinates. So, the pinhole camera may be seen as a linear mapping from a 3-D projective space to a 2-D projective space, $\mathbb{P}^3 \rightarrow \mathbb{P}^2$, unlike homography, which is a linear mapping from a 2-D projective space to another 2-D projective space, $\mathbb{P}^2 \rightarrow \mathbb{P}^2$. As we discuss in Chapter 10, the homography is invertible, which makes it a one-to-one mapping. Whereas, the pinhole camera imaging is not invertible, since its projection matrix is noninvertible. Multiple scene points lying on the ray passing through the center of camera map to the same image point.

In the canonical form of representation, it is initially assumed that both the world and image coordinate systems are mutually aligned in the sense that, x-axis and y-axis of the image plane are parallel to X-axis and Y-axis of the 3-D space, respectively. The Z-axis of the 3-D space intersects at the origin of the image plane. However, if the origin of the image coordinate system is not aligned with the world coordinate system, the principal point is shifted by an offset of (p_x, p_y), which corresponds to a shift of every image point in the image plane as $(x + p_x, y + p_y)$. The projected image point, (x', y'), is then evaluated as $(p_x + \frac{fX}{Z}, p_y + \frac{fY}{Z})$, which is equivalent to, $[f_x + p_x Z \quad f_y + p_y Z \quad Z]^\top$, where, $f_x = fX$ and $f_y = fY$. This transformation is accommodated in the third column of the projection matrix, which is given by Eq. 11.4.

$$\begin{bmatrix} x' \\ y' \\ 1 \end{bmatrix} \equiv \begin{bmatrix} f & 0 & p_x & 0 \\ 0 & f & p_y & 0 \\ 0 & 0 & 1 & 0 \end{bmatrix} \begin{bmatrix} X \\ Y \\ Z \\ 1 \end{bmatrix} \tag{11.4}$$

The decomposition of the projection matrix $\mathbf{P}$ as a product of two matrices, similar to Eq. 11.3, is given by Eq. 11.5.

$$\mathbf{P} = \begin{bmatrix} f & 0 & p_x \\ 0 & f & p_y \\ 0 & 0 & 1 \end{bmatrix} \begin{bmatrix} 1 & 0 & 0 & 0 \\ 0 & 1 & 0 & 0 \\ 0 & 0 & 1 & 0 \end{bmatrix} = \mathbf{K}[\mathbf{I}|\mathbf{0}] \tag{11.5}$$

where, $\mathbf{K}$ is known as the *camera calibration matrix*. The corresponding image of $\mathbf{X}$ in the image plane is given by Eq. 11.6.

$$\boldsymbol{x} = \mathbf{K}[\mathbf{I}|\mathbf{0}]\mathbf{X} \tag{11.6}$$

This results in a shift in the origin of image coordinate system, as observed in Fig. 11.3.

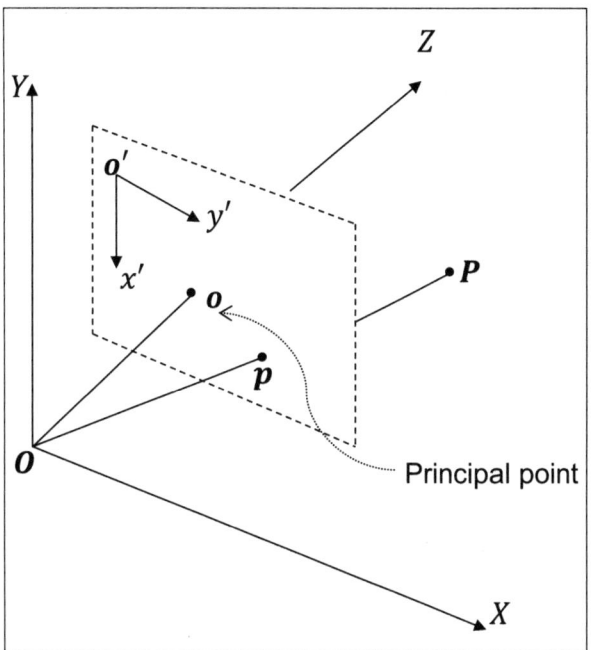

Figure 11.3 The origin of the image plane is at a different point than the principal point.

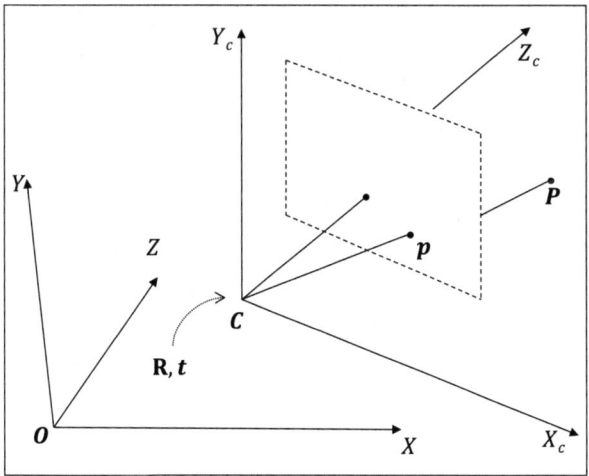

Figure 11.4 Origins of the camera and the world coordinate systems.

If the world and image coordinate systems are not mutually aligned as assumed before, this relationship becomes more generalized. In this case, the origin of the camera and the world coordinate systems are different, as shown in Fig. 11.4. A *homogeneous coordinate representation* of a 3-D world point is given by, $\boldsymbol{X} = \begin{bmatrix} \widetilde{\boldsymbol{X}} \\ 1 \end{bmatrix}$, where $\widetilde{\boldsymbol{X}}$ is its *nonhomogeneous coordinate representation* that is given by $\widetilde{X} = [X \quad Y \quad Z]^{\top}$. This convention is followed throughout this chapter. Here, the realization of the canonical representation of the projection matrix involves a cascade of translation and rotation operations. In order to align the camera coordinate system with the world coordinate system, $\widetilde{X}$ is shifted by $\widetilde{C}$ and then rotated to align the axes with the axes of camera centric coordinate system. The latter operation is equivalent to multiplication by a 3×3 orthonormal matrix $\mathbf{R}$. Hence the transformation of world coordinates to camera centric coordinates is given by Eq. 11.7.

$$\widetilde{X_c} = \mathbf{R}(\widetilde{X} - \widetilde{C}) \tag{11.7}$$

In nonhomogeneous representation, the shifted camera coordinate point, X_c, is given by Eq. 11.8.

$$X_c = \begin{bmatrix} \mathbf{R} & -\mathbf{R}\widetilde{C} \\ 0 & 1 \end{bmatrix} \begin{bmatrix} X \\ Y \\ Z \\ 1 \end{bmatrix} \tag{11.8}$$

From Eqs. 11.5 and 11.8, the relation between the image point, x, and the corresponding coordinate in the camera centric coordinate system, X_c, is given by Eq. 11.9.

$$x = \mathbf{K}[\mathbf{I}|\mathbf{0}]X_c = \mathbf{K}[\mathbf{I}|\mathbf{0}] \begin{bmatrix} \mathbf{R} & -\mathbf{R}\widetilde{C} \\ 0 & 1 \end{bmatrix} \begin{bmatrix} X \\ Y \\ Z \\ 1 \end{bmatrix} \tag{11.9}$$

The dimensions of $\mathbf{K}$, $[\mathbf{I}|\mathbf{0}]$, $\begin{bmatrix} \mathbf{R} & -\mathbf{R}\widetilde{C} \\ 0 & 1 \end{bmatrix}$, and $[X \quad Y \quad Z \quad 1]^{\top}$ are 3×3, 3×4, 4×4, and 4×1, respectively. The product of these matrices eventually results in a 3×1 image point, x, in the 2-D projection space. Also, the projection matrix is represented as in Eq. 11.10.

$$\mathbf{P} = \mathbf{K}\mathbf{R}[\mathbf{I}| - \widetilde{C}] = \mathbf{K}[\mathbf{R}|t] \tag{11.10}$$

where, t is the translation vector.

Numerical Example

If the principal point is located at $(2, 3)$ in the coordinate system of the image plane, what would be the image coordinates of the world point $(3, 4, 5)$ in a camera centric coordinate, using a pin hole camera with focal length $f = 0.5$?

Solution

If the origin of image plane is not at the principal point, then the mapping from world coordinates (X, Y, Z) to image coordinates (x, y) with principal point at (p_x, p_y) is given by $((fX/Z) + p_x, (fY/Z) + p_y) = (2.3, 3.4)$.

11.1.1 | CCD camera model

In a typical digital image, the light ray that gets reflected from a 3-D world point passes through the camera center to form its image on the sensor. The arrangement of sensors in a camera are usually made by charge-coupled device (CCD) sensors or CMOS sensors to form a digital image. This is referred to as CCD camera arrangement. Here each sensor corresponds to an image pixel. In order to relate physical dimensions with pixel coordinates, it is necessary to interpret the underlying parameters that are involved in digitization of the image points. Toward this, resolution is a parameter that denotes the number of sensor elements per unit length, for example, m_x and m_y sensor elements per unit length along x-axis and y-axis, respectively. The focal length, f, is a multiplicative factor of the resolution along x-axis and y-axis. By considering the resolution, the camera calibration matrix, $\mathbf{K}$, is given as in Eq. 11.11.

$$\mathbf{K} = \begin{bmatrix} \alpha_x & 0 & p_x \\ 0 & \alpha_y & p_y \\ 0 & 0 & 1 \end{bmatrix} \tag{11.11}$$

where, $\alpha_x = fm_x$ and $\alpha_y = fm_y$. Here, the diagonal elements of $\mathbf{K}$ are modified version of Eq. 11.5.

During the manufacturing of image sensors, the alignment of sensors may not be perfectly rectilinear. There is a possibility of minor angular deviation between the true vertical position with the placement of sensors along the vertical direction. However, the sensor rows are parallel and they are equally spaced along both the directions. In such cases, a very small skew parameter is used that shows up as a slight deviation in the orientation between x-axis and y-axis from 90°, which is supposed to be 90° in ideal case. This skew parameter is computed as, $s = \tan(\theta)$, where θ is the skew angle. With the inclusion of the skew parameter, the camera calibration matrix is given as in Eq. 11.12.

$$\mathbf{K} = \begin{bmatrix} \alpha_x & s & p_x \\ 0 & \alpha_y & p_y \\ 0 & 0 & 1 \end{bmatrix} \tag{11.12}$$

Using the form of Eq. 11.12 in Eq. 11.10, $\mathbf{K}$, $\mathbf{R}$, and $\widetilde{C}$ have five, three, and three parameters in them, respectively. Thus, there are 11 degrees of freedom or unknowns in projection matrix $\mathbf{P}$. Since the five parameters in $\mathbf{K}$ are related to the camera properties, they are referred to as the *intrinsic parameters*. The parameters in $\mathbf{R}$ and t are related to the transformation of 3-D coordinates between the camera and the world coordinate systems, which are referred to as the *extrinsic parameters*.

11.1.2 | General projective camera

The camera calibration matrix, $\mathbf{K}$, is an upper triangular matrix, whose determinant is given by, $\alpha_x \alpha_y$, a positive value. The matrix representation of $\mathbf{P}$ may be reorganized and expressed as in Eq. 11.13.

$$\mathbf{P} = \begin{bmatrix} \mathbf{M} \mid \boldsymbol{p}_4 \end{bmatrix} \tag{11.13}$$

where, $\mathbf{M}$ is a 3×3 matrix, and $\boldsymbol{p}_4$ is a 3×1 column vector corresponding to the last column of $\mathbf{P}$. Eq. 11.13 is also expressed as in Eq. 11.14.

$$\mathbf{P} = \mathbf{M} \begin{bmatrix} \mathbf{I} \mid \mathbf{M}^{-1}\boldsymbol{p}_4 \end{bmatrix} = \mathbf{KR} \begin{bmatrix} \mathbf{I} \mid -\widetilde{C} \end{bmatrix} \tag{11.14}$$

From the representations in Eq. 11.13 and 11.14, we observe that $\mathbf{M}$ may be decomposed into two 3×3 sub matrices as $\mathbf{M} = \mathbf{KR}$, where $\mathbf{K}$ is the camera calibration matrix and $\mathbf{R}$ is the rotation matrix. Also, $-\widetilde{C}$, in nonhomogeneous coordinates, is expressed as $\mathbf{M}^{-1}\boldsymbol{p}_4$. Since $\mathbf{K}$ is an upper triangular matrix, its inverse exists, which is given by Eq. 11.15.

$$\mathbf{K}^{-1} = \begin{bmatrix} \frac{1}{\alpha_x} & -\frac{s}{\alpha_x \alpha_y} & \frac{s p_y - \alpha_y p_x}{\alpha_x \alpha_y} \\ 0 & \frac{1}{\alpha_y} & -\frac{p_y}{\alpha_y} \\ 0 & 0 & 1 \end{bmatrix} \tag{11.15}$$

The inverse of the camera calibration matrix in Eq. 11.15 is used to compute the image coordinate of $\boldsymbol{x}$ in canonical form. In that case the normalized image coordinate in the canonical imaging configuration would be $\mathbf{K}^{-1}\boldsymbol{x}$. It may be noted that, in the canonical coordinate system, for a general projective camera, the projection (or image) plane is at a unit distance from the camera center, which is also the world origin. Also, the x and y axes of the image coordinate system are parallel to the X and Y axes of the camera centric world coordinate system.

11.1.3 | Estimation of the projection matrix

A homogeneous 3-D world point is mapped to a point in the 2-D projection plane by using the projection matrix, $\mathbf{P}$. The projection matrix is decomposed into (i) a camera calibration matrix, $\mathbf{K}$, of five intrinsic parameters, (ii) a rotation matrix, $\mathbf{R}$, with three parameter, and (iii) a translation vector, $\boldsymbol{t}$, with three parameters. The matrix $\mathbf{P}$ is a rank 3 matrix with 11 degrees of freedom. A pair of point correspondence gives three linear equations corresponding to the relation, $\boldsymbol{x} = \mathbf{P}\boldsymbol{X}$. But, two of them are linearly independent with nonhomogeneous coordinates of points to take care of scale factors of the homogeneous coordinate systems. So, in order to solve for 11 unknowns, at least 6 pairs of point correspondences are necessary. With six point correspondences, 12 equations are obtained by which the unknowns of the $\mathbf{P}$ are computed, which is mathematically represented by Eq. 11.16.

$$\mathbf{P}\boldsymbol{X}_i = \boldsymbol{x}_i = \begin{pmatrix} x_i & y_i & w_i \end{pmatrix}^{\top} \text{ for } i = 1, 2, \ldots, n \geq 6 \tag{11.16}$$

But, $\boldsymbol{x}_i$ has a scale factor, w_i, which restricts the use of equality while solving for $\mathbf{P}$ by point correspondences. So, $\boldsymbol{x}$ and $\mathbf{P}\boldsymbol{X}$ cannot be simply equated without considering the scale factors. In this context, an equivalence relation is used which symbolizes only the necessity of a scale adjustment, provided that the directions of $\boldsymbol{x}$ and $\mathbf{P}\boldsymbol{X}$ are the same. That is, the cross product of the two 3-vectors is a zero vector (when they are parallel). This is given by Eq. 11.17.

$$\boldsymbol{x}_i \equiv \mathbf{P}\boldsymbol{X}_i \implies \mathbf{P}\boldsymbol{X}_i \times \boldsymbol{x}_i = \boldsymbol{0} \tag{11.17}$$

In Eq. 11.17, $\mathbf{P}$ is represented in the form of, $\mathbf{P} = \begin{bmatrix} \boldsymbol{r}_1^\top & \boldsymbol{r}_2^\top & \boldsymbol{r}_3^\top \end{bmatrix}^\top$, where transpose of the column vectors, $\boldsymbol{r}_1$, $\boldsymbol{r}_2$, and $\boldsymbol{r}_3$, are the first, second, and third rows of $\mathbf{P}$, respectively. An expansion of Eq. 11.17 by including the scale factors is given in Eq. 11.18.

$$\implies \begin{bmatrix} \boldsymbol{0}^\top & -w_i\boldsymbol{X}_i^\top & y_i\boldsymbol{X}_i^\top \\ w_i\boldsymbol{X}_i^\top & \boldsymbol{0}^\top & -x_i\boldsymbol{X}_i^\top \\ y_i\boldsymbol{X}_i^\top & x_i\boldsymbol{X}_i^\top & \boldsymbol{0}^\top \end{bmatrix} \begin{bmatrix} \boldsymbol{r}_1 \\ \boldsymbol{r}_2 \\ \boldsymbol{r}_3 \end{bmatrix} = \boldsymbol{0} \tag{11.18}$$

where, each element of the left matrix represents a 1×3 vector, so that, the size of the whole matrix is 3×12.

In Eq. 11.18, though there are three rows, they effectively form only two equations due to a redundancy in it. In this case, the third row of the left matrix may be expressed as a linear combination of the first two rows as, $x_i\langle\text{first row}\rangle + y_i\langle\text{second row}\rangle = w_i\langle\text{third row}\rangle$. Since the third row is dependent on the first two rows, only two independent equations are formed by a pair of point correspondences. Hence, at least 6 point correspondences are necessary to solve for $\mathbf{P}$. The 2×12 modified matrix form of Eq. 11.18 with only two rows, by eliminating the third row, is given by Eq. 11.19.

$$\begin{bmatrix} \boldsymbol{0}^\top & -w_i\boldsymbol{X}_i^\top & y_i\boldsymbol{X}_i^\top \\ w_i\boldsymbol{X}_i^\top & \boldsymbol{0}^\top & -x_i\boldsymbol{X}_i^\top \end{bmatrix} \begin{bmatrix} \boldsymbol{r}_1 \\ \boldsymbol{r}_2 \\ \boldsymbol{r}_3 \end{bmatrix} = \boldsymbol{0} \tag{11.19}$$

For n point correspondences, the matrix form of equations in Eq. 11.19 are stacked to form a $2n \times 12$ matrix, $\mathbf{A}$, which is given by Eq. 11.20.

$$\mathbf{A}_{2n \times 12} \begin{bmatrix} \boldsymbol{r}_1 \\ \boldsymbol{r}_2 \\ \boldsymbol{r}_3 \end{bmatrix} = \boldsymbol{0} \tag{11.20}$$

In Eq. 11.19, since there are 12 equations for 11 unknowns, it is solved by a least squares error technique by minimizing the objective function, $\|\mathbf{A}\boldsymbol{p}\|$, subject to the constraint, $\|\boldsymbol{p}\| = 1$, where $\boldsymbol{p} = [\boldsymbol{r}_1^\top \boldsymbol{r}_2^\top \boldsymbol{r}_3^\top]^\top$. Direct linear transformation (DLT) may also be used to solve the unknowns in $\mathbf{P}$, as discussed in Section 10.3 of Chapter 10.

11.2 | Properties of the projection matrix

The 3×4 projection matrix, $\mathbf{P}$, may be described in various structures, such as in the form of row vectors, $\boldsymbol{r}_1$, $\boldsymbol{r}_2$, and $\boldsymbol{r}_3$, and column vectors, $\boldsymbol{p}_1$, $\boldsymbol{p}_2$, $\boldsymbol{p}_3$, and $\boldsymbol{p}_4$, as shown below.

$$\mathbf{P} \equiv \begin{bmatrix} \boldsymbol{p}_1 & \boldsymbol{p}_2 & \boldsymbol{p}_3 & \boldsymbol{p}_4 \end{bmatrix} \equiv \begin{bmatrix} \boldsymbol{r}_1^\top \\ \boldsymbol{r}_2^\top \\ \boldsymbol{r}_3^\top \end{bmatrix} \tag{11.21}$$

In the above, $\mathbf{P}$ is expressed as a stack of three 1×4 row vectors, or as an appending of four 3×1 column vectors.

Finite camera

It is not possible to form an image of the camera center, $\boldsymbol{C}$, because the ray emerges, passes through, and ends at the same point. This is a characteristic of singularity. Mathematically, it implies that the projection of the camera center results in a zero vector, as given by Eq. 11.22.

$$\boldsymbol{PC} = \mathbf{0} \tag{11.22}$$

Here, $\boldsymbol{C} = \begin{bmatrix} \widetilde{\boldsymbol{C}} \\ 1 \end{bmatrix}$ is a 1-D right zero vector of $\mathbf{P}$. Also, it has been observed that, the 3×3 sub-matrix, $\mathbf{M}$, is nonsingular for a finite camera, while it is singular for the camera at infinity. From Eq. 11.23, we compute the camera center for the finite camera as follows.

$$\begin{bmatrix} \mathbf{M} & | & \boldsymbol{p}_4 \end{bmatrix} \begin{bmatrix} \widetilde{\boldsymbol{C}} \\ 1 \end{bmatrix} = \mathbf{0} \implies \widetilde{\boldsymbol{C}} = -\mathbf{M}^{-1}\boldsymbol{p}_4 \tag{11.23}$$

Vanishing points of principal coordinate axes

A *vanishing point* is the image of a 3-D world point that is at an infinite distance from the camera along a direction. A vanishing point is represented by a direction, $\boldsymbol{d}$. In fact, any point in the space at infinity is expressed as a direction in the homogeneous coordinates representation, $\begin{bmatrix} \boldsymbol{d} \\ 0 \end{bmatrix}$. The vanishing points corresponding to X, Y, and Z-axes of world coordinate system are given by the column vectors $\boldsymbol{p}_1$, $\boldsymbol{p}_2$, and $\boldsymbol{p}_3$, respectively. They can be computed by multiplying the respective points at infinity along those directions with $\mathbf{P}$ as,

$$\mathbf{P} \begin{bmatrix} 1 \\ 0 \\ 0 \\ 0 \end{bmatrix} = \boldsymbol{p}_1; \qquad \mathbf{P} \begin{bmatrix} 0 \\ 1 \\ 0 \\ 0 \end{bmatrix} = \boldsymbol{p}_2; \qquad \mathbf{P} \begin{bmatrix} 0 \\ 0 \\ 1 \\ 0 \end{bmatrix} = \boldsymbol{p}_3 \tag{11.24}$$

where p_1, p_2, and p_3 are the first three columns of $\mathbf{P}$ that correspond to the vanishing points of X, Y, and Z-axes, respectively. Note that all the three points are in homogeneous coordinates. To get their real coordinates, it is necessary to divide the first two elements of a column vector by its third element.

Image point of world origin

The image of the coordinate origin is given by, $\mathbf{P} \begin{bmatrix} 0 & 0 & 0 & 1 \end{bmatrix}^{\top} = p_4$. This is the image point given by the fourth column of the projection matrix. Here, p_4 is also expressed in homogeneous coordinates.

Principal plane and principal axis

The principal plane of an imaging configuration is defined as the plane that is parallel to the image plane, which contains the camera center. This geometric definition of principal plane is independent of any coordinate convention. A point on the principal plane does not correspond to any physical image point, since any ray emanating from this point to the camera center does not intersect the image plane. In other words, it intersects the image plane at infinity. So, for any point, x, on the principal plane, its third coordinate is always zero, such that, it is in the form of $x = \begin{bmatrix} x & y & 0 \end{bmatrix}^{\top}$. Hence, $r_3^{\top} X = 0$. This is the principal plane described in the world coordinate system. The normal to the principal plane is the principal axis. The principal plane is represented by the third row, r_3, of $\mathbf{P}$, which is a 4×1 vector, i.e., a 3×1 vector and a scale factor.[1] This 3×1 column vector, with the scale factor removed from r_3, is represented as mr_3, which is the third row of $\mathbf{M}$. The direction of the normal of the principal plane is provided by mr_3.

The principal axis is the optical axis of the lens in the optical camera. In the canonical imaging configuration, it is the Z-axis of the camera centric coordinate system. The principal ray or the principal axis is the line passing through the camera center along the direction of mr_3. This direction may be toward points along the z-axis of the canonical configuration of the camera or it may be oriented along its opposite direction. The determinant of the transformation matrix, along with its sign, represents the actual direction of the principle ray. So, the vector, mr_3, is either represented by the sign of the determinant of $\mathbf{M}$, or the vector is scaled with determinant of the matrix.

As the y-axis in the image plane contains all the points whose x-coordinate is zero, the plane containing the camera center and the y-axis of the image plane is represented by, $r_1^{\top} X = 0$. This plane intersects the image plane at the y-axis of the image coordinate system. Similarly, the plane containing the camera center and the x-axis of the image plane is given by, $r_2^{\top} X = 0$. These planes corresponding to x-axis and y-axis are known as *axes planes*.

---

[1] In the standard equation of a plane, $ax + by + cz + d = 0$, the normal is given by the direction ratio, $a : b : c$, and d is the scale factor.

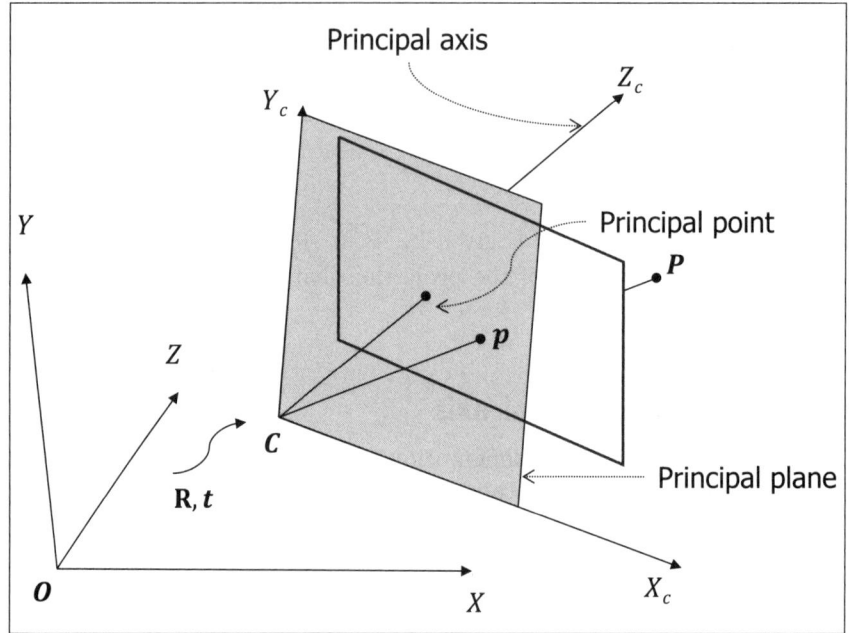

Figure 11.5 Geometric entities defining the configuration of an imaging system.

Principal point

Principal point is the image of the point that is lying in the direction of $\boldsymbol{m r}_3$ at infinity. That is, the principal point is the intersection of the normal of the principal plane with the image plane. The principal point, x_0, which is the image of a point at infinity along the direction of the normal of $\boldsymbol{r}_3^{\top} \boldsymbol{X} = 0$, is given by Eq. 11.25.

$$x_0 = \mathbf{P} \begin{bmatrix} p_{31} \\ p_{32} \\ p_{33} \\ 0 \end{bmatrix} = \mathbf{M} \, \boldsymbol{m r}_3 \tag{11.25}$$

The principal plane, principal axis, and principal point are diagrammatically shown in Fig. 11.5.

11.2.1 | Back projection

To understand how the image points on the image plane are back-projected to form a ray, it is necessary to map an ideal point, $[\boldsymbol{d} \; 0]^{\top}$, lying on the plane at infinity, π_∞ of a 3-D projective space. In a particular direction, $\boldsymbol{d}$, the product of the projection matrix and the vector, $[\boldsymbol{d} \ 0]^\top$, is given by Eq. 11.26.

$$x = \begin{bmatrix} \mathbf{M} \mid \boldsymbol{p}_4 \end{bmatrix} \begin{bmatrix} \boldsymbol{d} \\ 0 \end{bmatrix} = \mathbf{M}\boldsymbol{d} \tag{11.26}$$

That is, the vanishing point for the direction $\boldsymbol{d}$ is the image of the point at infinity lying in that direction. From Eq. 11.26 we observe that vanishing points are only affected by $\mathbf{M}$.

A back projection is defined as the ray that is formed by the camera center and a point on the image plane, which is expressed in the world coordinate system as in Eq. 11.27.

$$\begin{bmatrix} \mathbf{M} \mid \boldsymbol{p}_4 \end{bmatrix} \begin{bmatrix} \mathbf{M}^{-1}\boldsymbol{x} \\ 0 \end{bmatrix} = \boldsymbol{x} \tag{11.27}$$

where, $\mathbf{D} = \begin{bmatrix} \mathbf{M}^{-1}\boldsymbol{x} \\ 0 \end{bmatrix}$ is a point lying at infinity along the direction of $\mathbf{M}^{-1}\boldsymbol{x}$. Thus, $\mathbf{D}(= \mathbf{M}^{-1}\boldsymbol{x})$ provides the direction of the projection ray passing through the image point $\boldsymbol{x}$ and the camera center $\widetilde{C}$. A parametric form of the equation of a straight line in 3-D space along a direction, $\mathbf{M}^{-1}\boldsymbol{x}$, passing through a point, C, is expressed as a linear combination of the point at infinity, $\boldsymbol{D}$ and $\boldsymbol{C}$ in the homogeneous coordinate system, as given by Eq. 11.28.

$$\boldsymbol{X}(\mu) = \mu\boldsymbol{D} + \boldsymbol{C} \tag{11.28}$$

where, μ is a scalar parameter ranging from 0 to ∞. In the context of back-projected ray, this is expressed as in Eq. 11.29.

$$\begin{aligned} \boldsymbol{X}(\mu) &= \mu \begin{bmatrix} \mathbf{M}^{-1}\boldsymbol{x} \\ 0 \end{bmatrix} + \begin{bmatrix} \widetilde{C} \\ 1 \end{bmatrix} \\ &= \mu \begin{bmatrix} \mathbf{M}^{-1}\boldsymbol{x} \\ 0 \end{bmatrix} + \begin{bmatrix} -\mathbf{M}^{-1}\boldsymbol{p}_4 \\ 1 \end{bmatrix} \\ &= \begin{bmatrix} \mathbf{M}^{-1}(\mu\boldsymbol{x} - \boldsymbol{p}_4) \\ 1 \end{bmatrix} \end{aligned} \tag{11.29}$$

Eq. 11.29 represents the points that are lying on the projection ray that connects the camera center.

Depth of points The depth of a point is defined as the length of projection of a ray that connects the scene point and the camera center on the principal axis. Consider a point, $\widetilde{\boldsymbol{X}}$, in a 3-D space, as shown in Fig. 11.6. The projection of this vector on the principal axis, which is the Z-axis of the canonical form in the camera centric system, is

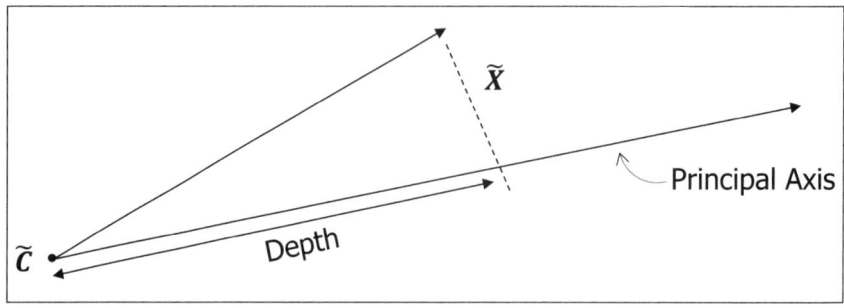

Figure 11.6 Depth of a point.

the depth of $\widetilde{\boldsymbol{X}}$. This is expressed by a scalar dot product of two vectors, as in Eq. 11.30.

$$\text{Depth} = \hat{m\boldsymbol{r}}_3^{\top} \cdot (\widetilde{\boldsymbol{X}} - \widetilde{\boldsymbol{C}}) \tag{11.30}$$

where $\hat{m\boldsymbol{r}}_3$ is the unit vector along the direction of principal axis.

11.2.2 | Computing camera center and camera parameters from $\mathbf{P}$

Another representation of the camera center is obtained by solving the set of equations involving the projection matrix, $\mathbf{P}$. This requires a set of three equations to be solved, since the camera center is represented by three coordinates, $[X_c \quad Y_c \quad Z_c]^{\top}$. The three coordinates of the camera center are expressed in terms of the column vectors of $\mathbf{M}$ by using Cramers' rule (Lay et al., 2015), which are given by Eq. 11.31.

$$
\begin{aligned}
X_c &= \frac{|-\boldsymbol{p}_4 \quad \boldsymbol{p}_2 \quad \boldsymbol{p}_3|}{|\boldsymbol{p}_1 \quad \boldsymbol{p}_2 \quad \boldsymbol{p}_3|} \\
Y_c &= \frac{|\boldsymbol{p}_1 \quad -\boldsymbol{p}_4 \quad \boldsymbol{p}_3|}{|\boldsymbol{p}_1 \quad \boldsymbol{p}_2 \quad \boldsymbol{p}_3|} \\
Z_c &= \frac{|\boldsymbol{p}_1 \quad \boldsymbol{p}_2 \quad -\boldsymbol{p}_4|}{|\boldsymbol{p}_1 \quad \boldsymbol{p}_2 \quad \boldsymbol{p}_3|}
\end{aligned}
\tag{11.31}
$$

where, $\boldsymbol{p}_1$, $\boldsymbol{p}_2$, $\boldsymbol{p}_3$, and $\boldsymbol{p}_4$ are the column vectors of $\mathbf{P}$, and $|a \quad b \quad c|$ denotes the determinant of the 3×3 matrix formed by 3×1 column vectors a, b and c, respectively.

Different representations of the projection matrix, $\mathbf{P}$, are given in Eq. 11.32.

$$
\begin{aligned}
\mathbf{P} &= \left[\mathbf{M} \mid \boldsymbol{p}_4\right] \\
&= \left[\mathbf{M} \mid -\mathbf{M}\widetilde{C}\right] \\
&= \mathbf{K}\left[\mathbf{R} \mid -\mathbf{R}\widetilde{C}\right]
\end{aligned}
\tag{11.32}
$$

By applying any of the standard QR-decomposition techniques on $\mathbf{M} = \mathbf{KR}$, an upper triangular camera calibration matrix, $\mathbf{K}$, and an orthogonal rotation matrix, $\mathbf{R}$ are obtained.

Though this solution by matrix decomposition technique is not unique, it is still considered as one of the possible solutions.

Numerical Example

Consider the following projection matrix.

$$\mathbf{P} = \begin{bmatrix} -9 & 2 & 3 & 1 \\ 3 & -9 & 6 & 1 \\ 2 & 6 & -10 & 1 \end{bmatrix}$$

Compute the following:

- camera center,
- vanishing point of x-axis,
- image point of origin, and
- vanishing point of the line with the direction ratios $2 : 3 : 4$.

Solution

The camera center is given as,

$$\widetilde{\mathbf{C}} = -\mathbf{M}^{-1}\boldsymbol{p}_4$$

where, the 3×3 matrix formed by the first three columns of $\mathbf{P}$ is $\mathbf{M}$, and the last column of $\mathbf{P}$ is $\boldsymbol{p}_4$. In order to find $\mathbf{M}^{-1}$, the cofactor matrix of $\mathbf{M}$ is computed as,

$$\text{Cofactor}(\mathbf{M}) = \begin{bmatrix} 54 & 42 & 36 \\ 38 & 84 & 58 \\ 39 & 63 & 75 \end{bmatrix}$$

$$\Rightarrow \mathbf{M}^{-1} = \frac{1}{\det(\mathbf{M})} \begin{bmatrix} 54 & 38 & 39 \\ 42 & 84 & 63 \\ 36 & 58 & 75 \end{bmatrix}$$

where, $\det(\mathbf{M}) = -294$ is the determinant of $\mathbf{M}$. The camera center in world coordinate system is then computed as,

$$\widetilde{\mathbf{C}} = \frac{1}{294} \begin{bmatrix} 131 \\ 189 \\ 169 \end{bmatrix}.$$

The vanishing point of x-axis is computed by multiplying the projection matrix with the direction along the x-axis, which is given by,

$$\mathbf{P}\begin{bmatrix}1\\1\\1\\0\end{bmatrix} = \boldsymbol{p}_1 = \begin{bmatrix}-9\\3\\2\end{bmatrix}$$

The vanishing point in 2-D coordinate system is given by $\left(\frac{-9}{2}, \frac{3}{2}\right)$.

The image point of the origin is computed as,

$$\mathbf{P}\begin{bmatrix}0\\0\\0\\1\end{bmatrix} = \boldsymbol{p}_4 = \begin{bmatrix}1\\1\\1\end{bmatrix}$$

The direction ratios are used to find out the point at infinity along the considered direction. It is given by, $\begin{bmatrix}2 & 3 & 4 & 0\end{bmatrix}^T$. The corresponding vanishing point is given by,

$$\mathbf{P}\begin{bmatrix}2\\3\\4\\0\end{bmatrix} = \begin{bmatrix}0\\3\\-18\end{bmatrix}.$$

The Vanishing point of the line with the direction ratios $2:3:4$ in 2-D coordinate system is given by, $\begin{bmatrix}0\\-\frac{3}{18}\end{bmatrix}$.

Numerical Example

Consider the following projection matrix of an optical camera based imaging system.

$$\mathbf{P} = \begin{bmatrix}8 & 5 & 4 & 0\\7 & 8 & 9 & 0\\1 & -5 & 8 & 1\end{bmatrix}$$

Answer the following with respect to $\mathbf{P}$:

(i) Given an image point, $(2, 7)$ in $\mathbb{R}^2$, compute its corresponding scene point, if it is known that the point is at a distance of 40 units from the center of the camera.

(ii) Compute the principal plane of the imaging system.

Solution

In order to back project the image point and find its scene point, it is necessary to compute the camera center. Hence, as discussed in Ex. 2, compute $\mathbf{M}^{-1}$ and determinant of $\mathbf{M}$ as,

$$\mathbf{M}^{-1} = \frac{1}{465}\begin{bmatrix} 109 & -60 & 13 \\ -47 & 60 & -44 \\ -43 & 45 & 29 \end{bmatrix}.$$

$$\Rightarrow \widetilde{\mathbf{C}} = -\mathbf{M}^{-1}\boldsymbol{p}_4 = \frac{1}{465}\begin{bmatrix} -13 \\ 44 \\ -29 \end{bmatrix}.$$

To find the direction of the ray along the given point, it is required to compute the direction ratios, $l : m : n$, which is given as follows.

$$\begin{bmatrix} l \\ m \\ n \end{bmatrix} = \mathbf{M}^{-1}\begin{bmatrix} 2 \\ 7 \\ 1 \end{bmatrix} = \frac{1}{465}\begin{bmatrix} -189 \\ 282 \\ 258 \end{bmatrix}.$$

As the projection ray, which contains all the 3-D scene points corresponding to a given image point, is computed as,

$$\widetilde{\mathbf{X}}(\mu) = \widetilde{\mathbf{C}} + \frac{\mu}{\sqrt{l^2 + m^2 + n^2}}\begin{bmatrix} l \\ m \\ n \end{bmatrix} = \begin{bmatrix} -17.76 \\ 26.55 \\ 24.14 \end{bmatrix}.$$

where, μ is given as a distance of 40 units from $\widetilde{\mathbf{C}}$.

The image point of a point in a principal plane is given by,

$$\boldsymbol{r}_3^\top \mathbf{X} = 0,$$

where $\boldsymbol{r}_3$ is the last row the projection matrix $\mathbf{P}$. Hence the equation of the principal plane is given by $X - 5Y + 8Z + 1 = 0$.

11.3 | Affine camera

A camera at infinity is another scenario where the camera center is at infinity and $\mathbf{M}$ is singular. In this case, there are two specific situations, the camera may be an affine camera or a nonaffine camera. Consider the case of an affine camera, which is more valid in the present context. One of the characteristics of the affine camera is that the last row of $\mathbf{P}$ is in the form of $[0 \quad 0 \quad 0 \quad 1]$, or any scaled factor of $[0 \quad 0 \quad 0 \quad 1]$. With the minimal representation of the third row by $[0 \quad 0 \quad 0 \quad 1]$, every other element is fixed with respect to the scale of 1. From the properties of an affine camera, its principal plane is the *plane at infinity*. So, all the points that are at infinity along different directions, lie on the principal plane. Naturally, the camera center also lies on this principal plane. Also, the images of the points at infinity are mapped to points at infinity. That is, the vanishing points are also at infinity in the image plane. All the points with their scale value of 0, i.e., the intersection of parallel lines of nonhomogeneous coordinates in the context of Euclidean geometry, are those points at infinity. These lines, after the projection by the imaging system, still remain parallel because the images of these lines have their intersection at infinity in the image plane. They lie on the line at infinity of the corresponding 2-D projective space.

11.3.1 | Affine projection

An *affine projection* of a 3-D scene point, $\widetilde{\boldsymbol{X}}$, is given by Eq. 11.33.

$$
\begin{bmatrix} \widetilde{\boldsymbol{x}} \\ 1 \end{bmatrix} = \begin{bmatrix} m_{11} & m_{12} & m_{13} & t_1 \\ m_{21} & m_{22} & m_{23} & t_2 \\ 0 & 0 & 0 & 1 \end{bmatrix} \begin{bmatrix} \widetilde{\boldsymbol{X}} \\ 1 \end{bmatrix}
$$

$$
\implies [\widetilde{\boldsymbol{x}}] = \begin{bmatrix} m_{11} & m_{12} & m_{13} & t_1 \\ m_{21} & m_{22} & m_{23} & t_2 \end{bmatrix} [\widetilde{\boldsymbol{X}}] + \boldsymbol{t}
$$

$$
\implies \widetilde{\boldsymbol{x}} = \mathbf{M}_{2 \times 3} \widetilde{\boldsymbol{X}} + \boldsymbol{t}
$$

(11.33)

where, $\begin{bmatrix} m_{11} & m_{12} & m_{13} & t_1 \\ m_{21} & m_{22} & m_{23} & t_2 \\ 0 & 0 & 0 & 1 \end{bmatrix}$ is the affine projection matrix, $\mathbf{M}_{2 \times 3}$ is the 2×3 sub-matrix formed from the first two rows, and $\boldsymbol{t}$ is the corresponding 2×1 column vectors denoting translation of image coordinates from those in canonical configuration. Here, $\widetilde{\boldsymbol{x}}$, a 2×1 vector, is in the nonhomogeneous coordinate system. This simple relationship in affine geometry depicts a transformation from a 3-D Euclidean space to a 2-D Euclidean space. In the *affine projection matrix* expressed in Eq. 11.33, there are eight independent parameters or degrees of freedom. The computation of the affine matrix requires *four* point correspondences, since every point correspondence gives two equations, one each for x and y coordinates. So, with four point correspondences, eight equations are formed, which is the minimum requirement to solve for eight unknowns. If more than four point correspondences are provided, then a least squares approach is used to estimate the affine projection matrix.

The affine camera center lies at infinity, which is the direction of the parallel rays that intersect at infinity. Its geometric interpretation is that, in an affine camera the imaging takes place using parallel rays, instead of considering a center where all the rays converge, as in the perspective projection geometry. The relationship between $\mathbf{M}$ and the direction of parallel rays, $\boldsymbol{d}$, is given by Eq. 11.34.

$$\mathbf{M}\boldsymbol{d} = \mathbf{0} \tag{11.34}$$

From the above, $\boldsymbol{d}$ is the right zero vector of the matrix $\mathbf{M}$. From Eq. 11.33 and 11.34, the image of the origin of world coordinate system is $\boldsymbol{t}$, and the principal plane of the affine projection matrix, $\mathbf{P}_A$, is the plane at infinity. The principal plane for $\mathbf{P}_A$ is represented by $[0 \ \ 0 \ \ 0 \ \ 1]^T$ as its last row. This ensures that the sub-matrix, $\mathbf{M}_{2\times3}$, is of rank 2, and $\mathbf{P}_A$ is of rank 3.

Numerical Example

Given the left and upper 2×3 matrix M of a 3×4 affine projective matrix $\mathbf{P}$, as $\begin{bmatrix} 8 & 5 & 4 \\ 1 & 8 & 9 \end{bmatrix}$, compute the direction of parallel projection.

Solution

Direction of parallel projection is given by the right null vector of $\mathbf{M}$ as $\mathbf{M}_{2\times3}[\boldsymbol{d} \ 1]^\top = \mathbf{0}$, where $[\boldsymbol{d} \ 1]$ is the direction of parallel projection, and is computed as $(13/59, -68/59, 1)$.

Estimation of an affine camera

For estimating an affine camera, a minimum of four point correspondences are necessary. However, more number of point correspondences make the estimation robust. A mapping between a scene point, $\boldsymbol{X}_i$ and its image point, $\boldsymbol{x}_i$, is given by $\boldsymbol{X}_i \leftrightarrow \boldsymbol{x}_i = (x_i, y_i, 1)$, where, $i = 1, 2, 3, \dots, n$. By considering the concatenation of row vectors as the representation of the projection matrix, $\mathbf{M}_{2\times3}$, the transformation between a point correspondence is expressed as in Eq. 11.35.

$$\begin{bmatrix} \boldsymbol{X}_i^\top & \boldsymbol{0}^\top \\ \boldsymbol{0}^\top & \boldsymbol{X}_i^\top \end{bmatrix} \begin{bmatrix} \boldsymbol{r}_1^\top \\ \boldsymbol{r}_2^\top \end{bmatrix} = \begin{bmatrix} x_i \\ y_i \end{bmatrix} \tag{11.35}$$

where, each element of the left matrix is 1×4 vector, and $\boldsymbol{r}_1$ and $\boldsymbol{r}_2$ are 1×4 row vectors.

For n point correspondences, the $2n$ equations are obtained in the matrix form by stacking forms in Eq. 11.35 of each point correspondence, which is given by Eq. 11.36.

$$\mathbf{A}_{2n \times 8} \begin{bmatrix} \boldsymbol{r}_1^{\top} \\ \boldsymbol{r}_2^{\top} \end{bmatrix} = \boldsymbol{b}_{2n \times 1} \tag{11.36}$$

The corresponding dimensions of every matrix or vector are also shown in Eq. 11.36 as their subscript. This set of nonhomogeneous equations are solved by using the standard least squares error method, whose solution is given by Eq. 11.37.

$$\begin{bmatrix} \boldsymbol{r}_1^{\top} \\ \boldsymbol{r}_2^{\top} \end{bmatrix} = [\mathbf{A}^{\top} \mathbf{A}]^{-1} \mathbf{A}^{\top} \boldsymbol{b} \tag{11.37}$$

11.4 | Imaging induced homography

There are various scenarios of constrained imaging which induces homography. For example, scene points may be constrained to lie on a plane or on a line, images of the same scene may be related by only changing camera views, etc. Some of such specific scenarios are discussed below.

11.4.1 | Imaging of a plane

Without the loss of generality, consider the XY-plane $Z = 0$, as shown in Fig. 11.7. By appropriate coordinate transformation, any plane may be considered as XY plane to hold this principle applicable. Any point on the XY plane is expressed as $\begin{bmatrix} X & Y & 0 & 1 \end{bmatrix}$. As shown in the figure, consider a scene point, $\boldsymbol{Q}$, the center of projection, $\boldsymbol{C}$, and an image

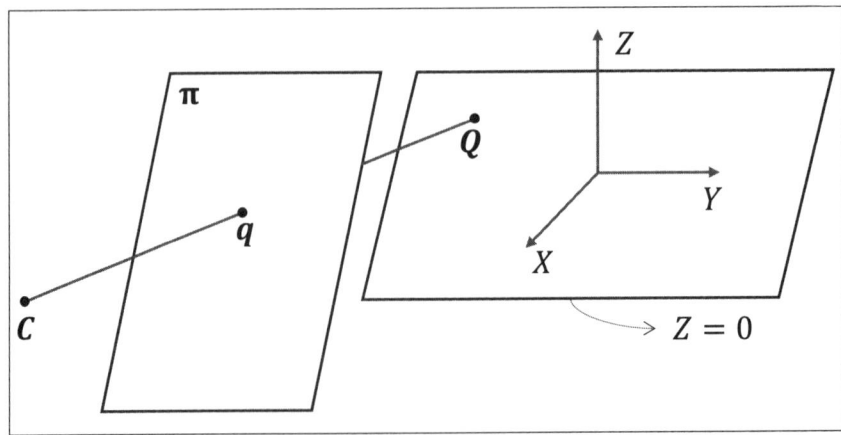

Figure 11.7 Imaging of a plane.

plane, $\boldsymbol{\pi}$. The intersection of the ray formed by $\boldsymbol{C}$ and $\boldsymbol{Q}$ with the image plane is the image point, $\boldsymbol{q}$, which is given by Eq. 11.38.

$$q = \mathbf{P}Q = \begin{bmatrix} \boldsymbol{p}_1 & \boldsymbol{p}_2 & \boldsymbol{p}_3 & \boldsymbol{p}_4 \end{bmatrix} \begin{bmatrix} X \\ Y \\ 0 \\ 1 \end{bmatrix} = \begin{bmatrix} \boldsymbol{p}_1 & \boldsymbol{p}_2 & \boldsymbol{p}_4 \end{bmatrix} \begin{bmatrix} X \\ Y \\ 1 \end{bmatrix} = \mathbf{H}Q_\pi \qquad (11.38)$$

where, $\mathbf{H} = \begin{bmatrix} \boldsymbol{p}_1 & \boldsymbol{p}_2 & \boldsymbol{p}_4 \end{bmatrix}$ and $Q_\pi = \begin{bmatrix} X & Y & 1 \end{bmatrix}$. The relationship between projection matrix, $\mathbf{P}$, and the 3-D point in the homogeneous coordinate system is reduced to a homography between points on two planes, namely the XY plane and the image plane. The points are also expressed in homogeneous coordinates of 2-D projective spaces. We may note that the homography $\mathbf{H}$ in Eq. 11.38 is a 3×3 matrix. Since perspective projection of points lying on the same plane is a projective transformation, the imaging of a plane establishes the homography between the image points and the scene points.

11.4.2 | Imaging of a line

Consider a 3-D line segment, $\boldsymbol{L}$ and an image plane, $\boldsymbol{\pi}$, with the camera center at $\boldsymbol{C}$, as shown in Fig. 11.8. In order to project $\boldsymbol{L}$ onto an image plane, the end points of the line

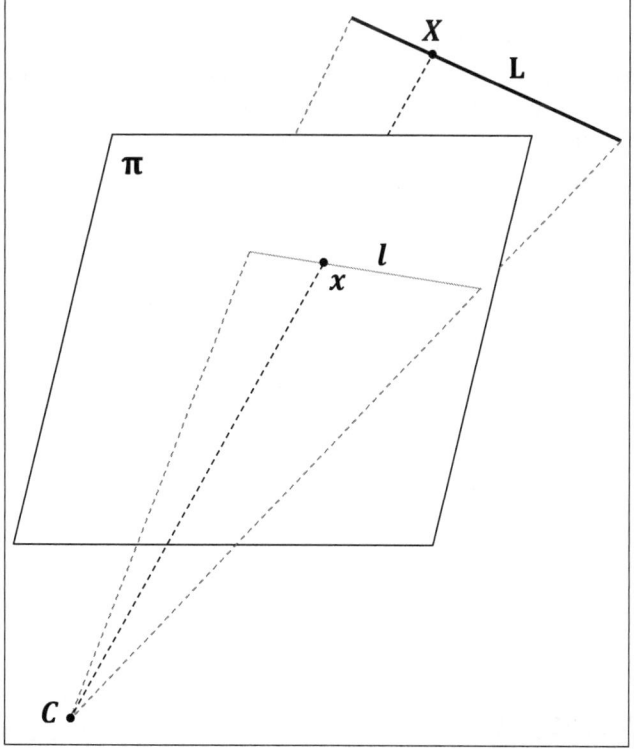

Figure 11.8 The plane formed by the camera center and a line in the image.

segment are first projected on image plane. The line formed between the two projected image points of the end points of L is the imaged line, l. The imaged line, l, lies in a 2-D projective space, $\mathbb{P}^2$. A point, X, on L, and its corresponding image point x on l are shown in the figure as a projected ray. The relationship between x and l is a point containment relation. The image of L lies on the 3-D plane that connects the camera center and L. This point containment relationship is expressed by Eq. 11.39.

$$x^\top l = 0 \tag{11.39}$$

Since the transformation of points are expressed by $x = \mathbf{P}X$, Eq. 11.39 is simplified as given by Eq. 11.40.

$$
\begin{aligned}
(\mathbf{P}X)^\top l &= 0 \\
\implies X^\top \mathbf{P}^\top l &= 0
\end{aligned} \tag{11.40}
$$

Here, $X^\top \mathbf{P}^\top l = 0$, expresses the point containment relationship of the 3-D point, X in homogeneous coordinates in a plane, where the plane is given by $\pi \equiv \mathbf{P}^\top l$. Thus, given a line l in the image plane, it is possible to determine the plane on which the 3-D line L whose image is l, and the camera center lie.

11.4.3 | Fixed camera center and moving image plane

To understand the relationship between the image points when the image plane is moving while the camera center is fixed, consider an example as shown in Fig. 11.9. The figure depicts two scenarios, where camera center, C, is at the same position and two images of a world point, X, are captured at two different positions of a moving image plane. In one of the image plane, the image point is denoted by x_1, and in the other plane the image point

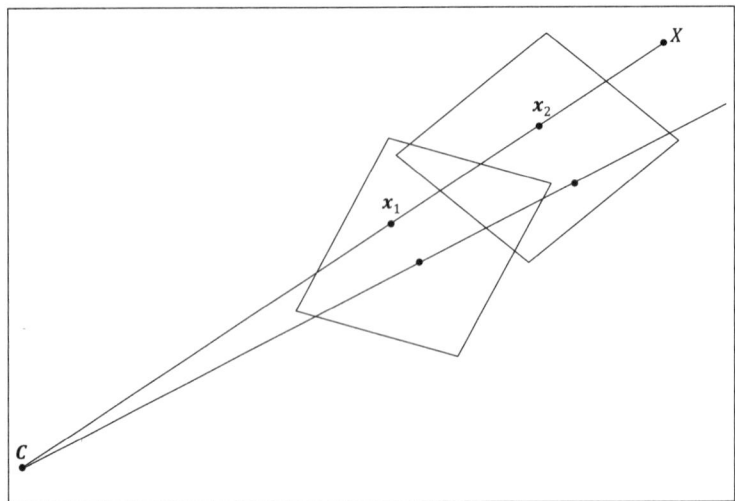

Figure 11.9 Fixed camera center but moving image plane.

is denoted by x_2, as shown in the figure. The camera projection matrix, $\mathbf{P}_1$, corresponding to the image plane that contains x_1 is given by Eq. 11.41.

$$\mathbf{P}_1 = \mathbf{K}_1\mathbf{R}_1[\mathbf{I}| - \widetilde{C}] \tag{11.41}$$

Similarly, the camera projection matrix, $\mathbf{P}_2$, corresponding to the image plane that contains x_2 is given by Eq. 11.42.

$$\mathbf{P}_2 = \mathbf{K}_2\mathbf{R}_2[\mathbf{I}| - \widetilde{C}] \tag{11.42}$$

The relation between $\mathbf{P}_1$ and $\mathbf{P}_2$ is expressed in the form as in Eq. 11.43.

$$\mathbf{P}_2 = \mathbf{K}_2\mathbf{R}_2(\mathbf{K}_1\mathbf{R}_1)^{-1}\mathbf{P}_1 \tag{11.43}$$

The transformation between the image point, x_2, and the scene point, X, is expressed as, $x_2 = \mathbf{P}_2 X$ which is expanded as in Eq. 11.44 using Eq. 11.43.

$$
\begin{aligned}
x_2 &= \mathbf{P}_2 X \\
&= \mathbf{K}_2\mathbf{R}_2(\mathbf{K}_1\mathbf{R}_1)^{-1}\mathbf{P}_1 X \\
&= \mathbf{K}_2\mathbf{R}_2(\mathbf{K}_1\mathbf{R}_1)^{-1}x_1 \\
&= \mathbf{H}x_1
\end{aligned}
\tag{11.44}
$$

For the expression in Eq. 11.44 to be valid, the matrix $\mathbf{K}_1\mathbf{R}_1$ must be invertible. From Eq. 11.44, it is inferred that the image points, x_1 and x_2 are related by a projective transformation or homography between them.

11.4.4 | Zooming

In the setup of Fig. 11.9, when the two image planes are parallel, the phenomenon is observed like zooming of images, shown in Fig. 11.10. Here, the image point in one of the planes is denoted by x, and the image point in the other plane is denoted by x'. In effect, the parallel image planes are observed as if the focal length is being varied, i.e., as if the distance between the camera center and the image plane is changing. Let the ratio of the focal lengths of the two planes be k. This situation establishes a homography between the two views, since there is no rotation between these two cameras. This is a condition where the rotation matrix is an identity matrix, and the relationship between the two views is expressed as a homography, which is given by Eq. 11.45.

$$x' = \mathbf{K}_2\mathbf{K}_1^{-1}x = \mathbf{H}x \tag{11.45}$$

where, $\mathbf{H} = \mathbf{K}_2\mathbf{K}_1^{-1}$.

This relationship is further elaborated by using the ratio of their focal lengths, k. Let x_0 be the principal point. Then the deviation of the projected ray from x_0 is also scaled by the same amount, k. The direction remains the same, but it is scaled by this k, which is given by Eq. 11.46.

$$\widetilde{x'} = \widetilde{x_0} + k(\widetilde{x} - \widetilde{x_0}) = (1 - k)\widetilde{x_0} + k\widetilde{x} \tag{11.46}$$

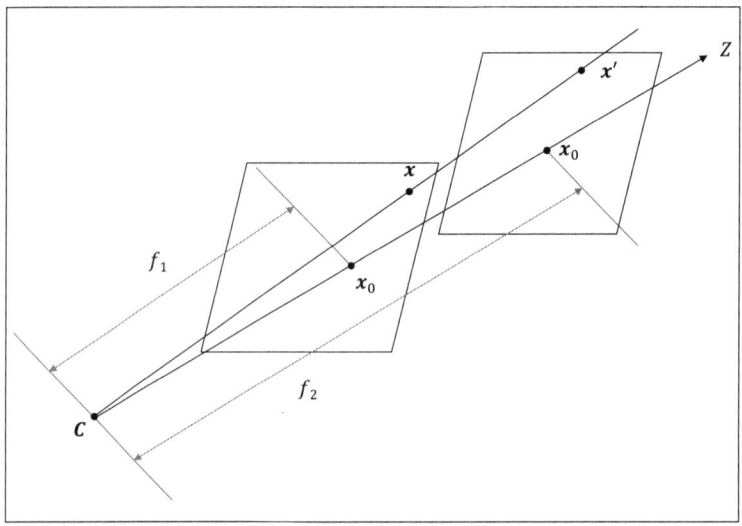

Figure 11.10 Homography induced by zooming.

The homography matrix between x and x', $\mathbf{H} = \mathbf{K}_2\mathbf{K}_1^{-1}$, is further elaborated by using Eq. 11.46, which is given by Eq. 11.47.

$$
\mathbf{H} = \begin{bmatrix} k\mathbf{I} & (1-k)\widetilde{\boldsymbol{x}_0} \\ \mathbf{0} & 1 \end{bmatrix} = \mathbf{K}_2\mathbf{K}_1^{-1}
$$

$$
\implies \mathbf{K}_2 = \begin{bmatrix} k\mathbf{I} & (1-k)\widetilde{\boldsymbol{x}_0} \\ \mathbf{0} & 1 \end{bmatrix} \mathbf{K}_1
$$

$$
= \begin{bmatrix} k\mathbf{I} & (1-k)\widetilde{\boldsymbol{x}_0} \\ \mathbf{0} & 1 \end{bmatrix} \begin{bmatrix} \mathbf{A} & \widetilde{\boldsymbol{x}_0} \\ \mathbf{0} & 1 \end{bmatrix} \tag{11.47}
$$

$$
= \begin{bmatrix} k\mathbf{A} & k\widetilde{\boldsymbol{x}_0} + (1-k)\widetilde{\boldsymbol{x}_0} \\ \mathbf{0} & 1 \end{bmatrix}
$$

$$
= \begin{bmatrix} k\mathbf{A} & \widetilde{\boldsymbol{x}_0} \\ \mathbf{0} & 1 \end{bmatrix}
$$

$$
= \mathbf{K}_1 \begin{bmatrix} k\mathbf{I} & \mathbf{0} \\ \mathbf{0} & 1 \end{bmatrix} = \mathbf{K}_1 \, \mathrm{Diag}(k,k,1)
$$

where, $\mathrm{Diag}(k,k,1)$, represents a 3×3 diagonal matrix with its elements as k, k, and 1. The effect of zooming by a factor of k is to multiply the calibration matrix, $\mathbf{K}$, on the right side by $\mathrm{Diag}(k,k,1)$. The set of expressions in Eq. 11.47 represent the effect of zooming in terms of the camera projection matrices of the two image planes with different focal lengths.

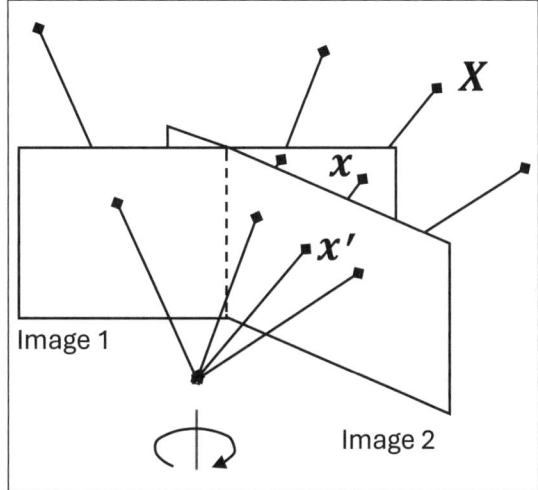

Figure 11.11 Rotation about an axis passing through the camera center.

11.4.5 | Rotation of image plane about an axis

Consider a scenario, where the camera center is fixed, but the image plane is rotated about its vertical axis, as shown in Fig. 11.11. Let the camera center be C, and the image formed by the 3-D world point, X, on the image plane be x, whose transformation is expressed as $x = \mathbf{K}[\mathbf{I}|0]X$. If the image plane is rotated by an angle, θ, about an axis, it begets another image plane due the rotation. Let the image point of X formed on the rotated image plane be x', which is expressed as in Eq. 11.48.

$$
\begin{aligned}
x' &= \mathbf{K}[\mathbf{R}|0]X \\
&= \mathbf{K}\mathbf{R}\mathbf{K}^{-1}\mathbf{K}[\mathbf{I}|0]X \\
&= \mathbf{K}\mathbf{R}\mathbf{K}^{-1}x \\
\implies \mathbf{H} &= \mathbf{K}\mathbf{R}\mathbf{K}^{-1}
\end{aligned}
\tag{11.48}
$$

As implied from Eq. 11.48, x and x' are related by a homography matrix, which is expressed in terms of the camera parameters. The transformation, $\mathbf{H} = \mathbf{K}\mathbf{R}\mathbf{K}^{-1}$ establishes the relation between the two rotated views, with their corresponding image points of the same scene point.

Numerical Example

Consider the following camera matrix.

$$
\mathbf{P} = \begin{bmatrix} 7 & 4 & 9 & 0 \\ 2 & 3 & 6 & 0 \\ 1 & 5 & 8 & 0 \end{bmatrix}
$$

Consider four image points $x_1 = (2,5)$, $x_2 = (7,9)$, $x_3 = (-1,3)$, and $x_4 = (4,-1)$. Let the camera center be denoted as O. Compute the dihedral angle between planes Ox_1x_2 and Ox_3x_4. *Hint: A dihedral angle between the planes is the angle between their normals.*

Solution

To compute the normals to the planes Ox_1x_2 and Ox_3x_4, it is necessary to compute the respective planes first. Since the plane Ox_1x_2 is formed by x_1 and x_2 with O, the projection of the line formed by those points defines the plane $\Pi_1 = Ox_1x_2$, which is given as,

$$\Pi_1 = \mathbf{P}^\top x_1 \times x_2 = \begin{bmatrix} 35 \\ 86 \\ 142 \\ 0 \end{bmatrix}.$$

Similarly, for plane $\Pi_2 = Ox_3x_4$,

$$\Pi_2 = \mathbf{P}^\top x_3 \times x_4 = \begin{bmatrix} -27 \\ 24 \\ 22 \\ 0 \end{bmatrix}.$$

The corresponding normals of the planes are computed as,

$$\hat{n}_1 = \frac{1}{\sqrt{35^2 + 86^2 + 142^2}} \begin{bmatrix} 35 \\ 86 \\ 142 \end{bmatrix}$$

$$\hat{n}_2 = \frac{1}{\sqrt{27^2 + 24^2 + 22^2}} \begin{bmatrix} -27 \\ 24 \\ 22 \end{bmatrix}.$$

The angle, θ, between the normals, $\hat{n}_1$ and $\hat{n}_2$, are computed as the inverse of the cosine of the dot product between the two unit normal vectors, which is given as,

$$\theta = cos^{-1}(\hat{n}_1 \cdot \hat{n}_2) = 53.752°.$$

11.4.6 | Applications of imaging induced homography

There are various practical applications of this homography, associated with single view camera geometry, for example, generation of synthetic view, planar panoramic mosaicing, etc.

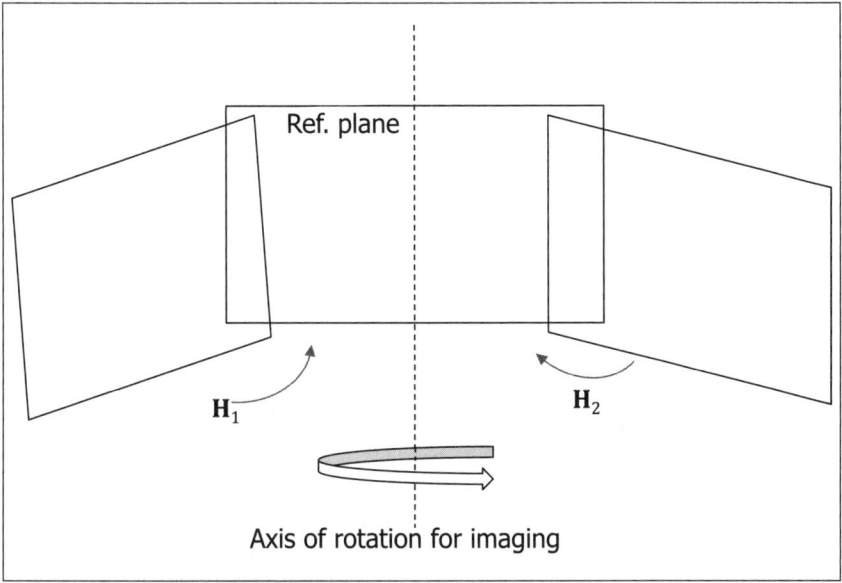

Figure 11.12 Planar panoramic mosaicing.

Consider a situation of a wider panoramic view of the world scene, but the image of only a limited view can be captured with a single camera at a time. In order to cover the view of a wide scene, a series of images are captured by rotating the camera about an axis. Then, the respective homographies due to rotation as discussed in Section 11.4.5, are estimated and applied to these multiple views. Effectively all rotated images of the scene are projectively transformed to a reference plane and the pixels are mapped to points under the same 2-D coordinate system of the reference plane, as shown in Fig. 11.12. Thus, all the points in the overlapping region are registered to the same coordinate system. This registration of image points from multiple overlapping views are used to render the panoramic view of the complete visual scene.

11.5 | Vanishing points of imaging

Vanishing points are the images of points that are at infinity. They are defined with similar analogy with respect to homography or projective transformation. A depiction of vanishing points using an analogy with respect to an 1-D scene is shown in Fig. 11.13. The 1-D scene is assumed to be an infinite line, L, with infinite number of points on it. According to the projection rule, a ray connecting each point, X_i, and the center of projection, C, intersects the image line to form its image at a point, x_i.

The projection of all the points onto the image line forms an image of the line. That is, the points of intersection of all the rays emerging from the 1-D world points, X_1, X_2, and so on, with image line forms the image of that particular set of scene points. If those 1-D points are imaged one after the other, eventually, the image line does not go beyond a point,

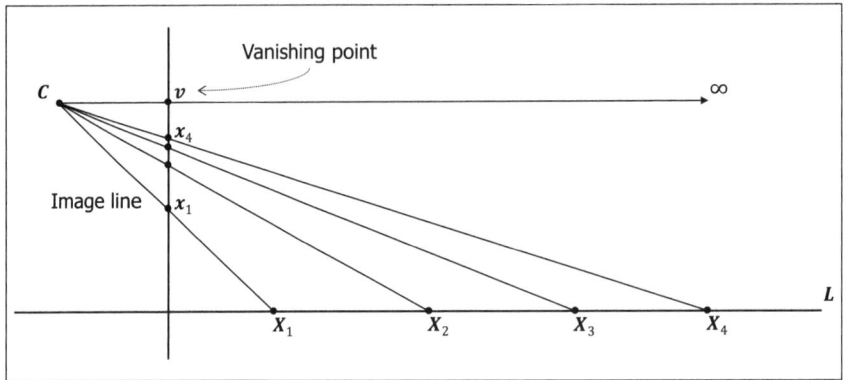

Figure 11.13 Depiction of vanishing points.

which is the intersection of a line passing through C and parallel to L, with the image line. This is the limiting point beyond which there are no more intersection points, because once the projection ray becomes almost parallel to the 1-D world line, they intersect at a point at infinity. This limiting point, v, is defined geometrically, as shown in Fig. 11.13. A line that is parallel to L, which passes through C, intersecting the image line at point v defines the vanishing point, because the image of any other point in L cannot go beyond v.

Consider two points in the image plane, r and q, that lie on a straight line, as shown in Fig. 11.14. Since these points are images of points on a straight line L, they lie on the image of L. Moving any further never crosses the point v in that respective directions, since v is the vanishing point of the straight line L. Let the direction of L be d. As established earlier, a point at infinity in a particular direction, d, is denoted as $\begin{bmatrix} d & 0 \end{bmatrix}^\top$. Its projected point is given as in Eq. 11.49.

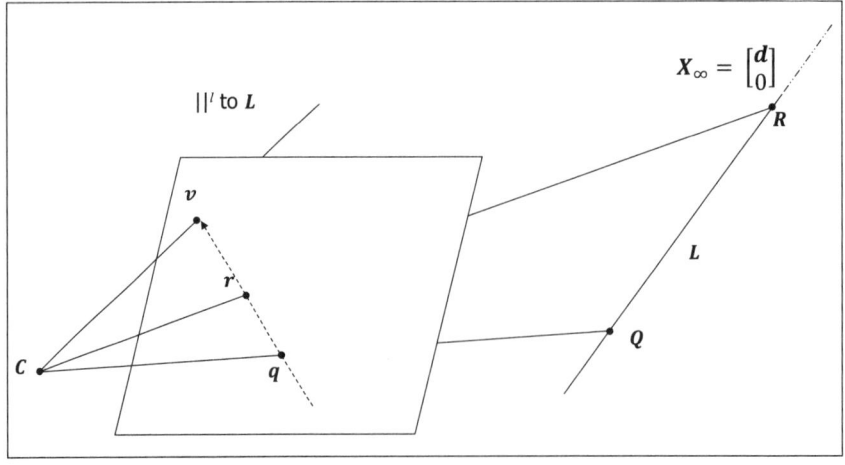

Figure 11.14 Illustration of point at infinity.

$$\mathbf{K}[\mathbf{I}|\mathbf{0}]\,[d \quad 0]^{\top} = \mathbf{K}d \qquad (11.49)$$

Thus, $\mathbf{K}d$ expresses the vanishing point. In this case, the vanishing point is independent of the position of the camera center. C.

Intuitively, this forms an important mathematical explanation to the perception of far away points. At very large distances from human observers, the points appear like relatively moving along the same direction of the observer. This observation is valid even if the movement of the observer is with respect to the observer's frame of reference, and not of the distant points' reference. For example, watching the moon, which is at a large distance from earth, while moving gives a perception that the moon always remains at the same point from the observer's frame of reference. This is because the motion involved with the observer is a simple translation, which does not involve any rotation.

If the camera is rotated, the projection matrix, $\mathbf{P}$, is expressed as $\mathbf{KR}$, and the vanishing point is defined as $v' = \mathbf{KR}d$. If the corresponding projection matrix after applying a rotation, $\mathbf{R}$, and moving it at a camera center, C is known, the projection of a point at infinity is given by Eq. 11.50.

$$\mathbf{K}[\mathbf{R} - \mathbf{R}\widetilde{C}]\begin{bmatrix} d \\ 0 \end{bmatrix} = \mathbf{KR}d \qquad (11.50)$$

One of the interesting implications of Eq. 11.50 is that, if the vanishing points, v and v', and the camera parameters, $\mathbf{K}$, are known, $\mathbf{R}$ is computed by using the relations in Eq. 11.51.

$$
\begin{aligned}
\hat{d} &= \frac{\mathbf{K}^{-1}v}{\|\mathbf{K}^{-1}v\|} \\
\hat{d}' &= \frac{\mathbf{K}^{-1}v'}{\|\mathbf{K}^{-1}v'\|} \\
\hat{d}' &= \mathbf{R}\hat{d}
\end{aligned}
\qquad (11.51)
$$

If the directions obtained by the first two equations in Eq. 11.51 are related with the same $\mathbf{R}$, they form two independent constraints on $\mathbf{R}$, which is computed using the third equation.

Numerical Example

Compute a homography induced by the plane at infinity $\mathbf{H}_\infty$ between images planes of two cameras with their projection matrices $\mathbf{P} = \begin{bmatrix} 1 & 0 & 0 & 0 \\ 0 & 1 & 0 & 0 \\ 0 & 0 & 1 & 0 \end{bmatrix}$, and

$\mathbf{P}' = \begin{bmatrix} 4 & 4 & 6 & 1 \\ 3 & 5 & 7 & 7 \\ 2 & 6 & 9 & 1 \end{bmatrix}$.

Solution

Plane induced homography $\mathbf{H}_\infty = \mathbf{M}'\mathbf{M}^{-1}$, where $\mathbf{M}$ and $\mathbf{M}'$ are the left 3×3 sub-matrices of $\mathbf{P}$ and $\mathbf{P}'$, respectively.

Hence, $\mathbf{H}_\infty = \begin{bmatrix} 4 & 4 & 6 \\ 3 & 5 & 7 \\ 2 & 6 & 9 \end{bmatrix}$.

11.5.1 | Vanishing lines

To understand another kind of geometric interpretation with respect to imaging, the vanishing line, consider a plane, $\boldsymbol{\pi}$, which is specified by its unit normal, $\hat{\boldsymbol{n}}$, as shown in Fig. 11.15. Consider a set of straight lines in $\boldsymbol{\pi}$ and another plane, $\boldsymbol{\pi}_{ll}$, which is parallel to $\boldsymbol{\pi}$ and contains the center of the camera $\boldsymbol{C}$. The normal of $\boldsymbol{\pi}_{ll}$ is the same as that of $\boldsymbol{\pi}$, $\hat{\boldsymbol{n}}$. Consider two lines $\boldsymbol{L}$ and $\boldsymbol{M}$ on $\boldsymbol{\pi}$. Let the vanishing point in the direction of $\boldsymbol{M}$ be $\boldsymbol{v}_m$. That is, the point of intersection of all lines that are parallel to $\boldsymbol{M}$ is denoted by $\boldsymbol{v}_m$. Similarly, let the vanishing point in the direction of $\boldsymbol{L}$ be $\boldsymbol{v}_l$. A vanishing line is formed by connecting these two points, $\boldsymbol{v}_m$ and $\boldsymbol{v}_l$. This line is interpreted as the line formed by all

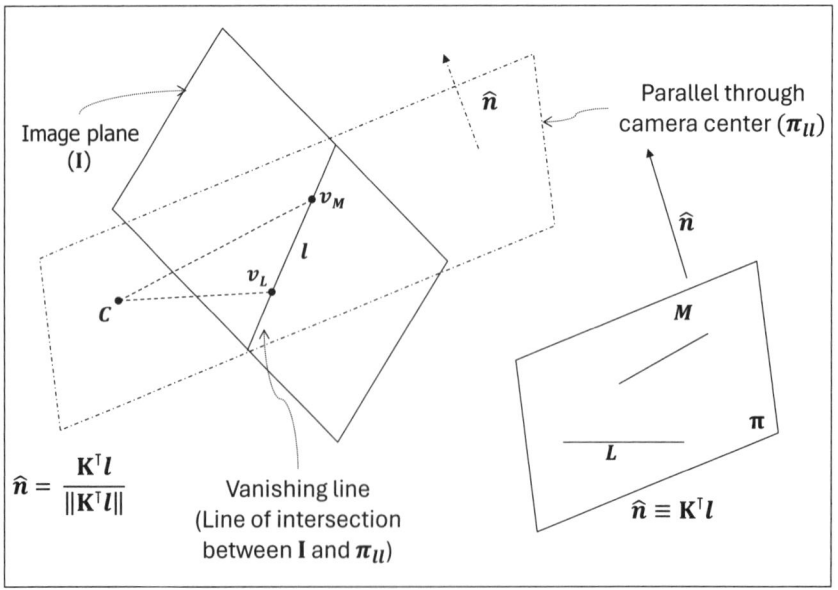

Figure 11.15 Geometric interpretation of vanishing lines.

the vanishing points of the 3-D lines lying on the plane π. Likewise, any plane parallel to π has the same vanishing line. So, the vanishing line l is defined as an intersection of two planes, π_{ll} and the image plane I_p. The normal of the plane, π_{ll}, is computed by back-projecting the vanishing line, l, which is given by Eq. 11.52.

$$\hat{n} \equiv \mathbf{K}^\top l \tag{11.52}$$

In the above, the projection matrix is taken as $[\mathbf{K}|0]$. Also, given the equation of the plane, the corresponding vanishing line is computed by the following steps.

- Identify groups of sets of parallel lines in a plane at different directions.
- Obtain their vanishing points.
- Compute the line joining the vanishing points.

Numerical Example

Consider that the camera projection matrix $\mathbf{P} = \begin{bmatrix} 8 & 5 & 4 & 0 \\ 1 & 8 & 9 & 0 \\ 2 & 1 & 1 & 0 \end{bmatrix}$, two image points $x_1 = (3, 2)$, $x_2 = (5, 7)$ and the camera center O. Find the unit normal to plane Ox_1x_2.

Solution

The plane Ox_1x_2 is given as $P^\top(x_1 \times x_2 = [-16 \quad 2 \quad 9 \quad 0]^T$. Hence the direction ratios of the normal is $-16 : 2 : 9$. The unit vector obtained by dividing the normal vector with its magnitude $= (-0.866, 0.1083, 0.4874)$.

Numerical Example

Given a projection matrix $\mathbf{P} = \begin{bmatrix} 1 & 0 & 1 & 0 \\ 2 & 1 & 2 & 0 \\ 1 & 0 & -1 & 1 \end{bmatrix}$, compute the vanishing point of a line with direction ratio $5 : 4 : 3$ in $\mathbb{R}^2$.

Solution

The vanishing point of the line with direction ratio $a : b : c$ is $(d, e, f)^\top = \mathbf{P}(a, b, c, 0)^\top$. In $\mathbb{R}^2$, it is given as $(d/f, e/f) = (4, 10)$.

Numerical Example

Suppose a camera has the following projection matrix **P**.

$$\mathbf{P} = \begin{bmatrix} 8 & 5 & 4 & 0 \\ 7 & 8 & 9 & 0 \\ 1 & -5 & 8 & 1 \end{bmatrix}$$

A line, l, is given in the image coordinate space, which is defined by the equation, $3x + 4y = 5$. Compute the normal of the plane for which the line appears as a horizon (vanishing line).

Solution

The given equation of the line equation is canonically represented as, $l = \begin{bmatrix} 3 & 4 & -5 \end{bmatrix}^{\top}$. The plane formed by the camera center and the line l is given by $\mathbf{P}^{\top}l$.

$$\mathbf{P}^{\top}l = \begin{bmatrix} 8 & 7 & 1 \\ 5 & 8 & -5 \\ 4 & 9 & 8 \\ 0 & 0 & 1 \end{bmatrix} \begin{bmatrix} 3 \\ 4 \\ -5 \end{bmatrix} = \begin{bmatrix} 47 \\ 72 \\ 8 \\ -5 \end{bmatrix}.$$

The line, l, is a vanishing line for all the planes that are parallel to the plane $\mathbf{P}^{\top}l$, which may also be expressed as, $47x + 72y + 8z - 5 = 0$. The normal (unit normal vector) to this plane is given by,

$$\hat{n} = \frac{1}{\sqrt{47^2 + 72^2 + 8^2}} \begin{bmatrix} 47 \\ 72 \\ 8 \end{bmatrix} = \begin{bmatrix} 0.54 \\ 0.83 \\ 0.09 \end{bmatrix}.$$

Summary

Pinhole camera model provides a projection matrix, **P**, which maps a 3-D point to an image point. The projection matrix is a 3×4 matrix of 11 degrees of freedom, which consists of five intrinsic parameters and 6 extrinsic parameters. So, a minimum of six point correspondences are necessary for the estimation of **P**.

The projection matrix is an affine projection matrix, if the last row of **P** is of the form $[0 \ 0 \ 0 \ 1]$. The affine projection matrix has eight degrees of freedom. So, a minimum of four point correspondences are necessary for the estimation of an affine projection matrix. The geometry of imaging is inherently encoded in a projection matrix, which may be expressed as, $\mathbf{P} = [\mathbf{M}|\mathbf{p}_4]$ or $\mathbf{P} = [\mathbf{p}_1 \ \ \mathbf{p}_2 \ \ \mathbf{p}_3 \ \ \mathbf{p}_4]$ or $\mathbf{P} = [\mathbf{r}_1^\top \ \ \mathbf{r}_2^\top \ \ \mathbf{r}_3^\top]$. Here, $-\mathbf{M}^{-1}\mathbf{p}_4$ represents the camera center. Particularly for the affine projection matrix, this corresponds to the right zero of $\mathbf{M}$ (a direction). The vanishing points of X, Y, and Z axes are given by $\mathbf{p}_1$, $\mathbf{p}_2$, and $\mathbf{p}_3$, respectively. The image of the world origin is given by $\mathbf{p}_4$. The principal plane of imaging is given by $\mathbf{r}_3^\top \mathbf{X} = 0$. The vector, $\langle r_{31} \ \ r_{32} \ \ r_{33} \rangle$, represents the direction of the optical axis. The corresponding principal point is given by $\mathbf{M}[r_{31} \ \ r_{32} \ \ r_{33}]^\top$. The plane formed with x and y axes of the image coordinate system are represented by, $\mathbf{r}_1^\top \mathbf{X} = 0$ and $\mathbf{r}_2^\top \mathbf{X} = 0$, respectively.

The projection ray formed at image point, $\mathbf{x}$, is one of the geometric derivatives from projection matrix $\mathbf{P} = [\mathbf{M}|\mathbf{p}_4]$. Its direction ratio is computed as, $\mathbf{M}^{-1}\mathbf{x}$. The camera center, $-\mathbf{M}^{-1}\mathbf{p}_4$, is a point on this projection ray. The plane formed with a line, $\mathbf{l}$, in the image plane with the camera center is obtained as, $\mathbf{P}^\top \mathbf{l}$.

Exercises

(i) Consider a camera with camera matrix $\mathbf{P} = \begin{bmatrix} 4 & 4 & 6 & 0 \\ 3 & 5 & 7 & 0 \\ 2 & 6 & 9 & 0 \end{bmatrix}$. Given an image point

$(5, 8)$, compute the direction cosines of the projection ray formed at that point in the world coordinate system.

(ii) Consider the following camera matrix.

$$\begin{bmatrix} 2 & -2 & 4 & 1 \\ 1 & 0 & -1 & 0 \\ 3 & 1 & -3 & 1 \end{bmatrix}$$

(a) Compute the camera center in world coordinate.

(b) Compute the direction of unit normal of the plane formed by the camera center and a straight line in the image plane given by $(1, 0, 1) \in \mathbb{P}^2$.

(c) Compute the image point of $(100, 100, -150) \in \mathbb{R}^2$.

(iii) Consider the following camera matrix. $\begin{bmatrix} 3 & 6 & 7 & 1 \\ 5 & 2 & 1 & 1 \\ 1 & 2 & 1 & 1 \end{bmatrix}$

(a) Compute the camera center in world coordinate.

(b) Compute the principal point in the image plane.

(c) Compute the image of the origin of the world coordinate.

(iv) If the principal point is located at $(2, 3)$ in the coordinate system of the image plane, what would be the image coordinates of the world point, $(3, 4, 5)$, using a pin hole camera with focal length $f = 0.5$?

(v) If the principal point $((p_x, p_y))$, focal length (f), orientation $(\mathbf{R})$ and the camera center $(\mathbf{C})$ of a pin hole camera are given by $(2, 3)$, 0.5, $\begin{bmatrix} 0.36 & 0.48 & -0.8 \\ -0.8 & 0.6 & 0 \\ 0.48 & 0.64 & 0.6 \end{bmatrix}$, and $(1, 2, 1)$, respectively, compute the 3×4 projection matrix $\mathbf{P}$.

(vi) Consider a projection matrix $\mathbf{P} = \begin{bmatrix} 8 & 5 & 4 & 0 \\ 7 & 8 & 9 & 0 \\ 1 & -5 & 8 & 1 \end{bmatrix}$.

   (a) Evaluate the camera center, $\mathbf{C}$, in homogeneous coordinates.

   (b) Given an image point $(3, 6)$ in $\mathbb{R}^2$, compute its scene point if the camera is at a distance of 20 units from the camera center.

(vii) Compute the principal point in 2-D real space and principal axis of the camera matrix $\mathbf{P} = \begin{bmatrix} -3 & -6 & -8 & 0 \\ 2 & 5 & 7 & 0 \\ 1 & 2 & 0 & 1 \end{bmatrix}$.

(viii) Given a projection matrix $\mathbf{P} = \begin{bmatrix} 1 & 0 & 1 & 0 \\ 2 & 1 & 2 & 0 \\ 1 & 0 & -1 & 1 \end{bmatrix}$, compute the vanishing point of a line in image coordinates with direction ratios $5 : 4 : 3$.

(ix) A projective camera $\mathbf{P} = \begin{bmatrix} 8 & 5 & 4 & 0 \\ 1 & 8 & 9 & 0 \\ 2 & 1 & 1 & 0 \end{bmatrix}$ images a 3-D line $\mathbf{L}$ as $\mathbf{l} = (1, 2, 3)$. Compute the plane formed by projected line $\mathbf{l}$ and the camera center.

(x) Consider a camera projection matrix $\mathbf{P} = \begin{bmatrix} 8 & 5 & 4 & 0 \\ 1 & 8 & 9 & 0 \\ 2 & 1 & 1 & 0 \end{bmatrix}$, two image points $(x_1 = (3, 2)$ and $x_2 = (5, 7))$, and the camera center $\mathbf{O}$. Find the unit normal to plane $\mathbf{O}x_1 x_2$.

(xi) Given a camera calibration matrix $\mathbf{K} = \begin{bmatrix} 4 & 2.5 & 2 \\ 0 & 4 & 3 \\ 0 & 0 & 1 \end{bmatrix}$, compute the aspect ratio, skew, and principal point.

(xii) Consider the projection matrix for pinhole camera as, $\mathbf{P} = \text{diag}(10, 10, 1)[\mathbf{I}|0]$. It is assumed that the origin of coordinates in the image plane is at the principal point.

   (a) Compute the camera calibration matrix if the coordinates of the principal point becomes $(15, 25)$.

(b) If the projection matrix for pinhole camera is $\mathbf{P} = \mathrm{diag}(f, f, 1)[\mathbf{I}|0]$ and the principal point is shifted to (p_x, p_y), then compute the calibration matrix.

(c) Compute the image point for the world co-ordinate $(60, 90, 30)$.

(d) Compute the image point for the world co-ordinate $(60, 90, 30)$, when the coordinates of the principal point is $(15, 25)$.

(e) Compute the image point for the world co-ordinate $(60, 90, 30)$, when the coordinates of the principal point is $(15, 25)$ and camera coordinate is rotated by $90°$ and translated by $(10, 20)$.

(xiii) Given the projection matrix as,

$$\mathbf{P} = \begin{bmatrix} -3 & 2 & 4 & 1 \\ 4 & -3 & 5 & 1 \\ 2 & 5 & -10 & 1 \end{bmatrix}$$

(a) Compute the vanishing point of x-axis.

(b) Compute the principal point of the camera.

(c) Compute the image point of the origin.

(d) Compute the vanishing point of the line with the direction cosines $1 : 3 : 5$.

(e) Given an image point $(2,7)$ in $\mathbb{R}_2$, compute its corresponding scene point if it is known that the point is at a distance of 40 units from the center of camera.

(f) Compute the principal plane of the imaging system.

(xiv) Consider the following camera matrix.

$$\begin{bmatrix} 8 & 5 & 4 & 0 \\ 7 & 8 & 9 & 0 \\ 1 & -5 & 8 & 0 \end{bmatrix}$$

Consider four image points, $x_1 = (2, 5)$, $x_2 = (7, 9)$, $x_3 = (-1, 3)$, and $x_4 = (4, -1)$. Let the camera center be denoted as $\mathbf{O}$. Compute the dihedral angle between planes of $\mathbf{O}x_1x_2$ and $\mathbf{O}x_3x_4$. Note: A dihedral angle of two planes is the angle between their normals.

(xv) Suppose a camera has the following projection matrix $\mathbf{P}$.

$$\begin{bmatrix} 8 & 5 & 4 & 0 \\ 7 & 8 & 9 & 0 \\ 1 & -5 & 8 & 1 \end{bmatrix}$$

Given a line l in the image coordinate space that is defined by $2x + 5y = 3$, compute the normal of the plane for which the line appears as a horizon (vanishing line).

(**xvi**) Verify the correct statement/s about projection matrix among the following.

(**a**) Projection matrix is of size 3×4.

(**b**) Degree of freedom is 11.

(**c**) There are 6 intrinsic parameters.

(**d**) There are 5 extrinsic parameters.

(**e**) A minimum of 6 point correspondences are required for estimation.

(**f**) Last row is $\begin{bmatrix} 0 & 0 & 0 & 1 \end{bmatrix}^\top$.

(**xvii**) Consider a camera matrix $\mathbf{P}$ and projecting a point $\mathbf{X} = (\frac{12}{98}, \frac{1}{14}, \frac{20}{98}, 1)$ in 3-D space to the image point $\mathbf{x} = w(x_1, y_1, 1)^\top$.

$$\mathbf{P} = \begin{bmatrix} 8 & 5 & 4 & 0 \\ 7 & 8 & 9 & 0 \\ 1 & -5 & 8 & 1 \end{bmatrix}$$

Compute the depth of the point $\mathbf{X}$ from the camera center $\mathbf{C}$ in the direction of the principal ray.

(**xviii**) Consider a camera placed at $(-10, 10, 6)$ with a focal length of 5 unit and optical axis parallel to Z-axis, axes in image plane parallel to X and Y axes respectively of the world coordinate system. An area of 1×2 square unit in image is represented by an array of 1600×700 pixels along X and Y axes respectively. Answer the following questions assuming there is no skew in the arrangement of the sensor array.

(**a**) Compute the projection matrix of the above camera.

(**b**) Discuss the extrinsic and intrinsic parameters with their values for the above imaging system.

(**c**) Compute the image coordinate of the origin of the world coordinate system.

(**d**) Which point in the world coordinate system does not have an image point?

(**e**) Define a vanishing line in the image plane. Compute the vanishing line of the plane in world coordinate system given by the equation, $4X + 3Y - 7Z = 15$.

(**xix**) Consider the following projection matrix of an optical camera based imaging system:

$$\mathbf{P} = \begin{bmatrix} 2 & 1 & 5 & -10 \\ 6 & 1 & 3 & 5 \\ 4 & 2 & 1 & 4 \end{bmatrix}$$

Compute the camera center and vanishing point of a straight line in $\mathbb{R}^3$ with direction ratios as $2 : 5 : 3$.

(**xx**) Derive the camera projection matrix for mapping a world coordinate of a 3-D point into its corresponding image pixel coordinate by showing the intrinsic and extrinsic parameters of camera geometry.

(**xxi**) Given a projection matrix how are the intrinsic parameters computed?

(xxii) Consider the following projection matrix of an optical camera based imaging system:

$$\mathbf{P} = \begin{bmatrix} -6 & 1 & 1 & -15 \\ 2 & -7 & 3 & 25 \\ 2 & 3 & -7 & 10 \end{bmatrix}$$

Compute the following.

(a) Camera center.

(b) Principal point.

(c) The plane formed by the camera center and the line in the image space given by $(1, 2, 3) \in \mathbb{P}^2$.

(d) Image of the origin of the world coordinate.

(e) Whether the 3-D point $(-2, -5, 10) \in \mathbb{R}^3$ is in front of the camera?

(f) Back projected ray formed by the image point $(8, 3) \in \mathbb{R}^2$.

(xxiii) Consider a camera matrix given by $\mathbf{P} = [\mathbf{A}^{-1}|\boldsymbol{b}]$, where $\boldsymbol{b} = (b_1, b_2, b_3) \in \mathbb{R}^3$ and

$$\mathbf{A} = \begin{bmatrix} a_{11} & a_{12} & a_{13} \\ a_{21} & a_{22} & a_{23} \\ a_{31} & a_{32} & a_{33} \end{bmatrix}$$

Answer the following.

(a) Given an image point $(p, q) \in \mathbb{R}^2$ and its depth (distance from the principal plane) d, prove that the corresponding scene point is at $(X, Y, Z) \in \mathbb{R}^3$, so that

$$X = \frac{(a_{11} - b_1 a_{31})p + (a_{12} - b_1 a_{32})q + (a_{13} - b_1 a_{33})}{D} \tag{11.53}$$

$$Y = \frac{(a_{21} - b_1 a_{31})p + (a_{22} - b_1 a_{32})q + (a_{23} - b_1 a_{33})}{D} \tag{11.54}$$

$$Z = d \tag{11.55}$$

where $D = a_{31}p + a_{32}q + a_{33}$.

(b) Given a straight line $\boldsymbol{l} \in \mathbb{P}^2$ as the image of a line $\boldsymbol{L}$ in 3-D world coordinate, prove that the unit normal to the plane formed by the camera center and $\boldsymbol{L}$ in the world coordinate is $\dfrac{\mathbf{A}^{-\top}\boldsymbol{l}}{\|\mathbf{A}^{-\top}\boldsymbol{l}\|}$.

(xxiv) Consider the following projection matrix of an optical camera based imaging system:

$$\mathbf{P} = \begin{bmatrix} -6 & 1 & 1 & -15 \\ 2 & -7 & 3 & 25 \\ 0 & 0 & 1 & 0 \end{bmatrix}$$

Answer the following w.r.t. **P**.

(a) Camera center in $\mathbb{R}^3$ (the world coordinate system).

(b) The equation of the image plane in $\mathbb{R}^3$ (the world coordinate system).

(c) The vanishing point in the image coordinates ($\mathbb{R}^2$) of the line in the world coordinate system ($\mathbb{R}^3$) with direction ratios $1 : 1 : 1$.

(d) Describe an algorithm for finding the focal length of the camera from **P** given the pixel resolutions (dots per cm) in horizontal and vertical directions.

(e) Given an image point $(5, -8)$ of a 3-D point p, which lies in a plane parallel to the image plane and at a distance of 35 unit compute its 3-D world coordinate.

(xxv) Consider the following projection matrix of an optical camera based imaging system:

$$\mathbf{P} = \begin{bmatrix} 8 & 5 & 4 & 0 \\ 7 & 8 & 9 & 0 \\ 1 & -5 & 8 & 1 \end{bmatrix}$$

Answer the following w.r.t. **P**.

(a) Given an image point $(2, 7)$ in $\mathbb{R}^2$, compute its corresponding scene point if it is known that the point is at a distance of 40 units from the center of camera.

(b) Compute the principal plane of the imaging system.

(c) How is the camera calibration matrix of **P** is computed?

(xxvi) Consider the following projection matrix of an optical camera based imaging system:

$$\mathbf{P} = \begin{bmatrix} 3 & 4 & 6 & 1 \\ 2 & 8 & -3 & 4 \\ -7 & 0 & 4 & 2 \end{bmatrix}$$

Compute the following from **P**.

(a) The camera center.

(b) The direction of principal axis toward the scene viewed by the camera.

(c) The principal plane of the camera.

(d) The horizon or the vanishing line in the image corresponding to the horizontal plane of the world coordinate system.

(e) The area of the triangle formed by the images of the following points in $\mathbb{R}^3$: $(2, 3, 4)$, $(1, 10, 8)$, and $(-7, -8, 2)$.

(xxvii) Define the following terms related to imaging in a pin-hole camera in a camera centric coordinate system:
Principal plane, image plane, principal axis, camera center, and principal point. Provide the respective diagram of the imaging system and label them. Relate a 3D coordinate point (α, β, γ) to its image coordinates for the above imaging system.

(xxviii) Given the projection matrix of a camera $\mathbf{P}$, compute the homography matrix between the corresponding points lying on XY-plane and on its image plane.

$$\mathbf{P} = \begin{bmatrix} 3 & 4 & 2 & -10 \\ 1 & 2 & 1 & 5 \\ 1 & 3 & 1 & 3 \end{bmatrix}$$

(xxix) Consider the below camera matrix, $\mathbf{P}$.

$$\mathbf{P} = \begin{bmatrix} 2 & 1 & 5 & -10 \\ 6 & 1 & 3 & 5 \\ 4 & 2 & 1 & 4 \end{bmatrix}$$

(a) Given the above camera matrix $\mathbf{P}$ and a line in the image $\begin{bmatrix} 2 & -3 & 4 \end{bmatrix}^{\top}$, compute the plane Π containing that line and the camera center.

(b) Define vanishing line of a plane in monocular camera geometry.

(c) Compute the vanishing line of the plane Π in this case.

(d) Compute the vanishing point of the normal of the plane Π.

(xxx) Consider a camera placed at $(-10, 10, 6)$ with a focal length of 5 unit and optical axis parallel to Z-axis, axes in image plane parallel to X and Y axes respectively of the world coordinate system. An area of 1×2 square unit in image is represented by an array of 1600×700 pixels along X and Y axes respectively. Answer the following questions assuming there is no skew in the arrangement of the sensor array.

(a) Compute the projection matrix of the above camera.

(b) What are the extrinsic and intrinsic parameters (with their values) for the above imaging system.

(c) Compute the image coordinate of the origin of the world coordinate system.

(d) Which point in the world coordinate system does not have an image point?

(e) Compute the vanishing line of the plane in world coordinate system given by the equation, $4X + 3Y - 7Z = 15$.

(xxxi) Consider the following projection matrix of an optical camera based imaging system:

$$\mathbf{P} = \begin{bmatrix} 10 & -1 & 1 & -15 \\ 7 & -2 & 3 & 15 \\ 0 & 0 & 1 & 1 \end{bmatrix}$$

Answer the following with respect to $\mathbf{P}$.

(a) Compute the image point of the origin of the world the world coordinate system in image coordinates ($\mathbb{R}^2$).

(b) The equation of the principal plane in $\mathbb{R}^3$ (the world coordinate system).

(c) The vanishing point in the image coordinates ($\mathbb{R}^2$) of the line in the world coordinate system ($\mathbb{R}^3$) with direction ratios $1 : 1 : 1$.

(d) Show that parallel lines in the XY plane in the world coordinate system remains parallel in the image plane of this camera.

(e) Given an image point $(5, -8)$ of a 3-D point p, at a distance of 35 unit from the camera center compute its 3-D world coordinate.

(xxxii) Consider the following projection matrix of an optical camera based imaging system:

$$\mathbf{P} = \begin{bmatrix} 3 & 4 & 6 & 1 \\ 2 & 8 & -3 & 4 \\ -7 & 0 & 4 & 2 \end{bmatrix}$$

Compute the following from $\mathbf{P}$.

(a) The camera center.

(b) The direction of principal axis toward the scene viewed by the camera.

(c) The principal plane of the camera.

(d) The horizon or the vanishing line in the image corresponding to the horizontal plane of the world coordinate system.

(e) The area of the triangle formed by the images of the following points in $\mathbb{R}^3$: $(2, 3, 4)$, $(1, 10, 8)$, and $(-7, -8, 2)$.

(xxxiii) Why does the moon in the sky move with the same velocity of a viewer while walking straight?

(xxxiv) Consider the following camera matrix $\mathbf{P}$.

$$\mathbf{P} = \begin{bmatrix} 1 & 9 & 3 & 12 \\ 5 & 6 & 7 & 8 \\ 2 & 10 & 4 & 1 \end{bmatrix}$$

Compute the following for the imaging system.

(a) The center of the camera in $\mathbb{R}^3$ (world coordinates).

(b) Vanishing points of X, Y, and Z axes in $\mathbb{R}^2$ (image coordinates).

(c) The image coordinate of the origin of the world coordinate system in $\mathbb{P}^2$.

(d) The direction ratios of the optical axis.

(e) The principal point in $\mathbb{P}^2$.

(f) The image point of the point at the coordinate position $(10, 10, 10)$.

(g) The algebraic equation of the plane in the world coordinate system formed by the camera center and the line $(1, -4, 3) \in \mathbb{P}^2$ in the image.

12

Stereo Vision

In the single view camera geometry it is not possible to resolve the ambiguity of depth of the scene point from its image point even with a calibrated camera, whose projection matrix is known. It is only possible to construct the ray in the 3-dimensional (3-D) world coordinate system passing through the image point from the center of the camera. But in an optical image a viewer can distinguish the object point which forms the image. It is the optical energy received from that point in a surface of the object and their distribution over its neighborhood that provide the key information to a viewer in interpreting the object point and judging the distances from the camera. In this chapter, we discuss how the depth ambiguity in a single view camera geometry can be resolved with the help of another additional camera. The combined setup of two cameras is called stereo camera setup and the geometry defined by them is referred to as *stereo geometry*.

12.1 | Epipolar geometry

A stereo setup consists of two cameras and a scene point, X, whose image is captured by the cameras, as illustrated in Fig. 12.1. The first (left) and the second (right) cameras are specified by their camera centers, C and C', respectively, which capture the images of the scene point on their respective image planes. In convention, the first camera or left camera is considered as the reference camera of the stereo setup. By the rule of projection, let the image of the scene point, X, in the first camera be x. Similarly, the image of X in the image plane of the second camera is represented by x'. The two images, x and x', correspond to the same scene point, X. Thus, for every scene point, there will be two image points in the image planes of the two cameras, if the scene point is visible from both the cameras.

This particular construct has certain characterizations or geometric properties, which are as follows.

(i) The image points, x and x', lie on the plane, π, that is formed by the points, C, X, and C', which is known as the *epipolar plane*, as shown in the illustration of the stereo setup.

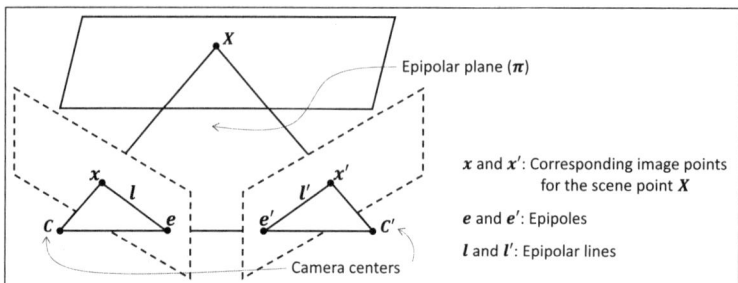

Figure 12.1 Illustration of a stereo camera setup.

(ii) In this stereo setup, the line formed by the points C and C' is called the *base line*. This line intersects the two image planes at e and e', respectively, as shown. Consider the projection ray formed by the first camera center, C, and the image point, x. Then, geometrically, any point lying on this ray is a possible candidate for projecting on the same image point, x.

(iii) These two points of intersection between the base line and the image planes are called *epipoles*. As a convention, epipoles of left and right cameras are called *left epipole* and *right epipole*, respectively. These points are interpreted as the images of the camera centers, C and C' on their respective image planes.

(iv) An epipole in an image plane is geometrically interpreted as the projection of camera center in the other image. For example, e' is the image of camera center C, which is a projection center (camera center) of the first camera.

(v) An epipole may also be interpreted as a vanishing point in the camera motion direction. A camera motion direction is a direction of translation of the camera center, which is given by its baseline. In the camera motion direction, the point of intersection of the ray along the baseline and the image plane is the vanishing point along that direction. Hence, the epipole is the vanishing point in the camera motion direction.

(vi) The lines, l and l', formed by the epipoles and image points in both the cameras are known as *epipolar lines*. They are the lines formed by the intersection of epipolar plane and the image planes, as seen in the Fig. 12.1.

(vii) The epipolar lines always come in corresponding pairs, l and l', in a stereo setup.

(viii) Geometrically, the images of all the possible candidates of the same image point, x, in the first camera lie on the epipolar line l'. Similarly, the images of all the points along the projection ray of the second camera lie on l. Thus, the corresponding points of x and x' lie on the epipolar lines, l' and l, respectively.

(ix) All the points on the epipolar plane are projected only on the corresponding pair of epipolar lines. For example as shown in Fig. 12.2, any point on π is projected on l and l', respectively.

(x) An *epipolar plane* is the plane that contains the baseline. The camera centers, base line, epipoles, epipolar lines, and scene point and its image points lie on the same plane, the epipolar plane.

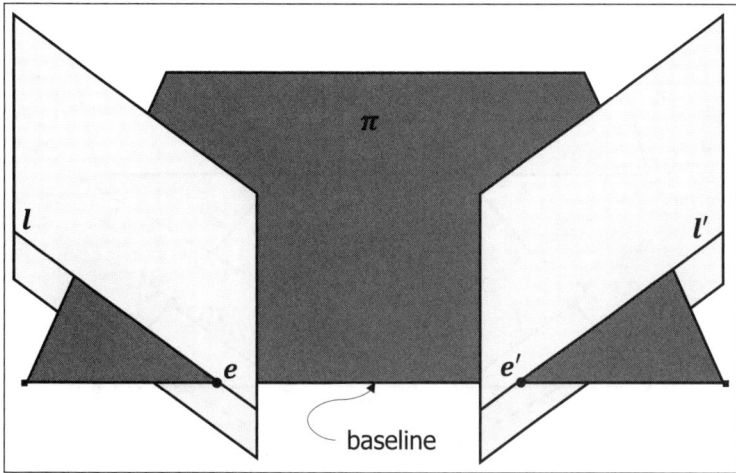

Figure 12.2 All points on π project on l and l'.

(xi) The baseline is a one-dimensional (1-D) family, in the sense that, it acts like a pencil and all the planes (family of planes, Π) centering around the baseline define the epipolar planes. This is illustrated in Fig. 12.3. In a family of epipolar planes, intersection of any of the epipolar planes with the image planes results in the corresponding pairs of epipolar lines.

(xii) All the epipolar lines meet at the respective epipoles in each of the image planes, as seen in Fig. 12.3.

These are the constraints that are imposed by this particular configuration of stereo setup. In general, this geometry is referred to as the *epipolar geometry*.

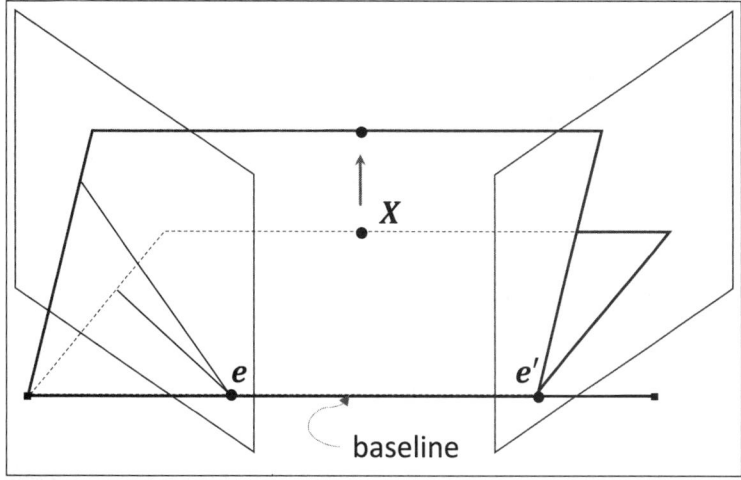

Figure 12.3 Family of planes Π and lines l and l' intersecting in e and e'.

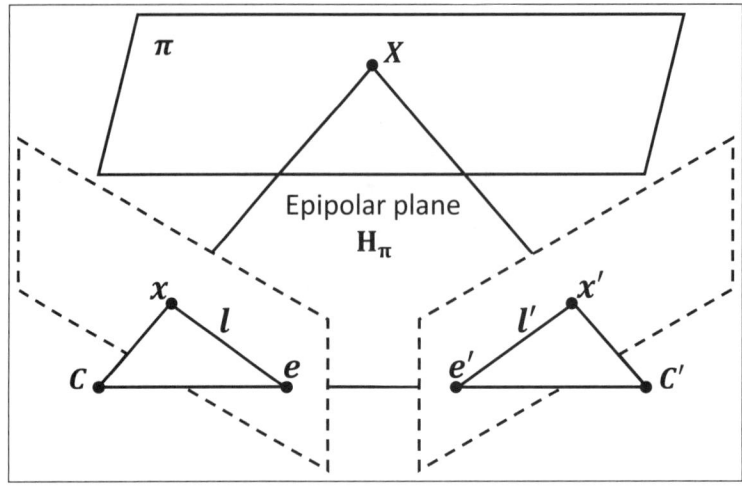

Figure 12.4 A stereo camera setup.

To provide mathematical formulations of different concepts involving various entities of the stereo geometry, consider the stereo setup in Fig. 12.4 (reproduced from Fig. 12.1 for the ease of accessibility). Here, the first (left) and second (right) cameras are represented by their centers, C and C', respectively. Also, the projection matrix of the first camera, which is the reference camera, is given by $K[I|0]$ in camera centric coordinate system. With respect to the reference camera, the projection matrix of the second camera is given by $K'[R|t]$, where R and t are rotation and translation matrices, respectively.

In the structure shown in Fig. 12.4, the two image points, x and x', correspond to the same world point X. Considering all the points in the plane π, their corresponding image points induce a homography. Using the relations in camera geometry, that x' is expressed as in Eq. 12.1 in the homogeneous coordinate systems of the projective geometry.

$$x' = P'X \tag{12.1}$$

For every scene point X lying on the plane π, two such corresponding points (e.g., x and x') are formed in the left and the right image planes. As they satisfy the conditions of projective transformation, they are related by a homography. We call this homography *plane induced homography* and denote it by H_π for the inducing plane π.

Next we consider a special inducing plane for defining a homography. A point lying at infinity along the ray formed by the image point, x, with respect to its respective camera center, is given by P^+x, where $P^+ = \begin{bmatrix} K^{-1} \\ 0^\top \end{bmatrix}$. Here, the direction of the ray is given by $K^{-1}x$ and any point that is lying at infinity on this line is given by $\begin{bmatrix} K^{-1}x \\ 0 \end{bmatrix}$. For every image point on the image plane, there is a corresponding point that is lying at infinity, which is formed by the scene point and the image point. The plane that contains all these points at the infinity is called the *plane at infinity*, π_∞. The formation of corresponding points in the image planes, only with respect to the plane at infinity, has a homography between them, which is also referred to as *homography at infinity*, $\mathbf{H}_\infty$. This homography matrix is computed as in Eq. 12.2.

$$\mathbf{H}_\infty = \mathbf{P}'\mathbf{P}^+$$

$$= \mathbf{K}'[\mathbf{R}|\mathbf{t}] \begin{bmatrix} \mathbf{K}^{-1} \\ \mathbf{0}^\top \end{bmatrix}$$

$$= [\mathbf{K}'\mathbf{R}|\mathbf{K}'\mathbf{t}] \begin{bmatrix} \mathbf{K}^{-1}\mathbf{0}^\top \end{bmatrix} \tag{12.2}$$

$$= \mathbf{K}'\mathbf{R}\mathbf{K}^{-1} + \mathbf{K}'\mathbf{t}\mathbf{0}^\top$$

$$= \mathbf{K}'\mathbf{R}\mathbf{K}^{-1}$$

12.2 | Fundamental and essential matrices

Given the point $\boldsymbol{x}'$, the line, $\boldsymbol{l}'$, is reconstructed in the projective space as the cross product of $\boldsymbol{e}'$ and $\boldsymbol{x}'$, which is expressed by Eq. 12.3.

$$\boldsymbol{l}' = \boldsymbol{e}' \times \boldsymbol{x}' \tag{12.3}$$

Let $\boldsymbol{e}' = \begin{bmatrix} e'_x & e'_y & e'_z \end{bmatrix}^\top$. Then the above operation can also be expressed in terms of a matrix multiplication as given below.

$$\boldsymbol{e}' \times \boldsymbol{x}' = [\boldsymbol{e}']_\times \boldsymbol{x}' \tag{12.4}$$

where, $[\boldsymbol{e}']_\times = \begin{bmatrix} 0 & -e'_z & e'_y \\ e'_z & 0 & -e'_x \\ -e'_y & e'_x & 0 \end{bmatrix}$.

We may check this equivalence as follows.

Consider in the homogeneous coordinates, $\boldsymbol{x}' = \begin{bmatrix} x' & y' & z' \end{bmatrix}^\top$, where z' is some scale value.

So, $\boldsymbol{e}' \times \boldsymbol{x}' = \begin{bmatrix} i & j & k \\ e'_x & e'_y & e'_z \\ x' & y' & z' \end{bmatrix} = (z'e'_y - y'e'_z)i + (x'e'_z - z'e'_x)j + (y'e'_x - x'e'_y)k.$

This can be represented as a vector, $\begin{bmatrix} (z'e'_y - y'e'_z) \\ (x'e'_z - z'e'_x) \\ (y'e'_x - x'e'_y) \end{bmatrix}$, which is the same as the result obtained by $[\boldsymbol{e}']_\times \boldsymbol{x}'$.

$[e']_\times$ is a skew symmetric matrix, whose diagonal elements are 0 and its transpose is negation of the matrix elements. It is further simplified by substituting $x' = \mathbf{H}_\pi x$, as given in Eq. 12.5.

$$
\begin{aligned}
l' &= [e']_\times x' \\
&= [e']_\times \mathbf{H}_\pi x \\
&= \mathbf{F}x
\end{aligned}
\tag{12.5}
$$

where $\mathbf{F} = [e']_\times \mathbf{H}_\pi$. We may note that $\mathbf{H}_\pi$ is some plane induced homography relating x and x'. This relation of l', the epipolar line in the second camera, with x, the image point in the first camera, is a very fundamental relationship in stereo geometry. This implies, there exists a 3×3 matrix, $\mathbf{F}$, such that, multiplying the image point in the first camera in its homogenous coordinate system with it provides the epipolar line l' of the second camera. This matrix is called the *fundamental matrix*, which is the characteristic matrix of a stereo setup that converts an image point to the epipolar line on which its corresponding image point of the second camera lies. The transformation from a point to a line as expressed in Eq. 12.5 is called *correlation*. By using Eqs. 12.2 and 12.5, the fundamental matrix can be expressed using the camera matrices and epipoles, as given in Eq. 12.6.

$$
\mathbf{F} = [e']_\times \mathbf{K}'\mathbf{R}\mathbf{K}^{-1}
\tag{12.6}
$$

When the fundamental matrix is multiplied with any image point in the projective space in the first camera, it results in the epipolar line in the second camera and vice versa. Hence, the point containment relationship between the corresponding point and the epipolar line exists here. By applying the point containment relationship to the epipolar line, l', using fundamental matrix, the following expressions are obtained.

$$
\begin{aligned}
l' &= \mathbf{F}x \\
\Longrightarrow x'^\top l' &= 0 \\
\Longrightarrow x'^\top \mathbf{F}x &= 0 \\
\Longrightarrow x^\top \mathbf{F}^\top x' &= 0
\end{aligned}
\tag{12.7}
$$

The above equation implies, if a pair of corresponding points are computed from two images, there exists a 3×3 matrix, $\mathbf{F}$, which satisfies the relations expressed in Eq. 12.7. This relationship is also very fundamental to the epipolar geometry. The epipoles can be considered as the images of the camera centers. The left epipole, e, can be expressed as the product of projection matrix of the first camera with C', which is given by,

$$
e = \mathbf{P}C' = -\mathbf{K}\mathbf{R}^\top t \equiv \mathbf{K}\mathbf{R}^\top t
\tag{12.8}
$$

Similarly, e' is the image of the first camera center, which is expressed in Eq. 12.9.

$$
e' = \mathbf{P}'C = -\mathbf{K}'t
\tag{12.9}
$$

In the stereo setup, if the left camera is considered as the reference camera with respect to the right camera and the fundamental matrix is $\mathbf{F}$, $\mathbf{F}^\top$ becomes the fundamental matrix for a stereo setup whose cameras interchange their roles from the left to the right. For a calibrated camera,[1] the relationship between the fundamental matrix and the camera parameters is given in the form of Eq. 12.10.

$$\mathbf{F} = [e']_\times \mathbf{P}'\mathbf{P}^+ = [\mathbf{K}'t]_\times \mathbf{K}'\mathbf{R}\mathbf{K}^{-1} \tag{12.10}$$

Here, $\mathbf{P}$ is given in its normalized canonical form as $\mathbf{P} = [\mathbf{I}|\mathbf{0}]$, (i.e., $\mathbf{K} = \mathbf{I}$), and $\mathbf{P}' = \mathbf{K}'[\mathbf{R}|t] = [\mathbf{K}'\mathbf{R}|\mathbf{K}'t] = [\mathbf{M}|m]$. So, Eq. 12.10 is expressed as the following.

$$\mathbf{F} = [m]_\times \mathbf{M} \tag{12.11}$$

where $\mathbf{M} = \mathbf{K}'\mathbf{R}$ and $m = \mathbf{K}'t$. In a particular case where $\mathbf{K} = \mathbf{I}$ and $\mathbf{K}' = \mathbf{I}$, Eq. 12.10 gets further simplified as in Eq. 12.12.

$$\mathbf{F} = [t]_\times \mathbf{R} \tag{12.12}$$

This particular form of the fundamental matrix is called the *essential matrix*, $\mathbf{E}$.

12.2.1 | Properties of the fundamental matrix

The fundamental matrix of a stereo configuration has certain properties, which are as follows.

- Given the fundamental matrix $\mathbf{F}$ of a stereo setup, a pair of corresponding image points, (x', x), of the same scene point satisfy the following relation.

$$x'^\top \mathbf{F}x = x^\top \mathbf{F}^\top x' = 0, \ \forall (x', x) \tag{12.13}$$

- As also observed in Eq. 12.13, if $\mathbf{F}$ is the fundamental matrix of a stereo configuration, $\mathbf{F}^\top$ is also the fundamental matrix of the stereo configuration that is obtained by interchanging the roles of the reference camera and the second camera. This is true for any pair of corresponding image points. Hence, if $\mathbf{F}$ is the fundamental matrix of a stereo setup defined by a pair of camera matrices, $(\mathbf{P}, \mathbf{P}')$, where $\mathbf{P}$ is the camera matrix of the reference camera, $\mathbf{F}^\top$ is the fundamental matrix of the stereo setup defined by the pair of camera matrices, $(\mathbf{P}', \mathbf{P})$.

- Epipolar lines: If x is an image point in the image plane of the left camera of the stereo setup, the epipolar line of the right camera is expressed as $l' = \mathbf{F}x$. Similarly, if x' is an image point in the image plane of the right camera, then the epipolar line of the left camera is expressed as $l = \mathbf{F}^\top x'$.

- Rank deficiency: From the transformation of a point to a line using the matrix $\mathbf{F}$, we also infer that, it is not possible to perform inversion on $\mathbf{F}$ as the mapping of a point to a line is not one to one. A different point lying on the epipolar line l will also map to l' by being premultiplied with $\mathbf{F}$. Hence $\mathbf{F}$ is singular. Thus $\mathbf{F}$ is a rank deficient matrix and its determinant, $\text{Det}(\mathbf{F}) = 0$.

---

[1] A camera is said to be calibrated, if its calibration matrix is known.

- Every property related to $\mathbf{F}$ is also true for $k\mathbf{F}$, where k is a scalar quantity. For example epipolar line l and kl are equivalent in the projective space. Hence, $\mathbf{F}$ is a projective element of 3×3 matrix. One of its nonzero element can act as the proportional scale factor for the remaining 8 elements. Further the constraint on the singularity reduces its degree of freedom (d.o.f.) by one. Hence, it has seven independent parameters or d.o.f.

- Epipoles: The epipoles lie on the respective epipolar lines. The epipoles are the intersections of all the epipolar lines of the respective camera. The relation of epipoles, (e, e'), with fundamental matrix are given by the point containment relationships of epipoles on their respective epipolar lines, which is expressed in Eq. 12.14.

$$e^\top (\mathbf{F}^\top x') = (\mathbf{F}e)^\top {x'}^\top = 0 \tag{12.14}$$

This implies, $\mathbf{F}e = 0$. Hence, e is the right null vector of $\mathbf{F}$. Likewise, $e'^\top \mathbf{F} = 0$, which implies, e' is the left null vector of $\mathbf{F}$.

Numerical Example

Consider the following fundamental matrix $\mathbf{F}$. A point in 3-D $\mathbf{X}$ is imaged as $(1,-1)$ in the first view, and $(6, 6)$ in the second view.

$$\mathbf{F} = \begin{bmatrix} 1 & 6 & 1 \\ 5 & 3 & 1 \\ 4 & 2 & 4 \end{bmatrix}$$

Can you check whether the above statement is true?

Solution

If $x'^T F x = 0$, then statement should be correct. But, It is to be noted that F is not singular. Hence, it is False.

Numerical Example

Consider the following stereo imaging matrices given by $\mathbf{P} = [\mathbf{I}|\mathbf{0}]$ (the reference camera) and $\mathbf{P}'$ as follows.

$$\begin{bmatrix} 3 & 2 & 1 & 4 \\ 6 & 1 & 5 & 2 \\ 1 & 2 & 3 & 1 \end{bmatrix}$$

Compute the fundamental matrix of the system.

Solution

$$M = \begin{bmatrix} 3 & 2 & 1 \\ 6 & 1 & 5 \\ 1 & 2 & 3 \end{bmatrix} \qquad [m]_\times = \begin{bmatrix} 0 & -1 & 2 \\ 1 & 0 & -4 \\ -2 & 4 & 0 \end{bmatrix}$$

$$F = [m]_\times M = \begin{bmatrix} -4 & 3 & 1 \\ -1 & -6 & -11 \\ 18 & 0 & 18 \end{bmatrix}$$

Numerical Example

Consider the following stereo imaging matrices given by P (the reference camera) and P'.

$$P = \begin{bmatrix} 5 & 7 & 1 & 2 \\ 1 & 6 & 3 & 5 \\ 9 & 3 & 2 & 6 \end{bmatrix} \qquad P' = \begin{bmatrix} 3 & 4 & 1 & 2 \\ 1 & 7 & 4 & 6 \\ 6 & 2 & 5 & 1 \end{bmatrix}$$

Answer the following.

   I) Find camera center C for the given P.

  II) Compute the right epipole e'.

 III) Find the homography induced by plane at infinity, (H_∞), for mapping each x_i to x'_i .

 IV) Find the fundamental matrix F.

  V) Given an image point $(10, 30)$ of the reference camera (P), compute the epipolar line of P'.

 VI) Given an image point $(10, 30)$ of the reference camera (P), compute its two end image points of P'.

Solution

   I)

$$C = -M^{-1}p_4 = -\frac{1}{139} \begin{bmatrix} 41 \\ -29 \\ 276 \end{bmatrix}$$

II)

$$e' = P' \begin{bmatrix} C \\ 1 \end{bmatrix} = \begin{bmatrix} 0.0035 \\ 0.0756 \\ 1.0 \end{bmatrix}$$

III)

$$H_\infty = M'M^{-1} = \frac{1}{139} \begin{bmatrix} 58 & 19 & 12 \\ -26 & 188 & 9 \\ -187 & 176 & 177 \end{bmatrix}$$

IV)

$$F = [e']_\times H_\pi = \begin{bmatrix} -0.8777 & 12.9209 & -0.3237 \\ 4.3381 & -1.3597 & -0.8417 \\ 0.3309 & 0.0576 & 0.0647 \end{bmatrix}$$

V)

$$l = F \begin{bmatrix} 10 \\ 30 \\ 1 \end{bmatrix} = \begin{bmatrix} 74.2102 \\ -16.6671 \\ 1 \end{bmatrix}$$

VI) One of the end points is the right epipole e'. The other endpoint is the transformation of the point using the Homography at infinity H_∞.

$$x' = H_\infty \begin{bmatrix} 10 \\ 30 \\ 1 \end{bmatrix} = \begin{bmatrix} 0.3239 \\ 1.5024 \\ 1 \end{bmatrix}$$

Numerical Example

Consider the following fundamental matrix of a stereo imaging system.

$$F = \begin{bmatrix} 2 & 3 & 7 \\ 5 & 7 & 17 \\ 19 & 26 & 64 \end{bmatrix}$$

Suppose an image point in the left camera is given by $(5, 6)$ in $\mathbb{R}^2$. Find the corresponding epipolar line in the image of right camera.

Solution

$$l' = \mathbf{F}[5\ 6\ 1]^\top = \begin{bmatrix} 35 \\ 84 \\ 315 \end{bmatrix}$$

12.2.2 | Properties of an essential matrix

The fundamental matrix defines a stereo configuration, even when the cameras are not calibrated. For calibrated cameras, the fundamental matrix gets simplified to an essential matrix. Consider the projection matrix of the reference camera, expressed in the canonical form as $\mathbf{P} = \mathbf{K}[\mathbf{I}|\mathbf{0}]$. The projection matrix of the other camera is defined by its rotation and translation parameters, as $\mathbf{P}' = \mathbf{K}'[\mathbf{R}|\mathbf{t}]$. Considering the image coordinates in normalized image coordinate system, the coordinates in the calibrated image planes are given by Eq. 12.15 by applying the inverses of the respective calibration matrices.

$$\begin{aligned} \mathbf{x}_c &= \mathbf{K}^{-1}\mathbf{x} \\ \mathbf{x}'_c &= \mathbf{K}'^{-1}\mathbf{x}' \end{aligned} \tag{12.15}$$

Then, the relationship of the fundamental matrix (in this case, the essential matrix, $\mathbf{E}$) with the image coordinates is given by Eq. 12.16.

$$\mathbf{x}'^\top_c \mathbf{E}\mathbf{x}_c = 0 \tag{12.16}$$

To compute the essential matrix from the fundamental matrix, consider the relationship of the fundamental matrix with the image coordinates, $\mathbf{x}'^\top \mathbf{F}\mathbf{x} = 0$. Using this with Eq. 12.15, the relationship between the fundamental and essential matrices is expressed by Eq. 12.17.

$$\begin{aligned} \mathbf{x}'^\top \mathbf{F}\mathbf{x} &= 0 \\ \implies (\mathbf{K}'\mathbf{x}'_c)^\top \mathbf{F}(\mathbf{K}\mathbf{x}_c) &= 0 \\ \implies \mathbf{x}'^\top_c \mathbf{K}'^\top \mathbf{F}(\mathbf{K}\mathbf{x}_c) &= 0 \\ \implies \mathbf{x}'^\top_c (\mathbf{K}'^\top \mathbf{F}(\mathbf{K})\mathbf{x}_c) &= 0 \\ \implies \mathbf{E} &= \mathbf{K}'^\top \mathbf{F}\mathbf{K} \end{aligned} \tag{12.17}$$

Similarly, the fundamental matrix can be computed from the essential matrix by using Eq. 12.19.

$$\mathbf{F} = \mathbf{K}'^{-\top}\mathbf{E}\mathbf{K}^{-1} \tag{12.18}$$

Using Eq. 12.12 and 12.19, the fundamental matrix can be expressed as in Eq. 12.19.

$$\mathbf{F} = \mathbf{K}'^{-\top}[t]_\times \mathbf{R}\mathbf{K}^{-1} \tag{12.19}$$

where $\mathbf{E} = [t]_\times \mathbf{R}$ is the form of essential matrix.

Here, the essential matrix, $\mathbf{E}$ has only six elements, three parameters related to the translation of camera center and three parameters related to the rotation of axes. Among them, one of the parameters represents the scale factor. So, the d.o.f. of $\mathbf{E}$ is five. Also, the relationship of epipoles, in their canonical representation, with the essential matrix is given by Eq. 12.20.

$$\mathbf{E}e_c = e_c'^{\top}\mathbf{E} = 0 \tag{12.20}$$

The rank of $\mathbf{E}$ is 2 and $\text{Det}(\mathbf{E}) = 0$.

Numerical Example

Compute the essential matrix $\mathbf{E}$, provided the calibration matrices of two cameras in a stereo setup as $\mathbf{K} = \begin{bmatrix} 4 & 3 & 2 \\ 0 & 4 & 3 \\ 0 & 0 & 1 \end{bmatrix}$ and $\mathbf{K}' = \begin{bmatrix} 1 & 1 & 2 \\ 0 & 2 & 3 \\ 0 & 0 & 1 \end{bmatrix}$ along with fundamental matrix $\mathbf{F} = \begin{bmatrix} 1 & 2 & -1 \\ -1 & 1 & -1 \\ -1 & -2 & 1 \end{bmatrix}$.

Solution

Essential matrix $\mathbf{E} = \mathbf{K}'^{\top}\mathbf{F}\mathbf{K} = \begin{bmatrix} 4 & 11 & 7 \\ -4 & 13 & 7 \\ -8 & 14 & 7 \end{bmatrix}$.

12.3 | Pure translation

Consider a special case of the stereo setup, where only translation is involved in the positioning of the cameras without any rotation, which is illustrated in Fig. 12.5. The projection matrices, in this case, are expressed as in Eq. 12.21.

$$\mathbf{P} = [\mathbf{K}|0]$$
$$\mathbf{P}' = \mathbf{K}'[\mathbf{I}|t] = [\mathbf{K}'|\mathbf{K}'t] \tag{12.21}$$

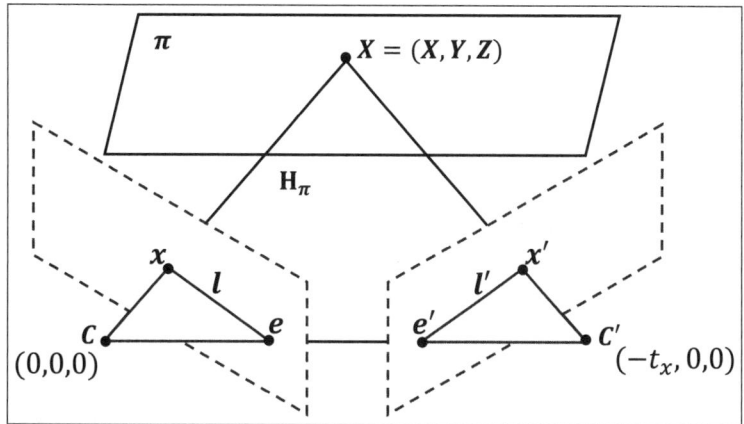

Figure 12.5 Illustration of stereo camera setup with pure translation.

where $\mathbf{K}'t$ represents the translation of the camera. The corresponding fundamental matrix is given by Eq. 12.22.

$$\mathbf{F} = [e']_\times \mathbf{K}'\mathbf{I}\mathbf{K}^{-1} = [e']_\times \mathbf{K}'\mathbf{K}^{-1} \tag{12.22}$$

For $\mathbf{K} = \mathbf{K}'$, Eq. 12.22 further reduces to Eq. 12.23.

$$\mathbf{F} = [e']_\times = \begin{bmatrix} 0 & -e'_z & e'_y \\ e'_z & 0 & -e'_x \\ -e'_y & e'_x & 0 \end{bmatrix}. \tag{12.23}$$

For the stereo setup with camera matrices as in Eq. 12.21, the first (reference) camera is at the origin. The translation, t, between the two cameras is given by Eq. 12.24, where the rotation matrix is an identity matrix.

$$t = \begin{bmatrix} t_x \\ 0 \\ 0 \end{bmatrix} \tag{12.24}$$

For 3-D reconstruction of a scene, it is necessary to compute the depth under the condition of pure translation, t. In general, the translation vector is expressed as $t = -\mathbf{R}\tilde{C}$, where $\tilde{C}$ is the camera center in world coordinates. Since $\mathbf{R} = \mathbf{I}$, center of the camera is given by, $\tilde{C} = -t$. That is, with respect to the reference camera, the camera center of the second camera is $[-t_x \ \ 0 \ \ 0]^\top$. The scene point, $\tilde{X} = [X \ Y \ Z]$, in nonhomogenous world coordinate system, from the first and the second cameras is given in Eq. 12.25.

$$\tilde{X} = Z\mathbf{K}^{-1}x$$
$$\tilde{X} + t = Z\mathbf{K}'^{-1}x' \tag{12.25}$$

Since there is no rotation involved, the principal plane is the same XY-plane. So, the Z-coordinate can be computed as the corresponding depth by subtracting the two equations in Eq. 12.25 and assuming $\mathbf{K} = \mathbf{K}'$, which is given by Eq. 12.26.

$$Z\mathbf{K}^{-1}(\boldsymbol{x}' - \boldsymbol{x}) = (\tilde{\boldsymbol{X}} + \boldsymbol{t}) - \tilde{\boldsymbol{X}} = \boldsymbol{t} \implies \boldsymbol{x}' = \boldsymbol{x} + \frac{\mathbf{K}\boldsymbol{t}}{Z} \tag{12.26}$$

Further, by considering the focal length, f, as the only parameter in the calibration matrix, where other parameters are initialized to 0 (i.e., the principal point is the center of the image coordinates and there is no skew), the calibration matrix can be expressed in the form of Eq. 12.27.

$$\mathbf{K} = \begin{bmatrix} f & 0 & 0 \\ 0 & f & 0 \\ 0 & 0 & 1 \end{bmatrix} \tag{12.27}$$

Using Eqs. 12.24, 12.26, and 12.27, the depth parameter can be computed as in Eq. 12.28.

$$Z = \frac{ft_x}{x' - x} \tag{12.28}$$

Here, the value $x' - x$, is the spatial distance or shift along the X-axis between the two camera centers, which is called *disparity*. The depth of the world point can be computed from the stereo camera configuration by evaluating the disparity at each pixel location in corresponding stereo images.

Numerical Example

Suppose the motion of the cameras is a pure translation with no rotation and no change in the internal parameters. One may assume that the two cameras are: $\mathbf{P} = \mathbf{K}[\mathbf{I}|\mathbf{0}]$ and $\mathbf{P}' = \mathbf{K}[\mathbf{I}|\boldsymbol{t}]$. If the camera translation is parallel to the x-axis, then $\boldsymbol{e}' = (1, 0, 0)^{\top}$. Compute fundamental matrix from the given information. Consider $\boldsymbol{x} = (3, 5)$ is an image point on the first image. Compute the corresponding epipolar line in the second image.

Solution

$$\mathbf{F} = [\boldsymbol{e}']_{\times} = \begin{bmatrix} 0 & 0 & 0 \\ 0 & 0 & -1 \\ 0 & 1 & 0 \end{bmatrix}$$

$$\boldsymbol{l} = \mathbf{F}\boldsymbol{x} = [\boldsymbol{e}']_{\times}\boldsymbol{x} = \begin{bmatrix} 0 \\ -1 \\ 5 \end{bmatrix}$$

12.4 | General motion of camera

The case of pure translation can be generalized to address general motion of camera, where two cameras are arbitrarily configured, as shown in Fig. 12.6. Here, the cameras are not necessarily in parallel stereo configuration. Consider the reference camera with a projection matrix, $\mathbf{P} = \mathbf{K}[\mathbf{I}|\mathbf{0}]$, and the second camera with a projection matrix, $\mathbf{P}' = \mathbf{K}'[\mathbf{R}|\mathbf{t}]$. Here, $\mathbf{K} \neq \mathbf{K}'$, which have different focal lengths, rotation, and translation parameters. The camera center $\mathbf{C}'$ is rotated and translated with respect to $\mathbf{C}$. This problem can be mapped to a parallel stereo problem by performing some simple geometric transformation.

Consider an imaginary camera that has the same center of the reference camera, $\mathbf{C}$, but it is related to it by only the rotation with the same rotation matrix $\mathbf{R}$ in the second camera. Let the projection matrix of the imaginary camera be $\mathbf{P}^{(2)}$. Then, the homography between the two image planes, reference camera and imaginary camera, can be computed. Consider a point, $\boldsymbol{x}$ in the image of the reference camera, whose corresponding point in the second camera is $\boldsymbol{x}'$. Due to the rotational homography, let another corresponding point of $\boldsymbol{x}$ be $\boldsymbol{x}^{(2)}$ in the image plane of the imaginary camera. Since the $\mathbf{R}$ is applied to both imaginary and the second cameras, their image planes form a parallel stereo configuration. Then with the corresponding pair of points, $(\boldsymbol{x}^{(2)}, \boldsymbol{x}')$, the depth can be computed. Also, let the calibration matrix of the imaginary camera be the same as the reference camera, $\mathbf{K}$. So, the projection of a world point, $\boldsymbol{X}$, on the imaginary plane is given by Eq. 12.29.

$$\begin{aligned}
\boldsymbol{x}^{(2)} &= \mathbf{K}[\mathbf{R}|\mathbf{0}]\boldsymbol{X} \\
&= \mathbf{K}\mathbf{R}[\mathbf{I}|\mathbf{0}]\boldsymbol{X} \\
&= \mathbf{K}\mathbf{R}\mathbf{K}^{-1}\mathbf{K}[\mathbf{I}|\mathbf{0}]\boldsymbol{X} \\
&= \mathbf{K}\mathbf{R}\mathbf{K}^{-1}\boldsymbol{x}
\end{aligned} \tag{12.29}$$

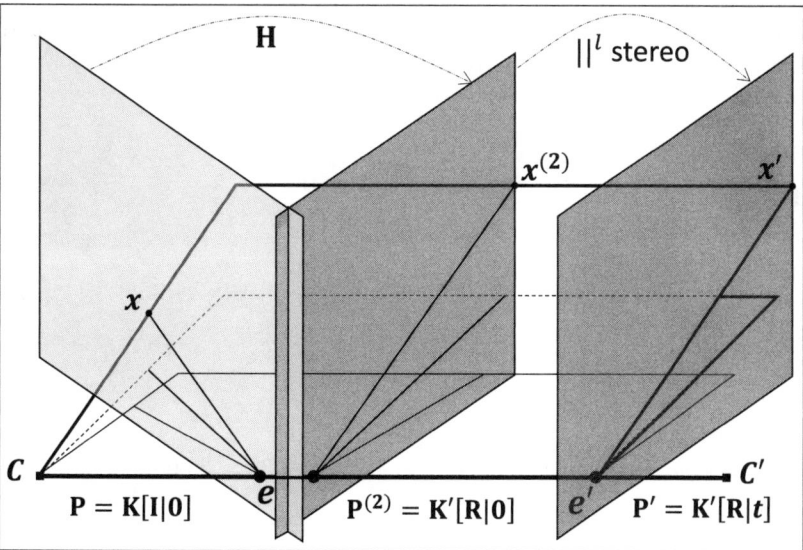

Figure 12.6 Illustration of a stereo setup with arbitrary configuration of cameras.

where $x = K[I|0]X$ is the image of the world point in the reference image plane. Also, $x^{(2)} = KRK^{-1}x$ is of the form $x^{(2)} = Hx$, where H is the rotational homography between x and $x^{(2)}$. That is, the rotational homography between x and $x^{(2)}$ is given by Eq. 12.30.

$$H = KRK^{-1} \tag{12.30}$$

Then, applying the treatment of pure translation in stereo system between the corresponding points $x^{(2)}$ and x', the relationship between x and x' can be established as in Eq. 12.31.

$$x' = x^{(2)} + \frac{K't}{Z} = KRK^{-1}x + \frac{K't}{Z} \tag{12.31}$$

The depth can be computed from Eq. 12.31 using simple algebraic operations.

Numerical Example

Consider a stereo setup with P and P' (camera matrices for left and right camera) as given below:

$$P = \begin{bmatrix} 5 & 0 & 0 & 0 \\ 0 & 5 & 0 & 0 \\ 0 & 0 & 1 & 0 \end{bmatrix} \quad P' = \begin{bmatrix} 5 & 0 & 0 & 10 \\ 0 & 5 & 0 & 0 \\ 0 & 0 & 1 & 0 \end{bmatrix}$$

If the image coordinates of a 3-D point are (4, 6) and (7.33, 6) in left and right cameras, compute its depth (Z-coordinate) in the 3-D.

Solution

$P = K[I|0]$ and $P' = K[I|t]$

$$K = \begin{bmatrix} 5 & 0 & 0 \\ 0 & 5 & 0 \\ 0 & 0 & 1 \end{bmatrix} \quad t = \begin{bmatrix} 10/5 \\ 0 \\ 0 \end{bmatrix}$$

$x' = x + (Kt)/Z \quad Z = (5 * 10/5)/(7.33 - 4) = 10/3.33 = 3.003$

12.5 | Estimation of fundamental matrix

Given a pair of corresponding two-dimensional (2-D) image points of left and right cameras from a stereo system, $(\boldsymbol{x}, \boldsymbol{x}')$, their relationship with the fundamental matrix, $\mathbf{F}$, is expressed by Eq. 12.32.

$$\boldsymbol{x'}^{\top}\mathbf{F}\boldsymbol{x} = 0 \tag{12.32}$$

The 3×3 fundamental matrix can be expanded in the form as given below.

$$\mathbf{F} = \begin{bmatrix} f_{11} & f_{12} & f_{13} \\ f_{21} & f_{22} & f_{23} \\ f_{31} & f_{32} & f_{33} \end{bmatrix} \tag{12.33}$$

With this form, Eq. 12.32 can be represented as,

$$\begin{bmatrix} x' & y' & 1 \end{bmatrix} \begin{bmatrix} f_{11} & f_{12} & f_{13} \\ f_{21} & f_{22} & f_{23} \\ f_{31} & f_{32} & f_{33} \end{bmatrix} \begin{bmatrix} x \\ y \\ 1 \end{bmatrix} = 0 \tag{12.34}$$

Eq. 12.34 can be further expanded as a transformation equation, as given by Eq. 12.35.

$$x'xf_{11} + x'yf_{12} + x'f_{13} + y'xf_{21} + y'yf_{22} + y'f_{23} + xf_{31} + yf_{32} + f_{33} = 0 \tag{12.35}$$

In the matrix notation, this is represented as in Eq. 12.36.

$$\begin{bmatrix} x'x & x'y & x' & y'x & y'y & y' & x & y & 1 \end{bmatrix} \begin{bmatrix} f_{11} \\ f_{12} \\ f_{13} \\ f_{21} \\ f_{22} \\ f_{23} \\ f_{31} \\ f_{32} \\ f_{33} \end{bmatrix} = 0 \tag{12.36}$$

This equation is represented for only one pair of corresponding points. For n pairs of point correspondences, n such equations are formed, which can be represented in the matrix form as given by Eq. 12.37.

$$
\begin{bmatrix}
x_1'x_1 & x_1'y_1 & x_1' & y_1'x_1 & y_1'y_1 & y_1' & x_1 & y_1 & 1 \\
x_2'x_2 & x_2'y_2 & x_2' & y_2'x_2 & y_2'y_2 & y_2' & x_2 & y_2 & 1 \\
\vdots & \vdots & \vdots & \vdots & \vdots & \vdots & \vdots & \vdots & \vdots \\
x_n'x_n & x_n'y_n & x_n' & y_n'x_n & y_n'y_n & y_n' & x_n & y_n & 1
\end{bmatrix}
\begin{bmatrix}
f_{11} \\ f_{12} \\ f_{13} \\ f_{21} \\ f_{22} \\ f_{23} \\ f_{31} \\ f_{32} \\ f_{33}
\end{bmatrix} = \mathbf{0}
\tag{12.37}
$$

This can be generalized and represented in a concatenated matrix form as in Eq. 12.38.

$$
\begin{bmatrix} \mathbf{A} \end{bmatrix}_{n \times 9} \begin{bmatrix} \boldsymbol{f} \end{bmatrix}_{9 \times 1} = \begin{bmatrix} \mathbf{0} \end{bmatrix}_{n \times 1}
\tag{12.38}
$$

where $\mathbf{A}$ is the data matrix and $\boldsymbol{f}$ is a vectorized form of the fundamental matrix.

Let the scaling element f_{33} be assigned to 1. With this constraint, the number of independent parameters is now eight. Also, the data matrix, $\mathbf{A}$, and the vector of fundamental matrix, $\boldsymbol{f}$, are reduced in their dimensions. In other words, the element f_{33} is removed from $\boldsymbol{f}$ and the last column is removed from $\mathbf{A}$. So, Eq. 12.38 is now represented by, Eq. 12.39.

$$
\begin{bmatrix} \mathbf{A} \end{bmatrix}_{n \times 8} \begin{bmatrix} \boldsymbol{f} \end{bmatrix}_{8 \times 1} = \begin{bmatrix} -\mathbf{1} \end{bmatrix}_{n \times 1}
\tag{12.39}
$$

In the above, there are n equations for n different pairs of corresponding points. The solution of this system of nonhomogeneous equations is obtained by performing the least squares estimate (LSE). Let the column vector in the right hand side of Eq. 12.39 be $[\boldsymbol{b}]_{n \times 1}$. Then, Eq. 12.39 is rewritten as,

$$
\mathbf{A}\boldsymbol{f} = \boldsymbol{b} = \begin{bmatrix} -\mathbf{1} \end{bmatrix}
\tag{12.40}
$$

Here, since the size of $\mathbf{A}$ is 8×8, it minimally requires eight pairs of corresponding points. When $n = 8$, the solution, $\tilde{\boldsymbol{f}}$, if $\mathbf{A}$ is nonsingular, is given by Eq. 12.41.

$$
\tilde{\boldsymbol{f}} = \mathbf{A}^{-1}b
\tag{12.41}
$$

When the number of corresponding points $n > 8$, the least squares estimate is performed to compute the solution of the system of equation in Eq. 12.39. In this case, the error term to be minimized is given as,

$$
||\mathbf{A}\boldsymbol{f} - \boldsymbol{b}||^2 = 0
\tag{12.42}
$$

The solution of Eq. 12.42 is the optimal $\boldsymbol{f}$, $\tilde{\boldsymbol{f}}$, that minimizes the norm of the matrix difference. This is computed by evaluating the pseudo inverse of the matrix, $\tilde{\mathbf{A}}$, that corresponds to minimum error, which is given by Eq. 12.43.

$$\tilde{\boldsymbol{f}} = \left[\tilde{\mathbf{A}}^\top \tilde{\mathbf{A}}\right]^{-1} \tilde{\mathbf{A}}^\top \boldsymbol{b} \tag{12.43}$$

For the set of nonhomogeneous equations, Eq. 12.43 provides the least squares estimate. This solution for the system of equations defined in Eq. 12.39 is, (1) up to the scale, and (2) solvable with minimum number of 8 point correspondences.

There is another constraint that is imposed on $\mathbf{F}$ by the property of singularity, $\text{Det}(\mathbf{F}) = 0$. With this constraint, along with the constraint of $f_{33} = 1$, the number of independent parameters in $\mathbf{F}$ is seven. Another approach to the above problem considers using seven point correspondences, since there are only seven independent parameters. This system of equations may also be solved using the technique called *direct linear transformation* (DLT) by considering only seven point correspondences from a linear combination of eigenvectors, to be discussed later in this chapter.

One of the major problems with this representation is the large range of the coordinates of the points. When the products of these coordinates are computed, they too become very large. So, the dynamic range of the coefficients in these equations of the unknown parameters vary widely. Usually, the variation is in the order of magnitudes ranging between $[1, 10000]$. Therefore, the numerical stability is relatively less in these computations, which may yield poorer results.

12.5.1 | Normalized 8-point algorithm

The normalized 8-point algorithm is a technique of solving the problem of estimation of fundamental matrix from point correspondences. Here, due to wide variations in the magnitudes of the coordinate values, the image coordinates are normalized so that they remain within the range of $[-1, 1]$. Consider that the linear transformations of 3×3 matrices $\mathscr{T}'$ and $\mathscr{T}$ are applied to coordinates of right and left images respectively, so that the coordinates in the image remain in $[-1, 1] \times [-1, 1]$. Thus, the transformation of the coordinates $\boldsymbol{x}$ and $\boldsymbol{x}'$ are given by,

$$\begin{aligned} \boldsymbol{y} &= \mathscr{T}\boldsymbol{x} \\ \boldsymbol{y}' &= \mathscr{T}'\boldsymbol{x}' \end{aligned} \tag{12.44}$$

Hence,

$$\begin{aligned} \boldsymbol{x} &= \mathscr{T}^{-1}\boldsymbol{y} \\ \boldsymbol{x}' &= \mathscr{T}'^{-1}\boldsymbol{y}' \end{aligned} \tag{12.45}$$

From the algebraic representation of the fundamental matrix in Eq. 12.32 and the representations in Eq. 12.45,

$$\begin{aligned} (\mathscr{T}'^{-1}\boldsymbol{y}')^\top \mathbf{F}(\mathscr{T}^{-1}\boldsymbol{y}) &= 0 \\ \Longrightarrow \boldsymbol{y}'^\top \mathscr{T}'^{-\top} \mathbf{F}\mathscr{T}^{-1}\boldsymbol{y} &= 0 \end{aligned} \tag{12.46}$$

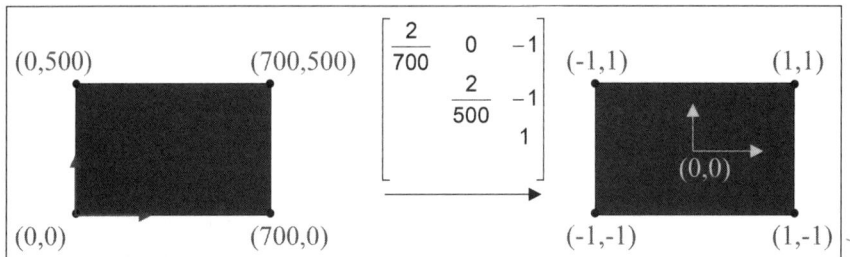

Figure 12.7 Normalizing the coordinates of an image.

From Eq. 12.46, the fundamental matrix is seen to be equivalent to the form shown in Eq. 12.47

$$\widehat{\mathbf{F}} = \mathscr{T}'^{-\top} \mathbf{F} \mathscr{T}^{-1} \tag{12.47}$$

An example of this operation is shown in Fig. 12.7. As seen in the figure, the transformation of the coordinates in the original image can be transformed to the normalized representation by multiplying the image coordinates in homogeneous representation with the matrix $\begin{bmatrix} \frac{2}{700} & 0 & -1 \\ 0 & \frac{2}{500} & -1 \\ 0 & 0 & 1 \end{bmatrix}$. It is seen that, the least squares error method yields relatively good results when the estimation of fundamental matrix is performed with normalization.

12.5.2 | The singularity constraint

The estimation of the fundamental matrix from a set of point correspondences is discussed using the constraint of setting the scale factor, $f_{33} = 1$, of the fundamental matrix, which results into estimation of eight parameters. The singularity constraint is not enforced in this case. So, the estimated 3×3 matrix is most likely to be a nonsingular matrix and then not truly a fundamental matrix. The singularity constraint is expressed by equating the determinant of $\mathbf{F}$ to 0. In this case, $\mathbf{F}$ is rank deficient, with the rank two. The objective is to get the estimation of $\mathbf{F}'$, which is very close to $\mathbf{F}$. This can be achieved by minimizing the Frobenius norm between $\mathbf{F}$ and $\mathbf{F}'$, which is expressed as in Eq. 12.48.

$$\min \|\mathbf{F} - \mathbf{F}'\|_F \tag{12.48}$$

A close approximation of a singular matrix of rank 2 from the estimated $\mathbf{F}$ is obtained by the singular value decomposition (SVD) of the matrix. Let the SVD of $\mathbf{F}$ be given by,

$$\mathbf{F} = \mathbf{U} \begin{bmatrix} \sigma_1 & & \\ & \sigma_2 & \\ & & \sigma_3 \end{bmatrix} \mathbf{V}^{\top} \tag{12.49}$$

where $\Sigma = \begin{bmatrix} \sigma_1 & & \\ & \sigma_2 & \\ & & \sigma_3 \end{bmatrix}$ is a diagonal matrix with $\sigma_1 \geq \sigma_2 \geq \sigma_3$, $\mathbf{U} = [\boldsymbol{u}_1\ \boldsymbol{u}_2\ \boldsymbol{u}_3]$ is the left orthogonal matrix, and $\mathbf{V} = [\boldsymbol{v}_1\ \boldsymbol{v}_2\ \boldsymbol{v}_3]$ is the right orthogonal matrix. Here, with normalization, both $\mathbf{U}$ and $\mathbf{V}$ can also be formed by orthonormal column vectors. Since we are dealing only with square matrix, $\mathbf{F}$, Eq. 12.49 can be decomposed in the form of Eq. 12.50.

$$\mathbf{F} = \boldsymbol{u}_1 \sigma_1 \boldsymbol{v}_1{}^\top + \boldsymbol{u}_2 \sigma_2 \boldsymbol{v}_2{}^\top + \boldsymbol{u}_3 \sigma_3 \boldsymbol{v}_3{}^\top \tag{12.50}$$

By the above SVD, the given matrix is expressed as a superposition of three rank-1 matrices.

In a singular matrix, one of the singular values is zero. The number of nonzero singular values provides the rank of the corresponding matrix. Since the considered $\mathbf{F}$ is seen to be of rank-2 and all the singular values are enforced to be positive, the minimum singular value, σ_3 is set to 0. Thus, by assigning the third singular value $\sigma_3 = 0$, an approximation of $\mathbf{F}$ is obtained. Hence, the closest rank-2 approximation of $\mathbf{F}$ is given by,

$$\mathbf{F}' = \mathbf{U} \begin{bmatrix} \sigma_1 & & \\ & \sigma_2 & \\ & & 0 \end{bmatrix} \mathbf{V}^\top = \boldsymbol{u}_1 \sigma_1 \boldsymbol{v}_1{}^\top + \boldsymbol{u}_2 \sigma_2 \boldsymbol{v}_2{}^\top \tag{12.51}$$

We may note that if $\mathbf{F}$ is not singular, the epipolar lines do not converge for the estimated $\mathbf{F}$ from the data set of point-correspondences. Ideally, all the epipolar lines should converge to a single point in the image plane, which is the epipole of that stereo system.

Singularity constraint for the essential matrix

As discussed earlier, the essential matrix is the same as the fundamental matrix, when the camera is calibrated. In this case, all the image coordinates are converted into the canonical form and the fundamental matrix is expressed only by the parameters of rotation and translation of the world coordinates to the camera coordinate system. So, extrinsic parameters are the only constraints in this case. Since there are six parameters in the essential matrix, $\mathbf{E}$, where one of them may be taken as the scale factor, there are only five independent parameters. Since the cameras are calibrated, their calibration matrix is known. By using the required transformations, $\mathbf{E}$ can also be estimated by any of the techniques that are used in the estimation of $\mathbf{F}$. Here, the estimation of $\mathbf{E}$ is also refined by the SVD to enforce the constraints of singularity.

Let the SVD of $\mathbf{E}$ be given by,

$$\mathbf{E} = \mathbf{U}\mathbf{D}\mathbf{V}^\top \text{ where } \mathbf{D} = \text{Diag}(a, b, c) \text{ with } a \geq b \geq c \tag{12.52}$$

An interesting property of essential matrix is to have two equal singular values. This is enforced by assigning the average of the two singular values to both a and b, and then computing the approximate essential matrix. The closest rank-2 approximation of $\mathbf{E}$ is computed by using the two singular values, a and b, as given by Eq. 12.53.

$$\widehat{\mathbf{E}} = \mathbf{U}\widehat{\mathbf{D}}\mathbf{V}^{\top} \text{ where } \widehat{\mathbf{D}} = \mathrm{Diag}(\frac{a+b}{2}, \frac{a+b}{2}, 0) \tag{12.53}$$

The minimum case: estimation from seven point correspondences

As the number of independent parameters in a fundamental matrix is seven (refer to Section 12.2.1), the fundamental matrix can be computed using a minimum of seven point correspondences. Consider the set of characteristic equations formed by the seven pairs of corresponding points. Let the coefficient matrix be denoted by $\mathbf{A}$ with dimension 7×9 (refer to Section 12.5.2). Let the SVD of $\mathbf{A}$ be given by Eq. 12.54.

$$\mathbf{A} = \mathbf{U}_{7\times 7}\mathrm{Diag}(\sigma_1, ..., \sigma_7, 0, 0)\mathbf{V}_{9\times 9}^{\top} \tag{12.54}$$

The SVD in Eq. 12.54 results in the last two columns of $\mathbf{V}$ as zero vectors, $\boldsymbol{F}_1$ and $\boldsymbol{F}_2$. The solution is computed as a linear combination of $\boldsymbol{F}_1$ and $\boldsymbol{F}_2$, which is given by Eq. 12.55.

$$\mathbf{F}_1 + \lambda\mathbf{F}_2 = 0 \tag{12.55}$$

However, the form of the matrix obtained by Eq. 12.55 is a rank-2 matrix. Since it is a rank deficient matrix, its determinant has to be 0. The value of λ is evaluated for $|\mathbf{F}_1 + \lambda\mathbf{F}_2| = 0$. Since both F_1 and F_2 are 3×3 matrices, the determinant results in a cubic polynomial, where a real valued solution for λ is desired. Since the determinant is a cubic polynomial, there are one or three possible solutions. Hence, there may be three possible solutions of fundamental matrices. In essence, at first, the eigen-decomposition of the $\mathbf{A}^{\top}\mathbf{A}$ matrix is performed. λ, which is the coefficient of linear combination of the eigen vectors, is solved by enforcing the equality of determinant of the linear combination to 0. Then from the values of λ the solutions of the fundamental matrix are obtained.

12.5.3 | Parametric representation of $\mathbf{F}$

The fundamental matrix can also be represented in a different parametric form. Though there are seven independent parameters in $\mathbf{F}$, not necessarily its representation includes all the intrinsic characteristics. If $\mathbf{F}$ has to be represented with more number of parameters, the dependencies among the parameters are to be enforced through specification of the necessary constraints. This is not always ensured, in which case, such constraint enforcing operations are taken care of in a post-estimation process, similar to equating the determinant of the matrix with 0. The over parameterized representation of $\mathbf{F}$ is observed in its following factors.

$$\mathbf{F} = [e]_{\times}\mathbf{M} \tag{12.56}$$

where e is an epipole. For the above expression, $\mathbf{F}$ can be described by 12 parameters, namely three parameters of e and nine parameters of $\mathbf{M}$. A left epipolar parameterization of $\mathbf{F}$ is given in Eq. 12.57.

$$\mathbf{F} = \begin{bmatrix} a & b & \alpha a + \beta b \\ c & d & \alpha c + \beta d \\ e & f & \alpha e + \beta f \end{bmatrix} \tag{12.57}$$

Here, $e = \begin{bmatrix} \alpha & \beta & -1 \end{bmatrix}^{\top}$ is the left epipole. In this representation also, there are eight independent parameters, a, b, c, d, e, f, α, and β. Interestingly, the singularity constraint on $\mathbf{F}$, enforced by $|\mathbf{F}| = 0$, is realized here, as the third column of $\mathbf{F}$ is the linear combination of its first and second columns. The representation of $\mathbf{F}$ using both the epipoles as parameters is given by Eq. 12.58.

$$\mathbf{F} = \begin{bmatrix} a & b & \alpha a + \beta b \\ c & d & \alpha c + \beta d \\ \alpha' a + \beta' c & \alpha' b + \beta' d & \alpha' \alpha a + \beta' \alpha c + \alpha' \beta b + \beta' \beta d \end{bmatrix} \tag{12.58}$$

where $e = \begin{bmatrix} \alpha & \beta & -1 \end{bmatrix}^{\top}$ and $e' = \begin{bmatrix} \alpha' & \beta' & -1 \end{bmatrix}^{\top}$ are the left and right epipoles, respectively, and the eight independent parameters are a, b, c, d, α, β, α', and β'.

12.6 | Retrieving the camera matrices from $\mathbf{F}$

Given the camera matrices, computation of the fundamental matrix is straight and simple, as seen in Section 12.5. However, given the fundamental matrix, estimating the camera matrices requires more analysis. Let us consider that the projection matrices of left and right cameras are, $\mathbf{P}$ and $\mathbf{P}'$, respectively. Then the fundamental matrix, $\mathbf{F}$, is uniquely computed, and it is independent of the choice of the world frame. We denote this relationship using the notations, $(\mathbf{P}, \mathbf{P}') \to \mathbf{F}$.

$\mathbf{F}$ is also an intrinsic entity corresponding to a stereo system if the relative position and orientation of the two cameras remain the same. Thus, for a fixed world coordinate system, if the stereo system is moved to any point by keeping relative orientation and positions of the two cameras the same, the fundamental matrix stays unchanged. But. it is not true for the projection matrices. If the corresponding image coordinate points and the world coordinate points change, with the movement of the stereo system, the projection matrices get affected. But in this case too, even the world coordinate changes, as the stereo system remains stationary, the fundamental matrix remains the same, since the corresponding pairs of points for a scene point are the same pairs in left and right image planes. The fundamental matrix solely depends on the image coordinates. A translation of the stereo setup, including changes in the world coordinate system, does not perturb $\mathbf{F}$. Thus we can say that, for a given pair of projection matrices $(\mathbf{P}, \mathbf{P}')$, a unique fundamental matrix, $\mathbf{F}$, exists. But the reverse is not true. There exists a family of pairs of projection matrices having the same fundamental matrix for their stereo setup. This is explained by a homography matrix, $\mathbf{H}$ (a 4×4 nonsingular matrix), in $\mathbb{P}^3$, such that,

$$(\mathbf{P}, \mathbf{P}') \to \mathbf{F} \implies (\mathbf{PH}, \mathbf{P}'\mathbf{H}) \to \mathbf{F} \tag{12.59}$$

Consider a scene point $\mathbf{X}$, which is a 4×1 column vector in its homogeneous coordinates. The corresponding pair of points in the stereo system are $\mathbf{PX}$ and $\mathbf{P}'\mathbf{X}$. The relationship is represented using the notations, $\mathbf{PX} \leftrightarrow \mathbf{P}'\mathbf{X}$. Consider a linear transformation of the scene point by a homography matrix, $\mathbf{H}$, which is a 4×4 nonsingular matrix, as given by Eq. 12.60.

$$\mathbf{X}' = \mathbf{H}^{-1}\mathbf{X} \tag{12.60}$$

Consider another pair of projection matrices, $\mathbf{PH}$ and $\mathbf{P}'\mathbf{H}$, so that, the corresponding pairs of points are now given by Eq. 12.61.

$$(\mathbf{PH})(\mathbf{H}^{-1}\mathbf{X}) \leftrightarrow (\mathbf{P}'\mathbf{H})(\mathbf{H}^{-1}\mathbf{X}) \implies \mathbf{PX} \leftrightarrow \mathbf{P}'\mathbf{X} \tag{12.61}$$

Which results in the same pair of corresponding points, $\mathbf{PX}$ and $\mathbf{P}'\mathbf{X}$. Similarly, a set of projection matrices in the form of $(\mathbf{PH}, \mathbf{P}'\mathbf{H})$ and the corresponding scene points as $\mathbf{H}^{-1}\mathbf{X}$ also results in a unique fundamental matrix between them, as given in Eq. 12.59. Hence, a fundamental matrix $\mathbf{F}$ does not uniquely map to a pair of $(\mathbf{P}, \mathbf{P}')$. It corresponds to a family of pairs of projection matrices as discussed above.

The canonical representations of the projection matrices and the corresponding fundamental matrix are given by Eq. 12.62.

$$((\mathbf{P} = [\mathbf{I}|\mathbf{0}]), (\mathbf{P}' = [\mathbf{M}|\boldsymbol{m}])) \to (\mathbf{F} = [\boldsymbol{m}]_\times \mathbf{M}) \tag{12.62}$$

In this stereo system, $\boldsymbol{m}$ is the right epipole and $\mathbf{M}$ denotes the homography at infinity. The relationship between the d.o.f. of $\mathbf{F}$ and the d.o.f. of projection matrices, $(\mathbf{P}, \mathbf{P}')$, can also be established from Eq. 12.62. The number of independent parameters of a projection matrix, (i.e., the d.o.f. of $\mathbf{P}$) is 11. So, in a stereo setup, with a pair of projection matrices, the maximum number of independent parameters is given by d.o.f. of $\mathbf{P}$ + d.o.f. of $\mathbf{P}' = 22$ (combining two projection matrices). These projection matrices are related by a homography matrix $\mathbf{H}$, that is derived from the projective elements, where d.o.f. of $\mathbf{H} = 15$. Effectively, d.o.f. of $\mathbf{F}$ is $22 - 15 = 7$, which is the number of independent parameters in $\mathbf{F}$.

It can also be shown that, $\mathbf{F}$ corresponds to $(\mathbf{P}, \mathbf{P}')$ if and only if $\mathbf{P}^\top \mathbf{FP}$ is a skew symmetric matrix.[2] This is also a way to check the compatibility between $\mathbf{F}$ and $(\mathbf{P}, \mathbf{P}')$. A $n \times n$ skew symmetric matrix, $\mathbf{S}$, has the following property.

$$\mathbf{X}^\top \mathbf{SX} = 0, \ \forall \mathbf{X} \in \mathrm{R}^n \tag{12.63}$$

---

[2] A matrix, $\mathbf{A}$, is a skew symmetric when the transpose of the matrix is equal to negative of the matrix. That is, $\mathbf{A}^\top = -\mathbf{A}$.

The above property for a skew symmetric matrix is both necessary and sufficient. It implies that if $\boldsymbol{X}^\top \mathbf{S} \boldsymbol{X} = 0$, $\forall \boldsymbol{X}$, $\mathbf{S}$ is a skew symmetric matrix. For a fundamental matrix $\mathbf{F}$, we show that $\mathbf{P'}^\top \mathbf{F} \mathbf{P}$ is a skew symmetric matrix by the following argument.

The expression in Eq. 12.63 can be rewritten in the following form.

$$\boldsymbol{X}^\top \mathbf{P'}^\top \mathbf{F} \mathbf{P} \boldsymbol{X} = (\mathbf{P'} \boldsymbol{X})^\top \mathbf{F} (\mathbf{P} \boldsymbol{X}) = \boldsymbol{x'}^\top \mathbf{F} \boldsymbol{x} = 0 \qquad (12.64)$$

The above is true for any $\boldsymbol{X}$ in $\mathbb{P}^3$. The expression in Eq. 12.63 holds true iff $\mathbf{P'}^\top \mathbf{F} \mathbf{P}$ is skew symmetric.

Another relationship that associates $\mathbf{F}$ with a skew symmetric matrix $\mathbf{S}$ is that the projection matrices of the form $\mathbf{P} = [\mathbf{I}|\mathbf{0}]$ and $\mathbf{P'} = [\mathbf{SF}|\boldsymbol{e'}]$, correspond to the fundamental matrix $\mathbf{F}$, where $\boldsymbol{e'}$ is any three vector and $\mathbf{S}$ is a skew symmetric. We may note that $\boldsymbol{e'}$ is the right epipole of $\mathbf{F}$, such that, $\boldsymbol{e'}^\top \mathbf{F} = 0$. A good choice[3] of $\mathbf{S}$ could be $[\boldsymbol{e'}]_\times$. Thus, given a fundamental matrix $\mathbf{F}$, it is always possible to get a pair of projection matrices. However, there exist a family of pairs of projection matrices for a given $\mathbf{F}$. The representation of this family of pairs of projection matrices is given in Eq. 12.65

$$([\mathbf{I}|\mathbf{0}], [[\boldsymbol{e'}]_\times \mathbf{F} | \boldsymbol{e'}]) \rightarrow \mathbf{F}$$
$$([\mathbf{I}|\mathbf{0}], [[\boldsymbol{e'}]_\times \mathbf{F} + \boldsymbol{e'} \boldsymbol{v}^\top | k\boldsymbol{e'}]) \rightarrow \mathbf{F} \qquad (12.65)$$

where $\boldsymbol{v}$ is a 3-D vector, k is a constant, $k\boldsymbol{e'}$ is the epipole (similar to $\boldsymbol{e'}$), and $\boldsymbol{e'} \boldsymbol{v}^\top$ is a 3×3 matrix.

Numerical Example

Compute the left epipole of following fundamental matrix of a stereo imaging system.

$$\begin{bmatrix} 2 & 3 & 7 \\ 5 & 7 & 17 \\ 19 & 26 & 64 \end{bmatrix}$$

---

[3] The epipole, $\boldsymbol{e'}$, can also written as $\boldsymbol{e'} = \begin{bmatrix} e'_x \\ e'_y \\ e'_z \end{bmatrix}$. From $\boldsymbol{e'}$, the operator $[\boldsymbol{e'}]_\times$ is expressed in the form of

$[\boldsymbol{e'}]_\times = \begin{bmatrix} 0 & -e'_z & e'_y \\ e'_z & 0 & -e'_x \\ -e'_y & e'_x & 0 \end{bmatrix}$. Here, $[\boldsymbol{e'}]_\times$ is also a skew symmetric matrix.

Solution

Right zero of **F**

$$\begin{bmatrix} 2 & 3 & 7 \\ 5 & 7 & 17 \end{bmatrix} \begin{bmatrix} e_{L_1} \\ e_{L_2} \\ 1 \end{bmatrix} = 0;$$

$$\begin{bmatrix} e_{L_1} \\ e_{L_2} \end{bmatrix} = -\begin{bmatrix} 2 & 3 \\ 5 & 7 \end{bmatrix}^{-1} \begin{bmatrix} 7 \\ 17 \end{bmatrix} = -\begin{bmatrix} -7 & 3 \\ 5 & -2 \end{bmatrix} \begin{bmatrix} 7 \\ 17 \end{bmatrix} = \begin{bmatrix} -2 \\ -1 \end{bmatrix}$$

Hence, the left epipole $= \begin{bmatrix} -2 \\ -1 \end{bmatrix}$.

Numerical Example

Compute the right epipole of the following fundamental matrix of a stereo imaging system.

$$\begin{bmatrix} 2 & 3 & 7 \\ 5 & 7 & 17 \\ 19 & 26 & 64 \end{bmatrix}$$

Solution

$$\mathbf{F}^\top = \begin{bmatrix} 2 & 5 & 19 \\ 3 & 7 & 26 \\ 7 & 17 & 64 \end{bmatrix}$$

Right zero of $\mathbf{F}^\top$

$$\begin{bmatrix} 2 & 5 & 19 \\ 3 & 7 & 26 \end{bmatrix} \begin{bmatrix} e_{R_1} \\ e_{R2} \\ 1 \end{bmatrix} = 0$$

$$\begin{bmatrix} e_{R1} \\ e_{R2} \end{bmatrix} = -\begin{bmatrix} 2 & 5 \\ 3 & 7 \end{bmatrix}^{-1} \begin{bmatrix} 19 \\ 26 \end{bmatrix} = -\begin{bmatrix} -7 & 5 \\ 3 & -2 \end{bmatrix} \begin{bmatrix} 19 \\ 26 \end{bmatrix} = \begin{bmatrix} 3 \\ -5 \end{bmatrix}$$

Hence, the right epipole $= \begin{bmatrix} 3 \\ -5 \end{bmatrix}$.

Numerical Example

Consider the following fundamental matrix.

$$\begin{bmatrix} -4 & 0 & 0 \\ 2 & 4 & 6 \\ 2 & -4 & -6 \end{bmatrix}$$

(i) Compute the left epipole in the image coordinate.

(ii) Compute the right epipole in the image coordinate.

(iii) Compute the epipolar line in the right image plane for the image point $(1, 2)$ of the left camera.

Solution

(i) $(0, -1.5)$

(ii) $(1, 1)$

(iii) $(1, -4, 3)$

12.6.1 | Retrieving camera matrices from $\mathbf{E}$

A matrix, $\mathbf{E}$, is an essential matrix if and only if two of its singular values are equal and the third singular value is zero. By matrix decomposition, $\mathbf{E}$ can be decomposed into two matrices, as given in Eq. 12.66.

$$\mathbf{E} = [\boldsymbol{t}]_\times \mathbf{R} \tag{12.66}$$

where $[\boldsymbol{t}]_\times$ is a skew symmetric matrix and $\mathbf{R}$ is a rotation matrix, which is also an orthogonal matrix. With this decomposition of $\mathbf{E}$, at least a pair of projection matrices are obtained as, $\mathbf{P} = [\mathbf{I}|\mathbf{0}]$, and $\mathbf{P}' = [\mathbf{R}|\boldsymbol{t}]$.

The decomposition of the essential matrix from Eq. 12.66 may be as follows.

$$\mathbf{E} = \mathbf{S}\mathbf{R} \tag{12.67}$$

which is a product of a skew symmetric matrix, $\mathbf{S}$, and an orthonormal matrix $\mathbf{R}$ (also called the *rotation matrix*, in this context). By SVD, $\mathbf{E}$ is expressed as in the form of Eq. 12.68.

$$\mathbf{E} = \mathbf{U}\,\mathrm{Diag}(1,1,0)\mathbf{V}^\top \tag{12.68}$$

where $\mathrm{Diag}(1,1,0)$ is a 3×3 diagonal matrix whose principal diagonal elements are 1, 1, and 0. From Eq. 12.67 and 12.68, there are two possible decompositions of $\mathbf{E}$ with the representations of the skew-symmetric matrix and the rotation matrix as in Eq. 12.69.

$$\mathbf{S} = \mathbf{U}\mathbf{Z}\mathbf{U}^\top, \text{ and}$$
$$\mathbf{R} = \mathbf{U}\mathbf{W}\mathbf{V}^\top \text{ or } \mathbf{R} = \mathbf{U}\mathbf{W}^\top\mathbf{V}^\top \tag{12.69}$$

One particular solution to this is given in the forms of $\mathbf{Z}$ and $\mathbf{W}$ matrices as given in Eq. 12.70.

$$\mathbf{Z} = \begin{bmatrix} 0 & 1 & 0 \\ -1 & 0 & 0 \\ 0 & 0 & 0 \end{bmatrix} \text{ and } \mathbf{W} = \begin{bmatrix} 0 & -1 & 0 \\ 1 & 0 & 0 \\ 0 & 0 & 1 \end{bmatrix} \tag{12.70}$$

We may note that, any skew symmetric matrix, $\mathbf{S}$, is decomposed as $\mathbf{S} = k\mathbf{U}\mathbf{Z}\mathbf{U}^\top$, where k is the scaling factor. It can be seen that $\mathbf{W}$ is orthogonal and $\mathbf{Z} = \text{Diag}(1, 1, 0)\mathbf{W}$. By exploiting the properties of these decompositions, there are four possible configurations of the projection matrix, $\mathbf{P}'$, of the second camera, given the projection matrix of the first camera is chosen as $\mathbf{P} = [\mathbf{I}|\mathbf{0}]$ in the canonical form. These four possible configurations are given in Eq. 12.71.

$$\begin{aligned} \mathbf{P}' &= [\mathbf{U}\mathbf{W}\mathbf{V}^\top | + \boldsymbol{u}_3], \\ \mathbf{P}' &= [\mathbf{U}\mathbf{W}\mathbf{V}^\top | - \boldsymbol{u}_3], \\ \mathbf{P}' &= [\mathbf{U}\mathbf{W}^\top \mathbf{V}^\top | + \boldsymbol{u}_3], \text{ and} \\ \mathbf{P}' &= [\mathbf{U}\mathbf{W}^\top \mathbf{V}^\top | - \boldsymbol{u}_3] \end{aligned} \tag{12.71}$$

where $\boldsymbol{u}_3$ is the last column of $\mathbf{U}$, with respect to the decomposition given in Eq. 12.69. Out of these four possibilities, only one configuration is valid, so that the corresponding pair of points correspond to the same scene point, which lies in front of both the cameras. It is sufficient to test a single point in this case. The form of the projection matrix that has the same frontal direction as of $\mathbf{P} = [\mathbf{I}|\mathbf{0}]$ is the solution from the essential matrix.

Numerical Example

Consider a stereo imaging setup camera with left calibration matrix $\mathbf{K} = \begin{bmatrix} 4 & 3 & 2 \\ 0 & 4 & 3 \\ 0 & 0 & 1 \end{bmatrix}$

and a right calibration matrix $\mathbf{K}' = \begin{bmatrix} 1 & 1 & 2 \\ 0 & 2 & 3 \\ 0 & 0 & 1 \end{bmatrix}$. The right camera is rotated and

translated by $\mathbf{R} = \begin{bmatrix} 0.36 & 0.48 & -0.8 \\ -0.8 & 0.6 & 0 \\ 0.48 & 0.64 & 0.6 \end{bmatrix}$ and $\boldsymbol{t} = (1, 1, 1)$, respectively with respect to

the left camera. In this context, compute the fundamental matrix $\mathbf{F}$.

Solution

Fundamental matrix $\mathbf{F} = [e']_\times \mathbf{H}_\pi$, where $e' = \mathbf{K}'t$ and $\mathbf{H}_\pi = \mathbf{K}'\mathbf{R}\mathbf{K}^{-1}$. Hence,

$$\mathbf{F} = \begin{bmatrix} 0.64 & -0.46 & 1.3 \\ -0.35 & 0.21 & -1.94 \\ -0.81 & 0.77 & 4.49 \end{bmatrix}.$$

12.7 | Computing the scene points

In the stereo geometry, another key task is the computation of the scene point, given a pair of corresponding points. The computational problem is stated as follows:
Given the corresponding pair of scene points, $(\boldsymbol{x}_i, \boldsymbol{x}'_i)$, the task is to compute the world point, $\boldsymbol{X}_i$.

This is performed using the triangulation method, where the equation of the projection ray in 3-D is evaluated, given the camera center $\boldsymbol{C}$ and an image plane. Using the image point, $\boldsymbol{x}_i$, in the image plane corresponding to the camera with its center at $\boldsymbol{C}$, the equation of the projection ray is formed by knowing its projection matrix, $\mathbf{P}$.

In a stereo setup, the projection rays are formed for the two image planes. Both of these projection rays ideally intersect at the 3-D scene point. In practice, the two back projection rays may not have a perfect intersection due to the observation and computation errors. Hence, the point closest to the exact point is computed. That is, the line segment perpendicular to both the projection rays is used to compute their mid-point, which is the 3-D world point, as illustrated in Fig. 12.8. The computational steps involved in this method are as follows.

(i) Compute $\mathbf{F}$.

(ii) Compute $\mathbf{P}$ and $\mathbf{P}'$.

(iii) For each $(\boldsymbol{x}_i, \boldsymbol{x}'_i)$, compute $\boldsymbol{X}$ by the triangulation method as follows:

    (a) Compute the intersection of $\boldsymbol{C}\boldsymbol{x}_i$ and $\boldsymbol{C}'\boldsymbol{x}'_i$.

    (b) Compute the segment perpendicular to both the rays.

    (c) Get the mid-point, which is the 3-D scene point.

This approach does not result in projection matrices that are projective invariant. This is because the camera projection matrices could also be $(\mathbf{PH}, \mathbf{P}'\mathbf{H})$ but the estimated scene point may not be the same as $\mathbf{H}^{-1}\boldsymbol{x}$, where x is obtained from the pair of projection matrices $\mathbf{PH}$ and $\mathbf{P}'\mathbf{H}$.

Another method to compute the 3-D scene point is to minimize an objective function by considering the projection of the scene points by applying the projection matrices. This method starts with an initial estimate and tries to reduce the error with respect to the ideal image point. This method is a constraint based nonlinear optimization problem, and the result is projective invariant. That is, the set of projection matrices $(\mathbf{PH}, \mathbf{P}'\mathbf{H})$ also satisfy for $\mathbf{H}^{-1}\boldsymbol{x}$ and $\mathbf{H}^{-1}\boldsymbol{x}'$. The computational steps of this method are as follows.

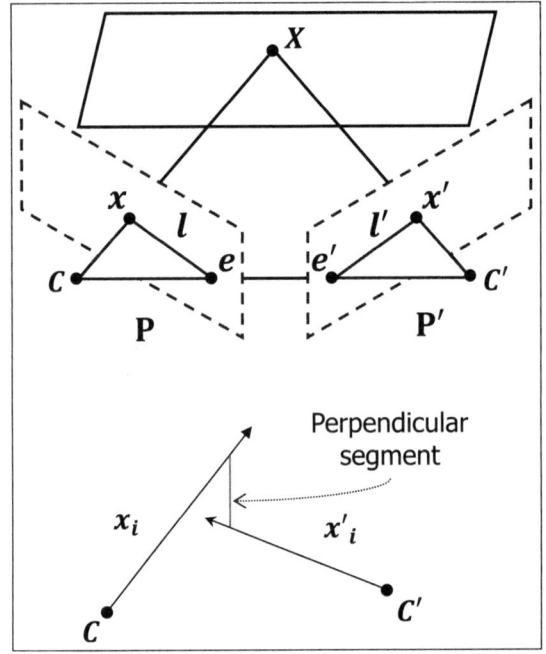

Figure 12.8 Illustration of computing the mid-point of the line segment perpendicular to the projection rays.

(i) Estimate $\hat{X}$ such that $\mathbf{P}\hat{X} = \hat{x}$ and $\mathbf{P}'\hat{X} = \hat{x}'$.

(ii) Minimize the reprojection error (E_{rp}).

$$E_{rp} = d(x, \hat{x})^2 + d(x', \hat{x}')^2 \text{ subject to } x^\top \mathbf{F} x = 0 \tag{12.72}$$

where $d(\cdot)$ is a distance function.

12.7.1 | Linear triangulation methods

Unlike the geometric methods of computation for estimating the projection matrices, the linear triangulation methods use algebraic operations and equations for estimation. An image point, x, corresponding to a world point, X, is computed using the projection matrix, $\mathbf{P}$ as, $\mathbf{P}X$. As x and $\mathbf{P}X$ in the projective space are parallel vectors having the same direction but different magnitudes due to variation of scale factors in them, they satisfy the following relation:

$$x \times \mathbf{P}X = 0 \tag{12.73}$$

The above relation uses cross products of three vectors. Similarly, another set of linear equations, with the projection matrix $\mathbf{P}'$, is given by Eq. 12.74.

$$x' \times \mathbf{P}'X = 0 \tag{12.74}$$

The projection matrix can be represented with their row vectors as follows.

$$\mathbf{P} = \begin{bmatrix} \boldsymbol{r}_1^{\top} \\ \boldsymbol{r}_2^{\top} \\ \boldsymbol{r}_3^{\top} \end{bmatrix} \tag{12.75}$$

Using this form of $\mathbf{P}$, $\mathbf{P}\boldsymbol{X}$ can be expressed as in Eq. 12.76.

$$\mathbf{P}\boldsymbol{X} = \begin{bmatrix} \boldsymbol{r}_1^{\top} \boldsymbol{X} \\ \boldsymbol{r}_2^{\top} \boldsymbol{X} \\ \boldsymbol{r}_3^{\top} \boldsymbol{X} \end{bmatrix} \tag{12.76}$$

The vectors in Eq. 12.76 are 3-D vector. For compatibility, $\boldsymbol{x}$ is also denoted by its homogenous form, $\boldsymbol{x} = \begin{bmatrix} x \\ y \\ 1 \end{bmatrix}$. Using this form $\boldsymbol{x}$, Eq. 12.76 can be expanded as in Eq. 12.77.

$$\begin{aligned} y\boldsymbol{r}_3^{\top} \boldsymbol{X} - \boldsymbol{r}_2^{\top} \boldsymbol{X} &= 0 \\ \boldsymbol{r}_1^{\top} \boldsymbol{X} - x\boldsymbol{r}_3^{\top} \boldsymbol{X} &= 0 \\ x\boldsymbol{r}_2^{\top} \boldsymbol{X} - y\boldsymbol{r}_1^{\top} \boldsymbol{X} &= 0 \end{aligned} \tag{12.77}$$

Here, in Eq. 12.77, the third equation can be expressed as a linear combination of the first two equations. So, there are only two independent equations. Also, considering the constraint in Eq. 12.73 and 12.74, another pair of equations can be formed. That is, given a pair of corresponding points four independent equations are obtained. But, with a scale factor, there are only three unknowns in $\boldsymbol{X}$. For estimating $\boldsymbol{X}$, the least squares error estimate technique is applied. The expression of the form $\mathbf{A}_{4 \times 4} \boldsymbol{X} = 0$ is optimized with a constraint of $\|\boldsymbol{X}\| = 1$, as given by Eq. 12.78.

$$\begin{bmatrix} \text{Minimize } \|\mathbf{A}\boldsymbol{X}\| \\ \text{subject to } \|\boldsymbol{X}\| = 1 \end{bmatrix} \tag{12.78}$$

Similar to the estimation of the projective matrix or homography as discussed in Section 10.3 of Chapter 10, $\boldsymbol{X}$ can also be estimated using the DLT, which is not projective invariant. This problem can be generalized and solved using this technique. For example, if there are three point correspondences in a three-camera system, $(\mathbf{P}_1, \mathbf{P}_2, \mathbf{P}_3)$, each camera provides a similar form of equations. So, there are six equations and three unknowns corresponding to a scene point. This is also solved using the same DLT technique.

12.7.2 | Computation of structure

Consider a stereo system with the projection matrices, $\mathbf{P}$ and $\mathbf{P}'$, for the left and the right cameras, respectively, as shown in Fig. 12.9. Let the images of a scene point be formed

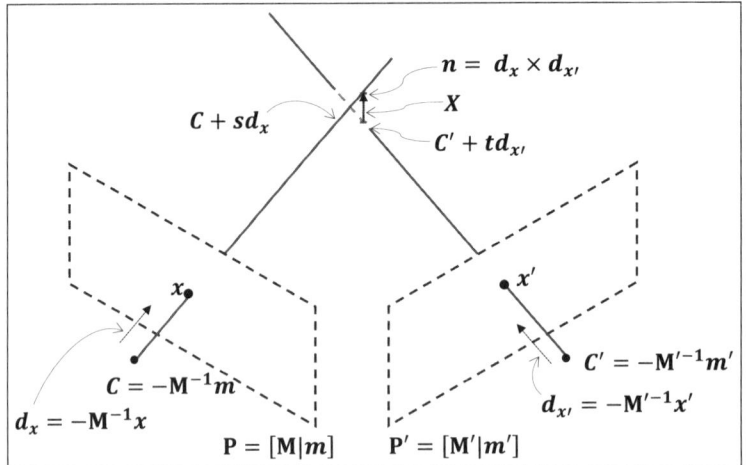

Figure 12.9 Illustration of the stereo setup for the computation of the scene point.

at $\boldsymbol{x} = (x, y)$ and $\boldsymbol{x}' = (x', y')$, in the left and the right cameras, respectively. Here, the objective is to compute the 3-D coordinate of the scene point. Let, the projection matrices be represented as, $\mathbf{P} = [\mathbf{M}|\boldsymbol{m}]$ and $\mathbf{P}' = [\mathbf{M}'|\boldsymbol{m}']$. By applying the geometric approach of triangulation, the back projection rays for the two cameras are obtained and their point of intersection is computed. Due to some noise in the observations, the rays may not exactly intersect at a point. In such a case, a very close estimate of the point of intersection has to be computed. This is achieved by considering a perpendicular segment for both the rays, and its midpoint is the solution.

Let $\boldsymbol{C}$ be the center of the first camera and $\boldsymbol{C}'$ be the center of the second camera, which are given by Eq. 12.79.

$$\boldsymbol{C} = -\mathbf{M}^{-1}\boldsymbol{m}$$
$$\boldsymbol{C}' = -\mathbf{M}'^{-1}\boldsymbol{m}'$$

(12.79)

Given the image points, $\boldsymbol{x}$ and $\boldsymbol{x}'$, the direction ratios, $\boldsymbol{d}_x$ and $\boldsymbol{d}_{x'}$, of their respective projection rays are computed as given in Eq. 12.80.

$$\boldsymbol{d}_x = -\mathbf{M}^{-1}\boldsymbol{x}$$
$$\boldsymbol{d}_{x'} = -\mathbf{M}'^{-1}\boldsymbol{x}'$$

(12.80)

These computations reveal all the 3-D constructs of the straight lines passing through image points. Then, 3-D coordinate geometry is used to solve the perpendicular segment between the projection rays and their point of intersection, which is the required solution. The direction ratios of this perpendicular segment is obtained by the cross product of $\boldsymbol{d}_x$ and $\boldsymbol{d}_{x'}$, since it is perpendicular to the projection rays. A point lying on the projection ray that passes through $\boldsymbol{x}$ and $\boldsymbol{C}$ is given by the parametric representation of a straight line, as in Eq. 12.81.

$$\boldsymbol{X}^{(1)} = \boldsymbol{C} + s\boldsymbol{d}_x$$

(12.81)

where s is any positive value. Similarly, a point lying on the projection ray that passes through $\boldsymbol{x}'$ and $\boldsymbol{C}'$ is given by Eq. 12.82.

$$\boldsymbol{X}^{(2)} = \boldsymbol{C}' + t\boldsymbol{d}_{\boldsymbol{x}'} \tag{12.82}$$

where t is any positive value. The values of s and t are chosen such that they satisfy the constraint of joining the corresponding projection rays. That is, the line obtained by the values of s and t, which joins the points of the rays $(\boldsymbol{x}, \boldsymbol{C})$ and $(\boldsymbol{x}', \boldsymbol{C}')$, is perpendicular to both the rays. The direction ratios, $\boldsymbol{n}$, of this line segment is given by Eq. 12.83.

$$\boldsymbol{n} = \boldsymbol{d}_{\boldsymbol{x}} \times \boldsymbol{d}_{\boldsymbol{x}'} \tag{12.83}$$

Since $\boldsymbol{n}$ is perpendicular to $\boldsymbol{d}_{\boldsymbol{x}}$ and $\boldsymbol{d}_{\boldsymbol{x}'}$, s and t are solved by applying this constraint.

12.7.3 | Line reconstruction

Consider that a straight line, $\boldsymbol{L}$, is projected onto the two corresponding image planes of a stereo system, as shown in Fig. 12.10. The images of the line in the left and the right image planes are also straight lines, $\boldsymbol{l}$ and $\boldsymbol{l}'$, respectively. The projection matrices of the two corresponding cameras are $\mathbf{P} = [\mathbf{I}|\mathbf{0}]$ and $\mathbf{P}' = [\mathbf{R}|\boldsymbol{t}]$, respectively. The equations of the planes, $\boldsymbol{\pi}$ and $\boldsymbol{\pi}'$, in which $\boldsymbol{L}$ and its respective images lie are given by Eq. 12.84 (refer to Section 11.4 of Chapter 11).

$$\begin{aligned} \boldsymbol{\pi} &= \mathbf{P}^{\top}\boldsymbol{l} \\ \boldsymbol{\pi}' &= \mathbf{P}'^{\top}\boldsymbol{l}' \end{aligned} \tag{12.84}$$

The solution to this reconstruction problem is the line of intersection of the two planes, $\boldsymbol{\pi}$ and $\boldsymbol{\pi}'$, which result is a 3-D line that is represented by Eq. 12.85.

$$\boldsymbol{L} = \begin{bmatrix} \boldsymbol{\pi} \\ \boldsymbol{\pi}' \end{bmatrix} \tag{12.85}$$

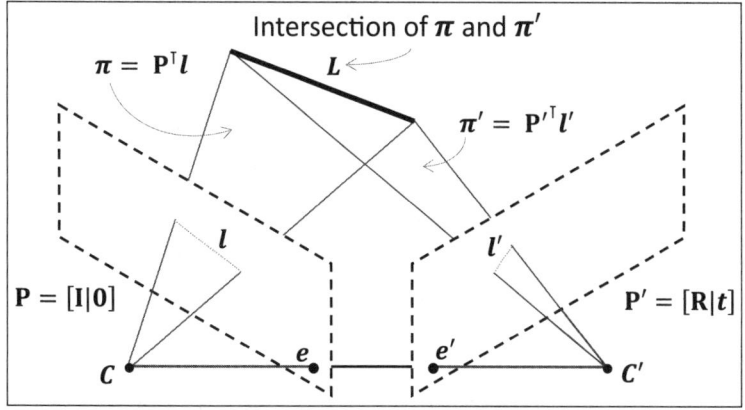

Figure 12.10 Illustration of the stereo setup for reconstructing a line.

12.8 | Plane induced homography

In a stereo system, the homography or projective transformation can be established among a pair of corresponding points for which the scene point lies on a particular plane, as shown in Fig. 12.11. This kind of transformation is called the *plane induced homography*. Let the two camera matrices of a stereo system be given by, $\mathbf{P} = [\mathbf{I}|\mathbf{0}]$ and $\mathbf{P}' = [\mathbf{A}|\mathbf{a}]$. Let the plane containing the scene point be represented by Eq. 12.86.

$$\boldsymbol{\pi} = \begin{bmatrix} [\boldsymbol{v}]_{3\times1} \\ 1 \end{bmatrix} \tag{12.86}$$

where $\boldsymbol{v} = \begin{bmatrix} v_1 \\ v_2 \\ v_3 \end{bmatrix}$. That is, the equation of a plane is expressed by,

$v_1 x + v_2 y + v_3 z + 1 = 0$.

Given a world point $\boldsymbol{X}$, its corresponding image points, $\boldsymbol{x}$ and $\boldsymbol{x}'$ are given by Eq. 12.87.

$$\begin{aligned} \boldsymbol{x} &= \mathbf{P}\boldsymbol{X} = [\mathbf{I}|\mathbf{0}]\boldsymbol{X} \\ \boldsymbol{x}' &= \mathbf{P}'\boldsymbol{X} = [\mathbf{A}|\mathbf{a}]\boldsymbol{X} \end{aligned} \tag{12.87}$$

Also, any point lying on the line $\boldsymbol{CX}$ is given by, Eq. 12.88.

$$\boldsymbol{X}_\rho = \begin{bmatrix} \boldsymbol{x} \\ \rho \end{bmatrix} \tag{12.88}$$

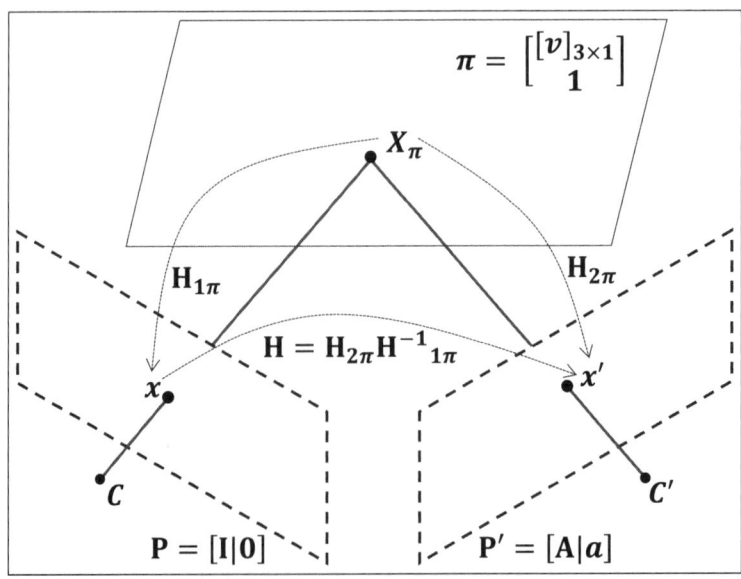

Figure 12.11 Illustration of plane induced homography in a stereo system.

where ρ is the scale factor. The value of ρ is determined by its point containment relationship on the plane $\boldsymbol{\pi}$, which is expressed by Eq. 12.89.

$$\boldsymbol{\pi}^{\top} \boldsymbol{X}_{\rho} = \boldsymbol{\pi}^{\top} \begin{bmatrix} \boldsymbol{x} \\ \rho \end{bmatrix} = 0$$

$$\implies \begin{bmatrix} \boldsymbol{v} \\ 1 \end{bmatrix}^{\top} \begin{bmatrix} \boldsymbol{x} \\ \rho \end{bmatrix} = 0 \qquad (12.89)$$

$$\implies \boldsymbol{v}^{\top} \boldsymbol{x} + \rho = 0$$

$$\implies \rho = -\boldsymbol{v}^{\top} \boldsymbol{x}$$

From Eqs. 12.87, 12.88, and 12.89,

$$\boldsymbol{x}' = \mathbf{P}' \boldsymbol{X} = [\mathbf{A}|\boldsymbol{a}] \begin{bmatrix} \boldsymbol{x} \\ -\boldsymbol{v}^{\top} \boldsymbol{x} \end{bmatrix}$$

$$= \mathbf{A}\boldsymbol{x} - \boldsymbol{a}\boldsymbol{v}^{\top} \boldsymbol{x} \qquad (12.90)$$

$$= (\mathbf{A} - \boldsymbol{a}\boldsymbol{v}^{\top})\boldsymbol{x}$$

Let the homography matrix associating the plane containing the world point and the first image plane be denoted by $\mathbf{H}_{1\boldsymbol{\pi}}$. Similarly, the homography matrix associating $\boldsymbol{\pi}$ with the second image plane be denoted by $\mathbf{H}_{2\boldsymbol{\pi}}$. Then, the homography associating the two corresponding image planes is given by Eq. 12.91.

$$\mathbf{H} = \mathbf{H}_{2\boldsymbol{\pi}} \mathbf{H}_{1\boldsymbol{\pi}}^{-1} \qquad (12.91)$$

The relationship of projective transformation between the corresponding points is represented by Eq. 12.92.

$$\boldsymbol{x}' = \mathbf{H}\boldsymbol{x} \qquad (12.92)$$

From Eq. 12.90 and 12.92, the plane induced homography is also expressed by Eq. 12.93.

$$\mathbf{H} = \mathbf{A} - \boldsymbol{a}\boldsymbol{v}^{\top} \qquad (12.93)$$

where $\boldsymbol{v}$ is the direction ratio of the normal of the plane $\boldsymbol{\pi}$. There is an interesting relationship between the fundamental matrix, $\mathbf{F}$, and the plane induced homography, $\mathbf{H}$. A transformation $\mathbf{H}$ between two stereo images is plane induced homography if $\mathbf{F}$ is decomposed into $[\boldsymbol{e}']_{\times}\mathbf{H}$. In that case, the projective matrices are given by $\mathbf{P} = [\mathbf{I}|\mathbf{0}]$, and $\mathbf{P}' = [\mathbf{H}|\boldsymbol{e}']$. Consequently, given $\mathbf{P} = [\mathbf{I}|\mathbf{0}]$, $\mathbf{P}' = [\mathbf{A}|\boldsymbol{a}]$, and a plane induced homography $\mathbf{H}$, the plane is recovered by solving $k\mathbf{H} = \mathbf{A} - \boldsymbol{a}\boldsymbol{v}^{\top}$, which is a set of linear equations for unknowns k and $\boldsymbol{v}$.

12.8.1 | Homography compatible stereo geometry

We may compute homography $\mathbf{H}$ from any arbitrary four pairs of corresponding points in a stereo imaging system. But the four scene points corresponding to these pairs may not lie on the same plane. Hence the computed homography $\mathbf{H}$ is not a plane induced homography, and is not compatible to the fundamental matrix $\mathbf{F}$. Only a plane induced homography $\mathbf{H}$ is compatible to $\mathbf{F}$ implying that, for a point $\boldsymbol{x}$, its transformed point, $\mathbf{H}\boldsymbol{x}$, lies on the epipolar line $\mathbf{F}\boldsymbol{x}$. The compatibility of the fundamental matrix $\mathbf{F}$ with a homography $\mathbf{H}$ may be checked by the following property.

$\mathbf{H}$ is compatible if and only if $\mathbf{H}^{\top}\mathbf{F}$ is skew symmetric, i.e., $\mathbf{H}^{\top}\mathbf{F} + \mathbf{F}^{\top}\mathbf{H} = 0$. The above can be proved as follows. For a pair of corresponding points, $\boldsymbol{x}$ and $\boldsymbol{x}'$,

$$\boldsymbol{x'}^{\top}\mathbf{F}\boldsymbol{x} = 0 \quad \text{and} \quad \boldsymbol{x}' = \mathbf{H}\boldsymbol{x}$$
$$\Longrightarrow (\mathbf{H}\boldsymbol{x})^{\top}\mathbf{F}\boldsymbol{x} = 0 \tag{12.94}$$
$$\Longrightarrow \boldsymbol{x}^{\top}\mathbf{H}^{\top}\mathbf{F}\boldsymbol{x} = 0$$

which is true for all $\boldsymbol{x}$. Following the property of the skew symmetric matrix, as discussed in Section 12.6, $\mathbf{H}^{\top}\mathbf{F}$ is a skew symmetric matrix.

12.8.2 | Plane induced homography and epipolar constraints

The existence of a plane induced homography, $\mathbf{H}$ in stereo geometry means, all the corresponding pairs of points satisfying the homography relationship are from the scene points of the same plane. However, points in an epipolar plane are projected on a line (epipolar line) in an image plane. This is a degenerate case, for which we do not have any plane induced homography. But if we consider the epipoles, $\boldsymbol{e}$ and $\boldsymbol{e}'$, they are related by any arbitrary plane induced homography $\mathbf{H}$ as follows.

$$\boldsymbol{e}' = \mathbf{H}\boldsymbol{e} \tag{12.95}$$

This is true since epipoles are the images of the point on the plane where the baseline intersects it, as shown in Fig. 12.12. Similarly, epipolar lines are mapped by the homography, as given in Eq. 12.96.

$$\mathbf{H}^{-\top}\boldsymbol{l}'_e = \boldsymbol{l}_e \tag{12.96}$$

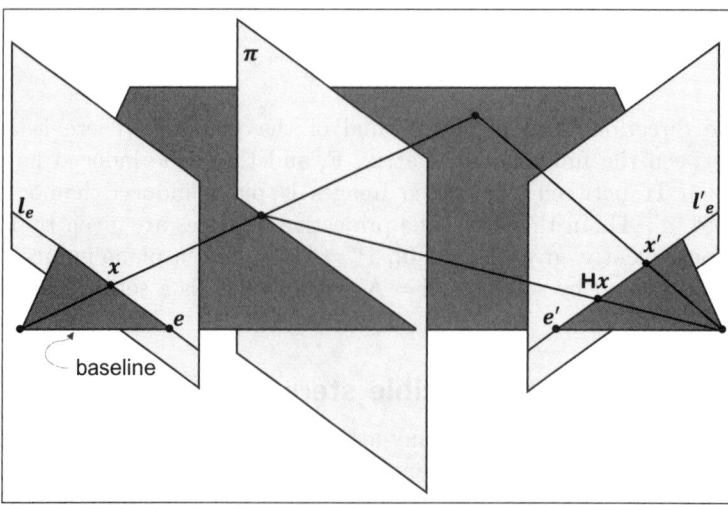

Figure 12.12 Epipolar constraints in plane induced homography.

where l'_e and l_e are right and left epipolar lines. Here, the points are lying on the plane that is inducing homography. So, the intersection of this plane with respect to the epipolar plane naturally satisfies the constraint of Eq. 12.96. Also, $\mathbf{H}x$ lies on epipolar line of l'_e. This is another constraint, which is expressed by Eq. 12.97.

$$l'_e = \mathbf{F}x = x' \times (\mathbf{H}x) \tag{12.97}$$

Numerical Example

Given the point x', and the epipolar line l' passing through x' and the epipole e'. x' may be written as $x' = \mathbf{H}_\pi x$. Compute the fundamental matrix given the following:

$$\mathbf{H}_\pi = \begin{bmatrix} 2 & 3 & 1 \\ 1 & 4 & 5 \\ 2 & 3 & 4 \end{bmatrix} \quad e' = \begin{bmatrix} 2 \\ 1 \\ 1 \end{bmatrix}$$

Solution

$$[e']_\times = \begin{bmatrix} 0 & -1 & 1 \\ 1 & 0 & -2 \\ -1 & 2 & 0 \end{bmatrix}$$

Hence, $\mathbf{F} = [e']_\times \mathbf{H}_\pi = \begin{bmatrix} 1 & -1 & -1 \\ -2 & -3 & -7 \\ 0 & 5 & 9 \end{bmatrix}$.

12.8.3 | Computing F from six points, out of which four are coplanar

Estimation of the fundamental matrix under certain constrained scenarios simplifies its estimation. Suppose $\mathbf{F}$ has to be evaluated using six corresponding points, (x_i, x'_i) where $i = 1, 2, \ldots, 6$. In this set of six corresponding points, four points, (x_j, x'_j) where $j = 1, 2, \ldots, 4$, are coplanar. The estimation of $\mathbf{F}$ is performed using the following steps of computation, which is illustrated by Fig. 12.13 for reference.

(i) At first, the plane induced homography, $\mathbf{H}_\pi$ is computed using the 4 coplanar points.

(ii) Using one of the other two corresponding points, say (x_5, x'_5) an epipolar line $l_1 = \mathbf{H}_\pi(x_5) \times x'_5$ is computed.

(iii) Similarly, another epipolar line, $l_2 = \mathbf{H}_{\pi}(\boldsymbol{x}_6) \times \boldsymbol{x}_6'$ is computed using the other set of corresponding points, $(\boldsymbol{x}_6, \boldsymbol{x}_6')$.

(iv) Then, an epipole is computed using the cross product, $\boldsymbol{e}' = l_1 \times l_2$.

(v) Finally, the fundamental matrix is estimated as, $\mathbf{F} = [\boldsymbol{e}']_{\times} \mathbf{H}_{\pi}$.

12.8.4 | Computing H from F and three point correspondences

In this computational problem, the fundamental matrix, $\mathbf{F}$, and three pairs of corresponding points are given. The objective is to compute the homography matrix, $\mathbf{H}$, induced by the plane containing the three scene points of the corresponding pairs. Two typical approaches are discussed here.

(i) Method-1: By computing 3-D scene points using the projection matrices (refer to Section 12.7), the world plane is computed. Then, plane induced homography is estimated from it. The computational steps are summarized below.

    (a) From the given $\mathbf{F}$, obtain the projection matrices, $\mathbf{P} = [\mathbf{I}|\mathbf{0}]$ and $\mathbf{P}' = [\mathbf{A}|\boldsymbol{a}]$. Then, construct three scene points, $\boldsymbol{X}_1$, $\boldsymbol{X}_2$, and $\boldsymbol{X}_3$.

    (b) Compute the world plane, $(\boldsymbol{v}^{\top}, 1)^{\top}$.

    (c) Finally, compute the plane induced homography, $\mathbf{H} = \mathbf{A} - \boldsymbol{a}\boldsymbol{v}^{\top}$.

(ii) Method-2: Estimation of homography matrix requires a minimum of four point correspondences. Since three of them are given, the fourth point correspondence is computed from $\mathbf{F}$ as the epipoles in the corresponding image planes. Then, using

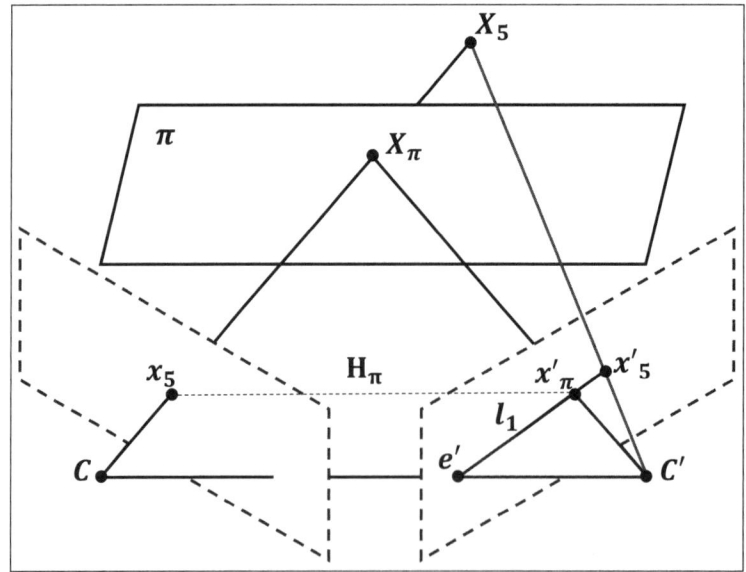

Figure 12.13 Computing $\mathbf{F}$ from 6 corresponding points, out of which 4 are coplanar.

these four corresponding points, $\mathbf{H}$ is estimated. The following computational steps summarize this approach.

(a) Obtain the two epipoles, (e, e') from the given $\mathbf{F}$.

(b) Use the four point correspondences (given three corresponding points and the computed epipoles) to obtain the plane induced homography $\mathbf{H}$.

We may note here that, any three corresponding points can bipartition the image space, with respect to the plane formed by them.

12.8.5 | Homography at infinity

The homography at infinity is the homography induced by the plane at infinity. Consider the camera matrices in the form, $\mathbf{P} = \mathbf{K}[\mathbf{I}|\mathbf{0}]$, and $\mathbf{P}' = \mathbf{K}'[\mathbf{R}|\mathbf{t}] = \mathbf{K}'[\mathbf{A}|\mathbf{a}]$. With the 3-D world plane, $\begin{bmatrix} v^{\top} \\ 1 \end{bmatrix}$, the general plane induced homography is given by $\mathbf{H} = \mathbf{A} - \mathbf{a}v^{\top}$. Let the world plane be represented as in Eq. 12.98.

$$\pi = \begin{bmatrix} [n]_{3 \times 1} \\ d \end{bmatrix} \tag{12.98}$$

where n is a 3-D normal vector and d is the scaling factor. Then, the plane induced homography at infinity is expressed in form as given by Eq. 12.99.

$$\mathbf{H}_{\pi} = (\mathbf{K}'\mathbf{R} - e'v^{\top})\mathbf{K}^{-1} \tag{12.99}$$

where $v = \frac{n}{d}$, and $e' = \mathbf{K}'t$. The expression in Eq. 12.99 can be simplified, as given in Eq. 12.100.

$$\begin{aligned} \mathbf{H}_{\pi} &= \mathbf{K}' \left(\mathbf{R} - \frac{tn^{\top}}{d} \right) \mathbf{K}^{-1} \\ &= \mathbf{K}'\mathbf{R}\mathbf{K}^{-1} - \mathbf{K}'\frac{tn^{\top}}{d}\mathbf{K}^{-1} \end{aligned} \tag{12.100}$$

Further, from Eq. 12.100, the plane induced homography at infinity, $\mathbf{H}_{\infty}$ is given by Eq. 12.101.

$$\text{as } d \to \infty, \ \mathbf{H}_{\pi} \to \mathbf{H}_{\infty} = \mathbf{K}'\mathbf{R}\mathbf{K}^{-1} \tag{12.101}$$

Also, the image, $\boldsymbol{x}'$, of the point on the world plane is given by Eq. 12.102.

$$\boldsymbol{x}' = \mathbf{K}'\mathbf{R}\mathbf{K}^{-1}\boldsymbol{x} + \frac{\mathbf{K}'t}{Z} \tag{12.102}$$

where Z is the distance of the plane from the cameras. From the representation of $\mathbf{H}_{\infty}$ in Eq. 12.101, $\boldsymbol{x}'$ can be expressed as in Eq. 12.103.

$$\boldsymbol{x}' = \mathbf{H}_{\infty}\boldsymbol{x} + \frac{\mathbf{K}'t}{Z} \tag{12.103}$$

Here, as $Z \to \infty$, $\boldsymbol{x}'$ will be the image of the point on the plane at infinity, $\boldsymbol{\pi}_\infty$. In fact, $\boldsymbol{x}'$ is the vanishing point over the epipolar line, since the points at infinity are projected on the image plane. The respective $\mathbf{H}_\infty$ maps the vanishing points between two images from a stereo setup.

Hence, $\mathbf{H}_\infty$ is computed by identifying three noncollinear points, given $\mathbf{F}$, or from four corresponding points. Consider the projection matrices of the two cameras in the form of $\mathbf{P} = [\mathbf{M}|\boldsymbol{m}]$ and $\mathbf{P}' = [\mathbf{M}'|\boldsymbol{m}']$, and a point at infinity in the form of $\boldsymbol{X} = \begin{bmatrix} \boldsymbol{x}_\infty^{\mathsf{T}} & \mathbf{0} \end{bmatrix}^{\mathsf{T}}$, then its corresponding image points are given by Eq. 12.104.

$$\begin{aligned}
\boldsymbol{x} = \mathbf{P}\boldsymbol{X} = \mathbf{M}\boldsymbol{x}_\infty \implies \boldsymbol{x}_\infty = \mathbf{M}^{-1}\boldsymbol{x} \\
\boldsymbol{x}' = \mathbf{P}'\boldsymbol{X} = \mathbf{M}'\boldsymbol{x}_\infty \implies \boldsymbol{x}' = \mathbf{M}'\mathbf{M}^{-1}\boldsymbol{x}
\end{aligned} \tag{12.104}$$

Since $\boldsymbol{x}$ and $\boldsymbol{x}'$ are related by $\boldsymbol{x}' = \mathbf{H}_\infty \boldsymbol{x}$, from Eq. 12.104, the expression for $\mathbf{H}_\infty$ can also be given in the form of Eq. 12.105

$$\mathbf{H}_\infty = \mathbf{M}'\mathbf{M}^{-1} \tag{12.105}$$

12.8.6 | Affine epipolar geometry

In an affine camera, the center of projections or the camera center lies at infinity. In this case, the projection rays are parallel to certain directions and the imaging mechanism takes place through the parallel projection of rays. Consider a stereo setup with two affine cameras where the second camera gets parallel projection of rays, as shown in Fig. 12.14. The projection rays form an epipolar plane, whose image on the second image forms an epipolar line. That is, the set of points lying on these projection rays form the epipolar line. Here, the set of all the epipolar lines and planes are parallel, which is the characteristic of an affine epipolar

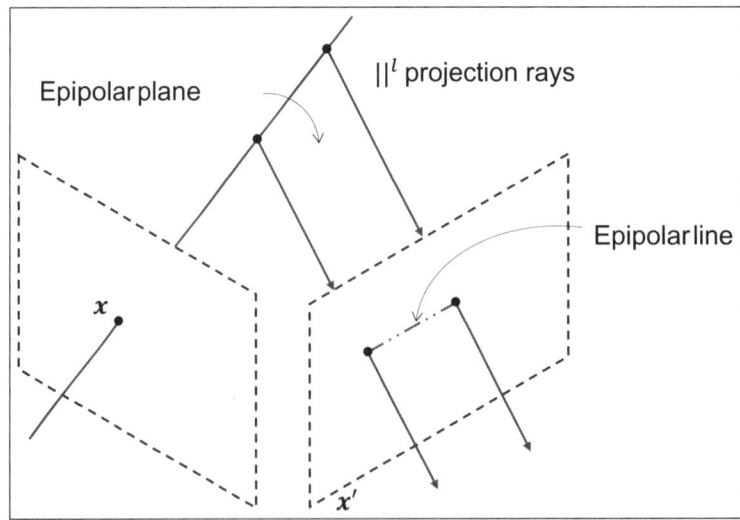

Figure 12.14 Computing $\mathbf{F}$ from 6 corresponding points, out of which 4 are coplanar.

geometry. As epipolar lines are parallel, the epipoles are in the form of $\begin{bmatrix} e_1 & e_2 & 0 \end{bmatrix}^{\top}$ This can also be represented as in Eq. 12.106.

$$[e']_{\times} = \begin{bmatrix} 0 & 0 & e'_2 \\ 0 & 0 & -e'_1 \\ -e'_2 & e'_1 & 0 \end{bmatrix} = \begin{bmatrix} \mathbf{0} & \mathbf{b} \\ -\mathbf{b}^{\top} & 0 \end{bmatrix} \quad (12.106)$$

Here, four elements of the matrix are 0. So, there are five parameters, which also includes the scale factor. Hence, there are only four independent parameters in this representation. Also, since the epipolar lines are parallel, they intersect at a point at infinity. Hence, the value of the third dimension, which represents the scale is 0. In general, in this kind of geometry, the form of the fundamental matrix gets simplified into a structure, as given by Eq. 12.107, which has only five nonzero elements.

$$\mathbf{F} = \begin{bmatrix} 0 & 0 & a \\ 0 & 0 & b \\ e & d & c \end{bmatrix} \quad (12.107)$$

Affine stereo

Consider an affine stereo, as shown in Fig. 12.15, where $\boldsymbol{x}$ is corresponding to $\boldsymbol{x}'$ and $\boldsymbol{y}$ is corresponding to $\boldsymbol{y}'$, which are the images of points that are lying on a particular plane, $\boldsymbol{\pi}$. Then, the plane induced homography between them is given by Eq. 12.108.

$$\mathbf{H_A} = \begin{bmatrix} \mathbf{A} & \boldsymbol{t} \\ \mathbf{0}^{\top} & 1 \end{bmatrix} \quad (12.108)$$

The epipolar line, corresponding to the right epipole, $\begin{bmatrix} e'_1 & e'_2 & 0 \end{bmatrix}^{\top}$, is given by Eq. 12.109.

$$\boldsymbol{l}' = \boldsymbol{e}' \times \mathbf{H_A}\boldsymbol{x} = [\boldsymbol{e}']_{\times}\mathbf{H_A}\boldsymbol{x} \quad (12.109)$$

Also, the affine fundamental matrix, $\mathbf{F_A}$, is given by Eq. 12.110.

$$\mathbf{F_A} = [\boldsymbol{e}']_{\times}\mathbf{H_A} \quad (12.110)$$

From Eq. 12.106, 12.108, and 12.110, the fundamental matrix, $\mathbf{F_A}$, is given by Eq. 12.111.

$$\mathbf{F_A} = \begin{bmatrix} \mathbf{0} & \boldsymbol{b} \\ -\boldsymbol{b}^{\top}\mathbf{A} & -\boldsymbol{b}^{\top}\boldsymbol{t} \end{bmatrix} = \begin{bmatrix} 0 & 0 & e'_2 \\ 0 & 0 & -e'_1 \\ e & d & c \end{bmatrix} \quad (12.111)$$

where e, d and c are nonzero elements, and the left epipole is represented by $\begin{bmatrix} -d & e & 0 \end{bmatrix}^{\top}$ and the right epipole is represented by $\begin{bmatrix} e'_1 & e'_2 & 0 \end{bmatrix}^{\top}$. From the structure of affine fundamental matrix, the epipoles can be easily determined using the form of Eq. 12.111.

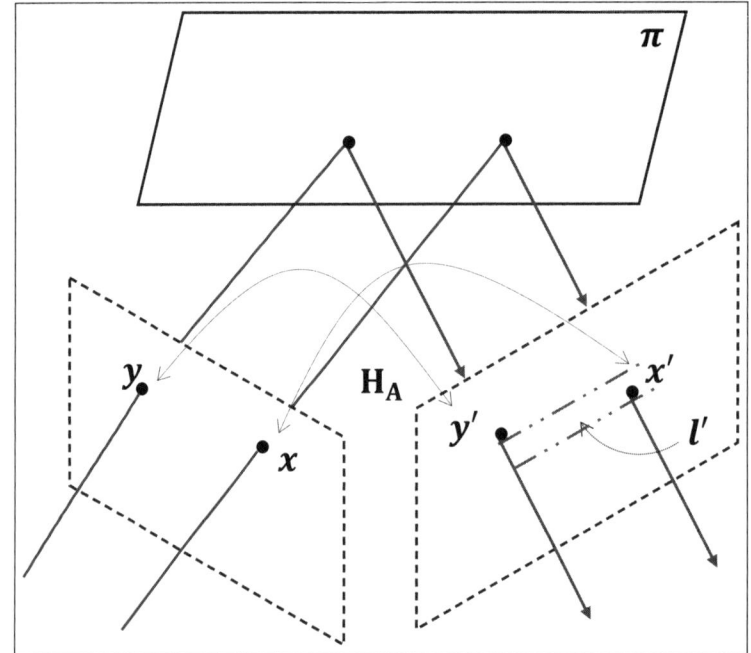

Figure 12.15 Computing $\mathbf{F}$ from 6 corresponding points, out of which 4 are coplanar.

Estimating $\mathbf{F_A}$

For the form of fundamental matrix in Eq. 12.107, the corresponding epipolar lines are represented by Eq. 12.112.

$$
\begin{aligned}
l' &= \mathbf{F_A} x = \begin{bmatrix} a & b & ex + dy + c \end{bmatrix}^\top \\
l &= \mathbf{F_A}^\top x' = \begin{bmatrix} e & d & ax' + by' + c \end{bmatrix}^\top
\end{aligned}
\tag{12.112}
$$

The set of linear equations in Eq. 12.112 is represented in a matrix form and solved using DLT. Since there are four independent parameters, only four point correspondences are required to estimate $\mathbf{F_A}$. Also, from the structure of the matrix, where all the elements in the upper 2×2 sub-matrix are 0, the singularity constraint is satisfied with no explicit enforcement. In this approach of estimating $\mathbf{F_A}$, the constraints of epipolar geometry are exploited.

Another approach of estimating $\mathbf{F_A}$ requires four point correspondences, (x_i, x_i'), $i = 1, 2, 3, 4$. The computations involved in this method are as follows.

   (i) Compute the homography, $\mathbf{H_A}$, induced by a plane using three point correspondences.

   (ii) Compute the epipolar line, which is given by Eq. 12.113.

$$
l' = \mathbf{H_A} x_4' \times x_4'
\tag{12.113}
$$

In this case, it is sufficient to compute the epipolar line, l', because the epipoles can be computed from it. Thus, the directions of the epipolar line provide the epipoles.

(iii) Compute the epipole, e', from l' in form of $\begin{bmatrix} l'_1 & l'_2 & 0 \end{bmatrix}$, which is the direction cosine of l'. The epipole is the point at infinity along the direction (l'_1, l'_2).

(iv) Finally, compute the fundamental matrix, $\mathbf{F_A} = [e']_\times \mathbf{H_A}$.

Summary

Epipolar geometry is characteristics of a stereo imaging system. The epipolar plane is the plane containing the epipoles, scene points, corresponding image points, and camera centers. This geometry, also called stereo geometry, is intrinsically characterized by a 3×3 singular matrix called fundamental matrix. The properties of the fundamental matrix, $\mathbf{F}$ are,

- It is invariant to transformation of world coordinates.
- It is a 3×3 rank-2 singular matrix with seven d.o.f.
- The epipolar line of an image point x is given by $l = \mathbf{F}x$.
- ${x'}^\top \mathbf{F}x = 0$ is true for any pair of corresponding points (x, x').
- $\mathbf{F}e = {e'}^\top \mathbf{F} = 0$ for the epipoles (e, e').
- $\mathbf{F}$ is unique for a pair of camera matrices $(\mathbf{P}, \mathbf{P}')$. For example,
  $(\mathbf{P} = [\mathbf{I}|0], \mathbf{P}' = [\mathbf{M}|m]) \implies \mathbf{F} = [m]_\times \mathbf{M}$, and $(\mathbf{P} = [\mathbf{M}|m], \mathbf{P}' = [\mathbf{M}'|m']) \implies$
  $\mathbf{F} = [m' - \mathbf{M}'\mathbf{M}^{-1}m]_\times \mathbf{M}'\mathbf{M}^{-1}$.
- Any arbitrary plane, except an epipolar plane, induces homography between corresponding image points in a stereo setup.
- Given a 4×4 homography $\mathbf{H}$, if $(\mathbf{P}, \mathbf{P}') \implies \mathbf{F}$, then $(\mathbf{PH}, \mathbf{P}'\mathbf{H}) \implies \mathbf{F}$.
- For a fundamental matrix $\mathbf{F}$, there exists a family of stereo setups (pair of camera matrices), i.e., $([\mathbf{I}|0], [[e']_\times \mathbf{F} + e'v^\top | ke'])$, where v is any arbitrary 3-vector, and k is a scalar constant.
- For a pair of camera matrices $(\mathbf{P}, \mathbf{P}')$ in a stereo setup and a corresponding pair of image points (x, x'), it is possible to reconstruct the respective 3-D scene point X.
- The fundamental matrix of calibrated cameras is called essential matrix $\mathbf{E}$.
- $\mathbf{E}$ can be an essential matrix, if and only if two of its singular values are equal and the third singular value is zero.
- Given a set of corresponding points, it is possible to estimate $\mathbf{F}$ with a minimum of 7 point correspondences.
- Given a set of corresponding points, it is possible to estimate the camera matrices and scene points up to projective (4×4 homography matrix) ambiguity
- Given a pair of corresponding lines, l and l' and camera matrices $(\mathbf{P}, \mathbf{P}')$, it is possible to reconstruct the respective 3-D line L, which is the intersection of the planes $\mathbf{P}^\top l$ and ${\mathbf{P}'}^\top l'$.
- Affine epipolar geometry simplifies the structure of the fundamental matrix.

Exercises

(i) Consider the following fundamental matrix $\mathbf{F}$. A point in 3-D, $\mathbf{X}$, is imaged as $(1, -2)$ in the first view, and $(1, 1)$ in the second view.

$$\mathbf{F} = \begin{bmatrix} 1 & 2 & 3 \\ 4 & 5 & 6 \\ 7 & 8 & 9 \end{bmatrix}$$

Verify whether the above statement is true.

(ii) Let the projection matrices for the left and right, cameras of a stereo system $\mathbf{P}$, and $\mathbf{P}'$ respectively, be given as:

$$\mathbf{P} = \begin{bmatrix} 1 & 0 & 0 & 0 \\ 0 & 1 & 0 & 0 \\ 0 & 0 & 1 & 0 \end{bmatrix} \quad \mathbf{P}' = \begin{bmatrix} 3 & 2 & 4 & 6 \\ 8 & 6 & 1 & 3 \\ 9 & 5 & 7 & 2 \end{bmatrix}$$

Compute the fundamental matrix of the stereo system.

(iii) Compute the left and right epipoles of the following fundamental matrix.

$$\mathbf{F} = \begin{bmatrix} 8 & 2 & 0 \\ 5 & 1 & 2 \\ -4 & 3 & -11 \end{bmatrix}$$

(iv) Consider a stereo imaging setup with two cameras.

$$\mathbf{P} = \begin{bmatrix} 1 & 0 & 0 & 0 \\ 0 & 1 & 0 & 0 \\ 0 & 0 & 1 & 0 \end{bmatrix} \text{ (left camera)}$$

and

$$\mathbf{P}' = \begin{bmatrix} 1 & 2 & 1 & 1 \\ -1 & -2 & 1 & 0 \\ 2 & 1 & 2 & 11 \end{bmatrix} \text{ (right camera).}$$

Compute the fundamental matrix $\mathbf{F}$.

(v) Consider a calibrated stereo rig with its two camera matrices and the world origin at the center of the first camera given as $\mathbf{P} = \mathbf{K}[\mathbf{I}|\mathbf{0}]$, $\mathbf{P}' = \mathbf{K}'[\mathbf{R}|\mathbf{t}]$, where

$$\mathbf{K} = \begin{bmatrix} 468.2 & 91.2 & 300 \\ 0 & 427.2 & 200 \\ 0 & 0 & 1 \end{bmatrix}, \quad \mathbf{K'} = \begin{bmatrix} 368.2 & 71.2 & 200 \\ 0 & 327.2 & 100 \\ 0 & 0 & 1 \end{bmatrix},$$

$$\mathbf{R} = \begin{bmatrix} 0.414 & 0.909 & 0.047 \\ -0.573 & 0.220 & 0.789 \\ 0.707 & -0.354 & 0.612 \end{bmatrix}, \text{ and } \mathbf{t} = \begin{bmatrix} 3 \\ 1 \\ 1 \end{bmatrix}$$

Answer the following questions.

I) Compute the epipole in the first image.

II) Compute the epipole in the second image.

III) Which of the following are the characteristics of the given rotation matrix.

    (a) Dot product of two different columns is 1.

    (b) Columns are orthonormal vectors.

    (c) Dot product of two different columns is 0.

    (d) Dot product of a column vector with itself is 1.

(vi) Consider a stereo imaging setup with two cameras $\mathbf{P} = \begin{bmatrix} 1 & 0 & 0 & 0 \\ 0 & 1 & 0 & 0 \\ 0 & 0 & 1 & 0 \end{bmatrix}$ (left camera)

and $\mathbf{P'} = \begin{bmatrix} 1 & 2 & 1 & 1 \\ -1 & -2 & 1 & 0 \\ 2 & 1 & 2 & 11 \end{bmatrix}$ (right camera), compute the right and the left epipoles of the stereo system.

(vii) Consider the following fundamental matrix.

$$\begin{bmatrix} 0 & 0 & 0 \\ 0 & 0 & 6 \\ 2 & -4 & -6 \end{bmatrix}$$

    I) Compute the left epipole in $\mathbb{P}^2$.

    II) Compute the right epipole in $\mathbb{P}^2$.

    III) Compute the epipolar line in the right image plane for the image point $(1, 2)$ of the left camera.

(viii) Consider a stereo imaging setup camera with left calibration matrix $\mathbf{K} = \begin{bmatrix} 2 & 1 & 0 \\ 0 & 2 & 2 \\ 0 & 0 & 1 \end{bmatrix}$ and a right calibration matrix $\mathbf{K}' = \begin{bmatrix} 1 & 1 & 2 \\ 0 & 5 & 3 \\ 0 & 0 & 1 \end{bmatrix}$. The right

camera has $\mathbf{R} = \begin{bmatrix} 0 & 0 & 1 \\ 1 & 0 & 0 \\ 0 & 1 & 0 \end{bmatrix}$

Answer the following.

  I) Given translation vector $\boldsymbol{t}$ as $(1, 1, 1)$, compute the right epipole.

  II) Compute the fundamental matrix $\mathbf{F}$.

  III) Compute the essential matrix $\mathbf{E}$

(ix) Answer the following questions.

  (a) Explain why and how the singularity of the projection of camera center is expressed mathematically.

  (b) Explain why and how the singularities at epipoles in a stereo setup are expressed mathematically.

  (c) Justify why an epipolar line is a finite line segment.

  (d) How many independent parameters are there in an essential matrix? Justify.

(x) Why does the use of our both eyes help us resolving relative distances among objects in front of us better than our viewing with a single eye only (i.e., either left or right eye)?

(xi) Consider the following fundamental matrix.

$$\begin{bmatrix} 0 & 0 & 0 \\ 0 & 0 & 6 \\ 2 & -4 & -6 \end{bmatrix}$$

  (a) Compute the left epipole in $\mathbb{P}^2$.

  (b) Compute the right epipole in $\mathbb{P}^2$.

  (c) Compute the epipolar line in the right image plane for the image point $(1, 2)$ of the left camera.

(xii) Consider the following stereo imaging system with camera matrices given by $\mathbf{P}$ (reference camera) and $\mathbf{P}'$.

$$\mathbf{P} = \begin{bmatrix} 3 & 2 & 4 & -2 \\ 8 & -6 & 0 & 4 \\ -9 & 5 & 7 & 3 \end{bmatrix} \qquad \mathbf{P}' = \begin{bmatrix} 3 & -8 & 5 & 2 \\ 2 & 7 & 6 & -3 \\ 6 & -4 & 9 & 8 \end{bmatrix}$$

Answer the following questions:

(**a**) Compute the fundamental matrix of the system.

(**b**) Given an image point $(10, 20)$ of the reference camera (**P**), compute the epipolar line and its two end image points of **P'**.

(**xiii**) Consider the following fundamental matrix of a stereo imaging system.

$$\mathbf{F} = \begin{bmatrix} 2 & 3 & 33 \\ 4 & 5 & 59 \\ 52 & 69 & 795 \end{bmatrix}$$

Answer the following questions.

(**a**) Compute the left and right epipoles of the stereo setup.

(**b**) Suppose an image point in the left camera is given by $(3, 4)$ in $\mathbb{R}^2$ and another point $(4, 3)$ in the right camera. Find the corresponding epipolar lines of these points in the other image.

(**c**) Check whether $(0, 11) \in \mathbb{R}^2$ in the right images can be a corresponding point of $(1, 0)$ in the left image.

(**d**) Provide the family of camera matrices given the camera matrix of the left camera as $[\mathbf{I}|\mathbf{0}]$.

PART THREE

NONOPTICAL VISION

13

Range Imaging

Intensity images are limited in capturing surface geometry. Range imaging refers to an aggregation of techniques to capture the surface topology as a collection of points that represent depths using different kinds of range sensors. Range images form a special class of digital images that require different processing techniques in their analysis. This chapter provides an overview of range imaging and processing.

13.1 | Range image

A *range image* is a $2\frac{1}{2}$-D or 3-D representation of the scene. It is sometimes called $2\frac{1}{2}$-D representation because it captures only the surface information of an object or scene as discretized points to represent it as an image. A range image, $f(i,j)$, records the distance, d, to the corresponding scene point at (x,y,z) for each image pixel, (i,j), as shown in Fig. 13.1. In the array representation of a range image, the pixel values correspond to the distances of the surface points, unlike conventional RGB camera image pixels that represent intensities. The distribution of all the recorded values of d forms the functional distribution of the surface points over the discretized space of the image, which is known as range data or depth data. This depth information may also be represented as a set of 3-D scene points, also called a *point cloud*. For a given functional value, $f(i,j)$, of an image array at an index position of (i,j), the corresponding pixel value of a scene point (x,y,z) in the discrete 3-D space is represented as $(i,j,f(i,j))$. An example of a range image is shown in Fig. 13.2, where the intensity image is captured as an RGB color image and its corresponding range image is captured using Microsoft™ Kinect sensor.

13.2 | Range imaging techniques

Primarily there are two types of range imaging systems. The images could be captured by (i) passive range sensing, or (ii) active range sensing. *Passive range sensing* is similar to conventional imaging using cameras, for example, as in stereo imaging systems. In *active*

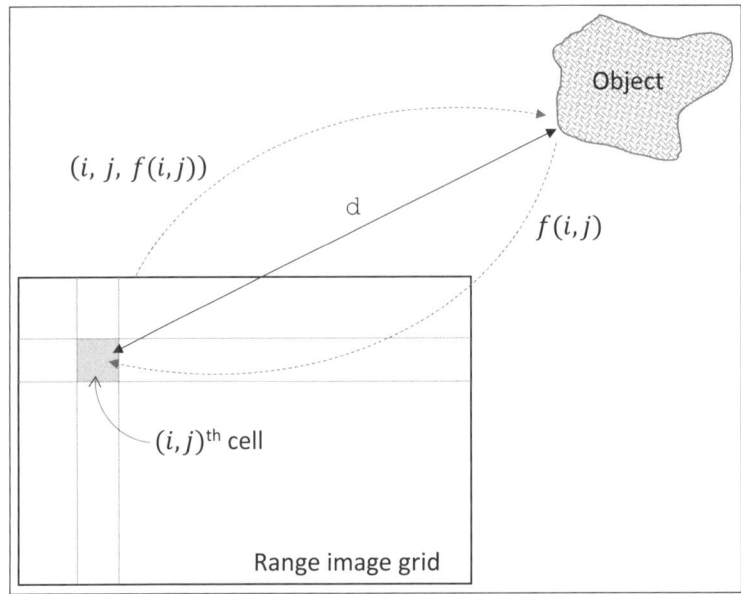

Figure 13.1 Range image formation.

Figure 13.2 An example of a range image. (a) Intensity image captured as RGB color image, and (b) its range image captured using Microsoft™ Kinect sensor.

range sensing, a ray of illumination is projected from an energy source over the scene and specific computations are performed for measuring the depth. Three different types of active range sensing mechanisms which beget high resolution range images using active range sensors discussed in this chapter are, *time-of-flight sensors*, *triangulation-based sensors*, and *structured light sensors*.

13.2.1 | Time-of-flight range sensors

A time-of-flight range sensor, in its simplest form, consists of a light source, usually a pulsed laser light source, which is transmitted toward the scene and the reflected laser signal is captured, as depicted in Fig. 13.3. By detecting the reflected pulses at the detector, the time of flight or duration of the transmission-reflection process, t, is measured. Here, both the source and detector are co-located to have the same location as the point of transmission and detection. Having a common point of transmission and detection gives the shortest path of the object from the imaging point, which is the depth, since light travels through the shortest path in the direction of the object. Then, by multiplying the time of flight by the velocity of light in the given medium, v, the depth, d, is computed as twice the distance between the object and the light source, which is given by Eq. 13.1.

$$d = \frac{vt}{2} \tag{13.1}$$

The popular laser sensors that are used in time-of-flight range sensing are based on *light detection and ranging* (LIDAR) and *laser radar* (LADAR) systems. Since each projected laser ray measures the depth of only one surface point at a given direction, the depths at all the discrete points over the whole surface are obtained by maneuvering the direction of the laser beam across the entire given surface. The surface is scanned by light beams by moving mirror mechanisms, where the mirror angles are varied in accordance with the required direction of laser beams in a given predetermined path. The depth at every point is determined by the reflected beam at the corresponding direction from the surface points.

A major limitation of the time-of-flight range sensing is the minimum observation time that is constrained by the laser pulse duration and the sampling interval of pulse laser emitter. This minimum observation time, which is restricted by the mechanism of detecting a pulse laser, also limits the minimum distance that is observable.

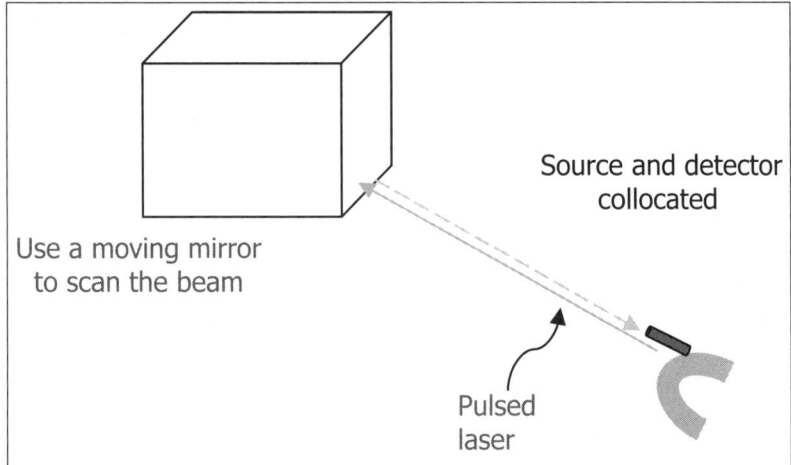

Figure 13.3 A basic time-of-flight range sensor.

13.2.2 | Triangulation-based range sensors

The triangulation-based range sensing consists of a light source, which is usually a laser source (Hsieh, 2001). The light from this source is projected on a surface point of an object, which is reflected and captured by a camera. A depiction of triangulation-based range sensing is shown in Fig. 13.4. The point of the reflected path is obtained from the image captured by the camera. By using a properly calibrated system of camera and light sources, the equations of the two lines that are formed by the light source and the surface point, and the surface point and the camera center, respectively, are obtained.[1] Then, the corresponding 3-D point is computed as the intersection of these two lines.

In this imaging system that is shown in Fig. 13.4, almost all the measurements are calibrated. From the camera calibration, the pixel at location (u, v) in the image plane, which is illuminated from the reflected light toward the camera, is obtained. The equation of this line (direction of the ray from the surface point to the camera center) is obtained from the calibrated camera parameters in the 3-D coordinate system. Similarly, the equation of the line between the light source and the surface point is encoded by the coordinate location of the laser beam source and the point (i, j) of the transmitting direction, which are obtained by calibrated laser source. The three dimensional scene information is obtained by solving this system of equations. The scanning paths or the directions along which the rays are transmitted by laser source are predetermined, which gives the equation of each transmitted ray. The observation of each illuminated surface point in the camera gives the equation of reflected ray. By applying triangulation, the respective 3-D point is computed.

For each transmitted beam in a given direction, only one 3-D surface point is computed. To obtain the surface information of the entire scene, the directions of the projected rays are varied in a calibrated path and the whole surface is illuminated. The distribution of all

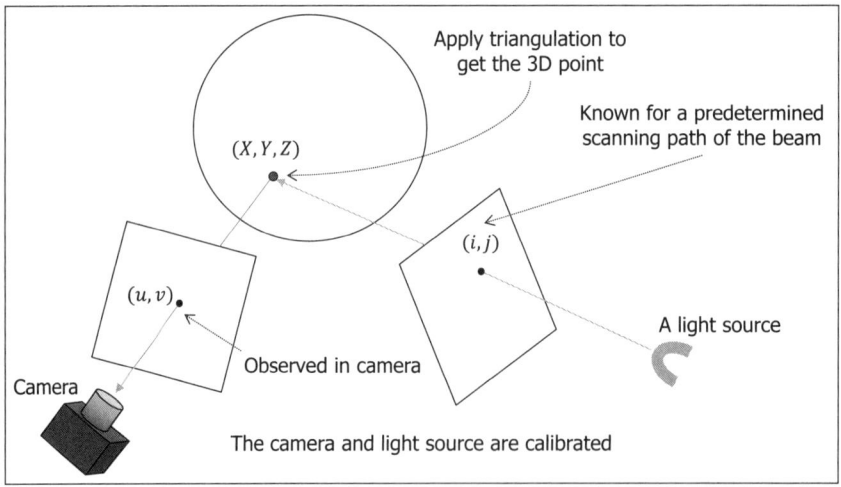

Figure 13.4 Triangulation-based range sensor.

---

[1] Refer to Chapter 12 for detail of computations.

the 3-D surface points obtained from all the projected beams form the range information of the given surface.

13.2.3 | Structured light range sensors

The technique of triangulation becomes very slow when it is projecting a ray for every point in its corresponding image plane. In this case, the plane, where each projected direction is identified, acts like a recording plane, which is traversed by one point at a time. To speed up the process, a vertical stripe of light is projected on the surface, instead of a single ray of light, as depicted in Fig. 13.5. So, all the directions along the vertical line, $p_{l_1} p_{l_2}$, are encoded into the stripe, $s_{l_1} s_{l_2}$. This stripe may be sensed in a distorted fashion, depending upon the surface geometry, which may not be a straight line. In a calibrated imaging system, the points p_{l_1} and p_{l_2} in the image plane correspond to s_{l_1} and s_{l_2}, respectively, which are predetermined in the system. Similarly, every point in the line $p_{l_1} p_{l_2}$ can be interpolated to a corresponding point in the light stripe $s_{l_1} s_{l_2}$.

   In this mechanism, it is not necessary to project a single ray multiple times. The information of all the surface points that lie on a projected light stripe is obtained by a single projection of a stripe of light. This technique is called *structured light range sensing system*, since the light is structured in specific patterns; the example of vertical stripe in Fig. 13.5 is one of the very familiar patterns. In such structured patterns, the 3-D positions of projected rays are already encoded, which are used to determine the surface points.

Space encoding

The utility of structured lighting is improved by encoding the vertical stripes in terms of m projected patterns, as shown in Fig. 13.6, instead of scanning over the entire surface by

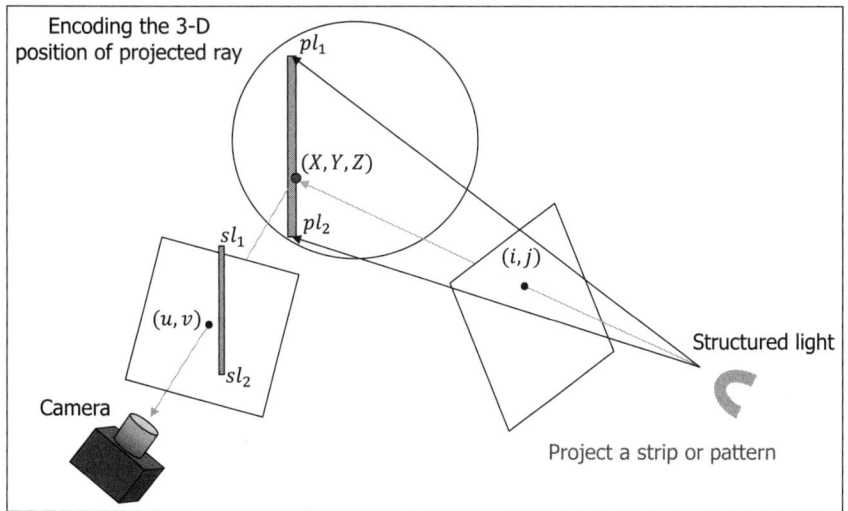

Figure 13.5 Structured light range sensor.

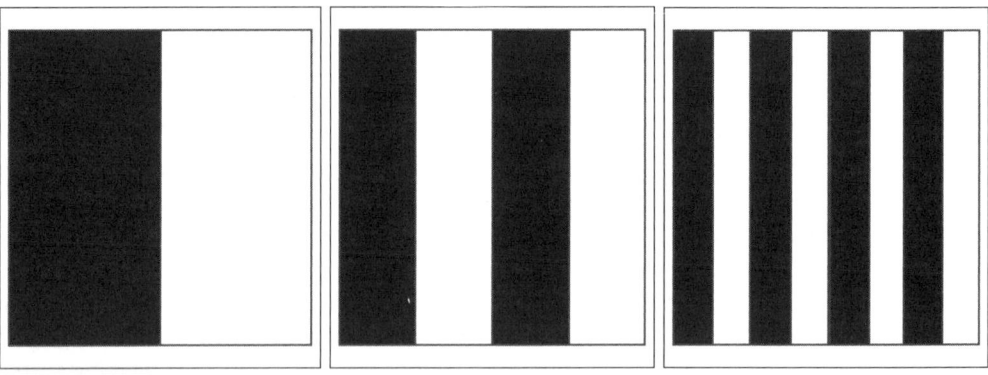

Figure 13.6 Examples of vertical stripes that are space encoded to improve the utility of structured lighting.

projecting a single vertical stripe at a time that requires more number of projections. A specific zone of the surface is identified by each of the patterns. In this particular structured light pattern, the number of stripes on the surface is doubled with every new pattern, and each light point, (i, j) in Fig. 13.5, is associated with an m-bit binary code whose image is observed by the camera. By observing the illumination of pixels using the stripes by the corresponding projection rays in m patterns, 2^m stripes are distinguished on the projected surface. For each of these stripes, the method of triangulation is applied and the respective 3-D points are obtained.

An example to demonstrate this mechanism is shown in Fig. 13.7 with $m = 3$ patterns. Consider a vertical line across a ray in each of the patterns, as shown in the figure, which will give m stripes corresponding to the m patterns that resolves 2^m discriminating patterns. With m patterns, each stripe is represented by an m-bit binary string. The binary string depends upon the kind of patterns that are used in identifying the corresponding stripes. In this example, there are three stripes for the considered vertical line. So, each line is represented by a binary string of 3-bits, which is 101 for the ray position shown in the figure. From each of the stripes, the depth information of all the scene points lying within the stripe on the surface is obtained by triangulation.

Spatial codification

Although projection of stripe patterns reduces the number of projections considerably, it still requires multiple projections to obtain all the 3-D points over a given surface. There are other kind of codifications of spatial structure or direction of the projected ray which does not require such multiple projections. Such mechanisms illuminate the surface only once, which need particular variations of spatial patterns on the grid of projected rays that uniquely appear at particular locations.

This technique also consists of calibrated light source that is used to identify the directions of the projected rays. Fig. 13.8 depicts this mechanism, where the surface illumination is modulated by different shapes of patterns through which the light rays are projected. These rays are captured by the camera sensors, where the patterns that may vary in shape, color,

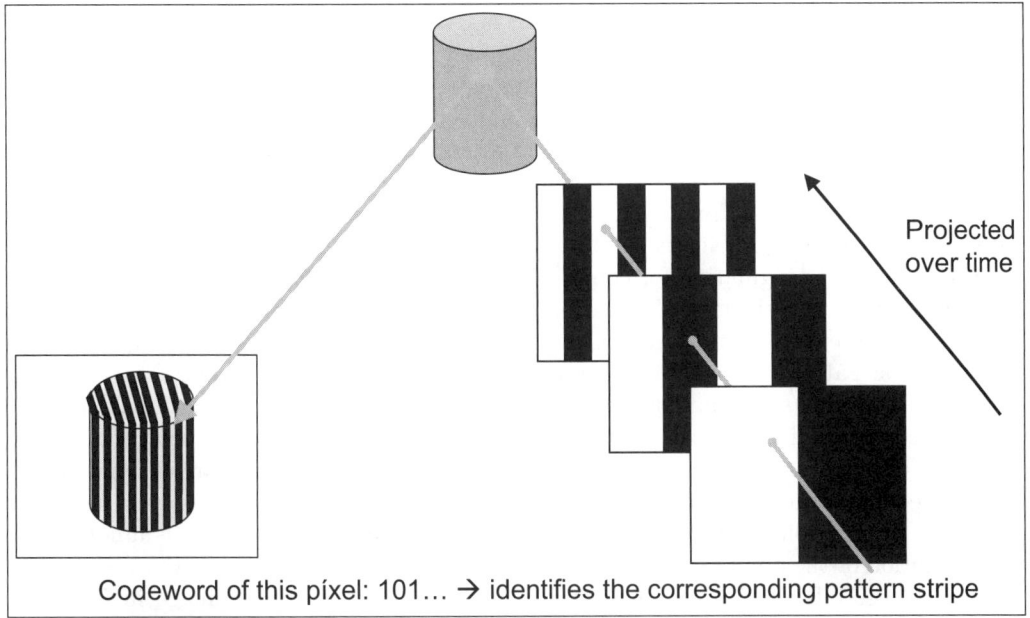

Codeword of this pixel: 101... → identifies the corresponding pattern stripe

Figure 13.7 An example demonstrating the mechanism of space encoding.

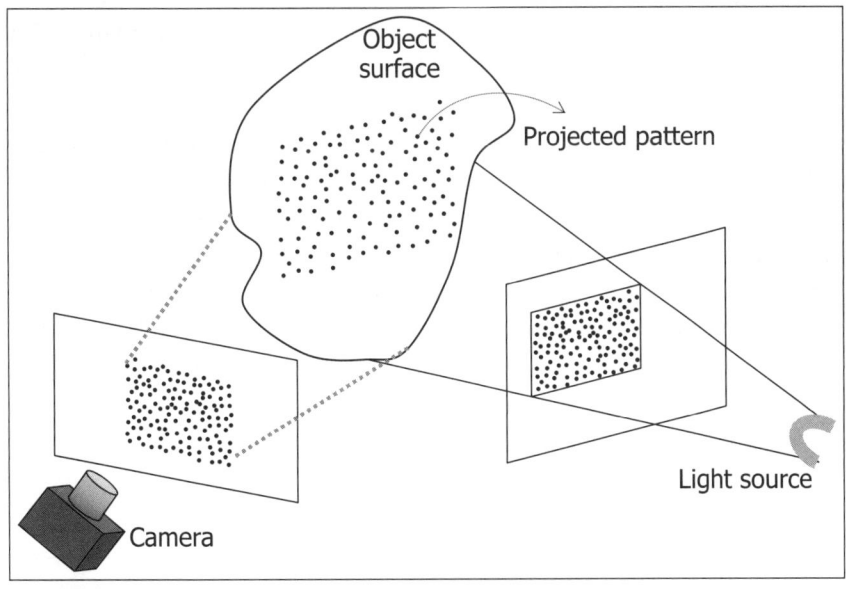

Figure 13.8 A typical example of spatial codification in range imaging.

and size are detected. The patterns in spatial neighbourhood uniquely identify the central point, so that all points on the surface are uniquely identified by different patterns.

In this approach, there is a minimum spatial resolution at which the directions are encoded, which is a limitation of this mechanism. However, as an advantage, all the encoded rays that are illuminating the object are obtained by a single projection only. So, all the encoded rays are projected simultaneously in a pattern and their reflections are observed in the corresponding image. The observed pattern in the image is then matched with the expected pattern in the pattern library to distinguish images of rays from each location to apply triangulation for computing the 3-D surface points.

With a comparatively lesser resolution than most other techniques, this technique of imaging is very effective and fast, which also makes the imaging system cheaper. In this case a spatial pattern uniquely characterizes the neighborhood by a spatial arrangement of dots with varying sizes and colors. There are different ways to design such patterns and when the corresponding patterns are detected in the camera, the respective images of surface points are also captured. Each pattern provides a set of code words that are associated with a calibrated light source, which removes the necessity of multiple projections over the object. A code word of a point that is obtained from a neighborhood of the point is unique in its representation of the point.

The Microsoft Kinect^{TM}, which is employed to capture the range image in Fig. 13.2, uses infrared laser light source with speckle pattern that encodes the corresponding light points using the spatial pattern to get the surface points. Both optical and range images in Fig. 13.2 are captured by the Kinect, which consists of an optical RGB camera and a depth sensor that uses range imaging principle. The images captured by the Kinect are known as RGBD images, which stand for Red-Green-Blue (optical components) and Depth (range component), respectively.

For range imaging, mostly laser (Light Amplification by Stimulated Emission of Radiation) lights are used as the light sources. The reasons for using laser light over ordinary light sources are as follows:

- Time-of-flight range sensing mechanism requires a coherent light source, which is a property of laser sources.

- It is easy to generate bright beams with lightweight sources.

- Infrared lasers are used unobtrusively without disturbing the viewers by visible speckle patterns while using the range cameras in day-to-day applications.

- It is easier and more flexible to precisely focus the light for obtaining narrow beams.

- Lasers are mostly single frequency sources that are easy to detect and do not disperse much due to refraction in the medium.

- Semiconductor devices efficiently generate short pulses of laser.

13.3 | Parametric curves and surfaces

Differential geometry is a useful tool in processing range images. Some of the key concepts of differential geometry that characterize the curves and surfaces are introduced in this section.

13.3.1 | Parametric curves

To explain the concepts of differential geometry, let us discuss first the mathematical representation of *parametric curves*. In this context, a parameter is taken as a subset of the real space, $\mathbb{R}$.

Parametric curves in 2-D

A function, $\boldsymbol{X}$, maps the parameter values to the coordinates of a 2-D space, as expressed by Eq. 13.2.

$$\boldsymbol{X} : I \subset \mathbb{R} \to \mathbb{R}^2 \tag{13.2}$$

In a parametric form, this is represented by a parameter, t, which is a variable that takes values from an interval of real space. For example, the parameter value may vary in an interval from 0 to 1, and for each parameter value, a coordinate within that interval is mapped. For a 2-D coordinate point, denoted by $\boldsymbol{X}(t)$, its x-coordinate, $u(t)$, and y-coordinate, $v(t)$ are also the functions of t, as given by Eq. 13.3.

$$\boldsymbol{X}(t) = (u(t),\ v(t)) \tag{13.3}$$

The parametric description is a simple way to describe a curve as a set of points. The parametric curves are continuous curves, where the parameters vary continuously and the respective functions are also continuous over the defining parameter, t. The curve may be continuous in the order of one or higher. Attributing to the continuity of the curve, tangents may be computed by taking derivatives at respective points of the curve that are used to describe it. The tangents, $\boldsymbol{T}(t)$, are also denoted by the corresponding derivatives of those parametric curves, $u'(t)$ and $v'(t)$, as given in Eq. 13.4, which are used in computing the tangent information that gives the directions of the vector with respect to the point of derivative.

$$\boldsymbol{T}(t) = (u'(t),\ v'(t)) \tag{13.4}$$

Also, the curvature of the curve, $k(t)$, at a specific point is computed by using the first derivative $\boldsymbol{X}'$, and the second derivative $\boldsymbol{X}''$, of the parametric curve, as given by Eq. 13.5.

$$k(t) = \frac{|\boldsymbol{X}' \times \boldsymbol{X}''|}{|\boldsymbol{X}'|^3} \tag{13.5}$$

where, the first and second derivatives are expressed as $\boldsymbol{X}' = [u'(t)\ v'(t)]^{\top}$ and $\boldsymbol{X}'' = [u''(t)\ v''(t)]^{\top}$, respectively. Here, the numerator on the right side of the equation is computed by a determinant operation, as given by Eq. 13.6.

$$|\boldsymbol{X}' \times \boldsymbol{X}''| = \begin{vmatrix} \frac{\partial u}{\partial t} & \frac{\partial v}{\partial t} \\ \frac{\partial^2 u}{\partial t^2} & \frac{\partial^2 v}{\partial t^2} \end{vmatrix} \tag{13.6}$$

For a particular value of t, the determinant of the matrix in the right side of Eq. 13.6 is computed by the respective scalar elements in it. Similarly, the denominator in the right side of Eq. 13.5 is computed as the cube of the magnitude of the tangent vector. For the tangent term in Eq. 13.4, this is given by Eq. 13.7.

$$|\boldsymbol{X}'|^3 = |\boldsymbol{T}(t)|^3 = \left(\sqrt{u'(t)^2 + v'(t)^2}\right)^3 \tag{13.7}$$

The curvature at any parameter value is computed using Eqs. 13.5-13.7.

Parametric curves in 3-D

Extending the definitions and notations of representation of a 2-D parametric curve, a 3-D parametric curve, $\boldsymbol{X}(t)$, and its tangent at a point $\boldsymbol{T}(t)$, for the 3-D mapping $\boldsymbol{X} : I \in \mathbb{R} \rightarrow \mathbb{R}^3$, with t as the parameter, are given by Eq. 13.8.

$$\begin{aligned} \boldsymbol{X}(t) &= (u(t),\ v(t),\ w(t)) \\ \boldsymbol{T}(t) &= (u'(t),\ v'(t),\ w'(t)) \end{aligned} \tag{13.8}$$

Here, $u(t)$, $v(t)$, and $w(t)$ represent the functions of x-coordinate, y-coordinate, and z-coordinate of t.

Similarly, the curvature of the curve at any point is computed using Eq. 13.5 with the first and second derivatives as $\boldsymbol{X}' = [u'(t)\ v'(t)\ w'(t)]^\top$ and $\boldsymbol{X}'' = [u''(t)\ v''(t)\ w''(t)]^\top$, respectively. In case of 3-D parametric curve, the numerator and denominator of the right side of Eq. 13.5 are computed as the magnitude of cross product of corresponding $\boldsymbol{X}'$ and $\boldsymbol{X}''$, and cube of the magnitude of the 3-D tangent, $|\boldsymbol{T}(t)|^3 = \left(\sqrt{u'(t)^2 + v'(t)^2 + w'(t)^2}\right)^3$, respectively, for a given value of t.

Parametric curves lying on a surface

A parametric curve lying on a surface and its tangent are represented in the same form as given in Eq. 13.8. The curvature of the curve is also computed in the same way, as in the case of generalized 3-D parametric curve, as the ratio of the magnitude of cross product of the first and second derivatives, and the cube of the magnitude of the first derivative.

In Fig. 13.9, a parametric curve lying on a surface is shown. Consider a point, $\boldsymbol{p} = \boldsymbol{X}(t)$, on this curve, where the tangent is represented by $\boldsymbol{T}(t)$. The plane in which both the tangent and the curve lie is called the *osculating plane*. The line, $\boldsymbol{N}(t)$, that is perpendicular to the tangent of the curve at $\boldsymbol{p}$ and lies on the osculating plane is known as the *normal* at $\boldsymbol{p}$. The plane on which the curve normal, $\boldsymbol{N}(t)$, lies and is perpendicular to the osculating plane is called the *normal plane*. The curvature at the point $\boldsymbol{p}$ is shown by a circle in the figure, whose radius is the inverse of the curvature. The center of this circle, C, which is formed at that point due to the curvature, lies on the normal, as shown in Fig. 13.9. Another plane that is perpendicular to both osculating and normal planes is called the *rectifying plane*. The line that is formed by the intersection of normal and rectifying planes, which lies in both of these planes, is called the *binormal*, $\boldsymbol{B}(t)$. The direction of the binormal is perpendicular to both the normal and the tangent of the curve.

The three planes, osculating, normal, and rectifying planes, are defined with respect to a point, $\boldsymbol{p}$, by considering the directions of tangent and normal of the curve at $\boldsymbol{p}$. As observed from Fig. 13.9, this defines a coordinate system at every point of the curve. There are three

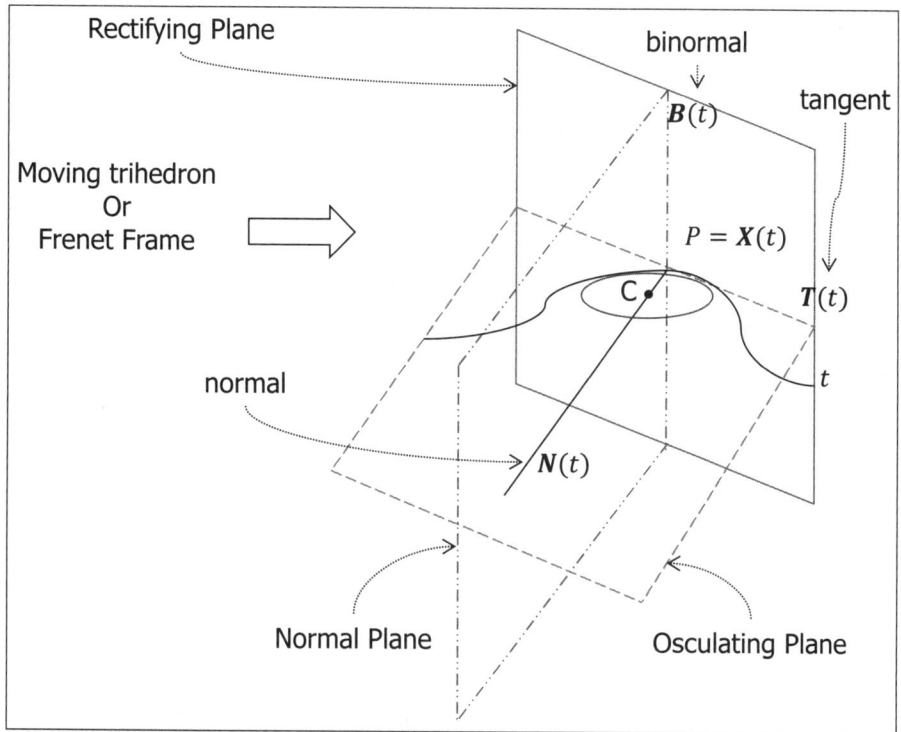

Figure 13.9 Illustration of a 3-D parametric curve lying on a surface.

axes which are perpendicular to each other and they define the local coordinate system at p. This particular configuration is called a *moving trihedron* or a *frenet frame*. In this configuration, three specific relationships between tangents, normals, binormals, and their derivatives are expressed, as given by Eqs. 13.9–13.11.

$$\widehat{T'(t)} = k(t)\widehat{N(t)} \tag{13.9}$$

where, $\widehat{T'(t)}$ is the unit vector along the derivative of the tangent of the curve, $k(t)$ is the curvature of the curve, and $\widehat{N(t)}$ is the unit vector along the normal at the given point.

$$\widehat{B'(t)} = -\tau(t)\widehat{N(t)} \tag{13.10}$$

where, $\widehat{B'(t)}$ is the unit vector along the derivative of the binormal and the quantity, τ, is known as *torsion of the curve*.

$$\widehat{N'(t)} = -k(t)\widehat{T(t)} + \tau(t)\widehat{B(t)} \tag{13.11}$$

where, $\widehat{N'(t)}$ is the unit vector along the derivative of the normal, $\widehat{T(t)}$ is the unit vector along the tangent of the curve, and $\widehat{B(t)}$ is the unit vector along the binormal of the curve at the given point. So, the derivatives of tangent and binormal are directed along the normal of the curve. The magnitude of the gradient vector of the tangent provides the curvature of the curve at that point. We also observe from Eq. 13.10 that the magnitude of the gradient of the binormal provides the torsion at that point. The derivative of the normal is related with the directions of tangent and binormal in a linear form. The relationships between the change of the directions of tangent, binormal, and normal, with respect to its curvature and torsions of the curve, as expressed in Eqs. 13.9–13.11, are the fundamental relationships in parametric curves lying on a surface.

13.3.2 | Parametric surfaces

The range data is mostly surface data, which may be represented in the form of a parametric surface for its analysis. Since a surface is a two dimensional entity, the parametric surface representation requires two parameters. It is a mapping from a 2-D real space to a 3-D real space, which is expressed as $\boldsymbol{X} : \boldsymbol{U} \subset \mathbb{R}^2 \to \mathbb{R}^3$. Here, the two parameters, denoted by u and v, may vary within certain finite ranges in real space, which are mapped to a three dimensional real space. A parametric 2-D surface is represented as in Eq. 13.12.

$$\boldsymbol{X}(u,v) = (x(u,v),\ y(u,v),\ z(u,v)) \tag{13.12}$$

Consider a curve, $\boldsymbol{C}_u$, that is lying on a surface, $\boldsymbol{X}(u,v)$, as shown by a solid curve in Fig. 13.10. The curve, $\boldsymbol{C}_u$, is formed on the surface by varying u, at a constant value of v, to obtain a single parametric description of points that define a curve. Consider another curve, $\boldsymbol{C}_v$, lying on the surface, $\boldsymbol{X}(u,v)$, which is formed by varying v, by keeping u constant at a value. It is shown as a dashed curve in the figure. Let the tangents of $\boldsymbol{C}_u$ and $\boldsymbol{C}_v$ be $\boldsymbol{X}_u = (x_u(u,v),\ y_u(u,v),\ z_u(u,v))$ and $\boldsymbol{X}_v = (x_v(u,v),\ y_v(u,v),\ z_v(u,v))$, respectively, at a particular point, $\boldsymbol{p}$, as shown in the figure. The plane in which the tangents, $\boldsymbol{X}_u$ and $\boldsymbol{X}_v$, lie, which also touches the surface at $\boldsymbol{p}$, is called the *tangent plane*, $\boldsymbol{S}$. The normal to the

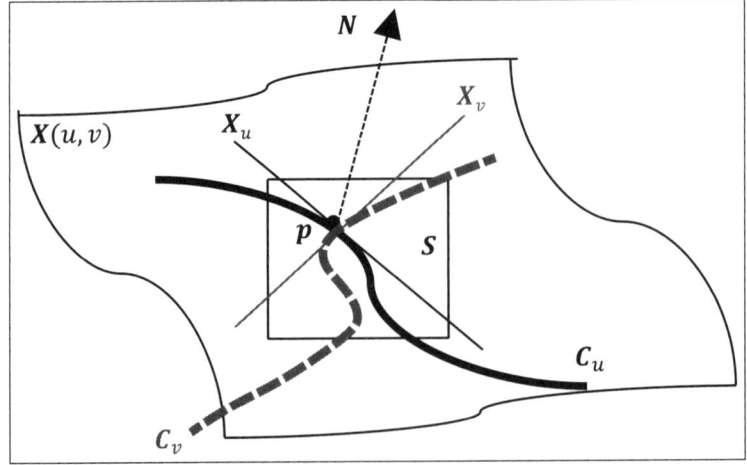

Figure 13.10 An illustration of a parametric surface.

tangent plane at that point is called the *surface normal*, $\hat{N}$, which is perpendicular to both X_u and X_v. A unit vector along the surface normal is computed by using the cross product of the corresponding two tangents, as given in Eq. 13.13.

$$\hat{N} = \frac{X_u \times X_v}{|X_u \times X_v|} \tag{13.13}$$

In general, even the parameters, u and v, are described as functions of another single parameter, t. It is a mapping of the values from an interval of a real space to a 2-D real space, which are coordinate values given by $(u(t),\ v(t))$. The function, $\beta(t)$, represents a parametric curve using the values of u and v for a particular t, which is given as $\beta(t) = (u(t),\ v(t))$. Unlike defining the curves on a surface in Fig. 13.10, the curve, $\beta(t)$, is a representation of a general curve on a surface, which is defined without the necessity to keep one of the parameters constant and vary the other parameter. But, there is a functional relationship in the variation between the parameters, u and v, that is denoted by the variable function, $\beta(t)$, which also denotes the parametric curve.

On expanding this notation, the curve on a surface with coordinates x, y, and z corresponding to $\beta(t)$ is given by Eq. 13.14.

$$\beta(t) \equiv (x(u(t), v(t)),\ y(u(t), v(t)),\ z(u(t), v(t))) \tag{13.14}$$

By applying the chain rule of differentiation, the tangent vector, t, to the curve defined by $\beta(t)$, is given by Eq. 13.15.

$$t = u'(t)X_u + v'(t)X_v \tag{13.15}$$

That is, the tangent is a weighted combination of the two vectors, X_u and X_v, since $u'(t)$ and $v'(t)$ are scalar values corresponding to their functional values for a particular t.

Numerical Example

Consider the three dimensional function $v(t) = \begin{bmatrix} \cos(t) \\ \sin(t) \\ \frac{t}{5} \end{bmatrix}$. Compute the parametric description of unit tangent vectors of $v(t)$.

Solution

The derivative $\frac{dv}{dt} = \begin{bmatrix} -\sin(t) \\ \cos(t) \\ \frac{1}{5} \end{bmatrix}$.

The magnitude of it is $\sqrt{(-\sin(t))^2 + (\cos(t))^2 + (\frac{1}{5})^2} = \frac{\sqrt{26}}{5}$.

Hence, the unit tangent vector is its derivative $\frac{dv}{dt}$ divided by its magnitude. It is given by $\frac{5}{\sqrt{26}} \begin{bmatrix} -\sin(t) \\ \cos(t) \\ \frac{1}{5} \end{bmatrix}$.

Numerical Example

Consider the set of parametric equations $x = t^2 + t$ and $y = 2t - 1$ representing a 2-D curve. Compute the tangent vector $(x'(t), y'(t))$ at $t = 1$.

Solution

Perform single derivative operation on x and y to compute the tangent at $t = 1$ and the vector is given by $(2t + 1, 2)$ at $t = 1$, which is $(3, 2)$.

Numerical Example

Compute the unit normal vector to the surface given by $S(u, v) = (x(u, v), y(u, v), z(u, v))$, $x(u, v) = u$, $y(u, v) = 2v^2$ and $z(u, v) = u^2 + v$ at the surface point given by $u = 1$ and $v = 1$.

Solution

The unit surface normal is given by $\frac{S_u \times S_v}{|S_u \times S_v|}$, where S_u, and S_v are partial derivatives with respect to u and v, respectively. Thus, $S_u = (1, 0, 2u)$, and $S_v = (0, 4v, 1)$. $S_u \times S_v = (-8uv, -1, 4v)$. Hence, the surface normal$= (-8, -1, 4)$. The unit surface normal: $\frac{1}{\sqrt{69}}(-8, -1, 4)$.

13.3.3 | First fundamental form

The first fundamental form relates to the change of magnitudes or the gradient directions at a point on a curve on the surface. The *first fundamental form* is a bilinear form that associates two vectors in the tangent plane in the form of a dot product. Thus, the dot product of two vectors, u and v, in the tangent plane gives the corresponding first fundamental form, as given by Eq. 13.16.

$$I(u, \ v) = u \cdot v \tag{13.16}$$

When both the vectors, u and v, are chosen as t in the derivation of the first fundamental form, $I(t, \ t) = t \cdot t$.

With respect to a parametric curve, $\beta(t)$, this is expressed as the dot product of the tangential directions, $\boldsymbol{t} \cdot \boldsymbol{t}$. Using Eq. 13.15, this is given by Eq. 13.17.

$$I(\boldsymbol{t},\ \boldsymbol{t}) = \boldsymbol{t} \cdot \boldsymbol{t} = (u'(t)\boldsymbol{X}_u + v'(t)\boldsymbol{X}_v) \cdot (u'(t)\boldsymbol{X}_u + v'(t)\boldsymbol{X}_v)$$

$$= (\boldsymbol{X}_u \cdot \boldsymbol{X}_u){u'}^2 + 2(\boldsymbol{X}_u \cdot \boldsymbol{X}_v)u'v' + (\boldsymbol{X}_v \cdot \boldsymbol{X}_v){v'}^2 \qquad (13.17)$$

$$= E{u'}^2 + 2Fu'v' + G{v'}^2$$

where, $\boldsymbol{X}_u$ and $\boldsymbol{X}_v$ are the partial derivatives of the function, $\boldsymbol{X}(u,v) = (x(u,v),\ y(u,v),\ z(u,v))$, with respect to u and v, respectively.

The parameters, E, F and G characterize the first fundamental form that are expressed as dot products of the corresponding partial derivatives of the functions with respect to u and v, and are given as follows.

$$E = \boldsymbol{X}_u \cdot \boldsymbol{X}_u$$
$$F = \boldsymbol{X}_u \cdot \boldsymbol{X}_v \qquad (13.18)$$
$$G = \boldsymbol{X}_v \cdot \boldsymbol{X}_v$$

The first fundamental form, $I(\boldsymbol{t},\ \boldsymbol{t})$ along the tangential vector $\boldsymbol{t}$ expresses the magnitude of the tangent vector of a curve at a surface point.

Numerical Example

Consider a hyperbolic paraboloid represented as parametric surface $x(u,v) = (u,v,uv)$. Consider a parametric curve on it with $u(t) = t^2$ and $v(t) = 2t$. Compute the quantity related to the first fundamental form at $t = 2$.

Solution

$E = x_u \cdot x_u = 1 + v^2$, $F = x_u \cdot x_v = uv$, $G = x_v \cdot x_v = 1 + u^2$.

At $t = 2$, $u(2) = 4$, and $v(2) = 4$. Hence, $E = 17$, $F = 16$, and $G = 17$. At $t = 2$, $u'(2) = 4$ and $v'(2) = 2$.

First fundamental form, i.e., the magnitude of the tangent vector at $t = 2$ for the parametric curve $u(t) = t^2$ and $v(t) = 2t$ on the surface: $E.(u')^2 + 2F.(u')(v') + G.(v')^2 = 17 \times 16 + 2 \times 16 \times 4 \times 2 + 17 \times 4 = 596$.

13.3.4 | Second fundamental form

Another concept, that is used in characterizing the surface points and local surface geometry, is the *second fundamental form*, which is related to the curvatures. Consider a curve, $\boldsymbol{X}(u,v) = (x(u,v),\ y(u,v),\ z(u,v))$, lying on a surface, as shown in Fig. 13.11. This curve is defined by varying along the parameter v, as represented by dv, while keeping the parameter u a constant. At a considered point, as in the figure, let $\boldsymbol{t}$ be the tangent of the curve, $\boldsymbol{n}$ be the normal of the curve, and $\boldsymbol{N}$ be the surface normal. Also, let the change in

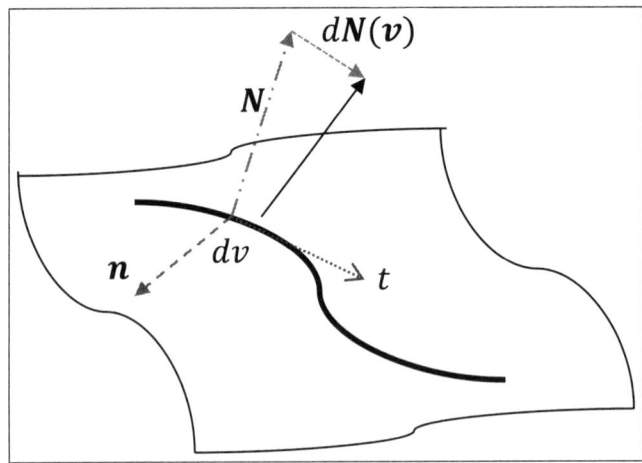

Figure 13.11 A parametric curve depicting the second fundamental form.

the surface normal with variations of the curve along the direction $\boldsymbol{v}$. be denoted by $d\boldsymbol{N}(\boldsymbol{v})$. The second fundamental form is defined by functions of two tangential vectors, $\boldsymbol{u}$ and $\boldsymbol{v}$, at the given point, which is given by Eq. 13.19.

$$II(\boldsymbol{u},\ \boldsymbol{v}) = \boldsymbol{u} \cdot d\boldsymbol{N}(\boldsymbol{v}) \tag{13.19}$$

where, both the vectors, $\boldsymbol{u}$ and $\boldsymbol{v}$, are chosen as $\boldsymbol{t}$ in the derivation of the second fundamental form, $II(\boldsymbol{t},\ \boldsymbol{t}) = \boldsymbol{t} \cdot d\boldsymbol{N}(\boldsymbol{t})$.

Since $\boldsymbol{t}$ and $\boldsymbol{N}$ are perpendicular to each other, their scalar dot product is given by Eq. 13.20.

$$\boldsymbol{t} \cdot \boldsymbol{N} = 0 \tag{13.20}$$

Taking the derivative of the terms in Eq. 13.20 with respect to the parameter v along the direction $\boldsymbol{v}$, it can be equated as in Eq. 13.21.

$$\frac{d\boldsymbol{t}}{dv} \cdot \boldsymbol{N} + \boldsymbol{t} \cdot d\boldsymbol{N}(\boldsymbol{v}) = 0 \tag{13.21}$$

Since the derivative of the tangent is a vector along the normal of the curve with its magnitude equal to the curvature at that point, substituting Eq. 13.9 in Eq. 13.21,

$$k\widehat{\boldsymbol{n}} \cdot \hat{\boldsymbol{N}} + \boldsymbol{t} \cdot d\boldsymbol{N}(\boldsymbol{v}) = 0 \tag{13.22}$$

where k is the curvature and $\widehat{\boldsymbol{n}}$ is the unit vector along the normal, $\boldsymbol{n}$, of the curve. From Eq. 13.19 and Eq. 13.22, the second fundamental form is expressed by Eq. 13.23,

$$II(\boldsymbol{t},\ \boldsymbol{t}) = -k\,\cos(\phi) \tag{13.23}$$

where ϕ is the angle between the curve normal, $\hat{\boldsymbol{n}}$, and the surface normal, $\hat{\boldsymbol{N}}$.

As an interpretation of the second fundamental form, since the vectors, the curve normal and the surface normal, are chosen to be unit vectors, Eq. 13.22 is expressed by the curvature and the angle between the vectors. In the particular case of a normal section, where the curve lies on the normal plane, the angle, ϕ, between the curve normal and surface normal becomes $0°$ or $180°$, depending on the topology. Then, for the case of a normal section, $II(\boldsymbol{t},\ \boldsymbol{t}) = \pm\,k_{\boldsymbol{t}}$, where $k_{\boldsymbol{t}}$ is the normal curvature.

By using the parametric representation of the curve that is given by Eq. 13.12, and defining the surface points with $\beta(s) = (u(s),\ v(s))$, with s in a certain range of interval of real values, the tangent of the curve is computed by taking the derivative of the curve with respect to s, as in Eq. 13.15, $\boldsymbol{t} = u'(s)\boldsymbol{X}_u + v'(s)\boldsymbol{X}_v$. The second fundamental form, $II(\boldsymbol{t},\ \boldsymbol{t}) = \boldsymbol{t}\cdot d\boldsymbol{N}(\boldsymbol{t})$, is represented as in Eq. 13.24,

$$II(\boldsymbol{t},\ \boldsymbol{t}) = e{u'}^2 + 2fu'v' + g{v'}^2 \tag{13.24}$$

where the parameters, e, f and g characterize the second fundamental form that are expressed as scalar dot products of the normal at a particular surface point and the second derivative vectors of the respective functions with respect to u and v parameters, which are given in Eq. 13.25.

$$\begin{aligned}
e &= \hat{\boldsymbol{N}}\cdot\boldsymbol{X}_{uu}\\
f &= \hat{\boldsymbol{N}}\cdot\boldsymbol{X}_{uv}\\
g &= \hat{\boldsymbol{N}}\cdot\boldsymbol{X}_{vv}
\end{aligned} \tag{13.25}$$

The *normal curvature*, $k_{\boldsymbol{t}}$, is computed by normalizing the second fundamental form by the magnitude of the tangent. That is, the ratio of the second fundamental form and the first fundamental form measures the normal curvature, which is given by Eq. 13.26.

$$k_{\boldsymbol{t}} = \frac{II(\boldsymbol{t},\ \boldsymbol{t})}{I(\boldsymbol{t},\ \boldsymbol{t})} = \frac{e{u'}^2 + 2fu'v' + g{v'}^2}{E{u'}^2 + 2Fu'v' + G{v'}^2} \tag{13.26}$$

where, the quantities, E, F, and G are defined by Eq. 13.18, and the quantities, e, f and g are defined by Eq. 13.25.

13.3.5 | Principal curvatures

A linear map, which contains all the necessary information for the computation of the curvature, is defined by the parameters of first and second fundamental forms, as given by Eq. 13.27.

$$\text{Linear map:}\quad \begin{bmatrix} e & f\\ f & g \end{bmatrix}\begin{bmatrix} E & F\\ F & G \end{bmatrix}^{-1} \tag{13.27}$$

where the E, F, and G are the elements of the first fundamental form that are given by Eq. 13.18, and e, f and g are the elements of the second fundamental form that are given by Eq. 13.25. The eigenvalues and eigen vectors of the linear map provide the *principal curvatures*, k_1 and k_2, that are associated with the respective principle directions.

Among the two principal curvatures, one of them is the dominant curvature, whose magnitude is relatively larger than the other.

The curvature is a very critical information in understanding the local topology or geometry of a surface. Toward this, two particular entities, *Gaussian curvature* and *mean curvature*, define the important intrinsic properties of the surface geometry. The Gaussian curvature, K, is computed as the determinant of the linear map, which is the product of the two principal curvatures, as given by Eq. 13.28.

$$K = k_1 k_2 = \frac{eg - f^2}{EG - F^2} \tag{13.28}$$

The mean curvature, H, is computed as half of the trace of the linear map, which is the mean of the two principal curvatures, as given by Eq. 13.29.

$$H = \frac{k_1 + k_2}{2} = \frac{Eg + Ge - 2Ff}{2(EG - F^2)} \tag{13.29}$$

The Gaussian curvature and the mean curvature also provide alternative descriptions of the local curvatures, besides the principal curvatures. By relating the theory of quadratic equations with the familiar form in Eqs. 13.28 and 13.29, a quadratic equation is expressed to reflect these relation, as given in Eq. 13.30.

$$k^2 - 2Hk + K = 0 \tag{13.30}$$

As a solution to Eq. 13.30, the roots of the quadratic equation provide the principal curvatures, which are given by Eq. 13.31.

$$k_{1,2} = H \pm \sqrt{H^2 - K} \tag{13.31}$$

In this way, given the mean curvature and the Gaussian curvature, the principal curvatures are computed.

Numerical Example

Consider the following representation of a surface $(x(u,v), y(u,v), z(u,v))$, where, $0 \leq (u,v) \leq 1$.

$$\begin{bmatrix} f_1(u) \\ f_2(u) \\ f_3(u) \end{bmatrix} = \begin{bmatrix} 3 & 2 & 4 \\ -5 & 6 & 2 \\ 1 & 4 & -3 \end{bmatrix} \begin{bmatrix} u^2 \\ u \\ 1 \end{bmatrix}, \text{ and } \begin{bmatrix} g_1(v) \\ g_2(v) \\ g_3(v) \end{bmatrix} = \begin{bmatrix} 4 & 3 & 2 \\ 1 & 7 & 8 \\ -5 & 6 & 3 \end{bmatrix} \begin{bmatrix} v^2 \\ v \\ 1 \end{bmatrix}$$

$$x(u,v) = f_1(u)g_1(v), y(u,v) = f_2(u)g_2(v), and\ z(u,v) = f_3(u)g_3(v).$$

Compute the surface normal, and Gaussian and mean curvatures at $(u,v) = (0.5, 0.5)$.

Solution

From the given data, let,

$$
\boldsymbol{F}(u) = \begin{bmatrix} f_1(u) \\ f_2(u) \\ f_3(u) \end{bmatrix} = \begin{bmatrix} 3 & 2 & 4 \\ -5 & 6 & 2 \\ 1 & 4 & -3 \end{bmatrix} \begin{bmatrix} u^2 \\ u \\ 1 \end{bmatrix}
$$

$$
\boldsymbol{G}(v) = \begin{bmatrix} g_1(v) \\ g_2(v) \\ g_3(v) \end{bmatrix} = \begin{bmatrix} 4 & 3 & 2 \\ 1 & 7 & 8 \\ -5 & 6 & 3 \end{bmatrix} \begin{bmatrix} v^2 \\ v \\ 1 \end{bmatrix}
$$

Taking the derivatives of the above functions with respect to the corresponding independent variables,

$$
\boldsymbol{F}'(u) = \begin{bmatrix} f_1'(u) \\ f_2'(u) \\ f_3'(u) \end{bmatrix} = \begin{bmatrix} 3 & 2 & 4 \\ -5 & 6 & 2 \\ 1 & 4 & -3 \end{bmatrix} \begin{bmatrix} 2u \\ 1 \\ 0 \end{bmatrix}
$$

$$
\boldsymbol{G}'(v) = \begin{bmatrix} g_1'(v) \\ g_2'(v) \\ g_3'(v) \end{bmatrix} = \begin{bmatrix} 4 & 3 & 2 \\ 1 & 7 & 8 \\ -5 & 6 & 3 \end{bmatrix} \begin{bmatrix} 2v \\ 1 \\ 0 \end{bmatrix}
$$

Evaluating the above expressions at $u = v = 0.5$,

$$
\boldsymbol{F}(0.5) = \begin{bmatrix} 5.75 \\ 3.75 \\ -0.75 \end{bmatrix} ; \qquad \boldsymbol{F}'(0.5) = \begin{bmatrix} 5 \\ 1 \\ 5 \end{bmatrix}
$$

$$
\boldsymbol{G}(0.5) = \begin{bmatrix} 4.5 \\ 11.75 \\ 4.75 \end{bmatrix} ; \qquad \boldsymbol{G}'(0.5) = \begin{bmatrix} 7 \\ 8 \\ 1 \end{bmatrix}
$$

Consider the tangents, $\boldsymbol{X}_u$ and $\boldsymbol{X}_v$, which are given by,

$$
\boldsymbol{X}_u = \boldsymbol{F}'(u) \odot \boldsymbol{G}(v) = \begin{bmatrix} 22.5 \\ 11.75 \\ 23.75 \end{bmatrix} , \text{ and } \boldsymbol{X}_v = \boldsymbol{F}(u) \odot \boldsymbol{G}'(v) = \begin{bmatrix} 40.25 \\ 30 \\ -0.75 \end{bmatrix} .
$$

where, $\odot$ represents element-wise multiplication operation. Also, $\boldsymbol{X}_u$ is independent of v, and the function $\boldsymbol{X}_v$ is independent of u. The surface normal, $\widehat{\boldsymbol{n}}$ is computed from $\boldsymbol{X}_u$ and $\boldsymbol{X}_v$ as,

$$\widehat{n} = \frac{X_u \times X_v}{||X_u \times X_v||} = \begin{bmatrix} -0.587 \\ 0.792 \\ 0.164 \end{bmatrix}_{\text{at } u=v=0.5}$$

To compute the mean curvature and Gaussian curvature, it is necessary to compute the elements of the *linear map*, which is given by,

$$\text{Linear map: } \mathbf{L} = \begin{bmatrix} e & f \\ f & g \end{bmatrix} \begin{bmatrix} E & F \\ F & G \end{bmatrix}^{-1}$$

Then, half of the trace of matrix of linear map is the mean curvature, and the determinant of the matrix is the Gaussian curvature. Similar to the computation of the first derivatives of given functions, $F'(u)$ and $G'(v)$, the second derivatives, $F''(u)$ and $G''(v)$, are computed, which are given by,

$$F''(0.5) = \begin{bmatrix} 6 \\ -10 \\ 2 \end{bmatrix} ; \qquad G''(0.5) = \begin{bmatrix} 8 \\ 2 \\ -10 \end{bmatrix}$$

Similar to X_u and X_v, X_{uu}, X_{uv} and X_{vv} are computed as,

$$X_{uu} = F''(u) \odot G(v), \ \ X_{uv} = F'(u) \odot G'(v), \text{ and } X_{vv} = F(u) \odot G''(v).$$

Also, the elements of the linear map are computed as,

$$\begin{aligned} E &= X_u \cdot X_u & e &= X_{uu} \cdot \widehat{n} \\ F &= X_u \cdot X_v & f &= X_{uv} \cdot \widehat{n} \\ G &= X_v \cdot X_v & g &= X_{vv} \cdot \widehat{n} \end{aligned}$$

At $u = v = 0.5$, the values of the elements of linear map are,

$$\begin{aligned} E &= 1208.375 & e &= 107.352 \\ F &= 1240.312 & f &= 13.389 \\ G &= 2520.625 & g &= 19.832 \end{aligned}$$

So, the corresponding linear map is given by,

$$\text{Linear map: } \mathbf{L} = \begin{bmatrix} 0.168 & -0.077 \\ 0.006 & 0.005 \end{bmatrix}$$

The principal curvatures are obtained by the Eigenvalues of the linear map, k_1 and k_2. Then, the required curvatures are given by,

$$\text{Gaussian curvature: } K = k_1 k_2 = \frac{eg - f^2}{EG - F^2} = \text{Det}(\mathbf{L}) = 0.0013$$

$$\text{Mean curvature: } H = \frac{k_1 + k_2}{2} = \frac{Eg + Ge - 2Ff}{2(EG - F^2)} = \frac{\text{Trace}(\mathbf{L})}{2} = 0.086.$$

13.3.6 | Surface types from signs of curvatures

Characterization of the topology of the local surface curvatures is one of the techniques for understanding the usefulness of the analysis of curvatures (Besl and Jain, 1986). There are various kinds of local shapes that could be attributed by the signs of curvatures. In Fig. 13.12, eight visible types of surfaces are shown that are characterized by the signs of the Gaussian curvature and the mean curvature.

From the elementary knowledge of differential calculus, it is known that, for a given function, $f(x)$, the derivative of the function, $f'(x)$, is zero, if it happens to be a peak or a pit value (maximum or minimum), at a particular value of x. Also, the double derivative at that point, $f''(x)$, is less than zero, if it is a maximum (peak). Similarly, if it is a minimum (pit), $f''(x)$ is greater than zero. Also, the curvature is closely proportional to the double derivative of the functional value. For example, consider the peak surface that is shown in Fig. 13.12 (a). For the peak surface, both the principal curvatures are negative valued, $k_1 < 0$ and $k_2 < 0$, since the surface is characterized by a shape similar to the Gaussian shape with a maximum peak. This can also be proved mathematically, which is left as an exercise for the reader to work out. Since mean curvature, H, is defined as the mean of the two principal curvatures, which are of negative values for the peak surface, $H < 0$. Similarly, the Gaussian curvature, K, which is the product of the two principal curvatures that are of negative values for the peak surface, $K > 0$. Hence, the surface characterized by $H < 0$ and $K > 0$ is a peak surface, as shown in the Fig. 13.12.

Similarly, for a pit surface, which is in Fig. 13.12 (b), both the principal curvatures are positive valued, $k_1 > 0$ and $k_2 > 0$, since the surface is characterized by a shape similar to the inverted Gaussian shape with a minimum (pit). So, as a mean of two positive values, $H > 0$; and, as a product of two positive values, $K > 0$. Hence, the surface characterized by $H > 0$ and $K > 0$ is a pit surface, as shown in the figure. For the surface that is shown in Fig. 13.12 (c), both the curvatures are zero, since the radius of curvature is infinite for the flat surface. Therefore, the surface characterized by $H = 0$ and $K = 0$ is a flat surface. Such observations are extended to other kinds of 3-D surfaces that are characterized, which are shown in Fig. 13.12 (Besl and Jain, 1986). These characteristic local properties of the surfaces are used as features in various applications like detection and segmentation of surfaces.

Although the directions or signs of principal curvatures can be used to characterize the surfaces, it is observed that, the characterization by mean curvature and Gaussian curvature are more elaborate in discriminating the surfaces. A summary of characterization of surface by the principal curvatures, and the mean and Gaussian curvatures is provided in Tables 13.1 and 13.2, respectively. Table 13.2, which summarizes the characterization by Gaussian and mean curvatures, is more elaborate with comparatively better discrimination of the surfaces.

13.3.7 | Monge patches

In a particular kind of surface description, which is akin to the range data discussed in Section 13.1, the x-coordinate and y-coordinate are described by the parameters u and v, and the z-coordinate is a function of the two parameters, $h(u, v)$, as given by $\boldsymbol{X}(u, v) = (u, v, h(u, v))$. An example of such representation is shown figuratively in Fig. 13.13. The figure shows a surface patch with independent parameters as u and v, which are equivalent to x-axis and y-axis, respectively, and the z-axis is given by the height of the surface point

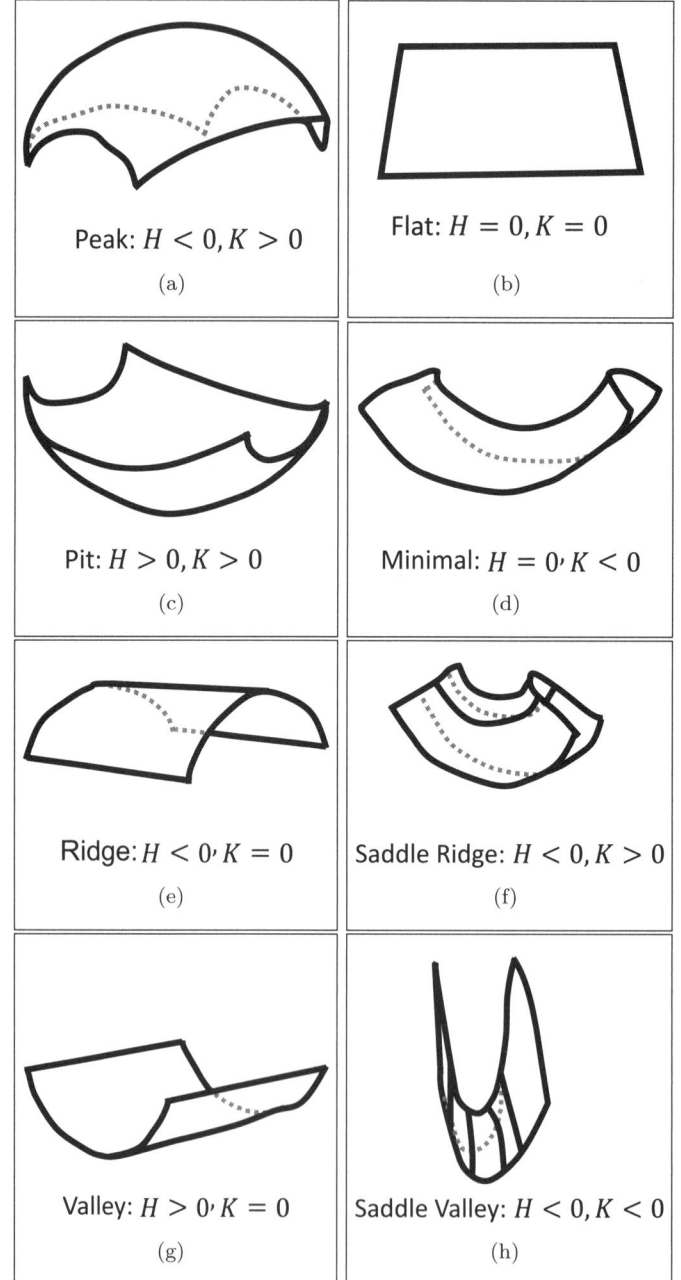

Figure 13.12 The eight visible types of surfaces that are characterized by the signs of Gaussian and mean curvatures.

Table 13.1 Characterization of a surface by the principal curvatures.

Principal curvatures		k_1		
		$-$	0	$+$
	$-$	peak	ridge	saddle
k_2	0	ridge	flat	valley
	$+$	saddle	valley	pit

Table 13.2 Characterization of a surface by the mean and Gaussian curvatures.

Gaussian and mean curvatures		K		
		$-$	0	$+$
	$-$	saddle ridge	ridge	peak
H	0	minimal surface	flat	none
	$+$	saddle valley	valley	pit

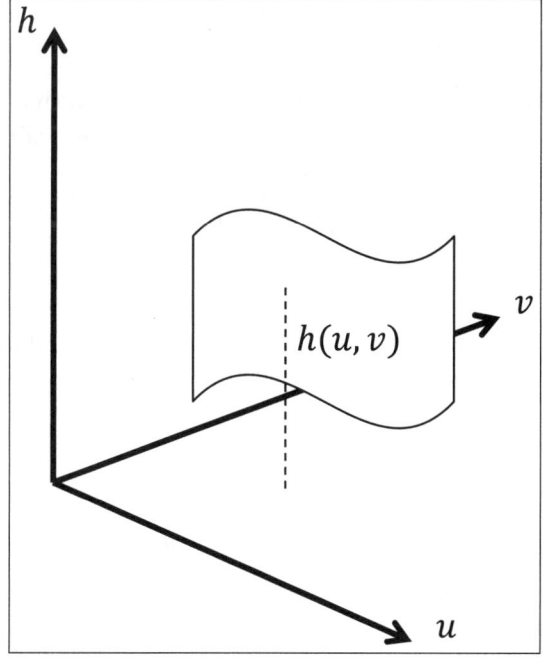

Figure 13.13 A figurative representation of a surface patch.

from the uv-plane. The surface patches with this kind of description are attributed as *Monge patches*. For any given description of a parametric surface, the surface normal, and all the elements of first and second fundamental forms are computed as in Eq. 13.18 and Eq. 13.25, which are reproduced in Eq. 13.32 for a reference.

$$
\begin{array}{cc}
2^{\text{nd}}\text{ fundamental form} & 1^{\text{st}}\text{ fundamental form} \\[4pt]
e = \hat{\boldsymbol{N}} \cdot \boldsymbol{X}_{uu} & E = \boldsymbol{X}_u \cdot \boldsymbol{X}_u \\[4pt]
f = \hat{\boldsymbol{N}} \cdot \boldsymbol{X}_{uv} & F = \boldsymbol{X}_u \cdot \boldsymbol{X}_v \\[4pt]
g = \hat{\boldsymbol{N}} \cdot \boldsymbol{X}_{vv} & G = \boldsymbol{X}_v \cdot \boldsymbol{X}_v
\end{array}
\tag{13.32}
$$

That is, the first fundamental form matrix elements, which are related to magnitude of tangents, are computed using the derivatives of corresponding functions. The second fundamental form matrix elements, which are related to curvatures, are computed using the double derivatives of the corresponding functions.

For the surface shown in Fig. 13.13, the partial derivatives and double partial derivatives of the corresponding function, with respect to u and v, are computed to find the respective matrix elements of Eq. 13.32. The gradient of $\boldsymbol{X}(u,v)$ with respect to u, $\boldsymbol{X}_u$, is represented as column vector given in Eq. 13.33.

$$
\boldsymbol{X}_u = \begin{bmatrix} 1 \\ 0 \\ h_u \end{bmatrix}
\tag{13.33}
$$

where, h_u is the partial derivative of $h(u,v)$ with respect to u, which is given by $h_u = \frac{\partial h(u,v)}{\partial u}$. Similarly, the gradient of $\boldsymbol{X}(u,v)$ with respect to v, $\boldsymbol{X}_v$, is represented by Eq. 13.34.

$$
\boldsymbol{X}_v = \begin{bmatrix} 0 \\ 1 \\ h_v \end{bmatrix}
\tag{13.34}
$$

where, $h_v = \frac{\partial h(u,v)}{\partial v}$. Then, the elements of the first fundamental form, E, F, and G, are computed using the vectors, $\boldsymbol{X}_u$ and $\boldsymbol{X}_v$, by their appropriate dot products, which are given in Eq. 13.35.

$$
\begin{aligned}
E &= \hat{\boldsymbol{N}} \cdot \boldsymbol{X}_{uu} = (1 + h_u^2) \\
F &= \hat{\boldsymbol{N}} \cdot \boldsymbol{X}_{uv} = h_u h_v \\
G &= \hat{\boldsymbol{N}} \cdot \boldsymbol{X}_{uv} = (1 + h_v^2)
\end{aligned}
\tag{13.35}
$$

The surface normal, $\hat{\boldsymbol{N}}$, is computed using the normalized cross product of $\boldsymbol{X}_u$ and $\boldsymbol{X}_v$ as in Eq. 13.13. The cross product of $\boldsymbol{X}_u$ and $\boldsymbol{X}_v$ is given by Eq. 13.36.

$$
\boldsymbol{X}_u \times \boldsymbol{X}_v = \begin{vmatrix} i & j & k \\ 1 & 0 & h_u \\ 0 & 1 & h_v \end{vmatrix} = (-h_u i) + (-h_v j) + k \equiv \begin{bmatrix} -h_u \\ -h_v \\ 1 \end{bmatrix}
\tag{13.36}
$$

So, the surface is normal is computed as,

$$\hat{\boldsymbol{N}} = \frac{\boldsymbol{X}_u \times \boldsymbol{X}_v}{|\boldsymbol{X}_u \times \boldsymbol{X}_v|} = \frac{(-h_u, \, -h_v, \, 1)^\top}{\sqrt{1 + h_u^2 + h_v^2}} \qquad (13.37)$$

The double derivatives, $\boldsymbol{X}_{uu}$, $\boldsymbol{X}_{uv}$, and $\boldsymbol{X}_{vv}$, are computed by taking the derivatives of $\boldsymbol{X}_u$ and $\boldsymbol{X}_v$ in Eqs. 13.33 and 13.34, with respect to u and v, which are represented by column vectors as given in Eq. 13.38.

$$\boldsymbol{X}_{uu} = \begin{bmatrix} 0 \\ 0 \\ h_{uu} \end{bmatrix}, \quad \boldsymbol{X}_{uv} = \begin{bmatrix} 0 \\ 0 \\ h_{uv} \end{bmatrix}, \quad \boldsymbol{X}_{vv} = \begin{bmatrix} 0 \\ 0 \\ h_{vv} \end{bmatrix} \qquad (13.38)$$

where, $h_{uu} = \frac{\partial^2 h(u,v)}{\partial u^2}$, $h_{uv} = \frac{\partial^2 h(u,v)}{\partial u \partial v}$, and $h_{vv} = \frac{\partial^2 h(u,v)}{\partial v^2}$. Then, the elements of the second fundamental form, e, f, and g, are computed using the vectors, $\hat{\boldsymbol{N}}$, $\boldsymbol{X}_{uu}$, $\boldsymbol{X}_{uv}$, and $\boldsymbol{X}_{vv}$, by their appropriate dot products, which are given in Eq. 13.39.

$$e = \hat{\boldsymbol{N}} \cdot \boldsymbol{X}_{uu} = \frac{-h_{uu}}{\sqrt{1 + h_u^2 + h_v^2}}$$

$$f = \hat{\boldsymbol{N}} \cdot \boldsymbol{X}_{uv} = \frac{-h_{uv}}{\sqrt{1 + h_u^2 + h_v^2}} \qquad (13.39)$$

$$g = \hat{\boldsymbol{N}} \cdot \boldsymbol{X}_{vv} = \frac{-h_{vv}}{\sqrt{1 + h_u^2 + h_v^2}}$$

The linear map is formed, as in Eq. 13.27, using the elements of the first and the second fundamental forms. Also, by Eqs. 13.28 and 13.29, the Gaussian curvature and the mean curvature are computed using these elements, which are given by Eqs. 13.40 and 13.41, respectively.

$$H = \frac{-h_{uu}(1 + h_u^2) - h_{vv}(1 + h_v^2) + 2h_{uv}h_u h_v}{2(1 + h_u^2 + h_v^2)^{\frac{3}{2}}} \qquad (13.40)$$

$$K = \frac{h_{uu}h_{vv} - h_{uv}^2}{(1 + h_u^2 + h_v^2)^2} \qquad (13.41)$$

Range data is a simplified form of surface description, where the parameters are directly described by x-coordinates and y-coordinates in their respective directions, and the depth value is a function of these coordinates which is along the z-axis. So, the expressions in Eqs. 13.40 and 13.41 may be readily used to compute the curvatures. Also, as discussed in Chapter 1 on fundamentals of image processing, various kinds of masks may be used for efficient computation of the derivatives and double derivatives in range images, which is then followed by computation of the curvatures. Using the curvatures and their signs, the local topology of the considered surface is obtained.

13.4 | Characterizing edges in range images

In intensity images, the edges usually appear as short changes of brightness values, which are almost like zeroth order discontinuity, and such edges are called *step edges*. Whereas in range images, there are some discontinuities which are not very sharp. This happens when the functional values change continuously across edges. In such cases, an edge is formed by the intersection of two planes in the functional map that produces the range image, which also gives the sense of depth variation, and these edges are called *roof edges*. A range image consists of both step and roof types of edges. As an example, a rectangular bar is shown in Fig. 13.14, where examples of step and roof edges are distinctly labeled at different junction transitions (Brady et al., 1985). Since the step and the roof edges are processed in different ways, let us discuss how they are distinguished and characterized.

Examples of edge models for step and roof edges (Brady et al., 1985) are shown in Fig. 13.15. In the step edge model, shown in Fig. 13.15, a sharp jump of h in the functional values can be observed, which are denoted by the slopes, k_1 and k_2, before and after the edge point, respectively. A model of the step edge is given by Eq. 13.42.

$$z = \begin{cases} k_1 x + c & \text{when } x < 0, \\ k_2 x + c + h & \text{when } x > 0 \end{cases} \qquad (13.42)$$

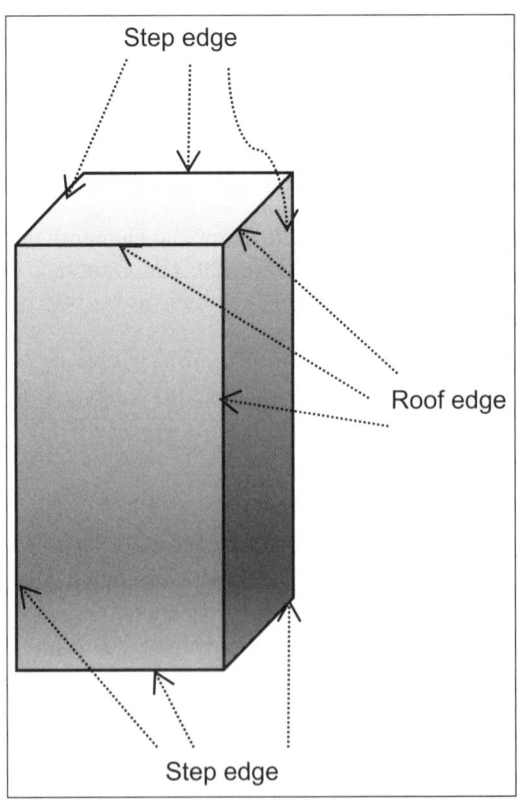

Figure 13.14 Example of a step and a roof edges formed in a range image of a structure.

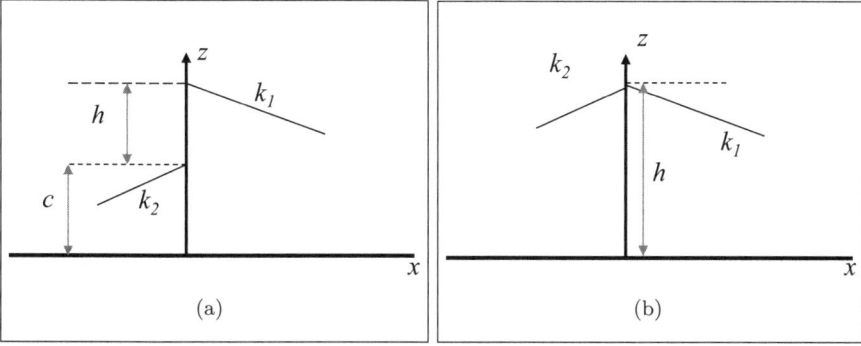

Figure 13.15 Edge models for step and roof edges. (a) Step edge, and (b) roof edge.

where, c and h are the height intercepts, as shown in the Fig. 13.15 (a). Whereas for the roof edge, as shown in Fig. 13.15 (b), there is no such distinct jump in the functional values. But there is a continuous gradation of the functional values in a linear form at different proportions around the edge point, as shown in the figure. A model of the roof edge is given by Eq. 13.43.

$$z = \begin{cases} k_1 x + h & \text{when } x < 0, \\ k_2 x + h & \text{when } x > 0 \end{cases} \tag{13.43}$$

where, h is the height intercept, as shown in the Fig. 13.15 (b). For the sake of simplicity, the analysis on the functional definitions of edges have been shown with respect to one dimensional function in Fig. 13.15.

To characterize the step and the roof edges in a particular function, the signal is smoothened with Gaussian mask and then its derivatives are computed. The signal is smoothened before computing the derivatives of higher orders to reduce noise in the signal, since the presence of spurious changes or noise in the signal results in errors while computing the gradients. There is an advantage of using a Gaussian mask in smoothing and computing the second derivatives of the signal. Instead of performing Gaussian smoothing of the signal and then taking its derivatives, the derivatives of the Gaussian mask may be directly used in the convolution operation with the signal, which is computationally more efficient, as given by an example in Eq. 13.44.

$$z''_\sigma(x) = \frac{\partial^2 G(x; \sigma)}{\partial \sigma^2} * z(x) \tag{13.44}$$

where, $z(x)$ is the considered signal, $G(x; \sigma)$ is the Gaussian function with scale σ, and $z''_\sigma(x)$ is the double derivative of Gaussian smoothened signal. A particular characteristic of this analysis is the ratio of second and first derivatives of curvature, which behaves differently across the scale of Gaussian mask.

For a given signal $z(x)$, the curvature, $k_\sigma(x)$, of the Gaussian smoothened signal, $z_\sigma(x)$, at a scale of σ, is given by Eq. 13.45.

$$k_\sigma(x) = \frac{z_\sigma''}{(1 + z_\sigma')^{\frac{3}{2}}} \qquad (13.45)$$

where z_σ' and z_σ'' are the first and second derivatives of $z_\sigma(x)$, respectively. From Eq. 13.45, it is observed that the curvature is directly proportional to the second derivative of the smoothened signal. So, the ratio of the second derivative of the curvature, $k_\sigma''(x)$, to the first derivative of the curvature, $k_\sigma'(x)$, is computed as the ratio of the fourth derivative of $z_\sigma(x)$, $z_\sigma''''(x)$, and the third derivative of $z_\sigma(x)$, $z_\sigma'''(x)$, at the scale of σ, as given by Eq. 13.46.

$$\frac{k_\sigma''(x)}{k_\sigma'(x)} = \frac{z_\sigma''''(x)}{z_\sigma'''(x)} \qquad (13.46)$$

For a step edge this ratio across the scales remains almost constant, whereas for a roof edge, this ratio is inversely proportional to the scale. Given a detected edge point, it is validated as a genuine edge point if it holds these characteristics. If the edge point does not follow these properties, it is considered as a spurious edge point.

An edge point is detected by using the curvatures of the smoothened function. The probable candidates of step edge points are detected by the zero crossings of one of the principal curvatures. Then, each of these points are observed across the scales to check if the points preserve the property of invariance of the ratio of second and first derivatives of curvature, with varying scales. In other words, for a step edge, $\frac{k_\sigma''(x)}{k_\sigma'(x)}$ is roughly a constant across σ.

The probable candidates of roof edge are characterized by local maximum of curvature that is sought in the direction of dominant (in the sense of magnitude) principal curvature, which roughly remains constant across the scales. Since the ratio of second and first derivatives of curvature is inversely proportional to the scale for a roof edge, the product of this ratio and the scale remains roughly a constant, which is captured by the maximum of curvature along the dominant principal direction. Thus, for a roof edge, $\sigma \frac{k_\sigma''(x)}{k_\sigma'(x)}$ is a constant across σ, the scale. These observations are combined in developing an algorithm of edge detection (Brady et al., 1985), which is given in Algorithm 18.

This analysis is also used to explain the mechanism of multi-scale edge tracking to track the edge pixels at different scales of the images that are obtained by smoothing the image at different scales of Gaussian functions. If the respective properties of step and roof edges are retained at higher scales for certain points, those points are considered as multi-scale edge points. However, the points represented at their finest scale are retained to avoid spatial shifts due to smoothing operations.

13.5 | Segmentation of range images

Segmentation of range images is also one of the key tasks in the analysis of range images. Though there are various approaches for range image segmentation, the discussion in this book has been restricted to only the techniques on segmentation of planar patches.

Algorithm 18 Algorithm for finding candidate edge points in range images

Input: Acquired range image.
Output: Candidate points of step and roof edges.
1: Compute a set of Gaussian smoothed images at multiple scales.
2: Compute the principal directions and curvatures at each point of the smoothed images.
3: Compute zero crossings of the Gaussian curvature for candidate step edge points and extreme of the dominant principal curvature in the corresponding principal direction candidate roof edge points.
4: Use the analytical models across the scales to select the candidate points for the respective edges.

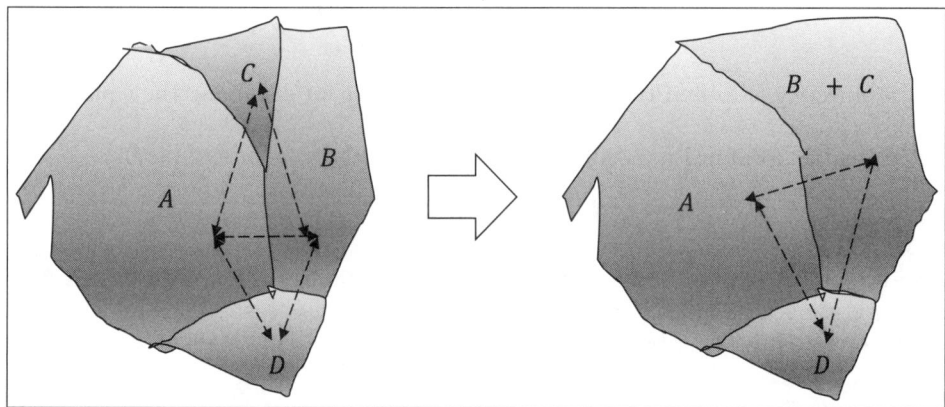

Figure 13.16 Illustration of segmentation of range images using region growing approach.

Segmentation of range images into planes via region growing One of the approaches is to consider small planar patches in the image, which are then integrated into a larger surface. This approach considers the planar faces in the images, as shown in Fig. 13.16. At first, very small patches are locally fit by the equations of the plane. Also, for each patch, a node of a graph is formed with edges between all the neighboring patches. Then, an average distance to the plane best fitting them is obtained as the cost of fitting of the total patches. If any of the patches are merged, then the costs of fitting would give the average fitting of the merged patch (Faugeras and Hebert, 1986).

Given a set of N data points, $S = \{(x_i, y_i, z_i)\}_{i=1,2,3,\ldots,N}$, with an objective to find a plane, a plane is fitted using the data points with the general expression for the plane, as given by Eq. 13.47.

$$z = a_1 x + a_2 y + a_3 \qquad (13.47)$$

The Eq. 13.47 is just a reformulation of the familiar equation of a plane, $ax + by + cz + d = 0$, where, $a_1 = -\frac{a}{c}$, $a_2 = -\frac{b}{c}$, and $a_3 = -\frac{d}{c}$, which is expressed with z as a function of x and y, a usual form of range data. A matrix form of Eq. 13.47 is expressed by Eq. 13.48.

$$z = [x \quad y \quad 1] \begin{bmatrix} a_1 \\ a_2 \\ a_3 \end{bmatrix} \tag{13.48}$$

So, a set of N linear equations are formed by N data points in S, which is expressed by Eq. 13.49.

$$\begin{bmatrix} z_1 \\ z_2 \\ z_3 \\ \vdots \\ z_N \end{bmatrix} = \begin{bmatrix} x_1 & y_1 & 1 \\ x_2 & y_2 & 1 \\ x_3 & y_3 & 1 \\ & \vdots & \\ x_N & y_N & 1 \end{bmatrix} \begin{bmatrix} a_1 \\ a_2 \\ a_3 \end{bmatrix} \tag{13.49}$$

Here, the objective is to find the values of a_1, a_2, and a_3 for obtaining the equation of the plane.

Let the matrix form in Eq. 13.49 be represented concisely as in Eq. 13.50.

$$\boldsymbol{Z} = \mathbf{X}\boldsymbol{A} \tag{13.50}$$

So, now the objective is to find a particular $\boldsymbol{A}$ that minimizes the norm, $\|\boldsymbol{Z} - \mathbf{X}\boldsymbol{A}\|$. This is solved by using a nonhomogeneous method of solving the least squares error estimate, where the error, $\boldsymbol{E}$, is given by Eq. 13.51.

$$\boldsymbol{E} = \|\boldsymbol{Z} - \mathbf{X}\boldsymbol{A}\| \tag{13.51}$$

From Eq. 13.50, $\boldsymbol{A}$ is computed by the expression in Eq. 13.52.

$$\boldsymbol{A} = \left(\mathbf{X}^\top \mathbf{X}\right)^{-1} \mathbf{X}^\top \boldsymbol{Z} \tag{13.52}$$

So, from Eqs. 13.51 and 13.52, the error is expressed in form given by Eq. 13.53.

$$\boldsymbol{E} = \left\| \boldsymbol{Z} - \mathbf{X}\left(\mathbf{X}^\top \mathbf{X}\right)^{-1} \mathbf{X}^\top \boldsymbol{Z} \right\| \tag{13.53}$$

The error expressed in Eq. 13.53 is called *arc cost*. The error of planar fit is an arc cost between two nodes of the graph.

For the graph considered in Fig. 13.16 (a), there are four nodes labeled A, B, C and D. The neighboring edges corresponding to these nodes represent the fitting of planes to them with an arc cost given by Eq. 13.53. The nodes of the edge corresponding to the minimum cost are fitted to transform the graph of Fig. 13.16 (a) to Fig. 13.16 (b). That is, each pair of planar regions are iteratively merged by minimizing the average distance to the plane best fitting them. A greedy approach is applied for selecting the best (minimum) arc cost and merge the nodes iteratively. The process of merging is repeated until all the patches are merged or the error is greater than a preset threshold. In the illustration of Fig. 13.16, the merging of B and C is indicated.

13.6 | Registration of range data

Given two images that are related by a certain transformation, the problem of image registration is to compute the transformation between the images, so that one of the images is obtained from the other image by applying the transformation. In the context of range data, it may be considered that a pair of views of a surface are captured individually from two different views. So, these data are related by the corresponding coordinate transformations between the two views and it is supposed to be a kind of rigid body transformation. To perform registration of a pair of range data, the following assumptions are made on the data:

- The surface data belongs to the same object.
- The two views are captured from different viewing directions.
- The coordinates of the corresponding points in the data are related by rigid body transformation.
- Same scale is assumed for the coordinate axes.

In this context, the coordinate transformation is attributed by translation and rotation between the views. The computational problem is to estimate the rotation and translation parameters.

Consider two corresponding point sets, $\{m_i\}$ and $\{d_i\}$, where $i = 1, 2, ..., N$, which correspond to the point sets of two different views of an object. Since the two point sets are related by a rigid body transformation with corresponding rotation and translation, they are expressed in nonhomogeneous coordinate system as given by Eq. 13.54.

$$d_i = \mathbf{R}m_i + \mathbf{T} + v_i \tag{13.54}$$

where, v_i is a 3×1 noise vector, $\mathbf{R}$ is a 3×3 rotation matrix, $\mathbf{T}$ is a 3×1 translation matrix, and the points, d_i and m_i, are represented as 3×1 vectors. The objective is to compute the parameters of $\mathbf{R}$ and $\mathbf{T}$ in presence of the noise. To solve for $\mathbf{R}$ and $\mathbf{T}$, the error of the model fitting, $\boldsymbol{E}$, is minimized, which is expressed by the sum of squared errors as given in Eq. 13.55.

$$\boldsymbol{E} = \sum_{i=1}^{N} \left\| d_i - \widehat{\mathbf{R}}m_i - \widehat{\mathbf{T}} \right\|^2 \tag{13.55}$$

where $\widehat{\mathbf{R}}$ and $\widehat{\mathbf{T}}$ represents the estimated rotation and translation matrices, respectively. In fact, this is not a simple least squares error estimation based minimization problem. It is a constrained optimization problem; the rotation matrix is constrained by its property of being an orthonormal matrix, so that, $\widehat{\mathbf{R}}^{\top}\widehat{\mathbf{R}} = \mathbf{I}$ or $\widehat{\mathbf{R}}^{\top} = \widehat{\mathbf{R}}^{-1}$. In this case, $\boldsymbol{E}$ in Eq. 13.55

is to be minimized, subject to this constraint on $\widehat{\mathbf{R}}$. A simplification by taking the partial derivatives of $\boldsymbol{E}$ in Eq. 13.55 with respect to $\widehat{\mathbf{T}}$ is given as follows.

$$\frac{\partial \boldsymbol{E}}{\partial \widehat{\mathbf{T}}} = 0 \implies -\sum_{i=0}^{N} \left(\boldsymbol{d}_i - \widehat{\mathbf{R}} \boldsymbol{m}_i - \widehat{\mathbf{T}} \right) = 0$$

$$\implies \widehat{\mathbf{T}} = \overline{\boldsymbol{d}} - \widehat{\mathbf{R}} \overline{\boldsymbol{m}}$$

(13.56)

where, $\overline{\boldsymbol{d}}$ and $\overline{\boldsymbol{m}}$ are the average of $\boldsymbol{d}_i$s and $\boldsymbol{m}_i$s, respectively. From Eq. 13.56, though $\widehat{\mathbf{T}}$ cannot be computed yet, the relation between $\widehat{\mathbf{T}}$ and $\widehat{\mathbf{R}}$ is known in terms of $\overline{\boldsymbol{d}}$ and $\overline{\boldsymbol{m}}$. So, an estimator of $\widehat{\mathbf{R}}$ resolves $\widehat{\mathbf{T}}$ as well.

A simple coordinate transformation given in Eq. 13.57 removes the translation term from the expression in Eq. 13.55, so that the minimization is considered only with respect to $\mathbf{R}$ and thus the task is to compute $\widehat{\mathbf{R}}$ with the constraint of $\widehat{\mathbf{R}}^\top \widehat{\mathbf{R}} = \mathbf{I}$.

$$\boldsymbol{d}_{c_i} = \boldsymbol{d}_i - \overline{\boldsymbol{d}}$$

$$\boldsymbol{m}_{c_i} = \boldsymbol{m}_i - \overline{\boldsymbol{m}}$$

(13.57)

where, $\boldsymbol{d}_{c_i}$ and $\boldsymbol{m}_{c_i}$ are the transformed coordinates. By applying the transformations in Eq. 13.57, Eq. 13.55 is expressed in terms of transformed coordinates and $\widehat{\mathbf{R}}$, which is given by Eq. 13.58.

$$\boldsymbol{E} = \sum_{i=1}^{N} \left\| \boldsymbol{d}_{c_i} - \widehat{\mathbf{R}} \boldsymbol{m}_{c_i} \right\|^2$$

(13.58)

The right hand side term of Eq. 13.58 can be expanded as $\| \boldsymbol{d}_{c_i} - \widehat{\mathbf{R}} \boldsymbol{m}_{c_i} \|^2 = (\boldsymbol{d}_{c_i} - \widehat{\mathbf{R}} \boldsymbol{m}_{c_i})^\top (\boldsymbol{d}_{c_i} - \widehat{\mathbf{R}} \boldsymbol{m}_{c_i})$ using matrix algebra. This simplification reduces the expression of the error estimate to be minimized, as given by Eq. 13.59.

$$\boldsymbol{E} = \sum_{i=1}^{N} (\boldsymbol{d}_{c_i}^\top \boldsymbol{d}_{c_i} + \boldsymbol{m}_{c_i}^\top \boldsymbol{m}_{c_i} - 2\boldsymbol{d}_{c_i}^\top \widehat{\mathbf{R}} \boldsymbol{m}_{c_i})$$

(13.59)

Minimizing the expression in Eq. 13.59 is equivalent to maximizing the last term in the equation, $2\boldsymbol{d}_{c_i}^\top \widehat{\mathbf{R}} \boldsymbol{m}_{c_i}$. This solution is the same as maximizing the trace of $\widehat{\mathbf{R}} \mathbf{H}$, where $\mathbf{H} = \sum_{i=1}^{N} (\boldsymbol{d}_{c_i} \boldsymbol{m}_{c_i}^\top)$ is the correlation matrix which is defined as covariance between the corresponding coordinates that are translated by their means. The solution for this maximization in $\widehat{\mathbf{R}}$ is given by singular value decomposition of $\mathbf{H}$ as $\mathbf{H} = \mathbf{U} \mathbf{D} \mathbf{V}^\top$, where $\mathbf{U}$ and $\mathbf{V}$ are orthogonal matrices and $\mathbf{D}$ is a diagonal matrix. Then, $\widehat{\mathbf{R}}$ and $\widehat{\mathbf{T}}$ are computed by the expressions given by Eq. 13.60.

$$\widehat{\mathbf{R}} = \mathbf{V} \mathbf{U}^\top$$

$$\widehat{\mathbf{T}} = \overline{\boldsymbol{d}} - \widehat{\mathbf{R}} \overline{\boldsymbol{m}}$$

(13.60)

Here, $\widehat{\mathbf{R}}$ is an orthonormal matrix. In fact, these forms of solutions for a scene point are also associated by an error of fit. So, these solutions are refined by performing an iterative fitting of the data points, since such an iterative process removes the outliers in the set of points. An algorithm known as *iterative closest point* (ICP) registration algorithm for removing the outliers is described in Algorithm 19 (Besl and McKay, 1992).

Algorithm 19 Iterative closest point registration algorithm

Input: A pair of range images that are to be registered
Output: Transformed and registered set of range images

1: Initialize the registration parameters as $\mathbf{R}_0$ and $\mathbf{T}_0$. Compute initial error of model fitting as $\boldsymbol{E}_0$.
2: Repeat the steps 3–5 till the error converges to become very small.
3: Apply transformation to the source scene (or point clouds).
4: Compute closest pairs of points between source and target scenes by selecting the corresponding data points that are nearest neighbors to the considered point both before and after the transformation.
5: Re-compute registration parameters and error of fitting.

Summary

In this chapter, some of the basic techniques of range image representation, acquisition, and processing are discussed. Different methods of range sensing have been discussed, viz., stereo imaging, time-of-flight range sensing, triangulation through scanning beams, and structured light range sensing. In characterizing range images, local features of a point are extracted using differential geometry. These local features include, surface normal, principal curvatures, Gaussian curvature, and mean curvature. The local topology of the surface is characterized by the signs of curvatures.

Characterization of edges in a range image into step and roof edges is discussed. This is found to be useful in multi-scale tracking of edge points. A step edge is determined by detecting zero crossings of Gaussian curvature, and a roof edge is characterized by extremum of the dominant curvature along its direction. Range images are segmented into planar patches using different approaches. Segmentation by region growing approach is a greedy approach, which is performed by fitting local surface patches and merging them. Registration is another important processing in the analysis of range images. A technique of rigid body registration using least squares error estimation for rotation and translation transformation matrices is discussed in this chapter. There is also a technique, called the ICP registration algorithm, which iteratively improves the estimates of the registration parameters by computing closest matches between predicted locations using the current estimated parameters and data points of target images. The technique uses these new estimated parameters in the next iteration and continues till the convergence.

Exercises

(i) Derive the first fundamental form for the surface $z = xy$.
(Note: Consider parametrization of the curve by $Z(u,v) = (u, v, uv)$.)

(ii) Consider a 3-D parametric curve, $x(t) = t^3 + 2t$, $y(t) = 2t - 1$, $z(t) = 3t$. Compute the tangent vector and curvature at $t = 2$.

(iii) Consider the set of parametric equations $x(t) = t^2 + t$ and $y(t) = 2t - 1$ representing a 2-D curve. Compute the tangent vector $(x'(t), y'(t))$ at $t = 1$.

(iv) Compute the normal vector at (u, v) to the surface given by $S(u, v) = (x(u, v), y(u, v), z(u, v))$, $x(u, v) = u$, $y(u, v) = 2v^2$ and $z(u, v) = u^2 + v$. What would be the unit surface normal at $u = v = 0$.

(v) Explain the principle of depth imaging using Microsoft Kinect Camera.

(vi) Consider a depth image given by $D(x, y) \in \mathbb{R}$. How are the principal curvatures at any point of this image computed? How are these curvatures used in characterizing the local geometry of the surface?

(vii) Consider the following parametric representation of a surface,
$(x(u, v), y(u, v), z(u, v)), 0 \le u, v \le 1$.

$$
\begin{bmatrix} f_1(u) \\ f_2(u) \\ f_3(u) \end{bmatrix} = \begin{bmatrix} 3 & 2 & 4 \\ -5 & 6 & 2 \\ 1 & 4 & -3 \end{bmatrix} \begin{bmatrix} u^2 \\ u \\ 1 \end{bmatrix}
$$

$$
\begin{bmatrix} g_1(v) \\ g_2(v) \\ g_3(v) \end{bmatrix} = \begin{bmatrix} 4 & 3 & 2 \\ 1 & 7 & 8 \\ -5 & 6 & 3 \end{bmatrix} \begin{bmatrix} v^2 \\ v \\ 1 \end{bmatrix}
$$

$$ x(u, v) = f_1(u).g_1(v) \quad y(u, v) = f_2(u).g_2(v) \quad z(u, v) = f_3(u).g_3(v) $$

Compute the surface normal, Gaussian curvature and mean curvature at $(u, v) = (0.5, 0.5)$.

(viii) Given a parametric representation of a 3-D surface explain how surface normal and principal curvatures at a point could be computed.
How can the curvature information be used for characterizing the local topology of the surface point?
What are the types of images in a range image?
How curvature information can be further used for finding and characterizing these edge points?

(ix) Define the following terms for a twisted curve in 3-D at a point on it and provide their analytical expressions following a parametric representation of the curve: Osculating plane, rectifying plane, binormal, curvature, and torsion.
Describe a technique for detecting edges in a range image.

(x) Explain how edges in range images are distinguished from an optical image.
Given a range image, discuss how the Gaussian and mean curvatures at an image point are computed.
How is the local surface geometry characterized by these two curvatures? Describe an algorithm for computing step edges in a noisy range image.

(xi) Write an algorithm for registering two range images using ICP method.

14

Medical Imaging

Medical imaging mostly deals with the visualization of internal organs, tissues, etc., using noninvasive or semi-invasive methods. The primary motive is to understand any anomalies in the anatomies and their functions. The signals are acquired in one-dimensional (1-D), two-dimensional (2-D), three-dimensional (3-D), or as videos, depending on the purpose and mode of imaging. There are various modalities in medical imaging. The major modalities are as follows.

- Projection X-ray (radiography)
- X-ray computed tomography (CT scan)
- Nuclear medicine images (emission tomographies like, single photon emission computed tomography (SPECT) and positron emission tomography (PET))
- Magnetic resonance imaging (MRI)
- Ultrasound

There are also several other modalities of medical imaging. In this chapter, only the above mentioned techniques are discussed.

14.1 | Projection X-ray imaging

The X-ray imaging technique was discovered by Wilhelm Conrad Rontgen (inaugural Nobel Prize, 1901) in 1895 in Wurzburg, Germany. In its basic form, the mechanism for generation of X-ray consists of a vacuum tube with a cathode and an anode appropriately placed as illustrated in Fig. 14.1 (a). A beam of electron that emanates from the cathode hits the anode at a very high speed. Depending upon the material of the surface in the anode, there are sub-atomic interactions due to the striking of sub-atomic particles, which release energy in the form of electromagnetic waves of a certain wavelength band, called *X-rays*. In the Fig. 14.1 (b), an image of a vacuum X-ray tube from the early stages of its development is shown for its relevance with the illustration shown in Fig. 14.1 (a). The first X-ray image, captured by Wilhelm Rontgen (1845–1923) in 1895, is shown in Fig. 14.2. It was the image of the left hand of his wife, Anna Bertha Ludwig (1839–1919).

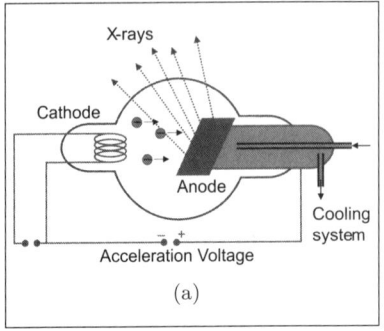 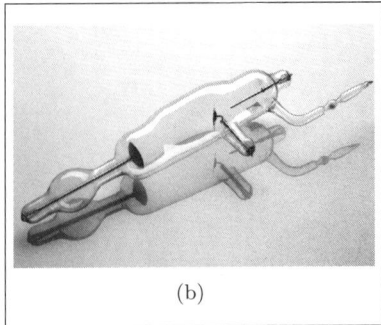

(a) (b)

Figure 14.1 Basic form of an X-ray system. (*Source*: (a) Adapted from Martin Berger, Qiao Yang, and Andreas Maier, Chapter 7 of "Medical Imaging Systems: An Introductory Guide", Springer Open, 2018; `https://creativecommons.org/licenses/by/4.0/`.
(b) `https://commons.wikimedia.org/wiki/File:`
`Potash_regulated_X-ray_tube,_England,_1897-1907_Wellcome_L0065141.jpg`;
`https://creativecommons.org/licenses/by/4.0/`, via Wikimedia Commons.)

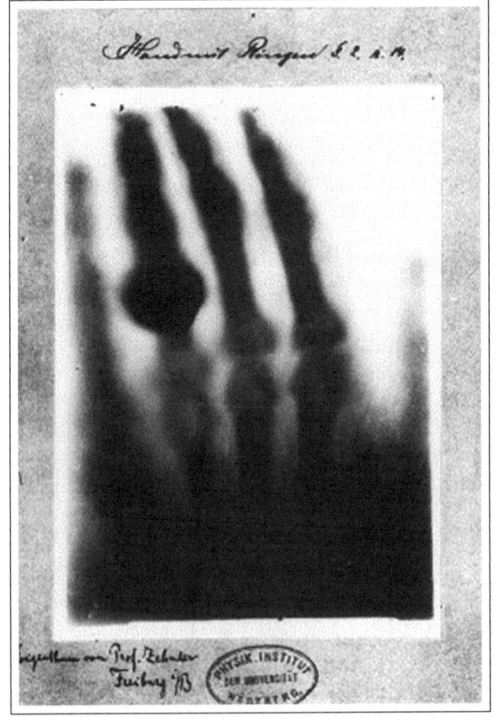

Figure 14.2 First X-ray image captured on December 22, 1895. (*Source*: Image in Public domain, via Wikimedia Commons, `https://commons.wikimedia.org/wiki/File:`
`First_medical_X-ray_by_Wilhelm_R%C3%B6ntgen_of_his_wife_Anna_Bertha_Ludwig%`
`27s_hand_-_18951222.gif`.)

For imaging, the X-rays are transmitted through an object to be imaged. The transmitted rays hit the corresponding detectors at the other end, where the intensities of the transmitted rays form an image. This is illustrated in Fig. 14.3. As shown in the figure, a parallel X-rays are transmitted through an object in this imaging technique. The image of the object is obtained on the image plane at a distance of d from the transmission point, which is shown by $I_d(x, y)$ in the figure. This is a parallel projection of the object on to a plane. Since the rays are transmitted through the object, the internal structures of the object have an effect on the production of the image.

The transmission of the energy in X-rays through the medium in the object is governed by the physical law known as *Lambert–Beer's law*, which was observed much before the discovery of X-rays. According to this law, the transmitted intensity of radiation decreases in proportion to the product of the intensity and the distance traveled by the ray. This is mathematically expressed in Eq. 14.1.

$$\delta I = -\mu I \delta z \tag{14.1}$$

where, δI is the change in the intensity, which is proportional to the product of the intensity, I, of the respective ray and the distance traveled, δz, by it. The proportionality constant, μ, is known as *X-ray attenuation coefficient*, which depends on the property of the medium (in the object) through which the ray is getting transmitted. Here, as per the conventions, the direction of the rays is denoted by the z-axis, and the imaging plane, spatially denoted by x and y axes, is perpendicular to it. Using the relationship in Eq. 14.1, the intensity of the transmitted ray, I_d, at the detection plane is expressed using the initial intensity, I_0, at the transmitter, which is given by Eq. 14.2.

$$I_d = I_0 e^{-\int \mu(x,y,z)dz} \tag{14.2}$$

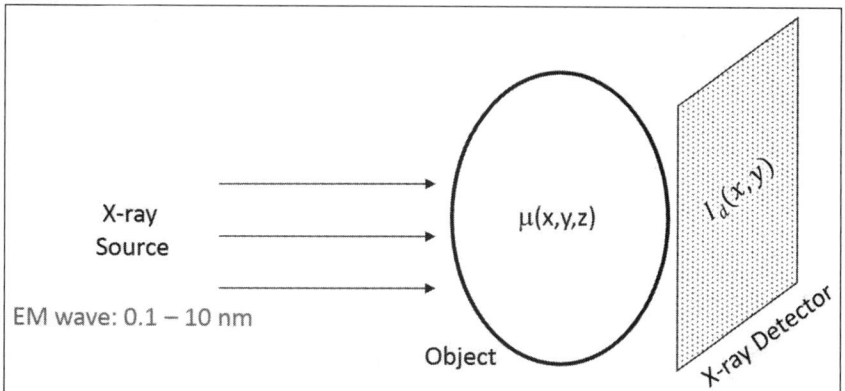

Figure 14.3 Illustration of projection X-ray imaging. (*Source*: Adapted from the slide set of Prof. D.C. Noll, Univ. of Michigan, Ann Arbor, USA, https://web.eecs.umich.edu/~fessler/course/516/l/noll,516,intro-jf.ppt.)

Here, the coefficient, $\mu(x, y, z)$, which depends on the property of the tissue being imaged, is mainly responsible for the variations in the X-ray image that gives a perception of different structures. The formed image is a function of transmitted electron density, atomic number of the material used, and the physical parameter $\mu(x, y, z)$, of the imaged object. As seen in the equation, the intensity of the X-ray decays exponentially when it travels through the given medium. It should be noted that, integration in Eq. 14.2 is a line integral over the distance. This has its critical use in the tomographic reconstruction of images. By taking the logarithm of Eq. 14.2, it is observed that, the logarithm of the ratio of the initial intensity and the detected intensity of the transmitted X-ray is proportional (or same) to the line integral of the attenuation coefficient along this path, as given in Eq. 14.3.

$$\ln\left(\frac{I_0}{I_d}\right) = \ln(I_0) - \ln(I_d) = \int \mu(x, y, z)dz \qquad (14.3)$$

Diagnostic X-ray imaging takes place due to the interaction of the X-ray photons with the imaging object. Physically, this happens in a specific energy band that is defined by the wavelengths of operation, known as the *diagnostic X-ray band* of the electromagnetic wavelengths. This is typically shown in Fig. 14.4. The projection X-ray imaging in medical application is operated in the diagnostic X-ray band of wavelengths between 0.1 nm to 10 nm. If the operation is above this band, the object appears too transparent for imaging, which causes the lack of variation over the line integral. In this case, the internal structures cannot be observed as well, and remain indistinguishable, because every point of the object behaves almost similar by transmitting most of the incident energy. If the operation is below the diagnostic X-ray, the image becomes too dark, because the intensity is not sufficient to reach the detector. Also, the wavelengths are too long to consider for operating well below this band.

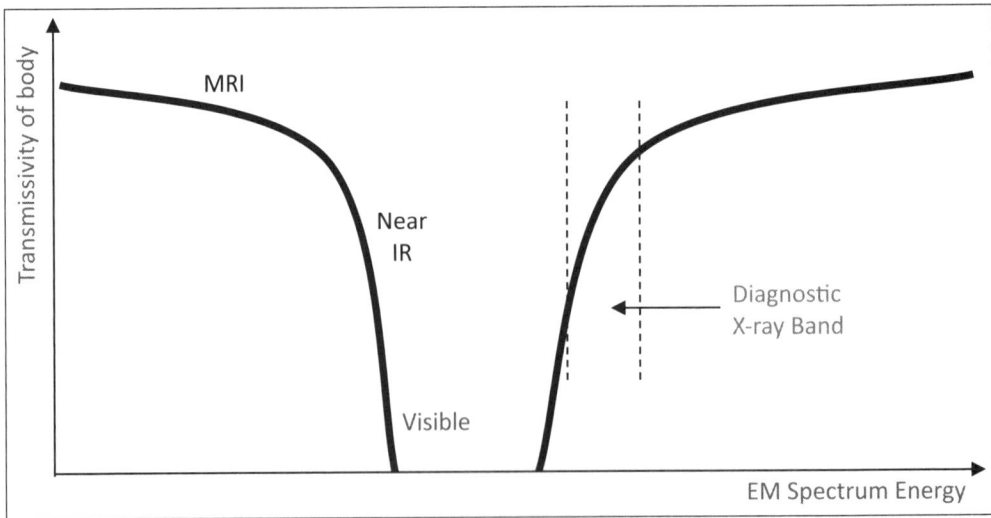

Figure 14.4 Wavelengths of operation of diagnostic X-ray imaging. (*Source*: Adapted from the slide set of Prof. D.C. Noll, Univ. of Michigan, Ann Arbor, USA, https://web.eecs.umich.edu/~fessler/course/516/l/noll,516,intro-jf.ppt.)

Numerical Example

The half-value thickness is the thickness of a given material of defined density that can reduce the intensity of incident radiation by one-half. Compute the half-value thickness $w_{\frac{1}{2}}$ of a material if the linear attenuation coefficient per unit length is μ.

Solution

Let the intensity of the incident radiation and the transmitted radiation be I_0 and I_d, where $I_d = \frac{I_0}{2}$. Hence following the Lambert–Beer's law $ln I_d - ln I_0 = -\mu w_{\frac{1}{2}}$. Hence, $ln \frac{I_d}{I_0} = -\mu w_{\frac{1}{2}} \longrightarrow w_{\frac{1}{2}} = \frac{ln2}{\mu}$.

Emission of X-ray   To understand the physics behind the emission of X-rays, consider a basic X-ray tube in which the electron beams from cathode hit the material surface of anode to produce the X-ray beam. The emission happens due to the interaction of the electrons with the atoms on the surface of the anode. It is known that an atom has a nucleus and electrons revolve around it. There are two different processes by which X-rays are emitted:

(i) through interactions with an inner shell electron, and

(ii) through interactions with the nucleus.

These interactions are prevalent because of the attraction of nucleus and the behavior of the electrons. The electron beam that passes through the inner shell of the atom, deviates from its path and loses some photon energy in the presence of the nucleus. But, this energy is relatively low in intensity. This phenomenon is called *Bremstrahlung*, where the speed of the electron beam is slowed down and the corresponding radiated energy is also of low intensity. However, when the electron beam hits an electron directly, it causes a quantum jump to its energy level and the electron beam deviates from its path by losing a part of energy. In this case, the electron, hit by an electron of the beam, moves out of the orbital system around its atom. Since an electron is ejected from the atom, such an atom becomes a positive ion. While the electron gets ejected from an inner shell, it leaves a hole in the inner shell, which makes an electron in the outer shell to move in. As the electron in the outer shell is of higher energy, its moving in to the inner shell emits significant energy. The higher intensity photons emitted in this process produce the characteristic radiation that is primarily used for diagnostic X-rays. This is depicted in Fig. 14.5. Similarly, when the electron beam interacts with the nucleus, the colliding electrons slow down and get deviated. The loss in kinetic energy in this process reappear as X-ray photons. But, in this case, the amount of energy of such photons is much lower than the energy being emitted due to the interaction with the inner shall electrons.

Absorption of X-ray   When X-ray passes through an object (or a body), it essentially passes through atoms in it. During this process, the energy of the X-ray gets absorbed

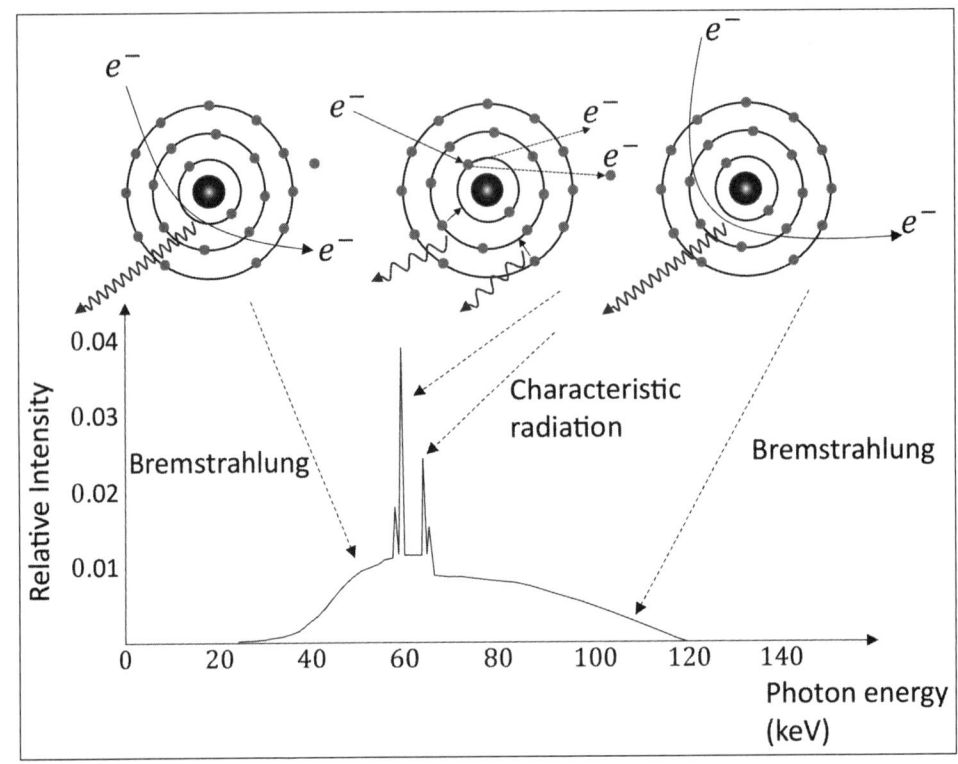

Figure 14.5 Processes of emission of X-ray. (*Source*: Adapted from Martin Berger, Qiao Yang, and Andreas Maier, Chapter 7 of "Medical Imaging Systems: An Introductory Guide", Springer Open, 2018; `https://creativecommons.org/licenses/by/4.0/`.)

through various interactions. There are three ways by which the X-ray is absorbed:

(i) If the energy of the X-ray beam is very high, it behaves differently with the atomic electrons and different kinds of scattering may occur. There are mainly two phenomena of high energy interaction with atomic electrons, which are as follows.

- The X-ray excites an electron in the inner shell and the energy is fully absorbed by it. Since the electron in the inner shell gets higher energy, it gets ejected by absorbing the energy. This is known as *photoelectric absorption*. In photoelectric absorption, since a photon of the X-ray beam gives off its complete energy to eject an electron to create a positive ion, it leaves a hole in the inner shell. This also results in emission of a photon due to the movement of an electron from an outer shell to inner shell. Photoelectric absorption also emits X-ray, but its path of emission is not very directed. Since imaging follows the principle of parallel projections, it requires the line of propagation in the same direction toward the detector. So, it cannot be used as diagnostic X-ray.

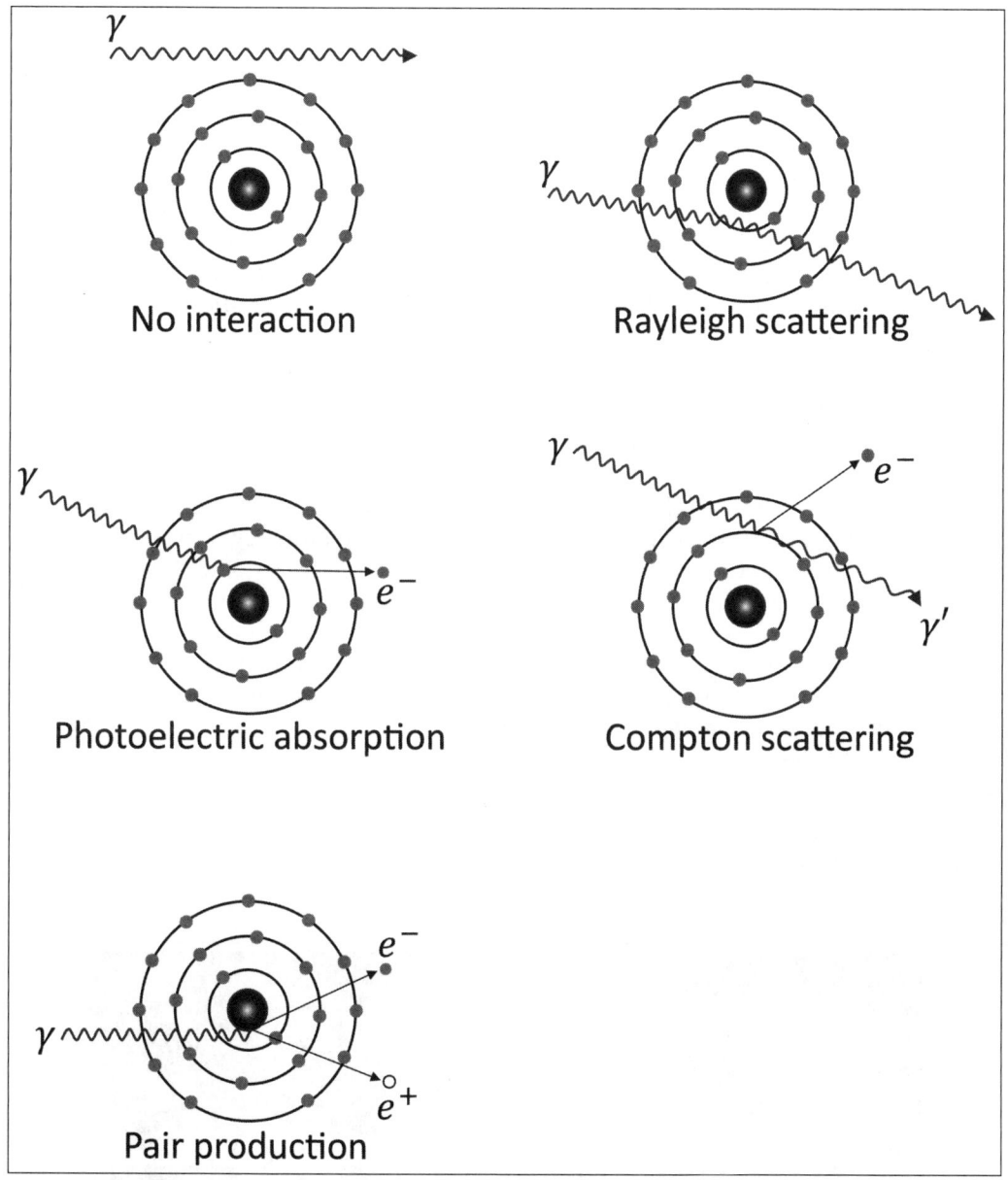

Figure 14.6 Processes of absorption of X-ray. (*Source*: Adapted from Martin Berger, Qiao Yang, and Andreas Maier, Chapter 7 of "Medical Imaging Systems: An Introductory Guide", Springer Open, 2018; https://creativecommons.org/licenses/by/4.0/.)

- The energy is partially absorbed by the electron. This results in the electron getting ejected and the X-ray gets transmitted along its path with significant attenuation. This is known as *Compton scattering* (Pattison, 1975). This is the major phenomena that contributes to the diagnostic imaging through X-ray. In Compton scattering, the transmitted X-ray has considerably higher energy than the binding energy of electron. Since the electron absorbs the energy partially and gets ejected to produce an ion, the X-ray also loses some of its energy and gets some deflection to its path with an attenuated energy. So, the X-rays may not be strictly parallel due to these minor deflections, which usually does not affect their usability in practical applications.

(ii) When very high energy is absorbed by a nucleus, two types of particles are emitted from it: electrons and positrons. These are always produced in pair. However, the resulting radiation is not relevant to the diagnostic X-ray.

(iii) A very low energy in the X-ray beam may be absorbed due to *Rayleigh scattering* effect. In Rayleigh scattering, the X-ray simply goes through the shells and get deviated. During this process, it loses relatively smaller amounts of energy. The energy absorbed in Rayleigh scattering is considerably lower than the binding energy of electrons. So, the electron may absorb the energy and it may move from its inner shell to outer shell if it is sufficiently strong, otherwise it may simply vibrate. This vibration may also be transferred by a photon at any arbitrary angle and it may result in the formation of an ion. However, the X-ray that is transmitted by this phenomenon is harmful for humans, since it can significantly damage the molecular structure of the tissues, and it is not used in diagnostic applications.

These absorption phenomena are illustrated in Fig. 14.6.

An example of an X-ray radiographic image is shown in Fig. 14.7. As it can be seen in the figure, the image shows a structure of the bones in a fractured hand. The anatomy

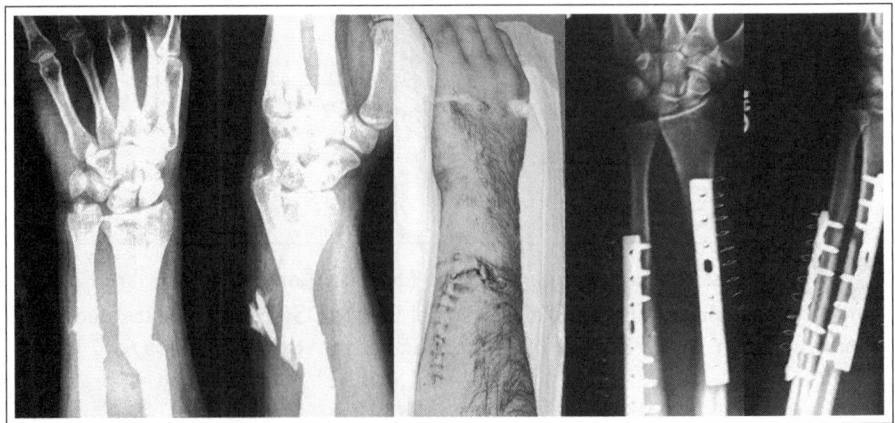

Figure 14.7 An example of X-ray radiographic image. (*Source*: Sjbrown at English Wikipedia, Public domain, via Wikimedia Commons, https://commons.wikimedia.org/wiki/File:Broken_fixed_arm.jpg.)

of the broken bones is visible in the X-ray images. After the surgery, the metal plates are inserted for support, which are also visible through X-ray imaging. This allows physicians to check on the location and extent of the fracture. Even after the surgery, it is used to verify whether the treatment is according to the plan.

14.2 | X-ray computed tomography

The X-ray imaging discussed in the previous section may be applied in various ways. One of the specialized extensions of X-ray imaging is *X-ray computed tomography* (CT). The principle behind this imaging technique is driven by the line integral relationship of X-ray propagation. It provides a good mathematical basis for reconstructing 3-D images through parallel projections. The CT deals with reconstruction of 3-D images of internal human anatomy through X-ray projections. There are different kinds of CT, depending on the way the X-rays are projected. The two main types are the *fan beam computed tomography* (fan beam CT) and the *cone beam computed tomography* (CBCT).

14.2.1 | Fan beam CT

In the fan beam CT, X-rays are projected on the body through a collimator, where the propagation of X-rays is allowed only at certain directions through a plane. These X-rays, after passing through a cross section of a body, reach the detectors. Assuming a cylindrical model of the body (object being imaged), the detectors are placed in a circular ring, where the propagated X-rays are detected. However, a linear form of a detector is also very much valid, depending on the usage of the system. This configuration is shown in Fig. 14.8. Here, the positions of the source of X-ray and the detector are exactly known. By rotating the imaging system around the fixed object, as indicted by the arrows in the figure, multiple detections from various directions in the same plane are performed. Since the body is fixed while the imaging source and detector are rotated, the respective paths of propagation give the line integrals of absorption of energy in the propagated rays at various directions. Here, only the respective lines that carry energy along the line of projection are detected in the fan

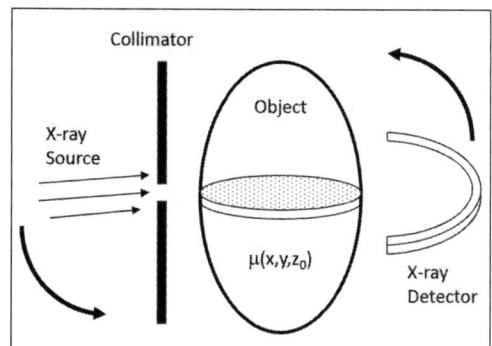
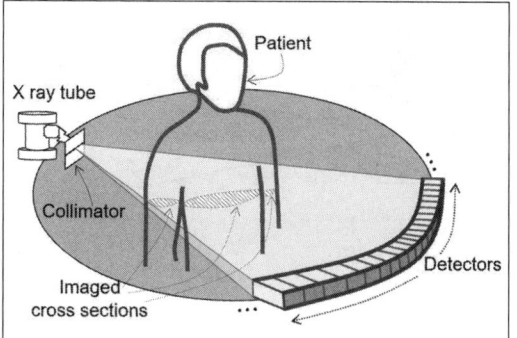

Figure 14.8 Basic configuration of fan beam computed tomography. (*Source*: Adapted from the slide set of Prof. D.C. Noll, Univ. of Michigan, Ann Arbor, USA, https://web.eecs.umich.edu/~fessler/course/516/l/noll,516,intro-jf.ppt.)

beam CT. The mathematical basis by which the image of the cross section is reconstructed is discussed in Section 14.2.4. In the fan beam CT, the exposure is limited to a slice by the collimator. This is the basic imaging principle of fan beam CT. The objective of the fan beam CT is to get the image of the cross section, where the distribution of the tissue properties may be studied at a particular cross sectional plane. So, at every step, only one 2-D cross sectional plane is subjected for the circular scan of parallel X-ray beams, and then it gets reconstructed in the fan beam CT.

14.2.2 | Cone beam CT (CBCT)

In the cone beam CT, the X-rays are propagated as a conical beam. Here, the propagated X-rays are detected by a planar array of detectors. The object to be imaged is placed between the X-ray source and the detector. This configuration is shown in Fig. 14.9. Similar to the fan beam CT, the whole system is rotated around the fixed object. Due to the rotation of the system, multiple planar projections of the object are obtained from different directions. In this case, the whole volume of the object is projected on different projection planes that are detected at various angles by rotating the system. Here, a 3-D reconstruction of the object is performed by considering the respective projections over the planes at different angles.

14.2.3 | Principles of computed tomography

It has been shown by Johan Radon (1887–1956) in 1917 that it is possible to reconstruct a complete function from its line integrals along all the possible lines through the function.

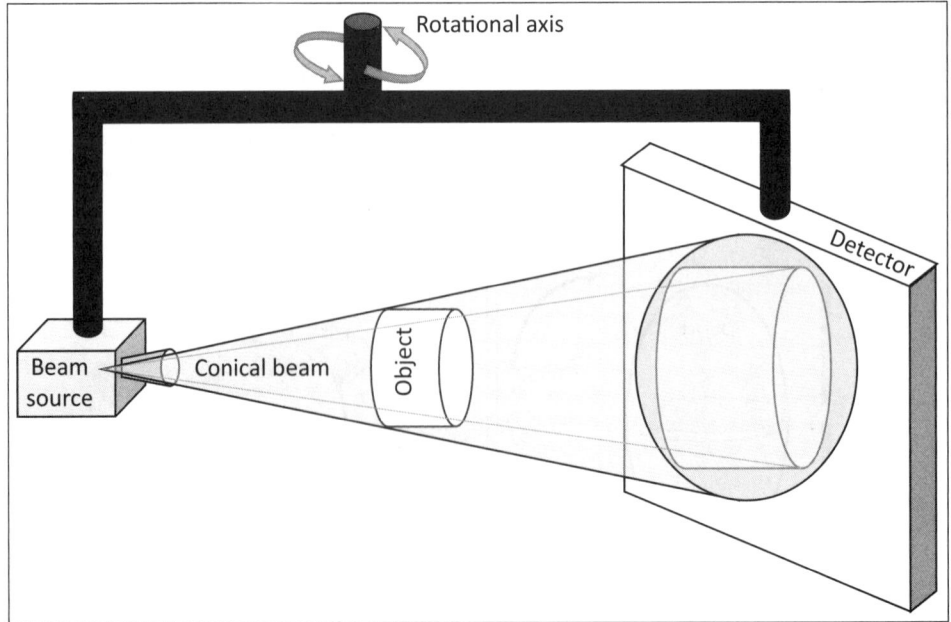

Figure 14.9 Basic configuration of cone beam computed tomography.

For example, consider the illustration in Fig. 14.10. Here, $f(x,y)$ is a 2-D function of x and y. Consider the line $\mathbf{L}$, as shown in the figure, that theoretically extends from $(-\infty, \infty)$. Any point on this line is represented by the parameter l. So, the parametric description of this straight line is denoted by $(x(l), y(l))$. The integration of all the functional values, $f(x(l), y(l))$, along $\mathbf{L}$, where l is a parameter, is the line integral, $p(\mathbf{L})$, along $\mathbf{L}$. This is a 2-D integration where the functional values are considered only at points $(x(l), y(l)) \in \mathbf{L}$. This line integral is given by Eq. 14.4.

$$p(\mathbf{L}) = \int_{-\infty}^{\infty} f(x(l), y(l)) dl \ \forall (x(l), y(l)) \in \mathbf{L}$$
$$= \int_{-\infty}^{\infty} \int_{-\infty}^{\infty} f(x,y) \delta\left((x(l), y(l)) \in \mathbf{L}\right) \ dx \ dy \tag{14.4}$$

where, $\delta(\cdot)$ is the Dirac delta function.[1]

Consider the representation of the straight line as shown in Fig. 14.11. Here, the normal of the straight line makes an angle θ with the x-axis and the straight line is at a distance s from the origin. Then, the equation of the straight line is given as follows.

$$x\cos(\theta) + y\sin(\theta) = s \tag{14.5}$$

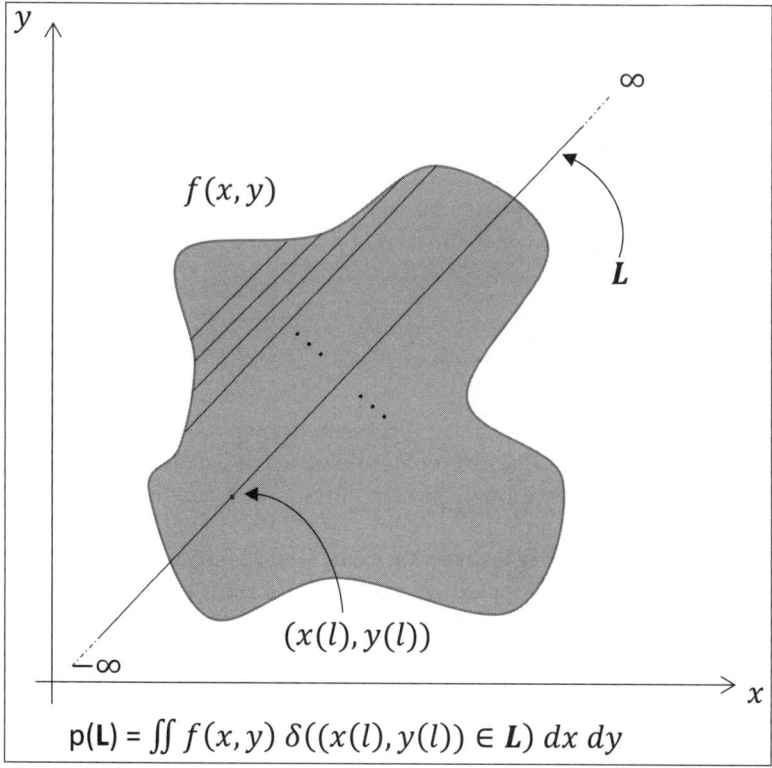

Figure 14.10 Illustration of line integral of a 2-D function.

---

[1] It implies that it samples $f(x,y)$ at a point on $\mathbf{L}$.

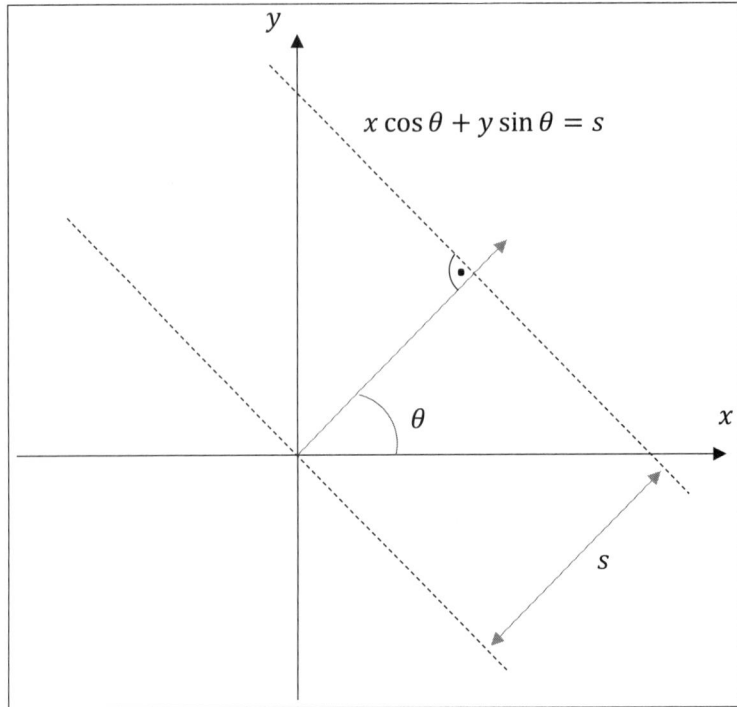

Figure 14.11 Representation of straight line with s and θ as parameters (Maier et al., 2018).

Now, the straight line is expressed using the parameters, θ and s. Similar to the expression in Eq. 14.4, the line integral of the functional values on this straight line is given by Eq. 14.6.

$$p(\theta, s) = \int \int f(x,y)\delta\left(x\cos(\theta) + y\sin(\theta) - s\right) \; dx \; dy \qquad (14.6)$$

The line integral in Eq. 14.6 may be represented as $\boldsymbol{p}_\theta(s)$, which is a function of s, at any given θ. Since $\boldsymbol{p}_\theta(s)$ is a scalar value along a particular line, by considering the functional values at each point along different lines (for different values of s, parallel to $\boldsymbol{L}$), the function of the line integral by varying s is obtained, which is shown in Fig. 14.12. These line integrals, $\boldsymbol{p}_\theta(s)$, are in a direction that is perpendicular to the line making an angle θ with the x-axis and passing through the origin of the space., as shown in Fig. 14.11. By varying θ and computing $\boldsymbol{p}_\theta(s)$ for each θ, a 2-D function of θ and s is obtained, as illustrated in Fig. 14.12. The stack of these integrals provides $p(\theta, s)$ that encodes $f(x,y)$. For a bounded $f(x,y)$, There exist finite ranges of θ and s in which $p(\theta, s)$ is nonzero, and it is zero outside these ranges, as seen in the $s\theta$-plot in Fig. 14.12. The envelope in Fig. 14.12, that is obtained by varying θ and placing all the projections, i.e., line integrals $\boldsymbol{p}_\theta(s)$, side-by-side as a 2-D image is called a *sinogram*. This sinogram is also referred to as the *Radon transform* of the given function $f(x,y)$ in the 2-D space.

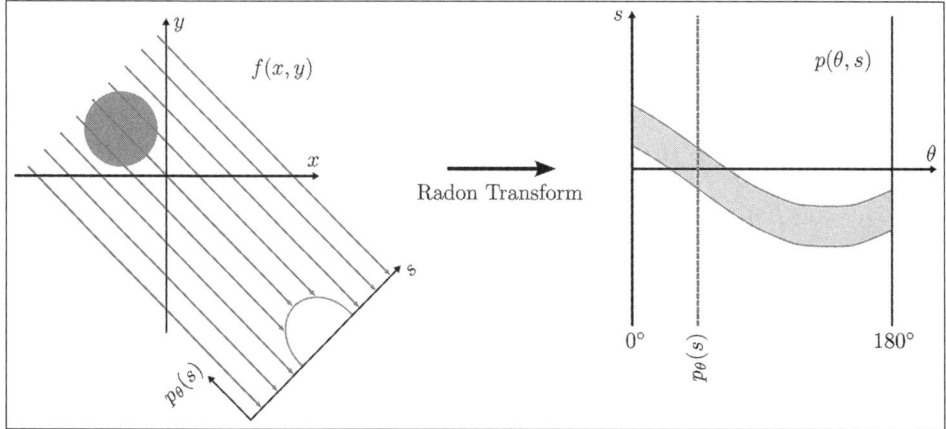

Figure 14.12 Radon transform from line integrals. (*Source*: Martin Berger, Qiao Yang, and Andreas Maier, Chapter 8 of "Medical Imaging Systems: An Introductory Guide", Springer Open, 2018; `https://creativecommons.org/licenses/by/4.0/`.)

14.2.4 | CT image reconstruction

There are certain methodologies that are developed to reconstruct the images from the sinograms. Three such techniques are discussed here.

Fourier slice theorem

A theorem called *Fourier slice theorem* defines the relationship between the projections, $\boldsymbol{p}_\theta(s)$, and the corresponding 2-D function in the frequency domain. By this theorem, it is shown that, the Fourier transform of $\boldsymbol{p}_\theta(s)$ is a part of the Fourier transform of $f(x, y)$. Let the frequency spectrum of the function $f(x, y)$ be expressed by $F(u, v)$, where u and v are the spatial frequencies. This is given by the Fourier transform of the 2-D function, as shown in Eq. 14.7.

$$F(u, v) = \mathscr{F}(f(x, y)) = \int \int f(x, y)e^{-j2\pi(ux+vy)} \, dx \, dy \qquad (14.7)$$

The parameter for direction of projection is θ, which is perpendicular to the direction of line integral. Let ψ be, the spatial frequency along the line passing through the origin of the 2-D frequency space in the direction of θ. Over this direction of θ, if the parameter ψ is varied, the Fourier transform is obtained at every sampled point. This is expressed as a function of ψ and θ, which is related to $\boldsymbol{p}_\theta(s)$. A function of line integrals for varying parameters of s and then θ is obtained by considering rotated $\boldsymbol{p}_\theta(s)$ in all possible directions. Thus the coefficients of the Fourier transform of $f(x, y)$ over a linear segment in the 2-D spatial frequency spectrum are obtained from the Fourier transform of each of these $\boldsymbol{p}_\theta(s)$. The Fourier transform of the line integral function, $\boldsymbol{p}_\theta(s)$, which is a 1-D function, is given Eq. 14.8.

$$P_\theta(\psi) = \int_{-\infty}^{\infty} \boldsymbol{p}_\theta(s)e^{-j2\pi\psi s} \, ds \qquad (14.8)$$

In this 1-D Fourier transform, ψ is the corresponding spatial frequency perpendicular to L. From Eq. 14.6, the expression in Eq. 14.8 can be written as Eq. 14.9.

$$P_\theta(\psi) = \int_{-\infty}^{\infty} \int \int f(x,y)\delta\left(x\cos(\theta) + y\sin(\theta) - s\right)\ dx\ dy\ e^{-j2\pi\psi s}\ ds$$
$$= \int \int f(x,y) \int_{-\infty}^{\infty} \delta\left(x\cos(\theta) + y\sin(\theta) - s\right) e^{-j2\pi\psi s}\ ds\ dx\ dy \tag{14.9}$$

In the Dirac delta function $\delta(\cdot)$, only certain sample values of x and y satisfy the condition for $\delta(0)$. Using this condition in Eq. 14.9 by substituting $s = x\cos(\theta) + y\sin(\theta)$,

$$P_\theta(\psi) = \int \int f(x,y)e^{-j2\pi\psi(x\cos(\theta)+y\sin(\theta))}\ dx\ dy$$
$$= \int \int f(x,y)e^{-j2\pi(\psi\cos(\theta)x+\psi\sin(\theta)y)}\ dx\ dy \tag{14.10}$$

The expression in Eq. 14.10 gives the values of Fourier transform at frequencies $\psi\cos(\theta)$ and $\psi\sin(\theta)$. That is,

$$P_\theta(\psi) = F(\psi\cos(\theta), \psi\sin(\theta)),\ \forall\psi \tag{14.11}$$

Actually, this is a 2-D Fourier transform at certain spatial frequencies defined by ψ. The relationship given by Eq. 14.11 is known as Fourier slice theorem. Using these 2-D Fourier coefficients, the original function can be reconstructed.

For a particular direction, θ, the 1-D transform coefficients at different values of ψ correspond to the 2-D transform coefficients along a line in the 2-D frequency space, which makes an angle of θ with the x-axis and passes through the origin of the space. This establishes an equivalence between the Fourier transform of the projection, $p_\theta(s)$, and a line in Fourier transform, $F(u,v)$ of $f(x,y)$. Consider the illustration shown in Fig. 14.13. As shown in the figure, the Fourier transform of $p_\theta(s)$ is the same as the Fourier transform of $f(x,y)$ over a line segment which makes an angle θ at the origin with the x-axis. Thus, the Fourier transform of the actual 2-D function in the frequency domain is reconstructed by computing the Fourier transform of $p_\theta(s)$ in all the directions of θ varying from 0° to 180°. By computing the inverse Fourier transforms of $P_\theta(\psi)$ for all θ's, the original 2-D function is retrieved. In this way, a 2-D function is reconstructed by the Radon transform using the Fourier slice theorem.

The principle discussed above is used in computed axial tomography for image reconstruction. The functional relationship of the X-ray projections (i.e., the respective intensity modulation of projection that are transmitted and detected) with the line integrals follows Beer's law. This is expressed as the ratio of log values of detected intensity on the body and the source intensity at the source, whose negation is equal to

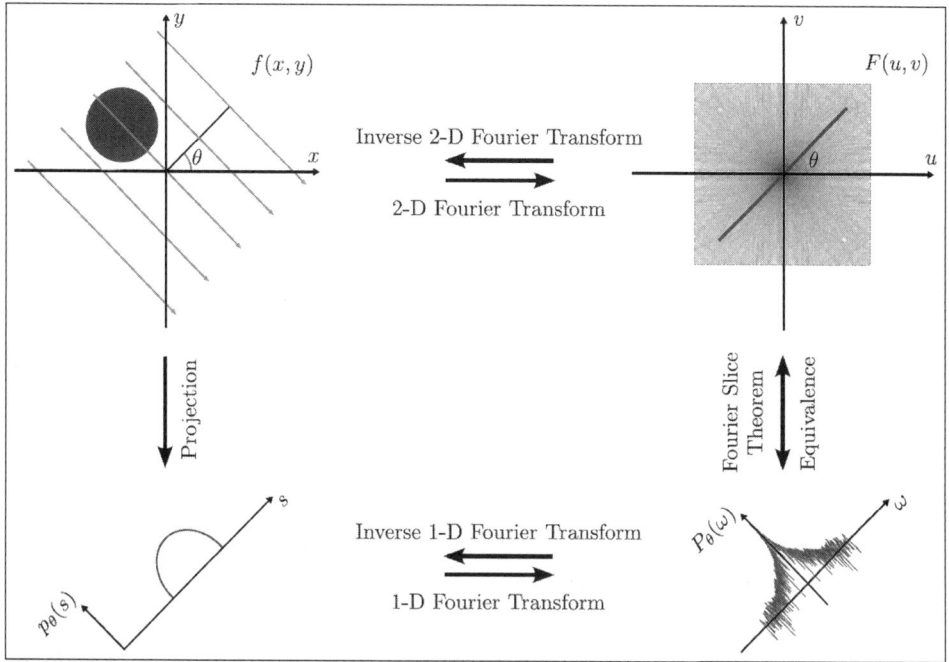

Figure 14.13 Illustration of Fourier slice theorem. (*Source*: Martin Berger, Qiao Yang, and Andreas Maier, Chapter 8 of "Medical Imaging Systems: An Introductory Guide", Springer Open, 2018; `https://creativecommons.org/licenses/by/4.0/`.)

the integration of the attenuation coefficients for the X-ray transmission, which is given by Eq. 14.12.

$$-\ln\left(\frac{I_d}{I_0}\right) = \int \mu(x, y, z)\, dz$$

$$\implies \int \mu(x, y, z)\, dz = \ln(I_0) - \ln(I_d)$$

(14.12)

where, I_0 is the incident intensity, I_d is the detected intensity, and $\mu(x, y, z)$ is the attenuation coefficient for the X-ray transmission. Thus, X-ray imaging captures the distribution of the attenuation coefficients over the space. In a rotating coordinate system, as in Fig. 14.9, the line integrals are computed along all the lines in each of the rotations made to the system. Thereby, $p_\theta(s)$ for a cross section is obtained by computing the line integrals in all possible directions.

This is how we get the image of a cross section of the object, which is reconstructed from $p_\theta(s)$ along all possible directions using the Fourier slice theorem. With reference to Fig. 14.9, this cross section corresponds to a plane parallel to XY-plane at a particular value of z_0. By moving the collimator window to different values of z_0 and using controlled X-ray exposures, different cross sections are computed using the Fourier slice theorem. A stack of these cross sections or slices provides the 3-D image of the object. In this 3-D

Table 14.1 Typical Hounsfield units of some generally encountered materials.

Material	Hounsfield units
Water	0
Air	−1000
Fat	−100 to −60
Lung	−600 to −400
Muscle	10 to 40
Blood	30 to 45
Soft tissue	40 to 80

image, the functional value at each voxel,[2] is proportional to the respective attenuation coefficients. When these coefficients are expressed in a normalized form, they relate to the characteristics of the underlying tissues. The normalized unit that is used to express these coefficients is called *Hounsfield unit* (HU), which expresses the attenuation coefficients with a linear transformation relative to the coefficients of water. The computed axial tomography using X-ray was invented by Godfrey Hounsfield (1919–2004) in 1971, which got him the Nobel Prize in 1979. The first clinical CT image was obtained in 1972. In the honor of Godfrey Hounsfield, the normalized unit of coefficients is named HU. The transformation of the attenuation coefficients in HU is given by Eq. 14.13.

$$\mu^* = 1000 \left(\frac{\mu}{\mu_{water}} - 1 \right) \qquad (14.13)$$

where, μ is the actual attenuation coefficient, μ^* is the transformed attenuation coefficient, and μ_{water} is the attenuation coefficient of water. With this transformation, the typical HU values of some of the generally used materials is given in Table 14.1. By knowing the values of coefficients in HUs, the physicians relate the respective tissues in the anatomy.

Numerical Example

For the incident radiation of an X-ray beam of 100 KeV, attenuation coefficients of water and a tissue of muscles are $0.1835/cm$ and $0.1892/cm$, respectively. Convert the attenuation coefficient of the tissue in the HU.

Solution

Attenuation coefficient of the tissue in HU = $1000 \left(\frac{\mu_{tissue}}{\mu_{water}} - 1 \right)$ HU = 31.06 HU.

---

[2] Similar to a *pixel* in a 2-D image, an element of a 3-D discrete array is called *voxel*.

Filtered backprojection

There is another approach for reconstruction where it is directly computed in the spatial domain, instead of computing in the frequency domain. This is also derived from the Fourier slice theorem, but computationally faster than the method of computing in frequency domain. Here, a type of filter, $h(s)$, known as a *ramp filter*, is applied on the line integral function, $\boldsymbol{p}_\theta(s)$, over s to get the functional values. Then, integrating the filtered function over θ reconstructs the actual function, $f(x, y)$, such that $s = x\cos(\theta) + y\sin(\theta)$. This is expressed by Eq. 14.14.

$$f(x, y) = \int_0^\pi \boldsymbol{p}_\theta(s) * h(s)|_{s=x\cos(\theta)+y\sin(\theta)} \, d\theta \qquad (14.14)$$

The frequency spectrum of the filter $h(s)$, $H(\xi)$, is shown in Fig. 14.14. It is a 1-D filter that performs computation in the original space of the image. This filter is convolved with $\boldsymbol{p}_\theta(s)$ for any angle θ, and the values of (x, y) belong to a set that satisfy $x\cos(\theta) + y\sin(\theta) = s$ for every s. This is repeated for all $\theta \in [0°, 180°]$, at every (x, y), and the values are summed up. The computation is described in the following.

Let, $g(s) = \boldsymbol{p}_\theta(s) * h(s)$.
At a particular value of $s = s_0$, $v = g(s_0) = \boldsymbol{p}_\theta(s) * h(s)|_{s=s_0}$, all those points that satisfy $x\cos(\theta) + y\sin(\theta) = s_0$ is a line in the functional space. Thus, the contributions from $g(s_0)$ is a line of constant values in the functional space, which is shown in Fig. 14.15. For every θ, there is a particular s for which a particular point, (x, y), on $g(s_0)$ is satisfied, which is shown in the figure as the point of intersection of various lines. All the functional values are accumulated at this point. By summing the values for all θ at each (x, y), and repeating it for every (x, y), the function $f(x, y)$ is obtained. This is the principle of *filtered backprojection*.

The ramp filter, $h(s)$, shown in Fig. 14.14 extends between $(-\infty, \infty)$. A practical implementation of this filter is realized by a *Ram-Lak filter*, where the responses are truncated at a maximum cut-off of ξ_{max}, as shown in Fig. 14.16. The filter response of Ram-Lak filter is given by Eq. 14.15.

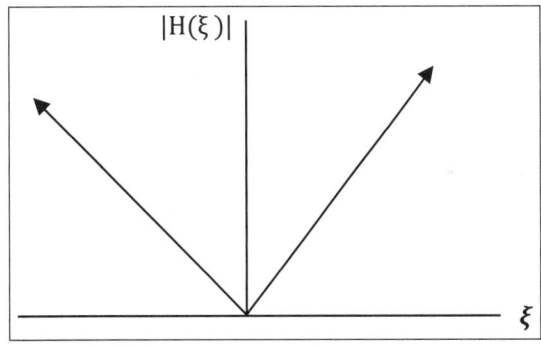

Figure 14.14 Frequency response of a ramp filter.

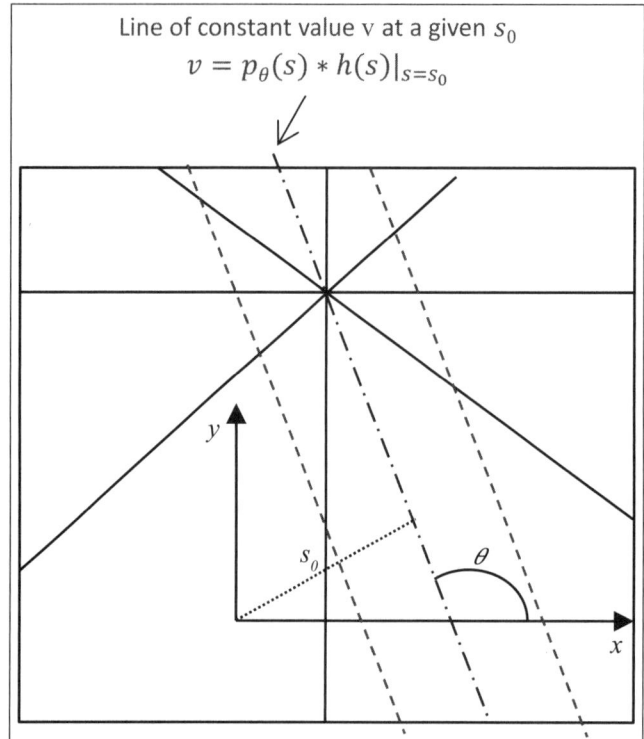

Figure 14.15 Line of constant value, $g(s_0)$, at a given s_0.

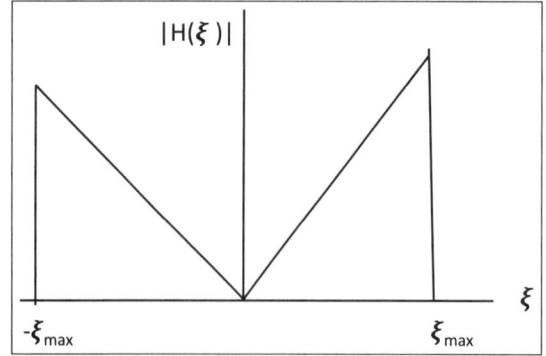

Figure 14.16 Frequency response of a Ram-Lak filter.

$$h(s) = \frac{\text{sinc}\left(\frac{s}{\Delta s}\right)}{2(\Delta s)^2} - \frac{\text{sinc}^2\left(\frac{s}{2\Delta s}\right)}{4(\Delta s)^2} \tag{14.15}$$

where, $\Delta s = \frac{1}{2\xi_{max}}$ and sinc functioned is defined as $\text{sinc}(x) = \frac{\sin(\pi x)}{\pi x}$.

Algebraic reconstruction technique (ART)

In the ART (Gordon et al., 1970), a system of linear equations is solved, where each linear equation expresses a line integral. A cross section results in a set of line integrals that form a set of linear equations. These equations are solved to retrieve the actual functional value. Consider the familiar form of a system of linear equations given in Eq. 14.16.

$$\mathbf{AX} = \mathbf{P} \tag{14.16}$$

Here, $\mathbf{A}$ is the set of coefficients, $\mathbf{X}$ is the set of functional values at the points of the cross section, and $\mathbf{P}$ is the set of respective line integrals. In this case, the 2-D or the 3-D function is linearized in the form of a 1-D function, $\mathbf{X}$, to simplify computations. By re-arranging $\mathbf{X}$, the respective 2-D or 3-D function is recomposed. This algebraic construction technique is equally applicable to both 2-D image and 3-D volume reconstruction, because it considers a system of linear equations that basically represent line integrals. So, it is irrespective of whether the line lies on a 2-D plane or over a 3-D volume, which makes this technique more general and flexible in application to image reconstruction. Here, a row, $\boldsymbol{a}_i$, of the matrix $\mathbf{A}$ is formed by the coefficients of the corresponding equation. For any line integral, its corresponding functional value is expressed now as a variable. That is, if a point of $\mathbf{X}$, x_j, lies on the line of projection, its corresponding coefficient is 1, otherwise, it is 0, as expressed in Eq. 14.17.

$$a_{ij} = \begin{cases} 1, & x_j \in \text{path of projection} \\ 0, & \text{otherwise} \end{cases} \tag{14.17}$$

where, the element, a_{ij}, of $\mathbf{A}$ represents the coefficient of ith equation and j^{th} variable of the functional space. This system of equations is usually an over determined set of equations, since the number of line integrals present is more than the number of pixels involved. So, this problem is solved by using the least squares method, whose solution is given by Eq. 14.18.

$$\mathbf{X} = \left(\mathbf{A}^{\top}\mathbf{A}\right)^{-1}\mathbf{A}^{\top}\mathbf{P} \tag{14.18}$$

But in reality, the above computation is not feasible, as the size of $\mathbf{X}$ is very large. So, the inversion is computationally not feasible. There is also another computational challenge. In the system of equations (Eq. 14.16), each equation represents a hyperplane in the space. The solution is the intersection of hyperplanes. For example, in a 2-D space involving two variables, the solution is the point of intersection of two lines. In a 3-D space involving three variables, it is the intersection of 3-D planes. A precise point of intersection of hyperplanes is achieved only in ideal cases, when there is no noise in the data. However, in practice, when the data is usually noisy, the exact point of intersection cannot be attained.

To address these issues, an iterative method called *Kaczmarz method* (Gordon et al., 1970) is used. This technique starts with any particular value chosen randomly as an initial solution. Then, it is orthogonally projected on one of the hyperplanes to get the solution at first iteration, which geometrically moves the estimated solution closer to the desired solution. This solution of this first iteration is then projected on another hyperplane to get the solution of the next iteration. This process is iterated till convergence, when the solution does not change by some fixed threshold. The iterative updates of solution is mathematically expressed in Eq. 14.19.

$$\mathbf{X}^{k+1} = \mathbf{X}^k + \frac{p_i - \boldsymbol{a}_i \mathbf{X}^k}{\boldsymbol{a}_i \boldsymbol{a}_i^\top} \boldsymbol{a}_i^\top \tag{14.19}$$

where p_i is the ith element of $\mathbf{P}$ and $\mathbf{X}^k$ is the kth approximation of the solution.

The advantage of this method is its general applicability to different kinds of data. For example, in cone beam CT, the X-rays are formed as conical beams, which are used in planar projection of the object. For a conical beam, along each ray, a linear equation is formed, which collectively define a system of linear equations to be solved. Even in 3-D applications, the problem of reconstruction can be directly solved in the 3-D space. These examples demonstrate the generalized applicability of this technique.

A typical cross section of a CT image of human brain is shown in Fig. 14.17. The imaged cross section is called the axial view and the reference image shown in the inner sub-window is called the sagittal view of the brain. A line in the sagittal view indicates a

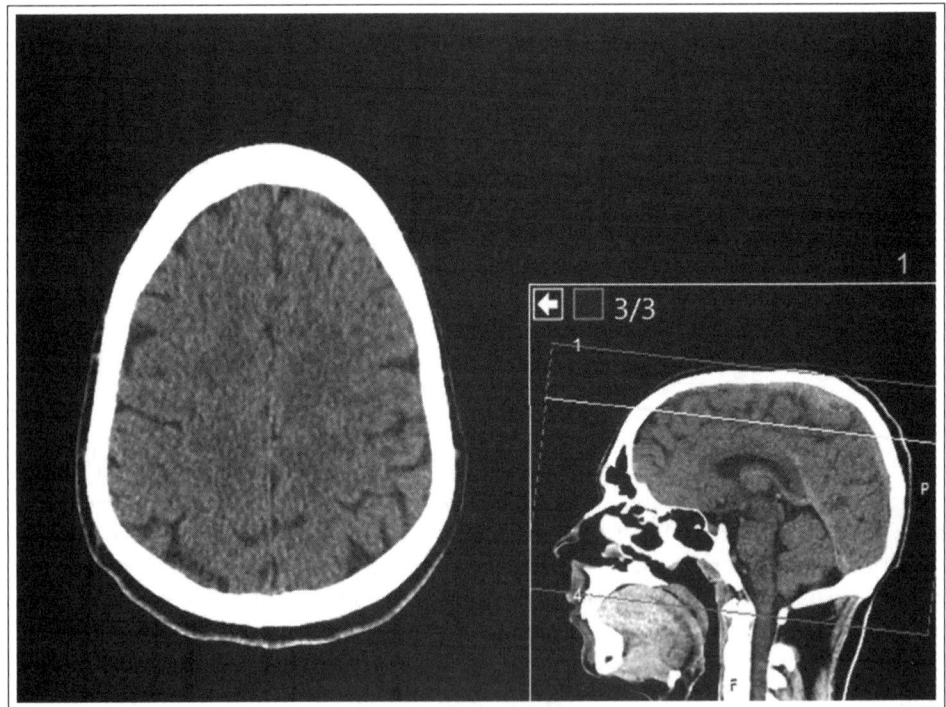

Figure 14.17 A typical cross section of a CT image of human brain. (*Source*: Mikael Haggstrom, M.D., https://commons.wikimedia.org/wiki/File: CT_of_a_normal_brain,_axial_10.png; Universal Public Domain Dedication, https://creativecommons.org/publicdomain/zero/1.0/deed.en via Wikimedia Commons.)

planar intersection of the respective axial view. This is a CT cross section of an 18 year old male with no injuries presented in the axial plane. Here, the physical thickness of the slice is 4 mm.

In Fig. 14.18, another example is shown, which is a typical cross section of a CBCT image of pelvis. This image is of a colorectal patient which was taken during radiotherapy. The physical dimension of the imaged volume is 450 mm × 450 mm × 157.5 mm. This is captured as a 3-D image of 384 × 384 × 64 voxels, where the voxel-to-voxel spacing along x and y axes is 1.1719 mm, and along z-axis is 2.5 mm. Although CBCT images are of low resolution, they require low energy in their acquisition, thereby reducing the radiation exposure to a patient.

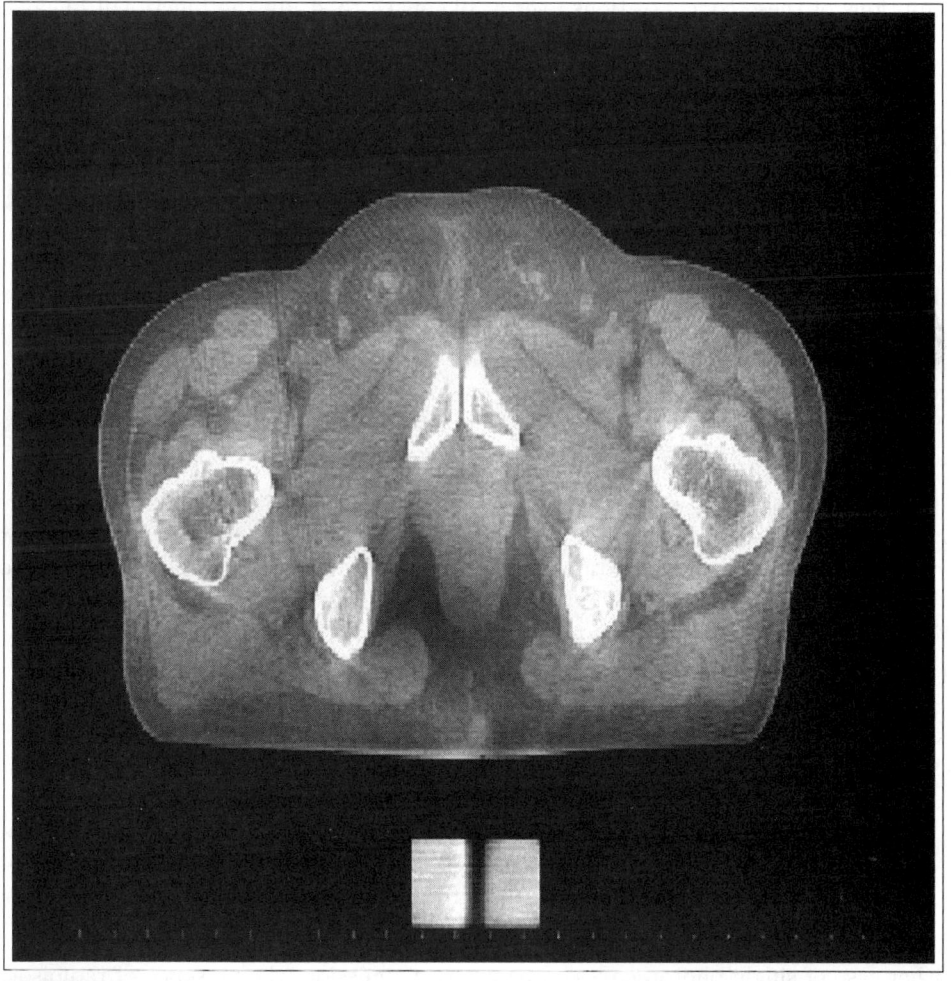

Figure 14.18 A typical cross section of a CBCT image of human pelvis. (*Source*: Dr Indranil Mallick, Tata Medical Center, Kolkata.)

14.3 | Emission tomography

Besides X-ray tomography, there are other different forms of tomography, where the physics behind the imaging principle are different. One such example in the field of nuclear medicine is to inject a patient with a radio-isotope. Then, the patient is subjected to imaging under *emission tomography* to visualize the underlying anatomy. This involves the emission of the radiation of certain isotopes, whose concentration in tissues are detected in imaging. In X-ray imaging, X-rays are externally projected on the body to pass through it and produce an image. In contrast, in emission tomography, the radiation source is within the body. The sources of radiation, such as radioisotopes, are injected into the body, which are digested by the metabolic system to distribute their concentration across different parts of the tissues. Here, the objective is to visualize the variations of the distributions of these concentrations over a 3-D space to study the functional behavior of different organs. The emission tomography is also known as *functional imaging* and *nuclear medicine*. There are different kinds of radioisotopes that are used as radiation sources. Some of the popularly used isotopes are of Phosphorous ($^{32}P_{15}$), Technetium ($^{99}Tc_{43}$), Fluorine ($^{18}F_9$), etc. These radioisotopes decay spontaneously, which is a desired property for emission tomography. Radioisotopes are not injected into the body directly. They are pushed as dyes of their compounds, like, ^{99m}Tc-Ethylcysteinat-Dimer (ECD), fluoro-deoxyglucose (FDG), etc. After injecting into the body, they are digested and distributed over the body with certain concentrations. By an initial calibration process, it is ensured that the acquired images conform to a known distribution under normal conditions. But in some cases, some of the cells may exhibit heavy concentrations, which are indications of some anomalies or diseases that have resulted in certain behavior or response of the body.

Primarily, there are two types of phenomena that are responsible for emission tomography:

(i) Single photon emission: When a radioisotope decays, it radiates a single photon, which is called γ-*ray*. Every event of such a γ-decay is an activity of the radioisotope that results in a single photon emission event. An illustration of this phenomenon is shown in Fig. 14.19. The imaging system that uses single photon emission is called *single photon emission computed tomography*.

(ii) Positron emission: When a radioisotope decays, the nucleus emits a positron that collides with an electron along its direction. In this process, the matter gets transformed into energy, which is emitted as two photons in opposite directions with equal energy of 511 keV. In this phenomena, after collision, two photons are simultaneously detected in opposite directions. A simultaneous detection of these photons indicate a β^+-decay, which is the activity of the radioisotope that results in positron emission. An illustration of this phenomenon is shown in Fig. 14.20. The imaging system that uses positron emission is called *positron emission tomography*.

In either case of single photon emission or positron emission, the presence of radioisotopes are verified only by the detection of photons, which are used in functional imaging for studying the biological processes.

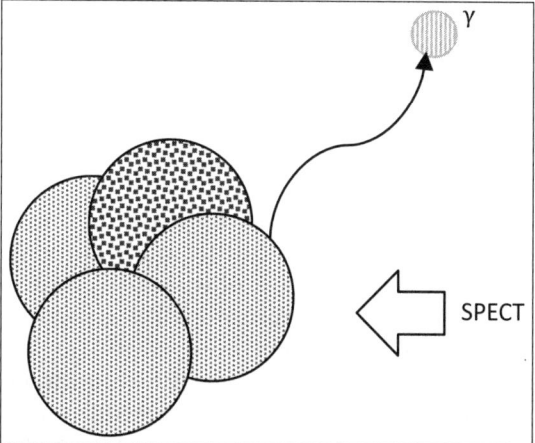

Figure 14.19 Illustration of single photon emission phenomenon.

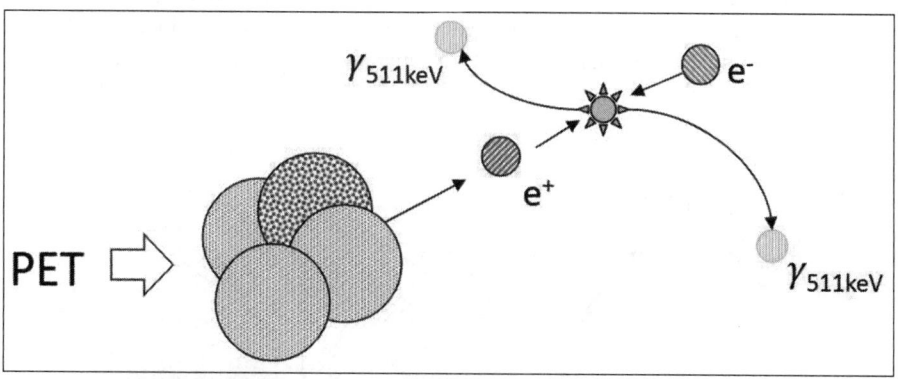

Figure 14.20 Illustration of positron emission phenomenon.

This phenomenon of radioactivity is a spontaneous and stochastic process by which an unstable atomic nucleus loses energy and subatomic particles by radiation. This is modeled by a Poisson process[3] with mean and variance of λ. Here, the rate of decay, i.e., the number of emissions in a particular interval of time, follows the Poisson probability distribution which is given by Eq. 14.20.

$$p(n) = e^{-\lambda}\frac{\lambda^n}{n!} \tag{14.20}$$

where, n is the number of emissions and λ is the average number of emissions. A radioactive decay is a discrete event that emits a single photon or simultaneously two photons per emission. The unit of radioactivity is expressed in terms of *Becquerel* (Bq), named after the renowned French scientist, Henri Becquerel (1852 - 1908), who discovered radioactivity. The amount of activity of an isotope is expressed by this unit. One radioactivity event per second is measured as one Becquerel, i.e.,

$$1 \text{ Bq} = 1 \text{ disintegration/second}$$

---

[3] For the Poisson distribution, the mean is equal to the variance.

Higher value of this unit implies a higher amount of radioactive dose. Typical doses of radioisotopes in patients range from 100 MBq to 1000 MBq, which is considered as a very small unit.

The radioactive decay follows an exponential decay process, which is given by Eq. 14.21.

$$S(t) = S_0 e^{-\ln\frac{2t}{T_h}} \tag{14.21}$$

where, S_0 is the initial radioactivity, $S(t)$ is the activity after time t, and T_h is the half-life period. The half-life period is the time interval in which the intensity of the amount of radioactivity gets halved. That is, the number of emissions gets reduced to half the initial number after the half-life period. Every radioisotope has a particular half-life period. For example, the half-life period of Technetium isotope (^{99m}Tc) is six hours. Consider a radioisotope with radioactivity level at 100, i.e., 100 disintegrations per second, whose half-life period is six hours. After six hours, the radioactivity level would be 50, i.e., 50 disintegrations per second. After another six hours, the radioactivity level would be 25. In this way, the isotope gets decayed exponentially.

For a SPECT, a γ-detector detects the γ-radiation through a collimator from the object, as shown in Fig. 14.21. Here, the γ-detector is an array of detectors. Since the directionality is an important aspect in tomography, the radiation from the object is passed through a collimator, which controls the direction of the radiation rays, so that, all the emissions

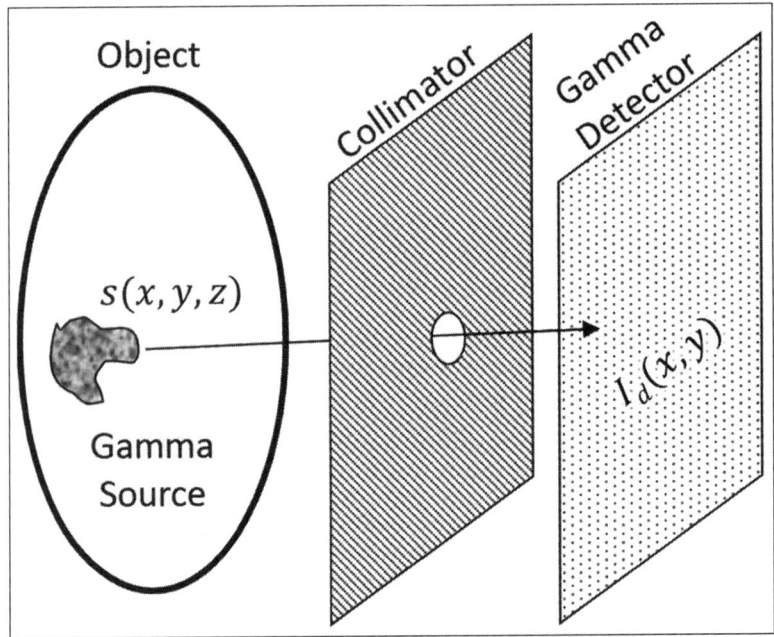

Figure 14.21 Basic form of an emission computed tomography system. (*Source*: Adapted from the slide set of Prof. D.C. Noll, Univ. of Michigan, Ann Arbor, USA, https://web.eecs.umich.edu/~fessler/course/516/l/noll,516,intro-jf.ppt.)

at the detector follow a common direction. The detector records the average number of emissions of γ photons at a given time, which represents the concentration of radioisotopes along the line of radiation. The γ-reconstruction is performed by the resulting line integral using the standard technique of computed tomography, particularly the ART, to form the respective image, as discussed in the previous section. For a positron emission, there may be some interference due to emission of two photons, which is either ignored when it is not significant, or statistically taken care of during the reconstruction.

In its basic form, the SPECT has an array of detectors, an array of collimators for passing the rays along the common line, and an array of multipliers. The weak radiation signal requires some amplification for detecting them. This amplification is achieved by the array of photon multipliers. A schematic representation of a SPECT system for a γ-camera is shown in Fig. 14.22. As shown in the figure, it involves three primary components, an array of Lead collimators, an array of Sodium Iodide crystal multipliers, and an array of photomultiplier tube detectors.

The PET consists of a ring detector to detect the photons that travel in opposite directions. The rays that are moving in opposite directions are detected by two elements of the detector, which is shown in Fig. 14.23. Here, the key is to check for the simultaneous detection of the photons. Only if a simultaneous detection is recorded, it is identified as a positron emission. If there is a detection, but not a simultaneous detection, it is considered noise. So, the PET has a better noise handling capability. The signals are simultaneously monitored from each of the detector blocks that are placed opposite to each other, as shown in Fig. 14.23. An event is counted as positron emission only when an impulse is detected from these two opposite blocks at the same time. For reconstruction of

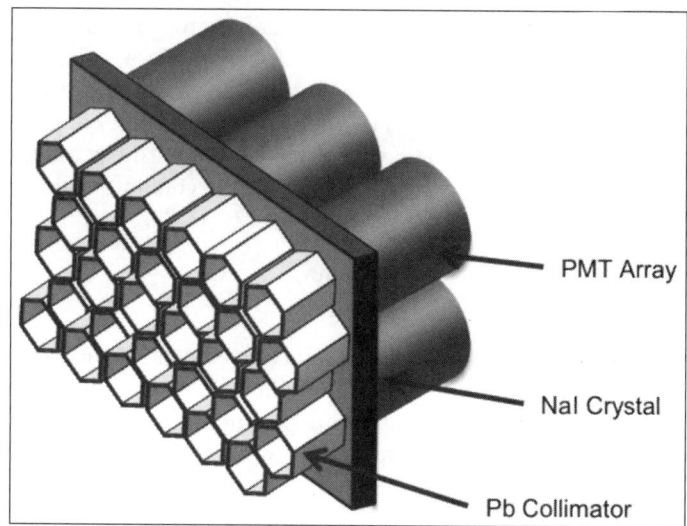

Figure 14.22 SPECT detector array. (*Source*: James Sander, Chapter 10 of "Medical Imaging Systems: An Introductory Guide", Springer Open, 2018; https://creativecommons.org/licenses/by/4.0/.)

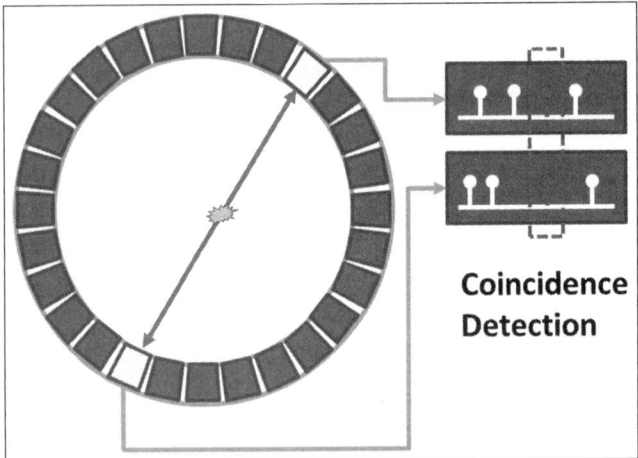

Figure 14.23 PET detector array. (*Source*: James Sander, Chapter 10 of "Medical Imaging Systems: An Introductory Guide", Springer Open, 2018; https://creativecommons.org/licenses/by/4.0/.)

images, there exist statistical methods like iterative maximum likelihood estimation, which is similar to ART. The information of the counts that represent the concentrations of radioactivity doses at various points, are used in the estimation.

Similar to reconstruction in X-ray imaging, where the intensities are converted to Hounsfield units, the intensities in emission tomography are converted to absolute units like kBq/ml for practical interpretations. Transforming to such absolute units of dose concentration is possible by strict calibration of the devices using phantoms. These phantoms are specialized medical devices that are built to mimic certain properties of tissues. By pushing the radioactive dye into those phantoms and capturing their images, the radioactivity is observed. Then, the device is calibrated with the known concentrations of doses. The volumetric sensitivity, α_{vol}, of the system is counts per minute and milliliter divided by the dose concentration, which is given by Eq. 14.22.

$$\alpha_{vol} = \frac{\text{counts}}{\text{minute} \cdot \text{ml}} \Big/ \frac{\text{kBq}}{\text{ml}} \tag{14.22}$$

There is another unit that is commonly used in practice, which is called *standardized uptake value* (SUV). This unit is normalized by the weight and dose of a patient. The SUV is expressed as the amount of dose in absolute units per milliliter in a *volume of interest* (voi) divided by the injected dose concentration and the weight of the person, which is given by Eq. 14.23.

$$\text{SUV} = \frac{\text{kBq}_{\text{voi}}}{\text{ml}_{\text{voi}}} \Big/ \frac{\text{MBq}_{\text{injected}}}{\text{kg}} \tag{14.23}$$

The expression of the concentration in terms of SUV is used for diagnostic purposes. As a standard, the SUV units are normalized by the maximum SUV, SUV_{max}, in the respective image. There are two main assumptions for SUV: (1) the tracer gets distributed uniformly in healthy tissues, and (2) the density of the body is almost equal to the density of water, which is 1 kg/liter. As an interpretation of this unit, if the SUV is significantly greater than 1, it indicates disproportionate amount of uptake and abnormal activity.

There are certain imaging systems which show both the functional and the anatomical perspectives of a subject. Such an imaging technique is called *hybrid imaging*, which is a combination of CT and PET, as shown in Fig. 14.24. Here, one portion of the system captures CT image of cross sections, while another portion of the system captures PET image. The subject is placed on a platform that slides in a particular direction to sequentially traverse through both the portions of the system. Thereby, both CT and PET images of the whole body of the subject are captured by a single system, which can be related with each other to gather more meaningful information.

An example is shown in Fig. 14.25. Here, Fig. 14.25 (a) is a differential SPECT scan using ^{99m}Tc-ECD to localize seizure epicenter. The image in Fig. 14.25 (b) is a FDG-PET scan of a patient with melanoma, where several small lesions are visible below liver and beside heart. By super-imposing such images from different modalities, it is easier to detect certain diseases or anomalous functional behaviors of various organs.

Numerical Example

Given the half life period of a Technetium isotope 6 hours, compute the amount of radioactivity in the body of a patient after 8 hours, if initially subjected to 500 MBq radiation dose of the same isotope.

Solution

$S(8) = 500e^{-ln\frac{2\times8}{6}}$ MBq = 187.5 MBq.

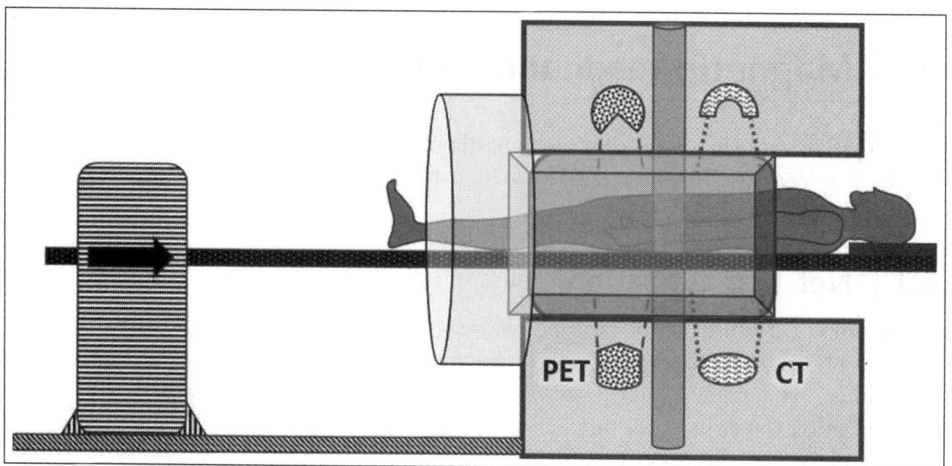

Figure 14.24 Illustration of a hybrid imaging system using CT and PET.

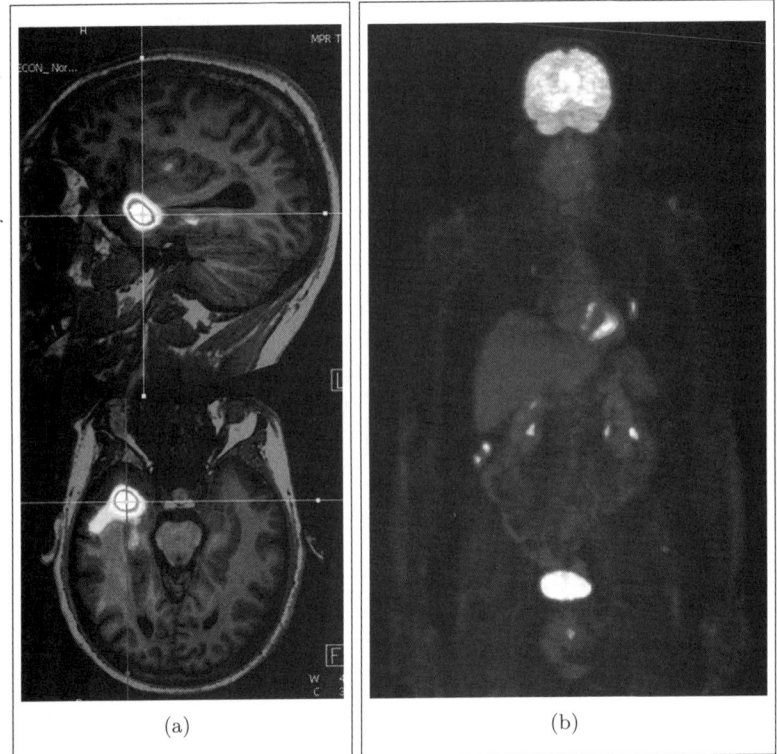

(a)   (b)

Figure 14.25 Example of diagnostic procedures in molecular imaging by (a) SPECT and (b) FDG-PET. Both the images are co-registered and displayed with superposition. (*Source*: James Sander, Chapter 10 of "Medical Imaging Systems: An Introductory Guide", Springer Open, 2018; `https://creativecommons.org/licenses/by/4.0/`.) See Color Plates (page 820).

14.4 | Magnetic resonance imaging

Another popular scan that is used in medical diagnosis is called *magnetic resonance imaging* (MRI). In this case, a 3-D image is formed using the phenomenon of nuclear magnetic resonance (NMR).

14.4.1 | Net magnetization

The behavior of tissues is observed by sensing the magnetic polarizations and the distribution of magnetization in the frequency space. Human body has a vast number of hydrogen ions, ^{1}H nuclei, which is in the order of 10^{27}. These ions behave like magnetic needles. Actually, the spin of the nucleus makes them act like a magnet. The directionality of the spin gives the direction of magnetization. In a normal human body, without the presence of any external field, the directions of spin in these ions are random, which neutralize the net magnetization to 0, as seen in Fig. 14.26 (a). However, in the presence

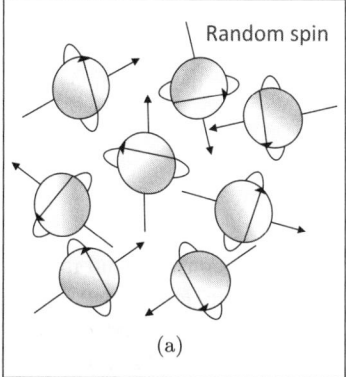 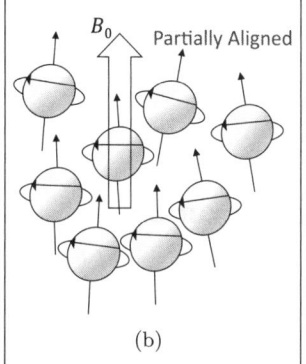 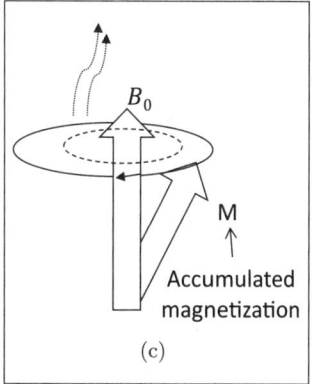

(a)   (b)   (c)

Figure 14.26 Spin of ^{1}H nuclei (a) at random, and (b) at an aligned direction from an external magnetic field. (c) The accumulated magnetization precesses around the external magnetic field B_0 and gets aligned with it to provide a net magnetization.

of an external magnetic field, B_0, the directions of the spin of ions get partially aligned with the external field and results in some positive net magnetization along the direction of B_0. As a magnetic needle oscillates in the presence of an external strong magnetic field before getting aligned with it, the direction of net magnetization also precesses around the external magnetic field before the alignment in its direction. During this precession, electromagnetic wave in the range of radio frequencies (RF) is emitted. After the alignment, there is no such radiation. This is illustrated in Fig. 14.26.

The frequency of the precession about the axis of the external magnetic field depends on the strength of the external magnetic field and the properties of the spinning nuclei. This is called the *Larmor frequency*, which is proportional to the inducing magnetic field, B_0. This is given by Eq. 14.24.

$$f_l = \gamma \|B_0\| \tag{14.24}$$

where, f_l is the Larmor frequency and γ is known as the *gyromagnetic ratio*, given a specific nucleus. Thus for a given nucleus, at a given magnetic field, the precession takes place at a particular frequency. For example, Larmor frequency of ^{1}H is 42.5676 MHz @ 1 Tesla of magnetic field and 64 MHz @ 1.5 Tesla of magnetic field. In magnetic resonance, the information of Larmor frequency is very crucial, which is used for sensing the magnetization. The precessing magnetic field radiates energy, whose frequency is also equal to the Larmor frequency or the resonant frequency.

Numerical Example

Compute the Larmor frequency of Hydrogen ion at the inducing magnetic field of 2 *Tesla* given the gyromagnetic ration $\gamma = 42.76$ MHz per Tesla.

Solution

Larmor frequency $= \gamma B_0$, where B_0 is the intensity of magnetic field. Hence, it is $42.76 \times 2 = 85.52$ MHz.

14.4.2 | Excitation and relaxation

Suppose the direction of the net magnetic field, M is modified by a weaker external magnetic field, B_1, that is orthogonal to B_0. This is realized by transmitting EM pulse in radio frequency (RF), the same as with the Larmor frequency. This process is called *excitation*. This is diagrammatically shown in Fig. 14.27 (a), where the direction of M is aligned to the direction shown by the dotted line after the excitation by B_1, which is orthogonal to B_0. This change of direction occurs like a rotating turntable, where the direction of net magnetization changes from vertical direction to horizontal direction along this imaginary turntable plane, as seen in the figure. If the magnetic field B_1 is withdrawn by removing the incident RF waves, then the direction of M returns back to its native alignment with B_0. It is called the process of *relaxation*. This is diagrammatically shown in Fig. 14.27 (b). The process of relaxation is relatively slower than the process of excitation. In fact, excitation is almost instantaneous compared to relaxation (which happens due to precession). At each point in the space, there are two components, a transversal component (along B_1) and a longitudinal component (along B_0). During the faster process of excitation, the longitudinal component decays due to the change in the angle of the magnetization and the transversal component gains. During the slower process of relaxation, the transversal component decays due to progressive dephasing of spinning dipoles and the longitudinal component regains due to the relaxation of the dipoles as they get aligned with B_0. During the relaxation process, polarized radiation is emitted which is also at the frequency of Larmor frequency. The amount of this radiation depends on the strength of magnetization. This polarized radiation of RF is detected at the Larmor frequency. Unlike tomographic scans, the directionality is not involved in magnetic resonance sensing.

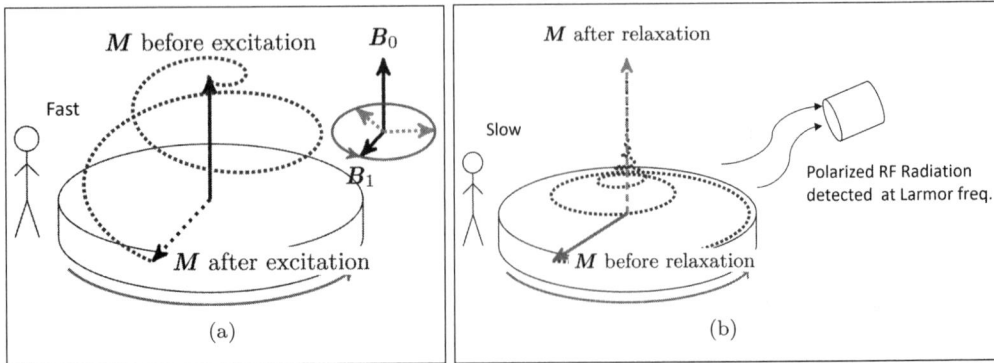

Figure 14.27 (a) Excitation, and (b) relaxation processes in magnetic resonance. (*Source*: Adapted from Felix Lugauer and Jens Wetzl, Chapter 6 of "Medical Imaging Systems: An Introductory Guide", Springer Open, 2018; https://creativecommons.org/licenses/by/4.0/.)

During relaxation, the decay and recovery components of magnetization follow a particular characteristic. There are two different time behaviors for longitudinal and transversal components. The longitudinal component recovers from 0 to the original state of its magnetization exponentially with a time constant T_1, which is shown in Fig. 14.28 (a) for arterial blood. This is given by Eq. 14.25.

$$||M_z(t)|| = ||M_0|| \left(1 - e^{-\frac{t}{T_1}}\right) \qquad (14.25)$$

where, $M_z(t)$ is the recovery at time t, and M_0 is the original state of magnetization. This recovery phenomena of the longitudinal component is called T_1 relaxation. Whereas, the transversal component decays from its original state of its magnetization to 0 exponentially with a time constant T_2, which is shown in Fig. 14.28 (b) for arterial blood. This is given by Eq. 14.26.

$$||M_{xy}(t)|| = ||M_0|| \left(e^{-\frac{t}{T_2}}\right) \qquad (14.26)$$

where, $M_{xy}(t)$ is the decay at time t, and M_0 is the original state of magnetization. This decay phenomenon of the transversal component is called T_2 relaxation. In practice, the transversal component decays faster than the theoretically defined T_2. These T_1 and T_2 are the parameters that vary over the properties of the tissue. As seen in Figs. 14.28 (a) and (b), the time constant for recovery period of longitudinal component, $T_1 = 2.5$ s, and the time constant for decay of transversal component, $T_2 = 45$ ms. Evidently, recovery is a slower process and decay is relatively a very fast process. These values are typical for arterial blood. However, these values vary with different types of tissues. The contrast imaging using MRI is about achieving contrast of these time constants. When a MRI image is taken, due to the variation of time constants, the amount of magnetization also varies, which indicates presence of different kinds of tissues and organs.

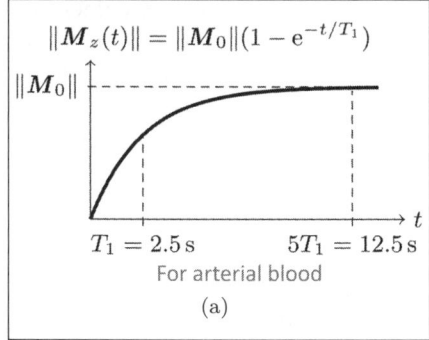
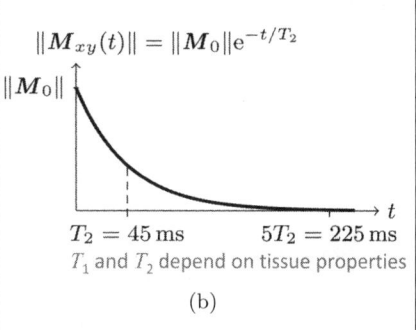

Figure 14.28 (a) Exponential recovery of longitudinal component for arterial blood. (b) Exponential decay of transversal component for arterial blood. (*Source*: Adapted from Felix Lugauer and Jens Wetzl, Chapter 6 of "Medical Imaging Systems: An Introductory Guide", Springer Open, 2018; https://creativecommons.org/licenses/by/4.0/.)

14.4.3 | Modes of imaging

There are three modes of forming images by NMR:

(i) T_1-weighted,

(ii) T_2-weighted, and

(iii) proton density (PD) weighted.

In T_1-*weighted images*, the contrasts due to recovery of longitudinal component are used, which include contrasts among the material, tissues and bones, arterial blood, etc. In T_2-*weighted images*, the contrasts due to decay of transversal component are used. In *proton density weighted images*, variations due to the proton density are considered, which are tissue specific properties that quantify the number of mobile hydrogen protons, ^1H, per unit volume.

There are two imaging control parameters by which one of the three modes of forming the images is selected. One of the imaging control parameters is called *echo time* (TE), which is the time delay between the middle of the excitation or the RF pulse and the measurement of magnetization. Another imaging control parameter is called *repetition time* (TR), which is the period of time between successive RF pulses of excitation. When the magnetic field is excited, the net magnetization through the tissues change from the longitudinal component to the transversal component. Following the excitation, if measurement is made too early, the recovery of longitudinal component of magnetization is not very high, since the recovery is a slower process. It provides better contrast in T_1-weighted image with the domination of transversal component. Longer TE provides better contrast for T_2-weighted images, but it results in a weaker signal since the transversal component decays fast. Shorter TR provides better contrast for T_1. For shorter TR, enough time for full recovery of the longitudinal component is not given. So, the signal is weak, but the variation of T_1 brings the contrast in the volume.

In brief, for a short TR and a short TE, T_1-weighted mode provides better contrast because the recovery is partial by that time. For a long TR and a long TE, T_2-weighted mode provides better contrast because most of the decay would have completed by that time. For a short TE and long TR, the effect of both recovery and decay does not provide a good contrast, but the net magnetization that varies over the tissues is reflected, which is the PD weighted mode. However, the PD weighted mode is a mixed mode where any conclusive contrast is not obtained, because any particular phenomena cannot be isolated. This is also summarized in Table 14.2.

Table 14.2 Modes of imaging defined by parameters TE and TR.

	Short TE	Long TE
Short TR	T_1-weighted	
Long TR	PD weighted	T_2-weighted

14.4.4 | Resolving spatial distribution

Sensing the amount of magnetization (in the form of the energy released by the molecules) from a volume by a detector does not provide any information about the precise location of the magnetization. Mere detection of magnetization does not resolve its source. The sensed magnetization may be from any part in the whole of the body being scanned. The phenomenon of magnetic resonance (MR) is used to resolve the source. Toward this, gradient coils are used for having a spatial variation of exciting magnetic field. Here, three gradient coils are used along the three orthogonal directions. A schematic diagram of a gradient coil is shown in Fig. 14.29. As shown in the figure, the z-direction is along the axis of the cylindrical structure along which the subject is placed lying horizontally. The magnet causes the magnetization B_0 along the z-direction. With reference to the figure, the gradient coil creates a spatial variation of the magnetic field along the z-direction, which is given by, $||B_0|| + z$. Also, an RF coil excites the magnetization to flip the dipoles, thereby creating transverse magnetization. Then, a slice selection is made along the z-axis, where the spatial variation of the magnetic field is present. At this slice, the device is excited by the RF wave with the respective Larmor's frequency for the selected value of z, which is given by Eq. 14.27.

$$f_l(z) = \gamma(||B_0|| + z) \qquad (14.27)$$

In the event of withdrawal of the excitation, the NMR phenomena occur only from the points of the tissues lying on that slice. Any observed measurement is related only to the selected

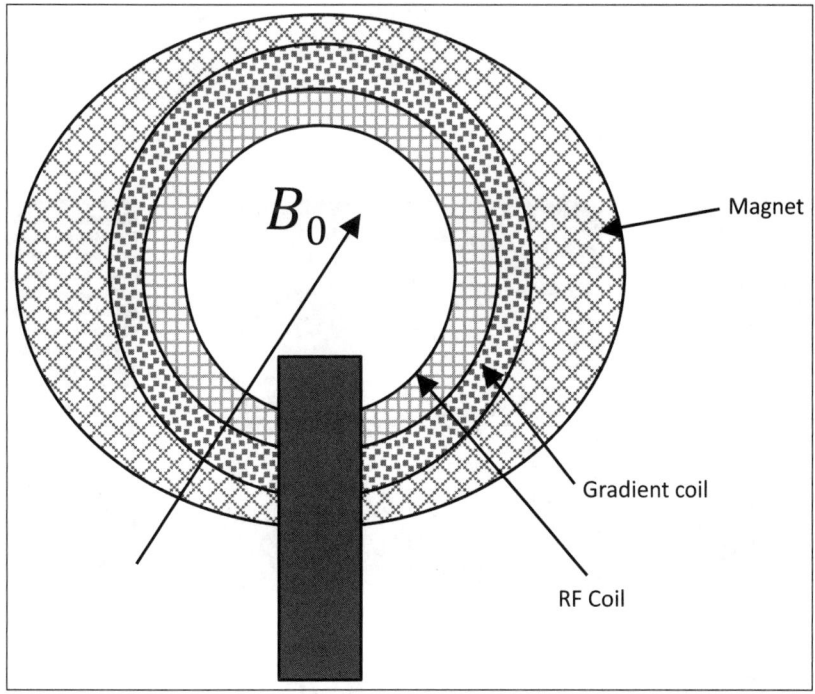

Figure 14.29 Schematic diagram of a gradient coil that are used to have spatial variation in exciting magnetic field.

cross section. However, this still does not resolve the 2-D distributions of magnetization across the cross section. To resolve it, encoding of spatial variation of magnetization is achieved using the linear gradient coils along x and y axes. A linear gradient of strength k along a direction, say x-axis, causes variation of phases of the directions of induced magnetization of the nuclei along that direction. Effectively, it can be shown that this variation is captured in the measurement of MR signal during relaxation as the correlation of the distribution of magnetization (or space varying function) with a spatially varying sinusoid along x with a frequency proportional to k. This effectively provides the coefficient of the Fourier transform of the distribution at that spatial frequency. For a 2-D distribution over the slice, the gradient coils along both x and y directions are used for measuring the coefficients of its 2-D Fourier transform at a point in the 2-D spatial frequency space, say (k_x, k_y). This measurement is called $\boldsymbol{k}$-*space measurement*, where $\boldsymbol{k}$ indicates the frequency in a multi-dimensional space. In the case of volume selective sensing, gradient coils along all the three orthogonal directions (x, y and z) are used to measure the Fourier coefficient at a point of 3-D spatial frequency space.

In $\boldsymbol{k}$-space imaging, the signal is sensed in the frequency space which provides the 2-D and 3-D Fourier spectrum directly. An example is shown in Fig. 14.30. Here, different sampled values of the frequency components are sensed by using the gradient coils by simulating the distribution of induced magnetic fields over a 2-D space.

An example of magnetic resonance image is shown in Fig. 14.31 The T_1 contrast image and the T_2 contrast image are shown in Fig. 14.31 (a) and (b), respectively. As it is seen in the figure, different tissues behave differently under the two relaxation processes. The PD weighted image is also shown in Fig. 14.31 (c).

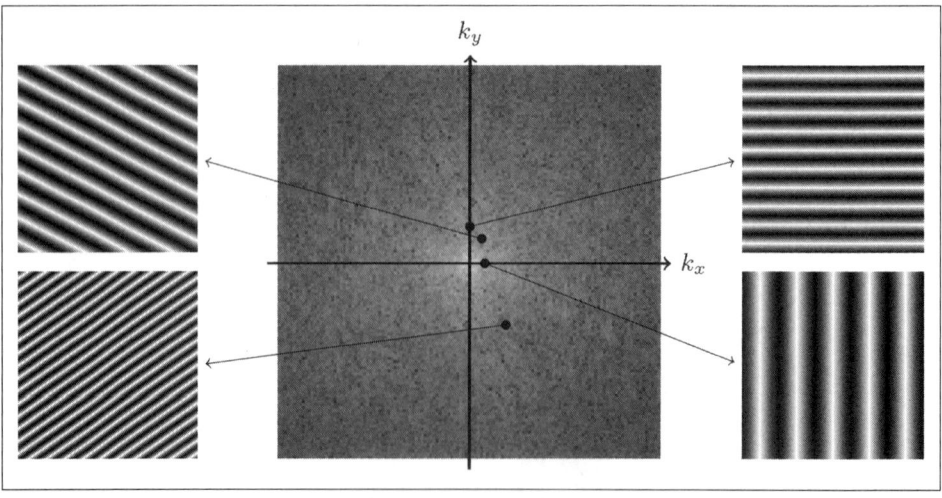

Figure 14.30 An example of k-space imaging. (*Source*: Felix Lugauer and Jens Wetzl, Chapter 6 of "Medical Imaging Systems: An Introductory Guide", Springer Open, 2018; https://creativecommons.org/licenses/by/4.0/.)

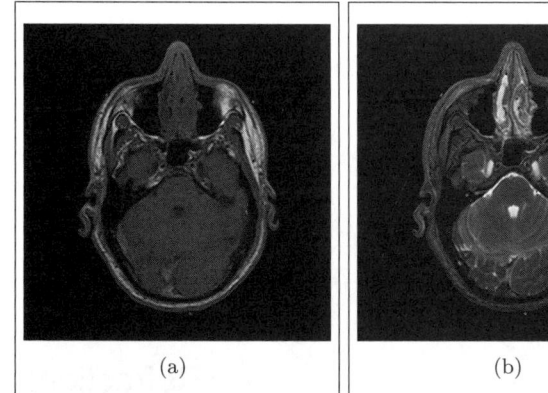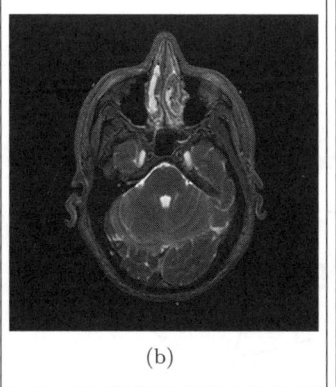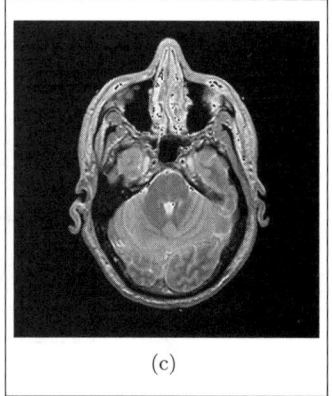

| (a) | (b) | (c) |

Figure 14.31 An example of MRI scanned image. (a) T_1-weighted, (b) T_2-weighted, and (c) PD weighted images. (*Source*: Courtesy of the U.S. National Library of Medicine through `https://www.nlm.nih.gov/research/visible/visible_human.html`. The images do not reflect the most current/accurate data available from National Library of Medicine (NLM).)

14.5 | Ultrasound

In ultrasound modality, the imaging is performed by the reflection of acoustic or sound waves. Here, a piezoelectric device is actuated by electric signals to generate sound waves. The piezoelectric device is a transducer that contains piezoelectric elements, which transmit and receive the signals. While transmitting, the electrical energy is converted to acoustic energy. While receiving, the acoustic energy is converted back to electrical energy. The sound waves are transmitted into the body. A significant proportion of the transmitted energy is reflected from various tissues and organs inside the body, while a part of it gets refracted. The reflected waves are received by the transducer. A schematic diagram illustrating the mechanism of an ultrasound imaging system is shown in Fig. 14.32. From these reflected waves, the depth and reflectivity of the boundary surface between various internal organs are measured. The amount of reflection provides information about various properties of the underlying tissues. In one of the ultrasound modes of operation, the Doppler shift of frequency in the reflected waves due to certain movements of organs or flow of fluids is measured, which provides the velocity of the target object. The ultrasound imaging also captures the temporal dynamics of objects under consideration. The ultrasound imaging is usually the first-resort clinical imaging modality due to its cost-effectiveness and lack of ionizing radiations, which makes it more safe to use. Typical frequency range of operation of an ultrasound system is between 2 MHz to 40 MHz.

The sound wave is characterized by certain parameters like, intensity (J), frequency (f), velocity (c), and wavelength (λ). The wavelength, frequency, and velocity are related by Eq. 14.28.

$$\lambda = \frac{c}{f} \tag{14.28}$$

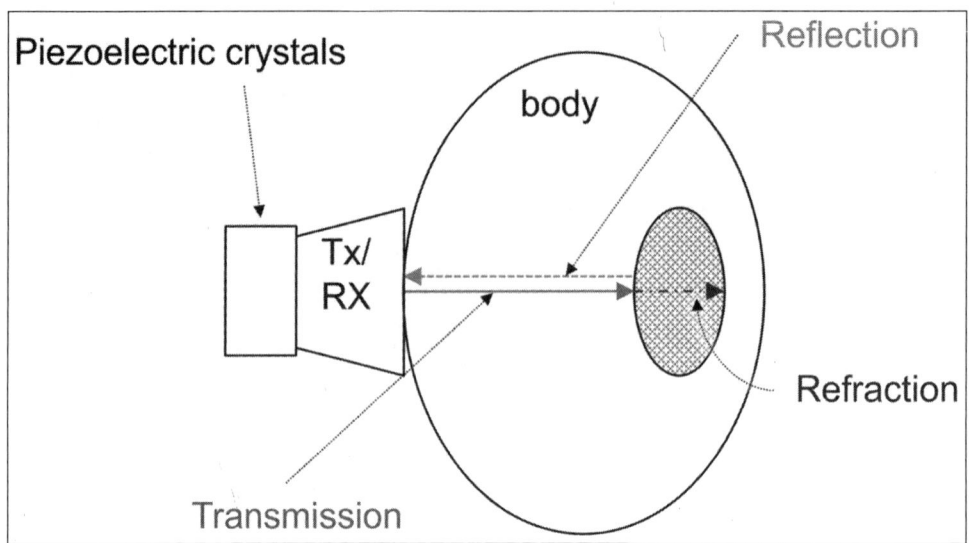

Figure 14.32 Schematic diagram of an ultrasound system.

During the propagation of acoustic wave, its attenuation takes place similar to Lambert Beer's law, which is expressed by Eq. 14.29.

$$J(x) = J_0 e^{-\mu x} \tag{14.29}$$

where, $J(x)$ is the intensity at depth x, J_0 is the transmitted intensity, and μ is the attenuation coefficient that depends on the propagating medium and the frequency. Higher frequencies result in higher attenuation and lower penetration through the medium. However, higher frequencies provide better resolution of the objects. In an ultrasound scan, the direction along the propagation of the acoustic waves is called *axial direction* and the direction perpendicular to the propagation of the acoustic waves in the same plane is called *azimuthal direction* or *lateral direction*. The resolution of the scanned images in the axial and lateral directions are known as axial resolution and lateral resolution, respectively. The axial resolution, Δz, is usually better than the lateral resolution Δx. If λ is the wavelength of the acoustic wave used in imaging, then the resolutions are given as in Eq. 14.30.

$$\Delta z = \frac{\lambda}{2}$$
$$\Delta x = 3\lambda \tag{14.30}$$

Smaller wavelengths provide better resolution because the reflected waves suffer lesser interference between them. The lateral resolution is relatively poorer than the axial resolution because the reflected waves get spread-out laterally resulting in lower resolving ability in lateral direction. Thus, higher frequencies provide better resolution, but low penetration.

14.5.1 | Modes of ultrasound imaging

There are mainly three modes of ultrasound imaging.

(i) Amplitude mode (A-mode): The amplitude of the reflected ultrasound wave at different depths are displayed over the sonic runtime in the sonic ray direction. This mode operates using an ultrasound beam only in one path, which is traced to understand the structures along the path.

(ii) Brightness mode (B-mode): A 2-D plane is scanned by transmitting several ultrasound beams and creating a plane using A-mode lines for each scanned beam. This mode provides a 2-D image of the cross section of an object. It is mainly used to visualize any anatomy as a sliced plane. Several B-mode images are stacked to generate a video, known as *cineclip*, by sweeping the ultrasound beam over the surface of the body.

(iii) Motion mode (M-mode): A-mode variations are traced on a single path of transmission with time in the form of a 2-D image. In this mode, the stack of temporal A-mode scans provide the temporal variations or temporal profile of a particular organ at the imaged point. It is used to study the functional behavior of moving structures like valves of heart.

There is another mode of operation known as Doppler mode, which primarily measures blood velocity using Doppler shift of the frequency of reflection. This mode is particularly useful in continuous monitoring of any condition involving pulsating structures. For example, it is used to monitor the heart rates of mother and foetus during labor and delivery procedure. It is also used for noninvasive screening to detect reverse-flow of blood in the cases of valve malfunction in heart.

Examples of B-mode ultrasound images of foetus are shown in Fig. 14.33. These images are sampled from a large dataset of routinely acquired maternal-fetal screening ultrasound images collected from two different hospitals by several operators and ultrasound machines (Burgos-Artizzu et al., 2020). Another example is shown in Fig. 14.34, which is acquired in Doppler mode (Kazci et al., 2023). Here, the flow pattern and Doppler ultrasound indices of the umbilical artery in a three-vessel cord fetus are illustrated.

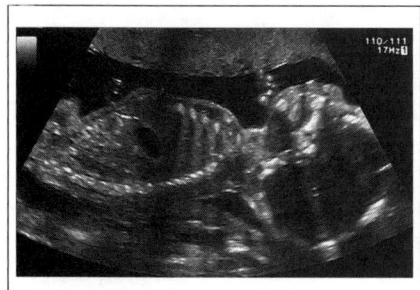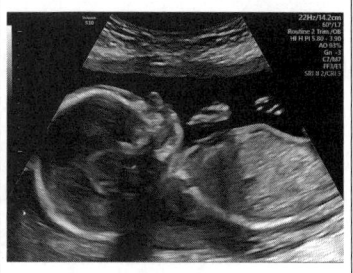

Figure 14.33 Examples of B-mode ultrasound images. (Sampled from https://zenodo.org/records/3904280 under http://creativecommons.org/licenses/by/4.0/.)

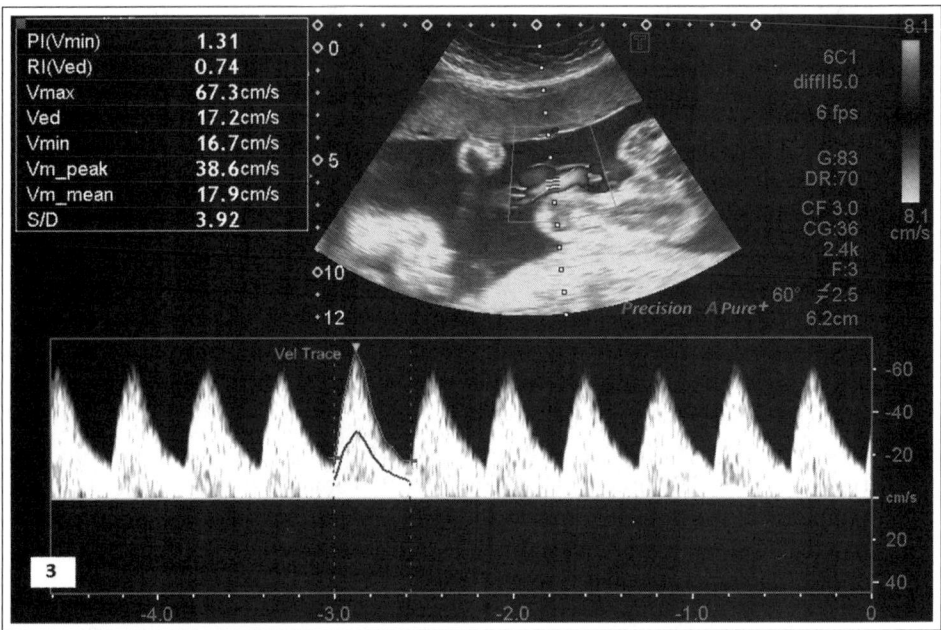

Figure 14.34 Example of Doppler mode ultrasound image. (Reproduced from (Kazci et al., 2023) under http://creativecommons.org/licenses/by/4.0/.) See Color Plates (page 821).

Particularly, this is a color Doppler image, where the flow velocities are coded by pseudo coloring for better visualization and understanding. The pseudo color coding is generally defined by a device manufacturer, which follows a standard code that help physicians to analyze and diagnose quickly. When the flow of blood in an organ is toward the sensor, a higher velocity is recorded, which results in a positive frequency shift. Similarly, the flow of blood away from the sensor results in a negative frequency shift.

Summary

In this chapter, various medical imaging techniques and their modalities are discussed. X-rays produced by the interaction of high energy electron beams with atoms of a metallic surface are capable of passing through tissues of our body and thus provide images of the medium with its compositions. The X-ray imaging technique records the attenuation of the transmitted X-rays through a human body and reflects the tissue properties in the path of propagation. Primarily the Compton scattering phenomenon is responsible for producing diagnostic X-ray images. As X-ray images record line integrals of absorption of energy along the path of propagation, the imaging technique is also used for imaging 3-D volumes using computed axial tomography. There are two types of CT imaging techniques, namely the fan beam CT and the cone beam CT. In a fan beam CT, the principles of Radon transform and Fourier slice theorem are used for reconstructing 2-D cross section of a 3D volume. In the CBCT imaging, there exist algebraic techniques for solving s set of simultaneous equations to reconstruct a volume. In nuclear medicine, similar mathematical principles are used for tomographic reconstruction using the phenomena of single photon emission and positron emission. Another distinguished modality of medical imaging is the MRI, which takes place by sensing the behavior of magnetization of hydrogen ions in our body under the presence of a strong magnetic field and with the events of excitation and withdrawal of transverse field. There are primarily three modalities of MR imaging technique, namely T_1-weighted, T_2-weighted and PD weighted. In MR imaging, the contrast of time constants of decay and recovery of transverse and longitudinal magnetic fields, respectively, across the volume is captured. The other modality of imaging discussed here is the ultrasound imaging, which takes place by transmitting ultrasound acoustic waves through a medium and recording its reflection. There exist various modes of ultrasound imaging, such as A-mode, B-mode, M-mode, and Doppler mode. Ultrasound imaging is a safe imaging modality for a human body as it does not involve radiation and ionization.

Exercises

(i) State Lambert–Beer's law on the behavior of radiation intensity as it travels through a medium over a distance. Show that given a constant attenuation of μ of a medium of thickness L, $\mu = \frac{ln(I_s) - ln(I_d)}{L}$, where I_s and I_d are intensities of X-ray at source and at detector, respectively.

(ii) What are the processes involved in emission of X-ray due to collision of a high energy electron with an atom? Describe how characteristics X-ray radiation is produced out of those processes?

(iii) Which scattering phenomenon is responsible for producing diagnostic X-ray? Describe briefly the phenomenon.

(iv) Describe how Raleigh and Compton scattering take place during absorption of X-ray in our tissues. Which scattering is less harmful and why?

(v) Describe the principles behind X-ray computed tomography.

(vi) How the imaging in fan beam CT differs from cone beam CT? Compare their relative merits and demerits.

(vii) Given a 2-D function $f(x, y)$ define its Radon transform. Discuss how it is possible to reconstruct the function from its Radon transform.

(viii) Describe the Fourier slice theorem relating the Fourier transform of a 2-D function to its Radon transform. Discuss how this theorem is used in reconstructing fan beam CT slices.

(ix) Name and define the unit used in measuring the attenuation coefficient of a medium in CT images. Which medium is taken as the reference in this measurement?

(x) Describe the filtered back projection technique for reconstructing CT images. Provide an example of a filter which is used in this technique.

(xi) Discuss the principle of ART for reconstruction of CT images.

(xii) Describe the Kaczmarz method to arrive at a solution iteratively following the principle of algebraic reconstruction.

(**xiii**) Describe the principle behind cone beam CT (CBCT) imaging. Describe an algorithm for the reconstruction of CBCT images.

(**xiv**) Discuss the principle of emission tomography. What is the purpose of this kind of imaging? Name a few radio-isotopes used for such imaging.

(**xv**) What is single photon emission computed tomography? How does the detection of radioactivity take place in this case?

(**xvi**) Name and define the unit of radioactivity.

(**xvii**) Consider a sample of 450 MBq radio-isotope is given to a patient for SPECT imaging. The half life of the radio-isotope is 8 hours. What would be the amount of radioactivity after 4 hours in the body of the patient?

(**xviii**) Describe the principle of a PET imaging system. What is the unit of reconstruction value in a PET imaging system? Define the standardized uptake value.

(**xix**) Explain why radio frequency wave is emitted from our body in the presence and withdrawal of a strong magnetic field. Name the factors on which the frequency of this wave is dependent.

(**xx**) What is the Larmor frequency? What is the Larmor frequency of a hydrogen ion under the magnetic field of 2 Tesla, given its gyromagnetic ratio 42.576 MHz/Tesla?

(**xxi**) Describe the excitation and relaxation processes in MRI. Describe how T_1-weighted, T_2-weighted, and PD weighted imaging take place using these processes.

(**xxii**) Discuss how a gradient coil in the MRI system is used to locate the slices of radiation.

(**xxiii**) Describe the method of K-space imaging and reconstruction of MRI images.

(**xxiv**) Describe the principle of ultrasound imaging of organs. How the velocity of an organ can be determined by using ultrasound imaging?

(**xxv**) Describe the principle of Motion (M)-mode ultra sound imaging and its usefulness in studying the movement of an organ.

(**xxvi**) Given an ultrasound imaging operating at 20 MhZ, find the lateral and axial resolution of the imaging system.

(**xxvii**) Compute the half-value thickness of lead given its linear attenuation at incident photon energy $0.1 MeV$ is $59.99\ cm^{-1}$. What would be the fraction of reduction in the intensity of transmitted radiation if the thickness is increased by 4 times?

(**xxviii**) Compute the required inducing magnetic field for a MRI machine, which operates with a detector of electromagnetic radiation at 78 MHz, given the gyromagnetic ratio $\gamma = 42.57$ MHz per Tesla.

(**xxix**) Suppose a patient is given a dye of Technetium isotope of dose 300MBq. After how long the SPECT imaging of the patient should be performed to observe the activity at 100 MBq, given the half life of Technetium 6 hours.

(**xxx**) Suppose that the attenuation coefficient of water at 100KeV XRay beam is $0.1707\ cm^{-1}$. If the Hounsfield unit of the liver is 50, what is its attenuation coefficient in absolute scale.

15

Remote Sensing

Remote sensing involves measurements on a target without getting in contact with it and it comprises techniques for collecting, storing, and processing georeferenced and geospatial data to extract valuable information. In this context, data refer to representations stored in computer memory, which can be manipulated using computers to derive meaningful insights. Remote sensing imaging systems primarily work with georeferenced images, capturing Earth's surfaces, environment, atmosphere, etc. These imaging systems may be carried by satellites or airborne platforms like airplanes or drones. For satellite-based imaging, revolution of the satellite around continuously rotating Earth allows periodic capture of images over the same area. There are two main types of imaging systems: passive and active. In passive systems, sensors detect reflected and emitted electromagnetic (EM) waves from Earth's surface, from mainly two types of energy sources, namely sunlight during the day and terrestrial heat at night. These sensors operate within specific spectral bands, converting energy into electrical signals stored as two-dimension (2-D) images. The principle is similar to optical cameras. Additionally, energy from Earth's thermal emission contributes to night time imaging, particularly in the thermal infrared (IR) or far IR bands. Passive remote sensing involves capturing images across various spectral bands, resulting in multispectral and hyperspectral images of specific regions on Earth.

In active imaging systems, microwave radar (RAdio Detection And Ranging) technology is utilized. A radar transmitter emits a pulse of an EM wave with a specific wavelength (in the microwave band). When this pulse strikes a target, some of its energy reflects back to the radar antenna to which the radar receiver is connected. The receiver captures information about the location and geometry of the target by recording the phase and amplitude of the returned signal. By scanning the radar beam over an area, an image of that region is formed. One of the limitations of radar imaging is that, the size of the transmitting antenna is required to be large for obtaining images of high spatial resolution. To address this, synthetic aperture radar (SAR) technology has been developed. In SAR imaging, the system moves along a straight path, and at regular intervals, a side-looking antenna transmits radar pulses toward the Earth's surface. The sensor receives the scattered signals from objects along the trajectory, which are then synthesized to create higher-resolution images. The SAR imaging offers additional advantages over passive multispectral imaging. First, radar waves are capable of penetrating clouds, unlike visible-IR and thermal bands. Therefore, it captures surface images even in cloudy conditions. In contrast, in a multispectral imaging system, the surface beneath the clouds remains occluded. There is another advantage of the radar imaging. It is capable of acquiring images at any time of the day, whether it is dark or bright. These are illustrated in Fig. 15.1.

Remote sensing imaging is widely applied in various critical applications. A few typical examples are as follows.

(i) Agriculture monitoring: Remote sensing of cultivated lands provides valuable information about crops and plants. By analyzing these images, we forecast overall agricultural production for large areas and estimate regional biomass production.

(ii) Telecommunication and infrastructure planning: Remote sensing imaging assists in determining optimal configurations for placing relay stations in telecommunication networks. High-resolution images of regions help assess terrain features and human settlements, aiding in strategic placement of microwave communication relay stations.

(iii) Climate and environmental analysis: Remote sensing is effective for understanding and analyzing climate and environmental processes. For instance, it may track phenomena like seasonal El Nino occurrences in South America.

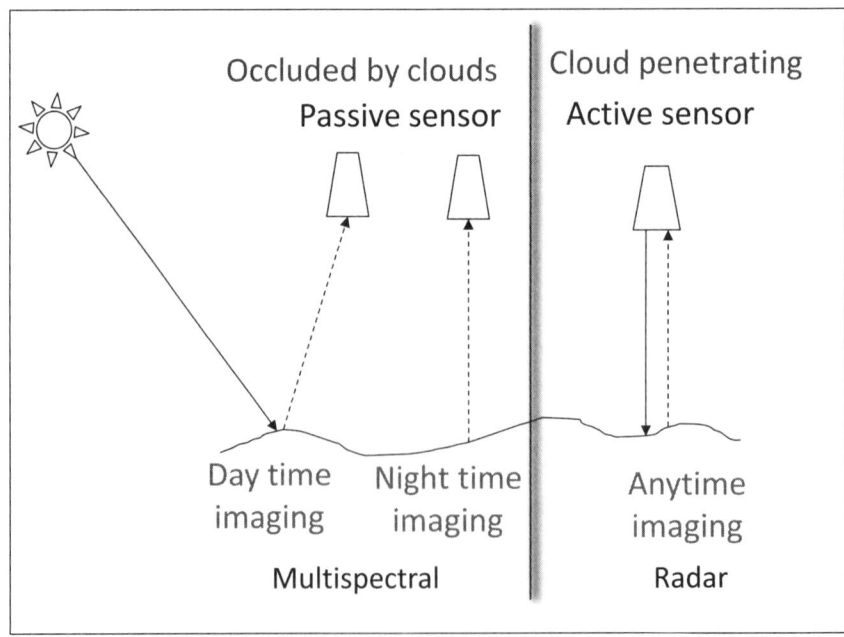

Figure 15.1 Remote sensing imaging systems.

15.1 | Spectral bands for remote sensing imaging

As the imaging takes place through sensing EM waves, the sensitivity of sensors to the spectral bands of this wave is very critical. Let us consider the full range of the EM spectrum, which is shown in Fig. 15.2. The wavelengths may range from as low as 10^{-6} μm of gamma rays to as high as of 100 meters of radio waves. However, the multispectral imaging takes place in a smaller range including the visible-IR optical bands and also the far IR bands of thermal emission. As mostly this energy comes from sun rays through reflection and refraction, and wavelengths of its radiation reaching to the Earth's surface span from 0.02 μm to 1000 μm (or 1mm), multispectral images are mostly captured in the visible, near IR, mid IR, and far IR bands. Within this range there are certain windows of spectral bands on which imaging takes place. This is due to the absorption of certain bands by gases and water vapor present in the atmosphere. For radar imaging, transmission and reception take place in microwave bands, where the wavelengths are in the order of centimeters. In this case, the signalling takes place by transmission of EM pulses of a single wavelength (pure or monochromatic EM wave).

15.1.1 | Interaction with atmosphere

There are three fundamental interactions of EM waves with the atmosphere, as shown in Fig. 15.3, namely, (i) the transmission, (ii) the scattering, and (iii) the absorption of the energy, while passing through the medium. In the process of transmission, the energy is carried to the target and the reflected energy is transmitted back to the sensor. The scattering involves reflection of energy in multiple directions by tiny particles, such as aerosols, water molecules in clouds, etc. that are present in the atmosphere. The amount of absorption depends upon the composition of the medium through which EM energy is propagated. It also depends on the frequency spectrum of EM waves. Energy in some of the spectral bands are absorbed more in certain materials. In the atmosphere, absorption primarily occurs due to the presence of ozone, carbon dioxide, and water vapor. The Sun serves as the source of EM energy, and the Earth's surface reflects this energy during the day while passively emitting thermal radiation at night. Satellite imaging sensors, positioned above the atmosphere, receive both reflected and emitted energy from the

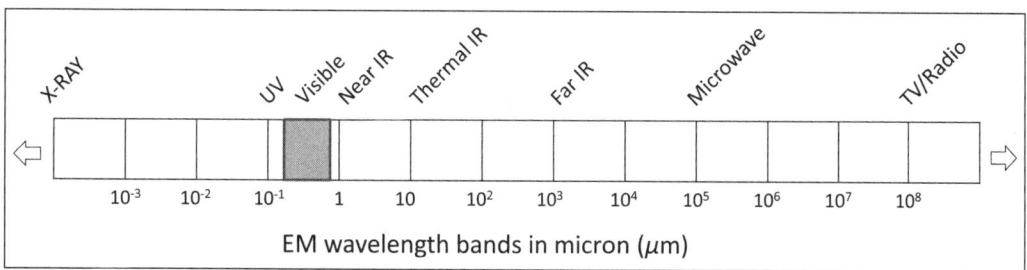

Figure 15.2 Electromagnetic spectrum.

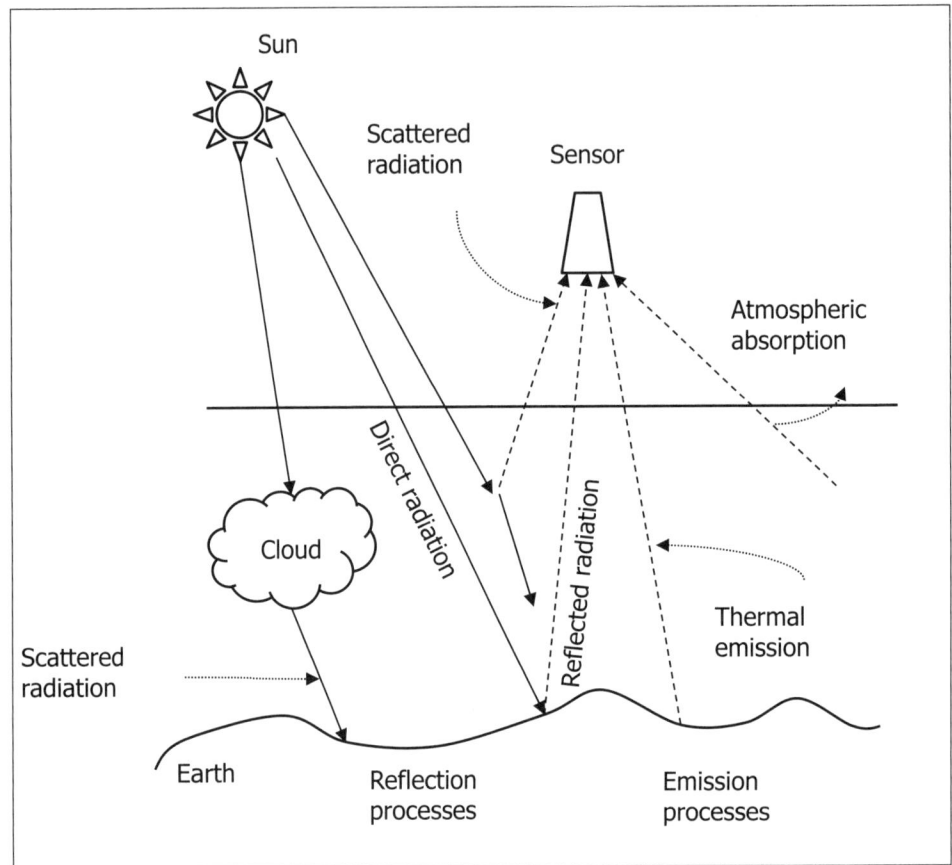

Figure 15.3 Interactions of EM waves with the atmosphere.

Earth's surface. Notably, direct sunlight passes twice through the atmosphere, whereas emitted thermal radiation makes a single journey to the sensor. Clouds also play a role in scattering, absorbing, and transmitting energy. Due to specific gases (such as ozone and CO_2) and water molecules, certain spectral bands experience dominant absorption, severely attenuating the energy reaching the sensor. Consequently, imaging does not occur effectively in those bands. However, there are a few transmission spectral windows of EM waves over which the passive imaging takes place. These windows belong to the visible and IR bands. These combined bands are referred to as the *optical bands*. It ranges from 0.4 to 2 μm for optical remote sensing. There are three such windows in the thermal IR bands, namely, very narrow bands of 3 μm, 5 μm and a wide band from 8 to 14 μm.

The presence of clouds affect the imaging in other ways. It occludes certain parts of the ground and it also casts shadow in visible objects in certain parts as shown in Fig. 15.4. The cloud also scatters EM waves in all possible wavelengths. That is why they mostly appear white.

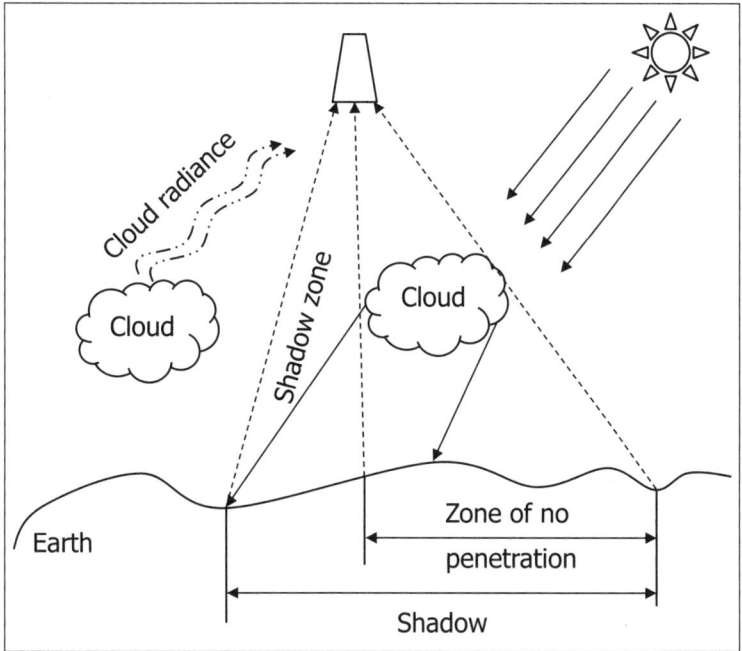

Figure 15.4 Occlusion of objects by clouds.

15.1.2 | Reflectance of the Earth's surface

The energy of the Sun reaching the Earth's surface is called *radiance*, while the reflected and emitted energy sensed by the sensor is referred to as *irradiance*. Both are measured in the same unit. For example, in the MKS system, it is Watts per square meter per steradian (Watt m^{-2} sr^{-2}). The fraction of incident energy that gets reflected in all directions (diffused reflection) depends on its frequency (or wavelength) and the properties of the interacting material. This fraction is called the *reflectance* of a material at a given wavelength. The variation of reflectance over wavelengths is known as the *reflectance curve* of a material, and it is a characteristic of that material. Since the passive imaging takes place in the optical range between 0.4 to 2.0 μm, the reflectance curves of materials within this range provide useful information about them. Water molecules exhibit a typical behavior in absorbing energy within this band. Water absorbs EM wave of wavelengths of 1.4 μm and 1.95 μm, respectively. Hence in many materials, where there is a significant amount of moisture content and presence of water molecules, the reflectance curve shows dips around these two wavelengths. The multispectral optical sensors also operate by employing filters within 0.4 to 0.8 μm.

It is important to study a few examples of reflectance curves of some of the materials which are present in the Earth's surface and observable in satellite remote sensing images. Spectral reflectance curves of some of the broad classes are shown in Fig. 15.5. The spectral behavior of the land cover by a broad class of vegetation, which include different kinds of crops, trees, plants, forest canopies, etc. exhibit a typical pattern of response. The reflectance

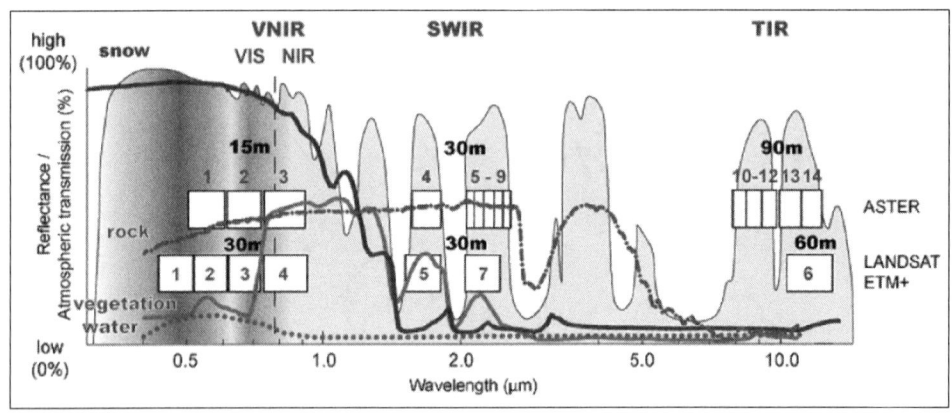

Figure 15.5 Spectral reflectance curves. (*Source*: ESA - Andreas Kaab, University of Oslo, https://www.esa.int/ESA_Multimedia/Images/2011/11/Reflectance_curves_of_ snow_vegetation_water_and_rock; ESA standard license.)

curve is mostly influenced by the reflectance properties of leaves, such as their orientations, thickness, leaf pigmentation, the structure of canopy, the cell structure, water present in the leaves, etc. All these produce an overall effect on the spectral behavior of vegetation in reflecting EM waves. It is observed that, the reflectance is highest in the near-infrared (NIR) band. However, the presence of water in leaves weakens the response in the middle IR band. In contrast, for dry leaves, the response is high in the middle IR due to less water. Particularly, the response is relatively higher in the red band, in comparison with the green and the blue bands.

Let us consider another two broad classes of land cover, namely the bare soil and water. The bare soil land cover class is void of vegetation and forms the Earth's upper surface containing clay, moisture, sand, and minerals, which gets exposed. In the reflectance curve of this class of material, two consecutive convex shaped segments are observed. It dips at its two ends, i.e., at 0.2 μm and 2.0 μm. In between there is another dip at 1.4 μm, which corresponds to one of the absorbing bands of moisture. It may be noted that the dip at 2.0 μm is also caused by the absorption of EM waves of wavelength 1.95 μm by the moisture.

On the other hand, water reflects visible band up to near IR bands, and beyond 1.2 μm all energy get absorbed by it. It has less reflectance compared to soil and vegetation in the optical bands of remote sensing. In the terrestrial land cover, roughly, vegetation accounts for 50%, soil accounts for 30%, and water accounts for 10% of the reflected energy. Contaminated water with silt, also called turbid water of river, ponds, and lakes, has higher reflectance than water.

15.2 | Multispectral imaging

Various imaging sensors are employed for recording and measuring EM energy. Passive sensors capture energy from external sources, such as the Sun or Earth. These sensors include aerial cameras, multispectral scanners, image spectrometers, hyperspectral cameras, and thermal scanners. On the other hand, active imaging systems uses own energy to illuminate a target and then sense the reflection within a specific time interval. Options for active imaging systems include laser scanner (namely, light detection and ranging (LIDAR)), radio detection and ranging (RADAR), and synthetic aperture radars (SAR). These imaging systems operate from flying vehicles like airplanes, drones, and satellites.

Multispectral scanners, which find application in various satellite remote sensing missions, sense the reflected EM wave energy, filtered within a spectral band in a particular direction. They record the reflected energy from a region of the Earth's surface associated with that specific direction relative to the sensor. The scanner scans an area by recording received energy from associated directions. Being onboard an airborne vehicle or a satellite, the scanner covers a rectangular strip known as a swath or scanning area. The longer side of the swath lies perpendicular or orthogonal to the direction of motion. The shorter side (width) of the strip may be divided into multiple scan lines by placing an array of detectors along the direction of the satellite's motion. The gap between adjacent scanlines determines the spatial resolution along the direction of the satellite's motion. The length of the swath is determined by the field of view (FOV) covered by the mirror along its longer side. The FOV represents the angle (in radians) spanned by the mirror from the start to the end of the scan line.

Two scanning mechanisms are commonly used: *whisk broom* and *push broom* scanners. In a whisk broom system, there is a single detector or sensor for each scan line. The EM radiation from the surface reaches the detector via reflection from the mirror. By rotating this mirror, the direction of incoming radiation varies, even though the detector remains fixed in its inertial frame. At each discrete rotating position of the mirror, energy detection occurs, forming image pixels along the scanning line. For every discrete rotating position of the mirror, reflected energy may be detected by a linear array of detectors. This is illustrated in Fig. 15.6. Multiple lines are scanned together in parallel while covering a single swath using the rotating mirror. For instance, in the Landsat imaging system, six detectors form six parallel scan lines along a single swath. The angle covered by a single instance of detection

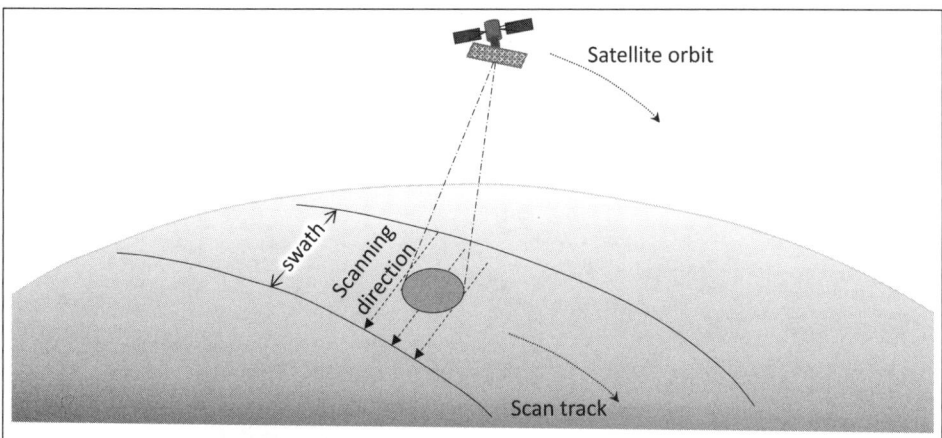

Figure 15.6 Functioning of a whisk broom sensor.

(i.e., the unit area covered by a single pixel of the image) defines the instantaneous field of view (IFOV) at the sensor or detector. The IFOV determines the ground resolution of the image. Suppose the height of the Satellite is H, and IFOV is β in radians, then the ground resolution is, $D = H\beta$. For example, let H be 4000 meters and β be 0.0025 radians. Then the spatial resolution is 10 m per pixel.

In the push broom scanning mechanism, the principles underlying optical image formation and acquisition by an ordinary camera are applied. In this case, an optical lens captures the image of a rectangular strip over a linear array of CCD sensors. These sensors scan and store the data to form a row (or column) of an image array. Here, the length covered by a single imaging instance along the track is referred to as the swath. This is illustrated in Fig. 15.7. Notably, the size of the sensing element can be as small as 2.5 μm, which results in images with relatively higher spatial resolution than those obtained by a whisk broom scanner. However, CCD sensors are sensitive only to optical and IR bands. Hence, this mechanism cannot be used for imaging at longer wavelength bands, such as thermal IR bands.

To relate a multispectral remote sensing image to physical measurements of various entities such as radiance or reflectance, spatial coordinates of corresponding area of a pixel, spectral information, and temporal instances, several metadata parameters are necessary. These parameters reside in the header of the image file and facilitate the interpretation of pixel values, which are expressed as positive numbers known as digital numbers (DN). To obtain the actual radiance value, the parameters like gain and bias, that are specified in the header file, are utilized. Additionally, L_{max} and L_{min} represent the maximum and minimum energy levels corresponding to the highest and lowest DN values in the image, respectively. These parameters play a role in relating pixel values to physical reflectance measurements, referred to as top-of-atmosphere (TOA) reflectance. Typical metadata includes the following details.

- *Radiometric resolution*: This parameter specifies the smallest difference between energy levels.

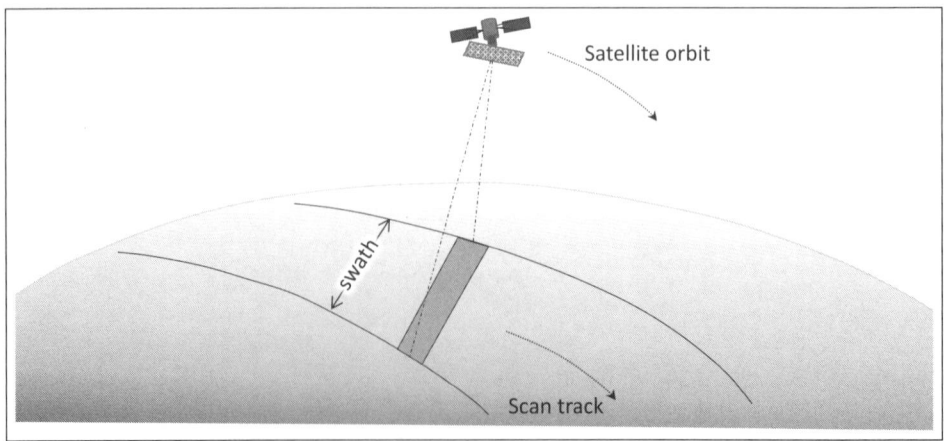

Figure 15.7 Functioning of a push broom sensor.

- *Spatial resolution*: It is described as the smallest unit area per pixel, which defines the spatial details in the image.

- *Spatial coverage*: It is the total area covered by the image.

- *Swath width*: Referring to the imaging system's coverage width, it runs orthogonal to the direction of motion.

- *Temporal latency*: The time interval between image recording and storage.

- *Revisit time*: Duration between capturing two successive images (temporal sequences) of the same locations.

15.3 | Satellite imaging

Satellite imaging has three broad applications. First, it is utilized for continuous monitoring of various phenomena and events in Earth's environment and atmosphere over specific regions, such as tracking cyclones. Second, it serves in global mapping of terrestrial objects, including land covers. Lastly, it plays a crucial role in applications that require selective imaging of specific regions, such as urban planning and development. The satellite's orbital motion determines the georeferenced locations or regions on Earth's surface for capturing images. An orbit of a satellite follows an elliptical path of revolution around the Earth. This path also lies on a plane, called *orbital plane*.

To characterize the *orbital motion* of a satellite, the following factors are considered:

(i) *Altitude* of the satellite from the Earth's surface (in km): It is the distance (measured in km) of the satellite from the Earth's surface. Since the altitude varies with the position of the satellite in its orbit, the mean altitude is used in this regard. The mean altitudes may vary from 150 km to 1000 km. For a *geostationary satellite*, which always remains at a fixed location with respect to Earth's surface as it rotates with the same speed of Earth's rotation, the altitude is 36000 km.

(ii) The *inclination angle*: It is the angle between the equatorial and orbital planes, and is measured in degrees. It provides the latitude coverage in the orbital motion. For example, if this angle is 60°, it covers the Earth's surface in the latitudes ranging from 60° N to 60° S. If the inclination angle is near 90°, the orbital motion also covers the pole and thus the full terrestrial surface can be covered by the imaging system. Satellites with this kind of orbital motion are called *polar satellites*. For polar satellites the inclination angle may vary between 80° to 100° and their altitudes range from 600 km to 1000 km. On the other hand, with the inclination angle 0°, it only covers the regions lying both the sides of the equator depending upon its FOV, which is determined by the altitude of the satellite. Geostationary satellites are placed with the inclination angle 0°, and have wide FOV to take images of the full visible disc of the Earth.

(iii) *Period*: It is the period of revolution or the time of a full orbital motion. It is typically expressed in minutes. For example, polar satellites at mean altitude of 860 km usually revolves with a period of 101 minutes.

(iv) *Repeat cycle*: It is the time between two successive identical orbits so that the imaging takes place on the same locations as of the previous orbital motion. Though the satellite travels across the same locations at regular time interval which is its period of motion, the imaging of a region depends upon the orientation or viewing direction of the camera. This viewing direction repeats with a different longer periodic interval, which is called repeat cycle of the imaging system of the satellite. This is typically in the order of few days.

Another aspect of characterizing the orbital motion of a polar satellite is its *sun-synchronous* nature. A sun-synchronous orbit ensures that the satellite consistently passes over the same location on the Earth's surface at the same local mean solar time. For example, most polar satellites pass the equator around 10:30 AM local time. Examples of *sun synchronous polar satellites* include Landsat, SPOT, IRS, etc.

A few examples of remote sensing satellites and their multispectral imaging systems, along with their orbital information are illustrated in Table 15.1.

15.4 | Preprocessing of multispectral imaging

Consider various preprocessing operations necessary for using multispectral images. Since the received signal is in analog form, it needs to be digitized through sampling and quantization. As the sensor sensitivity varies, calibration is necessary to apply a uniform quantization level when converting physical reflectance measures to DN. Next stage of preprocessing tasks involves radiometric and geometric corrections in an image. Radiometric correction aims to reduce random noise, occurrences of faults and biases in sensors, etc. Random noise may also occur due to atmospheric disturbances. Geometric corrections are required to straighten or dewarp the scanned lines of the images, which suffer from warping due to the curvature of Earth.

15.4.1 | Radiometric and atmospheric corrections

Broadly there are two kinds of processes that are mandatory before performing any data analysis: radiometric and atmospheric corrections. Radiometric correction is needed to handle noise, spikes and structural deformity such as periodic or random line dropouts, and line stripping, which may occur in the visible, NIR and SWIR bands. A noisy pixel is corrected using linear and non linear filters locally after detecting it as an outlier from its neighbors. A simple example of linear filter is the mean filter, which computes the average of the neighboring pixel values and replaces the noisy pixel by it. An example of nonlinear filter is the median filter.

15.4.2 | Radiometric corrections

An example of structural distortion of an image due to periodic line drop out is shown in Fig. 15.8. These are the drop out lines in the image, which occur after every k rows (scan lines), where k is the period of drop outs. This kind of error may occur in a whisk broom multiscanner imaging system, when a sensor of the linear array to scan along multiple

Table 15.1 A few examples of remote sensing satellites for multispectral imaging.

Name	Organization	Examples of orbiting satellites	Type	Inclination angle, mean alt., orbit period	Revisit time	Spectral bands (λ in μm)	Swath width and spatial resolution
Meteosat	WMO	Meteosat 9, 10, and 11	Geostationary	0°, 36000 Km, and 1436 min.	15 min.	Band 1: 0.56 - 0.71 Band 2: 0.74 - 0.88 Band 3: 1.50 - 1.78 Band 4: 3.48 - 4.36 Band 5: 5.35 - 7.15 Band 6: 6.85 - 7.85 Band 7: 8.30 - 9.10 Band 8: 9.38 - 9.94 Band 9: 9.80 - 11.80 Band 10: 11.00 - 13.00 Band 11: 12.40 - 14.40 Band 12: 0.4 - 1.1	Full earth disk and 1 to 3 km
NOAA	National Oceanic Atmospheric Administration, USA	NOAA 18	Polar sun synchronous	98.74°, 854 km, and 102.12 min.	1 day	Band 1: 0.58 - 0.7 Band 2: 0.7 - 1.0 Band 3A: 1.58 - 1.64 Band 3B: 3.5 - 4.0 Band 4: 10.2 - 11.5 Band 5: 11.4 - 12.5	2800 km and 1.1 to 4.2 km
Landsat	NASA	Landsat 8, and 9	Polar sun synchronous	98.2°, 705 km, and 98.9 min.	16 days (individual) or 8 days (combined)	Band 1: 0.43 - 0.45 Band 2: 0.450 - 0.51 Band 3: 0.53 - 0.59 Band 4: 0.64 - 0.67 Band 5: 0.85 - 0.88 Band 6: 1.57 - 1.65 Band 7: 2.11 - 2.29 Band 8: 0.50 - 0.68 Band 9: 1.36 - 1.38 Band 10: 10.30 - 11.30 Band 11: 11.50 - 12.50	185 km and 15 to 100 meters

(Continued)

Table 15.1 (*Continued*)

Name	Organization	Examples of orbiting satellites	Type	Inclination angle, mean alt., orbit period	Revisit time	Spectral bands (λ in μm)	Swath width and spatial resolution
Sentinel	ESA	Sentinel 2A and 2B	Two Polar sun synchronous 180° apart in the orbit	98.62°, 786 km, and 100.6 min.	10 days (individual) or 5 days (combined)	Band 1: 0.43 - 0.45 Band 2: 0.46 - 0.52 Band 3: 0.54 - 0.58 Band 4: 0.65 - 0.68 Band 5: 0.69 - 0.71 Band 6: 0.73 - 0.75 Band 7: 0.77 - 0.79 Band 8: 0.79 - 0.90 Band 8A: 0.86 - 0.88 Band 9: 0.94 - 0.96 Band 10: 1.36 - 1.39 Band 11: 1.57 - 1.66 Band 12: 2.10 - 2.28	290 km and 10 to 60 meters
Resourcesat	ISRO	Resourcesat 2 and 2A	Polar sun synchronous	98.689°, 817 km, and 101.35 min.	2 to 26 days	Band 2: 0.52 - 0.59 Band 3: 0.62 - 0.68 Band 4: 0.77 - 0.86 Band 5: 1.55 - 1.70	23 to 740 km and 5.8 to 56 meters

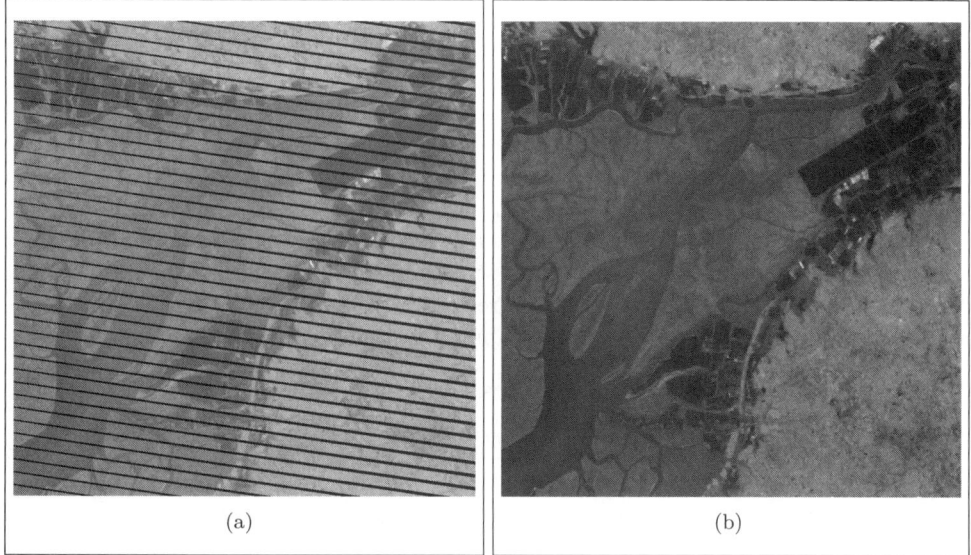

Figure 15.8 Structural distortion in an image due to periodic line drop out. (Image from USGS: WRS path 150, row 44, acq. 08-12-2023, Landsat-7, band-4.)

parallel lines, with the rotation of the reflecting mirror, becomes faulty. As a result, in every scan line along the swath, the pixel corresponding to the faulty sensor becomes dark. This produces a dark lines along the direction of the swath, implying in the perpendicular direction of the trajectory of the satellite. In the example shown in the figure, the image suffered due to a malfunction in the scanner in Landsat-7, which resulted in the periodic line drops.

For correcting line dropout, we may perform the computation in two steps. First, this error is identified and the dark lines are localized. After localization, the faulty scan lines are restored by taking averages of their 4-neighbor pixels in the neighboring scan lines. For detecting a faulty line, we may follow two different approaches: (i) a very specific approach to detect the periodic occurrence, and (ii) a more general context of detecting any random drop out. In both of these approaches, at first, the average DN for a scan line is computed, which corresponds to a row of the image (Fig. 15.8). Then, the sequence is checked for any periodic occurrence of a value (usually zero) along the row indices, which is the average DN for each scan line. For a single faulty detector this period is expected to be k, where k is the number of detectors in the linear array across the width of a swath. For example, for the Landsat image, the value of k is six. For handling random dropouts, the average value of a scan line may be compared with the scene average and by performing statistical tests (Evans and Rosenthal, 2009), such as z-test, it is checked whether it is an outlier, implying that it has a significant deviation from the scene average. The statistical test also requires computing of variance of the DNs in the scene or image.

The structural defect resulting in line striping occurs due to nonuniform gain of the sensors. When the satellite is launched, these sensors are properly calibrated to provide the same DN given the same energy level as the input to a sensor. However over the time of operation, a sensor's behavior changes and random drift occurs in gain and bias of the calibration. This gets reflected by the appearance of dark and bright stripes in the image, as the rows (along the direction of the satellite track) suffer from nonuniform scaling and shifting of pixel values. There is a difference in correcting these nonuniform stripes from the correction of periodic or random drop outs of rows. In this case, the DNs in these rows contain information about the radiance received from the Earth's surface. Hence they cannot be simply replaced by some value. To perform line striping, one of the rows may be chosen as the reference row. With respect to this reference row, the DNs of all other rows are corrected. This is done using histogram stretching technique. The mean and standard deviations (stdev) of the pixel values in the reference rows are computed. The pixel values of any other row are mapped to a value computed by the following expressions.

$$\text{DN}_{\text{out}} = \text{gain} \times \text{DN}_{\text{in}} + \text{offset}$$

$$\text{gain} = \frac{\text{stdev}_{\text{in}}}{\text{stdev}_{\text{ref}}} \qquad (15.1)$$

$$\text{offset} = \text{mean}_{\text{in}} - \text{mean}_{\text{ref}}$$

15.4.3 | Atmospheric correction

For performing atmosphere correction, the estimation of ground reflectance is necessary. This estimation involves deriving the true ground reflectance from the measured reflectance in an image. The measurement of reflectance by a sensor occurs at the top of the atmosphere, where the satellite is positioned. However, the phenomena of reflection and emission take place at the Earth's surface. As waves travel through the atmosphere, original surface reflectance undergo changes due to absorption by ozone, CO_2, water vapor, scattering by aerosols, and other factors. The estimation of the ground reflectance from the measured reflectance in an image is also called *top of atmosphere correction* of reflectance.

In the context of atmospheric corrections, there are two types of phenomena, namely, reflection and thermal emission, which are handled differently. In the case of reflection, solar rays travel twice through the atmosphere, whereas for thermal emission, EM waves travel only once to reach the sensor. The separate treatment for these two phenomena arises from the fact that their associated signals lie in different spectral bands. Reflected sunlight dominates the visible, NIR, and shortwave infrared (SWIR) bands, while thermal emission occurs in the longer wavelengths of the thermal IR spectrum. The attenuation factor also varies with wavelengths. Therefore, for atmospheric correction, it is necessary to model the interaction between the EM waves of a specific wavelength and the atmosphere to compute the attenuation factor. Once this factor is available, the measured (and estimated) reflectance components for each wavelength within a given spectral band are corrected by applying the inverse attenuation operation (dividing by the attenuation factor) and integrating them over the range. Various *radiation transfer models* (RTMs) have been proposed to describe the interaction with the atmosphere at different altitudes of a satellite. These models consider sensor types, atmospheric composition, pressure and temperature profiles, molecular behavior, and interactions. Examples of such models include LOWTRAN (Kneizys et al., 1988), MODTRAN,[1] Code 5S, 6S,[2] etc. Simplified models, like SMACK (a simplified method of atmospheric correction) derived from Code 5S and 6S, reduce computation by requiring only vertical profiling of compositions such as ozone, aerosols, and water vapor. Some models use lookup tables based on satellite track and Earth's atmospheric coverage. One such model is the *atmospheric and topographic correction model* (ATCOR).[3] A typical example of TOA correction with Landsat images is provided in the expressions below. The values of the parameters for the correction are provided in the header file of an image.

$$L_\lambda = \text{Gain}(\lambda) \times \text{DN} + \text{Bias}(\lambda)$$

$$\rho = \frac{(\pi L_\lambda d^2)}{(\text{ESUN}(\lambda)\cos(\theta))} \tag{15.2}$$

In this method, the DNs are converted to their respective received radiance measure, L, using two parameters, Gain and Bias. This value is modified further using the TOA correction, as given in Eq. 15.2, where ρ is the reflectance, d is the distance between Earth and Sun, $\text{ESUN}(\lambda)$ is mean solar exo-atmospheric irradiance, and θ is the solar zenith angle.

These models are used in applications where absolute atmospheric correction is required. These applications involve quantifying fluxes at the ground level. Examples of such applications include the quantification of evapotranspiration, CO_2 sequestration, the estimation of surface temperature and reflectivity, etc. For computing various spectral indices for characterizing land cover classes (discussed later), this kind of absolute correction is essential.

On the other hand, for some applications, a relative correction based on the ground reflectance properties is sufficient. The precise reflectance value in the ground level is not required. Examples that use their proportional measurements among the regions covered in the image include cartographic applications, qualitative visual interpretation, etc.

In this section, two techniques for relative correction are discussed: (i) the two reflectance measurement method, and (ii) the two reference surface method. In the first method, a portable radiometer is used to measure the reflectance of two different surface patches with contrastive reflectance, namely, bright and dark. These patches are carefully selected to be visible from the sensor and easily identifiable in the images. They should cover an area equivalent to at least three pixels in the image. Additionally, the reflectance values within these patches should remain roughly constant. It is important to ensure a consistent spectral sensitivity of the radiometer during measurements by using appropriate optical filters. The measurements should coincide with the satellite passing over these patches. By identifying the associated pixels, their corresponding DNs are obtained from the image. With two ground reflectance values and their respective pixel values in the image, a linear model is

---

[1] http://modtran.spectral.com/.
[2] https://salsa.umd.edu/6spage.html.
[3] https://atcor.com/.

constructed by fitting a straight-line equation to these observations. This model is then applied to all pixels in the image to estimate relative ground reflectance values.

In the two reference surface method, two contrastive regions are selected, uniform areas of dark (or brown) and bright values. The shifts in TOA reflectance values (measured in DNs) and ground reflectance values relative to a reference day are recorded for these two observations. Then, a linear model is constructed to describe the shift in DN values with respect to the DN measured on the reference day. This model is then applied to all pixels in the current image to correct their DN values.

15.5 | Characterizing material surfaces using reflectance curve

Reflectance curves are useful for characterizing material surfaces. The variation of reflectance of a material surface over different spectral bands is called its *spectral profile*. In a multispectral remote sensing image, this variation is observed across different spectral bands of its components or channels. These channels typically include visible optical bands such as blue, green, red, and a few IR bands such as NIR, SWIR, etc. Some multispectral images also incorporate thermal bands. In Fig. 15.9, examples of spectral profiles for different land cover surfaces in Landsat multispectral bands are shown. These curves reveal relative reflectance variations across various types of surfaces. For example, reflectance from bare land tends to be high across all the spectral bands considered, compared to other material surfaces. Also, it monotonically increases until the SWIR-1 band and then decreases toward the SWIR-2 band at longer wavelengths. Conversely, water exhibits an almost opposite trend in its spectral profile, with reflectance values decreasing monotonically as wavelength increases from blue to the SWIR-2 band. Proper vegetation, on the other hand, experiences a sudden rise in reflectance from the red to the NIR band, which is the band of its maximum response. This property has been exploited

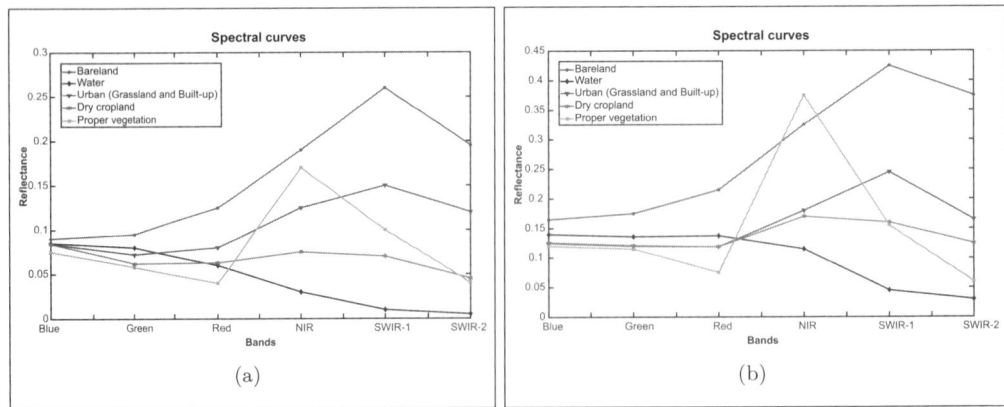

Figure 15.9 Spectral profiles for different land cover surfaces in Landsat imageries. (a) Landsat-7 and (b) Landsat-8.

in distinguishing vegetation land cover class from other types of surfaces from multispectral images.

15.5.1 | Spectral indices

The above fact is exploited by using a measure on the relative rise of reflectance values at a given spectral band with respect to that of a reference spectral band. For example, for the vegetation cover, the relative rise from Red to NIR band is measured. This measure is called *normalized difference vegetation index* (NDVI) which is defined as follows:

$$\text{NDVI} = \frac{(\text{NIR} - \text{Red})}{(\text{NIR} + \text{Red})} \tag{15.3}$$

Broadly the above type of measure is called the spectral index. For vegetation, there are also other variations, as it is a very broad class under which there are different kinds of plants and trees. Several other indices provide different shades of vegetation. A few such indices, *enhanced vegetation index* (EVI), *green ratio vegetation index* (GRVI), and *modified soil adjusted vegetation index* (MSAVI), are given below (Zurqani et al., 2020).

$$\text{EVI} = G_1 \times \frac{\text{NIR} - \text{Red}}{\text{NIR} + C_1 \times \text{Red} - C_2 \times \text{Blue} + L_1} \tag{15.4}$$

$$\text{GRVI} = \frac{\text{NIR}}{\text{Green}} \tag{15.5}$$

$$\text{MSAVI} = \frac{1}{2} \left(2\,\text{NIR} + 1 - \sqrt{(2\,\text{NIR} + 1)^2 - (8\,\text{NIR} - \text{Red})} \right) \tag{15.6}$$

For Landsat 7 and 8, $G_1 = 2.5$, $L_1 = 1$, $C_1 = 6$, and $C_2 = 7.5$.

Similar indices are also available for other types of material surfaces. For water, *normalized difference water index* (NDWI) is defined below.

$$\text{NDWI} = \frac{(\text{Green} - \text{NIR})}{(\text{Green} + \text{NIR})} \tag{15.7}$$

Similarly, there are *coal mine index* (CMI), *bare soil index* (BI), *clay mineral ratio* (CMR), *iron-oxide ratio* (IO), which are defined as follows (Mukherjee et al., 2019).

$$\text{CMI} = \frac{\text{SWIR2} - \text{SWIR1}}{\text{SWIR2} + \text{SWIR1}} \tag{15.8}$$

$$BI = \frac{(SWIR1 + Red) - (NIR + Blue)}{(SWIR1 + Red) + (NIR + Blue)} \quad (15.9)$$

$$CMR = \frac{SWIR1}{SWIR2} \quad (15.10)$$

$$IO = \frac{Red}{Blue} \quad (15.11)$$

It is observed that the CMI is also useful in detecting other minerals such as iron, copper, manganese, dolomite oxide, diamond, and gold. However, the other information about the region may require to be used to resolve ambiguities among these possible candidates, while using this index. Different kinds of spectral indices may be applied in a combination to characterize a material surface using machine learning techniques. In this case, a feature vector may be formed by computing several spectral indices and representing them as a vector. For example, EVI, GRVI, MSAVI, NDVI, and NDWI are computed at every pixel of a multispectral image and the values are used to form a feature vector of dimension 5. A feature vector represents the trend of the reflectance curve across the chosen bands, as demonstrated in Fig. 15.10 for various classes. Given the ground truth class information of the pixel, a set of training and test samples may be formed and a classifier may be trained to determine the land cover classes. In Zurqani et al. (2020), using this approach, a SVM classifier is trained for classifying the land surface into 11 land cover classes (refer to Fig. 15.10), such as open water, low-medium intensity urban, high intensity urban, barren land, deciduous forest, evergreen forest, shrub or scrub, grassland, pastures or hay, cultivated crops and wetlands. It is observed that it is more challenging to distinguish grass land among these classes, which is detected with a relatively less accuracy. On the other hand, water is easily detected with a relatively high accuracy.

15.5.2 | Spectral slopes

There may be simpler characterization of reflectance curves, instead of using these indices (Mattur et al., 2017). In a simplified form of representing the trend of the reflectance curve, a measure called *spectral slope*, is used. It is the slope of reflectance variation over the bands of increasing wavelengths. But the absolute value of the slope is not measured, instead the sign of the slope is considered. For example, let us consider only

Table 15.2 Spectral slope characterization of water, vegetation, and vegetation void classes.

Class	Slope(Red, NIR)	Slope(Red, SWIR1)	Slope(NIR, SWIR1)
Water	−	−	−
Vegetation	+	+	−
Vegetation void	+	+	+

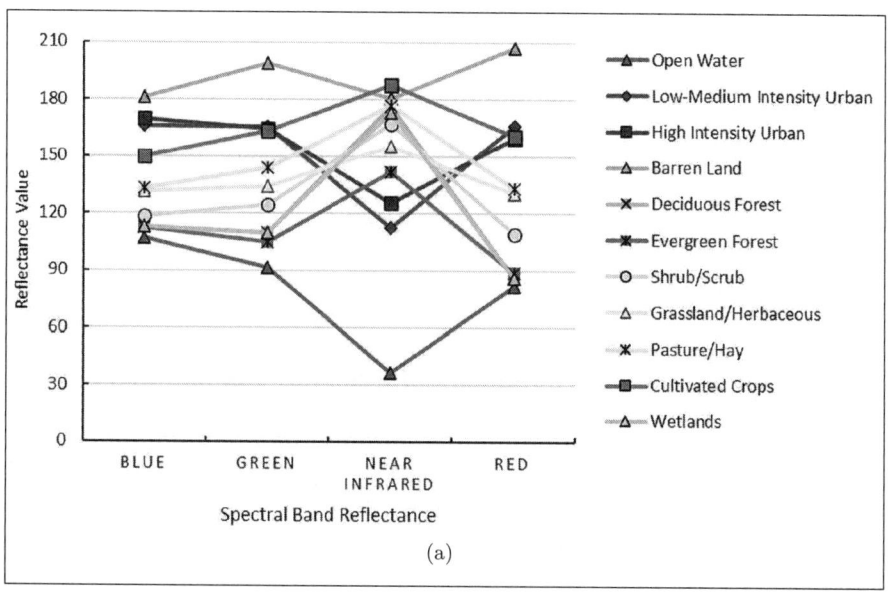

(a)

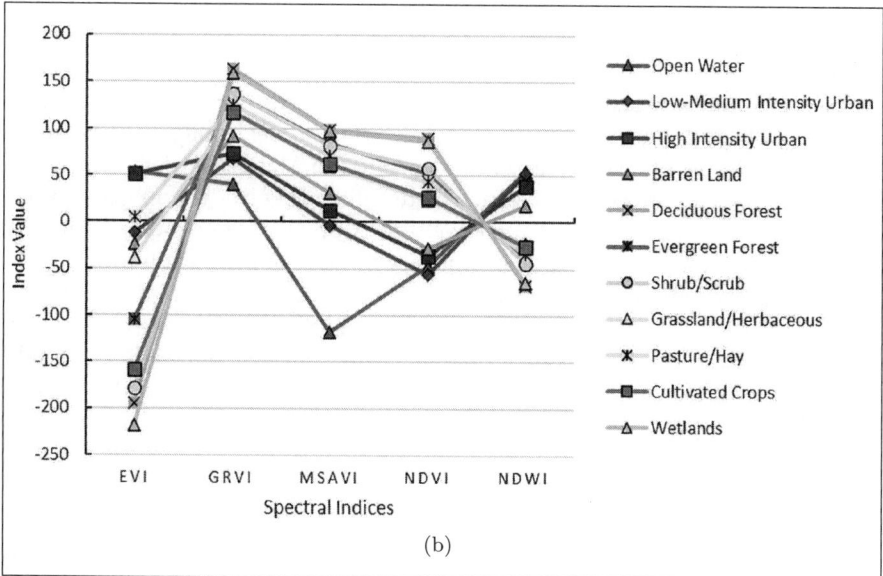

(b)

Figure 15.10 Reflectance curves and indices across a few bands. (*Source*: Reproduced fig. 3 of Zurqani et al. (2020), https://rdcu.be/dLS5v; http://creativecommons.org/licenses/by/4.0/.)

three broad classes of land cover, namely, water, vegetation, and vegetation-void. We may compute the signs of slope from Red and NIR bands for each of them. Similar computations are also done with the signs of slopes from Red to SWIR-1 and from NIR to SWIR-1 bands. In Table 15.2, the observations are summarized. It is observed that, for water, all these slopes are negative, which also confirms that the reflectance of water monotonically decreases from Blue to SWIR bands. On the other hand, for the vegetation void (bare land) the slopes are all positive confirming the trend of reflectance curve discussed previously. For vegetation, there is a fall in reflectance from NIR to SWIR bands, but it has sharp rise from Red to NIR. As the response is minimum among the visible spectral bands in the Red band for this class, the sign of the slope from Red to SWIR-1 is also positive. Using these three signs, we form rules to label pixels among these three classes.

These rules are quite robust because the absolute values of reflectance are not used in characterizing the classes. The relative increase or decrease of the reflectance among a pair of bands is used for this characterization. Hence the computation is more robust to presence of noise and also to variation in sensors of different imaging systems. However, these rules are not applicable to many pixels in an image, where different combinations of signs of slopes may occur. This may happen due to the fact that in the unit area corresponding to a pixel, there may be presence of mixed classes. As a unit area of the terrestrial surface may cover hundreds of square meter and may contain patches of vegetation, water and bare land. Hence the reflectance variation over the bands from this mixed region may not follow the pattern as observed for regions of pure classes. However, we may consider labeling of these pixels with the dominant land cover class present in the region. For doing this extension, machine learning based approaches may be useful as in the first stage of computation, a good number of pixels are labeled at a very high accuracy. They may be used for training and test samples for designing a classifier. Since no ground truth data is used from the beginning, and only the rules are applied to generate the ground truth for the next stage of computation, the technique is an example of a semi-supervised learning. In Mattur et al. (2016), a technique following this approach has been discussed. The technique involves training a support vector machine (SVM) using the labeled samples obtained by the application of three rules. It used a feature vector representation by computing spectral indices by all possible pairing of bands for a multispectral image. For example, in a Landsat image there are six bands under consideration namely blue, green, red, NIR, SWIR1, and SWIR2. Hence we may compute 15 distinct spectral indices from them and represent the information as a 15 dimensional feature vector. The feature vector is called *normalized difference spectral vector* (NDSV). Using this method an overall accuracy of around 93% is reported. The first phase of computation of rule based methods has the accuracy of 99.7%, though it covers around $\frac{2}{3}^{rd}$ pixels of an image.

The method also extends the computation by partitioning pixels belonging to a broad class to their subclasses. For example, pixels of vegetation are further classified into subclasses of proper vegetation and dry or sparse vegetation. Likewise, pixels of the vegetation void class are classified into classes such as urban land and bare land. To perform this partitioning K-means clustering technique with the value of $K = 2$, is applied for both the cases. For vegetation, the cluster corresponding to the higher mean magnitude is labeled to dry vegetation, else to proper vegetation. This association is derived empirically by observing some of the ground truth samples obtained by manual annotation. Likewise in the class of vegetation void, the cluster having the higher magnitude of the mean vector is labeled as bare land and otherwise to urban land. Typical results are demonstrated in Fig. 15.11.

Phase-1

Water
Vegetation
Vegetation-void

Phase-2

Water
Proper veg
Dry/Sparse veg
Grassland/Built-up
Bareland

Pseudo-RGB

Figure 15.11 An example of two-phase land cover classification. See Color Plates (page 821).

15.6 | SAR imaging

In active remote sensing, *radar imaging* is used to cover terrestrial surfaces. A radar antenna transmits a microwave pulse of a finite duration (5 - 100 μs) in a particular direction. The transmitted pulse is characterized by its amplitude, wavelength, and phase. The EM wave may also be polarized. The pulse propagates with a speed of EM wave in the free space (speed of light, 2.998×10^8 m/s) along the direction of transmission. After hitting a target, it gets reflected or scattered in all directions in the free space. In the context of radar imaging, the phenomenon is attributed as *back scattering*. A part of back scattered energy reaches the RADAR receiver, which is collocated with the transmitter. The receiver records the amplitude, phase, and frequency of the received signal, as well as the time interval between the transmission and reception, which provides the distance of the reflecting object. The relationship between the transmitted energy on the target and the back scattered energy is shown in the expression below.

$$P_r = \frac{G^2 \lambda^2 P_t \sigma}{(4\pi)^3 R^4} \tag{15.12}$$

In Eq. 15.12, it is shown that how different factors are involved in determining P_r, the part of transmitted energy, P_t, as received by the radar due to backscattering. One of them is the distance or range of the scattering point, R, from the radar. The other factors are antenna gain G, wavelength λ, and radar cross section σ. The radar cross section is a function of object characteristics, and it depends on its orientation.

15.6.1 | Principle of synthetic aperture radar imaging

In Fig. 15.12, the principle of *synthetic aperture radar imaging* is illustrated in a schematic diagram. The EM pulses of a finite duration, t_w (*pulse width*), are transmitted at a regular interval with a period T. The number of transmission pulses per second is called the *pulse repetition frequency* $(= \frac{1}{T})$. The pulse is not in the form of a pure sinusoid. It is transmitted with *linear frequency modulation* (LFM) over a *carrier frequency*. The beam of transmission covering a target region has also a spatial width, called *swath*. The back scattered continuous time varying signal is received at the receiver, which are sampled, quantized, digitized, and stored. The sampling instances provide the time of flight (say, t_i for i^{th} instance) of the transmitted and received signal from the scatterer. This is used to compute the range or distance of the scatterer as $r_i = c\frac{t_i}{2}$, where c is the velocity of the EM wave (or light). Hence each receiving signal produces a scan line of the image. After period T, another signal is transmitted. Meanwhile, the receiver would have moved to a new position. From there the next scan line is obtained. In this way, the 2-D image is formed. The direction

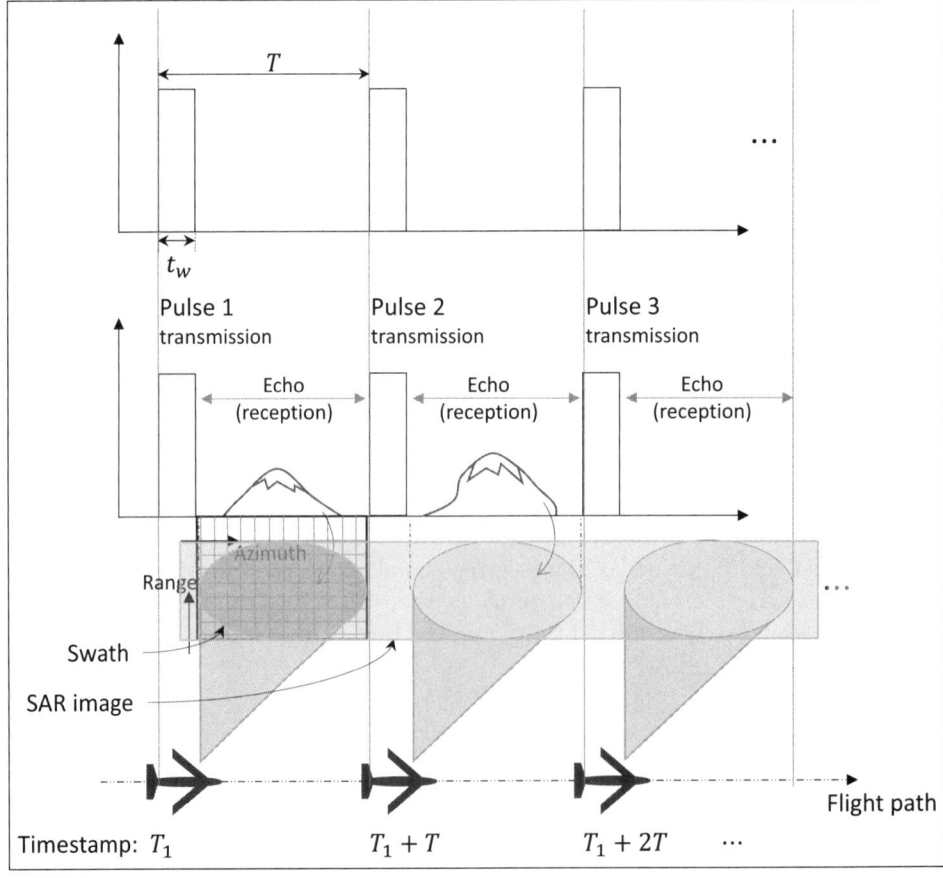

Figure 15.12 Pulse transmission in a radar system.

of the motion of the sensor is called *azimuth* and the direction of transmission of pulse is called *range*. In this process the resolution of the range is determined by the minimum time interval required to detect two distinct back scattered pulses (echoes). This time should be the same as the pulse width (when the LFM is not used). As the EM wave has to travel half the time of pulse width to produce a distinct echo at the receiver, the range resolution is given by $c\frac{t_w}{2}$, where t_w is the width of the pulse, and c is the velocity of the EM wave. When the LFM is used, range resolution is given by $\frac{c}{2B}$, where B is bandwidth of the transmitted signal. On the other hand the azimuth resolution is determined by the beam width, which is proportional to the wavelength and inversely proportional to the length of the antenna. Hence to get a narrow beam width it is required to have a very long antenna and small wavelength. However EM radiation of smaller wavelengths decreases the ability to penetrate through clouds. In overcoming these limitations, the SAR imaging becomes very effective, where a moving antenna of a small length provides a virtually long antenna. Thus, the imaging system operates with the desired cloud penetration wavelengths of signalling.

We also take advantage of the satellite motion in using SAR imaging system. With reference to Fig. 15.13, the SAR imaging process is briefly summarized. The onboard side looking radar of the SAR imaging system in a moving satellite illuminates a beam of coherent pulses over a target region. Then it receives the backscattered pulses from different objects lying in the illuminated region, and records the time interval from the temporal instance of transmission, amplitude, phase, and frequency of the signal. It also records the shift in carrier frequency (*Doppler shift*) of the received pulse as the sensor is moving with a constant velocity. By detecting the Doppler shift, the imaging system detects the locations of the target with higher resolution. The length of the footprint of the beam in the range direction is called the *swath width*. The range of the object is measured as its distance from the perpendicular drop of the satellite position on the ground, called *nadir*. The angle formed at the transmitting end is called the *illumination angle*. The distance of the closest point illuminated by the beam along the orthogonal direction of motion of the satellite, is called *near range*. Likewise the distance of the farthest illuminated point from the nadir lying on the same line is the *far range*. The swath width is the difference between these

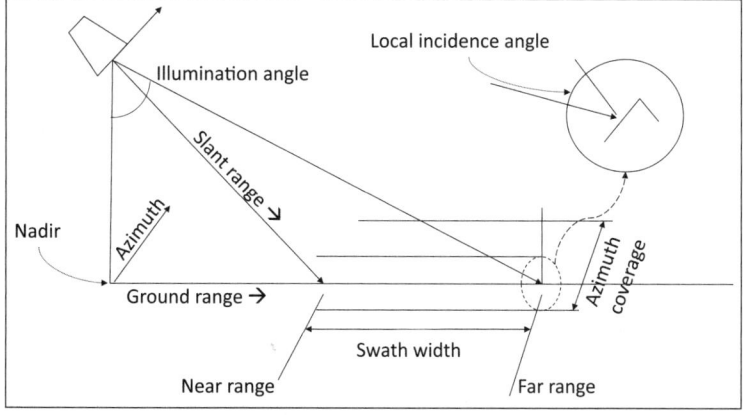

Figure 15.13 SAR imaging process.

two values. The direction of satellite motion is called the azimuth. It should also be noted that the incidence angle of the EM wave on the target is not the same as the angle of illumination. It is the angle between direction of propagation of incident EM wave and the surface normal at the point of incidence. We refer to it as the *local incidence angle*. We also assume that the sensor moves at a constant velocity during the imaging. The length of the area covered along the direction of the azimuth in a single image is called the *azimuth extent* or *azimuth coverage*. The distinct feature of the SAR imaging system is that the same back-scattered signal from a target is observed at different time instances at multiple positions of the sensor as it moves. All these observations are integrated and combined together by means of Doppler processing to increase the resolution of the range in the imaging system.

15.6.2 | SAR image data formats

There are different data formats in which a SAR image is available. In the lowest level of raw data format, it contains recording of all the discrete instances of back scatters at discrete sensor positions. In this case an object is included in many lines but their position varies for different slant regions. This data is called *raw* because it does not arrange target points in a single scan line with the varying range along the azimuths. The next level of representation is *single look complex* (SLC) data. In this case, many backscatters of the same target at different instances of sensor position are combined together into a single scan line containing the range of the target. The SLC image provides the highest spatial resolution.

An additional processing on the SLC representation results in *multi look complex* (MLC) data. In this case, the total azimuthal range along the track of sensors receiving echoes from the target is divided into a few segments, and their averages are computed. This representation reduces the spatial resolution, but it makes the measurement more robust to noise. In SAR images, the pixels are contaminated by speckle noise, which appears like grainy salt and pepper. The MLC representation reduces this speckle noise at the cost of reduced spatial resolution. Every point of SLC and MLC data is a complex value, which is usually represented in the rectangular form.

There is also another mode of representation, called the *intensity mode*. In this case, the complex data at every point is converted to its magnitude.

15.7 | Distortions in SAR images

There are various kinds of distortions that may occur in SAR images. These distortions may be broadly classified into two categories: (1) radiometric distortions, which occur due to the interference of coherent signals, and (2) geometric distortions that result from the limitations of the imaging system, since it uses side-looking antenna that introduces distortion in measuring the true ground range of a target under different conditions of terrestrial topography.

15.7.1 | Radiometric distortions

Under the class of radiometric distortions, the kind of noise that contaminates the pixel values occurs due to the interference of back scattered signals coming from closely spaced target points. It is called *speckle noise*. Here, multiple target points contribute to the formation of a single pixel in the SAR image. Their distances from the sensor vary in such a way that though the frequencies of the scattered signal from them remain the same, their phases vary and hence the wave interference happens. At some pixels they are in phase causing the increase of the strength of the received signal, and at some they are out of phase to make the superposed signal weak. The contamination of noise is modeled as a multiplicative process as shown in the following expression.

$$z(k,l) = x(k,l) \ v(k,l) \tag{15.13}$$

where $z(k,l)$, $x(k,l)$ and $v(k,l)$ are the measured value, true pixel value, and the noise at that pixel position, respectively. The noise, $v(k,l)$ is modeled by a probability distribution with unit mean and the standard deviation, as the ratio of standard deviation of z and expectation of z. That is, $v(k,l) \sim \mathcal{N}(1, \sigma_v)$, where $\mathrm{E}(v(k,l) = 1)$ and standard deviation of $v(k,l)$, $\sigma_v = \frac{\sqrt{\mathrm{var}(z)}}{\mathrm{E}(z)}$.

Speckle filters

There are different approaches to reduce the speckles in an image. The simpler approaches include mean (or box) filter and median filter. The size of the neighborhood for computing local mean and median is usually kept small such as 3×3 or 5×5. This is to reduce the effect of blurring of edges due to this computation. The computation of median is costlier than the mean, but it is more suitable for handling spot noise and also to preserve edges.

Using the statistics of the noise and the multiplicative model of its contamination there are several techniques to estimate the true pixel value by applying a regression model or local statistics filters. An example of such statistical model is provided below.

$$\hat{x} = \overline{x} + b\,(z - \overline{x})$$
$$\overline{x} = \frac{\overline{z}}{\overline{v}} = \overline{z} \ (\text{as } E(v) = 1)$$
$$\mathrm{var}(x) = \frac{\mathrm{var}(z) - \overline{z}^2 \sigma_v^2}{\sigma_v^2 + 1} \tag{15.14}$$
$$b = \frac{\mathrm{var}(x)}{\mathrm{var}(z)}$$

where $\hat{x}$ is the filtered value of noisy pixel value, x, $\overline{x}$ and $\mathrm{var}(x)$ represent the local mean and variance of x, respectively. This filter is called *Lee filter* (Lee, 1980), where the filtered pixel value is estimated by means of the local linear minimum mean square error (LLMMSE), which is given in Eq. 15.14. An example of application of Lee filter on different polarized components of the scattering matrix obtained from a SAR image (discussed in Section 15.10.2) is shown in Fig. 15.14.

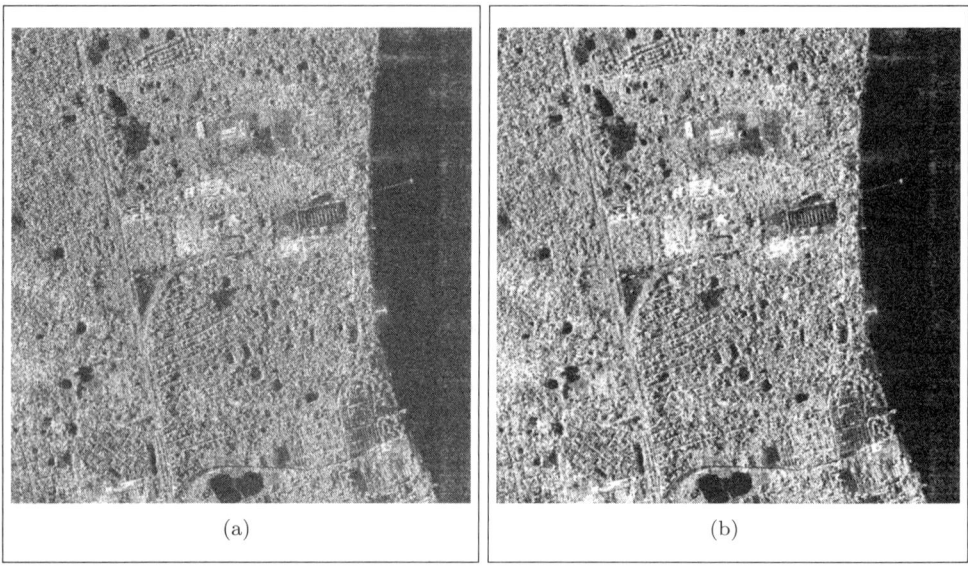

Figure 15.14 Example of despeckling on hybrid-pol RISAT data. (a) Original image and (b) despeckled image.

15.7.2 | Geometric distortions

There are various types of geometric distortions in SAR images. These distortions fall into two broad categories, namely, slant range scale distortion and terrain-induced distortion.

Slant range scale distortion

In the case of *slant range scale distortion*, the resolution of the image varies with the range. Objects in the near range appear more compressed than those in the far range. Thus, the resolution in the near range is lower than the resolution in the far range. To achieve uniform resolution, it is necessary to convert the data as a function of ground range and then uniformly sample the functional values at regular intervals. The ground range value, R_g is obtained from the slant range, R, by using the altitude of the sensor, H, as follows.

$$R_g = \sqrt{R^2 - H^2} \tag{15.15}$$

Terrain induced distortions

There are three types of terrain induced distortions, namely, foreshortening, layover, and shadow. In Fig. 15.15, the *foreshortening* phenomenon has been illustrated. As the imaging system measures the slant range, the uphill slope area facing the sensor gets compressed and its respective ground range gets shortened.

Fig. 15.16 illustrates the *layover* between two surface points, one at the bottom (point A) and the other at the top (point B), of a steep terrain. In this case the radar wave reaches

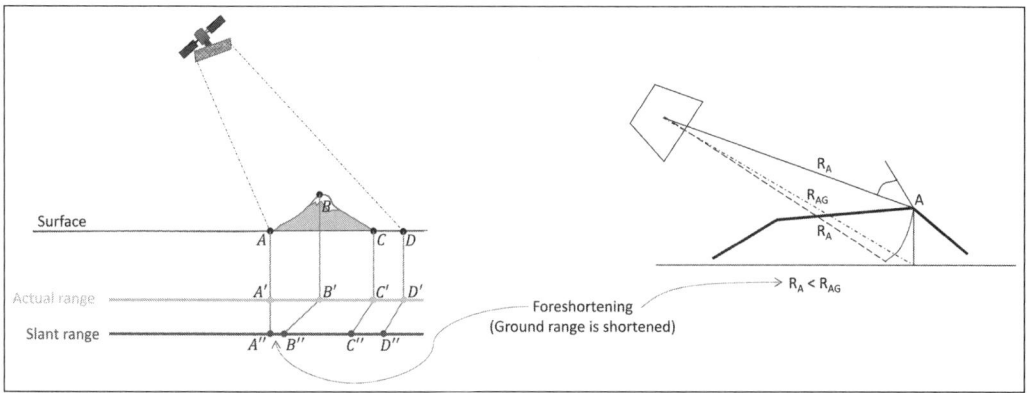

Figure 15.15 Foreshortening phenomenon in SAR imaging.

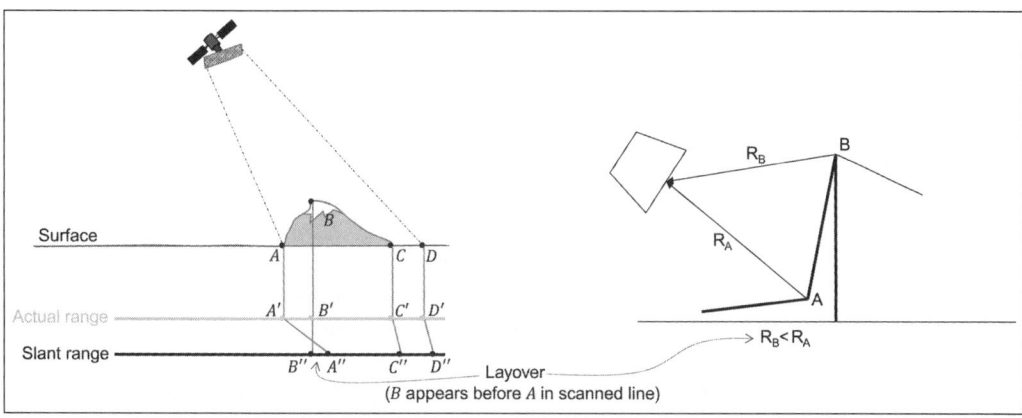

Figure 15.16 Layover phenomenon in SAR imaging.

the top (B) earlier than the bottom (A). Hence the slant range measured by the backscatter from B becomes smaller than that of A. This makes B appear before A, when arranged in the order of their ground range values. Thus the object looks upside down. For this kind of phenomenon, the layover region also shines brighter in the SAR image, which is an extreme case of foreshortening.

The other kind of terrain induced distortion is the *formation of shadow* due to the occlusion of a down hill terrain, which is illustrated in Fig. 15.17. The transmitted pulse does not reach any point of the occluded region. Hence, the backscatter values become nearly zero from those points. That region appears dark, which is due to the effect of a false shadow. It is very challenging to distinguish between low back scattered region and the shadow. For correcting terrain induced distortions, the digital elevation map (DEM) of the terrain is used to estimate the true ground range of surface points from the distorted range map.

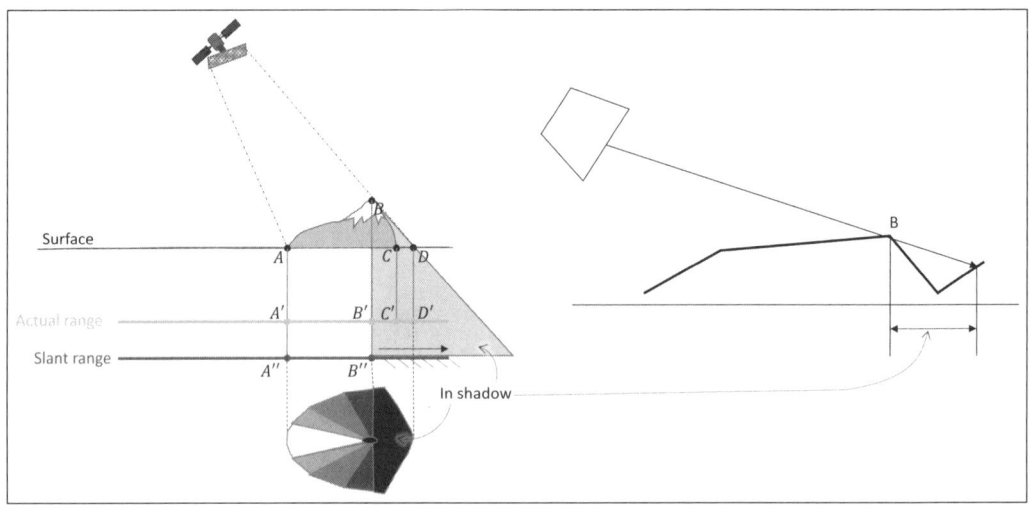

Figure 15.17 Shadowing in SAR imaging.

15.8 | Radar backscatter

The backscattering depends on surface characteristics and wavelength of EM waves. For polarized EM waves, the recording of amplitude, frequency, and phase of the backscatter occurs in both horizontal and vertical polarization components. The amount of backscatter depends on surface characteristics such as roughness, dielectric constant, orientation, and structure. Rough surfaces exhibit more backscatter than smooth areas. This may be observed in the backscatter from lakes and rivers, which is less compared to that from the ground. There are three broad types of backscattering depending on the geometry of the surface, namely single bounce surface scattering, double bounce or dihedral scattering, and volume scattering, as illustrated in Fig. 15.18. Surface scattering examples include scattering from water bodies (e.g., lakes, rivers, oceans) and flat, smooth planes (e.g., open grounds or grasslands). Dihedral scattering is usually observed in human settlements from buildings, bridges, etc. The volume scattering occurs from forests, canopies of trees, etc. Surface scattering exhibits the least backscatter, whereas dihedral scattering has the highest amount. On certain surfaces, depending on the roughness level, the backscatter may exhibit the characteristics between surface and volume scattering. Additionally, the composition of polarization components in the backscatter, given an incident polarized EM wave, also characterizes the surface.

15.8.1 | Wavelength of EM pulse

The wavelength of an EM pulse influences the level of penetration of the incident wave underneath the surface. In this case, the visibility of the surface through the backscatter

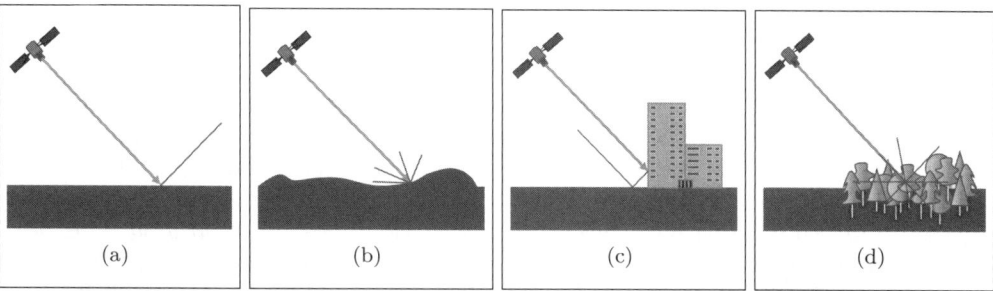

Figure 15.18 Types of backscatters. (a) Surface scatter, (b) rough surface scatter (surface/ volume scatter), (c) dihedral scatter, and (d) volume scatter.

Table 15.3 SAR imaging wavelengths.

Frequency Band	Frequency Range	Examples of Applications
VHF	300 kHz – 300 MHz	Foliage, ground penetration, biomass, etc.
P band	300 MHz – 1 GHz	Biomass, soil moisture, penetration, etc.
L band	1 GHz – 2 GHz	Agriculture, forestry, soil moisture, etc.
C band	4 GHz – 8 GHz	Ocean, agriculture, etc.
X band	8 GHz – 12 GHz	Ocean, agriculture, high resolution radar, etc.
Ku band	14 GHz – 18 GHz	Glaciology (snow cover mapping)
Ka band	27 GHz – 47 GHz	Very high resolution radar

depends on the wavelength of operation. Longer wavelengths penetrate deeper into the surface. However, the penetration is restricted to a few centimeters. The SAR carrier wavelengths are much longer than the wavelengths of the bands used in optical and thermal remote sensing, such as visible, IR, NIR, SWIR, Thermal IR, etc. The wavelengths of bands used in optical and thermal remote sensing range from 0.02 μm to 1 mm. But the SAR imaging uses EM wavelengths from 0.75 cm to 100 cm. The transmission bands are called by short names, usually a letter from the alphabet, such as K, Ku, X, C, S, L, and P. These are the names attributed to the era of secrecy, mostly during the period of cold war, that was maintained during the development of this technology by some of the countries. In Table 15.3, a list of such bands and their applications are illustrated. It may be observed that, in various applications related to agriculture, biomass prediction and estimation, forestry, soil moisture, etc., P and L band SAR imaging systems are used, as they operate with longer wavelengths, which have greater ability in penetrating a target. In this case, the imaging may take place through penetration of EM wave through forest canopy, upper surface of soil, etc.

15.9 | Polarized wave

A SAR imaging system uses *polarized EM waves*. In a polarized EM wave, its electric fields (and the magnetic fields in the orthogonal direction of the electric field) either oscillate along a single direction orthogonal to the direction of propagation, or rotate circularly or elliptically in a plane as the wave travels, as illustrated in Fig. 15.19. The wave with single directional oscillating field during its propagation is called *linearly polarized wave*. The polarization with rotating field is called *circular* or *elliptical polarization*. For the left hand rotation it is called *left-handed circular polarization* and likewise, for the right handed rotation, the polarization is *right-handed circular polarization*. A polarized electric field may be treated as an oscillating vector in a plane. If we define a coordinate system with Z-axis being the direction of propagation of the wave, the polarized electric field may be decomposed into horizontal components (along X-axis) and vertical components (along Y-axis) with the following representation.

$$\vec{E}(z,t) = \begin{bmatrix} E_{0x}\cos(\omega t - kz + \delta_x) \\ E_{0y}\cos(\omega t - kz + \delta_y) \\ 0 \end{bmatrix} \tag{15.16}$$

where the vector is represented in the form of a phasor with amplitude of the vector is given by $A = \sqrt{E_{0x}^2 + E_{0y}^2}$ and the phase angle $\theta = \tan^{-1}\left(\frac{E_{0y}}{E_{0x}}\right)$. The other qualifying parameter is the phase difference of the propagation of these two components, $\delta = \delta_x - \delta_y$. For different values of phase difference, the nature of polarization varies, as described below.

- Linear polarized wave: $\delta = \delta_x - \delta_y = n\pi$.
- Circular polarized wave: $\delta = \frac{\pi}{2} + n\pi$.
  Also, for this polarized wave, $E_{0x} = E_{0y}$.
- Elliptical polarized wave: The configuration of the wave other than the above two.

As seen from the above expressions, depending upon the phase differences the geometric feature of polarization varies. In a linear polarized wave, the phase difference is the multiple of π or 0. This implies that the two components are always either in phase or out of phase. In the case of a linear polarized wave, the wave may be considered as inscribed on a plane with an angle θ with the X axis. For circular polarized wave, the phase difference is effectively either $\frac{\pi}{2}$ or $-\frac{\pi}{2}$. In circular polarization, the electric field rotates about the direction of transmission on its every planar cross section (a plane orthogonal to the direction of propagation). The rotation is left handed or anticlockwise, if the phase of the horizontal component lags by $\frac{\pi}{2}$ from that of the vertical component. Otherwise, if the phase of the horizontal component leads by $\frac{\pi}{2}$, it is right handed or clockwise rotation. In a more general condition of phase difference other than 0 or multiple of π, the shape of the locus of the electric field is elliptical. This is expressed by the following relation.

$$\left[\frac{E_x(z_0,t)}{E_{0x}}\right]^2 - 2\frac{E_x(z_0,t)E_y(z_0,t)}{E_{0x}E_{0y}} + \left[\frac{E_y(z_0,t)}{E_{0y}}\right]^2 = \sin(\delta) \tag{15.17}$$

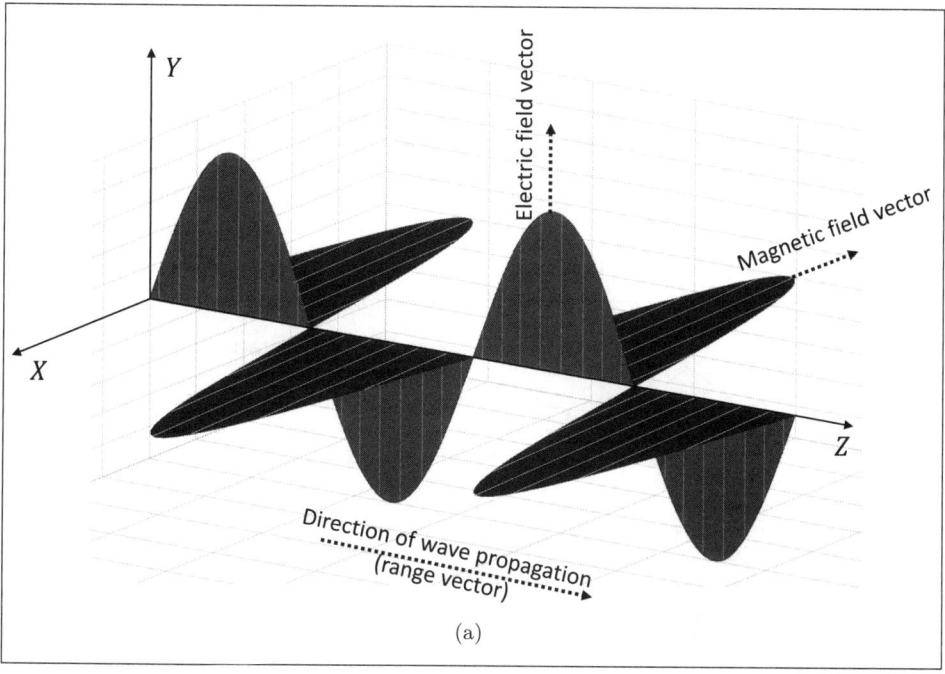

(a)

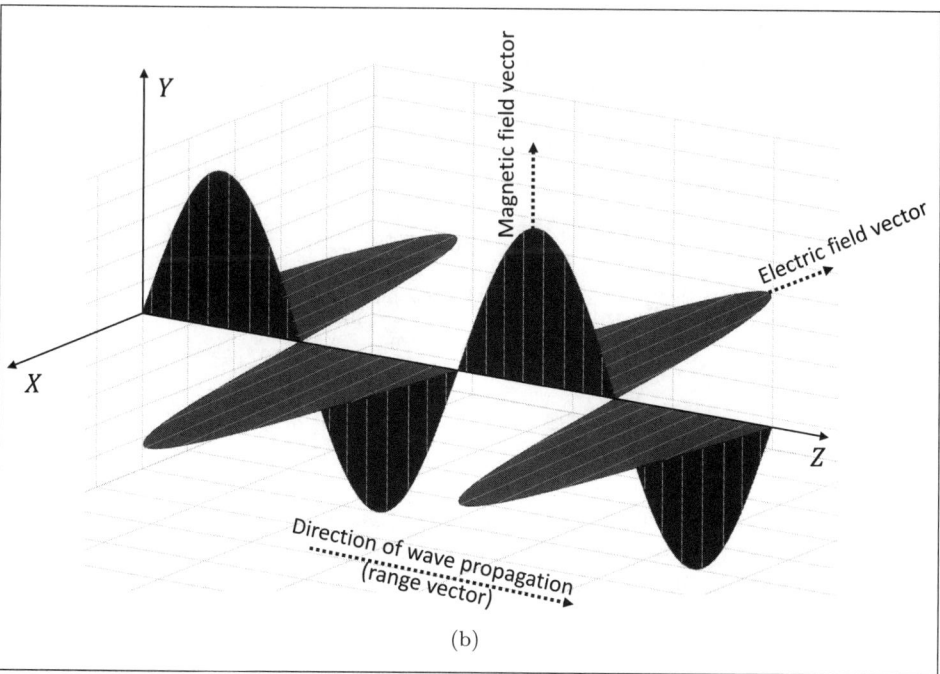

(b)

Figure 15.19 A polarized electromagnetic wave. (a) Vertically polarized signal (YZ plane corresponds to the plane defined by range and Earth normal vectors), and (b) horizontally polarized wave.

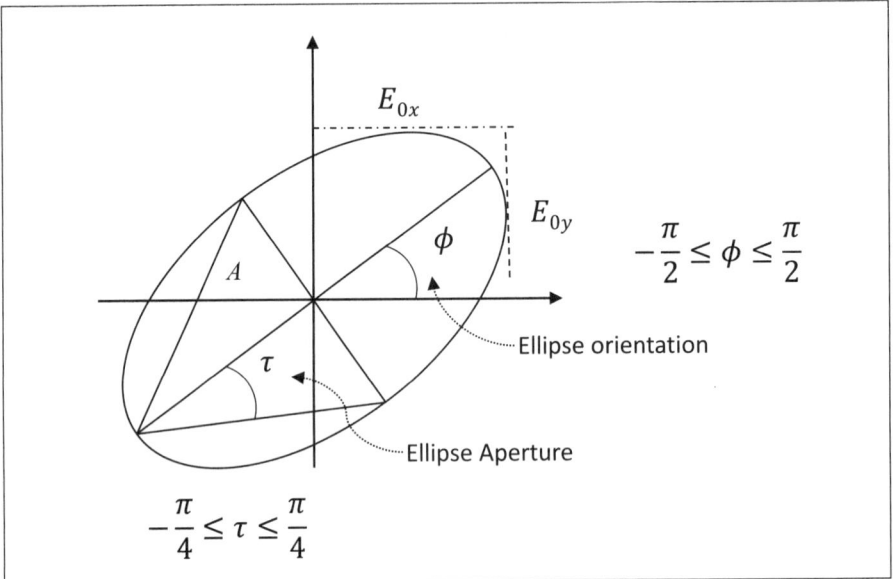

Figure 15.20 Parameters of a polarization ellipse.

We refer to this ellipse as *polarization ellipse*. From the above equation, different attributes of the polarization ellipse, such as *ellipse orientation* and *ellipse aperture*, are obtained. They are described in the following expressions and illustrated in Fig. 15.20.

$$A = \sqrt{E_{0x}^2 + E_{0y}^2}$$

$$\tan(2\phi) = 2\frac{E_{0x}E_{0y}}{E_{0x}^2 - E_{0y}^2} \tag{15.18}$$

$$|\sin(2\tau)| = 2\frac{E_{0x}E_{0y}}{E_{0x}^2 - E_{0y}^2}|\sin(\delta)|$$

15.9.1 | Jones vector

From the above discussion, it may be seen that it is convenient to represent a polarized electric field by a vector. This vector is called *polarization vector*, which is a time independent coherent representation of the electric field on the cross-sectional plane of the direction of propagation. It is also named *Jones vector*, which is given in Eq. 15.19.

$$\mathbf{E} = \begin{bmatrix} E_{0x}e^{j\delta_x} \\ E_{0y}e^{j\delta_y} \end{bmatrix} = \begin{bmatrix} E_x \\ E_y \end{bmatrix} \tag{15.19}$$

In a Jones vector the X and Y components are represented by the amplitude and the phase of the electric field along its direction.

15.9.2 | Stokes vector

There is another representation of the polarized EM wave, called *Stokes vector*, that is based on energy. The energy terms are obtained by the outer product of the Jones vector with its Hermitian transpose as given below.

$$
\mathbf{EE^{*^\top}} = \begin{bmatrix} E_x E_x^* & E_x E_y^* \\ E_y E_x^* & E_y E_y^* \end{bmatrix} = \frac{1}{2} \begin{bmatrix} g_0 + g_1 & g_2 - jg_3 \\ g_2 + jg_3 & g_0 - g_1 \end{bmatrix} \tag{15.20}
$$

The elements of the 4-D stokes vector are obtained from the above matrix as shown below.

$$
g_{\mathbf{E}} = \begin{bmatrix} g_0 \\ g_1 \\ g_2 \\ g_3 \end{bmatrix} = \begin{bmatrix} |E_x|^2 + |E_y|^2 \\ |E_x|^2 - |E_y|^2 \\ 2\mathrm{Re}(E_x E_y^*) \\ -2\mathrm{Imag}(E_x E_y^*) \end{bmatrix} = \begin{bmatrix} E_{0x}^2 + E_{0y}^2 \\ E_{0x}^2 - E_{0y}^2 \\ 2E_{0x}E_{0y}\cos(\delta) \\ -2E_{0x}E_{0y}\sin(\delta) \end{bmatrix} \tag{15.21}
$$

It may be noted that a Stokes vector is a noncoherent representation and all the elements of the vector are real values. It provides all necessary information regarding the polarization elements, except for the sense of rotation of the field about the direction of transmission. The representation of Stokes vector using the parameters of polarization ellipse is given in Eq. 15.22.

$$
g_{\mathbf{E}} = \begin{bmatrix} A \\ A\cos(2\phi)\cos(2\tau) \\ A\sin(2\phi)\cos(2\tau) \\ A\sin(2\tau) \end{bmatrix} \tag{15.22}
$$

The first component of the stokes vector provides the energy of the polarized wave. It is related to other three energy terms as follows:

$$
g_0^2 = g_1^2 + g_2^2 + g_3^2 \tag{15.23}
$$

15.10 | Polarimetric SAR

In a polarimetric SAR imaging system, the transmission of EM pulses takes place with controlled polarization, either with horizontal, with vertical, or with both (one after another) polarizations. The receiver performs detection of both the horizontal and vertical components coherently. During the transmission, if both the pulses are transmitted with both horizontal (H) and vertical (V) polarizations in alternate fashion, the system is called a *full polarimetric* or *quad-pol* system. In this case, for each type of transmitted polarized pulse, the receiver detects its horizontal and vertical components separately. Thus, a quad-pol imaging system produces image data in four channels, namely HH, HV, VH and VV. For example, the HH channel of the image is the component by detecting horizontal polarization of the scattering from a horizontally polarized transmitted pulse.

Likewise other channels are also named. In Fig. 15.21, an example of visual effect of polarimetric components in characterizing different types of surfaces is demonstrated. Here, the pseudocolor image of RISAT data is composed with magnitudes of HH, HV and VV components as RGB channels.

In a *dual polarimetric* or *dual-pol* SAR imaging system, either horizontally polarized or vertically polarized pulse is transmitted. Hence, in the receiver, there are two channels: either HH and HV, or VH and VV. There is another mode of SAR polarimetry, where the transmission takes place with circular polarization, denoted by either L or R, depending on the left-handed or right-handed rotation of the electric field. In this mode, there are two channels in the receiver either RH and RV or LH and LV. This mode is called *hybrid* or *compact polarimetry* (CP). In this book, we restrict our discussion to only full-pol or quad-pol polarimetry.

15.10.1 | Scattering process

Consider the modeling of the scattering process, where, given an incident polarized electric field, the scattered or reflected polarized electric field is produced. We assume that both the incident and reflected wave lie on a plane, which is orthogonal to the plane of incidence (see Fig. 15.22). This assumption is valid if the target is far from the transmitting end, which is the usual case. In Fig. 15.22, the incident wave travels along the direction Z', and it gets reflected along the direction Z''. Let us assume that the horizontal and vertical components of polarized incident wave are along X' and Y', respectively. Similarly, the horizontal and vertical components of reflected wave are along X'' and Y'', respectively. In the figure it may be noted that the vertical components lie on the plane of incidence and reflection, whereas the horizontal components are along the direction of normal of that plane. Without loss of generalization, the local coordinate directions of horizontal and vertical components may be attributed by the subscripts h and v, respectively. Also, in the Jones vector representation, the incident and scattered (reflected) polarized electric vectors are attributed by the superscripts i and s, respectively. This is illustrated in Fig. 15.23.

The mathematical relationship between these two vectors are given by Eq. 15.24.

$$\begin{bmatrix} E_h^s \\ E_v^s \end{bmatrix} = \frac{e^{-jkr}}{r} \begin{bmatrix} S_{hh} & S_{hv} \\ S_{vh} & S_{vv} \end{bmatrix} \begin{bmatrix} E_h^i \\ E_v^i \end{bmatrix} \tag{15.24}$$

where e^{-jkr} is the phase delay due to traveling of the wave, r is the distance between receiver and scatterer, $k = \frac{2\pi}{\lambda}$ is the wave number, and $\mathbf{S} = \begin{bmatrix} S_{hh} & S_{hv} \\ S_{vh} & S_{vv} \end{bmatrix}$ is the *scattering matrix*.

15.10.2 | Scattering matrix

In the relationship shown in Eq. 15.24, a 2×2 matrix, called the *scattering matrix*, converts the incident vector to the reflected vector as a linear superposition of reflections from each polarized component of the incident vector. For example, the element S_{hh} in the scattering matrix denotes the fraction of horizontal component of the incident vector that contributes to the horizontal component of the scattered polarized vector. Similarly, the other elements

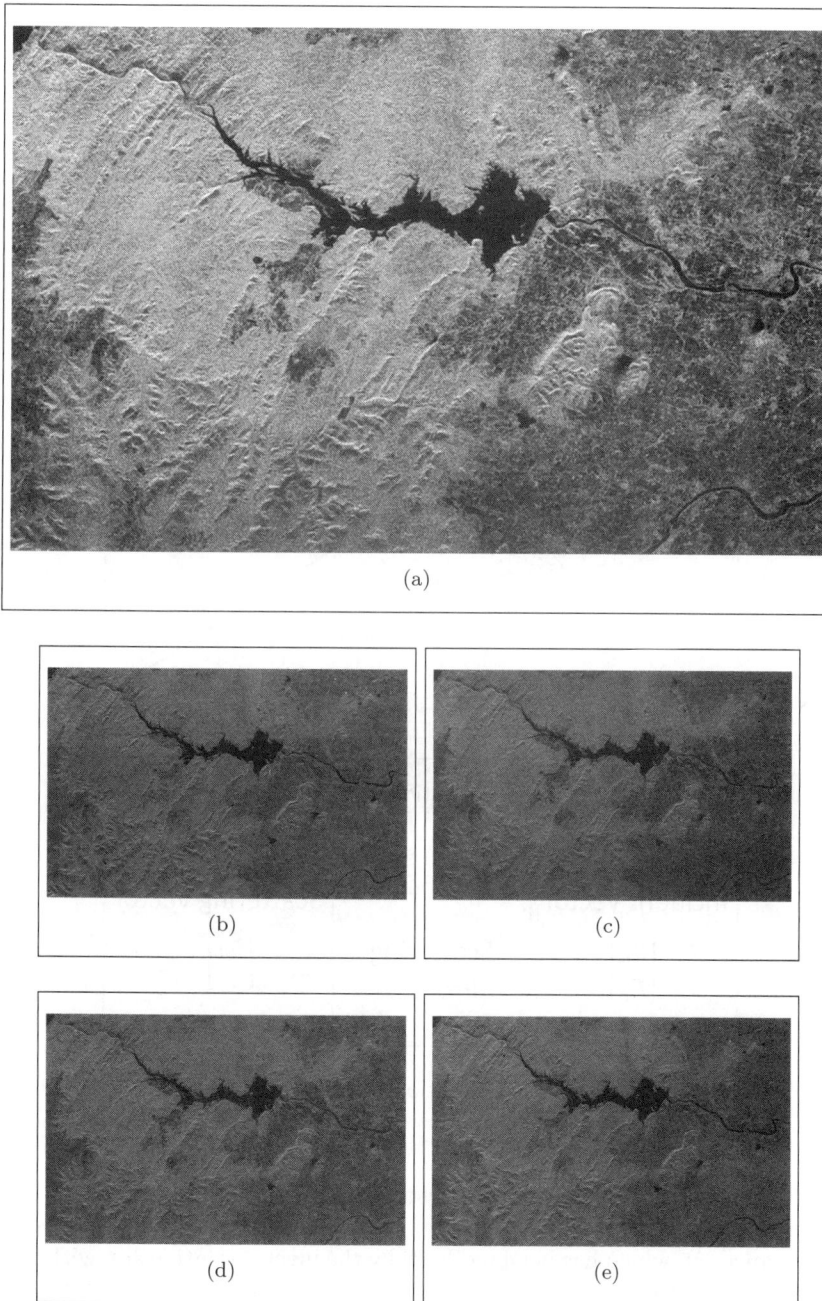

(a)

(b)   (c)

(d)   (e)

Figure 15.21 (a) Pseudocolor image of quad-pol RISAT data, (b) magnitude of HH component, (c) magnitude of HV component, (d) magnitude of VH component, and (e) magnitude of VV component. The pseudocolor image is formed by using the magnitudes of HH, HV, and VV components as RGB channels, respectively. See Color Plates (page 822).

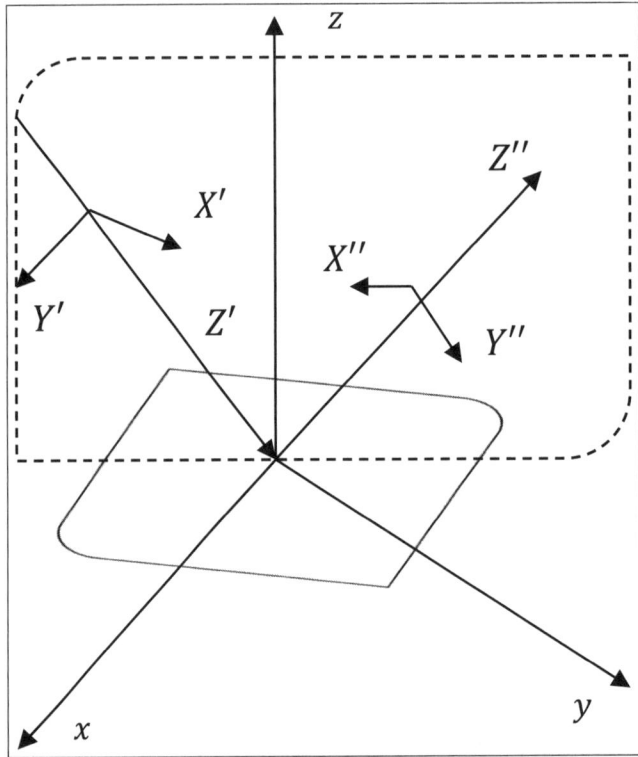

Figure 15.22 Illustration of planar scattering.

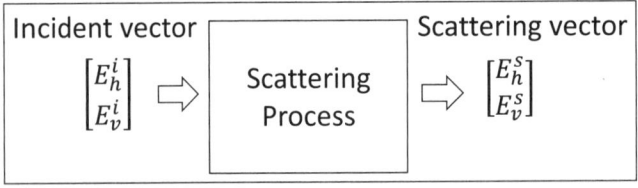

Figure 15.23 Representation of the scattering process.

of the matrix are defined. The reflected energy reaches the sensor after traveling a distance of r. Hence there is a phase delay from the point of scattering. Also, the energy gets attenuated due to the distance (r), which has been modeled by the inverse relationship with the distance between the sensor and the target.

Hence, the SAR imaging of a target may also be interpreted as the sensing of the elements of its scattering matrix. This is carried out in two steps of transmission of polarized pulses. In the first step, the transmitter may transmit a horizontally polarized wave and the receiver records both the horizontal and vertical components of the polarized back scattered pulse from a target. So in this case the first column of the scattering matrix is obtained. In the next step, a vertically polarized pulse is transmitted and likewise, the second column of the scattering matrix is obtained. Each element of the scattering matrix is a complex quantity as both the amplitude and phase of the received signal are recorded.

One of the key factors that influences the scattering matrix is the fixed imaging geometry defined by the positions of the transmitter, the receiver, and the target. This geometry, in turn, determines the directions of incident and scattered waves. The other influencing factors are surface geometry, material property, type of polarization, and the wavelength of the EM wave. It also depends upon the choice of basis vectors for the decomposition of polarized components. In a canonical configuration, the directions of horizontal and vertical polarized components, with respect to the plane of incidence, define the basis vectors. The total power of the scattered wave is expressed by the sum of squares of all the elements, i.e. $S_{hh}^2 + S_{hv}^2 + S_{vh}^2 + S_{vv}^2$. When the transmitter and receiver are collocated, the imaging system is called *monostatic*. In the monostatic case, $S_{hv} = S_{vh}$. This is usually satisfied in a SAR imaging system.

15.10.3 | Canonical surfaces of coherent scattering

Consider a few canonical surfaces whose scattering matrices can be analytically derived. In this case, a target appears to the sensor as a single coherent point scatterer. In Fig. 15.24, a list of such targets with their geometry and related scattering matrices are provided. The list includes a sphere (or a plane), a dihedral corner, a short thin cylinder, a left handed helix and a right handed helix. The parameters related to their geometry also are illustrated in the figure.

15.10.4 | Pauli basis decomposition

A target with an arbitrary scattering matrix may be modeled as a linear superposition of scattering of a few canonical scatterers. In this case, the target is assumed to be a single point coherent scatterer. There is a technique for coherent decomposition of an arbitrary scattering matrix, called *Pauli basis decomposition*. Suppose the scattering matrix **S** consists of elements as represented by the following complex numbers.

$$\mathbf{S} = \begin{bmatrix} a+b & c-jd \\ c+jd & a-b \end{bmatrix} \tag{15.25}$$

Then, a possible decomposition providing the linear superposition of canonical scattering matrices is given in the following form.

$$\mathbf{S} = a \begin{bmatrix} 1 & 0 \\ 0 & 1 \end{bmatrix} + b \begin{bmatrix} 1 & 0 \\ 0 & -1 \end{bmatrix} + c \begin{bmatrix} 0 & 1 \\ 1 & 0 \end{bmatrix} + d \begin{bmatrix} 0 & -j \\ j & 0 \end{bmatrix} \tag{15.26}$$

$$a = \frac{(S_{hh} + S_{vv})}{2}$$

$$b = \frac{(S_{hh} - S_{vv})}{2}$$

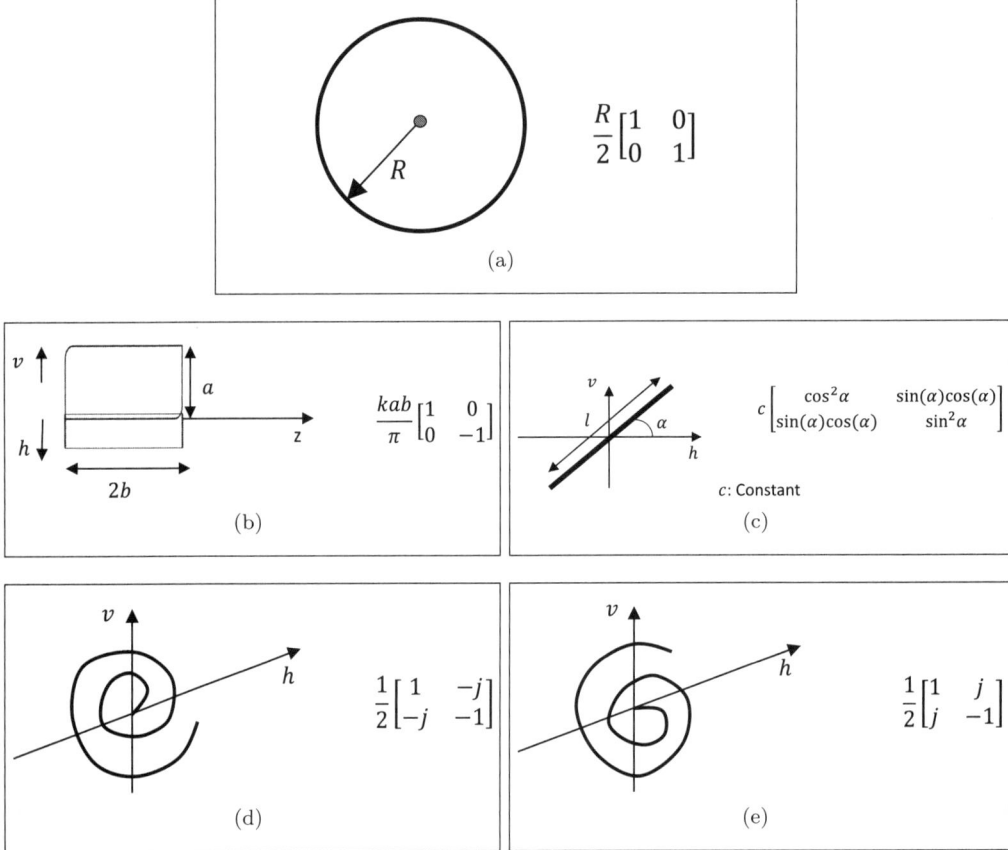

Figure 15.24 Canonical scatterers and their scattering matrices. (a) Sphere of radius R, (b) dihedral corner, (c) short thin cylinder, (d) left-handed helix, and (e) right handed helix.

$$c = \frac{(S_{hv} + S_{vh})}{2}$$

$$d = \frac{j(S_{hv} - S_{vh})}{2}$$

(15.27)

In Eq. 15.27, the coefficient a contributes to the phenomenon of single bounce scattering with the energy a^2. The coefficient b defines the mixing for the scattering by a dihedral corner and its associated energy term is b^2. The coefficient c attributes to the scattering by a diplane oriented at 45° with the direction of transmission. For monostatic imaging configuration, the contribution from a canonical right-helix scatterer is zero, since $S_{hv} = S_{vh}$. So, the coefficient $d = 0$. Hence there are only three decomposed components for any arbitrary scattering matrix in a monostatic imaging system. In Fig. 15.25, the Pauli's decomposition of a quad-pol ALOS PALSAR image is shown.

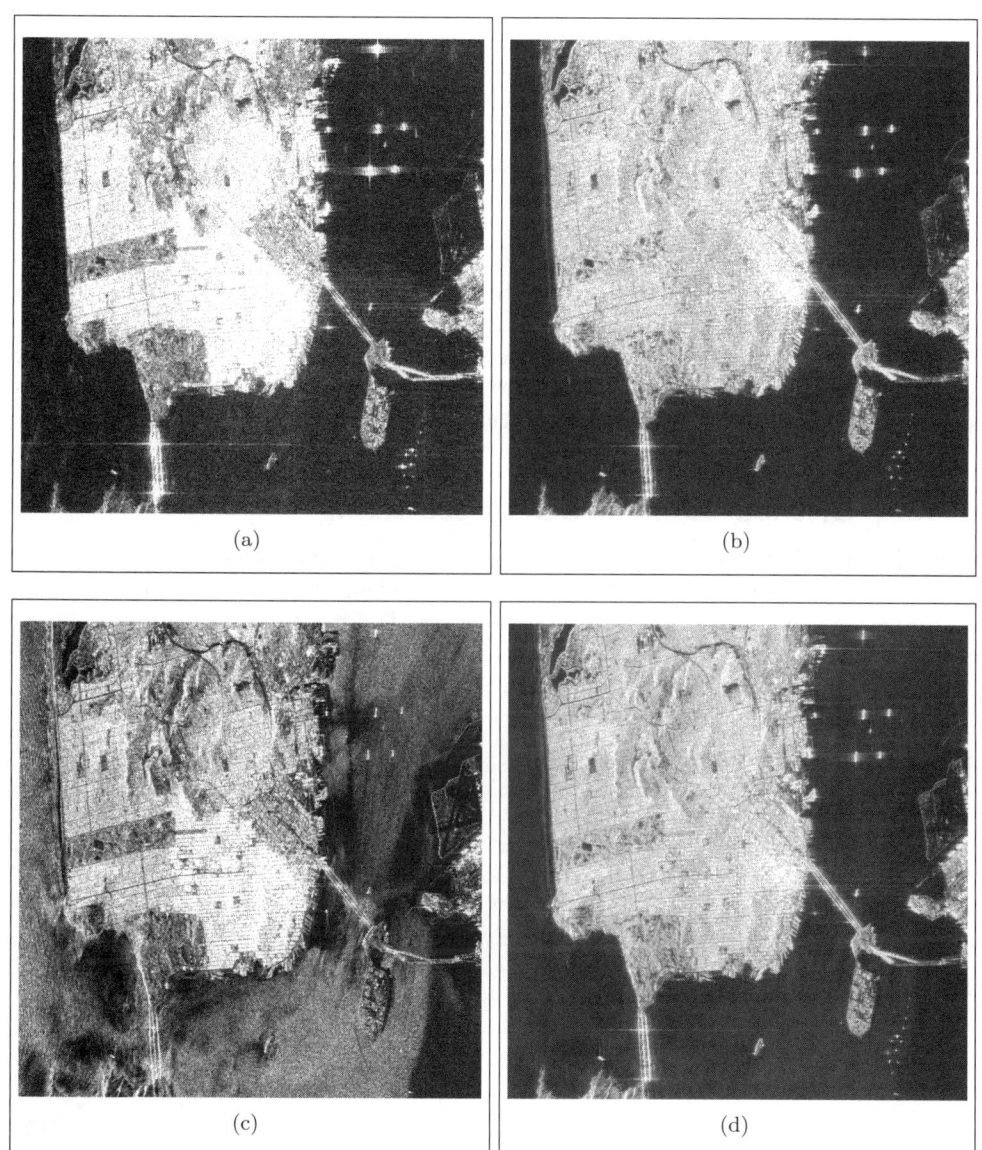

Figure 15.25 Pauli's decomposition of a quad-pol ALOS PALSAR image. (a) $|S_{hh} + S_{vv}|$, (b) $|S_{hh} - S_{vv}|$, (c) $|S_{hv}|$, and (d) RGB composite. The image is generated using the Polarimetric SAR data Processing and Education Toolbox (PolSARpro). See Color Plates (page 822).

15.10.5 | Other decomposition methods

There are also other methods to decompose the SAR image into factors of multiple canonical scatterers. In Krogager decomposition (Krogager, 1990), the scattering matrix is decomposed into a combination of the responses of a sphere, a diplane, and a helix. The Cameron decomposition (Cameron and Rais, 2006), decomposes the scattering matrix into two primary components, namely, symmetrical and asymmetrical. The symmetrical scattering component may include scattering from surfaces such as trihedral, dihedral, cylinder, etc., whereas the asymmetrical component may account scattering from right/left helixes and others.

The coherent decomposition method is only applicable to a scattering matrix characterizing a single coherent scatterer, as all the canonical scatterers are also of the same nature. The method does not work in the analysis of a scattering matrix sensed from a distributed scatterer. There are statistical tests by which it is possible to test whether a scattering matrix is produced from a single coherent scatterer or distributed scatterer. Roughly, the scattering from man made objects is attributed to be more pure than those coming from natural surfaces such as vegetation, water, tree cover in a forest, etc.

15.10.6 | Distributed noncoherent scattering

To factorize distributed scattering, a convenient representation of the scattering matrix in the form of a 4-D vector (constructed from its 4 elements) is used. It is mainly used for representing the interactions among components. There are two kinds of vectorization, namely, (i) lexicographic vectorization, and (ii) Pauli decomposition vectorization. These two representations on the scattering matrix **S** are shown below.

(i) Lexicographic vectorization:

$$\mathbf{K}_l = \begin{bmatrix} S_{hh} \\ S_{hv} \\ S_{vh} \\ S_{vv} \end{bmatrix} \tag{15.28}$$

(ii) Pauli decomposition vectorization:

$$\mathbf{K}_p = \frac{1}{\sqrt{2}} \begin{bmatrix} S_{hh} + S_{vv} \\ S_{hh} - S_{vv} \\ S_{hv} + S_{vh} \\ j(S_{hv} - S_{vh}) \end{bmatrix} \tag{15.29}$$

In both the representations, it is ensured that the total energy of polarization or the span of the scattering matrix implying the sum of squares of all its elements, remains the same. That is, $\text{SPAN}(\mathbf{S}) = |S_{hh}|^2 + |S_{hv}|^2 + |S_{vh}|^2 + |S_{vv}|^2$

As in the monostatic imaging configuration, $S_{hv} = S_{vh}$, there are three independent elements in the matrix. Hence its 4-D representations can be reduced to 3-D representations as follows.

$$\mathbf{K}_l = \begin{bmatrix} S_{hh} \\ \sqrt{2}S_{hv} \\ S_{vv} \end{bmatrix}$$

$$\mathbf{K}_p = \frac{1}{\sqrt{2}} \begin{bmatrix} S_{hh} + S_{vv} \\ S_{hh} - S_{vv} \\ 2S_{hv} \end{bmatrix}$$

(15.30)

For a distributed noncoherent scatterer, the scattering from the points in the target surface changes with time due to the change of incident angle, etc. For example, the incident angle over tree-covers in a forest gets affected by wind conditions. For characterizing the scattering phenomena, instead of directly using the elements of scattering matrix, we consider its representation by the energy and correlation of the components by using its second order moments. From the vectorized representations, their 3×3 outer product is shown below.

$$\mathbf{C}_3 = \mathbf{K}_l \mathbf{K}_l^{*\top} = \begin{bmatrix} |S_{hh}|^2 & \sqrt{2}S_{hh}S_{hv}^* & S_{hh}S_{vv}^* \\ \sqrt{2}S_{hv}S_{hh}^* & 2|S_{hv}|^2 & \sqrt{2}S_{hv}S_{vv}^* \\ S_{vv}S_{hh}^* & \sqrt{2}S_{vv}S_{hv}^* & |S_{vv}|^2 \end{bmatrix}$$

$$\mathbf{T}_3 = \mathbf{K}_p \mathbf{K}_p^{*\top} = \begin{bmatrix} |S_{hh} + S_{vv}|^2 & (S_{hh} + S_{vv})(S_{hh} - S_{vv})^* & 2(S_{hh} + S_{vv})S_{hv}^* \\ (S_{hh} - S_{vv})(S_{hh} + S_{vv})^* & |S_{hh} - S_{vv}|^2 & 2(S_{hh} - S_{vv})S_{hv}^* \\ 2S_{hv}(S_{hh} + S_{vv})^* & 2S_{hv}(S_{hh} - S_{vv})^* & 4|S_{hv}|^2 \end{bmatrix}$$

(15.31)

The $\mathbf{C}_3$ matrix obtained from $\mathbf{K}_l$ is called the *covariance matrix*, and the $\mathbf{T}_3$ matrix obtained from $\mathbf{K}_p$ is called the *coherency matrix*. For the distributed scatter to handle noise, instead of making point observations, a region around a point is observed. Hence, the expected values of the elements of these matrices is estimated. In a simplified computation, the average of scattering matrices over the region is computed, which is similar to multi look estimation.

15.10.7 | Factorization of a noncoherent distributed scatterer

Consider factorization of a noncoherent distributed scatterer using the known forms of covariance or coherency matrices of canonical distributed scatterers. Any of the two matrices, $\mathbf{C}_3$ or $\mathbf{T}_3$, may be used for this purpose. Here we illustrate with the decomposition of the $\mathbf{C}_3$ covariance matrix as a linear combination of canonical non coherent distributed scatterers.

In a decomposition technique called *Freeman-Durden decomposition*, three types of canonical distributed scattering phenomena are considered, namely volume scattering, single bounce or surface scattering, and double bounce or dihedral scattering. The example of a volume scattering phenomenon is the scattering from a canopy or a set of randomly oriented dipoles such as forest covers. For double bounce scattering, the surface is modeled as a dihedral corner, and for the single bounce or surface scattering, it is modeled as the first order Bragg surface. Generic forms of the covariance matrix, $\mathbf{C}_3$, for all the above types of scattering are given in the following expressions.

$$\mathbf{C}_v = \frac{f_v}{8} \begin{bmatrix} 3 & 0 & 1 \\ 0 & 2 & 0 \\ 1 & 0 & 3 \end{bmatrix}$$

$$\mathbf{C}_d = f_d \begin{bmatrix} |\alpha|^2 & 0 & \alpha \\ 0 & 0 & 0 \\ \alpha^* & 0 & 1 \end{bmatrix} \qquad (15.32)$$

$$\mathbf{C}_s = f_s \begin{bmatrix} |\beta|^2 & 0 & \beta \\ 0 & 0 & 0 \\ \beta^* & 0 & 1 \end{bmatrix}$$

The $\mathbf{C}_3$ matrix of a volume scatterer, which is modeled as an ensemble of thin dipoles, is denoted in Eq. 15.32 by $\mathbf{C}_v$. The scattering power due to this volume scatterer is given by $P_v = f_v$.

The $\mathbf{C}_3$ matrix of the double bounce scatterer is obtained by a generalized corner model, and it is denoted in Eq. 15.32 as $\mathbf{C}_d$. In this matrix α is a function of reflection coefficients of vertical and horizontal polarization for two intersecting surfaces and the phase difference between the polarized reflected waves from these surfaces. The power contributed from its scattering is given by $P_d = f_d(1 + |\alpha|^2)$

For the single bounce scatterer, a rough surface model is considered. Its $\mathbf{C}_3$ matrix is denoted by $\mathbf{C}_s$ in Eq. 15.32. In this matrix, β is a function of reflection coefficients of vertical and horizontal polarization of the surface. Its contribution to power is given by $P_s = f_s(1 + |\beta|^2)$.

The superposition of canonical scattering matrices is given by Eq. 15.33, which is compared with an arbitrary covariance matrix of a distributed noncoherent scatterer.

$$\mathbf{C}_3 = \begin{bmatrix} \frac{3f_v}{8} + f_d|\alpha|^2 + f_s|\beta|^2 & 0 & \frac{f_v}{8} + \alpha f_d + \beta f_s \\ 0 & 2\frac{f_v}{8} & 0 \\ \frac{f_v}{8} + f_d\alpha^* + f_s\beta^* & 0 & \frac{3f_v}{8} + f_d + f_s \end{bmatrix} \Leftrightarrow \begin{bmatrix} |S_{hh}|^2 & \sqrt{2}S_{hh}S_{hv}^* & S_{hh}S_{vv}^* \\ \sqrt{2}S_{hv}S_{hh}^* & 2|S_{hv}|^2 & \sqrt{2}S_{hv}S_{vv}^* \\ S_{vv}S_{hh}^* & \sqrt{2}S_{vv}S_{hv}^* & |S_{vv}|^2 \end{bmatrix}$$
$$(15.33)$$

For the above mixing, f_v, f_d and f_s are considered to be the factors of linear combination. The elements of this superposed matrix is related with an arbitrary $\mathbf{C}_3$ matrix expressed by the elements of scattering matrix obtained by the imaging system. By comparing the corresponding elements of these two matrices, a set of equations are formed, which are solved to get the values of the five unknowns of the superposed canonical models, namely, f_v, f_d, f_s, α, and β. It is expected that the elements of $\mathbf{C}_3$ corresponding to the zero entries of superposed form of $\mathbf{C}_3$ are negligible, and they are ignored in forming the equations.

On the other hand, as the equations formed by both the off-diagonal corner terms of these matrices are the same, as the terms are complex conjugates of each other, four equations are formed from these matrices. So, the additional constraints of preserving the total power is applied to form the fifth equation. These five equations are listed below.

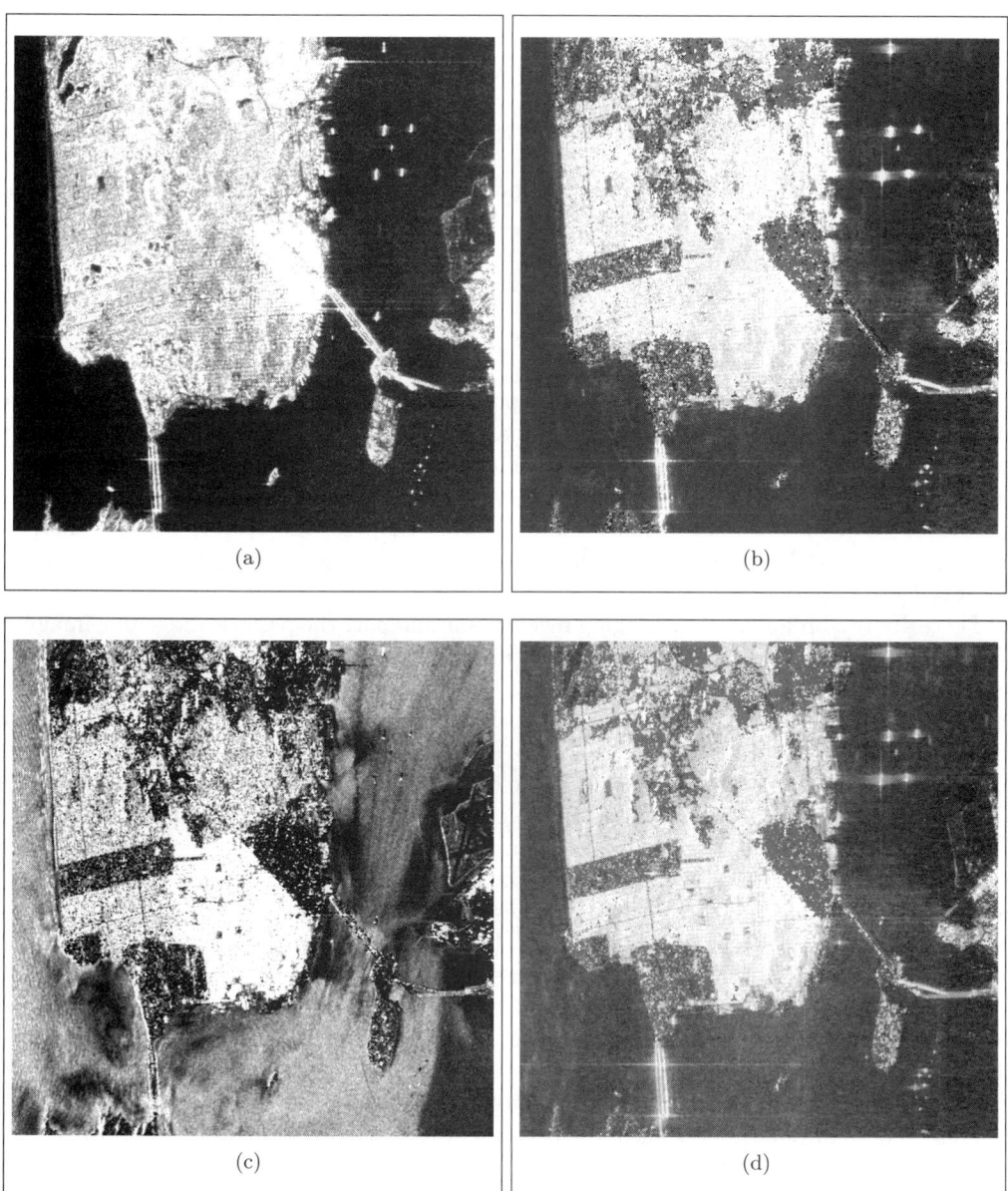

(a)

(b)

(c)

(d)

Figure 15.26 Freeman-Durden's decomposition of a quad-pol ALOS PALSAR image. (a) P_v, (b) P_d, (c) P_s, and (d) RGB composite. The image is generated using the Polarimetric SAR data Processing and Education Toolbox (PolSARpro). See Color Plates (page 823).

$$|S_{hh}|^2 = \frac{3f_v}{8} + f_d|\alpha|^2 + f_s|\beta|^2$$

$$|S_{hv}|^2 = \frac{f_v}{8}$$

$$|S_{vv}|^2 = \frac{3f_v}{8} + f_d + f_s \qquad (15.34)$$

$$S_{hh}S_{vv}^* = \frac{f_v}{8} + \alpha f_d + \beta f_s$$

$$P_v + P_d + P_s = |S_{hh}|^2 + 2|S_{hv}|^2 + |S_{vv}|^2$$

By solving the above equations, we may obtain values of the five parameters, and get the three canonical decomposed components. A typical result for the Freeman-Durden decomposition is shown in Fig. 15.26.

Summary

Remote sensing is the science of acquiring, processing and integrating images that record the interaction between EM energy and matter. The imaging system usually provides georeferenced images of a geospatial area, which are captured from satellite or by airborne cameras. This type of data, comprehensively illustrating various information related to terrestrial surfaces, is called synoptic data. In this chapter, the remote sensing imaging and processing of remote sensing images for characterizing terrestrial surfaces are discussed.

There are two broad types of imaging mechanisms, namely the passive and active imaging. In a passive imaging system, multispectral scanners are used to provide spectral bands of a region, mostly in the visible, IR and Thermal IR bands. In an active imaging system, radar imaging, in particular SAR imaging is used. Primarily, remote sensing images are meant for the upper-surface of the Earth. However, certain wavelengths of SAR imaging system, e.g., L and P band SAR imaging, are capable of penetrating a few centimeters underneath. Using these bands it is possible to study the growth and spread of roots of trees.

Multispectral images provide key information of reflectance of surfaces characterizing material objects such as vegetation, water, soil type, etc. SAR images characterize surface geometry from backscatters of polarized waves hitting a target such as volume or canopies, dihedral corners, smooth and rough surfaces, etc. Multispectral imaging senses reflected and emitted EM waves from objects on the Earth's surface in optical band of wavelengths from visible to IR (0.2 μm–2 μm) and in thermal IR bands (3 μm, 5 μm and 8 μm–12 μm). It uses spectral profile of reflectance of an object for characterizing objects by using measures such as spectral indices, signs of spectral slopes, etc.

Polarimetric SAR imaging system transmits and receives polarized EM waves. There are different modes of polarimetry such as quad-pol, dual-pol and compact or hybrid-pol. The imaging system essentially records the elements of a scattering matrix in multiple channels from the back scattered pulses. Polarimetric analysis involves characterizing geometry of targets from their scattering matrices. Toward this, decomposition of scattering matrices of coherent point scatterers and noncoherent distributed scatterers by factors of canonical scatterers are carried out.

Exercises

(i) Describe briefly the two phenomena of radiation responsible for passive remote sensing imaging of the surface of Earth. What are the ranges of spectral bands associated with these two phenomena. Explain why only a few windows in those spectral bands are available for multispectral imaging from the satellite.

(ii) How the radar imaging in remote sensing is different from the multispectral imaging?

(iii) Name and describe three fundamental interactions of EM waves with the atmosphere, which affect the passive imaging of Earth's surface. What are the substances in the atmosphere primarily responsible in these interactions? What are the atmospheric transmission widows for multispectral imaging?

(iv) Why does an ordinary cloud appear white in the day light?

(v) Which spectral index is used for identifying presence of vegetation in the Earth's surface and why?

(vi) Which spectral index is used for identifying presence of water in the Earth's surface and why?

(vii) Which spectral index is used for identifying presence of bare soil in the Earth's surface and why?

(viii) Describe the principles by which whisk-broom and push-broom multispectral scanners work. Consider the height of the satellite is 40 Km and the angle of IFOV of a whisk-broom scanner is 1.5 milliradian. Compute the ground resolution of the image.

(ix) Name and describe the orbital characteristics of a satellite.

(x) Consider the inclination angle of a satellite is 70°. What is the coverage of the Earth's surface by this satellite? Which type of orbital motion of a satellite covers the whole surface of the Earth?

(xi) What is meant by a sun-synchronous polar satellite? Give two examples of such satellite systems.

(xii) For what kind of remote sensing imaging tasks geostaionary satellites are used? Name a few examples of geostationary satellites.

(xiii) Explain how periodic line drop out may take place in a push-broom multispectral scanner. Describe a technique to restore an image suffering from such faults.

(xiv) Discuss why line stripping occurs in a multispectral scanner and describe a method to rectify the error.

(xv) Discuss the techniques for performing atmospheric corrections in a multispectral imaging system.

(xvi) Describe the two reflectance measure method for performing relative atmospheric correction in a multispectral image.

(xvii) Describe the two reference surface measure method for performing relative atmospheric correction in a multispectral image.

(xviii) Describe the method of rule based classification of land cover classes using multispectral images. How is the technique used in learning models for extending classification of pixels in an image, for which none of the rule is applicable?

(xix) Describe the principle of SAR imaging. Explain how the resolutions along the two directions of the image are determined.

(xx) What are meant by raw, SLC and MLC SAR data? Why do the SLC data suffer more from the speckle noise than the MLC data?

(xxi) Describe a method of reducing speckle noise in a SAR image.

(xxii) Discuss why the slant range scale distortion occurs in a SAR image. Describe the technique for removing this distortion in a SAR image.

(xxiii) Discuss why the foreshortening, layover and shadow occur in the formation of a SAR image.

(xxiv) Describe the method of polarimetric SAR and its use in characterizing the geometry of scattering element.

(xxv) What is meant by the backscatter of a SAR imaging system? Discuss how the polarized transmission of EM wave is used to characterize a target from its backscatter.

(xxvi) How it is possible to transmit linear, circular and elliptical polarized EM waves? How the state of polarization is described by the polarization ellipse?

(xxvii) How a polarized EM wave is represented by the Jones vector and the Stokes vector? What are the differences and motivations behind these two representations.

(xxviii) What is a scattering matrix in a full polarimetric SAR imaging system? How it is obtained from the imaging? Discuss how it is used for characterizing coherent and noncoherent targets?

(xxix) Describe Pauli's decomposition method for characterizing coherent scatters.

(xxx) Discuss how the vectorization of the scattering matrix helps in the analysis of noncoherent scattering phenomena.

(xxxi) Describe the Freeman decomposition method for understanding noncoherent phenomenon of scattering.

PART FOUR

APPLICATIONS

16

Document Processing

A document is an object which is primarily meant for human reading. It is not limited to only text. Besides text, which is primarily for reading, it may also contain figures, diagrams, photographs, tables, charts, etc. Many of these auxiliary components facilitate the reading experience. Document image processing involves processing of images of documents. Examples of documents comprise of scanned images of printed or handwritten pages, photographs of documents, etc. In general, images that contain different kinds of reading materials are considered as images of documents. In this context, the image of a text displayed in the environment is also an example of document, e.g., an image of a signboard. Such kinds of texts are referred to as scene texts.

A few examples of images of different kinds of documents are shown in Fig. 16.1. The document in Fig. 16.1 (a) contains printed text and graphics. Fig. 16.1 (b) is an example of an official document, which is a typical format of an official purchase order. Every organization usually has some standard template or format of each official form used in regular administrative routines, which belongs to this particular category of documents.

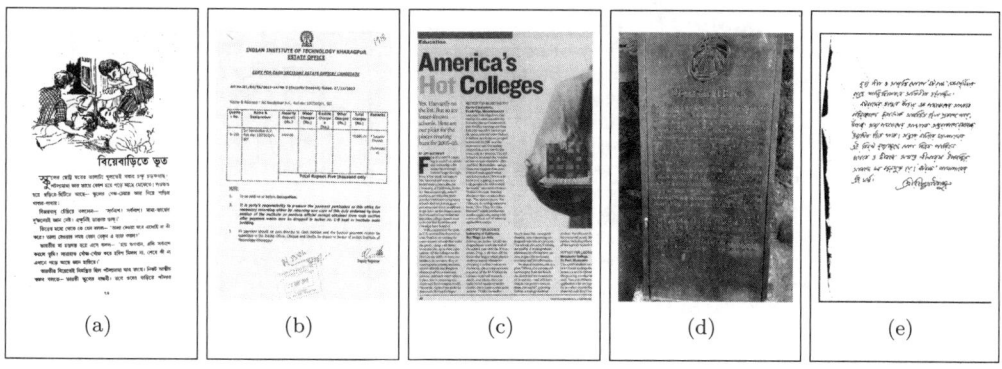

(a)   (b)   (c)   (d)   (e)

Figure 16.1 Examples of images of documents.

A page of magazine is shown in Fig. 16.1 (c), where the graphics and text are overlaid in a specific layout. In Fig. 16.1 (d), an example of scene text is shown, which is a photograph of a stone tablet describing a historical monument. The image shown in Fig. 16.1 (e) is a scanned document of a handwritten page, an example of writing of the famous Bengali poet and Nobel laureate, Rabindranath Tagore (1861–1941).

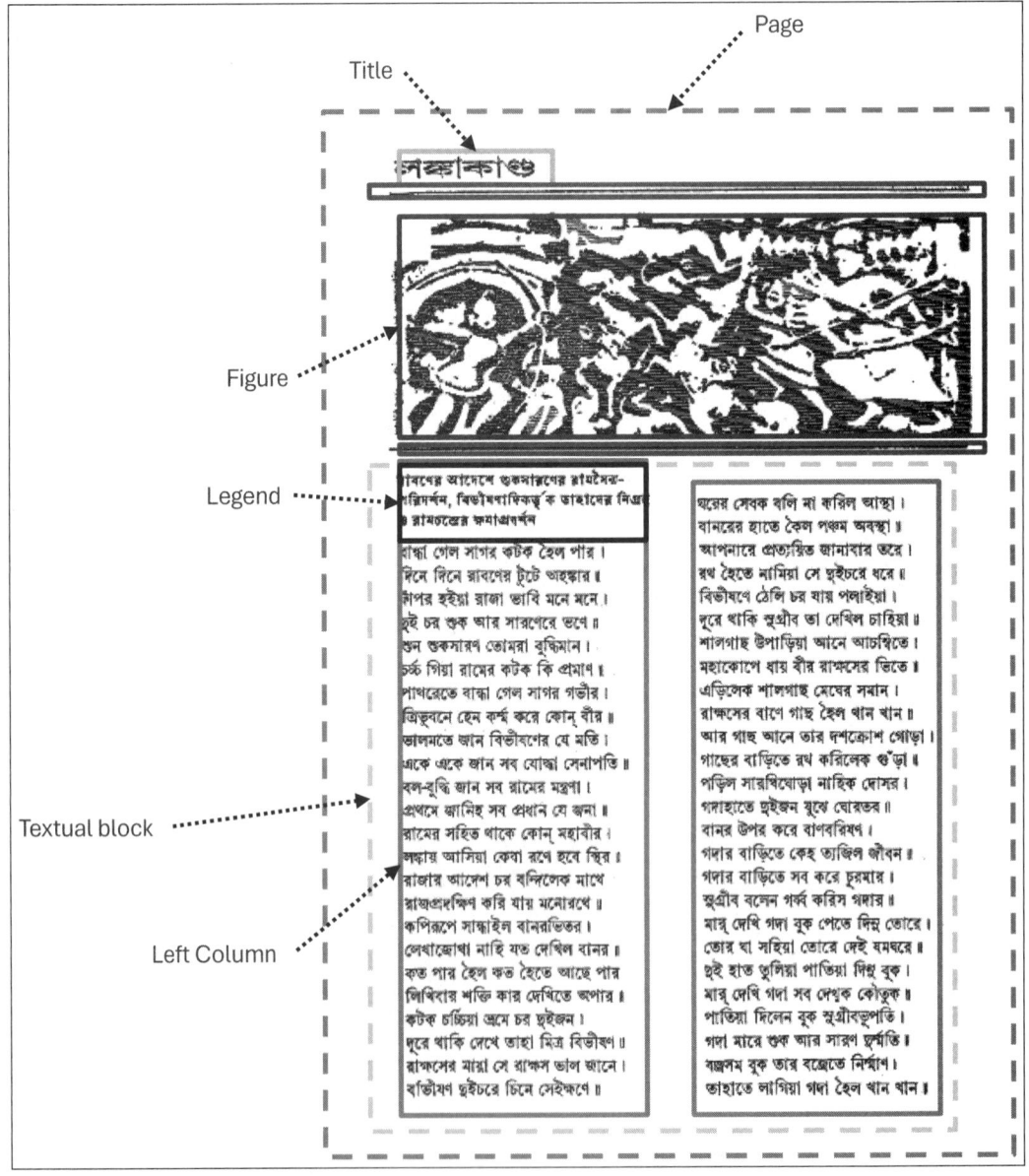

Figure 16.2 A sample document image with various elements.

16.1 | Document image processing

While considering the task of document comprehension, two types of structures are encountered. The first type pertains to the *geometric structure* or *layout* of the document. A geometric object in a document is an element of a specific geometric structure. For instance, the object may take the form of a rectangular block or a frame with composition of multiple blocks. It may also represent an entire page containing various distinct blocks. The second type of structure in a document is known as the *logical structure*. This structure is closely related to the geometric structure. It represents document elements based on their human-perceptible semantics and the relations among them. For example, logical structures result from dividing and sub-dividing content into smaller parts according to their meaningful context. These logical categories may include graphics, titles, chapters, paragraphs, lines, individual words, letters, etc. A sample document image is shown in Fig. 16.2, where the geometric and logical structures of various elements are shown.

The document image processing is usually performed in two stages, which are as follows.

(i) *Document analysis*: In this stage, the geometric structures are extracted.

(ii) *Document understanding*: In this stage, the geometric structures are mapped to a logical structure.

For example, in Fig. 16.2, the geometric structures, shown by the rectangular boxes of different parts of the document, are identified in document analysis. In document understanding, these geometric structures are mapped to a logical structure, which provides a meaningful context to the page. In the example, the elements like, title, figure, textual block, block of legend, two sub-blocks of text columns in the textual block, etc., are mapped appropriately in the composition of the page. Then, the semantics associated with the logical structures are derived. For instance, a page contains two columns of textual description labeled by a title, along with a figure for illustration. Here, the content of the title is written in Bengali script, `lankAkANDa`. Similarly, the graphic element is described by a legend, `rAbaNEr AdEshE shuk sAraNEr`. ... The text, starting as `bAndhA gEla sAgar` ... can also be decoded by the system in the document understanding stage.

16.2 | Document analysis

The geometric structure obtained in the analysis stage of the document processing is also called layout. Like rectangular boxes, there are different kinds of spatial arrangements of the geometric primitives. For instance, four distinct layouts are depicted in Fig. 16.3. In the *rectangular layout*, all components are positioned within nonoverlapping isothetic or axis-parallel rectangles.[1] This layout commonly occurs in research papers and official documents. In the *Manhattan layout*, it may not be always feasible to separate the components using an axis-parallel rectangle. Additionally, there can be polygons, whose sides are axis-parallel, but

---

[1] When the sides of the rectangular shape are parallel to the axes, they are referred to as axis-parallel rectangles.

do not form a rectangle. Such geometric regions are often found in newspapers, magazines, and in other similar contexts. There are other layouts, like *non-Manhattan layout*, where it may not be possible to place all components within a single polygon, and overlapping regions may occur. These layouts do not always adhere to isothetic conditions, and the sides may not be strictly axis-parallel. For instance, in magazines containing figures and tables, components might overlap with each other. There can also be component overlap in certain layouts with graphic elements, like a graphical magazine, where the text is embedded on the graphics (Fig. 16.3 (d)).

In the methodologies of layout analysis, it is important to understand how the document components are obtained. This process may also involve the classification of document components. The layout analysis is not merely a matter of extracting geometric primitives. Rather, it provides meaning for the classes associated with these geometric elements. Within a document, various types of objects may coexist. For instance, a document may consist of multiple pages, each containing text blocks, figures, tables, graphics, and other nontextual elements such as logos, stamps, and signatures. Each figure or table may possess both a legend and a body. The legend provides context for the figure, while the body contains the actual content, often in the form of image sketches. Similarly, tables may also have legends and bodies. Text blocks, on the other hand, may be further subdivided into text lines and individual characters, each enclosed within rectangular blocks. This structural arrangement defines the layout and adheres to specific semantics. Consequently, various computations are involved in this process. Furthermore, the text blocks may also encompass elements like titles, headers, footers, columns, and page numbers. A typical organization of document components is shown in Fig. 16.4.

Different stages of layout analysis are as follows.

  (i) Foreground-background separation,

  (ii) Separation of text and nontext content,

 (iii) Analysis of textual blocks, and

 (iv) Analysis of nontextual blocks.

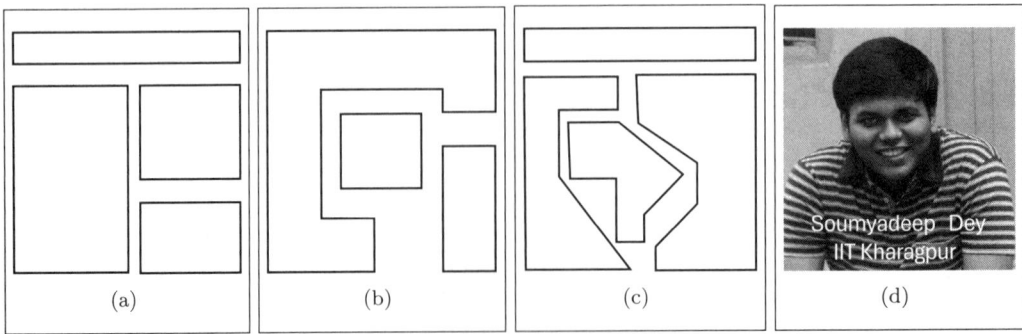

Figure 16.3 Examples of document layouts. (a) Rectangular layout, (b) Manhattan layout, (c) non-Manhattan layout, and (d) Overlapped text on image. (*Source*: Adapted from fig. 1.1 of Dey (2019).)

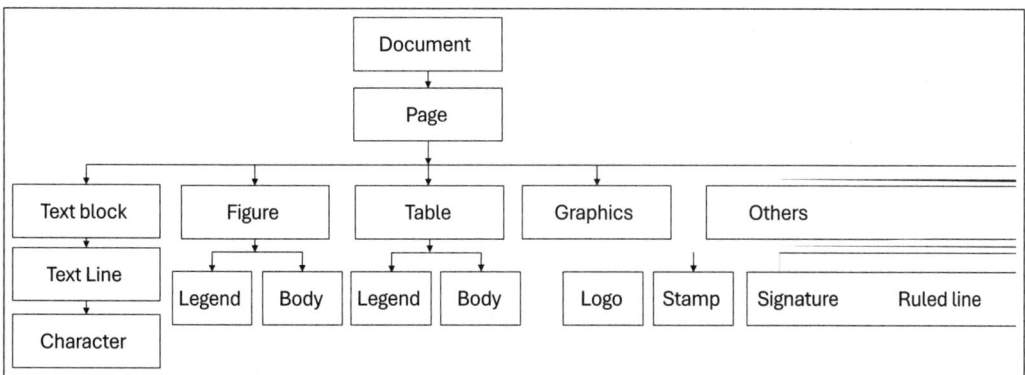

Figure 16.4 A typical organization of document components.

One of the tasks in initial computation involves determining how to separate the foreground and background. In the case of printed documents, a white page serves as the canvas for the content created using inks. Typically, the foreground appears darker or colored, while the background remains uniform or white. There are various techniques to achieve this objective of separating foreground and background. One of the popular approach is binarization, which is discussed in Section 1.3 of Chapter 1. Subsequently, the challenge of distinguishing text and nontext objects within the document is addressed. Then the focus is shifted to textual blocks, where the structures, such as text lines and characters, are identified. Simultaneously, nontextual blocks are also analyzed by examining their content. The nontextual blocks may include graphics, stamps, logos, and other elements. Overall, besides separating text from nontext, this process also involves categorizing different types of textual components and associating them with relevant semantics. A similar task is also applicable to nontextual components. This process is known as segmentation.

16.3 | Foreground-background separation

The foreground-background separation in document images is mostly performed using binarization technique. For binarization in document processing, one of the most commonly used methods is the adaptive thresholding technique. This approach selects a threshold based on local statistics, ensuring effective binarization of the local content. The general work-flow involves partitioning the image into rectangular blocks. For each block, a weighted average of intensity values is computed, which then serves as the threshold. These weights are assigned in various ways. For instance, one of the approaches is to consider a two-dimensional (2-D) Gaussian function centered on the block, with the weights proportional to the values of Gaussian function at the respective pixel locations. An example of binarization is shown in Fig. 16.5.

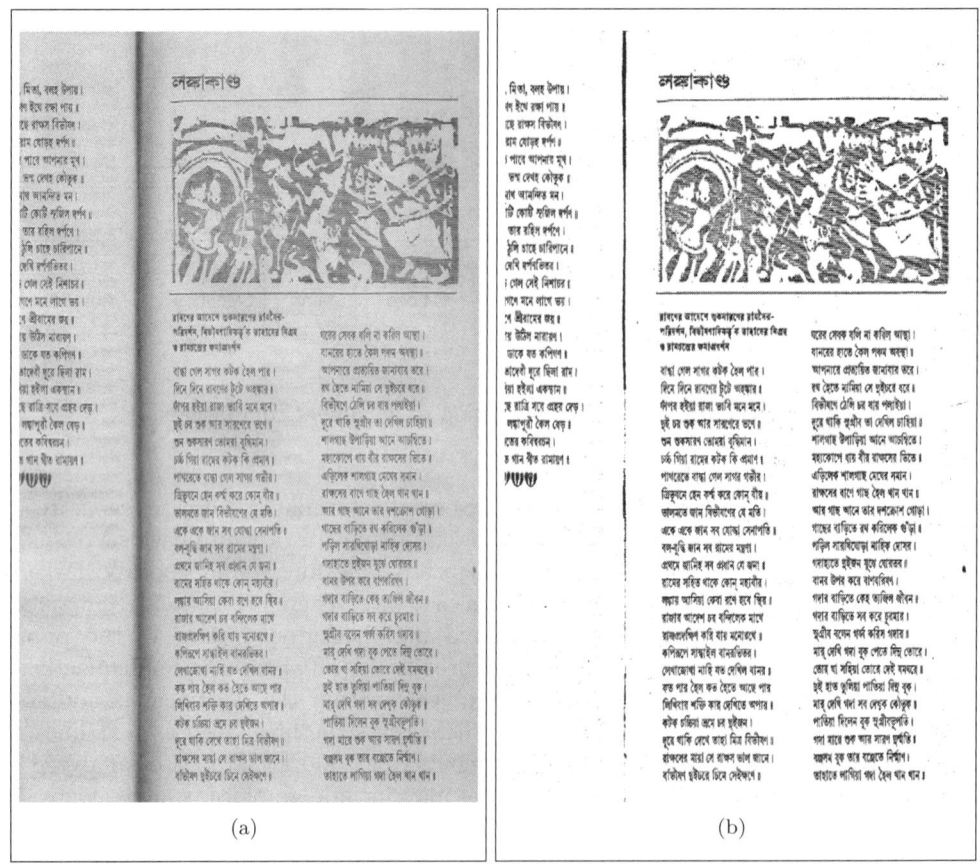

(a)

(b)

Figure 16.5 An example of binarization of a document image. (a) Original image of text. (b) Binarized image. (*Source*: Adapted from fig. 3.1 of Dey (2019).)

16.4 | Text and nontext content separation

One of the tasks for separating text and nontext elements in a document image involves extracting the connected components from the binarized document. The components are identified along straight lines using a technique reported by Fletcher and Kasturi in 1988 (Fletcher and Kasturi, 1988). This technique employs the Hough transform[2] to identify components with a linear arrangement. Those components falling along straight lines are considered as a part of the text, while the remaining portions are categorized as nontext elements. An illustration of this stage is shown in Fig. 16.6, where the text and nontext regions of the document are separated.

In document processing, the nontext objects also include stamps and logos, which are to be detected. While these elements are not the primary content of a document, identifying

---

[2] See Section 4.6.4 of Chapter 4.

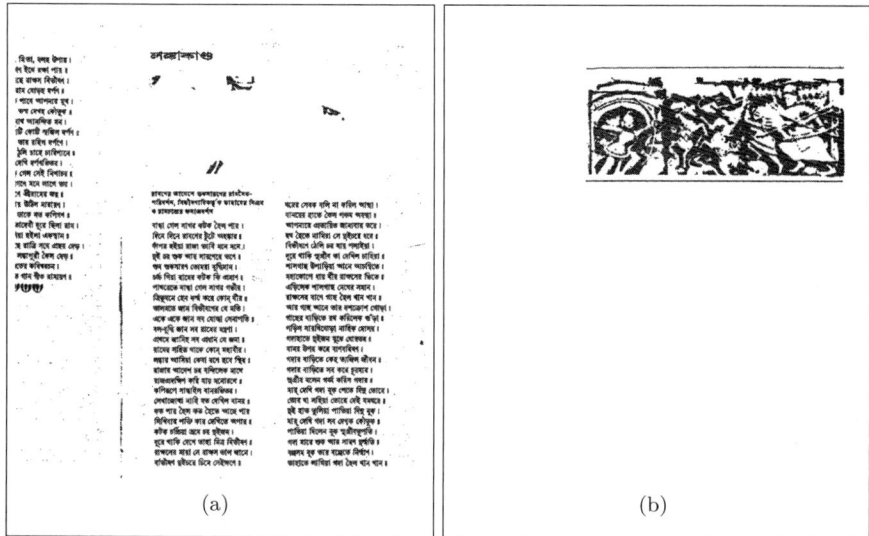

Figure 16.6 An example separating text and nontext components in a document image shown in Fig. 16.5. (a) Text components. (b) Nontext components. (*Source*: Adapted from fig. 3.7 of Dey (2019).)

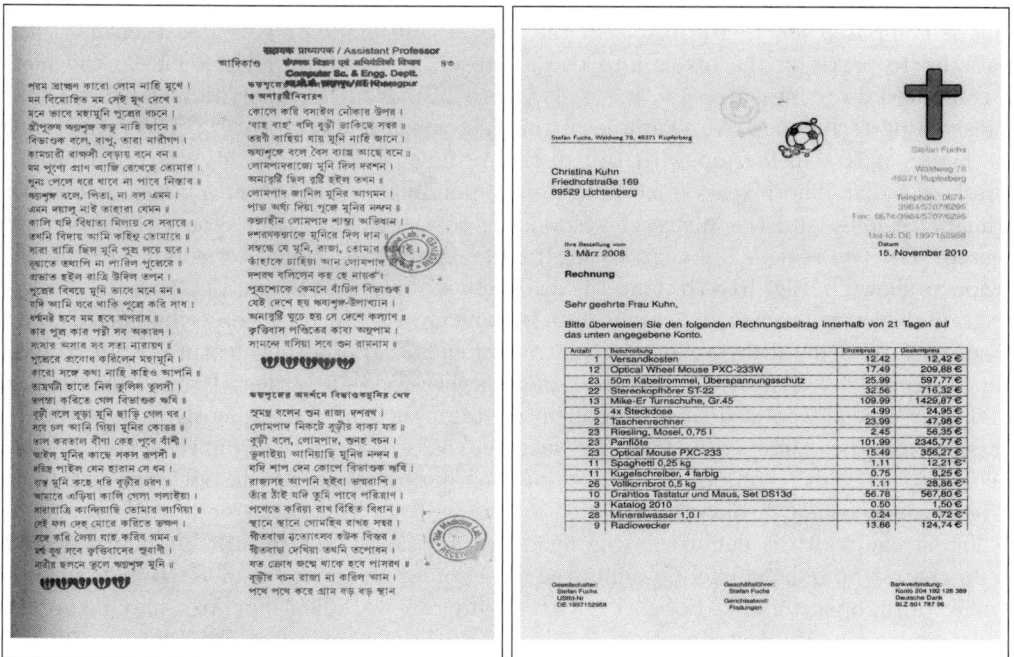

Figure 16.7 Typical examples of document images with stamps. (*Source*: Dr Soumyadeep Dey for sharing images from his PhD work (Dey, 2019). The right image is obtained from the StaVer Dataset (Micenkov and van Beusekom, 2011) available at http://madm.dfki.de/downloads-ds-staver.) See Color Plates (page 823).

them as outliers serves the crucial purpose of their separation. The typical approach involves detecting these stamps and logos, which may appear in color or black and white. Typical examples are shown in Fig. 16.7, where the documents contain stamps and logos of different colors and shapes. These document images are synthetically generated data using a set of logos and stamps placed on various scanned images of text.

The processing pipeline is as follows. At first, the foreground is separated from the background. Notably, the foreground exhibits two distinct colors: the primary color of the document and the secondary color associated with stamp and logo objects. Accordingly, the foreground is further divided into two distinct groups. Finally, the outlier components are identified by analyzing information related to location, stroke width, height of enclosing rectangles, pixel density, and other relevant factors.

16.4.1 | Stamp and logo detection

An example of a scanned page of a document containing colored stamp and logo is shown in Fig. 16.8 (a). The first step in the process of detecting stamps and logos is binarization of the document. Here, unlike thresholding, the color value of each binarized pixel is retained, so that, each colored pixel is a three-dimensional (3-D) vector. The eigenvectors are computed from the covariance matrix of all the colored pixel values. Then, the unit vector, e, along the direction of the principle eigenvector (eigenvector with dominant eigenvalue) is computed. Given the color vector, x, of a pixel, its component along e is computed as $z = x \cdot e$. This is computed for all the pixels in the image. The mode of z, z_m, is then used as a statistics to partition the pixels into two groups. The absolute deviation from the mode is computed as a measure, $y = |z - z_m|$, whose histogram is bipartitioned using Otsu's thresholding technique.[3] An example of this histogram is shown in Fig. 16.9. As seen in the figure, it is a histogram with two distinguishing peaks, which are separated using a threshold value. The pixels of the image corresponding to the lower values of y form the primary regions, and the pixels corresponding to the higher values form the secondary regions. The two regions are the two separated components, which correspond to the text region as shown in Fig. 16.8 (b), and the logos and stamps as shown in Fig. 16.8 (c). A block diagram depicting the flow of computation is shown in Fig. 16.10. As described in this block diagram, after separating secondary color components, appropriate features are extracted from a connected component to determine whether it is an outlier. If it is identified as an outlier, it is categorized as a component of stamp or logo. Subsequently each of them is classified as either a stamp or a logo. The features that are extracted from these components, include stroke width, component height, location and pixel density in both primary (color of text) and secondary color parts.

The stroke width is defined as the length of a straight line from a boundary pixel P to its nearest boundary pixel Q, along the direction of the gradient of P. To compute the stroke width, operators like Sobel, Prewitt, or any other gradient operator may be applied to determine the gradient direction. Then, Bressenham's algorithm (Bresenham, 1965) is employed to search the boundary pixel along the gradient. It follows the edge to locate the

---

[3] See Section 1.3.3 of Chapter 1.

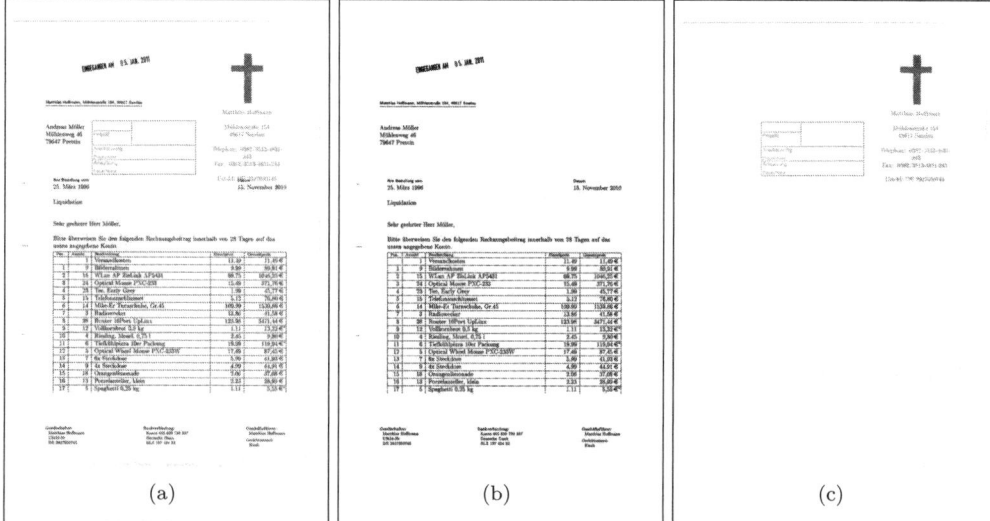

Figure 16.8 (a) An example of a document image containing colored logo and stamp, and separation of (b) text and (c) logo and stamp. (*Source*: Adapted from fig. 4.4 of Dey (2019). The original image is obtained from the StaVer Dataset (Micenkov and van Beusekom, 2011) available at http://madm.dfki.de/downloads-ds-staver.)

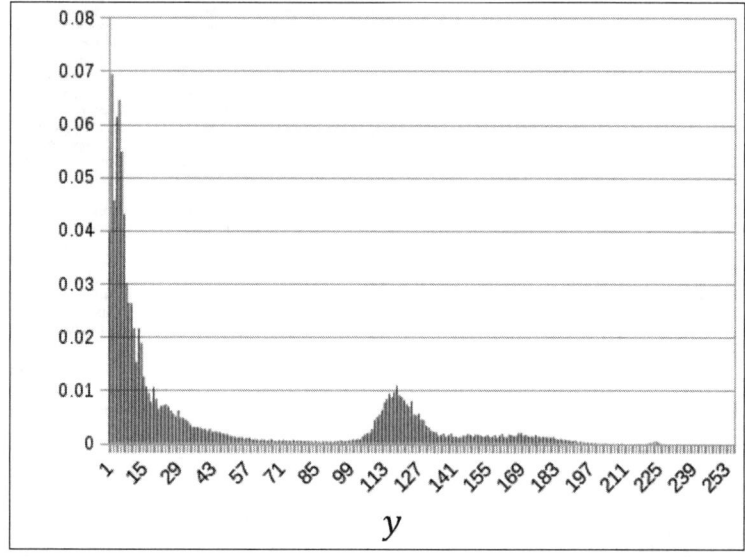

Figure 16.9 Typical histogram of the measure of deviation from mode, $y = |z - z_m|$.
(*Source*: Adapted from fig. 4.4 (b) of Dey (2019).)

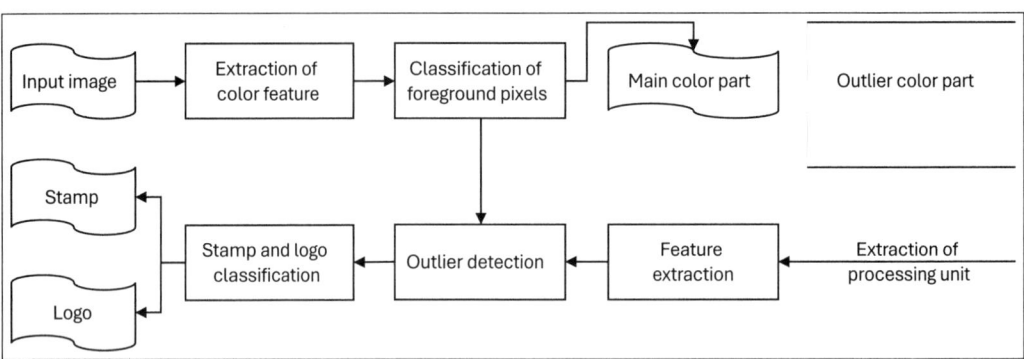

Figure 16.10 Block diagram of the process for separating logos and stamps in a document image. (*Source*: Adapted from fig. 4.2 of Dey (2019).)

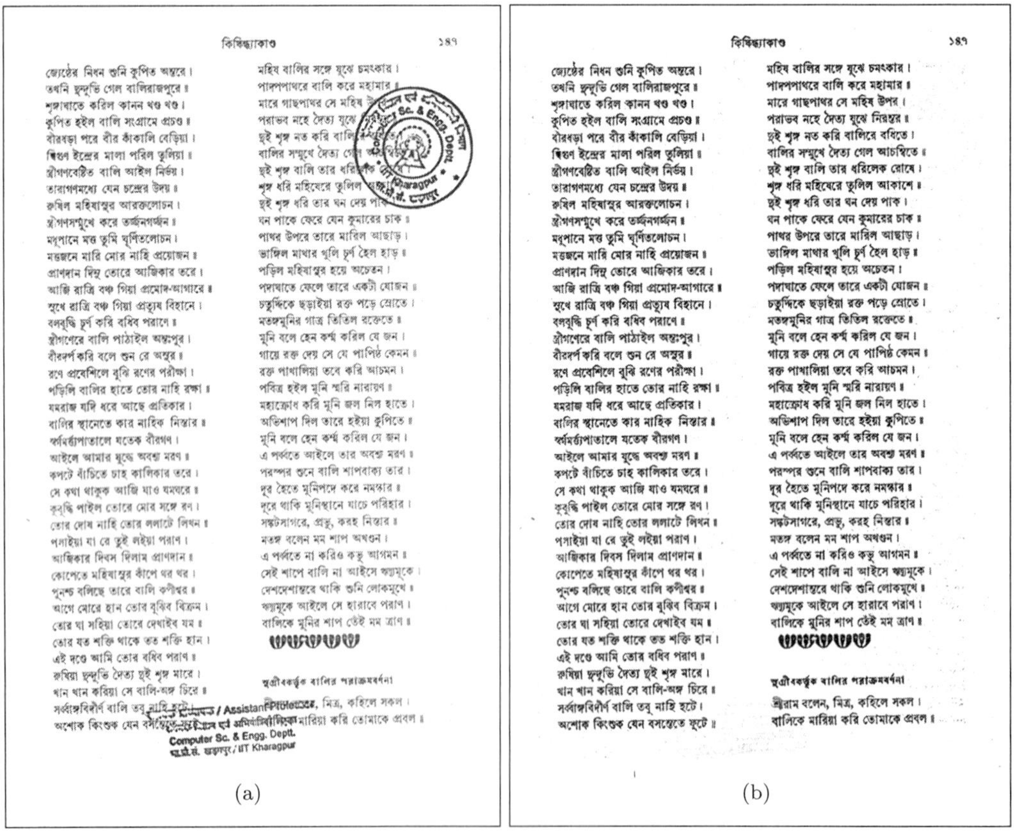

Figure 16.11 Example of stamp removal in a document image. (*Source*: Dr Soumyadeep Dey for sharing images from his PhD work (Dey, 2019).)

boundary pixel along the gradient. After computing the lengths of all stroke widths, the mean stroke width is used as a feature. Other features include the height of the component and its position within the document. Specifically, the height and center of only isothetic rectangular covers are computed. Then, pixel density-related features are extracted. There are two types of pixel densities, namely, (1) *type-I pixel density* measuring the fraction of foreground pixels in the rectangular cover, and (2) *type-II pixel density* measuring the fraction of foreground pixels in the area within the contour.

The rules employed for declaring outliers involve computing the modes of mean stroke widths and heights for the foreground components. An outlier is declared when a component significantly deviates from both the modes. To achieve this, Otsu threshold (refer to Section 1.3.3 of Chapter 1) is applied to the measures of deviation, similar to the approach used for separating primary and secondary color components of the foreground. Additionally, pixel density serves as a distinguishing factor between logos, stamps, and other outliers. Outliers identified by the type-I pixel density adhere to the same rules as those for stamps and logos. The position and type of pixel density are also used to differentiate between logos and stamps. Consequently, logos typically appear in the top, right, or left corners of a document, exhibiting higher pixel density, relative to the area enclosed by the contour of the component. This approach is also used for detecting stamps, then removing them, and performing inpainting in the removed segments.

An example shown in Fig. 16.11 demonstrates this application. In Fig. 16.11 (a), there are two components in the document, the primary color component (which contains an outlier) and the secondary color component (also containing outliers, but signifying text components). The detection of stamps can be leveraged for eliminating it from the document, as shown in Fig. 16.11 (b).

16.5 | Layout analysis of textual blocks

The analysis of textual blocks involves their processing and determination of their layout. Two assumptions are made during this process.

(i) It is assumed that there is no skew in document images. That is, the text lines are perfectly horizontal in the document.

(ii) There is no overlap of text lines in the document.

There are three main approaches for analyzing the textual blocks, such as, using projection, smearing, and connected component analysis.

In the *projection based approach*, horizontal and vertical projection profiles of the text lines within the corresponding textual section are utilized. These profiles are used to determine the gaps between the lines, indicating a separation between them. Additionally, the gaps between the characters are detected using vertical profiles of lines. By combining these two profiles, various rectangular areas are reconstructed and empty regions that do not contain any textual content are filtered out. These filtered areas constitute the textual part of the document.

In the *smearing based approach*, the gaps along the text lines (particularly, the horizontal gaps) are filled-up. The gap filling process provides rectangular bounding boxes around the respective text elements. Within the text region, there are horizontal rows and vertical columns. Among them, all the narrower gaps are filled. The gap filling may also be performed at multiple scales, which allows to identify individual characters and words. By filling the gaps between the characters, rectangular boxes representing the words can be obtained. Similarly, filling the gaps between the words and lines yield rectangular boxes corresponding to the lines and paragraph, respectively. The layouts of different textual entities are obtained by this approach.

In the *connected component based approach*, the connected components are first computed. Then, their spatial arrangement or layout is determined using geometric or graph based analysis, such as, Delaunay triangulation (Preparata and Shamos, 1985), minimum spanning tree (Cormen et al., 2009), etc., to build a hierarchy of the layout. Out of these approaches, let us typically elaborate the smearing based approach.

16.5.1 | Smearing based approach

In smearing based approach, certain thumb rules are employed to exploit the observed statistical relationships between the spatial heights of the characters and the words. For instance, let the mode of the distribution of height of characters in the text be denoted by h_m. Based on this modal height, the following thumb rules are applied in the computation.

- The minimum height of a word should exceed half of the modal height. i.e., minimum height of a word $> \frac{h_m}{2}$.

- The maximum height of a word should not exceed 1.5 times the modal height. Hence, maximum height of a word $< \frac{3h_m}{2}$.

- The maximum gap between the characters within a word should not exceed half of the modal height, Hence, maximum gap between characters within a word $< \frac{hm}{2}$.

- The maximum gap between the words within a line should not exceed the modal height. Therefore, the maximum gap between words within a line $< h_m$.

- The maximum gap between lines within a paragraph should not exceed twice the modal height. Hence, the maximum gap between lines within a paragraph $< 2h_m$.

By applying these rules, the thresholds for gap filling are determined. These parameters may also be computed adaptively by using projection profiles.

The smearing based technique is used for paragraph detection. At first, the connected components are obtained, and the distribution of their heights is noted. Typical distribution of heights of connected components is shown in Fig. 16.12. The mode of the heights, h_m is determined, which is assumed as the modal height of a character. Then, h_m is used to set the thresholds for smearing the gaps for respective components. By applying the horizontal and vertical gap filling operations successively, the connected components to form segments of words, lines, and paragraphs are extracted. Additionally, the page frame can also be recovered from these components.

An example of smearing at different stages is shown in Fig. 16.13. Results of word smearing, line smearing, and paragraph smearing are shown in Figs. 16.13 (a), (b), and (c), respectively. Typical result of the layout analysis of a scanned document page in Fig. 16.5 (a) is shown in Fig. 16.14. In the results, some of the blocks in the page are not

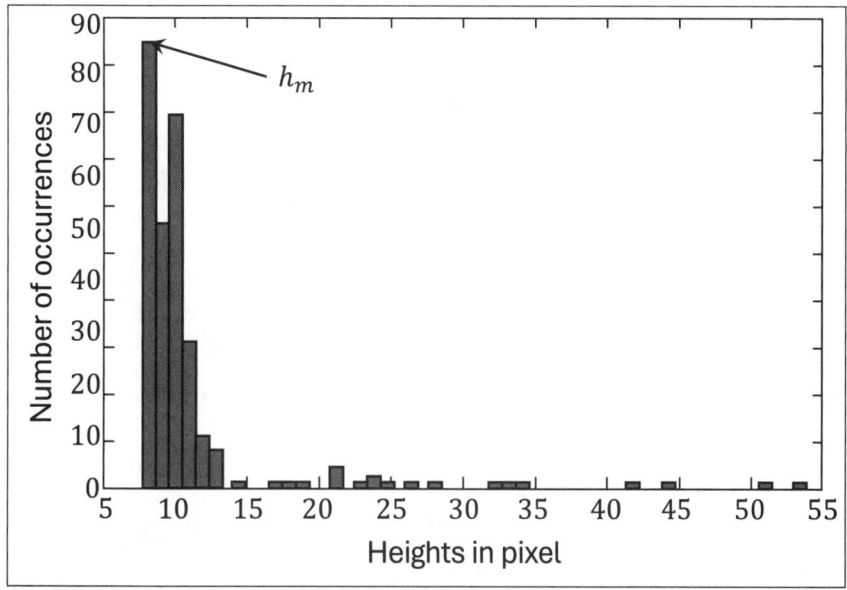

Figure 16.12 Typical distribution of heights of connected components. (*Source*: Adapted from fig. 3.2 of Dey (2019).)

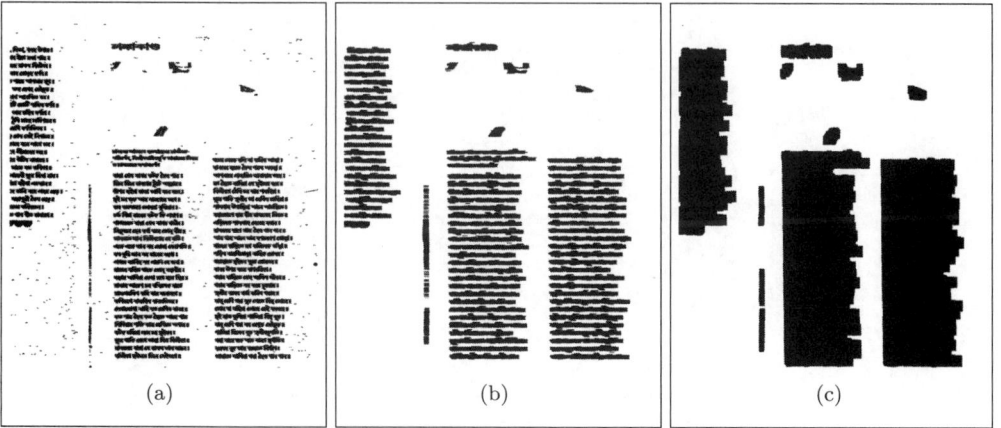

Figure 16.13 An example of smearing at different stages. (a) Word smearing, (b) line smearing, and (c) paragraph smearing. (*Source*: Adapted from figs. 3.9 and 3.11 of Dey (2019).)

shown, since those components are considered as not a part of the textual component. Also, some of the noisy components are removed to clean the document. For example, the component resulting from the junction of the book, as seen in the figure, is not included in the layout.

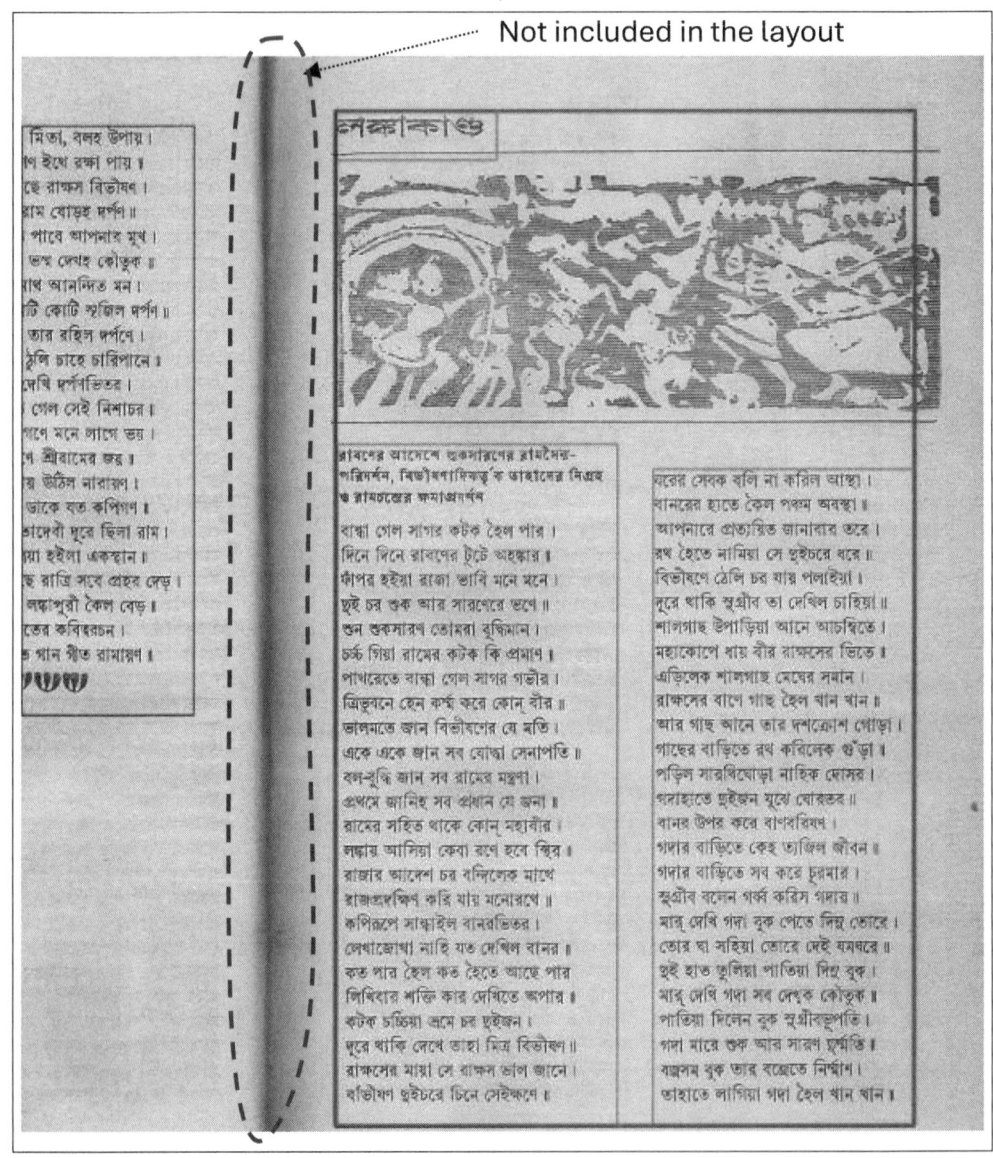

Figure 16.14 Result of layout analysis. (*Source*: Dr Soumyadeep Dey for sharing images from his PhD work (Dey, 2019).)

16.6 | Document understanding

Following document analysis, the next stage of document processing is the document understanding. This stage mostly involves various tasks related to text processing, like optical character recognition (OCR), language detection, script detection, font detection, etc. There exist other types of related tasks too, such as relating text and nontext segments using plots, charts, annotations, or other media elements. When considering these tasks, several other tasks also may require to be carried out. Other examples are recognition of the language, identification of the script and the font, etc. The language of the text in a document may be recognized either in the image or in OCR generated text. Scripts are used in writing or printing across multiple languages, e.g., Latin for English, German, French, Italian, Spanish; Devanagari for Hindi and Sanskrit; Kannada, Tamil, etc. Though all languages are not uniquely mapped to their respective scripts, detecting a script allows to identify a set of languages associated with it. For a given script, detecting the font involves analyzing the style and size of characters or graphemes. A *grapheme* refers to a specific atomic unit within a given writing system. Essentially, it represents the minimal significant orthographic component. For example, in English writing system, graphemes include basic letters of the English alphabet, punctuation marks, numerals, diacritics, and many other components.

16.6.1 | Script identification

Detecting script may assist in identifying a set of languages associated with it. For instance, the Roman script can be associated with English, German, French, and Spanish. With certain variations, most of the European languages primarily use the Roman script. Several Indian languages use the Devanagari script, including Sanskrit, Hindi, Marathi, etc. The Devanagari script has its own distinct characteristics. Similarly, the Bangla script is employed for various languages such as Bengali, Assamese, and Manipuri. The Arabic script serves as the writing system for a bunch of languages, like Arabic, Farsi, and Urdu.

The principle behind script identification is its characteristic of being distinguished by a collection of graphemes, allographs, glyphs, and other such elements. *Allographs*, are the variants of the same grapheme. *Glyphs* and signs are often used to describe the physical aspects and properties of a grapheme, allograph, or a diacritic symbol used in the script of a language. The glyphs are defined by a spatial arrangement of straight and twisted lines, strokes, curves, hooks, loops, etc. The direction of writing is also a key aspect of script identification. Most languages predominantly follow a left-to-right direction. However, for Arabic, the direction of writing is right-to-left. While some scripts incorporate both lowercase and uppercase letters, many languages do not have this convention. For example, the Latin script has the usage of lowercase and uppercase letters, but such practice does not exist in Devanagari.

Zone-wise character partition

There are some indicative principles for script identification. For example, consider Fig. 16.15, where two words written in the Roman script (left) and the Bangla script (right) are shown. From the figure, it is evident that both the scripts exhibit three distinct zones, which can be further partitioned. Specifically for these two scripts, the definitions of these zones are delineated as follows.

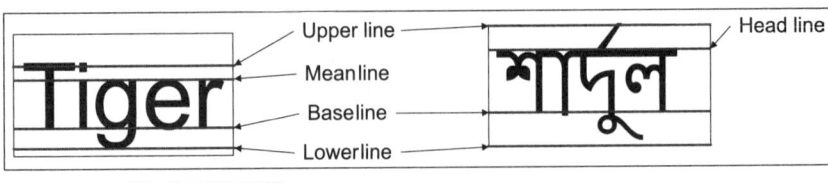

Figure 16.15 Examples of Roman and Bangla scripts.

Figure 16.16 Example of uppercase letters in Roman script.

(i) The first zone lies between the upper line and the mean line or head line.

(ii) The second zone is sandwiched between the mean line and the base line.

(iii) The third zone extends from the base line to the lower line.

These characteristics hold true for both the scripts.

In the case of the Bangla script, the lower line binding the upper zone is known as head line, which is analogous to the mean line for the Roman script. The headline serves as an uppermost boundary line for the text. Similarly, the lower line represents the lowermost boundary line. The mean line is an imaginary horizontal reference containing most of the uppermost points of the characters. The baseline predominantly encompasses the lowermost points of the characters. Additionally, a noteworthy feature of English or the Roman script is that, sometimes the words are written using only uppercase letters, where the mean line coincides with the upper line coincide, and so does the base line with the lower line. An instance is shown in Fig. 16.16. This provides an alternative method for identifying whether a script has been written using uppercase letters. Interestingly, this three-zone separation, which is inherent to both English and Bangla scripts, is not applicable to several other scripts, like Chinese and Arabic scripts.

Features for script identification

The distinguishing features used for identifying scripts can be analyzed through projection profiles of the partitioned zones. Different zones play distinct roles in distinguishing some of the scripts, such as, Latin, Devanagri, Bangla, etc. Several other features can also be utilized for this purpose. Among such features, two prominent profiles are as follows.

(i) Maximum run of 1's (or the object points) in rows of the horizontal profile.

In scripts like Bangla and Devanagari, due to the presence of a common head line (shirOrEkhA), the maximum run occurs in the top rows of the profile. For the Arabic text, the maximum run typically appears in the lower rows. For Chinese and Latin text, the maximum run is relatively small. If the value is small, the crossing counts in the rows of the horizontal profile is further examined.

(ii) The crossing count in rows of the horizontal profile.

The crossing count is the number of the transitions from object points to background points (1 to 0 and 0 to 1 in the rows of the horizontal profile). To address the insignificant gaps caused by noise, a run-length smoothing algorithm is applied, where runs of 0's between a pair of 1's are filled. The percentage of the character filled-up area of the smoothed text line, relative to its original version is significantly higher for Chinese and Arabic, compared to Latin.

Another distinct feature for script identification is defined using the *water reservoir principle*. In a given alphabet, hypothetical water may flood from any of its sides. That is, considering any specific alphabet, water is hypothetically poured onto it from four different sides: top, bottom, left, and right. The resulting effects of water flooding from the four directions yield various measures. The measures that are related to reservoir are used as features, such as, height, base line, area, profile of reservoir width, etc. For example, consider the letter "X". The resulting effects of water flooding from the four directions are shown in Fig. 16.17.

Interestingly, these widths usually exhibit monotonically increasing or decreasing behavior, with the rows, for English letters, as seen in Fig. 16.17. This trend may not be true for other scripts. For example, consider a letter of Bengali, "la", which is shown in Fig. 16.18. When filled from the bottom, the width shows nonmonotonic variation.

Counting the number of vertical runs provides another distinguishing feature for script identification. For instance, the number of thick vertical black runs is a feature, which is

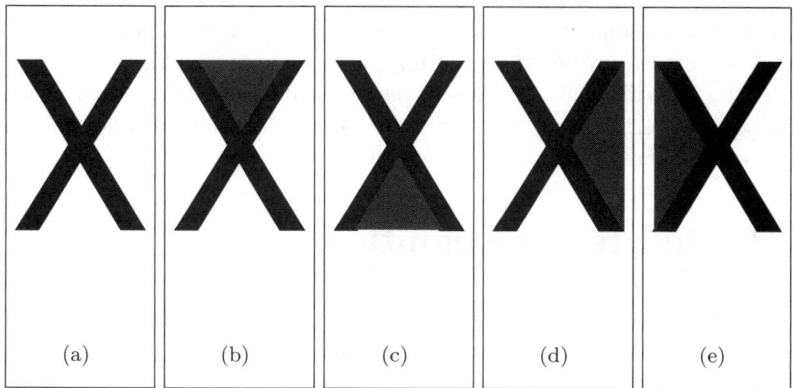

(a)　　　(b)　　　(c)　　　(d)　　　(e)

Figure 16.17 An example of water flooding from the four directions for the Roman letter "X". (a) The letter, and its flooding from (b) top, (c) bottom, (d) right, and (e) left directions.

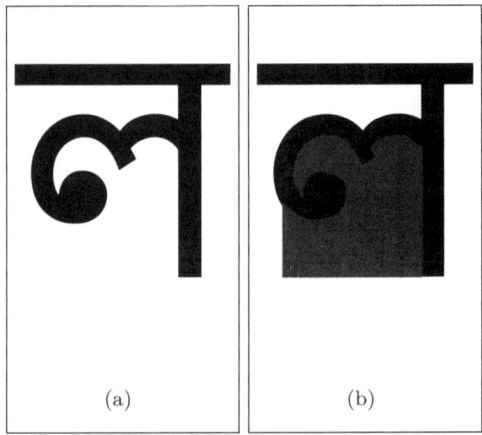

(a) (b)

Figure 16.18 Water flooding from the bottom direction for the Bengali letter "la".
(a) The letter, and (b) bottom reservoir.

particularly a distinguishing feature in Chinese scripts. Its value is high for Chinese script (typically 4 or more) and low for English (usually, 1 or 2).

A block of text may also be used to define features, since it forms a visual pattern distinctive for a script. Features like moments, the concavity distribution, textural features, fractal features, gray level coocurrence matrix (GLCM), wavelets, Gabor features, etc. can be extracted from a block of text. Subsequently, different kinds of classifiers, such as linear discriminant analysis (LDA), multi-layer perceptron (MLP), K-nearest neighbor (K-NN), Gaussian mixture model (GMM), support vector machine (SVM), etc., can be employed on these features for script identification.

16.6.2 | Font recognition

The features used for optical font recognition can be put into two categories, global and local features. Text density, size, orientation, spacing of letters, etc. are the examples of global features, which are representative of the entire document. On the other hand, local features are mostly the features from individual letters, whose characteristics effectively define the font. Fonts can be identified on the basis of particularities of letters, such as the shapes of serifs (coved, squared, triangular, etc.) and their representation in different angles. These features are used to identify both script and font.

16.7 | Printed text recognition

A general computational flow for printed text recognition consists of several processing units, which are depicted in Fig. 16.19. Before delving into the analysis, some preprocessing steps are executed. These preprocessing operations include denoising, deskewing, and dewarping. Then, the textual blocks are extracted. This involves binarization of the pages of the document, separation of text from nontext regions, and layout analysis. The text is further segmented into lines and characters using the techniques such as, smearing, and connected components. Subsequently, the characters are

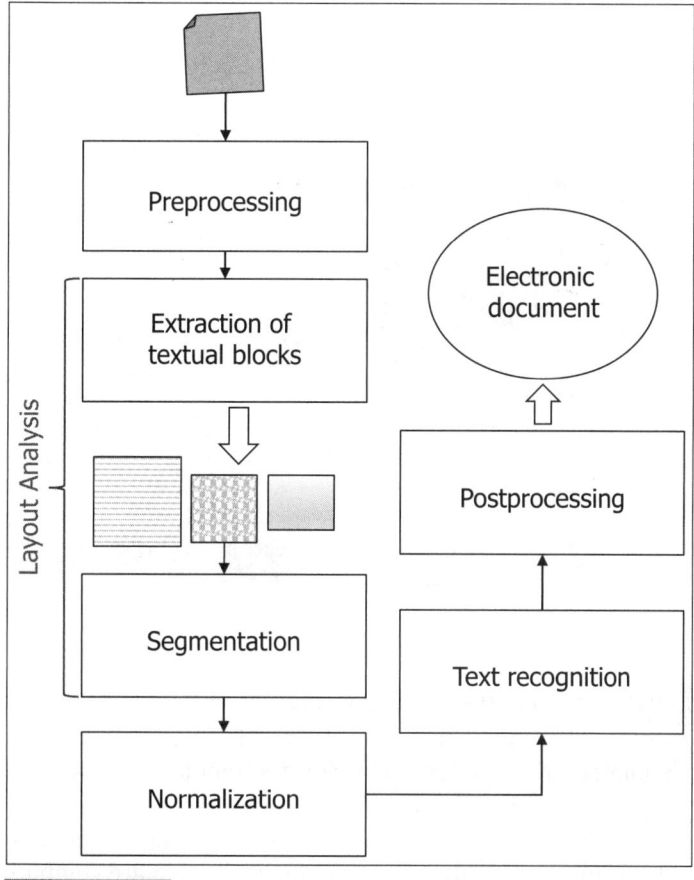

Figure 16.19 Processing pipeline for printed text recognition.

normalized to account for variations in fonts and sizes. The text recognition is then performed by recognizing isolated characters, consecutive characters, or entire words. Typically, the recognition process includes feature extraction, followed by classification. After obtaining a processed text string, post-processing techniques are applied using a language model to correct errors at the word level or sentence level.

16.7.1 | Skew detection and correction

Skew correction is one of the essential preprocessing techniques in the text recognition pipeline. The skew occurs when a document is not placed in the upright position in a scanner, effectively resulting in a rotation. The center of the rotation corresponds to one of the corners. An example of skew is shown in Fig. 16.20, where two types of rotations are shown, rotation centered at the bottom-left corner (Fig. 16.20 (a)) and rotation centered at the top-left corner (Fig. 16.20 (b)).

(a)   (b)

Figure 16.20 Examples of skew in documents, where center of rotation lies at (a) bottom-left corner, and (b) top-left corner. (*Source*: Prof. Sanjoy Pratihar, Indian Institute of Information Technology, Kalyani, for sharing images from his PhD work (Pratihar, 2015).)

The underlying principle of skew detection involves detecting the directions of text lines. To achieve this, the gradients and directions, and edge linking are computed. The discrete directions are estimated using Farey sequence (Pratihar et al., 2013) and the edge points are linked by Hough transform. By calculating the skew angle, the points in the image are rotated, centered at the respective corner, by the same amount in the opposite direction. The skew detection process applies to both horizontal and vertical skews. Detecting these lines enhances the robustness of computation. Examples of skew correction of images shown in Figs. 16.20 (a) and (b) are shown in Fig. 16.21 and Fig. 16.22, respectively.

There are also various other preprocessing operations that are necessary to account for scanning related issues for binarization. A few common examples are as follows.

- Pages may be warped, resulting in the text not being in a straight horizontal line. Instead, it may exhibit a curvilinear structure, where dewarping becomes essential.

- Differential fading may be present, where the intensity across the white page is not uniform.

- Ink bleed-through may occur, making the impression from opposite side of the pages visible on the other side.

- Sometimes, shadows may fill the document, causing nonuniform backgrounds, particularly in the documents imaged by cameras. Shadow removal becomes necessary in such cases.

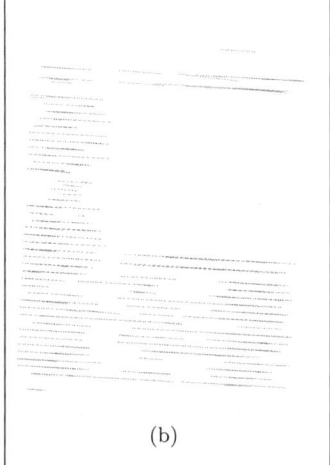

(a)   (b)   (c)

Figure 16.21 Example of skew correction of Fig. 16.20 (a). (a) Original image, (b) detected direction of text-line, and (c) skew-corrected document. (*Source*: Prof. Sanjoy Pratihar, Indian Institute of Information Technology, Kalyani, for sharing images from his PhD work (Pratihar, 2015).)

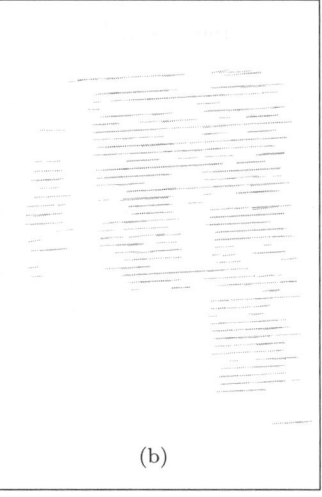

(a)   (b)   (c)

Figure 16.22 Example of skew correction of Fig. 16.20 (b). (a) Original image, (b) detected direction of text-line, and (c) skew-corrected document. (*Source*: Prof. Sanjoy Pratihar, Indian Institute of Information Technology, Kalyani, for sharing images from his PhD work (Pratihar, 2015).)

- Human activities during reading may introduce artifacts, such as underlining, striking out portions, or encircling. Artifact removal is needed to account for such undesired marks. This may also be in the form of annotations and comments, which often appear near the margins. Removing them ensures cleaner text. Certain lines of texts can be highlighted for reference. such highlights can also be eliminated during preprocessing.

16.7.2 | Normalization of character of grapheme

After preprocessing and binarization, the layout analysis is performed to get the respective components of characters, words and text lines. The core task of document recognition is isolated character recognition. A key challenge in this task is that same character may occur in different variants due to imaging, illumination, distortions, etc. So There are various kinds of normalization which enforce some uniformity to account for these variations and assist the recognition task. The moment based technique is one such popular normalization scheme. For an image, $f(x, y)$, in a rectangular box, its pq-th moment, m_{pq}, is defined by Eq. 16.1.

$$m_{pq} = \sum_x \sum_y x^p y^q f(x, y) \tag{16.1}$$

Using the pq-th moments the centroids, x_c and y_c, are defined as in Eq. 16.2.

$$x_c = \frac{m_{10}}{m_{00}}, \text{ and } y_c = \frac{m_{01}}{m_{00}} \tag{16.2}$$

Also, the central moments, μ_{pq}, are defined as in Eq. 16.3.

$$\mu_{pq} = \sum_x \sum_y (x - x_c)^p (y - y_c)^q f(x, y) \tag{16.3}$$

These moments provide an estimate of the stroke area of an input image. This is used to align the centroid of an input image and the boundary of the stroke area to the center and the boundary of a normalized box, respectively. Toward this, the stroke widths along x and y directions, δ_x and δ_y, are computed as in Eq. 16.4.

$$\delta_x = \alpha \sqrt{\frac{\mu_{20}}{m_{00}}}, \text{ and } \delta_y = \sqrt{\frac{\mu_{02}}{m_{00}}} \tag{16.4}$$

Using the stroke widths, δ_x and δ_y, and the centroids, x_c and y_c, the bounding rectangular box of any isolated character is mapped to a normalized box of size $W \times H$ as in Eq. 16.5.

$$x' = W \frac{x - x_c}{\delta_x} + \frac{W}{2}, \text{ and } y' = H \frac{y - y_c}{\delta_y} + \frac{H}{2} \tag{16.5}$$

where x' and y' are the coordinates of the normalized box.

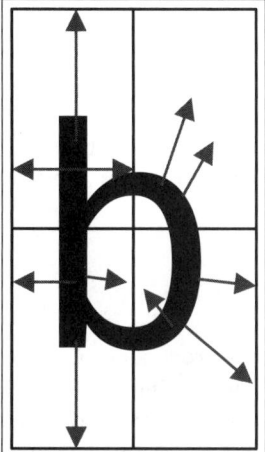

Figure 16.23 Illustration of histogram based feature.

16.7.3 | Feature extraction

There are various kinds of feature extraction methods to represent isolated characters, which are performed after normalization. Few of the popular features are histogram based methods such as, histogram of gradients, histogram of Gabor orientations, topological features such as, number of connected components and holes, Euler number, approximate Euler number, the count of number of vertical and horizontal lines, etc. Furthermore, local attributes can be captured by concatenating histograms of the partitioned blocks, representing the feature.

A typical example of histogram of gradients based feature representation is illustrated using the Roman letter 'b', which is shown in Fig. 16.23. The histogram of gradients is displayed with smaller partitions, such as a 2×2 partition, as shown in the figure. The gradients are denoted by the arrows in the figure, pointing their directions. In each of the four partitions, a histogram of certain number of bins is formed. The directions of the gradients contribute to the definition of the bins. Typically, 12 orientation bins are employed. The bins are accumulated by either unit values or the magnitude of the gradients to form the histogram. Similarly, histograms of Gabor filter responses may also be used to form features. Specifically, four orientations, $0°$, $45°$, $90°$, and $135°$, are considered for forming the histogram using the Gabor filter responses, which are used to classify the characters.

16.7.4 | Character recognition

Machine learning literature presents various classification schemes for isolated characters. These include techniques such as SVMs, decision trees, random forests, Bayesian classification, artificial neural networks, etc. A few classification techniques are also discussed in Chapter 7. Recent state-of-the-art methodologies include deep learning techniques for character recognition, particularly using convolutional neural network architectures (refer to Chapter 9). The advantage of deep learning architectures is its ability to facilitate end-to-end learning, encompassing both feature extraction module (convolutional layers) and classification module (a fully connected layer). Once trained appropriately, this model is applied for classification tasks. However, it is essential to have a substantial amount of data for training. Text recognition involves identifying sequences and spatial ordering of characters or words within a text. In this context, sequence-based deep neural models (Section 9.5 of Chapter 9), such as LSTM (Hochreiter and Schmidhuber, 1997) and Bi-LSTM (Thireou and Reczko, 2007) are found to be useful (Kantipudi et al., 2021).

Summary

In this chapter, we primarily discuss processing of printed documents. However, there are various other types of tasks for processing handwritten documents, scene text, stone inscriptions, and embedded text in images and videos. These tasks may necessitate different pipelines, not necessarily the same computational flow discussed for text recognition and related applications in this chapter. In the application specific context, the range of documents include historical documents, cinematographic texts, posters, number plates of cars, official document, medical prescriptions, diagnosis reports, filled-up forms, OMR answer sheets, etc. Their interpretations contribute to the diverse analysis within document processing.

In summary, document processing is applied across various aspects of human activity. Initially, the industry primarily focused on OCR and the conversion of scanned printed text into electronic text. Due to technological advancements, document processing now encompasses diverse domains and finds many applications in our social interaction, and in many other areas of science and technology. These applications include recognition of scene text, office automation, automatic scanning and reading of barcodes and batch numbers in manufacturing units, reading number plates of a vehicle, etc.

Exercises

(i) What is a document? In processing a document, what are meant by its geometric and logical structures? Give examples of various components of a document used in describing its structure.

(ii) Identify the major stages of processing of the layout of a document, and briefly describe the computation involved in these stages.

(iii) Describe a method of separating text and nontext using Hough transform.

(iv) Describe the method of detecting color stamps and logos by identifying the presence of primary and secondary colors in a document.

(v) How logos and stamps are detected as outliers among other regular components of a document?

(vi) Discuss various approaches of layout analysis.

(vii) Describe the smearing based method of detecting paragraphs, lines and words in a document.

(viii) Discuss various tasks involved in understanding a document.

(**ix**) Describe techniques of identification of Latin and Devanagari scripts.

(**x**) How fonts of printed English text are recognized in a document?

(**xi**) Describe a pipeline of processing a document for recognizing printed text.

(**xii**) What is meant by the skew of a document with reference to OCR? Describe techniques for detecting skew of a document and correcting it.

(**xiii**) What is a grapheme? Why normalization of a grapheme is required for recognizing it? Describe the method of moment based normalization.

(**xiv**) Describe various ways of extraction of features from an isolated character.

17

Biometry

Biometrics is the science and technology of uniquely identifying a person by the physical, physiological, genomic, or behavioral characteristics. For example, the biometric traits or signatures for unique characterization of a person may be obtained from fingerprint, palm print, face, iris, retina, shape of ear, voice, signature, gait, vein in the hand, odor, handwriting, DNA sequences, etc. Some of these traits are evidently visible and are often used in our social interactions to identify a person. But many of them may need use of technology and computational processing for extraction of biometric characteristic signatures from them and verifying them subsequently. For a unique identification of a person, the biometric data, also referred to as the biometric signature, should have the properties of uniqueness and permanence. The uniqueness is the characteristics that uniquely identifies an individual person and permanence implies that it should remain unchanged throughout the life of the individual. However, permanence in absolute sense is seldom true in practice. In view of that, it is pragmatic to use those biometric traits, which are expected to remain mostly unaltered for a significant period of time. During this period, there may be some marginal deviations that can be largely tolerated for a practical solution.

17.1 | Biometric system

A *biometric system* is primarily designed for managing the identity of a person. Identity management is required in almost every sphere of social interaction and activities like, border control, access control to certain resources, to avail conditional facilities (food, LPG connection, etc.), financial transactions, admission to examinations, certifying the qualification and competence, etc. There may also be various related tasks other than identifying a person like, determining age and gender of an individual, establishing kinship between two persons, etc. There are three main generic tasks that are involved in such a system of identity management.

(i) *Enrolment*: This is a kind of archival task where a person is enrolled by capturing and storing the biometric signatures. These signatures are indexed for fast retrieval.

741

The facility for updating the enrolment information or deleting them is also provided in the system. These are similar to different kinds of standard database transactions, that are operational in a biometric system.

(ii) *Verification*: This step is to verify a person given his/her biometric data and other personal (secondary) information. Usually, in the enrolled database, the biometric signature of a person is stored with other secondary information, such as enrolment id, name, address, etc. to identify the person. The acquired biometric signature is matched with the stored signature for this purpose.

(iii) *Recognition*: This is the process of identifying a person, given a biometric data from the database. In this case, any other secondary information, such as the personal details like name, date of birth, identity number, etc., is not provided. Only the biometric data is captured and it is searched for its availability in the database. The person is then identified or recognized as the candidate in the enrolled database whose signature matches with the queried biometric data.

When only the biometric data is taken as input, it is akin to the retrieval task of a content-based image retrieval system. In our context, only image-based biometry is considered here, which involves various modalities. The images of specific traits are captured and analyzed to obtain signatures, which are used for identification, verification, or enrolment. Some of these modalities include fingerprints, faces, iris scans, palm prints, etc. The biometric systems particular to three specific modalities, fingerprint, face, and iris, are discussed in this chapter.

17.1.1 | Building blocks of a biometric system

The fundamental building blocks of a biometric system are illustrated in Fig. 17.1. The system is built for a user who will be enrolled, verified, or identified with her biometric signature. Additionally, a system administrator oversees decisions related to system operation. In the basic system, the user's biometric data is sensed by a sensor. An

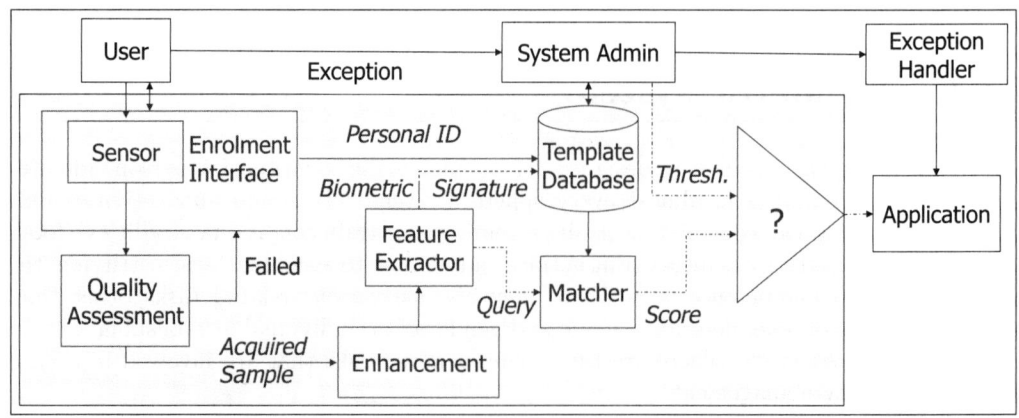

Figure 17.1 Building blocks of a biometric system (adapted from fig. 1.3 of Jain et al. (2011).)

enrolment interface captures the data. It is used for enrolment/verification/identification of the user. Within the system, a module called quality assessment plays a crucial role in ensuring the data quality. This is an essential component, since poor quality of data results in inaccurate decisions. By evaluating specific characteristics, the quality of the data is judged. If the quality is seen to be poor, the data is not accepted by the system, prompting the user to provide it again. This interaction with the system is necessary to forward the desired data to subsequent modules of processing. When the quality is assured, the data processing continues to further stages like, preprocessing stage that enhances the image quality and feature extraction that provides the *biometric signature*. This signature, also referred to as a *template*, digitally represents the underlying trait. Verification is performed by leveraging the template database and personal identity.

In the context of biometric systems, both verification and enrolment rely on user data. During enrolment, essential user information, including personal identity, is stored. Verification involves treating the user's signature as a query and matching it against corresponding signatures in the template database. For identification, the process is blind. In this case, the database is searched to identify templates that match the query. Thresholds, set by system administrators, differentiate verification and identification processes. If the matching score exceeds the threshold, it is considered as a match. Accepting the signature confirms the person's identity, allowing necessary applications to proceed.

17.1.2 | Issues in biometric system

Designing and implementing such systems involve addressing several critical issues. These include system's speed, accuracy, and the choice of feature representation. Ensuring high-quality of samples during their acquisition is also crucial, as poor-quality data can lead to inaccurate decisions. Here, interoperability across different domains and regions may also be required, making it necessary to standardize the templates that can be understood by all systems across different domains. The privacy and security considerations also play a vital role in the system.

For desired speed and accuracy, appropriate indexing schemes and matching algorithms have to be carefully selected. Additionally, the choice of features, with properties like uniqueness, performance, and universality, also plays an essential role. Universality ensures applicability to all individuals interacting with the system. Ensuring permanency is equally important, especially when dealing with factors like aging, disease, and injury. Regular template updates are necessary to mitigate these effects. Toward this, measuring feature characteristics is critical for efficient computations and user acceptance. Preventing forgery and circumvention emphasizes the need for robust security measures.

To ensure quality of acquired samples, the sensors should be properly calibrated. An appropriate resolution has to be determined to ensure proper interoperability. Standardizing template structures and matching algorithms promotes a consistency across systems. Privacy and security considerations include maintaining data integrity, preventing unauthorized access, and safeguarding digital identities. To preserve confidentiality and prevent illegitimate access, the verification from a user is made through a secondary communication channel. The necessary information should be available timely and reliably to provide authentication to only legitimate users.

17.2 | Characteristics of biometric features

Typical features for various image-based biometric signatures depend on the considered modalities. A crucial characteristic requirement of these features is their low inter-user similarity and low intra-user variations. Low inter-user similarity ensures that distinct users exhibit dissimilar features, preventing false matches during verification. Similarly, low intra-user variation ensures consistency for a specific individual. There are different kinds of features that are used in different modalities. For example,

- Fingerprint: Distinctive structural points on fingerprint maps form the feature sets, as shown in Fig. 17.2. These points, along with other attributes, contribute to the feature representation.
- Iris: The unique iris pattern is encoded into a feature vector, as shown in Fig. 17.3.
- Face: Various facial measurements yield a feature vector, as shown in Fig. 17.4, enabling further processing.

These features play a vital role in accurate biometric systems.

There are several potential sources of intra-user variability in biometric systems. Even when a user is properly enrolled and genuine, they may not be accepted by the system due to signature variations during verification. Some observed factors contributing to these variations are as follows.

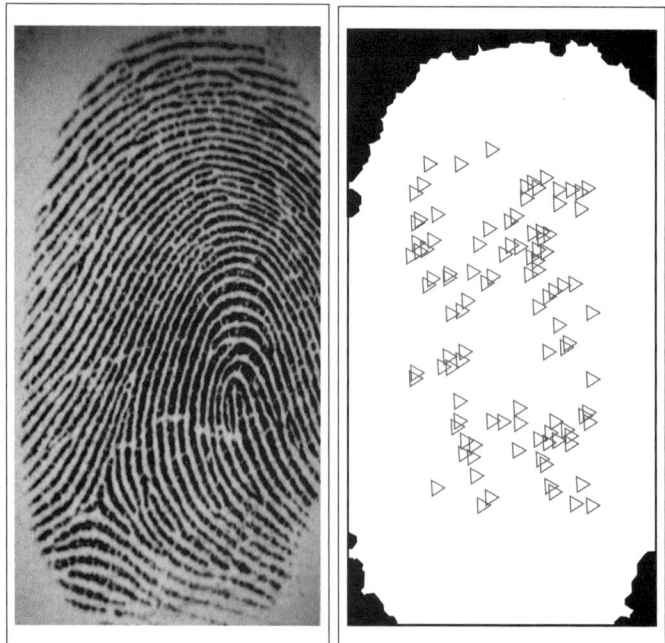

Figure 17.2 Example of a fingerprint image feature. (*Source*: A sample image from FVC2002 dataset (Maio et al., 2002).)

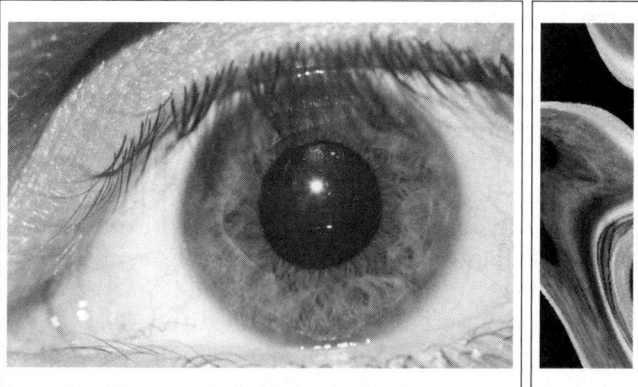

Figure 17.3 Example of an iris image feature. (*Source*: Getty Images/AlexTurton.)

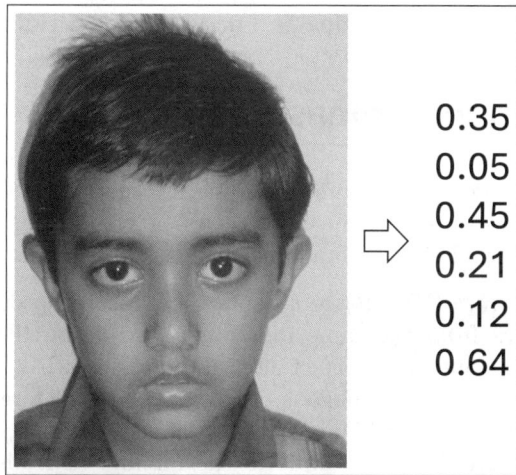

Figure 17.4 Example of a face image feature.

- Imperfect sensing conditions: Sensors may malfunction, resulting in noisy images (e.g., noisy fingerprints).

- Alterations to biometric characteristics: Events like finger injuries may alter biometric characteristics, affecting the features like fingerprints.

- Changes in ambient conditions: Changes in sensing conditions (e.g., imperfect illumination during face image capture) may lead to appear the same face as different images.

- Variations in user interaction: User interactions with sensors may impact the biometric signature. For example, varying pressure on fingerprint sensors or emotional fluctuations may influence biometric data during sensing.

- Genetic similarity: Similar biometric traits between different individuals (e.g., identical twins) may cause confusion or errors in the system.

Understanding this variability is key to design a robust biometric system.

17.2.1 | Feature matching

In the context of biometric systems, matching refers to computing a function that quantifies the similarity between two biometric descriptors. Here, matching does not necessarily look for a "perfect" match. Attributing to the variations in biometric signatures, a "close" match is usually considered as valid. So, higher scores of similarity measures or lower values of distance measures are desired. For verification, if the matching score is greater than a preset threshold, th_v, the signature is declared 'genuine'. Otherwise, an ambiguity of being 'imposter' is retained, which has to be verified by other means. Usually, th_v is set at a very high value. For identification, it is assessed whether the biometric signature ranks among the top N retrieved signatures, surpassing a predefined threshold, th_i. When N is greater than one, it constitutes *open set identification*, allowing multiple possibilities. In this case, there are several candidates and one of them is chosen by considering other identity bearing information. In contrast, if $N = 1$, only the top-ranking match is considered, which is a *closed set identification*. Here, the top match is the undisputed answer. At the end, the system determines whether the individual is a match or not, yielding a unique outcome.

17.3 | Performance measures

For assessing the performance of biometric systems, several performance measures are used. Understanding these performance measures is crucial for designing robust and reliable biometric systems. Two such fundamental measures are discussed below.

(i) *False nonmatch rate* (FNMR) represents the expected probability that two mate samples (samples from the same individual) are declared as a non-match. Such errors often arise due to incorrect user interactions with the sensors, leading to misidentification. It is analogous to mistyped or forgotten passwords. To accommodate these occasional errors, system designs allow user's multiple attempts. However, there is a limit to the number of trials to prevent imposters from exploiting the system by making as many attempts.

(ii) *False match rate* (FMR), in contrast to FNMR, quantifies the likelihood that nonmate samples (two samples from different individuals) are declared a match. This scenario resembles an imposter attempting to break into a system by guessing passwords.

Typically, for a dependable system, the FMR is lower than the FNMR.

17.3.1 | Verification measures

The FNMR and FMR measures are also used in the context of biometric verification, which are named differently. Here, *false rejection rate* (FRR) is equivalent to the FNMR and *false acceptance rate* (FAR) is equivalent to the FMR. Beyond these two fundamental measures, other error metrics also play a significant role in assessing the biometric systems. *Failure to enroll rate* (FTE) measures the proportion of users who cannot be successfully enrolled in the system. *Failure to acquire* (FTA) or *failure to capture* (FTC) error reflects the fraction of authentication attempts where the biometric sensor failed to capture valid samples. A high rate of FTA indicates the need for maintenance or replacement of the sensors. To holistically assess the performance of the task of verification by a biometric system, a combined measure of FTE, FTA or FTC, FRR, and FAR is used. Additionally, we may use the *receiver operating characteristic* (ROC) curve, a common characteristic curve used in binary classification systems for understanding the performance of the system. The ROC curve is obtained as a plot of FRR against the FAR, by varying the threshold of similarity measures. Key metrics derived from the ROC curve include the *area under curve* (AUC) and the *equal error rate* (ERR). The ERR represents the rate at which the FRR and FAR become the same in the ROC curve. It is a composite measure for comparing two systems.

17.3.2 | Identification measures

There are also similar performance measures for the identification task. In the identification task, the assessment is based on how well a system identifies individuals. Let there be N enrolled users in a system. Given a query Q, assume the system returns the top t matches, $1 \leq t << N$, with high scores, which depends on the preset threshold value on matching scores. With these considerations, the following measures are defined.

- *Identification rank*: It is the rank of the true identity among the top t retrieved identities, if the true identity exists among them.
- *False positive identification* (FPI): It occurs when the system wrongly identifies an unenrolled user. This is only applicable when $t > 0$. If $t = 0$, FPI is not valid.
- *False positive identification rate* (FPIR): It is the expected probability of FPI when the identity of an unenrolled user is returned with a high score.
- *False negative identification rate* (FNIR): It is the expected probability of false negative identification when the identity of an enrolled user is not returned.
- *True positive identification rate* (TPIR) or Rank-t accuracy (R_t): It is computed as TPIR $= 1 -$ FNIR. For example, Rank-1 accuracy corresponds to the TPIR rate when $t = 1$.
- *Cumulative match characteristic curve* (CMC): It is the plot of R_t against t, where t varies from 1 to N (total number of enrolled users). Instead of using the ROC curve, which is commonly used for verification, the CMC curve is used as a composite measure for identification task. Several meaningful performance measures are derived by analyzing this curve.

17.4 | Fingerprint biometry

Fingerprints are the oldest and the most reliable forms of personal identification trait that play a pivotal role in biometrics. A fingerprint is a distinctive pattern of interleaved *ridges* and *valleys* found on the tip of fingers of our hands. An example of a fingerprint pattern is shown in Fig. 17.5. The ridges are the darker lines that form the prominent features of a

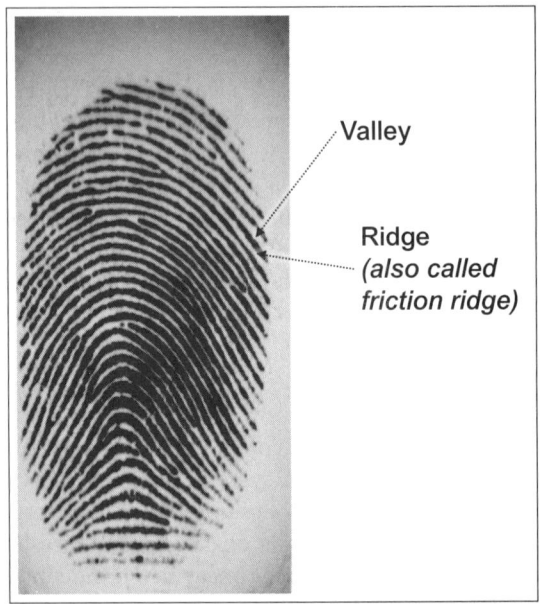

Figure 17.5 An example of fingerprint. (*Source*: A sample image from FVC 2002 database (Maio et al., 2002); http://bias.csr.unibo.it/fvc2002/download.asp.)

fingerprint. The valleys are the white lines between the ridges. These ridges are also referred to as friction ridges. Roughly, the number of ridges per centimeter for a young man is 21, and for a woman, it is 23.

Fingerprint recognition is preferred due to its following properties.

- Ease of capture: Fingerprint recognition has a relatively straightforward acquisition process. Unlike other biometric features (such as facial characteristics), fingerprints are not occluded by hair or affected by oily glands. However, sweating during capture may pose challenges.

- Uniqueness and immutability: Each person's fingerprint is remarkably unique. This uniqueness arises from the intricate ridge patterns. Even identical twins have distinct fingerprints. The pattern remains consistent over time, making it an immutable identifier.

- Recovery and healing: Superficial cuts or bruises do not significantly alter the fingerprint pattern. The natural healing process of the skin mostly restores the original ridges and valleys. However, deep cuts that penetrate the basal layer of the epidermis may result in permanent changes. In such cases, updating the fingerprint signature becomes necessary.

Understanding the science behind fingerprints allows in designing robust and secure identification systems. Whether for law enforcement, access control, or personal devices, fingerprints continue to be an enduring and reliable biometric marker.

17.4.1 | Features in fingerprint pattern

In fingerprint recognition, mainly three levels of features are used. Level-1 features represent the orientation field or ridge flow, and singular points. In Fig. 17.6 (a), the flow of ridges and their orientations can be distinctly seen. Singular points like loop or core and delta are also characterized by level-1 features. Level-2 features are based on ridge skeleton and minutiae, as shown in Fig. 17.6 (b). Two particular types of structures are characterized by level-2 features, bifurcation and ending of ridges. In level-3, more detailed features of the fingerprint, like ridge contours, pores, and dots, as shown in Fig. 17.6 (c), are considered for analysis. The pores are the white dots in the ridges and the dots are the dark points in their valleys. These distinguished features and their locations are used for identifying a fingerprint.

Level-1 fingerprint features

In fingerprint analysis, level-1 features provide essential information about the local characteristics of ridges and valleys. These features play a crucial role in identifying and distinguishing individuals. Here, at regular grids within the fingerprint, two critical

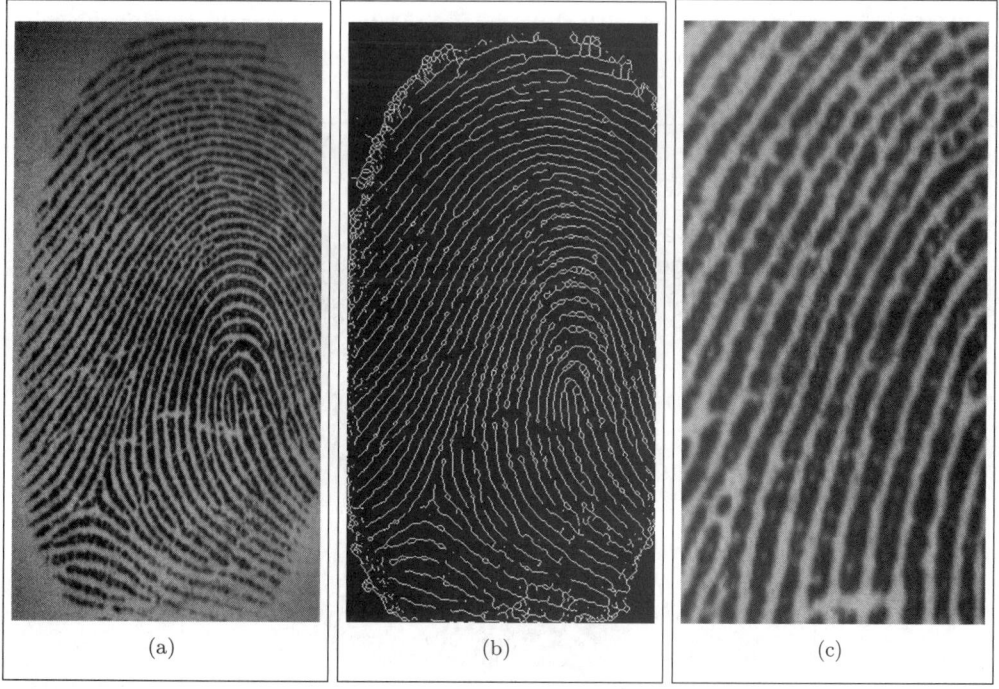

(a)   (b)   (c)

Figure 17.6 Examples of different levels of features in a fingerprint: (a) ridge flow and singular points forming loops and deltas (level-1), (b) ridge skeletons and minutiae (level-2), and (c) ridge contours, pores and dots (level-3). (*Source*: A sample image from FVC 2002 database (Maio et al., 2002); http://bias.csr.unibo.it/fvc2002/download.asp.)

attributes are recorded: (1) ridge frequency, which represents how frequently the ridges occur in a specific zone, and (2) ridge orientation, the tangential direction of ridges at discrete points. These information are stored for each grid point, creating a distribution that represents the fingerprint. Then, the ridge orientation map is generated, which is a visual representation of unit vectors along the ridge orientation at every point in the grid. It captures the directional alignment of ridges across the fingerprint. By identifying the changes in the ridge orientations, singular points are identified as the locations where ridge orientation changes abruptly. There are two common types of singular points, loop or core singularity and delta singularity. The loop or core singularity occurs when a set of ridges enters and exits along the same direction. The delta singularity appears where three ridge systems seem to meet. Typically, they occur in pairs within a full fingerprint. The ridge orientation, loop, and delta are illustrated in Fig. 17.7. Understanding level-1 features allows in extracting certain information from fingerprints that aid in accurate identification and distinguishing individuals, even identical twins.

There are different types of fingerprint patterns in level-1 features, which are as follows.

(i) Plain arch pattern: A simple arch pattern that is devoid of prominent loops or deltas. This is not so distinguishable for the purpose of recognition.

(ii) Tented arch pattern: An arch with slightly more pronounced loops and deltas. This is more recognizable than plain arch pattern, but still not highly distinctive.

(iii) Left loop pattern: A loop with the delta to its left. This is well recognizable with a distinguishing pattern.

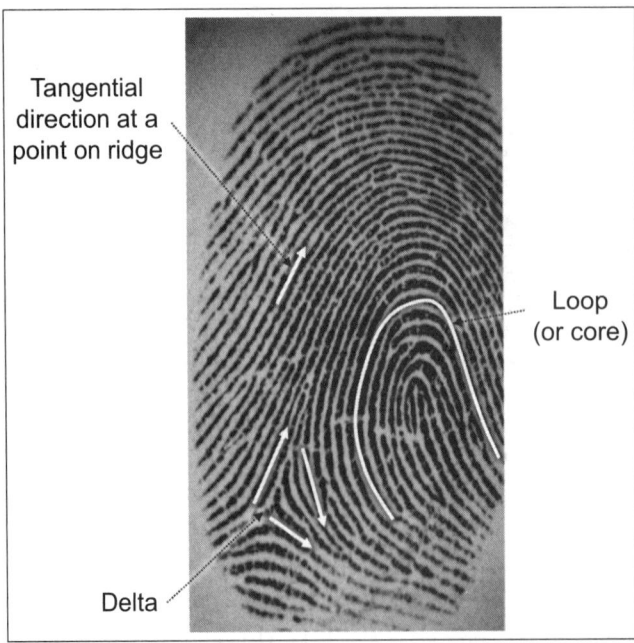

Figure 17.7 Illustration of ridge orientation, loop, and delta in a fingerprint. (*Source*: A sample image from FVC 2002 database (Maio et al., 2002); http://bias.csr.unibo.it/fvc2002/download.asp.)

(**iv**) Right loop pattern: A loop with the delta to its right. Similar to the left loop, this is also well recognizable with a distinguishing pattern.

(**v**) Twin loop pattern: Two closely spaced loops. This is not a very commonly occurring pattern.

(**vi**) Whorl pattern: Circular or spiral ridge arrangement. This is a common pattern and easily identifiable.

Understanding these patterns enhances our ability to decipher the unique language imprinted on the fingertips. A pictorial illustration of these patterns is shown in Fig. 17.8 (Watson, 2008). Based on extensive studies, it is observed that the loop pattern occurs in approximately 65% of cases, whorl pattern represents around 24% of cases, twin Loop pattern accounts for 4% cases, arch pattern is also found in 4% of cases, and tented arch pattern is less commonly observed in 3% of cases of fingerprints. To comfortably observe the level-1 features, a resolution of 250 pixels per inch (PPI) is suggested.

Level-2 fingerprint features

At level-2, the focus is on *minutiae*, which are critical points within a fingerprint. Minutiae are the locations where a ridge emerges or ends, and splits or merges. These minutiae provide unique and robust information for individual characterization. There can be two types of minutiae, which are as follows.

(**i**) Ending or emerging minutiae: Ending (termination) minutiae occurs where a ridge abruptly ends. Emergence minutiae identifies locations where ridges emerge.

(**ii**) Split or merging minutiae: Bifurcation minutiae represents a ridge splitting into two branches. Merging minutiae indicates two ridges converging into one.

An example of fingerprint image exhibiting these minutiae is shown in Fig. 17.9. The collective set of all minutiae within a full fingerprint is called *minutiae set*. The minutiae set is found to be very unique and robust for characterizing a person. It is also storage efficient and highly distinctive. Matching of minutiae set is similar to point set matching, where minutiae patterns are compared for identification. In cases where complete fingerprints are not available, subset matching enables recognition even from partial fingerprints. Minutiae play a pivotal role in the process of fingerprint recognition. For observing level-2 features, which capture finer details, a resolution of 500 PPI is recommended.

Level-3 fingerprint features

At level-3, the features are represented using inner holes (sweat pores) and outer contours (edges of a ridge). In this context, a resolution of 1000 PPI is necessary for observing these features. The example is shown in Fig. 17.10 (a), where the level-3 features, like contours, pores, dots, and incipient ridges, can be seen. Specifically, it illustrates an incipient ridge and a pore clearly. Though it is scanned at 500 PPI we may observe these features in an enlarged portion of the image in Fig. 17.10 (b). The level-3 features could potentially be utilized for latent fingerprint recognition (Feng et al., 2012).

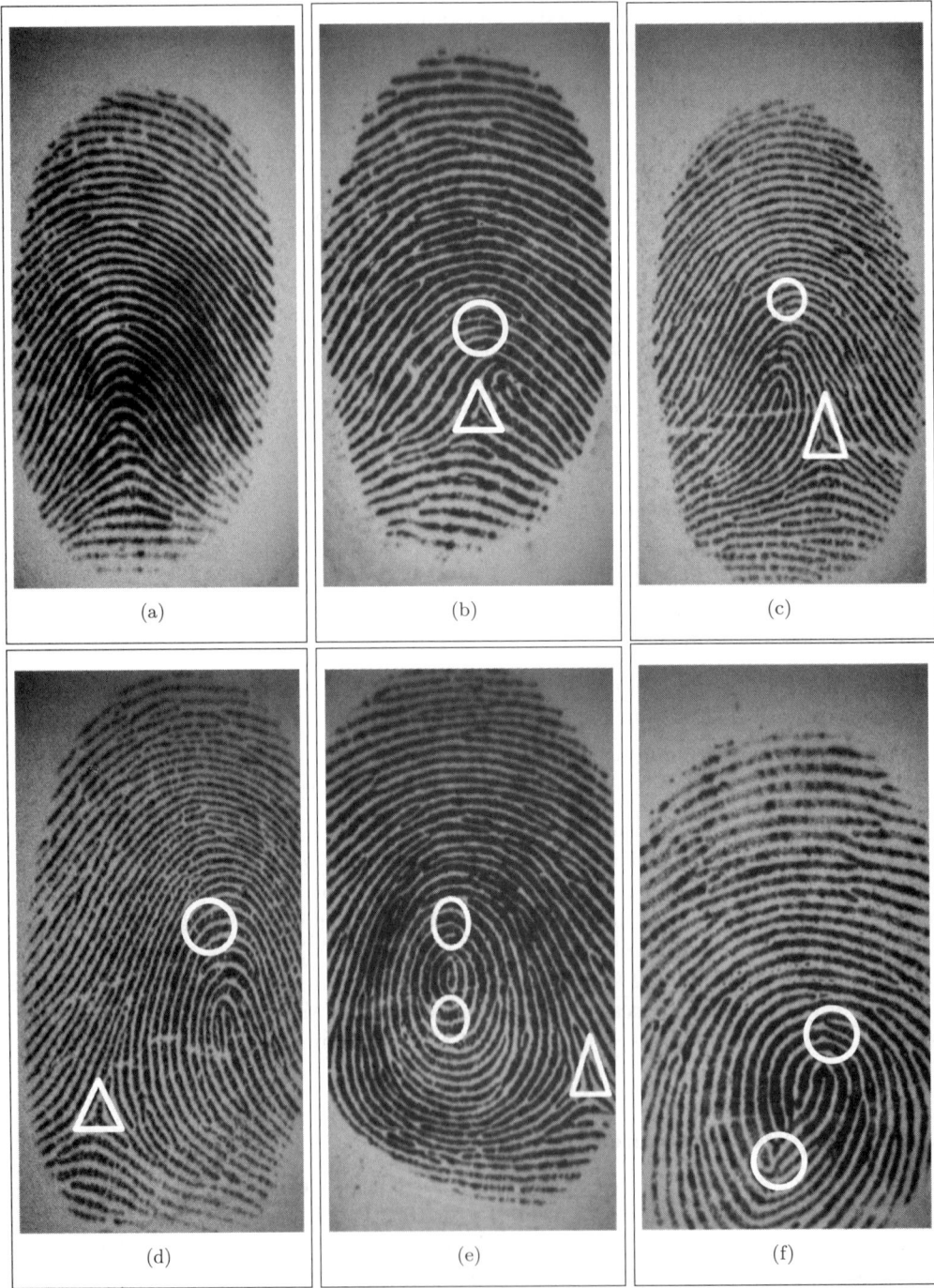

Figure 17.8 Pictorial illustration of level-1 fingerprint patterns. (a) Plain arch, (b) tented arch, (c) left loop, (d) right loop, (e) whorl, and (f) twin loop. (*Source*: Sample images from FVC 2002 database (Maio et al., 2002); http://bias.csr.unibo.it/fvc2002/download.asp.)

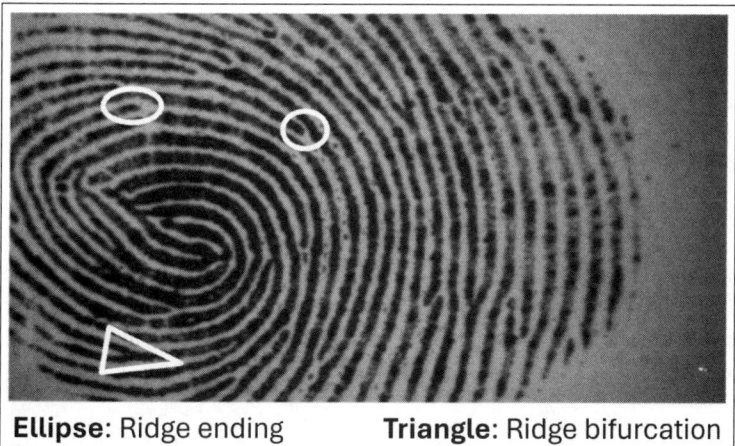

Ellipse: Ridge ending   **Triangle:** Ridge bifurcation

Figure 17.9 Minutiae in fingerprint image. (*Source*: A sample image from FVC 2002 database (Maio et al., 2002); http://bias.csr.unibo.it/fvc2002/download.asp.)

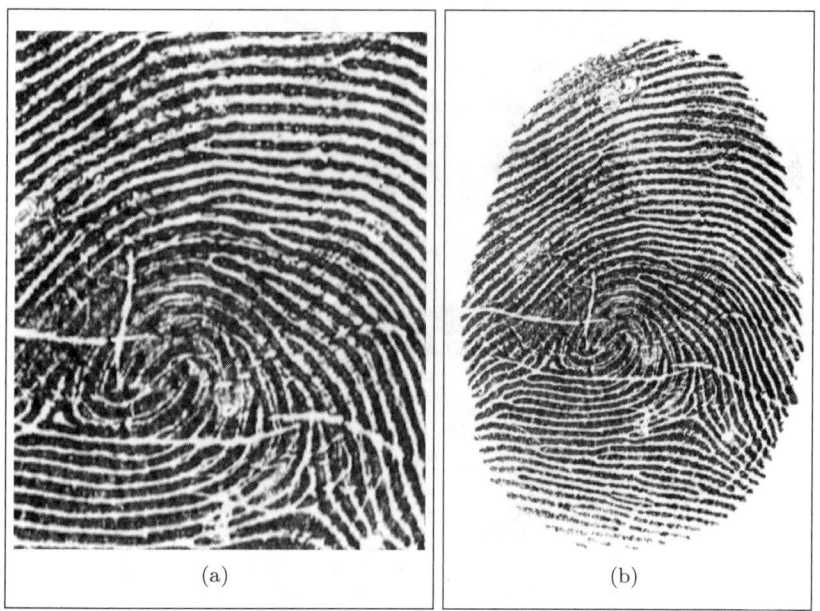

(a)   (b)

Figure 17.10 An example of level-3 features in fingerprint image. (*Source*: A template fingerprint image from the dataset reported in Feng et al. (2012).)

17.4.2 | Computing fingerprint features

There are various techniques to compute features from a fingerprint scan at each of the levels. Few such popular techniques are discussed here.

Computing level-1 fingerprint features

The computation of level-1 features is related to finding orientation and frequency of ridges. In the fingerprint scan, consider a specific zone where alternating ridges and valleys are observed, as shown in Fig. 17.11. Along a particular direction, the wavy pattern of local ridges and valleys is modeled as a cosine function, $w(x, y)$, as given in Eq. 17.1.

$$w(x, y) = A\cos\left(2\pi f(x\cos(\theta) + y\sin(\theta))\right) \tag{17.1}$$

where A is the amplitude, f is the frequency, θ is the orientation, and x and y are the spatial parameters. Here, orientation, θ, refers to the angle formed by the reference x-axis of these ridges. The amplitude corresponds to the average width of the ridges along θ. Frequency is the number of ridges along the considered direction.

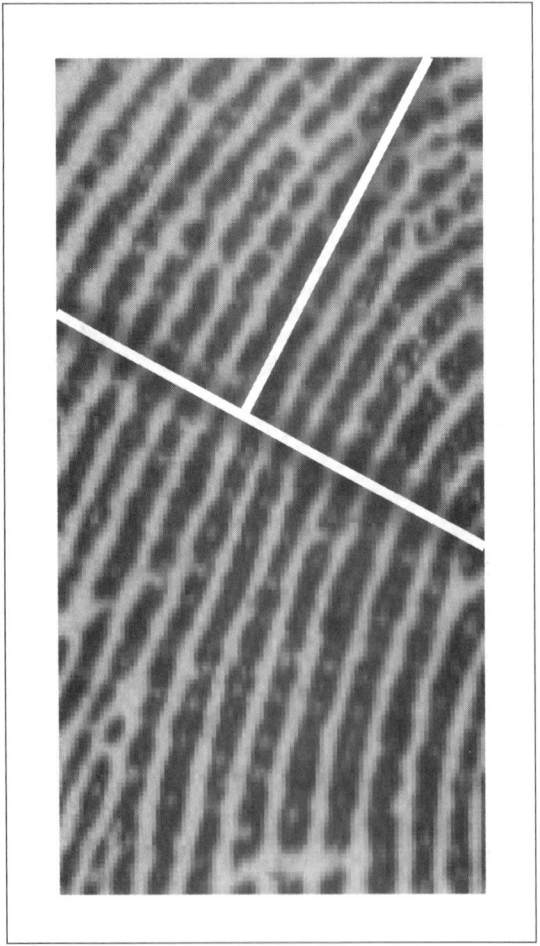

Figure 17.11 Pattern of alternating ridges and valleys in a fingerprint. (*Source*: A sample image from FVC 2002 database (Maio et al., 2002); http://bias.csr.unibo.it/fvc2002/download.asp.)

To detect these features, the 2-D Fourier transform is used, which is given by Eq. 17.2.

$$W(u, v) = \mathcal{F}(w(x, y)) = \tfrac{A}{2}(\delta(u - f\cos(\theta), v - f\sin(\theta)) + \delta(u + f\cos(\theta), v + f\sin(\theta))) \quad (17.2)$$

Since the pattern is modeled by a cosine function, ideally, it is expected to have 2-D impulses or Dirac delta responses. In the magnitude of the spectral transform of the cosine function, the location of the maximum magnitude occurs at $(\hat{u}, \hat{v}) = (\hat{f}\cos(\hat{\theta}), \hat{f}\sin(\hat{\theta}))$. Although the spectrum may not have a perfect peak, it would resemble a top-hat shape, which is sufficient to identify the global maximum magnitude. The location of this maximum value occurs at frequencies $(\hat{u}, \hat{v})$. Then, the required features are estimated in the Fourier transformed domain, as given by Eq. 17.3.

$$\hat{A} = |W(\hat{u}, \hat{v})|$$
$$\hat{f} = \sqrt{\hat{u}^2 + \hat{v}^2} \quad (17.3)$$
$$\hat{\theta} = \tan^{-1}\left(\frac{\hat{v}}{\hat{u}}\right)$$

where $\hat{\ }$ represents the estimated value of the underlying parameter. However, noise may impact the results significantly. To mitigate this, the magnitude spectrum is smoothed before estimating the global maximum. Notably, Gaussian smoothing is not appropriate values for orientations, since orientation angles wrap around from 0 to 360 degrees in circular order. Instead, the orientation angles are converted to unit vector fields along the direction of the angles and the vector fields are smoothed. Then, the orientation angles are recomputed from the smoothed vector components to obtain refined orientation angle.

The local orientations provide the basis for detecting the singularities using the *Poincare index* (Maltoni et al., 2022). Consider the local orientation at the ith neighbor of a pixel, which spans from 0 to π. Let the neighborhood be defined by a 3×3 grid around the center pixel, so that there are eight neighboring pixels. Let us denote the orientations at those neighboring pixels as, $o(i) \in [0, \pi)$, and $i = 0, 1, \ldots, 7$. Then the Poincare index (PI) is defined as the accumulated consecutive differences in the orientation angles of the pixels within this neighborhood, which is given by Eq. 17.4.

$$\text{PI} = \frac{1}{\pi} \sum_{i=0}^{7} \phi\left(o((i+1) \bmod 8) - o(i)\right) \quad (17.4)$$

where the ϕ function is given by $\phi(\theta) = \begin{cases} \theta - \pi & \theta > \frac{\pi}{2} \\ \theta, & -\frac{\pi}{2} < \theta < \frac{\pi}{2} \\ \theta + \pi & \theta < -\frac{\pi}{2} \end{cases}$.

These neighborhood orientations pertain to nearby pixels. The function ϕ operating on the differences in Eq. 17.4, constrains angles to lie between $-\frac{\pi}{2}$ and $\frac{\pi}{2}$. The computation of a singular point using the Poincare index is performed as follows: $PI = 0$ signifies a nonsingular point, $PI = 1$ corresponds to a loop singular point, $PI = -1$ denotes a delta singular point, and $PI = 2$ represents a whorl singular point. It is important to note that these values are typical, and approximations from real world data are necessary to identify singular points. When attributing characteristics of singular points to pixels, it is observed that clusters of similar singular points occur in close vicinity. Detecting these clusters and computing their respective cluster centers provide an estimation of singular points in the image. These constitute the level-1 features.

Computing level-2 fingerprint features

Detection of minutiae is the primary problem for the level-2 features. Here, ridges are extracted by enhancing them using some preprocessing techniques. Then thinning or skeletonization is performed on fingerprint scans and the number of neighboring ridge points are counted at each point. The characterization of the type of minutiae is based on this count. For the type of ending or emerging, the count is one. In the case of bifurcation or merging, the count is three, which indicates three neighbors in different directions. Typically, ridges are darker than valleys, necessitating binarization for thinning. To obtain desired binarized patterns, the image is enhanced and subjected to adaptive thresholding. Notably, applying Gabor filtering using the real part of the 2-D complex Gabor filter, tuned to the local ridge orientation of frequency, enhances the image. This filter acts as a bandpass filter, allowing certain image sharpening operations. The resulting binarized regions reveal white ridges against a dark background, representing the extracted ridges. Thinning further highlights these minutiae, as shown in Fig. 17.12.

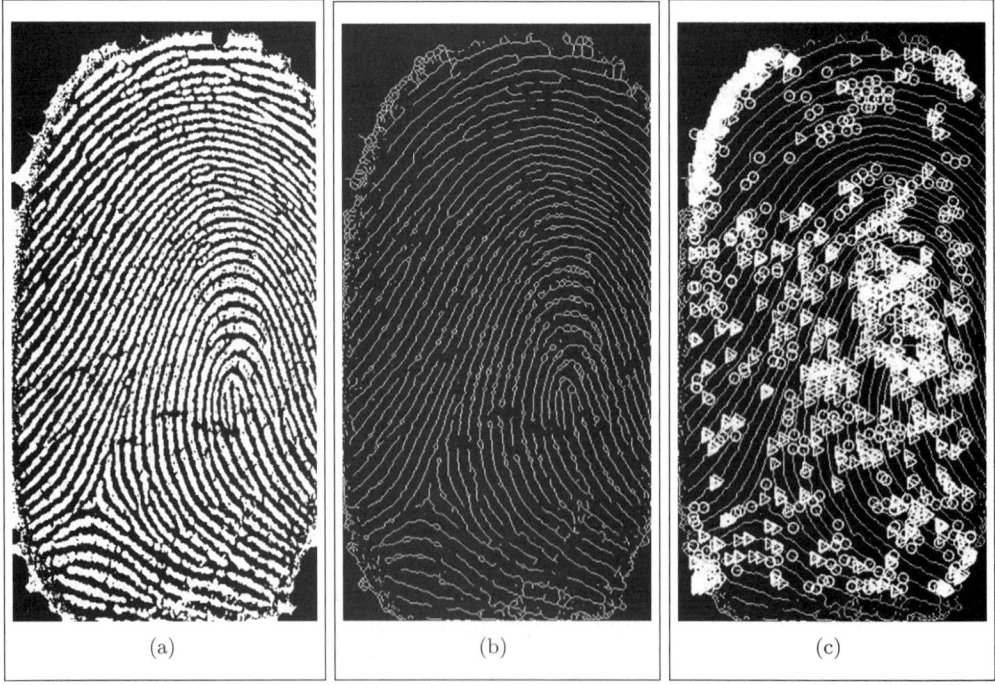

Figure 17.12 Minutiae in a fingerprint image. (a) Extracted ridges, (b) thinned, and (c) minutiae detected (from count only). (*Source*: A sample image from FVC 2002 database (Maio et al., 2002); http://bias.csr.unibo.it/fvc2002/download.asp.)

In this process, several spurious minutiae are detected, necessitating their filtering. Some minutiae lack adjacent ridges on both the sides, indicating their presence at the boundary. Such minutiae are removed. In some cases, the minutiae may be closely located, but in opposite directions. This is essentially due to an abrupt and noisy break along a specific ridge, which may have a continuation with a small gap. Such minutiae are ignored as endings. Additionally, an excessive number of minutiae in a small neighborhood often leads to the detection of too many bifurcations, which are also excluded. With these processes, the locations of the minutiae are obtained.

To make the representation robust, the directions of the minutiae are used. Specifically, the directions of the ridges, where the minutiae are located, are computed. For the ending type of minutiae, ridge points are traced over a fixed distance. The direction from the point to a point traced by a fixed length along the ridge is computed. Similarly, for the bifurcation type of minutiae, tracing along three directions is considered. The average of the two directions along the respective two ridges that meet or split at a bifurcation point is computed. The final fingerprint representation constitutes a set of minutiae, their locations, their types (either ending or bifurcations), and their directions. This representation is used for fingerprint recognition.

Computing level-3 fingerprint features

In fingerprint analysis, level-3 features also play a crucial role, when a very detailed and in-depth level of representation is necessary. These features delve into the dimensional aspects of the ridges, that include the elements like sweat pores, ridge contours, ridge edge protrusions, incipient edges, etc. Their significance lies in providing quantitative data that enhances the accuracy and robustness of fingerprint recognition systems. Level-3 features cannot be extracted from low resolution images. Also, some of the level-3 features are not strictly unique. For example, sweat pores, which are the tiny openings on the ridges of the skin, can be categorized into two distinct types, open and closed. A closed pore is neatly enclosed by a ridge, while an open pore intersects with the valley between two adjacent ridges. The state of a pore depends on various factors, like perspiration activity, physical strain, etc., which may make them appear inconsistent in images taken at different time-stamps. However, the pores exhibit a consistent behavior in their location of appearance. They naturally align themselves along friction ridges. So, regardless of whether they are open or closed, the locations of pores are identified with proper detection of ridges.

17.4.3 | Matching the fingerprints

In this task, the computation involves matching a query template, $Q = \{(x_i, y_i, \theta_i),$ $i = 1, 2, ..., N\}$, with a target template, $T = \{(x_j, y_j, \theta_j),\ j = 1, 2, ..., M\}$, where (x, y) represents the location, θ denotes the orientation, and N and M are the number of minutiae in query and target templates, respectively. The matching scores are computed by certain standard operations that are typically employed during this process, which are as follows.

The initial step is to align the query template with the target template. This alignment entails applying some transformation to template Q and bring it into the coordinate system of template T. Once proper alignment is achieved, the correspondences between a pair of feature points is established. Subsequently, the matching pairs are counted and the decision on whether a match exists or not is made on the basis of the count or number of matched pairs. A threshold is defined for this purpose.

During alignment, the generalized Hough transform is usually employed to compute the translation and the rotation parameters in 2-D transformations. For instance, the difference in orientations can be used to estimate the rotation parameter. This can be further used to estimate the translation parameters by computing the offset of the computed and the observed points. For each set of these parameter triplets, a count of their occurrences is maintained, which facilitates to compute the peak. To establish correspondences, the nearest neighbors in the template are identified. A matching correspondence is accepted, if the distance and difference of the orientation angles fall within specific limits. Occasionally, instead of an absolute count for scoring, the percentage of matched pairs in overlapping areas may also be used.

17.5 | Face biometry

Face biometry is a process that involves establishing the identity of a person based on her facial characteristics. However, face biometry is not immune to variations due to aging, which is one of the challenges in face biometry. Other issues involved in capturing the face images include factors like, illumination variations, applications of makeup, facial hair, use of accessories (such as sunglasses), etc., which can alter the appearance of a person. Consequently, achieving the same level of uniqueness in the feature representation as they are in fingerprint biometrics, may prove challenging. Additionally, there may be significant similarity between faces of two different individuals, which is not uncommon. Despite these challenges, face biometrics offers certain advantages too. Unlike fingerprint scanning, face images are captured noninvasively through simple imaging. Here, the sensor does not physically touch the face. Furthermore, face images can also be obtained remotely, making it advantageous for certain applications, especially in surveillance. There are various modalities for capturing face images. For example, commercial 2-D digital cameras for images, 3-D sensors that detect facial surfaces, video sequences that allow tracking a person across different frames, etc. Notably, sharing face data is more socially acceptable than sharing fingerprints. Numerous face databases already exist due to long-standing identity management systems run by various organizations and governments. These databases serve as valuable resources for research and system design.

Under certain applications, standardization of imaging is followed within constrained environment, especially for government-issued identities and mug shots (Jain et al., 2012). One of the applications in this context involves de-duplicating enrolments. That is, identifying duplicate faces in the database to prevent multiple enrolment of the same person under different names and to mitigate the risks of impersonation. However, in unconstrained environments, where images and videos capture human activities and interactions, the challenges are more pronounced. These challenges include variability due to the pose of a person, illumination of the environment, facial expressions, and age. Also, face biometrics has profound applications in forensics, such as matching sketches of suspects. In forensic applications, it is very difficult to have fully automated systems. Rather, various semi-automatic tools have been developed for accomplishing related tasks that require user intervention. Thus, face biometry encompasses various problem statements under different contexts.

17.5.1 | Features in face images

Face images are characterized by certain types of features, which are mostly based on face geometry, structure of organs in face, and properties of skin. Similar to fingerprint scans, the face images also use three levels of features. The *level-1 face features* serve as essential components in forensic investigations for identifying individuals based on their facial attributes. These features are mostly characterized by gross spatial aspects such as general geometry and global skin color, which are readily observable. Remarkably, level-1 features can be extracted from low resolution images, where the *interpupillary distance* (IPD) may be as low as 30 pixels. The IPD, which effectively quantifies the resolution of a face image, is measured by the number of pixels between the pupils of the two eyes in the given face image. The problem statements for using level-1 features depend on the context of usage. For example, distinguishing a short and round face from an elongated and thin face is a characteristics of individual faces, whereas identifying gender or racial category is a characteristics of a group of individuals. In the *level-2 features*, the structure of components in face, like eye, nose, etc., and the relationship between such facial components, like precise shape of the face, are considered. It may also use geometric and texture descriptors. The level-2 features are mainly used in identification or verification tasks. At level-2, the required resolution of a face image is between 30 to 75 IPD. The *level-3 features* mainly characterize the unstructured and micro level features, such as scars, freckles, moles, skin discoloration, pigmentation, etc. These features are critical to resolve challenging face identity discrimination, like identical twins.

Anthropometric facial landmarks play a significant role in facial analysis. In the *frontal view* of a face, as shown in Fig. 17.13 (a), specific points are marked on eyelids, nose, lips, chin, head, etc. Similarly, certain points are also marked in the *profile view*, as shown in Fig. 17.13 (b). These point sets are called anthropometric facial landmarks. These point sets are distinctive landmarks that serve as templates for representing individual faces with respective measurements among the key points.

17.5.2 | Face recognition system

In a face recognition system, several critical stages come into play, which are shown in Fig. 17.14. In the processing pipeline first a face is detected. It is essential for further processing. When dealing with a general image that has a face, the task involves precisely locating the face. This localization results in the selection of rectangular window that encapsulates the face, as shown in Fig. 17.14. Subsequently, the image is normalized using the rectangular window around the face. This normalization entails resizing the image by registering it with the key landmark points, such as the pupils in the frontal face. Then, various anthropometric facial landmarks and normalized measurements are leveraged to construct a feature representation. There are also other alternative forms of feature representations that can be used in recognition systems. Finally, matching algorithms

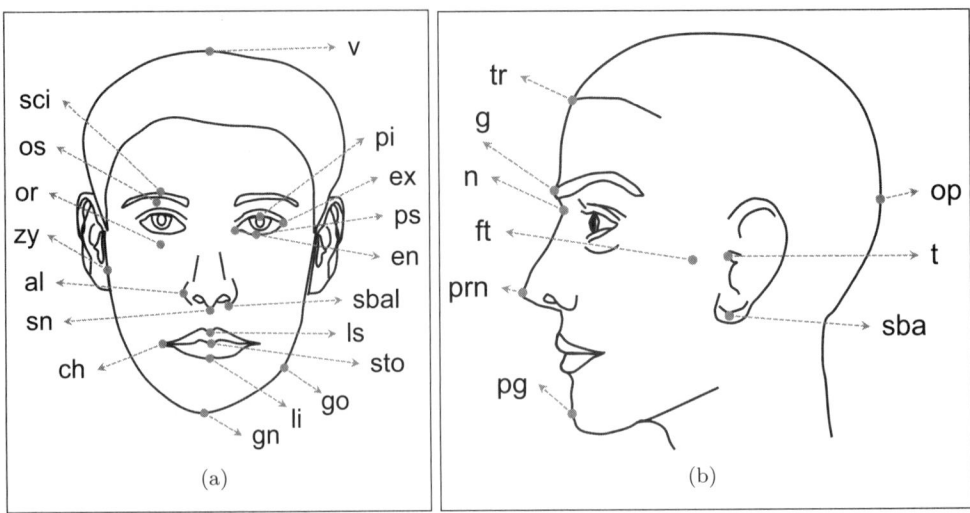

Figure 17.13 Anthropometric facial landmarks. (a) Frontal view, and (b) profile view.

utilize similarity or distance measures for identification of a person based on the feature representation.

Face detection

There are various techniques in the literature for face detection. In this chapter, two popular approaches are considered, namely the Viola–Jones face detection algorithm and a detection technique based on skin color.

Viola–Jones algorithm   Viola–Jones algorithm (Viola and Jones, 2004) is a well known face detection algorithm that systematically identifies potential face windows or regions within an image. It designs a classifier that evaluates various face features measured within these candidate windows to determine whether they correspond to a face or not. These features are computed using box filters that are similar to Haar wavelets. Typical examples of these windows are shown in Fig. 17.15. These filters use integral image representation (refer to Section 4.3.2 of Chapter 4) to enable fast and efficient computation of these features. By combining different rectangular filters, a diverse set of candidate features are obtained. The algorithm then selects the most suitable features and

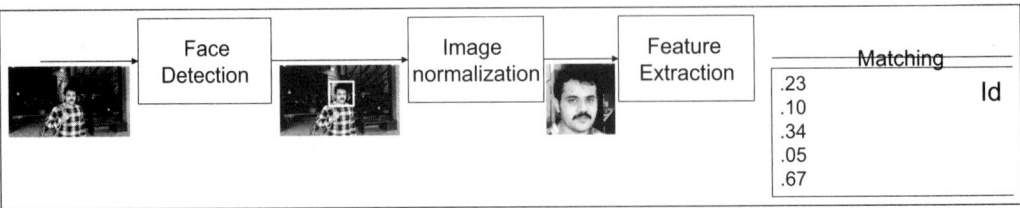

Figure 17.14 Typical face recognition system.

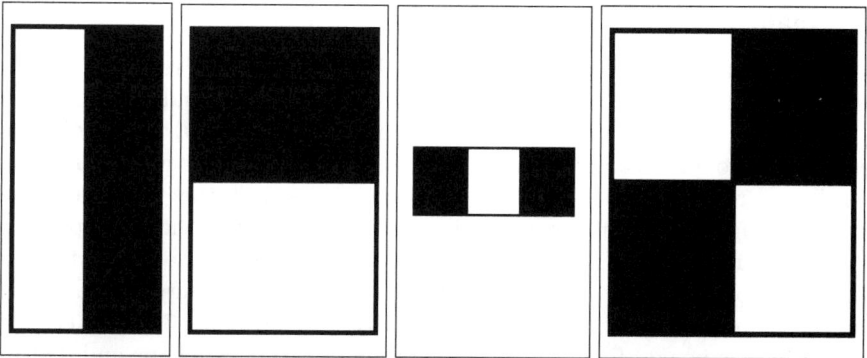

Figure 17.15 Box filters used in Viola–Jones face detection algorithm.

determines an optimal classification scheme. The Viola–Jones technique uses AdaBoost algorithm (Freund and Schapire, 1997), which selects the discriminating features and provides an ensemble of classifiers to successfully detect faces. Furthermore, this approach is also applied to identify facial components, such as eyes, lips, forehead, etc. The landmarks within the detected face can also be localized using this algorithm.

Face detection using skin color Another simple approach to face detection focuses on skin color, rather than directly identifying the faces. Since the facial regions are often more exposed than any other region of the body in images, associating skin color with the presence of a face is a simple and valid heuristic. This method uses colored imaging system, where the chroma values are normalized. By analyzing the distribution of the normalized chroma values across different color spaces, patterns commonly observed in human skin tones are identified. One of the first works in this direction was reported by James Crowley (Crowley, 1997), where a Bayesian classification-based approach was used by considering the normalized red and green colors. The normalization of red, r, and green, g, components are given by Eq. 17.5.

$$r = \frac{R}{R+G+B}; \; g = \frac{G}{R+G+B} \tag{17.5}$$

where R, G, and B are the raw pixel values of red, green, and blue components. Specifically, the probability of color given skin, $P(\text{color}|\text{skin})$, is computed empirically from the histogram of normalized red-green values as $P(r, g|\text{skin}) = \frac{H(r,g)}{N}$, where $H(r, g)$ is the histogram and N is the number of pixels. The objective is to determine the posterior probability of skin based on color information, $P(\text{skin}|\text{color})$. Using Bayesian theory, it can be expressed as, $P(\text{skin}|\text{color}) = \frac{P(\text{color}|\text{skin})P(\text{skin})}{P(\text{color})}$. Since $P(\text{skin})$ and $P(\text{color})$, or their ratio are considered as constants for practical considerations, the likelihood probability, $P(r, g|\text{skin})$, guides the identification of skin color intervals in the r-g space, ultimately leading to face detection. Similar approaches extend to other color spaces, including complementary blue and complementary red (of YCbCr color space), and hue and saturation (of HSI space) spaces (Singh et al., 2003).

Face normalization

For face normalization, appropriate views of the face may be required to obtain the anthropometric landmarks. For frontal views, pupil detection and subsequent rescaling based on a fixed IPD is performed. Some methods utilize a 3-D polygonal mesh representing the frontal face (Blanz and Vetter, 2003). Each point within this mesh has a 3-D coordinate relative to a specific coordinate system of the polygonal mesh. The objective is to align the landmark points in the query face with the corresponding points in the polygonal mesh of the frontal face. Once achieved, normalization of the face image is performed. For instance, the image may be rendered using calibrated pose and illumination parameters using the mesh. Alternatively, morphable 3-D models are trained on a dataset of face images to learn the distribution of 3-D facial shape and texture within a parameterized feature space (Park et al., 2010). These 3-D models, or certain parametric models developed using face images, facilitate the generation of facial images, accounting for different variations such as aging, pose, and illumination. The models are capable of normalizing the faces and taking care of the variation in representations.

Face feature extraction and representation

The features extracted from a face image may also be based on the appearance, parametric or nonparametric models and texture attributes. In appearance-based features, high-dimensional space is mapped to a low-dimensional subspace using dimension reduction techniques, such as, principal component analysis (PCA), independent component analysis (ICA), linear discriminant analysis (LDA), etc. In model-based approach, 2-D or 3-D models are developed to parameterize the given face image with respect to the model. *Face bunch graph model* or *active appearance model* is one of the popular 2-D face models (Wiskott et al., 1997; Cootes et al., 2001). Similarly, there are also certain models that provide 3-D modeling of the face, like the deformable models, which are used for handling pose variations and illumination (Yuille, 1991). In a texture-based approach, robust local features that are invariant to pose and lighting are computed, such as local binary pattern (LBP) (Ahonen et al., 2006), histograms of gradient orientations HoG (Dalal and Triggs, 2005), etc.

Eigen face representation Eigen face representation is one of the appearance-based feature techniques (Turk and Pentland, 1991). In this method, faces are mapped from their high-dimensional space to a lower-dimensional subspace. The process involves performing PCA on a given set of images (refer to Section 2.9 of Chapter 2). Here, each image is represented in a vectorized form. The PCA yields a set of N eigenvectors, each associated with nonzero eigenvalues. The images corresponding to these eigenvectors, known as eigen faces, correspond to specific facial variations. Any face is represented as a linear combination of these eigenvectors. In this way, the face is represented as a point in the feature space formed by the eigenvectors. This representation is useful for face identification and verification. Besides PCA, other techniques of decompositions like ICA, or LDA (a supervised technique; refer to Section 7.4.3 of Chapter 2) may also be used for feature representation.

Face bunch graph model Face bunch graph (FBG) model is a graph-based approach for facial representation, which provides a structured and efficient way to represent facial variations, making it valuable for tasks such as face recognition and analysis (Wiskott et al., 1997). Here, a face is represented as a labeled graph composed of nodes. Each node corresponds to a fiducial or landmark point on the face, characterized by certain attributes. The nodes are also attributed by a set of Gabor filtered coefficients called *Gabor jet*. The Gabor jet captures local texture information around each landmark point. Edges connect the landmark points within the graph. The distance between two nodes is determined by the weights of these edges. Each node is associated with a set of Gabor jets specific to individuals, considering different poses. The FBG model represents a collection of such individuals. Each node within this model holds the corresponding Gabor jets for those individuals. Edge weights represent the average distances between pairs of corresponding nodes. The FBG model essentially comprises of a stack of face graphs. Different poses yield distinct FBG models. For instance, a frontal pose may result in a specific FBG, while other poses would lead to different models. The similarity between two graphs is computed as the average similarity of corresponding fiducial points. There is an algorithm called *Elastic Bunch Graph Matching algorithm* (Wiskott et al., 2014), which computes the similarity between a query face image or face graph with the stored template face graphs in those FBG modules. It computes an image graph that best represents a given image from the available FBG models.

Texture representations   In texture representations, features like LBP, SIFT, HoG, SURF, etc., are used, similar to those used in the context based image retrieval (CBIR), which is discussed in the next chapter. In fact, the texture is represented as a histogram of such features. In block representation of images, a concatenated histogram of features in nonoverlapping blocks, similar to bag of visual word based representation of any of the features (refer to Section 4.4.3 of Chapter 4) is derived and used for face recognition.

17.6 | Iris biometry

The *iris* is a muscle within the eye that regulates the size of the pupil. An example of an image of an iris is shown in Fig. 17.16, where the organization of iris, pupil, and sclera in the eye is illustrated. The iris controls the amount of light that enters the eye. We may note that, the eye color is due to the color of the iris. The texture and patterns of iris in each person's eye are as unique as a fingerprint. So, it is a good candidate for its use in biometry.

17.6.1 | Iris recognition system

A typical iris recognition system consists of a pipeline with the same processing blocks as in the face recognition system shown in Fig. 17.14. The main modules are, acquisition of the iris image, detection and localization of the iris, normalization of the image, iris feature extraction and representation, and feature matching.

- Acquisition: Specialized cameras are used for the acquisition of an iris image. Generally, a monochrome CCD camera, which is sensitive to the near infrared range of the electromagnetic spectrum is used to capture the image of an iris. It typically captures multiple images in a sequence and retains the good ones.

- Localization: Localization of iris involves identifying the circular boundaries of the iris. This is achieved using background segmentation techniques. Here, the Hough

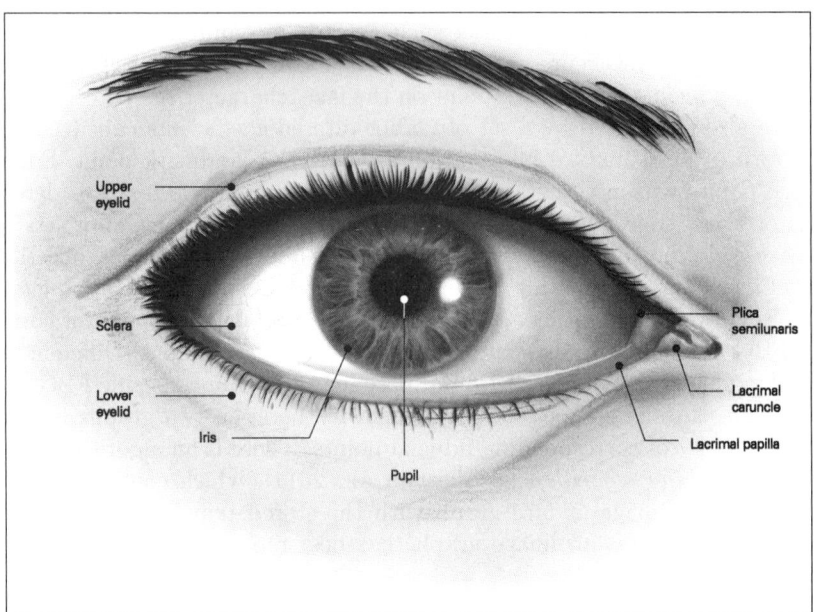

Figure 17.16 Image of an iris. (*Source*: Getty Images/Alan Gesek/Stocktrek Images.)

transform is applied on the edges that are computed from the iris image to extract circular patterns.

- Normalization: Given that the iris resembles a ring, it is normalized by unwrapping it into a rectangular window. The content within that circular ring are transformed into a discretized rectangular grid of polar coordinates. This transformation represents the circular iris region in a more structured format.

- Feature representation: The unwrapped iris pattern is encoded using multi-resolution wavelet filters. Typically, a set of complex Gabor filters are used for encoding. By considering only the phase of the filter responses (which consists of real and imaginary parts), relevant information is extracted. The phase is further quantized into quadrants within a coordinate space, with each quadrant represented by two bits. Since multiple Gabor filters are involved, the representations of the phases obtained from each filtered responses are concatenated. This concatenation yields a string of binary digits, which serves as the encoded representation of the iris. The binary string captures the essential features for subsequent matching.

- Matching: Given that the encoded representation is a binary string, a straightforward measure like the *Hamming distance* is used for matching. The Hamming distance computes the number of differing positions between a query string (from an observed iris) and a template string (from a stored reference iris). The template string with the smallest Hamming distance is considered the best match. These techniques enable robust iris recognition by effectively localizing the iris and extracting discriminative features

To illustrate the processing steps involved in iris recognition system, an example is shown in Fig. 17.17. This illustration uses an optical image of an iris as input. First the edge

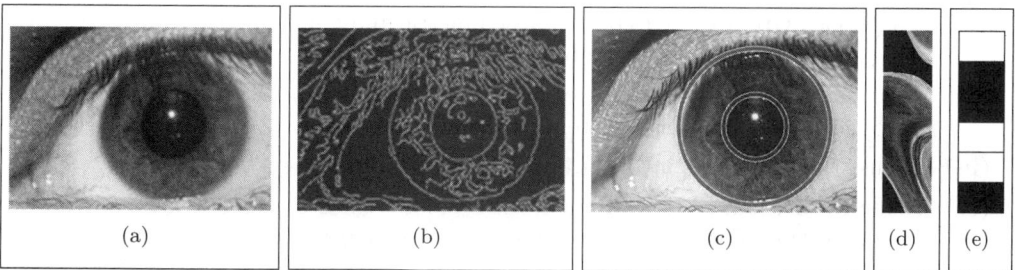

(a)   (b)   (c)   (d)   (e)

Figure 17.17 An example of processing steps involved in iris recognition system. (a) Input iris image, (b) Canny edge detection, (c) inner and outer circles, (d) unwrapped iris, and (e) encoded string. (*Source*: Getty Images/AlexTurton.)

detection is applied on the input image. Hough transform is used on the edge detected image to identify the circular rings between the inner and outer circles of the iris. Then the content in the circular iris region is unwrapped into a rectangular form. Lastly, using a set of Gabor filters, the phase of the response is represented in the form of an encoded string, which is used for matching.

Summary

In the realm of biometrics, the central objective is to establish unique identification based on an individual's physical, physiological, genomic, or behavioral traits. A biometric system serves as a tool for identity management. It finds applications in diverse areas, including border control, resource access, facility usage, financial transactions, examinations, and qualification certification. In this chapter, image based biometry is discussed, specifically from three primary modalities, fingerprint, face, and iris. Other modalities, such as palm print, sole print, and gait analysis in videos, can also be used for relevant biometric applications. Regardless of the modality, a generic pipeline is followed, which comprises of, image acquisition, enhancement/pre-processing, normalization, feature extraction, and enrolment/matching.

A biometric system performs three primary tasks, namely, (1) enrolment (capturing and storing of an individual's biometric data), (2) verification (confirming the identity during an authentication), and (3) identification (matching against a database to find the correct identity). There are various issues and challenges of biometric systems and metrics used in matching the biometric features. In biometrics it is required to ensure privacy and confidentiality of a user, and prevention of impersonation. The performance of the system should be robust and reliable. It is also desirable to have interoperability across systems.

Exercises

(i) What is biometry? How a biometric trait is distinguished from a nonbiometric trait of a person? Give examples of various biometric and nonbiometric traits of a human being. Give examples of image based biometric traits.

(ii) What are the generic tasks of a biometric system? Describe briefly various components of a biometric system performing these tasks.

(iii) Discuss the challenges involved in designing a biometric system.

(iv) Define FNMR and FMR of a biometric system. Which measure is more sensitive in the application of identity verification of a person and why?

(v) Define the following performance measures for verifying a person.

    (a) False acceptance rate (FAR).

    (b) False rejection rate (FRR).

    (c) Failure to enrolment rate (FTE).

    (d) Failure to acquisition rate (FTA).

    (e) ROC curve.

    (f) Equal error rate.

(vi) Define the following performance measures for identifying a person.

    (a) False Positive Identification Rate (FPIR).

    (b) False Negative Identification Rate (FNIR).

    (c) Failure to enrolment rate (FTE).

    (d) True Positive Identification Rate (TPIR).

    (e) Cumulative Match Characteristics Curve (CMC).

(vii) Illustrate the major types of fingerprint patterns. Define Poincare index (PI) for detecting singularities. Describe how PI is used to detect the singular points associated with these patterns.

(viii) What are minutiae? How they are extracted and used for matching a fingerprint?

(ix) Why face biometry is more popular even though it is less robust compared to other biometric traits.

(x) Describe the pipeline of processing in a face recognition system and briefly discuss each of these stages.

(xi) Describe the Viola–Jones method of face detection.

(xii) Describe a method of face detection through detection of skin color.

(xiii) How eigen faces are obtained and used for representing any arbitrary face.

(xiv) What is an iris in our eye? How it is represented uniquely as a biometric signature of a person.

18

Content Based Image Retrieval

Content based image retrieval (CBIR) is a search technique that uses similarity of visual features to compare images. It is also known as image based search process, where, given a query image (with or without an accompanying text), the system provides a set of images that are similar to the query. This provision is made available in most of the search engines, which enable us to search through the internet using a query image and get several images that are relevant to the query. The CBIR system has a lot of applications in various sectors, like education, research, tourism, health care, remote sensing, etc. In CBIR systems, while retrieving the results against a query, some domain specific information, like keywords, may also be provided to improve the quality of retrieval. The scope of such retrieval systems could be extended to videos and multimedia documents, which include text, audio, video, graphics, and images, as well.

Challenges and issues in building a CBIR system

Developing efficient CBIR systems is hurdled by several challenges. The image similarity computed for retrieving relevant images may not always satisfy the user's search intent. Often, objective criteria may not fill the semantic gap in the representation of similar images. Some images, that are similar to human understanding, may be outright rejected as dissimilar images by a computational model. Many objective models are sensitive to noise and the presence of a few outlier features may disturb the decision by rejecting seemingly similar images or accepting dissimilar images. In such cases of *similarity*, the system does not explain why a pair of images are similar. Such sparingly occurring instances may be acceptable in some domains, but there are various areas, like medicine and health care, where the verdict of a system is not acceptable without a proper explanation. Also, two images may be globally similar or they may have some local similarity between them. Capturing and localizing the local similarities for declaring a match between two images are also challenging. However, most of the CBIR systems work on global similarity.

A CBIR system is desired to provide relevant results in real time. So, it should be designed to make the search fast and accurate. This depends upon the choice of feature space and similarity measure. The choice of feature space should exploit the domain characteristics. It may also augment the information from other modalities to improve the quality of search. For example, it may use the domain ontology, text description, keywords, audio description etc. The data has to be indexed using an appropriate techniques, like, spatial tree indexing schemes (e.g., K-dimensional (K-D) tree, sphere/rectangle [SR] tree, etc.) or locality sensitive indexing (LSH) (refer to Section 4.5 of Chapter 4). Then the captured information and images are stored in the library with indexing. The redundancy in the data may be reduced by detecting the duplicate entries. For reporting the retrieved results, usually top K results are reported following a ranking strategy. The results may be visualized as either thumbnails or full size images. The search results are generally paginated and the corresponding link is used for accessing the search results.

18.1 | Computation of image similarity

In Fig. 18.1, the stages of computation of the similarity between two images is shown. The process works with two images: a query image and a target image from the image library. Both the images require intermediate representations. A similarity score is computed on features that are extracted to form these representations. Choice of an appropriate feature representation and determining the suitable similarity metric or distance function (which captures dissimilarity) are the key issues in the context of the CBIR.

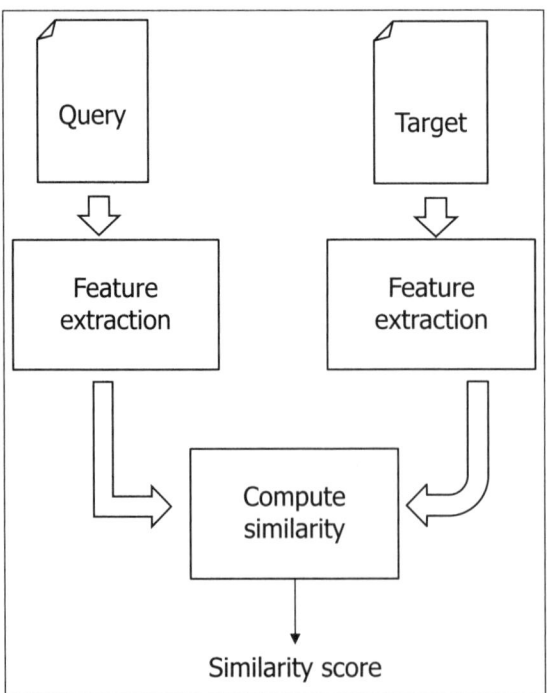

Figure 18.1 Process of computing similarity between two images.

18.1.1 | Feature descriptors in CBIR systems

In various systems, feature descriptors play a very crucial role. Typically, these descriptors are global in nature. For instance, histograms of different local features are used, such as local binary pattern (LBP) (Tobin et al., 2005), texture features, etc. Alternatively, feature descriptors may be generated using a code book. This involves forming a codebook or using a dictionary of reference feature vectors (or atoms). The *bag of visual words* (BoVW) and the *vector of locally aggregated descriptors* (VLAD)[1] are two of the popular codebook-based methods. The BoVW uses features like SIFT and SURF, which are quantized in a feature space, leading to histograms of visual words. In the VLAD, the offsets from various feature descriptors are accumulated, relative to the center of the quantized bin, for forming the codes. For a dictionary-based representation, sparse encoding using a dictionary of feature descriptors from a set of reference images is employed.

In specific domains, CBIR systems leverage certain domain-specific features. For instance, there are various CBIR systems reported in the literature to cater the needs of remote sensing applications (Aptoula, 2014). These systems utilize the features of multi-spectral images and combine the conventional descriptors such as the BoVW or the VLAD, with a bag of spectral value descriptors (Dai et al., 2018). In this case, the spectral value codebook is generated from the spectral vectors at pixels or histograms of the quantized spectral values in the neighborhood of a pixel. The *global morphological texture descriptor* is also one such example (Aptoula, 2014). There are various CBIR systems in medical imaging applications that use images from imaging modalities, like PET-CT CBIR system (Kumar et al., 2015). Here, the region properties, such as size and surface area, from the PET-CT images are used in addition to image texture and intensity information. The tumor *standardized uptake value* (SUV)[2] is also a relevant feature for retrieval in related cases. These techniques demonstrate the adaptability of CBIR systems under specific contexts within different domains.

18.1.2 | Similarity measures in CBIR systems

There are various measures of similarity (or dissimilarity) that are used in CBIR systems. A few of these metrics are discussed in Chapter 4. Here we present them again with a few other metrics used in a CBIR system.

- L_p norm: For the given two n-D vectors, $\boldsymbol{f} = \begin{bmatrix} f_1 & f_2 & ...f_n \end{bmatrix}$ and $\boldsymbol{g} = \begin{bmatrix} g_1 & g_2 & ...g_n \end{bmatrix}$, a general definition of L_p norm is given by Eq. 18.1.

$$L_p(\boldsymbol{f}, \boldsymbol{g}) = \left(\sum_{i=0}^{n} |f_i - g_i|^p \right)^{\frac{1}{p}} \tag{18.1}$$

- L_1 and L_2 norms: Two particular cases of L_p norm are, (1) L_1 norm ($p = 1$), which is the sum of differences of absolute values of the respective feature components, and

---

[1] Please refer to Section 4.4.3, Chapter 4.
[2] Refer to Section 14.3 of Chapter 14.

(2) L_2 norm $(p = 2)$, L_2 norm which is effectively the Euclidean distance between the two feature vectors. These norms are given by Eq. 18.2.

$$L_1(\boldsymbol{f}, \boldsymbol{g}) = \left(\sum_{i=0}^{n} |f_i - g_i| \right)$$

$$L_2(\boldsymbol{f}, \boldsymbol{g}) = \left(\sum_{i=0}^{n} |f_i - g_i|^2 \right)^{\frac{1}{2}}$$

(18.2)

- Cosine similarity measure: A normalized dot product of the unit vectors of the two feature descriptors is defined by cosine similarity, which is given by Eq. 18.3.

$$\text{Cosine similarity} = \frac{(\boldsymbol{f} \cdot \boldsymbol{g})}{||\boldsymbol{f}|| \, ||\boldsymbol{g}||}$$

(18.3)

- A probability distribution based measure similarity measure, known as Kullback–Leibler divergence (KLD), between two vectors, P and Q, is given by Eq. 18.4.

$$D_{KL}(P||Q) = -\sum_{\forall x} P(x)\ln\left(\frac{P(x)}{Q(x)} \right)$$

(18.4)

- The chi-square statistic is also a statistical measure used to measure the dissimilarity. This is given by Eq. 18.5.

$$\chi^2 = \frac{1}{2} \sum_{i=0}^{n} \frac{(f_i - g_i)^2}{f_i + g_i}$$

(18.5)

- Canberra distance (Lance and Williams, 1967) is another popular distance measure which is not a metric in strict sense, but found to be useful in the context of similarity. The Canberra distance is given by Eq. 18.6.

$$C(\boldsymbol{f}, \boldsymbol{g}) = \sum_{i=0}^{n} \frac{|f_i - g_i|}{|f_i| + |g_i|}$$

(18.6)

18.1.3 | Indexing methods in CBIR systems

Indexing methods consider the spatial proximity of the vectors in the feature space. There are different kinds of approximate nearest neighbor search, which are the basis of several indexing techniques that form certain kind of data structures, like K-D tree,[3] SR tree, etc. There are also certain hashing techniques that takes care of the local proximity during the generation of the hash value. One such technique is the locality sensitive hashing (LSH).[4] It is particularly found to be very useful in CBIR systems.

---

[3] See Section 4.5.4 of Chapter 4.
[4] See Section 4.5.4 of Chapter 4.

18.2 | Archival and query processing in CBIR systems

Though the heart of the system lies in computing the image similarity, it is also necessary to understand the overall architecture of a CBIR system. The CBIR system comprises of two primary processes, namely, the archival process and the query process. The archival process plays a pivotal role in organizing and managing image data in the database of a CBIR system. In the query processing stage, given a query it finds similar images from the archived database.

18.2.1 | Archival process in CBIR systems

The archival process archives information. It creates databases with indices to store relevant information. A block diagram of the archival process is shown in Fig. 18.2. Consider a set of n images, $I_1, I_2, \dots, I_n$. A codebook serves as a bag of visual words for this set. The technique for forming the visual words includes extraction of key points from the images. The feature descriptors (such as SIFT, SURF, etc.) associated with these key points form candidates for the codebook, which are then subjected to vector quantization. Techniques like K-means clustering[5] generate a finite set of codes (cluster centers) that constitute the visual words.

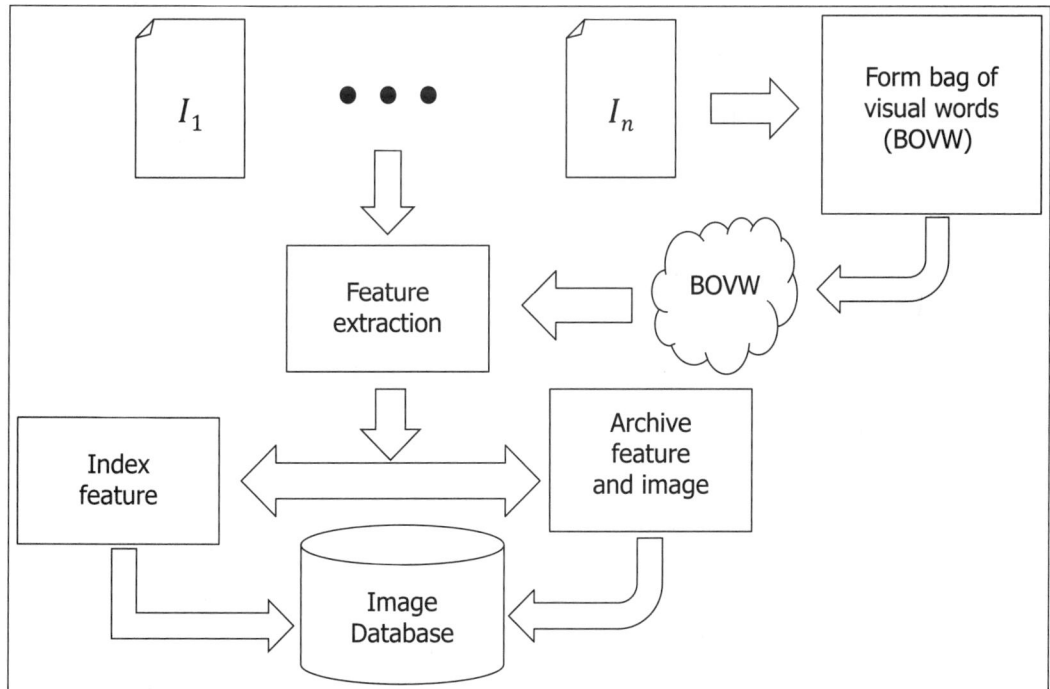

Figure 18.2 Archival process in CBIR systems.

---

[5] See Section 6.2 of Chapter 6.

Then, for each image, the features are extracted. The quantized cell of the codebook to which a feature descriptor belongs to is determined using nearest neighbor search. The count for that cell (representing the number of occurrences in the image) is incremented to construct a histogram of the visual words, which serves as a feature representation. This feature is indexed using an appropriate indexing scheme. Accordingly, the image is archived along with its associated features. This process generates the image database. Thus, the archival process involves forming a codebook, creating feature vectors, indexing, and storing images, enabling efficient retrieval in CBIR systems.

18.2.2 | Query processing in CBIR systems

When a query is provided, the goal is to identify similar images from that database. A block diagram of the query processing is shown in Fig. 18.3. Similar to the archival process, the query image is also represented by some kind of feature representation. The feature is extracted, key points are identified, and feature descriptors are captured. For example, the bag of visual words is used to form the feature descriptor, which is a histogram of visual words. Given a specific feature descriptor, an indexing scheme is applied to search for similar candidate feature vectors in the feature space. These vectors correspond to similar or neighboring features. Subsequently, similarity scores are computed for each of the candidate

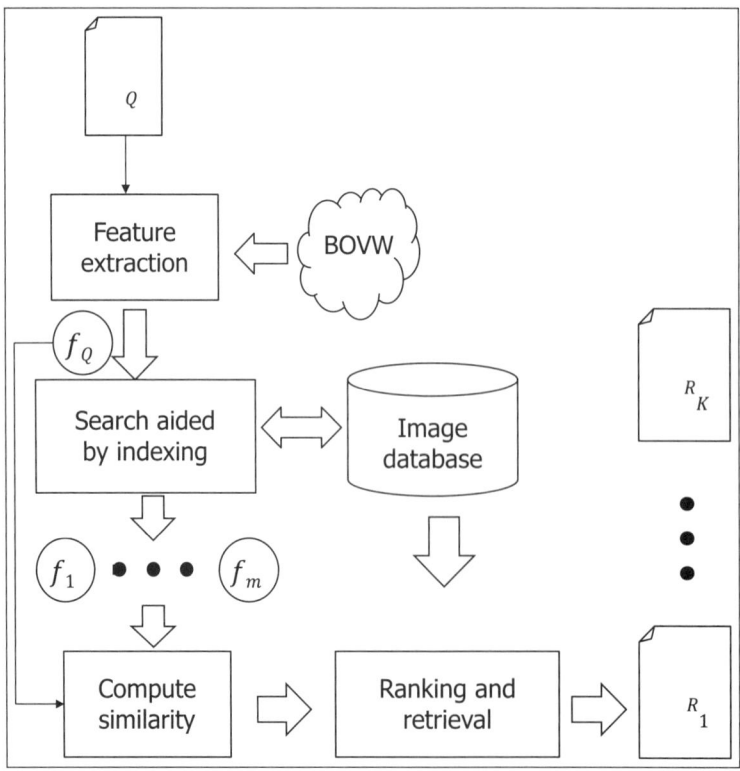

Figure 18.3 Query processing in CBIR systems.

vectors. Based on these scores, the vectors are ranked. Finally, using the image database and its corresponding feature representations, a list of top K ranked images are retrieved and reported. Thus, the query process involves extracting a feature vector from the query image, getting candidate feature vectors by approximate nearest neighbor search or LSH, computing similarity score for each of them, and rank them by its score to output top K results.

Typical results of query processing are shown in Fig. 18.4. The images shown in the figure belong to the *Indian Heritage Image Retrieval Dataset* (IHIRD)[6] (Podder, 2018), which are captured from the monumental sites of Hampi and Halebidu in Karnataka and some other

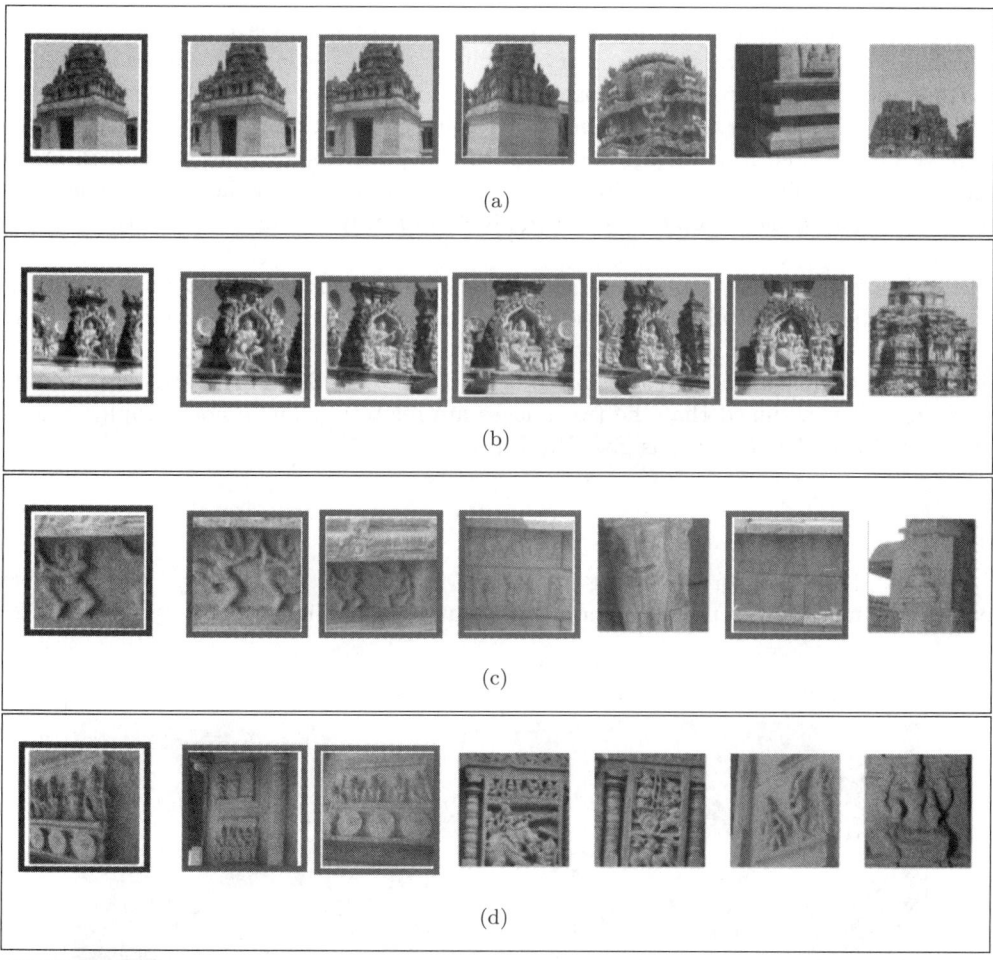

(a)

(b)

(c)

(d)

Figure 18.4 Retrieval results from the Indian Heritage Image Retrieval Dataset (IHIRD). (*Source*: Dipannita Podder, IIT Kharagpur, for sharing images from her MS thesis (Podder, 2018).) See Color Plates (page 824).

---

[6] http://www.facweb.iitkgp.ac.in/ jay/ihird/index.html.

places in India. The query images are shown by an encapsulated red rectangular box and the images in blue box are the correctly retrieved images. For example, the query image in Fig. 18.4 (a) represents a temple, showcasing its shape and appearance. By querying the database, several images are generated, which are visibly similar. It is observed that, even the temple's dome (referred to as the "Shikhara") exhibits visual similarities. Also, the results demonstrate scale invariance.

18.3 | Detection of duplicate images

In image databases, notably, the presence of near duplicate images is a common issue. When a database contains an excessive number of duplicate images, it leads to clutter, both in the database and the query results. For example, consider the two images shown in Fig. 18.5, which appear very similar, captures almost the same scene, yet they are not identical. These images were captured from slightly different camera positions and viewing angles. Due to their visual proximity, the user might prefer not to retain both of them. Such images fall into the category of near duplicates. There are certain ways to detect such near duplicate images.

Let us discuss a typical technique in detecting near duplicate images. In this technique (Mukherjee et al., 2014), the problem of duplicate image detection is considered as follows.

Given a pair of images, I_1 and I_2, it is to check if they are near duplicates capturing the same scene. It is assumed that the two images are related by affine homography (refer to Section 10.2.1 of Chapter 10), as given by Eq. 18.7.

$$x' = \mathbf{H}x \qquad (18.7)$$

where x and x' are corresponding points in I_1 and I_2, respectively, and $\mathbf{H}$ is the homography matrix. The points x and x' are related by the linear transform $\mathbf{H}$ in the 2-D

(a)   (b)

Figure 18.5 Example of a pair of near duplicate images.

Figure 18.6 Retrieval results from searches on duplicate images. (*Source*: Dr Jit Mukherjee of Birla Institute of Technology, Mesra, for sharing images from his MS thesis (Mukherjee, 2014).) See Color Plates (page 824).

projective space. The matrix, $\mathbf{H} = \begin{bmatrix} \mathbf{A} & \boldsymbol{t} \\ \mathbf{0}^{\top} & 1 \end{bmatrix}$, is an affine transformation matrix, where $\mathbf{A}$ is the 2×2 sub matrix whose rows are orthogonal, $\boldsymbol{t}$ is 2×1 translation vector, $\mathbf{0}$ is 1×2 zero vector, and 1 is a scalar value. Here, the properties of affine homography are exploited to establish existence of duplication. A ratio of distances between two points and their corresponding pairs in I_1 and I_2 is computed, which is used as a statistics to test for duplication. This ratio follows a distribution with a mean and standard deviation relating to the affine transform. Let $\mathbf{A}$ be expressed by its singular value decomposition in the form of $\mathbf{A} = \mathbf{U} \begin{bmatrix} \lambda_1 & 0 \\ 0 & \lambda_2 \end{bmatrix} \mathbf{V}^{\top}$, where λ_1 and λ_2 are the nonuniform scaling factors and $\mathbf{U}$ and $\mathbf{V}$ are orthonormal matrices. Then, μ, the mean of the ratios, and σ, their standard deviation, are given by Eq. 18.8.

$$\mu = \sqrt{\frac{\lambda_1^2 + \lambda_2^2}{2} \left(1 - \frac{\gamma^2}{16}\right)}$$

$$\sigma^2 = \frac{\lambda_1^2 + \lambda_2^2}{2} \left(\frac{\gamma^2}{8} - \frac{\gamma^4}{256}\right) \tag{18.8}$$

where $\gamma = \frac{\lambda_1^2 - \lambda_2^2}{\lambda_1^2 + \lambda_2^2}$. For two given images, performing a Z-test (Evans and Rosenthal, 2009) to check whether the average of the ratios follow the distribution given in Eq. 18.8 verifies if the images are duplicates. If the mean value of the observed distribution is close to the theoretical mean value, the null hypothesis of the Z-test is accepted as the two given images are near-duplicate images.

Examples of results of duplication check are shown in Fig. 18.6. Here, the query images are shown in red boxes. Among the retrieved results, some are duplicate images to the query image, which are shown by the blue boxes.

18.4 | Performance metrics in CBIR systems

Assessing the performance of a CBIR system is a critical task. It serves as a basis for comparing different CBIR systems. The fundamental objective lies in evaluating the relevance of retrieved images based on a query image. Here, the semantic gap is a challenge, making it difficult to determine what qualifies as relevant. Often, this judgment is subjective and user-driven. However, several methods exist to aggregate diverse opinions and establish a ground truth.

For testing CBIR systems, researchers create specialized test databases that contain labeled data. These labels indicate whether an image is relevant or nonrelevant, thereby establishing ground truths for the images in the dataset. Such labeled datasets are valuable for assessing system performance. Sometimes, when obtaining such annotated labels as ground truth is challenging, even unlabeled datasets are used. In such cases, user feedback during post-retrieval analysis contributes toward computing the performance metrics. There are various datasets that provide ground truths for evaluating CBIR systems, such as, INRIA Holidays dataset (Jegou et al., 2008), the University of Kentucky Recognition Benchmark (UKB) (Nister and Stewenius, 2006), and the Indian Heritage Image Retrieval Dataset (IHIRD) (Podder et al., 2018).

For evaluating CBIR systems, various performance metrics are used. Let top K images be retrieved for a given query image, q. Let X_r be a set of retrieved images, along with their ranks, such that, the number of images in this set is K, $|X_r| = K$. Also, let X_q be the set of ground truth labeled relevant images for the query q. That is, these considerations correspond to a labeled dataset.

Precision of a CBIR system is measured as the fraction of relevant images among the retrieved results. It is expressed as follows.

$$\text{Precision} = \frac{|X_q \cap X_r|}{|X_r|} \tag{18.9}$$

For the evaluation with top K ranked images, this is referred to as *precision@K*. Here, X_q is sometimes obtained from the user feedback, enabling the computation of precision.

Computing the *recall* of a query requires ground truth of relevant information. It represents the fraction of relevant images among the ground truth-labeled images. It is expressed as follows.

$$\text{Recall} = \frac{|X_q \cap X_r|}{|X_q|} \tag{18.10}$$

It should be noted that, recall is not defined for unlabeled datasets. With an increasing value of K (i.e., more number of retrieved results), recall may increase, but precision declines. To strike a balance, recall at certain precision (*recall@precision*) is defined. This composite measure is often used for assessing CBIR systems.

There is another widely used performance metric called *average precision* (AP) of a query, which is computed from the rank list of the query. For each relevant image in the ordered list, the precision at its ordinal position is computed. These precision values over the entire list are averaged to obtain the AP. Suppose the relevance of the jth retrieved image is denoted by $\text{Rel}(j)$. If the jth retrieved image is a relevant image then $\text{Rel}(j) = 1$, otherwise, $\mathrm{Rel}(j) = 0$. The precision of the top j retrieved images is denoted by $\mathrm{Prec}(j)$. Then, the *average precision* of a query, q, is given by Eq. 18.11.

$$AP(q) = \frac{\sum_{j=1}^{K} \mathrm{Rel}(j)\,\mathrm{Prec}(j)}{\sum_{j=1}^{K} \mathrm{Rel}(j)} \tag{18.11}$$

Thus, the AP of a query is a weighted average of precisions of relevant images. Also, when more number of queries are considered, then *mean average precision* is computed. The mean average precision of N queries, mAP, is given by Eq. 18.12.

$$\mathrm{mAP} = \frac{1}{N} \sum_{i=1}^{N} AP(q_i) \tag{18.12}$$

The rank based assessment of labeled datasets considers the number of available ground truth. Relevant images of a query q is expressed in this way. Let $\mathrm{NG}(q)$ represent the number of ground truth relevant images of q. Let the rank of the kth ground truth image for the query q be represented by $\mathrm{Rank}(k|q)$. A *rank* of k is modified to $\mathrm{Rank}^*(k|q)$, if $\mathrm{Rank}(k|q)$ is very high, i.e., $\mathrm{Rank}(k|q) \gg \mathrm{NG}(q)$. Then, the value of the rank is penalized with a penalization function that uses a query dependent threshold, $\mathrm{K}(q)$. Usually, $\mathrm{K}(q) = 2\,\mathrm{NG}(q)$. The modified rank is given by Eq. 18.13.

$$\mathrm{Rank}^*(k|q) = \begin{cases} \mathrm{Rank}(k|q), & \text{if } \mathrm{Rank}(k|q) < \mathrm{K}(q) \\ 1.25\,\mathrm{K}(q), & \text{otherwise} \end{cases} \tag{18.13}$$

Then the *average of the rank* of all the ground truths, normalized by the number of relevant images in the retrieved results, is given as follows.

$$AVR(q) = \frac{1}{\mathrm{NG}(q)} \sum_{k \in \mathrm{NG}(q)} \mathrm{Rank}^*(k|q) \tag{18.14}$$

Another measure that averages all the ranks for N number of queries is called *average normalized retrieval rank* (ANMRR), which is given by Eq. 18.15.

$$\mathrm{ANMRR} = \frac{1}{N} \sum_{q=1}^{N} \frac{AVR(q) - 0.5(1 + \mathrm{NG}(q))}{1.5\mathrm{K}(q) - 0.5(1 + \mathrm{NG}(q))} \tag{18.15}$$

The expression of ANMRR is adopted in MPEG-7 multimedia standard.[7]

---

[7] https://web.archive.org/web/20100420142306/http://mpeg.chiariglione.org/standards/mpeg-7/mpeg-7.htm.

18.5 | Improving the performance of CBIR systems

Several strategies are proposed for enhancing the performance of CBIR systems, particularly to tailor feature selection for specific domains. One of such approaches is to employ query based feature selection. Different techniques of query based feature selection are as follows.

- Using relevance feedback during feature selection (Jiang et al., 2006): In this approach, there is a provision for taking users' feedback during feature selection. Visual tools allow users to choose a relevant set of features or a projected feature subset. Overcoming the semantic gap is a key motivation here.

- Discriminative feature selection: By selecting k relevant images from the set of retrieved images, the gap between high-level and low-level features are bridged. Initially, discriminative features are extracted from the query images. User feedback on the relevance of retrieved images then guides the selection process. After classifying the query images, an appropriate feature set for each class is used.

- Class hierarchy and predefined features (Dy et al., 2003): A class hierarchy may be followed by using predefined features at every level of hierarchy. The hierarchical approach ensures relevance across different classes.

- Visual analytics in a low-dimensional space: Visual analytics may be applied through interactive exploration. Here, feature vectors are projected into a low-dimensional space. The goal is to choose an effective combination of discriminative features.

Another way of improving the retrieval performance is by including visual saliency[8] to guide the retrieval process. In this context, the effort is made to address a fundamental question, which is that whether the query intention can be discerned to retrieve relevant images (Rutishauser et al., 2004; Acharya and Devi, 2012; Wei et al., 2019). To illustrate this concept, consider a query image, as shown in Fig. 18.7. Depending on the intended object of focus in the image, the retrieved results may vary. For example, it can be the sea gull

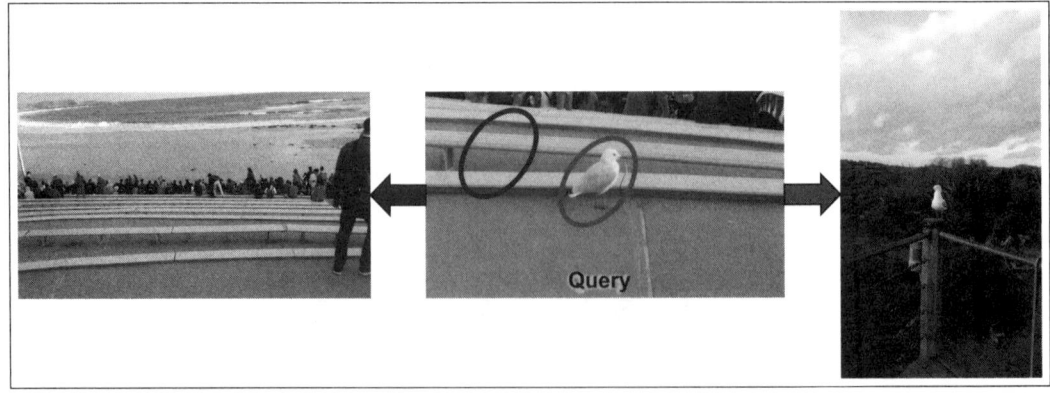

Figure 18.7 Illustration of visual saliency guided image retrieval.

[8] See Chapter 5.

or the bench. In this case, the central object, the single salient zone, holds the significance. By restricting feature representations to this salient zones, the retrieved results may be modified as desired. Extracting features solely from such regions and applying a saliency model enhances effectiveness of the retrieval.

Summary

CBIR involves searching similar images in an image database, given a query image. Images are generally represented using global descriptors. These descriptors may be generic by using codebook-based features, or domain-specific by incorporating features specific to different imaging modalities. Efficient search in CBIR systems faces several challenges to provide good quality of the results by keeping the search time short. To reduce search time, various techniques are suggested, including indexing schemes and hashing techniques. Mitigating the semantic gap is also a crucial step. Methods for feature selection based on queries, ontologies, and keywords are seen to play a significant role in bridging this gap. Avoiding near-duplicate images is also essential for creating a clean and clutter-free database and refining retrieved results. CBIR methodologies are evaluated using various performance metrics. These include precision, recall, precision@K, recall@precision, average precision, mean average precision, average rank and average normalized retrieval rank.

Exercises

(i) What is meant by the CBIR? What are the challenges involved in this computation.

(ii) Briefly describe various methods of describing the overall (global) content of an image.

(iii) Give examples of a few domain, whose specific features become useful in the CBIR.

(iv) Discuss different indexing methods used in storing the feature descriptors for reducing the time of search.

(v) Why is it needed to detect duplicate images in a CBIR system? Describe a method to detect duplicate images.

(vi) Suppose X_r is the top-K retrieved set of images for a query q in order of their ranks (from highest to the lowest rank), and $|X_r| = K$. Also X_q is the set of relevant images for the query q provides as the ground truth. Define the following performance metrics of a CBIR system.

(a) Precision of a query.

(b) Recall of a query.

(c) Recall @ precision of a query.

(d) Mean average precision (for N queries).

(e) Average rank of a query.

(f) Average normalized retrieval rank (ANMRR) (for N queries).

(vii) Discuss how visual saliency can guide the CBIR.

Bibliography

Acharya, Satrajit, and Devi, M. R. Vimala. 2012. Image Retrieval Based on Visual Attention Model. *Procedia Engineering*, **30**, 542–545. International Conference on Communication Technology and System Design.

Adams, James E. Jr., and Hamilton, John F. Jr. United States Patent 5 629 734, 1997. *Adaptive Color Plane Interpolation in Single Sensor Color Electronic Camera.*

Aharon, M., Elad, M., and Bruckstein, A. 2006. K-SVD: An Algorithm for Designing Overcomplete Dictionaries for Sparse Representation. *IEEE Transactions on Signal Processing*, **54**(11), 4311–4322.

Ahonen, T., Hadid, A., and Pietikainen, M. 2006. Face Description with Local Binary Patterns: Application to Face Recognition. *IEEE Transactions on Pattern Analysis and Machine Intelligence*, **28**(12), 2037–2041.

Andoni, Alexandr, and Indyk, Piotr. 2008. Near-optimal Hashing Algorithms for Approximate Nearest Neighbor in High Dimensions. *Commun. ACM*, **51**(1), 117–122.

Aptoula, E. 2014. Remote Sensing Image Retrieval With Global Morphological Texture Descriptors. *IEEE Transactions on Geoscience and Remote Sensing*, **52**(5), 3023–3034.

Arulampalam, M.S., Maskell, S., Gordon, N., and Clapp, T. 2002. A Tutorial on Particle Filters for Online Nonlinear/Non-Gaussian Bayesian Tracking. *IEEE Transactions on Signal Processing*, **50**(2), 174–188.

Badrinarayanan, Vijay, Kendall, Alex, and Cipolla, Roberto. 2017. SegNet: A Deep Convolutional Encoder-Decoder Architecture for Image Segmentation. *IEEE Transactions on Pattern Analysis and Machine Intelligence*, **39**(12), 2481–2495.

Barnard, Kobus, Martin, Lindsay, Funt, Brian, and Coath, Adam. 2002. A Data Set for Colour Research. *Color Research and Application*, **27**(3), 147–151.

Bay, H., Andreas Ess, A., Tuytelaars, T, and Gool, Luc Van. 2008. Speeded-Up Robust Features (SURF). *Computer Vision and Image Understanding*, **110**(3), 346–359.

Bazaraa, Mokhtar S., Sherali, Hanif D., and Shetty, C. M. 2006. *Nonlinear Programming: Theory and Algorithms.* New Jersy: John Wiley & Sons.

Bellman, Richard E. (ed). 2010. *Dynamic Programming.* New Jersey: Princeton University Press.

Besl, P. J., and McKay, N. D. 1992. A Method for Registration of 3-D Shapes. *IEEE Transactions on Pattern Analysis and Machine Intelligence*, **14**(2), 239–256.

Besl, Paul J., and Jain, Ramesh C. 1986. Invariant Surface Characteristics for 3D Object Recognition in Range Images. *Computer Vision, Graphics, and Image Processing*, **33**(1), 33–80.

Blanz, V., and Vetter, T. 2003. Face Recognition Based on Fitting a 3D Morphable Model. *IEEE Transactions on Pattern Analysis and Machine Intelligence*, **25**(9), 1063–1074.

Brady, Michael, Ponce, Jean, Yuille, Alan, and Asada, Haruo. 1985. Describing Surfaces. *Computer Vision, Graphics, and Image Processing*, **32**(1), 1–28.

Bresenham, J. E. 1965. Algorithm for Computer Control of a Digital Plotter. *IBM Systems Journal*, **4**(1), 25–30.

Buchsbaum, G. 1980. A Spatial Processor Model for Object Colour Perception. *Journal of the Franklin Institute*, **310**(1), 1–26.

Burgos-Artizzu, X.P., Coronado-Gutiérrez, D., Valenzuela-Alcaraz, B., Bonet-Carne, E., Eixarch, E., Crispi, F., and Gratacós, E. 2020. Evaluation of Deep Convolutional Neural Networks for Automatic Classification of Common Maternal Fetal Ultrasound Planes. *Nature Scientific Reports*, **10**, 10200.

Calonder, Michael, Lepetit, Vincent, Strecha, Christoph, and Fua, Pascal. 2010. BRIEF: Binary Robust Independent Elementary Features. Pages 778–792 of: Daniilidis, Kostas, Maragos, Petros, and Paragios, Nikos (eds), *Computer Vision – ECCV 2010*. Berlin, Heidelberg: Springer Berlin Heidelberg.

Cameron, William L., and Rais, Houra. 2006. Conservative Polarimetric Scatterers and Their Role in Incorrect Extensions of the Cameron Decompositions. *IEEE Transactions on Geoscience and Remote Sensing*, **44**(12), 3506–3516.

Canny, John. 1986. A Computational Approach to Edge Detection. *IEEE Transactions on Pattern Analysis and Machine Intelligence*, **PAMI-8**(6), 679–698.

Cao, Zhe, Simon, Tomas, Wei, Shih-En, and Sheikh, Yaser. 2017. Realtime Multi-person 2D Pose Estimation Using Part Affinity Fields. *IEEE Conference on Computer Vision and Pattern Recognition (CVPR)*, 1302–1310.

Carreira, J., and Zisserman, A. 2017. Quo Vadis, Action Recognition? A New Model and the Kinetics Dataset. *2017 IEEE Conference on Computer Vision and Pattern Recognition (CVPR)*, 4724–4733. IEEE Computer Society.

Chen, Fei, Wang, Xiaodong, Zhao, Yunxiang, Lv, Shaohe, and Niu, Xin. 2022. Visual Object Tracking: A Survey. *Computer Vision and Image Understanding*, **222**, 103508.

Cheng, Yizong. 1995. Mean Shift, Mode Seeking, and Clustering. *IEEE Transactions on Pattern Analysis and Machine Intelligence*, **17**(8), 790–799.

Cho, Kyunghyun, van Merrienboer, Bart, Gulcehre, Caglar, Bahdanau, Dzmitry, Bougares, Fethi, Schwenk, Holger, and Bengio, Yoshua. 2014. *Learning Phrase Representations using RNN Encoder-Decoder for Statistical Machine Translation*.

Clevert, Djork-Arné, Unterthiner, Thomas, and Hochreiter, Sepp. 2016. Fast and Accurate Deep Network Learning by Exponential Linear Units (ELUs). In: Bengio, Yoshua, and LeCun, Yann (eds), *International Conference on Learning Representations (ICLR)*.

Comaniciu, D., and Meer, P. 2002. Mean Shift: A Robust Approach Toward Feature Space Analysis. *IEEE Transactions on Pattern Analysis and Machine Intelligence*, **24**(5), 603–619.

Cootes, T.F., Edwards, G.J., and Taylor, C.J. 2001. Active Appearance Models. *IEEE Transactions on Pattern Analysis and Machine Intelligence*, **23**(6), 681–685.

Cormen, Thomas H., Leiserson, Charles E., Rivest, Ronald L., and Stein, Clifford. 2009. *Introduction to Algorithms, 3rd edition*. Cambridge, Massachusetts: MIT Press.

Crowley, James L. 1997. Vision for Man-machine Interaction. *Robotics and Autonomous Systems*, **19**(3), 347–358.

Dai, Jifeng, He, Kaiming, and Sun, Jian. 2016. Instance-Aware Semantic Segmentation via Multi-task Network Cascades. *IEEE Conference on Computer Vision and Pattern Recognition (CVPR)*, 3150–3158.

Dai, O.E., Demir, B., Sankur, B., and Bruzzone, L. 2018. A Novel System for Content-Based Retrieval of Single and Multi-Label High-Dimensional Remote Sensing Images. *IEEE Journal of Selected Topics in Applied Earth Observations and Remote Sensing*, **11**(7), 2473–2490.

Dalal, N., and Triggs, B. 2005. Histograms of Oriented Gradients for Human Detection. *IEEE Computer Society Conference on Computer Vision and Pattern Recognition (CVPR)*, **1**, 886–893.

Dey, Nilanjan, Pal, Gautam, Rudrapal, Dwijen, Acharjee, Suvojit, Ray, Ruben, and Chakraborty, Sayan. 2015. Video Shot Boundary Detection: A Review. *Advances in Intelligent Systems and Computing*, **338**, 119–127.

Dey, Soumyadeep. 2019. *Segmentation of Scanned Document Images and its Applications* (PhD Thesis). West Bengal: Indian Institute of Technology Kharagpur.

Dogra, D. P. 2012. *Algorithms for Video Assisted Analysis of Infant Neurological Examinations (PhD Thesis)*. West Bengal: Indian Institute of Technology Kharagpur.

Donahue, Jeff, Jia, Yangqing, Vinyals, Oriol, Hoffman, Judy, Zhang, Ning, Tzeng, Eric, and Darrell, Trevor. 2014. DeCAF: A Deep Convolutional Activation Feature for Generic Visual Recognition. Xing, Eric P., and Jebara, Tony (eds), *Proceedings of the 31st International Conference on Machine Learning*. Proceedings of Machine Learning Research, 32(1), 647–655. Bejing, China: PMLR.

Duda, Richard O., and Hart, Peter E. 1972. Use of the Hough Transformation to Detect Lines and Curves in Pictures. *Commun. ACM*, **15**(1), 11–15.

Duda, Richard O., Hart, Peter E., and Stork, David G. 2000. *Pattern Classification*. USA: Wiley-Interscience.

Dy, J. G., Brodley, C. E., Kak, A., Broderick, L. S., and Aisen, A. M. 2003. Unsupervised Feature Selection Applied to Content-based Retrieval of Lung Images. *IEEE Transactions on Pattern Analysis and Machine Intelligence*, **25**(3), 373–378.

Evans, M.J., and Rosenthal, J.S. 2009. *Probability and Statistics: The Science of Uncertainty*. W. H. Freeman.

Faugeras, O. D., and Hebert, M. 1986. The Representation, Recognition, and Locating of 3-D Objects. *International Journal of Robotics Research*, **5**(3), 27–52.

Feng, Jianjiang, Shi, Yuan, and Zhou, Jie. 2012. Robust and Efficient Algorithms for Separating Latent Overlapped Fingerprints. *IEEE Transactions on Information Forensics and Security*, **7**(5), 1498–1510.

Finlayson, G. D., Hordley, S. D., and HubeL, P. M. 2001. Color by Correlation: A Simple, Unifying Framework for Color Constancy. *IEEE Transactions on Pattern Analysis and Machine Intelligence*, **23**(11), 1209–1221.

Fischler, Martin A., and Bolles, Robert C. 1981. Random Sample Consensus: A Paradigm for Model Fitting with Applications to Image Analysis and Automated Cartography. *Commun. ACM*, **24**(6), 381–395.

Fisher, R. A. 1938. The Statistical Utilization of Multiple Measurements. *Annals of Eugenics*, **8**(4), 376–386.

Fletcher, L. A., and Kasturi, R. 1988. A Robust Algorithm for Text String Separation from Mixed Text/Graphics Images. *IEEE Transactions on Pattern Analysis and Machine Intelligence*, **10**(6), 910–918.

Forsyth, David A., and Ponce, Jean. 2011. *Computer Vision: A Modern Approach*. USA: Pearson Education.

Frazier, Michael W. 2005. *An Introduction to Wavelets Through Linear Algebra*. New York: Springer.

Freund, Yoav, and Schapire, Robert E. 1997. A Decision-Theoretic Generalization of On-Line Learning and an Application to Boosting. *Journal of Computer and System Sciences*, **55**(1), 119–139.

Fukunaga, K., and Hostetler, L. 1975. The Estimation of the Gradient of a Density Function, With Applications in Pattern Recognition. *IEEE Transactions on Information Theory*, **21**(1), 32–40.

Gatys, Leon A., Ecker, Alexander S., and Bethge, Matthias. 2016. Image Style Transfer Using Convolutional Neural Networks. *IEEE Conference on Computer Vision and Pattern Recognition (CVPR)*, 2414–2423.

Gershon, Ron, Jepson, Allan D., and Tsotsos, John K. 1987. From [R,G,B] to Surface Reflectance: Computing Color Constant Descriptors in Images. *International Joint Conference on Artificial Intelligence*, **2**, 755–758.

Girshick, Ross. 2015. Fast R-CNN. *2015 IEEE International Conference on Computer Vision (ICCV)*, 1440–1448.

Girshick, Ross, Donahue, Jeff, Darrell, Trevor, and Malik, Jitendra. 2014. Rich Feature Hierarchies for Accurate Object Detection and Semantic Segmentation. *2014 IEEE Conference on Computer Vision and Pattern Recognition*, 580–587.

Goodfellow, Ian, Warde-Farley, David, Mirza, Mehdi, Courville, Aaron, and Bengio, Yoshua. 2013. Maxout Networks. Dasgupta, Sanjoy, and McAllester, David (eds), Proceedings of the International Conference on Machine Learning. *Proceedings of Machine Learning Research*, **28**(3). 1319–1327. Atlanta, Georgia, USA: PMLR.

Gordon, Richard, Bender, Robert, and Herman, Gabor T. 1970. Algebraic Reconstruction Techniques (ART) for Three-dimensional Electron Microscopy and X-ray Photography. *Journal of Theoretical Biology*, **29**(3), 471–481.

Greff, Klaus, Srivastava, Rupesh K., Koutnk, Jan, Steunebrink, Bas R., and Schmidhuber, Jrgen. 2017. LSTM: A Search Space Odyssey. *IEEE Transactions on Neural Networks and Learning Systems*, **28**(10), 2222–2232.

Haralick, Robert M., Shanmugam, K., and Dinstein, Its'Hak. 1973. Textural Features for Image Classification. *IEEE Transactions on Systems, Man, and Cybernetics*, **3**(6), 610–621.

Harris, C., and Stephens, M. 1988. A Combined Corner and Edge Detector. *Proceedings of the Alvey Vision Conference*. Alvey Vision Club, pp. 23.1–23.6.

Hartley, Richard, and Zisserman, Andrew. 2003. *Multiple View Geometry in Computer Vision*. USA: Cambridge University Press.

Hastie, Trevor, Tibshirani, Rob, and Friedman, Jerry. 2017. *Elements of Statistical Learning*. Switzerland: Springer.

Haykin, Simon. 1998. *Neural Networks: A Comprehensive Foundation*. USA: Prentice Hall PTR.

He, Kaiming, Zhang, Xiangyu, Ren, Shaoqing, and Sun, Jian. 2016. Deep Residual Learning for Image Recognition. *IEEE Conference on Computer Vision and Pattern Recognition (CVPR)*, 770–778.

Heisenberg, W. 1927. On the Intuitive Content of Quantum Theoretical Kinematics and Mechanics. *Magazine for Physics*, **43**, 172–198.

Henriques, João F., Caseiro, Rui, Martins, Pedro, and Batista, Jorge. 2015. High-Speed Tracking with Kernelized Correlation Filters. *IEEE Transactions on Pattern Analysis and Machine Intelligence*, **37**(3), 583–596.

Hochreiter, Sepp, and Schmidhuber, Jurgen. 1997. Long Short-Term Memory. *Neural Computation*, **9**(8), 1735–1780.

Horn, Berthold K.P., and Schunck, Brian G. 1981. Determining Optical Flow. *Artificial Intelligence*, **17**(1), 185–203.

Howard, Andrew G., Zhu, Menglong, Chen, Bo, Kalenichenko, Dmitry, Wang, Weijun, Weyand, Tobias, Andreetto, Marco, and Adam, Hartwig. 2017. *MobileNets: Efficient Convolutional Neural Networks for Mobile Vision Applications*.

Hsieh, Yi-Chih. 2001. Decoding Structured Light Patterns for Three-dimensional Imaging Systems. *Pattern Recognition*, **34**(2), 343–349.

Hubel, D. H., and Wiesel, T. N. 1962. Receptive Fields, Binocular Interaction and Functional Architecture in the Cat's Visual Cortex. *The Journal of Physiology*, **160**(1), 106–154.

Hunt, R. W. G., and Pointer, M. R. 2011. *Measuring Colour*. USA: Wiley-Interscience.

Huo, Yi, Wang, Yanfeng, and Hu, Haihe. 2016. Effective Algorithms For Video Shot And Scene Boundaries Detection. *IEEE International Conference on Computer and Information Science*, **1**, 1–6.

Hutchinson, T.E., White, K.P., Martin, W.N., Reichert, K.C., and Frey, L.A. 1989. Human-computer Interaction Using Eye-gaze Input. *IEEE Transactions on Systems, Man, and Cybernetics*, **19**(6), 1527–1534.

Itti, L., and Koch, C. 2001. Computational Modelling of Visual Attention. *Nat Reviews Neuroscience*, **2**(3), 194–203.

Itti, L., Koch, C., and Niebur, E. 1998. A Model of Saliency-based Visual Attention for Rapid Scene Analysis. *IEEE Transactions on Pattern Analysis and Machine Intelligence*, **20**(11), 1254–1259.

Jain, Anil K. 2015. *Fundamentals of Digital Image Processing*. Chennai: Pearson Education.

Jain, Anil K., Ross, Arun A., and Nandakumar, Karthik. 2011. *Introduction to Biometrics*. New York: Springer-Verlag.

Jain, Anil K., Klare, Brendan, and Park, Unsang. 2012. Face Matching and Retrieval in Forensics Applications. *IEEE MultiMedia*, **19**(1), 20–20.

Jegou, H., Douze, M., and Schmid, C. 2008. Hamming Embedding and Weak Geometric Consistency for Large Scale Image Search. *European Conference on Computer Vision*, 304–317. Berlin: Springer-Verlag.

Jégou, Hervé, Douze, Matthijs, Schmid, Cordelia, and Pérez, Patrick. 2010. Aggregating Local Descriptors into a Compact Image Representation. 2010 IEEE Computer Society Conference on Computer Vision and Pattern Recognition, 3304–3311.

Jiang, W., Er, G., Dai, Q., and Gu, J. 2006. Similarity-based Online Feature Selection in Content-based Image Retrieval. *IEEE Transactions on Image Processing*, **15**(3), 702–712.

Kantipudi, M. V. V. Prasad, Kumar, Sandeep, and Jha, Ashish Kumar. 2021. Scene Text Recognition Based on Bidirectional LSTM and Deep Neural Network. *Comput. Intell. Neurosci.*, **2021**, 2676780:1–2676780:11.

Karpathy, Andrej, and Fei-Fei, Li. 2015. Deep visual-semantic alignments for generating image descriptions. *IEEE Conference on Computer Vision and Pattern Recognition (CVPR)*, 3128–3137.

Kaufman, Leonard, and Rousseeuw, Peter J. 2008. *Partitioning Around Medoids (Program PAM)*. John Wiley and Sons, Inc. 68–125.

Kazci, Omer, Aydin, Sonay, Fatihoglu, Erdem, Tokur, Oguzhan, Bahadir, Suzan, Karavas, Erdal, and Kantarci, Mecit. 2023. Normal Umbilical Artery Doppler Values in 18–22 Week Old Fetuses with Single Umbilical Artery. *Nature Scientific Reports*, **13**, 10477.

Kneizys, F. X., Shettle, E. P. snd Abreu, L. W., Chetwynd, J. H., and Anderson, G. P. 1988, Air Force Geophysics Lab Hanscom AFB MA, USA, August 16, *Users Guide to LOWTRAN 7*.

Koch, Christof, and Ullman, Shimon. 1985. Shifts in Selective Visual Attention: Towards the Underlying Neural Circuitry. *Human Neurobiology*, **4**(4), 219–227.

Krizhevsky, Alex, Sutskever, Ilya, and Hinton, Geoffrey E. 2012. ImageNet Classification with Deep Convolutional Neural Networks. In: Pereira, F., Burges, C.J., Bottou, L., and Weinberger, K.Q. (eds), *Advances in Neural Information Processing Systems*, vol. 25. Curran Associates, Inc.

Krogager, E. 1990. New Decomposition of the Radar Target Scattering Matrix. *IET Electronic Letters*, **26**(18), 1525–1527.

Kumar, A., Nette, F., Klein, K., Fulham, M., and Kim, J. 2015. A Visual Analytics Approach Using the Exploration of Multidimensional Feature Spaces for Content-Based Medical Image Retrieval. *IEEE Journal of Biomedical and Health Informatics*, **19**(5), 1734–1746.

Lance, G. N., and Williams, W. T. 1967. Mixed-Data Classificatory Programs I - Agglomerative Systems. *Aust. Comput. J.*, **1**(1), 15–20.

Land, Edwin H. 1977. The Retinex Theory of Color Vision. *Scientific American*, **237**(6), 108–128.

Lay, David C., Lay, Steven R., and McDonald, Judi J. 2015. *Linear Algebra and Its Applications*. USA: Pearson.

Lecun, Y., Bottou, L., Bengio, Y., and Haffner, P. 1998. Gradient-based Learning Applied to Document Recognition. *Proceedings of the IEEE*, **86**(11), 2278–2324.

Ledig, Christian, Theis, Lucas, Huszr, Ferenc, Caballero, Jose, Cunningham, Andrew, Acosta, Alejandro, Aitken, Andrew, Tejani, Alykhan, Totz, Johannes, Wang, Zehan, and Shi, Wenzhe. 2017. Photo-Realistic Single Image Super-Resolution Using a Generative Adversarial Network. *IEEE Conference on Computer Vision and Pattern Recognition (CVPR)*, 105–114.

Lee, Jong-Sen. 1980. Digital Image Enhancement and Noise Filtering by Use of Local Statistics. *IEEE Transactions on Pattern Analysis and Machine Intelligence*, **PAMI-2**(2), 165–168.

Li, Jun, Bioucas-Dias, Jos M., and Plaza, Antonio. 2011. A New Subspace Discriminant Analysis Approach for Supervised Hyperspectral Image Classification. *IEEE International Geoscience and Remote Sensing Symposium*, 3911–3914.

Ling, H., and Okada, K. 2007. An Efficient Earth Mover's Distance Algorithm for Robust Histogram Comparison. *IEEE Transactions on Pattern Analysis and Machine Intelligence*, **29**(5), 840–853.

Lipton, Zachary C., Berkowitz, John, and Elkan, Charles. 2015. *A Critical Review of Recurrent Neural Networks for Sequence Learning*.

Lloyd, S. 1982. Least Squares Quantization in PCM. *IEEE Transactions on Information Theory*, **28**(2), 129–137.

Long, J., Shelhamer, E., and Darrell, T. 2015. Fully Convolutional Networks for Semantic Segmentation. *2015 IEEE Conference on Computer Vision and Pattern Recognition (CVPR)*, 3431–3440. IEEE Computer Society.

Lowe, David G. 2004. Distinctive Image Features from Scale-Invariant Keypoints. *International Journal of Computer Vision*, **60**(2), 91–110.

Lucas, Bruce D., and Kanade, Takeo. 1981. An Iterative Image Registration Technique with an Application to Stereo Vision. IJCAI'81. San Francisco, CA, USA: Morgan Kaufmann Publishers Inc.

Lucchese, L., Mitra, S. K., and Mukherjee, J. 2001. A New Algorithm Based on Saturation and Desaturation in the XY Chromaticity Diagram for Enhancement and Re-rendition of Color Images. *International Conference on Image Processing*, **2**, 1077–1080.

Maas, A.L., Hannun, A.Y., and Ng, A.Y. 2013. Rectifier Nonlinearities Improve Neural Network Acoustic Models. *Proceedings of the International Conference on Machine Learning*.

Maier, Andreas, Steidl, Stefan, Christlein, Vincent, and Hornegger, Joachim (eds). 2018. *Medical Imaging Systems*. Switzerland: Springer.

Maio, D., Maltoni, D., Cappelli, R., Wayman, J.L., and Jain, A.K. 2002. FVC2002: Second Fingerprint Verification Competition. *2002 International Conference on Pattern Recognition*, **3**, 811–814.

Malladi, Sai Phani Kumar. 2022. *Study of Static and Dynamic Human Visual Saliency* (PhD Thesis). West Bengal: Indian Institute of Technology Kharagpur.

Malladi, Saiphani Kumar, Mukhopadhyay, Jayanta, Larabi, Mohamed-Chaker, and Chaudhury, Santanu. 2020. Eye Movement State Trajectory Estimator based on Ancestor Sampling. *IEEE International Workshop on Multimedia Signal Processing (MMSP)*, 1–6.

Maltoni, Davide, Maio, Dario, Jain, Anil K., and Feng, Jianjiang. 2022. *Handbook of Fingerprint Recognition*. Switzerland: Springer Nature.

Marr, D., and Hildreth, Ellen. 1980. Theory of Edge Detection. *Proceedings of the Royal Society of London. Series B, Containing papers of a Biological character. Royal Society (Great Britain)*, **207**(02), 187–217.

Mattur, Shashaank Aswatha, Mukhopadhyay, Jayanta, and Biswas, Prabir K. 2016. Spectral slopes for automated classification of land cover in landsat images. *2016 IEEE International Conference on Image Processing (ICIP)*, 4354–4358.

Mattur, Shashaank Aswatha, Mukherjee, Jayanta, Biswas, Prabir K., and Aikat, Subhas. 2017. Toward Automated Land Cover Classification in Landsat Images Using Spectral Slopes at Different Bands. *IEEE Journal of Selected Topics in Applied Earth Observations and Remote Sensing*, **10**(3), 1096–1104.

Micenkov, B., and van Beusekom, J. 2011. Stamp Detection in Color Document Images. *IEEE International Conference In Document Analysis and Recognition (ICDAR)*, 1125–1129.

Mikolajczyk, K., and Schmid, C. 2001. Indexing based on scale invariant interest points. *Proceedings Eighth IEEE International Conference on Computer Vision. ICCV 2001*, **1**, 525–531.

Mitchell, Tom M. 2017. *Machine Learning*. USA: McGraw Hill Education.

Mitra, Sanjit K. 2013. *Digital Signal Processing: A Computer-based Approach (Indian edition)*. New Delhi: McGraw Hill Education.

Morimoto, C.H., Koons, D., Amir, A., and Flickner, M. 2000. Pupil detection and tracking using multiple light sources. *Image and Vision Computing*, **18**(4), 331–335.

Mukherjee, J., Mukherjee, J., Chakravarty, D., and Aikat, S. 2019. A Novel Index to Detect Opencast Coal Mine Areas From Landsat 8 OLI/TIRS. *Journal of Selected Topics in Applied Earth Observations and Remote Sensing*, **12**(3), 891–897.

Mukherjee, Jit. 2014. *Archival and Retrieval of Heritage Images* (MS Thesis). West Bengal, India: Indian Institute of Technology Kharagpur.

Mukherjee, Jit, Mattur, Shashaank Aswatha, Mondal, Prasenjit, Mukherjee, Jayanta, and Mitra, Pabitra. 2014. Duplication Detection for Image Sharing Systems. *Indian Conference on Computer Vision Graphics and Image Processing*, 1–7. New York: Association for Computing Machinery.

Mukhopadhyay, Jayanta. 2011. *Image and Video Processing in the Compressed Domain*. USA: Chapman and Hall/ CRC Press.

Nister, D., and Stewenius, H. 2006. Scalable Recognition with a Vocabulary Tree. IEEE Conference on Computer Vision and Pattern Recognition. 2161–2168. Berlin: Springer-Verlag.

Nocedal, Jorge, and Wright, Stephen. 2006. *Numerical Optimization*. New York: Springer.

Noh, H., Hong, S., and Han, B. 2015. Learning Deconvolution Network for Semantic Segmentation. *IEEE International Conference on Computer Vision (ICCV)*. 1520–1528. IEEE Computer Society.

Ohta, Yu-Ichi, Kanade, Takeo, and Sakai, Toshiyuki. 1980. Color Information for Region Segmentation. *Computer Graphics and Image Processing*, **13**(3), 222–241.

Ojala, T., Pietikäinen, M., and Harwood, D. 1996. A comparative study of texture measures with classification based on featured distributions. *Pattern Recognition*, **29**(1), 51–59.

Ojala, T., Pietikainen, M., and Maenpaa, T. 2002. Multiresolution Gray-scale and Rotation Invariant Texture Classification with Local Binary Patterns. *IEEE Transactions on Pattern Analysis and Machine Intelligence*, **24**(7), 971–987.

Otsu, N. 1979. A Threshold Selection Method from Gray-Level Histograms. *IEEE Transactions on Systems, Man, and Cybernetics*, **9**(1), 62–66.

Pal, Rajarshi. 2011. *Modeling and Application of Visual Saliency* (PhD Thesis). West Bengal: Indian Institute of Technology Kharagpur.

Pal, Rajarshi, Mukherjee, Jayanta, and Mitra, Pabitra. 2009. An Approach for Preparing Groundtruth Data and Evaluating Visual Saliency Models. Chaudhury, Santanu, Mitra, Sushmita, Murthy, C. A., Sastry, P. S., and Pal, Sankar K. (eds), *Pattern Recognition and Machine Intelligence*. 279–284. Berlin, Heidelberg: Springer Berlin Heidelberg.

Pal, Rajarshi, Mukherjee, Animesh, Mitra, Pabitra, and Mukherjee, Jayanta. 2010. Modelling Visual Saliency Using Degree Centrality. *IET Computer Vision*, **4**(3), 218–229.

Pal, Rajarshi, Mitra, Pabitra, and Mukhopadhyay, Jayanta. 2012. Generation of groundtruth data for visual saliency experiments using image segmentation. *International Congress on Image and Signal Processing*, 889–893.

Palmer, Stephen E. 1999. *Vision Science: Photons to Phenomenolgy*. Boston: MIT Press.

Park, Unsang, Tong, Yiying, and Jain, Anil K. 2010. Age-Invariant Face Recognition. *IEEE Transactions on Pattern Analysis and Machine Intelligence*, **32**(5), 947–954.

Pattison, Philip. 1975. *X-ray and Gamma-ray Compton Scattering* (PhD Thesis). United Kingdom: University of Warwick.

Pei, Yan, Biswas, Swarnendu, Fussell, Donald S., and Pingali, Keshav. 2019. An Elementary Introduction to Kalman Filtering. *Communications of the ACM*, **62**(11), 122–133.

Pinker, Steven (ed). 1986. *Visual Cognition*. Cambridge: MIT Press.

Podder, Dipannita, Mukherjee, Jit, Mattur, Shashaank Aswatha, Mukherjee, Jayanta, and Sural, Shamik. 2018. Ontology-Driven Content-Based Retrieval of Heritage Images. *Heritage Preservation*, 143–160. Singapore: Springer Nature

Podder, Dippanita. 2018. *Content Based Retrieval of Heritage Images* (MS Thesis). West Bengal: Indian Institute of Technology Kharagpur.

Pratihar, Sanjoy. 2015. *On Farey Sequence and Farey Table with Digital-geometric Applications to Image Analysis* (PhD Thesis). West Bengal, India: Indian Institute of Technology Kharagpur.

Pratihar, Sanjoy, Bhowmick, Partha, Sural, Shamik, and Mukhopadhyay, Jayanta. 2013. Skew Correction of Document Images Using Rank Analysis in Farey Sequence. *International Journal of Pattern Recognition and Artificial Intelligence*, **27**(7), 1353004:35.

Preparata, Franco P., and Shamos, Michael Ian. 1985. *Computational Geometry - An Introduction*. Texts and Monographs in Computer Science. Springer.

Priya, G. G. Lakshmi, and Dominic, S. 2011. Video Shot Cut Detection Using Least Square Approximation Method. *International Conference on Image Processing: Computer Networks and Intelligent Computing*, **157**, 1–7.

Razavian, Ali Sharif, Azizpour, Hossein, Sullivan, Josephine, and Carlsson, Stefan. 2014. CNN Features Off-the-Shelf: An Astounding Baseline for Recognition. *2014 IEEE Conference on Computer Vision and Pattern Recognition Workshops*, 512–519.

Redmon, Joseph, Divvala, Santosh, Girshick, Ross, and Farhadi, Ali. 2016. You Only Look Once: Unified, Real-Time Object Detection. *IEEE Conference on Computer Vision and Pattern Recognition (CVPR)*, 779–788.

Reinhard, E., Adhikhmin, M., Gooch, B., and Shirley, P. 2001. Color Transfer Between Images. *IEEE Computer Graphics and Applications*, **21**(5), 34–41.

Reinhard, Erik, Khan, Erum Arif, Akyuz, Ahmet Oguz, and Johnson, Garrett. 2008. *Color Imaging: Fundamentals and Applications*. USA: AK Peters/ CRC Press.

Ren, Shaoqing, He, Kaiming, Girshick, Ross, and Sun, Jian. 2017. Faster R-CNN: Towards Real-Time Object Detection with Region Proposal Networks. *IEEE Transactions on Pattern Analysis and Machine Intelligence*, **39**(6), 1137–1149.

Rifkin, Ryan, Yeo, Gene, Poggio, Tomaso, et al. 2003. Regularized least-squares classification. *Nato Science Series Sub Series III Computer and Systems Sciences*, **190**, 131–154.

Rokach, Lior, and Maimon, Oded. 2005. *Decision Trees*. Boston, MA: Springer US. Pages 165–192.

Ronneberger, Olaf, Fischer, Philipp, and Brox, Thomas. 2015. U-Net: Convolutional Networks for Biomedical Image Segmentation. Navab, Nassir, Hornegger, Joachim, Wells, William M., and Frangi, Alejandro F. (eds), *Medical Image Computing and Computer-Assisted Intervention – MICCAI 2015*, 234–241. Cham: Springer International Publishing.

Rosten, Edward, Porter, Reid, and Drummond, Tom. 2010. Faster and Better: A Machine Learning Approach to Corner Detection. *IEEE Transactions on Pattern Analysis and Machine Intelligence*, **32**(1), 105–119.

Rublee, Ethan, Rabaud, Vincent, Konolige, Kurt, and Bradski, Gary. 2011. ORB: An efficient alternative to SIFT or SURF. *2011 International Conference on Computer Vision*, 2564–2571.

Russakovsky, Olga, Deng, Jia, Su, Hao, Krause, Jonathan, Satheesh, Sanjeev, Ma, Sean, Huang, Zhiheng, Karpathy, Andrej, Khosla, Aditya, Bernstein, Michael, Berg, Alexander C., and Fei-Fei, Li. 2015. ImageNet Large Scale Visual Recognition Challenge. *International Journal of Computer Vision (IJCV)*, **115**(3), 211–252.

Rutishauser, U., Walther, D., Koch, C., and Perona, P. 2004. Is bottom-up attention useful for object recognition? *IEEE Computer Society Conference on Computer Vision and Pattern Recognition* (CVPR 2004), 2, II–II.

Ryaben'kii, Victor S., and Tsynkov, Semyon V. 2006. *A Theoretical Introduction to Numerical Analysis.* Florida: Chapman and HAll/ CRC Press.

Serway, Raymond A., and Faughn, Jerry S. 2003. *College Physics.* Canada: Brooks/Cole; 6th edition.

Simonyan, Karen, and Zisserman, Andrew. 2015. Very Deep Convolutional Networks for Large-Scale Image Recognition. *International Conference on Learning Representations.*

Singh, Sanjay Kr., Chauhan, D. S., Vatsa, Mayank, and Singh, Richa. 2003. A Robust Skin Color Based Face Detection Algorithm. *Journal of Science and Engineering,* **6**(4), 227–234.

Sivic, J., Russell, B.C., Efros, A.A., Zisserman, A., and Freeman, W.T. 2005. Discovering objects and their location in images. *Tenth IEEE International Conference on Computer Vision (ICCV'05),* 1, 370–377.

Srivastava, Nitish, Hinton, Geoffrey, Krizhevsky, Alex, Sutskever, Ilya, and Salakhutdinov, Ruslan. 2014. Dropout: A Simple Way to Prevent Neural Networks from Overfitting. *Journal of Machine Learning Research,* **15**(56), 1929–1958.

Szegedy, Christian, Liu, Wei, Jia, Yangqing, Sermanet, Pierre, Reed, Scott, Anguelov, Dragomir, Erhan, Dumitru, Vanhoucke, Vincent, and Rabinovich, Andrew. 2015. Going deeper with convolutions. *IEEE Conference on Computer Vision and Pattern Recognition (CVPR),* 1–9.

Tan, Mingxing, and Le, Quoc V. 2020. *EfficientNet: Rethinking Model Scaling for Convolutional Neural Networks.*

Thireou, Trias, and Reczko, Martin. 2007. Bidirectional Long Short-Term Memory Networks for Predicting the Subcellular Localization of Eukaryotic Proteins. *IEEE/ACM Transactions on Computational Biology and Bioinformatics,* **4**(3), 441–446.

Tobin, Kenneth, Bhaduri, Leena, Bright, Eddie, Cheriyadat, Anil, Karnowski, Thomas, Palathingal, Paul, Potok, Thomas, and Price, Jeffery. 2005. Large-Scale Geospatial Indexing for Image-Based Retrieval and Analysis. *Symposium on Advances in Visual Computing,* **3804**, 543–552.

Tomasi, C., and Kanade, T. 1991. *Detection and Tracking of Point Features.* Shape and motion from image streams. School of Computer Science, Carnegie Mellon Univ.

Tran, Du, Bourdev, Lubomir, Fergus, Rob, Torresani, Lorenzo, and Paluri, Manohar. 2015. Learning Spatiotemporal Features with 3D Convolutional Networks. *2015 IEEE International Conference on Computer Vision (ICCV),* 4489–4497.

Tropp, J. A. 2004. Greed is Good: Algorithmic Results for Sparse Approximation. *Transactions on Information Theory,* **50**(10), 2231–2242.

Tsai, Yi-Hsuan, and Yang, Ming-Hsuan. 2014. Locality Preserving Hashing. *IEEE International Conference on Image Processing (ICIP),* 2988–2992.

Turk, Matthew, and Pentland, Alex. 1991. Eigenfaces for Recognition. *Journal of Cognitive Neuroscience,* **3**(1), 71–86.

Vajinepalli, Pallavi. 2007. *Trajectory Analysis and Video Summarization with Application to Soccer Videos* (PhD Thesis). West Bengal: Indian Institute of Technology Kharagpur.

Vajinepalli, Pallavi, Mukherjee, Jayanta, Majumdar, Arun K., and Sural, Shamik. 2008. Graph-Based Multiplayer Detection and Tracking in Broadcast Soccer Videos. *IEEE Transactions on Multimedia,* **10**(5), 794–805.

Viola, Paul A., and Jones, Michael J. 2004. Robust Real-Time Face Detection. *Int. J. Comput. Vis.*, **57**(2), 137–154.

Watson, Craig I. 2008 (2008-10-16 14:10:54). *NIST Special Database 14. NIST Mated Fingerprint Card pairs 2 (MFCP2)*.

Wei, S., Liao, L., Li, J., Zheng, Q., Yang, F., and Zhao, Y. 2019. Saliency Inside: Learning Attentive CNNs for Content-Based Image Retrieval. *IEEE Transactions on Image Processing*, **28**(9), 4580–4593.

Wiskott, L., Krger, Norbert, Kuiger, N., and von der Malsburg, C. 1997. Face Recognition by Elastic Bunch Graph Matching. *IEEE Transactions on Pattern Analysis and Machine Intelligence*, **19**(7), 775–779.

Wiskott, L., Wurtz, R. P., and Westphal, G. 2014. Elastic Bunch Graph Matching. *Scholarpedia*, **9**(3), 10587.

Witkin, A. P. 1983. Scale-Space Filtering. Bundy, Alan (ed), *Proceedings of the 8th International Joint Conference on Artificial Intelligence. Karlsruhe, FRG*, August 1983, 1019–1022. William Kaufmann.

Young, Thomas. 1802. The Bakerian Lecture. On the Theory of Light and Colours. *Philosophical Transactions of the Royal Society of London*, **92**, 12–48.

Yuille, A. L. 1991. Deformable Templates for Face Recognition. *Journal of Cognitive Neuroscience*, **3**(1), 59–70.

Zeiler, Matthew D., and Fergus, Rob. 2014. Visualizing and Understanding Convolutional Networks. Pages 818–833 of: Fleet, David, Pajdla, Tomas, Schiele, Bernt, and Tuytelaars, Tinne (eds), *Computer Vision – ECCV 2014*. Springer International Publishing.

Zhang, HongJiang, Kankanhalli, Atreyi, and Smoliar, Stephen W. 1993. Automatic Partitioning of Full-Motion Video. *Multimedia Systems*, **1**(1), 10–28.

Zhu, Zhiwei, and Ji, Qiang. 2007. Novel Eye Gaze Tracking Techniques Under Natural Head Movement. *IEEE Transactions on Biomedical Engineering*, **54**(12), 2246–2260.

Zurqani, H.A., Post, C.J., and Mikhailova, E.A. 2020. Evaluating the Integrity of Forested Riparian Buffers Over a Large Area using LiDAR Data and Google Earth Engine. *Sci. Rep.*, **10**(1), 14096.

Index

Color Plates

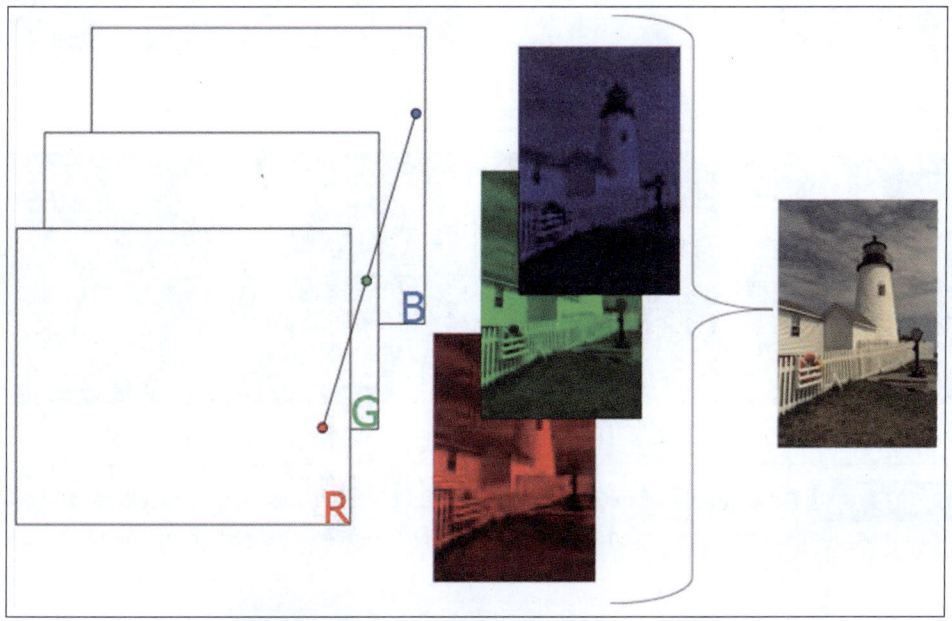

Figure 1.2 Representation of a color image.

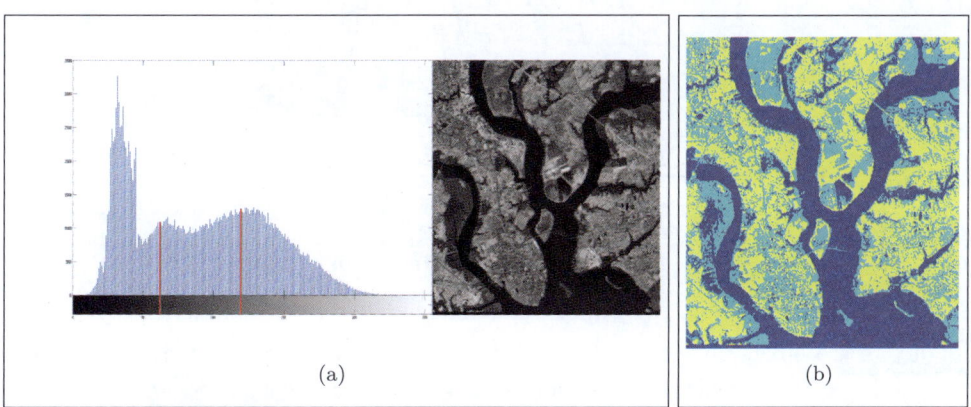

(a)

(b)

Figure 1.15 An example of multi-level threshloding of images.

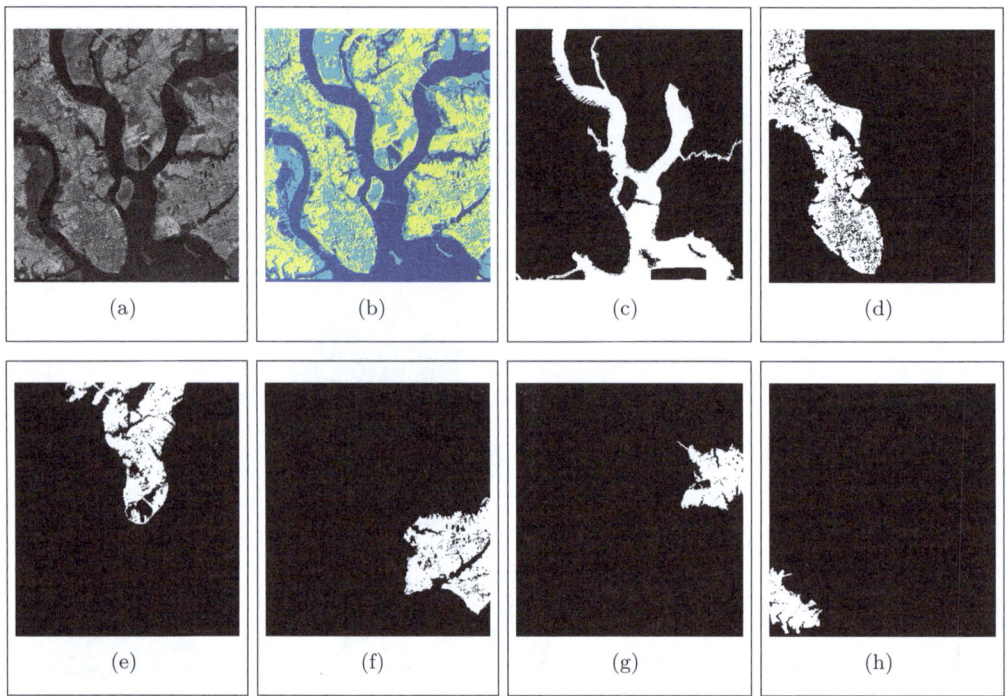

Figure 1.18 An example of extracting connected components from a satellite imagery. (a) Input image. (b) Segmented image. (c)–(h) Different connected components in (a).

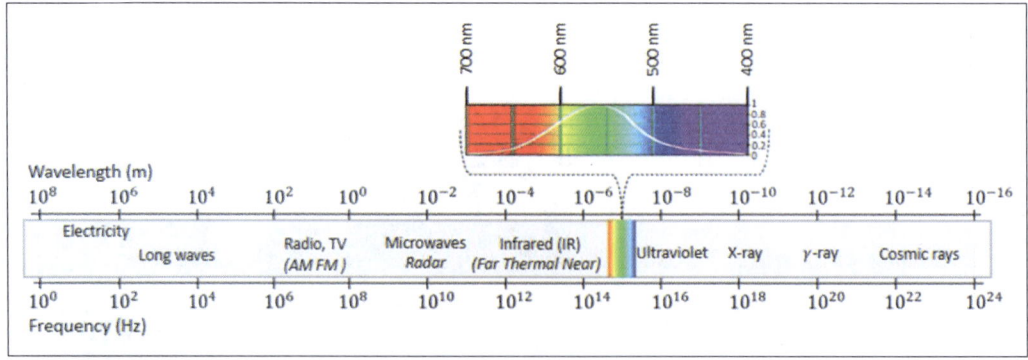

Figure 3.1 A broad range of electromagnetic spectrum and human luminance sensitivity function in the optical range of the spectrum.

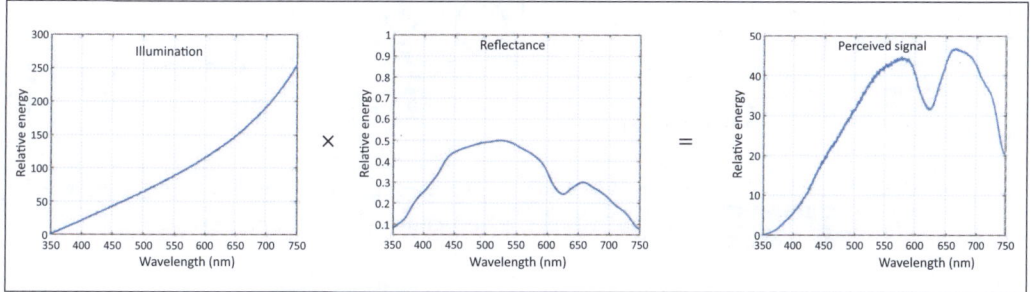

Figure 3.2 Components of a perceived signal.

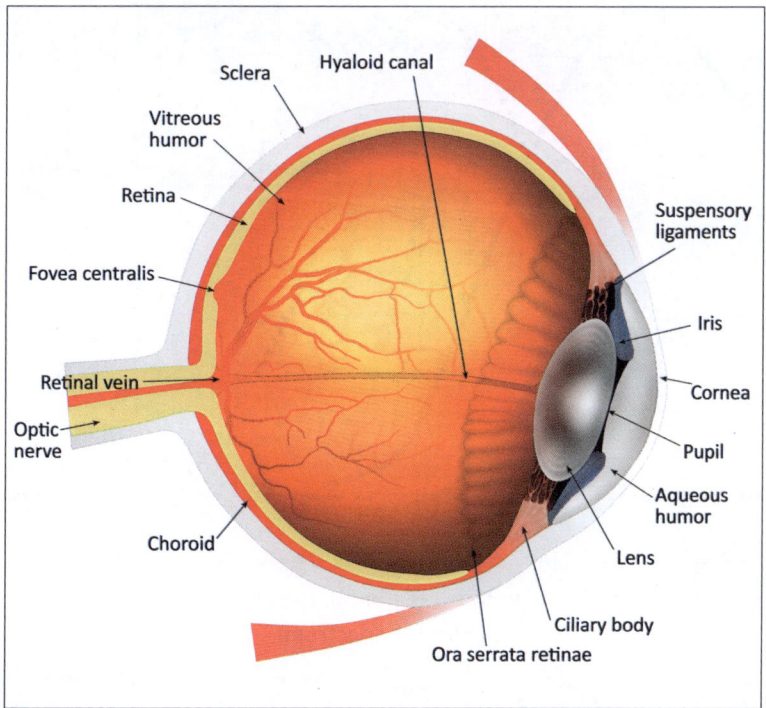

Figure 3.3 Basic anatomy of the human eye. (Courtesy: Getty Images/MARK GARLICK/SCIENCE PHOTO LIBRARY.)

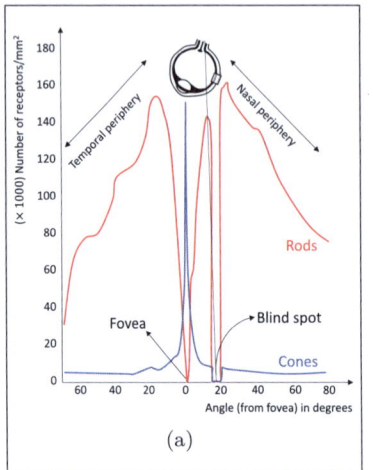

(a)

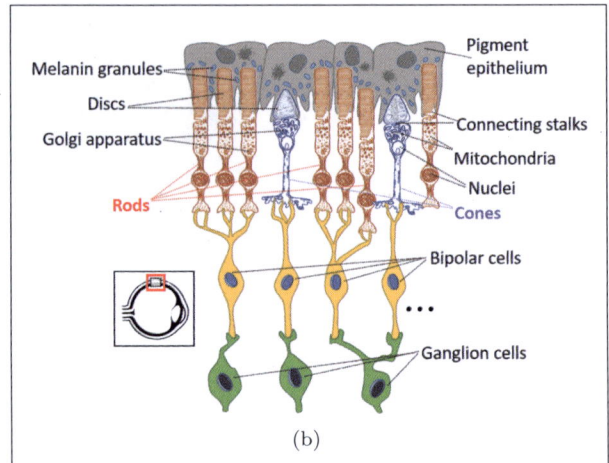

(b)

Figure 3.4 Distribution of rod and cone cells in human eye.

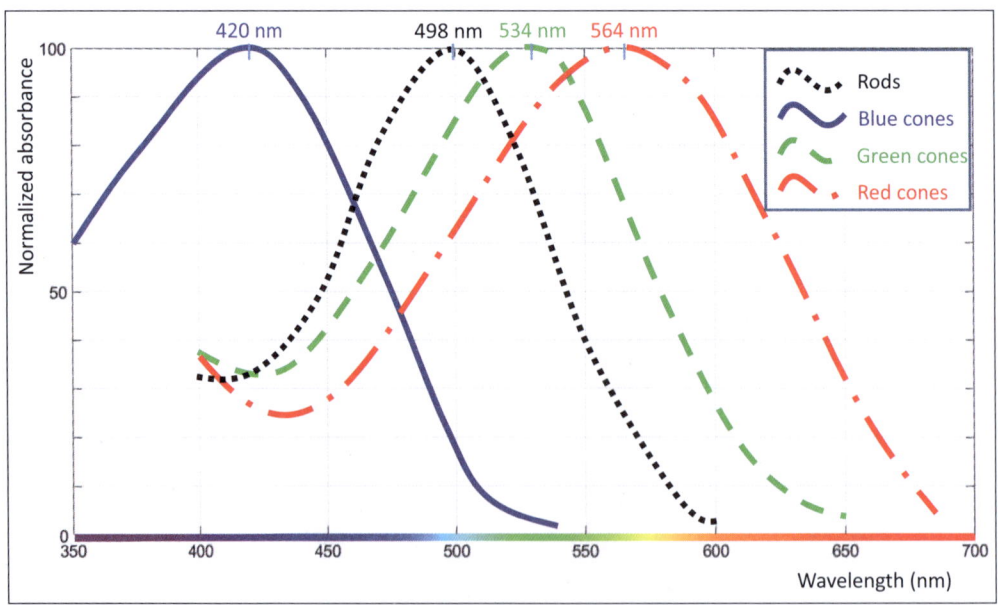

Figure 3.5 Responses of different cone cells in human visual system to a range wavelengths in visible spectrum.

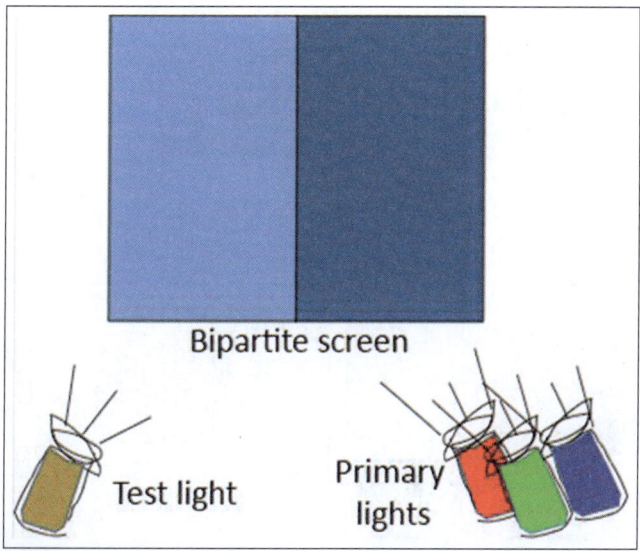

Figure 3.6 A typical setup for conduction of color matching experiments.

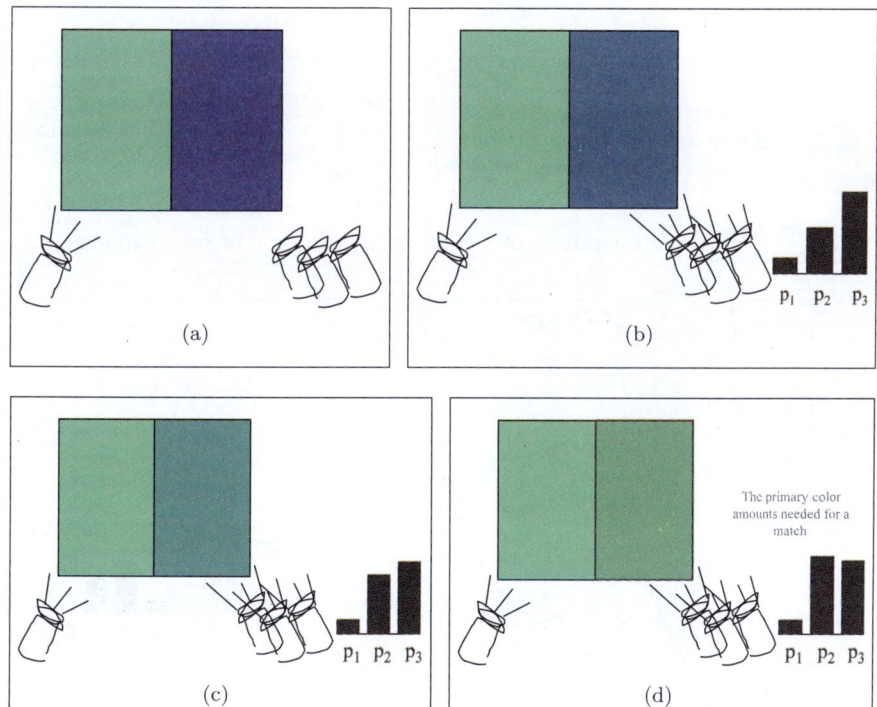

Figure 3.7 Diagrammatic illustration of the color matching experiment for additive mixing.

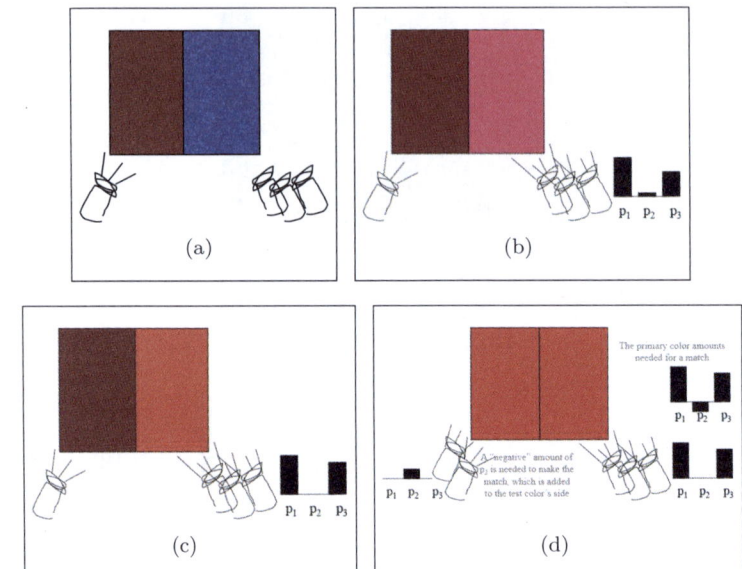

Figure 3.8 Diagrammatic illustration of the color matching experiment for subtractive mixing.

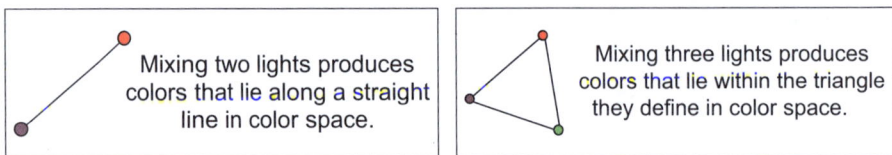

Figure 3.9 Representation of the linear combination of primary colors.

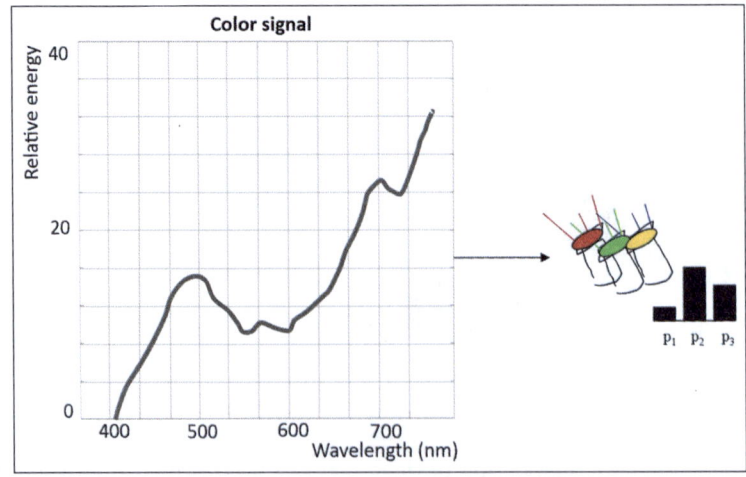

Figure 3.10 Representation of a test color signal as a linear combination of primary color signals.

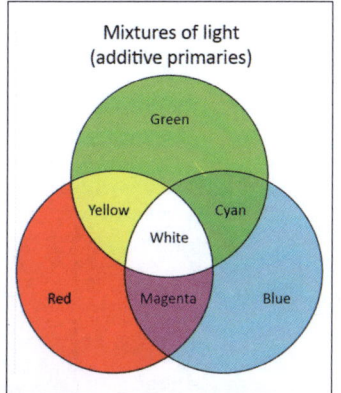
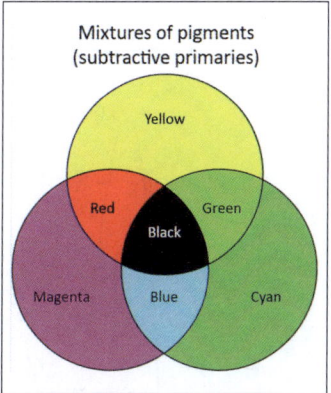

Figure 3.11 (a) Additive system of color mixing that depict mixtures of light. (b) Subtractive system of color mixing that depict mixtures of pigments. The labeled colors correspond to both primary and secondary colors of light and pigments.

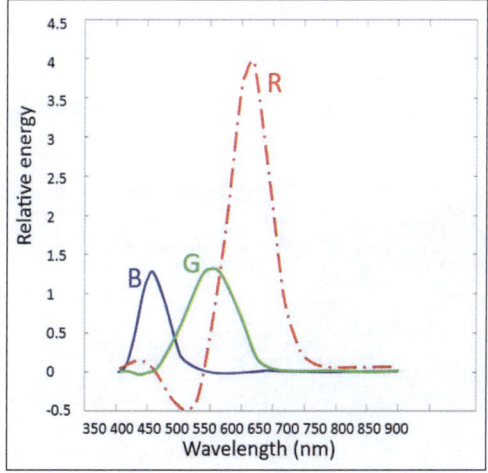

Figure 3.12 Curves of RGB matching function with respect to wavelengths. The curves labeled as "R", "G", and "B" correspond to the wavelengths of red, green, and blue, respectively.

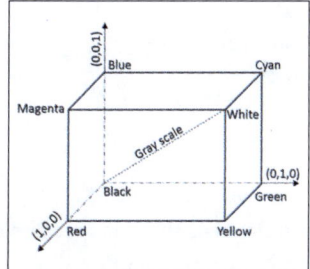
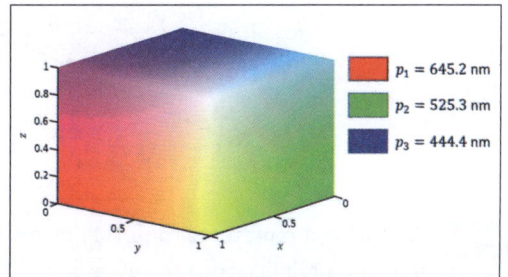

Figure 3.13 (a) RGB model in normalized form. (b) Representation of color vectors with the normalization cube.

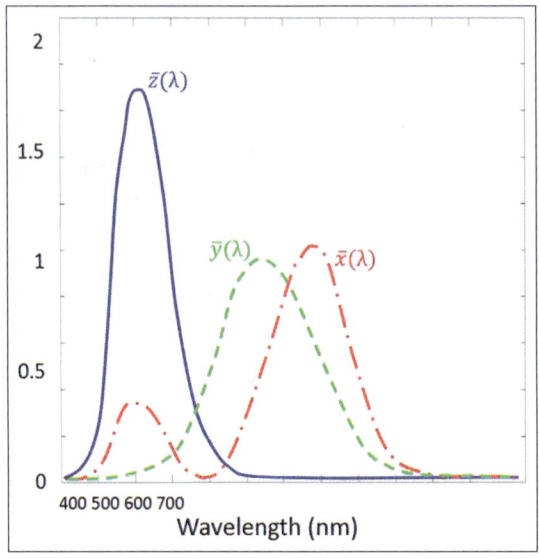

Figure 3.14 Curves of matching function of XYZ color space across wavelengths. Note that the functions are positive throughout the space, unlike the RGB matching functions.

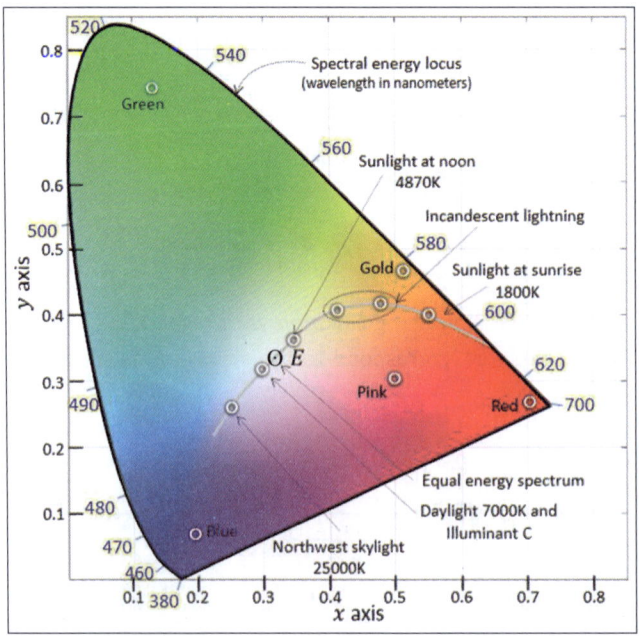

Figure 3.15 Normalized representation of all colors in a 2-D space. The wavelengths are shown at the periphery of the curve, and E represents the white point.

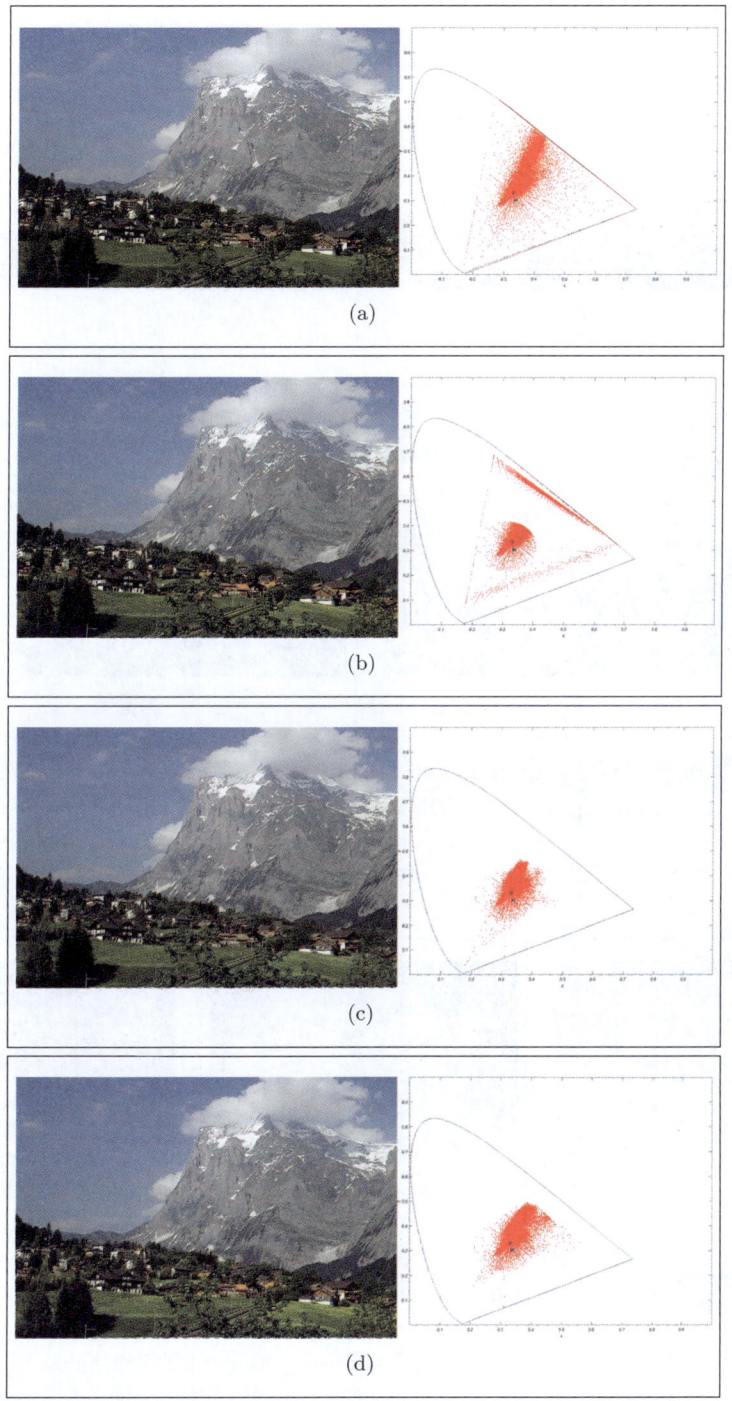

Figure 3.19 Examples of saturation and de-saturation processes on the image of the Alps. (a) Original image and its color gamut. (b) Saturated image and its color gamut. (c) De-saturated image and its color gamut. (d) Saturated–de-saturated image and its color gamut.

Figure 3.20 Examples of saturation and de-saturation processes on the image of the `Alps` (continued from Fig. 3.19). (a) De-saturated image with a negative value of k. (b) De-saturation by shifting the white point to $(0.5, 0.2)$. (c) De-saturation by shifting the white point to $(0.5, 0.4)$. (d) De-saturation by shifting the white point to $(0.2, 0.5)$.

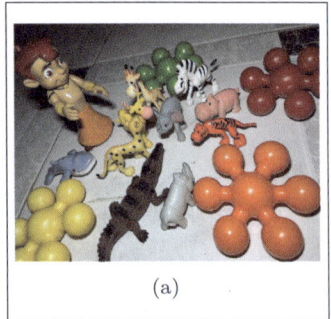

Figure 3.26 An example depicting the effect of illumination on the captured scene. (a) Image captured using the white camera flash. (b) Image captured using off-white LED light. (c) Image captured using orange filament light.

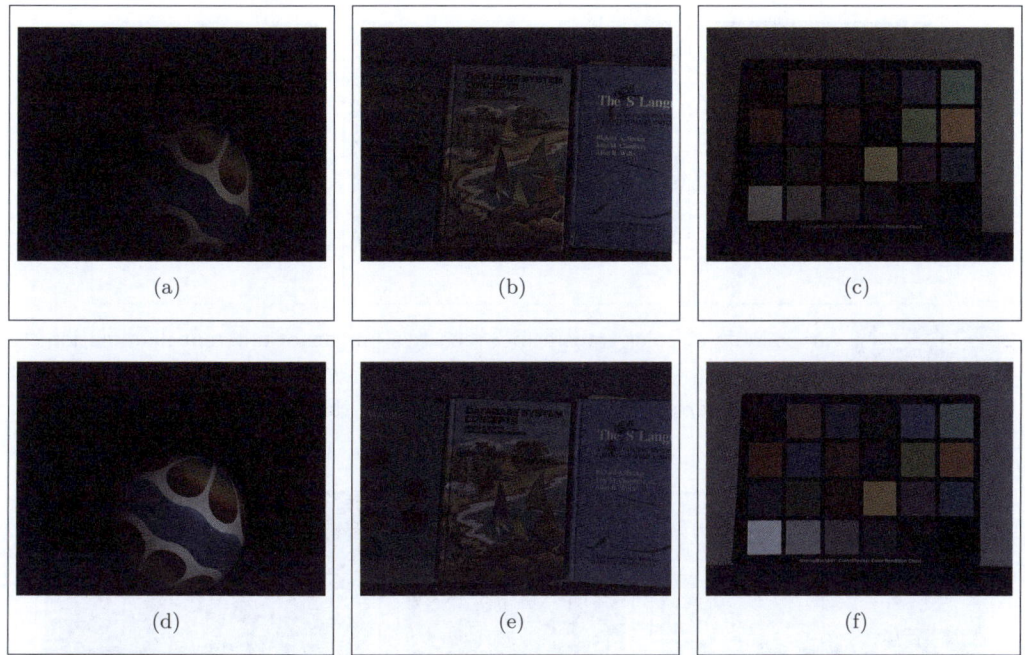

Figure 3.29 Examples of three different scenes that are captured under two different illumination conditions. Scenes: (a, d) `ball`, (b, e) `books`, and (c, f) `macbeth`. Scenes in (a, b, c) are captured by some reference illuminations, and their corresponding scenes in (d, e, f) are captured by different illuminations. (*Source*: Images obtained from https://www2.cs.sfu.ca/~colour/data/colour_constancy_test_images/mondrian/index.html (Barnard et al., 2002).)

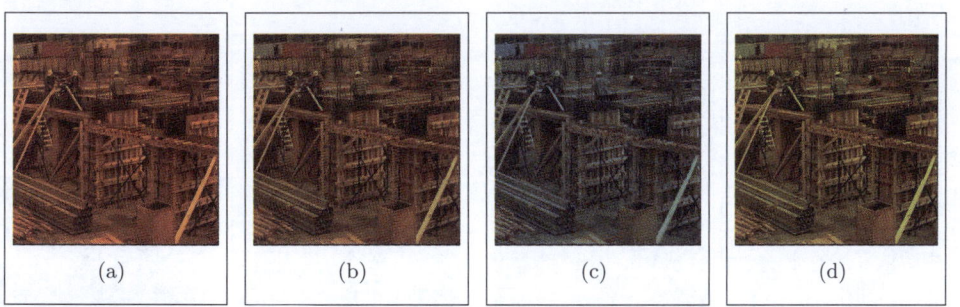

Figure 3.30 Examples of color correction. (a) Original image. (b) Color constancy computation using max-world assumption. (c) Color constancy computation using gray-world assumption. (d) Color constancy computation using gamut mapping approach.

(a)   (b)   (c)

Figure 3.31 An example of color transfer between two images of different illuminations. (a) Source image with reddish illumination, (b) target image with day light illumination, and (c) color transferred image (color transfer from target to source).

(a)   (b)   (c)

Figure 3.32 Another example of color transfer between two images of different illuminations. (a) Source image with day light illumination, (b) target image with reddish illumination, and (c) color transferred image (color transfer from target to source).

(a)   (b)   (c)   (d)

Figure 3.38 Example of demosaicing a color image. (a) Original color image, (b) bilinear interpolation, (c) averaging of red and blue hue interpolation, and (d) LCEC interpolation techniques.

(a)   (b)   (c)   (d)

Figure 3.39 Another example of demosaicing a color image. (a) Original color image, (b) bilinear interpolation, (c) averaging of red and blue hue interpolation, and (d) LCEC interpolation techniques.

Figure 3.40 An example of a zoomed portion of an interpolated image (from LCEC technique in Fig. 3.38) that shows blurred edges and appearance of false colors.

Figure 3.41 Another example depicting a severe appearance of false colors after reconstruction. (a) Original image. (b) Reconstructed using LCEC interpolation technique.

(a)   (b)   (c)

Figure 3.43 An example of suppressing false colors in reconstructed images using the pipeline depicted in Fig. 3.42. (a) Reconstructed image using LCEC interpolation, (b) LCEC with median filtering using 3×3 neighborhood, and (c) LCEC with median filtering using 5×5 neighborhood.

(a)   (b)   (c)   (d)

Figure 4.12 An example of pruning key points. (a) Input image, (b) initial 3312 key points, (c) pruned 2106 key points after gradient threshold, and (d) further pruned 1072 key points after ratio thresholding.

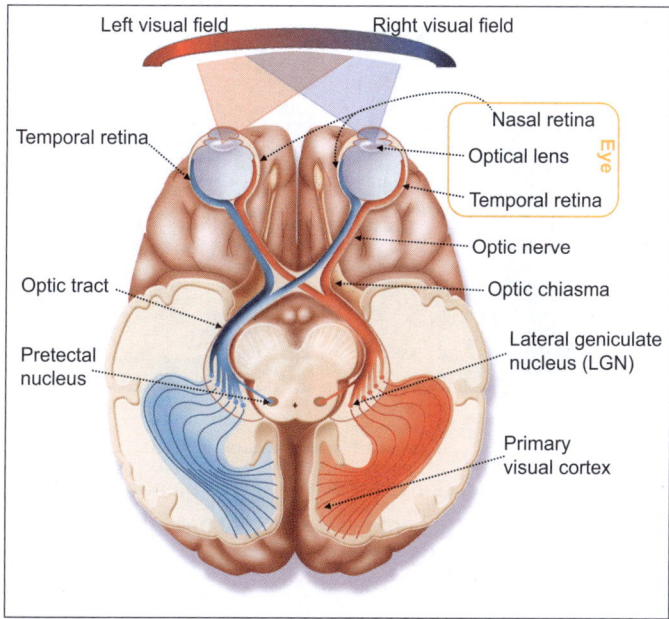

Figure 5.1 Representation of human visual pathway. (Courtesy: Getty Images/BSIP/Contributor.)

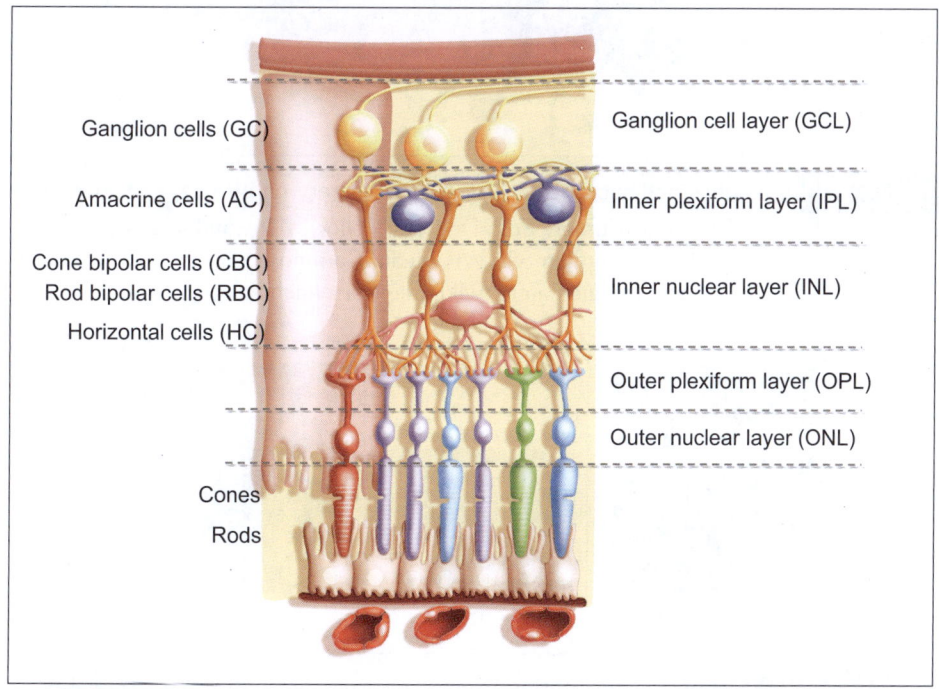

Figure 5.5 Synapse of rods and cones. (Courtesy: Getty Images/BSIP/Contributor.)

(a)   (b)

Figure 5.15 An example of eye tracking. (a) An image of painting by Picasso: `Tragedy`, and (b) its corresponding eye gaze. (*Source*: Dr Anup Kumar Roy, Post Doctoral Fellow, IIT Gandhinagar.)

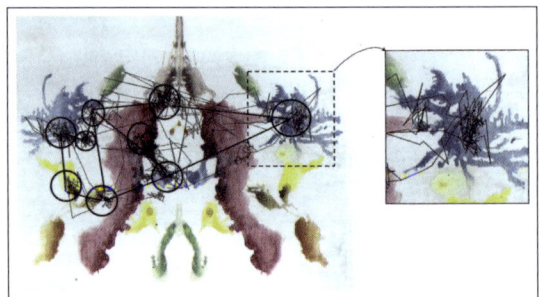

Figure 5.19 Fixations and saccades of eye gaze trajectory on an image of Rorschach test card. (*Source*: Dr. Anup Kumar, Post Doctoral Fellow, IIT Gandhinagar; Image in Public domain, via Wikimedia Commons https://commons.wikimedia.org/wiki/File:Rorschach_blot_10.jpg.)

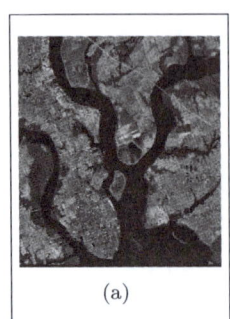 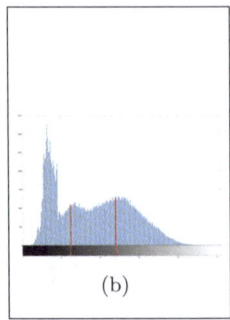 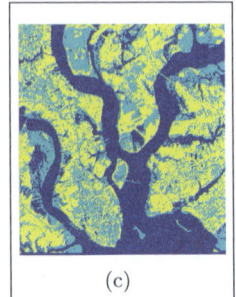

(a)   (b)   (c)

Figure 6.13 Example segmentation using expectation-maximization technique. (a) Input image, (b) histogram of the input image, and (c) segmented image with intervals [0, 60] as blue, [61, 119] as green, and [120, 255] as yellow.

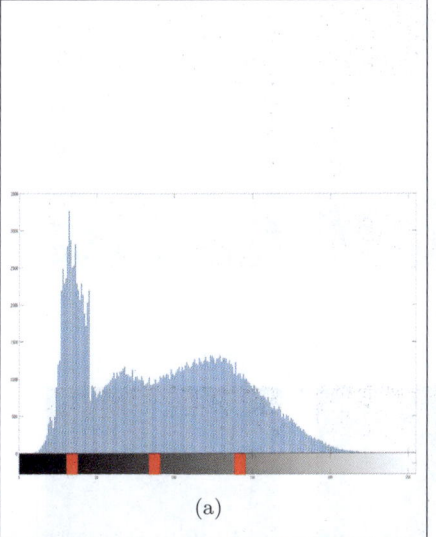
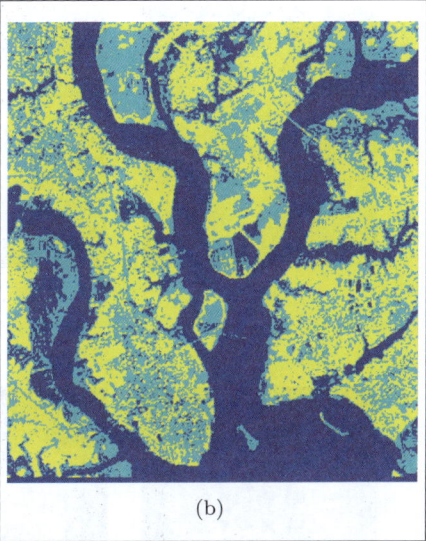

(a)   (b)

Figure 6.14 Example of K-means clustering based segmentation using histograms.
(a) Histogram of the input image, and (c) segmented image with $K = 3$. The cluster
centers are $m_1 = 39$, $m_2 = 90$, and $m_3 = 147$, with their corresponding intervals at
[0, 65] as blue, [66, 119] as green, and [120, 255] as yellow.

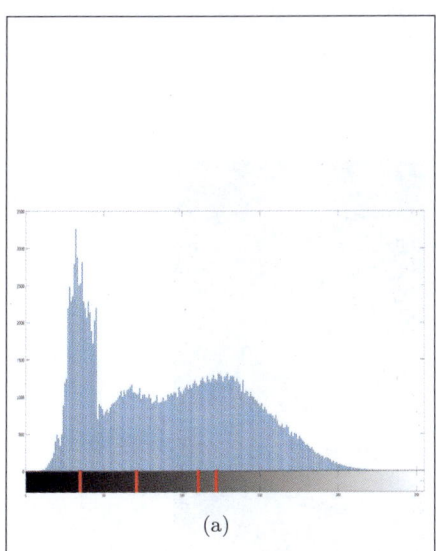
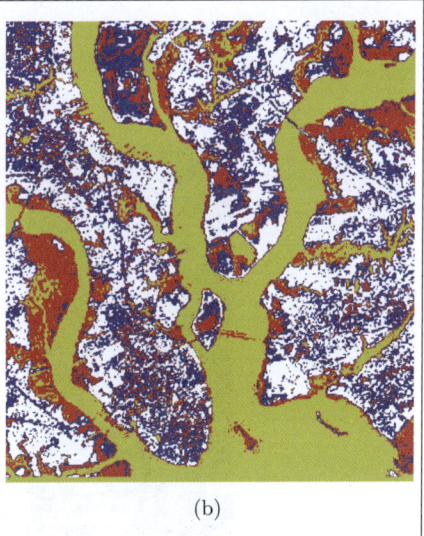

(a)   (b)

Figure 6.15 Example of mean shift clustering based segmentation using histograms.
(a) Histogram of the input image, and (c) segmented image with modes at 32, 67, 117, and
130. The corresponding intervals are [0, 51] as yellow, [52, 82] as red, [83, 128] as blues, and
[129, 255] as white.

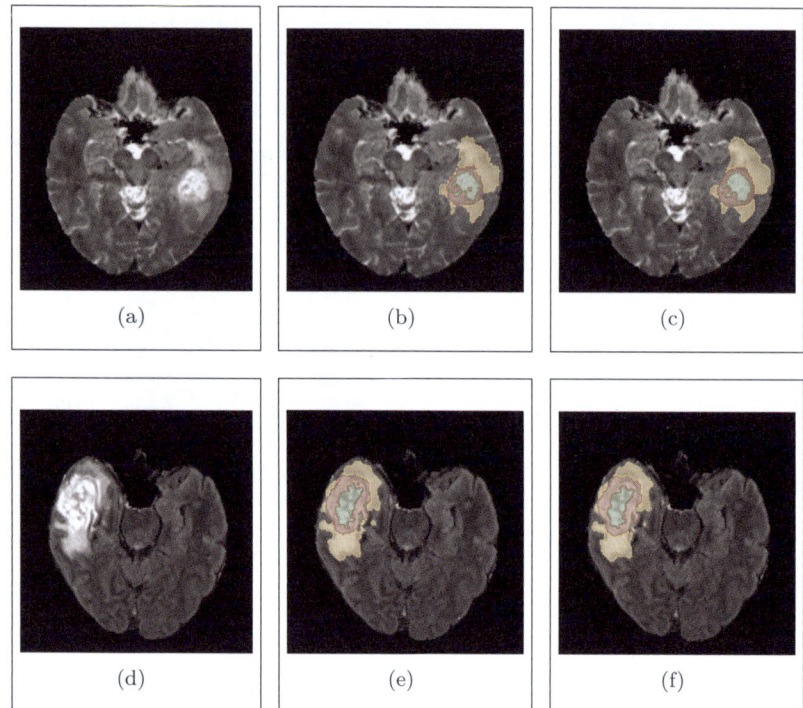

Figure 9.31 Example of image segmentation using UNet. (a, b) Original images, (c, d) ground truth images, and (e, f) segmentation results. (*Source*: Surajit Kundu, Research Scholar, IIT Kharagpur.)

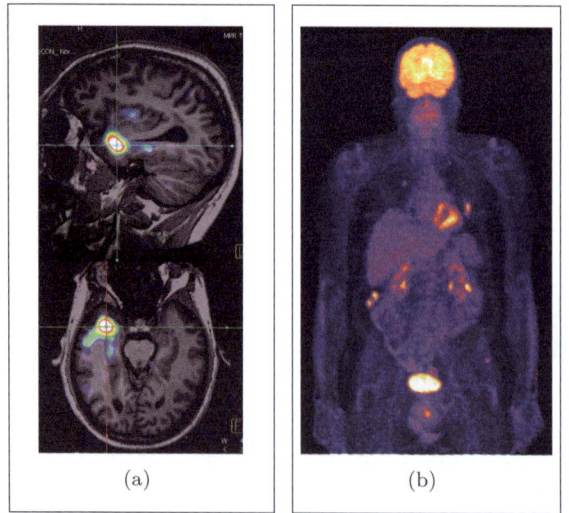

Figure 14.25 Example of diagnostic procedures in molecular imaging by (a) SPECT and (b) FDG-PET. Both the images are co-registered and displayed with superposition. (*Source*: James Sander, Chapter 10 of "Medical Imaging Systems: An Introductory Guide", Springer Open, 2018; https://creativecommons.org/licenses/by/4.0/.)

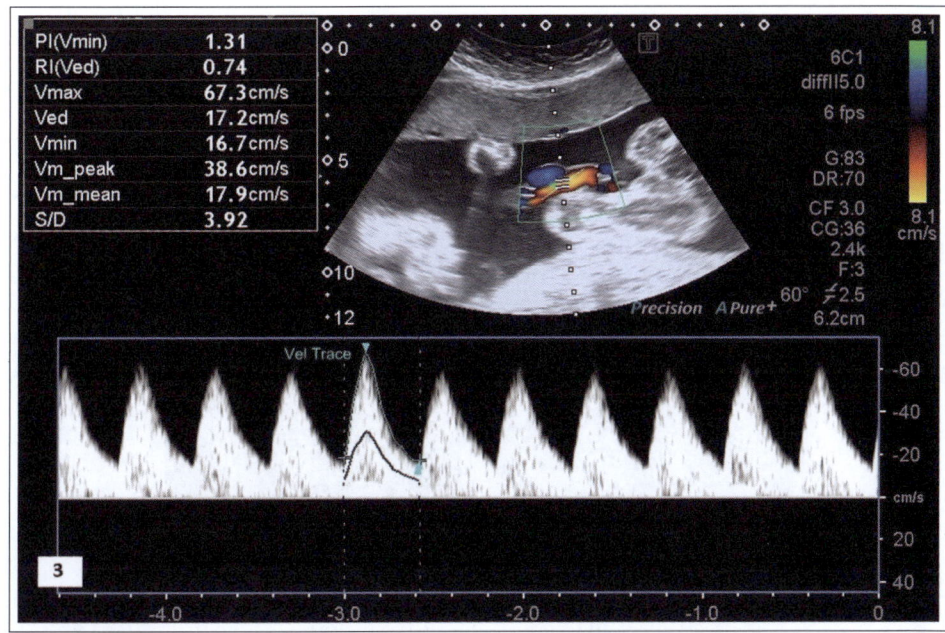

PI(Vmin)	1.31
RI(Ved)	0.74
Vmax	67.3cm/s
Ved	17.2cm/s
Vmin	16.7cm/s
Vm_peak	38.6cm/s
Vm_mean	17.9cm/s
S/D	3.92

Figure 14.34 Example of Doppler mode ultrasound image. (Reproduced from Kazci et al. (2023) under http://creativecommons.org/licenses/by/4.0/.)

Figure 15.11 An example of two-phase land cover classification.

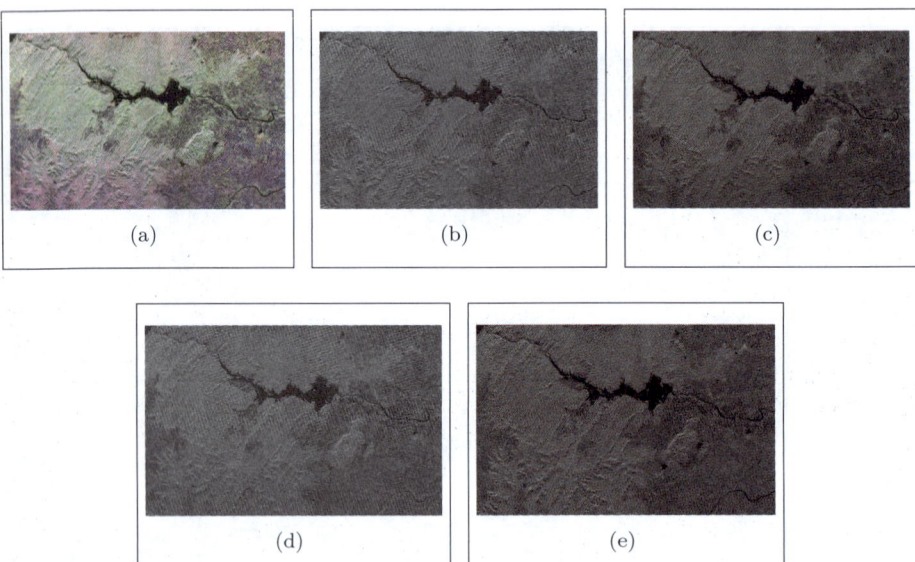

Figure 15.21 (a) Pseudocolor image of quad-pol RISAT data, (b) magnitude of HH component, (c) magnitude of HV component, (d) magnitude of VH component, and (e) magnitude of VV component. The pseudocolor image is formed by using the magnitudes of HH, HV, and VV components as RGB channels, respectively.

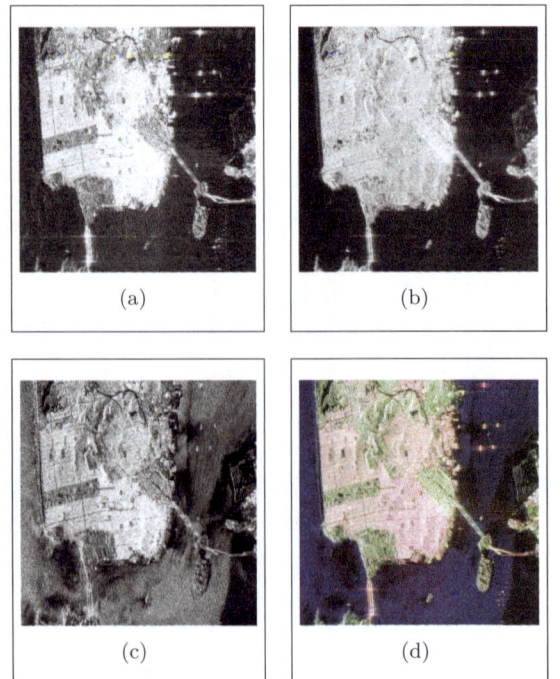

Figure 15.25 Pauli's decomposition of a quad-pol ALOS PALSAR image. (a) $|S_{hh} + S_{vv}|$, (b) $|S_{hh} - S_{vv}|$, (c) $|S_{hv}|$, and (d) RGB composite. The image is generated using the Polarimetric SAR data Processing and Education Toolbox (PolSARpro).

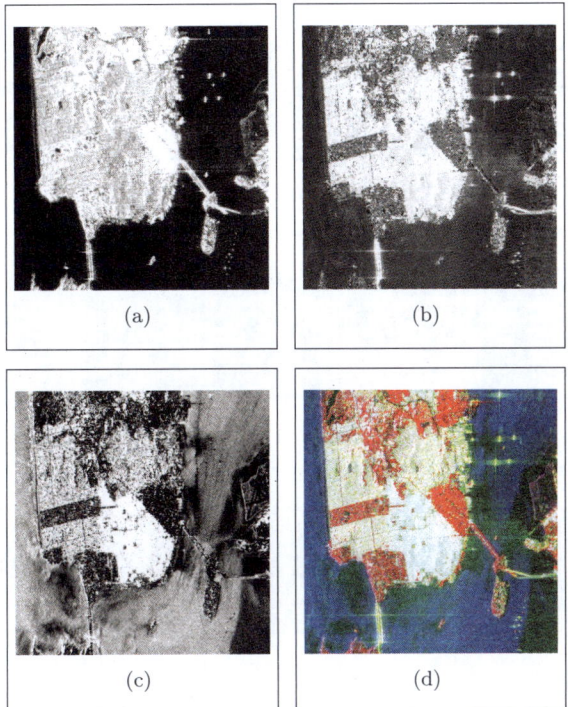

Figure 15.26 Freeman-Durden's decomposition of a quad-pol ALOS PALSAR image. (a) P_v, (b) P_d, (c) P_s, and (d) RGB composite. The image is generated using the Polarimetric SAR data Processing and Education Toolbox (PolSARpro).

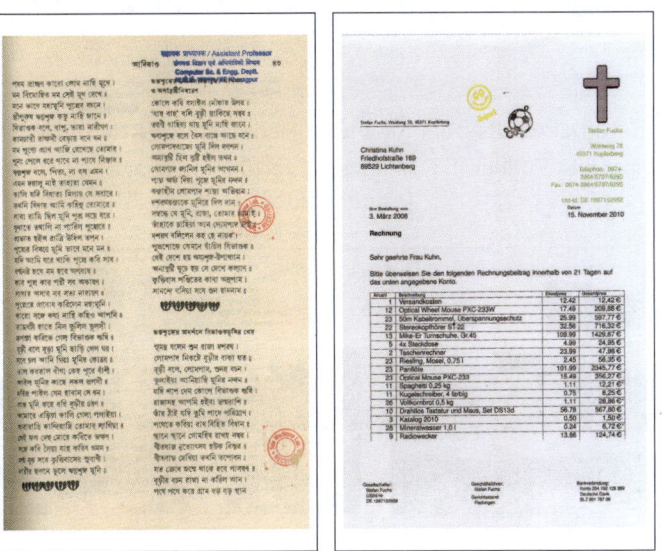

Figure 16.7 Typical examples of document images with stamps. (*Source*: Dr Soumyadeep Dey for sharing images from his PhD work (Dey, 2019). The right image is obtained from the StaVer Dataset (Micenkov and van Beusekom, 2011) available at http://madm.dfki.de/downloads-ds-staver.)

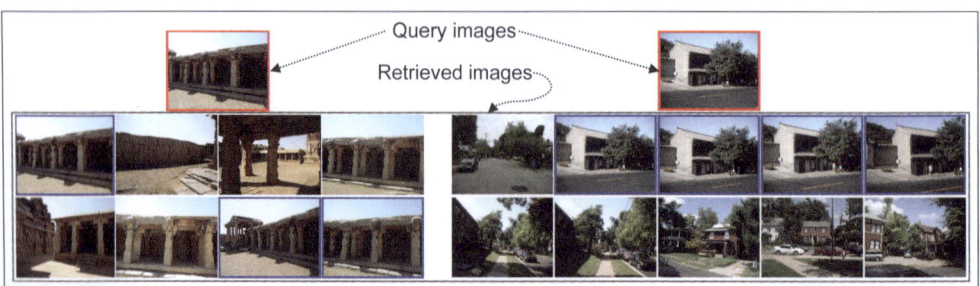

Figure 18.4 Retrieval results from the Indian Heritage Image Retrieval Dataset (IHIRD). (*Source*: Dipannita Podder, IIT Kharagpur, for sharing images from her MS thesis (Podder, 2018).)

Figure 18.6 Retrieval results from searches on duplicate images. (*Source*: Dr Jit Mukherjee of Birla Institute of Technology, Mesra, for sharing images from his MS thesis (Mukherjee, 2014).)